HANDBOOK OF PSYCHOLOGICAL AND EDUCATIONAL ASSESSMENT OF CHILDREN
Personality, Behavior, and Context

HANDBOOK OF PSYCHOLOGICAL AND EDUCATIONAL ASSESSMENT OF CHILDREN
Personality, Behavior, and Context

Edited by

Cecil R. Reynolds
Texas A&M University

Randy W. Kamphaus
University of Georgia

Foreword by George W. Hynd

THE GUILFORD PRESS
New York   *London*

© 1990 The Guilford Press
A Division of Guilford Publications, Inc.
72 Spring Street, New York, NY 10012

Printed in the United States of America

This book is printed on acid-free paper.

Last digit is print number: 9   8   7   6   5   4   3   2   1

Library of Congress Cataloging-in-Publication Data

Reynolds, Cecil R., 1952-
    Handbook of psychological and educational assessment of children:
Personality, behavior, and context / Cecil R. Reynolds, Randy W. Kamphaus.
        p.   cm.
    Includes bibliographical references.
    ISBN 0-89862-392-8
    1. Psychological tests for children.   2. Achievement tests.
I. Kamphaus, Randy W.   II. Title.
BF722.R49   1990
155.4'028'7—dc20   89-38018
                                                                          CIP

Foreword

Sixty-three years ago, David Wechsler wrote a section on psychometric tests in his brother's book, *A Textbook of Clinical Neurology* (Wechsler, 1927). Even with the degree of scholarship one would expect of David Wechsler, it took only 12 pages of text to comprehensively treat this vital topic. To place this in context, consider for a moment that the front matter to this handbook consumes more space than David Wechsler required to discuss the entire clinical appraisal of mental ability.

There has obviously been a proliferation of research regarding the measurement of human ability, achievement, and personality within the last century and the rate of test publication and usage increases exponentially. The relative explosion of knowledge regarding the multifaceted nature of human abilities, achievement, and personality has led, most understandably, to new and uniquely different conceptualizations of not only what to test, but how to test it.

Assessment procedures, regardless of theoretical formulation or format, invariably reveal that children's development can be seen as a constellation of emerging capabilities manifested in a highly variable and dynamic fashion. By studying empirically how abilities emerge (i.e., determining the factors that comprise ability or personality, or those predictor variables that might best explain test performance in children), it becomes evident that the more we learn about factors associated with human diversity, the more we need to objectively assess their unique expression in children.

The need for this two-volume handbook should be clear then when viewed in this context. The prismatic nature of the emerging personality and associated facets of intellectual ability have been revealed to be so complex that specialization in child assessment has become more the norm than the exception. It is now unreasonable to expect that any one psychologist or educator could possibly have a comprehensive grasp of all of the various approaches to assessment with children. For this very reason, there is an urgent need for these volumes.

Each chapter in each volume is a concise treatise of a particular subject relevant to the assessment of children. The value in advancing such diverse yet well-organized contributions is that the editors have constructed a rich tapestry which not only reflects the major topics and issues relevant today, but highlights the lacunae in our present state of knowledge regarding the assessment of children. In this sense, the contents of these volumes serve as a conceptual landmark from which to judge not only the state of our current knowledge but to embark on new directions in research and clinical practice in assessing ability, achievement, personality, and behavior in children.

Perhaps most importantly, the editors have provided an exceptionally balanced handbook in which various assessment procedures have been given equal weight in terms of their representation. Projective assessment procedures, procedures to assess social skills, clinical interview techniques, behavioral assessment procedures, and so on have all been equally addressed in both volumes. This fact alone will insure that they will indeed become widely cited resources among those who assess children as part of their efforts to more fully understand how to assist children in attaining a healthy and productive life in our dynamic and rapidly evolving society.

This two-volume handbook approaches psychological and educational assessment in a very appropriate fashion in that it is comprehensive in its coverage of the many complexities encompassed in the measurement of ability, personality, and exceptionality in children. Without question, the contributors to these volumes represent the most

knowledgeable scholars in their respective fields of endeavor. The individual chapters have been organized in such a logical manner that the final products represents an achievement of singular importance in the last decade of this century.

GEORGE W. HYND
University of Georgia

Wechsler, I.S. (1927). *A textbook of clinical neurology*. Philadelphia: W.B. Saunders.

Preface

The general area of psychological testing and assessment continues to be, as it has been for several decades, the most prolific of research areas in psychology as is evident by its representation in psychological journals. Although always controversial, psychological testing has nevertheless grown in its application to include evaluation and treatment of children's disorders of development, learning, and behavior. Tests are being published at an increasing rate as well. The scholarly literature on psychological testing of children has grown significantly over the past 2 decades and is rapidly becoming unmanageable. More than 40 different scholarly, refereed journals exist in North America alone that publish articles on psychological and educational assessment of children, making the task of the professor, the student, and the practitioner seem an impossible one. Hence, periodic comprehensive reviews of this massive literature seem necessary although onerous. Such tasks require the work and the thoughts of many authors. In undertaking this task, we endeavored to devise a work suitable for the professor as a reference, the student as a text, and the practitioner as a sourcebook and guide. In order to do this effectively it seemed reasonable to separate the two major areas of assessment—intelligence and personality—into their own volumes. This has allowed us the space for in-depth coverage, while retaining cohesion of topic in each book. The two volumes can thus be used in tandem or as separate units depending on need.

Thus, our hope for this two-volume hand-book was to develop a broad-based resource for those individuals who are charged with the assessment of children and adolescents. We also wanted to develop a comprehensive resource for researchers who are studying various aspects of children's assessment and psychodiagnostics, and to provide breadth and depth of coverage of the major domains of children's assessment in a single source. These include such diverse areas as academic achievement, intelligence, adaptive behavior, personality, and creativity assessment. Individual tests such as the WISC-R, the K-ABC, and the Rorschach are given their own treatments in addition to some general methods such as projective storytelling techniques. In each volume, the theoretical foundations and the measurement limitations of our approaches to these latent constructs are addressed.

In order to insure that the volumes are authoritative, we tried to identify and seek eminent scholars with a general command of assessment and a special expertise in research or practice in the area of their respective contributions. We think that we have been very successful in assembling such a group, which includes such luminaries as Wayne Holtzman, Alan Kaufman, David Lachar, Jeanne Chall, Paul Torrance, and June Tuma, just to name a few. The chapters purposely vary from an emphasis on specific applications in assessment to cutting-edge knowledge and critiques of research and statistical procedures. We hope that this will enhance the possibility of using this hand-book as a graduate level text. Because of its breadth we think that this text could be useful for courses in intellectual and personality assessment, practica and internship course work, and courses on psychodiagnostics, psychopathology, and special education.

We are deeply indebted to a number of individuals for assisting us with this, at times, overwhelming project. First of all, we wish to thank the authors of the various chapters for their extraordinary talent and patience with this arduous effort. We wish them continued success in all of their professional activities. We also owe a great debt to Sharon Panulla, our editor at Guilford Publications. We greatly appreciate her faith in giving us the opportunity to produce this work, along with her patience and support throughout the lengthy developmental process. We have had the opportunity to work with a number of editors in the past, but clearly none with the combination of talent and personable demeanor of Sharon. We also thank publisher Seymour Weingarten of Guilford for his concurrence, as well as his early thoughts on the organization and development of the work. We are very appreciative of the efforts of our staff and students: Angela Bailey, Mary Cash, Jana Dresden, Alison Lorys-Vernon, and Jerry Slotkin for their organizational and clerical assistance. Without the support of administrators such as Mike Ash of Texas A&M University and Roy Martin and Joe Wisenbaker of the University of Georgia, this book also would not have been possible.

Finally, we wish to thank all of the researchers of the last century dating back to and including Sir Frances Galton and his modern-day counterpart, Arthur Jensen, for the great strides they have made in enhancing our ability to measure and consequently understand the naturer of human behavior. To our common mentor, Alan S. Kaufman, we acknowledge a continuing debt for the superb model of scholarship that he continues to provide. However, it is to Julia and to Norma that we owe our greatest debts of gratitude. The strength they lend, the understanding they convey, and the support they give make our onerous schedules tolerable and enable us to be so much more than without them—thank you, again.

Contributors

JERRY C. ALLEN, Ed.D., Department of Educational Psychology, University of Georgia, Athens, Georgia

DAVID W. BARNETT, Ph.D., Department of Social Psychology and Counseling, University of Cincinnati, Cincinnati, Ohio

KAREN LINN BIERMAN, Ph.D., Department of Psychology, Pennsylvania State University, University Park, Pennsylvania

CINDY I. CARLSON, Ph.D., Department of Educational Psychology, University of Texas at Austin, Austin, Texas

LOUIS A. CHANDLER, Ph.D., Department of Psychology in Education, University of Pittsburgh, Pittsburgh, Pennsylvania

PAMELA R. CLINKENBEARD, Ph.D., Department of Educational Psychology, Research, and Measurement, University of Georgia, Athens, Georgia

LIZANNE DeSTEFANO, Ph.D., Department of Educational Psychology and Transition Institute, University of Illinois at Urbana, Champaign, Illinois

ROGELIO DIAZ-GUERRERO, M.D., Ph.D., Graduate Department of Social Psychology, National University of Mexico, Cuernavaca, Morales, Mexico

ROLANDO DIAZ LOVING, Ph.D., Graduate Department of Social Psychology, National University of Mexico, Cuernavaca, Morales, Mexico

JAMES L. DUPREE, M.A., Department of Educational Psychology, Humboldt State University, Arcata, California

JEAN C. ELBERT, Ph.D., Child Study Center, University of Oklahoma Health Sciences Center, Oklahoma City, Oklahoma

H. HILL GOLDSMITH, Ph.D., Department of Psychology, University of Oregon, Eugene, Oregon

RUTH ADOLF HAAK, Ph.D., Balcones Special Services Cooperative, Austin, Texas; Department of Educational Psychology, University of Texas at Austin, Austin, Texas

PATTI L. HARRISON, Ph.D., Area of Behavioral Studies, The University of Alabama, University, Alabama

ROBERT W. HEFFER, Ph.D., Children's Hospital of New Orleans, New Orleans, Louisiana

JILLAYNE HOLLIFIELD, Ph.D., Department of Psychology, University of North Carolina, Chapel Hill, North Carolina

WAYNE H. HOLTZMAN, Ph.D., Hogg Foundation for Mental Health and Department of Psychology, The University of Texas, Austin, Texas

JAN HUGHES, Ph.D., Department of Educational Psychology, Texas A&M University, College Station, Texas

PHILLIP C. KENDALL, Ph.D., Psychology Department, Temple University, Philadelphia, Pennsylvania

HOWARD M. KNOFF, Ph.D., Department of Psychological and Social Foundations, University of South Florida, Tampa, Florida

DAVID LACHAR, Ph.D., Department of Psychiatry and Behavioral Sciences, University of Texas Medical School at Houston, Houston, Texas

GREGG M. MACMANN, Ph.D., Institute of Clinical Training and Research, The Devereux Foundation, Devon, Pennsylvania

PATRICE McCLURE BUTTERFIELD, Ph.D., Department of Educational Psychology, Georgia Southern University, Statesboro, Georgia

MICHELLE P. MORAN, Ph.D., Private Practice, San Antonio, Texas

KEVIN L. MORELAND, Ph.D., National Computer Systems Professional Assessment Services, Minneapolis, Minnesota

SUE C. MURPHY, M.S.Ed., Department of Educational Psychology, Research, and Measurement, University of Georgia, Athens, Georgia

JAN PFEIFFER, M.S., Department of Psychology, Louisiana State University, Baton Rouge, Louisiana

ROBERT R. REILLEY, Ed.D., Department of Educational Psychology, Texas A&M University, College Station, Texas

LORETTA A. RESIER-DANNER, Ph.D., Department of Psychology, Villanova University, Villanova, Pennsylvania

KEVIN R. RONAN, M.S., Psychology Department, Temple University, Philadelphia, Pennsylvania

MARGARET SEMRUD-CLIKEMAN, M.S., Clinical Fellow, Massachusetts General Hospital, Harvard Medical School, Boston, Massachusetts

EDWARD S. SHAPIRO, Ph.D., Department of Counseling Psychology, School Psychology, & Special Education, Lehigh University, Bethlehem, Pennsylvania

CHRISTOPHER H. SKINNER, Ph.D., Department of Behavioral Studies, The University of Alabama, Tuscaloosa, Alabama

JON D. SWARTZ, Ph.D., Department of Education and Department of Psychology, Southwestern University, Georgetown, Texas

DEBRA S. THOMPSON, M.Ed., Department of Educational Psychology, University of Illinois at Urbana, Champaign, Illinois

JUNE M. TUMA, Ph.D., Department of Psychology, Louisiana State University, Baton Rouge, Louisiana

JOSEPH C. WITT, Ph.D., Department of Psychology, Louisiana State University, Baton Rouge, Louisiana

FRANCES F. WORCHEL, Ph.D., Department of Educational Psychology, Texas A&M University, College Station, Texas

Contents

PART III. MODELS AND METHODS OF PERSONALITY ASSESSMENT: OBJECTIVE EVALUATION OF CHILDREN'S PERSONALITY

PART V. SPECIAL TOPICS IN CHILDHOOD PERSONALITY ASSESSMENT

HANDBOOK OF PSYCHOLOGICAL AND EDUCATIONAL ASSESSMENT OF CHILDREN
Personality, Behavior, and Context

I

GENERAL ISSUES

1

Critical Issues and Current Practice in Personality Assessment of Children

JUNE M. TUMA
Louisiana State University

JEAN C. ELBERT
University of Oklahoma Health Sciences Center

Personality assessment of children is an important professional activity that is widely practiced by clinical child, pediatric, school, and developmental psychologists, as we shall see later in this chapter. In this chapter, we attempt to present an overview of the kinds of problems that come to the attention of psychologists, to indicate how these problems may be understood in the context of deviations from normal child development, and to show how these deviations influence the assessment process. In addition, we identify critical issues involved in the assessment process (preparing the child for evaluation, establishing a working rapport, keeping the child on task). Interpretation of assessment results, and consequences of personality assessment (labeling, diagnosis, feedback), are then considered.

We also review surveys of attitudes about and practice of personality assessment with both children and adults. In addition, we present child assessment training practices of general clinical and clinical child psychology academic and internship programs. Finally, we present some views about the future of personality assessment.

In this chapter, we use the terms "personality assessment" and "diagnostic assessment" synonymously. This process refers to the evaluation of children with problems in cognitive functioning, affective functioning, and conduct, as well as combinations of these problems.

Some critical issues, although relevant here (measurement and research issues, ethical issues, and detailed implications of assessment for treatment of choice), are not covered in this chapter because they are discussed in subsequent chapters. Likewise, this chapter includes only general references to various assessment models and instruments, since these are also discussed in detail in subsequent chapters.

THE REFERRAL QUESTION

Referrals for a personality evaluation of a child come to the attention of a professional following the detection of a problem in the child's adjustment in regard to school, home, or peer relations. Once the referral is made, the professional is required to proceed in a stepwise fashion to determine the best method of assessing the child's strengths and weaknesses, in order to produce a report delineating conclusions that lead to recommendations for remediation.

Almost everyone, including almost every child, has some sort of psychological problem and experiences periods of unhappiness and personal dissatisfaction; this is not, however, the determining factor in seeking help. Reisman (1973) identifies four factors that determine whether an adult seeks help: (1) the severity of the disorder; (2) the attitudes of the client toward psychological services and practitioners; (3) the attitudes of the client toward problems and feelings of adequacy in being able to deal with them; and (4) the availability of services.

When a child is the client, there are further considerations. Complicating the situation is that fact that the child is dependent on adults for arranging the help he or she needs. The child is a member of a family and is legally dependent on adults to provide whatever is necessary for survival. This parent–child dyad interaction shapes a child's future interpersonal relationships.

In the socialization process, parents or others responsible for the child reward some of the child's behaviors, are indifferent to others, and may be extremely punitive in regard to acts that they find objectionable. Their responses to the child shape much of the child's behavior, influence his or her concept of self and the world, color expectations of how people will treat him or her, and are important in determining the nature of the child's disturbance.

The disorder exhibited by the child usually indicates that the child has not been dealt with by adults effectively. Often adults have tried to compel the child to perform up to their standards in circumstances over which the adults actually have no control (e.g., by demanding better grades in school, then feeling personally defeated by anything else). Sometimes, they have subtly encouraged antisocial behaviors by their protestations of utter helplessness in being able to control their child. Many times they hear, but do not perceive, the child; they have talked to, but not with, him or her. The professional has to be sensitive to these issues.

The examiner may see the child's disorder in a number of ways: as an expression of inadequate parental training, as an assertion of individuality in a world of enforced obedience, or as a means of communicating the intensity and depth of emotions and wishes. Whatever the explanation the examiner may determine, he or she must assess the context in which it occurs and, in particular, the actions and attitudes of family members that can later be used to improve the child's adjustment.

The Child's View

The child's view may be quite different from views of parents or other adults. The child does not believe that his or her behavior is irrational and unreasonable; usually, the child believes that he or she has good reasons for the behavior in question. Like adults with characterological problems, children complain bitterly of the mistreatment inflicted by others and do not recognize their own responsibilites.

The child's denial of problems is often mentioned as a difference between the adult and the child patient (Freud, 1965). Sometimes the child really has no problem, other than being in a situation where parents are making unfair demands; at other times, the child's adjustment is relatively satisfactory, except that some adult is dissatisfied with it. There are children, however, who have problems, but steadfastly deny the existence of them. "Nothing is wrong; I have friends," such children may say, but the claims are made with little conviction, and the children express no indignation about being seen by the psychologist.

The actions of children often refute denials and demonstrate the difficulties they have. In the office, the psychologist often sees a child exhibit a violent temper tantrum resulting from some mild frustration, and the child still yells that there is nothing wrong and that he or she doesn't want to be seen; or a child may claim to love the mother while simultaneously hurling vicious curses at her.

Almost every child has complaints about siblings, or about parents not letting him or her grow up. Other children feel "nervous" but cannot explain why they are tense and anxious. They have no complaints, but they see their problems as centered around their own feelings. These children, who are inhibited and conflicted, usually welcome the prospect of being with a psychologist and experiencing a sense of safety and freedom.

The child's feelings regarding an evaluation are important because it is the child who is the psychologist's client. At the outset, the examiner should arrive at some understanding with the child about why the evaluation is being conducted and what its purposes or goals will be; it is the child's assessment of the disturbance that serves as the basis for this understanding.

The Parents' View

Referrals for the evaluation of a child come from adult caretakers who are confronted by others or are themselves dissatisfied with some aspect of their child's performance and/or behavior. Behaviors of concern to the parents should always receive careful attention from the professional. In general, parents are most troubled about child behaviors that increase the burdens and demands on them (Reisman, 1973). Parents who have a child who misbehaves in school but is good at home are sympathetic, but are inclined to believe that the school problem is the teacher's fault. Similar attitudes may be expressed by parents of a delinquent or antisocial child: They argue that if authorities would be more punitive, the child would behave. These parents are obviously reluctant to obtain professional services. They resent being sent for help; they may explain that they were urged or compelled by some authority in the community, but feel they do not need help.

Other parents display the opposite reaction with guilt. They tend to believe that the child's adjustment may signify the existence of covert problems within the family and are quick to assume that they have totally failed in their responsibilities as parents. This readiness to blame themselves can interfere with their abilities to attach the proper significance to events outside the family that may be damaging to their son or daughter. Both types of parents—those who resist consideration of the influence of parental actions on the child, and those who too easily accept the burden—are hampered in being of help. The former parents interfere by refusing to participate, and the latter do so by interposing themselves in the evaluation process to the exclusion of the child.

There are also parents who fear encounters with professionals because they dread having their own disturbances uncovered. They delay seeking help until the child is almost an adult. At this point, they hope the experts can do something with their child so that the child can become independent and assume adult responsibilities.

It is most constructive for parents to adopt a receptive and inquisitive attitude, in which they are willing to consider, to investigate, and to question the various possibilities that professionals may advance, while being willing to speculate about and to explore their own thoughts and hunches. The psychologist is well advised to work with parents to enable them to take a positive, receptive role in the evaluation process.

Defining the Problems

Upon referral, the psychologist must begin to define the question posed to enable an assessment of the child. The information caretakers provide usually takes a form that is understandable in a broad framework based upon knowledge of child development. There are three major indications of psychological problems in childhood: problems related to cognitive functioning, affective functioning, or conduct (Goldman, Stein, & Guerry, 1983). Each represents some disruption in the normal course of development, and therefore its assessment is predicated on knowledge of the patterns of human psychological growth. In any of these areas, they are generally reflected in any one of four categories: retardations, fixations, regressions, and deviations.

Retardations

"Retardation" in a child refers to a lack of or slower-than-normal development. The problem may simply be mental retardation, which is the basis of delay in other functions. However, children with intellectual retardation may have emotional problems unrelated to the retardation (Reisman, 1973). Retardations may also be thought of in more subtle and broad ways. Behaviors that are distressing to adults but are determined in part by failure to train the child adequately may be thought of as retardations (e.g., enuresis, encopresis, disobedience, and other acts of disturbance through behaviors that parents have handled ineffectually) (Reisman, 1973).

Fixations

"Fixations" occur when development is disrupted or fails to progress after a period of normal development. Usually, a fixation is indicated by an unreasonable persistence of some behavior, wish, emotion, or satisfaction beyond the age when it is tolerated and accepted. Fixations are pathological only when they are so extensive that they prevent the child from being able to deal with the problems and demands of the moment or when they persist in virtually unmodified and inflexible forms.

A professional must have knowledge of the range of variability for the behavior in question to distinguish between fixated and normal behavior. Temper tantrums and refusals to share are normal for a 3-year-old, but not for the child of 8. Likewise, bedwetting is common among 2-year-olds, but not for those aged 4 or over. Imaginary playmates are typical of nursery school youngsters, but not children who are entering first grade.

Regressions

"Regressions" are indicated when the child develops normally, then displays relatively immature behavior in the face of some crisis or change (e.g., birth of a sibling, separation of parents, death of a relative, requirements of attending school, demands to engage in heterosexual relations, breaking away from parents). Regressions can be normal (i.e., periodic relaxation and indulgence in less mature behavior; temporary reactions to stress, illness, fatigue). Pathological regression is distinguished from normal regression by its persistence, its maladaptive nature, its inappropriateness, and the child's feeling that the behavior is not under his or her control.

Deviations

"Deviations" occur when growth takes a distorted form. Deviations occur in the development of cognitive functions, affective functions, or conduct. Accordingly, different forms of psychopathology are manifested depending upon the area of deviation.

PLANNING THE ASSESSMENT

Once the psychologist considers the nature and content of the statements and questions posed by the referral sources, the questions can be defined in terms that will direct the nature and content of the assessment process. The first question confronting the professional is to determine the kind of assessment needed. The psychologist needs to make a decision about whether an intellectual assessment, a personality assessment, a family assessment, other specialized techniques, and/or further consultations are called for.

The problems children experience can be complex and demand an assessment to determine the primary difficulty that requires remediation. For example, if a child is doing poorly in school in spite of good intellectual potential, the psychologist would question whether emotional factors influence the learning difficulty. In this instance, a personality assessment would be indicated. Another scenario would involve poor intellectual potential in addition to poor conduct at school, which affects poor academic performance further.

Sometimes only cognitive evaluations are needed. Other times, regardless of the presenting problem, personality assessment only, or personality assessment in addition to cognitive assessment, is indicated. In the case of obvious psychopathology interfering with the child's adjustment, intellectual and achievement assessments are usually performed to provide a picture of the overall adjustment of the child or to give indications of those varieties of psychopathology that also affect cognitive functioning (e.g., schizophrenia, depression, etc.).

There are reasons for evaluating normal children as well, particularly when situational circumstances warrant them (Goldman et al., 1983). Normal children often are evaluated to address questions concerning placement (e.g., gifted programs, special reading classes, foster home and/or preadoption placement, parental custody). Sometimes a third party needs a description of the child even when the parents are satisfied with the child and his or her current adjustment (e.g., to evaluate effects of travel abroad on the child's educational progress; to provide an objective verification of the intelligence level that parents ascribe to the child; to evaluate a possible underlying disturbance following a traumatic event to which the child has apparently adjusted). Although some may question the motivation of parents in such cases, they do appear to be legitimate questions. Sometimes parents are seeking support or additional information that they do not have.

The nature of the referral, the initial interaction with the examiner, and the examiner's theoretical orientation all help determine the types of information gathered and the use and sequence of evaluation methods.

Assessment Paradigms

Achenbach (1985) has reviewed four major assessment paradigms that include most of the traditional and current methods in the evaluation of childhood psychopathology: (1) medical, (2) psychodynamic, (3) psychometric, and (4) behavioral paradigms, each of which has somewhat different objectives and methods.

In the "medical assessment paradigm" or "neurobiological model" (Knoff, 1986), the traditional approach has been primarily to identify organic correlates of disorder, which may then lead to an understanding of organic etiology. In the contemporary form of this approach, psychological tests may be employed in a fashion analogous to laboratory tests, and the goal is to determine a distinct disorder that explains the child's symptoms. Both disorders that appear related to a medical-disease-like condition (e.g., infantile autism, childhood psychosis) and others of unknown etiology (e.g., hyperactivity/attention deficit disorder) have been viewed as symptoms of organic abnormalities. Such a paradigm would also encompass neuropsychological and psychoeducational assessment, in which specific abilities and areas of competence are targeted for evaluation. Personality changes as a consequence of brain injury or pathology then call for personality assessment, in addition to assessment of specialized cognitive functions.

A second paradigm, the "psychodynamic assessment," evolved primarily out of psychoanalytic theory (Achenbach, 1985; Knoff, 1986) and led to the development of projective techniques, which use ambiguous stimuli to reflect internal needs, desires, motivation, affects, and conflicts (see Part II of this book). The goal of psychodynamic assessment is to yield information that presents an idiographic, or individual, formulation of the case (Achenbach, 1985). Projective tests, such as the Rorschach (Rorschach, 1921/1942) and the Thematic Apperception Test (TAT; Murray, 1943), were initially developed for adults and have been applied to or adapted for children (e.g., Children's Apperception Test [CAT], Bellak & Bellak, 1949; Michigan Picture Test—Revised, Hutt, 1980; Roberts Apperception Test for Children, McArthur & Roberts, 1982; Make-A-Picture Story Test [MAPS], Shneidman, 1952). Recently, there has been an expanding effort to develop nomothetic systems for scoring projective techniques (e.g., Exner & Weiner, 1982; Exner, Thomas, & Mason, 1985; Knoff, 1986).

A third paradigm, "psychometric assessment," has historical roots in the normative-developmental approach to the assessment of children's abilities relative to those of their age-matched peers. The factor that primarily distinguishes these objective personality approaches from the projective techniques is their basis in statistical methodology and objective norm-referenced comparisons. Multiscale/multidimensional approaches, such as the Minnesota Multiphasic Personality Inventory (MMPI; Hathaway & McKinley, 1943) and the Personality Inventory for Children (PIC; Lachar, Kline, & Boersma, 1986; Wirt, Lachar, Kleindinst, & Seat, 1977), are prototypical applications of the psychometric paradigm to psychopathology (Achenbach, 1985).

In addition to such multidimensional approaches to child assessment, the psychometric assessment paradigm has been applied to a single-trait personality construct or symptom such as anxiety and depression. Such measures abound in the area of adult psychopathology (Millon, 1984), and similar measures have been adapted for children, including the Revised Children's Manifest Anxiety Scale (RCMAS; Reynolds & Richmond, 1979, 1985), the State–Trait Anxiety Inventory for Children (STAIC; Spielberger, 1973), and the Children's Depression Inventory (CDI; Kovacs, 1981; Kovacs & Beck, 1977).

Finally, "behavioral assessment" represents a fourth paradigm of assessment of child psychopathology. This approach has developed more recently as a result of the behavioral revolution in clinical psychology. In contrast to both projective and objective personality paradigms, which focus only on the individual child, behavioral assessment also focuses on the environmental contingencies that serve to maintain the behavior. Behavioral assessment, with its direct link to intervention strategies, has evolved into an important area of subspecialization in child assessment.

In behavioral assessment (covered in Chapter 15 of this volume), primary data are gathered from the parent or other caregiver. Such assessment generally involves the use of objective behavior rating scales (see Chapter 16, this volume) endorsed by parent and/or teacher, together with attention to the environmental contingencies that are believed to reinforce inappropriate behavior.

Regardless of the paradigm chosen for a particular child, the examiner needs to know the nature of standardization data relative to the test if invalid results are to be avoided. Reliability data are also important for the examiner to review in order to make decisions about particular tests to administer. Clinicians should understand several aspects of each test used: theoretical orientation of the test, practical considerations, the appropriateness of the standardization sample, and the adequacy of its reliability and validity. The *Mental Measurements Yearbook*, the most recent edition of which was published in 1985 (Buros, 1985), provides essential reviews for tests in print as well as forthcoming ones. Similar reviews can be found in the various volumes of *Test Critiques* (Keyser & Sweetland, 1983–1987), as well as in Sattler (1987). These resources should be referred to frequently, since tests are being developed at a rapid rate (Reynolds & Elliott, 1983). The clinician should also have some familiarity with test theory and

construction; detailed treatment of these areas is provided by Anastasi (1982) and Kaplan and Saccuzzo (1982).

Preparing the Child

Children are brought for assessment with widely varying preparations by their caretakers; these preparations range from nothing to exasperated threats that the psychologists will "straighten you out" to empathic understanding that the children are suffering. The clinician should offer suggestions to the caretaker for preparing a child for the sessions. However, the clinician should understand that the child's cognitive understanding and motivational set will influence the manner in which the child will receive the assessment situation.

Very young children do not understand what a psychologist is nor the purpose of the visit. They may attribute the purpose to something that they have done to displease their parents or to their own shortcomings. Older children may appreciate parental frustration or concern, but may have a different view of the problem. Adolescents, especially those in extreme circumstances (such as those in conflict with the law or those entertaining suicide), will rarely have concordant views about the problems.

Cognitive development, as well, will determine the child's view of the problem. The child's understanding of causality in terms of time, space, and number may affect how that child interprets sequences of events that have taken place and caused concern among adults (Flavell, 1963; Piaget, 1950). In addition, the degree of egocentricity, which limits the child's ability to consider other points of view, will influence his or her understanding of problems.

The child's understanding is also affected by the social and emotional variables that characterize familial and peer relationships. The degree to which the child's need to be accepted, valued, and competent are frustrated, along with the strength of psychological defenses that protect the child from feelings of rejection, worthlessness, and incompetence, will affect the child's particular interpretations of the problems that lead to referral. Caretakers and teachers who have some appreciation of the child's understanding may be able to help the psychologist anticipate some of the child's responses to evaluation. There are times, however, when these adults do not understand or cannot accept the child's point of view. The reader is referred to Goldman et al. (1983) for a particularly sensitive account of cognitive and social development as it relates to assessment of children.

Establishing a Working Rapport

Since psychological assessment is an interactive process between examiner and child, problems can occur with either the examiner or the child. The psychologist may not feel comfortable relating to children; children may not be docile or cooperative; the instructions given and complied with by cooperative children will not work with shy, nonverbal, or noncomplaint children. The psychologist must be equipped to put a child at ease so that discomfort does not interfere with performance. Defensiveness on the part of the psychologist will not aid in this endeavor.

The sequence in which assessment instruments are given may vary, according to clinical judgments concerning whether the child is more comfortable with structured or unstructured tasks. It is generally wise to administer intellectual assessment procedures or achievement tests first to children who need structure. However, if the child is one who is very concerned about his or her performance (e.g., a shy or highly anxious child), less structured tasks (play, drawings, projective techniques, and other methods without right or wrong answers) may be advisable until the child warms up to the testing situation. An anxious child, in addition, may need to engage in tasks that permit a great deal of interaction with the examiner. Once the child masters some confidence, more independent tasks can be attempted.

Shy Children

Shy children often desire to enter new situations slowly. As the situation becomes familiar, they become more comfortable. One technique the psychologist may use with a shy child is to initially engage the child in a casual conversation about a nonpersonal topic. Once the child is engaged in a nonthreatening interchange, the psychologist can then ask for the child's understanding about the visit, clarify any confusion, and explain the child's role in the evaluation.

Unwilling Children

Unwilling children may be belligerent, defensive, angry, or simply determined not to be cooperative; a working relationship with these children is more difficult to establish. The strategy useful in this kind of situation is to acknowledge the child's obvious unhappiness about being in the situation and inquire why. The child may perceive the psychologist as being in the enemy camp (the parents') and may resist any effort to give the parents more power. If the psychologist explains that the child can be more in control by cooperating with the procedures that influence the outcome of the problem situation, the child is more likely to become cooperative.

Minimal Cooperation

Some children cannot trust the examiner enough to participate at all, while others merely go through the motions with only minimal performance. The decision the psychologist has to make in such a situation is whether to continue while attempting techniques to get a better performance or to terminate the session. Often it is better to suggest termination to the child. This action sometimes prompts the child to continue, but often the child accepts the offer to terminate. If a future appointment is possible, it should be suggested and arranged. However, if it is not possible, the psychologist should simply say so and accept the decision. The parents should be advised about the reasons for termination or delay, and all adult parties should discuss the value of a new session and, if it is determined to be possible, when it should be scheduled.

Keeping the Child on Task

The examiner has to strike a balance between being task-oriented and establishing a friendly personal relationship with the child. Taking an extreme position either way will not help the child's performance. On the one hand, if the examiner is distant, the child may believe the examiner is not interested at all in him or her. On the other hand, if the examiner is too personal, the child becomes preoccupied with how the examiner responds on a personal basis, and the task becomes irrelevant.

Clear instructions help the child. Instructions should be given only for the immediate task at hand. If the child shows hesitation or shows signs of discomfort at any time during the session, the examiner should take time to determine whether the child understands the task. Shy children often falsely claim to understand because the admission of not understanding may be embarrassing. Signs of discomfort may also indicate that a child needs a bathroom visit or needs some other kind of attention not related to the assessment.

The physical environment influences the child's on-task behavior. Obviously, a distractible child will be especially influenced by poor conditions in the surroundings. The room should be well lighted, but not too brightly; furniture should comfortably correspond to the child's size; the room can be pleasant, but should not be decorated so that it provides distractions to the child.

The examiner should sit near the child to facilitate manipulation of materials. However, unused materials should not provide distractions for young or distractible children. It is wise to keep material out of view so that a neutral background focuses attention on the task at hand.

The Examination

The examiner should be thoroughly familiar with instructions for administration of the tests within bounds of a standardized procedure. Not only will familiarity with the administration of particular instruments achieve more reliable results, but it will allow the examiner more opportunities for observation of a child's behavior. It is obvious that an examiner who fumbles with materials or who is more concerned with reading instructions from the manual than with observing the child as he or she is performing is going to miss important qualitative variables

related to that child's performance on the task.

The examiner should give instructions to the child so that the child is prepared for what will follow. A general statement concerning the procedure of giving the child a number of differing tasks should precede instructions for individual tasks. It is helpful to make analogies to tasks the child is familiar with. All children know what is involved when descriptions contain items such as "drawing," "answering questions," "solving puzzles," "copying drawings," or "making up stories to pictures." Jargon used to describe these same tasks should be avoided with children (e.g., "intelligence test," "projectives," "the Bender," etc.).

The examiner needs to be aware of fatigue factors and should adjust sessions and breaks within sessions to the age of the child. Test sessions for young children should not be as long as those for older children. Sessions should be scheduled during hours when the child is likely to be fresh and unfatigued. This implies that the child has to be removed from school for the sessions to insure an accurate estimate of the child's ability to function. Even when parents object to this arrangement, most are able to comprehend the advisability of this procedure. If parents are made to understand that school will only be missed for those few sessions required for the evaluation and that getting an accurate estimate of performance is more important at this point than the liability incurred by the child's missing some school, most parents will acquiesce.

During the sessions, the child should be permitted to work as long as performance remains satisfactory. Breaks requested by the child should be permitted as long as such requests are not an avoidance tactic. When fatigue or distraction interferes with performance, the examiner should stop and either restructure the situation or take a break. Sometimes it is necessary to make water or rest breaks contingent upon the child's satisfactory performance on tasks. Special reinforcement is not necessary for most children, but some children require it. In particular, children with attentional, resistance, or dependency problems respond well to reinforcers. The most effective reinforcer for most children is social approval, which may be easily administered by expressing approval of the child's performance. Retarded children and some exceptional or handicapped children with more pervasive problems may need reinforcers of a special sort; time to play with a desired toy or food reinforcers following satisfactory performance may be effective. Prior to using food, however, the examiner should be assured that there are no medical contraindications.

Even if reinforcers are used, the examiner should be in control of the session; thus, the child should not be in control of the reinforcement schedule. The examiner should be aware of when he or she is in danger of losing control; for example, the examiner should break for lunch or rest at the first indication of the child's becoming sleepy, uncooperative, or irritable because of either hunger or fatigue.

If the child is taking medication, particularly to control either a seizure disorder or attentional problems, performance may vary in relation to the time since the last dose. The examiner should attend to changes in attentiveness, quality of performance, and activity level. In the case of a child with attentional problems, the examiner may be interested in examining a child with and/or without medication.

Scheduling several appointments, especially with very young children, children with attentional problems, or children with pervasive problems, may be preferable to attempting to accomplish the entire evaluation in one sitting. Scheduling this way may have the disadvantage of necessitating delays in getting the results and making intervention decisions, but has the advantage of permitting observation of the child's performance over time, especially as it is affected by familiarity with the examiner and the procedures. Information obtained in this way is often important for the evaluation. The initially wary child who warms up to the task and is able to establish a warm relationship with the examiner is differentiated from the child who is unable to relate and adjust to the situation. Several sessions also offer the opportunity to retest the child on selected tasks that appear to have been affected by situational variables.

Interpretation

Obviously, any assessment procedure provides a picture of an individual's strengths and weaknesses along the dimension measured by some standardized method. Assessment involves comparing the individual to all those who have previously been evaluated on the same instrument during its development. Thus, it appears to be simply a psychometric question as to whether a person has any particular kind of "problem." However, inconsistencies both across and within tests make the procedure more complicated. In addition, the psychologist needs to know how development affects the child's abilities. It is not enough to know about assessment instruments and procedures; the psychologist must know about normal and deviant development, as well as possess clinical judgment that enables him or her to make valid interpretive statements about the individual. The psychologist who works with children should integrate material concerning cognitive, social, and emotional development. When cognitive growth is understood, an examiner is more acute in observation of interpersonal interaction and is less likely to overinterpret behavior in terms of social meaning (e.g., an infant is not oppositional when an object is not retrieved if he or she has not yet attained object constancy). The psychologist needs cognitive landmarks in order to make an accurate interpretation of compliance, for example.

The psychologist is an expert in human behavior who must deal with complex processes and understand test scores within the context of a person's life. The clinician must have a knowledge of problem areas that guides his or her observations of behavior and selection of areas in which to collect relevant data.

The clinician must also have knowledge of specific areas, including personality theory, abnormal psychology, psychology of adjustment, test construction, and basic statistics. In addition, familiarity with the main interpretive hypotheses in psychological testing, and identification, sorting, and evaluation of a series of hypotheses, are necessary. Furthermore, knowledge of what each assessment device taps is important in its context (e.g., influence of cultural, situational factors). And, in addition to being thoroughly familiar with traditional content areas in psychology and the nature of what is being tested, the clinician must be able to integrate the test data into a relevant description of the person. The description should focus on the individual, but should also account for the complexity of his or her social environment, personal history, and behavioral observations. The ultimate goal is to develop relevant answers to specific questions, aid in problem solving, and facilitate decision making.

Assessment should yield a description of the client's present level of functioning; considerations relating to etiology; prognosis; and treatment recommendations (Woody, 1969). Etiological descriptions should focus on the influence exerted by several interacting factors, which can be divided into "primary," "predisposing," "precipitating," and "reinforcing" causes (Coleman, 1980). An attempt should be made to assess the person from a systems perspective, in which patterns of interaction, mutual two-way influences, and the specifics of circular information feedback are evaluated. Thus, the description should provide a deep and accurate understanding of the person, not just a mere labeling or classification.

The clinician puts together a description of the person by making inferences from test data. The data are objective and empirical, but the process of developing hypotheses, obtaining support for these hypotheses, and integrating the conclusions is not; it is dependent on the experience and training of the clinician. Making inferences usually follows a sequence of developing impressions, identifying relevant facts, making inferences, and supporting them with relevant and consistent data.

A seven-phase approach has been developed by Maloney and Ward (1976). The first phase consists of initial data collection. This phase includes the referral question, review of the client's history and records, and actual client contact (interview, psychological tests, client behavior). Development of inferences is the second phase. Multiple tentative inferences are developed; these serve to guide future investigation to obtain additional information, which will confirm, modify, or negate later hypotheses.

Phase 3 is concerned with either accepting or rejecting the inferences. The meaning or emphasis of an inference can be altered, or entirely new ones can develop, depending upon the consistency and strength of the data that support a particular inference. The amount of evidence to support an inference directly affects the amount of confidence that a clinician can place in this inference. Phase 4 involves moving from specific inferences to general statements about the client. In this phase, each inference is elaborated to describe trends or patterns of the client (e.g., frequency, etc.).

In Phase 5, further elaboration of a wide variety of the individual's personality traits takes place, in an attempt to integrate and correlate the client's characteristics (e.g., need for achievement, dynamics involved in symptoms, level of anxiety, conflicting needs, intellectual potential, problem-solving style, and relative level of social skills) is made. Phase 5 provides a more comprehensive picture of the person than Phase 4 (although the two phases are similar).

Phase 6 places the comprehensive description of the person into a situational context, and Phase 7 makes specific predictions regarding his or her behavior. This last phase is crucial to making decisions concerning the patient and must take into account the interaction between personal and situational variables.

Since psychological inferences cannot be physically documented, as in the case of medical diagnoses, the validity of inferences presents a challenge for clinicians. Also, feedback regarding validity rarely comes to clinicians. Despite this situation, psychological descriptions should strive to meet four basic criteria: reliability, adequate descriptive breadth, descriptive validity, and predictive validity (Blashfield & Draguns, 1976). "Reliability" of descriptions essentially refers to interdiagnostician agreement (whereby the description or classification can be replicated by another clinician) as well as intradiagnostician agreement (whereby the description can be replicated by the same clinician on different occasions). "Adequate descriptive breadth" refers to breadth of coverage encompassed by the classification (e.g., broad enough to encompass a wide range of individuals and yet specific enough to provide useful information regarding the individual being evaluated). "Descriptive validity" involves the degree to which individuals classified are similar on variables external to the classification system (e.g., similar on PIC profiles and also similar on other relevant attributes of family history, demographic variables, legal difficulties, etc.). Finally, "predictive validity" is the confidence with which test inferences can be used to evaluate future outcomes (e.g., academic achievement, job performance, or treatment outcome); predictive validity is essential if the inferences are to contribute to effective decision making. These criteria are difficult to achieve and to evaluate accurately; they represent an ideal standard for which assessment should strive (Werry, 1979).

CONSEQUENCES OF PERSONALITY ASSESSMENT

Diagnosis

There is disagreement about the value of making a diagnosis. It does not matter if the child's problem is a fixation or a regression if the treatment recommendation is the same for either (Rogers, 1951) or if making the distinction delays getting the necessary remedial help. With adults, the argument for determining diagnosis may have validity, but a different situation pertains to children. When a child is referred, it is because of failure to satisfy expectations of others; this failure may be determined by the expectations' being unreasonable, as well as by a host of other variables (Reisman, 1973). Whereas poor performance by a college student usually implies psychological conflicts, failures of young children in school suggest a number of determinants.

The examiner is obliged to evaluate the behavior in question within the situation or context in which it occurs and in which the child lives, in order to determine remedial action. This does not imply that every case requires the same procedures, psychological tests, or means of assessment in making this determination. Personality assessment is always important as a means to an end, not an end in itself. The purpose of it is generally to aid in the formulation of a treatment plan. Since individuals differ, the procedures differ.

Taxonomy of Childhood Disorders

Only in recent years has there been systematic attention to the development of a taxonomy for children. Most diagnostic and taxonomic classification schemes used with children originated in the study of adult disorders (Achenbach, 1982, 1985; Achenbach & Edelbrock, 1978; Edelbrock & Achenbach, 1980). Until the publication of the *Diagnostic and Statistical Manual of Mental Disorders*, second edition (DSM-II; American Psychiatric Association, 1968), the only categories provided for children were Adjustment Reaction and Childhood Schizophrenia. A national survey in 1964 (Rosen, Badn, & Kramer, 1964) indicated that 70% of children seen in the psychiatric clinics were either unclassified or classified as having Adjustment Reaction according to the DSM-I system (American Psychiatric Association, 1952).

Several classification systems emerged in the 1960s, all of which followed a psychiatric tradition of formulating classifications through consensual committee work. Dissatisfied with the lack of attention to children in the DSM-I, the Group for the Advancement of Psychiatry (GAP) in 1966 proposed an elaborate system of classification of childhood disorders, which included three basic tenets: (1) the psychosomatic concept, involving the interrelatedness between psychological and somatic processes; (2) the developmental dimension; and (3) the psychosocial aspects of the child's existence in the family and society. Ten major categories were proposed, ranging from healthy responses (developmental and situational crises) to psychotic disorders.

The DSM-II (American Psychiatric Association, 1968) provided a category of Behavioral Disorders of Childhood (Hyperkinetic, Withdrawing, Overanxious, Runaway, Unsocialized, Aggressive, and Group Delinquent Reactions). These additions improved the DSM classification system, but there were still problems. In a study of child and adolescent psychiatric patients ($n = 330$) diagnosed with DSM-II, Cerreto and Tuma (1977) found 37.8% labeled as having Transient Situational Disturbance and 30.3% designated as having Behavior Disorder; most of the remaining youngsters received some adult diagnosis. It appears that in actual practice, DSM-II had the shortcoming of permitting fairly frequent use of adult diagnoses for young people, without providing specific criteria for identifying these conditions in children and adolescents. In addition, the narrow range of diagnostic categories available for children led to almost 40% being labeled in very general terms as having an Adjustment Reaction. Cerreto and Tuma (1977), along with many other authors, concluded that the Transient Situational Disturbance diagnosis was overutilized with children, and especially with adolescents, at the expense of calling adequate attention to developing and potentially serious patterns of specific psychopathology (Fard, Hudgens, & Welner, 1978; Meeks, 1973; Weiner, 1980; Weiner & Del Caudio, 1976).

Finally, the ninth edition of the *International Classification of Diseases* (ICD-9) was developed by the World Health Organization (Rutter, Shaffer, & Shepherd, 1975); while it contains an elaborate system of classification of "mental" as well as physical disorders, it has been more widely used in Europe and other parts of the world than in the United States (Rutter & Shaffer, 1980).

The most recent revisions of DSM by the American Psychiatric Association are the DSM-III (American Psychiatric Association, 1980) and DSM-III-R (American Psychiatric Association, 1987), which enjoy widespread use among those who are making clinical diagnostic classifications of children. Considerable discussion heralded the publication of the DSM-III. This system considerably broadened the number of child diagnostic categories, and the provision of a multiaxial approach recognized that different frames of reference (e.g., medical/neurological, cognitive, psychosocial) may be taken into account in diagnosis (Rutter & Shaffer, 1980). However, criticisms have included the dubious labeling of children with "mental disorders" (Garmezy, 1978), the proliferation of unvalidated diagnostic categories, and the extension of research diagnostic criteria to categories that lack empirical justification (Achenbach, 1980; Rutter & Shaffer, 1980).

Achenbach (1985; see his Ch. 18) has described all of these efforts at classification of childhood disorders as examples of the Kraepelinian paradigm of taxonomies (i.e., those that translate clinical concepts into categorical criteria). He and others have judged the DSM-III categories of childhood disorders as having a weak empirical basis without reliable research diagnostic criteria. As an alternative, Achenbach (1978, 1982, 1985) has proposed a taxonomy based upon empirical data regarding frequencies of symptoms in clinically referred children, and has developed a means of categorization of children according to a broad-band Undercontrolled–Overcontrolled dichotomy. These syndromes, together with the narrow-band syndromes (Aggressive, Delinquent, Hyperactive, Schizoid, Anxious, Depressed, Somatic, and Withdrawn) have been compiled in a diagnostic scale known as the Child Behavior Profile (Achenbach, 1978; Achenbach & Edelbrock, 1979).

Much attenton has been paid in recent years to the developmental foundations of both normal and deviant child behavior (Garber, 1984; Gelfand & Peterson, 1985; Knoff, 1986; Sroufe & Rutter, 1984). The recently expanding area of applied developmental psychology has contributed much insight into the issue of individual differences and normal developmental variation versus deviance; such data will probably find greater application in the area of child personality assessment (Gelfand & Peterson, 1985). At the same time, efforts are being made to describe age norms within an empirical classification system (e.g., Achenbach & Edelbrock, 1981).

Labeling

The classification systems available permit the psychologist to diagnose the child and provide feedback to parents and the child, as well as other involved adults. The issue about whether a child should be labeled is controversial (Goldman et al., 1983). After an adult labels a child in any manner, the child may begin to identify with and internalize a negative self-image that sets up expectations for future problems. Even though the process is at work outside the professional's office (e.g., when peers call a child names; when parents disregard differentiating behavior that they disapprove of from the child himself or herself), any label emanating from a professional evaluation carries more weight. The psychologist is wise to weigh the positives (e.g., the extent to which correct classification delineates and makes possible correct remediation) against the negatives (alerting the child and others of a severe problem) before deciding upon a classifiable problem.

The Psychological Report

The written report of the assessment procedures and results, along with the feedback conference, often determine the success of the personality assessment process (Knoff, 1986). Knoff (Chapter 15; 1986) outlines the goals of the report and feedback conference: (1) to answer and discuss the initial referral's questions and concerns; (2) to analyze the intrapersonal and interpersonal issues and circumstances that cause, support, or maintain the identified referral behaviors or affects; (3) to communicate this analysis clearly and effectively to relevant and/or concerned parties such that (4) these parties are motivated and able to work cooperatively on a comprehensive intervention program; and (5) to provide an additional component to the lasting and documented history of the referred child.

Although philosophies, models, and approaches to report writing have been presented (Hollis & Donn, 1979; Huber, 1961; Tallent, 1976), they have not addressed the individual tailoring of reports to unique issues and contents. Recently, however, articles have reflected many different perspectives and orientations in regard to children and adolescents: special education (Bagnato, 1980; Isett & Roszkowski, 1979; Ownby, Wallbrown, & Brown, 1982), pediatric psychology (Seagull, 1979), parents (Tidwell & Wetter, 1978), and school psychology (Sattler, 1982; Shellenberger, 1982). Of all the different types of reports possible, the personality assessment report is the most criti-

cized (Isett & Roszkowski, 1979; Shellenberger, 1982) and the most difficult to write and present effectively (Knoff, 1986).

Most authorities who have addressed the subject (e.g., Knoff, 1986; Sattler, 1982; Shellenberger, 1982; Tallent, 1976) recommend that the report contain the following sections:

1. Report heading (all identifying information; examiner and his or her degree, title, and certification/licensure number; and a conspicuous note as follows: "Confidential—Not to be Reviewed Without a Mental Health Pracititioner Present").
2. Tests administered/assessment procedures (names of all formal assessment tools written out in full, with notations about special forms or scoring systems used; behavior rating scales, etc., completed with someone other than the referred child; relevant conferences, interviews, or reviews of past records).
3. Reason for referral.
4. Background information (previous assessments, reports, observations, and clinical and conference notes; psychological, educational, medical, developmental, and social histories and impressions).
5. Assessment observations (observations during assessment procedures, home or school observations, and other informal assessments such as individual or family interviews, play interviews, etc.) and examiner's estimation of the validity of each assessment.
6. Test results and interpretations (description, analysis, and discussion of strengths and weaknesses of the child, including characteristics, dynamics, and resources of the child himself or herself, significant others, and the specific ecosystem; and the issues and/or variables that support, cause, maintain, or otherwise interact with the referred child, situation, or environment).
7. Summary and recommendations (review of the major aspects of the assessment process—the assessment goals, analyses, and conclusions—and presentation of an individually tailored intervention according to an overall comprehensive plan).

The report should be written according to the intended audience of the report (e.g., parent, school, professional, etc.) (Seagull, 1979). Care should be taken to include only material relevant to the referral question; that is, important but irrelevant information should not be included (see Knoff, 1986, for an excellent discussion of these issues). The report is an organized summary of material to be presented and discussed during feedback conferences with the child, parents, and other concerned parties.

Feedback Conferences

The feedback/planning conference occurs after all of the assessments, interviews, and observations have been completed. Although the assessment process includes ongoing conferences (including preassessment and follow-up conferences), we concentrate here on feedback/planning conferences with the parents and/or other concerned parties and the referred child. See Knoff (1986) for an excellent discussion of other forms of conferences.

Feedback to Child

Many professionals (e.g., Goldman et al., 1983; Reisman, 1973) stress the importance of giving the child a chance to discuss the testing session. During the final discussion, the examiner should ask the child how the session was for him or her and give a little feedback in regard to effort exerted, feelings of dislike for some tasks, and so forth. If the child was uncooperative or difficult, the examiner should acknowledge that it was not the child's best day and should indicate how the child dealt with it (e.g., worked hard in spite of dislike vs. not giving it the effort required), all in a matter-of-fact way. The examiner should answer any questions the child has, including the frequent query "Am I crazy?" At this point, the examiner should once again explain the purpose of the examination and the role the child played in the process. This aspect of the test sessions is important and can prevent any unnecessary discomfort the child may experience as a result of misconceptions and confusions about the process.

Feedback to Parents

The goals of the feedback conference with the parents are to discuss the diagnostic findings and the family- or child-oriented recommendations, and to prepare the parents for conferences with other concerned individuals (e.g., the school personnel). The conference has four components: (1) the initial conference analysis (in which the parents are asked about observations of and/or concerns about the child during the assessment process); (2) problem discussion (formal presentation and discussion of the implications of the assessment); (3) recommendations and intervention planning (family- or child-oriented recommendations and a summary of school or agency recommendations); and (4) summary (a brief review of the major concerns that initiated the referral, the primary assessment findings, and the specific recommendations and intervention directions) (Knoff, 1986). In a mental health setting where the parents have initiated the assessment, this may be the only feedback conference with adults. However, if the referral has been instigated by the school or other agency, a larger conference including all concerned individuals should be arranged, following the parent conference. By no means should the larger conference be scheduled prior to conferring with the parents. The parents need preparation for it, and also need to have the opportunity to discuss aspects of the assessment that are inappropriate in the larger conference because of violation of the child's privacy and confidentiality and family considerations. Discussion of these issues is, however, appropriate in the parental conference.

ATTITUDES TOWARD CHILD PERSONALITY ASSESSMENT

A number of reports over the past two decades have indicated a downward trend in commitment to the role of testing in general, and growing criticism of psychodiagnostic testing in particular (Berger, 1968; Bersoff, 1973; Cleveland, 1976; Holt, 1967; Ivnik, 1977; Korchin & Schuldberg, 1981; Lewandowski & Saccuzzo, 1976; Mischel, 1968;

Petzelt & Craddick, 1978; Piotrowski & Keller, 1984; Thelen, Varble, & Johnson, 1968).

The reasons for the decline of interest have been attributed to a number of factors. First, there has been a gradual broadening of the roles of practicing clinical/counseling psychologists from testing to teaching, research, administration, consultation, and psychotherapy. Another reason is that considerable time and economic constraints are involved in the administration, scoring, and interpretation of tests, which may thus become less cost-effective within the context of rising professional fees. Third, a rigorous scientific model led to disappointing research results when psychometric properties of many assessment measures were evaluated (Reynolds, 1979). Fourth, because of consumers' increased sophistication, tests have been subjected to public criticism and to litigation in some cases (Bersoff, 1973; Cleveland, 1976; Coles, 1978; Lewandowski & Saccuzzo, 1976; Millon, 1984). Fifth, there has been theoretical or pragmatic opposition to testing from behavioral, humanistic, and community psychology (Korchin, 1976). Finally, clinical testing was de-emphasized in graduate programs as faculties saw less value in it (Pruitt, Smith, Thelen, & Lubin, 1985; Shemberg & Keeley, 1970; Thelen et al., 1968), despite the fact that clinicians did not share these views (Levy & Fox, 1975; Wade & Baker, 1977). Even when testing was taught, masterful testers were not available to teach and serve as role models; courses were assigned to young faculty members whose skills, competence, and commitment to the field had not yet matured (Korchin, 1976; Korchin & Schuldberg, 1981).

In the face of these reasons for the decline in psychodiagnostic testing, there remain a need and a demand for clinical assessment in clinical settings, including internship settings (Garfield & Kurtz, 1973; Levitt, 1973; Shemberg & Keeley, 1970; Shemberg & Leventhal, 1981; Tuma & Pratt, 1982; Wade & Baker, 1977). The importance of diagnostic testing is emphasized by many (Gouth, 1971; Holt, 1967, 1968; Rabin, 1981; Rabin & Hayes, 1978; Small, 1972; Weiner, 1972), but evidence abounds to indicate that diagnostic testing has become of lesser importance in the work and identity of clinical psychologists.

The reported professional time spent in psychological assessment by clinicians in various types of mental health agencies was reported to decline from 44% to 22% between 1959 and 1982 (Lubin, Larsen, Matarazzo, & Seever, 1986; Lubin & Lubin, 1972; Sundberg, 1961). By 1976, members of Division 12 (Clinical Psychology) of the American Psychological Association (APA) reported spending only 24% of their professional time in diagnosis and assessment (Garfield & Kurtz, 1976). However, a larger proportion of such time was reported by those working with children: Clinical child psychologists spent 33% (Tuma & Pratt, 1982), master's-level school psychologists spent 47%–54%, and PhD-level school psychologists spent 34% (Goh , Teslow, & Fuller, 1981; Smith, 1984) of their professional time in assessment. In a survey of all advertising employers for clinicians in the APA Employment Bulletin during 1971–1972, 91% of the 334 settings responding expected their job applicants to have testing skills, and 84% reported that these skills should include projective techniques (Levy & Fox, 1975). Only 17% of the 500 surveyed members of APA's Division 12 (Wade & Baker, 1977) and 4% of members of the Section on Clinical Child Psychology (Tuma & Pratt, 1982) indicated that they did not use any tests.

When Wade and Baker (1977) asked respondents what recommendations they would make to students, 85% said that students should learn one test well; almost 75% suggested that young clinicians should be familiar with a number of tests, both objective and projective. The tests recommended were those found in previous surveys of actual clinical practice (Brown & McGuire, 1976; Lubin, Wallis, & Paine, 1971; Sundberg, 1961). Although there has been some variation in rank order over the years, surveys of how frequently tests are used typically include the following in the first 10: the Wechsler Intelligence Scale for Children (WISC), the Bender–Gestalt, the Wechsler Adult Intelligence Scale (WAIS), the MMPI, the Rorschach, the TAT, sentence completion tests of various sorts, Draw-A-Person Test (DAP), and the Stanford–Binet. With the exception of the high ranking of the MMPI and the WAIS, the same list has been obtained in surveys of child clinicians (Brown &

McGuire, 1976; Tuma & Cohen, 1981; Tuma & Pratt, 1982; Tuma & Salcedo, 1982). The available survey data indicate that projective techniques continue to be used extensively by practicing clinicians (Lubin et al., 1986; Piotrowski & Keller, 1984; Wade, Baker, Morton, & Baker, 1978).

Not surprisingly, attitudes toward projective personality assessment vary among groups of applied psychologists with differing theoretical orientations. In a survey of the membership of the Society for Personality Assessment (Piotrowski, 1984), more than 90% of the respondents believed that the professional practitioner should be competent in the use of the Rorschach and TAT; of projective measures specifically designed for children, 23% endorsed competence with the CAT as being important. These individuals similarly endorsed competence with the MMPI (87%), and predicted that objective personality assessment would increase in the near future. In a similar survey of membership of the Association for Advancement of Behavior Therapy (Piotrowski & Keller, 1984), both behavioral and objective personality assessment were viewed as continuing in usefulness, whereas competence in projective assessment was viewed as being unimportant. Of the children's measures mentioned in the survey, only 4% and 6% of respondents endorsed the importance of competence with the PIC and CAT, respectively. (However, because of the low response rate of 32%, generalizability of results in the latter survey is questionable.)

Wade and Baker (1977) investigated the reasons for usage of tests in spite of the lack of empirical support. They found that (1) respondents used tests because they are familiar and trusted; (2) their own experience was valued over published research; (3) testing was viewed "more as an insightful process than as an objective technical skill" (p. 879); and (4) there are no better alternatives for clinical decision making. Thus, it appears that some psychologists have decided to abandon assessment altogether, while others have continued using tests in spite of empirical evidence about their suspect psychometric qualities.

From the survey data above, it is apparent that reported trends represent attitudes toward and practice of personality assessment in general, and most surveys did not differentiate between child and adult clients in their samples of respondents. Those who are involved in personality assessment of children are likely to include three general categories of individuals: (1) school psychologists, whose evaluation of children is focused on the presence of emotional or behavioral problems that interfere with school comportment or adjustment (such evaluations are frequently the result of Public Law 94-142 mandates for assessment prior to special education placement); (2) clinical and/or counseling psychologists who function within state, community, private hospitals, and private practice settings, and whose assessment of children's personality represents the evaluation of psychopathology and intervention planning; and (3) developmental and child specialists whose evaluations represent personality and/or developmental psychopathology research.

Although specific practices in child personality assessment are not reported in many of the surveys of clinical psychologists, more data are available regarding the practice of psychological assessment among clinical child and school psychologists. As noted earlier, surveys show that clinical child psychologists spent 33% (Tuma & Pratt, 1982) and school psychologists spent from 34% to 54% (Goh et al. 1981; Smith, 1984) of total work time in assessment. The PhD respondents of the Goh et al. data ($n = 45$) were more nearly comparable (34% of time in assessment) to the predominantly doctoral-level respondents (91% of the sample) of the Tuma and Pratt data.

These two groups of child specialists also differed in kinds of assessments and tests used. School psychologists indicated that only a mean of 14% of the assessment measures they used were for personality assessment (Goh et al., 1981), whereas a majority of the clinical child psychologist sample used tests for this purpose (Tuma & Pratt, 1982). Further differences in practices between these two child specialties within psychology concern the frequency of usage of various tests. The personality measures most frequently used by the clinical child psychologists (after intelligence scales, used by 81% of respondents) were as follows, in order of preference: drawings (DAP, Kinetic Family

Drawing [K-F-D], House–Tree–Person Test [H-T-P], etc.), Rorschach, TAT (and CAT), Bender–Gestalt, and sentence completion (Tuma & Pratt, 1982). The measures most often used by school psychologists were in essentially the opposite order: Bender–Gestalt, sentence completion, H-T-P, TAT, CAT, DAP (Machover), Rorschach, and Self-Concept Scales (Goh et al., 1981).

TRAINING IN CHILD PERSONALITY ASSESSMENT

Within the general field of child psychology, because of lack of standards for training child clinicians, considerable attention has been focused on the adequacy of training, including training child assessment. The idea of minimal competencies in the delivery of services to children was first presented in a task force report prepared for the Division of Children, Youth, and Family Services (Division 37) of APA (Erickson, Roberts, & Tuma, 1985; Roberts, Erickson, & Tuma, 1985). Included in the general recommendations of this group was the suggestion that basic levels of competency in understanding the etiology of disorders, conducting assessment, and developing diagnoses for a wide range of childhood emotional and behavioral disorders should be expected of clinical child psychologists.

Surveys of Assessment Training

Two professional groups, Section 1 (Section on Clinical Child Psychology) and Section 5 (Society of Pediatric Psychology) of APA's Division of Clinical Psychology (Division 12), have addressed the issue of training in these subspecialities of clinical psychology. In the context of this concerted interest in training, several surveys provide data regarding both attitudes and practices in assessment training. In preparation for the National Conference on Training Clinical Child Psychologists sponsored by Section 1 (Tuma, 1985), attitudes toward and recommendations for training, including assessment training, were surveyed.

In a survey of 100 nonrandomly selected clinical child psychologists who had distinguished themselves in training, research,

and/or clinical activities (Johnson, 1985), 69 respondents rated items concerning personality assessment at the graduate and predoctoral internship training levels. The majority of the respondents indicated that graduate coursework and practica in child personality assessment should be required prior to internship (69% and 77%, respectively). Respondents also believed that clinical experience and didactic seminar training in child personality assessment should be required during internship (68% and 38%, respectively), either in the form of a separate seminar (15%) or as a seminar topic (23%).

LaGreca (1985) surveyed members of the Society of Pediatric Psychology and found similar results. Child personality assessment coursework achieved the highest rank order in importance, and 76% of respondents indicated that it was essential for training pediatric psychologists. Although clinical experience during graduate training achieved a lower ranking in importance, 76% of respondents likewise indicated it was essential for training. The results on attitudes are clear: Coursework (and seminars) appear more important at graduate levels and less so during internship, while clinical experience assumes greater importance at the internship level of training. Tuma and her colleagues also obtained a prescription for an ideal graduate training program for clinical child psychology: The ideal program is one that emphasizes coursework in clinical skills applicable to children, within the context of a great deal of experience with children under close supervision (Tuma & Cohen, 1981; Tuma & Pratt, 1982; Tuma & Salcedo, 1982).

Augmenting the opinions of experts and those in the field is a survey of training practices in child personality assessment. Tuma and Grabert (1983) conducted a survey of the practices of 57 internship and 14 postdoctoral training programs in pediatric psychology, clinical child psychology, and a combination of the two. The majority of these training programs required that applicants have a course in child personality assessment (76%), in projectives (67%), and in behavioral assessment (31%) at the graduate level of training. During the internship or fellowship years, seminars were offered in child development/pathology (28%) and child assessment (26%). Most of the programs (72%) provided practicum training in projective techniques, and some provided training in objective assessment techniques (40%). These respondents, then, appear to reflect the same balance of emphasis on didactic versus clinical experience in assessment as Johnson's (1985) experts and those in the field.

The high value placed on training in child personality assessment is further documented by two surveys of training practices in child assessment in graduate (Elbert, 1984) and internship programs (Elbert & Holden, 1987). The first included all programs ($n = 238$) listed as offering a formal degree in clinical psychology in 1982–1983 (American Psychological Association, 1982). A return rate of 45% ($n = 107$) resulted in a sample of programs that represented both master's-level (32%) and doctoral-level (68%) training, 59% of which were APA-approved programs. In the analysis, data from programs providing specialized clinical child psychology (CCP) training were distinguished from those programs offering general clinical psychology (GCP) training.

In contrast to required coursework in child intellectual assessment in 80% of the sample, specific coursework in child personality assessment was apparently viewed as less important; it was noteworthy that coursework in this area was not offered in nearly one-third (30%) of all programs surveyed. In CCP programs, child personality assessment was required in 43%, was an elective or was strongly recommended in 27%, and was not offered by 30%. In the total sample, a slightly greater percentage (54%) of programs required coursework in child personality assessment, 16% either recommended or offered it as an elective, and 30% of programs did not offer such coursework. The MMPI, Rorschach, and TAT received the most detailed coursework exposure (in 72%–85% of programs) and were administered most frequently (in 37%–57% of programs). Specific tests that received somewhat less detailed coursework exposure (25%–48% of programs) and administration experience (11%–28% of programs) were the following: sentence completion, H-T-P, CAT, and the California Psychological Inventory (CPI).

Although both projective and objective measures of personality are represented among this listing, it is noteworthy that

specific narrow band instruments to assess such personality traits as anxiety and depression were not frequently taught or administered; such behavioral rating scales as the Peterson–Quay Problem Behavior Checklist and the Conners Parent and Teacher Rating Scales were also infrequently included in assessment training.

In the second survey (Elbert & Holden, 1987), both CCP and GCP internship programs listed in the 1984–1985 Association of Psychology Internship Centers Directory (Association of Psychology Internship Centers, 1984) ($n = 294$) were surveyed. Forty-five percent ($n = 133$) of the questionnaires were returned. The questionnaire was designed to obtain information regarding didactic seminar experience, types of cases seen, and level of clinical experience with individual assessment instruments. No significant differences were found between the didactic seminar experiences in child personality assessment for CCP and GCP interns.

Almost half of interns (41%–49%) from both types of programs had exposure to child personality assessment as a topic area in general assessment seminars; few programs (11% to 16%) offered child personality assessment as a separate seminar; and among interns in GCP programs, nearly one-half (48%) received no seminar training in child personality assessment. Similar results were obtained for seminar training in child behavioral assessment.

In test adminstration, a moderately wide range of both objective and projective personality tests were endorsed as being administered by interns in both program types. For the CCP programs, in order of their frequency of use (at least four administrations during the internship) were the following tests: TAT (88%), Rorschach (81%), K-F-D (65%), CAT (56%), a sentence completion test (56%), H-T-P (47%), Vineland Adaptive Behavior Scales (40%), MMPI (26%). Other tests were apparently less frequently administered by child interns. For GCP interns, frequency of administration was high for the Rorschach (77%) and TAT (75%), and less frequent for the following measures: MMPI (57%), sentence completion (52%), H-T-P (51%), and K-F-D (41%).

Relatively little experience in administra

tion was reported with narrow-band measures (e.g., the CDI, which was not administered in 67% of CCP internships and 84% of GCP internships) or with global objective personality measures (56% of CCP internships and 72% of GCP internship programs offered no administrative experience with the PIC). At least in this study, the reported trends toward objective narrow-band (Glaser, 1981) and composite personality (Millon, 1984) measures are not apparent in the training experience of clinical psychology interns.

Thus, again, we find more emphasis on coursework in child personality assessment at graduate than at internship levels; although Elbert (1984; Elbert & Holden, 1987) did not survey test use at the graduate level, use of personality measures at the internship level is comparable to that found in earlier surveys in both child and general internship settings.

Conclusions: Attitudes and Practice in Child Assessment Training

Although at least two-thirds of the experts (Johnson, 1985; LaGreca, 1985) endorse the advisability of required child assessment coursework and 76% of clinical child and pediatric psychology internships require it (Tuma & Grabert, 1983), only 43% of CCP and 54% of GCP graduate programs provide this training (Elbert, 1984). Furthermore, over three-quarters of the experts (Johnson, 1985) also endorse required clinical experience (practica) in child assessment at the graduate level and 69% endorse it at the internship level; however, a wide range of graduate programs and internships (37%–57% and 40%–88%, respectively, depending on the technique) provide it (Elbert, 1984; Elbert & Holden, 1987).

When these training practices are viewed against findings that 91% of employers of psychologists expect testing skills of psychologists (Levy & Fox, 1975) and, moreover, that 83% of clinical psychologists (Wade & Baker, 1977) and 96% of clinical child psychologists (Tuma & Pratt, 1982) administer tests, training practices in child personality assessment appear to be insufficient. Even if the total time spent in assessment—approximately one-third of time for PhD-level clinical child and school psychologists (Goh et al., 1981;

Tuma & Pratt, 1982) and up to one-half for master's-level school psychologists (Goh et al., 1981—has declined from the time spent 20 years ago (about one-half; Lubin et al., 1986) in favor of other clinical activities and administration, not providing skills seems ill-advised.

It should be noted that the Lubin et al. study did not separate out psychologists who work with children; most respondents probably did not work with children. It is likely that assessment occurs more frequently among those working with children, because of the special requirements for assessment of children for a multitude of purposes. Those studies that surveyed child psychologists (Goh et al., 1981; LaGreca, 1985; Tuma & Pratt, 1982) appear to support this notion. Only in one survey (Piotrowski & Keller, 1984) of a specialized group of behavior therapists did assessment appear to be seen as unimportant; however, graduate programs appear to align with this very selectively chosen group. The proliferation of new tests (Reynolds & Elliott, 1983) also indicates psychologists' basic interest and work in assessment for a variety of purposes. From the available data, the call appears to be for more, not less, training in child assessment with the various techniques.

FUTURE OF PERSONALITY ASSESSMENT

Obviously, the demise of psychological assessment has been predicted over the past few years; however, continued development and practice are also strongly advocated. Korchin and Schuldberg (1981) note five new approaches to clinical assessment that indicate a future of renewed vitality.

Projective Techniques

Throughout time, projective tests have probably generated more research than any other assessment technique (Korchin & Schuldberg, 1981); now, however, there is a steady decline in research (Klopfer & Taulbee, 1976; Reynolds & Sundberg, 1976). Clinically, projectives are still widely used, although they are used by proportionally fewer clinicians with fewer patients than in former years

(Korchin & Schuldberg, 1981). Weiner (1972) points out, however, that actual usage is probably up because of the greater number of clinical psychologists currently in practice. Thus, surveys account for a greater number of respondents and, proportionally, a greater number of recipients of psychological assessment.

Important developments in projective testing are of two types: (1) a narrowing trend, seen in development of more focused, psychometrically refined, and theoretically relevant scales; and (2) a broadening focus, seen in a reconceptualization of the Rorschach as a type of interview that studies interpersonal transactions (Korchin & Schuldberg, 1981). The first focus is exemplified by the Klopfer Rorschach Prognostic Rating Scale (which assesses and predicts psychotherapeutic outcomes of various kinds), Friedman's Developmental Level Scoring (which is meaningfully related to personality dimensions and psychopathology) (Goldfried, Stricker, & Weiner, 1979), and the development of Exner's Comprehensive System for scoring of the Rorschach (Exner, 1974).

In the second development, the Rorschach is used more like an interview than like a psychological test. An example of this approach is Singer's (1977) use of it as a transaction. Communication deviances (language anomalies, disruptions, change of referent, etc.) are scored quantitatively, and the test is used to study family communication styles.

Objective Personality Tests

In adult personality assessment, the most popular test is the MMPI, which has been developed from use as an aid in differential psychiatric diagnosis into a broad-spectrum assessment device with new scales evolved in research. In addition, the rapid growth of computer programs for the MMPI has increased its utility; however, computer interpretation systems are mainly based on clinical guesses rather than on actuarial systems, they are difficult to modify, the output contains generalities, and the systems typically neglect local norms and base rates. Butcher and Owen (1978) warn that computer programs are not substitutes for clinical

judgment and are best considered a source of hypotheses.

In addition to the MMPI, new broad-band clinical inventories have been proposed (e.g., the Millon Multiaxial Clinical Inventory; Millon, 1977). Narrow-band instruments (e.g., measures of anxiety, depression, ego strength, self-concept, skills deficits, and problem behaviors or symptoms) to answer specific questions of importance for the care of particular clients have also received focused attention (Dana, 1984; Glaser, 1981; Korchin & Schuldberg, 1981; Millon, 1984; Petzelt & Craddick, 1978).

Behavioral Assessment

There is increasing concern not only with what clients say they do, but also with their feelings, thoughts, goals, and personal meanings. Behavioral assessment generally is moving toward greater theoretical and methodological sophistication as it broadens its base (Korchin & Schuldberg, 1981) to include cognitive–behavioral assessment.

Clinical Interview and Informal Assessment

Research has recently addressed the interview as an instrument of assessment (e.g., Matarazzo, 1978) as well as one of informal assessment (the processes by which we judge the qualities of other people without the use of explicit measures) (Korchin, 1976). Similarly, more objective semistructured or structured interviews of demonstrable reliability are increasingly being used in clinical settings and research. For example, the Schedule for Affective Disorders and Schizophrenia (Endicott & Spitzer, 1978) was developed to gather information to facilitate the making of a psychiatric diagnosis in the DSM-III nosological system.

Environmental Assessment

In a fifth approach, greater importance is placed on the environment—on decentering the individual and looking at the broader conditions in which he or she is embedded. This approach is also a part of a movement to consider the social system (e.g., the family, reference groups, society at large), advocated by such fields as family therapy, community psychology, and cross-cultural psychology.

Dana (1984) has espoused the need to devise new instruments that are relevant to changing cultural and environmental needs. In particular, coping with stress has become an increasingly important ecological aspect of personality assessment. Dana argues that measures of general life stress (e.g., Holmes & Rahe, 1967; Sarason, Johnson, & Siegel, 1978), situational life stress, and existing coping resources cannot be omitted from one's battery of important assessment tools. Dana (1984) additionally argues that we can no longer afford to be bound to our professional history of assessing only psychopathology. Some recent attention to social adjustment, social skills, and family and school climate is an example of the evaluation of competent behaviors within the context of specific environmental settings—family, school, work, interpersonal/social.

These developments indicate considerable activity in the development of methods of assessing personality. Personality theory and assessment appear to be experiencing a period of revitalization following the epoch of empiricism and clinical behaviorism in psychology in the 1960s and 1970s (Millon, 1984). During this period, activity centered on the development of narrow-band instruments, such as objective measures of anxiety, depression, ego strength, self-concept, skill deficits, and specific symptoms (Glaser, 1981).

The current re-emerging theoretical movement is toward viewing personality as a construct (e.g., believing that people exhibit distinctive and abiding characteristics) (Block, 1977). Correspondingly, various newer tools are being developed to analyze the "whole" personality. This trend has paralleled the continuing work in developing an accurate taxonomy of psychopathology; the DSM-III-R represents the most recent effort. Millon (1982), for example, developed a set of "holistic" personality scales; these scales, in a single inventory, measure major coping styles, psychosomatic correlates, and prognostic indices of all the DSM-III personality disorders.

The magnitude of interest in personality assessment is indexed by the development and commercial publication of tests. In the Reynolds and Elliott (1983) survey of the number of tests published between *The Eighth Mental Measurements Yearbook* (Buros, 1978) and the end of 1981, the most substantial change in test publication occurred in the development of personality tests; 29.6% (141 tests) of the total number of 477 new tests were tests of personality. The increase in personality testing corresponds to the increase in personality theories developed by individuals (Mitchell, Reynolds, & Elliott, 1980).

It is apparent that personality assessment is undergoing rapid development in all areas: projective, objective, and behavioral assessment; clinical interviewing and informal assessment; and environmental assessment. The developments outlined above encompass observable behavior, structured and unstructured use of tests and interviews, and assessment of broad- and narrow-band aspects of personality, all within the context of a person's situation/environment. Thus, in spite of various criticisms and some apparent decrease in the use of personality assessment instruments, all indications point to vigorous activity in the area that promises to continue.

SUMMARY

Even though most children, like most adults, have some sort of psychological problem and experience periods of unhappiness, the determining factors in seeking help for children are somewhat different from those that influence adults' seeking help. Notably, seeking help for a child is usually prompted by the dissatisfaction of adults (usually the parents or school officials) with the child's behavior in areas of school, home, or peer relations. Because the parents are the ones bringing the child in for evaluation, often the child perceives the situation differently: He or she does not see that the particular behavior is a problem and has explanations for it. Sometimes the child really has no problem, but at other times the child denies the problems with no conviction, and the child's actions often refute the denials. Even though most children have various complaints about siblings and parents, others feel nervous, are inhibited and conflicted, and welcome the prospect of receiving help.

Parents usually are most concerned with child behaviors that increase the burdens and demands on them. Three types of parents may be uncooperative in the quest for help for a child. Parents who blame others (e.g., the school teacher, laxness of authorities, etc.) for the child's misbehavior, parents who perceive the child's behavior as a reflection of their own failures as parents, and parents who are reluctant to uncover their own disturbances, which they construe as being contributory to their child's difficulties.

Once the child is referred, the psychologist must start to assess the general areas of difficulties: problems in cognitive functioning, affective functioning, or conduct, all of which can be seen as disruptions in the normal course of development. To make an accurate assessment of these disruptions, the psychologist requires a thorough knowledge of the patterns of human psychological growth. These disruptions of development can be categorized within one of four categories: retardations, fixations, regressions, and deviations of any of the three areas of functioning.

Problems children experience can be complex and demand an assessment to determine the primary difficulty that requires remediation. Thus, the first question confronting the psychologist is to determine the kind of assessment needed. The psychologist, at this point, decides whether to make use of an intellectual assessment, a personality assessment, a family assessment, other specialized techniques, and/or further consultations. At times, it is also appropriate to evaluate normal children, especially for certain types of placement in schools (e.g., gifted programs), for foster home or preadoption purposes, and sometimes for custody hearings.

The various phases of the assessment process include initial interview with the child and parent(s); obtaining background information concerning development and prior adjustment as well as current adjustment; assessing parenting behaviors and methods; conducting the examination (preparing the child, establishing rapport, planning the assessment in terms of selection and sequence of instruments administered, and keeping the child on task); evaluating the child's behavior on tests and test results; writing a report; and giving feedback to child, parents, and professionals and/or school personnel, as appropriate.

The child's cognitive understanding and motivational set will influence the manner in which he or she will receive the assessment situation. Both cognitive and social development are important and determine how the child sees the problems. The degree of egocentricity, which limits the child's ability to consider other points of view, will also influence his or her understanding of problems.

The psychologist has to determine the paradigm of assessment he or she will follow. There are four major approaches: medical, psychodynamic, psychometric, and behavioral assessment. Tests used will be determined by the assessment paradigm, the theoretical orientation of the examiner, and especially the demands of the case (whether an intellectual assessment is needed in addition to personality assessment; whether background history and presenting problems clearly delineate or obscure the factors responsible for the problems; etc.).

The sequence of testing instruments (along dimensions of structured–unstructured) is determined by the response style of the child, which also is reflective of the presenting problems. For example, the highly anxious or shy child usually needs more unstructured tasks without right or wrong answers until rapport is established. The examiner establishes rapport by assessing the response style of the child and offering variations of technique, including sequence of test instruments as well as interpersonal relating. Shy, unwilling, and minimally cooperative children will need different variations of technique.

Once the examiner begins the session, he or she must keep the child on task within the context of establishing a friendly personal relationship with the child. Clear instructions, presented without use of jargon; recognitions of signs of discomfort; design of the testing room, with good light and appropriately sized furniture; and minimal decorative distractions aid in eliciting valid functioning. Materials used in the test administrations should also be arranged to minimize distractions, especially when testing young or distractible children.

The examiner should be thoroughly familiar with the administration procedures of the instruments used, to allow for maximal interaction with the child and to permit observation of the child's behavior. Breaks should be tailored to the age and fatigability of the child. If reinforcers are used (they are particularly useful with children who have attentional, resistance, or dependency problems) to maintain productivity, the examiner should remain in control of the reinforcement schedule. Very young children or those with attentional problems should be scheduled for several appointments. Scheduling several sessions also permits retesting on selected tasks, should this be informative.

After the child is tested, the psychologist scores all materials and makes a series of interpretations and conclusions that comprise the content of the psychological report. The assessment role requires knowledge of traditional content areas in psychology and the nature of what is being tested, as well as the ability to integrate the test data into a relevant description of the child. The description should focus on the individual, as well as account for the complexity of his or her social environment, personal history, and behavioral observations. The ultimate goal is to develop relevant answers to specific questions, aid in problem solving, and facilitate decision making. Assessment should yield a description of the child's present level of functioning; considerations relating to etiology; prognosis; and treatment recommendations. The description should provide a deep and accurate understanding of the child, not just a mere labeling or classification.

In addition to giving feedback to the parents and professionals involved in the case, it is important to give feedback to the child. Immediately after the session, it is advisable to talk to the child about how he or she functioned in terms of cooperation, attitudes exhibited, reactions to difficult items, and so on, to help him or her maintain a positive attitude. In addition, any questions the child has should be answered. Finally, the examiner should again explain the purpose of the examination and the role the child played in the process. This feedback session may prevent any unnecessary discomfort the child may experience as a result of misconceptions and confusions about the process.

Among psychologists attitudes toward personality assessment in general have shown a decrease in commitment to the role of testing and a growing criticism of psychodiagnostic testing in particular. Reasons for the decline have been attributed to (1) the broadening of roles of practicing clinical/counseling psychologists; (2) time and economic constraints' making assessment less cost-effective; (3) disappointing research results concerning the psychometric properties of many assessment measures; (4) increased sophistication and criticism by consumers, together with court litigation; (5) theoretical or pragmatical opposition to testing from behavioral, humanistic, and community psychology; and (6) reduction of emphasis on clinical testing in graduate programs.

Professional time spent in psychological assessment by clinicians in various types of mental health agencies was reported to decline from 44% to 22% between 1959 and 1982; however, these reports did not differentiate between adult and child assessment practice. A larger proportion of time was reported in several surveys of those working with children. In spite of the decrease of time spent in assessment activities, 91% of employers expect job applicants to have testing skills, and 84% expect projective testing skills. Surveyed clinical psychologists also report a high usage rate, as do clinical child psychologists.

Most practitioners advise young clinicians to know one or several tests well. Although there is some variation in rank order over the years, surveys of how frequently tests are used in practice typically include the WISC, Bender–Gestalt, WAIS, MMPI, Rorschach, TAT, sentence completion tests, DAP, and the Stanford–Binet. The same responses have been obtained from practicing child clinicians, with the exception of the WAIS and the MMPI. Projective testing appears to vary in usage rates according to clinicians' theoretical orientations.

Psychologists indicate that they continue using some tests in spite of poor empirical support because (1) they are familiar and trusted; (2) they value their own experience over published research; (3) they view testing as an insightful process more than an objective technical skill; and (4) there are no better alternatives for clinical decision making.

There is some difference in the use of personality assessment instruments by child specialties. School psychologists use personality assessment measures infrequently, while the majority of clinical child psychologists use them. They also differ in the order of frequency of usage: Clinical child psychologists prefer drawings (DAP, K-F-D, H-T-P, etc.), Rorschach, TAT (and CAT), Bender–Gestalt, and sentence completion, in that order, whereas school psychologists rank them in essentially the opposite order.

Since personality assessment is an important professional activity for clinical child and school psychologists, data concerning training in assessment are of interest. At least two-thirds of experts in clinical child psychology training and practice endorse the idea of required child assessment coursework and three-quarters of clinical child and pediatric psychology internships require it, yet only 43% of clinical child psychology and 54% of general clinical psychology graduate programs surveyed provide this training. In addition, over three-quarters of the experts also endorse required clinical experience (or practica) in child assessment at the graduate level and 69% endorse it at the internship level, but only 37%–57% (depending on the technique) of graduate programs and 40%–88% of internships provide it.

When these training practices are viewed against findings of employers' expectations and clinicians' actual use of tests, training practices in child personality assessment appear to be insufficient. Even if the total time spent in assessment has declined from the time spent 20 years ago, in favor of other clinical activities and administration, not providing skills seems ill-advised. From the available data, the call appears to be for more, not less, training in child assessment with the various techniques.

What does the future hold for personality assessment? The demise of psychological assessment has been predicted over the past few years; however, continued development and practice are also strongly advocated. Korchin and Schuldberg (1981) note five new approaches to clinical assessment that indicate a future of renewed vitality.

In spite of the fact that psychologists have increased the time they devote to other professional activities, we have to conclude that personality assessment (especially of children) is a viable activity of professional psychologists. This conclusion is indexed by the continued practice and training in assessment, by vigorous theoretical activity concerning assessment, and by the rapid development of personality instruments.

REFERENCES

Achenbach, T. M. (1978). The Child Behavior Profile: I. Boys aged 6–11. *Journal of Consulting and Clinical Psychology, 46,* 478–488.

Achenbach, T. M. (1980). DSM-III in light of empirical research on the classification of child psychopathology. *Journal of the American Academy of Child Psychiatry, 19,* 395–412.

Achenbach, T. M. (1982). *Developmental psychopathology* (2nd ed.). New York: Wiley.

Achenbach, T. M. (1985). *Assessment and taxonomy of child and adolescent psychopathology.* Beverly Hills, CA: Sage.

Achenbach, T. M., & Edelbrock, C. S. (1978). The classification of child psychopathology: A review and analysis of empirical efforts. *Psychological Bulletin, 85,* 1275–1301.

Achenbach, T. M., & Edelbrock, C. S. (1979). The Child Behavior Profile: II. Boys aged 12–16 and girls aged 6–11 and 12–16. *Journal of Consulting and Clinical Psychology, 47,* 223–233.

Achenbach, T. M., & Edelbrock, C. S. (1981). Behavior problems and competencies reported by parents of normal and disturbed children aged four through sixteen. *Monographs of the Society for Research in Child Development, 46* (Serial No. 188).

American Psychiatric Association. (1952). *Diagnostic and statistical manual of mental disorders.* Washington, DC: Author.

American Psychiatric Association. (1968). *Diagnostic and statistical manual of mental disorders.* (2nd ed.). Washington, DC: Author.

American Psychiatric Association. (1980). *Diagnostic and statistical manual of mental disorders.* (3nd ed.). Washington, DC: Author.

American Psychiatric Association. (1987). *Diagnostic and statistical manual of mental disorders.* (3rd ed., rev.). Washington, DC: Author.

American Psychiatric Association. (1982). *Graduate study in psychology.* Washington, DC: Author.

Association of Psychology Internship Centers. (1984). *Directory of internships in clinical and counseling psychology* (13th ed.). Washington, DC: Author.

Bagnato, S. J. (1980). The efficacy of diagnostic reports as individualized guides to prescriptive goal planning. *Exceptional Children, 46,* 554–557.

Bellak, L., & Bellak, S. S. (1949). *The Children's Apperception Test.* New York: C.P.S.

Berger, L. (1968). Psychological testing: Treatment and research implications. *Journal of Consulting and Clinical Psychology, 32,* 179–181.

Bersoff, D. N. (1973). Silk purses into sow's ears: The decline of psychological testing and a suggestion for its redemption. *American Psychologist, 28,* 892–899.

Blashfield, R. K., & Draguns, J. G. (1976). Toward a taxonomy of psychopathology: The purpose of psychiatric classification. *British Journal of Psychiatry, 129,* 574–583.

Block, J. (1977). Advancing the psychology of personality: Paradigmatic shift or improving the quality of research. In D. Magnussen & N. S. Endler (Eds.), *Personality at the crossroads: Current issues in interactional psychology.* Hillsdale, NJ: Erlbaum.

Brown, W. R., & McGuire, J. M. (1976). Current psychological assessment practices. *Professional Psychology, 7,* 475–484.

Buros, O. K. (1978). *The eighth mental measurements yearbook.* Highland Park, NJ: Gryphon Press.

Buros, O. K. (1985). *The ninth mental measurements yearbook.* Lincoln: University of Nebraska.

Butcher, J. N., & Owen, P. L. (1978). Objective personality inventories: Recent research and some contemporary issues. In B. B. Wolman (Ed.), *Clinical diagnosis of mental disorders: A handbook* (pp. 475–545). New York: Plenum.

Cerreto, M. C., & Tuma, J. M. (1977). Distribution of DSM-II diagnoses in a child psychiatric setting. *Journal of Abnormal Child Psychology, 5,* 147–155.

Cleveland, S. E. (1976). Reflections on the rise and fall of psychodiagnosis. *Professional Psychology, 7,* 309–318.

Coles, G. S. (1978). The learning disabilities test battery: Empirical and social issues. *Harvard Educational Review, 48,* 313–340.

Coleman, J. C. (1980). *Abnormal psychology and modern life* (6th ed.). Glenview, IL: Scott, Foresman.

Dana, R. H. (1984). Personality assessment: Practice and teaching for the next decade. *Journal of Personality Assessment, 48,* 46–57.

Edelbrock, C. S., & Achenbach, T. M. (1980). A typology of Child Behavior Profile patterns: Distribution and correlates for disturbed children ages 6–16. *Journal of Abnormal Child Psychology, 8,* 441–470.

Elbert, J. C. (1984). Training in child diagnostic assessment: A survey of clinical psychology graduate programs. *Journal of Clinical Child Psychology, 13,* 122–133.

Elbert, J. C., & Holden, E. W. (1987). Child diagnostic assessment: A survey of training in clinical child psychology internships. *Professional Psychology: Research and Practice, 18,* 587–596.

Endicott, J., & Spitzer, R. L. (1978). A diagnostic interview: The Schedule for Affective Disorders and Schizophrenia. *Archives of General Psychiatry, 35,* 837–844.

Erickson, M. T., Roberts, M. C., & Tuma, J. M. (1985). Guidelines for training psychologists to work with children, youth, and families. In J. M. Tuma (Ed.), *Proceedings: Conference on Training Clinical Child Psychologists* (pp. 164–167). Baton Rouge, LA: Section on Clinical Child Psychology, Division of Clinical Psychology, American Psychological Association.

Exner, J. E. (1974). *The Rorschach: A comprehensive system. Vol. 2. Current research and advanced interpretation.* New York: Wiley.

Exner, J. E., & Weiner, I. B. (1982). *The Rorschach: A comprehensive system. Vol. 3. Assessment of children and adolescents.* New York: Wiley.

Exner, J. E., Thomas, E. A., & Mason, B. (1985). Children's Rorschachs: Description and prediction. *Journal of Personality Assessment, 49,* 13–20.

Flavell, J. H. (1963). *The developmental psychology of Jean Piaget.* New York: Van Nostrand Reinhold.

Fard, K., Hudgens, R. W., & Welner, A. (1978). Undiagnosed psychiatric illness in adolescents. *Archives of General Psychiatry, 35,* 279–282.

Freud, A. (1965). *Normality and pathology in childhood.* New York: International Universities Press.

Garber, J. (1984). Classification of childhood psychopathology: A developmental perspective. *Child Development, 55,* 30–48.

Garfield, S. L., & Kurtz, R. (1973). Attitudes toward training in diagnostic testing: A survey of directors of internship training. *Journal of Consulting and Clinical Psychology, 40,* 350–355.

Garfield, S. L., & Kurtz, R. (1976). Clinical psychologists in the 1970s. *American Psychologist, 31,* 1–9.

Garmezy, N. (1978). DSM-III: Never mind the psychologists—is it good for the children? *Clinical Psychologist, 31,* 4–6.

Gelfand, D. M., & Peterson, L. (1985). *Child development and psychopathology.* Beverly Hills, CA: Sage.

Glaser, R. (1981). The future of testing: A research agenda for cognitive psychology and psychometrics. *American Psychologist, 36,* 923–936.

Goh, D. S., Teslow, C. J., & Fuller, G. B. (1981). The practice of psychological assessment among school psychologists. *Professional Psychology: Research and Practice, 12,* 696–706.

Goldfried, M. R., Stricker, G., & Weiner, I. B. (1979). *Rorschach handbook of clinical and research applications.* Englewood Cliffs, NJ: Prentice-Hall.

Goldman, J., Stein, C. L., & Guerry, S. (1983). *Psychological methods of child assessment.* New York: Brunner/Mazel.

Gough, H. G. (1971). Some reflections on the meaning of psychodiagnosis. *American Psychologist, 26,* 160–167.

Group for the Advancement of Psychiatry. (1966). *Psychopathological disorders of childhood: Theoretical considerations and a proposed classification.* Washington, DC: Author.

Hathaway, S. R., & McKinley, J. (1943). *Manual for the MMPI.* New York: Psychological Corporation.

Hollis, J. W., & Donn, P. A. (1979). *Psychological report writing: Theory and practice* (2nd ed.). Muncie, IN: Accelerated Development.

Holmes, T. H., & Rahe, R. (1967). The Social Readjustment Rating Scale. *Journal of Psychosomatic Research, 11,* 213–218.

Holt, R. R. (1967). Diagnostic testing: Present situation and future prospects. *Journal of Nervous and Mental Disease, 144,* 444–465.

Holt, R. R. (Ed.). (1968). Editor's foreword. In D. Rapaport, M. M. Gill, & R. Schafer, *Diagnostic psychological testing* (rev. ed., pp. 1–44). New York: International Universities Press.

Huber, J. T. (1961). *Report writing in psychology and psychiatry.* New York: Harper & Row.

Hutt, M. L. (1980). *The Michigan Picture Test—Revised: Manual.* New York: Grune & Stratton.

Isett, R., & Roszkowski, M. (1979). Consumer preferences for psychological report contents in a residential school and center for the mentally retraded. *Psychology in the Schools, 16,* 402–407.

Ivnik, R. J. (1977). Uncertain status of psychological tests in clinical psychology. *Professional Psychology, 8,* 206–213.

Johnson, J. H. (1985). General program related issues in clinical child specialty training: Survey input from child oriented clinicians. In J. M. Tuma (Ed.), *Proceedings: Conference on Training Clinical Child Psychologists* (pp. 78–81). Baton Rouge, LA: Section on Clinical Child Psychology, Division of Clinical Psychology, American Psychological Association.

Kaplan, R. M., & Saccazzo, D. P. (1982). *Psychological testing: Principles, applications, and issues.* Belmont, MA: Wadsworth.

Keyser, D. J., & Sweetland, R. C. (Eds.). (1983–1987). *Test critiques* (Vols. 1–5). Kansas City, MO: Test Corporation of America.

Klopfer, W. G., & Taulbee, E. S. (1976). Projective test. *Annual Review of Psychology, 27,* 543–567.

Knoff, H. M. (Ed.). (1986). The personality assessment report and the feedback and planning conference. In Howard M. Knoff (Ed.), *The assessment of child and adolescent personality.* New York: Guilford Press.

Korchin, S. J. (1976). *Modern clinical psychology.* New York: Basic Books.

Korchin, S. J., & Schuldberg, D. (1981). The future of clinical assessment. *American Psychologist, 36,* 1147–1158.

Kovacs, M. (1981). Rating scales to assess depression in school-aged children. *Acta Paedopsychiatrica, 46,* 305–315.

Kovacs, M., & Beck, A. T. (1977). An empirical–clinical approach toward a definition of childhood depression. In J. G. Schulterbrandt & A. Raskin (Eds.), *Depression in childhood: Diagnosis, treatment, and conceptual models* (pp. 43–57). New York: Raven Press.

Lachar, D., Kline, R. B., & Boersma, D. C. (1986). The Personality Inventory for Children: Approaches to actuarial interpretation in clilnic and school settings. In H. M. Knoff (Ed.), *The assessment of child and adolescent personality* (pp. 245–271). New York: Guilford Press.

LaGreca, A. (1985). Training survey results. *Newsletter of the Society of Pediatric Psychology, 9(3),* 19–21.

Levy, M. R., & Fox, H. M. (1975). Psychological testing is alive and well. *Professional Psychology, 6,* 420–424.

Lewandowski, D. G., & Saccuzzo, D. P. (1976). The decline of psychological testing. *Professional Psychology, 7,* 177–184.

Levitt, E. E. (1973). Internship versus campus: 1964 and 1971. *Professional Psychology, 4,* 129–132.

Lubin, B., Larsen, R. M., Matarazzo, J. D., & Seever, M. F. (1986). Selected characteristics of psychologists and psychological assessment in five settings: 1959–1982. *Professional Psychology: Research and Practice, 17,* 155–157.

Lubin, B., & Lubin, A. W. (1972). Patterns of psychological services in the U.S.: 1959–1969. *Professional Psychology, 3,* 63–65.

Lubin, B., Wallis, R. R., & Paine, C. (1971). Patterns of psychological test usage in the United States: 1935–1969. *Professional Psychology, 2,* 70–74.

Maloney, M. P., & Ward, M. P. (1976). *Psychological assessment: A conceptual approach.* New York: Oxford University Press.

Matarazzo, J. D. (1978). The interview: Its reliability and validity in psychiatric diagnosis. In B. B. Wolman (Ed.), *Clinical diagnosis of mental disorders: A handbook* (pp. 47–96). New York: Plenum.

McArthur, D. S., & Roberts, G. E. (1982). *Roberts Apperception Test for Children manual.* Los Angeles: Western Psychological Services.

Meeks, J. E. (1973). Group delinquency reactions. In A. M. Freedman, H. I. Kaplan, & B. J. Sadock (Eds.), *Comprehensive textbook of psychiatry* (Vol. 2, pp. 2136–2142). Baltimore: Williams & Wilkins.

Millon, T. (1977). *Millon Multiaxial Clinical Inventory.* Minneapolis: National Computer Systems.

Millon, T. (1982). On the nature of clinical health psychology. In T. Millon, C. J. Green, & R. B. Meagher (Eds.), *Handbook of clinical health psychology* (pp. 1–28). New York: Plenum.

Millon, T. (1984). On the renaissance of personality assessment and personality theory. *Journal of Personality Assessment, 48,* 450–466.

Mischel, W. (1968). *Personality and assessment.* New York: Wiley.

Mitchell, J. V., Reynolds, C. R., & Elliott, S. N. (1980, March). Test news from the Buros Institute. *Measurement News,* pp. 4, 6, 9, 16.

Murray, H. A. (1943). *Thematic Apperception Test manual.* Cambridge, MA: Harvard University Press.

Ownby, R. L., Wallbrown, F. H., & Brown, D. Y. (1982). Special education teachers' perceptions of reports written by school psychologists. *Perceptual and Motor Skills, 55,* 955–961.

Petzelt, J. T., & Craddick, R. (1978). Present meaning of assessment in psychology. *Professional Psychology, 9,* 487–591.

Piaget, J. (1950). *Psychology of intelligence.* New York: Harcourt, Brace & World.

Piotrowski, C. (1984). The status of projective techniques: Or, "wishing won't make it go away." *Journal of Clinical Psychology, 40,* 1495–1502.

Piotrowski, C., & Keller, J. W. (1984). Psychodiagnostic testing in APA-approved clinical psychology programs. *Professional Psychology: Research and Practice, 15,* 350–356.

Pruitt, J. A., Smith, M. C., Thelen, M. H., & Lubin, E. (1985). Attitudes of academic clinical psychologists toward projective techniques: 1968–1983. *Professional Psychology: Research and Practice, 16,* 781–788.

Rabin, A. I. (Ed.). (1981). *Assessment with projective techniques.* New York: Wiley.

Rabin, A. I., & Hayes, D. L. (1978). Concerning the rationale of diagnostic testing. In B. B. Wolman (Ed.), *Clinical diagnosis of mental disorders: A handbook* (pp. 579–599). New York: Plenum Press.

Reisman, J. M. (1973). *Principles of psychotherapy with children.* New York: Wiley.

Reynolds, C. R., & Elliott, S. N. (1983). Trends in development and publication of educational and psychological tests. *Professional Psychology: Research and Practice, 14,* 554–558.

Reynolds, C. R., & Richmond, B. O. (1979). Factor structure and construct validity of "What I Think and Feel": The Revised Children's Manifest Anxiety Scale. *Journal of Personality Assessment, 43,* 281–283.

Reynolds, C. R., & Richmond, B. O. (1985). *Revised Children's Manifest Anxiety Scale: Manual*. Los Angeles: Western Psychological Services.

Reynolds, W. M. (1979). Psychological tests: Clinical usage versus psychometric quality. *Professional Psychology, 10*, 325–329.

Reynolds, W. M., & Sundberg, N. D. (1976). Recent research trends in testing. *Journal of Personality Assessment, 40*, 228–233.

Roberts, M. C., Erickson, M. T., & Tuma, J. M. (1985). Addressing the needs: Guidelines for training psychologists to work with children, youth and families. *Journal of Clinical Child Psychology, 14*, 70–79.

Rogers, C. (1951). *Client-centered therapy*. Boston: Houghton Mifflin.

Rorschach, H. (1942). *Psychodiagnostics: A diagnostic test based on perception*. (P. Lemkau & B. Kronenberg, Trans.) New York: Grune & Stratton. (Original work published 1921)

Rosen, B. M., Badn, A. K., & Kramer, M. (1964). Demographic and diagnostic characteristics of psychiatric clinic outpatients in the U.S.A., 1961. *American Journal of Orthopsychiatry, 34*, 455–468.

Rutter, M., & Shaffer, D. (1980). DSM-III: A step forward or back in terms of the classification of child psychiatric disorders? *Journal of the American Academy of Child Psychiatry, 19*, 371–394.

Rutter, M., Shaffer, D., & Shepherd, M. (1975). *A multi-axial classification of child psychiatric disorders*. Geneva: World Health Organization.

Sarason, I. G., Johnson, J. H., & Siegel, J. M. (1978). Assessing the impact of life changes: Development of the Life Experiences Survey. *Journal of Consulting and Clinical Psychology, 46*, 932–946.

Sattler, J. M. (1982). *Assessment of children's intelligence and special abilities* (2nd ed.). New York: Allyn & Bacon.

Seagull, E. A. W. (1979). Writing the report of a psychological assessment of a child. *Journal of Clinical Child Psychology, 8*, 39–42.

Shellenberger, S. (1982). Presentation and interpretation of psychological data in educational settings. In C. R. Reynolds & T. B. Gutkin (Eds.), *The handbook of school psychology* (pp. 51–81). New York: Wiley.

Shemberg, K., & Keeley, S. (1974). Psychodiagnostic training in the academic setting: Past and present. *Journal of Consulting and Clinical Psychology, 34*, 205–211.

Shemberg, K. M., & Leventhal, D. B. (1981). Attitudes of internship directors toward preinternship training and clinical training models. *Professional Psychology: Research and Practice, 12*, 639–646.

Shneidman, E. S. (1952). MAPS test. *Projective Techniques Monograph, 2*, 1–92.

Singer, M. T. (1977). The Rorschach as a transaction. In M. A. Rickers-Ovianskina (Ed.), *Rorschach psychology*. Huntington, NY: Krieger.

Small, L. (1972). The uncommon importance of psychodiagnosis. *Professional Psychology, 3*, 111–119.

Smith, D. K. (1984). Practicing school psychologists: Their characteristics, activities, and populations served. *Professional Psychology: Research and Practice, 15*, 798–810.

Spielberger, C. (1973). *State–Trait Anxiety Scale for Children*. Palo Alto, CA: Consulting Psychologists Press.

Sroufe, L. A., & Rutter, M. (1984). The domain of developmental psychopathology. *Child Development, 55*, 17–29.

Sundberg, N. D. (1961). The practice of psychological testing in clinical services in the United States. *American Psychologist, 16*, 79–83.

Tallent, N. (1976). *Psychological report writing*. Englewood Cliffs, NJ: Prentice-Hall.

Thelen, M. H., Varble, D. L., & Johnson, J. (1968). Attitudes of academic clinical psychologists toward projective techniques. *American Psychologist, 23*, 517–521.

Tidwell, R., & Wetter, J. (1978). Parental evaluations of psychoeducational reports: A case study. *Psychology in the Schools, 15*, 209–215.

Tuma, J. M. (Ed.). (1985). *Proceedings: National Conference of Training Clinical Child Psychologists*. Baton Rouge, LA: Section on Clinical Child Psychology, Division of Clinical Psychology, American Psychological Association.

Tuma, J. M., & Cohen, R. (1981). *Pediatric psychology; An investigation of factors relative to practice and training*. Unpublished manuscript.

Tuma, J. M., & Grabert, J. (1983). Internship and postdoctoral training in pediatric and clinical child psychology: A survey. *Journal of Pediatric Psychology, 8*, 245–260.

Tuma, J. M., & Pratt, J. M. (1982). Clinical child psychology training and practice: A survey. *Journal of Clinical Child Psychology, 11*, 27–34.

Tuma, J. M., & Salcedo, R. (1982). *Training and practice of Division 37 members: A survey*. Unpublished manuscript.

Wade, T. C., & Baker, T. B. (1977). Opinions and use of psychological tests: A survey of clinical psychologists. *American Psychologist. 22*, 874–882.

Wade, T. C., Baker, T. B., Morton, T. L., & Baker, L. J. (1978). The status of psychological testing in clinical psychology: Relationships between test use and professional activities and orientations. *Journal of Personality Assessment, 42*, 3–9.

Weiner, I. B. (1972). Does psychodiagnosis have a future? *Journal of Personality Assessment, 36*, 534–546.

Weiner, I. B. (1980). Psychopathology in adolescence. In J. Adelson (Ed.), *Handbook of adolescent psychology*. New York: Wiley.

Weiner, I. B., & Del Gaudio, A. C. (1976). Psychopathology in adolescence: An epidemiological study. *Archives of General Psychiatry, 33*, 187–193.

Werry, J. S. (1979). The childhood psychoses. In H. C. Quay & J. S. Werry (Eds.), *Psychopathological disorders of childhood* (2nd ed., pp. 43–89). New York: Wiley.

Wirt, R. D., Lachar, D., Kleindinst, J. K., & Seat, P. D. (1977). *Multidimensional descripton of child personality: A manual for the Personality Inventory for Children*. Los Angeles: Western Psychological Services.

Woody, R. H. (1969). *Behavioral problem children in the schools: Diagnosis and behavioral modification*. New York: Appleton-Century-Crofts.

2

Personality Assessment: Critical Issues for Research and Practice

DAVID W. BARNETT
University of Cincinnati

GREGG M. MACMANN
Institute of Clinical Training and Research,
The Devereux Foundation

P ersonality assessment has had a tentative status within professional psychology for the past several decades, and an initial question for some readers may be "Why hold on?" At the same time, many psychologists are concerned with what appear to be shallow approaches to assessment and intervention, and perhaps all would agree that the most important criteria for the overall evaluation of clinical and educational decisions are those related to enhanced personal and social development, rather than lesser but more easily measurable objectives.

Instead of a review of what amounts to a vast, often inconclusive, and weighty literature, our focus is more narrow: We offer an opinion on what would be helpful for professional practices associated with the topic. An underlying theme of the chapter is the need for new research consistent with the goal of defining an "epistemology of practice" (Schön, 1983)—research that involves the analysis of successful practice in real-life situations.

AN OVERVIEW OF THE CHAPTER

Despite the enormous controversies, personal and social development *is* the broadest

context for assessment and intervention design across a broad array of child and adolescent practices involving clinical, educational, and vocational decisions (Barnett, 1986). Procedures are needed to enable effective outcomes in difficult and ambiguous situations, when professionals would like to apply the tools of their trade with confidence. However, almost since their inception, personality measures have been subject to extensive criticism as summarized in the following paragraphs.

First, the inherent difficulties in "knowing" the personality of an individual are fundamental. Competing theories and measurement differences make any consensus unlikely. The question becomes one of demonstrating useful information through probabilistic statements, a process defined in part by error rates as well as by meaningful predictions. However, the need to account for "person" variables is unassailable—an important distinction.

Second, personality assessment for children has special difficulties, both theoretical and practical. The issues are made evident by research that deals with the continuity of personal and social development, and the processes of psychosocial change. Evidence exists for both coherence and continuity of development, and significant change within limits that are not easily defined for individuals (Block & Block, 1980; Emmerich, 1966; Moss & Sussman, 1980; Plomin, 1987; Rutter, 1984). When viewed from the perspective of individual development, Emmerich's (1966) review has stood the test of time: "Impressive as the evidence for the early determination of personality may seem, there are also grounds for believing that personality ordinarily remains open to change over extended periods" (p. 237). The issue in professional practice is one of enhancing the developmental trajectory of high-risk or maladapted children, and surprisingly little is known about the process (Gallagher & Ramey, 1987). A major goal of personality research has been the identification of traits or person variables that would improve the selection of specific and effective treatments, but such attributes have remained elusive thus far. Intervention design is in its infancy, and the course of personal and social development is complexly determined by psychological, biological, and accidental events (Bandura, 1985, 1986; Rutter, 1984).

A third issue has been the debate concerning the relative importance of situational versus personal determinants of behavior. The focal points have been the obvious control that situations exert on behavior, and the relatively modest predictive power of many "person" variables. War was waged over this issue in the 1960s (Mischel, 1968; Peterson, 1968), but most assume an interactionist position at present (Magnusson & Endler, 1977). Perhaps Bandura (1986) has put the debate to rest: "[B]ehavior, cognitive and other personal factors, and environmental influences all operate interactively as determinants of each other" (p. 23). However, the relative influence of specific factors in unique situations will vary with persons, situations, and behaviors (Bandura, 1985).

It would be easy simply to state that more basic research is needed in personality development and the design of corresponding assessment techniques. We stretch the analysis of needed research to the consideration of potential applications of personality measurement to individual children and intervention design—by far the most critical gap at present.

In this chapter, we first analyze personality measurement within the traditional categories of reliability and validity. The focus is on central theoretical and practical issues defined in terms of *decision* outcomes related to test usage. Second, we present fundamental dilemmas for research and professional practices associated with personality measurement. Third, we make suggestions in the form of component strategies for personal and social assessment. The challenges of behavioral assessment are integrated into the discussion as well, because they are inherently related to child intervention outcomes.

RELIABILITY

"Reliability" generally pertains to the consistency of measurement, and enables the estimation of test error. The classical model developed by Spearman at the turn of the 20th century assumed that each score has two components: a "true score," which is estimated from a person's obtained or "observed score" on a measure, and "test error." Traits are assumed to be stable, and error is assumed to be random or uncorrelated. The reliability of a test may be defined by the variation (or variance) in true scores divided by the variance in observed scores, or the ratio of true-score to observed-score variance (e.g., Thorndike, 1982). The definition of reliability from classical test theory makes the assumption of repeated measurements of an individual's performance on parallel tests, so that fluctuations in scores enable the estimation of error.

Although intuitively attractive and amenable to statistical manipulations, the classical model has significant complexities that have been debated for nearly as long as the model has dominated measurement theory (Lord & Novick, 1968). The greatest concern is that there is no direct link between the actual obtained score and the hypothetical true score. In psychology, the true score is always inferred, and for many traits critics have argued that the true score often seems to exist more vividly in the minds of test developers than in behavioral evidence. The definition of reliability based on classical test theory cannot be directly tested, and there are significant theoretical divisions in reliability theory. Further, there is no single reliability estimate for a test. A range of reliability estimates is determined on the basis of logic and through specific statistical and experimental procedures.

Some think that the concept of true score should be abandoned (e.g., Lumsden, 1976). However, the classical model and its derivatives have dominated test theory, and therefore test development (Ghiselli, Campbell, & Zedeck, 1981). Thus, many contemporary practices associated with test usage are based on the assumptions that stem from this model.

For any test, reliability can be examined in numerous ways; the methods account for different sources of error. Traditionally, experimental and statistical procedures are used to present reliability data in four ways: internal consistency, test–retest reliability, alternate forms, and analysis-of-variance procedures.

Internal Consistency

The reliability of a scale can be estimated from a single administration. Statistical analyses are used to determine the degree of "internal consistency" of responses to test items. An early procedure was (1) to "split" the test into equivalent parts, (2) to correlate the halves, and (3) to "correct" the obtained correlation that resulted from the briefer scale to estimate the reliability coefficient for the full-length test. The Spearman–Brown prophecy formula, the basic method to estimate the resulting reliability from the test halves, has other uses as well, and is discussed in a subsequent section concerned with aggregation (see Equation 2, below). A basic problem is that the resulting reliability coefficients derived from splitting the test in various ways (e.g., odd–even; first half–second half) will vary.

Coefficient alpha (Cronbach, 1951) provides a more general solution for internal-consistency reliability, in effect, representing the average of all possible item splits. It is derived from the variance of the items relative to the variance of the total test, or from the average interitem correlations, and establishes the "upper limit" for the test's reliability based on content sampling (Nunnally, 1978, p. 230). If coefficient alpha for a measure is low, the items have little in common and/or are too few in number.

Internal-consistency estimates are widely used in practice and are especially important for constructs hypothesized to change or fluctuate over time. Although it appears straightforward, coefficient alpha does present interpretive difficulties. Since coefficient alpha increases as a function of the magnitude of interitem correlations and number of correlated items, scales with similar reliabilities may have very different properties. High reliabilities may be achieved through a small number of highly correlated items or through large numbers of items with modest or even low interitem correlations. Tests that have very high estimates of internal consistency may be measuring a very homogeneous trait, may be asking redundant questions, or may be asking highly related questions repeatedly.

Test–Retest Reliability and Alternative Forms

Equally straightforward in description, the test–retest method involves a second administration of a scale within a specified interval (usually about 2 weeks). The results of the two administrations are correlated; thus, an estimate of the stability of the measurement is provided. It has been argued that test–retest reliability is less important to personality measurement because of a number of confounding variables: the unknown effects of two administrations of the questions or test stimuli; unknown changes in life circumstances during the retest interval; changes that occur in the testing situations; and the unknown influence of these factors upon estimates of the stability of the trait.

Reliability estimates also can be derived from alternative or equivalent forms of a scale, although this method is less frequently used in personality measurement. Simply, two (or more) measures of a trait are developed from an item pool. When this method is used to examine test–retest reliability, the effects of memory in responding to specific items are eliminated.

From the viewpoint of professional practices, the stability estimates based on test–retest procedures are often important. Practitioners are quite concerned about potential fluctuations of trait estimates over brief time periods, and the corresponding degree to which intervening variables may influence interpretations of various constructs and thus decisions that stem from test usage. Time-limited decisions are troublesome (even embarrassing) for many professional practices. A low test–retest reliability coefficient is only problematic if the behavior measured is presumed to be relatively stable. In this case, questions can be raised about the measurement procedure, the trait, or the power of intervening variables.

Analysis-of-Variance Procedures

Related to the classical model, analysis-of-variance procedures (Thorndike, 1967, 1982) and generalizability theory, advanced by Cronbach and associates (Cronbach, Gleser, Nanda, & Rajaratnam, 1972), have been proposed. Logically, the procedures enable questions to be raised about both the true-score and error components. Thorndike (1982) writes from a psychometric perspective:

What is included under the heading "error variance" depends on how the universe that the test score is presumed to represent is defined, with certain sources of variance being treated as error under one definition . . . and as true score under another definition. (p. 157)

The *realities* are that when tests are administered on different occasions, under different conditions, or through different procedures, variation in true-score estimates is a rule rather than an exception. Generalizability theory recasts the reliability problem "into a question of accuracy of generalization" (Cronbach et al., 1972, p. 15): An analysis is made of how test scores that result from a particular measure *generalize* to other subjects and to the universe of possible conditions. The conditions that are potentially examined include tasks, time of observations, situations or settings, and the performance of different raters.

Classical notions of test error have been challenged in a similar way by behaviorists. The questions raised are important because the criteria typically used *are* tied directly to issues of usefulness by way of intervention design. Concerns related to classical

measurement assumptions are described in the following way by Cone (1981):

Error is just a blanket way of referring to a host of "don't knows," none of which are random. . . . [T]he term "random" is really a pseudonym for "haven't found out yet" . . . since all behavior is lawful whether we know the controlling variables or not. (p. 61)

Analysis-of-variance procedures were for a time deemed potentially helpful in many aspects of behavioral assessment, although their overall contribution is likely to be limited, since the central tenets are different (Hayes, Nelson, & Jarrett, 1986). Behavioral assessment approaches have not resolved the basic measurement dilemmas, but the topics are dissimilar. In general, the most critical reliability and validity questions in behavioral assessment apply to (1) problem identification, (2) treatment selection, and (3) outcome measures of the therapeutic process (Barrios & Hartmann, 1986). These are not well treated through analysis-of-variance procedures. However, some studies are quite useful. For example, Hansen, Tisdelle, and O'Dell (1985) used generalizability procedures to establish the overall equivalence of audio versus direct observation of parent–child interactions, although low-frequency behaviors likely to have clinical significance had to be dropped from the analysis (e.g., crying, destructiveness).

The generalizability studies pertinent to professional practices are few (cf. Jones, Reid, & Patterson, 1975), and the methods based on analysis-of-variance procedures typically have rigorous design requirements that hamper many applications. Multifaceted studies require large samples, and other clinical realities introduce the potential for confounding design factors that are difficult to control, especially with more than two facets (Thorndike, 1982). The conceptual issues, however, are clearly critical to individual assessment. With generalizability theory, the distinction between reliability and validity is deliberately blurred. The model enables questions to be raised about "error." Sources of error become information from an experimental view. The study by Hansen et al. (1985) illustrates both the power of the techniques associated with analysis-of-variance procedures, and their difficulties: General relationships may be studied, but specific behaviors may require idiographic measurements.

Other Reliability Issues

Standards for Reliability

Well-established conventions for reliability coefficients have been described as follows (Nunnally, 1978; Stagner, 1948). Reliabilities for research purposes should range from .70 to .80 in order to be deemed "acceptable." For individual decisions, it has been argued that reliabilities should be .90 at a minimum, with coefficients of .95 the desirable standard.

Reliabilities can be directly interpreted as explained or true variance. However, for individual decisions, the "standard error of measurement" is a more meaningful representation of precision. Conceptually, the standard error of measurement is the standard deviation or variability of observed scores, given a true score, which is based on the hypothetical repeated measurement of an individual with parallel tests. In practice, an individual's true score is not known, but is estimated from a fallible observed score. The appropriate statistic for this situation is the "standard error of estimation," or standard deviation of true scores, given an observed score (Dudek, 1979). The standard error of estimation is used to establish a "confidence interval," which indicates the probability that an individual's true score lies within a specified range. Over repeated "theoretical" test occasions, estimates of true score (based on obtained scores) vary around the actual true score because of error, and thus presumably because of chance factors.

Three issues concerning standards for reliability are of primary importance for professional practices. The first two are considered here; the third bridges the gap between reliability and validity and is discussed in a subsequent section.

First, confidence intervals that apply to the prediction of true scores should be established around the "estimated true score." Nunnally (1978) points out that "obtained scores are biased estimates of true scores.

Scores above the mean are biased upward, and scores below the mean are biased downward" (p. 217). More extreme scores contain more "error" (i.e., a score that is two standard deviations from the mean contains twice as much error as a score that is one standard deviation from the mean), and thus are more biased. Obtained scores easily can be adjusted to enable the use of an estimated true score for creating confidence intervals, as follows:

$$X' = \bar{X} + (r_{XX})(X - \bar{X})$$

where $\bar{X}$ is the mean of X, r_{XX} is the reliability of X, and X is the observed score. Although this issue is often trivial in a numerical and statistical sense (scores may be "adjusted" by small amounts), an important exception to the triviality is when specific *cutting* scores are used for professional decisions—implicitly or explicitly, a common practice.

Second, the calculation of standard error of measurement should be placed within the context of a specific reliability estimate, intended for a specific function (Sechrest, 1984). Many test authors use internal estimates of reliability (e.g., coefficient alpha) to establish confidence intervals for test users[1]. This type of reliability only takes into account the consistency and number of items. Confidence intervals to describe the stability of the behavior over time, and the generalizability of estimates across potential raters, are often unexamined. For these situations, the "standard error of prediction," or standard deviation of expected scores across raters or occasions, is the appropriate statistic (Dudek, 1979; Lord & Novick, 1968; Schulte & Borich, 1985).

Third, and most important, reliability must be viewed within a context of validity. For example, the standard errors of prediction associated with independent estimates of the construct or behavior of interest need to be considered—a discussion resumed below in regard to multitrait–multimethod analyses.

Aggregation

The fundamental method to increase the reliability of a measure is simply to increase the number of items. The relationship between test length and reliability is defined by the Spearman–Brown formula:

$$r_{XX}' = \frac{kr_{XX}}{1 + (k - 1)r_{XX}}$$

where r_{XX}' is the reliability of expanded test form, r_{XX} is the original reliability of X, and k is the proportionate increase in test length. For example, in determining split-half reliability, $k = 2$.

Through a series of widely cited studies, Epstein (1984) has applied this basic relationship to issues concerning personality measurement. Rushton, Brainerd, and Pressley (1983) also have reviewed the principle of aggregation and have reached a similar conclusion: Many weak or unconvincing correlational relationships found in the personality, social, and cognitive development literature are "consequences of failure to aggregate" (p. 18).

Epstein (1984) theorized that "personality coefficients," a disparaging term applied to low but significant correlations of .20–.30 often found in personality research, might be the results of a failure to aggregate based on the analysis of units of behavior that were simply too small; these results might be similar to the results achieved when looking at item correlations. He summarized the effects of different aggregation strategies in the following manner:

1. Aggregation over stimuli and situations reduces error variance associated with the uniqueness of particular stimuli and situations. . . .
2. Aggregation over occasions and over trials within occasions reduces error variance associated with changes over time. . . .
3. Aggregation over judges or raters reduces error variance associated with individual differences among judges. . . .
4. Aggregation over modes of responses reduces error variance associated with different response modes. . . . (pp. 260–261)

Through aggregation, Epstein was able to achieve respectable correlations (as high as .80 and .90) for traditional constructs associated with personality measurement. Epstein (1984) summarized the results in the following way: "[S]table response dispositions can be demonstrated when responses are averaged over adequate samples of behavior but not necessarily when single instances of behavior are observed" (p. 214). The respectable stability coefficients obtained through aggregation of responses, he argued, lead to improved evidence for validity across a number of constructs and measures. Through aggregation, Epstein (1984) found support for the following statements: "(a) behavior is situationally specific, (b) behavior is general across situations, and (c) people have broad cross-situational response dispositions" (p. 263).

Of course, nothing is this simple in personality measurement, and aggregation is not a panacea, as pointed out by Epstein (1984) and others (Bandura, 1986; McFall & McDonel, 1986; Mischel, 1984a; Mischel & Peake, 1982). First, aggregation leads to a corresponding loss of information. If observations are aggregated over any of the four dimensions listed above, variance attributed to the dimensions is termed "error." For example, if observations are aggregated over situations, then information related to the potential variance of situations may be less readily apparent. Second, Mischel (1984a) argues that Epstein's research does not deal with the central issues of "the classic personality debate": the manner in which individuals *discriminate* situations in relationship to their social behavior, and the usefulness of inferring traits in predicting actions in a given context. In Bandura's (1986) words, "Aggregation inflates correlations but yields indeterminate or empty predictions" (p. 10). Furthermore, a high degree of behavioral consistency logically cannot be used to argue for the existence of traits without other considerations pertaining to validity (see McFall & McDonel, 1986, for a discussion of these concerns in addition to other related problems).

Aggregation may elucidate one area of difficulty but, in doing so, obscure others. Although aggregation may better reveal the coherence in some behaviors related to personality constructs, social and cognitive behaviorists argue that personality processes should be linked to psychological processes that result in a better understanding of individual patterns of behavior within socially important contexts.

The Reliability of Differences

The error involved in interpreting a difference between two measures is larger than the error in each measure, because the difference is influenced by both sets of errors. The "difference-score" problem is widely known in the field of psychological and educational measurement. The basic question is this: Given two measures for an individual, how reliable are any differences that may be identified? The reliability of a difference is related to (1) the reliability of each measure, (2) the intercorrelations between measures, and (3) possible normative difference between the measures. As the average reliability of the two measures approaches the intercorrelation between the two measures, the reliability of the difference score approaches zero:

$$r_{\text{DIFF}} = \frac{[\frac{1}{2}\,(r_{XX} + r_{YY})] - r_{XY}}{1 - r_{XY}}$$

where r_{XX}, r_{YY} are the reliabilities of X and Y, and r_{XY} is the correlation between X and Y.

The problem of the reliability of differences has been discussed primarily in terms of learning disabilities (Salvia & Ysseldyke, 1985; Thorndike, 1963; Thorndike & Hagen, 1961), but it is also a serious problem in profile interpretation (Macmann & Barnett, 1985), in which the objective is to identify "severe discrepancies" between correlated variables, as discussed in the next section. In addition to the determination of statistical significance, the psychological meaning of the differences must be determined.

The Interpretation of Profiles

Profile interpretation is the hallmark of many techniques, yet it raises a host of thorny issues. Profile interpretation is dependent upon scale construction employing appropriate methods and upon validity studies, although neither may be sufficient to enable one to interpret individual profiles with great confidence.

We define "profile interpretation" in two related ways: the meaning that can be attributed to the pattern of scores, and whether or not the pattern is related to a defined taxonomic group. A "taxonomic group" refers to "psychologically" similar individuals who occur with sufficient frequency in a population to permit reliable predictions and thus meaningful comparisons (Wiggins, 1973). Three dimensions of profiles are important (Nunnally, 1978): (1) the level or elevation of scores, (2) the dispersion or scatter of scores, and (3) the shape or features of the profile.

The following difficulties are associated with profile interpretation in professional practice (Barnett & Zucker, 1990):

1. The reliability of subscales, the validity of subscales, and the reliability and validity of patterns are likely to vary *within* a scale. Some profiles or patterns may ultimately be useful; others may require further research or may lack validity support.

2. The reliability of the difference between two correlated scores is lower than the reliability of either score alone (see the preceding section on the reliability of differences).

3. The stability of the profile may be unknown. Because of all of the factors described above, the overall pattern may be quite unstable. If there is an important general factor in a scale, peaks and valleys in the profile may connote trivial differences.

4. As the number of comparisons increases, differences due to chance are more likely to occur. Furthermore, most comparisons are unplanned. Profile interpretations for individuals capitalize on chance occurrences of behavior.

5. Extreme scores are most often interpreted; these have the most error.

6. Subscales may have very different meanings (a) at different elevations, and (b) within unique or overall profile patterns.

7. Unusual or idiographic patterns will not be represented in taxonomies.

8. Empirical support for the utility of profiles in intervention decisions should be evaluated.

9. Profile "classification" must also be understood in terms of error rates.

One of the best examples of profile development is that of Achenbach and Edelbrock (1983). They write: "Practitioners should adapt our materials to their own situations and integrate them with other types of data. . . . The essence of clinical creativity is to synthesize diverse and imperfect tools and data into practical solutions suited for each individual case" (p. 113). We agree with their analysis and provide suggestions toward this end in the concluding section of this chapter. Suffice it to say that the difficulties in personality measurement have not been redressed by profile development.

The Reliability of Projectives

An interesting review by Karon (1968) challenged the classical assumptions associated with the reliability of projective instruments, and the topic merits further analysis. Karon argued that traditional notions of reliability have resulted in a "paradox": Reliability estimates associated with temporal consistency are not applicable because the experiences are *expected* to fluctuate, and similar arguments may be applied to internal-consistency estimates. Thus, Karon argued that the validity of projective techniques are not necessarily bound by reliability.

Although projectives have been widely criticized for their limited success in reliably assessing personality traits or structures, a gap still exists in the study of "private" thought processes, fantasies, impulses, affect, defenses, and automatic or unconscious influences. The topic of projective measures has been introduced in different guises by those interested in cognitive processes (e.g., Ellett & Bersoff, 1976; Meichenbaum, 1977; Sobel, 1981). Furthermore, there continues to be interest in subjective inner experiences and potential causal factors including motivational, emotional, and unconscious processes from very diverse sources (Bandura, 1986; Dana, 1984; Denzin, 1984; Mahoney, 1980; Meichenbaum & Gilmore, 1984; Scherer & Ekman, 1984). The potential contributions of projective-like devices cannot be readily dismissed;' to do so would be to deny the significance of inner states not amenable to direct report, as well as creative applications of cognitive and affective theory. Unfortunately, the term carries negative connotations for many, based on years of high hopes followed by devastating research and subsequent reviews.

Although the development of some projective techniques has yielded reliability estimates that approximate those of so-called "objective" measures, and the interest in "covert processes" remains lively, many challenges to their use in professional practice still exist. For example, despite the fact that some reliability estimates (e.g., interrater reliabilities) reach satisfactory levels, the interpretations that result require study as well. Moreover, the use of the information for intervention design is a necessary and independent criterion. Major advances are less likely to be based on new instruments that follow tradition than on procedural safeguards and research-based methods for incorporating the information that projective strategies may reveal, concerning private thoughts and those out of awareness, into testable plans for professional practices (American Educational Research Association [AERA], American Psychological Association [APA], & National Council on Measurement in Education [NCME], 1985).

Decision Reliability

Although the issue of test reliability is addressed by the *Standards for Educational and Psychological Testing* (AERA, APA, & NCME, 1985), more attention should be given to the reliability of decisions. "Decision reliability" (or the reliability of classification) is amenable to study and merits formal practical consideration (e.g., Cronbach & Gleser, 1965; Livingston, 1977). Standard 2.12 (AERA, APA, & NCME, 1985) states: "For dichotomous decisions, estimates should be provided of the percentage of test takers who are classified in the same way on two occasions or on alternate forms of the test" (p. 50). Although Standard 2.12 is given a "conditional rating," it is "primary" for the purposes of classification decisions and intervention design. To examine the reliability of professional decisions, one can dichotomize (or simplify) the decisions to represent two choices or outcomes (e.g., the child fits a classification or does not; the child would benefit from intervention or would not).

Procedures for analyzing the reliability of decisions are flexible. Alternate forms, raters, observational systems, and decisions implied by test outcomes can be compared (e.g., parent vs. teacher ratings; parent vs. clinician ratings) with the outcomes dichotomized (e.g., eligible vs. not eligible for services). For example, Ronka and Barnett (1986) investigated the reliability of decisions based on different adaptive behavior instruments and raters and found kappa coefficients ranging from .00 to .51. In another example, the kappa coefficients revealed in comparisons of parents' versus clinicians' ratings of profiles and of Internalizing and Externalizing syndromes ranged from .30 to .90 (Achenbach & Edelbrock, 1983). Decisions based on multifactored evaluations can also be subjected to analysis. It is reasonable to require criterion levels for decision reliability that are equal to those for other areas of reliability (e.g., .90).

VALIDITY

"Validity" focuses on what a test measures and on the generalizations that can be made from test results. Research results validate a specific use for a test, not the test itself (Nunnally, 1978). Consequently, validity takes many forms. It is examined conceptually, logically, and through experimental procedures. There is no consensus on methods that are used to validate a test. Tests do not have "high" or "low" validity in a general sense; rather, general guidelines and principles for validation have been developed. Validity information must be qualified and scrutinized through consideration of the specific purposes of the technique, the standardization procedures and samples, and the actual experimental procedures used by the test developers.

Personality scales were intended as a short-cut method, to save time and money in contrast to other intensive methods (Peterson, 1968). However, in considering major scales, one often finds that test development has occurred over decades through the efforts of many—a process clearly revealed through the history of any major personality test, such as the Thematic Apperception Test or the Rorschach. It is an expensive endeavor

(Burisch, 1984). Validation efforts are conducted not only by test developers, but sometimes, even more importantly, by independent researchers. Therefore, validity evidence is subsumed by the body of research that follows the publication of a scale. However, Cronbach and Meehl (1955) pointed out that there is no one "scientific approach" that can completely legitimize a construct in a manner that would rule out scientific disputes and varying viewpoints.

Discussions concerning validity are typically organized according to the traditional categories of construct, content, and criterion-related validity (AERA, APA, & NCME, 1985). The distinctions are often difficult to make in practice. We discuss construct and criterion-related validity because of their primary importance to personality measurement. In addition, other forms of validity especially pertinent to professional practices associated with scale usage are reviewed: content validity, incremental validity, and subjective validity. The section concludes with an analysis of the relationship between reliability and validity.

Construct Validity

"Construct validity" is central to test development (Messick, 1980). Construct validity also may be thought to subsume other validities. It defines "theoretical constructions about the nature of human behavior" from the test developer's viewpoint (AERA, APA, & NCME, 1985, p. 9). Test developers should place the construct measured by a scale within a conceptual framework that defines the meaning of the construct and its relationships to other constructs and observable behaviors or variables—a process referred to as the construction of a "nomological network" (Cronbach & Meehl, 1955; see also Messick, 1989). Two methods typically used in construct validation studies are discussed here: the multitrait–multimethod matrix and factor analysis.

The Multitrait–Multimethod Correlation Matrix

A logical approach that stems from a classic paper by Campbell and Fiske (1959), the "multitrait–multimethod correlation matrix,"

(MTMM) can be employed whenever at least two constructs are measured by two methods. An MTMM analysis includes two features of validity. First, it examines "convergent validity." Logically, the correlations between the methods intended to measure the same trait should "converge" or be higher than those developed to measure different traits. "Discriminant validity" provides an indication of the predicted divergence of the traits. Dissimilar traits should have lower intercorrelations than those found for similar traits.

Each measurement procedure yielding a score is considered to be a "trait–method" unit in order to evaluate the possible contributions of various methods used to estimate the trait. "Method bias" is indicated when correlations between different traits (measured by the same method) are higher than the correlations between different traits (measured by different methods). Correlations between supposedly related traits may be substantial because of shared method variance (e.g., self-report methods), and ideally the correlation between two traits should not be a function of the methods. In contrast, the use of distinctly different methods (e.g., observations, behavior ratings) may attenuate (or minimize) estimates of the same trait (Campbell & O'Connell, 1982).

Validity coefficients are represented by correlations across methods for the same trait. To demonstrate evidence for construct validity, same-trait or validity coefficients must be higher than correlations between different traits. A number of alternative statistical approaches to MTMM analysis have been proposed (Kenny, 1979; Schmitt, Coyle, & Saari, 1977; Schmitt & Stults, 1986).

The MTMM analysis is quite appropriate to professional practice issues associated with the interpretation of psychological constructs. Given two (or more) methods of measuring various developmental skills, children's self-concepts, or anxiety, one basic question pertains to the decisions that would be made depending upon the various alternative assessment methods. Typically, the MTMM analysis has revealed a number of measurement problems when employed (e.g., Macmann & Barnett, 1984; Poth & Barnett, 1988). The validity coefficients,

even when significant, may be low or moderate, and logical or expected relationships may not be upheld. The effects of method similarities and differences may be pronounced.

In Fiske's (1982) review of the frequent disappointments revealed by the MTMM procedure, he pointed out that convergent–discriminant validation represented "*modest criteria*" (p. 90; emphasis added). The ultimate goal is convergence not only across different methods, but also across different research strategies. Campbell and O'Connell (1982) argued that the MTMM matrix may overemphasize problems with traits and that measurement methods require the same scrutiny as traits when one is analyzing the disappointing results of construct validation.

Factor Analysis

"Factor analysis" represents a family of techniques that have as the common goal the simplification of complex correlation matrices, or interrelationships between items (or behaviors), in order to reveal the major dimensions that underlie a set of items. Factor analysis can also be used to test theory. The logic is easy to comprehend, but the use of the techniques requires a great deal of sophistication. Furthermore, the statistical approaches that are used rely on the judgments and assumptions made in carrying out the necessary steps, and ultimately in interpreting and giving meaning to the results.

A "factor" is a construct that seems to best represent the structure or relationship between variables or clusters of variables. Factors are named by the researcher or scale developer through a subjective labeling or judgment process. "Factor analysis is only a prelude to more systematic investigations of the constructs" (Nunnally, 1978, p. 330). Despite the vast array of techniques, there is increasing agreement on the basic procedures. Stevens (1986) recommends the use of principal-components analysis to first describe and enumerate the underlying constructs for a set of variables—a procedure that requires fewer assumptions but often yields results similar to other statistical procedures. Confirmatory methods such as structural equation modeling (e.g., Judd, Jessor, & Donovan, 1986), may be used to

evaluate the degree of correspondence between obtained factor structure and theory.

There are two major areas in which the use
of factor analysis is relevant to the topics
subsumed in the present chapter: research in
personality and research in psychopathology.
One overarching difficulty is the variation in
terms (defined by the results of factor analysis with different samples, items, methods,
and researchers) that have been used to describe similar behaviors (Sells & Murphy,
1984).

One of the best examples of factor analysis
for the purpose of personality description
stems from decades of research by Cattell
(e.g., Cattell, 1982; Dielman & Barton,
1983). In numerous studies, Cattell has factor-analyzed self-report inventories, biographical inventories, and observations. The
work is based on Allport and Odbert's (1936)
research on basic descriptive adjectives that
define human characteristics. Cattell has
typically discussed 16 source traits of normal
personality for adults, and 14 for children.
However, other researchers stress far fewer
factors (e.g., Costa & McCrea, 1986), which
they think describe fundamental features of
personality in a reasonable manner.
Although there are important sources of
agreement, the descriptive research has
been tangential to professional practices
associated with the diagnosis or classification
of psychopathology, and especially with research concerning intervention design.

The study of childhood psychopathology
through the use of factor-analytic procedures
is exemplified by the work of Achenbach and
Edelbrock (e.g., Achenbach, 1985; Achenbach & Edelbrock, 1978, 1983). (For other
similar lines of research, see Quay & Peterson, 1987, and Wirt, Lachar, Klinedinst, &
Seat, 1984.) In a comprehensive review,
Achenbach and Edelbrock (1978) examined
the literature for empirical syndromes used
in classifying childhood psychopathology.
The studies included ratings by mental
health workers, teachers, and parents. Syndromes with at least five items and with "factor loadings or average intercorrelations of
.30 or higher" were included in the analysis
(p. 1284). They found four "broad-band" syndromes that were replicated across studies,
or that had "counterparts" in at least two
studies. Sex differences were found to be

important, with the findings most often
based on boys. Empirically based syndromes
found in two or more studies included the
following: Overcontrolled, Undercontrolled,
Pathological Detachment, and Learning Problems. In addition, 14 "narrow-band" syndromes were identified (e.g., Aggressive,
Depressed, Hyperactive, Anxious, etc.).

Achenbach and Edelbrock (1983) developed the Child Behavior Checklist
(CBCL) and the associated Child Behavior
Profile to provide "standardized descriptions" of problems and social competencies of children. A principal-components analysis with a sample of clinically
referred children (n = 2,300) yielded Internalizing and Externalizing syndromes,
and narrow-band scales varying by age and
sex (e.g., Depressed, Uncommunicative, Social Withdrawal, etc.). This methodology has
also been extended to the analysis of teachers' ratings (Achenbach & Edelbrock, 1986)
and adolescent self-reports (Achenbach &
Edelbrock, 1987).

From this brief review, a number of professional practice questions concerning factor
analysis become evident. The first involves
determining the primary purpose of the factor analysis. Some purposes involve basic research and are tangential to professional
practice issues. Second, the technical adequacy of the procedures should be evaluated.
Whether the factor structure is stable and
replicable is partly determined by the adequacy of the measure, but also by sample size
and other sample characteristics. Evidence
for cross-validation should be presented (replications on an independent sample). Third,
the importance of each factor should be considered, estimated by the percentage of variance explained by the factor solution.
Fourth, evidence to support various interpretations of the factors should be presented. Factor solutions that result in glee for
researchers may imply headaches for practitioners when the magnitude of support for
various interpretations is translated into actual professional practice decisions and corresponding error rates. Last, although factor-
analytic procedures represent an important
contribution to childhood psychopathology,
applications to intervention design have
not been directly addressed (see Haynes,
1986).

Basic research in childhood psychopathology is clearly needed, and empirical research will permit a better study of etiology and of the relationship among differentiable traits, syndromes, and well-developed interventions. Relatedly, Kazdin (1985a, 1985b; see also Quay, 1986) points out the need to study *constellations* of behaviors (or syndromes). The term "constellation" refers "to multiple characteristics that co-occur and encompass different behaviors, affect, cognition, and psychophysiological responses" (Kazdin, 1985b, p. 36). Multiple sources of evidence are required to derive the meaning of syndromes for children, including family studies, and it is further necessary to identify "the stability or predictability of dysfunction" (Kazdin, 1985a, p. 38).

Criterion-Related Validity

"Criterion-related validity" focuses attention on the degree to which a test predicts behavior (or classification status) on an independent criterion. The term "concurrent validity" is used to describe studies involving the child's status at the time of testing (e.g., a diagnosis), whereas the term "predictive validity" is used to examine the relationship between a score and future status (e.g., temperament and later adjustment). "Postdictive studies" examine the relationship between a score and past status on a criterion.

Criterion-related validity thus involves predictions between one set of variables (the predictor) and a second set (the criterion). Correlations typically used to estimate the association between variables are termed "validity coefficients." In addition to estimation of the correspondence between variables, the correlation coefficient permits estimation of the standard error of prediction. The Pearson correlation, perhaps most often used, indicates the strength of a linear relationship. When squared, it reveals the proportion of accountable variation between two variables, or the variance that may be reliably predicted (Wiggins, 1973). Factors that limit validity coefficients are the same as those that influence correlations: whether the measures have a linear relationship, are normally distributed, and have equal variances throughout the range of scores ("homoscedasticity"). Furthermore, sample characteristics can limit (or exaggerate) the size of the correlations (Nunnally, 1978).

The professional practice issues in studying criterion-related validity are formidable, but are more easily defined than those associated with construct validity. Criterion-related validity also lies at the heart of many professional practice questions.

A fundamental issue may be referred to as the "criterion problem." Wiggins's (1973) warning still applies: "[C]riterion analysis has proved to be the most recondite and vexing issue confronting personality assessment" (p. 39). The reasons are obvious. Many of the inherent problems in scale construction have counterparts in criterion construction. The criterion must be evaluated in terms of its reliability and validity. Criteria often include such ambiguous and ill-defined behaviors as "adjustment," "emotional disturbance," or "risk." Some relationships have proven to be limited because of moderating variables apart from the predictor or criterion measure. For example, fantasy or other indirect indications of "aggressiveness" may not predict overt aggressive behaviors because of social sanctions or inner controls, not because they do not exist or because they are trivial. Moreover, forms of aggression may be varied and subtle in their expression. Because of these and other theoretical factors, modest correlations are expected (e.g., Barnett & Zucker, 1980).

Other Validities

Incremental Validity

The correlations between a test and a criterion measure applied in the analysis of criterion-related validity can be misleading to a large degree. Other factors have to be taken into account. There should be clear benefits for the targeted measure over alternative procedures in terms of cost, intrusiveness, acceptability, concordance with intervention design, and other factors. The outcomes of actual decisions based on a comparison of procedures should be assessed.

"Incremental validity" (Sechrest, 1963) suggests the need to evaluate the contributions that a test makes, over and above information that is already known or readily available. Incremental validity is concerned with the improvements in predictions that are made through the use of a procedure, compared to those that can be made without it. The question is critical to personal and social assessment. For example, after interviewing parents, teachers, and child, and conducting observations across settings, the professional psychologist would ask: "What nonredundant information will be gained by adding additional procedures?" and "Will adding these procedures help my client?"

Among a number of factors, the incremental validity of an assessment procedure is dependent upon base rates for the problem to be identified, evaluated within an appropriate population. Mischel (1968) offered the following example: "If 95 percent of the in-patients of a particular hospital are diagnosed 'schizophrenic,' a test-derived statement that predicts this label correctly 80 percent of the time is less useful than systematically calling every patient in the hospital schizophrenic" (p. 106). Thus base rates limit the association that can be demonstrated between a predictor and criterion. Alternatively, modest validity coefficients may be useful in certain situations, because the "usefulness" is dependent upon information that is actually gained through a measurement procedure.

The criterion-related validity "problem" can also be refocused to that of "decision accuracy and validity," or the analysis of correct and incorrect decisions. Decision theory is concerned not only with accuracy, but also with the utility of decisions, and ultimately with values that can be tied to different outcomes. The decisions with respect to personal and social assessment are typically in the form of diagnostic systems: whether groups or individuals differ in measurable ways, and whether the groups or individuals should receive special "treatments." The prototypic study of decision accuracy is depicted in a 2 × 2 matrix whereby valid positives are successfully screened, with high scores on both the screening measure and criterion; valid negatives are also successfully screened, with low scores on both measures; false positives have high scores on the screening measure, but do not "succeed" according to the criterion measure; and false negatives have low scores on the screening measure, but do "succeed" according to the

criterion measure. "Cutting scores" on the test or predictor are used to guide decisions. The empirical basis for cutting scores should be clearly specified (AERA, APA, & NCME, 1985). As the cutting score is "moved" either higher or lower by the investigator, the type of errors change. Important sources for decision theory include Cronbach and Gleser (1965), Cronbach et al. (1972), von Winterfeldt and Edwards (1986), and Wiggins (1973).

Content Validity

Content validity is concerned with the adequacy of the items and is based on the systematic examination of content, selected from an identifiable "universe" of content. Typically, content validity has been applied to academic tests, or tests with similar properties, because of the difficulties of sampling items from a universe or domain related to personality or social constructs. In its traditional sense, content validity "is usually inappropriate and may . . . be misleading" when applied to personality tests (Anastasi, 1982, p. 135). When the point of emphasis is shifted to the functional analysis of behavior, however, principles associated with content validity can have considerable relevance for personal and social assessment (see Linehan, 1980; Strosahl & Linehan, 1986).

Subjective Validity

Although "subjective validity" is not a traditional topic in measurement theory, the personal or subjective elements of test usage are a major feature of the recent revision of the *Standards for Educational and Psychological Testing* (AERA, APA, & NCME, 1985). There are many lines of reasoning necessary for the consideration of subjective validities, but most point toward an increasing ecological perspective (Cronbach, 1984, p. 571). We mention three viewpoints.

Messick (1980, 1989) pointed out that tests are evaluated on the basis of measurement characteristics, whereas test applications require evaluation through potential social outcomes that include both normative and subjective comparisons. Social outcomes cannot be studied without reference to actual behaviors in real-life settings, followed over long time periods. In a related formulation, Bronfenbrenner (1977) defined ecological validity as an extension of classical validity: "the extent to which the environment experienced by the subjects in a scientific investigation has the properties supposed or assumed to have by the investigator" (p. 516). Lastly, in assessment related to intervention design, social validity (Kazdin, 1977; Wolf, 1978; see also the critique by Fuqua & Schwade, 1986) has been described through the identification of (1) socially significant problems for behavior change, and (2) socially acceptable methods with respect to the immediate social community. The results of the intervention should have practical significance (Baer, Wolf, & Risley, 1968), and should be evaluated in multiple ways (Willems, 1977). As broad and ill-defined as they appear in contrast to other measurement topics, subjective validities are necessary and basic considerations in the assessment–intervention process.

The Relationship between Reliability and Validity

As discussed earlier, the relationship between reliability and validity can be quite hazy, depending on the measurement model. The analysis by Campbell and Fiske (1959) is frequently cited: "Reliability is the agreement between two efforts to measure the same trait through maximally similar methods. Validity is represented in the agreement between two attempts to measure the same trait through maximally different methods" (p. 83). Cronbach and his associates recast the problem to one of generalizability.

Theoretically, based on the classical measurement model, the square root of the reliability coefficient (termed the "index of reliability") establishes the upper limit of validity for a measure (Gulliksen, 1950). As the reliability drops, so does the validity. Thorndike (1982) points out that a predictor cannot be expected to predict error variance in the criterion. The "effectiveness" of a measure in relationship to a criterion measure can be described by the ratio of (1) the correlation between the test and criterion measure (the validity coefficient) to (2) the index of reliability for the criterion measure:

$$r_{XY'} = \frac{r_{XY}}{\sqrt{r_{YY}}}$$

where $r_{XY'}$ is the correlation between X and Y (if Y were perfectly reliable), r_{XY} is the correlation between X and Y, and r_{YY} is the reliability of Y.

High reliability is necessary for, but does not guarantee, high validity in a traditional sense. Many important behaviors (e.g., covert processes) may not be measured reliably; correspondingly, it has been difficult to convincingly establish their validity or practicality. Furthermore, increasing reliability (e.g., through adding test items) may have quite modest effects on validity. The reliability of the criterion also limits the overall extent of the relationship between variables. Based on generalizability theory, there is not one reliability coefficient for a test, or one validity coefficient; considerations for both are linked to specific questions that may be asked. Some behaviorists have recast the problem as one of accuracy (e.g., Cone, 1981).

Modern Test Theory

"Modern test theory" involves the latent-trait approach to test development (e.g., Lord, 1980). The procedure involves the study of the relationship between individual items and an underlying (thus latent) trait through mathematical models. Two major aspects of latent-trait models include (1) the assumption of a unidimensional trait with homogeneous items, and (2) mathematical functions that depict the relationship between item choices and the trait or ability measured (Ghiselli et al., 1981). A "latent attribute" refers to "the hypothesized but unobserved characteristics that accounts for a particular set of consistencies within and differences among persons" (Thorndike, 1982, p. 5). The mathematical functions are expressed as item–characteristic curves. In test design, items are selected that satisfactorily are related to the latent attribute, and represent different levels of the trait. Thorndike (1982) presents an introductory but comprehensive description of the latent-trait approach to test construction.

Although modern test theory has been used increasingly for test construction, the potential issues on a practical level remain unknown. Psychometrically, the theory has attractive features. Items developed through latent-trait procedures can be thought of as "calibrated," presumed to be a major advantage. Nunnally (1978) points out that although the theory is termed "modern," its basic principles were developed in the 1950s, with the ideas present long before that period. More importantly, basic validity issues and child outcomes still remain as questions.

PERSONALITY MEASUREMENT, RESEARCH, AND PROFESSIONAL PRACTICES

The purpose of this section is to review major themes in personality measurement that have created dilemmas for both researchers and professional psychologists. In the final section, we turn to component strategies for sound professional practices associated with personal and social assessment.

Idiographic or Nomothetic?

Unique life experiences combined with inherited characteristics lead to "idiographic" patterns of behavior. "Nomothetic" pertains to general lawfulness of behavior. Although some view the relationship between the two as conflicted (Nunnally, 1978), the differences (as in many "dilemmas" in psychology) often define various goals in research and professional practices, and not fundamental conflicts. Allport (1937) argued for the importance of both approaches. Although "nomothetic" defines basic goals of behavioral research, there has been an "enduring interest" in idiographic approaches and their relationships to general laws, "and one that deserves renewed attention" (Runyan, 1983, p. 414). Furthermore, it is also viewed as a "false dichotomy" in a sense (McFall & McDonel, 1986, p. 234). All assessments involve idiographic and nomothetic objectives and procedures.

The Idiographic Approach

An interest in the in-depth understanding of individuals is shared by psychodynamic, phe-nomenological, behavioral, and cognitive–social learning theorists (Cone, 1986; Runyan, 1983). Mischel (1968, 1973, 1984a, 1984b) has developed the most coherent description of the idiographic approach to the study of personality from a social and cognitive viewpoint, as well as of its relationship to nomothetic principles. Mischel (1984a) writes:

> Deeply impressed by George Kelly's (1955) thinking, I was sensitive to the fact that clients—like other people—don't describe themselves with operational definitions. They invoke motives, traits, and other dispositions as ways of describing and explaining their experiences and themselves. Much of the assessor's task . . . should be to help people in the search for such referents for their own personal constructs, instead of forcing the assessor's favorite dispositional labels on them. (p. 280)

Mischel (1973, p. 265) suggests five "person" variables that serve as guidelines for assessment–intervention design: (1) the individual's competencies to construct (generate) diverse behaviors under appropriate conditions; (2) the encoding or categorization of events; (3) expectancies about outcomes; (4) the subjective values of different outcomes; and (5) self-regulatory systems and plans.

The Nomothetic Approach

Two very distinct lines of research can be identified within the nomothetic approach: those that have been concerned with the identification of traits (e.g., Costa & McCrea, 1986), and those that have been concerned with lawful behavioral principles (e.g., Cone, 1986; Mischel, 1968). We briefly describe the "trait" approach here. The applications from behavioral and from social and cognitive–behavioral approaches are integrated into the suggested components discussed in the final section of this chapter.

From Allport's early work, Stagner (1984) defines a trait in the following manner: "A trait is a consistent and persistent pattern of behavior and experience (cognitive and affective) characteristic of a particular individual" (p. 7). Theoretically, traits may be unique to the individual, or may be shared with others, or may be common. They are hierarchically structured, and function to control lower-level processes in behavior. Thus, a trait is associated with various probabilities of occurrences of specific behaviors or classes of behaviors in situations. "Trait–situation interactions are considered to be the rule" (Stagner, 1984, p. 34).

Although there are far too many traits (or factors) to review, convergence has been a recent goal of researchers (Sells & Murphy, 1984; Costa & McCrea, 1986). A well-established taxonomy similar to one proposed a number of years ago by several researchers (e.g., Fiske, 1949; Norman, 1963; Tupes & Christal, 1961) is presented by Costa and McCrea (1986, p. 410): Neuroticism (e.g., Calm–Worrying), Extraversion (e.g., Reserved–Affectionate), Openness (e.g., Down-to-Earth–Imaginative), Agreeableness (e.g., Ruthless–Softhearted), and Conscientiousness (e.g., Negligent–Conscientious).

Potential effects of a better understanding of traits include (1) more adequate research in personal and social development, (2) a better understanding of expressions and meanings of various symptoms, and (3) further insights into mechanisms of stability and change (e.g., Block & Block, 1980; Costa & McCrea, 1986). Costa and McCrea (1986) argue for stability in personality development through adulthood, and for the proposition that "human nature is by no means easily changed" (p. 420). This "proposition" has been well analyzed (e.g., Moss & Sussman, 1980), and while no one would disagree with the difficulties of change, others would argue that the complexities of intervention design and execution have hampered unequivocal statements regarding possibilities for change.

Interviews, Observations, or Ratings?

Interviews?

Many regard the interview as the most important "instrument" in assessment (Korchin & Schuldberg, 1981). An extensive and diverse literature on interviews stresses anything from communication skills, unstructured (Greenspan, 1981) or structured clinical diagnosis (Rapoport & Ismond, 1984), private experiences (Denzin, 1984), and in-

tervention roles (e.g., Glenwick & Jason, 1984), to therapeutic approaches (Cormier & Cormier, 1979). The topic has also been addressed with respect to interviews directed to children and to all others associated with the assessment–intervention process; these vary widely by function (Barnett & Zucker, 1990; Gutkin & Curtis, 1982). Many questions persist concerning the technical adequacy and use of interview procedures (Gresham, 1984). Despite problems in describing the interview in a way that would satisfy all uses, it may be best to state that it is integral to assessment and intervention, and all stages therein. All sources of assessment error are potentially relevant as well.

A prototypic behavioral interview was described by Peterson (1968). He pointed out that the distinguishing feature of the interview is the relationship dimension. Without the relationship, the assessment–intervention process is impaired and ultimately terminated. The future of the interview with respect to studies of technical adequacy rests with the study of the interview's interrelated but specialized functions: (1) as a technique of behavior analysis (e.g., Kanfer & Grimm, 1977; Peterson, 1968); (2) as a formal diagnostic tool; (3) as a method to study private experiences; and (4) as a data-gathering technique necessary to the assessment–intervention process.

Ratings or Observations?

As a reaction against the use of both projective and objective techniques for the study of personality structures and processes, there has been renewed interest in behavior rating scales and direct observations. They are *not* alternative ways of assessing the same information, nor are they complements of each other; they have different objectives (Cairns & Green, 1979). Rating scales have been developed to assess a broad range of factors: "personality, maladjustment, problem behavior, psychopathology, and social emotional functioning" (Edelbrock, 1983, p. 294). "Direct observations . . . can be the key for identifying how actual behaviors are elicited, maintained, and organized" (Cairns & Green, 1979, p. 222). Observations are essential for the analysis of interactions (Bakeman & Gottman, 1986). Cairns and Green

(1979) have examined the issue in depth. In their words,

> The distinguishing characteristic of rating scales is that they involve a social judgment on the part of the observer, "or rater," with regard to the placement of an individual on some psychological dimension. (p. 210)

> The distinguishing property of behavior observations is that they involve an attempt to record the actual activities of children as opposed to offering a judgment about children's personal dispositions or the quality of their relationships. (p. 213)

Professional Practice Issues

In summarizing the topics presented in this section, one problem stands out: The use of all the techniques described above must be guided by a template that defines decisions related to use, including interpretations and outcomes. "Professional judgment" is the pervasive term used to bridge the gap between the knowledge base and actual decisions concerning the usage of various techniques (Barnett, 1988). Professional judgment itself involves a host of unknowns and is dependent upon a personal model of professional practice. Unfortunately, professional judgment has not served well as a template, because the decision process has not been successfully explicated (e,g., Arkes, 1981; Hogarth, 1987; Kleinmuntz, 1984; Nisbett & Ross, 1980) and has not been amenable to study. Although concerns have been voiced most often about projectives, the same arguments apply in varying degrees to all techniques, including interviews, observations, "objectives," and behavior rating scales (e.g., Edelbrock, 1983; Kanfer, 1985; Wiggins, 1973).

COMPONENT STRATEGIES FOR PERSONAL AND SOCIAL ASSESSMENTS

Throughout the previous sections, many questions have been raised concerning personality measurement and professional practice issues. The final section addresses two underlying themes: the need for appropriate theory, and the need for analysis of problem-solving procedures that serve as the basis for professional practices.

The Need for a Coherent Theoretical Model

What factors guide decisions in ambiguous and complex real-life assessment situations? Whether this is obvious or not, decisions are guided by theory. Practitioners' theories may be deliberate and formal; they may be internalized and personalized adaptations of a venerable theory (e.g., Freudian theory, social–cognitive behaviorism); or they may be eclectic, accidental, or ad hoc. To the degree that factors that guide the assessment of personality remain unspecified, the process cannot be studied. Within any endeavor related to the assessment of personal and social functioning from the interpretations of projectives, objectives, rating scales, and interviews, the potential exists for significant judgmental differences that can lead to idiosyncratic outcomes for clients.

There are many personality "theories" that remain viable in the literature or in the minds of professional psychologists (see Loevinger, 1987). For the purposes of the present chapter, they warrant appraisal to the extent that they guide actual professional practice decisions. Bandura's (1986) criterion is pertinent: "The value of a theory is ultimately judged by its usefulness as evidenced by the power of the methods it yields to effect psychological changes" (p. 4).

Problem-Solving Components

Problem solving has been widely discussed in terms of steps, but not in terms of the components that guide the process. Social and cognitive behaviorism is presently viewed by many as a consensus position (Kazdin, 1984; Reynolds, Gutkin, Elliott, & Witt, 1984). While having a substantial history (Woodward, 1982), it has been recently and comprehensively described by Bandura (1986), and has been developed in personality assessment through the writing of Mischel (1968, 1973, 1981, 1984a, 1984b). Within a framework of social and cognitive behaviorism, we briefly summarize two interrelated problem-solving components: reflective practices (Kanfer, 1985; Schön, 1983), and empirical practices (e.g., Barlow, Hayes, & Nelson, 1984; Kazdin, 1985a).

Reflective Practice

"In real-world practice, problems do not present themselves to the practitioner as givens. They must be constructed from the materials of problematic situations which are puzzling, troubling, and uncertain" (Schön, 1983, p. 40). The tools include (1) self-questioning, and cognitive appraisals of professional behaviors in the representation of child systems; and (2) the development of assessment and intervention plans based on systems representation (Barnett, 1988; Evans, 1985).

Empirical Practice

Although it is limited, the intervention-related research that does exist is expanding rapidly and requires careful analysis, an important element of professional judgment. Two facets are identified: (1) empirically based syndromes (Achenbach, 1985; Kazdin, 1985b), and (2) interventions found in the literature that have established validity support. An aspect of professional judgment is to determine the correspondence between personality constructs (or syndromes, traits) that appear to apply to the client and those that have an empirical foundation. Many personality variables suggested by idiographic techniques are widely researched (e.g., anxiety, depression, aggression), and logical comparisons can be made between the idiographic client-based understanding of the construct and its researched dimensions, the most likely nomothetic link for professional practices. A major "criterion" with respect to the adequacy of plans is that of resulting changes in behaviors, as follows.

The Criterion of Planned Changes in Behaviors

Reflective and empirical practices lead to plans for assessment and intervention design. A useful concept is that of "decision frames," which "refer to the decision-maker's conception of the acts, outcomes, and contingencies associated with a particular choice" (Tversky & Kahneman, 1984, p. 25). When it is re-

lated to various potential outcomes and risks, the adoption of a particular decision frame is "an ethically significant act" (Tversky & Kahneman, 1984, p. 40). Therefore, the plans require evaluation with respect to child outcomes, including those that are unintended (Willems, 1977).

Sequential Decision Making

Intervention design typically involves a process of *sequential* decisions (Bandura, 1969), in contrast to diagnostic or classification decisions:

> By retaining flexibility in the selection, sequencing, and timing of objectives, the treatment program remains highly sensitive to feedback from resultant changes. . . . Successful treatment . . . requires the selection and attainment of a variety of specific objectives rather than a single omnibus outcome. (pp. 103–104)

Time-series methods associated with single-case experimental designs can be used flexibly to analyze the effects of plans with a wide range of problem behaviors, interventions, and even "philosophies" (Barlow et al., 1984). Based on the characteristics of one's client, logical generalizations can be made from researched interventions with children having similar characteristics. Replications are critical to the process (see Kazdin, Kratochwill, & VandenBos, 1986). Hayes et al. (1986) discuss specific research strategies that enable the analysis of the effects of assessment information on intervention decisions.

CONCLUSION: NEEDED RESEARCH FOR PROFESSIONAL PRACTICES

Long sought after, a major goal of personality research has been the identification of trait × treatment interactions. The difficulties are numerous: (1) limited consensus on the classification and measurement of traits; (2) limited consensus on intervention design; (3) treatment integrity issues; (4) experimental design issues, including the development of adequately sized groups for relatively rare syndromes, adequate control goups, and random assignment to groups; and (5) unique moderating effects for individuals and sub-groups even within defined taxonomic groups or classifications. Furthermore, assessment practices need to encompass methods of assessing the potential impact of life events that alter developmental trajectories, including those that are accidental or unplanned (e.g., Bandura, 1986; Lefcourt, Martin, & Ebers, 1981; Rutter, 1984). Important features of the family environment may often be discontinuous and nonshared (Plomin, 1987).

A different strategy is to study the intervention implications of syndromes through single-case designs. Single-case designs are of interest because (1) child characteristics can be well described in both idiographic and nomothetic ways; (2) interventions are correspondingly well described; and (3) the effects of interventions can be documented. Behaviors associated with various aspects of personal and social development, as well as covert experiences, can be studied using time-series methods.

Research into the art of practice is necessary. Schön (1983) refers to an "epistemology of practice which places technical problem solving within a broader context of reflective inquiry . . . and links the art of practice in uncertainty and uniqueness to the scientist's area of research" (p. 69). At the focal point of research and personality measurement is professional judgment, a highly vulnerable personal process used to arrive at decision frames or plans for professional action. Alternative research strategies are needed to help accomplish the valuable goals associated with the assessment of personality from the viewpoint of professional practices.

REFERENCES

Achenbach, T. M. (1985). *Assessment and taxonomy of child and adolescent psychopathology*. Beverly Hills, CA: Sage.

Achenbach, T. M., & Edelbrock, C. S. (1978). The classification of child psychopathology: A review and analysis of empirical methods. *Psychological Bulletin, 85*, 1275–1301.

Achenbach, T. M., & Edelbrock, C. (1983). *Manual for the Child Behavior Checklist and Revised Child Behavior Profile*. Burlington: University of Vermont, Department of Psychiatry.

Achenbach, T. M., & Edelbrock, C. (1986). *Manual for the Teacher's Report Form and Teacher Version of the Child Behavior Profile*. Burlington: University of Vermont, Department of Psychiatry.

Achenbach, T. M., & Edelbrock, C. (1987). *Manual for the Youth Self-Report and Profile*. Burlington: University of Vermont, Department of Psychiatry.

Allport, G. W. (1937). *Personality: A psychological interpretation*. New York: Wiley.

Allport, G. W., & Odbert, H. S. (1936). Trait-names: A psycholexical study. *Psychological Monographs, 47* (1, Whole No. 211).

American Educational Research Association, American Psychological Association, & National Council on Measurement in Education. (1985). *Standards for educational and psychological testing*. Washington, DC: Author.

Anastasi, A. (1982). *Psychological testing* (5th ed.). New York: Macmillan.

Arkes, H. R. (1981). Impediments to accurate clinical judgment and possible ways to minimize their impact. *Journal of Consulting and Clinical Psychology, 49*, 323–330.

Baer, D. M., Wolf, M., & Risley, T. R. (1968). Some current dimensions of applied behavior analysis. *Journal of Applied Behavior Analysis, 1*, 91–97.

Bakeman, R., & Gottman, J. M. (1986). *Observing interaction: An introduction to sequential analysis*. New York: Cambridge University Press.

Bandura, A. (1969). *Principles of behavior modification*. New York: Holt, Rinehart & Winston.

Bandura, A. (1985). Model of causality in social learning theory. In M. J. Mahoney & A. Freeman (Eds.), *Cognition and psychotherapy* (pp. 81–99). New York: Plenum.

Bandura, A. (1986). *Social foundations of thought and action: A social cognitive theory*. Englewood Cliffs, NJ: Prentice-Hall.

Barlow, D. H., Hayes, S. C., & Nelson, R. O. (1984). *The scientist–practitioner: Research and accountability in clinical and educational settings*. New York: Pergamon Press.

Barnett, D. W. (1986). Personality assessment and children: A critical appraisal and emerging trends. In R. E. Bennett & C. A. Maher (Eds.), *Emerging perspectives on assessment of exceptional children* (pp. 121–139). New York: Haworth Press.

Barnett, D. W. (1988). Professional judgment: A critical appraisal. *School Psychology Review, 17*, 656–670.

Barnett, D. W., & Zucker, K. B. (1980). The others-concept: Explorations into the quality of children's interpersonal relationships. In H. C. Foot, A. J. Chapman, & J. R. Smith (Eds.), *Friendships and social relations in children* (pp. 65–86). Chichester, England: Wiley.

Barnett, D. W., & Zucker, K. B. (1990). *The personal and social assessment of children: Current status and professional practice issues*. Boston: Allyn & Bacon.

Barrios, B., & Hartmann, D. P. (1986). The contributions of traditional assessment: Concepts, issues, and methodologies. In R. O. Nelson & S. C. Hayes (Eds.), *Conceptual foundations of behavioral assessment* (pp. 81–110). New York: Guilford Press.

Block, J. H., & Block, J. (1980). The role of ego-control and ego-resiliency in the organization of behavior. In W. A. Collins (Ed.), *Development of cognition, affect, and social relations* (pp. 39–101). Hillsdale, NJ: Erlbaum.

Bronfenbrenner, U. (1977). Toward an experimental ecology of human development. *American Psychologist, 32,* 513–531.

Burisch, M. (1984). Approaches to personality inventory construction: A comparison of merits. *American Psychologist, 39,* 214–227.

Cairns, R. B., & Green, J. A. (1979). How to assess personality and social patterns: Observations or ratings? In R. B. Cairns (Ed.), *The analysis of social interactions: Methods, issues, and illustrations* (pp. 209–226). Hillsdale, NJ: Erlbaum.

Campbell, D. T., & Fiske, D. W. (1959). Convergent and discriminant validation by the multitrait–multimethod matrix. *Psychological Bulletin, 56,* 81–105.

Campbell, D. T., & O'Connell, E. J. (1982). Methods as diluting trait relationships rather than adding irrelevant systematic variance. In D. Brinberg & L. Kidder (Eds.), *Forms of validity in research* (pp. 93–111). San Francisco: Jossey-Bass.

Cattell, R. B. (1982). *The inheritance of personality and ability: Research methods and findings.* New York: Academic Press.

Cone, J. D. (1981). Psychometric considerations. In M. Hersen & A. S. Bellack (Eds.), *Behavioral assessment: A practical handbook* (pp. 38–68). New York: Pergamon Press.

Cone, J. D. (1986). Idiographic, nomothetic, and related perspectives in behavioral assessment. In R. O. Nelson & S. C. Hayes (Eds.), *Conceptual foundations of behavioral assessment* (pp. 111–128). New York: Guilford Press.

Cormier, W. H., & Cormier, L. S. (1979). *Interviewing strategies for helpers: A guide to assessment, treatment, and evaluation.* Monterey, CA: Brooks/Cole.

Costa, P. T., & McCrea, R. R. (1986). Personality stability and its implications for clinical psychology. *Clinical Psychology Review, 6,* 407–423.

Cronbach, L. J. (1951). Coefficient alpha and the internal structure of tests. *Psychometrika, 16,* 297–334.

Cronbach, L. J. (1984). *Essentials of psychological testing* (4th ed.). New York: Harper & Row.

Cronbach, L. J., & Gleser, G. C. (1965). *Psychological tests and personnel decisions* (2nd ed.). Urbana: University of Illinois Press.

Cronbach, L. J., Gleser, G. C., Nanda, H., & Rajaratnam, N. (1972). *The dependability of behavioral measurements: Theory of generalizability for scores and profiles.* New York: Wiley.

Cronbach, L. J., & Meehl, P. E. (1955). Construct validity in psychological tests. *Psychological Bulletin, 52,* 281–302.

Dana, R. H. (1984). Personality assessment: Practice and teaching for the next decade. *Journal of Personality Assessment, 48,* 46–57.

Denzin, N. K. (1984). *On understanding emotion.* San Francisco: Jossey-Bass.

Dielman, T., & Barton, K. (1983). *Child personality structure and development: Multivariate theory and research.* New York: Praeger.

Dudek, F. J. (1979). The continuing misinterpretation of the standard error of measurement. *Psychological Bulletin, 86,* 335–337.

Edelbrock, C. (1983). Problems and issues in using rating scales to assess child personality and psy-chopathology. *School Psychology Review, 12,* 293–299.

Ellett, C. D., & Bersoff, D. N. (1976). An integrated approach to the psychosituational assessment of behavior. *Professional Psychology, 7,* 485–494.

Emmerich, W. (1966, March). Stability and change in early personality development. *Young Children,* 233–243.

Epstein, S. (1984). The stability of behavior across time and situations. In R. A. Zucker, J. Aronoff, & A. I. Rabin (Eds.), *Personality and the prediction of behavior* (pp. 209–268). New York: Wiley.

Evans, I. M. (1985). Building systems models as a strategy for target behavior selection in clinical assessment. *Behavioral Assessment, 7,* 232.

Fiske, D. W. (1949). Consistency of the factorial structures of personality ratings from different sources. *Journal of Abnormal and Social Psychology, 44,* 329–344.

Fiske, D. W. (1982). Convergent–discriminant validation in measurements and research strategies. In D. Brinberg & L. Kidder (Eds.), *Forms of validity in research* (pp. 77–92). San Francisco: Jossey-Bass.

Fuqua, R. W., & Schwade, J. (1986). Social validation of applied behavioral research: A selective review and critique. In A. Poling & R. W. Fuqua (Eds.), *Research methods in applied behavior analysis* (pp. 265–292). New York: Plenum.

Gallagher, J. J., & Ramey, C. T. (Eds.). (1987). *The malleability of children.* Baltimore: Paul H. Brookes.

Ghiselli, E. E., Campbell, J. P., & Zedeck, S. (1981). *Measurement theory for the behavioral sciences.* San Francisco: W. H. Freeman.

Glenwick, D. S., & Jason, L. A. (1984). Locus of intervention in child cognitive behavior therapy: Implications of a behavioral community psychology perspective. In A. W. Meyers & W. E. Craighead (Eds.), *Cognitive behavior therapy with children* (pp. 129–162). New York: Plenum.

Greenspan, S. I. (1981). *The clinical interview of the child.* New York: McGraw-Hill.

Gresham, F. M. (1984). Behavioral interviews in school psychology: Issues in psychometric adequacy and research. *School Psychology Review, 13,* 17–25.

Gulliksen, H. (1950). *Theory of mental tests.* New York: Wiley.

Gutkin, T. B., & Curtis, M. J. (1982). School-based consultation: Theory and techniques. In C. R. Reynolds & T. B. Gutkin (Eds.), *Handbook of school psychology* (pp. 796–828). New York: Wiley.

Hansen, D. J., Tisdelle, D. A., & O'Dell, S. L. (1985). Audio recorded and directly observed parent–child interactions: A comparison of observational methods. *Behavioral Assessment, 7,* 389–399.

Hayes, S. C., Nelson, R. O., & Jarrett, R. B. (1986). Evaluating the quality of behavioral assessment. In R. O. Nelson & S. C. Hayes (Eds.), *Conceptual foundations of behavioral assessment* (pp. 461–503). New York: Guilford Press.

Haynes, S. N. (1986). The design of intervention programs. In R. O. Nelson & S. C. Hayes (Eds.), *Conceptual foundations of behavioral assessment* (pp. 385–429). New York: Guilford Press.

Hogarth, R. (1987). *Judgement and choice* (2nd ed.). New York: Wiley.

Jones, R. R., Reid, J. B., & Patterson, G. R. (1975).

Naturalistic observations in clinical assessment. In P. McReynolds (Ed.), *Advances in psychological assessment* (Vol. 3, pp. 42–95). San Francisco: Jossey-Bass.

Judd, C. M., Jessor, R., & Donovan, J. E. (1986). Structural equation models and personality research. *Journal of Personality, 54,* 149–198.

Kanfer, F. H. (1985). Target selection for clinical change programs. *Behavioral Assessment, 7,* 7–20.

Kanfer, F. H., & Grimm, L. G. (1977). Behavioral analysis: Selecting target behaviors in the interview. *Behavior Modification, 1,* 7–28.

Karon, B. P. (1968). Problems of validities. In A. I. Rabin (Ed.), *Projective techniques in personality assessment* (pp. 85–111). New York: Springer.

Kazdin, A. E. (1977). Assessing the clinical or applied significance of behavior change through social validation. *Behavior Modification, 1,* 427–452.

Kazdin, A. E. (1984). *Behavior modification in applied settings* (3rd ed.). Homewood, IL: Dorsey Press.

Kazdin, A. E. (1985a). Alternative approaches to the diagnosis of childhood disorders. In P. H. Bornstein & A. E. Kazdin (Eds.), *Handbook of clinical behavior therapy with children* (pp. 3–43). Homewood, IL: Dorsey Press.

Kazdin, A. E. (1985b). Selection of target behaviors: The relationship of treatment focus to clinical dysfunction. *Behavioral Assessment, 7,* 33–47.

Kazdin, A. E., Kratochwill, T. R., & VandenBos, G. R. (1986). Beyond clinical trials: Generalizing from research to practice. *Professional Psychology: Research and Practice, 17,* 391–398.

Kelly, G. A. (1955). *The psychology of personal constructs* (Vols. 1 & 2). New York: Basic Books.

Kenny, D. A. (1979). *Correlation and causality.* New York: Wiley.

Kleinmuntz, B. (1984). The scientific study of clinical judgment in psychology and medicine. *Clinical Psychology Review, 4,* 111–126.

Korchin, S. J., & Schuldberg, D. (1981). The future of clinical assessment. *American Psychologist, 36,* 1147–1158.

Lefcourt, H. M., Martin, R. A., & Ebers, K. (1981). Toward a renewed integration of personality research and clinical practice. In I. Silverman (Ed.), *New directions for methodology of social and behavior science: Vol. 8. Generalizing from laboratory to life* (pp. 21–37). San Francisco: Jossey-Bass.

Linehan, N. M. (1980). Content validity: Its relevance to behavioral assessment. *Behavioral Assessment, 2,* 147–159.

Livingston, S. A. (1977). Psychometric techniques for criterion-referenced testing and behavioral assessment. In J. D. Cone & R. P. Hawkins (Eds.), *Behavioral assessment: New directions in clinical psychology* (pp. 308–329). New York: Brunner/Mazel.

Loevinger, J. (1987). *Paradigms of personality.* San Francisco: W. H. Freeman.

Lord, F. M. (1980). *Applications of item response theory to practical testing problems.* Hillsdale, NJ: Erlbaum.

Lord, F. M., & Novick, M. R. (1968). *Statistical theory of mental test scores.* Reading, MA: Addision-Wesley.

Lumsden, J. (1976). Test theory. *Annual Review of Psychology, 27,* 251–280.

Macmann, G. M., & Barnett, D. W. (1984). An analysis of the construct validity of two measures of adaptive behavior. *Journal of Psychoeducational Assessment, 2,* 239–247.

Macmann, G. M., & Barnett, D. W. (1985). Discrepancy score analysis: A computer simulation of classification stability. *Journal of Psychoeducational Assessment, 4,* 363–375.

Mahoney, M. J. (1980). Psychotherapy and the structure of personal revolutions. In M. J. Mahoney (Ed.), *Psychotherapy process: Current issues and future directions* (pp. 157–180). New York: Plenum.

Magnusson, D., & Endler, N. S. (1977). *Personality at the crossroads: Current issues in interactional psychology.* Hillsdale, NJ: Erlbaum.

McFall, R. M., & McDonel, E. C. (1986). The continuing search for units of analysis: Beyond persons, situations, and their interactions. In R. O. Nelson & S. C. Hayes (Eds.), *Conceptual foundations of behavioral assessment* (pp. 201–241). New York: Guilford Press.

Meichenbaum, D. (1977). *Cognitive-behavior modification.* New York: Plenum.

Meichenbaum, D., & Gilmore, J. B. (1984). The nature of unconscious processes: A cognitive–behavioral perspective. In K. S. Bowers & D. Meichenbaum (Eds.), *The unconscious reconsidered* (pp. 272–298). New York: Wiley.

Messick, S. (1980). Test validity and the ethics of assessment. *American Psychologist, 35,* 1012–1027.

Messick, S. (1981). Constructs and their vicissitudes in educational and psychological measurement. *Psychological Bulletin, 89,* 575–588.

Messick, S. (1989). Validity. In R. Linn (Ed.), *Educational measurement* (3rd ed., pp. 13–103). New York: MacMillan.

Mischel, W. (1968). *Personality and assessment.* New York: Wiley.

Mischel, W. (1973). Toward a cognitive social learning reconceptualization of personality. *Psychological Review, 80,* 252–283.

Mischel, W. (1981). A cognitive–social learning approach to assessment. In T. V. Merluzzi, C. R. Glass, & M. Genest (Eds.), *Cognitive assessment* (pp. 479–502). New York: Guilford Press.

Mischel, W. (1984a). On the predictability of behavior and the structure of personality. In R. A. Zucker, J. Aronoff, & A. I. Rabin (Eds.), *Personality and the prediction of behavior* (pp. 269–305). New York: Academic Press.

Mischel, W. (1984b). Convergences and challenges in the search for consistency. *American Psychologist, 39,* 351–364.

Mischel, W., & Peake, P. K. (1982). Beyond déjà in the search for cross-situational consistency. *Psychological Review, 89,* 730–755.

Moss, H. A., & Sussman, E. J. (1980). Longitudinal study of personality development. In O. G. Brim, Jr. & J. Kagan (Eds.), *Constancy and change in human development* (pp. 530–595). Cambridge, MA: Harvard University Press.

Nisbett, R., & Ross, L. (1980). *Human inference: Strategies and shortcomings of social judgment.* Englewood Cliffs, NJ: Prentice-Hall.

Norman, W. T. (1963). Toward an adequate taxonomy of personality attributes: Replicated factor structure in peer nomination personality ratings. *Journal of Abnormal and Social Psychology, 66,* 574–583.

Nunnally, J. (1978). *Psychometric theory* (2nd ed.). New York: McGraw-Hill.

Peterson, D. R. (1968). *The clinical study of social behavior*. New York: Appleton-Century-Crofts.

Plomin, R. (1987). Behavior genetics and intervention. In J. J. Gallagher & C. T. Ramey (Eds.), *The malleability of children* (pp. 15–24). Baltimore: Paul H. Brookes.

Poth, R. L., & Barnett, D. W. (1988). Establishing the limits of interpretive confidence: A validity study of two preschool developmental scales. *School Psychology Review, 17*, 322–330.

Quay, H. C. (1986). Classification. In H. C. Quay & J. S. Werry (Eds.), *Psychopathological disorders of childhood* (3rd ed., pp. 1–34). New York: Wiley.

Quay, H. C., & Peterson, D. R. (1987). *Manual for the Revised Behavior Problem Checklist*. Miami, FL: Authors.

Rapoport, J. L., & Ismond, D. R. (1984). *DSM-III training guide for diagnosis of childhood disorders*. New York: Brunner/Mazel.

Reynolds, C. R., Gutkin, T. B., Elliott, S. N., & Witt, J. C. (1984). *School psychology: Essentials of theory and practice*. New York: Wiley.

Ronka, C. S., & Barnett, D. W. (1986). A comparison of adaptive behavior ratings: Revised Vineland and AAMD-ABS-SE. *Special Services in the Schools,2,* 87–96.

Runyon, W. M. (1983). Idiographic goals and methods in the study of lives. *Journal of Personality, 51*, 413–437.

Rushton, J. P., Brainerd, C. J., & Pressley, M. (1983). Behavioral development and construct validity: The principle of aggregation. *Psychological Bulletin, 94*, 39–53.

Rutter, M. (1984). Continuities and discontinuities in socioemotional development: Empirical and conceptual perspectives. In R. Emde & R. Harmon (Eds.), *Continuities and discontinuities in development* (pp. 41–68). New York: Plenum.

Salvia, J., & Ysseldyke, J. E. (1985). *Assessment in special and remedial education* (3rd ed.). Boston: Houghton Mifflin.

Scherer, K. R., & Ekman, P. (Eds.). (1984). *Approaches to emotions*. Hillsdale, NJ: Erlbaum.

Schmitt, N., Coyle, B. W., & Saari, B. B. (1977). A review and critique of analyses of multitrait–multimethod matrices. *Multivariate Behavioral Research, 12*, 447–478.

Schmitt, N., & Stults, D. M. (1986). Methodology review: Analysis of multitrait–multimethod matrices. *Applied Psychological Measurement, 10*, 1–22.

Schön, D. A. (1983). *The reflective practitioner: How professionals think in action*. New York: Basic Books.

Schulte, A. C., & Borich, G. D. (1985). *Using confidence intervals appropriately*. Paper presented at the meeting of the American Psychological Association, Los Angeles.

Sechrest, L. (1963). Incremental validity: A recommendation. *Educational and Psychological Measurement, 23*, 153–158.

Sechrest, L. (1984). Reliability and validity. In A. S. Bellack & M. Hersen (Eds.), *Research methods in clinical psychology* (pp. 24–54). New York: Pergamon Press.

Sells, S. B., & Murphy, D. (1984). Factor theories of personality. In N. S. Endler & J. M. Hunt (Eds.), *Personality and the behavior disorders* (2nd ed., Vol. 1, pp. 39–72). New York: Wiley.

Sobel, H. J. (1981). Projective methods of cognitive analysis. In T. V. Merluzzi, C. R. Glass, & M. Genest (Eds.), *Cognitive assessment* (pp. 127–149). New York: Guilford Press.

Stagner, R. (1948). *Psychology of personality* (2nd ed.). New York: McGraw-Hill.

Stagner, R. (1984). Trait psychology. In N. S. Endler & J. M. Hunt (Eds.), *Personality and the behavior disorders* (2nd ed., Vol. 1, pp. 3–38). New York: Wiley.

Stevens, J. (1986). *Applied multivariate statistics for the social sciences*. Hillsdale, NJ: Erlbaum.

Strosahl, K. D., & Linehan, M. M. (1986). Basic issues in behavioral assessment. In A. R. Ciminero, K. S. Calhoun, & H. E. Adams (Eds.), *Handbook of behavioral assessment* (2nd ed., pp. 12–46). New York: Wiley.

Thorndike, R. L. (1963). *The concepts of over- and underachievement*. New York: Teachers College, Columbia University.

Thorndike, R. L. (1967). Reliability. In D. N. Jackson & S. Messick (Eds.), *Problems in human assessment* (pp. 217–240). New York: McGraw-Hill.

Thorndike, R. L. (1982). *Applied Psychometrics*. Boston: Houghton Mifflin.

Thorndike, R. L., & Hagen, E. (1961). *Measurement and evaluation in psychology and education* (2nd ed.). New York: Wiley.

Tupes, E. C., & Christal, R. E. (1961). *Recurrent personality factors based on trait ratings*. (USAF-ASD Technical Report No. 61-97). Lackland Air Force Base, TX: U.S. Air Force.

Tversky, A., & Kahneman, D. (1984). The framing of decisions and the psychology of choice. In G. Wright (Ed.), *Behavioral decision making* (pp. 25–41). New York: Plenum.

von Winterfeldt, D., & Edwards, W. (1986). *Decision analysis and behavioral research*. New York: Cambridge University Press.

Wiggins, J. S. (1973). *Personality and prediction: Principles of personality assessment*. Reading, MA: Addison-Wesley.

Willems, E. P. (1977). Steps toward an ecobehavioral technology. In A. Rogers-Warren & S. F. Warren (Eds.), *Ecological perspectives in behavioral analysis* (pp. 39–61). Baltimore: University Park Press.

Wirt, R. D., Lachar, D., Klinedinst, J. K., & Seat, P. D. (1984). *Multidimensional description of child personality: A manual for the Personality Inventory for Children*. Los Angeles: Western Psychological Services.

Wolf, M. M. (1978). Social validity: The case for subjective measurement, or how applied behavior analysis is finding its heart. *Journal of Applied Behavior Analysis, 11*, 203–214.

Woodward, W. R. (1982). The "discovery" of social behaviorism and social learning theory 1870–1980. *American Psychologist, 37*, 396–411.

II

MODELS AND METHODS OF PERSONALITY ASSESSMENT: PROJECTIVE TESTING

3

The Projective Hypothesis and the Development of Projective Techniques for Children

LOUIS A. CHANDLER
University of Pittsburgh

It should be stated at the outset that this chapter is concerned with the use of projective techniques *with children*. A number of unique characteristics make children different from adults as experimental subjects and as participants in the projective experience. Too often, researchers and writers have ignored this important variable when generalizing about the use of projective techniques. It is within that context that the statements made here, both critical and supportive, must be evaluated.

HISTORICAL OVERVIEW

In order to understand the current status of projective techniques, a brief historical overview is helpful. The history of personality assessment prior to the 1930s followed a fairly direct evolutionary path (see Figure 3.1). Its roots can be traced to the experiments of Wundt, Galton, and Cattel around the turn of the century. Indeed, Sattler (1982) has called the period from 1890 to 1905 the "laboratory period" in mental measurement, since it was during that time that tests were devised for measuring individual responses—tests that were gradually to find application in the emerging practice of psychology. These early efforts developed the methods and techniques that would be employed in the study of individual differences.

From these laboratory tasks, the line extended through such pioneering psychometric instruments as the Woodworth Personal Data Sheet of 1919 and the Bernreuter Personality Inventory of 1931. These instruments, based on face or content validity, contained items thought to represent the traits or dimensions under study. The items were arranged in a test format, allowing a subject's response to be scored and quantified. Quantification allowed one subject's scores to be compared to another's. It was thus possible to examine similarities and differences in test performance. It was also possible to compare the individual's score against some group average or norm.

But while psychometric techniques continued to develop along one track, a radically new approach was being proposed by the 1930s. This involved methods that had their theoretical foundations in psychoanalysis—at that time, a growing influence on psychiatry and psychology. These new methods were exemplified by the technique introduced by Hermann Rorschach as a means of personality appraisal.

In Rorschach's (1921) technique, a subject is presented with a set of 10 inkblots and asked to provide associations and interpretations. No attempt is made to structure or limit the response; rather, the subject is encouraged to generate his or her own

55

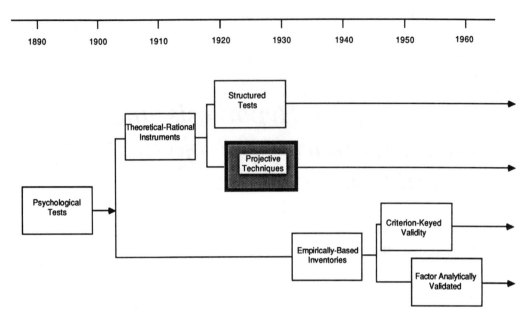

FIGURE 3.1.   The historical development of personality assessment methods.

unique response pattern. L. K. Frank (1939) is generally credited with coining the term "projective technique" for those methods that employ a relatively ambiguous stimulus to which the subject is asked to give meaning. The Rorschach technique, with its emphasis on the idiographic features of each individual's response pattern, stood in contrast to the psychometric focus of the comparative or nomothetic aspects. This was to become a fundamental point of difference between the two approaches.

Rorschach's technique was introduced in America by Samuel Beck in the 1930s. Also during that decade, Henry Murray and his colleague Christiana Morgan, while engaged in the study of personality, conceived of the idea of using stories generated by subjects to a standard set of relatively ambiguous pictures. The resulting technique, the Thematic Apperception Test (TAT; Murray, 1943) has subsequently found use in clinical practice.

At about the same time, there arose a growing interest in the use of creative drawings in psychological assessment. The clinical use of drawings can be traced back to Florence Goodenough (1926), who first proposed assessing children's intellectual maturity from their drawings of a person. Goodenough noted variations in the drawings that could not be accounted for by age, and pro-

posed that factors such as anxiety might influence drawings. But it was Karen Machover (1949) who was to emphasize the psychodynamic aspects of the drawing of a person in terms of the child's self-image. She suggested that a qualitative assessment might be done using drawings that could be examined for emotional indicators.

These major projective techniques were to spawn a number of others during the 1930s and 1940s. Such approaches to the study of personality, focusing as they did on individual responses, made few attempts to compare group responses. Unlike psychometric tests, these techniques did not easily lend themselves to quantification and statistical treatment.

The different approaches to the study of personality have led to misunderstanding and controversy. As a result, within the last few decades projective techniques have come in for considerable criticism from those who advocate psychometric, or, more recently, behavioral approaches to assessment. One result has been a recent decline in the number of published articles dealing with projective techniques (O'Leary & Johnson, 1979; Polyson, Norris, & Ott, 1985). Yet, while research interest appears to have waned, projective techniques continue to be popular among practicing psychologists

(Lubin, Larsen, & Matarazzo, 1984; Piotrowski, 1984), particularly among those who conduct personality assessments with children (Goh & Fuller, 1983). It is worth examining these techniques more closely to see what it is that makes them so compelling in that context.

THE PROJECTIVE HYPOTHESIS AND ITS USE WITH CHILDREN

The Projective Hypothesis

Two fundamental questions need to be addressed in a discussion of projective techniques: What is the nature of the mechanism of projection, and how does it work?

The projective hypothesis is based on the tendency of human beings to view and interpret their world in terms of their own experience. This anthropomorphic quality influences all our perceptions to a greater or lesser degree, and we can never totally escape it. For the same reason, every human production, from the most mundane to the most creative, reflects some aspect of the self. It is this tendency to interpret our world and to express ourselves in our productions that led Murray (1943) to explain the ability of TAT stories to reveal the personality as "the tendency of people to interpret an ambiguous human situation in conformity with their past experiences and present wants, and the tendency of those who write stories to do likewise" (p. 1).

Although there is some agreement on the fundamental nature of projection, there are differences of opinion as to how the mechanism operates. Part of the problem lies in the fact that the term "projection" has two meanings. "Projection," in common usage, means to cast forward. In this sense, projection implies a direct extension of psychological characteristics onto the outer world.

But "projection" also has a specific meaning within psychoanalytic theory. Freud (1936) used the term to refer to the process that occurs when the ego, faced with unacceptable wishes or ideas, thrusts them out onto the external world as a means of defense. In projection the individual attributes his or her own thoughts and actions to someone else. Thus, if one's own faults or feelings are unacceptable to the ego, they may be seen as belonging to someone else; in the process, the material may become distorted or remain partially repressed. From such a perspective, projective material would not be seen as direct representations of aspects of the personality—certainly not with the sort of one-to-one correspondence that the first meaning of "projection" implies. Hammer (1958) reflects this point of view when he writes that "distortions enter into the process of projection to the extent to which the projection has a defensive function . . . qualities are ascribed to the object the presence of which the subject denies in himself" (pp. 53–54).

This dual function of projection—as a psychological tendency to extend inner attributes to the outer world, and as a defense—creates problems in interpreting projective material. For example, if a child's story contains frequent references to violence, are we to interpret that as an actual reflection of an aggressive personality, or perhaps of a personality wherein aggression is latent and unlikely to find behavioral expression? After several decades of research with projective techniques, the crucial issue of the correspondence between fantasies and behavior remains poorly understood (Klinger, 1971; McNeil, 1976; Megargee & Cook, 1967; O'Leary & Johnson, 1979).

The Use of Projective Techniques with Children

In spite of these interpretive difficulties, projective techniques continue to be widely used, especially with children. Some of the reasons for this popularity are found both in the nature of childhood and in the nature of projective techniques. There are two sides to the coin. First, we must examine the developmental features of children that recommend them as ideal candidates for projective techniques; then we must examine the features of projective techniques that make *them* particularly useful with children.

As they struggle with the developmental task of gradually constructing a world view in consonance with adult reality, children's thinking processes undergo considerable change. Piaget has reported in great detail the changes in thinking that occur in the developing child. One such process involves externalization.

For Piaget, "externalization" is a process by which we attribute to things in the external world the products of our own mental activity. According to Elkind (1976), this attribution is immediate and unconscious. Elkind makes the point that this process differs from the psychoanalytic notion of "projection" in that it is a normal process common to everyone (thus, it is closer to "projection" as commonly used).

While externalization is a relevant facet of a child's thinking in terms of the projective experience, it is especially useful when combined with another childlike quality—egocentrism. "Egocentrism" refers to the young child's inability to put himself or herself in another's position and to adopt the other's point of view. Unlike the egocentric adult who can take another's point of view but chooses not to, the child is incapable of the perceptual shift.

Kessler (1966) has pointed to the similarity between childlike egocentrism and the projection of the paranoid patient. Like that of the paranoid patient, the child's narcissism is overwhelming. And like the paranoid individual, "[the child] interprets the universe as revolving around him, either to hurt him or help him, and he personifies all happenings in terms of his own projected wishes and fears" (p. 33). These two tendencies—toward externalization (with its immediate and unconscious aspects) and egocentrism (with its personification)—mean that children, who tend to rely heavily on both, are naturally good candidates for projective techniques.

The systematic study of childhood has also pointed to other relevant factors. We know, for example, that langauge acquisition is a gradual process, and that many crucial events occur in the life of the child before full mastery of speech and language. Even when they have acquired some language, children remain unable to express their feelings directly in words, and often resort to the more primitive means of motoric expression. We find a similar phenomenon when, as adults, we are confronted with one of those rare experiences where words fail us. In attempting to describe such situations, we find ourselves groping for analogies or metaphors to express what seems beyond logical narrative (Kenniston, 1965).

Even when speech and language are fairly well developed, verbal expression does not remain the sole or even the preferred way in which the child communicates. The difficulties found in conducting interviews with children illustrate the complexity of the problem. Ginsburg and Opper (1979) detail how, in the course of the interview, the child is asked to perform several tasks. He or she must interpret the examiner's question, make a special effort to comprehend the crucial aspects of the question, and express his or her response in words. It is not surprising that children, especially young children, may prefer to express themselves by projective techniques, which employ visual stimuli and/or motor or visual–motor response modes, as opposed to techniques that rely more on language.

Along with those language and associated cognitive limitations that make children poor subjects for interviews, a number of conscious factors intervene to influence their responses. Social desirability, motivation, and degree of cooperation all may influence the interviewing process. Unlike the self-report measures of personality assessment used with adults, projective techniques do not depend on higher levels of language development and conceptual understanding, and they require only minimal cooperation. The latter point may make them especially attractive, since children seldom find themselves being assessed as a result of a self-referral.

One further aspect of children's suitability for projective techniques needs to be mentioned. This has to do with the observation that children are in transition from prelogical to logical thought, from a magical to a realistic world view. Freud (1911/1959) explicated the developmental shift in terms of primary-process thinking versus secondary-process thinking. Primary-process thinking operates in accordance with the pleasure principle; secondary-process thinking in accordance with the reality principle.

Primary process thinking can be seen in dreams, where anything is possible, often in defiance of the laws of logic. It is also present to some extent in symptom formations of neurotic patients, and, of course, it dominates the thought processes of the young child. Primary-process thinking operates at the level of symbols. It is primitive and pre-verbal. Gradually, more of a child's thinking processes come to be dominated by the reality principle, although lapses and regression are common, especially in times of emotional distress.

Using magical thinking in the context of the adult real world leads to inevitable misunderstandings, frustrations, and conflict, often to the detriment of the child. This difference in thinking can also play a key role in children's emotional problems. The difference may be observed, for example, when a child, in appraising some event or situation, perceives the threat of harm or loss. If this perception results from magical thinking, it may well happen that an observing adult will see the child simply as being unrealistic (this is literally true, from the adult's point of view). The dark at the top of the stairs provides a case in point: Adult assurances, and even reality testing (turning on the light), may not be enough to eliminate the child's fears.

To understand a child's emotional status, a method of assessment is needed that allows us access to this inner world of childhood. Projective techniques hold the promise of being such a method.

VALIDITY

Several writers have stated that projective techniques are not tests, and should not therefore be subjected to the constraints normally applied to psychometric devices (Frank, 1939; Holt, 1978; Schwartz & Lazar, 1979). Yet fundamental validity and reliability issues cannot be avoided. Certain basic questions may legitimately be asked of any assessment method: Does it do what it purports to do, and does it do so with consistency?

The validity of projective techniques rests, in the first instance, on the projective hypothesis. Thus initial validity is based on the assumption that one's productions reflect qualities of the personality, although it may be argued that these techniques, specifically designed to elicit externalization, are at best only partially successful (Anastasi, 1982). The relative proportion of externalization manifested may vary among individuals, and even within the same individual if he or she is administered the same technique on two different occasions (Lindzay & Herman, 1955). This calls into question whether projective techniques are capable of accurately identifying relatively stable personality traits, or are more sensitive to situational variables.

If the purpose of using projective techniques is to obtain some global picture of the individual's personality (Anastasi, 1982), then the issue of whether they can identify enduring personality traits becomes a critical one. If, on the other hand, the purpose is to estimate the individual's *current* motivational and emotional status (Obrzut & Cummings, 1983), perhaps in terms of certain specified factors (Chandler, 1985), then the issue becomes less critical. These and other problems associated with projective techniques beg the question as to the purpose of the assessment. If the validity question is "Does this method do what we want it to do?", then we must be clear as to what it is we wish these techniques to do in the context of the personality assessment. The question as to what constitutes an appropriate outcome—in this case, what criteria the technique's performance can be measured against—is ultimately a question of criterion-related validity.

Beginning in the 1950s, a number of validation studies were performed on projective techniques (e.g., Little & Shneidman, 1959). Most of these studies were concerned with some aspect of criterion-related validity-that is, discriminative and/or predictive validity. Typically, such studies tested how well the techniques could discriminate between groups or predict membership in various psychiatric diagnostic categories. The results were generally negative; projective techniques were found to do poorly in discriminating between groups (Gittleman-Klein, 1978) and to do little better than chance in predicting diagnostic group membership (Chambers & Hamlin, 1957). This poor performance led some critics to conclude that the techniques were not valid. However, another interpretation is that these experiments were ill conceived because the hypothesis that they were designed to test was inappropriate. It has been argued that the purpose of projective techniques is not to determine psychiatric group membership, but to increase understanding (Exner, 1983; Holt, 1970; Knoff, 1983) or to provide information useful in developing interventions (Batsche & Peterson, 1983).

Wiggins (1980) finds the distinction proposed by Prelinger and Zimet (1964) to be an useful one. Those writers distinguish between "assessment for" and "assessment of." The former implies a predictive aspect of assessment; the latter implies the "understanding" that characterizes psychoanalytic investigations. Wiggins points out that the validation of each approach is established by recourse to different sources of evidence. For predicting diagnostic categories, such methods as those measuring the number of correct decisions are appropriate. For psychoanalytic investigations, interpretations are evaluated within the context of internal consistency among multiple sources of evidence.

Until there is some agreement as to what constitutes an appropriate outcome when projective techniques are used in clinical assessment, validity problems will remain, and projective techniques will continue to be poorly understood.

RELIABILITY

Although validity continues to be a concern with projective techniques, an issue of equal if not greater importance is reliability, since an assessment system that is unreliable must be invalid (McDermott, 1980; Spitzer & Fleis, 1974).

"Reliability" is a psychometric concept that can be approached in several ways. There are unique considerations associated with various types of reliability when applied to projective techniques. One index of reliability is agreement between two administrations of the same test with the same subject. But test–retest reliability poses problems with projective techniques, since if the interval between administrations is short, recall may affect the results; if the interval is long, the changes found may reflect actual changes that have occurred in the personality over time (Lanyon & Goodstein, 1982). Then, too, if projective techniques assess *current* emotional and motivational variables, test–retest reliability may be an inappropriate method to use (Obrzut & Cummings, 1983).

Still another index of consistency is split-half reliability, normally obtained by computing the correlation between scores on comparable halves of a test. But here, too, there are problems when applied to projective techniques. It can be argued that the cards used in the Rorschach technique, for example, are not comparable, so that this measure of internal consistency is not applicable (Anastasi, 1982). Although split-half reliability may be of limited value with projective techniques, Wagner and his colleagues have recently proposed a new technique for optimizing internal reliability estimates of the Rorschach that takes into account split-half distributional anomalies. They have also suggested that their method may be applied to other projective techniques (Wagner, Alexander, Roos, & Adair, 1986.)

One commonly used test of reliability for projective techniques is interjudge agreement, although there are difficulties with this as well. For an adequate test of interjudge agreement, some standardized scoring procedure is necessary. Over the years there have been a number of attempts to develop scoring procedures for projective techniques; Hughes (1983), in her review of the literature, identified nearly 40 methods that had been proposed for analyzing and interpreting thematic apperception techniques. These efforts have met with varying degrees of success. (Because there are different issues associated with the various techniques, these are discussed in the section below devoted to the major techniques.)

In general, the effort has been to develop relatively objective, quantitative scoring systems that can supplant or supplement the traditional methods of analysis and interpretation. Here, too, there are obstacles that make the task of developing a scoring system difficult. A lack of standardized procedures for administering some techniques, along with variations between different examiners, may influence the results. The stimulus material may not be standardized, as in the case of the TAT, where examiners may select which cards to present. The varying lengths of response, and the representativeness of the scoring constructs throughout the stimulus material, cause further difficulties (Lanyon & Goodstein, 1982). Finally, there remains some degree of subjective judgment—if not in the scoring, then in the interpretation of the response.

Because of these difficulties and the problem of controlling for the relevant variables in reliability studies, it is not surprising to find a wide range reported among the reliability data on projective techniques. For example, Magnusson (1960) has reported interjudge reliability on Children's Apperception Test (CAT) protocols as ranging from .17 to .72.

MAJOR PROJECTIVE TECHNIQUES USED WITH CHILDREN

Although a considerable number of projective techniques have been developed since the 1930s, most have been variations on a few major types. Of these, three major techniques have been widely used with children: creative drawings, thematic apperception techniques, and the Rorschach technique (Goh & Fuller, 1983; Prout, 1983).

The Projective Aspects of Drawings

Creative drawings, like other forms of artistic production, have long been seen as expressing some aspect of the artist's personality. Yet the systematic use of drawings in clinical assessment is a modern development. As pointed out above, drawings were initially proposed as a means of estimating the level of children's mental development (Goodenough, 1926; Harris, 1963), but from the beginning writers have observed that drawings are influenced by emotional factors (Buck, 1948; Hammer, 1958; Machover, 1949).

One of the first to call attention to the projective aspects of drawings was Karen Machover. Machover's task, like Goodenough's, was to ask the child to draw a person (the Draw-A-Person technique). A number of other drawing techniques have since been developed, including the House–Tree–Person (H-T-P; Buck, 1948), Human Figure Drawing (Machover, 1949), Draw-A-Family (Hulse, 1951), and Kinetic Family Drawing (K-F-D; Burns & Kaufman, 1970) techniques.

In analyzing drawings, the formal aspects as well as the content are considered. The formal aspects of drawings include such elements as the size and placement of items; the quality of lines and the amount of pressure used; erasures, distortions, and omissions; and undue emphasis on or unusual treatment of details.

In general, the approach is to interpret content elements of the drawings by referring to associated personality features. Such associations are derived from clinical experience and/or research studies that have hypothesized or demonstrated a relationship between the drawings' elements and various aspects of personality. For example, Buck (1971) suggests that high placement of a figure on the page may be interpreted as a high level of aspiration. Hammer (1958) maintains that a fence drawn around a house suggests defensiveness on the part of the individual.

Various checklists of such associated features have been compiled to aid in interpreting drawings (Jolles, 1971; Ogden, 1977; Urban, 1963). There is general agreement that while drawings may be helpful as aids in understanding children, they are best used in combination with other assessment instruments, and are never recommended as the sole method of personality assessment (Klopfer & Taulbee, 1976; Koppitz, 1983).

One frequently used drawing method is Buck's (1948) H-T-P technique, wherein the subjects is asked to draw a house, a tree, and a person, in that order. It is hypothesized that the house drawing elicits associations concerning home life and the family situation, whereas the tree and person drawings reflect aspects of self-concept and self-image (Hammer, 1985). According to Hammer, the tree represents the more unconscious aspects of the self-concept; the person represents those that are more conscious.

There are differing opinions as to what the person drawing actually represents. Hammer (1985) maintains that three types of person drawings are possible: self-portrait, self-ideal, or a representation of a significant other. Koppitz (1968), commenting on children's person drawings, has hypothesized that they represent the self-portrait and reflect the self-concepts, attitudes, and concerns of the moment. Yet she goes on to say that some children do not identify with the person they draw, but may depict a person who concerns them most at the time they make the drawing.

DiLeo (1973) also speculates on the meaning of the person when drawn by a child. He points out that often the figure the child tends to draw is an adult, a significant figure in his or her life. He goes on to make the interesting observation that a child who is relatively well adjusted is more interested in the external world; hence the drawing is more a concept of humankind with the self incorporated. In such a case, the product is more likely to be a significant adult. On the other hand, the child who is beset by worries and anxiety is more likely to be self-absorbed and tends to produce a self-image.

Koppitz (1968, 1984) has proposed analyzing children's drawings of the human figure in a six-step procedure. This includes the examination of the drawing for the presence of what she has termed "emotional indicators." These clinical signs are unusual features that have been found to occur significantly more often in the drawings of children with serious emotional problems. Koppitz originally identified these signs by examining the drawings of more than 1,800 school children. The criteria for inclusion of a sign as an emotional indicator were as follows: The sign was not present in more than 6% of the drawings of normal children; it differentiated between children with and without emotional problems; and it did not increase in frequency solely as a function of age. Using these criteria, Koppitz was able to identify 30 emotional indicators. Koppitz warns that these signs can only be interpreted as tendencies and must be viewed in the context of a more comprehensive assessment.

Another popular drawing technique requires the child to "draw a picture of your family." This Draw-A-Family technique (Hulse, 1951) results in a sort of family portrait, which is then analyzed by reference to the relative size, proximity, and placement of figures, and the significant additions, omissions, and elaborations of various family members.

A more recent variation on this technique is the K-F-D, in which the child is asked to "draw a picture of everyone in your family *doing* something" (Burns & Kaufman, 1970). The K-F-D is designed to assess a child's self-concept and perception of interpersonal relations. Family dynamics are suggested by the interaction among figures, and drawings are examined in terms of action, style, and symbols.

A number of interesting scoring systems have been proposed for the K-F-D (Cummings, 1981; Knoff & Prout, 1985). For example, a promising system developed by Mostroff and Lazarus (1983) consists of 20 variables on which the drawing may be rated. These researchers report interjudge agreement of 86 to 100 percent with a mean agreement of 97. Their data has also led them to conclude that the K-F-D probably measures state rather than trait characteristics.

Other interpersonal and situational dynamics may be explored by such techniques as school drawings (Prout & Phillips, 1974). And recently, Knoff and Prout (1985) have suggested integrating the K-F-D and school drawings into a single approach.

The use of children's drawings in assessment raises validity issues similar to those found with other projective techniques. Falk (1981) has examined the validity question by analyzing the research on one popular technique, the Draw-A-Person. Falk asks why an intuitively obvious way of understanding children has not been documented as such. He concludes that there are three reasons, all having to do with the approach of research studies that purport to examine validity. These are (1) a poor understanding of the theory of projection (and hence unrealistic outcomes for such studies); (2) the relatively small number of studies using children as subjects, and generalizations that take place from adult studies; and (3) poorly conceived psychiatric categories, which make predictive studies difficult.

Finally, Falk (1981) suggests some reasons for using drawing techniques with children. They tend to communicate indirectly, often by giving clues about what they think and feel. They often cannot express their feelings in words, especially their fears. Lastly, drawings are seen as a more "natural" activity for children than for adults. For these reasons drawings seem useful with children, and, if used appropriately, may help in furthering the understanding of children.

Thematic Apperception Techniques

Undoubtedly, the thematic projective technique that has had the most profound effect on applied psychology has been Henry Murray's TAT. The TAT was originally developed in the 1930s as a means of applying Murray's "need–press" theory of personality (Dana, 1985).

Murray conceived of personality theory as a theory of motivation. He proposed a set of motives as antecendents of personality traits and types; these motives could be assessed by analyzing the stories told by subjects viewing a set of pictures. After some experimentation, Murray and his colleagues came up with 31 plates—30 black-and-white illustrations and 1 blank card—which were to comprise the standard TAT set. Certain cards were designated for use with males, females, boys, and girls. The illustrations were meant to be rather ambiguous and to represent a wide variety of life situations: some common and everyday, others unusual and bizarre.

Murray (1938) advocated that the stories be examined by using a need–press analysis—that is, by interpreting them in terms of the needs of the hero or heroine of the story and the environmental forces or presses to which he or she was subjected. Murray suggested that the interpretation of TAT stories should include consideration of unusually high or unusually low frequencies of motives and feelings in the set of stories. With this method, scores could be tallied, and a rank order of needs and presses could be established. However, Murray's scheme proved cumbersome, requiring many hours of examiners' time, so that it was not practical for clinical work (Bellak, 1971). (At one point, Murray [1943] had identified some 40 needs and "thirty or more" presses that could be applied to each story.)

As the popularity of the TAT grew, various schemes were proposed for analyzing, scoring, and interpreting the TAT protocol. Murstein (1963) has reviewed a number of these in some detail. In a more recent review, Hughes (1983) has identified 39 such methods, which she has classified as "structured psychodynamic," "unstructured psychodynamic," "response productivity," and "formal characteristics" methods.

One of the more promising approaches was proposed by Cox and Sargent (1950), whose scoring method was designed as a research tool for analyzing the normative aspects of selected TAT cards. Cox and Sargent proposed that the cards be analyzed in terms of

six broad categories: needs, threats, feelings, heroes, action, and outcomes. A number of possible variables were to be considered within each category. With the exception of the action category, interjudge reliability ranged from .67 to 1.00, prompting the researchers to conclude that a scoring system for thematic material based on such "adaptive" aspects of the stories could be reliably employed.

In more recent years, the scoring systems have tended to focus on a few specific factors, moving away from broad general categories. As Thomas and Dudek (1985) have pointed out, the TAT scoring systems that have been the most successful have been those tailored for a specific purpose. Their own system was designed to examine interpersonal affect. Other scoring systems of this type include the well-known work of McClelland and his colleagues on achievement motivation (McClelland, Atkinson, Clark, & Lowell, 1953), and recent attempts by Kaliopska (1982) to assess empathy and by McAdams (1980) to assess intimacy motivation, all using the TAT.

Another recent development is a scoring system for the TAT and similar thematic techniques that places the responses in the context of the child or adolescent's experience of life stress. This system, called the Need–Threat Analysis (NTA), was developed as part of a stress assessment system for children designed specifically as a way of providing information on sources of perceived stress (Chandler, 1985; Chandler, Shermis, & Lempert, 1989). The NTA uses two categories derived from Murray's concepts through Cox and Sargent (1950); needs and threats. In this context, "stress" is defined as emotional tension arising from unmet needs and/or environmental threats, so that the purpose of the projective technique within the assessment is to identify those underlying needs and threats that are likely to make a particular event or situation especially meaningful, and hence stressful to an individual child.

Preliminary findings suggested that forcing motivations into a dichotomy of needs or threats was unrealistic, since motives generally contain some proportion of each. Therefore, selected needs and threats from the Cox and Sargent (1950) system were paired to provide five need–threat combinations, or "binaries": Independence–Domination, Affiliation–Rejection, Security–Insecurity, Achievement–Failure, and Aggression–Punishment. Each story is checked for the presence of each binary, and a tally is kept. The relative percentage of the occurrence of each binary throughout the set of cards is then calculated and the binaries are rank-ordered, so that the more important ones can be identified.

Two studies were conducted using the CAT, an instrument similar to the TAT (Hughes, 1983; Lempert, 1986). Both studies used graduate students as judges. After a brief orientation, they were asked to score a number of CAT protocols. Interjudge reliability correlations of .68 and .69 were found in the Hughes and Lempert studies, respectively. In addition, the percent of agreement with respect to the dominant binary ranged from 80 to 100. Intrajudge reliability correlation over a 1-month interval ranged from .76 to .85.

While various researchers were at work designing scoring systems for the TAT, another track of development was being followed by those who were developing TAT-like instruments. For example, Symonds (1948) published a picture–story test with TAT-like cards that were specifically designed to be relevant to adolescents. Symonds, like Murray, urged that the interpretation of TAT stories take into account the frequency of themes occurring over the entire set of stories. He maintained that from this frequency "one may logically assume that the theme has special significance for the subject" (1948, p. 2).

Even as Symonds found the TAT lacking in relevance for the adolescent population, so Bellak and Bellak (1949) found it to be of questionable usefulness with children, particularly younger children. These authors, in response to the need for an instrument more suited for the expression of the needs, emotions, and drives of children, developed the CAT. Like the TAT, this technique consists of a set of pictures about which the child is asked to tell a story. The authors recommend its use with children between the ages of 3 and 10 years.

In constructing the stimulus cards, the authors chose situations that they felt reflected critical issues of childhood, such as sibling rivalry, oral problems, attitudes toward parents, Oedipal concerns, and aggression. In this way the development of the CAT differed, at least in degree, from that of the TAT, where the attempt was to make the situation depicted relatively ambiguous. The degree of ambiguity of the stimulus in projective tests varies along a continuum from the abstract forms of the Rorschach through the relatively ambiguous situations of the TAT to the more blatant situations of the CAT, and finally to specifically oriented techniques such as the Blacky Pictures (Blum, 1950), which are explicitly designed to elicit comments on situations of psychoanalytic relevance (e.g., the Oedipal situation, castration anxiety, etc.).

Another important difference between the CAT and the TAT is the use of animal figures in the pictures, based on the assumption that children would identify more readily with animals.

In discussing analysis and interpretation, the authors of the CAT suggest that 10 aspects of the protocol be examined: main theme, hero, needs of the hero, concept of the environment, parental figures, significant conflicts, nature of anxieties, main defenses, severity of superego, and integration of ego. The authors resist providing a quantitative method of scoring, justifying their position by insisting that when one is using projective techniques, the focus should be on semantics and not statistics.

Recently, there have been several attempts to develop new thematic techniques that might be shown to be more valid and reliable. The Tasks of Emotional Development (TED) is a technique developed to provide a more objective method that could include normative data on the emotional development of children (Cohen & Weil, 1975). The purpose of the TED is to assess the degree to which developmental tasks are met and mastered at various age levels. The test consists of a set of 13 photographs, each of which depicts a different task of emotional development. The stories children produce in response to the photographs are scored using a set of objective rating scales that have five dimensions (perception, outcome, affect, motivation, and spontaneity), each of which permits the assessment of certain aspects of the mastery process. Pollak, Cohen, and

Weil (1981) have provided a review of research applications of the TED.

Still another recent development is the Roberts Apperception Test for Children (RATC; McArthur & Roberts, 1982). The RATC consists of a set of 27 stimulus cards (of which only 16 are administered to a given child). These cards depict common situations, conflicts, and stresses in children's lives. They are intended to measure areas of interpersonal interaction and are scored in terms of adaptive scales (eight), clinical scales (five), and other indicators (three). In the recommended scoring procedure, each story is scored separately on all the rating categories by checking whether the category applies to that story. The authors also recommend that both qualitative and quantitative aspects be taken into account when interpreting stories.

Vane (1981), in a review of the TAT, draws some conclusions relevant to thematic apperception techniques in general. He notes that the TAT's popularity as a clinical instrument remains high in spite of criticisms of its validity. He then goes on to urge the development of more standardized approaches to the TAT, because "research experience suggests that the TAT method elicits material regarding attitudes and motivation that is not adequately elicited by other methods" (p. 319).

The Rorschach Technique

The Rorschach technique consists of a set of 10 symmetrical inkblots (5 achromatic, 5 chromatic) printed on white cards, to which the respondent is asked to give associations. After all 10 plates have been presented, the examiner goes back over each response with the respondent to determine the precise area of the blot that elicited the response. The response is then scored (minimally) in terms of four categories: Location, Determinants, Content, and Originality. Location refers to the part of the blot that elicited the response; Determinants to the features of the blot that contributed to the formation of the percept; Content to the object represented in the response; and Originality to the uniqueness of the response. In some scoring systems, additional scoring categories are provided. Once scoring has been completed, an interpreta-

tion is made in terms of personality characteristics that are purported to be associated with certain scores or configurations of scores when placed in the context of the whole protocol.

There is an extensive literature on the Rorschach; much of it is devoted to validity issues, and much of that has used adult populations as subjects. Some of these validity issues have already been considered in the discussion of other projective techniques, although some are unique to the Rorschach (Exner, 1974; Lanyon & Goodstein, 1982). Although the preponderance of studies have used adults as subjects, the Rorschach has been used with children and adolescents in clinical practice. Some believe that the Rorschach can be used effectively with children as young as 5 years of age (Erdberg, 1985); others maintain that it can be used with even younger preschoolers, although extensive modifications may be necessary (Ames, Metraux, Rodell, & Walker, 1974; Halpern, 1971).

An important concern in the Rorschach literature on children and adolescents has to do with the developmental aspects of the Rorschach protocols. In general, the effort has been to focus more closely on development and the deviations in development than on the more crystallized traits and symptomatic conditions normally associated with adult psychopathology. There have been a few attempts to document developmental changes as reflected in Rorschach protocols by developing norms for children and adolescents (Ames, Metraux, Rodell, & Walker, 1974; Ames, Metraux, & Walker, 1971; Hertz, 1961). Adoption and use of such norms depend upon which one of the several scoring methods the examiner follows. And this lack of an agreed-upon scoring system has caused problems for Rorschach use over the years.

As the Rorschach gained acceptance in this country, five major approaches evolved for scoring and interpreting the technique. During the 1960s, Exner (1969) began a study of each of the extant systems to develop his Comprehensive System, in which he hoped to combine the best elements of each. Exner's goal was to develop a data-based system that could be standardized. By 1974 he and his colleagues had completed more than 150 studies, establishing the data base and supporting empirical evidence that he presented in his first volume on the Comprehensive System (Exner, 1974). A later volume was devoted to assessing children and adolescents (Exner & Weiner, 1982).

Exner believes it is an error to refer to the Rorschach as a "projective technique," because it is much more than that (Exner, 1983). He conceives of the Rorschach in two ways: as a perceptual–cognitive task, and as a stimulus to fantasy. The dual nature of the technique means that in interpretation different information is used in each context.

When the Rorschach is seen as a perceptual–cognitive task, the respondent must impose structure and organization on an ambiguous stimulus. From an analysis of this task, certain structural aspects of the personality may be inferred, such as cognitive styles, tendencies, and traits. These are seen as aspects of the personality that are relatively stable across time and situations, as well as ones that are more nearly representative of actual behavior (i.e., the approach the respondent uses in dealing with life experiences). Exner maintains that inferences based on structural responses can be made with some certainty.

When the Rorschach is seen as a stimulus to elicit fantasy, it provides information on personality dynamics. Information is provided on such aspects as needs, attitudes, and conflicts. Here the focus is on the content of the protocol—*what* the respondent says, not *how* he or she says it. Whereas perceptual–cognitive interpretations are representative of behavior, fantasy interpretations are seen as symbolic. Because there are a number of possible ways of understanding how fantasied material may be employed, inferences drawn from this aspect must remain more speculative.

These two levels of interpretation point to an important distinction, and one with implications not only for how much confidence the examiner can put in the interpretations of various aspects of the protocol, but also for the design and execution of research on the validity of the Rorschach (Exner & Weiner, 1982).

As for using his system with children, Exner argues that "Rorschach behavior means what it means regardless of the age of the subject" (Exner & Weiner, 1982, p. 14). The age of the subject becomes important, however, in interpreting the findings. Here a knowledge of developmental psychology and developmental psychopathology is essential. For example, a certain constellation of scores may indicate that the respondent lacks emotional control. This finding can only be interpreted by knowing what constitutes appropriate emotional control for a child of a certain age.

Exner provides normative data for children and adolescents, as well as extensive evidence on reliability of various aspects of the scoring system. In general, the reliability studies have taken a temporal-consistency approach using a test–retest design. This allows the examiner to view the relative stability of various scores and constellations over time. Exner reports good results, with most reliabilities above .70 and some exceeding .90 (Exner, 1983). He also interprets those few scores that are very unstable over both short and long periods of time as of questionable significance, but as clearly correlated with external factors such as situational stress.

Clearly, Exner's work represents a major contribution to the development of the Rorschach. With his data on the construct validity and temporal stability of Rorschach variables, he has provided a solid empirical foundation upon which to build. Anastasi (1982) has summarized Exner's efforts thus:

> A major contribution of Exner's work is the provision of a uniform Rorschach system that permits comparability among the research findings of different investigators. The availability of this system, together with the research completed thus far, has injected new life into the Rorschach as a potential psychometric instrument. (p. 569)

CONCLUSIONS

Projective techniques have been used for more than 50 years, and for most of that time they have been the subject of controversy. Critics have questioned the validity, the value, and even the ethics of using them. Although a number of issues are involved in the controversy, it seems that the more fundamental questions have to do with the place of projective techniques within the personality assessment, and, ultimately, the purpose of that assessment. The confusion arises from differing opinions as to what kind of information is expected and what kind of information the selected technique can best provide.

If projective techniques are seen as capable of contributing toward a global personality assessment by providing information on traits, characteristics, motivation, tendencies, intelligence, coping style, needs, temperament, defenses, fears and anxieties, ego strength, conflicts, adjustment, and psychopathological deviations, then the goal may be too ambitious, in which case projective techniques are bound to be disappointing. Advocates who claim such sweeping goals must assume the burden of proof. It may be because of such ambitious goals that projective techniques were originally oversold. If this is the case, then what we are seeing now is a necessary correction as more modest goals are being proposed, refined, and validated.

Similarly, if the goal is to provide data relevant to a dichotomous decision on membership in a psychiatric category—a category that may itself be of questionable validity—then projective techniques will fail to achieve that goal with any consistency, a finding amply demonstrated. On the other hand, if the goal is to contribute toward understanding a child by providing specific information for the psychological assessment, if that information is made relevant by some theoretical context, and if that information is of the type that is best provided by the selected technique, then the probability of success is considerably enhanced. After decades of experience, it is becoming increasingly clear that each of the major techniques best provides different types of information when used with children (see Table 3.1).

A final word should be said about the nature of the inferences drawn from projective techniques. As Exner and Weiner (1982) have pointed out, some projective technique data are more speculative than others. The challenge for researchers in the years ahead will be to sort out which conclusions will be the best justified, and which will have to remain speculative. The results of such research should enable the clinician to know

TABLE 3.1. Major Projective Techniques as Information Sources

Major technique	Best used to provide information on:
Creative drawings	Self-image Interpersonal relations Overall level of adjustment
Thematic apperception techniques	Current concerns Motivations, needs, and threats Perception of significant others
Rorschach technique	Perceptual–cognitive aspects, cognitive style, behavioral tendencies Psychodynamic aspects

how much confidence can be placed in children's responses to projective techniques, so that the techniques can be judiciously and appropriately used with children.

REFERENCES

Ames, L. B., Metraux, R., Rodell, J. L., & Walker, R. (1974). *Child Rorschach responses* (rev. ed.). New York: Brunner/Mazel.

Ames, L. B., Metraux, R., & Walker, R. (1971). *Adolescent Rorschach responses: Developmental trends from ten to sixteen years*. New York: Brunner/Mazel.

Anastasi, A. (1982). *Psychological testing* (5th ed.). New York: Macmillan.

Batsche, G. M., & Peterson, D. W. (1983). School psychology and projective assessment: A growing incompatibility. *School Psychology Review, 12,* 440–445.

Bellak, L. (1971). *The TAT and CAT in clinical use* (2nd ed.). New York: Grune & Stratton.

Bellak, L., & Bellak, S. (1949). *A manual for the Children's Apperception Test*. Larchmont, NY: CPS.

Blum, C. S. (1950). *The Blacky Pictures: A manual of instructions*. New York: Psychological Corporation.

Buck, J. N. (1948). The H-T-P technique: A qualitative and quantitative scoring manual. *Journal of Clinical Psychology, 4,* 317–396.

Buck, J. N. (1971). *The House–Tree–Person manual supplement*. Los Angeles: Western Psychological Services.

Burns, R. C., & Kaufman, S. H. (1970). *Kinetic Family Drawing (K-F-D)*. New York: Brunner/Mazel.

Chambers, G. S., & Hamlin, R. W. (1957). The validity of judgments based on "blind" Rorschach records. *Journal of Consulting Psychology, 21,* 105–109.

Chandler, L. A. (1985). *Assessing stress in children*. New York: Praeger.

Chandler, L. A., Shermis, M. D., & Lempert, M. E. (1989). The need–threat analysis: A scoring system for the children's apperception test. *Psychology in the Schools, 26*, 47–52.

Cohen, H., & Weil, G. R. (1975). *Tasks of Emotional Development*. Brookline, MA: TED Associates.

Cox, B., & Sargent, H. (1950). Brief reports: TAT responses of emotionally disturbed and emotionally stable children: Clinical judgments versus normative data. *Journal of Projective Techniques, 14*, 60–74.

Cummings, J. A. (1981, August). *An evaluation of objective scoring systems for Kinetic Family Drawings*. Paper presented at the meeting of the American Psychological Association, Los Angeles.

Dana, R. H. (1985). Thematic Apperception Test. In C. S. Newmark (Ed.), *Major psychological assessment instruments* (pp. 89–135). Boston, MA: Allyn & Bacon.

DiLeo, J. H. (1973). *Children's drawings as diagnostic aids*. New York: Brunner/Mazel.

Elkind, D. (1976). *Child development and education*. New York: Oxford University Press.

Erdberg, P. (1985). The Rorschach. In C. S. Newmark (Ed.), *Major psychological assessment instruments* (pp. 65–89). Boston, MA: Allyn & Bacon.

Exner, J. E. (1969). *The Rorschach systems*. New York: Grune & Stratton.

Exner, J. E. (1974). *The Rorschach: A comprehensive system. Vol. 1*. New York: Wiley.

Exner, J. E. (1983). The Rorschach: A history and description of the comprehensive system. *School Psychology Review, 12*, 407–413.

Exner, J. E., & Weiner, I. B. (1982). *The Rorschach: A comprehensive system. Vol. 3. Assessment of children and adolescents*. New York: Wiley.

Falk, J. D. (1981). Understanding children's art: An analysis of the literature. *Journal of Personality Assessment, 45* 465–472.

Frank, L. K. (1939). Projective methods for the study of personality. *Journal of Psychology, 8*, 389–413.

Freud, S. (1936). *The problem of anxiety* (J. Strachey, Trans.). New York: Norton.

Freud, S. (1959). Formulations regarding the two principles in mental functioning. In *The Collected papers of Sigmund Freud* (Vol. 4, pp. 13–22). New York: Basic Books. (Original work published 1911)

Ginsberg, H., & Opper, S. (1979). *Piaget's theory of intellectual development* (2nd ed.). Englewood Cliffs, NJ: Prentice-Hall.

Gittleman-Klein, R. (1978). Validity of projective tests for psychodiagnosis in children. In R. L. Spitzer & D. F. Klein (Eds.), *Critical issues in psychiatric diagnosis*. New York: Raven Press.

Goh, D. S., & Fuller, G. B. (1983). Current practices in the assessment of personality and behavior by school psychologists. *School Psychology Review, 12*, 240–243.

Goodenough, F. L. (1926). *Measurement of intelligence by drawings*. New York: Harcourt, Brace & World.

Halpern, F. A. (1971). The Rorschach test with children. In A. I. Rabin & M. R. Haworth (Eds.), *Projective techniques with children*. New York: Grune & Stratton.

Hammer, E. F. (1958). *The clinical application of projective drawings*. Springfield, IL: Charles C. Thomas.

Hammer, E. F. (1985). The House–Tree–Person Test. In C. S. Newmark (Ed.), *Major psychological assessment instruments* (pp. 135–164). Boston, MA: Allyn & Bacon.

Harris, D. B. (1963). *Children's drawings as measures of intellectual maturity*. New York: Harcourt, Brace & World.

Hertz, M. R. (1961). *Frequency tables for scoring Rorschach responses*. Cleveland, OH: Case Western Reserve University.

Holt, R. R. (1970). Yet another look at clinical and statistical prediction. *American Psychologist, 25*, 337–349.

Holt, R. R. (1978). *Methods in clinical psychology* (Vol. 1). New York: Plenum Press.

Hughes, C. A. (1983). *Reliability of the need–threat scoring system for projective material*. Unpublished master's thesis, University of Pittsburgh.

Hulse, W. C. (1951). The emotionally disturbed child draws his family. *Quarterly Journal of Child Behavior, 3*, 152–174.

Jolles, I. (1971). *A catalogue for the qualitative interpretation of the House–Tree–Person (H-T-P)*. Los Angeles: Western Psychological Services.

Kaliopska, M. (1982). Empathy as measured by Rorschach and TAT. *British Journal of Projective Psychology and Personality Study, 27*, 5–11.

Kenniston, K. (1965). *The uncommitted*. New York: Dell.

Kessler, J. W. (1966). *Psychopathology of childhood*. Englewood Cliffs, NJ: Prentice-Hall.

Klinger, E. (1971). *Structure and functions of fantasy*. New York: Wiley.

Klopfer, W., & Taulbee, E. (1976). Projective tests. *Annual Review of Psychology, 27*, 543–569.

Knoff, H. M. (1983). Personality assessment in the schools: Issues and procedures for school psychologists. *School Psychology Review, 12*, 391–398.

Knoff, H. M., & Prout, H. T. (1985). The Kinetic Family System: A review and integration of the Kinetic Family and School Drawing Techniques. *Psychology in the Schools, 22*, 50–59.

Koppitz, E. M. (1968). *Psychological evaluation of children's Human Figure Drawings*. New York: Grune & Stratton.

Koppitz, E. M. (1983). Projective drawings with children and adolescents. *School Psychology Review, 12*, 421–427.

Koppitz, E. M. (1984). *Psychological evaluation of Human Figure Drawings by middle school pupils*. New York: Grune & Stratton.

Lanyon, R. I., & Goodstein, L. D. (1982). *Personality assessment* (2nd ed.). New York: Wiley.

Lempert, M. E. (1986). *The need–threat scoring system: A study of reliability and agreement*. Unpublished manuscript, University of Pittsburgh.

Lindzay, G., & Herman, P. S. (1955). Thematic Apperception Test: A note on reliability and situational validity. *Journal of Projective Techniques, 19*, 36–42.

Little, K. B., & Shneidman, E. S. (1959). Congruencies among interpretations of psychological tests and anamnestic data. *Psychological Monographs, 73* (No. 476).

Lubin, B., Larsen, R. M., & Matarazzo, J. D. (1984). Patterns of psychological test usage in the United

States: 1935–1982. *American Psychologists, 39*, 451–454.

Machover, K. (1949). *Personality projection in the drawings of a human figure*. Sprinfield, IL: Charles C Thomas.

Magnusson, D. (1960). Some personality tests applied on identical twins. *Scandinavian Journal of Psychology, 1*, 55–61.

McAdams, D. P. (1980). A thematic coding system for the intimacy motive. *Journal of Research in Personality, 14*, 413–432.

McArthur, D. S., & Roberts, G. E. (1982). *Roberts Apperception Test for Children: A manual*. Los Angeles: Western Psychological Services.

McClelland, D. C., Atkinson, J. W., Clark, R. A., & Lowell, E. L. (1953). *The achievement motive*. New York: Appleton-Century-Crofts.

McDermott, P. A. (1980). A systems–actuarial method for the differential diagnosis of handicapped children. *Journal of Special Education, 14*, 7–22.

McNeil, E. (1976). *The psychology of being human*. San Francisco: Canfield.

Megargee, E., & Cook, P. E. (1967). The relationship of TAT and inkblot aggression content scales with each other and with criteria of overt aggression in juvenile delinquents. *Journal of Projective Techniques and Personality Assessment, 31*, 48–60.

Mosrtoff, D. L., & Lazarus, P. J. (1983). The Kinetic Family Drawing: The reliability of an objective scoring system. *Psychology in the Schools, 20*, 16–20.

Murray, H. (1938). *Explorations in personality*. New York: Oxford University Press.

Murray, H. (1943). *Thematic Apperception Test manual*. Cambridge, MA: Harvard University Press.

Murstein, B. I. (1963). *Theory and research in projective techniques*. New York: Wiley.

Obrzut, J. E., & Cummings, J. A. (1983). The projective approach to personality assessment: An analysis of thematic picture techniques. *School Psychology Review, 12*, 414–420.

Ogden, D. P. (1977). *Psychodiagnosis and personality assessment: A handbook* (2nd ed.). Los Angeles: Western Psychological Services.

O'Leary, K. D., & Johnson, B. (1979). Psychological assessment. In H. Quay & J. S. Werry (Eds.), *Psychopathological disorders of childhood* (2nd ed.). New York: Wiley.

Piotrowski, C. (1984). The status of projective techniques: Or, "wishing won't make it go away." *Journal of Clinical Psychology, 40*, 1495–1502.

Pollak, J., Cohen, H., & Weil, G. (1981). The Tasks of Emotional Development: A survey of research applications. *Psychology: A Quarterly Journal of Human Behavior, 18*, 2–11.

Polyson, J., Norris, D., & Ott, E. (1985). The recent decline in TAT research. *Professional Psychology: Research and Practice, 16*, 26–28.

Prelinger, E., & Zimet, C. N. (1964). *An ego-psychological approach to character assessment*. New York: Free Press.

Prout, H. T. (1983). School psychologists and social–emotional assessment techniques: Patterns in training and use. *School Psyhology Review, 12*, 377–383.

Prout, H. T., & Phillips, P. D. (1974). A clinical note: The Kinetic School Drawing. *Psychology in the Schools, 11*, 303–306.

Rorschach, H. (1921). *Psychodiiagnostik*. Bern:Bircher.

Sattler, J. M. (1982). *Assessment of children's intelligence and special abilities*. Boston: Allyn & Bacon.

Schwartz, F., & Lazar, A. (1979). The scientific status of the Rorschach. *Journal of Personality Assessment, 43*, 3–11.

Spitzer, R. L., & Fleis, J. L. (1974). A re-analysis of the reliability of psychiatric diagnosis. *British Journal of Psychiatry, 125*, 341–347.

Symonds, P. (1948). *A manual for the Symonds Picture–Story Test*. New York: Columbia University Press.

Thomas, A. D., & Dudek, S. Z. (1985). Interpersonal affect in TAT responses: A scoring system. *Journal of Personality Assessment, 49*, 30–37.

Urban, W. (1963). *The Draw-A-Person catalogue for interpretive analysis*. Los Angeles: Western Psychological Services.

Vane, J. R. (1981). The TAT: A review. *Clinical Psychology Review, 1*, 319–336.

Wagner, E. E., Alexander, R. A., Roos, G., & Adair, H. (1986). Optimum split-half reliabilities for the Rorschach: Projective techniques are more reliable than we think. *Journal of Personality Assessment, 50*, 107–112.

Wiggins, J. S. (1980). *Personality and prediction: Principles of personality assessment*. Reading, MA: Addison-Wesley.

4

Projective Storytelling Techniques

FRANCES F. WORCHEL
Texas A&M University

JAMES L. DUPREE
Humboldt State University

Despite decades of criticism regarding their poor psychometric properties, projective storytelling methods continue to be among the most popular and frequently used assessment techniques. Beginning with Murray's introduction of the Thematic Apperception Technique (TAT) in the mid-1930s, close to a dozen similar methods have been developed in the intervening 50 years. These variations, all very similar to the original TAT, have been attempts to expand storytelling techniques for use with children, various ethnic groups, or school-age pupils, or simply to "modernize" the original drawings. Because the different techniques generally have some grounding in the "projective hypothesis," this theory is discussed first.

THE PROJECTIVE HYPOTHESIS

A concept from early Freudian psychoanalytic theory, "projection" is a defense mechanism in which anxiety-producing thoughts or feelings are transferred or attributed to external events or individuals. However, more recently, projection in relation to thematic storytelling techniques has taken on a less stringent definition. According to Rabin (1986), projection is a common everyday occurrence, a part of the normal thought process by which all individuals tend to "externalize" as they interpret the environment and respond to it. Rabin goes on to state:

In a sense, people are projecting all the time; when perceiving and responding to the environment they are expressing their personal needs, motivations, and unique characteristics. When a person faces a particular stimulus or situation she responds . . . in her own particular manner. (p. 5)

Thus, in this light, projection is seen as less of an unconscious defensive maneuver and more of a normal cognitive operation. Projective responses are viewed differently from responses given on more structured tasks, in that projection allows the child to pull from a wide range of experiences and fantasy material, while being relatively unaware of the manner in which the responses will be interpreted.

In TAT-type techniques, the child is asked to make up a story and is assured that there is no right or wrong answer. Depending on the ambiguity of the picture (ranging from a blank card to a boy huddled on the floor with a gun-like object beside him), any number of stories are possible. Although the latter picture pulls more for a story with a sad or aggressive theme than does the blank card, it nonetheless remains up to the subject to interpret the picture. That interpretation will necessarily borrow on events, feelings, and important needs in the subject's own life. Just as a young child is unlikely to tell a story involving a kibbutz in Israel if he or she has never personally or indirectly known of such a thing, the projective hypothesis assumes

70

that a child is unlikely to recite numerous stories involving being rejected or unloved if that experience is not in some way important to that child.

Therefore, we come to a definition of "projection" as an apperceptive process by which the child integrates a stimulus (the picture) with both past experiences and current psychological concerns (Kagan, 1960). The ability to indulge in make-believe or fantasy, rather than to give a factual description of this picture, will vary across children. Of course, the child's fantasy should be bound by the reality constraints inherent in the picture. A child who gives only a factual description may be manifesting some resistance or inhibition, whereas a child who reports themes consistently unrelated to the scene portrayed in the picture may be reacting with fewer controls to his or her own internal needs or anxieties. It is believed that when both this and other aspects of the child's stories are examined, storytelling techniques lead to an assessment of defensiveness, ego strength, assets and liabilities, coping styles, interpersonal relationships, and problem solving, as well as basic organizing principles of the subject's personality (Rabin, 1960).

Although there is general agreement that projection is the cornerstone of most thematic storytelling techniques, there has been constant criticism that techniques based on this theory are psychometrically untenable. Numerous review have stressed the lack of empirical support for the reliability or validity of storytelling techniques in particular and projective assessments in general (Anastasi, 1982; Cleveland, 1976; Dean, 1984; Holmen & Docter, 1972; Lanyon, 1984; Munter, 1975). Defenders of projective techniques generally resort to one of two claims: (1) that negative research findings were often due to methodologically flawed studies, and (2) that projectives should be evaluated differently from more objective assessment techniques. Blatt (1978) characterizes the former view, charging that many negative findings failed to consider the configural approach needed to interpret projective test data, studied variables in isolation (e.g, the relationship between TAT stories and aggression rather than TAT stories and overall personality), or used imprecise diagnostic classifications (e.g., attempted to use the TAT to distinguish conduct-disordered from hyper-

active subjects, but used questionable criteria to diagnose the two groups). The second viewpoint continues to flourish, as stated by Schwartz and Lazar (1979):

> Although projectives may have poor psychometrics by some standards, interpretation deals with the possible meanings of a response, not probabilistic status. Over an extensive projective battery, the clinician is more interested in common themes or consistencies generated from responses than in psychometric properties. (cited in Obrzut & Cummings, 1983, p. 189)

More specifically directed at the TAT are the claims that, although it does not fulfill the requirements of a psychometric instrument, it is indeed a method of describing personality that provides rich idiographic data (Aronow, Reznikoff, & Rauchway, 1979; Dana, 1985; Goldman, Stein, & Guerry, 1983).

Surprisingly, although projective storytelling techniques consistently receive poor empirical support, they continue to enjoy widespread use in clinical practice and applied settings (Piotrowski, 1983). In the survey by Lubin, Larsens, and Matarazzo (1984), the TAT remained among the top 10 most frequently used tests. Wade and Baker (1977) attribute the continued employment of the TAT and other projectives to the facts that assessment continues to be a critical need, and that as yet there are few practical alternatives to projective tests. In addition, they stress that clinicians give greater weight to personal clinical experience than to experimental evidence.

FACTORS RELEVANT TO EVALUATING CHILDREN

Before moving on to a discussion of specific storytelling techniques, we first review several general factors relevant when evaluating children. Of course, it is important to consider a child's age, developmental status, and verbal ability when interpreting thematic stories. In using any type of age norms for test variables, one must realize that the norms mask a good deal of unevenness in the profiles of individual children (Rabin, 1960). Thus, a child's actual performance is likely to spread over several age levels, reflecting the lability of his or her ego development and cognitive capabilities. For example, a 4- or 5-year-old is just beginning to exercise control over impulses; thus impulsivity and poor judgment would be expected in a child by this age, and would not necessarily be indicative of emotional problems (Obrzut & Cummings, 1983). It becomes quite difficult, when working with young children, to distinguish between aberrant and merely immature responses (Altman, 1960). One can not expect to see patterns that reflect general coping styles until at least age 6 or 7. The length of thematic stories tends to increase with age, with girls telling longer stories than boys from age 6 up until early adolescence (Kagan, 1960). Kagan also contends that the fantasy productions of younger children contain more distortions and omissions, while 9- to 10-year-olds tend to give more concrete, descriptive stories. Thus, before assessing any young child, one should have an idea of normative development for children of different ages.

In the following sections, we review several storytelling techniques, with emphasis on specific usage, scoring systems, and psychometric qualifications. A number of variations on basic storytelling techniques are also discussed, although in less detail. Although our coverage is not exhaustive, we hope that the techniques selected for inclusion in this chapter will provide the reader with a solid historical base, as well as coverage of some of the more recent developments in the field.

THE THEMATIC APPERCEPTION TEST

The TAT was the first widely used thematic technique, with most other methods being modifications of this test. Developed by Henry Murray (1938, 1943), the TAT was based on psychoanalytic theory and was originally intended to hasten the process of therapy. It was expected that, through projection, the therapy client would reveal personality characteristics that might otherwise take months to uncover. In particular, the TAT was presumed to reveal the individual's dominant drives, emotions, traits, and conflicts by identifying significant needs, presses, and themes (Murray, 1943). As such, the TAT was intended to explore personality dynamics rather than to provide a differential diagnosis.

After a number of revisions, Murray's TAT contained 31 pictures: 11 suitable for both sexes, 7 for girls and women, 7 for boys and men, and 1 blank card for both men and women. Administration occurred over two sessions a week apart, with 10 cards used each session in a particular order. The cards were purposefully varied in content, in order to elicit fantasies concerning most areas of importance in the subject's life. They were structured enough to allow easy storytelling, yet ambiguous enough to allow for a variety of possible stories (Karon, 1981). Murray (1943) gave the following instructions:

> Tell me what has led up to the event shown in the picture, describe what is happening at the moment, what the characters are feeling and thinking, and then give the outcome. Since you have 50 minutes for 10 pictures, you can devote 5 minutes to each story. (p. 3)

Murray allowed for a reminder of the instructions after the first card. After this, nothing was to be said except to inform the subject of the time limits, give occasional praise, and give brief prompts such as "What led up to this situation?" if crucial details were omitted.

Although Murray intended that 20 cards be utilized, the TAT as currently administered is more likely to include only 10 cards. There is no general consensus as to which cards should be administered. Some argue that each examiner should become familiar with a certain set of 10 cards and use those cards exclusively. Others argue for specific cards, depending on the client's particular referral issue. Table 4.1 presents a summary of cards suggested for particular age groups and psychological concerns.

Some investigations have focused on administration factors affecting story production. Dana (1985) reports that cards of medium ambiguity are most useful in eliciting relevant personality data, at least for a college student population. Obrzut and Boliek (1986) raise the issue of whether clarifying questions should be asked, and conclude that the more questions asked, the less projective the material solicited will be. Finally, there is the issue of how stories

TABLE 4.1. Suggested Cards for TAT Administration

Cards	Suggested use	Source
1, 2, 3BM, 4, 6BM, 7BM, 11, 12M, 13MF	Standard administration: males	Bellak (1971)
1, 2, 3BM, 4, 6GF, 7GF, 9, 11, 13MF	Standard administration: females	Bellak (1971)
1, 3BM, 3GF, 4, 6, 7, 10, 11, 12M, 13MF, 14, 16, 20	Standard administration	Karon (1981)
1, 2, 5, 7GF, 12F, 12M, 15, 17BM, 18BM, 18GF	Standard administration: adolescents	Rabin & Haworth (1960)
1, 8BM, 14, 17BM	7- to 11-year-olds: achievement and status goals	Obrzut & Boliek (1986)
3BM, 8BM, 12M, 14, 17BM	7- to 11-year-olds: aggression	Obrzut & Boliek (1986)
3BM, 7GF, 13B, 14	7- to 11-year-olds: concern for parental nurturance and rejection	Obrzut & Boliek (1986)
1, 3BM, 7GF, 14	7- to 11-year-olds: parental punishment and attitudes toward parents	Obrzut & Boliek (1986)
7GF, 18GF, 3GF, 8GF	5- to 10-year-olds	Gerver (1946)
1, 3, 6, 7, 12M, 14, 16	Suicidal ideation	Karon (1981)
12M, 12F	Subject's reaction to therapy/therapist	Karon (1981)

should be recorded. Dana (1986) contends that when the examiner leaves the room and asks the subject to record his or her own stories, there is a tendency for more negative stories to be produced. However, when the examiner remained in the room, Baty and Dreger (1975) found no differences in tape-recorded, subject-written, or examiner-written stories. It should be noted that both these studies involved college students. Most examiners find that for younger age groups, it is often infeasible to have the child write his or her own stories.

According to Karon (1981), there is no scoring system for the TAT that is both usable and sufficiently inclusive to be clinically relevant. Although a number of systems have been developed, they either tend to be too lengthy and cumbersome to be practical, or lack any sound psychometric basis. Dana (1985) suggests that current TAT interpretation is most often based on "trained intuition and disciplined creativity." Karon (1981) proposes a similar approach whereby, for each story, the examiner inquires as to why a person would give that answer out of all the possibilities that exist.

The first systematic approach was developed by Morgan and Murray (1935). They suggested that, after the stories had been related, the examiner should inquire generally as to the source of the stories. A content analysis was then conducted, with each event analyzed for "needs" (forces emanating from the hero) and "presses" (forces emanating from the environment). Next, each story was analyzed for the following:

1. Characteristics of the hero.
2. Motives, trends, needs, and feelings of the hero, as measured by their intensity, duration, frequency, and importance to the plot. These included such variables as achievement, aggression, dominance, and nurturance.
3. Forces in the hero's environment, such as traits of others, their effect on the hero, aggression by others, dominance, seduction, rejection, or physical danger.
4. Outcomes to each story.
5. Themes, defined as the interaction of the hero's needs and presses combined into a pattern that is played out in the person's story. For example, the need for nurturance and the press of parental rejection might be portrayed in themes centering on children being left behind by parents.
6. Interests and sentiments, such as the positive or negative value of the older woman (mother figure), father figure, or same-sex figure.

Bellak's (1947) system is essentially a content analysis, focusing on the content and dynamics of interpersonal relationships, themes, heroes, needs and drives, conception of the environment, significant conflicts, anxieties, defenses, punishments, and ego integration. According to Karon (1981), this system is too simple to be clinically useful, whereas Tomkins's (1947) system, developed at about the same time, is too time-consuming to be useful. Other TAT scoring systems examine a single dimension or characteristic, such as hostility and agression (Davids & Rosenblatt, 1958; Hafner & Kaplan, 1960), need for achievement (McClelland, Atkinson, Clark, & Lowell, 1953), or depression (Aaron, 1967).

In a more recent attempt at an objective scoring system, Newman, Newman, and Sells (1974) devised a scaling procedure for distinguishing psychological deviance from normal behavior. Their measures included verbal fluency, conceptual maturity, dysphoric mood, emotionality, and narrative fluency, and were standardized on a national cross-section of children and adolescents. However, it was concluded that the objectively scored TAT is inappropriate for assessing personal adjustment (Krahn, 1985). Finally, Dana (1986) has argued for the development of five major areas that he feels tap the structure and content of TAT stories with "fidelity and completeness." These are ego strength, needs, sex role/sexual identity, assessee control, and content. However, he provides no systematic method for such an analysis.

Vane (1981) presents an interesting review of the major TAT standardization attempts. She surveyed 91 directors of American Psychological Association (APA)-accredited doctoral programs in clinical, school, and counseling psychology regarding usage of the following TAT scoring systems: Arnold, Eron, McClelland/Atkinson, Murstein, Murray, Dynamic, Psychoanalytic, and Other. She reports that 12% of the programs did not teach the TAT. Of the remainder, 44 programs used the Dynamic analysis, 25 used the Psychoanalytic approach, 20 used Murray's system, and fewer than 10 used Murstein, Eron, McClelland/Atkinson, or Arnold.

Whether using a structured scoring system or merely scoring the TAT informally, many clinicians include an analysis of themes present in the stories. Karon (1981) lists common TAT themes, including relations with parents, relations between mother and father, heterosexual relationships, suicidal ideation, tenderness and affection, and loneliness. Bellak (1971) includes such themes as autonomy versus compliance, depression, aggression, sexual conflicts, childhood issues, and ambitions.

Also used in more informal scoring systems are some general scoring principles. Dana (1985) discusses the principal of distance, stating that less acceptable drives are more likely in stories containing characters who differ from the client in some way, such as age, sex, race, or social status. Dana further suggests that the examiner consider how well the client is able to adhere to directions. For example, if the client is instructed to give an ending to every story, but does so on only eight out of ten cards, the examiner should determine whether cards eliciting certain themes have been left unfinished.

Karon (1981) suggests that bright people and healthy people tend to give longer stories. Therefore, disturbing material in a very brief protocol should be given more credence than disturbing material embedded in a longer, more elaborate story. Karon also suggests that the less the content "fits" the card, the more meaningful it will be. For example, a story about a man killing someone is more suggestive of pathology or anxiety if the picture depicts a woman and a girl sitting on a sofa. Finally, Karon believes that a subject's behaviors are predicted by behaviors of characters in the story, that a subject's verbalizations are predicted by characters who say things, and that a subject's thoughts are predicted by characters who think things. For example, a story about a man who considers suicide is more likely to be predictive of *thinking* about suicide than of actually *attempting* suicide. This last-mentioned scoring principle attempts to resolve a common criticism of the TAT—namely, that story content is not necessarily related to a client's actual behaviors. Many investigators have suggested that a need or personality characteristic exhibited on the TAT may never be acted upon in real life; rather, it exists only in the client's fantasies or unconscious (Dana, 1986; Lanyon & Goodstein, 1982; Vane, 1981). Santostefano (1970) contends that a need expressed in a TAT story may be manifested in the client's later verbalizations, thoughts, or behaviors, but that there is no way of determining which relationship will actually exist. Thus, there seems to be concurrence that a client who produces a number of agressive stories may either actually *be* agressive, *say* aggressive things, or merely *think* aggressive thoughts.

Overall, the literature on the TAT leads to a rather curious conclusion: Despite the fact that there appears to be no consistently used, psychometrically sound scoring system for it, the TAT continues to enjoy widespread usage in academic training programs, internships, and clinical practice. Even the administration of cards and specific instructions are flexible, and are generally left to the discretion of the individual examiner. Some general scoring principles are often adhered to, such as examining the cards for consistent needs, presses, and themes; however, interpretation almost certainly depends more on the clinical skills of the examiner than on the psychometric properties of the test.

THE CHILDREN'S APPERCEPTION TEST

The Children's Apperception Test (CAT) was designed by Bellak and Bellak (1949) as a downward extension of the TAT suitable for children aged 3–10. The CAT consists of 10 pictures of animal characters. An alternate form, the CAT-H, contains human figures. The original CAT pictures were designed from preconceived ideas about problems, situations, and roles that would be especially relevant to children. Animals were used for three reasons: (1) Most animals with which children are familiar are small and below children in "pecking order"; (2) animals are not as threatening as humans, and thus it is thought to be easier for children to ascribe unacceptable traits or emotions to them (e.g., jealousy, aggression); and (3) it is easier to draw animal figures of an ambiguous sex and age (Bellak & Adelman, 1960).

Administration of the CAT is similar to that of the TAT: Children are asked to make up stories for each card with a beginning, middle, and end, and to tell what the characters might be thinking or feeling. All 10 cards are used, with a set order maintained. As with

most tests given to children, it is important to establish good rapport before initiating the CAT. In one of the few recent empirical studies of the CAT, Passman and Lautman (1982) examined factors affecting responsiveness to the CAT. They evaluated rates of responding to the CAT by preschoolers when the mother, the father, or a security blanket was present during administration. They found that responsiveness was enhanced by either the mother's or the father's presence if the parent was initially with the child, but then left during the actual administration. Alternately, the parent's presence *during* administration seemed to facilitate rapport, but actually decreased speech output of the child.

The CAT pictures were designed to elicit responses to typical childhood concerns, such as sibling rivalry, relations with parents, aggression, fear of being lonely at night, toilet behavior, feeding problems, and problems of growth. Interpretation is similar to that for the TAT; Bellak and Bellak (1961) analyzed the stories for the following:

1. Main theme.
2. Main hero and his or her self-image.
3. Main needs and drives of the hero.
4. Concept of the environment.
5. The way figures are seen and reacted to (e.g., supportive, competitive).
6. Conflicts.
7. Nature of child's anxieties.
8. Defenses utilized.
9. Adequacy of the child's superego as manifested by the punishment received for wrongdoings.
10. Integration of the ego as manifested by the compromise between drives and demands of the ego.

Another major attempt at a standardized scoring system for the CAT is provided in Haworth's (1965) book, *A Schedule of Adaptive Mechanisms in CAT Responses*. This system, based on psychoanalytic theory, was intended to evaluate defense mechanisms evident in CAT responses. These included reaction formation, ambivalence and undoing, isolation, repression and denial, symbolism, projection, and introjection. Also included was a measure of same-sex versus opposite-sex identification. For each of the measures above, 6–10 specific types of responses were given as scoring criteria. If one of the criteria appeared in a story, that measure received a critical-score checkmark. Five or more critical scores were considered to be serious enough to warrant further investigation. Unfortunately, insufficient research has been done on Haworth's system to evaluate its psychometric usefulness.

A longitudinal study of 80 children aged 3–11 years also used psychoanalytic principles to develop a CAT scoring system (Witherspoon, 1968). Factor analysis was used to derive the following developmental behavioral categories: Schizothymia (antisocial, aggressive, socially undesirable), Emotionality, Character Integrity (self-disclosure, responsibility), Basic Needs (sleeping, eating), Sex Role, Activity (ongoing movement, verbal behavior), Description (enumeration, naming), Self-Reference (I, me, we), and Evasion (no response, card rejection, conversation with the examiner). The first four categories were found to occur only very rarely. Sex Role and Activity were categories that increased with age, whereas Description, Self-Reference, and Evasion decreased with age.

In a more recent work, Haworth (1986) reviews the research on the CAT over the past 20 years. Almost none of these studies dealt with the psychometric properties of the CAT. Most investigations had to do with aspects of the testing situation, such as effects of child anxiety on responses, the role of the examiner, coping style of children when taking the CAT, sex differences, and differences in the CAT and CAT-H. Three of the studies reported by Haworth involved attempts to differentiate diagnostic groups by means of the CAT: stutterers from nonstutterers, emotionally disturbed from normal children, and psychotics fron nonpsychotics. Differences on some scoring criteria were found in all three studies; however, different scoring systems were used in each of the studies.

Several early investigators reported that the animal figures were preferable, particularly with younger children, because identification with animals was less threatening and would result in greater responsiveness. However, later studies failed to support this. Haworth (1986) found no significant differences in the animal and human CAT forms in terms of eliciting responsiveness. Krahn (1985) confirms this, finding thematically meaningful stories to both sets of cards. Interestingly, Krahn also reports that both CAT and CAT-H evoke more responses than does the TAT with children.

As with the TAT, one of the major criticisms of the CAT is that contents given in the stories are not necessarily indicative of behaviors exhibited by subjects. Bradley and Caldwell (1976) confirm this, noting that children whose CAT responses contained achievement imagery did not always act in an achievement-oriented manner in real life. However, the CAT is also like the TAT in that it continues as a frequently used assessment device for children, despite its psychometric limitations.

THE ROBERTS APPERCEPTION TEST FOR CHILDREN

The Roberts Apperception Test for Children (RATC; McArthur & Roberts, 1982) is a recently developed storytelling technique designed for children and adolescents aged 6–15. The RATC is intended as a projective test with a standardized scoring system. McArthur and Roberts state that various weaknesses in the TAT and CAT led to the development of the RATC. They contend that many older children feel infantilized by the CAT animal figures and that this results in stereotyped responses. Alternately, only 2 of the 31 TAT cards actually depict children, thus making this test unsuitable for older children. Finally, McArthur and Roberts feel that the TAT and CAT cards contain unfamiliar, unrealistic, or ambiguous stimuli, which again lead to stereotyped or descriptive answers. The RATC consists of 27 cards, 11 of which have parallel forms for males and females. Sixteen cards are administered during a testing, which takes about 20–30 minutes. The examiner queries the subject on the first two cards only, asking what happened in the story, what happened before, what the characters are feeling and talking about, and how the story ends.

The RATC appears to have significant advantages over its predecessors (Worchel, 1987). The test manual includes comprehensive information on the RATC's psychometric properties, administration, and scoring, as well as a number of case studies. The pictures, designed to be more modern than those in the TAT and CAT, depict scenes intended to elicit common concerns. For example, specific cards portray family confrontation, family conference, parental depression, parental limit setting, parental affection, physical aggression, sibling rivalry, school issues, peer and racial interactions, and observation of nudity.

The test has a standardized scoring system, with scores converted to normalized T-scores based on data from a sample of 200 well-adjusted children. The following scores may be obtained from the RATC:

1. Adaptive scales: Reliance on Others, Support Others, Support Child, Limit Setting, Problem Identification, Resolution (three types).
2. Clinical scales: Anxiety, Aggression, Depression, Rejection, Unresolved.
3. Critical indicators: Atypical Response, Maladaptive Outcome, Refusal.
4. Supplementary measures: Ego Functioning, Aggression, Levels of Projection.

The scoring manual gives detailed instructions and examples for scoring each of these measures. It is possible to do a profile plot of the adaptive and clinical scales (about 20–30 minutes) without completing the more detailed and time-consuming Interpersonal Matrix.

A recent review of the RATC in *The Ninth Mental Measurements Yearbook* (Sines, 1985) cited validity data as being unimpressive. In perhaps the most substantial study to date, 200 well-adjusted children were compared with 200 children evaluated at guidance clinics. The normal children scored higher than the clinic children on all eight adaptive scales; however, the two groups could not be reliably differentiated on the clinical scales for Aggression, Anxiety, or Depression. Obrzut and Boliek (1986) state that the RATC has acceptable interrater and split-half reliabilities. They conclude that the profile scales do seem useful in differentiating adaptive from maladaptive functioning of children at different ages.

McArthur and Roberts (1982) agree that the current psychometric information is only a "first step" in establishing the RATC as a useful clinical tool. Overall, the RATC appears to be well-designed, easy-to-use technique for children and young adolescents. The standardized scoring system, while admittedly lacking in validity evidence compared to systems for more objective personality tests, appears to be relatively good compared to scoring systems for similar projective techniques (Worchel, 1987).

THE MAKE-A-PICTURE STORY TEST

The Make-a-Picture Story Test (MAPS; Shneidman, 1952, 1960) was designed to provide more choices for respondents and examiners than those provided by the TAT. The test consists of 22 background cards and 67 figure cards to be superimposed over the backgrounds. Most of the background cards are easily identifiable scenes, such as a living room, bridge, or street. A few background cards have less structure, such as a "dream" card. Of the 67 figures, most are human, varying in gender, age, race, pose, and clothing. Two animal and six fictitious figures (e.g., Superman and a pirate) are included.

The test was designed for children and adults and can be used with children as young as 6 years old. Test time may vary from 45 minutes to 3 hours, depending on the purpose of the evaluation and the abilities of the child.

Usually 10 backgrounds are utilized, with the examiner selecting the first 8 and the child selecting the last 2 from the remaining cards. A suggested alternative is to let the child look over all the material and pick his or her own backgrounds (Koppitz, 1982). Upon presentation of each background, the child selects one or more of the 67 figures and, after placing them on the background, tells a story. After the story is finished, the child is asked to give a title to the story. Although general prompting is acceptable, more detailed inquiry is discouraged in diagnostic usage. The examiner records the responses verbatim, including the title and incidental remarks, and also indicates the choice and placement of the figures on a location sheet provided with the test.

The test is psychodynamically based, although examiners may also gain information regarding cognitive distortions and interpersonal relationships. Story analysis may be accomplished in a manner similar to that for the TAT, such as noting the main character, needs, motivations, affect, and conflicts. No objective scoring system is typically used with children. The manual addresses diagnostic usage only, although the author considers therapeutic and research applications feasible. The original observations used in the development of the test were based on responses by adults, and many representative responses are presented in the manual. Only a few child responses are presented, although elsewhere Shneidman (1960) provides a case illustration with a 13-year-old Mexican-American girl.

For some hyperactive children, the MAPS may be an alternative to the more passive TAT format (Obrzut & Boliek, 1986), although the administration may need to be more controlled to avoid having the large number of materials strewn about (Goldman et al., 1983). The MAPS test has been considered useful in studying identification patterns in retarded and nonretarded children. Ward (1973) found that nonretarded boys projected themselves more readily into the stories, more often chose boys as main characters, and more often identified the main characters as themselves.

Schneidman admits to the difficulties in establishing reliability and validity for the MAPS, and Jensen (1965) does not recommend the use of the MAPS for this very reason. However, researchers may find the MAPS materials useful, since one or more scenes with preselected characters can be easily constructed to create a projective stimulus that is custom-made for the purpose of the study.

THE PICTURE–STORY TEST

The Picture–Story Test was developed from a study conducted by Percival Symonds (1949) on adolescent imagination and fantasy. Influenced by the TAT, Symonds established his own set of 42 cards, which included adolescent characters and themes that might elicit adolescent concerns. The drawings were done in black-and-white crayon. His report of that study in *Adolescent Fantasy* (Symonds, 1949) included norms, thematic data, and an exhaustive analysis of the responses of 20 male and 20 female high school students in New York City. This book includes a good review of the literature, discussion of apperception techniques, and more than a hundred sample stories. It has historical significance for the interested reader.

From the original drawings, 20 cards were chosen (two sets of 10 each) as the final test (Symonds, 1948). The cards are not segregated for gender. In administration, the child is invited to imagine being a story writer for a magazine that would use the picture as an illustration. The examiner stresses that the study can be silly or fantastic and that it will be confidential.

Card content includes family and peer interaction, adult interactions, street scenes, and a hint at school themes with the presence of books in a few of the cards. Facial expressions, however, appear grim or morose, and the shadowly nature of the cards is likely to evoke stories of gloom, depression, or aggression. Clothing is very dated, with some of the adolescent characters in suit and tie, and the characters would probably appear more like college students than teenagers to the modern adolescent.

Because of limited normative data and limited reliability and validity studies, the test is not recommended for current use. However, it may prove to be a productive historical background for anyone attempting to create an up-to-date apperception test for adolescents.

THE TASKS OF EMOTIONAL DEVELOPMENT TEST

The Tasks of Emotional Development Test (TED; Cohen & Weil, 1975a, 1975b) consists of 12 photographs for children aged 6–11 and 13 photographs for adolescents aged 12–18. Separate sets are presented to males and females, with an additional card eliciting heterosexual adjustment themes for adolescents. The four sets have nearly identical content, varying only by age group and gender.

Photos are somewhat outdated and mainly depict white, middle-class persons from the early 1960s. The TAT-style administration includes an explantion of what is meant by "feelings."

Each card represents one of 13 developmental tasks purported by the authors to be common across child personality development. Tasks include separation issues, socialization with peers, and the establishment of positive attitides toward school and parents. The theorectical background for the test is based on the ego-oriented, psychoanalytic thinking of Erik Erikson (1950) and George Gardner (1959); the cards, however, seem amenable to any orientation.

The tasks depicted are clear, structured, and concerned with everyday events such as watching television or joining a play group. Kohlbert (cited in Cohen & Weil, 1975a) applauds the pictures as allowing the children to project their needs and motives without getting sidetracked in the cognitive complexity of ambiguous stimuli. The authors claim that the lack of ambiguity is more apt to bring out responses pertinent to the real lives of children and their actual, rather than fantasized, emotions. They add that responses may be shorter than those given to the TAT.

The test is intended by the authors to be scored on five dimensions: Perception (the ability to accurately see what the story is supposed to be about), Outcome (the level of maturity implied by the developmental "solution" to the presented task), Affect (an indicator of the appropriateness of the feelings as related to the outcome; a successful outcome should have positive feelings and an unsuccessful outcome should have negative feelings), Motivation (the maturity of reasoning associated with the outcome), and Spontaneity (related to the comfort and completeness with which a respondent tells the story).

Norms are given for boys and girls from a wide variety of socioeconomic backgrounds, who were either "normal" or referred to a psychological clinic. Unfortunately, norms are given for only 6 of the 13 developmental tasks. No adolescents were included in the norming sample, and the norm statistics are not broken down by age. Levitt (1975) considers the TED to be a poorly developed test with questionable validity. The validity of the TED has also been questioned (Ammons & Ammons, 1972), and the rating scale has been described as "tedious" and "cumbersome" in terms of the test's potential use by dynamically oriented clinicians (Wise, 1975). The authors report good interrator reliability for scoring, but have not assessed the test reliability because of the difficulties of establishing test reliability in thematic projective-style tests (Cohen & Weil, 1975b).

Since 1970, the TED has been used in research to study abused children (Kinard, 1980, 1982), obese adolescents (Karpowitz & Zeis, 1975), and battered adult women (Koslof, 1984). Gotts (1974) is enthusiastic about its use with all children and claims to have received good clinical material from children with mental ages of 5 and above. A survey of some research applications can be found in Pollack, Cohen, and Weil (1981, 1982).

The strengths of the TED are in its theoretical base, in the lack of picture ambiguity for some examiners, and in an objective scoring system. The weaknesses of the test may be in the lack of data to support validity or test reliability, in photos that are outdated and middle-class, and in limited norms on only half the test. Anyone intending to use this test for research or for extended clinical use is encouraged to regard the book by Cohen and Weil (1975b) as an extension of the manual. This book provides seven full cases and the use of the TED with other tests. Many sample stories are given, demonstrating a variety of scoring issues, but again only for the first six tasks.

THE MICHIGAN PICTURE TEST—REVISED

The Michigan Picture Test—Revised (MPT-R; Hutt, 1980, 1986) was first developed through the Michigan State Department of Mental Health in 1953. A primary goal was to develop an assessment technique to differentiate adjusted from maladjusted children that would offer quantified approaches for clinicans rather than simple reliance on clinical intuition and skill of interpretation. This purpose is laudable, and the efforts are extensive, but the final product as presented in this revised edition is of limited success.

The present test consists of a total of 15

cards: 7 general cards, 4 cards for girls, and 4 cards for boys. A "full series" administration consists of 11 cards; a briefer "core series" version utilizes only four of the general cards when the purpose of the test is for general screening. The content of the four core cards is as follows: (1) a breakfast scene, (2) children playing checkers, (3), a lightning scene without human characters, and (4) a blank card.

Administration is similar to that for the TAT: requesting a story that includes what is happening and how it will turn out. Although the stories are not timed, inordinate reaction or story length is to be noted. Electronic recording is encouraged. Suggested ages are 8–14.

Four indices are presented in the manual that purport to discriminate between adjusted and maladjusted children. A "Tension Index" is based on the frequency of four needs expressed. A "Tense" variable relates to the percentage of past- versus present-tense verbs used in the stories. A "Direction of Forces" score tabulates and weighs references to action in the story, noting whether the main character is acting or being acted upon or whether there is an absence of action. The "Combined Maladjustment Score" is a checklist of the number of times scores on the first three variables are at or above the critical scores or norms provided in the manual.

The responsible test user will note many of the following observations before deciding on whether to utilize the MPT-R. The standardization sample remains that of children in the early 1950s, with a limited description of population demographics. The "maladjusted" children were identified as such because they either scored in the lower third of a teacher rating scale or were undergoing treatment at child guidance clinics; 90% of the clinic group were boys. The samples were third-, fifth-, seventh-, and ninth-grade children. The manual has grouped the seventh- and ninth-grade data, without any statistical or theoretical explanation that we could find. Despite the large number of subjects ($n = 700$) used in developing the test over a series of studies, some of the tables from which one must assess maladjustment have a limited number of subjects per group. The norms for discrimination are based on the four "core" cards for only two of the scorable indices. Two additional cards must be presented to assess the Direction of Forces index. We found no clearly demonstrated reason for using the four cards as the "core series." The use of the critical scores on the Tension Index can give false positives at a hit rate worse than chance (55%). The Tense variable only discriminated between the fifth-graders and seventh-/ninth-graders in the standardization sample, and research (Hartwell, Hutt, Andrew, & Walton, 1951) casts doubt as to how well it does at the fifth-grade level. The Combined Maladjustment Score has no statistical support, as admitted by the author, other than correlational data between the other three variables.

Bauserman (1985) questions whether the MPT-R has demonstrated any "clear or significant" gain over the TAT and CAT. Bischoff (1985) complains that the cards are dated, that ethnic variability is lacking, that good clinical judgments in assessing responses to these cards may be more accurate than utilizing the limited data in the manual, and that the changes in the MPT-R appear more "cosmetic" than substantial. The test user who assumes that he or she can objectively discriminate between maladjusted and adjusted children with only four cards may be greatly overestimating the assessment qualities of the MPT-R.

THE SCHOOL APPERCEPTION METHOD

The School Apperception Method (SAM; Solomon & Starr, 1968) was developed to provide a projective thematic test to assess a child's emotional and academic adjustment to school. Prior to the introduction of the SAM, tests for children failed to adequately address the milieu in which children spend most of their time and in which children may gain or lose in the areas of self-concept, self-esteem, and social relations outside the home.

The 22 cards are clear black-and-white drawings, with degrees of shading reminiscent of water colors. Backgrounds are vague and nonintrusive; the characters (dress and hair) are depicted in such a way that the test is not as likely to appear dated as photographs are.

A variety of school-oriented situations are presented. There are 12 main or standard cards depicting children, often with adult figures (teacher, principal), in active situations that seem to call for some kind of resolution. For example, in one card a boy is reading while two pupils off to the side appear to be whispering about him. In another card, one boy is holding back another while the teacher talks to a third boy. In addition to the 12 main cards, 10 additional cards are provided, 5 of which include black students or black adults. The additional cards may be substituted when the examinee is black or when the school is racially integrated. The remaining 5 cards depict situations that are less common but may need to be explored, depending on the purpose of the testing.

The intended main characters are children in the middle grades of elementary school and are predominantly boys. The test can be used with children in elementary or junior high school.

Administration is similar to that for the TAT, and inquiry is encouraged following the primary response if the test is used for assessment purposes. Analysis may be accomplished through several approaches, but the authors also provide nine categroies suggested for assessment:

- Formal Qualities (general manner and length of stories)
- Attitudes toward Teachers and Other Authorities
- Attitudes toward Schoolmates
- Attitudes toward Academic Activity
- Aggression
- Frustration
- Anxiety and Defense Mechanisms
- Home and School
- Punishment

Sample responses are included in the manual, but without norms. The authors suggest that the SAM responses may be used to communicate more easily with school personnel in explaining a child's problems and in supporting recommendations. The SAM should be used with other assessment measures, interviews, and observations, and not alone as a basis for decision making.

An elementary school child may have quite different sets of feelings, attitudes, and self-concepts, depending on whether the child is considering the home or school environment. Many authors suggest utilizing at least some SAM cards in a full child assessment to make up for the lack of school-oriented cards in other projective tests (Koppitz, 1982; Peterson, Kroeker, & Torshen, 1976).

THE TELL-ME-A-STORY TEST

The Tell-Me-A-Story Test (TEMAS) was developed out of the need for a culturally sensitive thematic projective test (Costantino, Malgady, & Rogler, 1985). Most of the work on the test to date has been done under the auspices of the Hispanic Research Center of Fordham University. A manual for the TEMAS (Costantino, Malgady, & Rogler, 1988) has recently been published.

The test has two parallel sets, one for Hispanics and black children depicting minority characters and one for white children. Each set consists of 23 chromatic drawings with contemporary inner-city settings. Scene contents include home and family, peer interactions, street experiences, school, and fantasy or daydreaming. Generally the cards present psychological dilemmas that are familiar to urban children and require some resolution. For example, one card draws on the conflict of whether to obey parents or play with friends. In another card, the main character must decide between putting money in a piggy bank or buying ice cream. Scenes may juxtapose antithetical material, in that part may be primarily positive (a group helping to repair a bicycle) and part primarily negative (children fighting).

Twelve cards are used with both sexes, and 11 are sex-specific. Full administration of the 23 cards, which is conducted similarly to the TAT, may take 2 hours; a short form of 9 cards, taking about 45 minutes, is available. Standardization and other studies have been done on children from kindergarten through sixth grade. We found no studies using adolescents as subjects. Normative data, for both the full form and the short form, are reported to be available in the manual on Hispanic, black, and white children up to age 14. The Hispanic norms are divided into Puerto Rican and non-Puerto Rican; the latter category includes Dominican Republic,

South American, and Mexican-American respondents.

The theoretical basis of the TEMAS is less psychodynamic than that of most other thematic apperception tests; it is based on the developmental and personality theories of Piaget, Kohlberg, McClelland, Atkinson, and Bandura. The intent is not to draw out the unconscious so much as the inner verbal and imaginal processes (Costantino et al., 1985). The developers have attempted to present situations that will evoke one or more of the following nine categories of ego functioning (Costantino, 1982). The categories are scored on a 4-point scale, ranging from "very maladaptive" to "mature and responsible."

• Interpersonal Relations
• Aggression
• Anxiety/Depression
• Achievement
• Delay of Gratification
• Self-Concept of Competence
• Sexual Identity
• Moral Judgment
• Reality Testing

In addition to being scored on the nine personality variables, the responses are scored on a variety of descriptive devices, including number of words per story, length of time used to tell each story, perceptual style, and affect of the main character.

Face validity for the "pull" of each card to the nine categories is high (Malgady, 1982). Interrater reliability in scoring the TEMAS is reported as moderate to high, depending on the personality category being tested; there is also moderate support for concurrent validity and ability to predict treatment outcome (Malgady, Costantino, & Rogler, 1984). There is support for the ability of the TEMAS to discriminate between clinical and nonclinical samples of minority children (Costantino et al., 1985).

Hispanic children tend to be more responsive, as measured by verbal output, in the TEMAS than on the TAT (Costantino, Malgady, & Vasquez, 1981). Interestingly, in comparing the output of Hispanic, black, and white elementary school children to the minority form, the nonminority form, and the TAT, researchers found that Hispanics and blacks were more verbally fluent on the TEMAS, but not significantly more fluent on the ethnic form than on the nonminority form. The authors suggest that the richness of the TEMAS may be due as much to the themes and settings as to the ethnicity of characters (Costantino & Malgady, 1983).

In many of the studies conducted in the development of the TEMAS, the children were tested by a bilingual examiner in their dominant language. Many of the children were more likely to respond in Spanish to the TEMAS than to the TAT (Costantino et al. 1981). We do not know whether a non-Spanish-speaking psychologist who is examining a bilingual Hispanic will obtain the same results in a nondominant language. As for generalization, most of subjects reported in the published support research came from inner-city settings and lower-socioeconomic-status families. To our knowledge, the population has not included rural children or Hispanics from the western or southwestern United States. A critical evaluation of the demographic characteristics of the black and white normative sample must still be done, as must further validity studies.

G. Costantino (personal communication, July 21, 1987) reports that attempts to include Hispanics of the western United States have unfortunately not worked out yet, but that this population needs to be included in future norms. He adds that another planned step will be to expand the standardization to age 18.

The TEMAS appears to be a promising projective tool for the assessment of inner-city school children and particularly those of ethnic minority. Whether it could be appropriate, or even should be, for general assessment remains to be seen.

THEMES CONCERNING BLACKS

Themes Concerning Blacks (TCB; Williams, 1972) is a thematic apperception test consisting of 20 black-and-white drawings, 10 of which include children or adolescents. Although the intended age range for the test is kindergarten through adulthood, most of the support data have been obtained from child populations, and most research studies have been conducted with children as subjects. Administration is similar to that for the TAT, with the additional availability of open-ended story questions to assist the more hesitant child.

The TCB has been compared with the TAT; results suggest that black children are more attracted to the TCB, more likely to give a wider range of affect, and more likely to give stories with a positive tone and outcome (Dlepu & Kimbrough, 1982; Triplett & Brunson, 1982; Weaver, 1981). The user should understand that the content of the TCB is different from that of the TAT. Weaver (1981) points out that the type of scenes may have influenced responses in that, compared to the TAT, the TCB contains more positive situations, includes more children of the same economic class and age as the respondents, is more culturally up-to-date and relevant, and offers more scenes of maternal nurturance.

Because of the wider range of emotional responses on the TCB and the tendency of blacks to give sad or remorseful stories to the TAT, Williams, Williams, and Williams (1981) give little credence to pathological responses given by blacks on the TAT. They consider that the TCB provides a more accurate assessment, and they have more confidence in assessing true pathology when abnormal responses are given to the TCB, because the chance for false positives is less.

Daum (1985) warns that the inner-city themes in the TCB may not be relevant to rural or middle-class blacks and calls for an update of the manual if more recent and broader data on reliability, validity, and norms are presently available.

Although no one argues that cultural and experiential differences exist between the inner-city black respondent and the mainstream white respondent, Ness (1985) points out that there is no theoretical basis for a personality difference based on racial lines and calls for more experimental research if the TCB is to be applied as an assessment tool. We found no studies comparing white and black responses to the TCB.

The psychologist who is assessing urban black children may find the TCB more helpful in evoking a wider range of themes and feelings than the TAT, and more helpful in some clinical decisions, but the user should bear in mind that the test construction as reported has psychometric shortcomings.

VARIATIONS ON THEMATIC APPERCEPTION TECHNIQUES

Full story responses are sometimes difficult to obtain from younger children. The psychologist who wishes to use projective techniques with children 5–8 years old has an alternative with story completion methods. In such methods, a brief story or scene is presented and the child is asked either to complete the story or to respond to a question at the end of the story. Norms, reliability studies, and validity studies are generally unavailable, and the tester must rely on clinical skills alone in evaluating the responses. These methods take about 10–20 minutes, and three are briefly described below.

The Despert Fables (Despert, 1946) were originally developed by Louisa Duss of Switzerland. Ten short stories, some with animal characters, are intended to elicit psychoanalytic themes. For example, in one story a mother, a father, and a baby bird are asleep in their nest. A wind knocks the nest to the ground. The two parents fly to separate trees, and the child is asked what the little bird is going to do. Fine (1948) expanded the number of stories to 20 and categorized them according to such variables as dependency, hostility, identification, sibling rivalry, Oedipal issues, and fears.

The Madeleine Thomas Stories (Mills, 1953) are 15 quite brief scenarios that create suspenseful situations and are followed by a direct question. For example, in one story the child is simply asked to tell what a mother will do on finding two brothers fighting. Mills (1953) introduced these stories (originally written in French; Helmut Wursten, translator) to the American psychological community. He offers a way to organize a clinical analysis, and lists recurring themes common to particular stories.

As part of a larger study in the 1950s, Elizabeth Koppitz (1982) developed what she calls the Munsterburg Incomplete Stories. There are 12 incomplete stories, to be varied by gender-identifiable names (e.g., "Sammy [Sandra] wakes . . ."), each setting up a scene that the child is asked to finish. The author suggests an analysis that includes positive and negative feelings or attitudes of the child toward self and others, positive and negative attitudes of others toward the child, coping mechanisms, and the quality of language.

Other thematic apperception methods have been designed to explore particular areas of development or concern rather than to assess general personality. The Adolescent Separation Anxiety Test (Hansburg, 1980) was developed, starting in the mid-1960s, to assess the intensity of feelings and patterns of responses to experiences of separation, individuation, and attachment in children and adolescents. It is not, strictly speaking, a thematic test. The test consists of 12 black-and-white drawings of mild (going to camp) to strong (death of parent) separation scenarios. Two parallel forms are available, differing only in the genders of the children in the pictures. For each picture, the child is asked to chose one or more of 17 written statements as to how the child in the picture is feeling. The statements are intended to reflect reactions such as withdrawal, anxiety, somatization, adaptation, or denial. Norms are presented for ages 11–14, although the intended use is for ages 11–18. Use of this test, in its present stage of development, for diagnostic or child placement decisions is not recommended by some reviewers (Bailey-Richardson, 1985; Hartsough, 1985).

The Blacky Pictures (Blum, 1950) are a series of cartoon drawings of dogs, wherein Blacky is the main character, appearing at times with a mother, a father, and a sibling (Tippy). Administration is comparable to that for the TAT. The content is specifically designed to elicit themes directly related to the psychoanalytic theory of psychosexual development. These cards are generally out of favor because of advances in formulations of personality development.

Some practicing child therapists use a storytelling technique that is primarily designed for therapeutic purposes but can also be used as an informal and ongoing assessment barometer. In the "mutual storytelling technique" (Gardner, 1971), the child is drawn into a "game" and invited to make up an exciting story, while talking into a tape recorder, for an imaginary television audience. Older children are asked to end with a moral to the story; younger children may simply title it. While the child tells the story, the therapist makes personal note of the needs, conflicts, and possible psychodynamic interpretations, and then in turn tells a story to the child. The story told by the therapist will utilize the same characters, plot, and setting as the child's, but will be changed to provide alternative reactions or behaviors for the character with whom the child has identified. The therapist also ends with a moral to the story. The alternate story by the therapist is meant to be a therapeutic communication that bypasses direct insight or interpretation of the unconscious. Gardner (1971, p. 25) claims that the projective nature of the child's stories is free of "contaminating and distracting stimuli" such as drawings, puppets, or other means to elicit stories.

Some methods are apperceptive, in that they ask for a projective response to visual stimuli, but are not truly thematic, in that only brief responses are required or responses are based on the selection of one or more provided responses. An example of the former is the Rosenzweig Picture-Frustration Test (Rosenzweig, 1977, 1978). Much of the work with this test has been done with the adult form, but a child's form is also available. The child is presented with 24 comic-strip-like scenes, with one person saying something in the "balloon" that might cause frustration to the other character in the picture. The child is to write as quickly as possible a response in an empty "balloon" that sits over the other character. The test may be read to younger children.

Two interesting variations of apperception methods simply show a hand or pair of hands; both have child forms. The Hand Test (Wagner, 1983) is used to explore such areas as aggression and withdrawal. The child is presented with a series of drawings of hands in different positions and is asked to describe what the hands might be doing. The Paired Hands Test (Zucker & Barnett, 1977; Zucker & Jordan, 1968), a series showing a black and white hand interacting, is better suited to explore attitudes toward or expectations of others.

It is beyond the scope of this chapter to mention the abounding variations available in the literature. Many techniques developed in Great Britain, especially through the Tavistock Institute, are not well known in this country and can be reviewed in *Projective Techniques* (Semeonoff, 1976).

CONCLUSIONS

When one is reviewing the numerous thematic storytelling techniques currently available, several issues become apparent. Foremost is the ongoing debate as to whether storytelling techniques should be evaluated as psychometric instruments or as a means of exploring personality dynamics. One should bear in mind that the TAT was originally developed as an aid to therapy, with no intention that it be used to compare individuals or lead to a diagnosis. Continuing in this tradition, many therapy-oriented clinicians and practitioners defend storytelling techniques as emphasizing the uniqueness of individuals. Although the test is still used to compare individuals, clinicians do so by means of their clinical intuition, which is often based on their particular experience with a wide range of individuals and personality types. Although this usage can often be quite accurate and helpful, and even appears wonderously convincing to students learning the technique, it unfortunately cannot be taught in any systematic fashion. In addition, the TAT is now used almost exclusively for purposes of assessment. Thus, it is only fair to assume that current evaluations of the TAT and similar instruments will focus on psychometric properties of the tests.

Of the psychometric problems mentioned in this chapter, two seem to stand out. First, most storytelling techniques have normative information that is at worst nonexistent, and at best based on inadequate samples. Second, in terms of validity, the major problem appears to be with content interpretations: Do events portrayed in stories relate to the subject's actual behaviors, repressed personality characteristics, or mere fantasies? These and similar difficulties must be addressed before storytelling techniques can be considered as psychometric instruments.

As should be evident from our review, several older techniques are still enjoying widespread popularity. Unfortunately, little or none of the current research attempts to improve the scoring systems of these techniques. Any number of reviews concur that instruments such as the TAT and CAT are psychometrically untenable, should not be used for placement decisions or diagnosis, and should never be used except as part of an assessment battery. Fortunately, some of the more recent storytelling variations are continuing to be researched and have good potential for future use. We were most impressed with the present status of the RATC and the TEMAS, although we emphasize that both instruments need refinement. We hope that these and other new measures signal a growing compatibility between the scientist and the practitioner, with an understanding that useful assessment tools require the wisdom of both.

REFERENCES

Aaron, N. S. (1967). Some personality differences between asthmatics, allergic and normal children. *Journal of Clinical Psychology, 23*, 336–340.

Altman, C. H. (1960). Projective techniques in the clinical setting. In A. I. Rabin & M. Haworth (Eds.), *Projective techniques with children* (pp. 329–349). New York: Grune & Stratton.

Ammons, C. H., & Ammons, R. G. (1972). [Review of the Tasks of Emotional Development Test]. *Psychological Reports, 31*, 679.

Anastasi, A. (1981). *Psychological testing* (5th ed.). New York: Macmillan.

Aronow, E., Reznikoff, M., & Rauchway, A. (1979). Some old and new directions in Rorschach testing. *Journal of Personality Assessment, 43* (3), 227–234.

Bailey-Richardson, B. (1985). Review of Separation Anxiety Test. In J. V. Mitchell, Jr. (Ed.), *The ninth mental measurements yearbook* (pp. 53–54). Lincoln: Buros Institute of Mental Measurements, University of Nebraska.

Baty, M. A., & Dreger, R. M. (1975). A comparison of three methods of record TAT protocals. *Journal of Clinical Psychology, 31*, 348.

Bauserman, D. N. (1985). Review of the Michigan Picture Test—Revised. In J. V. Mitchell, Jr. (Ed.), *The ninth mental measurements yearbook* (pp. 970–971). Lincoln: Buros Institute of Mental Measurements, University of Nebraska.

Bellak, L. (1947). *A guide to the interpretation of the Thematic Apperception Test*. New York: Psychological Corporation.

Bellak, L. (1971). *The TAT and CAT in clinical use*. New York: Grune & Stratton.

Bellak, L., & Adelman, C. (1960). The Children's Apperception Test. In A. I. Rabin & M. Haworth (Eds.), *Projective techniques with children* (pp. 62–94). New York: Grune & Stratton.

Bellak, L., & Bellak, S. S. (1949). *The Children's Apperception Test*. New York: C.P.S.

Bellak, L., & Bellak, S. S. (1961). *Children's Appercep-tion Test (C.A.T.) manual* (4th ed.). Larchmont, NY: C.P.S.

Bischoff, B. G. (1985). Review of Michigan Picture Test. In J. V. Mitchell, Jr. (Ed.), *The ninth mental measure-ments yearbook* (pp. 971–972). Lincoln: Buros In-stitute of Mental Measurements, University of Ne-braska.

Blatt, S. J. (1978). [Review of E. Aronow and M. Rezni-koff, *Rorschach content interpretation*]. *Contempo-rary Psychology, 23,* 251–253.

Blum, G. S. (1950). *The Blacky Pictures: Manual of Instructions*. New York: Psychological Corporation.

Bradley, R. H., & Caldwell, B. M. (1976). Early home environments and changes in mental test performance in children from 6–36 months. *Developmental Psy-chology, 12,* 93–97.

Cleveland, S. E. (1976). Reflections on the rise and fall of psychodiagnosis. *Professional Psychology, 7,* 309–318.

Cohen, H., & Weil, G. R. (1975a). *Tasks of Emotional Development test manual*. Brookline, MA: Tasks of Emotional Development Associates.

Cohen, H., & Weil, G. R. (1975b). *Tasks of Emotional Development: A projective test for children and adolescents*. Brookline, MA: Tasks of Emotional De-velopment Associates.

Costantino, G. (1982). TEMAS: A new technique for personality assessment and psychotherapy for Hispan-ic children. *Research Bulletin, Hispanic Research Center, 5,* 3–6.

Costantino, G., & Malgady, R. G. (1983). Verbal fluency of Hispanic, black and white children on TAT and TEMAS, a new thematic apperception test. *Hispanic Journal of Behavioral Sciences, 5,* 199–206.

Costantino, G., Malgady, R. G., & Rogler, L. H. (1985, August). *Cross-cultural validation of TEMAS, a minority projective test*. Paper presented at the 93rd Annual Meeting of the American Psychological Association, Los Angeles.

Costantino, G., Malgady, R. G., & Rogler, L. H. (1988). *Tell-Me-A-Story (TEMAS): Manual*. Los Angeles: Western Psychological Services.

Costantino, G., Malgady, R. G., & Vazquez, C. (1981). A comparison of the Murray-TAT and a new thematic apperception test for urban Hispanic children. *Hispanic Journal of Behavioral Sciences, 3,* 291–300.

Dana, R. H. (1985), Thematic Apperception Test. In C. S. Newmark (Ed.), *Major psychological assessment instruments* (pp. 89–134). Boston: Allyn & Bacon.

Dana, R. H. (1986). Thematic Apperception Test used with adolescents. In A. I. Rabin (Ed.), *Projective tech-niques for adolescents and children* (pp. 14–36). New York: Springer.

Daum, J. M. (1985). Review of Themes Concerning Blacks. In J. V. Mitchell, Jr. (Ed.), *The ninth mental measurements yearbook* (p. 1617). Lincoln: Buros In-stitute of Mental Measurements, University of Ne-braska.

Davids, A., & Rosenblatt, D. (1958). Use of the TAT in assessment of alienation. *Journal of Projective Tech-niques, 22,* 145–152.

Despert, J. L. (1946). Psychosomatic study of fifty stuttering children. *American Journal of Ortho-psychiatry, 16,* 100–113.

Dean, R. S. (1984). Commentary on "Personality assess-ment in the schools: The special issue." *School Psy-chology Review, 13*(1), 95–98.

Dlepu, O., & Kimbrough, C. (1982). Feeling-tone and card preferences of black elementary children for the TCB and TAT. *Journal of Non-White Concerns, 10,* 50–56.

Erikson, E. H. (1950). *Childhood and society*. New York: Norton.

Fine, R. (1948). Use of the Despert Fables (revised form) in diagnostic work with children. *Rorschach Research Exchange and Journal of Projective Tech-niques, 12,* 106–118.

Gardner, G. E. (1959). Psychiatric problems of adoles-cence. In S. Arieti (Ed.), *American handbook of psychiatry* (Vol. 1, pp. 870–892). New York: Basic Books.

Gardner, R. A. (1971). *Therapeutic communication with children: The mutual storytelling technique*. New York: Science House.

Gerver, J. M. (1946). *Level of interpretation of children on the Thematic Apperception Test*. Unpublished master's thesis, Ohio State University, Columbus, Ohio.

Goldman, J., Stein, C., & Guerry, S. (1983). *Psycholog-ical methods of child assessment*. New York: Brunner/ Mazel.

Gotts, E. (1974). Reviews of school psychology materi-als. *Journal of School Psychology, 12,* 84–85.

Hafner, A. J., & Kaplan, A. M. (1960). Hostility content analysis of the Rorschach and TAT. *Journal of Pro-jective Techniques, 24,* 137–143.

Hansburg, H. G. (1980). *Adolescent separation anxiety* (2 vols.). Melbourne, FL: R. E. Krieger.

Hartsough, C. S. (1985). Review of Adolescent Separa-tion Anxiety Test. In J. V. Mitchell, Jr. (Ed.), *The ninth mental measurements yearbook* (pp. 54–55). Lincoln: Buros Institute of Mental Measurements, University of Nebraska.

Hartwell, S. W., Hutt, M. L., Andrew, G., & Walton, R. E. (1951). The Michigan Picture Test: Diagnostic and therapeutic possibilities of a new projective test in child guidance. *American Journal of Orthopsychiatry, 21,* 124–137.

Haworth, M. R. (1965). *A schedule of adaptive mech-anisms in CAT responses*. Larchmont, NY: C.P.S.

Haworth, M. R. (1986). Children's Apperception Test. In A. I. Rabin (Ed.), *Projective techniques for adolescents and children* (pp. 37–72). New York: Springer.

Holmen, M. G., & Docter, R. (1972). *Educational and psychological testing*. New York: Russell Sage Foundation.

Hutt, M. L. (1980). *The Michigan Picture Test—Revised*. New York: Grune & Stratton.

Hutt, M. L. (1986). The Michigan Picture Test—Revised. In A. I. Rabin (Ed.), *Projective techniques for adolescents and children* (pp. 73–84). New York: Springer.

Jensen, A. R. (1965). Review of the Make-A-Picture Story. In O. K. Buros (Ed.), *The sixth mental measurements yearbook* (pp. 468–470). Highland Park, NJ: Gryphon Press.

Kagan, J. (1960). Thematic apperceptive techniques with children. In A. Rabin & M. Haworth (Eds.), *Projective techniques with children* (pp. 105–129). New York: Grune & Stratton.

Karon, B. P. (1981). The Thematic Apperception Test. In A. I. Rabin (Ed.), *Assessment with projective techniques* (pp. 85–120). New York: Springer.

Karpowitz, D. H., & Zeis, F. R. (1975). Personality and behavior differences of obese and nonobese adolescents. *Journal of Consulting and Clinical Psychology, 43,* 886–891.

Kinard, E. M. (1980). Emotional development in physically abused children. *American Journal of Orthopsychiatry, 50,* 686–696.

Kinard, E. M. (1982). Experiencing child abuse: Effects on emotional adjustment. *American Journal of Orthopsychiatry, 52,* 82–91.

Koppitz, E. M. (1982). Personality assessment in the schools. In C. Reynolds & T. Gutkin (Eds.), *The handbook of school psychology* (pp. 273–295). New York: Wiley.

Koslof, K. E. (1984). The battered woman: A developmental perspective. *Smith College Studies in Social Work, 54,* 181–203.

Krahn, G. L. (1985). The use of projective assessment techniques in pediatric settings. *Journal of Pediatric Psychology, 10,* 179–193.

Lanyon, R. I. (1984). Personality assessment. *Annual Review of Psychology, 35,* 667–701.

Lanyon, R. I., & Goodstein, L. (1982). *Personality assessment* (2nd ed.). New York: Wiley.

Levitt, E. E. (1975). A methodological review. *Professional Psychology, 6,* 101–102.

Lubin, B., Larsen, R. M., & Matarazzo, I. D. (1984). Patterns of psychological test usage in the United States: 1932–1982. *American Psychologist, 39,* 451–453.

Malgady, R. G. (1982). Reliability and validity of TEMAS: A new thematic apperception test for urban ethnic minority children. *Research Bulletin, Hispanic Research Center, 5,* 10–13.

Malgady, R. G., Costantino, G., & Rogler, L. H. (1984). Development of a thematic apperception test (TEMAS) for urban Hispanic children. *Journal of Consulting and Clinical Psychology, 52,* 986–996.

McArthur, D. S., & Roberts, G. E. (1982). *Roberts Apperception Test for Children: Manual.* Los Angeles: Western Psychological Services.

McClelland, D. C., Atkinson, J. W., Clark, R. A., & Lowell, E. L. (1953). *The achievement motive.* New York: Appleton-Century-Crofts.

Mills, E. S. (1953). the Madeline Thomas Completion Stories Test. *Journal of Consulting Psychology, 17,* 139–141.

Morgan, C. D., & Murray, H. A. (1935). A method for investigating phantasies: The Thematic Apperception Test. *Archives of Neurology and Psychiatry, 34,* 289–306.

Munter, P. O. (1975). The medical model revisited: A humanistic reply. *Journal of Personality Assessment, 39,* 344.

Murray, H. A. (1938). *Explorations of personality.* New York: Oxford University Press.

Murray, H. A. (1943). *Thematic Apperception Test manual.* Cambridge, MA: Harvard University Press.

Ness, M. K. (1985). Review of Themes Concerning Blacks. In J. V. Mitchell, Jr. (Ed.), *The ninth mental measurements yearbook* (pp. 1618–1619). Lincoln: Buros Institute of Mental Measurements, University of Nebraska.

Newman, R. S., Newman, J. F., & Sells, S. B. (1974). Language and adjustment scales for the Thematic Apperception Test for youths 12–17 years. *Vital and Health Statistics* (Series 2), *62,* 1–84.

Obrzut, J. E., & Boliek, C. A. (1986). Thematic approaches to personality assessment with children and adolescent. In H. Knoff (Ed.), *The assessment of child and adolescent personality,* (pp. 173–198). New York: Guilford Press.

Obrzut, J. E., & Cummings, J. A. (1983). The projective approach to personality assessments: An analysis of thematic picture techniques. *School Psychology Review, 12,* 414–420.

Passman, R. H., & Lautman, L. A. (1982). Fathers', mothers', and security blankets' effects on the responsiveness of young children during projective testing. *Journal of Consulting and Clinical Psychology, 50,* 310–312.

Peterson, R. A., Kroeker, L., & Torshen, K. (1976). Predicting clinical judgment for a primary grade apperception battery. *Journal of Personality Assessment, 40,* 378–382.

Piotrowski, C. (1983). *The status of projective techniques: Or, "wishing won't make it go away"* (Report No. CG-017-178). Pensacola: University of West Florida. (ERIC Document Reproduction Service No. ED 239 134)

Pollack, J., Cohen, H., & Weil, G. (1981). The Tasks of Emotional Development Test: A survey of research applications. *Psychology: A Quarterly Journal of Human Behavior, 18*(4), 2–11.

Pollack, J., Cohen, H., & Weil, G. (1982). The Tasks of Emotional Development Test: A survey of research applications. *Psychology: A Quarterly Journal of Human Behavior, 19*(4), 42–44.

Rabin, A. I. (1960). Projective methods and projection in children. In A. I. Rabin & M. Haworth (Eds.), *Projective techniques with children* (pp. 2–11). New York: Grune & Stratton.

Rabin, A. I. (1986). Concerning projective techniques. In A. I. Rabin (Ed.), *Projective techniques for adolescents and children* (pp. 3–11). New York: Springer.

Rabin, A. I., & Haworth, M. (Eds.). (1960). *Projective techniques with children.* New York: Grune & Stratton.

Rosenzweig, S. (1977). *Manual for the children's form of the Rosenzweig Picture-Frustration [P-F] Study.* St. Louis: Rana House.

Rosenzweig, S. (1978). *Aggressive behavior and the Rosenzweig Picture-Frustration Study.* New York: Praeger.

Santostefano, S. (1970). Assessment of motives in children. *Psychological Reports, 26,* 639–649.

Semeonoff, B. (1976). *Projective techniques.* New York: Wiley.

Shneidman, E. S. (1952). *Manual for the Make-A-Picture Story method* (Projective Techniques Monographs No. 2). The Society for Projective Techniques and Rorschach Institute.

Shneidman, E. S. (1960). The MAPS Test with children. In A. I. Rabin & M. R. Hayworth (Eds.), *Projective techniques with children* (pp. 139–148). New York: Grune & Stratton.

Sines, J. O. (1985). Review of the Roberts Apperception Test for Children. In J. V. Mitchell, Jr. (Ed.), *The ninth mental measurements yearbook* (pp. 1289–

1291). Lincoln: Buros Institute of Mental Measurements, University of Nebraska.

Solomon, I. L., & Starr, B. D. (1968). *School Apperception Method: SAM*. New York: Springer.

Symonds, P. M. (1948). *Picture–Story Test: Manual and set of 20 pictures*. New York: Columbia University Press.

Symonds, P. M. (1949). *Adolescent fantasy: An investigation of the picture–story method of personality study*. New York: Columbia University Press.

Tomkins, S. S. (1947). *The Thematic Apperception Test*. New York: Grune & Stratton.

Triplett, S., & Brunson, P. (1982). TCB and TAT response characteristics in black males and females: A replication. *Journal of Non-White Concerns, 10*, 73–77.

Vane, J. R. (1981). The Thematic Apperception Test: A review. *Clinical Psychology Review, 1*, 319–336.

Wade, T. C., & Baker, T. B. (1977). Opinions and use of psychological tests: A survey of clinical psychologists. *American Psychologists, 32*, 874–882.

Wagner, E. E. (1983). *The Hand Test manual: Revised 1983*. Los Angeles: Western Psychological Services.

Ward, J. (1973). Self identification in the Make-A-Picture Story protocols of a group of retarded boys. *American Journal of Mental Deficiency, 77*, 469–471.

Weaver, V. (1981). Racial attribution, story length, and feeling-tone of young black males to the TCB and TAT. *Journal of Non-White Concerns, 10*, 31–43.

Williams, R. L. (1972). *Themes Concerning Blacks*. St. Louis: R. L. Williams and Associates.

Williams, Y., Williams, R. L., & Williams, A. L. (1981). Suicidal themes in the TCB: Two case studies. *Journal of Non-White Concerns, 10*, 23–29.

Wise, A. J. (1975). Clinical review. *Professional Psychology, 6*, 102–103.

Witherspoon, R. L. (1968). Development of objective scoring methods for longitudinal CAT data. *Journal of Projective Techniques and Personality Assessment, 32*, 406–412.

Worchel, F. (1987). The Roberts Apperception Test for Children. In C. R. Reynolds & L. Mann (Eds.), *The encyclopedia of special education* (p. 1367). New York: Wiley.

Zucker, K. B., & Barnett, O. W. (1977). *The Paired Hands Test manual*. Dallas: McCarron-Dial Systems.

Zucker, K. B., & Jordan, D. C. (1968). The Paired Hands Test: A technique for measuring friendliness. *Journal of Projective Techniques and Personality Assessment, 32*, 522–529.

5

Evaluation of Projective Drawings

HOWARD M. KNOFF
University of South Florida

I n the context of modern psychology and personality assessment, projective drawings have had a significant impact and history. Originally used as tests of creativity and intellectual maturity, projective drawings have been used as personality assessment techniques since the 1920s and continue to be used frequently in the field (Fuller & Goh, 1983; Lubin, Larsen, & Matarazzo, 1984; Prout, 1983), most appropriately within multisetting, multisource, multi-instrument personality assessment designs (Knoff, 1986). Significantly, projective drawing approaches and adaptations continue to be developed, refined, and introduced into the field. Therefore, it is important to understand their historical and theoretical development, approaches toward their psychometric and clinical evaluation, and their use in the context of a comprehensive personality assessment battery. This chapter addresses these three major components that are necessary in the evaluation of projective drawings, while recommending "best-practice" approaches toward their interpretation and use by psychologists and other mental health professionals.

HISTORICAL DEVELOPMENT AND THEORETICAL CONTEXTS

Historical Review

As noted above, drawings were first used to assess creativity and intellectual maturity. In fact, the use of drawings to evaluate children's intellectual functioning continues to the present. Goodenough (1926, 1931) was the first to develop and standardize an approach to evaluating children's intelligence through their drawings of a man (i.e., the Goodenough Draw-A-Man Test). By crediting children at different chronological ages with points for the characteristics or details included in their drawings, and, separately, for their drawings' qualitative maturity, Goodenough was able to quantitatively assess their intellectual functioning and derive individual intelligence estimates. This technique was updated by Harris (1963), whose Goodenough–Harris scoring system provides a more recent standardization and standard scores related to children's intellectual maturity.

In the Goodenough–Harris scoring system, children's drawings of a man and/or woman are given points for the presence of specific characteristics (e.g., parts of the body, clothes, accessories); for the quality of the drawing (e.g., appropriate and well-drawn lines and angles within the figure, good proportionality between different body parts such as head and trunk); and for the integration of figures into whole, recognizable persons. These points are entered as raw scores into norm tables, which are separated by the sex of the figure drawn (i.e., male vs. female), the sex of the child completing the drawing, and the chronological age of the child. The resulting standard scores represent an evaluation of the child's intellectual maturity (as opposed to his or her "intelligence"), which Harris (1963) defines as the "ability to form concepts of increasingly abstract character" (p. 5). Clearly, the Draw-A-Man technique assesses only one type of intellectual maturity—that which is operationalized by a visual–motor task requiring the cognitive, experiential, and environmental recognition of people's physical characteristics and the ability to represent them pictorially during a test/demand situation. Other techniques or tests operationalize intellectual maturity differently; thus, an understanding of the Draw-A-Man versus these other techniques is critical to sound assessment and interpretation.

A separate qualitative component of the Goodenough–Harris approach involves evaluating a child's drawing against 12 criterion drawings that represent increasing levels of drawing sophistication and intellectual maturity. This more global assessment component integrates a developmental perspective into the evaluation. This perspective recognizes that children's drawing maturity (and therefore intellectual maturity) changes over time, and that it must be evaluated periodically if a child is to be accurately assessed. Without this developmental perspective, some drawings might be interpreted projectively when they actually represent good developmental approximations of the child's current drawing maturity and/or chronological age. It would be a grave error to interpret the lack of a drawing's detail as some manifestation of an "apparent" emotional trauma or dysfunction when the absence of that detail is developmentally appropriate and expected.

Although the Goodenough–Harris Draw-A-Man scoring system has been used for many years, it has also been criticized for its outdated scoring standards, norms, and standardization, and approach toward deriving standard scores. Recently, Naglieri (1987) developed an improved scoring system with norms based on a standardization sample of 5- through 17-year-old children matched to the 1980 census data. This quantitative Draw-A-Person scoring system evaluates students' Man, Woman, and Self drawings using a less subjective approach than the Goodenough–Harris system, with 14 scoring criteria rating the presence of specific body parts, the detail of the body parts, the proportions of the body parts, and other elaborations for bonus credit. Described as a nonverbal measure of intellectual ability, Naglieri's Draw-A-Person system has been reported to have good test–retest, interrater, and internal reliabilities, and factor analyses suggest that scoring items are correlated strongly with g. Standard scores from matched pairs of males and females, blacks and whites, and Hispanics and non-Hispanics also did not significantly differ. As a relatively new scale, the Naglieri system needs more use and critical analysis in the field. At the present time, however, it appears to offer a well-developed updating of the Goodenough and Goodenough–Harris scoring systems—one that continues the historical use of drawings as measures of intelligence.

Besides the Draw-A-Man, the Bender–Gestalt Test (BGT) also has a significant history as a technique evaluating children's intellectual development and/or visual–motor integration. Developed by Bender (1938), the test consists of nine geometric drawings that are presented individually to children in a standard order, with directions to reproduce them on paper with pencil as accurately as possible. The Koppitz scoring system for the BGT (Koppitz, 1963, 1975) is probably the best-known and most widely used system for intellectual and visual–motor assessment, and its use in studies correlating BGT performance with neurological development, the presence of brain injury, math and reading skill, and other academic areas is documented in a number of reviews (e.g., Eno & Deichmann, 1980; Koppitz, 1975; Tolor & Brannigan, 1980). Still an extremely popular technique with psychologists (Prout, 1983), the BGT remains an important part of most assessment batteries. There is, however, significant debate (e.g., Bigler & Ehrfurth, 1981) as to its utility beyond its very basic visual–motor integration assessment—a fact that is discussed in relation to personality assessment below.

The use of drawings to evaluate children's personality characteristics and functioning has a history that parallels their use in the assessment of intelligence, intellectual maturity, and visual–motor and other development. In fact, with the publication of Goodenough's Draw-A-Man Test, a number of individuals noted the impact of personality variables, characteristics, and influences on the clinical drawing process. This interest in the projective use of drawings culminated in the late 1940s with a number of significant works, one related to the House–Tree–Person (H-T-P) technique (Buck, 1948) and one related to Human Figure Drawings (HFDs) (Machover, 1949). The H-T-P technique involves having children complete separate drawings of a house, a tree, and a person, with opportunities to ask them questions that clarify and expand the apparent information in each picture after each has been drawn. Although Buck (1948) published his H-T-P monograph to expand the use of drawings as intellectual assessment measures, he also provided a host of personality-related hypotheses concerning the global and specific characteristics of the H-T-P figures and their relationship to a child's personality dynamics. Since that seminal work, Hammer (1958, 1980), Burns (1987), and Buck again (1970) have published major works that have summarized and expanded on the clinical use of the H-T-P in evaluating children's personality dynamics and dimensions.

Machover's (1949) work on the projective uses of HFDs, which could involve any drawing of a person for the purposes of personality assessment (including the Draw-A-Man or Draw-A-Person), was based on her work with emotionally disturbed adolescents and adult psychotics. Expanded by Hammer (1958), Koppitz (1968, 1984), Schildkraut, Shenker, and Sonnenblick (1972) and others, HFDs now have an extensive projective literature on both child and adult drawings, yielding information on their relationships to self-concept, personality style and orientation, sexual and other development, and inter- and intrapersonal conflicts (Handler, 1985), Koppitz's (1968) work is especially significant, in that she analyzed the HFDs of boys and girls aged 5 through 11 and 12 to identify developmentally expected and unusual items and characteristics. As noted above, this developmental perspective helps the psychologist to differentially analyze HFDs; this insures that drawings characteristic of a child's chronological or maturational age are not interpreted projectively, thereby resulting in

inappropriate interpretations and improper clinical conclusions and recommendations.

Another strand of projective drawing history relates to drawings that involve more complex or interactive subject matter—that is, drawings that go beyond simply "Draw me a house," "Draw me a tree," or "Draw me a person." Initially, these more complex drawings involved asking children to draw specific events or groups of people, most notably their families (Hulse, 1951, 1952). Although these "nonkinetic" drawings were helpful in discerning children's perceptions of their families, they also were often portrait-like, with noninteracting figures and elements. Burns and Kaufman (1970, 1972), therefore, saw the need for and utility of demanding that the figures in their complex projective drawings be actively engaged. Their Kinetic Family Drawing (K-F-D) technique asked children to "draw a picture of everyone in your family, including you, *doing* something." These directions resulted in significantly more extensive projective data for interepretation—data that extended their social–emotional hypotheses beyond simple child-focused, intrapersonal concerns to complex, ecologically focused, interpersonal, multisetting, and multidimensional concerns and issues.

After the K-F-D, a number of other books and monographs describing additional kinetic drawing approaches were published. Prout and Phillips (1974) and Sarbaugh (1983) developed separate variations of Kinetic School Drawing (K-S-D) techniques asking children to "draw a school picture. . . . Put yourself, your teacher, and a friend or two in the picture. . . . Make everyone doing something." These projective drawing techniques tap children's school-based problems, issues, expectations, and/or concerns, while also evaluating their relationships with peers and adult models. However, the K-S-D was not found to differentiate meaningfully between school-based issues and home issues that were being manifested in school. In a projective sense, this need was addressed by integrating the K-F-D and K-S-D techniques into a combined system, the Kinetic Drawing System (Knoff & Prout, 1985), which facilitates this differential analysis while also updating and reviewing the literature specific to both techniques in one place.

Although the major works and trends in projective drawing have been described above, the discussion is far from exhaustive. For example, Burns (1987) has recently published a book describing the Kinetic House-Tree-Person technique. And other techniques, such as the Draw-A-Person-in-the-Rain and the Kinetic Drawing—School: First Memory Technique abound in the literature. The history of projective drawings will continue, but the context and theoretical interpretations of projective drawings will change as the zeitgeist of psychology changes. This fact is exemplified below, first in a discussion of the possible theoretical perspectives of projective drawings, and later in a discussion of best-practice approaches for their use in comprehensive personality assessment.

Theoretical Perspectives on Projective Drawings

Among the many psychological trends and movements that have occurred during the modern history of projective drawing techniques (i.e., from the 1920s to the present), four important psychological perspectives or orientations are particularly relevant: the psychodynamic, the cognitive-developmental, the behavioral, and the cognitive–behavioral orientations. These four orientations are discussed below, with emphasis on the way in which projective drawings are interpreted in each one.

The Psychodynamic Orientation

The psychodynamic orientation has its roots in Freudian psychoanalysis, where projective drawings are seen as symbolic representations of a child's world of perception of reality. In this context, the paper on which any figure is drawn corresponds to the child's environment; figures represent significant people in the child's life (past, present, or future) or significant role figures (e.g., father or authority figures, sibling figures, perceived self figures); and objects may be symbolic of specific conflicts, attitudes toward or between figures, or behavioral tendencies (e.g., spiders are said to suggest conflicts with dominant or threatening mothers, and monsters are thought to indicate specific

power issue related to male or authority figures). The drawing process, according to this orientation, involves the presentation of an ambiguous task. For example, the child is told to draw a house, but is not told what type of house, how to hold the paper, how many elaborations to put onto the house, or whether to put people or objects in or around the house. The child therefore must "project" his or her feelings, attitudes, strivings, and/or perspectives into the drawing process, thereby allowing the examiner to see a particular facet of his or her personality and/or personality functioning.

At times, children will draw distorted figures or scenes in their projective drawings. For example, given the K-F-D instructions, a child who comes from a physically abusive home may draw a very close-knit family unit with everyone participating together in a joyous birthday celebration. Psychodynamically, this scene may be analyzed as a distortion of reality; the child, it is believed, is using this defense mechanism to deny his or her current reality so as to deal with a very torturous, anxiety-provoking situation. At other times, children may draw their perceptions or interpretations of how their lives exist, despite the fact that these perceptions do not quite mesh with actual situations or events. Psychodynamically, these drawings may not be considered distorted; rather, they may be interpreted as depictions of the children's actual (albeit inaccurate) interpretation of a life situation that has idiographically traumatized them and affected their social–emotional or psychological development.

Because of the symbolic nature of the psychodynamic approach, many of the projective drawings have both global and specific aspects that are interpreted in fairly consistent ways. Below are brief psychodynamic interpretations of the H-T-P and Kinetic Drawing System techniques to exemplify this point.

Psychodynamically, the house drawing is said to reflect a child's perception of his or her home life and the quality of the relationships among family members. Although the house drawing may represent a child's past, present, future, ideal, or fantasized home, it also provides information about his or her feelings about the home environment and his or her approach toward dealing with home- and family-related issues (e.g., to be defensive, aggressive, withdrawing, insecure, regressive). Within the house, the door and windows reflect a child's openness to direct contact with the environment or individuals in the environment; windows, in addition, may indicate whether a child is controlled by family or home issues or is excluded because of those same issues. Roofs relate to a child's need for and type of fantasy, while walls provide a measure of the child's ego strength and stability.

Tree drawings are said to reflect the unconscious, underlying personality dynamics of a child, along with indications as to the child's ability to adjust to intrapersonal, interpersonal, and environmental crises, events, and issues. The tree drawing is considered symbolic of life and growth. It may suggest traumas that the child has experienced, deep-seated self-concepts and self-attitudes, and resources that are available to the child and whether or not they will be utilized. With respect to specific components, the tree's roots generally reflect the child's reality testing or need to hold onto reality; the trunk relates to the child's ego strength and feelings of psychological control and power; the branches suggest the child's ability to derive satisfaction from the environment and ability to interact interpersonally in appropriate and socially successful ways; and the crown symbolizes the child's inter- and intra-active style—his or her use of fantasy, emotional lability, reactions to environmental pressure, and ability to deal with reality.

Person drawings can usually be categorized as drawings of the self, the ideal self, and/or significant others. Self-drawings tend to reflect children's feelings or self-concepts at the time of the drawings; these self-concepts may range from body image issues to issues related to a child's interpersonal, intellectual, behavioral, vocational, religious, extracurricular, and/or familial self. Drawings of the ideal self tend to reflect children's aspirations, needs, and/or desires—whether realistic, fantasized, troubled, or irrational. These drawings can also specifically focus on the self-concept areas noted above, and they can depict another person who in actuality symbolizes the child doing the drawing. Drawings of significant others often identify specific individuals (e.g., a sibling, peer, or adult) or individuals who symbolize specific roles or issues (e.g., a vice-principal as an authority figure, a doctor as a helping figure) for the purpose of communicating some strong past, present, or expected negative or positive affect, experience, or interaction. Parent figures are the most typical drawings of significant others, and a child's choice in drawing such a figure is not considered random; it is thought to indicate some significant conscious or unconscious psychological issue specific to the individual drawn, with which the child is currently dealing.

Relative to other specific parts of the figure, the head of a person drawing is considered, psychodynamically, to provide hypotheses about the child's intellect, fantasy activity, ability to control impulses and emotional lability, and ability to interact socially in appropriate ways. Facial features help to assess the potential quality of the child's interactions with the environment, as well as the child's overall affect and feelings toward self and/or others. Characteristics of the neck are considered symbolic of relations between the child's cognitive, intellectual, and problem-solving capabilities and his or her ability to enact those capabilities so that emotional impulses are controlled. The body or trunk is often related to children's basic drives, while arms, fingers, legs, and toes provide information on the qualitative nature of children's social and interpersonal adjustments (e.g., friendly, constructive, hostile, destructive), their interactive styles (e.g., rigid, flexible, relaxed, stilted), and their openness or closedness to interpersonal relationships and dealing with significant social–emotional issues or developmental circumstances.

Globally, the Kinetic Drawing System's family (K-F-D) and school (K-S-D) drawings look at children's perceptions of the psychological warmth and support within their home and school environments, respectively, as well as potential themes and issues in those settings that may be interfering with a child's ongoing social, emotional, personality, or other development. Also suggested within the drawings may be specific events that have distressed the child, and when and how the distress might have occurred and interfered with the ongoing development noted above. More specifically, both the family and school drawings are evaluated for the (1) actions of and between drawn figures; (2) characteristics of specific figures; (3) position, distance between, and barriers between figures; (4) drawing style; and (5) psychodynamic or other symbols present in the drawings. All of these areas have potential psychodynamic interpretations. For example, in K-F-D drawings, activities such as a father mowing a lawn or chopping wood may indicate some fears of castration of an overly dominant father/authority figure. If the father's pants are excessively darkened, it may suggest the child's conflict with some aspect of sexual development or impulse. In K-S-D, the presence of a prominent "X" shape within a drawing suggests the influence of a strong superego, which may be needed by the child to control specific aggressive or other inappropriate id impulses. The child's use of heavy and overworked lines in drawing this "X" may suggest an excessive amount of anxiety specific to that need for superego involvement. Finally, the presence of light bulbs, lights, or electricity in either K-F-D or K-S-D may indicate that the child has such a great need for psychological warmth or love such that all thoughts and activities are directed toward that need.

This overview of some of the psychodynamic interpretations of various projective drawing techniques is necessarily brief and simplistic. For a broader review of other psychodynamic interpretations and analyses, books by Buck (1948), Hammer (1958, 1980), Schildkraut et al. (1972), Handler (1985), Machover (1949), and Burns (1987) are recommended. In addition, two thorough literature reviews (Ogdon, 1977, 1982) for the H-T-P and BGT, and one (Knoff & Prout, 1985) for the Kinetic Drawing System, are suggested.

The Cognitive–Developmental Orientation

The cognitive–developmental orientation emphasizes that figure drawings are first and foremost reflections of children's developmental and cognitive characteristics, and that they should be evaluated in this context before any projective or personality-related interpretations are hypothesized. Further-more, the effects of the environment on the child's cognitive development (e.g., the amount of sensory stimulation at home, the availability of preschool and play groups) should be analyzed as part of these characteristics, and again should be evaluated prior to projective considerations. All of this is accomplished in five ways: by evaluating (1) the child's developmental and health history, including specific prenatal, perinatal, and postnatal milestones and events; (2) the child's cognitive and intellectual development, through IQ and other processing tests; (3) the child's visual–motor ability, through measures developed for that purpose (e.g., the Developmental Test of Visual–Motor Ability); (4) relevant and critical components of the child's socioeconomic status that interact with the cognitive, intellectual, visual–motor, and other developmental skills that are apparent in figure drawing tasks; and finally (5) the child's visual–motor drawing skill as compared to same-age peers from some standardization or norm group.

Theoretically, this orientation has been best conceptualized by Jean Piaget (Wadsworth, 1989), with his emphasis on cognitive development as a central and determining feature of most other areas of development. Historically, this orientation has been best operationalized by the writings of Goodenough (1926, 1931), Harris (1963), and Kopitz (1968). Piaget would say that the child's cognitive perspective of his or her world, and his or her schema of a "person" within that cognitive perspective, should significantly determine (1) how a child being given a Draw-A-Person Test will complete a requested drawing, (2) what details will be in that drawing, and (3) to what degree it compares with drawings of same-age peers. Although the schema may be influenced by social–emotional experiences, it is first and foremost a cognitive structure that is based on an interaction of intelligence and experience. That is, children's drawings of a "person" will most reflect their cognitive conceptualizations of those physical or other characteristics possessed by their prototypical person. If they have not assimilated the fact that all people have feet, their drawings will lack that characteristic.

Koppitz, taking a more normative perspective on cognitive and visual–motor development, summarized her analyses of children's expected and unusual HFD characteristics in 1968. Looking separately at boys' and girls' drawings from ages 5 through 11 and 12, Koppitz defined an expected drawing characteristic as one present in 86%–100% of the drawings for a specific sex at a specific age, and an unusual characteristic as one present in fewer than 15% of the drawings. According to these criteria, a typical 5-year-old boy would be expected to draw a head, eyes, nose, mouth, body, and legs on his HFD. A typical 11- or 12-year-old girl's drawing would contain these same six characteristics plus two-dimensional arms and legs (with the arms attached at the shoulder and positioned downward), feet, hair, a neck, and at least two articles of clothing. Exceptional HFD characteristics for 5-year-old boys would include knees, elbows, two lips, nostrils, arms drawn at the shoulder, two-dimensional feet, five fingers, pupils in the eyes, at least four articles of clothing, a figure drawn in profile, and a figure drawn in appropriate body proportions. For 11- or 12-year-old girls, only the presence of knees would be considered exceptional.

According to these norms and this cognitive-developmental perspective, characteristics of drawings that are not expected, given a child's chronological and/or maturational age, may not be accurately interpreted projectively when they are missing from a drawing. Thus, this perspective must be considered prior to projective interpretations so as to prevent the overinterpretation and inappropriate interpretation to projective drawings. Naturally, the presence of these expected and exceptional characteristics differ across the 5–12 age span and for boys versus girls. At this time, an updating of these norms, using a national stratification and sampling process, would be most welcome.

To summarize, the cognitive-developmental orientation suggests that a child's intellectual ability and experiential development must be considered before projective drawings can be interpreted in personality-related ways. Therefore, information about a child's IQ and his or her home environment and developmental opportunities is critical as an evaluative baseline. This baseline facilitates an analysis of a child's cognitive × personality style, abilities, and status, so that projective interpretations are as accurate as possible. For example, if a 12-year-old girl who has grown up in a low-socioeconomic-status background with very little sensory and environmental stimulation is asked to draw a person, the absence of feet, two-dimensional arms and legs, and hair may suggest one or more of the following:

1. The child simply has not attended appropriately to environmental stimuli and does not yet cognitively perceive (or have the schema of) people as having those characteristics.
2. The child is delayed, compared to same-age peers, because she has not had the necessary and sufficient environmental and/or sensory experiences that result in those features' being cognitively included in the concept of "person."
3. The child has not had the necessary and sufficient environment and/or sensory experiences that result in those features' being motorically reproduced in person drawings—whether or not the child has an accurate cognitive perspective of a "person."
4. The child does not have the intellectual ability to benefit from any experiential learning, and the missing features result from this deficiency.
5. The child does not want to reproduce the person completely, because of culturally or socioeconomically related poor motivation or a situational fear of the testing situation.
6. The child has some social–emotional difficulty (as hypothesized from the projective literature) related to the absence of feet, two-dimensional arms and legs, and hair.

These are just hypotheses that will need to be validated more objectively; doing this, however, is further discussed in a later section.

The Behavioral Orientation

Within the behavioral orientation, the projective drawing task represents an ambiguous task, completed in a formal assessment situation, with an examiner who may or may not be familiar, under conditions that are inherent both to the child (e.g., defensiveness, anxiety, resistance to authority) and to the environment (e.g., a comfortable room that is quiet and with no chance of interruptions). Thus, the projective task allows an examiner to sample a child's behavior under specific task, situational, and environmental conditions and to make innumerable behavioral observations and analyses across a number of dimensions. With enough appropriate and representative behavioral samples during projective testing, the examiner may hypothesize about and then determine how the child reacts, for example, in similar ambiguous situations or under similar evaluative conditions. And with enough appropriate and representative multimethod, multisetting, and multisource behavioral samples, the examiner may formulate and validate hypotheses about the child's general behavioral style and functioning (i.e., personality trait patterns) and the child's differential style and functioning under more specific ecological circumstances (i.e., personality state patterns).

In essence, behavioral observations during projective test administration are no different from behavioral observations during any other testing situation. What differ, as noted above, are the task demands, the reactions and responses of the child to the task demands, the examiner's reactions and responses to the task demands, and the complex behavioral effects that occur because of child–test–examiner interactions. Possible behavioral observations during projective testing, then, include the child's (1) behavior or physical reactions during the test performance or inquiry process; (2) speech and language; (3) attitude and behavior toward the examiner; (4) reaction to the examiner's style, questions, and comments; (5) reaction to the test situation and demands; (6) problem-solving and behavioral or work style in completing the task demands; and (7) comments to himself or herself as a reflection of self-concept and self-confidence (Knoff, 1986). Many of these observation areas are also used to assess the child's general mental status (Sattler, 1987). Among the additional mental status areas available for observation during projective testing and not yet mentioned are the child's (1) content of thought, (2) sensory

and motor functioning, (3) intellectual and cognitive processing functioning, and (4) insight and judgment. All of these observation areas focus on overt behavioral functioning, interactions within interdependent facets of the behavioral ecology, and representative samples of behavior that can be used to predict future behavior under similar or more generalized circumstances.

The Cognitive–Behavioral Orientation

The cognitive–behavioral orientation represents a theoretical extension of the behavioral orientation that includes children's cognitions as part of their behavior. In this context, projective drawing techniques provide information that permits hypotheses about children's thoughts, beliefs, expectations, self-statements, aspirations, attributions, needs, and perceptions. Within the research related to this orientation, these cognitions have been shown to cause, encourage, support, reinforce, change, and/or influence behavior. Thus, the identification of consistent and significant cognitions may help to predict a child's behavioral actions or reactions, a critical component of any personality evaluation.

Unfortunately, projective drawings provide a fairly unsystematic and disorganized assessment of a child's cognitions. Unlike the situation in a structured or semistructured interview, the psychologist is dependent on the social–emotional themes and cognitions that a child reveals in his or her drawings. The requested drawings do not systematically survey a broad range of possible problem areas, such that the assessment process can then focus on and fully analyze those areas that are identified. Furthermore, because of the ambiguity inherent in each drawing technique, a child can reveal information about *any* of the possible cognitive areas listed above, and then from any number of perspectives. For example, a child may reveal cognitions that are related (1) to past, present, or future issues or events; (2) to a specific person or to a myriad of people or roles; (3) to a specific setting or to multiple settings or circumstances; and/or (4) to specific social–emotional processes or to more generalized social–emotional or personality processes. Although it is assumed that children generally will reveal their most troubling cognitions within the themes present in their projective drawings, this assumption must be tested with every case. The psychologist's job, then, is to analyze any cognitive hypothesis across all of the personality assessment data in the comprehensive battery, and to systematically expand on and validate the most relevant cognitive information through additional interviews, observations, and/or objective processes. Potential problem areas that are not assessed should be addressed in other parts of the assessment battery.

Despite the possible weaknesses of projective drawings within this orientation, one of the variables that does provide some cognitive organization to the various drawing techniques is the "stimulus pull" of each. Stimulus pull is the phenomenon that explains why certain projective drawings tend to elicit certain themes, cognitions, or types of responses. For example, the request to draw a house tends to elicit a drawing or a story about the drawing that reveals a child's remembrances, beliefs, or expectations related to a house he or she has experienced, either in real life or in fantasy. The house may be a past house (e.g., where the child was last happy), a present house (e.g., depicting the current conflicts between family members), or a future house (e.g., alluding to the child's expectation that his or her future home also will contain significant conflictual relationships). But, according to this orientation, the drawing will represent some cognition that has been stimulated by the task demand. Similarly, the person drawing in H-T-P tends to uncover children's cognitions about themselves or significant others; the K-F-D obviously provides the children's perceptions of their real or idealized family life; and the K-S-D elicits reflections about academics, the school environment and interactions, or the schooling process. Thus, although they are unsystematic, projective drawings' stimulus pulls do provide a sample of some important areas and environments of children's lives. Moreover, if the stimulus pull does not elicit a child's particular cognitive conflict or concern, there is sufficient ambiguity within the drawing techniques that he or she can freely express these issues if desired.

Summary

It is important to re-emphasize that projective drawings can be interpreted within any combination of the four theoretical orientations described above. The tenets and beliefs of the theory, then, drive the interpretation of the projective drawings, rather than vice versa. In practice, all four orientations may be useful for a comprehensive analysis. The cognitive-developmental orientation may provide information on the impact of cognitive, visual–motor, and developmental variables and experiences on the projective drawing process, and thus the degree to which the drawing can be interpreted from a social–emotional perspective. The psychodynamic orientation can offer hypotheses as to the inner dynamics and conflicts that may be represented within the projective drawings—hypotheses that should be objectively evaluated before their acceptance. The cognitive–behavioral orientation can provide insight into the child's self-statements, beliefs, expectations, and other perceptions, so that the psychologist then can explore how these cognitions translate into behavior and social–emotional functioning for the child. Finally, the behavioral orientation analyzes the drawing process and the child's interactions within the behavioral ecology, making predictions when appropriate as to how the child might respond to similar situations in his or her day-to-day functioning.

Analyses of projective drawings, regardless of the theoretical orientation used, generate hypotheses about personality and social–emotional functioning. Many of these hypotheses are reported in the professional literature. The next section reviews a number of these studies, analyzing their methodological strengths and weaknesses and commenting on the utility of their results and implications.

A PSYCHOMETRIC AND CLINICAL EVALUATION OF SELECTED STUDIES

A psychometric and clinical analysis of the hundreds of projective drawing studies available in the literature necessarily involves an evaluation of each individual study. This is primarily because of the vast differences in psychometric and experimental quality among these studies, and because these studies provide such widely differing methodological details that one cannot assume that results are clinically accurate and socially valid without additional validation and replication. Despite this need for individual evaluations, few critical reviews of the literature are available for projective drawings. More common are (1) collections of projective characteristics and interpretations based on the work of individual clinicians, who have investigated self-selected populations and truncated samples that often are nonrandomly distributed; and/or (2) reviews that fail to integrate projective drawings into a multitrait, multisetting, multimethod assessment approach (Campbell & Fiske, 1959), which would demonstrate their ability to generate integrated hypotheses rather than isolated, relative meaningless results. The lack of a comprehensive literature review leaves the clinician without an objective and useful measure of the current status of projective research, and the field without a clear direction as to what future directions are most necessary and relevant.

Cummings (1986) has completed the most recent review of the psychometric qualities of projective drawings. Evaluating a dozen studies between 1968 and 1981 with respect to interjudge reliability, he reported reliabilities ranging from .75 to .97, with the critical determinants of good interjudge agreement being (1) the specificity of the items, characteristics, or drawing styles to be scored and (2) the training and supervision of the various judges to insure similar scoring criteria and conditions. With respect to test–retest stability, Cummings critically reviewed nine studies with retest intervals from 1 day to 3 months and stability coefficients ranging from .69 to .91. With stability generally decreasing as the test–retest interval increased, the importance of simultaneously evaluating psychometric quality and clinical utility becomes apparent. That is, this decrease in stability should not immediately suggest that projective drawing techniques are unreliable over time, or that they should be immediately purged from the personality assessment battery. Instead, it should be noted that the decrease in stability may be

accurately reflecting a child's change in social–emotional status. Or the decrease in stability may be due to a scoring system that attends more to structural changes in the test versus retest drawings (e.g., the presence of excessive shading in the first drawing and lack of shading in the second drawing), than to an accounting of the clinical hypotheses that are generated by the two drawings (e.g, the presence of anxiety), regardless of their derivation from qualitatively different structural characteristics. The difficulty in accommodating the traditional psychometric assessment of projective drawings with their *clinical* reliability must be acknowledged in the evaluation of these techniques. An emphasis on the latter reliability explains why the use of projective drawing techniques in hypothesis generation may be the most defensible and the most helpful, as the consistent presence of similar interpretations within the multitrait–multimethod approach is tracked and used for psychometric evaluation.

The validation of projective drawing techniques has been extremely difficult to document, and an extremely variable research literature exists in this area. Three types of validity are commonly found in this literature: concurrent validity, construct validity, and incremental validity. There are very few studies of concurrent validity in the projective drawing literature. These studies typically correlate specific diagnostic indicators in projective drawings with more objective scales or indices that already are validated with respect to these indicators. Conceptually, this is a very acceptable method of validation. Pragmatically, however, its success is based on the integrity of the methodological procedures used and the ability of the researchers to choose samples that have some level of generalizability to specific and important clinical groups or to more universal populations. More concurrent validity research with projective drawings is needed before definitive conclusions can be made as to their utility. Although the issue of interpretation accuracy is important with projective drawings, this issue is equally critical in the interpretation of many so-called "objective" personality assessment tools.

Studies of construct validity with projective drawing techniques have often focused on the "known-groups" method, which uses a validated anchor scale to separate a large sample of children into clinically differentiated subgroups. These subgroups then complete a projective drawing battery, which is analyzed for its ability to approximate the same clinical separations. This type of construct validity has been used in numerous studies of the K-F-D, demonstrating its ability to discriminate groups of children from intact versus divorced homes, with versus without delinquent characteristcs, and from abusing versus nonabusing homes (see Knoff & Prout, 1985, for a review). Once again, this type of validity becomes dependent on the scales or procedures used to initially separate a sample into clinical subgroups; the methodological characteristics and reliability of the projective drawing administration and scoring, respectively; and the statistical analyses used to assess the diagnostic "hit rates" and false-negative and false-positive decisions. Again, far more research in this validity area is needed before conclusive statements can be made.

Studies of incremental validity with projective drawings have focused on their ability to facilitate more accurate diagnostic and clinical judgments when used in conjunction with other assessment tools and approaches in a stepwise decision-making process. To date, few studies have demonstrated this type of validity with projective drawings, and some studies have reported that various clinicians were unable to discriminate clinically unremarkable versus clinically identified populations beyond the chance level with projective drawings (Cummings, 1986). Although this may discourage the use of projective drawings as diagnostic tools, Hammer (1969) defends their use and minimizes the results of the incremental validity studies to date, noting (1) that projective drawings provide hypotheses that are more descriptive than diagnostic, especially when many clinical groups share similar psychological characteristics and behavioral patterns; and (2) that projective drawings should not be used independently to discriminate clinical groups, but as part of an integrated assessment battery involving numerous objective and other diagnostic approaches.

Thus, the psychometric debate with respect to projective drawings continues. Some researchers decry their lack of psychometric integrity, while others argue that projective drawings should not and cannot be fairly evaluated in a traditional statistical and psychometric manner. This argument aside, the hypothesis-generating use of projective drawings and their ability to be interpreted within various psychological orientations remain both viable and defensible. But, as noted above, the validity of hypotheses tied to specific drawing characteristics must still be determined, preferably by means of an analysis of the individual studies that have generated those hypotheses. This analysis process and a review of many of the studies most often cited in the projective drawing literature are shown in Appendices 5.1 and 5.2 in this chapter. These tables analyze the predominant interpretations of projective drawing techniques and the BGT according to their experimental designs, their statistical and methodological characteristics, their dependent variables and results, and their generalizability to other clinical situations in the field.

Although exhaustive descriptions and evaluations of the studies in Appendices 5.1 and 5.2 are beyond the scope of this chapter, some descriptive analyses of these studies are possible as one way to analyze the state of projective research to date. Within the projective drawing studies described in Appendix 5.1, 50% utilized *ex post facto* designs, 37% used descriptive "designs," 9% used experimental designs, and 4% used case study designs. Sixty-eight percent of the studies did no systematic type of sampling, whereas 22% used some type of randomized sampling and 10% used some type of matched sampling. Seventy-two percent of the studies did not use control groups, while 28% did; 56% analyzed their data using nonparametric statistics, whereas the other 44% used some type of parametric analysis. Finally, in an external analysis, 20% of the studies were deemed to have good generalizability to other samples, 51% of the studies were considered to have fair generalizability, and 29% of the studies were felt to have limited or no generalizability. Of the BGT studies described in Appendix 5.2, 53% utilized *ex post facto* designs, 44% used descriptive "designs," 3% used experimental designs, and no case study designs were reviewed. Sixty-three percent of the studies did no systematic type of sampling, whereas 22% used some type of matched sampling and 15% used some type of randomized sampling. Fifty-three percent of the studies used control groups, while the other 47% did not; 62% analyzed their data using parametric statistics, whereas the other 38% used some type of nonparametric analysis. Finally, in the same type of external analysis, 22% of the studies were deemed to have good generalizability to other samples, 51% of the studies were considered to have fair generalizability, and 27% of the studies were felt to have limited or no generalizability.

It is important to note the significant number of descriptive "designs" used in both the projective drawing and BGT studies, even though they were outnumbered by the *ex post facto* designs. Even more notable is the dearth of experimental studies, a gap that points to the need for far more sophisticated research in the future—research that should especially target the validity and clinical utility of projective drawings. Furthermore, the studies' general lack of appropriate sampling and control groups, and their dependence on the less robust nonparametric statistical analyses, suggest that research on projective drawings has yet to fully evaluate their real potential and their actual impact. Finally, the relatively small percentage of studies considered to have good generalizability indicates that much of the projective drawing research cannot be used for differential diagnosis, or even for validation of specific clinical characteristics within a referred individual or an identified group. This reinforces the use of projective drawings as hypothesis-generating tools, rather than as hypothesis-validating tools. This use and perspective are further explicated below. Two final points, however, remain.

First, it is interesting to note that the BGT studies (Appendix 5.2) used significantly more control groups and parametric statistical analyses than the projective drawing studies (Appendix 5.1). Although this may be due to the BGT's more explicit and investigated scoring systems, which have been standardized and normed around the country, the real reasons are not otherwise apparent. Second, few if any of the studies reviewed

utilized multitrait–multimethod designs. This is a significant flaw that again, in summary, points out the relative weakness of current projective drawing research. For the future, the areas of potential and needed research are both apparent and unlimited. Projective drawings cannot be evaluated on the basis of the present research; only after a great number of experimentally sound studies have been completed can these assessment tools and techniques be fairly critiqued.

INTEGRATING PROJECTIVE DRAWINGS INTO COMPREHENSIVE PERSONALITY ASSESSMENT

When projective drawings are being integrated into a comprehensive personality assessment, the primary goals of such an evaluation need to be considered. Elsewhere (Knoff, 1986), in discussing the comprehensive personality assessment process and its goals, I have identified two critical conceptualizations of that process: (1) Personality assessment is a hypothesis-testing, problem-solving process that works within a probability model; and (2) personality assessment uses a multitrait, multisetting, multi-method assessment approach, which is sensitive to the ecological and reciprocally determined nature of personality and behavior. Personality assessment, in its most basic form, exists to evaluate children who have been referred for some behavioral, affective, intrapersonal, and/or interpersonal difficulty that threatens some critical domain or facet of their development (e.g., social–emotional, academic, cognitive). The process involves systematic problem solving as it attempts, first, to identify and analyze the primary referred (and other relevant) problems from a multifaceted, ecological perspective; and second, to intervene in the problem with appropriate and effective interventions. Evaluation of these identification, analysis, and intervention components occurs throughout as a way to maintain both the integrity and the utility of the entire process.

During problem analysis, the psychologist evaluates the referred problem and situation, using multitrait, multisetting, multimethod assessment approaches to generate hypotheses that best explain and facilitate an understanding of the significant variables that are causing, supporting, maintaining, and/or encouraging the problem. Once these hypotheses are identified and refined, the analysis process continues at a higher level as the hypotheses are tested, using the most objective, empirically proven methods, for their validity and reliability across people, settings, time, and ecological circumstances. Given their more clinical nature (both in the research and in actual practice), and their focus on children's covert processes, projective drawings probably are best used *to generate hypotheses* about the referral situation rather than *to validate those hypotheses*. Indeed, at times, projective drawings may be unnecessary in the assessment battery, because other tools or techniques can identify and validate the relevant hypotheses more efficiently. Ultimately, the problem is fully and accurately analyzed in such a way that intervention programs can be implemented and problem resolution can occur.

After the referred problem has been analyzed to the extent that its primary determinants or contingencies are clear and the necessary interventions are apparent, the process of psychological change can begin. Although the link between assessment and intervention is logical and methodologically necessary, the presence of unassessed and unknown intervening variables can decrease the predictive validity of intervention success. Thus, personality assessment in general and the development of effective interventions in particular must be based on a probability model. That is, given thorough and well-conceived analyses, we expect that our explanations of referred problems have the highest probability of accuracy, and that our interventions based on these analyses have the highest probability of success. At times, however, intervening variables (e.g., a teacher's covert lack of commitment to the intervention) are missed, and the efficiency and efficacy of the process are diminished. In most cases, the intervening and the disruptive variables will be identified through a formative evaluation of the ineffective intervention program. In other cases, the intervening variable may be the intervention program *itself*, and the decrease in program

effectiveness may indicate that some facet of the original referred problem has been solved and that a different problem, unaffected by the intervention, has taken its place. In both cases, the intervention must be reconceptualized, and the assessment-to-intervention link must be forged anew. At this juncture, problem analysis and intervention may focus only on observable and measurable behavior; beyond suggesting additional explanative hypotheses, projective drawings may be of little assistance at this level.

To summarize, personality assessment is a process, not a product. The real product, the primary goal of the process, is the treatment or resolution of referred behavioral or social–emotional problems so that a child's normal development and positive mental health can continue. Thus, it is not enough to *understand* a child's social–emotional problems; we must move from problem analysis to intervention by *using* this understanding. On a different level, given the goals of personality assessment above, it should be apparent that *not all personality assessment evaluations with a referred child necessitate the use of projective tests, or, more specifically, projective drawings*. In fact, psychologists should use only those personality assessment tools or techniques that are needed (1) to fully and validly identify and analyze the significant variables that are causing, supporting, maintaining, and/or encouraging the problem; and (2) to fully and validly identify those interventions that will effectively and efficiently resolve these significant variables and the referred problem. In most cases, these necessary and sufficient personality assessment tools and techniques will involve those that are behaviorally based, objective, standardized, and/or well researched. Projective drawings, then, may be used when a referred problem situation is particularly complex, when an in-depth evaluation of a child's intrapersonal and cognitive–behavioral status is needed, and/or when behavioral and objective assessments have not provided an understanding of the problem situation that makes intervention success highly probable. Projective drawings *are* important to the personality assessment process. They should be used strategically, however, and not randomly; they should be used to maximize problem understanding and treatment effectiveness, not to cloud the issues with unnecessary redundancies or irrelevancies.

On a more pragmatic level, when used in the personality assessment battery, projective drawing techniques do provide potentially unique information and samples of behavior that are unavailable through other approaches, be they behavioral, objective, or anecdotal. From a cognitive–behavioral perspective, projective drawings use administration approaches and test-related stimuli that allow children to introduce their own significant, egocentric beliefs, attitudes, expectations, or attributions into the assessment session. These cognitions generally are not elicited by the more standardized techniques, which often are so structured and so specific in the personality domains they are intended to evaluate that they either suppress children's more personal self-reflections and intricacies or assess in ways that appear not to relate to a child's actual or perceived difficulties. Projective drawings are among a handful of techniques that do not fully structure the assessment interaction, providing instead an opportunity for children to communicate, in their own way, the specific issues that are troubling them. In a sense, then, projective drawing techniques may be most similar to unstructured or semi-structured clinical interviews, except that the psychologist asks the child to draw (or, in a sense, to discuss *visually*) some event or facet of his or her life, rather than to discuss *verbally* important personality-related issues as in a clinical interview.

To expand on this idea briefly, the clinical interview can be just as "projective" as the projective drawings. On the one hand, some interview questions are more direct, and the interpretation of a child's "direct" responses may appear to be self-evident and objective. However, the child still can decide whether or not to answer these direct questions honestly or completely. Thus, like the projective drawings, interview responses may only generate hypotheses that need additional, external validation. On the other hand, many interview questions are purposely global and ambiguous, in the hope that they will trigger some important memory, emotional reaction, or relevant response by the child, and/or so that the child has the opportunity to respond with personal issues that are of real and current concern. Again, this is similar to the projective drawings, except that the drawings use a visual modality as compared to the interview's verbal modality. To continue, the success of the clinical interview in eliciting information of importance often depends on the rapport and trust between the child and the interviewer, and the ability of the interviewer to ask the right questions at the right time. The success of projective drawings is dependent on the same factors. Finally, and somewhat parenthetically, it is interesting to note that clinical interviews suffer the same potential problems with respect to reliability and validity as projective drawings, yet they seem to be more often included within the personality assessment battery because the psychologist somehow "has more control" over the interview. I would suggest that this logic is faulty, but not in order to recommend that the clinical interview be purged from our assessment procedures. Clearly, the clinical interview *is* an important, almost irreplaceable, procedure. Projective drawings, in certain cases, may be just as important; they cannot be categorically dismissed from the assessment battery, and their use should be at least considered for every referral that requires face-to-face testing with the referred child.

Although space considerations preclude a description of every projective drawing technique—its administration and scoring procedures, its interpretive approaches, and its integration into the comprehensive personality assessment battery (see Cummings, 1986, for a review)—a few generalizations are important. First, projective drawings can be analyzed from both structural and content perspectives. Specific structural characteristics of a drawing (e.g., actions of and between drawn figures; characteristics of specific figures; the position, distance between, and barriers between figures; the drawing style; symbols or objects present in the drawing) are interpreted depending on the psychological orientation being used for analysis. These interpretations are evaluated both *within* drawings and *across* drawings, such that recurrent themes and issues are identified. These recurrent themes, and not the random and isolated ones, are integrated into the broader diagnostic picture of the referred child, which includes all other assessments and pieces of data, all multisetting evaluations, and all multisource observations. These themes are what generate the projective hypotheses for further study and validation.

The content analysis is related to the second important generalization: the importance of an inquiry process during the projective drawing administration. Projective drawings are administered in two phases. The performance phase involves providing the child with the materials needed to complete the drawings and with the actual directions needed to proceed. After the drawing is completed, the inquiry phase begins, using a series of questions aimed (1) at clarifying the objects and actions in the actual drawing; and (2) at eliciting a broader description or story about the drawing, which expands into a semistructured interview focusing on the child's underlying decisions and cognitions in choosing to draw what was completed. The child's responses to the inquiry-phase questions are used in the content analysis.

The content analysis has the same goal as the structural analysis: to generate hypotheses that contribute to a comprehensive understanding of the referred child. Although the source of the data may differ slightly from that for the structural analysis, the content analysis should also evaluate themes within and across projective drawings, and integrate only recurrent themes in the broader assessment and interpretation process. In some ways, the content analysis can be conceptualized as similar to that done with the thematic techniques (e.g., as in the Thematic Apperception Test). That is, questions about the projective drawing can be put into story format, and important details about the characters in the pictures can be ascertained. This is not necessary; what is necessary is that the inquiry process be used to clarify and expand the information in the projective drawing. This process decreases the potential for misinterpretation, and increases the potential for eliciting significant cognitions and issues that are inherent in the material of the projective drawing.

The third important generalization relates to training and expertise with projective drawings. The administration, scoring, and interpretation of projective drawings take a great deal of training, practice, experience, and supervision. One does not simply read "the book" or take "the course" to become "expert" in projective drawing use. Instead, the effective utilization of projective drawings is an ongoing endeavor. It would be improper to require some specific amount of training or supervision before one can use projective drawings independently. In a sense, the only criterion of readiness is the same criterion upon which projective drawing interpretation should be evaluated as valid: whether or not the projective drawings elicit valid hypotheses that contribute significantly to a greater understanding of the referred child and to a subsequently successful intervention program. If a psychologist is able to utilize projective drawings consistently in this way under supervision, then he or she should be considered ready to use them independently. All of this, however, appears far too specific to projective drawing techniques. Clearly, if projective drawings are an integral part of the comprehensive personality assessment process (as I believe them to be), then psychologists need to be expert in the *entire process* before practicing it independently. Personality assessment is both a content- and a process-oriented skill. It is a skill that develops over time and experience. It is a practice that requires ongoing supervision and continuing education to best serve referred children and the settings where they live and interact.

CASE STUDY: INTEGRATING AND INTERPRETING PROJECTIVE DRAWINGS

In this section, a case study is presented that demonstrates the interpretation of projective drawings and their integration into a comprehensive personality assessment battery. A "stream-of-consciousness" format is used throughout this discussion to show the psychologist's thinking processes as numerous personality assessment tools and techniques were integrated and a complex case was fully analyzed. The projective drawings in this case were analyzed primarily as data providing behavioral and social–emotional hypotheses that would need to be confirmed using more objective and direct means. However, they did sample areas of personality and cognitive–behavioral functioning that other assessment mechanisms might evaluate only tangentially or in different ways. Finally, a multitrait, multisetting, multimethod assessment approach was used in this case. The number of multiple assessments, however, was limited to only those needed for reliable and valid evaluation of the various traits, settings, and methods unique to the referred child and situation. This number will vary from case to case and from psychologist to psychologist; with every case, however, there is a point of diminishing returns where another assessment tool or interview adds nothing new to the data of the analysis of the referred problem.

Referral and Background

David, at the time of referral and evaluation, was between 15 years, 4 months and 15 years, 8 months old. An athletically built white adolescent, David was placed during this assessment period in a full-time residential program for learning-disabled (LD) students, many of whom had associated behavioral and social–emotional difficulties. Indeed, David had recently been kicked out of school after numerous fights with other students and a serious confrontation with his high school principal, who eventually suspended him. In an initial interview, David spent a good deal of time bragging about how tough his high school was, and made allusions to his possible drug use. He complained that he was weak in spelling, English, and reading; that he could do better in math, but that he did not like to hand in assignments or study for exams; and that he did best in classes where he could listen to the course material rather than take a lot of class notes.

A developmental interview with David's mother indicated that David was an unhappy baby, that he cried constantly during his first months of life, and that he never stayed in his playpen for a very long period of time. The mother characterized him at 9 months as a "child who constantly defied authority— when he learned to walk, he would not stop grabbing things, even when he was told." She noted that he walked comparatively ear-

ly, and that "he always amazed everybody" with what he could do. For example, she noted that he would carry on a full conversation at a very young age.

Specific to their disciplinary styles, the mother noted that she and her husband never agreed on how best to discipline David. She would typically spank him, carry a specific punishment through for a period of time, and then give David back the privileges lost. The father would usually threaten David, but not carry through. Early on, however, the mother noted that David was quite facile at manipulating her and his father. This manipulation had continued to the present day, and the mother fully acknowledged that she was tired of dealing with David, that she was ineffective in controlling and structuring him, and that the residential placement was probably best for David *and* her.

Academically, David did appear to present a classic LD pattern. His problems began in second grade, when he was tested for reading and associated problems and considered "dyslexic." David's mother recalled many frustrations in trying to help David to learn how to read, especially since a significant number of behavioral problems were already surfacing, at home and in school, as a result of David's frustration with his academic failure. In school, David was exhibiting a lot of out-of-seat behavior, daydreaming, argumentativeness, and anger. He was eventually placed in an LD program for part of the year. At the same time, however, David also was considered lazy, and his parents would put him on restriction at home because he was not doing his work in school. After the special education placement, David's LD teacher actually blamed David and his behavior for a miscarriage that she experienced during the school year.

In fourth and fifth grades, David went on to a private school, where he was provided with special training and support as an LD student. In fact, during one of the summer programs at that school, David's mother recalled a "phenomenal" teacher who was particularly successful with him. It was during this summer that he made the most progress, academically and emotionally, during his school career. David's mother bemoaned the fact that he had never had as talented a teacher since that summer, and that David had never felt so positive about his academic accomplishments or future. Ultimately, David's family relocated to another state, and he returned to the public schools for his middle school and early high school years. During those latter years, David's mother noted that she lost control of him, that he was running with a crowd of underachievers who were involved with drugs and continually skipped school, and that the school administration was unresponsive to both his educational and his behavioral needs. David's mother saw the current program at the residential LD institution as David's "last chance"; she felt that his failure in that program would leave him as a dropout with no educational foundation to get an appropriate job in the work force.

As for his family life, David had a younger sister, but she did not seem to have any relevance to his referral problem or history. More significantly, David's parents experienced a number of marital problems as he was growing up. In fact, they divorced when David was 10 years old, but were separated only 3 months; they eventually remarried only 9 months after the divorce. David's mother noted that her husband's problems with alcohol were a significant reason for the divorce. She also noted that David blamed himself for the divorce and that he was very "lost" during it. Nonetheless, no one in the family was involved in any psychological counseling or support during the time immediately before or after the divorce and remarriage. In fact, the only counseling that the family every experienced occurred for only a month and a half and centered around David's LD problems when he was in third grade. David's mother noted that the psychologist involved was very negative and tried to blame her and her husband for many of the problems they were experiencing.

The psychologist's "blame" notwithstanding, it did appear that David's parents had unrealistic expectations for his behavior even when he was 9 months old (e.g., describing his behavior as "defying authority"), and that their inability to discipline him consistently had left David with little external structure, few explicit behavioral and interpersonal expectations, and no real consequences for either positive or inappropriate behavior.

David's parents did not fully understand his LD, nor were they prepared to deal with its academic and social–emotional characteristics. Finally, all of these situations had existed for such a long time that most of the familial behavioral patterns were ingrained and intractable—both for David's parents with respect to parenting, and for David with respect to his interactions both at home and in school. At the time of the interview, it appeared that a residential program was very appropriate for David, but that both he and his parents needed very specific counseling support to change their patterns of behaviors and expectations so that David could eventually and successfully be reintegrated into the family and community setting. The assessment goal, then, was to gain a full understanding of David's intrapersonal, interpersonal, academic, social–emotional, and familial behavior and self-concept, so that appropriate and comprehensive therapeutic directions could be developed and implemented.

Initial Assessments

The first part of this ongoing assessment process began when David was evaluated for entrance into the residential placement at 15 years, 4 months of age. At that time, a battery of intellectual (the Wechsler Intelligence Scale for Children—Revised [WISC-R]), academic achievement (the Wide Range Achievement Test, the Detroit Tests of Learning Aptitude, the Gates–MacGinitie Reading Tests, the Gilmore Oral Reading Test, the Metropolitan Achievement Tests, the Schonell Spelling Lists), processing (the Illinois Test of Psycholinguistic Abilities, the Frostig Visual Perceptual Tests), and personality tests (the Personality Inventory for Children [PIC], the Millon Adolescent Personality Inventory [MAPI]) were given.

On the WISC-R, David received a Verbal Scale IQ in the average to above-average range, a Performance Scale IQ in the average range, and a Full Scale IQ in the average range (100 ± 6). On the Verbal subtests, he demonstrated very consistent verbal skills— conceptually, expressively, with respect to academic information, and in arithmetic. Significantly, David achieved a scaled score of

13 on the Comprehension subtest, indicating that he understood societal expectations and appropriate behavior, even though he might not choose or might be unable to behaviorally meet those expectations.

On the Performance subtests, David did extremely well on the Picture Completion and Picture Arrangement subtests, less well and average on the Block Design and Object Assembly subtests, and extremely poorly on the Coding subtest. It appeared that David's strong verbal skills were helping him to "talk himself through" and score well on these first two subtests. Thus, David might be able to control his behavior and aggressive actions through cognitive, mediational processes, or through a "think-aloud" approach if motivated to do so. His low Coding subtest (scaled score, 4) and his low Digit Span subtest (scaled score, 4) suggested some significant distractibility, probably associated with his LD, and/or some significant anxiety and emotional lability. Actually, both of these hypotheses were found to be accurate. David scored in the at-risk range on the Gordon Diagnostic System, an objective attention and vigilance task that assesses for attention deficit disorders. And the personality tests (below) and interview with David's mother suggested that he had significant behavioral and emotional difficulties, especially when frustrated and stressed.

In the academic achievement areas, David's spelling achievement was measured at approximately the third-grade level, his oral reading at the fourth- to early fifth-grade level, and his math skills at the fifth- to early sixth-grade level. Significantly, his oral reading comprehension was at grade level or above when he was able to decode the specific words in the reading passage. In the processing area, David's auditory memory was almost age-appropriate when the stimulus material was concrete and relevant to him, and his ability to process and follow oral directions was excellent. But when the auditory material became abstract and/or novel, David had significantly more memory problems. David's visual memory and visual processing abilities, in contrast, were well developed. In fact, the visual modality in general appeared to be David's stronger processing area.

When this psychometric information was compared with his intellectual test results, it appeared that David was still manifesting an LD pattern: specific difficulties in reading, auditory memory, auditory processing, and spelling, and a potential attention deficit disorder. As for his social–emotional status, David's history of LD and its concomitant pattern of academic and social failure had clearly influenced his personality development, and in some cases his LD might be influencing how he saw and interpreted circumstances and events in his past and present worlds. Although his social–emotional status might be evaluated separately, it could not be analyzed without considering his academic history and its influence both on his self-concept and on the behaviors and expectations of his parents. This was not an attempt to explain all of David's behavior as a part of his LD; rather, it was an attempt to recognize the complexity of his behavior and the need for a complex analysis of his difficulties and a multifaceted intervention program.

David's social–emotional status initially was evaluated with the PIC, completed by his mother, and the MAPI, completed by himself. David's personality profile on the PIC (see Figure 5.1) indicated severely delinquent and hyperactive tendencies that were apparent to such a degree that significant antisocial, out-of-control, and irrational behavior could be expected. In addition, David was seen as an adolescent (1) who lacked appropriate interpersonal and social skills and the ability to deal with conflict-producing situations in the environment; (2) who had significantly withdrawn from his environment and who might exhibit periods of depression along with agitated, acting-out behavior; (3) who felt a great deal of anxiety and distrust in his world; and (4) who continued to have significant intellectual and academic achievement problems in the midst of all the social–emotional turmoil. All but three of the PIC's clinical scales reached significance, suggesting a very disturbed, emotionally labile individual. Two of those nonsignificant scales related to David's overall development and his lack of somatic concerns. The other scale was the Family Relations scale, a scale that assesses the relationship between family and parental variables and the child's psychological difficulties. This

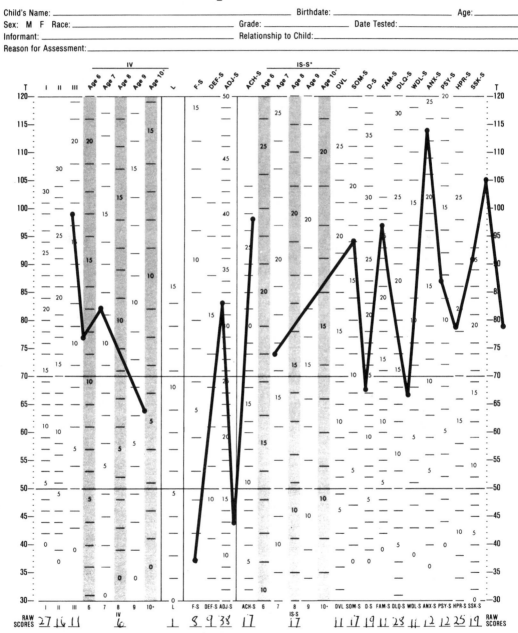

FIGURE 5.1. David's personality assessment profile on the PIC.

result suggests (1) that many of David's problems were thought to be specific to him, rather than related to family problems or issues; (2) that many of David's problems influenced characteristics that did exist within the family unit; and (3) that David's absence from the home because of his placement in the residential program was having a positive effect on the atmosphere and intrafamily relationships at home.

The MAPI (see Figure 5.2) reinforced many of the results from the PIC. On this scale, David was described as both fearful and apprehensive about his relationships with others, and as resentful and critical to those who had not supported him in the past. His profile reflected a person who was very

sensitive as to how others evaluated him as a person, and predicted that he would tend to withdraw and distance himself from close involvements in order to avoid further rejections or disappointments. The MAPI further indicated that David revealed feelings of low self-worth, expressing a minimal degree of self-acceptance and a great deal of difficulty with academic achievement and success. The family problems and David's perceived rejection by his parents were also evident in the profile, as were his indifference to others and his lack of empathy for others and their welfare. In total, the MAPI results predicted that David would have limited success in therapy and that he would probably withhold his innermost feelings, primarily because he

```
************************************************************************ೲ******************************
 SCALES      * SCORE *        PROFILE OF BR SCORES             ೲ
            *RAW  BR*    35  60       75         85      100  DIMENSIONS
*********+**+***+***+----+---+------+----------+--------+-------ᵥ********::********
        1   13  41 XXXXXXX                                          INTROVERSIVE
        +--+---+---+------+---+------+----------+--------+-------+---------------
        2   18  78 XXXXXXXXXXXXXXXXXXXXXXXX                         INHIBITED
        +--+---+---+------+---+------+----------+--------+-------+---------------
        3   19  65 XXXXXXXXXXXXXX                                   COOPERATIVE
        +--+---+---+------+---+------+----------+--------+-------+---------------
PERSNLTY 4  16  45 XXXXXXXX                                         SOCIABLE
        +--+---+---+------+---+------+----------+--------+-------+---------------
 STYLES 5   21  32 XXXXXX                                           CONFIDENT
        +--+---+---+------+---+------+----------+--------+-------+---------------
        6   18  72 XXXXXXXXXXXXXXXXXXX                              FORCEFUL
        +--+---+---+------+---+------+----------+--------+-------+---------------
        7   16  38 XXXXXXX                                          RESPECTFUL
        +--+---+---+------+---+------+----------+--------+-------+---------------
        8   25  91 XXXXXXXXXXXXXXXXXXXXXXXXXXXXXXXXXXXXX             SENSITIVE
*********+**+***+***+----+---+------+----------+--------+--------+*****************
        A   17  81 XXXXXXXXXXXXXXXXXXXXXXXXXXXXX                    SELF-CONCEPT
        +--+---+---+------+---+------+----------+--------+-------+---------------
        B   16  77 XXXXXXXXXXXXXXXXXXXXXXXXX                        PERSONAL ESTEEM
        +--+---+---+------+---+------+----------+--------+-------+---------------
        C    7  43 XXXXXXXX                                         BODY COMFORT
        +--+---+---+------+---+------+----------+--------+-------+---------------
EXPRESSD D   7  37 XXXXXXX                                          SEXUAL ACCEPTNCE
        +--+---+---+------+---+------+----------+--------+-------+---------------
CONCERNS E  11  75 XXXXXXXXXXXXXXXXXXXXXX                           PEER SECURITY
        +--+---+---+------+---+------+----------+--------+-------+---------------
        F   13  81 XXXXXXXXXXXXXXXXXXXXXXXXXXXX                     SOCIAL TOLERANCE
        +--+---+---+------+---+------+----------+--------+-------+---------------
        G    9  81 XXXXXXXXXXXXXXXXXXXXXXXXXXXX                     FAMILY RAPPORT
        +--+---+---+------+---+------+----------+--------+-------+---------------
        H   14  75 XXXXXXXXXXXXXXXXXXXXXX                           ACADEMIC CONFDNCE
*********+**+***+***+----+---+------+----------+--------+--------+*****************
        SS  17  67 XXXXXXXXXXXXXXX                                  IMPULSE CONTROL
        +--+---+---+------+---+------+----------+--------+-------+---------------
BEHAVIOR TT 17  70 XXXXXXXXXXXXXXXXX                                SOCIAL CONFORMITY
        +--+---+---+------+---+------+----------+--------+-------+---------------
 CORRE-  UU 18  76 XXXXXXXXXXXXXXXXXXXXXXXX                          SCHOLAST ACHVMNT
        +--+---+---+------+---+------+----------+--------+-------+---------------
 LATES   WW 19  72 XXXXXXXXXXXXXXXXXXXX                             ATTNDNCE CNSTNCY
*********+**+***+***+----+---+------+----------+--------+--------+*****************
```

FIGURE 5.2.   David's personality assessment profile on the MAPI.

would not believe that anyone could really care about him in the end.

Continuing Assessments

After the initial assessments, David was accepted by the residential program and placed in an individualized LD curriculum and a dorm with his own room. Over the next 4 months, he was behaviorally monitored and discussed at monthly meetings of the clinical staff. During the first of these staff meetings, David was described as hyperactive, sneaky, and nontrusting, and as continually breaking the no-smoking rules. It was noted that he did serve consequences when they were applied, but that he had put his head through a wall of his dorm room, had made additional holes there with some metal rods, liked to stare people down, and was making no progress in his academic program. At the second meeting, this pattern was described as continuing, with additional concerns about his manipulative behavior and his constant challenging of both school and residential staff. By the third meeting, David's belligerent attitude, lack of respect for adults, inability to work independently, and inability to be trusted during off-campus activities resulted in a call for additional diagnostic assessments to determine whether he was appropriate for the program or not. At this point, a more projectively oriented battery was completed to supplement the data already collected during the intake process. This battery consisted of the Rorschach, some incomplete-sentence blanks, the H-T-P, the Kinetic Drawing System (the K-F-D and K-S-D), and four sessions of diagnostic counseling and clinical interviews.

David's Rorschach evidenced a significantly high number of total responses; significantly high percentages of large blot area responses $(D\%)$ and Animal responses $(A\%)$; and significantly low percentages of small blot area responses $(Dd\%)$, high-quality Form responses $(F+\%)$, Animal Movement responses (FM), and Human responses $(H\%)$ as compared to same-age norms from Ogdon (1977). In addition, his responses qualitatively focused on aggressive activities, monsters, and "scary" scenes fairly often. The interpretation of the Rorschach suggested an above-average intellectual potential, anxiety, a suppression of emotions and spontaneity as a way to protect against rejection, social isolation, and an absence of empathy for others. The analysis also indicated that David would probably be a poor therapy candidate because of his inability to trust others and to overcome his feelings of vulnerability and cautiousness.

David's incomplete-sentence blank responses revealed the following issues: his desire to smoke on the grounds of the campus, his dislike for authority figures who told him what to do, his poor peer interpersonal relationships, his dislike for school and the residential school in particular, and his secret admiration for his father and his desire to graduate from high school to please him. Some of the more pertinent sentences were as follows (the stems are in roman, David's responses in italics):

People *suck—they are sometimes not the nicest things in the world.*
In the lower grades *I was always a very bad student.*
Other kids *annoy me.*
The future *holds alot for me—working with my father, marriage, owning a car.*
I am best when *I'm good.*
I hate *school.*
I wish *I were home right now.*
My father *is cool.*
I secretly *admire my father.*
My greatest worry is *that I graduate from high school.*

After the incomplete-sentence blanks, David was asked what he would do with three wishes. He wanted (1) "to be with Sharon [his girlfriend] whenever I want," (2) "to graduate from high school and go to college for a civil engineering degree," and (3) to be "rich off of life—and I don't mean just have money."

David's H-T-P drawings are shown in Figures 5.3, 5.4, and 5.5, and his Kinetic Drawing System drawings in Figures 5.6 and 5.7. As each drawing was completed, a series of inquiry questions was asked to describe and clarify the objects and actions within the drawing. (These are indicated below by [Q]:, but are not given in full.) David's verbatim responses to the questions were as follows:

FIGURE 5.3. House drawing (on the H-T-P) from David's comprehensive personality assessment battery.

House: [Q]: "This is the house I lived in for around 2 to 3 years when I was about 7 to 10 years old." [Q]: "This is a real house, a sketch of my old house in Tennessee." [Q]: "It is 7 years old." [Q]: "Me, my parents, and my sister live in the house." [Q]: "The house is in with a group of houses." [Q]: "It's thinking about running into the woods and going up to this huge cave—like an airplane hangar."

Tree: [Q]: "It's a treehouse in Tennessee— the same place as my house drawing." [Q]: "It's a hugh oak tree—4 feet in diameter." [Q]: "Me and my friends built the treehouse. I have good memories of this treehouse. It was in the backyard of my house on about 1½ acres of land."

Person: [Q]: "This is just something that I drew—it's a nothing, just a body—a 'he–she– it.' " [Q]: "It's anywhere from 5 to 90 years old." [Q]: "It lives alone—in the middle of the Alps. It's a hermit—it doesn't like society—it doesn't get along with crowds." [Q]: "In the Alps, it hunts, fishes—the usual." [Q]: "It's thinking, 'Where's my clothes? I'm freezing.' " [Q]: "It's feeling cold—and lonesome. Even hermits have to show some feeling. It has a dog—but it's been dead for 6 years."

K-F-D: "This is a happy picture— everyone is having a good time. It is a picture of us in a river near our house in Florida. We go water-skiing all the time. There is my father driving, my mother sitting behind him watching my sister ski, me sitting, and my sister skiing and saying "Wheeee!!' My father is saying, 'David, get me another beer.' I'm saying, 'Why do you want another beer? You just had one.' "

K-S-D: "This is my classroom with kids who are just doing their homework. There's the teacher. She thinks she can control everything—she thinks she's the dominant power. But that's not true—we just follow her for fear of being suspended. I respect her 'cause she's the teacher—you should respect adults."

From a structural perspective, the many characteristics in the H-T-P, K-F-D, and K-S-D provided numerous social–emotional and behavioral hypotheses that would later need to be tested more objectively. The most relevant hypotheses, based on the referral and background and the initial assessment

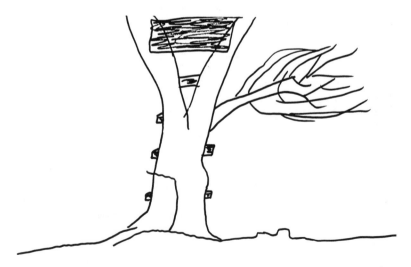

FIGURE 5.4. Tree drawing (on the H-T-P) from David's comprehensive personality assessment battery.

FIGURE 5.5. Person drawing (on the H-T-P) from David's comprehensive personality assessment battery.

FIGURE 5.7. K-S-D from David's comprehensive personality assessment battery.

FIGURE 5.6. K-F-D from David's comprehensive personality assessment battery.

information, are shown in Table 5.1 for each respective drawing.

From a qualitative or content perspective came other social–emotional and behavioral hypotheses (which would also need later objective validation) and information that might begin to confirm or strengthen some of the structural hypotheses above. Integrating the qualitative/content information for each projective drawing resulted in the following analyses:

House: It was interesting that David chose to draw a house that he had lived for 2–3 years in Tennessee, when he was about 7–10 years of age. Structurally, the house looked like a typical house, except that it was hard to tell whether the driveway led to a door or a garage (one of these was missing, in any case). Chronologically, this was the period of time when David's family was all together, although the parents were having marital problems that led to their divorce when David was 10. Immediately after the divorce, David and his family had to move from this house in Tennessee to another state. Thus, the fairly typical structure of the house might

suggest that David was secure with the nuclear family together. His comment about what the house was thinking ("It's thinking about running into the woods and going up to this huge cave—like an airplane hangar") might suggest that his parents' fighting made him want to excape from the house. It also might suggest that he wanted to escape blame for his parents' fighting, given his mother's interview comment that David blamed himself for his parents' divorce.

Tree: The tree drawing helped the examiner to continue the analysis of David's "Tennessee" years, because he chose to draw a tree that was in the backyard of his house in Tennessee. The tree had a treehouse that was built by David and his friends, and David had good memories about this treehouse. The tree appeared to be very strong, perhaps indicating that David used his peers as a support group while his parents were leading up to their divorce. However, there was some shading, a very shaky baseline grounding the tree, and a very barren-looking branch, collectively indicating that this peer group did not provide David suf-

TABLE 5.1. Social–Emotional and Behavioral Hypotheses Suggested by Structural Characteristics of David's Drawings

Hypotheses	Structural characteristics
General drawing styles and tendencies	
Insecurity	Sketchy drawing style
Poor self-concept	Sketchy drawing style
Low self-confidence	Sketchy drawing style
Possible character disorder	Sketchy drawing style
House	
Withdrawing tendencies	Distant-appearing house; small house; unusual door treatment
Feelings of inaccessibility	Distant-appearing house; elongated driveway
Feelings of rejection	Distant-appearing house; unusual door treatment
Home situation beyond subject's ability to handle effectively	Distant-appearing house
Inadequacy feelings	Small house
Vulnerable to environmental pressure	Horizontal dimension overemphasized
Tree	
Self-centeredness	Large tree
Poor environmental interactions	Poor branch quality
Perceives environment as bleak and unhappy	Bleak branch structure
Personality imbalance with excessive tendencies to avoid or delay emotional satisfactions	Emphasis on right-handed branches
Perceived loss of satisfaction-seeking resources in the environment	Dead branches
Lack of ego integration	No leaves present
Inner barrenness	No leaves present
Traumatic experiences	Scar on trunk
Person	
Possible character disorder	Dehumanized figure
Inadequancy	Wasted arms
Subject not interested in perceiving/ interacting with environment accurately	Vacant eyes, no ears
Depersonalization	Dehumanized figure
Inability to cope with others	Vacant eyes
Power needs	Large shoulders
Aggressive tendencies	Hand treatment; finger treatment
Insecurity	Feet treatment
K-F-D	
Conflict/anxiety over family issues, interactions, or expectations	Omissions of full bodies
Poor self-concept, feelings of insignificance	Treatment of self-drawing
Defensiveness and resistance with respect to family life	Poor figure quality; strange treatment of figures
Rivalry/anger with sister	Hanging sister figure; action between figures of boat and sister; sister drawn larger than parents
Thought pattern disturbances	Strange treatment of figures

(continued)

TABLE 5.1. (*continued*)

Hypotheses	Structural characteristics
Perceives self as apart from family system	Self-drawing in back of boat
Poor family communication processes	Lack of integration/interaction of figures
Perceives sister as psychologically safest or healthiest	Distance of sister figure with respect to others
Insecurity/inadequacy feelings	Light, broken, and uneven line quality
Need for or lack of power issues within the family significant	Motorboat presence
K-S-D	
Conflicts with teacher	Teacher compartmentalization
Power/dominance needs around school issues	Bird's eye view looking down at the classroom
Defensiveness in school/academics	Edging of figures around the paper
Emotional disturbance present	Edging of figures around the paper
Social isolation tendencies	Bird's eye view looking down at the classroom

ficient support to compensate him fully (in a social–emotional sense) for the turmoil at home. In addition, these characteristics suggested that David might have perceived this peer support as being stronger than in fact it was. The generalized barrenness of the tree also might reflect David's current emotional coldness, his social and interpersonal aloofness, and his lack of empathy toward others. This coldness might be accentuating his memories of Tennessee as "the last time I was really happy," thereby allowing him to ignore his current difficulties through fantasy and to blame his current situation on his parents' divorce and his move from his home in Tennessee.

Person: David's person drawing provided insight into how he was really feeling and into his current self-concept. First of all, the figure was "an it." David did not feel as if he had an identity at the present time. He had conflict all around him—with his family, at the residential school, with his peer group, in the classroom. Furthermore, he had lost all sense of control over his own life: Everyone was making decisions for him, and he was caught in a downward spiral in which his attempts to reassert his control were causing the adults in his life to make more restrictive and more controlling decisions. Thus, David wanted to be all alone ("a hermit"), but this was a forced isolation. The hermit (David) did not like "society"—that is, having all the adults forcing him to conform to their societal

rules and expectations—and he did not like having all the adults (both his parents and those at the residential school) working together to apply consistent expectations and consequences (the hermit "doesn't get along with crowds"). It was a forced isolation also in the sense that David described the hermit as "lonesome—even hermits have to show some feeling." His final comment about having a dog that had been dead for 6 years was very sad. It suggested that David really wanted to interact and share his feelings with others and that he wanted to be accepted, but the overall tone of the drawing indicated that this was a deep, underlying aspiration that would not soon be fulfilled. Finally, it was interesting that 6 years before drawing this picture, David was living in Tennessee and his parents were approaching their divorce. Perhaps David had never emotionally recovered from that traumatic event.

K-F-D: David's family drawing included all of the members of his family, but the figures were incomplete and poorly formed, and could not be differentiated from one another. This suggested that David felt a significant amount of conflict among the members of his family—conflict that he focused around his father. Indeed, the potential issue of and conflict around David's father's alcohol abuse was readily apparent: David had the father in the drawing asking for another beer and himself rejecting the request, saying, "You just had one." Significantly, the mother in the drawing was depicted as somewhat passive, and as an individual who often got in between David and his father to act as a buffer or intermediary. Finally, David's sister appeared to be the psychologically safest and healthiest one in the family—she was allowed to water-ski behind the boat, free from the conflict within the boat and was able to have fun.

It was interesting that David described the picture as a happy picture and as one taking place in Florida. No longer was David drawing pictures about himself or his family in Tennessee. He was now focused on his more recent experiences in Florida, and he still perceived his family as his father, mother, and sister despite his being placed in the residential program. The description of the picture as happy, despite the subtle indications of conflict and confrontation, might suggest that David perceived any family interaction where there was only limited conflict as "happy." This, then, might provide a baseline as to the amount of interpersonal conflict actually in the home setting, and might suggest that David had not recently experienced a truly supportive family environment, at least while living in Florida.

On a more positive note, David did include himself within the family unit. He had returned from "the Alps," although his drawing did reflect a sense of isolation within the family unit. It might be that, despite its faults, David felt most supported within his family, and that his perceptions of rejection and isolation were related more to peers, other adults, and school and community settings.

K-S-D: David's reaction to and need for control in the school setting were clearly apparent from his school drawing. His choice of the "bird's eye" view, looking omnisciently over the classroom, with the teacher's head drawn more heavily than those of the students, suggested his need to be even more powerful than the teacher and to be more of an "overseer" or authority. And the fact that he did not identify himself in the picture almost suggested that the teacher could not force him to be at one of the desks, the way the other students were depicted. David verbally expressed this power theme and need when he stated that the teacher thought she could control everything in the classroom

and that, from his perspective, she really could not. He then identified the powers that might control him most: the fear of being suspended (although he did not appear to fear that in reality), and the more moralistic power or reason that students should respect teachers and adults because they *are* adults. (Once again, this was a power that did not seem to curtail David's resistance to authority figures).

One interesting question not answered by the school drawing was the reason why David seemed to harbor these power issues. On the one hand, it might be that David's acting-out and controlling behavior countered his feelings of powerlessness with respect to his LD and his inability to achieve academically in school. That is, he needed to feel in control of something, and his negative behavior and ability to anger and frustrate others were the things that he could best control. Or, on the other hand, it might be that David had always exhibited this negative pattern of behavior, and that the behavior had affected his academic failure and his poor peer interrelationships and acceptance. Regardless of the answer, it was clear that the issues of power and conflict were well embedded in David's perceptions of school and family, and that these perceptions had to be considered in any intervention program that might hope to address David's social–emotional, behavioral, and academic needs.

A Final Integration

Objective tests such as the PIC and the MAPI, and behaviorally oriented measures such as behavior rating scales and behavioral observations, are clearly important to the personality assessment process; they provide reliable and valid samples of the student's functioning intrapersonally, interpersonally, ecologically, and across multiple settings. From a diagnostic perspective, David was correctly placed in the residential setting, according to these objective and behavioral assessments. In addition, the psychoeducational assessments relative to his intellectual and academic functioning were critical in developing an appropriate educational program with reasonable demands and expectations.

From a therapeutic perspective, however, the addition of the projective tests, and the drawing tests in particular, provided a more in-depth cognitive–behavioral view that contributed to a fuller understanding of David's attitudes, attributions, expectations, and perceptions. Who would have expected David to draw a figure in the Alps feeling lonesome and reflecting that it didn't like society and didn't get along with crowds, and what personality assessment measure could have elicited a feeling that descriptive and intense other than the projective drawings? Who would have predicted that David would have addressed his need for power and control so explicitly in response to the K-S-D inquiry? Obviously, no one. But these cognitions were what completed the diagnostic picture within a multitrait, multisetting, multimethod assessment approach. Furthermore, these cognitive beliefs and perceptions might be most instrumental in creating an intervention program that addressed both David's cognitions and his behaviors.

Integrating the projective drawings with all of the other assessments done with and for David resulted in a comprehensive personality picture. David had a long history of personality and adjustment difficulties, beginning with an interaction between his own behavior and his parents' perceptions of him being a child who "defied authority" at 9 months, and extending through a diagnosis of hyperactivity and numerous failure experiences at home and at school; parents with inconsistent disciplinary styles; a parental divorce and subsequent remarriage; a suspension from school; and a move to a residential school because of his behavior and active resistance. Qualitatively, David had serious feelings of negative self-concept, deep feelings of inadequacy and vulnerability, and a great need to be accepted by others. Behaviorally, however, he had very poor impulse control, and he lacked the social and conflict resolution skills to interact appropriately with peers. Thus, he was caught in a vicious cycle: He was rejected continually by peers and adults; he withdrew from them in anger and self-protection; he increasingly resented his rejection and isolation; and then he tried to interact again, only motivated by revenge, anger, and a self-fulfilling prophecy for another social failure. This vicious cycle had played itself out continually over the past several years, such that the behavioral pat-

tern was now occurring many times per day, and David's behavior was more and more out of control. David now presented himself as someone with serious conduct disorder and delinquency problems and behaviors, and as one with little internal self-control or trust in anyone who could help him to assert that self-control. David was not a good therapy prospect at this time, and unfortunately his parents were not either: They did not want to acknowledge their part in the broad, ecological problem, or their need to change their own behavioral styles and cognitive beliefs so that David could be fully reintegrated into the family system.

Therapeutically, the picture of David emerging from this assessment was quite distressing. It was, however, accurate. Within 2 months of the final diagnostic assessments, David's behavior was so far out of control that he was asked to leave the residential school. At last contact, David's parents were looking for a residential psychiatric setting for David, still disavowing their part and responsibility in the presenting problems and the needed comprehensive therapy and intervention process.

SUMMARY

This chapter has attempted to provide a comprehensive picture of projective drawing approaches: their historical and theoretical development, their psychometric and clinical strengths and weaknesses, and their use in the context of a comprehensive personality assessment battery. A case study has also been presented to exemplify the use of projective drawings in the comprehensive personality assessment process, and their contributions to that process. There is no doubt that projective drawing techniques—indeed, projective techniques as a whole—continue to be controversial and questioned (see Batsche & Peterson, 1983; Knoff, 1983). However, there is also no doubt that they continue to be discussed in graduate training, employed in the field, and useful to many. Projective drawings need more sophisticated research attention and evaluation. However, they should be evaluated as part of the entire personality assessment process, not in an isolated and out-of-context way, and their use should be strategic and well considered. Projective drawings are not needed in every assessment of a referred child, but when they are used, they should be used correctly and with an eye toward an accurate understanding of the referred child and an appropriate and effective intervention and service delivery program. This is the bottom line for all personality assessment: not that we complete our test with just a better understanding of a child, but that we implement our intervention programs and have a positive, lasting impact on the children, families, and systems who are referred to us as needing emotional and other supports.

APPENDIX 5.1. A METHODOLOGICAL SUMMARY AND ANALYSIS OF PROJECTIVE INTERPRETATIONS FOR SELECTED DRAWING TECHNIQUES

Authors	Type of design	Number of subjects	Control (Y/N)	Population sampled	Variables	Results	Scoring reliability	Sampling	Stats	Generalizability[a]
Adler (1970)	DESC	216	N	Pyschiatric patients of varying diagnoses, 18–65 years old	Subjected 32 scoring criteria to factor analysis	Yielded one large factor (Maturity of Body Image Concept) and three small factors; diagnostic categories were not differentiated by factors	—	—	P	2
Albee & Hamlin (1949)	EPF	10	N	Individuals with normal to severe psychological problems	HFDs rated by 15 clinicians in pairwise comparisons; clinicians were asked to pick better-adjusted individual from each pair	Ratings for clinicians split into two groups correlated .955 (reliability); rank-order correlation between rank by case records and rank by ratings on HFD = .624 (validity)	—	—	P NP	0
Beck (1959)	EPF	843	Y	805 normal children, 5–6 yrs. old; 25 organic MH children, 6–19 yrs. old; 13 nonorganic MH children	House drawing of H-T-P: recognizable or not, bizarre appearance, details present/or absent	Signif. diff between MH children and normals in recognizabilities and omissions; organic- nonorganic MH children were not diff.; 5- and 6-yr.-old normals signif. diff. on omissions	—	M?	NP	1
Berman & Laffal (1953)	EPF	88	N	Neuropsychiatric male patients	Subjects body-typed (endomorphic, mesomorphic, ectomorphic) and compared on whether self-drawing matched actual body type or not	Correlations between drawing and body types were signif.—patients did tend to draw themselves as they were	Body type rating $r =$ .73	—	P	0
Bieliauskas (1960)	EPF	1,000	N	Normal school children, 5–14 yrs. old, 50 male and 50 female for each age	Tested hypothesis that there would be no signif. diff. between boys and girls at various age levels in drawing figure as male or female	Males tended to draw males, females drew females; tendency increased with age	—	—	NP	2
Bodwin & Bruck (1960)	DESC	60	N	Children 10–17 yrs. old, 30 male and 30 female	Compared DAP Scores based on 13 characteristics thought to be associated with self-concept to clinical ratings of self-concept based on interviews	High correlation between ratings and scales	—	—	P	0

(continued)

APPENDIX 5.1. *(continued)*

Authors	Type of design	Number of subjects	Control (Y/N)	Population sampled	Variables	Results	Scoring reliability	Sampling	Stats	General-izability[a]
Bradfield (1964)	EPF	50	Y	Chronic schizophrenic women	Percentage of total height represented by the head	Signif. diff. (p < .01)	—	—	P NP	1
Bradfield (1964)	EPF	85	Y	Children identified by teachers as acting out, withdrawn, overachievers, underachievers, normals (n = 17 in each group)	Compared groups on size, location and degree of implied movement in DAPs	No signif. diff.	—	—	P NP	0
Britain (1970)	EPF	64	Y	Middle-class nursery school children	Four groups compared on family drawings: control, control free play, play therapy, play session designed to reduce self-esteem	Signif. diff. among groups on such things as sequence of self figure, colors, area of family figures, elaboration; predictable by emotional-evocative level induced	90% agreement	R	P	2
Burton & Sjoberg (1964)	EPF	98	Y	49 schizophrenic females, 49 normal females	Judges sorted random HFDs into two stacks to determine hit rate and identify their criteria for selection; also tested within method, anatomical distortions, and a checklist of 67 items	Trained clinicians were able to discriminate between schizophrenics and normals, but no clear agreement on characteristics used to distinguish	Interjudge r = .79	—	NP	1
Carlson, Quinlan, Tucker, & Harrow (1973)	DESC	59	N	Psychiatric patients: 28 schizophrenics, 11 personality-disordered, 8 neurotic, 13 mixed	Factor analysis of 14 specific features of HFD along with global ratings of sophistication and artistic skill; correlated results with other measures of body image disturbance and psychopathology	Two factors, Body Disturbance (BD) and Sexual Elaboration (SE); BD signif. correlated with artistic skill and sophistication; SE correlated with pathological thinking	Interrater r = .79	—	P	1
Cassel, Johnson, & Burns (1958)	EXP	130	N	White applicants for employment	Compared H-T-Ps of applicants where examiner remained in room with those where examiner was not present during drawing	Same comparisons statistically but not practically signif.	r > .90 on 16 pairs	—	P	1
Chase (1941)	EPF	150	Y	50 schizophrenic, 50 hebephrenics, 50 normal male adults	Compared on Goodenough drawings	Schizophrenics had signif. lower scores than normals; other variables, such as age, level of education, duration of psychosis, and mental age did not differentiate	—	—	P	1

Author (year)	Type	N		Purpose	Results	Reliability		P/NP	
Craddick (1963)	EPF	46 (23 pairs)	N	Compared DAP and self-portrait on size, no. of same-sex drawings, position on page, no. of subjects' correct pairing of pictures by judges	Signif. relationship of size and grades (p < .05); more females drew opposite sex on DAP (ANOVAs); most maintained same position on two drawings	95% agreement	—	P NP	0
Craddick (1964)	EXP	86	N	Subjects asked to draw a person, draw themselves, and draw a person the way someone who is "crazy" would	"Crazy" drawings signif. larger than other two, suggesting expansiveness as a perceived characteristic of craziness	NA	—	P	0
Craddick & Leipold (1968)	DESC	200	N	Compared size of male versus female figure drawing	Male drawings signif. smaller ($t = 3.4$, $p < .01$)	NA	NA	P	1
Datta & Drake (1968)	DESC	939	N	Head Start children: 487 males, 452 females aged 3 yrs. to 6 yrs., 11 mos.	Sex differentiation of DAP figure	Girls drew more sex-differentiated DAP, but dependent on sex of examiner	49 out of 50 agreements	R?	NP	2
Delatte (1985)	DESC	38	NA	Compared femininity ratings of HFDs with self-esteem on Rosenberg Self-Esteem Scale	Small but signif. correlation (.31) between femininity of HFD figures and self-esteem	Interjudge (on 38 drawings) r = .97	—	P	0
Delatte & Hendrickson (1982)	DESC	76	NA	Explored relationship between size (height, width, area) of HFD and Rosenberg Self-Esteem Scale scores	No signif. correlations for females; signif. correlation between self-esteem and HFD width and area for males (only .35 for width); some restriction of range (mostly high scores) in self-esteem scores	NA	—	P	0
DeMartino (1954)	DESC	100	N	DAPs analyzed on 39 characteristics and which sex drawn first	Most drew male first; more than 75 % had mouth open, front view, feet/shoes, large head, nose, arms, generally poor proportions, standing; fewer than 25% had mouth closed, teeth, arms perpendicular to body	—	—	NP	1
De Martino (1954)	EPF	74	N	DAPs analyzed as above	Homosexuals had signif. more eyelashes and high heels	—	—	NP	0

(continued)

APPENDIX 5.1. (*continued*)

Authors	Type of design	Number of subjects	Control (Y/N)	Population sampled	Variables	Results	Scoring reliability	Sampling	Stats	General-izability[a]
Dunleavy, Hansen, & Szasz (1981)	DESC	141	NA	Kindergarten students in six randomly selected schools representing three SES levels	Tested Koppitz scores of HFD in predicting school readiness of Kindergarten children (measured by Metropolitan Readiness Test)	42% of "nonready" children identified; 10% false positives, so HFD was a reasonable predictor	—	R?	P	2
Exner (1962)	EXP	80	Y	Psychoneurotics, character-disturbed, normals, and group experiencing induced fear conditions (n = 20 in each group); attributes not clearly defined	Compared groups on line pressure, sketchiness, shading movement, profiles, buttons, feet, holding object, using bottom edge of page as baseline	Character-disturbed group used lighter pressure, more shading than the rest; psychoneurotics used more unbroken lines. Altogether, 6 of 10 variables differentiated pathological groups from each other and other groups; nothing really conclusive, though	—	—	P	0
Fellows & Cerbus (1969)	EPF	278	N	Enrollment of parochial elementary grade school	Compared drawing and Drawing Completion Test (DCT); six variables of H-T-P between males and females	DCT scores not signif. diff. for males vs. females up to age 12; signif. diff. between males and females on sex of figure drawn first on HIP; strongest correlations at ages 11, 12, and 13	Only DCT reported; r = .89	—	P	1
Fielder & Siegel (1949)	EPF	46	N	15 "improved" psychotherapy clients, 19 "unimproved" clients; all male veterans	Used characteristics of Free Drawing Test to predict success or nonsuccess of therapy	Unimproved patients received signif. lower (poorer) scores on criteria for formation of head	92% agreement	—	NA	0
Fisher (1961)	DESC	1,154	N	White male adolescents jailed for delinquent behavior	Degree of nudity in figure drawings	Subjects drawing female first had signif. more nudity; low numbers of drawings contained nudity overall	—	NA	NP	1
Fisher (1968)	DESC	1,000	N	Male felons	Nudity in DAP, sex of figure drawn first	Drew male figure first less often than reported for normals in literature; twice as many adolescents indicated some nudity compared to adults	—	—	NP	2

Author (year)	Type	N		Subjects	Comparison	Findings	Reliability			
A. P. Goldstein & Rawn (1957)	EXP	39	Y	Male and female attendants in state mental hospital	Analyzed pre- and post-HFDs for control and experimental groups for increased aggression level by announcing they must work longer hours for same pay	No diff. in line pressure (no. of carbons imprinted) or figure size; other qualitative diff. were signif. (symbolic representation of aggression)	—	—	NP	0
H. S. Goldstein & Faterson (1969)	EXP	23	Y	Normal males	Shading differences between subjects' HFDs following high- and low-stress films	Signif. more shading following high-stress films	Interrater r = .90	—	NP	0
Goodman & Kotkov (1953)	DESC	8	Y	Obese vs. nonobese women (n = 4 in each group)	Rank-order correlations between judges' ordering of drawing and ordering based on scoring criteria	Signif. no. of high correlations, but also many nonexistent correlations	NA	R	NP	1
Graham (1956)	EXP	23	N	Graduate students: 12 males, 11 female	Compared subjects' initial figure drawings and their drawings following lectures emphasizing negative characteristics inferred from certain aspects of figure	Very few changes from first to second drawing	—	—	P	0
Granick & Smith (1953)	EPF	571	N	Male and female undergraduates	Compared sex drawn first on DAP to masculinity–femininity scale of MMPI	Most drew own sex first, but males signif. more than females; no relation between MMPI scores and sex drawn first	—	—	P	1
Gravitz (1966)	DESC	2,000	N	Normal adults; 1,088 males, 912 females	Drawing of same-sex, opposite-sex, or undifferentiated-sex figures	76% drew same sex, 21% opposite, 3% undiff.; more than twice as many women drew opposite sex	NA	R	Percentages only	2
Gravitz (1967)	DESC	800	N	Normal adults, 20-30 yrs. old; half single, half married	Sex of drawing	No differences between married people and singles on whether drawing was same-sex	NA	R	NP	2
Gravitz (1968)	DESC	200	N	100 male and 100 female job applicants	General characteristics of HFDs compared	Males, 85% same-sex, 15% opposite-sex; females, 67% same-sex; no diff. in mean heights of figures	NA	—	P	1
Gravitz (1969a)	EPF	200	N	Male and female adult job applicants divided into four groups: males with high Masculinity scores on the MMPI; males with low scores; females with high scores; females with low scores	Compared groups on drawing of same-sex figures	High-masculinity males, 85% signif.; low-masculinity males, 78%; both female groups were identical	NA	—	NP	1

(continued)

APPENDIX 5.1. (continued)

Authors	Type of design	Number of subjects	Control (Y/N)	Population sampled	Variables	Results	Scoring reliability	Sampling	Stats	Generalizability[a]
Gravitz (1969b)	EPF	469	N	328 men, 141 women; 40–60 yrs. old	Compared HFDs of married people and singles for percentage of same-sex drawings	Males drew same sex signif. more than females, but no diff. between male or female married people or singles	NA	—	NP	1
Gravitz (1971)	EPF	1,000	N	500 normal male adults, 500 normal female adults; 20–50 years old, job applicants	Compared on drawing of opposite or same sex, degree of nudity	No diff. on fully clothed same-sex figures; males drew more fully clothed females; males and females no diff. on opposite- and same-sex nude figures	By joint agreement	R	P NP	2
Gray & Pepitone (1964)	EXP	88	Y	College students: 25 high self-esteem (HSE), 25 low self-esteem (LSE), 38 controls	HSE took personality battery and received a report stating that they made unusually favorable scores; LSE got opposite report; controls didn't get report before doing HFD; groups compared on figure size, placement on page, emotional tone, activity level	LSE group drew smaller figures, but not signif.; LSE had signif. more isolated and smaller figures; HSE more similar to controls	Interjudge agreement 88–94%	R	P	1
Green, Fuller, & Rutley (1972)	EPF	55	Y	30 "feminine" boys, 4–10 yrs. old (judged to like dressing in girls' clothes); 25 control normals	Compared groups on sex drawn first in DAP; subjects matched on age, sex of children in family, and marital status and SES of parents	Feminine boys drew girl first (57%); controls drew boy first (76%)	NA	M	NP	1
Griffith & Peyman (1959)	EPF	76	Y	18 male mental patients selected on overemphasis of eyes and ears on DAP; 58 controls	Compared eye-ear emphasis to whether clinically judged "ideas of reference" were present	Signif. more of eye-ear group had ideas of reference	—	—	NP	0
Hamilton (1984)	DESC	55	NA	Male and female kindergarten through third-grade children in bilingual education programs (three groups; n's = 16, 17, and 22)	Compared HFD sample protocols across grades for presence of indicators of self-concept	ANOVAs revealed signif. diff. in growth of self-concept during kindergarten and remained stable through third grade	3 judges' agreement by discussion	R	P	1

Study	Method	N	Y/N	Sample	Procedure	Results	Reliability			
Hammer (1953a)	EPF	40	Y	Normal controls and eugenically sterilized males ($n = 20$ in each group)	Looked at H-T-Ps before and after operation (controls had other types of surgery)	Signif. diffs. suggested more genital symbolism and feelings of castration in sterilized group	—	—	NP	0
Hammer (1953b)	EPF	400	N	148 black children and 252 white children in first through eighth grades	Clinical judgments of H-T-P on 6-point scale from 0 (well adjusted) to 6 (psychotic); whites and blacks compared	Blacks got higher overall adjustment scores; whites and blacks got closer together as age increased	Among three judges, $r = .90$	—	P	1
Hammer (1954A)	EPF	64	N	All sex offenders: 31 adult rapists, 33 pedophiles	Compared H-T-Ps: age of tree, dead or alive, age of people, male or female figures	Pedophiles drew signif. younger trees; pedophiles drew signif. older females	NA	—	P	0
Handler & Reyher (1964)	EXP	57	Y	21 nonstressed control undergraduates; 36 stressed undergraduates	Compared DAPs for Hoyt–Baron scoring of anxiety indices; stressed subjects were hooked up to a polygraph in a small, dimly lighted room with experimenter looking over their shoulders	Signif. diff.	Percentage of agreement between two judges ranged from 67% to 100%	—	NP	1
Handler & Reyher (1966)	DESC	96	N	Male college students	Compared drawings of male, female, and automobile on GSR and Hoyt–Baron scoring indicators of anxiety	Auto yielded lowest measures of anxiety; female yielded highest measure of anxiety; low but signif. correlations between GSR and 10 of 23 graphic indicators	67%–97% agreement	R	P NP	1
Heberlein & Marcuse (1963)	EPF	160	N	Four groups of college females: those drawing same-sex figures on two DAPs; opposite-sex figures on two DAPs; opposite- then same-sex DAP figures; same- then opposite-sex DAP figures	Compared groups on Aggression, Heterosexuality, and Abasement scales of Edwards Personal Preference Schedule	Greater need for aggression in females who drew males	NA	R	P	1
Hiler & Nesvig (1965)	EPF	60	Y	30 adolescent psychiatric patients; 30 normal adolescents	Compared on criteria scores of DAP by six psychologists and eight nonpsychologists to determine valid criteria for differentiation	Valid criteria for pathology were bizarre, distorted, incomplete and transparent characteristics; criteria for normality were happy expression and no pathological characteristics present; nonpsychologists discriminated just as well as psychologists	—	R	NA	1

(continued)

Authors	Type of design	Number of subjects	Control (Y/N)	Population sampled	Variables	Results	Scoring reliability	Sampling	Stats	Generalizability[a]
Holzberg & Wexler (1950)	EPF	108	Y	Control group, 78 female student nurses; experimental group, 38 schizophrenic women	Comparisons between groups on checklist of 174 drawing variables	Signif. diffs. on 27 variables	Scored only items on which judges agreed	M?	NP	1
Hoyt & Baron (1959)	EPF	112	N	Female psychiatric patients	Subjects divided into two groups according to high or low Manifest Anxiety Scale (MAS)	Placement and size of drawing signif. related to MAS score but not eight other indicators	Mean absolute difference between	—	NP	1
Jensen (1985)	EXP	175	N	College students randomly assigned into mixed male and female groups	DAP administered by either male or female examiner; groups compared by sex on sex of first drawing	No diff. for male or female subjects according to sex of examiner when DAP administered in mixed-sex groups	NA	R	NP	2
Johnson (1971)	DESC	103	N	College students	Compared on IPAT Anxiety scale scores and anxiety indicator of upper left-hand placement of DAP	Signif. relationship: more upper left-hand placement as IPAT score higher	—	—	NP	1
Jolles (1952a)	DESC	8,500	N	Children in Illinois public schools, 5–12 yrs. old	Drawing of same-sex person (H-T-P)	Younger children drew opposite sex more than older; girls drew opposite sex more often than boys	NA	R?	NP	2
Jolles (1952b)	DESC	2,701	N	Same as Jolles (1952a)	Phallic-looking trees on H-T-P	More common in younger children; became more psychosexually signif. with age; more common in females	—	R?	NP	2
Jolles & Beck (1953)	DESC	2,083	N	Same as Jolles (1952a)	Horizontal placement of drawing as indicator of intellectual control over affect	Supported Buck's hypothesis that psychological center is to the left of geometric center; normal range varied with age	NA	R?	P	2
Jordan (1970)	CS	1	N	Child 9 yrs. old with cerebellar disorder	Analyzed HFD and Bender-Gestalt Test drawing	Case study: Drawings "floating in space"	NA	NA	NA	0
Judson & MacCasland (1960)	DESC	240	N	Psychology patients (mixed diagnoses)	Foliage present or absent on trees of H-T-P drawings drawn over the four seasons of the year	Signif. more bare trees drawn in winter by females but not males	Only 1 disagreement in 240 protocols	NA	NP	1

Study	Code	N		Sample	Procedure	Results				
Kamano (1960)	DESC	45	N	Institutionalized schizophrenic women	HFDs rated by subjects as to whether they were most like: ideal self, actual self, least-liked self; these compared to self-ratings on semantic differential scales	Signif. more rated drawing most like actual self; supported idea that HFD is a perception of drawer's self	NA	NA	P	1
Koppitz (1966a)	EPF	161	N	100 "good students," 61 "poor students"; first and second grade (by Metropolitan Achievement Test)	Analyzed HFDs on 30 Koppitz emotional indicators (EIs)	Five EIs were signif. more often present in poor-student group, including poor integration of parts, slanting	—	—	NP	1
Koppitz (1966b)	EPF	152	Y	76 children from guidance clinic; 76 normal school children	Compared HFDs on 30 EIs	11 EIs signif. more frequent in clinic group	95 % agreement on 25 protocols	M	NP	1
Koppitz (1966c)	EPF	62	N	Guidance clinic children; 31 identified as aggressive, 31 identified as shy	Compared HFDs on 30 EIs	Asymmetry of limbs, presence of teeth, long arms, big hands were present signif. more often in aggressive group; hands cut off, no mouth were more frequent in shy group	—	M	NP	1
Kotkov & Goodman (1953)	EPF	55 (pilot); 56 (experiment)	N	61 obese women, 40 normal-weight women; all matched on age, education, IQ, marital status, and employment status	Compared groups on 43 scoring items on the DAP	32 signif. diff. measures in pilot group led to seven combined signs that differentiated obese from normal women's drawings; primarily related to obese using more of page	—	M	NP	2
Kurtzberg, Cavior, & Lipton (1966)	EPF	125	Y	"Normal" inmates; inmates addicted to opiates	DAP; female drawn first, female larger than male	Signif. more addicts drew female first; addicts drew females signif. larger than males	NA	—	NP	1
Laird (1962)	EPF	303	N	132 male introductory psychology students; 100 male alcoholics, mean age 45 yrs, mean education 11th grade; 71 male psychiatric patients, mean age 42 yrs., mean education 9th grade	Compared HFDs on sex of figure drawn first	Percentage who drew same-sex figure first: normals, 94.7%; psychiatrics, 84.5%; alcoholics, 81.0%; (latter two groups signif. diff. from normals but not from each other)	NA	—	NP	1
Lakin (1956)	EPF	49	N	25 third-grade children; 24 elderly residents of a home for aged	Compared groups on area used, figure height, and centeredness of DAP as indicators of self-concept and body image	Supported hypothesis: Drawings by aged more constricted, shorter, and less centered	—	—	NP	0

(continued)

APPENDIX 5.1. (*continued*)

Authors	Type of design	Number of subjects	Control (Y/N)	Population sampled	Variables	Results	Scoring reliability	Sampling	Stats	Generalizability[a]
Lehner & Gunderson (1948)	DESC	421	N	College students; 229 males and 192 females	Subjects' age compared to age assigned to DAP	Men assigned slightly older ages to male and female DAPs as own age became greater; for females, the function was curvilinear—age of drawn figure increased with actual age until actual age of 35, then decreased	NA	—	Percentage only	1
Lewinsohn (1964)	EPF	100	N	Four groups of psychiatric patients rated as depressed male or female, or nondepressed male or female, by physicians (n = 25 in each group)	Compared groups on height of DAPs	Depressed patients had signif. shorter figures	NA	—	P	1
Lyons (1955)	EPF	50	N	Last 50 people the author tested at work	On H-T-Ps, asked subjects to imagine the tree had been struck by lightning and place an "X" where this might have occurred; compared height of mark on tree to relative age at time when "worst thing that ever happened to you" occurred and best thing"	Signif. correlation between "scar" height and age when "worst thing" occurred; not signif. for "best thing"	NA	—	NP	0
Mabry (1964)	CS	1	N	Patient with malignant brain tumor	DAP	Case study	NA	NA	NA	0
Marzolf & Kirchner (1970)	DESC	850	N	College students	List of 73 H-T-P characteristics: compared males and females, and diff. between first and second drawing	29 items were signif. diff. across sex	Median and agreement r = 91.8	—	NP	1
Marzolf & Kirchner (1972)	DESC	760	N	College males and females	Analyzed presence or absence of 108 drawing characteristics and compared to 16PF scores	Some signif. but low correlations; 347 signif. comparisons out of 3,672 correlations (17 16PF traits × 108 drawing characteristics × sex)	Interjudge agreement > 90%	R	P	2

Study	Design	N		Sample	Analysis	Findings	Reliability		Category	
McHugh (1963)	DESC	626	N	Male and female students, first through sixth grades	Analyzed whether same sex was drawn first and size of drawings	Overall tendency to draw same sex first; females drew female figure larger than males drew male figure	NA	—	NP	1
McHugh (1966)	EPF	108	N	Four groups ($r = 27$ each): two diagnosed with adjustment reaction of childhood (neurotic traits or conduct-disturbed); two diagnosed with adjustment reaction of adolescence (neurotic traits or conduct-disturbed); both sets matched on age and IQ	Groups compared on 23 variables on HFD	Children with neurotic traits drew first figure significantly shorter and both figures farther from bottom of page; neurotic boys drew opposite sex first more frequently than conduct-disordered children	—	—	NP	1
McPhee & Wegner (1976)	EPF	264	Y	102 ED children (male and female), 162 normals; no ages reported	Compared groups by sex on stylization of K-F-Ds	No sex diff.; signif. diff. between ED and normals on stylization	Five judges; $r = 66{-}1.00$	—	P	0
Melikian & Wahab (1969)	DESC	162	N	137 male and 25 female Moslem, African-born college students	Percentage drawing same-sex figure first on DAP	Women started signif. more often than males on opposite sex (females, 48%; males, 18%); similar to literature with American samples	NA	—	NP	0
Meyer, Brown, & Levine (1955)	CS	22	N	People undergoing a number of surgical procedures	Case study comparisons on pre- and postoperative HIPs	Various conclusions; many postoperative changes in drawings noted	NA	NA	NA	1
Michal-Smith (1953)	EPF	50	Y	25 individuals with normal EEG; 25 with abnormal EEG	H-T-P comparisons on six variables from Buck's scoring system	Only *line quality* differentiated	—	—	NP	0
Modell (1951)	DESC	28	Y	28 mental patients: 13 recovered, 8 unimproved, 7 uncertain	Subjective scoring of HFD on "body image maturation" and "sexual maturation" in patients returning from a regressed state	An illustrative case study is presented in full; recovered group showed diff. in body image maturation and sexual maturation	Tested by χ^2 for signif. diff.	—	NA	0
Modell & Potter (1949)	CS	32	N	Medical patients with hypertension, peptic ulcers, or bronchial asthma	Compared features of HFDs for diff. types of patients; qualitative descriptions and case study provided for each type presented	Made conclusions about various personality characteristics	NA	NA	NA	1

(continued)

APPENDIX 5.1. (continued)

Authors	Type of design	Number of subjects	Control (Y/N)	Population sampled	Variables	Results	Scoring reliability	Sampling	Stats	General-izability[a]
Mogar (1962)	DESC	123	N	Male psychiatric patients	Looked at relationship between Manifest Anxiety (MA) scores and Hoyt–Baron anxiety indicators on DAP, and same anxiety indicators with Rorschach Content Text (RCT) scores	No results with MA, thus supporting previous research; several RCT variables had signif. correlation with DAP anxiety indicators	Interrater r = .84–1.00	—	NP	1
Moll (1962)	DESC	269	N	Normal college students	Foilage or not on H-T-P trees; drawings done by subjects during all four seasons	Signif. no. of bare trees in fall and winter drawings	Agreement reached by two judges in all but three cases	NA	NP	1
Mostkoff & Lazarus (1983)	DESC	50	NA	25 male, 25 female students qualifying for Title I; second–fifth grade	Determined interrater and test-retest reliability of an objective scoring system for K-F-D	Signif. agreement on nine variables: self in picture, evasions, arm extensions, elevated figures, rotated figures, omission of body parts (self, other), barriers, drawings on back of page (out of 20 variables)	Interrater agreement 97%	—	NP	1
Nathan (1973)	EPF	72	Y	36 chronically obese children, 36 controls; 7, 10, and 13 yrs. old; matched on sex, IQ, SES	Compared on Goodenough–Harris scoring of HFD looking for diff. in detail and sex differentiation	Obese sample signif. more global and undifferentiated than controls; related to self-image/body image	—	M	P	1
Oas (1984)	EPF	214	Y	100 adolescent psychiatric patients, 114 "normal" adolescents from regular and special education classes	Tested Bender-Gestalt Test and HFD ability to discriminate between impulsive and nonimpulsive adolescents (Matching Familiar Figures Test, Behavioral Checklist, Impulsive Behavior Checklist used to discriminate groups)	Discriminant-function analyses of Bender-Gestalt and HFD variables indicated high relation; HFD variables slightly better at discriminating impulsives from nonimpulsives in each group; 79% of school sample correctly classified; 93% of hospitalized sample correctly classified	—	M	P	2

Otterbacher, Haley, Abbott, & Watson (1984)	DESC	40	NA	Male and female ID students, 59–146 months old	Investigated relation between HFD and postrotary nystagmus	All variables (age, nystagmus, IQ, sex) yielded sign; age and nystagmus were as predictive of HFD performance without IQ and sex added into equation; nystagmus was still predictive with age partialed out	Interrater r = .94	—	P	1
Paine, Alves, & Tabino (1985)	EPF	24	Y	12 pediatric oncology patients, 12 general pediatric surgery patients and students	Compared groups on Koppitz HFDs according to size of drawing	Cancer patients' drawings signif. smaller than those of surgery patient/student group; implied increased anxiety	NA	M	P	0
Pollitt, Hirsch, & Money (1964)	CS	7	N	Males with priapism (prolonged erection)	Case studies used Bender–Gestalt Test and DAP	Concluded that a "blind" investigator would find no clear signs in drawings to distinguish this group	NA	NA	NA	1
Prout & Celmer (1984)	DESC	100	NA	Normal male and female fifth-grade students	Examined relation between indicators of emotional conflict and negative affect on K-S-D and academic achievement	Modest but signif. correlations between achievement (SRA achievement test) and 6 of 10 variables; 26% of variance in achievement accounted for by K-S-D variables in stepwise multiple regression	—	—	P	1
Reznikoff & Tomblen (1956)	EPF	75	N	25 organic brain-impaired, 25 schizophrenic, 25 neurotic individuals	Compared HFDs on 17 indicators	Organics signif. diff. from other two groups on five to six indicators: weak synthesis, parts misplaced, shrunken appendages, etc.	Two scores, 91% agreement	—	P NP	1
Rosen & Boe (1968)	DESC	98	N	Male college students enrolled in weight-lifting class	Nudity in DAP	64% completely nude, 48% with penis; discussed as very unusual finding	NA	—	Percentage only	0
Saracho (1984)	DESC	480	NA	Random samples: 240 first graders, 240 third graders	Assessed interjudge, test-retest, and split-half reliability; tested relationship between Goodenough DAP and Children's Embedded Figures Test and Articulation of Body Concept Scale (measures of field dependence and independence)	High reliabilities found: Embedded Figures, .90s; body concept, .50s; Goodenough, .80s; high correlation with articulation of Body Concept Scale (.90s); low correlation with Embedded Figures Test; concluded DAP was good measure of field dependence–independence	Interjudge r = .91 for DAP	R	P	2

(continued)

APPENDIX 5.1. *(continued)*

Authors	Type of design	Number of subjects	Control (Y/N)	Population sampled	Variables	Results	Scoring reliability	Sampling	Stats	General-izability[a]
Schubert (1969)	DESC	22	N	Army enlisted mean	Compared three administrations of DAP (male and female) on a DAP quality scale (drawings once a week)	Revealed signif. linear trend toward poorer quality; indicated a motivation deficit that must be considered in studies where more than one administration is involved	Interrater r = .80s–.90s	—	P	0
Sobel & Sobel (1976)	EPF	40	Y	20 institutionalized male delinquents, 14–17 yrs. old; 20 normals from a public school, 15–17 yrs. old	Compared K-F-Ds on 16 traits	Only 3 of 16 traits showed signif. diff. between groups; questionable ability to diagnose delinquency	—	R	NP	1
Strumpfer (1963)	EPF	81	N	Psychotic inpatients; 45 male, 36 female	DAP compared by age and length of time since diagnosis; DAP variables included quality, height, sex differentiation	Most variables showed signif. negative correlations with chronicity (length of illness); the longer subjects had been sick, the poorer the performance	Interrater r = .85	—	P	1
Vane & Eisen (1962)	EPF	662	N	Kindergarten children divided into three groups by teacher adjustment ratings of good, fair, or poor behavior on a 9-item scale	Compared Goodenough Draw-A-Man on four signs and combinations	Poor group showed signif. more signs compared to other two groups	—	R?	NP	2
Vroegh (1970)	EPF	151	N	Preschoolers rated most masculine and most feminine, and least masculine and least feminine, by teachers	Sex of DAP	No diff. based on degree of gender; signif. diff. on percentage drawing same sex by biological sex (males, 76%; females, 58%); only 25% of figures sex-differentiated at all	—	—	NP	1
Weider & Noller (1950)	EPF	438	N	210 boys, 228 girls; 7–12 yrs. old	Compared HFD: Subject sex × sex of first figure; subject sex × larger figure drawn; location on page × age; subject sex × IQ × full face or Profile	Girls drew own sex more often; girls drew own sex larger more often; younger children placed drawing closer to upper left quadrant more often	NA	R?	NP	2

130

Study	Design	n		Sample	Procedure	Results	Reliability	R?	NP/P	Score
Weider & Noller (1953)	EPF	153	N	Children 8–11 yrs. old	For HFD: Divided subjects into upper, middle, lower SES; compared no. of characteristics drawn, size of figures, same or opposite sex, drawn first, overt drawing compared to covert things learned from interview but not in drawing	Girls drew own sex first more than boys; boys drew own sex larger; boys increased no. of characteristics drawn as SES increased, especially in same-sex figure; girls did too, but no signif. diff. depending on sex of figure; responses in interview did not differ from drawn	—	R?	NP	2
Wildman (1963)	EPF	60	N	Patients from psychiatric department of state hospital divided in two groups according to whether or not their knee/arm joints were present in H-T-Ps (n = 30 in each group)	Judges rated patient records on degree of paranoid pathology (little, moderate, high); compared across jointed and nonjointed groups	More than twice as many patients who had drawn joints were rated highly paranoid compared to no-joint patients; more than twice as many who didn't draw joints were rated low compared to joint patients	On ratings of paranoia, interrater r = .80	—	NP	0
Wisotsky (1959)	DESC	490	N	Black and white male incarcerated alcoholics	Compared percentage who drew male figure first between whole group and normative group from literature; also between blacks and whites	Whole group drew male figure first signif. more often than normals; no diff. between blacks and whites in sample	NA	R	NP	2
Woods & Cook (1954)	DESC	138	N	Eighth-grade students	Looked at relationship between detailing in drawing of hands in HFD and level of proficiency in drawing	Found signif. relationship; questioned use of detailing in hands as a measure of personality variables	Reported with χ^2 significance only	—	NP	0
Wysocki & Whitney (1965)	EPF	100	Y	50 crippled school children (due to polio, cerebral palsy, clubfoot, dislocated hips), 50 noncrippled school children; all 6–11 yrs. old	Machover DAPs compared on 15 variables	Eight variables showed signif. diff.—large head, opposite sex, large figure, placement, shading, pressure, paper rotation, and an area of insult	—	—	P	1
Yates, Beutler, & Crago (1985)	EPF	34	Y	17 females referred to psychiatric clinic as victims of incest; 17 referred for other reasons	Developed clinical rating scale of indicators of potentially disturbed functioning while comparing groups	Only two signif. diff. (dimensions of impulse control and quality of representative defenses); signif. diff. in *variability* of hypersexualization	Combined ratings of two raters	M	P	1

Note. EPF, *ex post facto* design; DESC, descriptive "design"; EXP, experimental design; CS, case study; LD, learning-disabled; ED, emotionally disturbed; MH, mentally handicapped; SES, socioeconomic status; HFD, Human Figure Drawing; DAP, Draw-A-Person Test; H-T-P, House–Tree–Person Test; K-F-D, Kinetic Family Drawing; K-S-D, Kinetic School Drawing; MMPI, Minnesota Multiphasic Personality Inventory; GSR, Galvanic skin response; IPAT, Institute for Personality and Ability Testing; 16PF, Sixteen Personality Factor Test; SRA, Science Research Associates; NA, not available; ANOVA, analysis of variance; (?), results questioned; R, random sample; R?, possible random sample; M?, possible matched sample; M, matched sample; P, parametric statistics used; NP, nonparametric statistics used.

[a]Generalizability rated on a scale of 2 (good), 1 (fair), or 0 (limited or none).

APPENDIX 5.2. A METHODOLOGICAL SUMMARY AND ANALYSIS OF PROJECTIVE INTERPRETATIONS FOR THE BENDER–GESTALT TEST (BGT)

Authors	Type of design	Number of subjects	Control (Y/N)	Population sampled	Variables	Results	Scoring reliability	Sampling	Stats	Generalizability[a]
Anderson & Rallis (1981)	DESC	100	NA	School children referred for ED or behavioral problems in metropolitan school district	Explored relationship between BGT recall scores and no. of emotional indicators	No signif. correlation found; children with signif. number of emotional indicators did not recall fewer BGT figures	—	—	NP	1
Baroff (1957)	EPF	76	N	Twins institutionalized as mental defectives (endogenous)	Compared results on Pascal–Suttell scoring with results from previous research	Similarities suggested feasibility of establishing clinical norms for endogenous retardates	—	—	P	0
Bensberg (1952)	EPF	322	N	161 organic brain damage MH, 161 familial etiology MH; matched on MA and CA, mean MA about 6 yrs., 6 mos.	Bender scoring of BGT	Familial group signif. more accurate in reproduction; reversals, parts repeated, and lines instead of dots signif. more frequent in brain-injured	—	M	P NP	2
Blaha, Fawaz, & Wallbrown (1979)	DESC	74	N	Male and female black first-graders	Examined relationship among BGT errors, BGT time, DAP scores, DAP time, Matching Familiar Figures errors & time, and Slosson IQ	16% of variance in BGT performance due to pre-processing and central processing with general IQ partialed out; conceptual tempo accounted for little variance	—	—	P	1
Billingslea (1948)	EPF	150	Y	100 male psychoneurotic patients, 50 normal males (all soldiers)	Compared groups on 38 factors in scoring and interdrawing reliability	Equivocal results	NA	R?	NP	0
Breen & Butler (1983)	EPF	59	Y	30 students diagnosed ED; 29 normal controls (ages 7–11 yrs.)	Compared groups on 12 Koppitz emotional indicators on BGT	No signif. diff.	—	—	P	1
Byrd (1956)	DESC	400	Y	200 children in need of psychotherapy; 200 children judged well adjusted; 8–16 yrs. old	15 interpretation factors developed by Hutt on BGT groups compared by age level	About half of factors signif. at each age level; pattern differed for these factors	—	M?	NP	1
Chorost, Spivack, & Levine (1959)	EPF	68	N	Children under 18 who had EEG and a scorable BGT	Compared BGT rotations to whether EEG was normal or abnormal	Correct prediction of abnormal EEG by rotations in 65% of cases; not a great increase over other clinical signs	—	—	NA	1

Curnutt (1953)	EPF	50	Y	25 males in Alcoholics Anonymous (AA); 25 control males matched on age, SES, occupation, education	Compared BGT scored using Pascal–Suttell method (scored by author, who knew which group each case was in)	Signif. diff. between mean scores; signif. indicators included rotations, counting dots; higher scores (poorer performance) in AA group	—	M	P	0
Fabian (1945)	DESC	692	Y	106 children with a variety of psychological problems who were all "retarded" in reading; 586 normal school-age children	Comparisons, descriptions of BGT rotations and reversals	Established developmental nature of rotation of horizontally oriented figures to the vertical; persistent "verticalization" concluded to be a clinical sign of problems	—	—	NA	1
Fuller & Chagnon (1962)	EPF	270	Y	Normals, ED, schizophrenic ($n = 90$ in each group)	Rotation of BGT drawings	Signif. diff. between each pairwise group comparison; also diff. depending on original orientation of figure, or figure–ground	—	—	P	2
Gavales & Millon (1960)	EXP	80	Y	40 undergrads with high Taylor Manifest Anxiety (TMA) scores; 40 undergrads with the lowest TMA scores (out of 195)	Subjects divided into experimental (anxiety-inducing tasks) and control groups; sizes of initial and recall BGT figures compared	Sign. greater diff. in size in high-TMA induced-anxiety group	—	R	P	1
Gobetz (1953)	EPF	393 118	Y	108 neurotic, 285 normal male adult veterans (validation study) 64 neurotic, 54 normal adult male nonveterans (cross-validation study)	Two BGTs from each subject; neurotics and controls compared using objective scoring system with 82 general categories and 312 specific signs	Result was a final scoring system of 30 signs that discriminated consistently between groups on both test and retest; test–retest reliabilities in the high .60s did not corroborate Hutt's "neurotic syndrome"; BGT recommended as a screening device and supplement to other instruments, not for elaborate interpretation	—	—	NP	1
Goldberg (1956–1957)	EPF	45	Y	White male children: 15 schizophrenic, 15 MH, 15 normals; ages 11–16	Looking for diff. among groups on BGT according to Pascal–Suttell scoring	Signif. diff. between normals and other two groups; concluded that objective scoring in conjunction with qualitative analysis effective for clinical diagnosis	—	M	P	0

(continued)

133

APPENDIX 5.2. (*continued*)

Authors	Type of design	Number of subjects	Control (Y/N)	Population sampled	Variables	Results	Scoring reliability	Sampling	Stats	General-izability[a]
Goldfried & Ingling (1964)	DESC	80	N	College undergrads; 40 male, 40 female	Rated BGT drawings on descriptive semantic differential scales (e.g., kind, strong, fast)	Generally negative findings; no "universal" symbolic meanings among individuals	NA	—	NP	1
Goodstein, Spielberger, Williams, & Dalstrom (1955)	EXP	114	N	54 male and 60 female undergrads	Exp. 1—effect of serial position on BGT design recall; Exp. 2—effect of where more difficult designs placed in presentation order on recall	Designs differed signif. on ease of recall; recall related to both difficulty and serial position; no diff. between males and females	86.3%–91.8% agreement	—	P	1
Griffith & Taylor (1960)	DESC	1,000	N	Matched neuropsychiatric patients; mean age 35.5 yrs.	Compared no. of BGT rotations to diagnostic category	Categories with signif. more rotations were chronic brain syndrome and mental deficiency	—	NA	NA	2
Griffith & Taylor (1961)	EPF	213	Y	56 neuropsychiatric patients; 157 control neuropsychiatric patients	Compared no. of BGT rotations for regular admission and paper presented lengthwise	Signif. fewer rotations when blank paper presented lengthwise instead of vertically	—	—	NP	1
Guertin (1952)	DESC	100	N	Male and female mental patients: organic brain-injured, nonpsychotic, and schizophrenic	41 BGT scoring characteristics from Billingslea method factor-analyzed	Six factors: propensity for curvilinear movement, poor reality contact, careless execution, constriction, poor spatial contiguity, unidentified	—	—	P	0
Guertin (1954a)	DESC	100	N	Male and female schizophrenics and nonschizophrenics	46 BGT scoring variables factor-analyzed	Six factors: unstable closure, curvilinear distortion, propensity of curvilinearity, fragmentation, irreg. propensity of curvilinear movement, experimental dependence; suggested using clusters of variables in scoring rather than single variables	—	—	P	0
Guertin (1954b)	DESC	37	N	Male schizophrenics	BGT scored on 100 items, factor-analyzed	Four types of schizophrenic performance factored out	—	—	P	0

Study	Type	N	Norm	Sample	Method	Results	Reliability	Agreement	P/NP	No.
Guertin (1954c)	DESC	27	N	Organic brain-diseased males	100 items as above factor-analyzed	Three factors: curvilinear distortions, spatial disability, construction and feelings of inadequacy	—	—	P	0
Guertin (1955)	DESC	30	N	Male schizophrenics	100 items as above factor-analyzed	Four types of schizophrenic performance factored out	—	—	P	0
Hain (1964)	EPF	101	Y	Patients in neuropsychiatric ward; 20 brain-damaged, 38 psychiatric, and 20 controls not diagnosed in either category	Compared groups on a scoring system designed to differentiate brain damaged group from others	High scores did differentiate, but low scores did not predict lack of brain damage	—	—	NP	1
Halpin (1955)	EPF	30	N	15 brain-damaged children; 15 familial retardates; ages 7–13 yrs. matched on CA, MA, IQ	Compared no. of rotations on BGT	No signif. diff.	M	96% agreement	P NP	1
Hammer (1954b)	EPF	40	Y	20 males undergoing sterilization; 20 males undergoing other surgeries	Numerous variables selected for each drawing indicative of castration anxiety before and after surgery	Many variables showed signif. diffs.	—	—	NP	1
Hanvik & Andersen (1950)	EPF	44	Y	20 patients with lesions in dominant hemisphere; 24 patients with lesions in nondominant hemisphere; control group of patients with low back pain	Compared groups on no. of BGT figures recalled from memory and no. of rotations	Dominant and nondominant groups not signif. different, but signif. more rotations than control group	—	—	P	0
Helgert (1985)	DESC	120	Y	60 severely ED children; 60 "normals"—referred but not placed	Compared traditional and digital computer methods of scoring BGT	Interrater reliability for computer, .99+; interrater reliability for traditional, .70s; small but signif. correlations between methods; computer method accurately placed 61.7% of subjects; traditional method accurately placed 70% of subjects	—	(?)	P	1
Hellkamp & Hogan (1985)	EPF	180	Y	Psychiatric patients, organic and nonorganic (functional) etiology	Investigated ability of Hutt BGT scoring system to diff. organic from functional group as a function of IQ	Signif. correlation between IQ and BGT errors for either group; no acceptable percentages of accuracy scores for groups across IQ ranges	M	—	P	2

(continued)

APPENDIX 5.2. (*continued*)

Authors	Type of design	Number of subjects	Control (Y/N)	Population sampled	Variables	Results	Scoring reliability	Sampling	Stats	Generalizability[a]
Hinkle (1983)	EPF	60	Y	30 institutionalized male delinquents, 30 nondelinquents	Compared BGT error scores; tested a cutoff criterion for discriminating delinq. from nondeling. adolescents	Signif. diff. in error scores between groups; cutoff criterion yielded 35% false positives and 47% false negatives; indicated need for further research	—	M	P	1
Holmes & Stephens (1984)	DESC	76	NA	Male and female college students	Investigated amount of edging on BGT, Memory for Design, and DAP	Not a consistent factor; very little edging found; signif. Q indicated *lack of* consistency	NA	—	NP	1
Hutt & Monheit (1985)	EPF	180	Y	Carefully screened normal male students (13–16 yrs. old) and children diagnosed ED	Compared on Hutt adaptation of BGT scoring	Signif. diff. in mean scores; the configuration score for disturbed adolescents signif. differentiated groups	Interrater	—	NP	1
Jernigan (1967)	EPF	779 206 247	N	Patients with central nervous system, psychiatric, physical, and unknown problems	Rotation of BGT figures compared on type of patient, education, direction of rotation	Three separate studies: Rotators were older, had lower IQ, had less education; 45% rotated in clockwise direction	—	—	NP P	2
Johnson (1973)	EPF	50	N	25 psychiatric patients with and 25 without constricted BGT figures, respectively	Constriction defined using less than half of page to complete figures; compared groups on MMPI Depression scores	t test yielded signif. diff.; constriction indicated depression, but low rate of occurrence detracted from its usefulness	NA	—	P	0
Koppitz (1958)	EPF	51	Y	Elem. students (first through fourth grades) divided into good and poor achievement groups (reading, writing, spelling)	Group comparison on 7 of 20 scoring categories that tested signif. on a first sample and cross-validated on second sample	Signif. discrimination in cross-validation group	93% agreement on 14 protocols	—	NP	1
Koppitz (1960)	DESC	1,055	N	School children; 5 to 10½ yrs. old, kindergarten–fourth grade	Blind scoring using Koppitz approach	Normative table with mean scores SDs by age groups and grade	—	R?	NA	2
Koppitz (1962)	EPF	384	Y	103 brain-damaged elem. students; 5–10 yrs. old; 281 normals	Compared groups on Bender scoring system	Signif. more "poor" BGT scores in brain-damaged group ($p < .001$) across ages	—	M	NP	1

Study		N		Sample	Purpose	Reliability			
Lachmann (1960)	EPF	120	Y	40 reading-retarded elem. students; 40 behavior disordered normal readers, 40 controls (no problems); all normal IQ, matched on age	Compared groups on BGT scores (Pascal–Suttell)	—	M	NP	2
McCormick & Brannigan (1984)	DESC	40	NA	Matched ED adolescents 12–17 yrs. old from day treatment and residential centers	Examined ability of emotional indicators on BGT to discriminate behavioral indicators of Devereaux Adolescent Behavior Rating Scale	—	NA	P	1
					Correlations between BGT and Devereaux indicated some signif. correlations for individual signs; overall BGT withdrawal and anxiety signs did not signif. correlate; caution indicated in using BGT to draw implications about behavior				
Moore & Zarske (1984)	DESC	452	Y	150 LD, 189 educationally disadvantaged, 113 nonhandicapped Navajo children; ages 6–11 yrs.	Compared normals to 1974 Koppitz and SCMPA norms for BGT; compared BGT scores across groups by age and sex	—	—	P	1
					Nonhandicapped compared favorably with Koppitz norms and SCMBA norms; nonhandicapped and LD groups showed signif. diff., with nonhandicapped having lower error rates across age and sex				
Mosher & Smith (1965)	EPF	262	Y	142 brain-damaged, hospitalized veterans (BD); 120 nonbrain-damaged controls (NBD)	Compared ability of two BGT scoring systems (Peek–Quast and Hain) in discriminating BD from NBD patients	On 30 protocols, interscorer $r = .84$–$.86$	—	P	1
					Each discriminated statistically, but not at clinically useful level				
Neale & McKay (1985a)	DESC	200	NA	School children 5–7 yrs. old	BGT (Koppitz) errors described; item difficulty analyzed	For three scores, $r = .90$s	R	P	2
					Reported percentage of each error type across figures; interjudge agreement across error categories in low .90s for total error scores (r's ranged from .71 to .98); angulation errors were the most frequent				
Neale & McKay (1985b)	DESC	195	NA	Kindergarten students followed through fourth grade	Explored relationship between kindergarten BGT performance and later reading and writing performance (Neale analysis of reading abilities) and (developed handwriting analysis system)	—	R	P	2
					BGT performance was predictive of overall school achievement; major error categories (e.g., circles for dots, distortion) more predictive than total errors; only predictive of one reading or writing variable (reading comprehension at end of first grade)				

(continued)

APPENDIX 5.2. (*continued*)

Authors	Type of design	Number of subjects	Control (Y/N)	Population sampled	Variables	Results	Scoring reliability	Sampling	Stats	Generalizability[a]
Peek (1953)	EPF	150	Y	75 neuropsychiatric patients who had certain characteristics on BGT Figure 5; 75 randomly selected patients from same population	Compared groups on frequency of list of 40 external characteristics of behavior and personality and complaints	27 variables were signif. diff. between groups	—	—	NP	0
Quast (1961)	EPF	100	N	50 suspected brain-damaged psychiatric patients, 50 ED psychiatric patients; all 10–12 yrs. old	Compared groups on 17 attributes of BGT drawings	10 of 17 signif. differentiated groups; low intercorrelations between these 10 differentiating attributes	—	M?	NP	1
Schulberg & Tolor (1962)	DESC	106	N	15 neurotics; 41 functional psychotics; 15 acute organic psychotics; 45 with character disorder	Wanted to see what connotative meaning psychiatric patients attached to BGT drawings using semantic differential scales	Not much difference by patient type	NA	—	P	0
Story (1960)	EPF	60	Y	Control, white male elem. and second. school teachers; exp., male in-patient alcoholics (n = 30 in each group)	Various characteristics of BGT drawings	Most characteristics showed signif. diff., including more counting of dots, nonintersections, "liquid" responses on Design 6	Interscorer $r = .99$	R	P NP	1
Suczek & Klopfer (1952)	DESC	48	N	Matched college students (male and female)	Subjects asked to free-associate to BGT figures	Compilation of more frequent symbolic associations to each of the figures	Disagreement resolved by discussion	NA	NA	1
Taylor, Kaufman, & Partanio (1984)	DESC	652	NA	Statewide school children, ages 5–11 yrs.	Subjected elements of Koppitz scoring of BGT to multiple regression by age	Variance associated with age for total sample was only 35% (for 9- to 11-yr.-olds, 3%); concluded BGT scores not valid developmental indicator beyond age 8	—	R	P	2
Thomas (1984)	DESC	66	NA	Children with low scores on horse puzzle of WISC-R Object Assembly	Assessed relationship between ratio of horse score and other three Object Assembly puzzles and BGT errors	BGT errors positively correlated to "horse ratio" (.35)	—	—	P	0

Study	Design	N	Cross-val.	Sample	Procedure	Results	Reliability note	Type	P/NP	Factors
Tolor (1957)	DESC	50	N	Matched male and female neuropsychiatric patients (Air Force pop.)	Had patients match Rorschach blots with BGT design that best represented or stood for each blot; rated them on type of response, or quality	Tried to establish associational stimulus value of the BGT figures; found that some produced signif. better associative responses than others	—	NA	NP	0
Tolor (1958)	EPF	54	N	Three groups ($n = 18$ each): Character-behavior-disordered, schizophrenic, organic brain-injured; all matched on IQ and age	Compared groups on ability to reproduce BGT designs from memory after standard testing	Some signif. diff. but not of clinical value	NA	M?	NP	0
Tolor (1960)	DESC	68	N	College undergrads; 41 males, 27 females	Ratings of BGT designs on descriptive semantic differential scales	79 out of 180 χ^2 comparisons of item ratings between pairs of figures were signif.; connotative meanings for each were different; no sex differences	NA	R	NP	2
Trahan & Stricklin (1979)	EPF	93	N	Male and female students, kindergarten through fourth grade	Investigated relation between 15 proposed indicators (emotional) on BGT and acting-out behavior in class as rated by teachers	No signif. correlations	Determined by χ^2 (?)	R?	P NP	2
Wagner & Murray (1969)	EPF	50	Y	25 children with organic brain damage; 25 normal controls	Clinicians (MDs, PhDs, MAs) made diagnoses (brain-damaged or not) based on BGT and design reproduction test	No signif. diff. between professional groups' high degree of correct diagnoses	—	—	NP	1
Wallbrown & Fremont (1980)	DESC	84	NA	Matched reading-disabled children referred from one school district	Examined test-retest reliability of Koppitz BGT scoring (12- to 24-day interval)	Pearson correlation was .83 for total error scores	Judges resolved differences by discussion	NA	P	1
Wiener (1966)	EPF	822	N	822 children from a Johns Hopkins study on prematurity, ages 8–10 yrs.; matched sample (race, sex, SES)	Compared BGT scores to neurological data to see whether BGT could predict minimal brain damage for premature and full-term groups	Some variables were signif.: ability to copy angles and curves, tendency to produce distortions	For 50 protocols, interrater $r = .92$	M	P	2

(continued)

APPENDIX 5.2. (*continued*)

Authors	Type of design	Number of subjects	Control (Y/N)	Population sampled	Variables	Results	Scoring reliability	Sampling	Stats	General-izability[a]
Wright & DeMers (1982)	DESC	86	NA	55 boys, 31 girls; ages 6–11 yrs.; referred for leaning or adjustment problems	Compared VMI and Koppitz scoring of BGT on ability to predict academic achievement (WRAT)	Partialing out variance assoc. with IQ yielded signif. correlations between VMI and WRAT Spelling and BGT and WRAT Reading and Spelling; absolute magnitude was very small; added little to predication beyond measure of general ability (WISC-R)	—	—	P	1
Zolik (1958)	EPF	86	Y	Two groups: delinquents and nondelinquents matched on age and IQ (roughly)	Compared on BGT scored by Pascal–Suttell method	Scores signif. diff. (delinquents higher) on all but Design 8; each item also further analyzed for specific characteristics	—	M?	P	1

Note. EPF, *ex post facto* design; DESC, descriptive "design"; EXP, experimental design; LD, learning-disabled; ED, emotionally disturbed; MH, mentally handicapped; MA, mental age; CA, chronological age; DAP, Draw-A-Person Test; SES, socioeconomic status; MMPI, Minnesota Multiphasic Personality Inventory; SOMPA, System of Multicultural Pluralistic Assessment; WISC-R, Wechsler Intelligence Scale for Children—Revised; VMI, Test of Visual Motor Integration; WRAT, Wide Range Achievement Test.

[a]Generalizability rated on a scale of 2 (good), 1 (fair), or 0 (limited to or none).

Acknowledgment. I gratefully acknowledge the assistance of Bill Carlyon in helping to review the projective drawing literature, and for his precision and dedication in helping to develop the appendices.

REFERENCES

Adler, P. T. (1970). Evaluation of the figure drawing technique: Reliability, factorial structure, and diagnostic usefulness. *Journal of Consulting and Clinical Psychology, 35*, 52–57.

Albee, G. S., & Hamlin, R. M. (1949). An investigation of the reliability and validity of judgments of adjustment inferred from drawings. *Journal of Clinical Psychology, 5*, 389–392.

Anderson, B., & Rallis, K. (1981). Relationship between Bender errors, emotional indicators and performance on Bender recall. *Perceptual and Motor Skills, 53*, 497–498.

Baroff, G. S. (1957). Bender–Gestalt visuo-motor function in mental deficiency. *American Journal of Mental Deficiency, 61*, 753–760.

Batsche, G. M., & Peterson, D. W. (1983). School psychology and projective assessment: A growing incompatibility. *School Psychololgy Review, 12*, 440–445.

Beck, H. S. (1959). A comparison of convulsive organics, non-conclusive organics, and non-organic public school children. *American Journal of Mental Deficiency, 63*, 866–875.

Bender, L. (1938). *A visual motor gestalt test and its clinical use* (American Orthopsychiatric Association Research Monograph No. 3). New York: American Orthopsychiatric Association.

Bensberg, G. (1952). Performance of brain-injured and familial mental defectives on the Bender-Gestalt Test. *Journal of Consulting Psychology, 16*, 61–64.

Berman, S., & Laffal, J. (1953). Body type and figure drawing. *Journal of Clinical Psychology, 9*, 368–370.

Bieliauskas, V. J. (1960). Sexual identification in children's drawings of human figure. *Journal of Clinical Psychology, 16*, 42–44.

Bigler, E. D., & Ehrfurth, J. W. (1981). The continued inappropriate singular use of the Bender Visual Motor Gestalt Test. *Professional Psychology, 12*, 562–569.

Blaha, J., Fawaz, N., & Wallbrown, F. (1979). Information processing components of Koppitz errors on the BVMGT. *Journal of Clinical Psychology, 35*, 784–790.

Billingslea, F. Y. (1948). The Bender–Gestalt: An objective scoring method and validating data. *Journal of Clinical Psychology, 4*, 1–27.

Bodwin, R. F., & Bruck, M. (1960). The adaptation and validation of the Draw-A-Person test as a measure of self concept. *Journal of Clinical Psychology, 16*, 427–429.

Bradfield, R. H. (1964). The predictive validity of children's drawings. *California Journal of Educational Research, 15*, 166–174.

Breen, M. J., & Butler, L. (1983). Applicability of Bender–Gestalt emotional indicators for emotionally disturbed and nonreferred students. *Psychological Reports, 52*, 569–570.

Britain, S. D. (1970). Effect of manipulation of children's affect on their family-drawings. *Journal of Projective Techniques and Personality Assessment, 34*, 234–237.

Buck, N. J. (1948). The H-T-P technique, a qualitative and quantitative method. *Journal of Clinical Psychology, 4*, 317–396.

Buck, J. N. (1970). *The House–Tree–Person Technique: Revised manual.* Los Angeles: Western Psychological Services.

Burns, R. C. (1987). *Kinetic House–Tree–Person Drawings (K-H-T-P): An interpretive manual.* New York: Brunner/Mazel.

Burns, R. C., & Kaufman, S. H. (1970). *Kinetic Family Drawings (K-F-D): An introduction to understanding children through kinetic drawings.* New York: Brunner/Mazel.

Burns, R. C., & Kaufman, S. H. (1972). *Actions, styles, and symbols in Kinetic Family Drawings (K-F-D).* New York: Brunner/ Mazel.

Burton, A., & Sjoberg, B. (1964). The diagnostic validity of human figure drawings in schizophrenia. *Journal of Psychology, 57*, 3–18.

Byrd, E. (1956). The clinical validity of the Bender–Gestalt Test with children: A developmental comparison of children in need of psychotherapy and children judged well-adjusted. *Journal of Projective Techniques, 20*, 127–136.

Campbell, D. T., & Fiske, D. W. (1959). Convergent and discriminant validation by the multitrait–multimethod matrix. *Psychological Bulletin, 56*, 81–105.

Carlson, K., Quinlan, D., Tucker, G., & Harrow, M. (1973). Body disturbance and sexual elaboration factors in figure drawings of schizophrenic patients. *Journal of Personality Assessment, 37*, 56–63.

Cassell, R. H., Johnson, A. P., & Burns, W. H. (1958). Examiner, ego defense, and the H-T-P test. *Journal of Clinical Psychology, 14*, 157–160.

Chase, J. M. (1941). A study of the drawings of a male figure made by schizophrenic patients and normal subjects. *Character and Personality, 9*, 208–217.

Chorost, S., Spivack, G., & Levine, M. (1959). Bender–Gestalt rotations and EEG abnormalities in children. *Journal of Consulting Psychology, 23*, 559.

Craddick, R. A. (1963). The self-image in the Draw-A-Person Test and self-portrait drawings. *Journal of Projective Techniques, 27*, 288–291.

Craddick, R. A. (1964). Size of drawings-of-a-person as a function of simulating "psychosis." *Perceptual and Motor Skills, 18*, 308.

Craddick, R. A., & Leipold, W. D. (1968). Note on the height of Draw-A-Person figures by male alcoholics. *Journal of Projective Techniques and Personality Assessment, 323*, 486.

Cummings, J. A. (1986). Projective drawings. In H. M. Knoff (Ed.), *The assessment of child and adolescent personality* (pp. 199–244). New York: Guilford Press.

Curnutt, R. H. (1953). The use of the Bender–Gestalt with an alcoholic and non-alcoholic population. *Journal of Clinical Psychology, 9*, 287–290.

Datta, L., & Drake, A. (1968). Examiner sex and sexual differentiation in preschool children's figure drawings. *Journal of Projective Techniques and Personality Assessment, 32*, 397–399.

Delatte, J. G. (1985). Significance of femininity in human figure drawings of girls. *Psychological Reports, 56*, 165–166.

Delatte, J. G., & Hendrickson, N. J. (1982). Human figure drawing size as a measure of self-esteem. *Journal of Personality Assessment, 46*, 603–606.

DeMartino, M. F. (1954). Human figure drawings by mentally retarded males. *Journal of Clinical Psychology, 10*, 241–244.

Dunleavy, R. A., Hansen, J. L., & Szasz, C. W. (1981). Early kindergarten identification of academically not-ready children by use of human figure drawing developmental score. *Psychology in the Schools, 18*, 35–38.

Eno, L., & Deichmann, J. (1980). A review of the Bender–Gestalt Test as a screening instrument for brain damage with school-aged children of normal intelligence since 1970. *Journal of Special Education, 14*, 37–45.

Exner, J. E. (1962). A comparison of the human figure drawings of psychoneurotics, character disturbances, normals, and subjects experiencing experimentally-induced fear. *Journal of Projective Techniques, 26*, 392–397.

Fabian, A. A. (1945). Vertical rotation in visual–motor performance: Its relationship to reading reversals. *Journal of Educational Psychology, 36*, 129–154.

Fellows, R., & Cerbus, G. (1969). HTP and DCT indicators of sexual identification in children. *Journal of Projective Techniques and Personality Assessment, 33*, 376–379.

Fiedler, F. E., & Siegel, S. M. (1949). The Free Drawing Test as a predictor of non-improvement in psychotherapy. *Journal of Clinical Psychology, 5*, 386–389.

Fisher, G. M. (1961). Nudity in human figure drawings. *Journal of Clinical Psychology, 17*, 307–308.

Fisher, G. (1968). Human figure drawing indices of sexual maladjustment in male felons. *Journal of Projective Techniques and Personality Assessment, 32*, 81.

Fuller, G. B., & Goh, D. S. (1983). Current practices in the assessment of personality and behavior by school psychologists. *School Psychology Review, 12*, 244–249.

Fuller, J. B., & Chagnon, T. (1962). Factors influencing rotation in the Bender–Gestalt performance of children. *Journal of Projective Techniques, 26*, 36–46.

Gavales, D., & Millon, T. (1960). Comparison of reproduction and recall size deviations in the Bender–Gestalt as measures of anxiety. *Journal of Clinical Psychology, 16*, 278–280.

Gobetz, W. (1953). A quantification, standardization, and validation of the Bender–Gestalt Test on normal and neurotic adults. *Psychological Monographs, 67*(356).

Goldberg, F. H. (1956–1957). The performance of schizophrenic, retarded, and normal children on the Bender–Gestalt Test. *American Journal of Mental Deficiency, 61*, 548–555.

Goldfried, M. R., & Ingling, J. (1964). The connotative and symbolic meaning of the Bender–Gestalt. *Journal of Projective Techniques, 28*, 185–191.

Goldstein, A. P., & Rawn, M. L. (1957). The validity of interpretive signs of aggression in the drawing of the human figure. *Journal of Clinical Psychology, 13*, 169–171.

Goldstein, H. S., & Faterson, H. F. (1969). Shading as an index of anxiety in figure drawings. *Journal of*

Projective Techniques and Personality Assessment, 33, 454–456.

Goodenough, F. L. (1926). *Measurement of intelligence by drawings*. New York: Harcourt, Brace & World.

Goodenough, F. L. (1931). Children's drawings. In C. Murchison (Ed.), *A handbook of child psychology* (pp. 480–514). Worcester, MA: University Press.

Goodman, M., & Kotkov, B. (1953). Prediction of trait ranks from Draw-A-Person measurements of obese and non-obese women. *Journal of Clinical Psychology, 9*, 365–367.

Goodstein, L. D., Spielberger, C. D., Williams, J. E., & Dahlstrom W. G. (1955). The effects of serial position and design difficulty on recall of the Bender–Gestalt Test designs. *Journal of Consulting Psychology, 19*, 230–234.

Graham, S. R. (1956). A study of reliability in human figure drawings. *Journal of Projective Techniques, 20*, 385–386.

Granick, S., & Smith, L. J. (1953). Sex sequence in the Draw-A-Person Test and its relation to the MMPI Masculinity-Femininity scale. *Journal of Consulting Psychology, 17*, 71–73.

Gravitz, M. A. (1966). Normal adult differentiation patterns on the figure drawing test. *Journal of Projective Techniques and Personality Assessment, 30*, 471–473.

Gravitz, M. A. (1967). Marital status and figure drawing choice in normal adults. *Journal of Projective Techniques and Personality Assessment, 31*, 86–87.

Gravitz, M. A. (1968). The height of normal adult figure drawings. *Journal of Clinical Psychology, 24*, 75.

Gravitz, M. A. (1969a). Direction of psychosexual interest and figure drawing choice. *Journal of Clinical Psychology, 25*, 311.

Gravitz, M. A. (1969b). Marital status and figure drawing choice in normal older Americans. *Journal of Social Psychology, 77*, 143–144.

Gravitz, M. A. (1971). Nudity and amount of clothing in the figure drawings of normal adults. *Journal of Genetic Psychology, 118*, 141–145.

Gray, D. M., & Pepitone, A. (1964). Effect of self-esteem on drawings of the human figure. *Journal of Consulting Psychology, 28*, 452–455.

Green, R., Fuller, M., & Rutley, B. (1972). It-scale for children and Draw-A-Person Test: 30 feminine vs. 25 masculine boys. *Journal of Personality Assessment, 36*, 349–352.

Griffith, A. V., & Peyman, D. A. R. (1959). Eye-ear emphasis in the DAP as indicating ideas of reference. *Journal of Consulting Psychology, 23*, 560.

Griffith, R. M., & Taylor, V. H. (1960). Incidence of Bender–Gestalt figure rotations. *Journal of Consulting Psychology, 24*, 189–190.

Griffith, R. M., & Taylor, V. H. (1961). Bender–Gestalt figure rotations: A stimulus factor. *Journal of Consulting Psychology, 25*, 89–90.

Guertin, W. (1952). A factor analysis of the Bender–Gestalt tests of mental patients. *Journal of Clinical Psychology, 8*, 362–367.

Guertin, W. (1954a). A factor analysis of curvilinear distortions on the Bender–Gestalt. *Journal of Clinical Psychology, 10*, 12–17.

Guertin, W. (1954b). A transposed factor analysis of schizophrenic performance on the Bender–Gestalt. *Journal of Clinical Psychology, 10*, 225–228.

Guertin, W. (1954c). A transposed analysis of the Bender–Gestalts of brain disease cases. *Journal of Clinical Psychology, 10,* 366–369.

Guertin, W. (1955). A transposed analysis of the Bender–Gestalts of paranoid schizophrenics. *Journal of Clinical Psychology, 11,* 73–76.

Hain, J. D. (1964). The Bender–Gestalt Test: A scoring method for identifying brain damage. *Journal of Consulting Psychology, 28,* 34–40.

Halpin, V. (1955). Rotation errors made by brain injured and familial children on two visual motor tests. *American Journal of Mental Deficiency, 59,* 485–489.

Hamilton, L. (1984). Human figure drawings as measures of self-concept development in bilingual children. *Journal of Instructional Psychology, 11,* 28–36.

Hammer, E. F. (1953a). An investigation of sexual symbolism: A study of H-T-P's of eugenically sterilized subjects. *Journal of Projective Techniques, 17,* 401–413.

Hammer, E. F. (1953b). Negro and white children's personality adjustment as revealed by a comparison of their drawings (H-T-P). *Journal of Clinical Psychology, 9,* 7–10.

Hammer, E. F. (1954a). A comparison of H-T-P's of rapists and pedophiles. *Journal of Projective Techniques, 18,* 346–354.

Hammer, E. F. (1954b). An experimental study of symbolism on the Bender–Gestalt. *Journal of Projective Techniques, 18,* 335–345.

Hammer, E. F. (Ed.). (1958). *The clinical application of projective drawings.* Springfield, IL: Charles C. Thomas.

Hammer, E. F. (1969). DAP: Back against the wall? *Journal of Consulting and Clinical Psychology, 33,* 151–156.

Hammer, E. F. (1980). *The clinical application of projective drawings.* Springfield, IL: Charles C Thomas.

Handler, L. (1985). The clinical use of the Draw-A-Person Test (DAP). In C. S. Newmark (Ed), *Major psychological assessment instruments* (pp. 165–216). Boston: Allyn & Bacon.

Handler, L., & Reyher, J. (1964). The effects of stress on the Draw-a-Person Test. *Journal of Consulting Psychology, 28,* 259–264.

Handler, L., & Reyher, J. (1966). Relationship between GSR and anxiety in projective drawings. *Journal of Consulting Psychology, 30,* 60–67.

Hanvik, L. J., & Andersen, A. L. (1950). The effect of focal brain lesions on recall and on the production of rotations in the Bender–Gestalt Test. *Journal of Consulting Psychology, 14,* 197–198.

Harris, D. B. (1963). *Children's drawings as a measure of intellectual maturity.* New York: Harcourt, Brace & World.

Heberlein, M., & Marcuse, F. L. (1963). Personality variables in the DAP. *Journal of Consulting Psychology, 27,* 461.

Helgert, L. D. (1985). A graphic analysis Bender–Gestalt Test. *Journal of Clinical Psychology, 41,* 505–511.

Hellkamp, D. T., & Hogan, M. E. (1985). Differentiation of organics from functional psychiatric patients across various IQ ranges using the Bender–Gestalt and Hutt Scoring System. *Journal of Clinical Psychology, 41,* 259–264.

Hiler, E. W., & Nesvig, D. (1965). An evaluation of criteria used by clinicians to infer pathology from figure drawings. *Journal of Consulting Psychology, 29,* 520–529.

Hinkle, J. A. (1983). Comparison of reproduction on the Bender–Gestalt and Memory-for-Design for delinquents and non-delinquents. *Perceptual and Motor Skills, 57,* 1070.

Holmes, C. B., & Stephens, C. L. (1984). Consistency of edging on the Bender–Gestalt, Memory-for-Design, and Draw-a-Person Test. *Journal of Psychology, 117,* 269–271.

Holzberg, J. D., & Wexler, M. (1950). The validity of human form drawings as a measure of personality deviation. *Journal of Projective Techniques, 14,* 343–361.

Hoyt, T. E., & Baron, M. R. (1959). Anxiety indices in same-sex drawings of psychiatric patients with high and low MAS scores. *Journal of Consulting Psychology, 23,* 448–452.

Hulse, W. C. (1951). The emotionally disturbed child draws his family. *Quarterly Journal of Child Behavior, 3,* 152–174.

Hulse, W. C. (1952). Child conflict expressed through family drawings. *Quarterly Journal of Child Behavior, 16,* 66–79.

Hutt, M. L., & Monheit, S. (1985). Effectiveness of the Hutt Adaptation of the Bender–Gestalt Test configuration scale in differentiating emotionally disturbed adolescents. *Psychological Reports, 56,* 439–443.

Jensen, K. W. (1958). Sex of the administrator as a variable affecting draw-a-person. *Perceptual and Motor Skills, 60,* 72–74.

Jernigan, A. J. (1967). Rotation style on the Bender–Gestalt Test. *Journal of Clinical Psychology, 23,* 176–179.

Johnson, J. H. (1971). Upper left hand placement of human figure drawings as an indicator of anxiety. *Journal of Personality Assessment, 35,* 336–337.

Johnson, J. H. (1973). Bender–Gestalt constriction as an indicator of depression in psychotic patients. *Journal of Personality Assessment, 37,* 53–55.

Jolles, I. (1952a). A study on the validity of some hypotheses for the qualitative interpretation of the H-T-P for children of elementary school age: I. Sexual identification. *Journal of Clinical Psychology, 8,* 113–118.

Jolles, I. (1952b). A study of the validity of some hypotheses for the qualitative interpretation of the H-T-P for children of elementary school age: II. The "phallic tree" as an indicator of psychosexual conflict. *Journal of Clinical Psychology, 8,* 245–255.

Jolles, I., & Beck, H. S. (1953). A study of the validity of some hypotheses for the qualitative interpretation of the H-T-P for children of elementary school age: IV. Vertical placement. *Journal of Clinical Psychology, 9,* 164–167.

Jordan, S. (1970). Projective drawings in a cerebellar disorder due to chicken pox encephalitis. *Journal of Projective Techniques and Personality Assessment, 34,* 256–258.

Judson, A. J., & MacCasland, B. (1960). A note on the influence of the season on tree drawings. *Journal of Clinical Psychology, 16,* 171–173.

Kamano, D. K. (1960). An investigation on the meaning of human figure drawing. *Journal of Clinical Psychology, 16,* 429–430.

Knoff, H. M. (1983). Justifying projective/personality

assessment in school psychology: A response to Batsche and Peterson. *School Psychology Review, 12,* 446–451.

Knoff, H. M. (Ed.). (1986). *The assessment of child and adolescent personality*. New York: Guilford Press.

Knoff, H. M., & Prout, H. T. (1985). *The Kinetic Drawing System: Family and School*. Los Angeles: Western Psychological Services.

Koppitz, E. M. (1958). The Bender–Gestalt Test and learning disturbances in young children. *Journal of Clinical Psychology, 14,* 292–295.

Koppitz, E. M. (1960). The Bender–Gestalt Test for children: A normative study. *Journal of Clinical Psychology, 16,* 432–435.

Koppitz, E. M. (1962). Diagnosing brain damage in young children with the Bender–Gestalt Test. *Journal of Consulting Psychology, 26,* 541–545.

Koppitz, E. M. (1963). *The Bender–Gestalt Test for young children*. New York: Grune & Stratton.

Koppitz, E. M. (1966a). Emotional indicators on human figure drawings of children: A validation study. *Journal of Clinical Psychology, 22,* 313–315.

Koppitz, E. M. (1966b). Emotional indicators on human figure drawings and school achievement of first and second graders. *Journal of Clinical Psychology, 22,* 481–483.

Koppitz, E. M. (1966c). Emotional indicators on human figure drawings of shy and aggressive children. *Journal of Clinical Psychology, 22,* 466–469.

Koppitz, E. M. (1968). *Psychological evaluation of children's human figure drawings*. New York: Grune & Stratton.

Koppitz, E. M. (1975). *The Bender–Gestalt Test for young children: Vol. 2. Research and application 1963–1973*. New York: Grune & Stratton.

Koppitz, E. M. (1984). *Psychological evaluation of human figure drawings by middle school pupils*. Orlando, FL: Grune & Stratton.

Kotkov, V., & Goodman, M. (1953). Draw-A-Person tests of obese women. *Journal of Clinical Psychology, 9,* 362–364.

Kurtzberg, R., Cavior, N., & Lipton, D. (1966). Sex drawn first and sex drawn larger by opiate addict and non-addict inmates on the Draw-A-Person Test. *Journal of Projective Techniques and Personality Assessment, 30,* 55–58.

Lachmann, F. M. (1960). Perceptual–motor development in children retarded in reading ability. *Journal of Consulting Psychology, 24,* 427–431.

Laird, J. (1962). A comparison of male normals, psychiatric patients and alcoholics for sex drawn first. *Journal of Clinical Psychology, 18,* 302.

Lakin, M. (1956). Certain formal characteristics of human figure drawings by institutionalized aged and by normal children. *Journal of Consulting Psychology, 20,* 471–474.

Lehner, G. F., & Gunderson, E. K. (1948). Height relationships in DAP test. *Journal of Personality, 17,* 199–209.

Lewinsohn, P. M. (1964). Relationship between height of figure drawings and depression in psychiatric patients. *Journal of Consulting Psychology, 28,* 380–381.

Lubin, B., Larsen, R. M., & Matarazzo, J. D. (1984). Patterns of psychological test usage in the United States: 1935–1982. *American Psychologist, 39,* 451–454.

Lyons, J. (1955). The scar on the H-T-P tree. *Journal of Clinical Psychology, 11,* 267–270.

Mabry, M. (1964). Serial projective drawings in a patient with a malignant brain tumor. *Journal of Projective Techniques, 28,* 206–209.

Machover, K. (1949). *Personality projection in the drawing of the human figure*. Springfield, IL: Charles C Thomas.

Marzolf, S. S., & Kirchner, J. H. (1970). Characteristics of House–Tree–Person drawings by college men and women. *Journal of Projective Techniques and Personality Assessment, 34,* 138–145.

Marzolf, S. S., & Kirchner, J. H. (1972). House–Tree–Person drawings and personality traits. *Journal of Personality Assessment, 36,* 148–165.

McCormick, T. T., & Brannigan, G. G. (1984). Bender–Gestalt signs as indicants of anxiety, withdrawal, and acting-out behavior in adolescents. *Journal of Psychology, 118,* 71–74.

McHugh, A. (1963). Sexual identification, size, and associations in children's figure drawings. *Journal of Clinical Psychology, 19,* 381–382.

McHugh, A. (1966). Children's figure drawings in neurotic and conduct disturbances. *Journal of Clinical Psychology, 22,* 219–221.

McPhee, J. P., & Wegner, K. W. (1976). Kinetic Family Drawing styles and emotionally disturbed childhood behavior. *Journal of Personality Assessment, 40,* 487–491.

Melikian, L. H., & Wahab, A. Z. (1969). First-drawn picture: A cross-culture investigation of the DAP. *Journal of Projective Techniques and Personality Assessment, 33,* 539–541.

Meyer, B. C., Brown, F., & Levine, A. (1955). Observations on the House–Tree–Person drawing test before and after surgery. *Psychosomatic Medicine, 17,* 428–454.

Michal-Smith, H. (1953). The identification of pathological cerebral function through the H-T-P technique. *Journal of Clinical Psychology, 9,* 293–295.

Modell, A. H. (1951). Changes in human figure drawings by patients who recover from regressed states. *American Journal of Orthopsychiatry, 21,* 584–596.

Modell, A. H., & Potter, H. W. (1949). Human figure drawing of patients with arterial hypertension, peptic ulcer, and bronchial asthma. *Psychosomatic Medicine, 11,* 282–292.

Mogar, R. E. (1962). Anxiety indices in human figure drawings. *Journal of Consulting Psychology, 26,* 108.

Moll, R. P. (1962). Further evidence of seasonal influences on tree drawings. *Journal of Clinical Psychology, 18,* 109.

Moore, C. L., & Zarske, J. A. (1984). Comparison of Native American Navajo Bender–Gestalt performance with Koppitz and SOMPA norms. *Psychology in the Schools, 21,* 148–153.

Mosher, D. L., & Smith, J. P. (1965). The usefulness of two scoring systems for the Bender–Gestalt Test for identifying brain damage. *Journal of Consulting Psychology, 29,* 530–536.

Mostkoff, D. L., & Lazarus, P. J. (1983). The Kinetic Family Drawing: The reliability of an objective scoring system. *Psychology in the Schools, 20,* 16–20.

Naglieri, J. A. (1987). *Draw-A-Person: A quantitative scoring system*. San Antonio, TX: Psychological Corporation.

Nathan, S. (1973). Body image in chronically obese children as reflected in figure drawings. *Journal of Personality Assessment, 37,* 456–463.

Neale, M. D., & McKay, M. F. (1985a). Scoring the Bender–Gestalt Test using the Koppitz Developmental System: Interrater reliability, item difficulty, and scoring implications. *Perceptual and Motor Skills, 60,* 627–636.

Neale, M. D., & McKay, M. F. (1985b). Predicting early school achievement in reading and handwriting using major "error" categories from the Bender–Gestalt Test for young children. *Perceptual and Motor Skills, 60,* 647–654.

Oas, P. (1984). Validity of the Draw-A-Person and Bender–Gestalt Test as measures of impulsivity with adolescents. *Journal of Consulting and Clinical Psychology, 52,* 1011–1019.

Ogdon, D. P. (1977). *Psychodiagnostics and personality assessment: A handbook* (2nd ed.). Los Angeles: Western Psychological Services.

Ogdon, D. P. (1982). *Handbook of psychological signs, symptoms, and syndromes.* Los Angeles: Western Psychological Services.

Ottenbacher, K., Haley, D., Abbott, C., & Watson, P. J. (1984). Human figure drawing ability and vestibular processing dysfunction in learning disabled children. *Journal of Clinical Psychology, 40,* 1084–1088.

Paine, P., Alves, E., & Tubino, P. (1985). Size of human figure drawing and Goodenough–Harris scores of pediatric-oncology patients: A pilot study. *Perceptual and Motor Skills, 60,* 911–914.

Peek, R. M. (1953). Directionality of lines in the Bender–Gestalt Test. *Journal of Consulting Psychology, 17,* 213–216.

Pollitt, E., Hirsch, S., & Money, J. (1964). Priapism, impotence and human figure drawing. *Journal of Nervous and Mental Disease, 139,* 161–168.

Prout, H. T. (1983). School psychologists and social-emotional assessment techniques: Patterns in training and use. *School Psychology Review, 12,* 35–38.

Prout, H. T., & Celmer, D. S. (1984). A validity study of the Kinetic School Drawing technique. *Psychology in the Schools, 21,* 176–180.

Prout, H. T., & Phillips, P. D. (1974). A clinical note: The Kinetic School Drawing. *Psychology in the Schools, 11,* 303–306.

Quast, W. (1961). The Bender–Gestalt: A clinical study of children's records. *Journal of Consulting Psychology, 25,* 405–408.

Reznikoff, M., & Tomblen, D. (1956). The use of human figure drawings in the diagnosis of organic pathology. *Journal of Consulting Psychology, 20,* 467–470.

Rosen, A., & Boe, E. E. (1968). Frequency of nude figure drawings. *Journal of Projective Techniques and Personality Assessment, 32,* 483–485.

Saracho, O. N. (1984). The Goodenough–Harris drawing test as a measure of field-dependence/independence. *Perceptual and Motor Skills, 59,* 887–892.

Sarbaugh, M. E. (1983). Kinetic Drawing-School (KS-D) technique. *Illinois School Psychologists' Association Monograph Series, 1,* 1–70.

Sattler, J. M. (1987). *Assessment of children's intelligence and special abilities* (3rd ed.). San Diego, CA: Sattler Associates.

Schildkraut, M., Shenker, I., & Sonnenblick, M. (1972). *Human figure drawings in adolescence.* New York: Bruner/Mazel.

Schubert, D. S. P. (1969). Decrease of rated adjustment on repeat DAP tests apparently due to lower motivation. *Journal of Projective Techniques and Personality Assessment, 33,* 34.

Schulberg, H., & Tolor, A. (1962). The "meaning" of the Bender–Gestalt Test designs to psychiatric patients. *Journal of Projective Techniques, 26,* 455–461.

Sobel, H., & Sobel, W. (1976). Discriminating adolescent male delinquents through the use of Kinetic Family Drawings. *Journal of Personality Assessment, 40,* 91–94.

Story, R. I. (1960). The revised Bender–Gestalt and male alcoholics. *Journal of Projective Techniques, 24,* 186–193.

Strumpfer, D. J. W. (1963). The relation of Draw-A-Person test variables to age and chronicity in psychotic groups. *Journal of Clinical Psychology, 19,* 208–211.

Suczek, R. F., & Klopfer, W. G. (1952). Interpretation of the Bender–Gestalt Test: The associative value of the figures. *American Journal of Orthopsychiatry, 22,* 62–75.

Taylor, R. L., Kaufman, D., & Partanio, A. (1984). The Koppitz developmental scoring system for the Bender–Gestalt: Is it developmental? *Psychology in the Schools, 21,* 425–428.

Thomas, A. D. (1984). Bender scores and the horse as a distinct item on Object Assembly on the WISC. *Perceptual and Motor Skills, 59,* 103–106.

Tolor, A. (1957). Structural properties of Bender–Gestalt Test associations. *Journal of Clinical Psychology, 13,* 176–178.

Tolor, A. (1958). Further studies on the Bender–Gestalt Test and the Digit-Span test as measures of recall. *Journal of Clinical Psychology, 14,* 14–18.

Tolor, A. (1960). The "meaning" of the Bender–Gestalt Test designs: A study in the use of the semantic differential. *Journal of Projective Techniques, 24,* 433–438.

Tolor, A., & Brannigan, G. G. (1980). *Research and clinical applications of the Bender–Gestalt Test.* Springfield, IL: Charles C Thomas.

Trahan, D., & Stricklin, A. (1979). Bender–Gestalt emotional indicators and acting–out behavior in young children. *Journal of Personality Assessment, 43,* 365–375.

Vane, J., & Eisen, V. (1962). The Goodenough Draw-A-Man Test and signs of maladjustment in kindergarten children. *Journal of Clinical Psychology, 18,* 276–279.

Vroegh, K. (1970). Lack of sex-role differentiation in preschoolers' figure drawings. *Journal of Projective Techniques and Personality Assessment, 34,* 38–40.

Wadsworth, B. J. (1989). *Piaget's theory of cognitive and affective development* (4th ed.). New York: Longman.

Wagner, E. E., & Murray, A. Y. (1969). Bender–Gestalts of organic children: Accuracy of clinical judgment. *Journal of Projective Techniques and Personality Assessment, 33,* 240–242.

Wallbrown, F. H., & Fremont, T. (1980). The stability of Koppitz scores on the Bender–Gestalt for reading disabled children. *Psychology in the Schools, 17,* 181–184.

Weider, A., & Noller, P. (1950). Objective studies of children's drawings of human figures: I. Sex awareness and socio-economic level. *Journal of Clinical Psychology, 6,* 319–325.

Weider, A., & Noller, P. (1953). Objective studies of children's drawings of human figures: II. Sex, age, intelligence. *Journal of Clinical Psychology, 9,* 20–23.

Wiener, G. (1966). The Bender–Gestalt Test as a predictor of minimal neurologic deficit in children eight to ten years of age. *Journal of Nervous and Mental Disease, 143,* 275–280.

Wildman, R. W. (1963). The relationship between knee and arm joints on human figure drawings and paranoid trends. *Journal of Clinical Psychology, 19,* 460–461.

Wisotsky, M. (1959). A note on the order of figure drawing among incarcerated alcoholics. *Journal of Clinical Psychology, 15,* 65.

Woods, W. A., & Cook, W. E. (1954). Proficiency in drawing and placement of hands in drawings of the human figure. *Journal of Consulting Psychology, 18,* 119–121.

Wright, D., & DeMers, S. T. (1982). Comparison of the relationship between two measures of visual–motor coordination and academic achievement. *Psychology in the Schools, 19,* 473–477.

Wysocki, B. A., & Whitney, E. (1965). Body image of crippled children as seen in Draw-A-Person test behavior. *Perceptual and Motor Skills, 21,* 499–504.

Yates, A., Beutler, L. E., & Crago, M. (1985). Drawings by child victims of incest. *Child Abuse and Neglect, 9,* 183–189.

Zolik, E. S. (1958). A comparison of the Bender–Gestalt reproductions of delinquents and non-delinquents. *Journal of Clinical Psychology, 14,* 24–26.

6

Using the Sentence Completion to Assess Emotional Disturbance

RUTH ADOLF HAAK
Balcones Special Services Cooperative

The sentence completion technique is over half a century old (Payne, 1928) and is a psychological procedure whose administration is almost standard in the practice of clinically oriented psychologists. Goh and Fuller (1983), for example, in a recent survey of the practices of school psychologists, found that the psychologists they surveyed used sentence completion as one of three main approaches to the assessment of personality in school children. Yet there is little uniformity in the types of sentence completion instruments that are available and little systematic research to support the use of most of them. Like most projective or semiprojective instruments, sentence completions suffer from a current lack of scientific popularity and investigation (e.g., see Pruitt, Smith, Thelen, & Lubin, 1985).

Nevertheless, as indicated by both its popular use in school psychology and its general usage level in all of assessment (Lubin, Larsen, & Matarazzo, 1984), those who use the sentence completion consider it an efficient and productive instrument. Like Jenkins and Gowdey (1981), sentence completion users find that the technique provides a "window" into the mind of the client, which allows the assessor both to explain and to predict behavior (Hart, 1986). Sentence completion information with children also provides strong evidence of their intellectual potential and functioning; their maturity and developmental levels; their major affective sources and identifications; their immobilizing conflicts, fears, and emotions; and, most importantly, their unique organization of experiences, attitudes, and action propensities. Sentence completion historically has been viewed as capable of contributing to the major decisions that must be made about children (see, for example, Malpass, 1953). These include the decisions that often must be made in schools today as to whether children are emotionally disturbed and, if so, what the major dimensions of the disturbance might be.

BRIEF HISTORY AND DISCUSSION OF THE TECHNIQUE

The sentence completion technique grew out of one of the oldest approaches in psychological assessment, the word association technique (Forer, 1960). The use of a partial sentence stem to stimulate the verbal production of a client obviously provides more direction and focus than the use of mere words themselves. A. F. Payne (1928) devised the first sentence completion instrument to overcome the limitations of simple word association, which were primarily the cultural and structural biases being experienced with word association procedures. Although these same biases also affect the sentence completion technique, the sentence completion is far more capable of providing a proper degree of set (or control) to responses that are elicited.

A review of the literature regarding the sentence completion technique shows that it has been, and still is, primarily used to assess attitudes and degree of adjustment to specific situations, conditions, and settings. (Though a complete review of the literature over time is not an intention of this chapter, examples of the statement above can be seen in Agesen, Brun, & Skovgaard, 1984; Cruikshank, 1951, 1952; Efron, 1960; Feldhusen, Thurstone, & Benning, 1966; Graham, Charwat, Honig, & Weltz, 1951; Hanfmann & Getzels, 1953; Irvin, 1967; Kimball, 1952; Kinzie & Zuniver, 1968; Kozmar, 1975; Mosher & Mosher, 1967; Peck & McGuire, 1959; Sanford, Adkins, Miller, & Cobb, 1943; Takala & Pitkanen, 1963; Wilson, 1949.) The sentence completion is used in many different countries, including Finland, Czechoslovakia, Germany, Denmark, India, Taiwan, Japan, and others. Purposes for the various sentence completions range from its major use as a measurement of adjustment in certain settings, including school adjustment, to effects of conditions upon performance, effects of interventions upon mental health, and the measurement of lasting effects of trauma over time. The use of the sentence completion with school populations has been a popular worldwide use of the instrument.

A number of forms of the sentence completion technique are in use today. One that has recently been developed in the United States for use in evaluating emotional disturbance in school-age children, the Hart Sentence Completion Test (Hart, 1986), has an unusual degree of psychometric sophistication. Hart feels that the measure is an "effective social–emotional screening instrument" that has the ability both to predict behavior and to suggest appropriate educational intervention strategies.

No matter what the setting in which the sentence completion is to be used, however, it is clear that the appeal of this technique has always been that it can provide a window into the mind of the client. The examiner wishes to know what the client thinks about certain situations, how he or she feels about these situations, and what he or she is likely to do about these situation. Some investigators feel that the sentence completion instrument, as such, functions somewhat like a structured interview (Dean, 1984; Hart, Kehle, & Davies, 1984; Knoff, 1983).

The very clinical nature of the instrument concerns many psychologists. The goal of providing more reliable and common methods of interpreting sentence completions, other than individual and clinical interpretation, has been an elusive goal for a number of researchers. Nothing uniform or highly satisfactory has been achieved in this effort. Most investigators eventually resort to a system of codification that depends upon the assigning of values to the sentence completion stems, such as "positive," "neutral," or "negative." (Examples of this approach over the years can be found in Baker, 1988; Costin & Eiserer, 1949; and Harris & Tseng, 1957.) Other approaches to codifying sentence completions include systems based upon theoretical conceptualizations, such as Murray's system of needs (Rohde, 1946); and special scoring for variable of concern, a very common procedure (e.g., prejudice, Hanfmann & Getzels 1953; violence, Jenkins & Gowdey, 1981).

The very complexity of sentence completions serves as a challenge to many investigators to devise scoring systems to reduce that complexity. Veldman, Menaker, and Peck (1968) attempted to solve the scoring–interpretation problem for one sentence completion form by reducing the response possibilities for each stem to one word. Later, we (Peck & Haak, 1973) attempted to convert the free responses of over 600 normal 10- and 14-year-old children to a classification system of responses that reduced the open-ended possibilities of the sentence completion to a multiple-choice response format. This process has also been used by others (Stahl, Grigsby, & Gulati, 1985). Such attempts to impose a scoring system upon the verbal responses to sentence completion invariably will verge over into norm generating. Though reliability and norming are separate psychometric functions, they can become completely enmeshed when psychometrically applied to the sentence completion format.

The problem with all of these standardization efforts is the amount of destruction they wreak on the essential nature of the sentence completion instrument. All such approaches result in a huge loss of the rich and complex information that is obtained by using the sentence completion format in the first place. This opinion seems supported by Baker's (1988) recent finding that certain positive factors that emerge from the Haak Sentence Completion (Haak, 1973b) after its content is scored by the negative–neutral–positive system can predict a judgment of nonemotional disturbance in school-age children; however, no factor from the Haak instrument can predict a judgment of emotional disturbance. The latter judgment, of course, is highly complex, must be made in an arbitrary fashion upon data that are essentially continuous, and is determined by agency criteria rather than categories of psychological conditions. It is precisely the unreduced complexity of the sentence completion itself that assists in making such a complex determination.

If a sentence completion is to be standardized, it is suggested that there be two levels of analysis. One would be the level of standard information—a screening level at best. This would provide some useful information regarding whatever major dimensions of concern the sentence completion is constructed to assess, particularly regarding levels of disturbance. This first level of information could also serve as a double-check on the clinician's basic perceptions regarding the major qualities of the instrument. The second level of analysis of the sentence completion should remain what it is (in fact, should be greatly improved)—that is, the clinical level of interpretation, which utilizes the wealth of information that the sentence completion can provide. If one is only interested in standardized information, there is no need to use a sentence completion, as there are far more efficient and satisfactory methods of obtaining such information.

Norming the sentence completion responses is another matter altogether. The experienced clinician, of course, has such norms, but they reside only within his or her own head and are not communicated to others, making them of limited value. There are ways to study "norms" for the sentence completion without so seriously truncating the information the format provides as to impose the positive–neutral–negative judgment system upon the data, though this system may also be involved. Our initial attempt grouped the most common responses to sentence stems. This approach resulted in some surprising clinical results in normal children aged 10 and 14, instructive in and of themselves: For example, 75% would problem-solve if they saw others doing well in school; 50% would ask for assistance with difficult work, attempt to resolve anger from a friend, or comply with a request; and 33% would comply with the need to perform something difficult, physically attack a class bully, or withdraw from parental anger. Such "norms" are useful, certainly in clinical interpretation. After all, one can profit from realizing that if only 50% of the normal children tested would comply with a request, 50% could hardly be passive–aggressive. Such a line of investigation shows that the absence of common positive responses that are often expected in the testing of children does not automatically justify an inference of pathology, at least not without further support. Unfortunately, this attempt at norming and most others have not been pursued to satisfactory completion.

All types of norms for children need to be understood by the assessor, not just norms directly related to the sentence completion. Particularly important are developmental norms and language development norms. For example, it is fairly typical of a 5-year-old to state that his or her favorite school activity is "playing"; this response is a red flag for an 8-year-old.

In short, the sentence completion technique could profit from a much higher degree of study than is presently being devoted to it, in standardization, norming and in clinical interpretation. An effort toward meeting the latter goal, improved clinical interpretation, is the primary focus of this chapter.

To substitute a type of purpose for the sentence completion other than its unique purpose—which is to secure from the client the information that is the result of the active processing (both highly conscious and less conscious) of both stored and current cognitions—would seem to be a basic error. It appears more productive to use sentence completion data in conjunction with other, more standardized, behaviorally based data (see later discussion on "Using the Sentence Completion as Part of a Test Battery"). The sentence completion is what it is: a clinical instrument that provides rich data with parsimonious effort, best utilized by a clinician who pursues the riches of the instrument rather than reducing them. A clinician who approaches the sentence completion in this frame of mid will seldom be disappointed.

THE SATISFACTORY SENTENCE COMPLETION FORM

Since there are many sentence completion forms available, or one may devise his or her own, the minimal conditions for a satisfactory clinical sentence completion instrument need to be considered. One needs to remind oneself that the sentence completion is neither wholly projective nor nonprojective in nature; it taps both areas of cognitive functioning. For this reason, the sentence completion format is best viewed as semiprojective in nature. It is also an instrument particularly adaptable to the needs of specific institutions and areas of functioning, as is shown by its history. Furthermore, it is easily geared to providing both a general and a specific level of information. Finally, though the stems of the sentence completion format provide a degree of orientation and set to the responses of the client, the client is still free to use or not to use the entire range of the language within his or her possession to express an endless choice of responses.

Features of the Satisfactory Instrument

A satisfactory sentence completion instrument should contain at least the following features:

1. The sentence completion form needs to be general enough in some of its examination of the client to elicit responses that can indicate a general judgment of mental health versus mental disturbance. It also needs to provide stems that tap the major categories of mental disturbance, such as anxiety and depression. There is hardly any child or other

client for whom this level of judgment will not be necessary.

2. The sentence completion form must be capable of yielding a personal range of information so that no matter what its specific concerns, the unique mental organization and motivational organization of the client can emerge from the data. This will allow the assessor to *reorganize* each individual sentence completion protocol according to the inherent organization that emerges from the client. This imposition of structure on structure is part of the richness of the sentence completion's possibilities.

3. The sentence completion form needs to be biased toward the population and the questions regarding this population that the examiner needs to assess. No instrument can assess all possible attitudes and problems, nor should the instrument provide a "fishing trip" of random possibilities. Instead, it needs to yield the type of information needed to make the judgments required in a particular setting.

4. The sentence completion form must provide a sufficient number of the types of stems discussed in paragraphs 1 and 2 above, so that some degree of confidence can be put in their interpretation. This is best achieved by organizing the instrument into subcategories of appropriate concerns and including several stems per category. As in all psychological testing, one response cannot be viewed as reliable information, though a single response may be highly pathognomonic and meaningful.

5. The sentence completion form must be appropriate to the age level with which it is being used. Clients, especially adolescents, will be "put off" by an inappropriate level of language in the sentence stems. Younger children will not be able to respond to long, involved stems. Direct language works best with all groups. By the manner in which it is written, the sentence completion will communicate to the client a level of serious or nonserious concern with him or her.

The Haak Sentence Completion Forms

I developed a sentence completion instrument in conjunction with the Learning Disabilities Center (as it was then called) of the University of Texas at Austin in 1973. This instrument is the one that is used for discussion and illustration in this chapter. Two forms of the "Haak" were developed (Haak, 1973a, 1973b) after an initial trial with only one form. The Haaks are appropriate for use with school-age children and adolescents (5–22 and probably older). The two forms were developed because it was discovered that the language level needed to be upgraded in the original form to meet the acceptance of secondary students.

The Haak Sentence Completion forms are partly based upon the earlier work of Robert Peck, who provided some of the original stems and the insight to organize the stems into content areas to improve reliability of interpretation. The first version of the Haaks was also influenced by the late Dr. Fern Williams, first director of the Learning Disabilities Center. It was she who requested my help to develop a relatively short procedure for the Learning Disabilities Center to use in ruling out emotional problems in the children they examined. It was she who also contributed some of the categories of the sentence completion, particularly the "openness to help" category, and she who first reproduced the sentence forms and named them the "Haaks." This sentence completion procedure has never been adequately studied, though a first doctoral dissertation has now been completed on these forms (Baker, 1988), but the forms are in wide use in the Texas area. There is a great deal of clinical experience available related to these forms. The Haaks are not claimed to be model forms of the sentence completion technique; however, they meet the conditions outlined above for a satisfactory format for this type of instrument.

USING THE SENTENCE COMPLETION TO ASSESS EMOTIONAL DISTURBANCE

The focus of the remainder of this chapter will be on the clinical interpretation of the sentence completion technique in evaluating school-age children for the condition of emotional disturbance. This is the primary task of school psychologists and clinicians today who utilize the technique in working with a school-age population.

To establish the simple-appearing matter of whether a person is "emotionally disturbed" or not is analogous to requiring a physician to certify someone as sick or well. Every professional person who deals in clinical settings knows that such arbitrary dichotomies are usually false. Some persons may be clearly sick, and others clearly well, but most would fall into some degree of what is often called the "worried well," neither free of concerns nor totally dysfunctional.

In addition to the fact that most functioning persons have some degree of identifiable disturbance or problem dynamics, there are further difficulties that appear with children: Children are always going through predictable changes and stresses, if only those associated with stages of development. Each of these stages presents its known challenges, which are probably the result of temporary imbalances in physical and psychological growth and maturity. In Western culture, these seemingly inherent problems associated with age have been variously conceptualized as "childhood stages" (Ilg & Ames, 1960; Spock, 1946), "psychosexual stages" (Freud, 1949), developmental tasks (Havighurst, 1953), and "psychosocial crises" (Erikson, 1959), all resting on more fundamental stages of neurological growth and development (Reinis & Goldman, 1980), cognitive accomplishments (Piaget & Inhelder, 1958), and the simpler matter of "on-time" developmental milestones (age of sitting, standing, walking, talking, etc.). No psychological examiner should attempt to evaluate children without a sound knowledge of all these developmental relationships.

Another complication of assessing children is that they are far less stable and predictable than adults. Assessors may have fairly constant notions of what capabilities to expect in a 30-year-old adult with an eighth-grade education, a Verbal IQ of 80, and a Performance IQ of 105. What to expect is far less clear in children for a number of reasons: (1) All test scores are less stable in children; (2) children's performances are more affected by environmental conditions than those of adults; (3) children have not formed stable work habits; (4) children's performances on verbal measures are affected by their stage of verbal development; and (5) children's performances are affected by the degree of pressure or stricture they feel from significant adults, especially on items they feel to be revealing or instrusive. Children's intellectual performance can be affected by emotional disturbance as well.

Finally, assessing "emotional disturbance" as a global condition of a child involves, to a great extent, a judgment about the general adequacy of the environment in which the child finds himself or herself. Every practicing school psychologist has had to label a child as "emotionally disturbed" when this disturbance was clearly the result and *only* the result of observable environmental deficiencies. There is *no* analogous problem in adult psychology or psychiatry. This is very disturbing to the clinician, for such children are genuinely disturbed and in need of services; nevertheless, the same children would be essentially normal if the pathological stressors were removed or altered in their effects. Not all emotionally disturbed children fit this description, but a large number do.

There are two major ways in which children today are classified in the global sense as "emotionally disturbed," usually for the purpose of qualifying a child for some institutional service: (1) A child is assessed according to the criteria of Public Law 94-142 (Education for All Handicapped Children Act, 1975) as emotionally disturbed; or (2) a child is assessed as having some condition listed in the revised third edition of the *Diagnostic and Statistical Manual of Mental Disorders* (DSM-III-R; American Psychiatric Association, 1987), which is accepted as evidence of emotional disturbance.

The six federal categories of emotional disturbance, which are based upon the work of Eli Bower (1969), are as follows:

(i) The term ["emotional disturbance"] means a condition exhibiting one or more of the following characteristics over a long period of time and to a marked degree, which adversely affects educational performance:
- (A) An inability to learn which cannot be explained by intellectual, sensory, or health factors;
- (B) An inability to build or maintain satisfactory interpersonal relationships with peers and teachers;
- (C) Inappropriate types of behavior or feelings under normal circumstances;

- (D) A general pervasive mood of unhappiness or depression; or
- (E) A tendency to develop physical symptoms or fears associated with personal or school problems.

(ii) The term includes children who are schizophrenic. The term does not include children who are socially maladjusted, unless it is determined that they are seriously emotionally disturbed. (Education for All Handicapped Children Act, 1975, § 300.5)

The matter of what constitutes "social maladjustment" has been the center of much discussion and some rule writing, but it has never been clearly settled. Also, recent legal and government opinions are beginning to make it clear that abnormal feelings (the affective component) must accompany abnormal behavior in order for behavior to be considered emotionally disturbed. Apparently, the condition of emotional disturbance was never intended to cover mere problem behavior.

In short, for a child to receive many services today, especially services provided by special education in the public schools, some professional must finally come down with a judgment that a child is emotionally disturbed (the "sick" or "well" question). The reliability problem inherent in this level of practice is so complicated that it boggles the mind. Unlike other categories of disability, which have clear-cut if not altogether professionally satifying criteria, emotional disturbance remains a matter for professional judgment alone. The only available "reliability" for this situation at present is to assure that such judgments are made by fully trained and experienced professional persons without conflicts of interest, using a range of instruments that provide as much information as possible about the condition in question. These professionals also need clear assistance in determining at what point on the continuum of emotional disturbance they are to determine that a condition has reached the stage defined by federal law or DSM-III-R. That judgment in the school setting is made upon the basis of "educational need." The effects of the proposed emotional disturbance upon the child's ability to learn, either academic material or the normal level of interactional (behavioral) skill, must be clear and serious.

I suggest that the sentence completion is a psychological instrument particularly adept at helping the professional person arrive at a judgment of emotional disturbance in a school-age child. The reasons for this position are that (1) the sentence completion is not purely behavioral in nature, and some believe that behavioral instruments supply information more appropriate for a diagnosis of behavioral than of emotional disorder; (2) the sentence completion is not completely projective in nature, and some would consider projective instruments too unsubstantiated by behavior to qualify as reliable material in diagnosing conditions of children. The sentence completion hits a middle ground between behavioral self-report and projection. Of course, the sentence completion has other appealing properties, such as face validity, ease of administration, efficiency of time usage, and acceptance by most children.

I do not agree with one property that is often advanced for the sentence completion, however, and that is its supposed ease of interpretation. The sentence completion is not "easy to interpret" if by the statement it is meant that all the information in the sentence completion is readily obvious to the naive user. The sentence completion is a mine of information to the most experienced user; no matter how long one has been interpreting sentence completions, it appears, there is always some new diagnostic skill that can be acquired. What could be more properly proposed is that the sentence completion is not easy to abuse diagnostically; that is, the naive user will simply not comprehend the information the sentence completion contains. I have not seen many instances of overinterpretation and endless diagnostic embroidery (e.g., such as one often sees in the interpretation of children's drawings) with sentence completions. There are a few such examples in case histories presented in books. For the most part, however, the inexperienced user will simply not be aware of most of the connotations of the sentence completion. The naive user will, however, be able to pick up the obvious, and many children make very obvious statements in the sentence completion. This still makes the instrument useful, for often there is no other place in the diagnostic battery where children will make such blatant state-

ments as they do on the sentence completion ("I am thinking about *killing myself*"; "I wish my father would not *drag me in the bathroom*"; "My parents *get drunk and fight every night*"). The sentence stem itself often impels the child to divulge information that he or she cannot or will not otherwise give (Derichs, 1977; Pernigotti, 1976).

In short, the sentence completion is a safe instrument. It is not easily abused by the inexperienced assessor, but it still provides a very useful level of information for the inexperienced assessor. The loss of information that the inexperienced user suffers is regrettable but at least not misleading.

Some of the judgments that can be made on the level of "emotional disturbance versus no emotional disturbance" from the sentence completion follow.

The "Rule-Outs"

Judgments regarding the following difficulties can often readily be made from the sentence completion material, and these judgments help to rule out emotional disturbance as a causative factor for the problems that caused the child to be referred.

Intellectual Difficulties

A clinician experienced with the sentence completion can often predict the child's IQ within a few points. This can be done primarily on the basis of fullness or poverty of language usage; articulateness; concreteness of language; complexity of language; perseveration in language; imagination; general level of expressiveness; empathy; openness versus defensiveness; social intelligence expressed; and qualification of responses. In particular, qualification of responses almost never occurs without good intellectual potential ("I am *generally nice but sometimes I am not*").

Certainly no emotional evaluation should be conducted without hard, recent data regarding intellectual potential and achievement status. But the sentence completion can act as a check upon other intellectual data, especially in the sense of indicating more potential than the child is presently able to demonstrate on testing. (This, however, should always be cautiously stated; a great deal of damage is done every day by careless or overconfident clinicians who lead parents to believe that their child is "much brighter than test scores indicate." Such statements sometimes lead to years of parental pressure on a child who is not having his or her needs met.)

It is also not enough to have simple intellectual "test scores" without considering which test is used, the subscores involved, and the reliability and validity of the test. Highly desirable are a full set of subscores from the Wechsler Intelligence Test for Children—Revised (Wechsler, 1974), the Stanford–Binet Intelligence Scale, fourth edition (Thorndike, Hagen, & Sattler, 1986), or the Kaufman Assessment Battery for Children (Kaufman & Kaufman, 1983). These subscores then need to be analyzed; if one is uncomfortable or inexperienced in this regard, an excellent assist can be provided by the Individual Ability Profile (Dean, 1983). A child with a great deal of within-child variance in important mental abilities, as represented by the subscores on the tests above, may be suffering from learning disabilities and other neuropsychological dysfunctions. This child will experience much stress and discomfort with school. It is also common to find children who have masked such intellectual difficulties for years behind a front of exceptional social competence; this particularly occurs with girls and breaks down at the high school level. Such children often present as "emotionally" disturbed.

A child experiencing intellectual difficulties may also be experiencing emotional disturbance; however, if the emotional symptoms being displayed can be directly related to the intellectual deficits and the stress these deficits cause with school performance, then it is improper to label the child as emotionally disturbed. The child requires other remedies than emotional remedies, though these also may help alleviate secondary symptoms.

Attention Deficit Disorder (Attention Deficit–Hyperactivity Disorder)

Symptoms of attention deficit disorder (or the newer DSM-III-R diagnosis, Attention Deficit–Hyperactivity Disorder) can easily be elicited from the sentence completion.

The child will commonly complain about his or her own attentional problems ("I have a hard time *paying attention*"; "My biggest problem is *understanding what the teacher wants*"). The child will also often complain that others shout at him or her, yell too much, lose their tempers at him or her, are too impatient, become exasperated, and are otherwise frustrated with the child (they are!). The child often seeks isolation, freedom, a high degree of personal movement (the life of a bird, motorcycles, high-speed cars)—that is, being alone, in control, and away from the "bugging" of others. He or she typically demonstrates a "thin-skinned" attitude and feels that other people are always picking on him or her. The child often feels acutely unfairly treated. No one understands this child. He or she nonetheless displays a paucity of empathy and can see nothing from any other point of view than his or her own. The empathetic and reflective processes are particularly deficient. (This does not mean that the child does not give positive social responses and attitudes; indeed, this is often the case. These attitudes are positive in the "conceptual" sense, however, and do not translate to concrete social skill.)

This child projects few plans, including plans of action; this is often a critical factor. When the child has not projected an action in the first place, he or she does not feel responsible for that action's occurring. (Indeed, the law agrees with this concept of premeditation.) Such children complain bitterly about other people's reactions to their impulsive misbehaviors. The other people rail about the child's lack of responsibility. Between the two points of view is a "moral" battleground. These issues will often be reflected in the sentence completions and in the referral originally received. "My father thinks I am *irresponsible*"; "My teacher thinks I am *stupid*"; "I wish that teachers would *leave me alone*"; "My friends expect me to *lead out on things*" (in other words, be the incautious one who gets into trouble first); "Most adults are *people who blame you for everything*"; "I am *always blamed*." The stems that refer to future plans will often be vague, undifferentiated, and obviously not previously considered.

As previously stated, social intelligence is often not lacking in the sentence completion expressions of such youngsters. They express social attitudes that persons dealing with them would scarcely believe (and often do not!). Rather than being immune to the effects of others, they seem hypersensitive to these effects. They are often in acute states of affective starvation, with perhaps the mother the only compensating factor in the picture ("My mother loves *me anyway*"). Their behavior, of course, is what puts them into this position. Attentional deficits lead to emotional double-binds for children. Many of these difficulties will be expressed as responses to the sentence completion stems.

How does one differentiate whether the symptoms displayed in the sentence completions of children with possible attention deficit disorder are attentionally or emotionally based, particularly when the child has not been previously diagnosed as having an attention deficit? This is a difficult and ongoing question even for research. The present answer appears to be that when most all of the troublesome sentence completion responses coalesce into what is known of the secondary symptom picture associated with attention deficit disorder (examples have been given above), one can clearly feel comfortable in assuming attention deficit disorder rather than something else to be the basic cause of the child's disturbing behaviors. When one has clustered the emotionally loaded sentence completion responses of the child with true attention deficit disorder, few such sentence stems will be left out of the picture.

Of course, a child can be both attentionally disordered and emotionally disturbed. In that case, the examiner will see the usual coalescence of secondary symptoms associated with attention deficit disorder; however, there will also be left over a large number of negatively emotionally loaded responses that do not neatly fit this picture. (One caution needs to be stated in this regard, however: A mild level of depression is common in attentionally disordered children.) But strong levels of emotional conditions, including strong depression, should usually not be viewed as deriving solely from attention deficit disorder. An emotionally based condition then needs to be searched for, with or without attention deficit disorder.

Stress

One of the major rule-out decisions facing the clinician who must decide the emotional condition of a child is a decision regarding the contribution of stress to the child's symptom picture. Sometimes this decision is very difficult, but more often it is not as difficult as it may at first appear. The clinician needs to consider the number and intensities of stressors upon the child, their recency, and their duration. Also important is the child's reaction(s) to the stressor(s). A child for whom multiple and strong stresses in the immediate past are found cannot safely be judged to be emotionally disturbed unless the emotional disturbance preceded the stressors or is itself very extreme. This is an instance, also, where the clinician will wish to depend a great deal upon outside information about the stressors in order to interpret the child's responses to them on the sentence completion. Yet outside information can serve only as a rough guideline; the degree of an individual's response to stress also tells one something about the individual. The makeup of the individual child is a multiplicand in such a formula, and the status of that individual makeup is precisely what one is looking for in an evaluation.

In the usual case, when multiple and/or strong stressors have persisted over time, they will almost inevitably erode the functional capacities of the child until that sad state is reached in which, even though all the causes of the child's emotional condition can be traced directly to the environment, the child is emotionally disturbed. His or her functional capacity is scarred as a consequence of the damaging conditions. Fortunately, the psychologist assessing school children often sees children before this state is reached.

As with attention deficit disorder, the sentence completion instrument can assist the clinician in making the decision regarding stress versus emotional disturbance by organizing the symptom picture. Children under great stress will indeed give indications in their sentence completions of the degree of discomfort they feel, though they may also give highly defensive and closed responses. But the essence of the differentiation of the two conditions will usually lie in the failure of the child to give responses on the sentence completion that are as disturbed as one might expect from reports of the child's overt behavior.

Stress most often produces physical and behavioral symptoms. These symptoms may be stronger in younger children, but they are almost invariably present in anyone. Usually, heavily stressed children strongly act out or strongly withdraw. Both sets of behaviors are obvious. But when the examiner begins to analyze the sentence completions of such children, the examiner will usually see preserved and positive social attitudes, even though spotty; preserved though damaged belief in oneself ("The one thing people need to understand about me is *I am really a good person*"); articulated coping strategies, even if effective only in the short run; some belief that things can get better; and some hope for the future, with scraps, at least, of future plans.

These cases are the "close calls" that the experienced psychologist hates. To call the child emotionally disturbed seems unfair to the child. To fail to call the child emotionally disturbed may be unrealistic and deny the child services. Most often the call will be resolved by the presence of depression, which almost invariably occurs at some point in these cases and, when strong, clearly qualifies the child as emotionally disturbed. When these cases are discovered earlier and at milder levels, fortunately they usually do not constitute cases of emotional disturbance. They still probably require some timely intervention, however.

In any case, the matter of effective school programming and appropriate psychological services is the issue. It behooves the clinician to explain the stress-based nature of the disturbances that have been observed; to recommend the exact types of interventions that are needed; to address the stressors (some of which the examiner legally must do something about himself or herself, such as reporting abuse); and to indicate a date for reevaluation of the emotional condition after a reasonable but relatively short period of time. The examiner may create a little stress himself or herself by specifying a reevaluation date, so that an expectation of positive change is established.

The "Rule-Ins"

What major factors, with or without the rule-outs above, constitute a state of general emotional disturbance in children? This is, of course, a highly debatable question, open to the various theoretical biases existing in the fields of psychology, medicine, psychiatry, social work, anthropology, biology, religion, and philosophy, to name a few. But the question must be answered in everyday practice.

Federal law (Education for All Handicapped Children Act, 1975) says, as previously discussed, that serious emotional disturbance in school children can be inferred from severe disturbances in forming or maintaining relationships; abnormal feelings and behaviors that occur under normal circumstances (strong anxiety, among other emotions, would appear to fit here); pervasive unhappiness (depression); abnormal fears and psychosomatic reactions; an inability to learn that cannot be explained by other handicapping conditions; and schizophrenia. Which of the conditions listed in the DSM-III-R meets the criterion of "emotional disturbance" is an issue not addressed by that system (American Psychiatric Association, 1987). The federal law specifies the use of no one system for establishing emotional disturbance. Most assessors working with school-age children are, however, heavily influenced by the outlines of the federal law, and indeed must be if they intend to qualify children for services.

Though the sentence completion can contribute strong evidence for any of the six criteria of emotional disturbance listed under the federal law or any of the major affective (and often cognitive) conditions listed in the DSM-III-R, it would not seem productive to try to organize the sentence completion responses into these (and no other) major categories. The sentence completion should contribute toward a diagnosis of emotional disturbance, but specifically qualifying the student for services is not its burden. An emotional evaluation should be composed of many parts, of which the sentence completion is one. (This is further discussed in the section "Using the Sentence Completion as Part of a Test Battery.") Perhaps the largest burden of the sentence completion is to assure that a true emotional disorder as opposed to a merely behavioral disorder is involved. A combination of emotional and behavioral data, as reported or observed, probably addresses the category-of-qualification question best.

(For those interested in this problem, the Joint Task Force on Emotional Disturbance of the Texas Education Agency/Texas Department of Mental Health and Mental Retardation has been working on this issue for several years. It is presently developing a set of ecologically oriented instruments that should provide information directly related to the federal law's specific qualifying criteria for emotional disturbance. I am a member of this group and may be contacted for further information, if desired.)

As stated, the sentence completion can and does provide evidence for any major emotional condition. Some of its more powerful contributions to the overall conclusion that an emotional disturbance is present can come from the following evidence.

Depression

A depressed child almost never completely "escapes" the sentence completion. Evidence for depression is found in the following instances:

1. Outright references to self-destruction (not rare).
2. Responses indicating that the child confuses (or responds alike to) anger and sadness ("When I am angry, *I cry*"; "When I am sad, *I am mad*").
3. A response to *either* of the following stems that indicates sadness: "I am always . . ."; "I am never . . ." The denial form of this particular stem often allows the child to express a depression he or she otherwise defends against.
4. Quite a number of expressions of anger combined with a number of expressions of positive social and moral attitudes (the socialized person is more often depressed).
5. A self-concept that is almost altogether negative except, at times, for the person's *own* view of himself or herself (i.e., the child/may report that others see him or her negatively, but he or she holds

on to a positive though perhaps defensive self-view; this varies).
6. Homicidal ideation (also not rare, but more rare than suicidal ideation and often quite intense and expressed in concrete, vivid images).
7. A gross level of anger in any child below the teenage years (and in some very immature teenagers); the younger the child, the stronger this is as evidence. Such children lack the controls to subvert their anger into adult-type depression. (All children do not lack these controls, however, and the self-depreciating qualities of an adult depression should not be overlooked.)
8. The expression of a conspicuous level of nonaffection and nonsupport from parental or adult figures, and a yearning for this support.
9. Premature sexual and romantic ideas; a young child thinking about getting married has usually given up on obtaining any immediate source of affection. (Again, this is not rare.)
10. A general paucity of expressiveness or high degree of defensiveness in completing the sentence completion stems; protests over having to complete the instrument or obvious upset in doing so; demands to stop the examination; obvious and building agitation; anger directed toward the examiner ("My biggest problem is *you*"). These behaviors in completing the instrument itself are indicative of the low tolerance of depression.
11. Intolerance of noise and stimulation ("Everyone *yells*").
12. A strong desire for activities combining escape, aloneness, and self-sufficiency, sometimes but not typically involving the element of speed ("Nothing feels as good as *being alone*"; "I would make a good *pilot*"; "If I were a king, I would *go skiing on a hidden, magic mountain—the tallest in the world*"; "I often daydream about *life on a little island*").

Of course, the quantity and intensity of such expressions as these will determine to what degree one suspects depression in a child. But the sentence completion is a productive place to look for depression, for its partial structuring of the responses is an aid to expression in the low-energy, depressed youngster.

Anxiety

The presence of strong anxiety in a child may exhibit itself in the sentence completions of the child as follows:

1. A large number of statements expressing fear and apprehension. One needs to be careful in evaluating fears, however, for some fears are known to be associated with certain developmental stages. Also, certain fears are related to real-life concerns; in such cases, these statements are indications of stress as well as realistic anxiety. Children, too, have certain fears blown out of proportion by television or increased by otherwise well-meaning TV ads. For example, because of the antismoking campaign, children who see their parents smoke can be very apprehensive that they may soon die. One child showed fear of eggs because of the TV ad that shows an egg being fried and states, "This is your brain on drugs."

The number or extent of fears expressed can be a valuable clue to an anxiety state. High anxiety tends to be generalized.

2. A number of statements that express vulnerability. Anxious students do not feel safe. One indication of vulnerablity does not constitute anxiety; however, several normally do.

3. Unexpected expressions of anxiety in response to stems. When a child responds anxiously to a stem designed to elicit anxiety, this is one thing; when the same child gives an anxious response to an otherwise innocuous or unrelated (to the examiner) stem, this is quite telling. An overreactive response of *any* kind is a strong indication of emotional disturbance, at the least. (A couple of examples: "If I had all the books in the world, *I would stack them up all around me and hide inside*" or ". . . *use them to throw at burglars*.")

4. Premature responding to an item (another instance of overreaction). Anxious students often cannot wait for the examiner to finish the sentence stem (if it is being read aloud) or do not read the stem carefully themselves. It is valuable for the examiner to

notice the content of a stem that receives this kind of overreactive response. What develops with such a sentence completion may be illogical in thought but will almost certainly be incorrect in grammatical structure. The latter is as indicative of anxiety as the former (e.g., "I often think of *that you are leaving*").

5. Overproduction of responses. The overproduction of the anxious (including the compulsive) student is mere verbal running on and not the same as the long, complex, and, most importantly, the *qualified* responses of the articulate, thoughtful student. The anxious student may repeat himself or herself over and over; go off on pointless tangents in a linear, compulsive manner; or simply run on and on, unable to put a stop to his or her verbalizing. (The all-time high for this behavior that I have seen was a three-page response in which the student told about nothing but running, getting up, getting killed, being resurrected, running again, *ad infinitum*.)

6. Lack of defensiveness. Most children are nondefensive in their responses to the sentence completion, but at a few points their own responses simply do not interest them. These occurrences can appear defensive. Consider this example: "When my father gives me a lot of work, *he gives me a lot of work*." If that is an isolated response, it may still mean something; but it also may mean, "So what!" (As Freud said, sometimes a cigar is just a cigar.) But the protocols of anxious children are overly void of defensiveness because control over their responses is simply not within their power.

7. Worry. Anxious children indicate in many responses that they are worried, even about sentence stems more often seen as pleasant.

The psychologist working with an anxious child will not lack for reports of agitated behavior in the child. But the sentence completion information will help the examiner to determine what the sources of this agitation may be: attention deficit disorder, stress, anxiety, or even physical disorders. The absence of many secondary symptoms of attention deficit disorder, the ruling out of major stresses, the ruling out of physical problems, the presence in the sentence completion of responses typical of anxiety—these leave a picture of a child experiencing more purely emotional anxiety states for whatever reason. Of course, it is possible also to suffer from anxiety and one or more of the above conditions simultaneously. And certainly any of them would feed an anxiety condition.

Thought Disturbance

Thought disturbance is certainly an indication of emotional disturbance, and a rather uncommon, severe one in a child at that. Children may truncate their responses, summarize their responses, respond with partial data, suppress their responses, convert their responses, and do all manner of things to try to avoid fully expressing how they feel or what they think. These maneuvers are generally unsuccessful if the testing instrument is of sufficient length. But thought disturbance is generally frankly expressed: The thought content is just outright disturbed. And it is usually expressed in a manner that is at odds with the context of the stimulation.

Indications of thought disturbance produced by the sentence completion include the expression of illogical ideas and the expression of these and other ideas in grammatically abnormal, fractionated sentence structure. The expression of one highly illogical thought does not constitute thought disturbance, but it should not be ignored either. One such blatant flag can alert the examiner to look for thought disturbance at a more subtle level in other expressions. Thought disturbance also has an intrusive quality. This can be overt, in the interruption of an otherwise appropriate response; or it can be inferred from a response incongruent with the sentence stem ("My father wants *I was a chicken in the Easter play*"; "If I were a king, I would *buy a whole truckload of toys. I would invite all the children. I would murder the queen. We would all get together in the park and have a good time*"; "In my family, I *the man came to see us*").

Thought disturbance must be differentiated from the premature responding of the anxious student. Even though the anxious student's response will not be grammatically smooth, the response will usually be in the same ballpark as the stem. In thought disturbance, the response has no obvious relationship to the stem, though there may be an illogical, personal relationship. In fact, discovering such relationships (if they exist) is a challenge to the examiner.

It is also wise to be sure that the student's auditory processes are intact when one suspects thought disturbance.

The use of highly convuluted grammar is often a sign of thought disturbance. Grammatical improprieties are rare in children, even uneducated children. The grammatical mistakes of uneducated children are fairly well known and mean nothing psychologically. But actual fracturing of basic grammatical structure should not be excused on the basis of lack of education. It may indicate brain damage, severe language dysfunctions, neuropsychological conditions, psychosis, or a combination of them all. This, of course, applies to repeated and consistent inability to express oneself in the basic grammatical forms of the native language.

Finally, in rare cases, a child may not be thought-disturbed but may be so psychologically pressured that he or she may construct a whole protocol of shifted, converted responses to hide his or her true expression. This is a case of extreme defensiveness, usually in response to extreme pressure. The child is very frightened to be giving responses to the threatening items in the sentence completion, but sees no way out of it. I have seen two protocols like this. In one, the child was the focus of an especially bitter divorce and custody suit. He was being pummeled by both sides for his loyalty. The child substituted animal figures for family members, actions for other actions, and so forth, and he was consistent in his substitutions. For example, one of his responses was "I love to *dance with a horse*." The examiner was sent back to have a talk with the boy; he produced another protocol, this time straightforwardly. It was possible to lay the two side by side and translate the substitutions. The occurrence of such an elaborate scheme is rare. Again the key was that the child could perform this type of exercise with consistency. A thought-disturbed child could not have done this. (Yes, the horse was the boy's mother.)

Defensiveness must always be considered when a child gives nonsense responses to sentence stems. Even more, the reason for the need to be defensive is important. But the thought-disturbed responses in the sentence completion will be more than merely defensive.

Defensiveness

For the most part, the sentence completion protocols of children are nondefensive. Even where there is the appearance of defensiveness, other possibilities need to be examined. The paucity or poverty of responses may be related to inferior intellectual ability, and this should always be checked. This kind of minimal production is also often associated with depression, for the student simply lacks the motivation and energy to be expansive.

Many times the sentence completion format brings forth a rich production of responses in an otherwise defensive student. A student who is remarkably hostile in behavior toward others, including toward psychological examiners, may flow forth in the sentence completion with the most blatant statements: exact plans for homicide, hatred of individuals, retaliatory schemes, injuries, fantasies, and exact feelings. This degree of revelation can also occur in the positive sense: A student who is having nothing but problems with other people will reveal a high level of conceptual social intelligence, plans for changing the world to a better place, personal dreams and plans for the future, and even a detached perspective on those with whom he or she is having difficulties. The results of a sentence completion are hard to predict, and this is one of the features that make it valuable.

But there are students who will react defensively to the sentence completion procedure. After all, the sentence completion is straightforward, not disguised. Students know exactly what is wanted. (That is why some take the opportunity to tell the examiner that they need help. Like hostile students, they can do this without being face to face; and they hope there is a small chance that the examiner actually may be there to aid them. This is the widely recognized "cry for help.")

No matter how defensively the student reacts to the sentence completion, he or she cannot get out of telling the examiner something. The student always has a *choice* of how to respond to the sentence stems; this provides the material that will keep the examiner busy with analysis. But not telling is also telling with the sentence completion.

Extreme defensiveness needs to be pursued. An analysis of the items to which the student is responding defensively can be instructive; an investigation into the daily life conditions of the student is warranted; and shifting to a more projective approach will often be useful. Although surveys of practicing school psychologists indicate that many of them do not find the use of projective tests useful or efficient (Vukovich, 1983), this appears to be one of those instances where at least the projective story approaches are useful. Children who are defensive toward the more straightforward stems in the sentence completion can be effusive in their responses to the Thematic Apperception Test (TAT) or the Chilren's Apperception Test (CAT). Conversely, and more strangely, some children respond openly to the sentence completion but clam up on the projectives. It may be that these children lack imagination, rather than that they are merely being defensive on this test. But it also appears that the projectives may not be productive in eliciting responses from some children, including some defensive children, because their ambiguity causes even more anxiety and thus the need to be even more defensive in such children.

Despite its potential for additional failure, the projective approach should be tried with a student who is consistently and highly defensive on the sentence completion (when other reasons for this apparent behavior, as discussed, have been ruled out). Defensiveness, no matter what its underlying causes, hardly ever emanates from mental health (though what appears to psychologists as "defensiveness" can also be a subcultural trait, and this should be considered). There is reason to suspect emotional disturbance in an extremely defensive youngster. Its causes need to be pursued.

Depression, anxiety, thought disturbance, and extreme defensiveness are major components of any general condition called "emotional disturbance." These factors can nearly always easily be determined from the evidence presented in the sentence completion format. The sentence completion is also capable of contributing evidence for more specific subtypes of emotional disturbance, whether these are categories of the DSM-III-R or the simpler categories of the federal law defining emotional disturbance in children. For example, one of the categories of the federal law is that of inability to form or maintain interpersonal relationships with peers or adults. The evidence from the sentence completion is so direct and extensive for this category that it really requires little discussion. Many sentence stems provide information that can be used to make a judgment regarding this specific problem.

I now turn, however, to the matter of how a more analytic approach to the sentence completion can provide definite, dynamic information about the nature and organization of a particular individual's problems. This should give the clinician the ability to tailor an effective treatment plan for the student.

UNDERSTANDING THE INDIVIDUAL CHILD AS A BASIS FOR TAILORING A TREATMENT PLAN

The sentence completion provides information that will allow an examiner to make a judgment about whether a child is emotionally disturbed or not, or where the child is represented on a continuum of emotional disturbance. The sentence completion can also contribute to a specific diagnosis of disturbance. But the sentence completion goes much further than providing such general levels of evidence; it is an instrument that can be analyzed at the level of the organization of the individual client. This is the level that leads to the type of understanding needed to plan a good treatment approach, including an efficient psychotherapeutic approach. Some dimensions of this individual analysis are discussed here.

Individual Qualities

The individuality of the client will emerge in the sentence completions in the form of humor, imaginativeness, insight, tolerance, forgiveness, ambition, social intelligence, talent, and many other qualities. These are not

"blips" to be ignored, but strengths and talents to be noted and exploited. Children often display highly realistic, surprisingly appropriate plans for their own futures, and they need feedback about these. Children divulge needs and dreams they are too shy to articulate anywhere else. Parents and teachers can often meet these needs if they realize them (this does not mean they should be told directly what the children have said). Many times the psychological examiner is the first person to suggest that a talent be developed, an activity be pursued, or a personality dimension be allowed. Not all class clowns are acting out of pathology; a few are real comedians.

What is suggested here is that the individuality of the student not be dismissed as of little concern. This individuality can be the heart of a positive treatment plan.

Idiosyncratic Reactions

For all kinds of idiosyncratic reasons, the meaning of one person's experience may be different from that of the majority of other people in the culture or subculture. For example, a sentence completion such as "People don't know that *I secretly enjoy missing parties*" is not the standard teenage response. But in the protocol of a child who is overscheduled with activities, pressured to be outstanding, and showing minor psychosomatic reactions, such a stem is revealing of the child's need for more solitude. Likewise, religious and philosophical teachings can also cause a student's responses to differ from typical cultural responses, and this can mislead the examiner. Consider these examples: "When others do well in school, I *praise them*"; "It is *wrong to compete with others*"; "When I do something well in school, I *am embarrassed*." On the surface of it, these appear to be the responses of an excessively reticent child. But many children come from families where they are taught that to compete or show pride in oneself is wrong.

Oversensitivity is another personal and idiosyncratic way of responding to sentence stems. This will be observed in sensitivity to stems that do not appear to affect other children in this manner. This style is often generalized to many stems. There is much evidence today that there may be a biologically based type of shyness, and such children do not need to be psychologically overinterpreted.

One also needs to be aware of the possibility of misunderstanding of American meanings for children arriving here from foreign countries and children of our own subcultures. Sentence responses that appear potentially pathological can rest on nothing more than misunderstanding in such children. Some of these idiosyncrasies may lead to concerns that need to be addressed in the treatment plan; others may be of little concern, once they are understood.

Personal Decisions and Strategies

Many persons have arrived at decisions and strategies as to how they will handle certain instances or classes of stimulation. Many of these decisions and strategies are hardly unique; this is what allows us to be able to understand common types of mental dysfunction. But often the decisions and strategies that a person uses are unique to the person, originate in childhood, and comprise the stuff of which therapy is made.

Many of these decisions and strategies can be apprehended from the sentence completion responses, particularly in comparing one response to another or to a cluster of other responses. For example, the stem "When my father gives me lots of work . . ." should be examined in relation to the stem "When my teacher corrects me, I . . ."; a common pattern of compliance or resistance may emerge to demands by authority. These responses, however, do not always appear with the stem designed to elicit them. For example, one young child who was quite deprived of affection produced this response: "If I had all the books in the world, *I would fill up my room to the ceiling and then I would get to sleep with my mother*." Almost any situation this child viewed was related back to his abject emotional need and was converted into strategies for meeting this need.

Decisions of the client can be picked up anywhere in the sentence completion, but one telling stem is "It is not use to . . .". If the response is *"act silly"* or some such inane and moralistic reply, it is not of the same level of meaning as the response *"think things will get better."* This implies that a decision has been reached.

Language Translations

Most persons have individualistic and unique ways of handling language. When these personal strategies become too bizarre, we become concerned about thought disturbance. But since language is the codification of experience, and all persons' experiences differ, language usage will always be somewhat personal and provide a window into the person's unique experience. The ability to *express* this experience is not, however, uniform among persons. A great deal of verbal ability is required for a person to be able to fully articulate his or her experience and point of view. Most persons can do this to at least some degree. But with many persons, the examiner must become a translator in order to get to a basic understanding of how these persons are using language.

The simplest translation is the individual word itself. "When I am afraid, I *hiccup*"; "When we have a math test, I *hiccup*." The personal definition of "hiccuping" with this student is "being afraid." Math tests induce a strong level of fear in this student.

Whole experiences can be translated. A teenage boy responds that "When I am mad, I *drive my car too fast*." He has been arrested for speeding several times of late. He also divulges that "at Christmas time *we never get much. My dad always drives us around town to see the lights after we have our tree but he drives so fast he scares me*." The translation is that the way the father handles depression has been picked up by the son.

Emotions themselves can be translated—a sign in itself of emotional disturbance. In a normally functioning adult, emotions stand alone; this is not altogether achieved by children. But even with children, major emotions should not be translatable if the child is in good mental health. The most common translation for children is the crossover of sadness and anger: "When I am sad, *I am mad*." Unhealthy translations also occur in how the emotions are handled. Far better the somewhat defensive "When I am sad, *I am sad*" than "When I am sad, *I am stupid*."

Translations can function as common denominators (they also do this in some of the examples above): "I am *childish and do not care enough about my grades*"; "My mother thinks I am *childish*." One would suspect a conflict with the mother over this child's school performance.

A single translation can tie a number of responses together. These translations are keys to understanding the individual client. They can hardly be overemphasized. One should have lines drawn all over a sentence completion protocol when analyzing it to tie these translations together. They often form major conclusions and provide the major insights of the assessment. Consider these examples: "I cannot work *when I am tired*"; "When my father yells at me, I *am tired*"; "When a dog comes toward me, I *feel tired*"; "I could be happy if I *wasn't so tired*." This is a child so threatened that he or she cannot work and wishes for relief. Some action needs to be taken to remedy the child's sense of threat. Parent consultation would appear to be a necessary part of this action.

Analyzing the individual dynamics of the sentence completion is a real challenge. Only a few of the dimensions of this individual analysis have been discussed above. This is the level of analysis that entices the examiner, for no two sentence completions are ever alike. There is always something new to be discovered in a sentence completion protocol. A lot of these individual discoveries will lead, in fact, to the discovery of relationships that exist on a dependable basis in other people. But their first function is to explain the behavior of the client in question, for whom it becomes much easier to plan an effective treatment plan once these dynamics are understood.

ASSESSING THE FUNCTIONAL ASPECTS OF THE CHILD IN THE SETTING

The status of a person is seldom judged out of its context. Acceptable Mardi Gras behavior occurring in a sedate business office would lead to predictable concerns. In school, Freud's old adage about the ability to love and to work as criteria of satisfactory functioning are acceptable criteria still. A child who is working satisfactorily and getting

along well with others will seldom be referred for an emotional evaluation.

In a sentence completion form to be used in a school setting, adequate stems must be provided to assess the student's work attitudes and performance and his or her interpersonal attitudes and performance. The degree to which children honestly report these conditions is amazing. And when what they report on the sentence completion is at variance with what is perceived by others, what they report usually explains what is perceived by others. For example, less motivation and work performance reported by a child than is observed will often be explained by the types of problems the child reports with his or her work deficits.

The Haak Sentence Completion (elementary form) contains the following categories of setting-related stems: School (actions, attitudes, locus of control, and goals); Authority (actions and attitudes); Peers (skill/relationships and attitudes); Adults (father, mother, and teacher relationships); Self-Concept; Emotional Status (state, routing, sources, fantasized needs, and comforters); Cognitive Status (general level and dimensions); Aspirations; Openness to Help; and Fillers (initial and concluding stems). The secondary form has similiar dimensions.

These categories of responses, related to making judgments about the fit of the student to his or her setting or the source of difficulty for the student in that setting are meant to help answer the kinds of questions that are involved in devising a treatment plan for a student in school. They are also grouped to provide more reliability of judgment about these dimensions (though they are not grouped on the form the child completes). Having several sentence stems available that are related to the same general area helps the examiner to make sound judgments.

It is desirable but not necessary that these categories of the sentence completion stand up in psychometric investigation. They should never be that rigidly interpreted by the examiner. Children violate the "structure" of these sentence completion arrangements all the time, as previously discussed, providing sentence completions to stems where they are least expected. But organizing the sentence completion instrument into categories provides the same kind of set and guidance to the interpreter that using sentence stems in the examination of the child does. It keeps the action of interpretation from wandering far afield of the concerns that have caused the child to be referred in the first place.

The point of assessing a child in school is to provide an efficient treatment plan with some hope of succeeding. Having stems specifically created to provide information about the setting in which the child is being assessed, and also organizing these stems into more predictable categories of response, are helpful toward attaing this desired end.

Anyone using a sentence completion form in the assessment of a client needs to examine the format selected, to be sure it offers information about dimensions of the setting in which the client is expected to function. This has historically been one of the strengths of the sentence completion, and it is not making the best use of the instrument to employ a format that fails to provide this information.

USING THE SENTENCE COMPLETION AS PART OF A TEST BATTERY

I have experimented with a number of approaches to the placement of the sentence completion within a test battery for the purpose of examining students for possible emotional disturbance. I have found the following procedure to be the most effective:

Assume a theoretical orientation to the assessment. The view I employ is that of general systems theory: The client, the school-age child, is viewed as a small system (actually an organization of subsystems) within several larger systems affecting him or her—the home, school, and community (and the larger world, for an older student). One needs an accurate assessment of the functioning of the subsystems within the child, and must equally understand the pressures and supports acting upon the child from the external systems. Only with such a comprehensive set of facts can a treatment plan be developed.

Consider the objective ("outside") facts and opinions about the child first. This is a debatable point with many professionals, who do not wish to be biased by having outside facts first. But admitting to bias shows a certain fear of gullibility, which the assessor can guard against as well as against bias. It appears helpful to work from the outside in, especially in a systems point of view, in analyzing a child. One knows what others think of the child. One has a full report of the behaviors of the child and can properly consider them. One has sound information about the intellectual capacity of the child and his or her achievement. All these data are part of a proper *emotional* evaluation. *Emotions are reactions*. One needs to have an idea of what the reactions may be directed toward. A full slate of facts about the child and the situation in which he or she lives also allows one to judge to what degree the emotions that may be discovered are primary or secondary effects. Emotions that are secondary symptoms associated with more fundamental problems will normally not be considered to be disturbed emotions per se.

The most objective data the examiner will gather will be the standardized test data, of course. It is my own practice to consider this information as fundamental to the assessment of emotional disturbance in the school setting. School is the child's job. The abilities of the child certainly affect how easy it is for the child to accomplish his or her job. But these data should be considered to contribute only the information they were devised to provide. Poor verbal performance is better explained by poor left-hemisphere functioning than either of them is explained by passive aggression, for example. (Both, however, may contribute to an explanation of apparent passive aggression.) For the child in school, learning potential and neuropsychological integrity are considered to be "what came first."

Less objective but still "outside" data are the behavioral reports gathered from teachers, parents, and administrators. Useful standardized forms are available at this level also—for example, the Achenbach Child Behavior Checklist (Achenbach, 1982). But it should be remembered that although many behavior scales have been standardized, they are not necessarily reliable or valid in the *individual case*. Their entire reliability and validity depends upon the individual raters filling out the protocol, and this has never been demonstrated for these raters. This is not altogether bad. One learns methods of evaluating the evaluators—a process that provides highly useful information about the major individuals with whom the child interacts. When teacher reports and parent reports agree, it is seldom the case that either one of them is very inaccurate in reporting behavior. When they do not agree, there are several possibilities. One possibility is that the child behaves differently in the two settings represented by the two reporters. Some assessors do not give full credence to this possibility. It is more likely that the school is the problem when this happens. Many children escape from school to a happier, more relaxed home life; few children escape from a disturbed home into school and function well there. But children do function differently in different settings, and when they do, this ability argues against generalized emotional disturbance.

There are other possibilities for differing results on parent and teacher standardized behavioral reports. Either of these reporters may be reflecting a present high level of concern about the child. In this case, the concerned reporter will elevate most scores. The profile of the child based upon these data will be elevated across the board, violating the factor structure that provided the profile. This is not liable to be a very realistic report of the child, but it is a report of the reporter's level of concern, either with the child or from other sources of stress. Either of the reporters may also have definite feelings about the child's eventual diagnosis, which they know is forthcoming. If they believe the child to be disturbed, one way to assure this diagnosis is to elevate scores. The reverse may also be true: A reasonably elevated profile with differentiated scores from one reporter, compared with a flat profile from the other reporter, usually argues for defensiveness on the part of the latter.

When all these possibilities are taken into consideration, the behavioral reports can be sifted. Maladaptive behavior by itself does not necessarily indicate emotional disturbance, as the federal law reminds us. On the other hand, many behaviors are known to be associated with certain emotional conditions. Behavioral reports are important to emotional assessment. The assessor can gain behavioral information and ecological information from the reports of both teachers and parents. All these data comprise the "outside" facts that one needs in a systems interpretation.

A behavioral observation in the classroom can also be a valuable piece of information. Some teachers are truly expert in performing these observations, providing an objective description of a child's behavior that answers many of the questions raised by the behavioral reports.

After the "outside" data are gathered and examined, one is prepared to go behind the scene—to see the world from the child's eyes. One now has a set. One knows what the world thinks and how the child is seen to behave. One has some ideas about the major interactors with the child and the conditions of the child's life (these come from routine school referral reports, parent questionnaires, health history, and work samples, which are part of the assessment and routinely examined, in addition to the behavioral reports discussed above). If the child is already receiving special services but is being examined for possible emotional disturbance for the first time, one should have reviewed the records and should know the course of treatment pursued with the child so far. Now one is ready to compare "inside" with "outside." The resolution of these two perspectives will lead to the diagnostic conclusions and the treatment plan, if needed.

I take the child data in the order of its projectiveness. This may not agree with other examiners' views of what is projective. Any productions included are viewed first; drawings next; sentence completion next; and projective stories last. (I use the Rorschach very infrequently.) The findings of these instruments are balanced against the major findings of the more objective data. Major conclusions are confined to what factors constitute the problems and what remedies are called for in the treatment plan. On another level, however, therapists who will work with the child will desire access to the more particular and individual dynamics of concern with this child, information the sentence completion is particularly adept at providing.

The sentence completion is part of a comprehensive emotional evaluation of a child. It is not an emotional evaluation in itself. Nevertheless, the sentence completion is a workhorse of an instrument, widely employed and delivering information on the level that the assessor is able to utilize. What remains to be discovered is that the sentence completion has the properties of a race horse as well. It is an instrument always full of potential.

REFERENCES

Achenbach, T. M. (1982). *Child Behavior Checklist*. Burlington: University of Vermont, Department of Psychiatry.

Agesen, N., Brun, B., & Skovgaard, B. (1984). [Rotter's Sentence Completion Test]. *Nordisk Psykologi* (Danish), *36*, 188–200.

American Psychiatric Association. (1987). *Diagnostic and statistical manual of mental disorders* (3rd ed., rev.). Washington, DC: Author.

Baker, D. (1988). *Establishing inter-rater reliability and criterion-related validity for the Haak Sentence Completion*. Unpublished doctoral dissertation, Texas A&M University.

Bower, E. M. (1969). *Early identification of emotionally handicapped children in school*. Springfield, IL: Charles C Thomas.

Costin, F., & Eiserer, P. E. (1949). Student's attitudes toward school life as revealed by a sentence completion test. *American Psychologist, 4*, 289.

Cruikshank, W. M. (1951). The effect of physical disability on personal aspiration. *Quarterly Journal of Child Behavior, 3*, 323–333.

Cruikshank, W. M. (1952). The relationship of physical disability to fear and guilt feelings. *Cerebral Palsy Review, 13*, 9–13.

Dean, R. S. (1983). *Individual Ability Profile*. Odessa, FL: Psychological Assessment Resources.

Dean, R. S. (1984). Commentary on "Personality assessment in the schools: The special issue." *School Psychology Review, 13*, 95–98.

Derichs, G. (1977). [Sentence completions as intake instruments]. *Praxis der Kindderpsychologie und Kinderpsychiatrie* (German), *26*, 142–149.

Education for All Handicapped Children Act, Pub. L. 94–142, 34 C.F.R. § 300.5 (1975).

Efron, H. (1960). An attempt to employ a sentence completion test for the detection of psychiatric patients with suicidal ideas. *Journal of Consulting Psychology, 24*, 156–160.

Erikson, E. H. (1959). Identity and the life cycle. *Psychological Issues, 1*, 1–171.

Feldhusen, J. F., Thustone, J. R., & Benning, J. J. (1966). Sentence completion responses and classroom social behavior. *Personnel and Guidance Journal, 45*, 165–170.

Forer, B. R. (1960). Word association and sentence completion methods. In A. I. Rabin & M. R. Haworth (Eds.), *Projective techniques with children* (pp. 210–224). New York: Grune & Stratton.

Freud, S. (1949). *An outline of psychoanalysis*. New York: Norton.

Goh, D., & Fuller, G. B. (1983). Current practices in the assessment of personality and behavior by school psychologists. *School Psychology Review, 12*, 240–243.

Graham, F. K., Charwat, W. A., Honig, S. A., Weltz, P. A. (1951). Aggression as a function of the attack and the attacker. *Journal of Abnormal and Social Psychology, 46*, 512–520.

Haak, R. A. (1973a). *Haak Finish the Sentence: Elementary form*. Unpublished instrument.

Haak, R. A. (1973b). *Sentence Completion: Attitudes and Interests (Secondary form)*. Unpublished instrument.

Hanfmann, E., & Getzels, J. R. (1953). Studies of the sentence completion test. *Journal of Projective Techniques, 17*, 280–294.

Harris, D. B., & Tseng, S. C. (1957). Children's attitudes toward peers and parents as revealed by sentence completions. *Child Development, 28*, 401–411.

Hart, D. H. (1986). The sentence completion technique. In J. Goldman, C. L. Englestein, & S. Giverny (Eds.), *Psychological methods of child assessment*. New York: Brunner/Mazel.

Hart, D. H., Kehle, T. J., & Davies, M. V. (1983). Effectiveness of sentence completion techniques: A review of the Hart Sentence Completion for Children. *School Psychology Review, 12*(4), 428–434.

Havighurst, R. J. (1953). *Human development and education*. New York: Longmans, Green.

Ilg, F. L., & Ames, L. B. (1960). *Child behavior*. New York: Dell.

Irvin, F. S. (1967). Sentence completion responses and scholastic success or failure. *Journal of Counseling Psychology, 14*, 269–271.

Jenkins, R. L., & Gowdey, E. B. (1981). *Prediction of violence: Attitudes as projected in sentence completion*. Springfield, IL: Charles C Thomas.

Kaufman, A., & Kaufman, N. L. (1983). *Kaufman Assessment Battery for Children*. Circle Pines, MN: American Guidance Service.

Kimball, B. (1952). The sentence completion technique in a study of scholastic underachievement. *Journal of Consulting Psychology, 16*, 353–358.

Kinzie, W., & Zuniver, H. (1968). On the measurement of hostility, aggression, anxiety, projection and dependency. *Journal of Projective Techniques and Personality Assessment, 32*, 388–391.

Knoff, H. M. (1983). School based personality assessment. *School Psychology Review, 12*, 391–398.

Kozmar, J. (1975). [Analysis of projection of psychosexually traumatized girls on a sentence completion test]. *Psychologia a Patopsychologia Dietata* (Czechoslovakian), *10*, 307–318.

Lubin, B., Larsen, R. M., & Matarazzo, J. D. (1984). Patterns of psychological test usage in the United States: 1935–1982. *American Psychologist, 39*(4), 451–454.

Malpass, L. F. (1953). Some relationships between students' perception of school and their achievement. *Journal of Educational Psychology, 44*, 475–482.

Mosher, D., & Mosher, J. B. (1967). Guilt in prisoners. *Journal of Clinical Psychology, 23*, 171–173.

Payne, A. F. (1928). *Sentence completions*. New York: New York Guidance Clinic.

Peck, R. F., & McGuire, C. (1959). Measuring changes in mental health with the sentence completion technique. *Psychological Reports, 5,* 151–160.

Pernigotti, P. (1976). [The application of the Sacks Test in ambulatory psychodiagnostics for children]. *Bollettino di Psicologia Applicata* (Italian), Nos. 136–138.

Piaget, J., & Inhelder, B. (1958). *The growth of logical thinking from childhood to adolescence.* New York: Basic Books.

Pruitt, J. A., Smith, M. C., Thelen, M. H., & Lubin, B. (1985). Attitudes of academic clinical psychologists toward projective techniques. *Professional Psychology: Research and Practice, 16,* 781–788.

Reinis, S., & Goldman, J. M. (1980). *The development of the brain.* Springfield, IL: Charles C Thomas.

Rohde, A. R. (1946). Explorations in personality by the sentence completion method. *Journal of Applied Psychology, 30,* 169–181.

Sanford, R. N., Adkins, M. M., Miller, R. B., & Cobb, E. A. (1943). Physique, personality and scholarship. *Monographs of the Society for Research in Child Development, 8*(1, Serial No. 34).

Spock, B. (1946). *The pocket book of baby and child care.* New York: Pocket Books.

Stahl, M. J., Grigsby, D. W., & Gulati, A. (1985). A choice exercise and the multiple choice version of the Miner Sentence Completion Scale. *Journal of Applied Psychology, 70,* 228–232.

Takala, M., & Pitkanen, L. (1963). [Level of activation and goal-directed behavior: The effect of chlorpromazine on aggressive, achievement-oriented and affiliation-oriented verbal responses]. *Scandinavian Journal of Psychology* (Finnish), *4,* 115–122.

Thorndike, R. L., Hagen, E. P., & Sattler, J. M. (1986). *Stanford–Binet Intelligence Scale* (4th ed.). Chicago: Riverside.

Veldman, D. J., Menaker, S. L., & Peck, R. F. (1968). *Computer scoring of the sentence completion data* (Research Methodology Monograph No. 3). Austin: University of Texas, Research and Development Center for Teacher Education.

Vukovich, D. H. (1983). The use of projective assessment by school psychologists. *School Psychology Review, 12,* 358–364.

Wechsler, D. (1974). *Wechsler Intelligence Scale for Children—Revised.* San Antonio, TX: Psychological Corporation.

Wilson, I. (1949). The use of the sentence completion test in differentiating between well-adjusted and maladjusted secondary school pupils. *Journal of Consulting Psychology, 13,* 400–402.

7

Using the Rorschach with Children and Adolescents: The Exner Comprehensive System

JERRY C. ALLEN
University of Georgia

JILLAYNE HOLLIFIELD
University of North Carolina

The Rorschach test has one of the most controversial histories of any instrument in the era of psychological testing. Although the controversy is still far from over, the Rorschach is currently gaining renewed popularity among psychologists as the instrument of choice when their purpose is to understand and describe the psychological features of an individual. This renewed popularity is evidenced in the increasing numbers of training institutions offering graduate courses in the Rorschach; in the number of internship sites requiring students to have training and skill in using the Rorschach; and in the increasing frequency with which the Rorschach is being used in clinics and hospitals—and yes, even in the schools. This renewed popularity is due in large measure to the continuing efforts of John E. Exner, Jr., and his associates at the Rorschach Research Foundation (Rorschach Workshops).

This chapter presents a brief introduction to the Rorschach, using the procedures and norms established in Exner's Comprehensive System (Exner, 1974, 1978, 1986; Exner & Weiner, 1982) and a discussion of the use of the test with special populations of children and adolescents. A thorough knowledge of the above-listed references is essential if one is to use the Rorschach properly and wisely, as are intensive study and training in administration, scoring, and interpretation.

THE EXNER COMPREHENSIVE SYSTEM

Three factors that contributed to the Rorschach controversy, according to Exner and Martin (1983), were "(1) confusion and disagreement concerning the theoretical underpinnings of the Rorschach, (2) the lack of a single, consistent administration, scoring, and interpretation procedure, and (3) the oversimplified classification of the Rorschach as a projective technique" (p. 407). Although there is still no one theoretical orientation underlying the Exner Comprehensive System (Exner, 1986, p. ix), Exner and his associates have expended much effort in addressing the second and third critical factors.

While projection may be present in an individual's verbalizations about what the inkblots might be, Exner defines the Rorschach test as a problem-solving (perceptual–cognitive) task, similar to the way Rorschach himself considered it to be a "form interpretation test" (Exner & Martin, 1983, p. 407). If projection is present, the examiner may wish to use that material as supplemental to the formal, psychometrically based data obtained from the Structural Summary of the Comprehensive System. Thus, the Rorschach may now be viewed as a test, administered under standard procedures and scored according to established criteria. These scores (or codes) may then be compared with the scores obtained by an appropriate reference group.

The Comprehensive System originated from Exner's attempt to develop a single, consistent procedure of administration, scoring, and interpretation of the Rorschach test, based upon empirically defensible data. The history of this endeavor can be found in Exner and Martin (1983). The outcome resulted in the development of the system (Exner, 1974, 1978, 1986; Exner & Weiner, 1982). The development is continuing today through efforts of the Rorschach Research Foundation and other professionals' research contributions.

ADMINISTRATION

Two skills are of prime importance to the Rorschach examiner who chooses to work with children and adolescents. The first is a thorough understanding of childhood developmental processes, and the second is a high level of knowledge and expertise with the instrument itself and with the Exner Comprehensive System. These skills are essential to obtain complete and accurate data during the administration phase, which, in turn, permit appropriate scoring and interpretation. Because of the differences in verbal skill levels inherent in the various developmental levels of childhood, and because Rorschach data collection is almost entirely dependent upon verbal exchange, the administration process can often be quite challenging. Nevertheless, the individual child's verbal skills are always uniquely revealing.

Preparing the Child

Because it is so important to be particularly careful in collecting Rorschach data from children, it is advisable for the examiner to spend adequate time with the child prior to administration to put the child at ease. Children generally have some idea as to why they are being tested, but often they do not know how the information gained in the assessment will be used. It is not uncommon for them to develop negative fears and expectations, resulting in various forms of resistance and, consequently, less than optimal performance. Thus, it is wise for the examiner to take as much time as possible with the child, explaining the nature and purpose of the test and indicating how the results will be used, as well as answering any questions the child or the parents may have. This should be done in as honest and straightforward a manner as the situation permits, and without unnecessary elaboration. Children value honesty and will generally respond with minimal resistance to an examiner who has taken adequate preparation time before the procedure begins.

The Response Process

It is vital that the examiner understand the nature of the Rorschach response process—what is involved in the formation of a response and its ultimate delivery. Exner and his colleagues have studied in detail the processes an individual goes through in making a response, from the moment the person is asked "What might this be?" and is handed the inkblot until the first response is delivered. Exner (1986) summarizes the operations as follows:

Phase I:	1. Visual input and encoding of the stimulus and its parts.
	2. Classification of the stimulus and/or its parts, and a rank ordering of the many potential responses that are created.
Phase II:	3. Discarding potential answers that have low rankings.
	4. Discarding other potential answers through censorship.
Phase III:	5. Selection of some of the remaining responses because of traits or styles.
	6. Selection of some of the remaining responses by reason of the state influences. (p. 51)

The crucial elements in assuring the cooperation of the child and a valid Rorschach protocol are, as in the case of all assessment procedures, the time and effort the examiner expends in putting the child at ease prior to the examination proper. Recognizing this, Exner and Weiner (1982) stress that the response process is a

complex interaction among at least three in-terrelated variables: (1) the set of the subject toward the test and the testing situation, (2) the evaluation of the subject regarding which of several perceived responses is most appropriate or "correct" in light of the set, and (3) the impact of the composite of response tendencies or styles plus the ongoing psychological operations of the subject. (p. 19)

Thus, the necessity of preparing the child adequately to yield the most appropriate test set is evident and will usually produce a valid record even when some amount of resistance to the task remains.

The next variable in the response process of the child involves his or her evaluation of which of all of the perceived responses is most appropriate to the established test set. Exner has noted that children, as well as adult subjects, see more potential responses than they are willing to verbalize. In fact, when a sample of children was encouraged to give as many responses to a card as they could in 60 seconds, they averaged slightly more than 94 total responses for the test (Exner, Armbruster, & Mittman, 1978). More-over, the Form Quality of the responses did not diminish, and in fact increased slightly over the 60-second time span. Nevertheless, most children, regardless of socioeconomic status or environmental setting, restrict the number of responses they deliver. This restriction is related to the evaluation process and involves both rank ordering and censor-ship operations (Exner, 1986). That is, on the basis of the established test set, the child selects from among numerous potential re-sponses those that seem most appropriate or correct and censors those that do not.

Not surprisingly, Leura and Exner (1978) found that examinees do not restrict as much and, in fact, give significantly greater num-bers of responses to examiners who are known to them. The largest increases are seen in Human Movement responses (M), Color responses $(FC, CF,$ and/or $C)$, and

Blends, with significant increases in Whole (W) and Uncommon Detail (Dd) locations. Nevertheless, the proportions of both M and C responses to total number of responses remains unaffected because of the increased number of responses generated overall. Leura and Exner found the greatest differ-ence in proportion occurring in the grey–black Shading responses. Persons whose ex-aminer was known to them gave about 11% Shading responses, while the control group gave about 15%. Consequently, examiners who test children they know well should be alert to the possibility that these children's profiles may reflect some or all of the features just described. Other studies related to re-sponse productivity have yielded mixed re-sults with regard to the potential influence of sex of the examiner. Tuma and McCraw (1975) found no relationship between sex of examiner and response productivity in the children in their study. However, Greenberg and Gordon (1983), who restricted their sam-ples to latency-age children, found that boys gave significantly more responses to male ex-aminers and girls gave significantly more re-sponses to female examiners. Consequently, examiners may wish to consider the potential for gender effects in Rorschach response pro-ductivity, particularly with latency-age chil-dren.

Another factor that will influence both the quantity and the quality of children's re-sponses is their need for reinforcement. Chil-dren are far more concerned than adults about giving correct responses. They are motivated by needs to please the examiner, to perform well, to do the socially acceptable thing, and to avoid potentially unpleasant outcomes. Reassuring a child that there are no right or wrong answers is not always suf-ficient to provide the reinforcement the child needs. Even adults have been shown to be strongly influenced by the perceived social acceptability of their responses. Exner and Leura (1976) demonstrated that adults would report that certain sexual and aggressive re-sponses were "easy to see" when they had received prior instructions that these re-sponses were frequently given by successful businessmen. A second group of adults in-dicated that these same sexual and aggressive responses were "difficult to see" when prior instructions implied that they were produced by seriously disturbed persons. Children, too, want to do the right thing and to gain approval for their performances—or, at the very least, to avoid any undesirable consequences.

The inherent lack of structure in the Rorschach is problematic for the child. Depending on the stage of development, or in some cases on developmental lag, children are to one degree or another concrete in their thinking and prefer situations in which there are rules or guidelines. Ambiguity is troublesome. As mentioned earlier, to attempt encouragement by telling the child that there are no right or wrong answers does not remove the necessity of dealing with an ambiguous situation. Exner and Weiner (1982) point out that, in fact, the only "right" answer is that it is an inkblot. By coaxing the child to report what it *might* be, or by encouraging the reluctant child with "Most children see more than one thing," the examiner engages the child's preferred problem-solving operations and coping mechanisms. Therefore, while the test itself causes the surfacing of test sets, it also requires that the child utilize his or her unique psychological response style in the perceptual, cognitive, and affective spheres. These will be apparent in the responses generated by the child, regardless of any residual resistance.

Children's psychological response styles tend to be relatively consistent, although far less so than those of adults. Their response styles tend to become increasingly stable over the developmental years and, like those of adults, are susceptible to situational variables. Stability of a psychological response style is determined by its utility in reducing stress for the child. Consequently, change in the cognitive, perceptual, and affective operations of the child is to be expected, and the younger the child at the time of initial testing, the more the psychological response style will change with time (Ames, Metraux, Rodell, & Walker, 1974).

The child's psychological response style is highly unique and individualistic, and determines which of the many responses that could be articulated will be selected in the child's problem-solving operations. For example, in giving the popular response to Card V, the child could report: "a butterfly" (Form, or F); "a black butterfly" (Form/

Achromatic Color, or FC', a response in which form is the primary determinant but achromatic color is also used); "a butterfly flapping its wings" (Animal Movement, FM); or "a soft, velvety-looking butterfly" (Form/Texture, or FT, a response in which form is the primary determinant but texture is also used). Moreover, expression of the child's unique psychological response style is not limited to what is actually articulated. It can be seen in the choice of location and whether the child prefers to respond to the blot as a whole or to common or unusual detail areas. It can also be seen in whether or not the child attempts to organize details of the blot in the response. Furthermore, the child's psychological response style is apparent in the use of pairs, reflections, or special scores or contents, or in the failure to use these. Since children's psychological response styles are at best only relatively consistent, it is of utmost importance that the examiner know which of the Rorschach test variables are relatively consistent and which are highly vulnerable to change over time.

A study by Exner, Rosenthal, and Thomas (1980) underscores the lack of consistency in many of the child's psychological operations. In this study, two groups of children, initially aged 6 and 9, were examined at specified intervals over time. The only variables with high test–retest correlations over a 2-year period were $X+\%$ (perceptual accuracy for the total record), frequency of Active Movement (M^a), and frequency of Popular (P) responses. All other variables showed great disparity over the same interval. Moreover, there were substantial differences between the two groups of children. Thus, the childhood development process has been found to exert considerable influence during the formation of the child's perceptual, cognitive, and affective operations. It is highly unlikely that a child's current protocol will predict accurately his or her future psychological response style.

Children change over time; as noted earlier, the younger the child at the time of initial testing, the more change is to be expected over even relatively short intervals. Older children and adolescents exhibit less change, and their records are apt to be more stable over longer intervals. In particular, $X+\%$ is consistent in the early years, perhaps even prior to school entry (Exner & Weiner, 1982), whereas Human Movement (*M*) production is not consistent until midadolescence. Thus, the preferred problem-solving or coping style tends to fluctuate during the child's first 10–12 years, and a dominant style is not formed until somewhere between 14 and 18 years of age.

Thus, it is apparent that knowledge of both the instrument and the developmental process are essential to competent Rorschach administration with children and adolescents. The examiner must spend adequate preparation time with the child to ease tensions and minimize resistance, so that a clear picture of the psychological operations of each child may be obtained. The examiner must be aware that children evaluate and censor potential responses on the basis of how they expect their test data to be used, and also on the basis of what sorts of responses they believe are "correct" or will please the examiner. Examiners must also be alert to the potential effects of testing children who are well known to them and to possible gender effects in Rorschach response productivity. Finally, the examiner must be aware of the high degree of inconsistency in children's Rorschach records over time and the considerable potential for change in this age group.

Administering the Rorschach

The actual formal administration of the Rorschach test is a relatively straightforward task; nevertheless, certain basic guidelines must be followed. The examiner must adhere to the standard administration practices in order to insure accurate scoring and interpretation. Practice is required so that the examiner can avoid inadvertently establishing unwanted test sets or reinforcing any particular type of response. The preferred seating is side by side. Seating can be altered to accommodate very young children or those with special needs (e.g., sitting on the floor), as long as standard administration is maintained.

The formal administration of the Rorschach consists of two phases: the "Administration Proper" and the "Inquiry." In the Administration Proper phase (often termed the "Free Association" phase), after appropriate preparation of the child for the test, the examiner hands each of the inkblots in sequence to the child, who is asked, "What might this be?" Responses are recorded verbatim; therefore, the examiner will need to develop some type of shorthand method for recording responses. After responses to all 10 cards have been obtained, the Inquiry phase begins. The purpose of the Inquiry is to allow the examiner to obtain all information needed so that the responses may be scored appropriately. (See Exner, 1986, pp. 70–78, for details on conducting the Inquiry.)

Since normally the Rorschach is just one of a battery of instruments given to the child, its description should be brief and similar to that given for other procedures. For example, the examiner may say, "And then we will be doing the inkblot test. Maybe you've heard of it." If the child's parents are present, the explanation should be delivered in a manner that insures understanding for both the parents and the child. Subsequent questions should be answered directly and honestly.

During the administration proper, there is no need to change the standard instructions, except in the case of very young children or children with language difficulties, for whom even more simplified instructions may be in order. The examiner should refer to the cards as inkblots; that is what they are. Typical instructions are as follows: "I am going to show you some inkblots, and I would like you to tell me what this might be."

Children tend to ask a lot of questions, and it is best to answer them in as direct and straightforward manner as possible. "Where did you get these?" "I bought them." "Do you think it looks like that?" "Right now I'm interested in what you think it looks like." "Did I get that one right?" "If that's the way it looks to you." "Do other kids say things like that?" "People say all sorts of things." "What kinds of kids do you show these pictures to?" "All sorts of kids." "Do you like this one?" "I'd rather know what you think it might be; I'll tell you later if you like." Some questions require lengthy explanations or are complex and should be deferred until the end of the test: "That's a pretty complicated question. Let's wait until we finish and then I'll explain. I'll write it down so I won't forget."

Instructions for the Inquiry should be equally straightforward and direct. "We are going to go through the cards again now, and I will read to you what you said. I want you to show me where on the blot you saw what you saw, and then tell me why it looks like that to you. I want to see it just the way you did." Generally, if the examiner has given clear instructions at the outset of the Inquiry, scoring can proceed without difficulty. Some children require more encouragement even when adequate instructions have been given: "Yes, I know it looks like that to you. But remember, I have to see it too. I have to see it just like you do." Younger children may need reminders from time to time: "Put your finger on the part that looks like _____ ." "What in the blot makes it look like that to you?" "I'm not sure what makes it look like that to you." "Draw a line around the ____ with your finger." Pursuing key words from the Administration Proper may serve to clarify a response: "You said it was pretty; what about it makes it look pretty to you?" The examiner should not become directive, however. If the attempt at clarification is not productive, examiner and child should move on to another response. It is important to avoid establishing test sets.

Some Typical Administration Problems

Occasionally, a child is extremely resistant and defensive. In this case, the examiner must decide whether to proceed with the test or to postpone it until a later date. Reviewing two areas of the administration process may be helpful in making this decision. First, have sufficient time and effort been spent in establishing rapport with the child? If not, it is possible that the problem can be remedied within the session. Second, and only in extreme cases, the examiner should consider the possibility of altering the administrative process to accommodate such difficulties as hyperactivity, unusual anxiety, and the like. Ames et al. (1974) and Halpern (1953), for example, advocate the use of the Inquiry immediately after each card, particularly with preschool and easily distracted children. However, Exner and Weiner (1982) caution that this procedure should be used only as a last resort, since Leura and Exner (1977) have found a resulting elevation in Common Detail (D) and Form (F) responses, espe-

cially on Cards VI and X, when immediate Inquiry is utilized.

Another problem frequently encountered by the examiner is the brief record. Young children tend to give relatively short records, and it is not uncommon for 5- and 6-year-olds to give 15 or fewer responses. Moreover, children generally give more pure F responses than adolescents or adults, although they usually give enough responses with a sufficient variety of determinants to be interpretively useful. When this is not the case, the examiner should consider several possibilities, including intellectual limitations, neurological impairment, and attitude problems. Other instruments in the psychological battery may be useful in ruling out the possibility of either intellectual or neurological difficulties. When defensiveness or resistance is present, the child is often able to control his or her affect sufficiently to yield a record that is not interpretively useful. The examiner will then need to assess whether sufficient time was spent in establishing rapport with the child or whether the utilization of other procedures might be more productive. When none of these possibilities is plausible, however, the presence of a brief and barren record signals the question of a psychological style in which the child copes by oversimplifying the stimulus field (Exner & Weiner, 1982). That is, the child may be ignoring important environmental cues and oversimplifying complexity to keep his or her world manageable, but at the price of almost inevitable conflict.

Occasionally, the examiner will find that a child who has been somewhat resistant or defensive in the Free Association phase will respond more freely in the Inquiry. Klopfer (1956) and Klopfer, Ainsworth, Klopfer, and Holt (1954) have indicated the importance of noting behavioral differences in the child's performance on the two portions of the test as providing valuable information to the interpretation. Exner and Weiner (1982) suggest that by the time the Free Association has been completed, and with the additional structure of the Inquiry, the child may have become more relaxed. Thus, it is advisable to record any additional responses generated in the Inquiry, while not including these as scored responses, to supplement the interpretation.

In some instances, when the scorable record is extremely brief and barren, it may be advisable to retest the child. Another instance where retesting is strongly indicated is the production of a very brief and impoverished record by a child who is apparently cooperative, signaling the possibility of a psychological style whereby the child copes with the environment by ignoring or oversimplifying complexity.

Many examiners are reluctant to retest a child after a short period, because they fear that recent exposure results in responses too similar to those of the original examination or that recent exposure affords the child an opportunity to change his or her responses and thus changes the interpretation. Studies by Hulsart (1979) and Exner (1980) have shown that this is not the case and that valid, interpretively useful records may be obtained after very brief intervals.

However, a viable and often preferable alternative in these cases is simply to say, at the completion of the Administration Proper, "Good. Now you've got the idea of how to do these, so let's go through them again. Most children see more than one thing, and you may too, now that you know how to do these." This procedure is often all that is necessary to yield an interpretively useful record.

NORMATIVE DATA

All of the major Rorschach methods currently in use in the United States include some mention of administrative procedures and interpretation guidelines for use with children. However, only two scoring systems provide normative data obtained from stratified samples of children at various ages and exclusively designed to facilitate interpretation of children's records (Ames et al., 1974; Ames, Metraux, & Walker, 1971; Exner, 1978, 1986; Exner & Weiner, 1982). Ames and her colleagues have based their work on the scoring system of Dr. Marguerite Hertz. Their method provides norms for children aged 2 through 16, with the advantage of norms at half-year intervals for children ages 2 through 5½ to accommodate the diversity in development common to children in that age range.

The Exner Comprehensive System provides norms for children aged 5 through 16, as well as adult norms, thus giving added flexibility to the examiner who works with both children and adults. The child and adolescent norms are based on a sample of 1,580 nonpatient children who were recruited through schools and other organizations. Sample selection was partially stratified for socioeconomic and geographic status (Exner, 1986, p. 255). Normative tables provide the following information for 70 of the scoring variables at each year level: mean, standard deviation, mode, minimum and maximum range, frequency, skewness, and kurtosis. These data, both for children and for adolescents, are helpful to the examiner in serving as baseline information.

Although the availability of normative data specifically designed for use with children is a substantial aid to interpretation, norms, like all other standards for normal performance, must be used intelligently. Digressions from the norms may be signs of uniqueness or idiographic ways of looking at the world and may be in no way abnormal. Conversely, a child can produce a normal record and still lack or be deficient in certain necessary adaptive skills. Moreover, the normative data itself may underrepresent certain groups or be insensitive to developmental differences, Finally, because many of the Rorschach scores occur infrequently, they are not normally distributed, and rigid application of the normative data is inappropriate. In these instances, the examiner should rely more heavily on either the mode or the frequency with which the response is likely to occur for the age of the child in question.

SCORING

General Considerations

A full explanation of the Comprehensive System's scoring procedures is beyond the scope of this chapter; the interested or unfamiliar reader might consult either of the Exner books describing the system (Exner, 1978, 1986). A summary of the scoring variables is given in Exner and Martin (1983, pp. 410–411).

The Comprehensive System currently includes approximately 90 possible scores (or codes) for the Rorschach responses. There are seven major categories into which the scores are placed:

1. Location (Where on the blot is the response or percept seen?)
2. Determinants (What features in the blot contributed to the formation of the percept?)
3. Form Quality (How "good a fit" is the percept to the area of the blot to which the percept was offered?")
4. Content (What is the content of the percept?)
5. Popularity (Is the percept one that is commonly given?)
6. Organizational Activity (To what degree does the response organize the blot elements?)
7. Special Scores (Does the response include unusual verbal material or unusual characteristics?)

Each response a child makes to the inkblots is scored according to specified criteria. These scores are then expressed as percentages, frequencies, or ratios on the "Structural Summary" and are compared to the normative data for purposes of interpretation.

One of the strengths of the Comprehensive System is its continuing research program investigating the psychometric qualities of the scores remaining on the Structural Summary. Exner (1986) reported that more than 30 reliability studies of temporal consistency of the variables had been completed at the Rorschach Research Foundation by 1983. Time intervals between test and retest have varied from a few days to 3 years. Exner and Martin (1983) report that in the longest test–retest study, using 100 nonpatient subjects, reliability coefficients for 20 critical variables were uniformly high for that amount of elapsed time: For 10 variables, the coefficients were between .80 and .90; for 7, between .73 and .80; and only 3 fell at or below .70. Short-term reliability coefficients are even higher. Many studies have also been conducted investigating interscorer reliability for each of the variables. Exner (1986, p. 89) reports that a standard of 90%

agreement among scorers or a .25 intercorrelation was used as a standard.

Notes on Scoring for Children and Adolescents

The examiner should also be aware that certain scoring differences are to be expected with children. Very young children give shorter records, and preschoolers will commonly give as few as 10 responses. Younger children also give more Whole (W) than Common Detail (D) location responses, and this tendency may continue through age 11 or so. By approximately age 12, however, more D than W responses are expected. Very few children give a Dd location response, and even fewer give more than one. Similarly, children seldom give large numbers of White Space responses (S), although almost all children give some of these; thus, the absence of S is conspicuous.

Children's ability to synthesize develops slowly and gradually, but is expected to appear by age 8 or 9. The production of Human Movement (M) increases with the age of the child, whereas Animal Movement (FM) is fairly consistent across age groups. Inanimate Movement (m) rarely appears before age 8 and continues thereafter to be low in frequency. Regardless of the type of movement, children consistently report more active than passive movement, although some passive movement appears in almost all records.

Young children are not expected to mediate their expressions of affect to any great extent, and this is generally reflected in a Form–Color ratio (FC:CF + C) that is weighted on the right side. The shift in weighting from the right to the left side is a gradual one, however, and is not expected to be complete until age 15 or 16. Nonetheless, pure C and Color-Naming responses (Cn) decline more rapidly beginning at about age 5. By age 8, only about one-third will give any of these responses.

Across all age groups, children generally give few grey–black or Shading responses. When they do, a Texture response (T) is twice as likely as any other. Achromatic Color (C') and Diffuse Shading (Y) responses are low in frequency for all youngsters, and Vista responses (V) are the least common of all. The *FD* score for dimension based on form, refered to as the Form-Dimension (Exner & Weiner, 1982) response, tends to increase with the age of the child, but is still expected to be relatively infrequent.[1] Young children between the ages of 5 and 8 commonly give Reflection responses *(Fr)*, but by age 9 they dramatically reduce the frequency. By age 15, Reflection responses appear in only about one of four records. Pair responses (2), on the other hand, appear at all age levels, although probably less so in the records of 5-year-olds.

Even very young children will generate one or more *P* responses, but the frequency of these is far greater by adolescence. Similarly, young children will demonstrate some ability to organize. However, in young children, the Organizational score (Z) tends to be associated with W responses, whereas in middle and later childhood, scores reflect more sophisticated organizational activity. Most children, regardless of age, will give at least one blend and one pure *H* (Human) response.

Perseveration responses *(PSV)* are not unusual in the records of very young children, but tend to decline by about age 8. Color Projection *(CP)*, too, is common among young children, but virtually disappears by age 6. Similarly, Confabulatory responses *(CONFAB)* and the Special Scores of the Exner Comprehensive System (Exner, 1978, 1986; Exner & Weiner, 1982) are often seen in young children's records, but generally disappear by middle childhood.

Several other scores unique to the Comprehensive System show a similar decline with age. Lambda *(L)*, the Affective Ratio *(Afr)*, and the Egocentricity Index $(3r + (2)/R)$ tend to be elevated in the very young child and to diminish over time. The *Zd* score for children is expected to be around 0 except for those aged 7 years and under, who commonly score negative values.[2] However,

the *X–%*, and to some extent the *F+%*, are highly consistent over time and change is unlikely. Finally, children's *EB* values frequently reflect an extratensive style, particularly in the early years. With age, the number of introversives tends to increase. Moreover, while very few children generate more shading responses than *Fm + m*, it is quite likely that children through ages 11 or 12 will have an *es* that is greater than *EA*.

INTERPRETATION OF CHILDREN'S RECORDS

General Considerations

Skilled interpretation demands a thorough understanding of the developmental process, together with a complete comprehension of what the normative data can be expected to provide. Rorschach data have essentially the same meaning at all ages; however, the particular frequency, percentage, or weight of a response varies in interpretive significance with age. Nevertheless, the examiner must not apply the normative data concretely, but instead must be sensitive to the unique qualities of the individual scores. Moreover, examiners must be familiar with psychopathology and with personality theory. This background is essential to making determinations regarding prognosis and the form of treatment or remediation most likely to elicit a positive response from the child.

Children's Rorschach scores are not consistent over time; thus, the examiner must think in terms of probabilities rather than predictions, except in the case of severe pathology. Exner, Thomas, and Mason (1985) have demonstrated that only the *X+%* is relatively stable from ages 8 through 16. In the same study, the majority of Rorschach variables were inconsistent until approximately ages 14 to 16, and even then the ability to modulate affect, the extent of self-focus, the effort expended in organizing, and some of

---

[1]*FD* and *V* are both scores for dimensionality, but *V* is based on the use of Shading whereas *FD* is based on the use of Form.

[2]*Zd* is a difference score, which is calculated by subtracting the *Zest* from the *Z Sum*. *F+%* refers to conventional pure form or perceptual accuracy in the Pure *F* responses only, whereas *X+%* and *X–%* refer to perceptual accuracy in the entire record. *EB* is the Erlebnistypus or preferred response style or problem-solving style. It is a ratio comprised of *M* on the left and all of

C responses on the right, the sum of which is expressed as the *EA*, or Experience Actual. A similar ratio is the *eb*, or Experience Base, which is comprised of *FM + m*, or all the nonhuman movement determinants on the left and all of the Shading and achromatic color determinants (Y, T, V, C') on the right. The sum of these is expressed as the *es* or Experienced Stimulation. (For further information on the composition and use of these ratios, see Exner, 1978, 1986.)

the factors involved in cognitive slippage remained unstable.

Among younger children, the *EB* generally reflects an extratensive style. When this persists beyond age 12, it is highly likely to become a stable feature. On the other hand, the establishment of an introversive style appears to occur somewhat earlier, and the child who demonstrates an introversive style at age 8 may well maintain it (Exner, Leura, Wylie, Armbruster, & Thomas, 1980).

Similarly, the *es* of young children frequently is greater than the *EA*; however, when the *EA* does become greater than the *es*, it tends to remain so in subsequent protocols. Depending on the age of the child, *EA > es* can be either a positive or a negative finding. This shift is expected during the developmental process and generally signals psychological maturity. A premature shift, however, could portend rigidity and inflexibility (Exner, Leura, et al., 1980). The *es* tends to be relatively stable, but since it is comprised of some highly unstable elements (*m* [Inanimate Movement] and *Y* [Diffuse Shading]), it warrants the examiner's careful attention. When any of the unstable elements of the *es* is present in a child's record, particularly if the element appears in greater than the expected number, the stability of the *es* and the direction of the *EA : es* are both suspect. The examiner must determine whether the scores are truly representative of the child or whether they reflect temporary situational phenomena.

The interpretation of the *EA : es* ratio, therefore, must take several factors into account. First, the age of the child must be considered in conjunction with the appropriate normative data to establish the expected directionality of the ratio and range of values for the component scores. The examiner should note the magnitude of the difference between the *EA* and *es* values, as well as the frequencies and kinds of variables that comprise the *es*, with particular attention to those that are transitory and situational. The directionality of the *eb* relative to the *es* should also be examined. The presence or absence of *T* (Texture) in a child's record is vital (Leura & Exner, 1976; Pierce, 1978). Elevations in *T* can signal personal loss, whereas the absence of *T* is highly uncommon and may indicate either a tendency toward defensiveness and guardedness in interpersonal relationships or the absence of a need for or expectation of interpersonal closeness. Finally, the examiner must integrate the child's history and background information with the data to insure meaningful and useful interpretation.

Another aspect of Rorschach interpretation where findings are unique to children is the *FC : CF + C* ratio. Young children do not (and are not expected to) modulate their expressions of affect, resulting in a ratio that is weighted on the right. As the development process progresses, the capacity for control increases, and a gradual shift from right to left generally occurs. The composition of the scores on the right side of the ratio, however, undergoes a rather dramatic change at about age 6, when the occurrence of pure *C* and Color-Naming responses diminishes markedly. Thus, while a *FC : CF + C* ratio weighted to the right is not uncommon at age 12, the majority of responses on the right side should be *CF*. When the capacity for affective modulation develops in the child, it tends to persist and is reflected in a shift in the weight of the ratio from right to left. Once again, the age of the child, the magnitude of the difference between the values for the right and left sides of the ratio, and the integration of the child's history and background are vital to accurate interpretation. An *FC* weighting in a child of 12 years of age or less is often premature and may signal overcontrol. Moreover, for certain youngsters, an *FC* weighting even at age 16 may be problematic (Exner, Leura, et al., 1980).

Another common occurrence in the records of children and adolescents is the Personalized response (PER). These tend to be frequent in the records of very young children, but disappear gradually through the course of development. The appearance of one such response in an adolescent record is not unusual; however, a high frequency of Personalized responses suggests defensiveness and a need to protect the self-image. Therefore, the examiner should note the frequency of these responses relative to the age of the child, as well as the overall quality of the child's personalized responses. Some responses are distinctly more defensive than others and yield substantial indications of the child's unique vulnerabilities.

The $W:M$ ratio will also show some characteristic variability in the records of children. Commonly, the left side of the ratio will be markedly higher—particularly in the very young child, where grandiosity and limitless aspirations prevail. During the course of normal development, the ratio is expected to decrease gradually until it approaches adult levels in late adolescence. The examiner should be alert for a $W:M$ ratio that is too constrained in relation to the age of the child.

Gordon and Tegtmeyer (1982) substantiate the use of the Egocentricity Index $(3r + (2)/R)$ as a measure of self-focusing as opposed to self-esteem in children. However, the authors indicate that possibly these results are an artifact produced by limiting the number of responses to two per card. These same authors (Tegtmeyer & Gordon, 1983) found that children who gave a high number of S responses also gave significantly more W and total Shading responses, and more blends and a greater number of Content categories, than children who gave no more than one S response. Tegtmeyer and Gordon (1983) concluded that relatively high frequencies of S responses appear to be related to cognitive complexity and active mastery in children.

In a somewhat different approach to the question of cognitive complexity, Smith (1981) found a positive relationship between children's cognitive-developmental stage and the number and percentage of W responses. In addition, the level of cognitive functioning and W production was found to vary with the complexity of the stimulus. That is, children who had achieved the developmental stage of formal operations showed a marked increase in the number and complexity of W responses to the broken blots, compared to children in the concrete stage.

The Rorschach and Children from Disadvantaged Backgrounds

Some special considerations are in order when interpreting the records of children from low-socioeconomic-status (low-SES) backgrounds. Exner and Weiner (1982) have delineated very specific findings for sex, age, and SES. Generally speaking, there appear to be some differences in the records of children from low-SES backgrounds, but these differences are not consistent across all of the samples. The authors caution that although the Structural Summary may not yield differences among the various SES groups in terms of location, determinant, or content category, substantial variation may be found in the verbal material or verbal expression of these children that is not reflected in their scores. Although a child's cognitive and perceptual operations certainly influence the content of his or her verbal material, interpretations of the verbal material should be done with extreme caution (Exner & Weiner, 1982).

A recent study of inner-city children (Krall et al., 1983) found a lower F accuracy level, a lower percentage of W responses, and a higher frequency of D responses among these children when compared to both the Ames et al. (1974) and the Exner and Weiner (1982) normative data. The authors also found, however, that the children in their study were very similar to those in both data bases with regard to response rate and development of the P response.

Although caution is always warranted in content interpretation, a study of the aggressive content in the Rorschach records of inner-city children (Crain & Smoke, 1981) yielded information that may be of use to the prudent examiner. Children in the control group gave aggressive content related to interpersonal interactions and equal power, such as fighting, whereas children in the clinical group gave aggressive responses characterized by vicitimization and feelings of being overwhelmed, such as devouring monsters.

Other studies involving content analysis of children's Rorschach records, although not limited to children from lower-SES backgrounds, have produced findings that may be used to augment the basic interpretation. Gordon and Tegtmeyer (1983) found that oral-dependent responses in the records of children do not have the same interpretive significance that they do in the records of adults. Rather, these responses in the records of children tend to be associated with various internalizing behaviors, such as withdrawal, somatic complaints, and obsessive and compulsive behaviors.

The Rorschach and Children with Learning Problems

The Rorschach test has been shown to be very sensitive to many of the variables that affect children's ability to learn. For example, Ames and Walker (1964) demonstrated that children with cognitive flexibility, as indicated on Rorschach protocols collected in their kindergarten years, were better readers in the fifth grade. These children were found to be more open to information in the environment and more able to use these cues in their learning. Conversely, Smock (1958) showed that when anxiety is artificially induced in children, it can promote perceptual rigidity and premature closure on cognitive tasks. Subsequently, Smock and Holt (1962) found significant negative correlations between perceptual rigidity and IQ, school achievement, and curiosity.

Although children with learning problems do not necessarily demonstrate diminished intelligence or curiosity, they frequently show marked perceptual difficulties and other impediments to school achievement. In addition to documented learning disabilities, learning problems can include limited intellectual functioning and various types of neurological impairment. When a child has demonstrated limited intellectual functioning, as indicated by a standardized individual IQ score in the 70s or 80s, the Rorschach may or may not be useful. Other measures may better address the education and training needs of these youngsters. On the other hand, the Rorschach can occasionally be useful, particularly with the higher-functioning of these children, in detecting personal assets that can be used to the best advantage in educational interventions. Certain Rorschach features are common to this group of children; they include low number of total responses, predominance of pure F, few or no M responses, few or no chromatic C responses with poor integration, few or no Synthesized responses, low $F+\%$ and $X+\%$, narrow range of Contents, low number of P responses, and a higher than usual occurrence of Color-Naming (CN) responses (Exner & Weiner, 1982).

When a child has a neurological impairment and/or attention deficit disorder, the Rorschach can be a very useful addition to the assessment battery because of the complex emotional and behavioral features attendant upon these difficulties. Testing can reveal the child's preferred coping mechanisms, level and availability of controls, ability to direct cognitions, interpersonal attitudes, and personality assets, all of which will be helpful in determining the most appropriate methods of intervention and education (Exner & Weiner, 1982).

Certain specific features of the Rorschach records of children with neurological impairment have been noted. One of these is a lower frequency of M responses. Gordon and Oshman (1981) suggest that this is related to the inability to delay in hyperactive children. Champion, Johnson, McCreary, and Doughtie (1984) propose that the lower-than-average Egocentricity Index frequently found in these children's records is related to the social stigma accompanying their learning problems. In addition, these authors attribute the lower $X+\%$ to problems with perceptual accuracy. Scott (1985) indicates that the data in the Four Square can be extremely useful in locating sources of problems as well as in formulating interventions.

Williams and Miles (1985) tested a small sample of dyslexic children on two occasions approximately 6 months apart. Eight of the children were American, and seven were from the United Kingdom. The authors found that the dyslexic children in their sample gave Rorschach records that were very similar to one another's but unlike those of other clinical populations or the matched control group. Specifically, the dyslexic children gave fewer responses (typically one per card), a high percentage of F responses, and a very limited range of Determinants; also, they rarely turned the cards. Although the generalizability of these findings is limited by the small number of youngsters in the sample, the authors note that there were essentially no differences between the responses of the dyslexic children from the United States and those of the children from the United Kingdom, regardless of age or type of school.

A study of two groups of learning-disabled children (Champion et al., 1984) revealed that the response patterns for children with learning disabilities were distinctly different from Exner and Weiner's (1982) normative data for nonpatients, behavior problems, or withdrawn children. Compared to nonpatients, children with learning disabilities had lower $F+\%$ and $X+\%$, lower Egocentricity Indices, higher Lambdas, more Dd and S, and more Shading responses. In the group of 8-year-old learning-disabled children, the mean number of H percepts was at least one standard deviation below the mean of the normative sample. This group also gave more C', V, and Y, and fewer T, than nonpatients of the same age. Dyslexic children in the 11-year-old group gave more of all types of Shading responses, and their mean Lambda was at least one standard deviation above the mean for the 11-year-old norm group.

In studies of learning-disabled children related to Rorschach content, Heinicke (1972) found no specific conflict or content category consistent across records. The author proposed, however, that learning disturbances were often associated with unresolved intrapsychic conflicts that were manifested in the unsuccessfully integrated primary-process material found in these children's records. Based on earlier findings in children with reading problems (Heinicke, 1969), the author asserted that children who can integrate and master primary-process material are more likely to be flexible thinkers and, therefore, better learners than those who defend against and repress this material. Subsequently, Russ (1980) found that the ability to integrate primary-process material successfully, in a socialized manner with good Form Quality, was significantly related to achievement, independent of intelligence. Although content interpretation is not recommended in exclusion of the psychometric data from the Rorschach, examiners may wish to use these findings to augment the Rorschach test data.

The Rorschach and Children with Depression

When depression is suspected in a child, critical information can be obtained from a thorough and dependable history and from the behavioral observations of the parents and teacher. Adults, however, are not always alert to the signs of childhood depression or are preoccupied with personal concerns and fail to attend sufficiently. Parents engrossed in personal concerns may overlook the child's cues. The teacher may misinterpret the child's "perfect" behavior. Consequently, from time to time, the child's Rorschach data will show signs of depression even when there is no report of substantiating evidence.

In adults, the two most common features found in the records of depressives are a low Egocentricity Index and elevation in the right side of the eb (Experience Base), or a sum of the shading responses that is greater than $FM + m$. Occasionally, the Egocentricity Index will be elevated rather than depressed. This is the exception rather than the rule, but in either case, there is a problem in self-focusing and evaluation of the self. When the depression is reactive rather than chronic, however, the Egocentricity Index frequently falls in the normal range (Exner, 1974, 1978). Adult depressives also frequently give more V and FD (Form-Dimension) responses than are normally expected.

The Rorschach records of children who are depressed show features similar to those of adults, although it is unusual to find both a depressed Egocentricity Index and a higher right-sided eb in the record of a child. When this occurs, it is also very likely that there will be an elevation in Morbid Content (MOR) responses (Exner & McCoy, 1981). Children who are depressed, whether chronic or situational, tend to give more MOR responses than those who are not. Nevertheless, MOR does appear in the records of children who are not depressed at all. Thus, the features commonly associated with childhood depression are more than one Vista or FD response, the presence of even one Color–Shading blend, a low Egocentricity Index, eb elevated on the right, and an unusually high frequency of MOR content responses (Exner & Weiner, 1982). Exner and Weiner state that when four of these five are present, the child is experiencing either distress or, more likely, depression.

The examiner must then decide whether the condition is reactive or chronic. Both V responses and the Egocentricity Index are not particularly responsive to situational effects and take a long time to form. Thus, if the child's record contains both V responses and a low Egocentricity Index, the condition is probably chronic. Conversely, if the child's record contains m and Y responses with no elevation in V or depression of the Egocentricity Index, the condition is more likely to be situational or reactive.

A more complex circumstance exists when an earlier situational stressor in the life of the child has not been effectively resolved. In these instances, both V responses and a low Egocentricity Index can appear together with m and Y in the child's record, even when there is no evidence of enduring problems.

There are several other Rorschach indices that may attend depression in children. The Affective Ratio may be low because of the child's tendency to withdraw and avoid emotional situations. The frequency of S responses may be elevated. A low Lambda indicates that the child has become too involved in complexity, which actually aggravates the depression. An elevated $W:M$ ratio signals that the child's aspirations exceed his or her abilities, leading to frequent experiences of frustration. The presence of this indicator can point to early intervention possibilities. An elevated $W:D$ ratio indicates that the child cannot or will not economize in using resources; this is confirmed by an elevated Zf. If only the Zf is elevated, it is important for the examiner to note how much of the elevation is accounted for by W and how much is comprised of more complex responses. Finally, when the child's $X+\%$ is below what is normally expected, the examiner should ascertain whether this is a function of unique and idiographic responses ($Xu\%$) or actual distortion ($X-\%$). The number of P responses in the child's record can be useful in determining the significance of a low $X+\%$ (Exner & Weiner, 1982).

Obviously, when a child is depressed, the question is not only whether the experience is situational or chronic, but also how acutely the distress is felt by the child. More precisely, what is the likelihood that the child will act on this experienced distress and attempt or succeed in committing suicide? Unfortunately, there are no infallible guidelines. Exner (1978) has constructed a Suicide Constellation for children, but admits to its limited usefulness and cautions examiners to use it only with a complete understanding of its limitations and in conjunction with information from the child's history, background data, and behavior. The Exner (1978) children's Suicide Constellation was based on a sample of only 39 cases. Using a criteria of seven or eight predictors, the constellation correctly identified only 23 of 39 attempted suicides and only 15 of 21 completed suicides. Moreover, using the same criteria, the Suicide Constellation did not identify any children in the nonpatient control group, but it *did* incorrectly identify 20% of the children and adolescents in the psychiatric group (Exner & Weiner, 1982).

The Rorschach Workshops (1987, p. 6) have issued a more severe caution concerning the children's Suicide Constellation. They ran a cross-validation study using a total sample of 51 cases, 36 of whom attempted and 15 of whom completed suicide. The results did not cross-validate, and Exner has concluded that the "constellation is psychometrically worthless" as it now exists for children. However, the adult constellation possesses a "true positive" hit rate of approximately 67% for the children ages 15 and 16. The same is not true for children below this age.

Finally, Blatt and Ritzler (1974) and Rierdan, Lang, and Eddy (1978) have found that the frequency of occurrence of Transparent, Translucent, and Cross-Sectional responses is a useful predictor of completed suicide in adults. Apparently, these types of responses represent an unsuccessful attempt to establish dimensionality or volume, with obvious implications for the sense of self. Unfortunately, the authors have as yet been unable to explain why individuals who commit suicide give more of these types of responses than do individuals who threaten or unsuccessfully attempt suicide; nor has either study specified a critical cutoff for the frequency of these responses. Furthermore, there is as yet no evidence to support the usefulness of this concept in evaluating children's Rorschach records. Nevertheless, the prudent examiner may wish to view the occurrence of any of these responses in a child's record as a "red flag" and proceed with appropriate follow-up measures.

The Rorschach and Childhood Schizophrenia

The diagnosis of schizophrenia is, of course, never made on the basis of the Rorschach record alone. A thorough and reliable history, and the behavioral observations of parents and teachers, are invaluable supplements to information obtained in the assessment battery. Part of that information will be the examiner's own observations of the child during the examination period. Thus, the examiner must be able to identify the salient behavioral features of schizophrenia. There are four major areas that pose difficulty for the schizophrenic individual: cognition, perception, interpersonal relationships, and the ability to exert appropriate controls in each of these endeavors (Exner & Weiner, 1982).

The cognitions of the schizophrenic child or adolescent are often marked by difficulties in maintaining clear and coherent associations, strained or deviant logic, and inappropriate levels of abstraction. Initially, and particularly in the younger child, these cognitive difficulties are extremely subtle, and the examiner may attribute their occurrence to inattentiveness, anxiety, and the like. However, the logic of the schizophrenic child tends to be highly circumstantial, with frank dissociations or associations that are tenuous at best. For example, when asked his name, a schizophrenic boy may respond, "My name is Bill, but my dog's name is Charlie. I don't know where he is, though." Although this sort of thinking is common in very young children, it usually disappears by age 7 (Exner & Weiner, 1982). Moreover, these children have marked deficiencies in their ability to abstract at appropriate levels. They are inclined to polarize, being either too concrete or too abstract. For example, in response to the comment "Time is money," the child may respond, "No, it's three o'clock." At the other extreme, these youngsters become preoccupied with abstraction, such as "This bat looks more peaceful, young, like he's got these big wings he doesn't know what to do with yet, just trying to experience."

Manifestations of these sorts of cognitive difficulties will appear in the language of the child during the Free Association and the Inquiry. Neither Ames and colleagues (Ames et al., 1971, 1974) nor any of the other major Rorschach systematizers deal with schizophrenia across children's age groups as succinctly as does the Comprehensive System (Exner, 1974, 1978, 1986; Exner et al., 1985;

Exner & Weiner, 1982). Therefore, Rorschach findings unique to the protocols of schizophrenic youngsters will be expressed in the scoring terminology of the Exner method.

In addition to evidence of cognitive disturbance in the child's general manner of expression, the response language of the child will contain scorable features that range on a continuum from mild to severe. At the mild extreme are slips of the tongue and Redundancies (DV) and Incongruous Combinations (INCOM), such as "blue chickens." Deviant Responses (DR), such as inappropriate or irrelevant phrases or circumstantial responses, and Fabulized Combinations (FABCOM), such as "two cats sitting on a rocket," are in the midrange of severity. At the severe extreme of the continuum are the Contamination (CONTAM) and Inappropriate Logic (ALOG) responses. CONTAM responses represent the fusion of two percepts into one, as exemplified in the response, "I see a kitty and a bird. It's a cat–bird." ALOG responses, on the other hand, contained strained or circumstantial logic, such as "They must be in love because this heart is between them." In terms of interpretive significance, the presence of one or even several of the milder responses is expected in the record of a child, but the presence of only one CONTAM is a serious indicator of pathology.

Moreover, each of these types of scores has an inherent range of possible responses from mild to severe. For example, "two cats sitting on a rocket" is far milder that "two giant bugs eating the Eiffel Tower." Of further interpretive significance is the child's ability to recognize a poor response. The youngster who is able to say, "That's not very good," is far less likely to have a disturbance in thinking than the child who persistently maintains, "That's just what they look like." Of course, INCOM, FABCOM, and ALOG are more common among children (particularly very young children) than adults, and appear with higher frequency in their records. Therefore, the examiner must make prudent use of the normative data in forming interpretive decisions.

The child's cognitive difficulties may include an inappropriate level of abstraction. On the Rorschach, this is often manifested in a preoccupation with abstraction and symbolism. It may take the form of an unusually high frequency of responses containing conventional symbolism, or may emerge in responses containing highly personalized, idiographic symbolism. In either case, the child's overuse of or preoccupation with symbolism increases the possibility of a thought disturbance. It should be noted, however, that in the intelligent and otherwise healthy child, moderate use of symbolism and/or abstraction is probably a positive indicator.

Schizophrenic youngsters also demonstrate distorted perceptions that lead to poor judgment. They tend to misperceive both themselves and others. An adolescent girl with no training or skills will insist that she is a highly talented designer who simply has no outlet for her superior gifts, for example, and will refuse to consider employment opportunities appropriate to her background. Or a casual remark, such as "It's been nice to see you," will be misconstrued as a serious romantic innuendo.

On the Rorschach, distortions in perception are measured by the Form Quality, the $F+\%$, the $X+\%$, and the $X-\%$ (Distorted Form). Scores below .70 for both the $F+\%$ and the $X+\%$ generally signal impaired perceptual functioning, and scores below .60 are almost always indicative of inaccuracy. In a brief Rorschach record, it is advisable to rely on the $X+\%$, because the $F+\%$ may be representative of only a few responses. When the $X+\%$ is below .70, the $X-\%$ will indicate whether the low $X+\%$ is the result of idiosyncratic responding (as represented in Form Quality scores of "unusual") or whether it is the result of frank distortion (as represented in "minus" Form Quality scores). Although it is true that an individual can be unique to the point of eccentricity, idiographic responding does not have the same prognostic implications as does seriously impaired perceptual accuracy. The examiner should scan the sequence of scores to determine whether clusters of "unusual" or "minus" responses occur in relation to particular determinants or contents. When patterns occur, it is highly likely that the impaired perception is linked to specific precursors as opposed to overall inaccuracy, and interventions are far more apt to be successful.

Another Rorschach indicator of perceptual accuracy is the P response, which measures the child's ability to see things as others do, or to respond conventionally. Youngsters aged 11 or older who deliver less than four P responses have an impaired ability to be conventional, which generally results in poor judgment. Before age 11 this is not always true, and the examiner must use the normative data carefully to determine the significance of a low number of P responses in the individual child. Moreover, P responses occur most frequently to Cards I, III, V, and VIII, so if the child gives only three or four P responses, they should occur on these cards. When the child does this, the concern regarding perceptual distortions and poor judgment is somewhat diminished. When the child delivers three or four P responses to cards *other* than I, III, V, and VIII, the concern is magnified considerably.

Because of their disordered thinking and their misperceptions of self and others, schizophrenic youngsters have poor social skills, and therefore great difficulty in forming and maintaining interpersonal relationships. Even when participating in group activities, these children tend to be distant and emotionally withdrawn. Often they are physically withdrawn as well. The child's history and the behavioral observations of parents and teachers will provide vital information regarding patterns of interpersonal functioning, as well as onset and duration of any deviations from established patterns. Naturally, the assessment process itself provides an opportunity for the examiner to engage the child in various interactions directly.

The primary Rorschach indicators of interpersonal difficulties are inferior M and H production. Although conservatism is warranted when interpreting the records of very young children, the absence of M in a child's record generally signals a serious withdrawal from interest in people. Moreover, M is expected to appear with good Form Quality. A child, even as young as age 5, who delivers an M response with "minus" Form Quality will tend to assign inaccurate and illusory meanings to social situations and to have deficient social skills (Exner & Weiner, 1982). Other, less severe indicators of the child's difficulty in dealing with people are M responses with (H), Hd, (Hd), A, (A), Ad, and (Ad) content.[3]

Since it is possible for the child to give a response with human content but without human movement, the presence of good H in the child's record is a positive sign in the very young child or in the child whose operations are not yet sufficiently complex to produce M. However, the absence of H or the presence of H in conjunction with M– is interpreted in essentially the same way as the absence of M or the presence of M– responses.

An additional problem for the schizophrenic child is his or her inability to exert appropriate controls in the cognitive, perceptual, and interpersonal spheres. These children are preoccupied with anxiety-provoking thoughts, largely of sexual and aggressive content. Moreover, they are unable to integrate their thoughts and feelings properly, resulting in either blunted or unsuitable expressions of affect. These difficulties are expressed in Rorschach contents of cruelty, violent aggression, and flagrant sexuality. Whereas the average child reports aggression in terms of "fighting" or some type of MOR, the schizophrenic child delivers responses that reflect gore and brutality. Similarly, although sexual responses are rare in a child, they normally tend to represent developmental concerns when they do occur. Sexual responses occur more frequently in the records of schizophrenic children and tend to reflect a disturbed preoccupation. These children's inability to exert effective controls is often apparent in an FC:CF + C ratio that is weighted to the right. Throughout the developmental process, there is a gradual shift of the weighting from the right to the left side of the ratio. Nevertheless, the appearance of pure C in the record after age 8 warrants investigation and signals the possibility of episodes of unmodulated affect.

Once the examiner has established substantial support for the presence of a thought disorder in a child, the question of an acute versus a chronic process remains. Generally

speaking, when the frequency of scores on variables measuring cognitive disturbance, perceptual inaccuracy, interpersonal difficulties, and problems with control are relatively low and do not deviate excessively from the norms, the process is likely to be an acute and reactive one, probably in the early stages. In this context, the presence of increased numbers of INCOM, FABCOM, and ALOG responses may be indicative of the child's attempt to manage and make sense of his or her world, in contrast to the apathy typical of the chronic process. Acute onset is usually related to a precipitating event or a situational precursor; the child is aware of his or her diminished capacities and is upset and anxious in this regard. As mentioned earlier, these youngsters often spontaneously recognize the inadequacy of their responses.

The chronic schizophrenic process, on the other hand, is characterized by Rorschach scores that are more markedly deviant on variables measuring cognitive disturbance, perceptual inaccuracy, interpersonal difficulties, and problems with control. Moreover, while these youngsters tend to become quite anxious with regard to external events, they are unconcerned about their own inappropriate thoughts and behaviors. This sense of apathy and resignation tends to become a permanent feature when the EA is greater than the es, indicating no particular distress.

The hallmarks of schizophrenia are disordered thinking and perceptual inaccuracy. Although bizarre contents and peculiar language may augment these findings, they may not substitute for concrete evidence of serious cognitive slippage and impaired perception. Moreover, in a recent study, Exner et al. (1985) have demonstrated that many of the cognitive and perceptual operations unique to schizophrenia are highly resistant to change, even with therapeutic intervention and even over extended periods of time.

Few other conditions exist in which both of these features, disordered thinking and perceptual inaccuracy, are present. However, examiners, particularly those who work with adolescents, should be aware that the Rorschach records of youngsters experiencing amphetamine-related and phencyclidine hydrochloride (PCP) psychoses frequently mimic those of schizophrenics. When amphetamine-related psychoses are involved,

---

[3](H) = Whole Human (fictional or mythological; Hd = Human Detail; (Hd) = Human Detail (fictional or mythological; A = Animal or Whole Animal; (A) = Whole Animal (fictional, mythological, including cartoons); Ad = Animal Detail; and (Ad) = Animal Detail (fictional, mythological, or cartoon).

retesting after approximately 30 days should yield a more accurate profile (Exner, 1978; Weiner, 1964). Almost all of the records of individuals experiencing PCP-induced psychoses show features concomitant with a diagnosis of schizophrenia. In the case of PCP-induced psychoses, however, these features do not disappear after 30 days, but persist for as yet undetermined lengths of time.

A LAST WORD

Now, a word of caution: While we are all familiar with the need to select and use instruments with current, up-to-date norms, we are also familiar with problems that arise when old tests are modified and new norms are established (e.g., the original vs. revised versions of the Wechsler Intelligence Scale for Children, or the Stanford–Binet, Form L-M, vs. the "new" Binet). As Exner (1986, p. 4) suggests, "It would be foolhardy to suggest that the work is finished. The Rorschach continues to pose many unanswered questions."

Research on the Exner Comprehensive System of the Rorschach is an ongoing process that results in modifications in scoring criteria, changes in norms for some scores, and refinement of definitions and scoring criteria for some variables. For example, Exner and his colleagues at the Rorschach Research Foundation are currently conducting studies in an attempt to differentiate levels among the Special Scores more clearly. The Rorschach Research Foundation (Rorschach Workshops) publishes periodic newsletters, updating for previous participants any changes that have been made in the system and keeping them abreast of ongoing research. However, not all individuals trained in the Exner system receive this information. The caution, then, is that all users of the system should keep current with the progress being made.

REFERENCES

Ames, L. B., Metraux, R. W., Rodell, J. L., & Walker, R. N. (1974). *Child Rorschach responses* (rev. ed.). New York: Brunner/Mazel.

Ames, L. B., Metraux, R. W., & Walker, R. N. (1971). *Adolescent Rorschach responses*. New York: Brunner/Mazel.

Ames, L., & Walker, R. (1964). Prediction of later reading ability from kindergarten Rorschach and I.Q. scores. *Journal of Educational Psychology, 55*, 309–313.

Blatt, S. J., & Ritzler, B. A. (1974). Suicide and the representation of transparency and cross-sections on the Rorschach. *Journal of Consulting and Clinical Psychology, 42*, 280–287.

Champion, L., Johnson, P. J., McCreary, J. H., & Doughtie, E. B. (1984). Preliminary investigation into the Rorschach response patterns of children with documented learning disabilities. *Journal of Clinical Psychology, 40*, 329–333.

Crain, W. C., & Smoke, L. (1981). Rorschach aggressive content in normal and problematic children. *Journal of Personality Assessment, 45*, 2–4.

Exner, J. E. (1974). *The Rorschach: A comprehensive system. Volume 1*. New York: Wiley.

Exner, J. E. (1978). *The Rorschach: A comprehensive system. Vol. 2. Recent research and advanced interpretation*. New York: Wiley.

Exner, J. E. (1980). But it's only an inkblot. *Journal of Personality Assessment, 44*, 562–577.

Exner, J. E. (1986). *The Rorschach: A comprehensive system. Vol. 1. Basic foundations* (2nd ed.). New York: Wiley.

Exner, J. E., Armbruster, G. L., Mittman, B. L. (1978). The Rorschach response process. *Journal of Personality Assessment, 42*, 27–38.

Exner, J. E., & Leura, A. V. (1976). *Variations in the ranking of Rorschach responses as a function of situational set* (Workshops Study No. 221). Unpublished manuscript, Rorschach Workshops.

Exner, J. E., Leura, A. V., Wylie, J. R., Armbruster, G. L., & Thomas, E. A. (1980). *A longitudinal Rorschach study with children* (Workshops Study No. 207). Unpublished manuscript, Rorschach Workshops.

Exner, J. E., & McCoy, R. (1981). *An experimental score for Morbid Content* (MOR) (Workshops Study No. 269). Unpublished manuscript, Rorschach Workshops.

Exner, J. E., & Martin, L. S. (1983). The Rorschach: A history and description of the Comprehensive System. *School Psychology Review, 12*, 407–413.

Exner, J. E., Rosenthal, M., & Thomas, E. (1980). *A Rorschach study involving retesting several times at brief intervals* (Workshops Study No. 270). Unpublished manuscript, Rorschach Workshops.

Exner, J. E., Thomas, E. A., & Mason, B. J. (1985). Children's Rorschachs: Description and prediction. *Journal of Personality Assessment, 49*, 13–20.

Exner, J. E., & Weiner, I. B. (1982). *The Rorschach: A comprehensive system. Vol. 3. Assessment of children and adolescents*. New York: Wiley.

Fisher, S., & Cleveland, S. E. (1958). *Body image and personality*. New York: Van Nostrand Reinhold.

Gordon, M., & Oshman, H. (1981). Rorschach indices of children classified as hyperactive. *Perceptual and Motor Skills, 52*, 703–707.

Gordon, M., & Tegtmeyer, P. F. (1982). The Egocentricity Index and self-esteem in children. *Perceptual and Motor Skills, 55*, 335–337.

Gordon, M., & Tegtmeyer, P. F. (1983). Oral-dependent content in children's Rorschach protocols. *Perceptual and Motor Skills, 57*(3, Pt. 2), 1163–1168.

Greenberg, R., & Gordon, M. (1983). Examiner's sex and children's Rorschach productivity. *Psychological Reports, 53*, 355–357.

Halpern, F. (1953). *A clinical approach to children's Rorschachs*. New York: Grune & Stratton.

Heinicke, C. (1969). Frequency of psychotherapeutic sessions as a factor affecting outcome: Analysis of clinical ratings and test results. *Journal of Abnormal Psychology, 74*, 553–560.

Heinicke, C. (1972). Learning disturbance in childhood. In B. Wolman (Ed.), *Manual of child psychopathology*. New York: McGraw-Hill.

Hulsart, B. (1979). *The effects of a second chance instructional set on the Rorschach of emotionally disturbed and culturally deprived children*. Unpublished doctoral dissertation, Long Island University.

Klopfer, B. (1956). *Developments in the Rorschach technique* (Vol. 2). Yonkers, NY: World.

Klopfer, B., Ainsworth, M. D., Klopfer, G., & Holt, R. (1954). *Developments in the Rorschach technique* (Vol. 1). Yonkers, NY: World.

Krall, V., Sacks, H., Lazar, B., Rayson, B., Growe, G., Navar, L., & O'Connell, L. (1983). Rorschach norms for inner city children. *Journal of Personality Assessment, 47*, 155–157.

Leura, A. V., & Exner, J. E. (1976). *Rorschach performance of children with a multiple foster home history* (Workshops Study No. 220). Unpublished manuscript, Rorschach Workshops.

Leura, A. V., & Exner, J. E. (1977). *The effects of Inquiry after each card on the distribution of scores in the records of young children* (Workshops Study No. 247). Unpublished manuscript, Rorschach Workshops.

Leura, A. V., & Exner, J. E. (1978). *Structural differences in the records of adolescents as a function of being tested by one's own teacher* (Workshops Study No. 265). Unpublished manuscript, Rorschach Workshops.

Pierce, G. E. (1978). The absent parent and the Rorschach "*T*" response. In E. J. Hunter & D. S. Nice (Eds.), *Children of military families*. Washington, DC: U.S. Government Printing Office.

Rierdan, J., Lang, E., & Eddy, S. (1978). Suicide and transparency responses on the Rorschach: A replication. *Journal of Consulting and Clinical Psychology, 46*, 1162–1163.

Rorschach Workshops. (1987). *1987 alumni newsletter*. Asheville, NC: Author.

Russ, S. W. (1980). Primary process integration on the Rorschach and achievement in children. *Journal of Personality Assessment, 44*, 338–344.

Scott, R. S. (1985). Exner's Four Square: Useful index in appraisal of LD? *Perceptual and Motor Skills, 60*, 525–526.

Smith, N. M. (1981). The relationship between the Rorschach Whole response and level of cognitive functioning. *Journal of Personality Assessment, 45*, 13–19.

Smock, C. (1958). Perceptual rigidity and closure phenomenon as a function of manifest anxiety in children. *Child Development, 29*, 237–247.

Smock, C., & Holt, R. (1962). Children's reactions to novelty: An experiential study of curiosity motivation. *Child Development, 33*, 631–642.

Tegtmeyer, P. F., & Gordon, M. (1983). Interpretation of White Space responses in children's Rorschach protocols. *Perceptual and Motor Skills, 57*, 611–616.

Tuma, J. A., & McCraw, R. K. (1975). Influences of examiner differences on Rorschach productivity in children. *Journal of Personality Assessment, 39*, 362–368.

Weiner, I. B. (1964). Differential diagnosis in amphetamine psychosis. *Psychiatric Quarterly, 38*, 707–716.

Williams, A. L., & Miles, T. R. (1985). Rorschach responses of dyslexic children. *Annals of Dyslexia, 35*, 51–66.

8

Use of the Holtzman Inkblot Technique (HIT) with Children

WAYNE H. HOLTZMAN
University of Texas

JON D. SWARTZ
Southwestern University

The Holtzman Inkblot Technique (HIT) was developed to overcome psychometric limitations in the Rorschach by constructing completely new sets of inkblots. Although much of the early research on the Rorschach was either irrelevant or poorly conceived, an impressive number of well-designed validity studies generally yielded negative results. The growing realization that the Rorschach had inherent psychometric weaknesses came to a head in a symposium on failures of the Rorschach that was sponsored by the Society for Projective Techniques (Zubin, 1954). The evidence to date seems to indicate that the HIT has answered most, if not all, of these criticisms of the Rorschach (Holtzman & Swartz, 1983). By the end of 1982, more than 650 publications using the HIT had appeared in the world literature (Swartz, Reinehr, & Holtzman, 1983a). When the Rorschach had been in use for the same period of time, Buros (1949) listed fewer than 500 publications using it. HIT research to date, therefore, generally verifies the initial promise of this newer inkblot technique (Sundberg, 1962).

DESCRIPTION OF THE TECHNIQUE

The HIT attempts to capture the best qualities of both the projective and the psychometric approaches to the Rorschach. Unlike the Rorschach, which has only 10 inkblots in a single form, the HIT consists of two parallel forms, A and B, each of which contains 45 inkblots constituting the test series and 2 practice blots (X and Y) that are identical in both forms. The inkblots were drawn from a large pool of several thousand, many of which were created by an artist working with special papers and inks that produced brilliant colors and rich shading. Only about 1 blot in 50 survived initial screening by a group of judges who were familiar with the Rorschach.

Selection of inkblots for the final version of the HIT was aimed at maximizing the reliability of these scores, as well as maximizing the discriminatory power of the final forms in differentiating superior normals from mental hospital patients in a series of standardization studies (Holtzman, Thorpe,

187

Swartz, & Herron, 1961a). The two parallel forms were constructed by pairing blots on stimulus qualities as well as item characteristics from the scores, and then randomly assigning members of each pair to either Form A or Form B. The final order of presentation for the 45 inkblots in each form was arranged so that most of the "best" inkblots appear rather early in the series.

In the major standardization program, using printed versions of the original inkblots, nearly 2,000 individual protocols were collected on samples ranging from 5-year-olds to mature adults and from chronic schizophrenic patients to mentally retarded individuals. Through the cooperation of psychologists in other settings across the country, 15 different, well-defined populations were sampled to provide the standardization data. Five of these samples were normal children—122 children aged 5 from nursery schools in Austin, Texas; 60 children in second through sixth grades from a middle-class, private school in Austin; 72 fourth-graders from Hamden, Connecticut; 197 seventh-graders from four Texas communities other than Austin; and 72 adolescents in 11th grade from Chicago high schools. This last sample was given both the Rorschach and HIT in a comparative study of the two methods (Bock, Haggard, Holtzman, Beck, & Beck, 1963).

Percentile norms subsequently were published for emotionally disturbed children and adolescents and for male juvenile delinquents (Hill, 1972). Additional normative data for four representative groups of children and adolescents seen in clinical practice have been published by Morgan (1968). The norms for emotionally disturbed children published by Hill are based upon HIT protocols collected by Conners (1965) in clinical studies of 99 emotionally disturbed children and 114 neurotic adolescents. The norms for male juvenile delinquents are based on 75 cases collected by Megargee (1965) and replicated and extended by Mullen, Reinehr, and Swartz (1983). When taken together with the earlier sets of norms for mentally retarded and normal children, the percentile norms that are available for the HIT provide a rich source of helpful information to be used in psychodiagnosis and personality assessment.

The standardization data also were used for a number of methodological studies, including investigations of scorer agreement, internal-consistency reliability, test–retest stabilities, and intergroup differences as a preliminary basis for differential diagnosis. The results of these studies, together with percentile norms and recommendations for use of the HIT in clinical assessment or for research, were published in 1961 (Holtzman et al., 1961a). While retaining the clinical sensitivity of the Rorschach, the HIT yields 22 standardized variables that can be objectively defined, reliably scored, and efficiently handled by statistical methods. For the first time, it allows the clinician, the psychometrician, and the experimentalist to work with the same projective technique.

Greater reliability and objectivity of scoring on the HIT are obtained because of the large number of inkblots and the fact that the subject is limited to one response per blot. A scoring guide (Holtzman, Thorpe, Swartz, & Herron, 1961b) further increases objectivity by making interscorer differences negligible on most of the major variables. The existence of two parallel forms of the same technique permits accurate retesting to evaluate change over time.

Since the publication of the individual version of the HIT by the Psychological Corporation in 1961, hundreds of studies have been reported in the world literature (Swartz et al., 1983a). Our own work has focused largely upon the development of a group version (Herron, 1963; Holtzman, Moseley, Reinehr, & Abbott, 1963; Swartz & Holtzman, 1963; Swartz, Witzke, & Megargee, 1970); a computer method for scoring and interpreting HIT variables (Gorham, 1967; Holtzman, 1975; Vincent, 1982); and a major cross-cultural study of over 800 children in Mexico and the United States, involving repeated measures with alternate forms of the HIT 6 years in a row (Holtzman, Diaz-Guerrero, & Swartz, 1975). Some of the HIT findings from the cross-cultural study that are particularly relevant in the assessment of children are presented later in this chapter.

TEST MATERIALS

Standard materials for the HIT consist of two parallel series, Form A and Form B; the accompanying printed Record Forms and Summary Sheets; and the *Guide for Administration and Scoring*. The inkblots are printed on thin but tough white cardboard 5½ × 8½ inches in size. Cards X and Y contain practice blots that usually are not scored. These two cards appear at the beginning of both Forms A and B. Card X is a massive achromatic blot that looks like a bat or butterfly to most people. Very few subjects reject this card, although some prefer to use a smaller area than the whole blot. Card Y is suggestive of a person's torso to most subjects. Red spots of ink introduce the subject to color and often evoke responses such as "spots of blood," either given alone or interpreted with the torso.

Cards 1 and 2 in both Forms A and B are achromatic and sufficiently broken up to make a whole response difficult unless there is integration of detail, or unless the subject gives a very vague concept or one in which the form of the concept fails to fit the form of the inkblot. Both cards have popular responses in smaller areas of the blots, helping to break up a response set to give only wholes. Card 3 is irregular in form and has a large red "sunburst" splotch overlaid on an amorphous black inkblot. It is very difficult to give a form-definite, form-appropriate whole response to Card 3 because of the chaotic, unstructured nature of this inkblot. Card 4 is just the opposite, containing several finely detailed popular concepts that can be interrelated, together with color and shading that produces a vista-like effect. "A battle scene" or "a cowboy watching a sunset" are typical responses to Card 4A, and "a knight carrying a spear and shield" is a typical response to Card 4B.

Cards 5A and 5B are asymmetrical, greyish-colored blots unlike any in the Rorschach. By penetrating the charcoal-like quality of these blots, one can distinguish a number of detailed objects. Together with several similar, rather wispy, amorphous, asymmetrical blots later in the series, these cards are difficult, particularly for the individual who is searching for definite concepts having good form or who wishes to use the entire blot.

The remaining inkblots cover a wide range of stimulus variation, giving the individual ample opportunity to reveal certain aspects of his or her mental processes and personality by projecting thoughts onto otherwise meaningless inkblots. Twelve of the inkblots in Form A are black or grey; 2 are monochromatic; 11 are black with a bright color also present; and the remaining 20 are multicolored. Most of the blots have rich shading variations, which help to elicit texture responses. A similar distribution of color, shading, and form qualities is present in Form B.

ADMINISTRATION AND SCORING

Standard procedures for administering the HIT have been developed so that published normative data may be used as aids to interpretation. Instructions to the subject have been designed to make the task as simple as possible while eliciting sufficient information to score major variables reliably. The instructions differ from those for the Rorschach in the following ways: (1) The examiner instructs the examinee to give only one response per card; (2) a brief inquiry is given immediately after each response; (3) permissible questions by the examiner during inquiry are limited both in number and in scope, and are asked rather routinely to avoid inadvertent verbal conditioning of certain determinants or content. Three kinds of questions are permissible as part of the brief inquiry in the standard administration. The actual wording used can vary a great deal, so that the inquiry becomes a natural part of the conversation between examiner and subject. Typical phrasing should be as follows:

"Where in the blot do you see a _____ ?"
"What is there about the blot that makes it look like a _____ ?"
"Is there anything else you care to tell me about it?"

After establishing rapport, the examiner picks up the cards one at a time, handing each one in an upright position to the subject. The instructions given to the subject should be informal and should stress the following points: (1) These inkblots were not made to look like anything in particular; (2) different people see different things in each inkblot; and (3) only one response for each card is desired. The examiner uses a Record Form for recording the responses and scoring. To facilitate the recording of the location of the response, schematic diagrams for the inkblots are included on the Record Form. As each response is given, the examiner outlines a specific area used. Adjacent to the diagram is a blank space for recording the verbatim response or a shortened version of it.

Usually the subject comprehends the nature of the task very quickly, and the actual inquiry can be kept to a minimum. A skilled examiner, sensitive to subtle nuances in the examiner–subject interaction, can control the flow of conversation by stimulating a reticent individual and slowing down a verbose person.

In spite of the many interesting variations in test administration that can be attempted, there is much to be said for adhering closely to the standard method of administration. This method has proved highly practical and yields objective, reliable scores on a number of important variables. Currently published normative data and statistical studies of value in the interpretation of the protocols assume close adherence to the standard method of administration.

One exception to the standard method of administration has been successfully developed for young children, whose attention span is short and who therefore may get restless halfway through the testing session. As in the case of the 122 Austin 5-year-olds, the examiner may temporarily interrupt the testing session after 20–30 cards, returning to finish the task after interpolated activity of a relaxing kind. In testing young children, the task can be structured as a playful, game-like activity, heightening the children's interest in attending to it. This technique has been used successfully for some children as young as 3 years of age, although no norms are available below the age of 5.

In the course of standardization, 22 quantitative variables were developed to cover nearly all of the important scoring categories and dimensions commonly employed with the Rorschach. The names, abbreviations, brief definitions, and scoring weights for these variables are given in Table 8.1. Summary scores for the individual variables are obtained by adding the weights for a given variable across the 45 inkblots in either Form A or Form B. Three of the variables routinely

are "corrected" for the number of rejections in order to provide an estimate of what the total score would have been if the subject had given a response to each of the 45 inkblots.

Scoring agreement is uniformly high when trained scorers are compared. Intercorrelations between two independent scorers ranged from .89 to .995, with a median value of .98 in a sample of 40 protocols from a schizophrenic sample. When beginning scorers were compared, average scoring reliability for all variables yielded a median value of .86 in a large sample of normal adolescents. The more difficult variables to score, such as Pathognomic Verbalization and Form Appropriateness, require a greater degree of training. Qualified clinicians and research investigators, however, have had little difficulty achieving satisfactory scoring reliability.

RELIABILITY OF HIT SCORES FOR CHILDREN

Both internal-consistency and parallel-forms reliability based on repeated testing have been reported in great detail elsewhere (Holtzman et al., 1961a; Holtzman et al., 1975). Split-half reliabilities, determined by computing the correlations between scores based on odd-numbered and even-numbered blots, are generally high. The four scores with highest internal consistency (generally about .90), regardless of populations sampled (ranging from 5-year-old children to schizophrenic adults), are Reaction Time, Rejection, Location, and Form Definiteness. Eight additional scores that have internal-consistency reliability generally higher than .80 are Form Appropriateness, Color, Shading, Movement, Pathognomic Verbalization, Human, Animal, and Anatomy. Odd–even reliability coefficients for the symbolic content scores—Anxiety, Hostility, Barrier, and Penetration—are only slightly lower on the average and more variable. Four scores— Space, Sex, Abstract, and Balance—occur too infrequently for accurate estimates of reliability, leaving only Popular as a score with relatively unsatisfactory internal consistency.

The most pertinent reliability measure for most clinical applications is the stability of an

TABLE 8.1. Names, Abbreviations, Brief Definitions, and Scoring Weights for 22 HIT Variables

Reaction Time (RT). The time in seconds from the presentation of the inkblot to the beginning of the primary response.

Rejection (R). Score 1 when subject returns inkblot to examiner without giving a scorable response; otherwise, score 0.

Location (L). Tendency to break down blot into smaller fragments. Score 0 for use of the whole blot, 1 for large area, and 2 for smaller area.

Space (S). Score 1 for true figure–ground reversals; otherwise, score 0.

Form Definiteness (FD). The definiteness of the form of the concept reported, regardless of the goodness of fit to the inkblot. A 5-point scale with 0 for very vague and 4 for highly specific.

Form Appropriateness (FA). The goodness of fit of the form of the percept to the form of the inkblot. Score 0 for poor, 1 for fair, and 2 for good.

Color (C). The apparent primacy of color (including black, grey, or white) as a response determinant. Score 0 for no use of color, 1 for use secondary to form (like Rorschach *FC*), 2 when used as primary determinant but some form present (like *CF*), and 3 when used as primary determinant with no form present (like *C*).

Shading (Sh). The apparent primacy of shading as response determinant (texture, depth, or vista). Score 0 for no use of shading, 1 when used in secondary manner, and 2 when used as primary determinant with little or no form present.

Movement (M). The energy level of movement or potential movement ascribed to the percept, regardless of content. Score 0 for none, 1 for static potential, 2 for casual, 3 for dynamic, and 4 for violent movement.

Pathognomic Verbalization (V). Degree of autistic, bizarre thinking evident in the response as rated on a 5-point scale. Score 0 where no pathology is present. The nine categories of V and the range of scoring weights for each is as follows: Fabulation, 1; Fabulized Combination, 2, 3, 4; Queer Response, 1, 2, 3; Incoherence, 4; Autistic Logic, 1, 2, 3, 4; Contamination, 2, 3, 4; Self-Reference, 2, 3, 4; Deterioration Color, 2, 3, 4; Absurd Response, 3.

Anatomy (At). Degree of "gut-like" quality in the content. Score 0 for none; 1 for bones, X-rays, or medical drawings; and 2 for visceral and crude anatomy.

Sex (Sx). Degree of sexual quality in the content. Score 0 for no sexual reference; 1 for socially accepted sexual activity or expressions (buttocks, bust, kissing); and 2 for blatant sexual content (penis, vagina).

Abstract (Ab). Degree of abstract quality in the content. Score 0 for none, 1 for abstract elements along with other elements having form, and 2 for purely abstract content ("Bright colors remind me of gaiety").

Anxiety (Ax). Signs of anxiety in the fantasy content as indicated by emotions and attitudes, expressive behavior, symbolism, or cultural stereotypes of fear. Score 0 for none, 1 for questionable or indirect signs, and 2 for overt or clear-cut evidence.

Hostility (Hs). Signs of hostility in the fantasy content. Scored on a 4-point scale ranging from 0 for none to 3 for direct, violent, interpersonal destruction.

Barrier (Br). Score 1 for reference to any protective covering, membrane, shell, or skin that might be symbolically related to the perception of body image boundaries; otherwise, score 0.

Penetration (Pn). Score 1 for concept that might be symbolic of an individual's feeling that his or her body exterior is of little protective value and can be easily penetrated; otherwise, score 0.

Balance (B). Score 1 where there is overt concern for the symmetry–asymmetry feature of the inkblot; otherwise, score 0.

Popular (P). Each form contains 25 inkblots in which one or more popular percepts occur. "Popular" in the standardization studies means that a percept had to occur at least 14% of the time among normal subjects. Score 1 for popular core concepts (or their precision alternatives) as listed in the scoring manual; otherwise, score 0.

Integration (I). Score 1 for the organization of the two or more adequately perceived blot elements into a larger whole; otherwise, score 0.

Human (H). Degree of human quality in the content of response. Score 0 for none; 1 for parts of humans, distortions, or cartoons; and 2 for whole human beings or elaborated human faces.

Animal (A). Degree of animal quality in the content. Score 0 for none (including animal objects and microscopic life); 1 for animal parts, bugs, or insects; and 2 for whole animals.

individual's score across time. Unlike the Rorschach, with which spuriously high results are obtained because of retesting with the same inkblots, the HIT has truly parallel forms that provide conservative but realistic estimates of reliability of measurement over time. The best measure of such stability is the intraclass correlation obtained in a Latin-square design, where half of the subjects are randomly selected to receive Form A before B, while the other half receive B before A. The most extensive studies of this kind on college students yielded stability coefficients ranging from a low of .36 for Popular to a high of .82 for Location, with an interval of 1 week between tests.

Similar studies on other normal subjects with time intervals between testing sessions ranging from 3 months to 5 years provide additional evidence of the stability of HIT scores across time. The most extensive data come from a major cross-cultural study of over 800 children in Mexico and the United States, involving repeated measures with alternate forms 6 years in a row (Holtzman et al., 1975). Beginning during the 1962–1963 school year in Austin, Texas, 133 first-graders, 142 fourth-graders, and 142 seventh-graders were tested with the HIT as part of a large battery of perceptual, cognitive, and personality tests. Annual testing took place on the anniversary date of the initial testing until 6 years of repeated measurement had been completed. The basic design of this study is given in Table 8.2.

A complete replication of the Austin longitudinal project was begun in Mexico City in

TABLE 8.2. Overlapping Longitudinal Design for 6 Years of Repeated Testing

Group	Initial age[a]	School grades covered
I	6.7 years	1 2 3 4 5 6
II	9.7 years	4 5 6 7 8 9
III	12.7 years	7 8 9 10 11 12

Note. From *Personality Development in Two Cultures: A Cross-Cultural Longitudinal Study of School Children in Mexico and the United States* by W. H. Holtzman, R. Diaz-Guerrero, and J. D. Swartz. 1975. Austin: University of Texas Press. Copyright 1975 by the Hogg Foundation for Mental Health. Reprinted by permission.

[a]The starting ages of 6 years, 8 months; 9 years, 8 months; and 12 years, 8 months were chosen when a pilot study revealed most children in the public schools of Texas reach these exact ages at some time during the school year. Actual testing took place within 30 days of the age specified.

1964 under the direction of Rogelio Diaz-Guerrero and his associates. (For more details on the Mexican research, see Chapter 21, this volume.) Split-half reliability coefficients for 17 HIT scores in the first year of testing for these large samples of children in Mexico and the United States are given in Table 8.3. From these statistics, it is clear that scores on the HIT generally have high reliability for school children of all ages as well as for adults.

The results for internal consistency of HIT scores among preschool children are equally high, as evidenced by the results obtained for the 122 children aged 5 who were tested in Austin nursery schools as part of the standardization sample. Split-half reliability coefficients ranged from .53 for Penetration to .97 for Reaction Time. The median or average reliability for all variables among the 5-year-olds was .86.

Scores on the HIT, the Human Figure Drawing Test, and the Vocabulary and Block Design subtests of the Wechsler Intelligence Scale for Children (WISC) in the cross-cultural longitudinal project provide an unparalleled opportunity to examine the degree of test–retest stability of these measures over time intervals varying from 1 to 5 years and for school children of all ages. On a theoretical basis, one would anticipate that the magnitude of such correlations would fall somewhere in the middle ranges—say, from .40 to .80. Correlations much higher than this would indicate rather rigid, unchanging personality characteristics; correlations much lower would reveal instability sufficiently serious to call into question the enduring nature of the measured personality traits over time. Among young children, one would expect lower stability coefficients than among adolescents or adults, since personality and cognitive development proceed more rapidly at the younger ages. And finally, on a theoretical basis, one would also expect that stability would gradually drop as the interval of time between testing increased from 1 to 5 years.

The most stable of all HIT scores is Location. The complete set of test–retest correlations for Location is presented in Table 8.4 to illustrate the power of this methodology for estimating stability across time. With the exception of the youngest children in the first

TABLE 8.3. Split-Half Reliability Coefficients for 17 HIT Variables

Variable	Mexico			United States		
	6 (147)[a]	9 (141)	12 (149)	6 (133)	9 (142)	12 (142)
Reaction Time	.94	.94	.96	.92	.97	.97
Rejection	.95	.87	.91	.90	.93	.88
Location	.94	.95	.95	.95	.97	.95
Form Definiteness	.91	.88	.89	.90	.80	.86
Form Appropriateness	.90	.82	.77	.86	.81	.67
Color	.94	.84	.78	.93	.83	.85
Shading	.61	.55	.58	.74	.58	.78
Movement	.84	.83	.85	.86	.87	.88
Pathognomic Verbalization	.86	.52	.87	.90	.76	.79
Integration	.57	.69	.77	.58	.85	.82
Human	.84	.81	.79	.82	.81	.83
Animal	.92	.83	.71	.80	.73	.72
Anatomy	.83	.86	.75	.91	.80	.69
Anxiety	.92	.73	.70	.78	.68	.80
Hostility	.95	.63	.66	.88	.72	.78
Barrier	.70	.57	.46	.75	.51	.52
Penetration	.52	.69	.63	.81	.75	.63

Note. From *Personality Development in Two Cultures: A Cross-Cultural Longitudinal Study of School Children in Mexico and the United States* by W. H. Holtzman, R. Diaz-Guerrero, and J. D. Swartz, 1975, Austin: University of Texas Press. Copyright 1975 by the Hogg Foundation for Mental Health. Reprinted by permission.
[a]Numbers outside parentheses indicate age of each group; numbers within parentheses indicate the number of children in each group.

year, the test–retest correlations for Location were high in both Mexico and the United States, ranging into the .80s for the older children even after several years of testing. It is interesting to note in Table 8.4 that even after an interval of 5 years, the stability of Location was still moderately high, averaging .46 for all six groups combined.

It should be pointed out that the availability of parallel forms for the HIT means that an interval of 2 years takes place before the child responds again to the identical form. Two years is a sufficiently long time for memory of the initial responses to fade almost completely. The use of a staggered longitudinal design with overlapping groups, as noted in Table 8.2, also makes possible the isolation of any practice or adaptation effects regardless of the form used. A detailed analysis of the differences that can be attributed to culture, age, sex, and trial of repeating testing has been reported elsewhere (Holtzman et al., 1975; see also Chapter 21, this

volume). Only selected highlights of the findings are presented here.

In a major analysis of variance of Location scores, noticeable adaptation to repeated testing was indeed found over the 6-year period. Mexican children tended to use smaller areas of the inkblot than did American children. Similarly, children of all ages in both cultures tended to use smaller detail areas more often than whole inkblots as the test was repeated. The amount of adaptation was much greater for the Mexican children in the first 2 years of testing. Of all the variables analyzed, only Location showed this adaptation effect over a year of testing, and even then the stability of individual differences through time was unusually high.

Close behind Location in stability were Reaction Time, Form Definiteness, Movement, and Human. These variables compared favorably with scores on Vocabulary and Block Design and with the Harris–Goodenough developmental score on Hu-

TABLE 8.4. HIT Location Test–Retest Correlations

Years correlated	Mexico			United States		
	I	II	III	I	II	III
1 & 2	.27	.57	.66	.28	.72	.76
1 & 3	.20	.49	.60	.27	.62	.70
1 & 4	.25	.49	.58	.26	.59	.69
1 & 5	.24	.46	.56	.26	.51	.67
1 & 6	.50	.26	.51	.33	.56	.59
2 & 3	.58	.70	.71	.50	.77	.84
2 & 4	.49	.73	.72	.54	.68	.81
2 & 5	.42	.64	.67	.46	.58	.76
2 & 6	.23	.57	.52	.49	.62	.75
3 & 4	.64	.75	.76	.68	.78	.82
3 & 5	.56	.70	.74	.70	.80	.80
3 & 6	.44	.63	.55	.64	.77	.75
4 & 5	.60	.77	.85	.71	.76	.86
4 & 6	.62	.73	.68	.68	.80	.86
5 & 6	.63	.76	.74	.79	.86	.85

Note. Table covers 6 years of repeated testing; Groups I, II, and III started in Year 1 at ages 6.7, 9.7, and 12.7, respectively. From *Personality Development in Two Cultures: A Cross-Cultural Longitudinal Study of School Children in Mexico and the United States* by W. H. Holtzman, R. Diaz-Guerrero, and J. D. Swartz, 1975, Austin: University of Texas Press. Copyright 1975 by the Hogg Foundation for Mental Health. Reprinted by permission.

man Figure Drawing, with respect to stability over a long period of time. Of the 17 HIT scores sufficiently well distributed to permit the use of product–moment correlation coefficients, 6 had generally low stability coefficients ranging from insignificant values into the .40s and .50s, with an occasional value into the .60s and .70s—Rejection, Form Appropriateness, Shading, Pathognomic Verbalization, Barrier, and Penetration. Four variables—Space, Sex, Abstract, and Balance—generally occurred too infrequently in samples of children to yield data amenable to treatment by correlation methods.

Several generalizations concerning the stability of inkblot variables among the children and adolescents tested can be drawn from these findings:

1. Test–retest stability increased generally with an increase in the age of children. Older adolescents tended to have the highest degree of stability, while children of any age showed higher test–retest stability in the later years of testing than in the initial years.

2. Test–retest stability dropped off in a regular fashion with increasing size of interval between tests.

3. Test–retest stability was generally slightly higher for American children than for Mexicans, regardless of age group. This cross-cultural difference was particularly marked for Integration, Hostility, and Barrier.

4. Most of the HIT scores showed a sufficiently high degree of stability across time, ranging from .40 to .80, to justify their use as predictors of later behavior. (A successful example of such a study over a 9-year period is reported later in this chapter.) At the same time, the test–retest correlations were not so high as to suggest any kind of fixed traits that remain relatively invariant as children grow older.

VALIDITY OF THE HIT FOR CHILDREN AND ADOLESCENTS

Several hundred studies have been published bearing upon the relationships between scores on HIT variables and independent measures of personality. Although most have been carried out with adults, many have dealt specifically with children or adolescents. Extensive reviews have appeared recently elsewhere (Holtzman, 1981; Holtzman & Swartz, 1983). A comprehensive annotated bibliography containing all known references to the HIT through 1982 (Swartz et al., 1983a) contains abstracts of these articles. Only representative highlights of these many findings as they pertain to use of the HIT with children and adolescents are provided here. Because factor analyses of intercorrelations among the 22 HIT variables have indicated that, with few exceptions, these scores tend to cluster into meaningful factors, the findings with respect to validity are arranged according to these more general dimensions.

Factor 1: Perceptual Maturity and Integrated Ideational Activity

Factor 1 is made up of these four variables: Movement, Integration, Human, and Barrier. High scores on these four variables taken together are indicative of well-organized ideational activity, good imaginative capacity, and well-differentiated ego boundaries. All four variables increase with age among children and are significantly higher among college graduates than average adults, indicating a strong component of cognitive ability and creativity (Swartz, Reinehr, & Holtzman, 1983b). Studies have shown repeatedly that these variables are indicative of creative potential. They show significant relationships with reading comprehension among children, even after general intelligence has been held constant (Laird, Laosa, & Swartz, 1973).

The energy level of movement ascribed to the percept, regardless of content, has some other interesting correlates. A high score on Movement is associated with perceived empathy in counselors, whereas low Movement is associated with the reverse (Mueller & Abeles, 1964). The degree of eye contact and smiling among psychiatric patients when interviewed is also related to high Movement scores (Lefcourt, Telegdi, Willows, & Buckspan, 1972). Movement is correlated with the discharge or inhibition of cognitive energy, according to Covan (1976). Increased perception of movement in inkblots follows experimental inhibition of cognitive responses, while discharge of cognitive processes in a series of free association tasks leads to a sharp decrease in reported perception of movement in inkblots. Studies of dream deprivation, whether induced by drugs (Lerner, 1966) or prevented by interrupting rapid eye movements (Feldstein, 1973), results in higher Movement scores. These findings support Rorschach's views on the fundamental similarity between movement and dreams because of the centrality of kinesthetic experience in both; the results are also consistent with Heinz Werner's sensory tonic theory of perception.

Movement has a particularly strong cognitive component among young children. In the first year of testing for 6-year-olds in the longitudinal study, the complete battery of tests for the WISC was given. Factor analyses of intercorrelations among the various cognitive tests were done with Movement included as an extra variable. Among the American children, Movement was clearly a major part of the first factor defined by the Verbal subtests from the WISC. Movement did not show up heavily loaded on a similar factor for the Mexicans until the 9-year-olds were analyzed. Similar results were found for the 12-year-old Mexican children. No complete analyses could be performed for the American 9- and 12-year-olds, since they had not been given the complete WISC test battery. Movement deals with that component of verbal ability characterized by a lively, active imagination and the ability to project outward from one's fantasies. In this sense, it deals particularly with the expressive, imaginative aspects of verbal ability, rather than with factual information, word meanings, and analytic problem solving.

Human content also has some special meaning worthy of note. As one would expect from projective theory, a high score on Human suggests high social interest, whereas lack of any Human content indicates the opposite (Fernald & Linden, 1966).

One of the most interesting of the symbolic content scores is Barrier, developed by Fisher and Cleveland (1958). The score is given for references to any protective covering, membrane, shell, or skin that might be symbolically related to the perception of body image boundaries. High Barrier is indicative of strong ego identity, whereas low Barrier suggests diffusion. High Barrier is related to being influential and independent in group processes (Cleveland & Morton, 1962), adjusting well to physical disablement (Fisher, 1963), being able to tolerate pain (Nichols & Tursky, 1967), and having a positive evaluation of one's own body (Conquest, 1963). These findings are consistent with others showing low Barrier related to juvenile delinquency (Megargee, 1965).

Factor 3: Psychopathology of Thought

Factor 3 consists of Pathognomic Verbalization, Anxiety, and Hostility. Dealing with unbridled fantasies, affective expressivity, and loose imagination, these three variables, frequently also associated with Movement, constitute an important cluster of scores indicative of psychopathology. Among children, moderately high scores on these three variables may be a good sign rather than a bad one. In most factor analyses of inkblot variables among children, this factor often proves to be highly correlated with Factor 1, indicating creativity and imaginative capacity rather than psychopathology. Even among children, however, very high scores on these variables are indicative of future emotional disturbance, as demonstrated by a long-term follow-up study of the 6-year-olds tested in Austin as part of the cross-cultural study.

Nine years after the initial testing of the first-graders in Austin, 46 of them (23 girls, 23 boys) were located within the Austin schools and rated on personal adjustment by school personnel (Currie, Holtzman, & Swartz, 1974). These 46 subjects constituted more than half the group ($n = 89$) that completed the 6-year period of testing and were all from families that had continued to live in Austin, Texas, over a 10-year span, thus representing a particularly stable sample in relation to current population mobility. Seven of the children were judged to have serious problems of adjustment; 7 were judged to have noticeable areas of maladjust-

ment; 18 were judged to be generally well adjusted but with some problems in relating to others; and 14 were judged to be well adjusted. The mean scores on Pathognomic Verbalization, Anxiety, and Hostility from HIT protocols 6 years earlier for the seven most disturbed children were two standard deviations higher than the means for children judged to be well adjusted. Low Form Appropriateness was also associated with emotional disturbance. Interestingly enough, from the many tests in the original battery, the only other one that correlated significantly with later emotional disturbance in these children was the Koppitz Scale of emotional indicators in Human Figure Drawings. (see Table 8.5).

Pathognomic Verbalization is the best single indicator of psychopathology. Among adults, the bizarre perception and autistic logic underlying high scores on this variable are characteristic either of schizophrenia or of extreme artistic license in responding to inkblots. Highly creative artists do tend to get much higher scores than average in-

TABLE 8.5. Mean Test Scores from the WISC, the Human Figure Drawing (HFD), and the HIT by Four Levels of Adjustment and Correlations between Test Variables and the Adjustment Index

| Test variable | Means by adjustment level | | | | | Total SD | r |
	A(3) ($n = 14$)	B(2) ($n = 18$)	C(1) ($n = 7$)	D(0) ($n = 7$)	Total ($n = 46$)		
WISC IQ	111.8	112.6	116.3	99.5	110.8	10.9	.21
HFD							
Koppitz indicators	0.6	0.9	1.4	2.0	1.0	1.1	−.44**
Goodenough–Harris	18.8	16.8	18.4	14.7	17.4	5.1	.21
HIT							
Form Appropriateness (FA)	35.0	35.3	35.7	25.6	33.8	9.2	.28*
Movement (M)	14.9	21.4	17.7	23.3	19.2	15.5	−.15
Pathognomic Verbalization (V)	6.8	6.8	6.3	18.4	8.5	8.3	−.38**
Integration (I)	1.0	1.3	1.6	0.6	1.2	1.1	.10
Human (H)	12.8	16.9	20.7	16.7	16.2	9.7	−.19
Anatomy (At)	4.1	4.8	6.4	7.7	5.3	6.3	−.19
Anxiety (Ax)	5.6	6.8	4.9	16.0	7.5	7.4	−.37**
Hostility (Hs)	6.2	6.7	5.7	19.3	8.3	9.1	−.39**
Penetration (Pn)	2.8	3.6	3.3	3.0	3.2	2.6	−.03

Note. From "Early Indicators of Personality Traits Viewed Retrospectively" by S. F. Currie, W. H. Holtzman, and J. D. Swartz, 1974, Journal of School Psychology, 12, 51–59. Copyright 1974 by the Journal of School Psychology. Reprinted by permission.

*Correlation of test variable and adjustment index significant beyond .05 level.

**Correlation of test variable and adjustment index significant beyond .01 level.

TABLE 8.6. Names, Abbreviations, Brief Definitions, and Scoring Weights for Nine Categories of Pathognomic Verbalization (V)

Fabulation (FB). A response in which there is associative elaboration having notable affective components (16A—"A kind monster . . . eyes, and he looks real sweet"). FB is scored 1 when present.

Fabulized Combination (FC). An impossible, fantastic combination of otherwise fairly acceptable parts, based largely on a spatial rather than a logical relationship (14B—"Some kind of get-together. Two caterpillars talking to each other in a sociable mood, don't seem to mind having the sheep around"). FC is scored 2, 3, or 4, depending on the judged severity of pathology evident.

Queer Response (QR). A response in which the subject employs peculiar or eccentric language and syntax in verbalizing the response (14A—"The male part of the back . . . like the muscles in the biceps formed in the V-shaped web"). QR is scored 1, 2, or 3, depending on judged severity.

Incoherence (IC). A response in which there is a complete breakdown of rational control (14A—"A dental of hell . . . under misunderstanding"). IC is scored 4 when present.

Autistic Logic (AL). The presence of faulty, fantastic reasoning given by the subject as justification for the response (43A—"A carbon copy of a person . . . because he's lying down on carbon paper"). AL is scored 1, 2, 3, or 4, depending on judged severity.

Contamination (CT). A response in which two conflicting interpretations are fused into one, or when the same area simultaneously stands for two or more interdependent but logically separate concepts (11B—"That looks like a stone stain . . . looks like a heart . . . well, a stained heart"). CT is scored 2, 3, or 4, depending on judged severity.

Self-Reference (SR). A response in which the subject draws himself or herself into the percept, giving the response a personal meaning (29B—"A person's face. Looks like my face . . . maybe I lost it"). SR is scored 2, 3, or 4, depending on judged severity.

Deterioration Color (DC). Loose, fantastic color associations having bizarre content are given with an air of reality (4B—"The yellow is a virulent disease, the yellow plague . . . the kiss of death"). DC is scored 2, 3, or 4, depending on judged severity.

Absurd Response (AB). A response is categorized as absurd when a subject assigns a form-definite concept to an area of an inkblot in which by no stretch of the imagination can the form be conceived of as appropriate, and the response is not an abstract one (36A—"The Empire State Building . . . whole card"). AB is scored 3 when present.

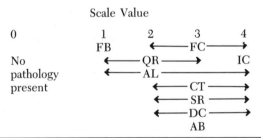

Note. The schematic diagram above shows the range of scoring weights for each of the nine V categories and the relationship of the FB and QR categories to the FC and IC categories, respectively.

dividuals on this variable (Holtzman, Swartz, & Thorpe, 1971), but the quality of the response is noticeably different.

Table 8.6 gives names, abbreviations, definitions, and scoring weights for the various categories of Pathognomic Verbalization. Normal individuals tend to give Fabulations with notable affectivity, mildly Fabulized Combinations of otherwise acceptable percepts, or even occasional Queer Responses that are often described in a playful manner.

Schizophrenics, on the other hand, manifest a loss of distance between themselves and the inkblots, often giving severely Fabulized Combinations, Contaminations, Queer Responses, or special kinds of Autistic Logic that show faulty, fantastic reasoning as a justification for the response. Embellishing a response with highly personal meaning by Self-Reference is particularly characteristic of psychotic thinking when manifested repeatedly (Swartz, 1969). A predominance of

Absurd Responses is characteristic of mentally retarded individuals, while a predominance of Deteriorated Color associations is indicative of severe disintegration.

Among young children, moderately high scores on Pathognomic Verbalization may simply indicate immature thought processes coupled with uncontrolled fantasies and loose imagination, rather than serious psychopathology. Although few of the cases in either the Mexican or the American sample received scores on this variable so high as to indicate serious psychopathology, the presence of some Pathognomic Verbalization among young children may indeed be taken as a good sign, provided that the qualitative nature of the disordered thinking reveals primarily Fabulized Combinations and invalid Integrations rather than bizarre perceptions.

In an analysis of longitudinal data on the three groups of American children from the Mexico–United States cross-cultural investigation discussed earlier, a highly significant curvilinear developmental trend was apparent for Pathognomic Verbalization (Swartz, 1969). Across the 11 years from 6 to 17, the lowest mean score on this variable occurred in 12-year-old children, with rising means both up and down the developmental order. When groups of children ($n = 180$)— 6, 9, and 12 years of age, respectively—were matched for sex and *total* Pathognomic Verbalization score (and HIT data only from initial testing sessions were used), it was found that with increasing age there was a significant increase in the number of children giving Fabulation responses and significant decreases in the numbers of children giving Austistic Logic, Contamination, and Absurd Responses. The numbers of children giving Fabulized Combination, Queer Responses, and Deteriorated Color responses remained quite steady across the 6-year age span (with about half in all three age groups giving Fabulized Combination responses, more than half giving Queer Responses, and only about 8% giving Deteriorated Color responses). Almost none produced verbalizations falling into the Incoherence or Self-Reference categories.

The importance of Pathognomic Verbalization in psychodiagnosis can best be illustrated by an individual case drawn from our files of school children in the Austin longitudinal study. While being tested with the HIT in the third year of repeated study, a young, apparently normal teenage boy shifted abruptly from normal responses one-third of the way through the test, thereafter giving responses heavily loaded with Pathognomic Verbalization. It is important to note that his responses to the first 12 inkblots and in the previous testing sessions over the past 2 years were generally normal, although under a high degree of self-control. Even in the remainder of this testing session, he continued to maintain an outward appearance of control, being polite, cooperative, and attentive. Although we were quite concerned about the sudden deterioration in the quality of his responses, nothing was said to his parents or authorities because of the research nature of the data collection. Some months later, we learned to our dismay that the boy killed his father and was hospitalized for treatment as a schizophrenic patient. The incipient psychosis was not apparent in his general behavior or other tests, although it was clearly revealed by his Pathognomic Verbalization score on the HIT.

Signs of anxiety or hostility in the fantasy content form the basis for the Anxiety or Hostility score. Moderate-level scores on both of these symbolic content scales are normal, particularly in young children, but very high scores should be interpreted as having likely clinical significance. Zero or low positive correlations can be expected between these two variables and anxiety or hostility scales in self-report inventories. The most important evidence of their validity comes from experimental studies. Subjects who rapidly acquire the conditioned eyelid response have higher Anxiety scores than those who do not condition easily (Herron, 1965). Individuals with high Anxiety are less tolerant of pain (Nichols & Tursky, 1967). Individuals who show a marked increase in Hostility score after a frustrating situation are those who also show a predisposition to hostility as measured by Factor 1 of the Buss–Durkee Inventory (Rosenstiel, 1973). Both Anxiety and Hostility scores are directly related to observed interpersonal distance characteristic of an individual in an experimental setting; the higher the inkblot scores, the greater the distance (Greenberg, Aronow, & Rauchway, 1977). These findings all are consistent with the theoretical conception of these symbolic content scores. In a series of studies, Kamen (1969, 1970, 1971) found several HIT variables related to State anxiety (but not Trait anxiety) as measured by the State–Trait Anxiety Inventory (STAI). A later study by Iacino and Cook (1974), however, found HIT Anxiety to be correlated positively with the STAI Trait scale. Auerbach and Edinger (1977) found that only HIT Barrier correlated significantly (negatively) with STAI Trait anxiety; no HIT variables were found to be related to STAI State anxiety.

Although the meaning of Anxiety and Hostility scores on the HIT undoubtedly is complex, it seems clear that very high scores, even among children, have sufficient validity to justify clinical interpretation for individuals. While cautioning that the HIT and other projective techniques are not direct behavioral measurements, but instead measure underlying processes based upon an individual's perception, Fehr (1983) sees the HIT as superior to the Rorschach in measuring both anxiety and hostility.

Factor 2: Perceptual Sensitivity

Factor 2 consists of Color, Shading, and Form Definiteness (reversed). The clustering together of these three variables is inevitable. As with scoring systems for the Rorschach, the greater the predominance of color or shading over form in a response, the higher the score. Among younger children, significant negative loadings on this factor also appear for Animal, suggesting that many children tend to use color and shading as a determinant only when they cannot find a familiar animal form. The positive pole on this factor indicates overreactivity to the stimulus determinants; the negative pole shows primary concern for form alone as a response determinant.

Among normal subjects, a high Color score has been found to be related to impulsivity (Holtzman, 1950) and to increased expression of affect (Mayfield, 1968). In her clinical use of the HIT, Hill (1972) recommends paying attention to the quality of the Color responses, particularly those given to inkblots having a high stimulus strength for Color, in making interpretations about the lability of affect.

There is little experimental evidence bearing upon the validity of Shading or Form Definiteness, the other two variables that measure degree of perceptual sensitivity. Nor is there much information from correlational studies with other personality measures that would indicate the independent meaning of these variables for assessment purposes. To be sure, there is a consensus among Rorschach clinicians concerning the use of these scores for personality assessment, but the scientific evidence is too tenuous at this time to justify any confident interpretations, particularly among children.

Other Factors

The remaining three factors are less important and vary somewhat in their patterning from one population to another. Location and Form Appropriateness generally appear as defining variables for Factor 4. A high score on Location results when an individual uses smaller areas of the inkblot while ignoring the rest. This perceptual style makes it easier to find percepts that have good form. The combination of low score on Location with high score on Form Appropriateness is less common and indicates a high level of perceptual maturity and organization, particularly when accompanied by high scores on Integration.

Reaction Time and Rejection tend to be associated in a single factor, because both measure the extent of inhibition or outright perceptual inability. Both variables must be taken into account with other inkblot scores rather than interpreted alone.

Three scores—Sex, Anatomy, and Penetration—deal with bodily preoccupation and are occasionally clustered together in one factor for this reason. Blatant Sex responses are relatively rare, but are significant when they do appear, especially among children. Very high Anatomy scores are also quite unusual and significant. High Anatomy scores have been found to be closely associated with a high degree of somatic preoccupation among hospitalized patients, confirming the theoretical interpretation of Anatomy (Endicott & Jortner, 1967). Penetration frequently loads also on Factor 3, Psychopathology of Thought, suggesting that high scores on Penetration should be generally interpreted as pathological.

Use of Scores for
Differential Diagnosis

Closely related to the clinical validity of individual variables within the HIT is the use of patterns of scores for differential diagnosis. The original standardization data on 15 different populations are presented in percentile norms for eight major reference groups ranging from 5-year-olds to superior adults and including psychiatric patients as well as mentally retarded individuals. Chronic schizophrenics differ from normal reference groups on almost all of the standard HIT variables.

Conners (1965) reported a number of highly significant differences between emotionally disturbed children seen in an outpatient clinic and normal controls of the same age and background. In Conners's study, disturbed children got higher scores on Rejection and Anatomy and lower scores on all other variables except Pathognomic Verbalization, Sex, Abstract, Hostility, Penetration, and Balance. Using HIT factor scores, Conners found that neurotic children appeared to be more differentiated in response and more inhibited than did hyperkinetic children. At the same time, it should be noted that neurotic children received higher scores on Form Appropriateness and Location than did children with conduct disorders.

Hill's (1972) handbook on clinical application of the HIT has provided detailed suggestions on how best to interpret HIT scores, as well as the qualitative aspects of content with respect to cognitive functioning, affective functioning, and self-identity. More recently, Aronow and Reznikoff (1976) compared Rorschach and HIT content scores and concluded that "the HIT is clearly the technique of choice for most research purposes" (p. 315).

CROSS-CULTURAL USE
OF THE HIT

Use of the HIT in research studies of differences in personality development among children of different cultures is particularly appropriate because of the more or less universal nature of the technique. The method has been translated into a number of languages and is relatively culture-free. The technique has been used successfully for both adults and children in cultures as widely varied as primitive groups in New Guinea, Aleutian Eskimos, peasant children in Latin America, and children from modern, industrialized societies. Our own work has concentrated upon factors related to personality and cognitive development among children in Mexico and the United States (Holtzman et al., 1975). Of all the measures used in the cross-cultural longitudinal study, the HIT yielded the most striking differences between Mexican and American children. One finding is of particular interest, since it sheds considerable light upon the possible use of the HIT for measuring an important coping style.

The most significant differences between Mexican and American children, regardless of age, sex, or socioeconomic status, were found for seven HIT scores—Reaction Time, Pathognomic Verbalization, Location, Movement, Integration, Anxiety, and Hostility. Mexicans had a slower response time; showed less pathology, anxiety, hostility, or movement in their fantasy expressions; tended to use more small details within the blots for their responses; and showed lower ability to integrate the parts into a meaningful whole than did the American children. These differences tended to narrow with increasing age.

Most of the differences between the Mexican and American children on the HIT can be understood better in terms of coping style than of any other concept. The American children produced faster Reaction Time, used larger portions of the inkblots in giving responses, gave more definite form to responses, and still were able to integrate more parts of the inkblots while doing so. In addition, they incorporated other stimulus properties of the inkblots, such as Color and Shading, into their responses more often than did the Mexican children, and elaborated their responses by ascribing more movement to their percepts. In attempting to deal with all aspects of the inkblots in such an active manner, however, they failed more often than the Mexican children; that is, the Mexican children gave responses with better form and less often produced responses that showed deviant thinking and anxious and hostile content. In general, U.S. children tried to deal with the testing situation in a much more active manner than the Mexican children, even when unable to do so successfully.

The work of Tamm (1967) in the American School in Mexico City allows for a deeper insight into the meaning of these cross-cultural findings with U.S. and Mexican school children. Tamm designed a study involving bilingual Mexican and U.S. children attending the same school. Thirty children in the first, fourth, and seventh grades were tested at 6 years, 8 months; 9 years, 8 months; and 12 years, 8 months of age, respectively, in order to provide precise parallels to the design employed in the larger cross-cultural study between Mexico and the United States. One-half of the children were native Mexicans for whom Spanish was the primary language. These children generally came from upper-class Mexican families in which there was a strong desire on the part of the parents for their children to obtain a U.S.-style education. The remainder of the children were Americans whose fathers were businessmen or government representatives in Mexico City. The U.S. families wanted their children to develop bilingual/bicultural skills and attitudes. The curriculum in the American School was taught half in English and half in Spanish.

Tamm administered the HIT and all the subtests of the WISC to each of the 90 school children 2 years in a row. The children's test performance was analyzed in a three-way analysis-of-variance design—by culture, age group, and year of testing. Of the WISC subtests, only Digit Span proved significant across cultures, the Mexican children doing slightly better than the Americans. The usual developmental differences were clearly apparent in both groups. On the HIT, however, marked differences were found between the Mexican and American children— differences that in every respect were essentially the same as the major differences found for HIT scores in the larger cross-cultural study. Mexican children used much more small detail and gave less Color, less Movement, less Pathognomic Verbalization, less Human content, less Anxiety, and less Hostility than did the American children.

The lack of any notable differences between the Mexican and American children on the intelligence tests in Tamm's study, regardless of the length of time the children had spent in the American School or the children's ages, provides convincing evidence that the combination of home environment and schooling is important in the development of these mental abilities. At the same time, the dramatic differences in personality and perceptual style reflected in the HIT—differences identical to those obtained when American children in Austin were compared with Mexican children in Mexico City—indicate that fundamental aspects of the American and Mexican personality or "national character" remain intact, in spite of common schooling and other forces within the immediate environment of the children that would tend to produce convergence of the two cultures. The sociocultural premises underlying the U.S. and Mexican societies, and the basically different styles of coping with the challenges of life in the two cultures, provide a key to the interpretation of these results. American children tend to be more actively independent and to struggle for a mastery of problems and challenges in their environment, whereas Mexican children are more passively obedient and adapt to stresses in the environment instead of trying to change them.

CONCLUSION

The value of the HIT for clinical and research use with children depends upon the reliability and validity of HIT scores for use in personality assessment and psychodiagnosis, as well as upon the efficiency and ease of administration, scoring, and interpretation. Although the HIT is still a relatively young technique, the evidence to date seems to indicate that it has answered most if not all of the criticisms of the Rorschach.

The availability of parallel forms and standardized variables, without sacrificing the qualitatively rich projective content of the Rorschach, provides clinicians and researchers alike with a powerful tool for the assessment of personality in children as well as adults, and explains the growing acceptance of the HIT throughout the world. Experts in assessment have been quick to point out its advantages over the Rorschach (Anastasi,

1982; Fehr, 1983; Kleinmuntz, 1982; Peterson, 1978). The HIT is more demanding of the clinician than the Rorschach; however, the time and effort involved in administering, scoring, and interpreting the HIT need not be any greater than for the Rorschach once the technique has been mastered. Those who have learned the method well have been enthusiastic about its value for both clinical and research purposes. Some find the HIT difficult because it has 45 inkblots rather than 10, or because it has only one response per card rather than as many as the child wishes to give. Yet these are the very features that produce superior psychometric qualities, rendering the HIT more suitable for rigorous scientific validity as well as for implementation by modern computer technology. As with any major test for the assessment of personality, the final verdict on the HIT will be reached only after many years of experimental and clinical work with children and adults.

Materials for the HIT can be obtained from the Psychological Corporation, 555 Academic Court, San Antonio, TX 78204-0952. The *Guide for Administration and Scoring* is an offprint of the sections on administration and scoring from Holtzman et al. (1961a). Sets of 35-mm slides are used with the group method of administration. An annotated bibliography of the HIT, and other monographs in addition to Holtzman et al. (1961a), are also available.

REFERENCES

Anastasi, A. (1982). *Psychological testing* (5th ed.). New York: Macmillan.

Aronow, E., & Reznikoff, M. (1976). *Rorschach content interpretation*. New York: Grune & Stratton.

Auerbach, S. M., & Edinger, J. D. (1977). The effects of surgery-induced stress on anxiety as measured by the Holtzman Inkblot Technique. *Journal of Personality Assessment, 41*, 19–24.

Bock, D. R., Haggard, E. A., Holtzman, W. H., Beck, A. G., & Beck, S. J. (1963). *A comprehensive psychometric study of the Rorschach and Holtzman inkblot techniques*. Chapel Hill: University of North Carolina, Psychometric Laboratory.

Buros, O. K. (Ed.). (1949). *The third mental measurements yearbook*. New Brunswick, NJ: Rutgers University Press.

Cleveland, S. E., & Morton, R. B. (1962). Group behavior and body image: A follow-up study. *Human Relations, 15*, 77–85.

Conners, C. K. (1965). Effects of brief psychotherapy, drugs, and type of disturbance on Holtzman Inkblot

scores in children. *Proceedings of the 73rd Annual Convention of the American Psychological Association, 1*, 201–202.

Conquest, R. A. (1963). *An investigation of body image variables in patients with the diagnosis of schizophrenic reaction*. Unpublished doctoral dissertation, Case Western Reserve University.

Covan, F. L. (1976). *The perception of movement in inkblots following cognitive inhibition*. Unpublished doctoral dissertation, Yeshiva University.

Currie, S. F., Holtzman, W. H., & Swartz, J. D. (1974). Early indicators of personality traits viewed retrospectively. *Journal of School Psychology, 12*, 51–59.

Endicott, N. A., & Jortner, S. (1967). Correlates of somatic concern derived from psychological tests. *Journal of Nervous and Mental Disease, 144*, 133–138.

Fehr, L. A. (1983). *Introduction to personality*. New York: Macmillan.

Feldstein, S. (1973). *REM deprivation: The effects of inkblot perception and fantasy processes*. Unpublished doctoral dissertation, City University of New York.

Fernald, P. S., & Linden, J. D. (1966). The human content response in the Holtzman Inkbolt Technique. *Journal of Projective Techniques and Personality Assessment, 30*, 441–446.

Fisher, S. (1963). A further appraisal of the body boundary concept. *Journal of Consulting Psychology, 27*, 62–74.

Fisher, S., & Cleveland, S. E. (1958). *Body image and personality*. Princeton, NJ: Van Nostrand.

Gorham, D. R. (1967). Computer use in psychological testing. In G. Gillespie (Ed.), *Memorias del XIth Congreso Interamericano de Psicologia* (Vol. 9, pp. 1–7). Mexico City: Universidad Nacional Autonoma de Mexico.

Greenberg, E., Aronow, E., & Rauchway, A. (1977). Inkblot content and interpersonal distance. *Journal of Clinical Psychology, 33*, 882–887.

Herron, E. W. (1963). Psychometric characteristics of a thirty-item version of the group method of the Holtzman Inkblot Technique. *Journal of Clinical Psychology, 19*, 450–453.

Herron, E. W. (1965). Personality factors associated with the acquisition of the conditioned eyelid response. *Journal of Personality and Social Psychology, 2*, 775–777.

Hill, E. F. (1972). *The Holtzman Inkblot Technique: A handbook for clinical application*. San Francisco: Jossey-Bass.

Holtzman, W. H. (1950). *The Rorschach test in the assessment of the normal superior adult*. Unpublished doctoral dissertation, Stanford University.

Holtzman, W. H. (1975). New developments in the HIT. In P. McReynolds (Ed.), *Advances in psychological assessment* (Vol. 3, pp. 243–274). San Francisco: Jossey-Bass.

Holtzman, W. H. (1981). Holtzman Inkblot Technique (HIT). In A. I. Rabin (Ed.), *Assessment with projective techniques: A concise introduction* (pp. 47–83). New York: Springer.

Holtzman, W. H., Diaz-Guerrero, R., & Swartz, J. D. (1975). *Personality development in two cultures: A cross-cultural longitudinal study of school children in Mexico and the United States*. Austin: University of Texas Press.

Holtzman, W. H., Moseley, E. C., Reinehr, R. C., & Abbott, E. (1963). Comparison of the group method and the standard individual version of the Holtzman Inkblot Technique. *Journal of Clinical Psychology, 19,* 441–449.

Holtzman, W. H., & Swartz, J. D. (1983). The Holtzman Inkblot Technique: A review of 25 years of research. *Zeitschrift für Differentielle und Diagnostische Psychologie, 4,* 241–259.

Holtzman, W. H., Swartz, J. D., & Thorpe, J. S. (1971). Artists, architects, and engineers: Three contrasting modes of visual experience and their psychological correlates. *Journal of Personality, 39,* 432–449.

Holtzman, W. H., Thorpe, J. S., Swartz, J. D., & Herron, E. W. (1961a). *Inkblot perception and personality: Holtzman Inkblot Technique.* Austin: University of Texas Press.

Holtzman, W. H., Thorpe, J. S., Swartz, J. D., & Herron, E. W. (1961b). *Administration and scoring guide.* New York: Psychological Corporation.

Iacino, L. W., & Cook, P. E. (1974). Threat of shock, state anxiety, and the HIT. *Journal of Personality Assessment, 38,* 450–458.

Kamen, G. B. (1969). Effects of a stress-producing film on the test performance of adults. *Journal of Projective Techniques and Personality Assessment, 33,* 281–285.

Kamen, G. B. (1970). *The effects of a stress-producing film on the test performance of adults.* Unpublished doctoral dissertation, University of Missouri.

Kamen, G. B. (1971). A second look at the effects of stress-producing film on adult test performance. *Journal of Clinical Psychology, 27,* 465–467.

Kleinmuntz, B. (1982). *Personality and psychological assessment.* New York: St. Martin's Press.

Laird, D. R., Laosa, L. M., & Swartz, J. D. (1973). Inkblot perception and reading achievement in children: A developmental analysis. *British Journal of Projective Psychology and Personality Study, 18,* 25–31.

Lefcourt, H. M., Telegdi, M. S., Willows, D., & Buckspan, B. (1972). Eye contact and the human movement response. *Journal of Social Psychology, 88,* 303–304.

Lerner, B. (1966). Rorschach movement and dreams: A validation study using drug-induced dream deprivation. *Journal of Abnormal Psychology, 71,* 75–86.

Mayfield, D. G. (1968). Holtzman Inkblot Technique in acute experimental alcohol intoxication. *Journal of Projective Techniques and Personality Assessment, 32,* 491–494.

Megargee, E. I. (1965). The relation between barrier scores and aggressive behavior. *Journal of Abnormal Psychology, 70,* 307–311.

Morgan, A. B. (1968). Some age norms obtained for the Holtzman Inkblot Technique administered in a clinical setting. *Journal of Projective Techniques and Personality Assessment, 32,* 165–172.

Mueller, W. J., & Abeles, N. (1964). The components of empathy and their relationship to the projection of human movement responses. *Journal of Projective Techniques and Personality Assessment, 28,* 322–330.

Mullen, J. M., Reinehr, R. C., & Swartz, J. D. (1983). Holtzman Inkblot Technique scores of delinquent adolescents: A replication and extension. *Journal of Personality Assessment, 47,* 158–160.

Nichols, D. C., & Tursky, B. (1967). Body image, anxiety, and tolerance for experimental pain. *Psychosomatic Medicine, 29,* 103–110.

Peterson, R. A. (1978). Holtzman Inkblot Technique. In O. K. Buros (Ed.), *The eighth mental measurements yearbook* (pp. 847–849). Highland Park, NJ: Gryphon Press.

Rosenstiel, L. von. (1973). Increase in hostility responses in the HIT after frustration. *Journal of Personality Assessment, 37,* 22–24.

Sundberg, N. D. (1962). The Rorschach Americanized. *Contemporary Psychology, 7,* 250–252.

Swartz, J. D. (1969). *Pathognomic verbalizations in normals, psychotics, and mental retardates.* Unpublished doctoral dissertation, University of Texas.

Swartz, J. D., & Holtzman, W. H. (1963). Group method of administration for the Holtzman Inkblot Technique. *Journal of Clinical Psychology, 19,* 433–441.

Swartz, J. D., Reinehr, R. C., & Holtzman, W. H. (1983a). *Holtzman Inkblot Technique, 1956–1982: An annotated bibliography.* Austin, TX: Hogg Foundation for Mental Health.

Swartz, J. D., Reinehr, R. C., & Holtzman, W. H. (1983b). Personality development through the lifespan: Assessment by means of the Holtzman Inkblot Technique. In C. D. Spielberger & J. N. Butcher (Eds.), *Advances in personality assessment* (Vol. 3, pp. 35–51). Hillsdale, NJ: Erlbaum.

Swartz, J. D., Witzke, D. B., & Megargee, E. I. (1970). Normative item statistics for the group form of the Holtzman Inkblot Technique. *Perceptual and Motor Skills, 31,* 319–329.

Tamm, M. (1967). *El Holtzman Inkblot Test, el Wechsler Intelligence Scale for Children y otros tests en el estudio psicologico transcultural de ninos de habla Espanola e Inglesa residentes en Mexico.* Unpublished doctoral dissertation, Universidad Nacional Autonoma de Mexico, Mexico City.

Vincent, K. R. (1982). The fully automated Holtzman interpretation. In K. Herman & R. M. Samuels (Eds.), *Computers: An extension of the clinician's mind, a reference book* (pp. 123–125). Norwood, NJ: Ablex.

Zubin, J. (1954). Failures of the Rorschach technique. *Journal of Projective Techniques, 18,* 303–315.

9

Using the Clinical Interview to Assess Children's Interpersonal Reasoning and Emotional Understanding

KAREN LINN BIERMAN
Pennsylvania State University

This chapter describes the purpose and techniques of open-ended clinical interviews with children. Very few studies have evaluated the reliability and validity of such interviews; nonetheless, many clinicians recommend them for inclusion in comprehensive psychological evaluations (Greenspan, 1981; Rutter & Graham, 1968). Three major factors support this recommendation. First, research suggests that the quality of children's social–emotional reasoning and their feelings about themselves and their relationships may have important implications both for case conceptualization (e.g., understanding the etiology or mechanisms maintaining a child's difficulties) and for treatment (e.g., selecting developmentally appropriate intervention strategies and goals). Second, empirical findings reveal that the self-reports given by young children about themselves and their interpersonal relations are often unrelated or only poorly related to external indicators such as observational data, test performance, or teacher/parent report. "Public" sources are insufficient to gather information about a child's "private" thoughts and feelings; the only way to gain access to such "private" information is to ask the child directly. Third, and most important, developmental research indicates that major transformations occur in children's thinking and communications about their relationships, their feelings, their self-understanding and self-evaluations during the preschool, grade school, and adolescent years. One cannot assume that even same-age children are functioning at similar developmental levels in terms of their social–emotional reasoning. Standardized and age-normed self-report instruments are useful supplements to open-ended interviewing, but cannot replace sensitive interviewing that can be adjusted to the developmental level and communication skills of the individual child. Apparently, information about a child's "private" experiences is important for clinical evaluation and treatment planning, but is accessible only via open-ended clinical interviews that are sensitive to the developmental capabilities of the individual child.

The chapter is divided into two major sections. The first section provides a brief developmental overview summarizing important transformations in children's social–emotional reasoning. Typical patterns of development are described, along with individual differences and deviations in development that may have important consequences for child adaptation. This section provides a framework for understanding the major purpose and goals of open-ended interviewing with children. In the second section specific techniques and strategies that are useful in clinical child interviewing are discussed. Procedures are presented that may help the clinician to establish rapport with children at various developmental levels and may promote the children's abilities to express and discuss their emotional concerns.

INTERPERSONAL REASONING AND EMOTIONAL UNDERSTANDING

Two aspects of a child's social–emotional reasoning are of particular interest to a clinician and can be assessed in a clinical child interview: (1) the developmental sophistication of the child's social–emotional reasoning; and (2) the child's emotional response to and affective evaluation of himself or herself, his or her abilities, and his or her relationships.

The first of these variables—the developmental sophistication of the child's social–emotional reasoning—is important because developmental research has shown that the manner in which children think about themselves and their relationships undergoes dramatic changes during the preschool, grade school, and preadolescent years (see Damon, 1983). Although children may show age-appropriate reasoning in many domains of cognitive functioning, they often show developmental delays or distortions in domains of emotional stress (Harter, 1977). Children's implicit personality theories and causal schemas may affect the manner in which they interpret interpersonal events; their interpretations of various social and emotional events may, in turn, affect their reactions to such events and their subsequent attitudes and behaviors (Bierman & Furman, 1981). Thus, the developmental sophistication of a child's social–emotional reasoning may have a direct impact on the child's behavioral reaction to and ability to cope with environmental stressors.

A child's responses to open-ended or semi-structured questions during a clinical child interview can provide a basis for the clinician to formulate and test hypotheses concerning the quality and developmental sophistication of the child's reasoning in social–emotional

domains. This knowledge, in turn, may enable the clinician to formulate hypotheses concerning ways in which the child's cognitive processing may be mediating behavioral difficulties, and it may also aid the clinician in the selection of developmentally appropriate intervention strategies.

The second set of variables—the child's emotional response to and affective evaluation of himself or herself, his or her abilities, and his or her relationships—provides information about the child's central subjective experiences and feelings. Since parents or teachers are typically the referral agents for child evaluations, it may be particularly important to assess the extent to which the children themselves are experiencing subjective distress, and to assess the quality of their awareness of, conceptualization of, and reaction to their difficulties or problem areas. As mentioned earlier, children's self-reports and self-evaluations are often poorly related to external indicators of their adjustment, such as observational data, test performance, or teacher/parent reports. For example, teachers and peers tend to agree when asked to rate a child's popularity with peers (correlations are typically about .50); however, prior to preadolescence, children's self-ratings of their popularity are not significantly correlated with the consensual external judgments of teachers and peers (Hymel & Rubin, 1985). Similarly, whereas teachers and peers agree quite well on ratings of children who show overt signs of depression, these observer ratings are not highly correlated with the children's own self-ratings of depression on the same scale (Lefkowitz & Tesiny, 1980). For a variety of reasons—including developmental limitations in cognitive reasoning and information-processing skills, as well as characteristic defenses associated with early personality development—children's perceptions of themselves and their feelings will often be "inaccurate" relative to more objective criteria.

Whether they are "accurate" or not, however, children's self-evaluations appear to be quite stable (Cairns & Cairns, 1984). Even in the early grade school years, children's self-reports of negative emotions and feelings of low self-efficacy or low self-esteem in various domains may predict their self-ratings several years later. Hence, regardless of their objective accuracy, such self-evaluations deserve closer attention in future clinical research, as well as close consideration in child assessments.

Since young children conceptualize their interpersonal interactions and emotional experiences in characteristic ways that are quite different qualitatively from the conceptualizations of adults, an understanding of the characteristics of developing social–cognitive processes is an important prerequisite for conducting and interpreting effective clinical child interviews. Such an understanding may enable the clinician to follow and understand the young child's communications more easily and may enable him or her to judge the extent to which a child's reasoning is developmentally appropriate, represents an immature reasoning style, or represents a significant deviation from typical child reasoning. A brief overview is included next, to highlight the basic trends and processes that characterize developmental changes in children's interpersonal reasoning and emotional understanding.

Developmental Overview

Development entails a gradual acquisition of a knowledge base—such as information about the characteristics, behavior, and motivations of other individuals; societal expectations associated with various social relationships and situations; language terms to describe various feelings and motivations; and so forth. In addition, development involves transformations in the child's cognitive capacities to integrate, organize hierarchically, and reason about multiple pieces of social information, enabling him or her to conceptualize increasingly complex representations of self and others. In the following sections, the general characteristics of children's social cognitive reasoning and emotional understanding are described for the developmental periods of early childhood (preschool years), middle childhood (grade school years), and adolescence.

Early Childhood

By the second year of life, children already demonstrate distinct mental images of themselves and of others. They are able to reliably classify unfamiliar individuals into broad groups by age and sex, and to respond differentially to a number of familiar individuals (see Edwards & Lewis, 1979). The toddler initially forms broad categories, classifying others on the basis of distinctive physical characteristics (e.g., age and sex). It is not until the preschool years, however, that most children become able to respond to a clinical interview situation, describing verbally or through play information about their self-image, their emotional understanding, and their representations of others.

In their emotional and interpersonal reasoning, preschoolers tend to focus on a few specific behaviors and concrete situational features (Harter, 1983). Their ability to manipulate concepts mentally is limited. Although they can consider one concept, they find it difficult to conceptualize relations between concepts. Hence, they focus on one dimension or attribute of an event, emotional state, or other individual at a time, and their conceptions are limited to ideas that can take concrete observable forms (Fischer, 1980). When asked to describe themselves or others, for example, preschool children focus on a few overt characteristics or behavioral features, such as their physical size, sex, or hair color (Livesley & Bromley, 1973). Similarly, children first identify social roles on the basis of concrete behaviors and salient physical features (Fischer & Watson, 1981). For preschoolers, a friend is someone who plays with him and lives nearby (Furman & Bierman, 1983); a mother is someone who takes care of children (Moore, Cooper, & Brickhard, 1977); boys are children who wear pants and have short hair, whereas girls wear dresses and have long hair (Fischer & Watson, 1981). As a result of their concrete basis, the social conceptions of preschoolers are rigid and inflexible. For example, preschoolers may feel that mothers who fix cars will become fathers (Moore et al., 1977) or that girls who wear pants will become boys (Fischer & Watson, 1981).

Since they find it difficult to consider multiple aspects of various concepts simultaneously, young children are unable to integrate conflictual information about others. For example, when Gollin (1958) showed children movies in which the central character performed "good" acts in two scenes and "bad" acts in two scenes, preschool children often remembered selectively that the character engaged in one type of act, either good or bad. They denied that the opposite behaviors happened, or else they attributed inconsistent actions to other movie characters. Similarly, when told that a good baseball player (one who caught well and hit many home runs) was a liar, young children denied that he could still be a good baseball player, and even denied that he could catch well or hit home runs (Saltz & Medow, 1971).

The person perceptions of young children are often characterized as "egocentric" (Peevers & Secord, 1973). Young children are unable to consider perspectives that differ from their own because they cannot mentally compare what they are thinking with information about other persons and deduce how others' thinking may differ from their own (Fischer, 1980). Hence, they remember best the characteristics of others that are highly salient and relevant to them.

Mental representations of the basic emotions of sadness, happiness, and anger emerge during the preschool years. Like their perceptions of themselves and others, however, young children's conceptions of emotions are behaviorally based and tied to situational cues. When asked to describe their emotions, preschool children often refer to particular situations or bodily reactions (e.g., happiness means "at a party" or "a smile") (Carroll & Steward, 1984). In fact, when young children (under the age of 6 or so) are asked to describe the emotions of characters in pictures when the characters' facial expressions are inconsistent with the situations (e.g., a child frowning at a birthday party), they base their inferences exclusively on the situational cues, often failing even to notice the facial cue inconsistencies (Burns & Cavey, 1957).

Similarly, emotions are viewed as externally determined (and not subject to internal manipulation or control). That is, a person feels a certain way because of the way he or she is treated or because of the situation. Only changes in the situation or treatment can induce changes in feelings. For example, sad feelings may be relieved when a person gets a present; angry feelings may change when a person gets what he or she wants (Carroll & Steward, 1984).

Finally, like their interpersonal concepts, preschool children's emotional concepts are unidimensional. They typically deny that one can have two opposing feelings at the same time (e.g., can be mad at someone and still love him or her). Just as preschoolers often use denial to deal with conflicting information about others, they focus on only one emotion and disregard the others when faced with their own conflicting feelings.

As illustrated by these examples, the cognitive limitations of young children result in social and emotional concepts that are more limited and unidimensional, more concrete and behavioral, and more externalized and inflexible than the conceptions of older children and adults.

Middle Childhood

During the early grade school years, children master the ability to consider relationships among concepts. They can then represent a series of actions (rather than just a single concept or action), describe concepts in relational terms (rather than in absolute terms), and consider part–whole relationships. Lawfulness, logic, and rules enter the social–emotional world as children become able to combine, integrate, and organize concepts and events along temporal and hierarchical dimensions.

Correspondingly, grade school children provide longer descriptions of themselves and others, and show more differentiation between descriptions of various others and themselves than do preschool children (Livesley & Bromley, 1973). Grade school children begin to compare behaviors across individuals and across time. They may recognize consistencies in their own and others' behavior, and may compare themselves and others to general norms of behavior (e.g., "Joe runs faster than Jim"; "I'm not as good in math as other kids in my class") (Barenboim, 1977). Such comparisons provide the foundation for the construction of abstract inferences about one's own and others' dispositions and personality traits, which begin to emerge in the later grade school years (e.g., "He's a real stubborn idiot"; "Randy . . . is always trying to boss other kids around") (Barenboim, 1977). The emerging ability to make inferences about covert psychological traits, in turn, enables children to construct more stable perceptions of themselves and others that can accommodate different (even conflicting) concrete behaviors (Gollin, 1958).

Similarly, grade school children begin to emphasize the relational and normative functions of social roles, rather than focusing on discrete behaviors (Fischer & Watson, 1981). For example, grade school children describe friendships as reciprocal, prosocial dyadic relationships (Furman & Bierman, 1983); they recognize that a person becomes a mother when she has children and that because she has children she remains a mother, regardless of her particular behaviors (Moore et al., 1977).

Children's understanding of emotions undergo similar transformations during the grade school years; increasingly, emotions are conceptualized as multidimensional, internally determined, and internally controlled. Grade school children begin to make finer discriminations among various negative emotions, such as sadness, fear, and anger, reliably (Borke, 1973). Children also become more able to conceptualize multiple and conflicting emotions, recognizing that one may experience more than one feeling at the same time—including feelings that are conflictual or ambivalent (see Harter, 1983). By 10–11 years of age, children begin to view emotions as linked to thoughts rather than as external cues. As such, they recognize that one may control feelings internally by reflecting or repressing thoughts or images associated with those feelings. Grade school children also recognize that they can conceal their real feelings from others by masking their facial displays (Carroll & Steward, 1948).

Adolescence

Finally, adolescents begin to consider abstract relationships among systems of logic and sets of concepts. This reasoning ability enables adolescents to generate and consider multiple solutions or perspectives for a given problem or situation; it makes possible sophisticated inductive logic and the consideration of a myriad of "what-if" hypothetical propositions about the world. Correspondingly, the descriptions of self and other given by adolescents may be well differentiated and well integrated, making use of abstract inferences to detect regularities in the diverse behaviors of self and others. Increasingly, adolescents are likely to show interest and concern about the expectations of peers. They may form opinions about the attitudes and values of various peer groups and then use these opinions as reference standards to guide their own behavior and to evaluate their self-worth. That is, they may adopt behaviors and attitudes similar to those ascribed to the peer groups with which they wish to identify, and avoid or devalue behaviors and attitudes they ascribe to disliked peers. In addition, their beliefs about their acceptance or rejection by highly valued peer groups may weigh heavily in their evaluations of their own social worth and personal likability (O'Brien & Bierman, 1988). As one adolescent explained:

> The trendies are fashion-conscious, you know, but the hicks just wear jeans. You have to dress like they dress if you want to be accepted, and each group has its own dress code more or less. It's important to be accepted because it gives you a sense of pride and belonging. Otherwise, you just feel tossed away. (quoted in O'Brien & Bierman, 1988, p. 1364).

Relationships in adolescence are defined on the basis of their abstract purpose and functions (Selman, 1980). For example, friendships are based upon loyalty, trustworthiness, and intimacy (Furman & Bierman, 1983); motherhood reflects an affective bond between mother and child that may supersede the biological connection (Moore et al., 1977). Adolescents may recognize that the specific behaviors exhibited by individual friends or mothers may vary; the essence of these relationships lies in the intentions, motivations, and mutual affections of the individuals involved.

The capacity for abstract and self-reflective thinking may have particular importance for the emotional experiences that accompany self-evaluation in adolescence. Because adolescents are more able to consider how they are viewed by various others, they may feel particularly self-conscious, as if others everywhere are interested in and judgmental of their thoughts, feelings, and actions (Damon, 1983). Correspondingly, they may increasingly begin to evaluate the legitimacy of their own thoughts and feelings.

Recursive cognitive–emotional experiences, such as anxiety, guilt, and self-reproach, may become more intense for some individuals during adolescence, as they become able cognitively to consider and reconsider thoughts and feelings internally without needing (and sometimes without reference to) an immediate external stimulus. Several investigators have posited that these advanced cognitive abilities may provide the foundation for the dramatic increases in internalizing disorders such as depression during adolescence (Cicchetti & Schneider-Rosen, 1986).

Clearly, important and significant developments take place in children's conceptions of themselves and others and in their understanding of emotions during the preschool, grade school, and adolescent years. Initially, the child's person perceptions and emotional constructs are simple, undifferentiated, and tied to concrete external cues. Increasingly, psychological processes such as thoughts and attitudes are inferred, and internal experiences are emphasized in conceptions of self and others.

As discussed in the next section, the manner in which individuals think about themselves and others may have dramatic effects on their subsequent attitudes and behavior. The quality of a child's interpersonal reasoning and emotional understanding may affect both the child's adaptation and adjustment, and may also determine the child's responsivity to various intervention strategies (Craighead, Meyers, Craighead, & McHale, 1982; Furman, 1980).

Developmental Capabilities and Child Adaptation

The ability to integrate information and reason flexibly about causal relations, which develops gradually during childhood with major transformations occurring around the ages of 4–7 and 11–14, has important implications for children's social understanding and consequent social behavior. The global, concrete, and limited social conceptions of young children provide little basis for the prediction or explanation of others' social behavior. Until children become able to compare and manipulate concepts mentally, they are not adept at inferring logical cause-and-effect sequences or predictable patterns, nor are they very good at anticipating others' thoughts, feelings, and actions. Thus, the young child's social world is quite unpredictable and magical.

The developing ability to integrate information about multiple concepts lays the foundation for logical causal reasoning about interpersonal behavior. That is, as children become able to compare diverse behavioral events and to construct concepts of thoughts and feelings, they increasingly make inferences about the internal factors (motives and dispositions) and external factors (rules, standards, consequences) that control or influence their own and others' behavior. The adaptive function of such causal reasoning is that it enables children to predict interpersonal events and to anticipate the behaviors of various others (Kelvin, 1970). Thus, children become more adept at anticipating the effects of their own actions on the responses of various others and regulating their behavior accordingly.

A corresponding developmental capacity involves children's abilities to use social norms and outcome feedback to evaluate the appropriateness of their own and others' behavior. The preschool child is just beginning to attach value labels to particular concrete actions. Some behaviors are "good" (e.g., sharing toys), whereas other behaviors are "bad" (e.g., hitting). The grade school child begins to combine and integrate various types of behavior and thus can evaluate himself or herself and others in terms of conventional rules or standards of behavior. That is, their social expectations involve principles of behavior, which include a variety of specific behavioral examples (e.g., it's good to play fair; it's bad to be a poor sport). As they are able to consider and integrate ideas about various standards, adolescents may then move beyond the rigid rule-based or conventional expectations of grade school children and recognize that the relevance or importance of particular standards may vary depending upon the circumstances and individuals involved.

The source of children's social expectations also varies developmentally. Young children depend upon direct social feedback (e.g., praise or rebuke) to establish their standards for behavior. By the grade school years, children begin to show an interest in peer progress and begin to evaluate their own achievement relative to information about peers' achievement (Ruble, Boggiano, Feldman, & Loebl, 1980). With increased life experience, children also gradually develop greater knowledge about social protocol and social roles, which allows them to predict and interpret the behavior of unknown individuals in various situations. That is, by knowing the attitudes and behaviors that individuals in various social positions typically direct toward individuals in other social positions, children "know about" many people who, as individuals, remain unknown (Edwards & Lewis, 1979). Such social knowledge also provides children with a guide for their own behavior in various social situations.

Young children, who have a limited understanding of social role relations, may show confused social behavior. For example, Fischer and Watson (1981) suggest that it is the child's developing understanding of the social relationships in his or her family that contributes to the "Oedipus complex." By age 4–5, children can label sex roles and recognize that male and female roles go together as "husband and wife" or "Mommy and Daddy." They may select the opposite-sex parent as the most available mate for themselves, and express the intention of marrying this parent when they grow up. Since young children are unable to consider relationships between multiple mental concepts, they fail to consider that, despite the "match" between themselves and their opposite-sex parent on the male–female dimension, coexisting "mismatches" on the dimensions of parent–child roles and age invalidate the selection of one's parent as one's spouse. By 6 or 7 years of age, children become cognitively capable of considering multiple role dimensions, realize that one must select a spouse who "matches" on multiple dimensions (e.g., opposite sex, not familially related, etc.), and thus resolve the "Oedipus complex."

Research on children who have poor peer relations suggests that deficits in social knowledge may lead to inappropriate social behavior and subsequently to interpersonal difficulties (see Putallaz & Gottman, 1983). That is, if children are not aware of peer-accepted standards of behavior, they may behave in a manner that leads to avoidance and ostracism from their peers.

Just as the development of abstract and flexible causal reasoning facilitates children's ability to evaluate and to make predictions about others' behavior, it may have important ramifications for their self-evaluations. Since young children cannot conceive of multiple and inconsistent concepts, they find it difficult to accept negative information about themselves and yet maintain a positive self-image (Harter, 1977). Even when faced with concrete evidence of their wrongdoings, they may deny them or blame those wrongdoings on others. Alternatively, they may waver moodily between global positive feelings about themselves and global negative feelings (Harter, 1977). The capacity to consider multiple concepts enables children to consider and evaluate the motivations associated with their various behaviors (including negative behaviors), and thus to utilize anticipatory problem solving to prevent or remediate similar problems in the future.

Even if a child's chronological age suggests that he or she should have the cognitive-developmental capacities to reason in a flexible and causal fashion about his or her misbehavior or emotional distress, the child may not actually be able to do so. Chronological age is a relatively poor marker of reasoning abilities in affectively charged domains, and children who have experienced a great deal of stress, conflict, or unpredictability in the social–emotional domain are particularly likely to show immature or variable reasoning. Regression in reasoning abilities in the face of stress is also not uncommon (Selman, 1980). The quality of a child's reasoning about social–emotional issues has important implications for treatment planning—for both the selection of treatment goals and the design of intervention approaches. To the extent that a child's social–emotional reasoning seems to represent a domain of relative cognitive delay for the child, the clinician may wish to design interventions to facilitate more sophisticated, developmentally appropriate reasoning. In general, however, the manner in which the clinician works with the child must be adapted to the child's current level of functioning in order to maximize treatment effectiveness. (See Craighead et al., 1982, and Furman, 1980, for more discussion on the tailoring of intervention strategies to the developmental level of the child.)

Summary

To summarize, the previous section has been concerned with the "what" and "why" of child interviewing. The value of the interview for evaluating the developmental sophistication of the child's social–emotional reasoning has been stressed. Importantly, the clinician should try to determine the extent to which a child shows social–emotional reasoning that is developmentally appropriate, or that represents a delay relative to development in other domains of reasoning, or that represents a distortion of clinical significance. In addition, the clinician should try to assess the content or quality of the child's feelings about himself or herself and his or her significant relationships. The type of defenses or responses to negative emotions and stressful situations shown by the child; the child's ability to use language and verbal problem solving to identify and regulate stressful emotions; and the extent to which the child feels control or can consider effective coping strategies for his or her problems are all topics of interest to the interviewer. Research reviewed in this section suggests that these topics are important because of their potential impact on other child attitudes and behaviors and their potential value as intervention targets.

In the next section, the "how" of the child interview is discussed in more detail. The phases and process of the child interview are presented, with an emphasis on how development may affect a child's responses to the interview and how the interviewer may adjust his or her interview strategies to match the developmental needs of particular children. Corresponding to the focus of the first part of this chapter, interview techniques that contribute to an assessment of the developmental sophistication and the quality of a child's interpersonal reasoning and emotional understanding are highlighted.

INTERVIEW TECHNIQUES

Four general phases of the child interview are presented here: (1) the "getting acquainted" (introductory and rapport-building) phase; (2) the exploratory phase, in which semistructured prompts and open-ended questions may be used to elicit and examine social–emotional themes and issues of particular importance to the individual child; (3) a phase in which more specific and standardized self-rating instruments may be administered to enable comparison with age-graded norms; and (4) closure. Not all interviews will incorporate all four phases, and the content of each phase will vary with the developmental level, verbal skills, and interpersonal responsivity of the particular child client. As stated earlier, a major advantage of child interviewing is that it provides the clinician with the flexibility to tailor his or her interviewing strategies in order to maximize the individual child's ability to communicate. Hence, the specific techniques presented below are intended to serve as ideas and guides, not mandatory procedures; they should be chosen as needed to facilitate each child's emotional expression.

Getting Acquainted

Before beginning the interview, the clinician should give some thought to the organization of the interview room. It is important to provide some space for free play and a table and chairs suitable for the child's size. Toys and materials should be carefully selected for each interview. It is best to have a cabinet to store toys and materials to allow the interviewer to select and display the appropriate subset of materials and thus "set the stage" for each interview. Too many available toys may distract the younger child or the child with poor behavioral controls; a few toys selected for their value for expressive play are preferable. For example, simple toys that foster communication, dramatic play, and interaction are best, including paper and crayons, a chalkboard, a doll house, a few dolls and cars, blocks, clay or Play-Doh, puppets, and toy telephones. Toys that enable many uses and foster creative expression are better than toys that elicit stereotypic play. For example, a punching bag will often elicit punching and a baby bottle will often elicit sucking; given the high "demand characteristics" of these toys, such behavior tells one more about the toy than about the child. More information about the child can be inferred when dramatic play involves toys with low "demand characteristics," such as when a child creates a punching interaction with puppets (when no external stimulus for punching is present) or when "playing baby" becomes a recurrent theme in doll play. When interviewing an older child (especially a preadolescent or young adolescent), it may be desirable to have a few toys available (such as clay or crayons), but to arrange them less conspicuously, so that the child does not feel demeaned by being interviewed in a "nursery."

In preparing for the interview, it will be useful to consider differences in the expectations and orientations that children at different developmental levels may bring to the interview. Most children have not had experience with a strange adult who is asking them difficult questions about their thoughts and feelings. Preschool children often need to be enticed and encouraged in the interview situation. They may become negativistic if the interviewer places many verbal or behavioral demands upon them. Hence, the interviewer may need to expend much energy in nurturing and supporting the young child and in moderating demands to maximize the child's responsivity. Typically, young children will warm up fairly quickly and respond well to an interviewer who is supportive, full of praise, and as energetic as a play partner. Although limited in their verbal expressive skills, preschool children are often quite open and willing to share their social perceptions and current concerns to the best of their communicative ability. Grade school children, on the other hand, are more skillful at conceptualizing and describing their thoughts and feelings than preschool children, but the older children also recognize that their thoughts and feelings are their own and can be consciously withheld,

concealed, or denied. Establishing a sense of trust is an important initial step in interviews with grade school and young adolescent children, along with fostering a sense of interpersonal comfort by sensitive and nonintrusive interviewing.

With any child, the interview usually begins with a statement of purpose for the child. Although parents may have explained the interview in advance, it is useful for the interviewer to give a brief and clear statement, such as the following: "This is a place where moms and dads and kids come to talk with a helper like me. Sometimes they tell me they wish things could go better at home or at school. I help them figure things out so that they can feel better." The interviewer may ask why the child thinks he or she needs to come to the interview. However, for many children this is a difficult or even embarrassing question. Therefore, the clinician may wish to save this question for later in the interview, when greater rapport has been established.

The initial goal is then to establish rapport with the child. With young children, this is often best done by giving them an opportunity to look around at the toys in the room and find something they would like to play with. The interviewer may learn about the child by observing the manner in which the child approaches the room and the play initiated by the child. That is, the organization and complexity of the child's play and the themes that arise provide a basis for some initial hypotheses about the child's thoughts and feelings, which can be followed up later in the interview. (See Greenspan, 1981, for more information about clinical observation in play interviews.)

The initial phase of the interview with an older grade school child or young adolescent, as with a younger child, is directed toward establishing rapport. These older children may not need toys to help them express their feelings, however, and in fact may find toys distracting or uninteresting. Simple interview tasks may facilitate "getting acquainted." Initial questions should focus on concrete topics that are not emotionally laden or overly personal, such as where the child goes to school, what grade he or she is in, who is in the family, and so on.

It is important not to assume that the

child's behavior in the interview situation is representative of his or her behavior in other, more familiar settings. Indeed, research suggests that children's behavior is quite variable across even familiar settings such as home and school. The strangeness of the interview setting and clinician and the unfamiliar interview demands, may lead to quite atypical child behavior. Some children, if anxious in this situation, may respond with less behavioral control and more immature behavior than in familiar settings; others may show considerably more than their typical amount of behavioral control. Therefore, interview behavior is *not* an accurate reflection of the child's typical interpersonal style or behavioral adjustment—parents, teachers, and observations in naturalistic settings are far better measures for such variables. However, interview behavior may provide the interviewer with clues and hypotheses about a child's concerns and feelings, which further observation and discussion may confirm or disconfirm.

Exploring Social–Emotional Themes

As children become more comfortable in the interview situation, the interviewer may want to expand upon his or her initial observations of the child by using more directive techniques to identify and explore social–emotional issues of significance for the child. Occasionally, the interviewer can explore social–emotional themes simply by entering into a child's dramatic play and encouraging the child to expand the interactions and feelings being displayed. For example, a child may begin playing with a doll house during the unstructured part of the interview. Perhaps the child has identified some family members and is selecting furniture for each room. The interviewer may attempt to stimulate more dramatic and expressive play by wondering aloud what a doll is saying or what events will happen next. The interviewer may even want to introduce events, such as a doll doing something bad, and then have the child "guess" what bad thing was done or what will happen next, encouraging the child to show the bad behavior and its consequences. Some children respond well to this type of play dialogue and are eager to play out family interactions and feelings; other children are not interested in story play or reject the interviewer's bid for play entry.

Other interview strategies to explore the child's thoughts and feelings involve the use of pictures and semistructured tasks. Each of these strategies can be modified to suit the conceptual and expressive skills of particular children. In general, children are able to recognize and identify concepts before they spontaneously describe and discuss them, and they can demonstrate mastery of a concept on a nonverbal task before they can articulate their reasoning (see Shantz, 1975). Young children may often lack the words or the organizational skills to describe their thoughts and feelings. Hence, designing these tasks so that they require nonverbal or less complex verbal responses often enables young children to communicate feelings that they might otherwise have trouble putting into words. Depending upon the developmental level of the child, these tasks can also be introduced and structured more like "games" or more like "school tasks." Three such general strategies are described: (1) affect labels, (2) picture–question techniques, and (3) drawing stories.

Affect Labels

The basic strategy of the "affect label" technique is to use concrete aids to enable children to discuss their negative and positive feelings. Using simple drawings depicting happy, sad, angry (and, for older children, frightened) expressions, the interviewer can ask the child about each emotion. In the easiest version of this task, the interviewer may ask the child to label each face and then to point to one of the faces to show how he or she feels in a particular situation (e.g., "How do you look when you go to school?" or "How do you look when you are with your baby brother?") When the faces are used in this fashion, no verbal response is required from the child, making the task easy and fairly nonthreatening even for young children. The task may be made more difficult but more informative by using the faces as open-ended prompts (e.g., "Tell me something that makes you feel like this") and asking the child to generate several things that make him or her feel happy, sad, mad, or afraid. If the child appears comfortable and capable of more extended verbal inquiry, the interviewer may explore the child's answers further with simple probes. For example, if a child lists "When my mom and dad fight" as something that makes him or her sad, the interviewer may ask follow-up questions such as these: "What about that makes you sad?", "Does it just make you sad, or does it make you a little bid mad or scared too?", "What do you feel like doing when that happens?", "What do you think might happen when you hear them fight?" The interviewer should pay close attention to the child's responsivity when conducting such follow-up probing. If the child seems responsive and eager to explain, the interviewer can continue probing and need not feel constrained to return to the concrete aid of the faces task. On the other hand, if the child seems stressed and responds with "I don't know," or appears uncomfortable (verbally or behaviorally), the interviewer should back off and return to a less threatening task such as the faces. However, the interviewer should note the issues that seem distressing to the child and should seek opportunities to explore them further with tasks that are less intrusive and less threatening than direct questioning.

Another example of the affect label technique of interviewing has been developed by Bene and Anthony (1957) in their Family Relations Test. Designed specifically to help the child express his or her feelings about various family members, this task presents children with feeling statements (e.g., "I like to hug this person"), which they deliver to one of the cardboard figures representing each member of the family. Statements include positive and negative feelings experienced toward and received from others.

Using pictures to help children label their feelings provides young children with a fairly easy task and can provide older children with a fairly nonthreatening initial interview task. For older children who have the verbal capabilities, pictures can also be used to elicit more elaborate responses, as in the picture–question interview techniques described next.

Picture–Question Techniques

In picture–question strategies, concrete stimuli such as dolls or pictures may be used to present familiar situations to children and to provide a focus for interview questions. The interviewer may choose pictures that display common affect-laden situations for children and ask children to make up a story that describes the situation, including the feelings experienced by the various story characters. By providing more or less structure and direction, the interviewer can control the difficulty level of this type of task for the child. For example, Biber and Lewis (1949) used pictures of various school situations to help first- and second-graders discuss their expectations and perceptions of school. To help these young children respond, familiar school situations were presented in pictures along with descriptions of events (e.g., "Oh, look, this little girl is crying—see her tears?") Then children were asked to predict what would happen (e.g., "What do you think the teacher is saying to her?") Older children may be asked to provide more of the structure themselves. That is, they may be shown the picture and asked to make up a story about the picture that has a beginning, a middle, and an end. They may then be asked to describe the feelings experienced by each of the story characters.

The interviewer may wish to select pictures most relevant for particular children from the several sets of projective pictures that depict typical and affect-laden familial, peer, and school situations, such as the Michigan Picture Test (Andrew, Hartwell, Walton, & Hutt, 1953), the School Apperception Method (Solomon & Starr, 1968), and the Make-A-Picture Story Test (Schneidman, 1952). Some of the pictures from the TAT (Murray, 1943) may also be selected, although the TAT was not designed for use with children and includes pictures which may not be appropriate for preschool and grade school children.

The use of projective techniques as interview strategies, which is being advocated here, must be distinguished from the use of projectives as personality tests (Oaklander, 1978). When used with adults, the traditional projective approach assumes that an indiviudal's perceptions of and responses to ambiguous or affect-laden stimuli will reveal basic personality characteristics, such as the nature and intensity of unconscious drives and desires, the integrity and quality of perceptions of reality, and the use of defense mechanisms. Such interpretations of projective responses may be inappropriate for children because children's verbal expressive abilities may not allow them to respond well to projective techniques; age-appropriate norms to guide interpretation of projective tests are often unavailable; and the personality theory guiding the interpretation of responses assumes adult development. Therefore, rather than assuming that children's responses to these various pictures can be interpreted with adult norms, I suggest that the pictures are simply one way of eliciting children's feelings about selected issues. At face value, children's responses may allow the interviewer to form hypotheses about issues and feelings of importance to the child, which can be confirmed or disconfirmed with further interviewing.

Rather than using standard pictures, the clinician may also choose pictures that reflect situations confronting particular children. For example, the interviewer may present a picture or doll situation to a child whose parents were recently divorced and say, "Here are a mom and dad and a little girl about your age. The mom and dad got divorced." The interviewer can then explore the child's conceptions of divorce with quetions such as these: "What do you think happened?", "What did the mom/dad/little girl say?", "What did the mom/dad/little girl feel?", and "What will happen next?"

The use of picture stimuli in these examples makes the interview task more concrete and less personally intrusive for the child. The interviewer can address issues relevant for the child with less anxiety-provoking directness and fewer demands on the child's conceptual and verbal expressive skills than direct open-ended questioning. Similarly, drawings may be used to focus the interview.

Drawing Stories

Like picture–question techniques, children's drawings can provide a concrete stimulus to help them focus on clinically relevant topics. For example, children may be asked to draw themselves and then to answer questions about their drawings, such as things they like or do not like to do, things they like or do not

like about school or the family, things that get them into trouble, or things that make them mad. After asking the child to draw himself or herself, for example, the interviewer can suggest, "What a nice drawing. Let's do something special with it. I'm going to put some numbers on the side here to help us tell all about this drawing. For the first list, I need to know something you like to do." This strategy takes the interviewer's direct (often intimidating) focus off the child and puts it onto the task, and it gives the child a concrete response demand. The interviewer can maintain a very positive and supportive attitude toward the child when using this technique, encouraging and praising the child for thinking of things, while enabling the child to express his or her hopes, fears, and frustrations.

Harter (1979) describes another drawing technique that she uses in her clinical interviews to help young children describe family interactions. First, she asks children to draw themselves and their families doing something together. She then draws a bubble above each figure to hold the words that each figure might be saying (as in comic strip). Children are encouraged and helped to construct a story by suggesting things that family members might say to each other. They are asked to think of one thing at a time that a family member could say—a method that reduces the verbal and organizational skill demands made on the children. Although young children may find it difficult to describe the nature of family interactions on an abstract level, this strategy allows them to represent concretely their views of typical family interaction patterns.

Any of these structured tasks (affect labels, picture–question techniques, or drawing stories) may provide a starting point for further interviewing with other children. Some children will feel more comfortable starting with these focused tasks, but will be able as the interview progresses to respond to open-ended interview probes about issues that emerge during the structured tasks. The phrasing and timing of open-ended interview questions is important, however; the interviewer must watch the responses of the child and must phrase questions carefully to stay within an optimal comfort level for the child.

Open-Ended Interviewing

Understanding and organizing coherent answers to open-ended questions require a fairly high level of comprehensive and expressive abilities. Young children may often fail to respond to such questions because they do not understand what or how to think about the interviewer's demands. Many interview procedures that are standard with adults, such as sitting face to face and asking exploratory open-ended questions, may be intimidating and ineffective for young children because they overwhelm their linguistic and cognitive processing abilities. When interview questions are structured to reduce verbal complexity and ambiguity by providing children with concrete referents, however, they are often more effective.

For example, Yarrow (1960) suggests several ways in which open-ended questions may be made easier for children: (1) suggesting that other children feel that way (e.g., "One kid I know told me that he wished more kids liked him. Do you ever feel that way?"); (2) giving two alternatives (e.g., "Do you ever wish that your dad spent more time with you, or do you think he spends enough time with you?"); (3) softening negative choices or phrasing questions to imply negatives (e.g., "What kind of things do your brother and you fight about?" rather than "Do you ever fight with your brother?"); and (4) combining questions about positive affects with those about negative feelings (e.g., "What's one thing your mom does that you really like? What's something she does that you don't like very much?"). Many of these questions can be extended with specific probes. Probes that provide concrete structure (e.g., "Tell me one thing that you don't like about school," "When was the last time you felt that way?") usually elicit better responses than do vague probes ("Can you tell me anything else?").

In addition to the content of the child's responses, the clinician will want to attend to the child's reasoning about his or her feelings and relationships. After noting the child's spontaneous description of a feeling or an event, the interviewer may wish to explore and gradually clarify exactly how the child was reasoning, asking for elaboration and confirmation until the child's logic becomes clear. For example, if a boy were to say that it makes him mad when his brother won't share, the interviewer may ask, "What about that makes you angry?" It may be that the boy simply covets a particular toy, or it may turn out that the child's perception of differential parental perference (his brother gets better toys and more parental affection than he himself does) is the real issue. Young children will often present spontaneous descriptions of interpersonal events, fantasies, or feelings that are vague or disorganized. If the clinician begins with the child's statements, and then gradually helps the child with probes to expand and explain each piece of his or her story, the clinician may gain a better understanding of the child's thought processes and may also help the child to clarify his or her understanding of the event in question.

Another structured way to interview is to phrase questions as sentence completions. That is, the interviewer may tell the child that he or she would like to make a story together. The interviewer may begin with a prompt designed to explore an issue of significance for the child. For example, with a learning-disabled girl, the interviewer may begin with a prompt such as this: "One day a girl was at school and she was feeling . . . (To child:) What should we say she was feeling at school?" The child may respond, "Sad." The interviewer may then continue, "She was feeling sad because . . . (To child:) What could we say she was sad about?" In this manner, the interviewer can encourage the child to explain the various feelings she may herself experience (or wish to experience) at school.

Similarly, an interviewer may wish to select some of the story beginnings provided in the Madeleine Thomas Stories, which are well suited for grade school children (Würsten, 1960). The themes that arise when a child completes these stories may provide the interviewer with insights concerning the child's perceptions and feelings, which again can be examined or pursued further in the interview.

In addition to these open-ended interview strategies, the clinician may at times wish to use more standardized self-report measures, particularly with grade school and older clients.

Standardized Self-Report Measures

Standardized self-report measures may enable the interviewer to examine certain aspects of the child's social–emotional adjustment more closely and may allow for a direct comparison with age-graded norms. With older children, the inclusion of such measures may provide an useful supplement to open-ended interviewing by broadening the surveyed scope of the children's feelings. A comprehensive review of the self-report measures that could contribute useful information in a clinical child interview is beyond the scope of this chapter (see Finch & Rogers, 1984, for a review). However, a few instruments are described here to illustrate the type of measure that may tap a child's feelings of their self-worth and well-being, and may thus be particularly useful as a "screening" device in initial child assessment interviews.

One such measure is the Perceived Competence Scale for Children (Harter, 1982; Harter & Pike, 1984). This scale is particularly useful for children for several reasons: (1) It provides separate forms and norms for grade school and preschool children; (2) it samples children's self-evaluations in specific competence domains, as well as feelings of general self-esteem; and (3) it uses a 4-point rating system (rather than a true–false format), which increases the variation in children's responding and reduces social desirability biases.

Another well-standardized measure is the Children's Depression Inventory (Kovacs, 1978). Children use a 3-point scale to describe the extent to which they experience various affective and vegetative symptoms of depression, including sad mood, fatigue, and eating and sleeping problems. Age-graded norms and clinical sample comparison norms are available.

A third measure that may be useful for screening is the Loneliness Scale developed by Asher, Hymel, and Renshaw (1984), which taps children's perceptions of their peer relations. The 16 items on this questionnaire have three foci: (1) loneliness (e.g., "I'm lonely"); (2) social adequacy (e.g., "It is easy for me to make new friends at school"); and (3) self-perceptions of peer status (e.g., "I

have a lot of friends"). Each item is rated on a 5-point scale ranging from "always true" to "never true," and norms are available for grade school children.

Standardized diagnostic interviews have also been developed for children to elicit information about child symptomatology that can contribute to formal diagnosis. Such interviews may provide useful information about a child's behavior and feelings, and may extend the breadth of the open-ended interview. For a more extensive review of child diagnostic interviews and their psychometric properties, the reader is referred to Edelbrock and Costello (1984). These structured techniques do not, however, allow the clinician to establish a relationship and a natural, reciprocal system of communication with the child that can become the foundation for subsequent therapeutic interaction. In addition, structured techniques may not provide the interviewer with sufficient information about areas or issues of particular concern to the individual child, or with a sense of the child's ability to describe and reason about his or her problems. For this reason, self-report questionnaires and structured diagnostic interviews may be best used within the context of, or as supplements to, open-ended clinical child interviews.

Closure

At the end of the child interview, the clinician may want to leave a period of time for "refueling" and closure. To the extent that the interview has explored areas of significant distress, the child may feel somewhat upset and disorganized. It is helpful then to provide the child with a period of nonthreatening free play or nonintensive activity to allow him or her to regain composure. In addition, the clinician may use this period to provide an atmosphere of positive regard and interpersonal support for the child.

SUMMARY

In summary, then, this chapter has presented interviewing strategies that may increase the effectiveness of open-ended clinical interviews with grade school and preschool children. The importance of developmental considerations has been stressed, both in selecting interview techniques and in interpreting children's interview responses. Clinicians are encouraged to consider the supplemental use of structured self-report rating scales to explore areas of clinical relevance for specific children and to enable comparison with developmental norms.

Although child interviews cannot replace parent and teacher interviews or behavioral observations as sources of information about children's behavioral adjustment, they can help the clinician assess the developmental sophistication of a child's interpersonal reasoning and emotional understanding, as well as survey his or her current thoughts, perceptions, and feelings. Moreover, child interviews can provide information useful for treatment planning. If individual child therapy is planned, the child interview can serve to establish initial rapport and to provide the clinician with information concerning the type of communication or expressive medium best suited for a particular child.

Acknowledgment. Preparation of this chapter was supported in part by a Scholars in Mental Health of Children Award from the W. T. Grant Foundation.

REFERENCES

Andrew, G., Hartwell, S. W., Hutt, M. L., & Walton, B. E. (1953). *The Michigan Picture Test*. New York: Science Research Associates.

Asher, S. R., Hymel, S., & Renshaw, P. D. (1984). Loneliness in children. *Child Development, 55,* 1456–1464.

Barenboim, C. (1977). Developmental changes in the interpersonal cognitive system from middle childhood to adolescence. *Child Development, 48,* 1467–1474.

Bene, E., & Anthony, J. (1957). *Manual for the Family Relations Test*. London: National Foundation for Educational Research in England and Wales.

Biber, B., & Lewis, C. (1949). An experimental study of what young school children expect from their teachers. *Genetic Psychology Monographs, 40,* 3–97.

Bierman, K. L., & Furman, W. (1981). Effects of role and assignment rationale on attitudes formed during peer tutoring. *Journal of Educational Psychology, 73,* 33–40.

Borke, H. (1973). The development of empathy in Chinese and American children between three and six years of age: A cross-cultural study. *Developmental Psychology, 9,* 102–108.

Burns, N., & Cavey, L. (1957). Age differences in empathic ability among children. *Canadian Journal of Psychology, 11,* 227–230.

Cairns, R. B., & Cairns, B. D. (1984). Predicting aggressive patterns in girls and boys: A developmental study. *Aggressive Behavior, 10,* 227–242.

Carroll, J., & Steward, M. (1984). The role of cognitive development in children's understanding of their own feelings. *Child Development, 55,* 1486–1492.

Cicchetti, D., & Schneider-Rosen, K. (1986). An organizational approach to childhood depression. In M. Rutter, C. E. Izard, & P. B. Read (Eds.), *Depression in young people: Developmental and clinical perspectives* (pp. 71–134). New York: Guilford Press.

Craighead, W. E., Meyers, A. W., Craighead, L. W., & McHale, S. M. (1982). Issues in cognitive–behavior therapy with children. In M. Rosenbaum, C. M. Franks, & Y. Jaffe (Eds.), *Perspectives on behavior therapy in the eighties* (pp. 234–205). New York: Springer.

Damon, W. (Ed.) (1983). *Social and personality development: Infancy through adolescence*. New York: Norton.

Edelbrock, C., & Costello, A. J. (1984). Structured psychiatric interviews for children and adolescents. In G. Goldstein & M. Hersen (Eds.), *Handbook for psychological assessment* (pp. 276–290). New York: Pergamon Press.

Edwards, C. P., & Lewis, M. (1979). Young children's concepts of social relations: Social functions and social objects. In M. Lewis & L. A. Rosenblum (Eds.), *The child and its family* (pp. 245–266). New York: Plenum.

Finch, A. J., Jr., & Rogers, T. R. (1984). Self-report instruments. In T. H. Ollendick & M. Hersen (Eds.), *Child behavioral assessment* (pp. 106–123). New York: Pergamon Press.

Fischer, K. W. (1980). A theory of cognitive development: The control and construction of hierarchies of skills. *Psychological Review, 87,* 477–531.

Fischer, K. W., & Watson, W. M. (1981). Explaining the Oedipus complex. In K. W. Fischer (Ed.), *New directions in child development: Vol. 12. Cognitive development* (pp. 79–92). San Francisco: Jossey-Bass.

Furman, W. (1980). Promoting social development: Developmental implications for treatment. In B. B. Lahey & A. E. Kazdin (Eds.), *Advances in clinical child psychology* (Vol. 3, pp. 1–40). New York: Plenum Press.

Furman, W., & Bierman, K. L. (1983). Developmental changes in young children's conceptions of friendship. *Child Development, 54,* 549–556.

Gollin, E. S. (1958). Organizational characteristics of social judgements: A developmental investigation. *Journal of Personality, 26,* 139–154.

Greenspan, S. I. (1981). *The clinical interview of the child*. New York: McGraw-Hill.

Harter, S. (1977). A cognitive-developmental approach to children's expression of conflicting feelings and a technique to facilitate such expression in play therapy. *Journal of Consulting and Clinical Psychology, 45,* 417–432.

Harter, S. (1979). *Play techniques for child therapy*. Lecture presented at the University of Denver.

Harter, S. (1982). The Perceived Competence Scale for Children. *Child Development, 53,* 87–97.

Harter, S. (1983). Developmental perspectives on the

self system. In *Handbook of child psychology* (4th ed.): *Vol. 4. Socialization, personality, and social development* (pp. 275–386). New York: Wiley.

Harter, S., & Pike, R. (1984). The Pictorial Scale of Perceived Competence and Social Acceptance for young children. *Child Development, 55,* 1969–1982.

Hymel, S., & Rubin, K. H. (1985). Children with peer relationships and social skills problems: Conceptual, methodological, and developmental issues. In G. J. Whitehurst (Ed.), *Annals of child development* (Vol. 2, pp. 251–297). Greenwich, CT: JAI Press.

Kelvin, P. (1970). *The bases of social behaviour: An approach to terms of order and value*. London: Holt, Rinehart & Winston.

Kovacs, M. (1978). Rating scales to assess depression in school aged children. *Acta Paedopsychiatrica, 46,* 305–315.

Lefkowitz, M. M., & Tesiny, E. P. (1980). Assessment of childhood depression. *Journal of Consulting and Clinical Psychology, 48,* 43–50.

Livesley, W. J., & Bromley, D. D. (1973). *Person perception in childhood and adolescence*. Chichester, England: Wiley.

Moore, N. V., Cooper, R. G., & Brickhard, M. H. (1977, March). *The child's development of the concept of family*. Paper presented at the meeting of the Society for Research in Child Development, New Orleans.

Murray, H. A. (1943). *Thematic Apperception Test Manual*. Boston: Harvard College Press.

Oaklander, V. (1978). *Windows to our children*. Moab, UT: Real People Press.

O'Brien, S., & Bierman, K. L. (1988). Conceptions and perceived influence on peer groups: Interviews with preadolescents and adolescents. *Child Development, 59,* 1360–1365.

Peevers, B. H., & Secord, D. F. (1973). Developmental changes in attribution of descriptive concepts to persons. *Journal of Personality and Social Psychology, 27,* 120–128.

Putallaz, M., & Gottman, J. (1983). Social relationship problems in children: An approach to intervention. In B. B. Lahey & A. E. Kazdin (Eds.), *Advances in clinical child psychology* (Vol. 6, pp. 1–43). New York: Plenum.

Ruble, D., Boggiano, A., Feldman, N., & Loebl, J. (1980). Developmental analysis of the role and social comparison in self evaluation. *Developmental Psychology, 16,* 105–115.

Rutter, M., & Graham, P. (1968). The reliability and validity of the psychiatric assessment of the child: I. Interview with the child. *British Journal of Psychiatry, 114,* 563–579.

Saltz, E., & Medow, M. L. (1971). Concept conservation in children: The dependence of belief systems on semantic representation. *Child Development, 42,* 1533–1542.

Selman, R. L. (1980). *The growth of interpersonal understanding: Developmental and clinical analyses*. New York: Academic Press.

Shantz, C. U. (1975). The development of social cognition. In E. M. Hetherington (Ed.), *Review of child development research* (Vol. 5, pp. 257–324). Chicago: University of Chicago Press.

Shneidman, E. S. (1952). *Manual for a Make-A-Picture Story method*. Portland, OR: The Society for Projective Techniques and Rorschach Institute.

Soloman, I. L, & Starr, B. D. (1968). *School Apperception Method*. New York: Springer.

Wursten, H. (1960). Story completions: Madeleine Thomas Stories and similar methods. In A. I. Rubin & M. Haworth (Eds.), *Projective techniques with children* (pp. 192–209). New York: Grune & Stratton.

Yarrow, L. H. (1960). Inverviewing children. In P. H. Mussen (Ed.), *Handbook of research methods in child development* (pp. 561–602). New York: Wiley.

III

MODELS AND METHODS OF PERSONALITY ASSESSMENT: OBJECTIVE EVALUATION OF CHILDREN'S PERSONALITY

10

Assessment of Children's Anxieties, Fears, and Phobias: Cognitive–Behavioral Models and Methods

PHILIP C. KENDALL
KEVIN R. RONAN
Temple University

Many of the fears and anxieties seen in children and adolescents are nothing more than intrinsic experiences within the developmental sequence, and accordingly are a normal part of growing up. Beyond the "normal" anxieties, there are often transitory affective stages that can serve an adaptive function in learning to cope with the stressors of everyday life (Morris & Kratochwill, 1985). Anxiety can, however, be more intense, more pervasive, and/or more persistent than preferred, and can lead to and be associated with unwanted psychological distress.

Interestingly, it was the very early investigations into children's pathological fears that played more than a minor role in several important conceptualizations of human behavior (Barrios, Hartmann, & Shigetomi, 1981). Freud's treatment of 5-year-old Little Hans's fear of horses was said to provide support for Freud's psychoanalytic concepts. Not long after, Watson and Raynor (1920) published a classic study concerned with utilizing behavioral techniques in the conditioning of phobic behavior: the conditioning of a rat phobia in 1-year-old Little Albert. In a related investigation, behavioral techniques were applied to the treatment of 3-year-old Peter's fear of furry animals and

other articles (Jones, 1924). These classic case reports and studies of childhood fears provided the initial foundation for the nascent psychoanalytic theory, as well as for the nascent theoretical concepts of behaviorism.

The advent of cognitive psychology generally and of information-processing approaches in particular, and their more recent integration with theories concerning clinically relevant aspects of human behavior (e.g., Ingram, 1986), have afforded us a potentially more complete picture of adaptive and maladaptive behavior in adults and children. Consequently, this chapter approaches the assessment of childhood fears, phobias, and anxieties from an integrative cognitive–behavioral viewpoint. Although the model is more fully explicated later, we briefly put forth the major tenets of this model here in order to provide an initial idea of its scope. The essential emphasis of this model of child psychopathology is upon (1) the learning process and the influence of behavioral contingencies and models encountered in the child's environment; and (2) the importance of information processing and mediation in the development, assessment, and treatment of childhood disorders such as children's fears and anxieties (Kendall, 1985).

Before this cognitive–behavioral model is discussed in greater detail, it is necessary to cover some salient issues with regard to assessing children's anxieties and fears. First, the goal of assessment is threefold: (1) selection/classification, (2) treatment evaluation, and (3) research (Kendall, Pellegrini, & Urbain, 1981). Unfortunately, it is beyond the scope of the present review to cover all three areas exhaustively. Accordingly, the goal of this chapter is in line with the goal of this section of the volume—models and methods of objective personality assessment. Throughout this review, however, we refer the interested reader to sources covering particular topics more extensively than space here permits. Second, there are important issues that revolve around definitional concerns and around the question, "What exactly are normal or maladaptive anxieties or fears in children?"

DEFINITIONS

Although there seems to be a general consensus regarding the specific working definitions of "fears," "phobias," and "anxieties," many commentators regard the actual utility of the separation of these constructs to be of limited heuristic and/or clinical utility (e.g., Barrios et al., 1981; Johnson & Melamed, 1979; Morris & Kratochwill, 1983). A childhood fear has typically been thought of as a discriminative response to a perceived environmental threat involving behavioral avoidance, cognitive distress, and physiological arousal. Anxiety is usually distinguished from fear, in that it is seen as a less differentiated response; some authors (e.g., Johnson & Melamed, 1979) have described it as "apprehension without apparent cause" (p. 107).

Childhood phobias, or specific clinical fears, are fears that are more persistent and disturbing and result in *maladaptive,* avoidant behavior (Marks, 1969; Miller, Barrett, & Hampe, 1974). Phobias, then, are generally regarded as behavioral reactions to specific environmental stimuli that have attained a level of clinical significance in terms not only of motoric reactivity, but also of various concomitant cognitive and physiological changes. In fact, there have been

suggestions that fears, anxieties, and phobias in children should be assessed exclusively in terms of defining the stimulus conditions that lead to avoidant responses and negative states for each individual child (e.g., Barrios et al., 1981; Johnson & Melamed, 1979).

Although we agree that it is necessary to define the antecedent conditions leading to avoidant behavior, we argue that this functional analysis may be enhanced by extending the pristine behaviorist interpretation of "stimulus conditions." It is necessary to assess behavioral specifics, and we feel that it is also necessary to examine the cognitive conditions (factors in information processing) leading to, maintaining, and/or remediating children's fearful or anxious behavior. A cognitive–behavioral analysis holds much promise for future theoretical developments, research projects, and treatment applications. For example, examination of "cognition" could facilitate distinct yet related definitions for the constructs of fear and anxiety. Fear would be conceptualized as behavioral and physiological arousal resulting from a cognitive representation of concrete external threat, whereas anxiety would be associated with a cognitive representation of an abstract internal threat. Furthermore, distinctions between normal and pathological cognitive processing and within cognitive analysis (e.g., distortions vs. deficiencies; Kendall, 1985) would be revealing. Fearful responsivity to an external condition may be either normal (e.g., running from a snarling dog) or a result of *distorted* thinking (e.g., a 15-year-old believing a cute puppy to be a safety threat). This hypothesized distinction is extended later in the review.

PREVALANCE AND NORMATIVE DATA

Some fears and anxieties are a normal part of child and adolescent development. In order to understand pathological fears and anxieties, it is necessary to define the upper and lower limits of what is considered normal. A number of normative studies since the 1930s have reported the content, incidence, and developmental aspects of childhood fears and anxieties, and some tentative conclusions may be drawn from these studies (despite potential methodological problems in many of them (see reviews by Graziano, De-Giovanni, & Garcia, 1979; Graziano & Mooney, 1984).

Childhood fears and anxieties, in general, are numerous and common throughout development. For example, Jersild and Holmes (1935) found an average of 4.6 mother-reported fears in preschool children. In addition, MacFarlane, Allen, and Honzik (1954) reported at least one specific fear in 90% of the normal children they studied between the ages of 2 and 14.

The developmental progression of the content of fears and anxieties seems to move in a somewhat predictable sequential fashion. Typically, the content of children's fears and anxieties moves from concrete external fears to increasingly abstract, internalized anxieties. For example, fears of loud noises and specific objects (e.g., strangers) in infancy give way to fears of nightmares, ghosts, and other imaginary objects in the pre- and early school years (Jersild & Holmes, 1935; Piaget, 1967). Later school years witness the arrival of more internalized, abstract, and future-oriented anxieties, such as those concerning health, school, or social issues (e.g., Kennedy, 1965; Simon & Ward, 1974).

It has been suggested that the fears of childhood remain relatively constant up to adolescence (Miller, 1983). Various factor-analytic studies have categorized the fears associated with childhood into a proposed classification scheme. Ollendick, Matson, and Helsel (1985) report a five-factor structure of the contents of these fears: (1) Fear of Failure and Criticism; (2) Fear of the Unknown; (3) Fear of Injury and Small Animals; (4) Fear of Danger and Death; and (5) Medical Fears. These factors are comparable to a three-factor structure found by Miller, Barrett, Hampe, and Noble (1972): Factor I consists of fears of injury (e.g., wars, being kidnapped, having an operation) and personal loss (e.g. death); Factor II is characterized by natural and supernatural events (e.g., storms, the dark); and Factor III is labeled as "psychic stress or tension" and reflects fears of such things as exams, making mistakes, being criticized, making others angry, social and school events, and doctors and dentists. These authors' results corroborate earlier work (e.g., Scherer & Nakamura, 1968) and

further suggest that fears such as being afraid of the dark and the supernatural decline with increasing age, whereas internalized anxieties appear and become more predominant toward adolescence and adulthood.

The frequency of childhood fears and anxieties appears to be a function of a developmental progression. There is evidence that fears seem to peak between 2½ and 4 years of age and then decline somewhat. Jersild and Holmes (1935), employing a cross-sectional sample of preschool children, reported an inverted-U relationship between the number of fears reported by mothers and the age of the child. These results were replicated in a recent longitudinal study (Draper & James, 1985). Other investigators have reported a similar interaction between age and number of fears in older children (e.g., Bauer, 1976; Lapouse & Monk, 1959; Mac-Farlane et al., 1954). Ollendick et al. (1985), while discussing a similar inverse relationship in 7- to 18-year-olds, nevertheless reported a surprisingly high number of fears across age groups: Adolescents aged 16–18 reported an average of 11.6 fears, compared to an average of 14.2 fears reported by 7- to 9-year-olds. It may be concluded from the bulk of evidence that fears are relatively short-lived and that they decline in number with age, but this decrease is not as great as one might expect, since evidence suggests that these fears are replaced by new fears or anxieties that are associated with a particular developmental level.

In addition to developmental differences, there are sex differences in the number of child and adolescent fears and anxieties. Fears have been found to be more prevalent in girls than in boys across a number of studies, both past and present (e.g., Bauer, 1976; Houston, Fox, & Forbes, 1984; Lapouse & Monk, 1959; Ollendick et al., 1985; Pratt, 1945). One possible explanation for this is what we might call "report bias": Girls may be more willing than boys to admit their fears and anxieties because of various sociocultural factors rather than any real gender differences (Bauer, 1976; Ollendick et al., 1985). In the same vein, parents may label the behaviors of girls as more fearful and anxious than the same behaviors in boys, possibly because they are more willing to accept this behavior in girls and/or are less able to perceive this type of behavior in boys (Harris & Ferrari, 1983). Of course, an additional explanation would be that there are genuine gender differences in the frequency of fears and anxieties.

Little is known, unfortunately, about the intensity of fears or their relation to cognition or behavior, although it is often assumed that younger children have more global and intense fears than do their older counterparts. Graziano et al. (1979), however, found no data either to support or to refute this contention. In addition, Ollendick et al. (1985) found no differences in intensity of fear across four age groups (7–9, 10–12, 13–15, and 16–18). Clearly, more research is needed to investigate any systematic differences in fears and anxieties between different age cohorts. Empirical efforts of this sort will assist in providing the normative data base necessary to delineate normal from clinical levels of fear and anxiety.

CLINICAL FEARS AND ANXIETIES

It appears to be widely accepted that although fears and anxieties are quite common in childhood, the incidence of severe fears and anxieties is not pervasive. Miller et al. (1974) reported the incidence of excessive fears in 7- to 12-year-olds to be about 5%. Marks (1969) reports a similar percentage (i.e., 4%) being referred to a clinic for treatment. In their review, Morris and Kratochwill (1985) noted that although various incidence studies have differing definitions of clinical fears, not one of them reports the prevalence to exceed 8% of the general child population. However, Johnson and Melamed (1979) review studies that have found a much greater incidence of children in a clinic population (as high as 26%) exhibiting not only fears specifically, but also a cluster of symptoms including excessive anxiety, worrying, self-consciousness, crying, and social withdrawal (Frommer, Mendelson, & Reid, 1972; Wolff, 1971).

In addition, little is known about the developmental trajectory of severe fears and anxieties, although one study found a 100% improvement rate (10 of 10) over 5 years for children initially identified as phobic (Agras,

Chapin, & Oliveau, 1972). Hampe, Noble, Miller, and Barrett (1973) report that most of the children in their study who were experiencing severe fears overcame them without treatment within 2 years. However, studies looking at children treated for school phobia have reported that in many cases there are major adjustment problems (Coolidge, Brodie, & Feeney, 1964; Waldron, 1976), although children with acute onset earlier in life seem to have a better prognosis (Johnson & Melamed, 1979).

Barrios et al. (1981) concluded that, given the bulk of evidence, researchers and clinicians would be best advised to maintain a developmental perspective when investigating children's fears, phobias, and anxieties. For example, a normal fear for a 4-year-old (e.g., fear of the dark) may be quite another matter if seen in an older child or adolescent. Moreover, given that many fears are short-lived and quite often are phenomena peculiar to a particular developmental level, treatment may or may not be deemed appropriate for a particular child's fears or anxieties. As a result, we recommend that the decision to label a fear as maladaptive and in need of treatment be based not only on normative, developmental data, but also on the particular features of each child's discomfort. We agree with Graziano et al. (1979) and Morris and Kratochwill (1983) that developmental appropriateness is one factor needed to label a child's fears or anxieties as pathological. We would add, however, that it is necessary to examine cognitive information-processing factors, so that we may better understand behavioral avoidance.

A COGNITIVE–BEHAVIORAL MODEL OF CHILDHOOD ANXIETY

Numerous models of child psychopathology have arisen to explain and guide theory, research, and treatment for childhood disorders (Kendall, 1985). These models, in general, have paralleled those of adult psychopathology: psychodynamic, humanistic, and behavioral. Davids (1975) argued that pre-eminent among those explanatory domains, until recently, have been behavioral models (e.g., King, Hamilton, & Ollendick,

1988) and treatment methods. However, examinations of the roles of distorted cognitive processing, of the failure to engage in cognitive mediation during problem solving, and of expectational and attributional factors in the development and maintenance of behavioral disorders have demonstrated the need for a shift to a theoretical model that preserves the efficacy of the learning environment while consolidating the role of cognitive activity in anxieties and fears (Kendall & Ingram, 1987).

As noted earlier, this model places a major emphasis not only on (1) the child's learning environment, along with the attendant influences of external contingencies and models; but also on (2) the prominence of information processing and mediation in the development, maintenance, and treatment of childhood disorders such as anxiety (Kendall, 1985). Accordingly, the model does not seek to uncover unconscious trauma of early life; nor does it place undue emphasis on biological, neurological, and genetic factors in explaining psychopathology. These latter characteristics are considered of greater importance in some disorders but of less primacy in others. Although affective processes, family and social contexts, and developmental considerations are not the sole primary focus on the model, they are integrated into it. Thus, a cognitive–behavioral model of childhood anxiety represents an integrated and consolidated consideration of numerous aspects of the child's environment, both external and internal. The role of the external environment in the etiology and maintenance of children's fears and anxieties has been thoroughly reviewed elsewhere (e.g., Barrios et al., 1981; Johnson & Melamed, 1979; Morris & Kratochwill, 1983); because of space limitations, these factors are not discussed further here. Instead, we focus our attention on the internal cognitive variables implicated in childhood fear and anxiety, which, until recently, have not been taken into consideration by most explanatory models and treatment methods.

Cognitive Features

An increasing number of theorists have focused on "unseen" cognitions as an information-processing system (e.g., Ingram & Kendall, 1986; Marzillier, 1980; Turk & Speers, 1983). One such model (Ingram & Kendall, 1986; Kendall & Ingram, 1987) based on this processing system distinguishes among the conceptual heuristics of cognitive structures, cognitive contents (events), cognitive processes (operations), and cognitive products. "Cognitive structures" may be defined as the means by which information is internally represented. A potentially useful metaphor for understanding cognitive structures is the hardware of a system of indexing and filing. "Cognitive content," (or "propositions") refers to the actual information that is represented and stored within the cognitive structures. "Cognitive processes" are the means by which the information-processing/cognitive system carries out its various operations (e.g., input, processing, and output). Finally, cognitive interplay among new information, cognitive structures, content and operations results in the conclusions/attributions that we assign to our experiences in everyday life.

A further conceptual tool that is available for understanding this complex system lies within the construct of the "schema." Representing the essential interdependence between cognitive structures and cognitive content, schemata constitute a person's point of reference—the unique base from which the person constructs his or her own particular view of himself or herself, others, the environment, and the past, present, and future. Cognitive schemata have been implicated as playing a distinctive role in the study of depression (e.g, Beck, 1967; Ingram, 1984). Only more recently, however, have theoretical views of the anxiety disorders afforded a potentially significant place for the role of schemata (Ingram & Kendall, 1986).

One notable exception to the earlier lack of attention to schemata was provided by Beck (1967), who suggested that an anxious individual's cognitive functioning is characterized by a schema centered on contents of internal and/or external danger to the person or to an object valued by that particular person. This formulation has led Beck and Emery (1985) to propose that *threat* is the dominant theme upon which anxious (and fearful) individuals will center. Building upon not only this and other theoretical foundations (e.g., Kendall, 1985), but also on empirical work with adult populations (e.g., Ingram, Kendall, Smith, Donnell, & Ronan, 1987; Merluzzi, Rudy, & Krejer, 1986; Smith, Ingram, & Brehm, 1983), Kendall, Howard, and Epps (1988) have proposed two distinct yet interrelated hypotheses concerning the cognitive functioning of the anxious, fearful child.

The first formulation, delineated by Kendall and Ingram (1987), has been labeled as the "schematic-content hypothesis." This supposition states that two intricately linked schemata are operating in anxious, fearful individuals. One schema, the "self-schema," is focused on the internal environment, while the related schema, the "other-schema," focuses on the external world. The self-schema represents the anxious individual's "routine" ("normal") level of functioning and contains anxious and questioning propositions. Ingram et al (1987) used an incidental-recall paradigm containing depressive, anxious, or neutral stimulus objectives. In order to test the specificity of the hypothesis, subjects were psychometrically screened and classified into anxious (not depressed), depressed (not anxious), depressed and anxious, and neither depressed nor anxious groups. Pertinent to this discussion, results indicated that the content-specific hypothesis was supported: Anxious subjects were found to recall more of the anxious-content adjectives, whereas depressed subjects recalled more of the depressive-content adjectives. It would appear that the anxious self-schema contains contents that are quite specific to anxiety.

Whereas the self-schema associated with anxious individuals represents an "everyday" level of functioning, the other-schema is activated by evaluative/stressful situations, in which the schema's content is focused on other individuals' potentially hurtful judgments and/or harmful reactions. Smith et al. (1983) presented subjects with an incidental-recall paradigm that gave information about the self or others' views of the subject. In a socially anxiety-provoking situation, no evidence was found to indicate enhanced recall of personally relevant content in socially anxious subjects; however, these same individuals did display an increased recall of propositions related to how others evaluated them. Thus, it appears that this schema is focused on external determinants (i.e., others) of internal states, while the self-schema centers on internal propositions relating to these internal states. As proposed earlier, the former is associated with our conceptualization of both adaptive and maladaptive fears, whereas the latter is associated more with the seemingly diffuse anxiety experienced in everyday functioning. With regard to the fearful other-schema, the questions of what factors create a maladaptive (as opposed to an appropriate or normal) fear, and what factors raise the self-schema's content above normal limits, constitute the subject of the next section. One last point that requires mention is the fact that current research restricts generalizations to adult populations. However, it is thought that this theoretical formulation indeed holds great promise in future investigations with children and adolescents.

A second explanatory construct applicable to childhood psychopathology in general, and to childhood anxieties and fears specifically, is the type of cognitive malady related to the interface between cognitive processing and cognitive products. The potentially significant distinction has been referred to by Kendall (1985) as "cognitive distortions versus cognitive deficiencies." As the term suggests, deficiencies denote a general lack of mental activity required by situations in which engagement in this activity (e.g., forethought) would be quite beneficial (e.g., perspective taking, interpersonal problem solving). As deficiencies point to a lack of cognitive planning and execution in the child, the manifest problems, then, are associated with a correlated lack of verbal mediation and a resultant lack of self-control. These disorders point to the undercontrolled, acting-out nature of impulsive, aggressive behavioral patterns (Fuhrman & Kendall, 1986).

Cognitive distortions, on the other hand, point to dysfunctional thinking processes and their products, manifested as some form of excessive negative self-talk (e.g., questioning, hopelessness). Whereas childhood disorders resulting from cognitive deficiencies invite undercontrolled behavior, cognitive distortions summon a tendency toward overcontrolled behavior. Thus, childhood anxiety includes misperceptions of environmental demands, excessive self-criticism, and an undervaluation of abilities, and is associated more with anxious, depressed, withdrawn, and/or isolated patterns of behavior.

Although it is believed that there are a number of important processes yet to be implicated in explaining childhood anxiety, the current theory implicates cognitive distortions reflected in dysfunctional processing as critical in the etiology and maintenance of pathological childhood anxieties and fears. One specific manifestation of these distorted thinking operations is seen in the form of excessive self-focused attention (Kendall & Ingram, 1987). The notion of anxious self-preoccupation (Sarason, 1975; Wine, 1971) emphasizes increased levels of attention directed toward internal schematic factors. In order to avoid potential confusion, a distinction between "self-focused attention" and "self-preoccupation" (i.e., *excessive* self-focused attention) is made. On the one hand, self-focused attention is typically seen as a variable that covaries with numerous situational determinants (e.g., Carver & Scheier, 1981). On the other hand, self-preoccupation refers to a perseveration of the self-focused states that is maladaptive. The key to this distinction lies in the relative inability of the cognitive operations to switch to a more external focus as needed.

In sum, the cognitive–behavioral model requires a delineation between (schematic) *content* and (cognitive) *process*. For example, a 12-year-old girl is known to her teachers and parents as a generally anxious youngster (excessive focus on content of self-schema). She is asked to give a speech in front of her sixth-grade class. In order to quell her fear of how her teacher and fellow students will judge her (i.e., excessive focus on content or other-schema), she practices for many hours. As she stands up to give the speech, she simply cannot stop focusing on her fears or her fear of fears (anxiety), and she runs out of the room. She is now not only generally anxious, but also specifically and excessively fearful of others' evaluations. Whereas the content of this girl's attention consists of cognitions centering on both internal and external determinants, the process is characterized by excessive and detrimental self-focus rather than by a "speech-related" focus. These two interrelated factors contribute to the girl's freezing up cognitively and avoiding behaviorally. She is unable to attend to task-relevant factors, but instead focuses negatively on her anxieties and fails to perceive her arousal within a more positive and coping-related framework. Treatments from a cognitive–behavioral perspective (e.g., Kane & Kendall, 1989; Kendall, Kane, Howard, & Siqueland, 1989) address distorted processing and teach coping skills.

Affective, Contextual, and Developmental Concerns

"Cognitive–behavioral theory" communicates a great deal about the system, but the term may not be inclusive enough to fully articulate the system's complexities. The phrase may imply that affect, social context, and developmental considerations seem to be excluded from a model of childhood anxieties and fears. Such a belief is simply inaccurate. The phrase "cognitive–behavioral" is used to describe the synthesis of cognitive, behavioral, affective, and social perspectives in addition to a developmental perspective in looking at childhood psychopathology (Kendall, 1985). Such a model moves beyond a purely behavioral model: Cognitions and behaviors are seen as functionally related to each individual's affective states and his or her functioning in the social environment. Cognitive–behavioral theory thus provides an integrationist approach to various issues involved in the assessment and treatment of clinical phenomena such as the anxieties and fears of childhood.

Affect has been assigned many roles in childhood disorders, with recent theorizing placing it both in primary (Bernard & Joyce, 1984) and in ancillary (Santestefano & Reider, 1984) roles. Cognition and affect are certainly interrelated, we believe. When dysfunction is affective in nature, as is the case in childhood anxieties and fears (e.g., as compared to conduct disorder or attention deficit disorder), the child's affective state is of great importance. Thus, attention to affect is indeed warranted within a cognitive–behavioral model and should be assessed and monitored, with improved affect used as a criterion indicating therapeutic gains.

Relevant social context is essential in understanding childhood adjustment. The fact is that cognitive, behavioral, and affective concerns have little or no meaning except in regard to social/interpersonal functioning, and the cognitive–behavioral perspective endorses not only the importance of the family, but also the salience of peer relationships (Hartup, 1983; Howard & Kendall, 1987) in the psychological adjustment of children.

A particularly crucial concern in the understanding and assessment of childhood fears and anxieties is the developmental level of the child in question. As previously noted, the fact that certain fears are quite common at different stages suggest they play an important, if not a functional, role in normal development. We have earlier recommended the need to assess and evaluate normative data, so that a fair judgment can be made of the appropriate or maladaptive nature of anxieties and/or fears. We again stress the need to critically examine the child's level of development not only in terms of age, but also with respect to his or her developmental status in memory, attention span, comprehension of verbal instructions, self-report skills, reasoning, and metacognitive abilities.

ASSESSMENT METHODS

This section is devoted to a discussion of the commonly used methods and measures in childhood fear and anxiety assessment. Within a cognitive–behavioral model, we agree with Lang (1968) and Morris and Kratochwill (1985), who stress the need for assessing children's fears and anxieties both across various methodologies and across the cognitive, behavioral (motoric), and physiological response channels.

Interview Assessment

Child clinical interviews are perhaps the most commonly utilized technique for assessing anxieties, fears, and related concerns (Miller et al., 1974). This format provides valuable information about children that is not readily available from any other source. For example, this strategy allows the cognitive–behavioral assessor not only to elicit a child's thoughts, feelings, and perceptions, but also to determine his or her developmental sophistication (see also Bierman

& Schwartz, 1986, and Chapter 9, this volume).

Interview formats range from unstructured, open-ended formats to more highly structured versions in which only a relatively preordained flowchart of questions is allowed. Along this continuum are semistructured formats, where the exact wording and phrasing of questions is not specified. There are strengths and weaknesses associated with those various types of interviews (Bierman & Schwartz, 1986). Relatively unstructured formats allow for greater flexibility in examining the scope and content of a particular problem. In addition, these types of interviews are useful in establishing the rapport with a child that may prove helpful in a future treatment environment. However, what the unstructured design gains in flexibility, it loses with respect to objectivity—namely, the reliability and validity of the procedure. Structured formats, on the other hand, potentially lack flexibility, but do offer the advantages of increased reliability and data that are easily quantifiable; in addition, they may be administered by less experienced personnel (Wiens, 1976). Furthermore, stuctured interviews such as the Schedule for Affective Disorders and Schizophrenia for School-Aged Children (Kiddie-SADS; Puig-Antich & Chambers, 1978), the Diagnostic Interview for Children and Adolescents (Herjanic & Reich, 1982), the Diagnostic Interview Schedule for Children (Costello, Edelbrock, Kalas, Kessler, & Klaric, 1982), and the Anxiety Disorders Interview Schedule for Children (Silverman, 1987) can greatly assist the researcher/ clinician in making a formal diagnosis based on various psychiatric classification schemes (e.g., the revised third edition of the *Diagnostic and Statistical Manual of Mental Disorders*, or DSM-III-R). It is beyond the scope of this chapter to provide a comprehensive review of these psychiatric diagnostic criteria, but the reader is referred to some excellent reviews (e.g., Morris & Kratochwill, 1983; Werry, 1986).

Bierman and Schwartz (1986) reported that although psychiatric interviews are sufficient for detecting the global indices associated with a particular disorder, they often do not provide *reliable* information about specific thoughts or behaviors (Edelbrock & Costello,

1984). This point is particularly salient because of the highly individualized nature of children's anxieties and fears. Morris and Kratochwill (1983) add that, given the present state of research, one must be cautious and perhaps even skeptical of the available interview data in the area of children's fears and anxieties.

In view of the foregoing discussion, we recommend that the interview be used in conjunction with other assessment methods or as a preliminary screening tool for guiding future assessments aimed at gaining more specific information about a child's fears and anxieties. We also recommend the use of more structured formats, which in fact do allow for some flexibility and rapport building, and have some specific advantages in the assessment of children's fears and anxieties. First, this strategy can elicit the developmental level of a child's social-cognitive reasoning abilities. We have stressed the importance of developmental considerations throughout, and this procedure allows for assessing this crucial dimension. Second, specific fears/anxieties might be identified from a structured interview and later form the basis of an assessment of coping—such as a coping questionnaire on which the child (and parents) reports the extent to which he or she can cope with a particular situation. Such "coping" data can be used diagnostically, as well as after readministration, as an indicant of therapeutic gains (Kendall, 1989). Finally, a structured interview can examine anxiety and fear across the three response channels. Specifically, it may be utilized as one method of assessing not only the behavioral and physiological parameters of anxiety, but also the specific cognitive characteristics of the fearful, anxious child. In a later section dealing specifically with cognitive assessment, we report on the use of a stuctured format to assess cognitions in fearful children.

Self-Report Measures

Three self-report measures are most often utilized in the process of assessing child and adolescent anxiety. The present discussion focuses on these three measures; some other inventories are briefly mentioned at the end of this section.

Children's Manifest Anxiety Scale

The Children's Manifest Anxiety Scale (CMAS), developed by Castaneda, McCandless, and Palermo (1956), is a downward extension of the instrument used to measure general or chronic states of anxiety in adults (Taylor, 1951). There are over 100 published studies utilizing this scale in the literature (Reynolds, 1977). More recently, Reynolds and Richmond (1978) revised the scale in response to criticism that the original scale took too long to administer, its items lacked clarity, the reading level was not suitable for younger children, and some of its items did not qualify as a good test item (Flanigan, Peters, & Conry, 1969).

The revision of the CMAS (RCMAS) resulted in the "What I Think and Feel" measure, a 37-item scale containing 28 Anxiety and 9 Lie scale items. Factor analysis yielded three subscales of anxiety (Reynolds & Richmond, 1979), designated (1) Physiological Anxiety, (2) Worry and Oversensitivity, and (3) Concentration Anxiety. These factors are quite consistent with those of an earlier study of the CMAS (Finch, Kendall, & Montgomery, 1974). In addition, further analysis has provided evidence for a Generalized Anxiety factor (Reynolds & Paget, 1981; Scholwinski & Reynolds, 1985).

Reynolds and his associates have devoted much research attention to establishing the reliability and validity of the RCMAS. Internal-consistency estimates have been reported to be in the middle to upper .80s (Reynolds & Richmond, 1978; Reynolds & Paget, 1983). Reynolds and Paget (1983) also report test–retest reliabilities ranging from .68 to over .90. Correlations with the State–Trait Anxiety Inventory for Children (STAIC: Spielberger, 1973; see below) have provided further evidence supporting the concurrent and construct validity of the measure as an indicator of chronic, generalized anxiety. Correlations of up to .85 with the A-Trait scale of the STAIC and nonsignificant correlations with the A-State scale have been offered as supportive of the convergent and divergent validity of the scale, respectively (Reynolds, 1980, 1982). Finally, low though positive correlations of up to .31 were reported between the RCMAS and teachers' ratings of the anxiety-related behaviors of withdrawal and distractibility (Reynolds, 1982).

Normative data have also been provided (Reynolds & Richmond, 1978; Reynolds & Paget, 1983). Reynolds and Paget (1983) used a sample of almost 5,000 children from 13 states and established norms for children from 6 to 19 years of age. In addition, good reliability coefficients and preliminary norms have been established for Mexican-American children (Argulewicz & Miller, 1984), Nigerian children (Pela & Reynolds, 1982), and high-IQ children (Scholwinski & Reynolds, 1985).

Although cross-cultural use of the instrument is advocated, one study found differences among Canadian, Japanese, and American children in reported levels of anxiety (Richmond, Sukemune, Ohmoto, Kawamoto, & Hamazaki, 1984). These findings indicate the need for establishing separate norms for separate groups (including separate age cohorts). The RCMAS has proceeded nicely in this direction.

State–Trait Anxiety Inventory for Children

The STAIC was developed by Spielberger (1973) to assess not only relatively enduring tendencies to experience anxiety (A-Trait), but also temporal and situational variations in levels of perceived anxiety (A-State). The STAIC is quite similar in conception to the State–Trait Anxiety Inventory (STAI), which measures state and trait anxiety in adolescents and adults (Spielberger, Gorsuch, & Lushene, 1970; see also Kendall, Finch, Auerbach, Hooke, & Mikulka, 1976). Spielberger states that although the STAIC is recommended for use with 9- to 12-year-old children, it may also be used with younger children of average or above-average reading ability and with older children of below-average reading ability.

Spielberger (1973) provides normative data based on the completed protocols of approximately 1,500 fouth- through sixth-grade students. Spielberger states that although the norms reported are not based on representative or stratified samples, they are useful nonetheless as a large sample to which comparisons can be made. Reliability and validity data are provided in the manual

and in several other studies. Internal consistency of both scales has been found to be reasonably good. Alpha coefficients reported by Spielberger (1973) were .78 or above for both scales. Finch, Montgomery, and Deardorff (1974) found split-half reliabilities of .89 for the A-State scale and .88 for the A-Trait scale. However, the test–retest reliability of both scales was considerably lower over a 3-month period (A-State, .63; A-Trait, .44; Finch, Montgomery, & Deardorff, 1974) and even over the same day (A-State, .72; A-Trait, .65; Finch, Kendall, Montgomery, & Morris, 1975). One study, however, has reported a test–retest reliability coefficient of .94 for the A-Trait scale (Bedell & Roitzsch, 1976).

Validity studies have demonstrated highly divergent results and, while positive, have not been overwhelmingly supportive of the state–trait distinction *in children* (Finch & Kendall, 1979). It would be expected that the A-Trait scale would correlate more highly with other measures of chronic generalized anxiety (e.g., the CMAS, the RCMAS) than would the A-State scale (Johnson & Melamed, 1979). Speilberger (1973) and Reynolds (1980, 1982) did indeed report such findings supporting the state–trait distinction, but other research has been less definitive (e.g, Finch et al., 1975; Finch & Nelson, 1974; Montgomery & Finch, 1974). Whereas Bedell and Roitzsch (1976) and Newman, Wheeler, Newmark, and Stabler (1975) both found increases in A-State scores but not A-Trait scores following experimental stress induction, Finch et al. (1975) found an increase in both A-State and A-Trait scores. One possible explanation for these discrepant results may be in the types of populations studied. Unfortunately, although Finch, Montgomery, and Deardorff (1974), Finch and Nelson (1974), and Montgomery and Finch (1974) found results suggesting that emotionally disturbed children score higher on both dimensions and respond in a different manner than do normal children, other studies have reported that disturbed subjects respond in the direction of support for the state–trait distinction (e.g., Bedell & Roitzsch, 1976; Finch, Kendall, Dannenburg, & Morgan, 1979). The issue seems to be the ability of children, especially emotionally disturbed children, to distinguish between their present emotional state and more transitorial or characteristic emotional traits. When children are emotionally aroused (heightened A-State), self-reports of trait anxiety appear to be heightened.

Factor-analytic research with single-administration data supports a state–trait distinction: Items from the A-State scale and the A-Trait scale loaded on separate factors (Finch, Kendall, & Montgomery, 1976). For both emotionally disturbed and normal children, A-State factors were distinct but comparable to the A-State scale, in that they both contained factors with items loading on either positive thoughts or negative ruminations. The A-Trait factor contained items dealing with worry or with rumination and obsessive characteristics. An additional factor for normals loaded on items dealing with sweaty hands or insomnia.

Gender differences, with girls typically scoring higher than boys (e.g., Finch & Nelson, 1974), are often but not always found (e.g., Newmark et al., 1975). Anomalous findings are confusing and may point to subtle distinctions, such as differences in experimental instructions (Finch & Kendall, 1979). Finch et al. (1976) concluded that subject populations must be considered when evaluating findings, as there are indications of qualitiative as well as quantitative differences across different types of children. This conclusion is in accord with our general belief in the necessity of acquiring separate psychometric data for separate populations.

Fear Survey Schedule for Children

The Fear Survey Schedule for Children (FSSC), an 80-item, 5-point scale, was developed by Scherer and Nakamura (1968) to assess specific fears in children. The scale was adapted from adult fear survey schedules (e.g., Wolpe & Lang, 1964) and includes several of the same items contained in these scales. The categories under which items were developed for the FSSC are as follows: School, Home, Social, Physical, Animal, Travel, Classical Phobia, and Miscellaneous. Ollendick (1983) notes that although the instrument has been widely used in clinical and research settings, few data are available regarding its psychometric properties. Furthermore, impaired children have trouble

understanding or discriminating the responses on the 5-point format utilized by the scale (Ollendick, 1983). Ollendick (1978) revised the original scale (FSSC-R) to a 3-point response format while leaving the specific items intact. Ollendick (1983) has provided psychometric data for the FSSC-R, utilizing 242 normal and school-phobic children between the ages of 7 and 12 years. Internal-consistency estimates ranged for .92 to .95. Test–retest reliability was good over a 1-week interval (.82) and moderate over a 3-month interval (.55).

Validity was assessed by comparing the scores to related instruments, by comparing the scores of normal and clinical samples, and through further analysis. The FSSC-R shows moderate positive correlations of approximately .50 with the A-Trait scale of the STAIC, and significant negative correlations with self-concept and internal locus of control in girls but not in boys. Girls scored significantly higher than boys, a finding that is consistent with other studies using the FSSC or FSSC-R (Ryall & Dietiker, 1979; Ollendick et al., 1985; Scherer & Nakamura, 1968). In addition, total scores discriminated between normal children and their school-phobic counterparts. Finally, factor analysis yielded factors similar to those found by Scherer and Nakamura (1968) and also similar to those reported by Miller et al. (1972).

Ollendick (1983) has suggested that the FSSC-R may be efficaciously employed for selecting children for treatment, as a pre- and post-treatment measure of therapeutic effectiveness, and as a research tool to identify fear sensitivities in children. Johnson and Melamed (1979) review studies that have shown the original FSSC to be somewhat sensitive to therapeutic interventions (e.g., Melamed, Hawes, Heiby, & Glick, 1975; Melamed, Yurcheson, Fleece, Hutcherson, & Hawes, 1978); however, only one of these studies reported statistically significant differences between the treated and nontreated groups (Melamed et al., 1978). Further research is needed to elucidate the possible roles suggested for this instrument.

Other Self-Report Measures

Before launching into a discussion of the issues surrounding self-report measures, we mention a few other scales available to the researcher/clinician. First, the Generalized Anxiety Scale for Children (GASC: Sarason, Davidson, Lighthall, Waite, & Ruebush, 1960) is a measure designed, like the CMAS, to assess chronic levels of anxiety. A specialized version of the GASC, the Test Anxiety Scale for Children (TASC), was designed to identify specific anxiety levels in children in the school setting (Sarason et al., 1960). Second, the Louisville Fear Schedule for Children (LFSC; Miller et al., 1972), designed in the manner of the FSSC, examines specific reactions to fear stimuli. Lastly, the efficacy of an intervention can be examined by assessing clients' self-perception of their ability to cope in specific fearful/anxious situations both before and after treatment (e.g., coping questionnaire; see Kendall, 1989).

Considerations Regarding Self-Reports

A number of general issues have been raised regarding the utility of self-report measures in the assessment of children's anxiety and fear (Barrios et al., 1981; Johnson & Melamed, 1979; Morris & Kratochwill, 1983). One problem with the use of self-report measures is that they do not adequately measure the situation-specific aspects of anxiety and fear in children. In the same vein, specific fear schedules utilizing endorsement procedures may not always reflect a child's sometimes quite specific and individualized fear. Another potential limitation of some of these measures is the lack of adequate psychometric data for various ages and genders. Also, children's self-reports may not always accurately reflect their internal states. This problem may be due to various factors, such as therapists' inability to identify subtle changes in affect, cognition, and behavior, and/or childrens' need to appear socially desirable. Anxious children, in particular, often present in a manner that appears nondistressed. That is, a part of the anxious child's processing of social and evaluative situations includes perceiving threat, and he or she presents nonanxiously to reduce this threat. We have seen diagnosed children worry and labor to answer a self-report question such as "Do you have difficulty making up your mind?", only to then

reply "No." The inaccuracy of child reports may in turn contribute to discrepancies between data from self-report measures and those obtained from parents and/or teachers. Research is needed to examine convergence of agreement across alternate sources of information and, relatedly, to examine the predictive validity of each of the sources of information.

The continued use of self-report scales in research and clinical settings is probably due to the economy and convenience involved in their administration and scoring (data are easily quantifiable). Consequently, they offer great utility as a screening device. A potential advantage of some of these measures over others (e.g., the RCMAS, the STAIC) is their examination of more than one response channel, making possible the correlation of items with data obtained via more specific methods (e.g., direct observation).

The cognitive–behavioral model holds that self-report measures have utility for screening children for anxieties and specific fears. Children identified with various levels of anxiety and/or fear can then be followed up with a more specific cognitive and behavioral assessment procedure. Furthermore, the hypothesized distinctions between cognitive deficiencies and cognitive distortions, and between internal (i.e., anxious self-schema) and external (i.e., fearful other-schema) determinants of behavioral and physiological arousal can be evaluated using such measures.

Cognitive Assessment

A relatively unexplored approach holding great promise in assessing children's fears and anxieties is the application of the cognitive–behavioral model to the assessment process. The cognitive characteristics that have potential utility in the assessment process and in treatment applications are cognitive contents, cognitive schemata, cognitive processes, and cognitive products, which as we know, have been implicated as playing a distinctive role in the etiology, maintenance, and remediation of childhood anxiety and fear. The optimal goal in cognitive assessment is to look not only at these specific constructs, but also at the relationships among the cognitive factors themselves and between these characteristics and the behavioral and physiological response channels associated with anxiety.

Assessing self-statements, irrational beliefs, current concerns, images, problem-solving capacities, expectancies, and attributions has much potential in elucidating the cognitive characteristics associated with the anxious/fearful child. The actual methods and measures available to the cognitive–behavioral assessor have been reviewed elsewhere (Kendall & Braswell, 1982a, 1982b; Kendall & Hollon, 1981; Merluzzi, Glass, & Genest, 1981). Among the array of methods available are self-monitoring techniques, unobstrusive recordings of spontaneous speech, recording of self-talk following specific instructions (e.g., "think aloud"), role playing, imagery assessment, thought-sampling and thought-listing methods, interviews, and endorsement measures.

Despite limitations, some recent empirical efforts point to the efficacy of assessing the cognitive correlates of childhood anxiety and fear. For example, Houston et al. (1984) examined the relationships among trait and state anxiety, performance, and cognitive activities in a stress-induced mathematics task. A total of 67 fourth-grade students were randomly assigned to high- and low-stress manipulation conditions, and within each condition were assigned to high- or low-trait-anxiety groups on the basis of their scores on the A-Trait portion of the STAIC. Subjects in the high-stress condition were told that they were to be given a math test on which their performance was to be evaluated and compared with other children's scores. Low-stress subjects were only told that they were going to play a game that most children liked. Prior to the task, the children's cognitions were assessed via two different methods. First, the children were asked to "think aloud" their thoughts and feelings into a tape recorder for 2 minutes while the experimenter left the room. Second, the subjects were given a measure and asked to indicate the degree to which each item (thought) reflected their thinking and feeling states during the think-aloud procedure. Following performance on a 1½-minute math task, children filled out the A-State portion of the STAIC.

Results pertinent to this discussion indicated that high stress subjects displayed significantly more negative self-talk—a less analytic attitude (e.g., "This is interesting"), and preoccupation concerning negative expectancies (e.g., "I'm not good on math tests") and affective arousal (e.g., "I'm feeling sort of scared")—in addition to making more errors. Interestingly, high-trait-anxiety subjects were also found to be significantly more preoccupied and made more errors than did their low-trait-anxiety counterparts.

These results, as well as similar findings by Fox, Houston, and Pittner (1983), point to the utility of assessing the cognitions of the anxious child; they also serve as positive evidence for the role of cognitive distortions manifested as negative self-talk in childhood anxiety disorders within and across stressful situations. Finally, from our conceptualization of fear and anxiety, these results make particular sense. That is, the high-trait-anxiety subjects' cognitive activity conformed to a greater degree with our definition of anxiety in terms of the tendency to focus on self-schematic representations of questioning and threatening content (e.g., preoccupied cognitively in the absence of perceived threat); the high-stress subjects' information-processing characteristics, on the other hand, corresponded to a greater degree with our description of fear, as their distorted processing was associated with more of an external threat (i.e., being evaluated).

Other empirical efforts have supported cognitive assessment methodology and the role of dysfunctional processing and negative self-talk in children's fears and anxieties (Kendall et al., 1988). Prins (1985, 1986) utilized a structured interview to compare high- and low-fear children's self-speech during a visit to the dentist, and high-, moderate-, and low-fear children identified by behavioral observations of their diving performance at a local pool. Both studies found a significant relationship between negative self-talk (e.g., preoccupation with fears of being hurt, negative expectancies, and escape fantasies) and high fear levels, but no relationship between the type of self-speech and low or moderate fear levels. In two studies of performance on a cognitive task, Zatz and Chassin (1983, 1985) found that children's improved performance was associated with an absence of negative, distorted thinking about themselves and the task, rather than the presence of positive cognitions, in both an analogue (1983) and a naturalistic testing situation (1985). In addition to providing support for the cognitive–behavioral model and pointing to the efficacy of the assessment methodology, these results buttress what Kendall (1984) has referred to as the "power of non-negative thinking" in nonpsychopathological conditions. Positive thinking accounts for relatively little systematic variance, whereas the presence of excessive negative thinking is related to psychopathological states.

Using a methodology with some success in assessing the negative thinking of adult depressives (e.g., Hollon & Kendall, 1980), Kendall and Ronan (1989) have developed a self-statement questionnaire to measure the content of anxiety-disordered cognition in children and adolescents. The 55 items on the scale were selected for their ability to separate known groups of anxious from nonanxious subjects. The items were cross-validated on a separate sample, and later tested for discriminative ability between clinical (diagnosed) cases and normals. The discriminative power of the scale is impressive. The Children's Anxious Self-Statement Questionnaire (CASSQ) has a .92 test–retest reliability, and a factor analysis suggests a two-factor solution (Negative Self-focused Attention; Positive Self-Concept and Expectations). While in the final stages of development, the CASSQ nevertheless has already shown meaningful discriminant validity and test–retest reliability, and is presently being used in treatment outcome evaluation.

In sum, the inclusion of cognitive measures to supplement the more traditional inventories (e.g., self-report measures), behavioral ratings and observations, and measures of physiological arousal is critical to assess the role of the actual thoughts of the anxious, fearful child. Failure to incorporate these measures in an assessment battery will drastically limit the clinician's ability to examine the role of cognitive mediation in childhood fear and anxiety. As a treatment evaluation tool, cognitive assessment can help to specify the mechanisms of therapeutic change (Kendall, 1981; Kendall & Korgeski, 1979). Furthermore, as we have stressed,

the assessment of children's thinking will guide the elucidation of the role of distorted cognitive processing from a developmental perspective. Addressing such issues as the appropriate or maladaptive nature of certain fears for children at various stages of development is of particular interest. Another interesting question lies within the developmental area: It could be hypothesized that fear develops prior to anxiety, and, moreover, that anxiety may be possible only with the inception of certain metacognitive capabilities. It would be expected that this time frame would correspond roughly to the onset of adolescence and the inception of Piagetian formal operational thinking. These questions merit theoretical and research attention; through the critical examination of the relevant cognitive correlates of behavior and physiological arousal, these questions may be answered more fully.

Behavioral Assessment

Behavioral assessment measures fall into four categories: behavioral avoidance tests, global ratings, rating scores and checklists, and direct observation.

Behavioral Avoidance Tests

A quite common procedure for assessing the motoric components of specific fears is the behavioral avoidance test (BAT). According to Morris and Kratochwill (1983), these measures have a long history (e.g., Jersild & Holmes (1935). Barrios et al. (1981) describe an example of a frequently employed BAT procedure (e.g., Lang & Lazovik, 1963). This generally involves the subject's entering a room containing a feared stimulus, with the experimenter requesting that he or she approach the stimulus. The subject's behavior is scored in objectively defined categories, such as how closely the stimulus is approached, the number of steps in the approach task that are completed, response latencies, and the time spent touching or handling the phobic stimulus.

BATs are used quite often in children's fear research and have also been shown to discriminate treated from nontreated subjects (Johnson & Melamed, 1979). In addition, the procedure can easily be administered by nonprofessionals. There are, however, several problems with these measures (see Barrios et al., 1981; Johnson & Melamed, 1979; Morris & Kratochwill, 1983). The fact that most investigations employ their own version of the BAT procedure makes comparison across studies and across fear-arousing stimuli quite difficult. For example, increasing the number of steps in the approach task has been suggested to produce greater approach behavior (e.g., Nawas, 1971). Other problems resulting from nonstandardized procedures are the variability in the types and natures of instructions, the actual "threat" of various stimuli (both real and as cognitively processed by subjects), and the lack of reliability and validity data on these measures. A most central problem, according to Morris and Kratochwill (1983), is the analogue nature of the procedure; this, of course, may dramatically limit the external validity of results.

The BAT procedure, however, also has several associated advantages, including a more structured environment that may increase the internal validity of investigations using the methodology. There are other advantages that make it desirable for future research use. It allows for assessment of the motoric mode that is not limited to just avoidance behavior (e.g., facial expression, trembling), and it has the advantage of detecting idiosyncratic behaviors that may have direct treatment implications (Barrios et al, 1981). Another advantage of the BAT procedure, from the cognitive–behavioral perspective, is its potential utility in being combined with cognitive measures (e.g. self-statement inventories, think-aloud procedures) in order to examine the relationship between cognitive mediation and behavioral approach–avoidance.

Global Ratings

As the name suggests, global ratings involve more general evaluations of behavior, usually on a dimensional rating scale (e.g., from never to always, from negative to positive). Several features of these scales make them desirable for use in children's fear and anxiety assessment (Morris & Kratochwill, 1983). Kazdin (1980) has reported such advantages of global ratings as their relative flexibility in

rating many behaviors, and their potential as summary indicants before, during, and after treatment. They also provide a standardized format for obtaining ratings from those involved with a child (e.g., therapist, parent). In addition, Johnson and Melamed (1979) cite several studies that have shown global ratings to be sensitive to treatment manipulations (e.g., Johnson & Machen, 1973; Melamed, Hawes, et al., 1975). Peterson and Shigetomi (1981) found treatment effects on various global indices in their study of modeling and self-control procedures in the prevention of anxiety and fear associated with hospitalization.

Several potential problems are also associated with these types of measures, however (Morris & Kratochwill, 1983). Kazdin (1980) has listed several of these, including the potential ambiguity of global, nonoperational ratings; observer drift and bias because of a lack of operational definitions for the behaviors being observed; difficulties in comparing studies when different global ratings are employed; and a potential lack of treatment sensitivity, as a general rating may not be sensitive to manipulation, whereas a more direct, specified measure of anxiety may be sensitive to change. We conclude that these measures should be used in conjunction with more specific procedures. For a review of some of the commonly utilized global indices, the reader is referred elsewhere (Barrios et al., 1981; Barrios & Hartmann, 1989; Johnson & Melamed, 1979).

Specific Rating Scales and Checklists

Rating scales and checklists constitute a form of behavioral assessment by someone well acquainted with a child (e.g., parents, teachers). They generally involve rating behaviors on an occurrence–nonoccurrence basis or on a dimensional scale.

Numerous rating scales have included components associated with children's fears and anxieties. These include the Devereux Elementary School Behavior Rating Scale (DESB; Spivack & Swift, 1967), the School Behavior Checklist (SBCL; Miller, 1972), the Child Behavior Checklist (CBCL; Achenbach & Edelbrock, 1983), and the Walker Problem Behavior Identification Checklist (WPBIC; Walker, 1970). For example, the

CBCL has items dealing with specific fears (e.g., fears going to school; fears certain animals, situations, or places other than school) and also with more general anxieties and related behaviors (e.g., too fearful and anxious; worrying; withdrawn; doesn't get involved with others). A real advantage of the CBCL and other checklists of this sort (e.g., the SBCL) is that the psychometric data available for many of them are generally quite good.

There are relatively few scales specifically designed for the assessment of children's anxiety and fear (Morris & Kratochwill, 1983). The TASC (Sarason et al., 1960) may be used as a rating scale of children's test anxiety, and the LFSC (Miller et al., 1972) may be filled out by parents in order to assess children's specific fears. There also have been scales designed to assess separation anxiety (e.g., Doris, McIntyre, Kelsey, & Lehman, 1971). Finally, Graziano and Mooney (1980) have reported the use of an instrument to assess the multidimensionality of children's fears. This 120-item structured questionnaire has parents respond to the many different dimensions of their children's fears, including frequency, intensity, duration, seriousness, degree of disruption, and degree of school interference.

Potential problems that have been identified for these instruments are numerous (see Saal, Downey, & Lahey, 1980); they include retrospective rather than direct data collection, the lack of situational specificity in rating behaviors, and a lack of agreement regarding conceptual and operational definitions. Moreover, most of the available rating scales aimed at assessing specific fears lack adequate reliability, validity, and norming data (Morris & Kratochwill, 1983).

With this last point in mind, use of more standardized scales, especially as a measure of generalized treatment outcome, is encouraged (Kendall et al., 1981). A researcher and/or clinician usually has limited resources with which to work (e.g., time, funding, personnel). In addition, the researcher may want to measure the "impact" of the treatment on parents and teachers, and these scales allow for just this form of evaluation. Another advantage of the specific rating scales (Morris & Kratochwill, 1983) is that they allow the researcher/clinician to identify related problems (e.g., academic problems)

that may be missed with other assessment techniques. Finally, as Kendall et al. (1981) point out, there are data that indicate the predictive validity of teacher ratings (reviewed in Strain, Cooke, & Apolloni, 1976) and positive correlations between these ratings and observed behavior (Greenwood, Walker, & Hops, 1977).

Direct Observation

Unlike the BAT, direct assessment often involves the direct observation of a child in naturalistic settings, such as school, medical, or dental environments. Measures of this type are normally scored in terms of explicitly defined behavioral categories (e.g., stammering, trembling). For example, in the school setting, Cradock, Cotler, and Jason (1978) report the use of the Timed Behavioral Checklist (Paul, 1966) in a treatment analogue study with junior high school girls identified as high in public speaking anxiety. This behavioral coding system records the frequency of 20 different indicators of public speaking anxiety during 30-second intervals (e.g., voice quivers, hand tremors). Although the interrater reliability was quite good (.93), this measure, unfortunately, was insensitive to treatment effects for either overall scores or specific items.

Observational codes implemented in school and other environments generally are designed and utilized for a particular study, and thus lack standardized formats, manuals, and validity data (Morris & Kratochwill, 1983). A good example of an observational code that *does* utilize standardized procedures and validity data is the Preschool Observational Scale of Anxiety (POSA), for use in the school environment (Glennon & Weisz, 1978). This measure is designed to assess 30 behaviors associated with anxiety (e.g., screaming, trembling, body contortions) in 30-second intervals while the child performs tasks with or without the mother present. Although there is no explicit manual for the POSA, Glennon and Weisz (1978) are quite specific in operationalizing behaviors. For example, the "expression of fear or worry" must be accompanied by the child's actually using the word "afraid," "scared," "worried," or a synonym.

Glennon and Weisz (1978) have also presented reliability and validity data for the coding system. Interrater agreement is adequate (.78). Validity data were of two types. First, Glennon and Weisz (1978) hypothesized that anxiety scores would be significantly higher without mothers present than with them nearby. The results supported their hypothesis and were viewed as supportive of the measure. Second, total POSA scores were significantly correlated with both teachers' and parents' ratings of children's anxiety. Efforts such as these are necessary to ensure both the utility and accuracy of these types of behavioral observation measures and to foster cross-study comparisons.

Behavioral coding systems have also been developed for use in dental and medical contexts (Johnson & Melamed, 1979; Morris & Kratochwill, 1983). For example, Melamed and Siegel (1975) have developed the Observer Rating Scale of Anxiety (ORSA) to assess the behavioral components of children's fear and anxiety prior to surgery. The coding system is designed to rate the presence or absence of 29 behaviors (e.g., crying, stuttering, trembling hands) during certain intervals. Melamed and Siegel (1975) have reported interrater agreement to be as high as .94. The OSRA also differentiated treated from untreated children. The Behavior Profile Rating Scale (BPRS) is a similar coding system for use in the dental setting, and has also been found to discriminate treated children from untreated children (e.g., Melamed, Weinstein, Hawes, & Katin-Borland, 1975).

The cognitive–behavioral model maintains the importance of the family and social contexts with regard to the etiology, maintenance, and remediation of childhood anxiety disorders. Consistent with this perspective, we feel it is optimal within direct observation to code the interactions of an anxious, fearful child with his or her peers and/or parents. A generalized format for this approach is seen in the Response-Class Matrix (Mash, Terdal, & Anderson, 1973), a coding system that assesses the antecedents and consequences of a child's behaviors (i.e., compliance, play, competing, negative, interaction, no response). A specific observational code designed for use in medical settings has been developed (Melamed & Bush, 1985). This coding system assesses specific anxiety-related behaviors of children and their mothers within an interactional environment. The four categories of children's behaviors rated are as follows: Distress, Attachment, Exploration, and Social–Affiliative. The six parenting behavioral categories include Ignoring, Reassurance, Distraction, Restraint, Agitation, and Informing. Efforts of this sort are crucial to determine the role that social and family interactions play in developing, maintaining, or remediating children's fears and anxieties. Finally, despite its various problems (e.g., Barrios et al., 1981), we encourage the use of direct observation both alone and in combination with other assessment modalities (e.g., cognitive and physiological measures), in order to examine the relationships among the three response channels.

Psychophysiological Assessment

Although the physiological measurement of anxiety has been widely investigated in adults (see Himadi, Boice, & Barlow, 1985), it has been accorded much less research attention in children (Johnson & Melamed, 1979). Physiological assessment of anxieties and fears in children, while a promising future, is a quite specialized, technical, and complex area for research (Wells & Vitulano, 1984). Not only does it require high levels of sophistication with expensive equipment, it also demands extensive knowledge of psychophysiology to record and interpret data in an accurate fashion. Despite such caveats, these assessment procedures are direct measures of the physiological response channel and can be included in the assessment process when possible.

The methods most commonly utilized in anxiety and fear assessment in children are cardiovascular and electrodermal measures (Barrios et al., 1981; Wells & Vitulano, 1984). Johnson and Melamed (1979) review some earlier studies that found increases in cardiovascular responsivity related to increases in stress (e.g., Darley & Katz, 1973; Stricker & Howitt, 1965). However, Tal and Miklich (1976) found equivalent levels of heart rate increase for children who imagined either a frightening experience or an anger-arousing situation. Increases in heart rate also are typically not highly correlated with other measures. For example, Melamed et al. (1978) found no correlations between heart rate and either self-report or behavioral measures, and although one study found significant correlations between heart rate and CMAS, they were in the opposite direction from that expected (Kutina & Fischer, 1977).

On the other hand, electrodermal responses (formerly referred to as galvanic skin responses) have correlated significantly with both self-reported general fears (.30) and self-reported specific fears (.31; Melamed & Siegel, 1975). These correlations were reported prior to treatment only, and it remains to be seem whether these types of measures covary in the same manner following treatment manipulation. Johnson and Melamed (1979) have reported, however, that palmar sweat prints, one index of electrodermal activity, are useful as a measure of both situational stress and treatment effects. In addition, these procedures have been shown to have reasonable test–retest reliabilities of .64 over a 1-day interval and .60 over a 15-day intervale (Lore, 1966). Unfortunately, as Barrios et al. (1981) point out, electrodermal responsivity is highly influenced by various environmental variables such as novel and interesting stimuli (Raskin, 1973; Sokolov, 1963). This fact points to the need for standardization as well as well-trained assessers in this area of fear and anxiety assessment.

Despite the limitations, there is a current advocacy of triple response measurement in adults (e.g., Himadi et al., 1985) and this form of assessment in youth is also called for and recommended. In addition, we believe that the physiological correlates of fear and anxiety are potentially quite useful when looked at from the cognitive–behavioral perspective. For example, what does a child say to himself or herself when experiencing physiological arousal? These self-statements reflect the child's understanding of the arousal and are very informative regarding beyond-normal levels of anxiety. Consider the following: A child jumps into a swimming pool; the water is cold, and the body reacts. A child who thinks, "I'm gonna die by freezing to death!" will behave differently than one who, after jumping into the same pool, thinks, "It's cold. I better move around

quickly to get warmed up." Both children experience heart rate increases associated with arousal, but the less detrimental self-explanation of the arousal is to avoid distorting and "catastrophizing." Successful treatment of anxiety disorders in children requires addressing the children's self-talk concerning this very arousal. It is not the case that children will never be aroused, but treatment can teach them to make proper sense of the arousal and to use the arousal as a cue for nonanxious coping rather than behavioral avoidance (e.g., Kane & Kendall, 1989). From this example, we see the utility of directly assessing the physiological response channel if we are to assess patterns of synchrony and desynchrony across the response modes.

CLOSING COMMENTS

Assessing anxious and fearful conditions in childhood and adolescence requires multi-method measurement: self-reports, behavioral observations, cognitive assessments, parent/teacher ratings, and indices of physiological arousal. Given the age and gender variations in anxiety and fear, there is a need for better standardization and normative data. These needs are buttressed by the fact that anxiety and fear routinely occur in most children and adolescents, and therefore may be needed for proper development. Greater attention to the cognitive features of anxiety/fear, such as examining the cognitive processing distortions associated with heightened anxious arousal is also needed. In addition to research on anxiety-focused attention, there is a need for research to differentiate anxiety from other related constructs (e.g., depression). Concepts such as "negative affectivity" (Watson & Clark, 1984) challenge the specificity of symptoms associated with anxiety and depression (see also Kendall & Watson, 1989; Wolfe et al., 1987).

REFERENCES

Achenbach, T. M., & Edelbrock, C. S. (1983). *Manual for the Child Behavior Checklist and Revised Child Behavior Profile*. Burlington: University of Vermont, Department of Psychiatry.

Agras, W. S., Chapin, H. H., & Oliveau, D. C. (1972). The natural history of phobia. *Archives of General Psychiatry, 26,* 315–317.

Argulewicz, E. N., & Miller, D. C. (1984). Validity of self-report measures of anxiety for use with Anglo-American, Mexican-American, and Black students. *Journal of Psychoeducational Assessment, 2,* 233–238.

Barrios, B. A., Hartmann, D. P., & Shigetomi, C. (1981). Fears and anxieties in children. In E. J. Mash & L. G. Terdal (Eds.), *Behavioral assessment of childhood disorders* (pp. 259–304). New York: Guilford Press.

Bauer, D. (1976). An exploratory study of developmental changes in children's fears. *Journal of Child Psychology and Psychiatry, 17,* 69–74.

Beck, A. T. (1967). *Depression: Clinical, experimental and theoretical aspects.* New York: Harper & Row.

Beck, A. T., & Emery, G. (1985). *Anxiety disorders and phobias: A cognitive perspective.* New York: Basic Books.

Bedell, J., & Roitzsch, J. (1976). The effects of stress on state and trait anxiety in emotionally disturbed, normal, and delinquent children. *Journal of Abnormal Child Psychology, 4,* 173–177.

Bernard, M. E., & Joyce, M. R. (1984). *Rational-emotive therapy with children and adolescents: Theory, treatment strategies, preventive methods.* New York: Wiley.

Bierman, K. L., & Schwartz, L. A. (1986). Clinical child interviews: Approaches and developmental considerations. *Journal of Child and Adolescent Psychotherapy, 3,* 267–278.

Carver, C. S., & Scheier, M. F. (1981). *Attention and self-regulation: A control-theory approach to human behavior.* New York: Springer.

Castaneda, A., McCandless, B., & Palermo, D. (1956). The children's form of the Manifest Anxiety Scale. *Child Development, 27,* 317–326.

Coolidge, J., Brodie, R., & Feeney, B. (1964). A ten-year follow-up study of sixty-six school phobic children. *American Journal of Orthopsychiatry, 34,* 675–684.

Costello, A. J., Edelbrock, C., Kalas, R., Kessler, M. D., & Klaric, S. (1982). *The NIMH Diagnostic Interview Schedule for Children (DISC).* Pittsburgh: Authors.

Cradock, C., Cotler, S., & Jason, L. A. (1980). Primary prevention: Immunization of children for speech anxiety. *Cognitive Therapy and Research, 2,* 389–396.

Darley, S., & Katz, I. (1973). Heart rate changes in children as a function of test versus game instructions and test anxiety. *Child Development, 44,* 784–789.

Davids, A. (1975). Therapeutic approaches to children in residential treatment: Changes from the mid 1950's to the mid 1970's. *American Psychologist, 30,* 809–814.

Doris, J., McIntyre, J. R., Kelsey, C., & Lehman, E. (1971). Separation anxiety in nursery school children. *Proceedings of the 79th Annual Convention of the American Psychological Association, 6,* 145–146.

Draper, T. W., & James, R. S. (1985). Preschool fears: Longitudinal sequence and cohort changes. *Child Study Journal, 15,* 147–155.

Edelbrock, C., & Costello, A. J. (1984). Structured psychiatric interviews for children and adolescents. In G. Goldstein & M. Hersen (Eds.), *Handbook of psychological assessment* (pp. 276–290). New York: Pergamon Press.

Finch, A. J., Jr., & Kendall, P. C. (1979). The measurement of anxiety in children: Research findings and methodological problems. In A. J. Finch, Jr., & P. C. Kendall (Eds.), *Clinical treatment and research in child psychopathology.* New York: Spectrum.

Finch, A. J., Jr., Kendall, P. C., Dannenburg, M., & Morgan, J. R. (1979). Effects of task difficulty on state–trait anxiety in emotionally disturbed children. *Journal of Genetic Psychology, 133,* 253–259.

Finch, A. J., Jr., Kendall, P. C., & Montgomery, L. (1974). Multidimensionality of anxiety in children: Factor structure of the Children's Manifest Anxiety Scale. *Journal of Abnormal Child Psychology, 2,* 311–334.

Finch, A. J., Jr., Kendall, P. C., & Montgomery, L. (1976). Qualitative difference in the experience of state–trait anxiety in emotionally disturbed and normal children. *Journal of Personality Assessment, 40,* 522–530.

Finch, A. J., Jr., Kendall, P., Montgomery, L., & Morris, T. (1975). Effects of two types of failure on anxiety. *Journal of Abnormal Psychology, 84,* 583–586.

Finch, A. J., Jr., Montgomery, L., & Deardorff, P. (1974). Reliability of state-trait anxiety with emotionally disturbed children. *Journal of Abnormal Child Psychology, 2,* 67–69.

Finch, A. J., Jr., & Nelson, W. (1974). Anxiety and locus of conflict in emotionally disturbed children. *Journal of Abnormal Child Psychology, 2,* 33–37.

Flanigan, P. J., Peters, C. J., & Conry, J. L. (1969). Item analysis of the Children's Manifest Anxiety Scale with the retarded. *Journal of Educational Research, 62,* 472–477.

Fox, J. E., Houston, B. K., & Pittner, M. S. (1983). Trait anxiety and children's cognitive behaviors in an evaluative situation. *Cognitive Therapy and Research, 7,* 145–154.

Frommer, E., Mendelson, W., & Reid, M. (1972). Differential diagnosis of psychiatric disturbance in pre-school children. *British Journal of Psychiatry, 121,* 71–74.

Fuhrman, M. J., & Kendall, P. C. (1986). Cognitive tempo and behavioral adjustment in children. *Cognitive Therapy and Research, 10,* 45–50.

Glennon, B., & Weisz, J. R. (1978). An observational approach to the assessment of anxiety in young children. *Journal of Consulting and Clinical Psychology, 46,* 1246–1257.

Graziano, A. M., DeGiovanni, I. S., & Garcia, K. A. (1979). Behavioral treatment of children's fears: A review. *Psychological Bulletin, 86,* 804–830.

Graziano, A. M., & Mooney, K. C. (1980). Family self-control instruction for children's nighttime fear reduction. *Journal of Consulting and Clinical Psychology, 48,* 206–213.

Graziano, A. M., & Mooney, D. C. (1984). *Children and behavior therapy.* Chicago: Aldine.

Greenwood, C. R., Walker, H. M., & Hops, H. (1977). Issues in social interactions/withdrawal assessment. *Exceptional Children, 43,* 490–499.

Hampe, E., Noble, H., Miller, L., & Barrett, C. (1973). Phobic children one or two years post treatment. *Journal of Abnormal Psychology, 82,* 446–453.

Harris, S. L., & Ferrari, M. (1983). Developmental

factors in child behavior therapy. *Behavior Therapy*, *14*, 54–72.

Hartup, W. W. (1983). Peer relations. In E. M. Hetherington (Ed.), *Handbook of child psychology* (4th ed.): *Vol. 4. Socialization, personality, and social development* (pp. 103–196). New York: Wiley.

Herjanic, B., & Reich, W. (1982). Development of a structured psychiatric interview for children: Agreement between child and parent on individual symptoms. *Journal of Abnormal Child Psychology*, *10*, 307–324.

Himadi, W. G., Boice, R., & Barlow, D. H. (1985). Assessment of agoraphobia: Triple response measurement. *Behaviour Research and Therapy*, *23*, 311–323.

Hollon, S. D., & Kendall, P. C. (1980). Cognitive self-statement in depression: Development of an Automatic Thoughts Questionnaire. *Cognitive Therapy and Research*, *4*, 383–395.

Houston, B. K., Fox, J. E., & Forbes, L. (1984). Trait anxiety and children's state anxiety, cognitive behaviors, and performance under stress. *Cognitive Therapy and Research*, *8*, 631–641.

Howard, B. L., & Kendall, P. C. (1987). *Child intervention: Having no peers?* Unpublished manuscript, Temple University.

Ingram, R. E. (1984). Toward an information processing analysis of depression. *Cognitive Therapy and Research*, *8*, 443–447.

Ingram, R. E. (Ed.). (1986). *Information processing approaches to clinical psychology*. New York: Academic Press.

Ingram, R. E., & Kendall, P. C. (1986). Cognitive clinical psychology: Implications of information processing perspectives. In R. E. Ingram (Ed.), *Information processing approaches to clinical psychology* (pp. 3–21). New York: Academic Press.

Ingram, R. E., Kendall, P. C., Smith, T., Donnell, C., & Ronan, K. (1987). Cognitive specificity in emotional distress. *Journal of Personality and Social Psychology*, *53*, 734–742.

Jersild, A. T., & Holmes, F. B. (1935). *Children's fears* (Child Development Monograph No. 20). New York: Teachers College, Columbia University.

Johnson, R., & Machen, J. (1973). Modification techniques and maternal anxiety. *Journal of Dentistry for Children*, *40*, 272–276.

Johnson, S. B., & Melamed, B. G. (1979). The assessment and treatment of children's fears. In B. B. Lahey & A. E. Kazdin (Eds.), *Advances in clinical child psychology* (Vol. 2, pp. 107–139). New York: Plenum Press.

Jones, M. C. (1924). A laboratory study of fear: The case of Peter. *Pedagogical Seminary*, *31*, 308–315.

Kane, M. T., & Kendall, P. C. (1989). Anxiety disorders in children: A multiple-baseline evaluation of a cognitive–behavioral treatment. *Behavior Therapy*, *20*, 499–508.

Kazdin, A. E. (1977). Assessing the clinical or applied importance of behavior change through social validation. *Behavior Change*, *1*, 427–452.

Kazdin, A. E. (1980). *Research design in clinical psychology*. New York: Harper & Row.

Kendall, P. C. (1981). Assessment and cognitive behavioral interventions: Purposes, proposals, and problems. In P. C. Kendall & S. D. Hollon (Eds.), *Assessment strategies for cognitive–behavioral interventions* (pp. 1–12). New York: Academic Press.

Kendall, P. C. (1984). Behavioral assessment and methodology. In G. T. Wilson, C. M. Franks, K. D. Brownell, & P. C. Kendall (Eds.), *Annual review of behavior therapy: Theory and practice* (Vol. 9, pp. 39–94). New York: Guilford Press.

Kendall, P. C. (1985). Toward a cognitive–behavioral model of child psychopathology and a critique of related interventions. *Journal of Abnormal Child Psychology*, *13*, 357–372.

Kendall (1989). Development and evaluation of cognitive–behavioral therapy for anxious children. NIMH Grant, in progress.

Kendall, P. C., & Braswell, L. (1982a). Assessment for cognitive–behavioral interventions in schools. *School Psychology Review*, *11*, 21–31.

Kendall, P. C., & Braswell, L. (1982b). Cognitive–behavioral assessment: Model, measures, and madness. In J. N. Butcher & C. D. Spielberger (Eds.), *Advances in personality assessment* (Vol. 1, pp. 35–82). Hillsdale, NJ: Erlbaum.

Kendall, P. C., Finch, A. J., Jr., Auerbach, S. M., Hooke, J. F., & Mikulka, P. J. (1976). The State–Trait Anxiety Inventory: A systematic evaluation. *Journal of Consulting and Clinical Psychology*, *44*, 400–412.

Kendall, P. C., & Hollon, S. D. (Eds.). (1981). *Assessment strategies for cognitive–behavioral interventions*. New York: Academic Press.

Kendall, P. C., Howard, B. L., & Epps, J. (1988). The anxious child: Cognitive–behavioral treatment strategies. *Behavior Modification*, *12*, 281–310.

Kendall, P. C., & Ingram, R. (1987). The future for the cognitive assessment of anxiety: Let's get specific. In L. Michelson & L. M. Ascher (Eds.), *Anxiety and stress disorders: Cognitive–behavioral assessment and treatment* (pp. 89–104). New York: Guilford Press.

Kendall, P. C., Kane, M., Howard, B., & Siqueland, L. (1989). *Cognitive–behavioral therapy for anxious children: Treatment manual*. Available from the author, Temple University.

Kendall, P. C., & Korgeski, G. P. (1979). Assessment and cognitive–behavioral interventions. *Cognitive Therapy and Research*, *3*, 1–21.

Kendall, P. C., Pellegrini, D. S., & Urbain, E. S. (1981). Approaches to assessment for cognitive–behavioral intervention with children. In P. C. Kendall & S. D. Hollon (Eds.), *Assessment strategies for cognitive–behavioral interventions* (pp. 227–285). New York: Academic Press.

Kendall, P. C., & Watson, D. (Eds.). (1989). *Anxiety and depression: Distinctive and overlapping features*. New York: Academic Press.

Kennedy, W. A. (1965). School phobia: Rapid treatment of fifty cases. *Journal of Abnormal Psychology*, *70*, 285–290.

Kutina, J., & Fischer, J. (1977). Anxiety, heart rate and their interrelation with mental stress in school children. *Activitas Nervos Superior*, *19*, 89–95.

Lang, P. J. (1968). Fear reduction and fear behavior: Problems in treating a construct. In J. M. Schlien (Ed.), *Research in psychotherapy*. Washington, DC: American Psychological Association.

Lang, P. J., & Lazovik, A. D. (1963). Experimental desensitization of a phobia. *Journal of Abnormal and Social Psychology*, *66*, 519–525.

Lapouse, R., & Monk, M. A. (1959). Fears and worries in a representative sample of children. *American Journal of Orthopsychiatry*, *29*, 223–248.

Lore, R. (1966). Palmar sweating and transitory anxieties in children. *Child Development, 37*, 115–123.

MacFarlane, J. W., Allen, L., & Honzik, M. P. (1954). *A developmental study of the behavior problems of normal children between 21 months and 14 years*. Berkeley: University of California Press.

Marks, I. M. (1969). *Fears and phobias*. New York: Academic Press.

Marzillier, J. S. (1980). Cognitive therapy and behavioural practice. *Behaviour Research and Therapy, 18*, 249–258.

Mash, E. J., Terdal, L. G., & Anderson, K. (1973). The Response-Class Matrix: A procedure for recording parent–child interaction. *Journal of Consulting and Clinical Psychology, 40*, 163–164.

Melamed, B. G., & Bush, J. P. (1985). Family factors in children with acute illness. In S. Auerbach & A. Stoberg (Eds.), *Crisis in Families*. New York: Hemisphere Publishing.

Melamed, B. G., Hawes, R. R., Heiby, E., & Glick, J. (1975). Use of filmed modeling to reduce uncooperative behavior of children during dental treatment. *Journal of Dental Research, 54*, 797–801.

Melamed, B. G., & Siegel, L. J. (1975). Reduction of anxiety in children facing hospitalization and surgery by use of filmed modeling. *Journal of Consulting and Clinical Psychology, 43*, 511–521.

Melamed, B. G., Weinstein, G., Hawes, R., & Katin-Borland, M. (1975). Reduction of fear-related dental management problems with use of filmed modeling. *Journal of the American Dental Association, 90*, 822–826.

Melamed, B. G., Yurcheson, R., Fleece, E. L., Hutcherson, S., & Hawes, R. (1978). Effects of film modeling on the reduction of anxiety-related behaviors in individuals varying in level of previous experience in the stress situation. *Journal of Consulting and Clinical Psychology, 46*, 1357–1367.

Merluzzi, T. V., Glass, C. R., & Genest, M. (Eds.). (1981). *Cognitive assessment*. New York: Guilford Press.

Merluzzi, T. V., Rudy, T. E., & Krejer, M. (1986). Social skill and anxiety: Information processing perspectives. In R. E. Ingram (Ed.), *Information processing approaches to clinical psychology* (pp. 109–129). New York: Academic Press.

Miller, L. C. (1972). School Behavior Checklist: An inventory of deviant behavior for elementary school children. *Journal of Consulting and Clinical Psychology, 38*, 134–144.

Miller, L. C. (1983). Fears and anxieties in children. In C. E. Walker & M. C. Roberts (Eds.), *Handbook of clinical child psychology* (pp. 337–380). New York: Wiley.

Miller, L. C., Barrett, C. L., & Hampe, E. (1974). Phobias of childhood in a prescientific era. In A. Davids (Ed.), *Child personality and psychopathology: Current topics* (Vol. 1, pp. 89–134). New York: Wiley.

Miller, L. C., Barrett, C. L., Hampe, E., & Noble, H. (1972). Factor structure of childhood fears. *Journal of Consulting and Clinical Psychology, 39*, 264–268.

Montgomery, L., & Finch, A. J. Jr. (1974). Validity of two measures of anxiety in children. *Journal of Abnormal Child Psychology, 2*, 293–296.

Morris, R. J., & Kratochwill, T. R. (1983). *Treating children's fear and phobias: A behavioral approach*. New York: Pergamon Press.

Morris, R. J., & Kratochwill, T. R. (1985). Behavioral treatment of children's fears and phobias: A review. *School Psychology Review, 14*, 84–93.

Nawas, M. M. (1971). Standardized scheduled desensitization: Some unstable results and an improved program. *Behaviour Research and Therapy, 9*, 35–38.

Newmark, C., Wheeler, D., Newmark, L., & Stabler, B. (1975). Test induced anxiety with children. *Journal of Personality Assessment, 39*, 409–413.

Ollendick, T. H. (1978). *The Fear Survey Schedule for Children—Revised*. Unpublished manuscript, Indiana State University.

Ollendick, T. H. (1983). Reliability and validity of the Revised Fear Survey Schedule for Children (FSSC-R). *Behaviour Research and Therapy, 21*, 685–692.

Ollendick, T. H., Matson, J. L., & Helsel, W. J. (1985). Fears in children and adolescents: Normative data. *Behaviour Research and Therapy, 23*, 465–467.

Paul, G. L. (1966). *Insight versus desensitization in psychotherapy*. Stanford, CA: Stanford University Press.

Pela, O. A., & Reynolds, C. R. (1982). Cross-cultural application of the Revised Children's Manifest Anxiety Scale: Normative and reliability data for Nigerian primary school children. *Psychological Reports, 51*, 1135–1138.

Peterson, L., & Shigetomi, C. (1981). The use of coping techniques in minimizing anxiety in hospitalized children. *Behavior Therapy, 12*, 1–14.

Piaget, J. (1967). *Six psychological studies*. New York: Random House.

Pratt, K. C. (1945). The study of the "fears" of rural children. *Journal of Genetic Psychology, 67*, 179–194.

Prins, P. J. M. (1985). Self-speech and self-regulation of high- and low-anxious children in the dental situation: An interview study. *Behaviour Research and Therapy, 23*, 641–650.

Prins, P. J. M. (1986). Children's self-speech and self-regulation during a fear-provoking behavioral test. *Behaviour Research and Therapy, 24*, 181–191.

Puig-Antich, J., & Chambers, W. (1978). *The Schedule for Affective Disorders and Schizophrenia for School-Aged Children*. Pittsburgh: Western Psychiatric Institute and Clinic.

Raskin, D. C. (1973). Attention and arousal. In W. F. Prokasy & D. C. Raskin (Eds.), *Electrodermal activity in psychological research* (pp. 125–155). New York: Academic Press.

Reynolds, C. R. (1977). *A bibliography of research employing the Children's Manifest Anxiety Scale: 1956–1977*. Unpublished manuscript.

Reynolds, C. R. (1980). Concurrent validity of "What I Think and Feel": The Revised Children's Manifest Anxiety Scale. *Journal of Consulting and Clinical Psychology, 49*, 774–775.

Reynolds, C. R. (1982). Convergent and divergent validity of the Revised Children's Manifest Anxiety Scale. *Educational and Psychological Measurement, 42*, 1205–1212.

Reynolds, C. R., & Paget, K. D. (1981). Factor analysis of the Revised Children's Manifest Anxiety Scale for blacks, whites, males and females with a national normative sample. *Journal of Consulting and Clinical Psychology, 49*, 352–359.

Reynolds, C. R., & Paget, K. D. (1983). National normative and reliability data for the revised Children's Manifest Anxiety Scale. *School Psychology Review, 12*, 324–336.

Reynolds, C. R., & Richmond, B. O. (1978). "What I

Think and Feel": A revised measure of children's manifest anxiety. *Journal of Abnormal Child Psychology, 6,* 271–280.

Reynolds, C. R., & Richmond, B. O. (1979). Factor structure and construct validity of "What I Think and Feel": The Revised Children's Manifest Anxiety Scale. *Journal of Personality Assessment, 43,* 281–283.

Richmond, B. O., Sukemune, S., Ohmoto, M., Kawamoto, H., & Hamazaki, T. (1984). Anxiety among Canadian, Japanese, and American children. *Journal of Psychology, 116,* 3–6.

Ryall, M. R., & Dietiker, K. E. (1979). Reliability and clinical validity of the Children's Fear Survey Schedule. *Journal of Behavior Therapy and Experimental Psychiatry, 10,* 303–309.

Saal, F. E., Downey, R. G., & Lahey, M. A. (1980). Rating the ratings: Assessing the psychometric quality of rating data. *Psychological Bulletin, 88,* 413–428.

Santestefano, S., & Reider, C. (1984). Cognitive controls and aggression in children: The concept of cognitive affective balance. *Journal of Consulting and Clinical Psychology, 52,* 46–56.

Sarason, I. G. (1975). Anxiety and self-preoccupation. In I. G. Sarason & C. D. Spielberger (Eds.), *Stress and anxiety* (Vol. 2, pp. 27–44). New York: Wiley.

Sarason, S., Davidson, K., Lighthall, F., Waite, R., & Ruebush, B. (1960). *Anxiety in elementary school children.* New York: Wiley.

Scherer, M. W., & Nakamura, C. Y. (1968). A Fear Survey Schedule for Children (FSS-FC): A factor analytical comparison with manifest anxiety (CMAS). *Behaviour Research and Therapy, 6,* 173–182.

Scholwinski, E., & Reynolds, C. R. (1985). Dimensions of anxiety among high IQ children. *Gifted Child Quarterly, 29,* 125–130.

Silverman, W. K. (1987). *Anxiety Disorders Interview Schedule for Children.* (Available from the author, Center for Stress and Anxiety Disorders, 1535 Western Ave., Albany, NY 12203)

Simon, A., & Ward, L. (1974). Variables influencing the sources, frequency and intensity of worry in secondary school pupils. *British Journal of Social and Clinical Psychology, 13,* 391–396.

Smith, T. V., Ingram, R. E., & Brehm, S. S. (1983). Social anxiety, anxious self-preoccupation, and recall of self-relevant information. *Journal of Personality and Social Psychology, 44,* 1276–1283.

Sokolov, V. N. (1963). *Perception and the conditioned reflex.* New York: Macmillan.

Spielberger, C. D. (1973). *Manual for the State–Trait Anxiety Inventory for Children.* Palo Alto, CA: Consulting Psychologists Press.

Spielberger, C. D., Gorsuch, R. L., & Lushene, R. E. (1970). *Manual for the State–Trait Anxiety Inventory.* Palo Alto, CA: Consulting Psychologists Press.

Spivack, G., & Swift, M. (1967). *Devereux Elementary School Behavior Rating Scale manual.* Devon, PA: Devereux Foundation.

Strain, P., Cooke, T., & Apolloni, T. (1976). *Teaching exceptional children: Assessing and modifying social behavior.* New York: Academic Press.

Stricker, G., & Howitt, J. W. (1965). Physiological recording during simulated dental appointments. *New York State Dental Journal, 31,* 204–213.

Tal, A., & Miklich, D. (1976). Emotionally induced decreases in pulmonary flow rates in asthmatic children. *Psychosomatic Medicine, 38,* 190–200.

Taylor, J. A. (1951). The relationship of anxiety to the conditioned eyelid response. *Journal of Experimental Psychology, 42,* 183–188.

Turk, D. C., & Speers, M. A. (1983). Cognitive schemata and cognitive processes in cognitive–behavioral interventions: Going beyond the information given. In P. C. Kendall (Ed.), *Advances in cognitive–behavioral research and therapy* (Vol. 2, pp. 1–32). New York: Academic Press.

Waldron, S., Jr. (1976). The significance of childhood neurosis for adult mental health: A follow-up study. *American Journal of Psychiatry, 133,* 532–538.

Walker, H. M., (1970). *Walker Problem Behavior Identification Checklist.* Los Angeles: Western Psychological Services.

Watson, D., & Clark, L. A. (1984). Negative affectivity: The disposition to experience aversive emotional states. *Psychological Bulletin, 96,* 465–490.

Watson, J. B., & Raynor, P. (1920). Conditioned emotional reaction. *Journal of Experimental Psychology, 3,* 1–14.

Wells, K. C., & Vitulano, L. A. (1984). Anxiety disorders in childhood. In S. Turner (Ed.), *Behavioral theories and treatment of anxiety* (pp. 413–433). New York: Plenum Press.

Werry, J. S. (1986). Diagnosis and assessment. In R. Gittelman (Ed.), *Anxiety disorders of childhood* (pp. 73–100). New York: Guilford Press.

Wine, J. (1971). Test anxiety and direction of attention. *Psychological Bulletin, 76,* 92–104.

Wiens, A. N. (1976). The assessment interview. In I. B. Weiner (Ed.), *Clinical methods in psychology* (pp. 3–60). New York: Wiley.

Wolf, M. F. (1978). Social validity: The case for subjective measurement or how applied behavior analysis is finding its heart. *Journal of Applied Behavior Analysis, 11,* 203–214.

Wolfe, V. V., Finch, A. J., Jr., Saylor, C. F., Blount, R. L., Pallmeyer, T. P., & Carek, D. J. (1987). Negative affectivity in children: A multitrait–multimethod investigation. *Journal of Consulting and Clinical Psychology, 55,* 245–250.

Wolff, S. (1971). Dimensions and clusters of symptoms in disturbed children. *British Journal of Psychiatry, 18,* 421–427.

Wolpe, J., & Lang, P. (1964). A fear survey schedule for use in behaviour therapy. *Behaviour Research and Therapy, 2,* 27–30.

Zatz, S., & Chassin, L. (1983). Cognitions of test anxious children. *Journal of Consulting and Clinical Psychology, 51,* 524–534.

Zatz, S., & Chassin, L. (1985). Cognitions of text-anxious children under naturalistic test-taking conditions. *Journal of Consulting and Clinical Psychology, 53,* 393–401.

11

Assessing Early Temperament

H. HILL GOLDSMITH
University of Oregon

LORETTA A. RIESER-DANNER
Villanova University

CHOOSING A TEMPERAMENT ASSESSMENT INSTRUMENT

Overview

As temperament researchers, we are tempted to begin this chapter with a theoretical overview and then to show how current temperament assessment instruments flow from the various theoretical orientations. However, as investigators who regularly answer their telephones and hear slightly frenzied questions from others needing the "best" temperament measure for a study that is scheduled almost immediately, we feel that another beginning is preferable. Because we hope that this handbook will serve as a first source for those interested in childhood assessment, our chapter's introduction is modeled after the diagrams that family medical encyclopedias provide for self-diagnosis of injury or illness. Like the disclaimers offered by medical encyclopedias, we suggest that the reader consult the original literature if symptoms (of indecision, skepticism, or curiosity) persist.

To serve readers who contemplate assessing temperament after the neonatal period and before adolescence, we offer Figure 11.1. Readers should enter Figure 11.1 at the upper left of Panel A and proceed along the various paths until arriving at the recom-

mendations. In a subsequent section, we provide brief descriptions of each of the instruments mentioned in the Figure.

Explanation of Figure 11.1

Temperament need not be assessed in every developmental study. The future of temperament research might best be served by investigators' carefully deciding whether to measure temperament in their studies. If temperament is assessed without a compelling conceptual reason ("Let's toss in a short temperament questionnaire and see whether it relates to anything"), the inevitable accumulation of negative findings will cast a shadow over the results of more carefully conceived studies. We agree with Bornstein, Gaughran, and Homel (1986) that "When temperament finds an integral rather than ancillary role in theories of child development, its significance as a contrast will be certain" (p. 196).

After a careful decision to assess temperament, the next decision is whether temperament will be evaluated directly by the investigator or indirectly via a respondent. Each strategy has its advantages and disadvantages, as we discuss later in this chapter. The most popular choice is to rely on economical questionnaires—that is, to assess

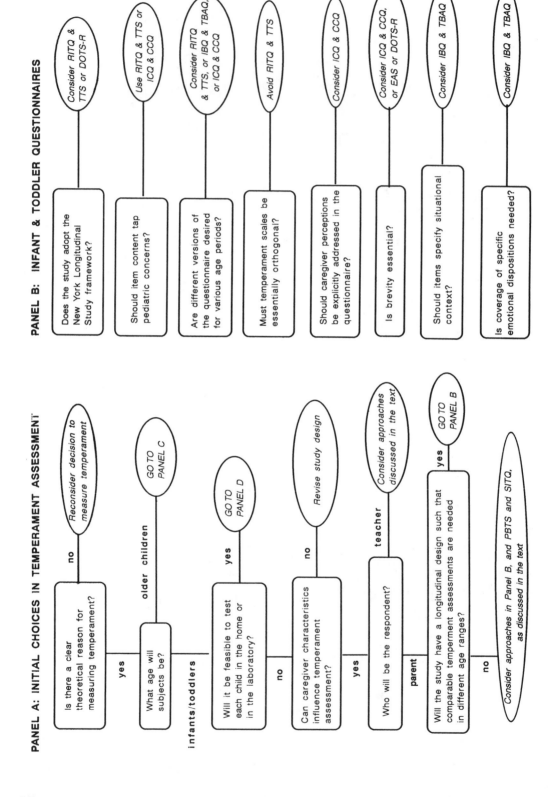

PANEL A: INITIAL CHOICES IN TEMPERAMENT ASSESSMENT

PANEL B: INFANT & TODDLER QUESTIONNAIRES

246

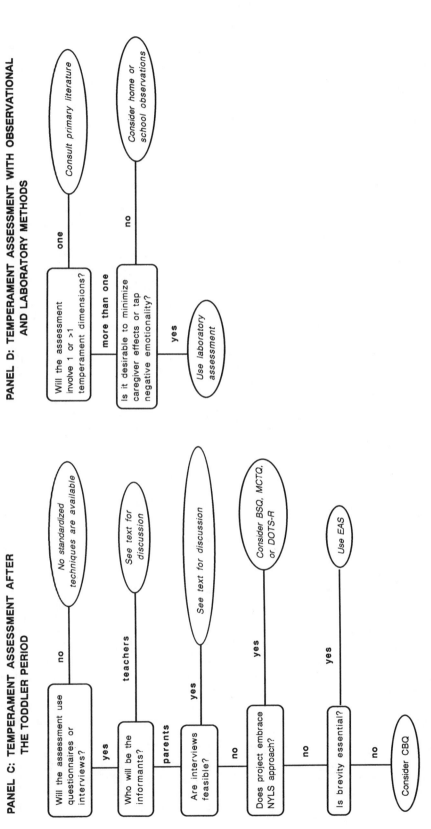

FIGURE 11.1. Flowchart illustrating the process of choosing a temperament assessment instrument. See text for details.

temperament indirectly via a respondent who can report his or her extensive observations of the child. We urge that this decision be based primarily on substantive reasons rather than simply on cost and convenience. If direct assessment is preferable, both laboratory and home observation measures are possible for infants and toddlers. Neither laboratory nor home observation methods are monolithic (see Panel D). In fact, relatively naturalistic observations can be done in laboratory settings, and relatively controlled situations can be arranged in the home. Of course, the age of subjects will dictate assessment options. Beyond the toddler stage, only questionnaire and interview techniques have been constructed, with the exception of observational measures of specific constructs (see Panel C).

Continuing to trace through the paths of Panel A, and assuming that indirect assessment via caregivers is chosen, the investigator must be prepared to accept the likelihood that caregiver characteristics influence the temperament reports to some degree. However, substantial evidence suggests that the caregiver influence need not invalidate the assessment; the evidence is reviewed in the last section of this chapter. Indeed, assessment via the caregiver may be the method of choice in certain designs. If caregiver report is used, the investigator should consider how biases resulting from the caregiver's personality or attitudes, history of interaction with the child, situational demands, or other factors may influence perception and/or report of temperament. The most likely of these biasing factors should perhaps be operationalized in the study, so that their impact can be ruled out or at least quantified.

Certain designs require infant or toddler temperament assessment by teachers or day care workers. In these cases, one can employ questionnaires designed specifically for teachers. However, most teacher report questionnaires are meant for older children. Another option is to administer questionnaires intended for parents to the teachers or day care workers. This option may be particularly attractive when comparisons of parents' and teachers' perceptions of temperament are needed. Because some items asked of parents typically involve situations that teachers do not witness, instructions for the teachers should be modified accordingly. Such modification of instructions is probably preferable to dropping items on an a priori basis. A subsequent section explains the differentiating features of the most prominent teacher report instruments.

Assuming that parental report methodology is chosen, several questionnaires are available. How does one choose among them? Of course, theoretical positions or predilections should play the most important role in the decision. Some temperament questionnaires operationalize their developers' theoretical ideas; others emerge from less well-formulated theoretical notions. In making this aspect of the decision of which questionnaire to use, reading the theoretical literature is essential. Goldsmith et al. (1987) provide an overview of four approaches to temperament theory, along with commentary. Several other review articles summarize current theoretical approaches (Bates, 1987; Bornstein et al., 1986; Buss & Plomin, 1984; Goldsmith & Campos, 1982; Lerner & Lerner, 1983; Seifer & Sameroff, 1986; Strelau, 1983).

Closely related to theoretical orientation is the relevance of item content. Although it seems so basic a suggestion that we hesitate to emphasize it, we recommend simply reading items carefully and considering whether they tap information needed for a particular study.

There are also practical aspects to the decision. Many studies of temperament encompass a longitudinal component. These studies call for questionnaires that have versions for different age periods (the questionnaires by Carey and his colleagues, by Bates, and by Rothbart and Goldsmith) or that are suitable for particularly broad age ranges (the questionnaires by Lerner and colleagues and by Buss and Plomin). The five questionnaires (or questionnaire series) just mentioned are also the most popular ones in current usage in the United States. This popularity allows users to relate their results to an existing literature. For these reasons, Panel B is devoted to factors that may aid in deciding among these five approaches to infant and toddler questionnaire assessment via caregivers.

On the other hand, if longitudinal or cross-sectional applicability and popularity are not important issues for an application, there are other infant and toddler questionnaires to consider. Some of the other choices are listed at the bottom of Panel A and described briefly in a later section.

In Panel B, a series of nonsequential questions might help the consumer choose among the five most prominent, English-language, infant and toddler parental report questionnaires. The suggestions in Panel B might not lead all investigators to a unique recommendation, but they should at least narrow the choices.

Panel C outlines some choices that those who study temperament in children beyond the toddler period must face. The temperament questionnaires for older children are of more recent vintage, and few data on reliability and validity have accumulated in most cases. In addition to the instruments mentioned in Panel C, other personality questionnaires are applicable to children in this age range. These other instruments, such as the Personality Inventory for Children (see Lachar, Chapter 13, this volume), include scales undoubtedly related to temperament, but they are not treated in this chapter.

As in the infancy and toddler periods, one of the major decisions facing the consumer is whether to subscribe to the New York Longitudinal Study (NYLS) framework or to consider alternative views. Within the NYLS framework, the conventional choice might be the Behavioral Style Questionnaire (BSQ) and the Middle Childhood Temperament Questionnaire (MCTQ), which tap each of the NYLS dimensions and yield difficulty scores. A worthwhile alternative that is more distantly related to the NYLS framework is the Dimensions of Temperament Scale— Revised (DOTS-R; Windle, 1988; Windle & Lerner, 1986).

Outside the NYLS framework, the best-known choice is Buss and Plomin's (1984) Emotionality, Activity, and Sociability (EAS), a brief instrument that assesses three broad temperamental dispositions. In stark contrast to the EAS is Rothbart's (1988) Childhood Behavior Questionnaire (CBQ), an instrument that has undergone considerable development and validation but that has not yet been formally published. The lengthy CBQ provides assessment of quite differentiated aspects of childhood behavioral patterns. The choice between the EAS and the CBQ is clear: The EAS is more general and easier to administer because of its short length; the CBQ dimensions are more specific and cover a greater portion of the child's behavioral repertoire. Of course, the CBQ derives from Rothbart's (in press) conception of temperament, and the EAS derives from Buss and Plomin's (1984).

Another issue concerns the assessment of temperament in even older children or adolescents. In our view, the assessment of temperament and personality become difficult to distinguish in older children, just as adult temperament and personality are not well differentiated. For example, despite its name, the venerable Thurstone Temperament Survey simply measures some of the salient dimensions of adult personality. It does not tap temperament independent of other influences on personality. Two of the instruments to be reviewed in this chapter, the EAS and DOTS-R, have adult forms. Thomas, Chess, and Korn (1982) have published an adult questionnaire form of their temperament assessment procedure. The reader should also be alerted to the future availability of an adult questionnaire based on Rothbart's theory of temperament (Derryberry & Rothbart, 1988).

Panel D outlines the options for direct assessment of temperament after the neonatal period. As a comprehensive enterprise, construction of laboratory and observational approaches is new, compared to construction of questionnaires. For many years, researchers have devised laboratory and home observation techniques for assessing certain facets of temperament in single projects. More recently, standardized techniques that can be exported to other sites have been developed. The techniques cited in Panel D are described in a later section.

BACKGROUND FOR ASSESSMENT: AN OVERVIEW OF TEMPERAMENT RESEARCH

Undoubtedly, the reason why one finds a temperament chapter in this handbook is that temperament research activity has increased dramatically. The concept of temperament has been revitalized in recent years by interdisciplinary research involving developmental and clinical psychologists, pediatricians, child psychiatrists, educators, and behavioral geneticists (Bates, 1987; Campos, Barrett, Lamb, Goldsmith, & Stenberg, 1983). In its new look, temperament no longer carries connotations of lack of malleability or a rigid association with body type. Instead, there are new emphases on developmental psychobiology and interactive social processes. Rather than a single characteristic roughly synonymous with "irritability" or "moodiness," temperament is now considered a multidimensional construct. Most researchers consider temperament to be the behavioral manifestation of biologically influenced processes determining both the infant's characteristic response to the environment and his or her style of initiating behavior.

Signs of Increased Interest in Temperament

The revitalization of temperament research is documented by a tremendous increase in publications in *Child Development, Developmental Psychology,* and other developmental journals; in papers and symposia at the Society for Research in Child Development and the International Conference on Infant Studies; and in the number of small conferences devoted to temperament. The upsurge of interest is clearly international in scope, with active contributors to the literature from Japan, Australia, and Eastern and Western Europe. Two comprehensive new handbooks on temperament are in preparation, with editors from the United States, the Netherlands, West Germany, and Poland (Kohnstamm, Bates, & Rothbart, in press; Angleiter & Strelau, in press). These handbooks follow earlier edited volumes by Kohnstamm (1986), Lerner and Lerner (1986), Plomin and Dunn (1986), and Porter and Collins (1982), among others. One can view the prominence of emotion in social psychologists' work and the increased interest in emotional effects on cognition, and vice versa, by cognitive psychologists as counterparts to developmentalists' new focus on temperament.

The Importance of Temperament Research

The fundamental significance of temperament lies in its proposed role as the "emotional substrate" of later personality, a role accorded it in both traditional (Allport, 1937; Cattell, 1946) and contemporary (e.g., Buss & Plomin, 1984) theories of personality. Indeed, Kagan (1982) suggests that aspects of temperament may be among the few behavioral characteristics that are relatively stable from infancy throughout the lifespan.

The societal significance of temperament research lies in its claimed predictive power (Rutter, 1987). In a chapter devoted to assessment, it is impossible to review the burgeoning empirical research on temperament and its developmental implications. A very selective listing of issues under study indicates the scope of recent efforts. In the realm of social development, an important but perhaps overdebated issue concerns the relationship between temperament and attachment. We have reviewed this issue from conceptual and assessment perspectives (Goldsmith, Bradshaw, & Rieser-Danner, 1986), as well as analyzing the data within a meta-analytic framework (Goldsmith & Alansky, 1987). Approximately 20 studies have addressed the temperament–attachment issue. Only a few projects have comprehensively assessed the links among temperament, attachment, and parenting (Belsky, Rovine, & Taylor, 1984; Van den Boom, 1988).

Several researchers have investigated infant temperamental influences on the developing mother–infant relationship, particularly on maternal caregiving behavior. Early evidence suggested that mothers of "difficult" infants were less responsive (Milliones, 1978). Furthermore, Kelly's (1976) results suggested that mothers of difficult infants responded more negatively to their infants' expression of negative emotion, and Sameroff (1977) reported that mothers of difficult infants avoided social interaction with their infants more than other mothers. In fact, some research suggests that infant negative emotionality is associated with less responsive, less contingent maternal behavior (see Crockenberg, 1986, for a review). Unfortunately, most of these studies cannot

claim complete independence between measures of infant and maternal behaviors. Furthermore, as Crockenberg (1986) has pointed
out, other research suggests that infants high
in negative emotionality or difficulty receive
higher levels of responsivity, social interaction, and stimulation than less negative infants.

Infant temperament has also been linked
to maternal control strategies (Lee & Bates,
1985), maternal teaching behavior (Maccoby,
Snow, & Jacklin, 1984), negative reaction to
the birth of a sibling (Dunn, Kendrick, &
McNamee, 1981), later aggressiveness (Kolvin, Nichol, Garside, & Tweddle, 1982), and
many facets of social development.

A few investigators have focused on the
role that temperamental differences play in
standard testing situations. Lamb (1982) reported a modest correlation between infant
sociability, measured by reactions to strangers, and performance on cognitive development tests. Rieser-Danner (1985) also found
a modest correlation between infant fearfulness, again measured by reaction to strangers, and performance on a series of Piagetian object permanence tasks at 12 months of
age. Also, Trieber (1984) and Wachs and
Smitherman (1985) observed that infants
classified as "difficult" were less likely to
complete a standard habituation procedure.
A smaller literature relates temperament to
cognitive variables. For instance, temperament has been associated with rates of learning in 2- to 3-month-olds (Dunst & Lingerfelt,
1985), as well as to cognitive achievements in
older children (Hall & Cadwell, 1984).

Best known to the clinical literature is
Thomas, Chess, and Birch's (1968; see also
Thomas & Chess, 1977) report that infants
described by their parents as "difficult"
tended to show a number of behavior problems during later childhood. Although
methodological problems existed in this research (Bates, 1980; Goldsmith & Campos,
1982; McNeil, 1976; Persson-Blennow &
McNeil, 1979; Rothbart & Derryberry,
1981), recent work reaffirms that some
aspects of temperament can be associated
with subsequent psychological disturbances
(Bates, 1987; Wolkind & Desalis, 1982).
However, these temperamental effects do
typically seem to interact developmentally
with other familial variables in predicting

subsequent behavior (Bates & Bayles, 1984;
Crockenberg, 1981; Lee & Bates, 1985).
Carey (1986) reviews numerous clinical implications of temperament, including associations of temperament with clinical phenomena such as sleep problems (Carey, 1981)
and impulsive accidents (Huttunen & Nyman, 1982).

In summary, there is little doubt that
temperament is a construct with potentially
broad predictive utility.

The Need for Improved Assessment

The current surge of interest in temperament
has not been without its pitfalls. There is
danger that easy-to-administer but in-
adequately validated caretaker report temperament questionnaires will be included in
studies without sufficient theoretical justification, giving rise to an uninterpretable
body of positive and negative results (some
serendipitous). At times, there has also been
a failure to appreciate the distinctions between parental reports and direct observational measures of temperament. Attention
to measurement issues should aid in avoiding
these and other pitfalls.

A few years ago, there were severe limits
to the progress possible in temperament research with existing assessment tools. An
accumulation of negative findings, perhaps
largely because of faulty assessment,
threatened to "short-circuit" a promising
field. For example, Hubert, Wachs, Peters-
Martin, and Gandor (1982) tabulated reliability and validity data for a number of questionnaires and concluded that "stability data are
inconsistent and interparent agreement coefficients were low. Validity data . . . showed
little convergence between instruments and
inconsistent findings regarding concurrent
and predictive validity" (p. 571). This conclusion was too global, because the Hubert et al.
"box score" allowed methodologically un-
sound studies to outweigh fewer well-
conceived ones.

Since the Hubert et al. (1982) review, the
status of temperament assessment has improved. For example, questionnaires derived
more or less directly from the Thomas and
Chess approach have been refined (e.g.,
Keogh, Pullis, & Cadwell, 1982; Martin,
1988; Sanson, Prior, Garino, Oberklaid, &

Sewell, 1987; Windle, 1988; Windle & Lerner, 1986) and extended to new age groups (e.g., Bates & Bayles, 1984). Most—but not all—scales from the more recent questionnaires show adequate internal consistency and a reasonable degree of independence when correlated with other scales on the same questionnaires. On the other hand, strong and extensive evidence for external validity remains to be garnered for most instruments.

TEMPERAMENT ASSESSMENT INSTRUMENTS: INTERVIEWS AND QUESTIONNAIRES

Parental Interviews

The initial temperament research of Thomas and Chess and their colleagues in the New York Longitudinal Study (NYLS) used parental interviews. The NYLS researchers began interviews when infants were approximately 3 months of age and conducted them at regular and gradually longer intervals throughout early development. These original interviews by skilled clinicians were relatively unstructured. They simply asked parents to describe recent events in their children's lives. After the initial interviews during infancy, they devised a coding system to score nine dimensions of temperament. These dimensions, identified by an "inductive content analysis," were Activity Level, Rhythmicity, Approach/Withdrawal, Adaptability, Intensity, Mood, Distractibility, Attention Span/Persistence, and Threshold. Each was rated on a 3-point scale. Later, Thomas and Chess (1977) suggested guidelines for clinical interviews to assess temperament. It is important to note that these NYLS dimensions were derived from early infant behavior. It is perilous to assume that the same nine dimensions would emerge from later developmental periods or that they represent the best structure for understanding later temperament. Nevertheless, these nine dimensions have served as the basis for interview assessment throughout childhood and adolescence and into early adulthood (Chess & Thomas, 1984).

Graham, Rutter, and George (1973) modified the NYLS interview approach for a British study with 4- to 5-year-old children. They dropped four dimensions and added assessment of Malleability and Fastidiousness. Garside et al. (1975) further standardized parental interviews. They designed a sequenced set of questions and probes to "elicit immediately rateable descriptions of how children do what they do, in specific situations" (p. 220). Their approach is directly related to the NYLS approach. Interviewers use 5-point rating scales to score the descriptions of behavior elicited by the 30 questions. All questions are related to four dimensions: (1) Withdrawal, Poor Adaptability, and Dependence; (2) High Activity, Intensity, and Distractibility; (3) Moodiness and Sulkiness; and (4) Irregularity. The interview was designed for 5- to 7-year-olds. The Garside et al. (1975) approach has found some acceptance by the field, being used, for example, in the work of Stevenson-Hinde, Hinde, and their colleagues (e.g., Stevenson-Hinde & Simpson, 1982).

Other researchers have also employed parental interviews. For instance, Wilson, Brown, and Matheny (1971) used interviews in assessing temperament in the early stages of the Louisville Twin Study, and Torgersen (1982) adapted the NYLS approach for temperament assessment in a Scandinavian twin study. Porter and Collins (1982) report a wide-ranging discussion of interview and questionnaire approaches by temperament researchers.

Parental Report Questionnaires

The most popular form of temperament assessment in infancy and childhood is the parental report questionnaire. Its popularity undoubtedly derives from its low cost and ease of administration. Questionnaires also take advantage of the caregiver's extensive observational data base, which is unavailable to observers in the home or laboratory. The various parental report questionnaires—even those with similarly named scales—are hardly interchangeable. For example, questionnaires vary in the number and specificity of dimensions included. Questionnaires derived from various theoretical approaches are described below, and advantages and disadvantages are outlined. These descriptions should be read in conjunction with the information presented in Figure 11.1.

In the questionnaire domain, there are two general strategies for dealing with situational context: one represented by Rothbart's approach on the Infant Behavior Questionnaire, and the other, for example, by Buss and Plomin's strategy in constructing their questionnaires (see below). Rothbart's approach specifies the situational context for every item, whereas Buss and Plomin's approach implicitly asks the respondent to generalize across many situations. Of course, the former approach assumes that the test designer has adequately sampled the situations relevant to the temperament dimension, and the latter approach assumes that the respondent attends to the relevant situations and weighs each appropriately in formulating responses. On a priori grounds, the specification of situational context in each item might be preferred as more objective; however, the final arbiter of the relative value of the two approaches should be evidence of superior external validity.

Respondent Bias in Questionnaires

In all attempts to measure temperament, the researcher must be aware of the constraints of the assessment situation that cannot be controlled and must attempt to assess the effects of these constraints. In questionnaire measures, one must accept that the parents' possibly biased perception is what is actually being assessed and must attempt to evaluate any distortion introduced by this perception (e.g., Bates & Bayles, 1984; Goldsmith, Bradshaw, & Campos, in press; Goldsmith, Rieser-Danner, & Pomerantz, 1983; Lyon & Plomin, 1981; Sameroff, Seifer, & Elias, 1982; Stevenson-Hinde & Simpson, 1982; Vaughn, Taraldson, Crichton, & Egeland, 1981). This evaluation may take the form of validity scales on the questionnaire; comparison with converging measures of temperament contaminated by fewer, less powerful, or different souces of bias; or direct attempts to measure biasing factors in the parents.

The remainder of this section provides brief descriptions of the most widely used temperament questionnaires. Within the descriptions, we discuss several important psychometric issues; this leads to considerable variation in lengths of the descriptions.

Questionnaire by Thomas and Chess

In their 1977 book, Thomas and Chess provided the Parent Questionnaire for assessment of temperament in 3- to 7-year olds. The 72 items of this questionnaire consist of sets of eight questions that tap each of the NYLS dimensions. In each eight-item set, four items inquire about behaviors indicative of upper extremes on the dimensions, and the other four assess behaviors at the lower end of the dimensions. For example, for the Threshold scale, one item is "My child quickly notices and comments on unpleasant smells," and another is "My child ignores loud noises. For example, he/she is the last to complain about music being too loud, sirens, etc." Each item is rated on a 7-point frequency scale.

Questionnaires by Carey and Colleagues

At least until recently, the most frequently used temperament questionnaires were those based on the original nine temperament categories outlined by the NYLS group (Thomas, Chess, Birch, Hertzig, & Korn, 1963). The NYLS research was already well known before Thomas and Chess provided a parental report questionnaire. Within the framework of the NYLS approach, Carey and his collaborators developed the first—and still best-kown—questionnaires. Carey's (1970, 1972) initial effort to capture the NYLS dimensions in a parental report instrument, while yielding some interesting findings, proved psychometrically inadequate on a number of grounds. Readers should not generalize any critiques of that early version to its substantial revision, the Revised Infant Temperament Questionnaire (RITQ; Carey & McDevitt, 1978). Companion questionnaires measure temperament at the toddler, preschool, and school-age levels. With each of these questionnaires, individuals receive scores on the nine NYLS dimensions and are classified as easy, difficult, slow to warm up, or intermediate-difficult in temperamental profile. The difficulty classification depends on scores on the dimensions of Intensity,

Mood, Adaptability, Approach/Withdrawal, and Rhythmicity.

The RITQ (Carey & McDevitt, 1978) includes 95 items and is suitable for infants from 4- to 8-months of age. An illustrative item from the Adaptability scale is "The infant accepts right away any change in place or position of feeding or person giving it." All items are rated on a 1–6 scale anchored by the phrases "almost never" and "almost always." Data on internal consistency, test–retest reliability, and other issues are available in the original publication (Carey & McDevitt, 1978).

The Toddler Temperament Scale (TTS; Fullard, McDevitt, & Carey, 1984) is quite similar to the RITQ in format, with content changed slightly to make the items appropriate for the 12- to 36-month age range. An illustrative item from the Adaptability scale is "The child accepts delays (for several minutes) for desired objects or activities (snacks, treats, gifts)." As in other questionnaires in this series, construction of the TTS involved fashioning items that seemed related to the NYLS dimensions, administering the items to a sample, and retaining items with higher item–total correlations.

McDevitt and Carey (1978) designed the Behavioral Style Questionnaire (BSQ) for use with 3- to 7-year-old children. Again, the items were revised to be age-appropriate. For instance, an Adaptability scale item is "The child is slow to adjust to changes in household rules." Like the RITQ and the TTS, the BSQ was designed to provide a profile of clinically relevant temperamental characteristics in a format that parents can complete in about 30 minutes.

Finally, Hegvik, McDevitt, and Carey (1982) constructed the Middle Childhood Temperament Questionnaire (MCTQ) for use with 8- to 12-year-old children. The characteristics of the newer MCTQ apparently parallel those of its predecessors.

Several problems have been associated with the NYLS approach. For instance, Bates (1987), Buss and Plomin (1984), and Goldsmith and Campos (1982) have argued that the definition of temperament as "behavioral style" may apply to some of the NYLS dimensions (e.g., Intensity), but that other dimensions are actually descriptions of the content of behavior (e.g., Approach/Withdrawal). Another problem is that the use of categories to describe general patterns of temperament results in a loss of valuable information. Furthermore, the item selection procedure used to construct the primary questionnaires did not ensure relative independence of the resulting cases.

Overview of Variations on the Thomas and Chess and the Carey Approaches

Just as Carey first operationalized the Thomas and Chess interview approach in questionnaire format about 20 years ago, other researchers have attempted to improve, shorten, or otherwise adapt the questionnaires devised by Carey and colleagues. Still other questionnaire designers have developed their approaches quite independently of the NYLS framework. Below, we first review those questionnaires related to the NYLS approach, and then describe more independent efforts.

Pedersen's Infant Questionnaire. Besides Carey's questionnaires, one of the earliest approaches to refining questionnaire assessment of the NYLS dimensions was that of Pedersen, Anderson, and Cain (1976; Pedersen, Zaslow, Cain, Anderson, & Thomas, 1980). Their Perception of Baby Temperament (PBT) scale is administered in a sorting format, with the items printed on cards. Although the questionnaire has not been widely used (however, see Affleck, Allen, McGrade, & McQueeny, 1983; Huitt & Ashton, 1982), some of its psychometric properties are promising. Because of the authors' interest in family interaction, all items are appropriate for response by fathers as well as mothers. To deal with possible bias due to social desirability, the authors attempted to write items so that the entire range of possible responses would be perceived as "normal" by parents; furthermore, the items were intended to be nonevaluative. To reduce the possible bias due to acquiescence response sets, half the items on each of the nine scales were worded in the negative direction. The PBT instrument merits additional attention from the field.

Factor Analysis Yielding a Short Form of the Revised Infant Temperament Questionnaire. Sanson et al. (1987) reported a factor analysis of the RITQ (Carey & McDevitt, 1978). After analyzing results from a sample of over 2,400 Australian infants, they adopted a nine-factor solution that accounted for about one-third of the total variance. Factors included Approach; Activity/Reactivity; Food Fussiness; Rhythmicity; Cooperation/ Manageability; Placidity; Threshold; Irritability; and Persistence. Both Rhythmicity and Persistence emerged as relatively pure factors, lending some support to the corresponding NYLS dimensions. However, the remaining factors (even those with labels similar to the original NYLS dimensions) are basically composites of the other seven NYLS dimensions. For example, the new Approach factor consists of items from both the RITQ Approach/Withdrawal and Adaptibility scales, and the new Threshold dimension comprises the original RITQ Distractibility and Threshold items. Items on the RITQ Approach scale contributed to both the new Approach and Food Fussiness factors. Original Adaptability items contributed to the new Approach factor and Cooperation/ Manageability factor. And both the RITQ Activity and Intensity scales split to create two new combinations: Activity/Reactivity and Placidity.

Five of the empirically derived factors (Approach, Cooperation/Manageability, Rhythmicity, Activity/Reactivity, and Threshold) were used by Sanson et al. (1987) to develop a short form of the RITQ (SITQ). The SITQ consists of 30 items and is intended for use with 4- to 8-month-old infants. The five-factor structure was further confirmed by factor analysis of this new short form, and standard measures of reliability were generally superior to those reported for the original RITQ (Carey & McDevitt, 1978).

Validation of the recently developed SITQ largely remains to be undertaken; investigators in need of a brief instrument that can be related to the NYLS framework might consider using it even at this stage of research. However, the reason why we have devoted substantial space to the SITQ research is that it illustrates that the traditional NYLS dimensions are not the most defensible partitions of RITQ item content from a factor-analytic viewpoint. Few other researchers besides Sanson et al. (1987) have used a sufficient number of subjects to justify

a factor analysis of the RITQ items (as opposed to the scales, which are frequently factor-analyzed). Below, we more briefly review other factor-analytic investigations of the NYLS framework. First, however, we should recognize that Thomas and Chess, Carey, and other investigators within their framework do not recognize the factor-analytic criteria of high intrascale and low interscale associations among items as crucial to their conceptualizations. Rather, they favor external criteria, such as evidence for clinical usefulness and predictive power of the existing scales, as much more important.

Other Factor-Analytic Approaches to the New York Longitudinal Study Dimensions. In addition to Sanson et al. (1987), other groups have reported item-based factor analyses of NYLS-derived item content (Bohlin, Hagekull, & Lindhagen, 1981; Lerner, Palermo, Spiro, & Nesselroade, 1982). Results of this work have typically yielded fewer than nine dimensions. For example, Rowe and Plomin (1977) started with the NYLS interview protocols (Thomas et al., 1968). From these descriptions, 54 questionnaire items were designed to assess each of the nine dimensions in children aged 2–6 years. Factor analysis yielded seven factors: Attention Span/Persistence; Sociability; Reactivity; Sleep Rhythmicity; Soothability; Reaction to Food; and Stubbornness. Although some of these seven factors are similar to the original NYLS dimensions, only the Attention Span/Persistence factor clearly matches a NYLS dimension. On the other hand, there are several specific matches in the factors identified by Bohlin et al. (1981), Sanson et al. (1987), and Rowe and Plomin (1977).

The Dimensions of Temperament Scale— Revised. Lerner et al. (1982) reported perhaps the most comprehensive analysis of the content of the original nine NYLS dimensions. Beginning with a pool of almost 500 items, the authors designed the Dimensions of Temperament Scale (DOTS), a temperament questionnaire with virtually the same factor structure for use in infancy, childhood, and adulthood. Items were provisionally retained if they were consistently categorized into the same dimension by a group of raters, if they were potentially useful across the wide age range of infancy through young adulthood, and if they were independent of any particular context. Following this, a second categorization task resulted in a total of 89 items covering nine dimensions. Analyses of variability across the age range and factor analyses resulted in the adoption of a 34-item questionnaire with five factors: Activity Level (limited to activity during sleep, unlike the NYLS dimension); Adaptability/Approach–Withdrawal; Attention-Span/Distractibility; Rhythmicity; and Reactivity (a combination of items from the Activity Level, Intensity, and Threshold dimensions).

The original DOTS was soon replaced by the 54-item Dimensions of Temperament Scale—Revised (DOTS-R; Windle & Lerner, 1986). This seven-scale questionnaire includes the following scales: Activity Level–General; Activity Level–Sleep; Approach–Withdrawal; Flexibility–Rigidity; Attention Span–Distractibility; Mood; Rhythmicity. The items are quite straightforward; for example, a Mood scale item is "My child's mood is generally cheerful." The DOTS-R is available in three forms: a child self-report, a parental report about the child, and an adult self-report. The DOTS-R is really only one component of a more encompassing system for the assessment of adaptive functioning. Included is a questionnaire that taps parents' ideas about temperamental difficulty. Other related instruments measure teachers' and peers' demands regarding temperament (Lerner, Lerner, & Zabski, 1985).

Summary of Approaches Related to the New York Longitudinal Study. Investigators who wish to assess temperament within the tradition of the NYLS have at least three major choices. They may use a combination of interviews and questionnaires developed by Thomas, Chess, and coworkers that cover development from early infancy to young adulthood (Chess & Thomas, 1984; Thomas et al., 1982). Alternatively, they may choose the series of questionnaires by Carey and his colleagues, described above. In choosing either of these options, investigators must recognize that item-based factor analyses have generally suggested that the tempera-

ment domain should be parsed somewhat differently than in the nine NYLS dimensions. They must also recognize that factor analyses of scales generally suggest fewer than nine independent dimensions (e.g., Maziade, Boudreault, Thivierge, Caperaa, & Cote, 1984; Persson-Blennow & McNeil, 1982). These psychometric issues are recognized in the DOTS-R framework, which is applicable throughout much of the lifespan after infancy (Windle, 1988). Most other existing questionnaires owe some of their inspiration to the NYLS, although many of these do not really adopt the NYLS framework. We now proceed to review some of these other instruments.

Bates's Approach

Bates and his colleagues have concentrated on the concept of infant difficulty. Bates, Freeland, and Lounsbury (1979) started with items from the five dimensions defined by Thomas and Chess as related to difficulty: Rhythmicity, Adaptability, Approach/Withdrawal, Mood, and Intensity. Additional items regarding soothability, sociability, and activity level were added. Finally, a single item asked mothers to rate the overall "degree of difficulty" their infants would present to the average mother. Factor analysis of these items yielded four factors. The primary factor, labeled Fussy/Difficult, concerned the degree of fussiness and soothability and contained the overall-degree-of-difficulty item. Other factors were named Unadaptable, Dull (items concerning social responsiveness and activity level), and Unpredictable (similar to Thomas and Chess's Rhythmicity dimension). Thus, in the Bates approach, the concept of difficulty is differentiated into four components, none of which should be equated with difficulty as measured in NYLS-related approaches. Bates's main factor concerns the frequency and intensity of negative affect expression. Unadaptability items and Rhythmicity items are relatively independent (Bates & Bayles, 1984).

The brief instrument that resulted from this factor-analytic approach, the Infant Characteristics Questionnaire (ICQ; 6-month version, used for ages 4–7 months), comprises 24 items, each rated on a 7-point scale. Unlike most other questionnaires, the ICQ is explicitly intended to measure parental perceptions of difficulty, rather than assuming that parental report directly reflects objective infant behavior. As such, Bates entertains the possibility that perceptions of infant difficulty are influenced by maternal personality and experience, and argues that these perceptions inevitably become part of reality for the child (Bates, 1987).

As Bates's research program has expanded longitudinally, the ICQ has also been adapted to yield 32-item versions for 13- and 24-month-olds. These instruments are similar in design and content to the ICQ; however, the scales' names and content vary slightly (Bates & Bayles, 1984; Lee & Bates, 1985). Despite developmentally appropriate changes in the item content of these versions of the ICQ, Lee and Bates (1985) reported a correlation of .57 between maternal perceptions of infant difficulty at 6 and 24 months.

Bates's temperament questionnaires should not be confused with the Maternal Perceptions Questionnaire, which was devised to measure certain aspects of social and cognitive development in 13- and 24-month-olds (Olson, Bates, & Bayles, 1984).

Buss and Plomin's Approach

Buss and Plomin's ideas about temperament are contained in two books published in 1975 and 1984. These books offer reviews of the literature, a theoretical orientation, critiques of other approaches, summaries of their own research, and—most pertinent to this chapter—an approach to assessment of temperament via parental report.

Based on their criteria of early appearance, genetic influence, and stability, Buss and Plomin (1984) suggest three specific dimensions of temperament—Emotionality, Activity, and Sociability (EAS). Impulsivity, a dimension proposed in their original theory (Buss & Plomin, 1975), was dropped after a review of the heritability evidence proved unconvincing. Emotionality is defined as strong arousal in response to environmental events. This arousal is expressed as general distress in early infancy, but becomes differentiated into fear and anger during the first year of life. This emphasis on negative affect closely resembles the concept of difficult temperament discussed by Bates. Activity concerns the preferred level of activity and its tempo. Sociability, the level of preference for being with other people, is similar to the social component of the Approach/Withdrawal dimension discussed by Thomas et al. (1963). According to Buss and Plomin, the sociable child prefers the presence of other individuals and seeks attention from them.

Questionnaire items were written for each of the three theoretical factors, including subcomponents of the Emotionality factor (i.e., items for distress, fear, and anger). Factor analysis verified the a priori assignment. The EAS Temperament Survey for Adults, then, consists of 20 items that are rated on a 5-point scale (see Buss & Plomin, 1984). For children, Buss and Plomin (1984) provided the EAS Temperament Survey for Children: Parental Ratings, which apparently measures the same dimensions as the adult EAS. Finally, the parental rating form has been modified to obtain teacher ratings of first- and second-graders.

Whereas the EAS represents a contraction of their original EASI, another related approach has expanded the EASI. Rowe and Plomin (1977) factor-analyzed a combination of EASI Temperament Survey items and items from the NYLS, yielding the Colorado Childhood Temperament Inventory (CCTI). The CCTI scales are Sociability, Activity, Attention Span/Persistence, Reaction to Food, Emotionality, and Soothability. The CCTI comprises 30 items, each rated on a 5-point scale, and is suitable for 1- to 6-year-old children.

In other related research, Plomin and DeFries (1983) factor-analyzed a short version of the BSQ for 3- to 7-year-old children (McDevitt & Carey, 1978). Nine factors resulted from this analysis, but only Distractibility and Persistence were similar to original NYLS dimensions. A third factor, Sociability/Shyness, was found to be similar to the NYLS dimension of Approach/Withdrawal, but the authors argued that it only involved approach in a social context. Three other factors were not as closely related to the original dimensions: Reaction to Discipline, Emotionality (Distress), and Emotionality (Anger).

Finally, three factors emerged that consisted of only two items each, and did not seem to tap any general behavioral dimension.

An investigator who wishes to adopt the Buss and Plomin approach to assess childhood temperament would now be advised to use the EAS questionnaire (Buss & Plomin, 1984). If a more differentiated picture of the child's temperament is needed, one might employ the longer version of the older EASI-III (Buss & Plomin, 1975) or the CCTI (Rowe & Plomin (1977).

Rothbart's Approach

Theoretical Background. Rothbart has offered a theoretical view of individual differences in temperament as the result of two basic processes: reactivity and self-regulation (Rothbart, in press; Rothbart & Derryberry, 1981). "Reactivity" refers to the physiological response systems, and "self-regulation" refers to basic processes such as attention and approach–avoidance that regulate expressions of individual differences in reactivity. Responses to environmental events are characterized, then, by the intensive and temporal parameters surrounding their expression (e.g., threshold of response, intensity of response, and rise time). Both before and after the construction of her theory, Rothbart devised techniques for temperament assessment.

Infant Behavior Questionnaire. Before the theory was fully elaborated, Rothbart (1981) developed a questionnaire with strong psychometric qualities that measured individual differences in various facets of temperament. She started with an item pool derived from the work of Thomas et al. (1963), Shirley (1933), and other temperament researchers. She added items based on interviews with parents of infants. On the basis of conceptual and item analyses, six relatively independent dimensions were retained: Activity Level; Smiling and Laughter; Fear; Distress to Limitations; Soothability; and Duration of Orienting. Independent, psychometrically adequate measures of the other dimensions (General Negative Emotionality; Threshold; Intensity; Rhythmicity) could not be constructed. In the final form of the Infant Behavior Questionnaire (IBQ),

Activity Level is the only scale that is directly related to the original NYLS conceptualization, in both its general orientation and item content. Among other notable features, the IBQ is the only infant questionnaire that captures positive affectivity independently of negative emotions.

To avoid the necessity of global judgments or problems with long-term recall, Rothbart worded all items to refer to specific behaviors in specific situations, and parents are asked to make judgments regarding the frequency of specific behaviors during the past week. The IBQ consists of 94 items rated on a scale of 1–7, and is designed for use with 3- to 12-month-old infants. The scales have also been used with infants somewhat older than 1 year (e.g., Thompson & Lamb, 1984).

Childhood Behavior Questionnaire. Rothbart (1988) has also developed the Childhood Behavior Questionnaire (CBQ), an unpublished parental report questionnaire for young children past the toddler period. Although the CBQ assesses dimensions similar to those tapped by the IBQ, it also includes more differentiated scales. These more differentiated scales measure typical patterns of attention, activity, and emotional reactivity differentiated into subcomponents (Rothbart, 1988).

Goldsmith's Approach

Using methods and concepts largely derived from Rothbart's approach in the IBQ, Goldsmith developed a questionnaire to measure temperament during the toddler period. The Toddler Behavior Assessment Questionnaire (TBAQ) assesses Activity Level, Social Fearfulness, Anger Proneness, (tendency to express) Pleasure, and Interest/Persistence (Goldsmith, Elliott, & Jaco, 1986). We designed the TBAQ primarily for use with 18- to 24-month-old children. It has been employed in a broader range of 16–36 months.

To illustrate the process of constructing a temperament questionnaire, we discuss the TBAQ here in some detail. We began by compiling a list of responses relevant to each construct that was to be included in the questionnaire. We also formed a list of situations, or contexts, that might elicit these responses. In developing both lists, we strove for a wide variety of content. We then joined responses with appropriate situations to form a preliminary item pool. In doing so, we attempted to minimize overt social desirability in item content, and we keyed a number of items in reverse direction to disrupt acquiescence response sets. We checked the face validity of these items by interviewing a few mothers of toddlers, and made appropriate revisions.

We then administered the set of candidate items to samples of mothers with children in the appropriate age range. Item statistics were computed, and items that showed low correlations with their intended scale (a correlation of .25 served as a general guideline) or that correlated relatively highly with another scale were eliminated. Examining the content of items eliminated led to slight revisions in how the underlying dimensions were conceptualized in the cases of Social Fearfulness and Interest/Persistence.

This process continued for a total of four waves of data collection, with more than one sample assessed in some waves. However, the Interest/Persistence and Anger Proneness scales were used in only the last two waves, which comprised a total of five samples. The samples varied in size, but totaled approximately 500 subjects. We generally considered item statistics in more than one sample before deciding whether to retain or eliminate an item. A consistent goal was to avoid undue narrowing of content while retaining high internal consistency.

Throughout the various phases of construction, estimates of internal consistency (Cronbach's alpha) clustered in the .80s, occasionally reaching the .90s and sometimes falling into the .70s. We adopted the view that interscale correlations should be low but not necessarily near zero. For example, we expected some inverse relationship between the positive- and negative-affect scales. Averaged across two samples, the absolute value of interscale correlations ranged from .01 to .32 ($M = .13$), with the highest correlation between the Pleasure and Interest/Persistence scales. Early results showed significant but modest agreement between fathers and mothers; sources of parental disagreement are under investigation.

In another sample, we used an earlier version of the TBAQ in conjunction with Fullard et al.'s (1984) TTS (which measures Thomas and Chess's nine dimensions of temperament), and Buss and Plomin's (1975) EASI. In the maternal report, the TBAQ Activity Level scales correlated highly with the Activity Level and Activity scales on the other two questionnaires, respectively. TBAQ Social Fearfulness correlated highly with TTS Approach and EASI Sociability when scores were reflected. TBAQ Social Fearfulness and TTS Mood showed a correlation in the .30s. In the reports of day care teachers on these same children, similar results held for activity, but correlations involving the TBAQ Social Fearfulness scale were weaker. The data also demonstrated substantial discriminant validity, in the sense that TBAQ scales were not associated with conceptually unrelated scales on other questionnaires.

To our knowledge, the TBAQ is the first childhood temperament questionnaire to include a validity scale. Our basic approach to avoiding biased responding derives from Rothbart's strategy in constructing the IBQ (see Rothbart, 1981). Rothbart's strategy involved asking the respondents to report behavioral frequencies during a recent, specified time interval rather than to make global judgments. Her items also carefully specify the situational context for each response. Furthermore, Rothbart sought to avoid language that would elicit a social desirability response set. We followed each of these practices but judged that a direct measure of social desirability response bias would be a useful addition.

A well-known dilemma in measuring social desirability is that some traits (such as Pleasure) are more valued by society (and caregivers) than others (such as Anger Proneness). To help unconfound biased responding from the desirability differences inherent in society's evaluation of different characteristics, we constructed a content-balanced Social Desirability scale. We borrowed the basic idea for this scale from Tellegen (1982), but implemented it differently than he did on the Multidimensional Personality Questionnaire. We chose two pairs of items from each of the five TBAQ scales. For the Social Desirability scale, all four items are keyed in the socially desirable direction. However, this keying results in two of the items (one from each pair) being keyed toward high scores on the temperamental dimension in question and the remaining member of each pair being keyed toward low scores. Furthermore, we attempted to match—very roughly—the situation and response for the members of each pair. If this strategy was successful, a high score on Social Desirability would be likely to be obtained only if a respondent contradicted himself or herself regarding the child's behavior.

To investigate the extent to which scale scores are affected by social desirability, we estimated correlations of Social Desirability with the five content scales of the TBAQ. Two samples yielded the following average correlations: −.22 (Activity Level); .45 (Pleasure); −.21 (Social Fearfulness); −.07 (Anger Proneness); and .32 (Interest/Persistence). These values should not be inflated by part–whole correlations, because half the items in common with each substantive scale were reversed, as explained above. (An exception to this generalization concerns a few items that are not scored on any substantive scale.) The results would appear to implicate social desirability response sets to some extent, particularly for the Pleasure scale. This conclusion is, of course, subject to the validity of the procedures we followed, and much additional research on the validity scales needs to be done.

The TBAQ would, of course, be the appropriate instrument to use when following a sample previously tested with the IBQ. The corresponding scales are as follows (IBQ scale vs. TBAQ scale): Distress to Limitations versus Anger Proneness; Smiling and Laughter versus Pleasure; Fear versus Social Fearfulness; Duration of Orienting versus Interest/Persistence; Activity Level versus Activity Level. There is no TBAQ counterpart to the IBQ Soothability scale. Despite the corresponding scales, the user should be aware that the TBAQ items were not derived from the IBQ items, with a few exceptions. The scale content varies in an age-appropriate fashion, and the underlying nature of the constructs is probably not identical. In general, the TBAQ contains a greater variety of item content. In particular, TBAQ Social Fearfulness has substantially more shyness-related content than IBQ Fear.

In addition to their questionnaires, Rothbart and Goldsmith have provided observa-tional and laboratory-based techniques to assess temperament. These are described in a later section.

Non-English-Language Temperament Questionnaires

Some of the best temperament research is done outside the United States, the United Kingdom, Canada, and Australia. Thus far (including the advice offered in Figure 11.1), we have neglected non-English-language questionnaires. However, some of these questionnaires are available in English translation, and the measurement research—in whatever language—is relevant to anyone who needs to assess temperament. Questionnaires from Chinese (e.g., Hsu, Soong, Stigler, Hong, & Liang, 1981), German (e.g., Meyer, 1985), Italian (e.g., Attili, Alcini, & Felaco, in press), Japanese (e.g., Windle, Iwawaki, & Lerner, 1988), Polish (e.g., Strelau, 1983), and Russian (e.g., Rusalov, 1987) investigators, as well as researchers of other nationalities, are beyond the scope of this chapter, in part because many of them are intended for adults and in part because some are translations and adaptations of questionnaires that we have discussed. See Kohnstamm (in press) for a review that relates temperament to culture. Some of the best non-English-language assessment work has been done in Sweden, where Persson-Blennow and McNeil (1979, 1982) developed brief questionnaires to assess the nine NYLS dimensions. However, we confine our more detailed treatment here to another program of research in Sweden.

Hagekull and her colleagues developed temperament questionnaires for the infancy and toddler periods (Hagekull, 1985; Hagekull, Lindhagen, & Bohlin, 1980). In an attempt to replicate empirically the nine NYLS dimensions, Bohlin et al. (1981) started with the original Infant Temperament Questionnaire (Carey, 1970). Principal-components analyses utilizing items with acceptable response frequencies yielded nine factors that were not very similar to the nine NYLS dimensions, according to the authors. This item base was expanded by adding items suggested during parental interviews to arrive at the 54-item Baby Behavior Questionnaire (BBQ), for use with 3- to 10-month-old infants. A seven-factor solution was adopted, accounting for one-third of the total item variance. These factors included Intensity/ Activity (a measure of the activity and intensity aspects of behavior in different situations); Regularity (involving the regularity of different behaviors and biological functions); Approach/Withdrawal (including positive and negative reactions to strangers and new situations); Sensory Sensitivity (involving the strength of reaction to strong sensory stimulation); Attentiveness (to environmental stimulation); Manageability (an interpretation of a group of items describing mood, endurance, activity, and acceptance of new situations); and Sensitivity (to new food). Most of the nine NYLS content dimensions can be discerned in this seven-factor solution. However, only two dimensions show direct correspondence: Regularity and Approach/ Withdrawal. Other NYLS dimensions combined or split. For example, the new Intensity/Activity dimension consists of items from the original dimensions of Intensity (of reaction) and Activity Level, and the new Manageability dimension contains items similar to the original Mood and Adaptability dimensions. On the other hand, both the new dimensions of Sensory Sensitivity and Attentiveness consist of items from the original Threshold dimension. The BBQ was standardized separately for younger and older infants. The Toddler Behavior Questionnaire is similar in structure and format to the BBQ, with age-appropriate changes in item content.

Teacher Report Questionnaires

In addition to their parent assessment of temperament, Thomas and Chess (1977) designed a 64-item Teacher Temperament Questionnaire (TTQ) to measure eight of the original NYLS dimensions in school children from 3 to 7 years old. The TTQ is a companion to Thomas and Chess's (1977) Parent Questionnaire. Many of its items refer to classroom situations: for example, "When class is promised something in the future (trip, party, etc.), this child keeps reminding the teacher of it" (Persistence); and "Child will get up and perform before the class (sing, recite, etc.) with no hesitation, even the first time" (Approach/Withdrawal).

Keogh's Approach

When study designs require teachers to rate the temperament of several children, brevity of the questionnaire becomes essential. In part to meet this requirement, Keogh and her colleagues revised the Thomas and Chess (1977) questionnaire. Their work in this area is some of the most complete and psychometrically sophisticated available. Keogh and colleagues improved item statement and attended to factor structure in constructing a short form of the TTQ. In the school setting, three temporally stable factors, interpreted as Task Orientation, Personal Social Flexibility, and Reactivity, accounted for the covariance among the eight original scales. A total of 23 items were selected to tap these three factors. Substantial research supports the utility of this revised teacher rating scale. For instance, temperamental factors (particularly Task Orientation) have been related to classroom decisions and teachability ratings of the young students, even when other relevant variables such as IQ were taken into account (Keogh, 1982; Pullis & Cadwell, 1982).

Martin's Approach

Martin has carried out another extensive program of instrument development for the school setting; his work also began with the NYLS approach. Martin, Nagle, and Paget (1983) investigated associations among temperament variables, classroom behavior, teacher attitudes, and academic achievement. Other studies have investigated longitudinal prediction of both achievement and later temperament from preschool temperament (Martin & Holbrook, 1985; Martin et al., 1986). The batteries used in these studies are published commercially, and well-documented manuals are available (Martin, 1988).

Other Options for Report of Temperament by Teachers

Other instruments have teacher forms that have been constructed without extensive derivation in the school setting. For instance, Buss and Plomin's EAS has a 20-item teacher version that is very similar to the parent version. Initial studies with this instrument are underway in the Colorado Adoption Project (Plomin, DeFries, & Fulker, 1988). In addition, the DOTS-R (discussed above) has a teacher version that has been used in research (Lerner et al., 1985). Of course, researchers also have the option of simply using instruments designed for parents and omitting items that the teacher has no opportunity to observe. This strategy may be defensible when school or day care behavior is not the focus of study. In such cases, the teacher is simply used as an informant to validate or supplement parental report or objective report (see Eaton, 1983; Goldsmith, Rieser-Danner, & Briggs, 1989). In a given study, one must also consider the virtues of employing a teacher report questionnaire that focuses on aspects of social behavior beyond temperament (e.g., Roper & Hinde, 1979).

Final Caveats about Questionnaire Assessment of Temperament

In summarizing issues about temperament assessment using the questionnaire approach, we would emphasize three psychometric concerns. First, selection of the initial item pool, always a rational decision, largely determines the characteristics of scales derived from the pool. If one begins with the NYLS content, there is no possibility of discovering aspects of temperament overlooked in the NYLS. Second, various scale construction approaches contain different assumptions about the independence of temperament dimensions "in nature," the correlation of individual differences in parameters of expression across dimensions, and the "breadth" of temperament dispositions. Third, some attempt should be made either to minimize or to assess parental response sets, especially when the poles of the dimensions being measured differ in social desirability.

In our judgment, questionnaire assessment of temperament—although often maligned—is a worthwhile enterprise. However, it must be conceded that certain classes of problems are common to questionnaire approaches. The ratings are somewhat subjective; they are subject to parental response sets; and the behaviors being rated, although intended to reflect infant characteristics, are

seldom independent of the interaction between caregiver and infant (Rothbart & Goldsmith, 1985). Several studies show that parental perceptions of temperament can be predicted to some degree by parental characteristics uncorrelated with actual infant behavior (e.g., Crockenberg & Acredolo, 1983; Bates et al., 1979). Thus, the need for alternatives to assessment via the parent is pressing.

LABORATORY AND HOME OBSERVATION TECHNIQUES

As objective assessment methodology becomes better established in many realms of social and developmental inquiry, the need for similarly objective temperamental measures of temperament increases. To address that need, researchers have begun to assess temperament not only in the home and school, but also in the laboratory. We begin our discussion of objective techniques with laboratory methods, defined by the investigator's attempt to elicit specific reactions thought to index temperamental dispositions. These methods are widely used to measure adaptive functioning during the neonatal period, and such measures are sometimes conceptualized as temperamental. We shall not treat this issue; however, investigators interested in neonatal temperament should consult Riese (1987) and references therein.

Issues in Laboratory Assessment

Laboratory assessment of temperament requires attention to a number of measurement issues; some of these issues have counterparts in questionnaire techniques whereas others are specific to the laboratory. In the laboratory, one can minimize the parents' role in temperament assessment, but this factor must be balanced against concerns about ecological validity. By its nature, temperament cannot be judged from single instances of behavior. However, researchers must guard against carryover effects in repeated laboratory testing. In addition, the desirability of incorporating measures of stability and cross-situational generality into the assessment process is also clear, from a consensus of temperament theorists (Goldsmith et al., 1987).

The laboratory approach has some problems that differ from those of more traditional experimental work in infant development. For example, to assess temperament, laboratory paradigms should be modified to maximize individual differences. This can be accomplished by devising graded measuring scales that show high variance for dependent variables and by adjusting the difficulty levels of dichotomous dependent variables. In addition, both internal-consistency reliability and stability should be computed for laboratory measures, just as one would do for questionnaire scales. To achieve satisfactory internal consistency and an adequate sampling for situations, a fairly extensive series of laboratory paradigms is necessary.

Situational context is crucial in laboratory assessment of temperament. As mentioned above, a given behavior that is expressive of temperament can also serve other functions unrelated to temperament. Therefore, in the laboratory, the aim of temperament assessment should be to focus both the stimulus situation and the behavioral coding so as to lessen the probability of the elicited behavior being unrelated to temperament. For example, if the researcher wishes to use crying as a measure of fearfulness, the infant should not be in a tired state that could produce fussiness. A slightly more complex precaution related to situational context involves discrimination among various dimensions of temperament. For example, in attempting to assess anger during a frustrating situation, it is important to avoid novel elements in the situation that might elicit fear. (Obviously, similar considerations apply to mixing novel and frustrating contexts in the construction of questionnaire items.)

Description of Multidimensional, Standardized Laboratory Assessments

Goldsmith and Rothbart's Battery

The Laboratory Temperament Assessment Battery (LAB-TAB) is an objective, behaviorally based, theory-oriented laboratory assessment battery for studying infant and toddler temperament. It comprises standardized procedures for eliciting and recording infant behavior, and can be conducted in typical videotape-equipped laboratories. The full LAB-TAB assessment sequence yields scores for the following dimensions of temperament: Fearfulness, Anger Proneness, Pleasure/Joy, Interest/Persistence, and Activity Level. There are two versions of LAB-TAB, one for prelocomotor infants who can reach and another for those who crawl proficiently or walk. A detailed manual describing LAB-TAB procedures is now available, and standardization, reliability, and validity data will be added to it (Goldsmith & Rothbart, 1988).

LAB-TAB is designed to be used in a developmental research laboratory without atypical or expensive equipment. The standard setting consists of two experimental rooms and one control room with windows suitable for videotaping. One of the rooms should be similar to a living room, whereas the other can be much smaller, perhaps like an interviewing room. To minimize distractions, some episodes are best carried out in a small, partially enclosed booth that has windows for the presentation of stimuli.

At least one video recording system is necessary. In our laboratory, a programmable timing light cues participants to change activities and aids scoring. For cuing the mother as to her role and instructing her about how to react to unexpected behavior from her child, we use a small FM transceiver for some episodes. We have rejected numerous ideas for "high-tech" enhancement of stimulus presentation and scoring, so that the episodes can be used widely and economically.

Two experimenters are sufficient to carry out most LAB-TAB episodes. One female experimenter interacts with the mother and child during a warm-up period, which typically lasts about 10 minutes, and then administers the five to seven episodes that can typically be completed during a single visit. Testing should cease if the child becomes fatigued or drowsy. The LAB-TAB procedures assume that the primary caregiver accompanies the child to the laboratory.

The Fearfulness episodes include (1) approach of a remote-controlled toy; (2) reaction to an unpredictable mechanical toy; (3) reaction to a stranger approach; and (4) reaction to display of facial masks. Anger episodes include reactions in the following situations: (1) gentle arm restraint by parent; (2) attractive toy placed behind barrier; (3) brief maternal separation; and (4) confinement in a car seat. Comparable episodes tap the temperamental dimensions of Pleasure/Joy, Interest/Persistence, and Activity Level. A subset of the episodes occur in a living-room-like setting with few constraints on the infant's behavior; these episodes are intended to give LAB-TAB some of the features of home observations.

In total, there are 20 settings or episodes, four per dimension, that form the context for assessment. Sometimes the stimulus is presented on multiple trials. To facilitate scoring, the longer episodes are typically divided into shorter intervals called "epochs." Within each epoch or trial, a number of infant responses, such as smiling, reaching, or crying, are scored. Sometimes the presence or absence of a response is simply noted; however, more often parameters of the response, such as latency, duration, and intensity, are scored.

With the availability of LAB-TAB, it no longer will be necessary to develop laboratory measures of temperament anew for every study, and it will be easier to compare results from different laboratories. Appropriate standardization data on large samples will allow researchers to assign more accurate scores, rather than to rely on standardization in individual samples. At its current early stage of development, the validity of LAB-TAB remains to be established.

The Louisville Twin Study Approach

Another general, laboratory-based approach to the assessment of temperament was designed for the Louisville Twin Study (Matheny & Wilson, 1981; Wilson & Matheny, 1983). Several brief vignettes confront the infant with specific opportunities for interaction with examiners and engagement in play. For instance, one vignette is standardized procedure for observing cuddling. Another is a visible barrier task in which an attractive toy is taken away from the infant. In these and other vignettes, several behavioral categories are rated; most relevant to temperament are emotional tone, attention, activity, and orientation to staff (social

avoidance vs. approach). Each of these dimensions is rated every 2 minutes from videotaped records; acceptable levels of interrater agreement have been obtained. The procedure yields summary scores reflecting both central tendency and variability across the rating intervals. Emotional tone has been the focus of the Louisville researchers, as well as others who have adopted this approach (Gunnar, Mangelsdorf, Kestenbaum, Lang, & Larson, 1988).

The same approach has been extended for use with 36- and 48-month-olds (Matheny, 1987). The 30-minute procedure begins with a brief period of mother–infant interaction, followed by a short separation and several short structured vignettes when an examiner interacts with the child. Ratings on scales of 1–9 are recorded every 2 minutes on the dimensions of Emotional Tone, Threshold (of responsiveness), Attentiveness, Surgency, Activity, Assertiveness, and Orientation to Cotwin (included for specific purposes of the original study). One might view these dimensions as encompassing not only temperament, but also early social aspects of childhood personality. These dimensions are not orthogonal; factor analysis yields two or three vectors, the most salient of which is labeled Surgency. High scorers on Surgency in the laboratory exhibited rapid responses, forceful interactions, high activity, attention, and positive emotional tone. Matheny (1987) observed moderate 1-year stability ($r = .45$) for the Surgency factor. At each age, Matheny found modest convergence with a similar broad Surgency-like factor from the BSQ.

Other Laboratory-Based Approaches

Approaches to the Study of Single Temperamental Constructs

In addition to the more comprehensive approaches, such as LAB-TAB and the Louisville procedure, several investigators have devised laboratory-based procedures to assess particular temperament-like characteristics. To represent this area of assessment research, we describe one such approach in substantial detail. Kagan, Reznick, and colleagues developed extensive laboratory procedures to assess temperamental inhibition (e.g., Kagan, Reznick, & Snidman, 1986). To identify children who vary in behavioral inhibition (increased withdrawal or longer latency to approach unfamiliar situations, people, etc.), they constructed a full set of laboratory procedures to be used at varying ages (e.g., Garcia-Coll, Kagan, & Reznick, 1984; Kagan, Reznick, Clarke, Snidman, & Garcia-Coll, 1984). At 21 months of age, infants are scored in terms of their reactions to a series of six episodes to be moderately unfamiliar to the age group. First, mother and infant are merely involved in a warm-up session that includes the presence of an experimenter collecting standard background information. Next, infant, mother, and experimenter participate in a 5-minute freeplay session, during which mother and experimenter interact with the infant as little as possible. At the end of this 5-minute period, the experimenter models three specific acts with toys (varying in complexity), and an additional 5 minutes of free play are observed. The fourth and fifth episodes include the infant's reactions to an unfamiliar adult and an unfamiliar object (a robot), respectively. Finally, the sixth episode includes separation from the mother. Each episode is scored for the presence of inhibited behaviors; based on the total number of such behaviors exhibited, each child is classified as inhibited, uninhibited, or neither. Furthermore, each child receives an inhibition score for each episode and an overall inhibition score. Garcia-Coll and colleagues (1984) reported significant positive correlations for inhibition scores across the six episodes within a testing session and a correlation of .63 for overall inhibition scores across a 1-month period. However, only 68% of infants classified as inhibited during the first session were also classified as consistently inhibited across the six episodes of the second session.

At 31 months of age, toddlers are observed both in the home and in a standard laboratory situation. The home visit consists of 30 minutes of free play with the mother and experimenter in the same room. The laboratory situation is also a 30-minute free-play session, but includes the presence of a peer and the peer's mother as compared to the presence of an experimenter. Based on seven variables coded during each of these two episodes, behavioral inhibition scores are calculated for each toddler for each session. Concurrent overall inhibition scores for the two sessions were not significantly related for the entire group, but behavioral inhibition scores from the home visit and the laboratory visit at 31 months of age were positively correlated with behavioral inhibition scores at 21 months of age's (r's = .39 and .66, respectively). Specifically, infants with higher inhibition scores at 21 months showed longer latencies to interact with unfamiliar home visitors at 31 months of age, interacted with them less frequently, and spent more time not playing at all.

Peer sessions have also been used by these investigators to classify the degree of behavioral inhibition shown by 4-year-olds (e.g., Kagan et al., 1984). Unlike the earlier peer session, however, behavioral inhibition scores at 4 years of age actually consisted of two clusters of variables: inhibited behavior scores and uninhibited behavior scores, each being derived from objectively scored behaviors. In a longitudinal follow-up, Kagan and colleagues (1984) reported that behavioral inhibition at 21 months of age predicted both inhibited and uninhibited behavior with peers (in the appropriate directions) and maternal Q-sort descriptions of their children at 4 years of age.

Finally, at 5½ years of age, a series of laboratory tasks, peer sessions, and school observation sessions yielded separate indices of behavioral inhibition, including peer play inhibition, laboratory inhibition, school inhibition, and risk avoidance (Reznick et al., 1986). An overall aggregate inhibition score was also calculated. Substantial predictability of these inhibition scores at 5½ years from inhibition scores at 21 months and 4 years of age has been reported (see Reznick et al., 1986).

Naturalistic Observation Techniques

Home observations are the primary form of naturalistic observation. Although such observations allow an assessment of behavior as it occurs in a relatively natural context, there are distinct problems associated with these measures. For example, the very presence of an observer in the home alters the environment in ways that are not easily measured. Furthermore, limited periods of observation often reduce the possibility of observing critical instances of specific behaviors (e.g., fear or anger). For a more complete discussion of the advantages and disadvantages associated with this method, see Rothbart and Goldsmith (1985).

Home observations typically involve 1–3 hours of observation by one or more trained observers. Observers are expected to remain unobtrusive at all times, and, in some instances, the observers simply apply the type of rating scales typically used in parental report questionnaires. Thus, trained observers rate infants and children on all relevant items after the observation period is over. On the other hand, observers are frequently trained to record the occurrence of specific infant/child behaviors according to a behavioral coding scheme.

Brief Illustrations of Observational Approaches

Rothbart (1986) reported home observations of Activity Level, Smiling and Laughter, Fear, Distress to Limitations, and Vocal Activity at 3, 6, and 9 months of age. These dimensions correspond closely to her IBQ scales. Observations were conducted for 3 days at each age, and the average score across all 3 days for each dimension was used as the observation score for each age. In assessing behaviors associated with each of these dimensions, Rothbart used three types of data: weighted frequencies, simple frequencies, and frequencies/durations involving context information. Interrater correlations for observation scores ranged from .56 (Distress to Limitations) to .90 (Activity Level).

In initial validity studies for the ICQ, Bates et al. (1979) collected home observations on infants 5–7 months of age. First, observers rated the frequency and duration of specific infant behaviors such as crying. Interrater agreement ranged from .57 to .99. Factor analysis of these observation variables yielded three factors: Fussiness, Negative versus Fun, and Soothability. In addition, observers rated infants on items from the ICQ. In a later study, Bates and Bayles (1984) used trained home observers both to record molecular events and to make more subjective ratings of the child's behavior

(similar to the ratings made by parents) at 6, 13, and 24 months of age. Composite scores based on factor analyses were used to summarize the molecular data. Infant behavioral factors at 6 months of age included Happy and Active, Reach and Gaze at Mother, Frown, and Fuss/Cry. At 13 months, the appropriate factors were Socially Demanding, Object Communication, Persists, and Happy Play. At 24 months, the corresponding factors were Verbal Communication, Trouble, Negative Emotion, Compliance, Disengaged, and Mastery Attempts. From these factor labels, one readily understands that Bates's home observations capture aspects of social and motivational behavior well beyond the usual boundaries of temperament.

Bornstein et al. (1986) reported promising preliminary results linking new home observation techniques to maternal reports of temperament. This approach is unique in that the same 62 behavioral items are assessed in three ways: in the typical questionnaire fashion (with items phrased in a general way—"My baby usually . . ."); by observers after a 2-hour observation session; and by mothers after the same 2-hour observation session. In the third case, the mother rates the infant on the basis of only the behaviors that occurred during the 2-hour session. The opportunity for deriving multisource measures is obvious. Borstein et al.'s approach capitalizes on some strengths of the laboratory approaches by alternating structured vignettes (during which behaviors are rated) and free-play periods (during which frequency counts are made). The 62 items comprise five a priori dimensions: Positive Affect, Negative Affect, Persistence, Motor Responsivity, and Soothability. Further evaluation of this promising approach awaits empirical investigation.

Activity level is a widely accepted dimension of temperament that is particularly easy to assess under naturalistic conditions. In addition to being measured by raters, activity level can also be measured by an "actometer," a self-winding, mechanical instrument that records frequency of movement. Eaton (1983) investigated the reliability and validity of actometer measures in a study of nursery school children who wore actometers during free-play periods. Average scores, based on a median of 4.7 hours of free play, were used as the activity level measure. Results suggested that activity level as measured by actometers is a valid individual-difference variable in young children. Variability between children accounted for much more of the variance in activity level scores than did variability between instruments or sessions. Furthermore, aggregation greatly improved reliability. Reliability of a single actometer reading was only .33, but reliability rose to .70 with five or more actometer readings, and with nine sessions reliability was approximately .80. Adequate reliabilities have been reported for an infant sample as well (Eaton & Dureski, 1986).

Results such as these support the use of objective measurement techniques under naturalistic conditions, but further point out the importance of aggregation of data points in the search for stable estimates of behavior (Epstein, 1980; Rushton, Brainerd, & Pressley, 1983).

Potential of Observational Measures of Temperament

Optimally, home observations of temperament would circumvent potential biases in parental report while drawing upon an extensive, ecologically valid base of behavior. There are several obstacles to realizing this potential. At least two and probably more sessions are needed for a representative sampling of behavior. And sometimes representative samples are not enough, because certain rarer behavioral reactions—such as angry protest or fearful withdrawal—may be particularly informative regarding temperament. Because temperament is conceived of more as an "individual" than as a "relational" construct (Stevenson-Hinde, 1986), it is desirable to disentangle infant actions from caregiver actions. This may be particularly difficult to accomplish in the home. Another obstacle is the difficulty of establishing that the observer's presence does not alter typical behavior in the home. Thus, we cannot strongly recommend unstructured observations in the home for temperament assessment. Of course, other aspects of socio-emotional development may be optimally captured in the home.

EMPIRICAL EVALUATION OF MEASUREMENT ISSUES

The most important evidence about any measurement device is how it fares empirically. Validation is a process that is never completed, and no existing temperament instrument can be considered extremely well validated. This section reviews current validity evidence. The review is by no means exhaustive; more literature appears each month. We have, however, attempted to gather representative data for instruments that researchers are most likely to use. We have confined our review to validity issues internal to the construct of temperament: agreement and convergence across different respondents and observers and across different measurement instruments. Because our focus is on assessment, we have not attempted to treat the more complex literature on external validity (see Bates, 1987).

Agreement across Respondents on Questionnaires

Mother–Father Agreement

Ten years ago, most investigators would undoubtedly have expected high agreement between mothers and fathers on the temperamental characteristics of their offspring. However, experience has tempered our expectations. Behavior that is expressive of early temperament seems to be more sensitive to contextual demands than a naive theory of temperament would have predicted. Correspondingly, the impact of different parents may be stronger than generally was supposed.

Overall, moderate levels of parental agreement have been found using infant temperament questionnaires; correlations seldom exceed the .40–.60 range. For example, Bates et al. (1979) observed moderate but significant agreement correlations for all four ICQ factors (.60, .40, .41, and .38 for Fussy/Difficult, Unadaptable, Dull, and Unpredictable, respectively). Furthermore, Bates and

Bayles (1984) reported average correlations between mother and father ICQ ratings (across 6- and 13-month ratings) that ranged from .39 for Dull to .61 for the Fussy/Difficult dimension.

In another investigation of mother–father agreement, Field, Vega-Lahr, Scafidi, and Goldstein (1987) asked parents of 8-month-old infants to complete the CCTI (Rowe & Plomin, 1977). Results revealed significant and low to moderately high correlations for all six dimensions (Emotionality, $r = .28$; Activity, $r = .33$; Attention Span/Persistence, $r = .33$; Reaction to Food, $r = .40$; Soothability, $r = .45$; and Sociability, $r = .72$). Lyon and Plomin (1981) investigated mother–father agreement on all 11 subscales of Buss and Plomin's (1975) EASI by asking both parents to rate both members of a set of twins. Agreement coefficients ranged from .16 to .57 (uncorrected for reliability). In a study with a much narrower focus on behavioral inhibition, Garcia-Coll et al. (1984) reported a correlation of .66 between mother and father reports of Approach/Withdrawal on McDevitt and Carey's (1978) TTS. The subjects in this study, however, had been selected as extreme on the inhibition dimension.

In the Denver Twin Temperament Study, Goldsmith and Campos (1986) observed low parental agreement on most of Rothbart's IBQ scales. Several precautions designed to guard against "contamination" of ratings might have contributed to the low agreement. In this study, there was moderate, significant agreement for scales that tapped hedonically negative or active motoric behavior. The authors suggested that these more overt aspects of temperament might elicit stronger consensus. In addition, they measured parental personality as a potential biasing factor in perception and report of infant temperament. No strong biases were uncovered. See Goldsmith et al. (in press) for details.

Parent–Teacher Agreement

We should not expect the reports of regular teachers, who see children only in the school setting with its strong behavioral constraints (where certain behaviors are not observable),

to agree strongly with parental reports based on more extensive experience.

Some examples of parent–teacher agreement illustrate the results. Eaton (1983) demonstrated particularly strong agreement; he found that parental and teacher ratings of Activity Level on Plomin and Rowe's CCTI correlated .73. Furthermore, actometer scores were significantly correlated wtih staff rankings ($r = .69$) to approximately the same extent that actometer readings correlated with parental ratings ($r = .75$). Field and Greenberg (1982) reported very low to moderate correlations between mother and/or father ratings and teacher ratings on Carey and McDevitt's RITQ. The average correlation between mothers and teachers for all nine NYLS dimensions was .20 for infants (range = .04–.33), and for fathers and teachers the average was .35 (range = .17–.54). The magnitude of the relations was a bit higher in the toddler and preschool age groups. That is, the mother–teacher agreement averaged .35 (range = .20–.56) and the father–teacher mean was .39 (range = .16–.67). Using Rothbart's IBQ, we (Goldsmith & Rieser-Danner, 1986) reported results similar to those observed by Goldsmith and Campos (1986) for parental agreement: moderate mother–teacher agreement for scales related to negative affect and activity, but virtually no agreement for the other scales. We (Goldsmith & Rieser-Danner, 1986) also examined teacher–mother agreement on Bates's ICQ and Carey and McDevitt's RITQ, with the same outcome of moderate to low convergence.

In summary, parents and teachers do agree about temperament, but only to a modest degree for most dimensions. Undoubtedly, different norms for temperamental behavior, different sets of behaviors in the home and school contexts, and the difficulty of designing an instrument that is appropriate for both teachers and parents contribute to the lack of agreement. Also, different child characteristics are salient for teachers versus parents. For example, the child's persistence and attention span are probably more salient to the teacher than the parent (Keogh, 1986), whereas negative affectivity is a more overriding concern for the parent.

Convergence across Methods of Assessment

A general principle of measurement is that observed scores should primarily be a function of the construct under study (temperament) rather than the method of measurement. Thus, it is essential to demonstrate convergence across different reliable methods of measuring the same temperamental construct (Campbell & Fiske, 1959). Of course, when we fail to find convergence between two methods in a given study, it is difficult to know which method (if not both) is at fault. As the validity literature grows, the nexus of successes and failures at demonstrating convergence suggests the flawed methods. One must also bear in mind the possibility that some putative temperamental characteristics may simply not possess the requisite stability or cross-situational applicability to show convergence in typical study designs.

In the following sections, we treat relationships across different assessment methods. As in previous sections, our review is representative rather than exhaustive.

Convergence across Questionnaires

In one of the first reports of questionnaire convergence, Bates et al. (1979) compared the ICQ with the original Carey ITQ (a 70-item questionnaire based on the content of the Thomas and Chess interview procedures). Six specific predictions regarding which particular scales should be correlated (based on item content) were all confirmed, with moderate correlations ranging in size from −.25 to .39. For example, the ICQ factor of Fussy/Difficult correlated with Carey ITQ scales of (low) Intensity and (negative) Mood.

Furthermore, the scales of the 13-month version of Bates's ICQ have been correlated with Rothbart's IBQ (Rieser-Danner, 1986). Infants rated higher on the ICQ Fussy/Difficult factor were viewed by their mothers as higher in gross motor activity, as more likely to show distress in a novel situation (Fear), and as higher on Distress to Limitations. Less adaptable infants (as rated by the ICQ) were also rated as higher on Activity

Level and Fear, and as lower on Soothability. Finally, an overall positive versus negative affect composite from the IBQ significantly predicted all of the global dimensions from Bates's questionnaire ($r's = -.37$ to $-.48$).

In the study mentioned above of children high or low on behavioral inhibition, Garcia-Coll et al. (1984) reported a correlation of .72 between maternal reports of Approach/Withdrawal on the TTS and an index of behavioral inhibition based on maternal interview responses.

The most extensive study of cross-questionnaire convergence thus far is our own (Goldsmith & Rieser-Danner, 1986; Goldsmith et al., 1989). Selected results are provided in Table 11.1. For the three sets of comparisons in the table, cross-questionnaire convergence tends to lie within the range of correlations between .50 and .75. The content area of temperament and the age of the children being rated seem not to affect the degree of convergence. This agreement is impressive, given that reliabilities of the scales seldom exceed .80. Of course, we have presented the results for only the pairs of scales that seem most directly comparable in content.

What can we conclude from these results and other similar results in the literature? Are scales of the same name more or less interchangeable? No, but they sometimes are. Unfortunately, so are some scales with different names.

Convergence between Parental Questionnaires and Various Types of Observer Ratings

Generally, correlations between parental reports and observer ratings of infant behavior are quite small, rarely accounting for more than 15% of the variance (Bates, 1987). However, one of the primary problems with this kind of research is the inability to provide an observer with an observational base that approximates the parent's extensive experience with the child. Research of this sort can be classified in several ways. Observer ratings may be made on scales similar to the usual questionnaires completed by parents. Alternatively, observer ratings may be more molecular in nature than the parental ratings,

TABLE 11.1. Cross-Questionnaire Correspondence Analyses

	Maternal report	Modified teacher report
Withdrawal- and fear-related scales		
IBQ Fear × ICQ Unadaptable	.60	.51
IBQ Fear × RITQ Approach/Withdrawal	.69	.73
IBQ Unadaptable × RITQ Approach/Withdrawal	.64	.66
TTS Approach/Withdrawal × EASI Sociability	−.46	−.56
BSQ Approach/Withdrawal × EASI Sociability	−.47	−.71
BSQ Approach/Withdrawal × DOTS Adaptability/ Approach–Withdrawal (negative)	.59	.46
EASI Sociability × DOTS Adaptability/Approach– Withdrawal (negative)	−.49	−.53
Negative-affect-related scales		
IBQ Distress to Limitations × ICQ Fussy/Difficult	.63	.66
IBQ Distress to Limitations × RITQ Mood (negative)	.54	.72
ICQ Fussy/Difficult × RITQ Mood (negative)	.44	.74
TTS Mood (negative) × EASI Emotionality	.52	.45
BSQ Mood (negative) × EASI Emotionality	.69	.68
BSQ Mood (negative) × DOTS Irritability	.35	.56
EASI Emotionality × DOTS Irritability	.55	.66
Activity-level-related scales		
IBQ Activity Level × RITQ Activity Level	.65	.65
TTS Activity Level × EASI Activity	.56	.77
BSQ Activity Level × EASI Activity	.50	.75
BSQ Activity Level × DOTS Activity Level[a]	.21	−.09
EASI Activity × DOTS Activity Level	.18	−.10

Note. Questionnaires used: Infants (4–8 months), Carey RITQ, Rothbart IBQ, Bates ICQ. Toddlers (18–24 months), Fullard TTS, Goldsmith TBAQ, Buss & Plomin EASI. Preschoolers (3–5 years), McDevitt BSQ, EASI, Lerner DOTS. From "Variation among Temperament Theories and Validation Studies of Temperament Assessment" by H. H. Goldsmith and L. A. Rieser-Danner, 1986. In G. A. Kohnstam (Ed.), *Temperament Discussed: Temperament and Development in Infancy and Childhood* (p. 6), Lisse, The Netherlands: Swets & Zeitlinger. Copyright 1986 by Swets & Zeitlinger. Adapted by permission.

[a]The original DOTS Activity Level scale used in this study contains primarily items related to activity while sleeping; this circumstance probably accounts for its lack of convergence with the other activity scales.

including the frequency of specific behaviors during defined time intervals. Sometimes observers rate temperament in the home under relatively natural conditions. At other times, observer ratings are completed during visits to some standard setting, where the child and accompanying parent are usually observed during free play or while engaged in relatively unstructured tasks. (This latter case is akin to actual laboratory-based measurements under controlled conditions, which we treat in the next section.) In evaluating the literature, one must bear in mind the similarity in both types of ratings (from global to molecular) and types of settings (from the home to the laboratory) in assessing the expected degree of convergence. Particular combinations of coding procedures and observational settings may predispose researchers to obtain higher or lower estimates of agreement. That is, investigators who utilize observer coding procedures very similar to those used by parents and who place their observers in situations similar to those parents experience will find higher levels of agreement.

For example, Bates and his colleagues (Bates et al., 1979; Bates, Olson, Pettit, &

Bayles, 1982; Pettit & Bates, 1984) have reported modest correlations between maternal perceptions of infant difficulty and observer reports of home behavior. Pertinent to the present discussion, they found that observer ratings of infants via relevant items on the ICQ (the same questionnaire used by mothers) were correlated with maternal perceptions at a slightly higher level than were observer reports of the frequency of fussing/crying behaviors. More specifically, Bates et al. (1979) reported low but significant correlations between parental and observer ratings on the Fussy/Difficult dimension of the ICQ. Mothers' and observers' questionnaire scores correlated .34; for fathers, the value was .40. Agreement between maternal ICQ ratings and home observation variables was lower but still significant. Two home observation variables were related to the ICQ dimension of Fussy/Difficult: Fussiness ($r = .22$) and low Soothability ($r = .18$). Bates et al. (1982) also reported a significant relation between maternal perceptions of infant difficulty and observed fussiness ($r = .30$). Bates and Bayles (1984) found similar results.

Rothbart (1986) reported low to moderate levels of convergence at 3, 6, and 9 months of age between maternal IBQs and home observations. When corrected for attenuation, these low to moderate correlations increased substantially; however, the pattern of correlations was inconsistent across ages. Results such as these suggest periods of developmental transition accompanied by individual differences in rates of development. Finally, general reactivity composites (positive, negative, and overall reactivity) derived from temperament dimensions from both assessment procedures showed more consistent levels of convergence across the three age groups (eight of nine correlations were significant and ranged from .28 to .46); this finding again emphasizes the importance of aggregation.

Based on the use of a maternal interview procedure (i.e., the Assessment of Temperamental Characteristics interview), Dunn and Kendrick (1980) found high levels of agreement between maternal responses to interview items and observer ratings using the same interview items (percentage of agreement ranged from 81% to 90% for dimensions of Malleability, Assertiveness, Intensity, Mood, Persistence, and Withdrawal). Only the dimension of Activity showed low convergence (i.e., 57% agreement). Furthermore, in comparisons of maternal interview responses and other observation variables, preschoolers rated as more intense by their mothers fussed more at home, and children rated as negative in mood spent more time sitting without playing, and in close proximity to their mothers.

Crockenberg and Acredolo (1983) found that maternal reports of overall distress on Rothbart's IBQ correlated slightly with fussing and crying at 3 months of age, but Crockenberg and Smith (1982) reported that the total amount of fussing and crying was more a function of the mother's behavior in the home than of the infant's characteristics.

Bates (1980) and Sameroff et al. (1982) have correctly suggested that limited observations contribute to low convergence. However, such negative results may also result from dissimilar content or lack of theoretical congruence between observed infant behaviors and the parental rating instrument. Moreover, poor psychometric properties of either the parental questionnaire or the observations may be at fault. For example, Bates (1987) argued that the report of weak convergence by Vaughn et al. (1981) is plagued by both problems—the poor psychometric properties of the original ITQ, and a choice of behavioral measures that were not well selected for comparative purposes.

In a highly informative Swedish study, Hagekull, Bohlin, and Lindhagen (1984) demonstrated that when observations were limited to situations addressed by the parental rating instrument, validity coefficients were high. Their data also suggested that mothers and observers can agree to the same extent that two trained observers typically do. Using situation descriptions from the BBQ (Bohlin et al., 1981), correlations between parent and observer data ranged from .60 to .83 (Attentiveness, $r = .60$; Approach/Withdrawal, $r = .67$; Intensity/Activity, $r = .68$; Manageability, $r = .76$; and Sensory Sensitivity, $r = .83$). This level of agreement obtained when mothers focused their attention on narrow selections of behavior in the same way that the observers did.

*Convergence between Parental Report
and Laboratory Observation*

Garcia-Coll et al. (1984) found significant agreement between paternal and maternal TTS Approach/Withdrawal scale scores and laboratory measures of behavior inhibition at 21 months of age (r's = .49 and .54 for fathers and mothers, respectively). Furthermore, infants classified as inhibited in laboratory sessions were rated by their mothers as less adaptable to new situations, as more likely to withdraw from new events, and as more likely to be negative in mood; fathers rated these infants as less likely to approach new events. Finally, measures of behavioral inhibition based on maternal interview responses predicted the laboratory index of inhibiton (r = .67). At 4 years of age, mothers' *Q*-sort descriptions of inhibited and uninhibited behavior were significantly related to measures of inhibited and uninhibited behavior with peers in the laboratory.

Bates and Bayles (1984) reported convergence between ICQ ratings of Unadaptability and infant responses to a Bayley examiner at 13 and 24 months of age. Similarly, parental ratings of Emotionality (on Buss & Plomin's original EASI) predicted more negative reactions to a stranger in the lab, while reports of higher Sociability were correlated with fewer negative and more positive reactions to the stranger at 2 years of age (Lemly & Schwarz, 1979). Berberian and Snyder (1982) reported moderate, significant correlations between RITQ scales and several objective measures of fearfulness during a series of stranger approach episodes for 8- and 9-month-olds. Moreover, overall temperament ratings (with high scores being linked to negative temperaments) were significantly related to these same behaviors (e.g., correlation between total negative temperament score and the appearance of unhappy facial expression during the approach was .50; correlation with fussing and crying during the episode was .49).

Using factors derived from their laboratory observations and from an analysis of Fullard et al.'s TTS, Wilson and Matheny (1983) found the two first factors to be modestly correlated (canonical r = .60) at 12 months of age. The laboratory factor consisted primarily of ratings of emotional tone, attention, and orientation to/cooperation with staff. The TTS factor strongly resembled the description of difficulty offered by Thomas and Chess (i.e., it included Adaptability, Attention Span/Persistence, Approach/Withdrawal, Mood, and Distractibility). At 18 and 24 months of age, first factors from the laboratory and questionnaire measures were designated "lab tractability" and "questionnaire tractability." At 18 months, the correlation between lab tractability and questionnaire tractability was .38, and by 24 months of age, the correlation was .52 (Matheny, Wilson, & Nuss, 1984).

Parental ratings of Activity Level on the CCTI correlated .75 with aggregate activity level scores (actometer readings) based on a series of observations in the nursery school (Eaton, 1983). However, in a similar study with 3- to 4-month-old infants, actometer readings and parental ratings via Rothbart's IBQ failed to converge (Eaton & Dureski, 1986). At the 6-month follow-up, Eaton (personal communication, April 1987) did observe positive actometer–IBQ Activity Level associations. Rothbart (1986) reported similar negative results for home observations of activity level at 3 months, but she found significant correlations at 6 and 9 months of age. Teacher ratings of overall activity level (via the California *Q*-sort) were compared to actometer composite scores in the preschool at ages 3 and 4 by Buss, Block, and Block (1980). Impressive consistency was obtained. The two measures of activity level correlated .61 and .50 for boys and girls, respectively, at age 3, and .53 and .48 for boys and girls at age 4. Furthermore, cross-method correlations between ages 3 and 4 were .66 and .56 for boys and .36 and .34 for girls. Thus, with the exception of the precrawling, prereaching phases of early infancy, there is substantial evidence for the validity of questionnaire assessment of activity level.

In another study of convergence, Rieser-Danner (1985) included three assessments of infant temperament. Mothers completed both Bates's ICQ (13-month version) and Rothbart's IBQ. Furthermore, laboratory episodes were used to assess activity level (percentage of time locomoting; percentage of time in active play; percentage of time in quiet play; ratio of active to quiet play), fear (peak intensity of distress to an approaching stranger and peak intensity of distress to pickup by stranger), and interest/attention span (percentage of time viewing a cartoon). Maternal reports of gross motoric activity significantly predicted the proportion of time infants engaged in active play behaviors in the laboratory ($r = .32$). Babies rated higher on the IBQ Fear scale showed a greater peak intensity of distress to an approaching stranger ($r = .35$) and to the stranger's attempts to pick them up ($r = .55$). This significant association was replicated with the ICQ Unadaptability scale (r's $= .28$ and $.23$). Maternal reports of the general motoric activity and duration of orienting (focused attention) also significantly predicted fear in the stranger approach episode (r's $= .28$ and $.26$, respectively). Discriminant analysis procedures, using the original six scales of Rothbart's IBQ, significantly predicted 87% of those babies who showed distress in the laboratory episodes versus those who showed no distress ($r = .56$, $p < .05$). Duration of Orienting, Fear, and Activity Level were most strongly weighted in making this discrimination. Finally, interest/attention span in the laboratory (i.e., percentage of time spent viewing a videotaped cartoon) was predicted by neither the IBQ Duration of Orienting nor the ICQ Persistence scales.

Goldsmith and Campos (1986, 1988) reported a pattern of IBQ–laboratory convergence generally comparable to that noted by Rieser-Danner (1985). One feature of their results was that convergence for fear-related behavior was higher than for positive-affect-related behavior. They also observed that mothers' and fathers' reports on the IBQ tended to predict different aspects of the infant's behavior in the laboratory; the mothers' reports, quite reasonably, better predicted infant reactions when the mother herself was part of the context of assessment.

Summary of Validity Evidence

The validity evidence, only part of which can be recounted here, can be framed to support several theoretical viewpoints about the nature and importance of temperament. The types of convergence predicted by most temperament theorists are indeed evident. However, the degree of convergence is modest enough to also encourage those who place an emphasis on situational and interpersonal influences on socioemotional development. It seems clear that temperamental differences, at least as currently measured, are not overwhelming influences on behavioral individuality. However, we would also emphasize, along with Kenrick and Funder (1988), that correlations across methods in the .30s and .40s can be practically significant.

The current state of validity evidence does not yield a clear winner among interview, questionnaire, observational, and laboratory techniques. We would place our highest bets on the ultimate utility of the questionnaire and laboratory approaches, but for the next decade, all four approaches deserve further refinement and application.

REFERENCES

Affleck, G., Allen, D. A., McGrade, B. J., & McQueeny, M. (1983). Maternal and child characteristics associated with mothers' perceptions of their high risk/developmentally delayed infants. *Journal of Genetic Psychology, 142*, 171–180.

Allport, G. W. (1937). *Personality: A psychological interpretation*. New York: Holt.

Angleitner, A., & Strelau, J. (in press). *Explorations in temperament: Contemporary conceptualizations, measurement and methodological issues*. New York: Plenum.

Attili, G., Alcini, P., & Felaco, R. (in press). Temperamento e percezione del temperamento: Differenze madre–padre nella valutazione delle caratteristiche individuali di bambini di 4 anni e stato emotivo materno. *Giornale Italiano di Psicologia*.

Bates, J. E. (1980). The concept of difficult temperament. *Merrill–Palmer Quarterly, 26*, 299–319.

Bates, J. E.(1987). Temperament in infancy. In J. D. Osofsky (Ed.), *Handbook of infant development* (2nd ed., pp. 1101–1149). New York: Wiley.

Bates, J. E., & Bayles, K. (1984). Objective and subjective components in mothers' perceptions of their children from age 6 months to 3 years. *Merrill–Palmer Quarterly, 30*, 111–130.

Bates, J. E., Freeland, C. A. B., & Lounsbury, M. L. (1979). Measurement of infant difficultness. *Child Development, 50*, 794–803.

Bates, J. E., Olson, S. L., Pettit, G. S., & Bayles, K. (1982). Dimensions of individuality in the mother–infant relationship at six months of age. *Child Development, 53*, 446–461.

Belsky, J., Rovine, M., & Taylor, D. G. (1984). The Pennsylvania Infant and Family Development Project: III. The origins of individual differences in infant–mother attachment: Maternal and infant contribution. *Child Development, 55*, 718–728.

Berberian, K. E., & Snyder, S. S. (1982). The relationship of temperament and stranger reaction for younger and older infants. *Merrill–Palmer Quarterly, 28*, 79–94.

Bohlin, G., Hagekull, B., & Lindhagen, K. (1981). Dimensions of infant behavior. *Infant Behavior and Development, 4*, 83–96.

Bornstein, M. H., Gaughran, J. M., & Homel, P. (1986). Infant temperament: Theory, tradition, critique and new assessments. In C. E. Izard & P. B. Read (Eds.), *Measuring emotions in infants and young children* (Vol. 2, pp. 172–202). Cambridge, England: Cambridge University Press.

Buss, D. M., Block, J. H., & Block, J. (1980). Preschool activity level: Personality correlates and developmental implications. *Child Development, 51*, 401–408.

Buss, A. H., & Plomin, R. (1975). *A temperament theory of personality development*. New York: Wiley.

Buss, A. H., & Plomin, R. (1984). *Temperament: Early developing personality traits*. Hillsdale, NJ: Erlbaum.

Campbell, D. T., & Fiske, D. W. (1959). Convergent and discriminant validation by the multitrait-multimethod matrix. *Psychological Bulletin, 56*, 81–105.

Campos, J. J., Barrett, K., Lamb, M. E., Goldsmith, H. H., & Stenberg, C. (1983). Socioemotional development. In M. M. Haith & J. J. Campos (Eds.), *Handbook of child psychology* (4th ed.): *Vol. 2. Infancy and developmental psychobiology* (pp. 783–915). New York: Wiley.

Carey, W. B. (1970). A simplified method for measuring infant temperament. *Journal of Pediatrics, 77*, 188–194.

Carey, W. B. (1972). Clinical applications of infant temperament measurements. *Journal of Pediatrics, 81*, 823–828.

Carey, W. B. (1981). The importance of temperament–environment interaction for child health and development. In M. Lewis & L. A. Rosenblum (Eds.), *The uncommon child* (pp. 31–55). New York: Plenum.

Carey, W. B. (1986). Clinical interactions of temperament: Transitions from infancy to childhood. In R. Plomin & J. Dunn (Eds.), *The study of temperament: Changes, continuities and challenges* (pp. 151–162). Hillsdale, NJ: Erlbaum.

Carey, W. B., & McDevitt, S. C. (1978). Revision of the Infant Temperament Questionnaire. *Pediatrics, 61*, 735–739.

Cattell, R. B. (1946). *Description and measurement of personality*. Yonkers-on-Hudson, NY: World Book Company.

Chess, S., & Thomas, A. (1984). *Origins and evolution of behavior disorders*. New York: Brunner/Mazel.

Crockenberg, S. B. (1981). Infant irritability, mother responsiveness, and social support influences on the security of infant–mother attachment. *Child Development, 52*, 857–865.

Crockenberg, S. B. (1986). Are temperament differences in babies associated with predictable differences in caregiving? In J. V. Lerner & R. M. Lerner (Eds.), *New directions for child development: Vol. 31. Temperament and social interaction in children,* (pp. 53–74). San Francisco: Jossey-Bass.

Crockenberg, S. B., & Acredolo, C. (1983). Infant temperament ratings: A function of infants, or mothers, or both? *Infant Behavior and Development, 6*, 61–72.

Crockenberg, S. B., & Smith, P. (1982). Antecedents of mother–infant interaction and infant irritability in the first three months of life. *Infant Behavior and Development, 5*, 105–119.

Derryberry, D., & Rothbart, M. K. (1988). Arousal, affect, and attention as components of temperament. *Journal of Personality and Social Psychology, 55*, 958–966.

Dunn, J., & Kendrick, C. (1980). Studying temperament and parent–child interaction: Comparison of interview and direct observation. *Developmental Medicine and Child Neurology, 22*, 484–496.

Dunn, J., Kendrick, C., & McNamee, R. (1981). The reaction of the first born children to the birth of a sibling: Mother's report. *Journal of Child Psychology and Psychiatry, 22*, 1–18.

Dunst, C. J., & Lingerfelt, B. (1985). Maternal ratings of temperament and operant learning in two- and three-month-old infants. *Child Development, 56*, 555–563.

Eaton, W. O. (1983). Measuring activity level with actometers: Reliability, validity, and arm length. *Child Development, 54*, 720–726.

Eaton, W. O., & Dureski, C. M. (1986). Parent and actometer measures of motor activity level in the young infant. *Infant Behavior and Development, 9*, 383–394.

Epstein, S. (1980). The stability of behavior: II. Implications for psychological research. *American Psychologist, 25*, 790–806.

Field, T., & Greenberg, R. (1982). Temperament ratings by parents and teachers of infants, toddlers, and preschool children. *Child Development, 53*, 160–163.

Field, T., Vega-Lahr, N., Scafidi, F., & Goldstein, S. (1987). Reliability, stability, and relationships between infant and parent temperament. *Infant Behavior and Development, 10*, 117–122.

Fullard, W., McDevitt, S. C., & Carey, W. B. (1984). Assessing temperament in one-to-three-year-old children. *Journal of Pediatric Psychology, 9*, 205–216.

Garcia-Coll, C., Kagan, J., & Reznick, J. S. (1984). Behavioral inhibition in young children. *Child Development, 55*, 1005–1019.

Garside, R. F., Birch, H., Scott, D. M., Chambers, S., Kolvin, I., Tweedle, E. G., & Barber, L. M. (1975). Dimensions of temperament in infant school children. *Journal of Child Psychology and Psychiatry, 16*, 219–231.

Goldsmith, H. H., & Alansky, J. A. (1987). Maternal and infant temperamental predictors of attachment: A meta-analytic review. *Journal of Consulting and Clinical Psychology, 55*, 805–816.

Goldsmith, H. H., Bradshaw, D. L., & Campos, J. J. (1989). *Parental personality as a predictor of infant temperament and attachment*. Manuscript submitted for publication.

Goldsmith, H. H., Bradshaw, D. L., & Rieser-Danner, L. A. (1986). Temperament as a potential developmental influence on attachment. In J. V. Lerner & R. M. Lerner (Eds.), *New directions for child development: Vol. 31. Temperament and social interaction in infants and childhood* (pp. 5–34). San Francisco: Jossey-Bass.

Goldsmith, H. H., Buss, A. H., Plomin, R., Rothbart, M. K., Thomas, A., Chess, S., Hinde, R. A., & McCall, R. B. (1987). Roundtable: What is temperament? Four approaches. *Child Development, 58*, 505–529.

Goldsmith, H. H., & Campos, J. J. (1982). Toward a theory of infant temperament. In R. N. Emde & R. J. Harmon (Eds.), *The development of attachment and affiliative systems* (pp. 161–193). New York: Plenum.

Goldsmith, H. H., & Campos, J. J. (1986). Fundamental issues in the study of early temperament: The Denver Twin Temperament Study. In M. E. Lamb, A. L. Brown, & B. Rogoff (Eds.), *Advances in Developmental Psychology*, (Vol. 4, pp. 231–283). Hillsdale, NJ: Erlbaum.

Goldsmith, H. H., & Campos, J. J. (1988). *Infant temperament: The structure of laboratory and questionnaire based assessment*. Manuscript submitted for publication.

Goldsmith, H. H., Elliott, T. K., & Jaco, K. L. (1986, April). Construction and initial validation of a new temperament questionnaire. *Infant Behavior and Development 9*, 144. (Abstract)

Goldsmith, H. H., & Rieser-Danner, L. A. (1986). Variation among temperament theories and validation studies of temperament assessment. In G. A. Kohnstamm (Ed.), *Temperament discussed: Temperament and development in infancy and childhood* (pp. 1–9). Lisse, The Netherlands: Swets & Zeitlinger.

Goldsmith, H. H., Rieser-Danner, L., & Briggs, S. (1989). *Evaluating convergent and discriminant validity of preschooler, toddler, and infant temperament questionnaires*. Manuscript submitted for publication.

Goldsmith, H. H., Rieser-Danner, L., & Pomerantz, S. (1983, April). *Maternal attitudinal structure as a correlate of perceived infant temperament*. Paper presented at the meeting of the Southwestern Psychological Association, San Antonio, TX.

Goldsmith, H. H., & Rothbart, M. K. (1988). *The Laboratory Temperament Assessment Battery (LAB-TAB): Locomotor Version, Edition 1.2* (Technical Report No. 88-01). Eugene, OR: Oregon Center for the Study of Emotion.

Graham, P., Rutter, M., & George, S. (1973). Temperamental characteristics as predictors of behavior disorders in children. *American Journal of Orthopsychiatry, 43*, 328–339.

Gunnar, M., Mangelsdorf, S., Kestenbaum, R., Lang, S., Larson, M., & Andreas, D. (in press). Stress and coping in early development. In D. Cicchetti (Ed.), *Process and psychopathology*. Hillsdale, NJ: Erlbaum.

Hagekull, B. (1985). The Baby and Toddler Behavior Questionnaires: Empirical studies and conceptual considerations. *Scandinavian Journal of Psychology, 26*, 110–122.

Hagekull, B., Bohlin, G., & Lindhagen, K. (1984). Validity of parental reports. *Infant Behavior and Development, 7*, 77–92.

Hagekull, B., Lindhagen, K., & Bohlin G. (1980). Behavioral dimensions in one-year-olds and dimensional stability in infancy. *International Journal of Behavioral Development 3*, 351–364.

Hall, R. J., & Cadwell, J. (1984). *Temperament influences on cognitive achievement in children with learning problems*. Paper presented at the annual conference of the American Education Research Association, New Orleans.

Hegvik, R. L., McDevitt, S. C., & Carey, W. B. (1982). The Middle Childhood Temperament Questionnaire. *Developmental and Behavioral Pediatrics, 3*, 197–200.

Hsu, C., Soong, W., Stigler, J. W., Hong, C., & Liang, C. (1981). The temperamental characteristics of Chinese babies. *Child Development, 52*, 1337–1340.

Hubert, N. C., Wachs, T. D., Peters-Martin, P., & Gandor, M. J. (1982). The study of early temperament: Measurement and conceptual issues. *Child Development, 53*, 571–600.

Huitt, W. G., & Ashton, P. T. (1982). Parents' perception of infant temperament: A psychometric study. *Merrill-Palmer Quarterly, 28*, 95–109.

Huttunen, M. O., & Nyman, G. (1982). On the continuity, change and clinical value of infant temperament in a prospective epidemiological study. In R. Porter & G. M. Collins (Eds.), *Temperamental differences in infants and young children* (Ciba Foundation Symposium No. 89, pp. 240–247). London: Pitman.

Kagan, J. (1982). *Psychological research on the human infant: An evaluative summary*. New York: W. T. Grant Foundation.

Kagan, J., Reznick, J. S., Clarke, C., Sniddman, N., & Garcia-Coll, C. (1984). Behavioral inhibition to the unfamiliar. *Child Development, 55*, 2212–2225.

Kagan, J., Reznick, J. S., & Snidman, N. (1986). Temperamental inhibition in early childhood. In R. Plomin & J. Dunn (Eds.), *The study of temperament: Changes, continuities, and challenges* (pp. 53–65). Hillsdale, NJ: Erlbaum.

Kelly, P. (1976). The relation of infant's temperament and mother's psychopathology to interactions in early infancy. In K. F. Riegel & J. A. Meacham (Eds.), *The developing individual in a changing world*. Chicago: Alpine.

Kenrick, D. T., & Funder, D. C. (1988). Profiting from controversy: Lessons from the person–situation debate. *American Psychologist, 43*, 15–34.

Keogh, B. K. (1982). Children's temperament and teachers' decisions. In R. Porter & G. M. Collins (Eds.), *Temperamental differences in infants and young children* (Ciba Foundation Symposium No. 89, pp. 141–154). London: Pitman.

Keogh, B. K. (1986). Temperament and schooling: Meaning of "goodness of fit"? In J. V. Lerner & R. M. Lerner (Eds.), *New directions for child development: Vol. 31. Temperament and social interaction in infants and childhood* (pp. 89–108). San Francisco: Jossey-Bass.

Keogh, B. K., Pullis, M. E., & Cadwell, J. (1982). A short form of the Teacher Temperament Questionnaire. *Journal of Educational Measurement, 19*, 323–329.

Kohnstamm, G. A. (Ed.). (1986). *Temperament discussed: Temperament and development in infancy and childhood*. Lisse, The Netherlands: Swets & Zeitlinger.

Kohnstamm, G. A. (in press). Cross-cultural, social, gender and other group differences. In G. A. Kohnstamm, J. Bates, & M. K. Rothbart (Eds.), *Temperament in childhood*. Chichester, England: Wiley.

Kohnstamm, G. A., Bates, J. E., & Rothbart, M. K. (Eds.). (in press). *Temperament in childhood*. Chichester, England: Wiley.

Kolvin, I., Nichol, A. R., Garside, R. F., & Tweddle, E. G. (1982). Temperamental patterns in aggressive boys. In R. Porter & G. M. Collins (Eds.), *Temperamental differences in infants and young children* (Ciba Foundation Symposium No. 89, pp. 252–268). London: Pitman.

Lamb, M. E. (1982). Individual differences in infant sociability: Their origins and implications for cognitive development. In H. W. Reese & L. P. Lipsett (Eds.), *Advances in child development and behavior* (Vol. 16, pp. 213–239). New York: Academic Press.

Lee, C., & Bates, J. (1985). Mother–child interaction at age two years and perceived difficult temperament. *Child Development, 56,* 1314–1326.

Lemly, E. B., & Schwarz, J. C. (1979). *Temperament and child-rearing antecedents of two-year-olds' reactions to male and female strangers.* Paper presented at the biennial meeting of the Society for Research in Child Development, San Francisco.

Lerner, J. V., & Lerner, R. M. (1983). Temperament and adaptation across life: Theoretical and empirical issues. In P. B. Baltes & O. G. Brim (Eds.), *Lifespan development and behavior* (Vol. 5, pp. 197–231). New York: Academic Press.

Lerner, J. V., & Lerner, R. M. (Eds.). (1986). *New directions for child development: Vol. 31. Temperament as a moderator of individual and social development in infancy and childhood.* San Francisco: Jossey-Bass.

Lerner, J. V., Lerner, R. M., & Zabski, S. (1985). Temperament and elementary school children's actual and rated academic abilities: A test of a "goodness of fit" model. *Journal of Child Psychology and Psychiatry, 26,* 125–136.

Lerner, R. M., Palermo, M., Spiro, A., & Nesselroade, J. R. (1982). Assessing the dimensions of temperamental individuality across the life-span: The Dimensions of Temperament Survey (DOTS). *Child Development, 53,* 149–159.

Lyon, M. E., & Plomin, R. (1981). The measurement of temperament using parental ratings. *Journal of Child Psychology and Psychiatry, 22,* 47–53.

Maccoby, E. E., Snow, M. E., & Jacklin, C. N. (1984). Children's dispositions and mother–child interaction at 12 and 18 months: A short-term longitudinal study. *Developmental Psychology, 20,* 459–472.

Martin, R. P. (1988). *The Temperament Assessment Battery for Children.* Brandon, VT: Clinical Psychology.

Martin, R. P., & Holbrook, J. (1985). Relationship of temperament characteristics for the academic achievement of first-grade children. *Journal of Psychoeducational Assessment, 3,* 131–140.

Martin, R. P., Nagle, R., & Paget, K. (1983). Relationships between temperament and classroom behavior, teacher attitudes and academic achievement. *Journal of Psychoeducational Assessment, 1,* 379–386.

Martin, R. P., Wisenbaker, J., Matthews-Morgan, J., Holbrook, J., Hooper, S., & Spalding, J. (1986). Stability of teacher temperament ratings over six and twelve months. *Journal of Abnormal Child Psychology, 14,* 216–232.

Matheny, A. P. (1987). Developmental research of twin's temperament. *Acta Geneticae Medicae et Gemellologiae, 36,* 135–143.

Matheny, A. P., & Wilson, R. S. (1981). Developmental tasks and rating scales for the laboratory assessment of infant temperament. *JSAS: Catalog of Selected Documents in Psychology, 11,* 81–82.

Matheny, A. P., Wilson, R. S., & Nuss, S. M. (1984). Toddler temperament: Stability across settings and over ages. *Child Development, 55,* 1200–1211.

Maziade, M., Boudreault, M., Thivierge, J., Caperaa, P., & Cote, R. (1984). Infant temperament: SES and gender differences and reliability in a large Quebec sample. *Merrill–Palmer Quarterly, 30,* 213–226.

McDevitt, S. C., & Carey, W. B. (1978). The measurement of temperament in 3–7 year old children. *Journal of Child Psychology and Psychiatry, 19,* 245–253.

McNeil, T. (1976). *Temperament revisited: A research-oriented critique of the New York Longitudinal Study of temperament.* Unpublished manuscript, Malmo, Sweden.

Meyer, H. J. (1985). *Zur emotionalen beziehung zwischen muttern und ihren erst- und zweitgeborenen kindern.* Regensburg, West Germany: S. Roderer Verlag.

Milliones, J. (1978). Relationship between perceived child temperament and maternal behaviors. *Child Development, 49,* 1255–1257.

Olson, S. L., Bates, J. E., & Bayles, K. (1984). Mother–infant interaction and the development of individual differences in children's cognitive competence. *Developmental Psychology, 20,* 166–179.

Pedersen, F. A., Anderson, B. J., & Cain, R. L. (1976). *A methodology for assessing parental perception of infant temperament.* Paper presented at Fourth Biennial Southeastern Conference on Human Development, Children's Hospital, Pittsburgh.

Pedersen, F. A., Zaslow, M., Cain, R. L., Anderson, B. J., & Thomas, M. (1980). A methodology for assessing parent perception of baby temperament. *JSAS: Catalog of Selected Documents in Psychology, 10,* 10. (Ms. No. 1517)

Persson-Blennow, I., & McNeil, T. (1979). A questionnaire for measurement of temperament in six-month-old infants: Development and standardization. *Journal of Child Psychology and Psychiatry, 20,* 1–13.

Persson-Blennow, I., & McNeil, T. (1982). Factor analysis of temperament characteristics in children at 6 months, 1 year, and 2 years of age. *British Journal of Educational Psychology, 52,* 51–57.

Pettit, G. S., & Bates, J.E. (1984). Continuity of individual differences in the mother–infant relationship from 6 to 13 months. *Child Development, 55,* 729–739.

Plomin, R., & DeFries, J. C. (1983). The Colorado Adoption Project. *Child Development, 54,* 276–289.

Plomin, R., DeFries, J. C., & Fulker, D. W. (1988). *Nature and nurture in infancy and early childhood.* New York: Cambridge University Press.

Plomin, R., & Dunn, J. (Eds.). (1986). *The study of temperament: Changes, continuities and challenges.* Hillsdale, NJ: Erlbaum.

Porter, R., & Collins, G. M. (Eds.). (1982). *Temperamental differences in infants and young children* (Ciba Foundation Symposium No. 89). London: Pitman.

Pullis, M., & Cadwell, J. (1982). The influence of children's temperament characteristics on teachers' decision strategies. *American Educational Research Journal, 19,* 165–181.

Reznick, J. S., Kagan, J., Snidman, N., Gersten, M., Baak, K., & Rosenberg, A. (1986). Inhibited and uninhibited children: A follow-up study. *Child Development, 57,* 660–680.

Riese, M. (1987). Longitudinal assessment of temperament from birth to 2 years: A comparison of full-term and preterm infants. *Infant Behavior and Development, 10,* 347–363.

Rieser-Danner, L. A. (1985). *The relations among measures of temperament and their correlations with cognitive test performance in infants*. Unpublished manuscript, University of Texas at Austin.

Rieser-Danner, L. A. (1986, April). *Subjective and objective measures of infant temperament: A convergent validity study*. Paper presented at the International Conference on Infant Studies, Los Angeles.

Roper, R., & Hinde, R. A. (1979). A teacher's questionnaire for individual differences in social behavior. *Journal of Child Psychology and Psychiatry, 20*, 287–298.

Rothbart, M. K. (1981). Measurement of temperament in infancy. *Child Development, 52*, 569–578.

Rothbart, M. K. (1986). Longitudinal observation of infant temperament. *Developmental Psychology, 22*, 356–365.

Rothbart, M. K. (1988). *Child Behavior Questionnaire*. Unpublished manuscript, University of Oregon.

Rothbart, M. K. (in press). Temperament and development. In G. A. Kohnstamm, J. Bates, & M. K. Rothbart (Eds.), *Temperament in childhood*. Chichester, England: Wiley.

Rothbart, M. K., & Derryberry, D. (1981). Development of individual differences in temperament. In M. E. Lamb & A. L. Brown (Eds.), *Advances in developmental psychology* (Vol. 1). Hillsdale, NJ: Erlbaum.

Rothbart, M. K., & Goldsmith, H. H. (1985). Three approaches to the study of infant temperament. *Developmental Review, 5*, 237–250.

Rowe, D. C., & Plomin, R. (1977). Temperament in early childhood. *Journal of Personality Assessment, 41*, 150–156.

Rusalov, V. M. (1987). *Object-related and communicative aspects of human temperament: A new questionnaire of the structure of temperament*. Moscow: Institute of Psychology, USSR Academy of Sciences.

Rushton, J. P., Brainerd, C. J., & Pressley, M. (1983). Behavioral development and construct validity: The principle of aggregation. *Psychological Bulletin, 94*, 18–38.

Rutter, M. (1987). Temperament, personality and personality disorder. *British Journal of Psychiatry, 150*, 443–458.

Sameroff, A. J. (1977). Concepts of humanity in primary prevention. In G. W. Albee & J. M. Joffe (Eds.), *Primary prevention of psychopathology* (pp. 42–63). Hanover, NH: University Press of New England.

Sameroff, A. J. (1983). Developmental systems: Context an evolution. In W. Kessen (Ed.), *Handbook of child psychology* (4th ed.): *Vol. 1. History, theory, and methods*. New York: Wiley.

Sameroff, A. J., Seifer, R., & Elias, P. K. (1982). Sociocultural variability in infant temperament ratings. *Child Development, 53*, 164–173.

Sanson, A., Prior, M., Garino, E., Oberklaid, F., & Sewell, J. (1987). The structure of infant temperament: Factor analysis of the Revised Infant Temperament Questionnaire. *Infant Behavior and Development, 10*, 97–104.

Seifer, R., & Sameroff, A. J. (1986). The concept, measurement, and interpretation of temperament in young children: A survey of research issues. In M. L.

Wolraich & D. Routh (Eds.), *Advances in developmental and behavioral pediatrics* (Vol 7, pp. 1–43). Greenwich, CT: JAI Press.

Shirley, M. M. (1933). *The first two years: A study of 25 babies*. Minneapolis: University of Minnesota Press.

Stevenson-Hinde, J. (1986). Towards a more open construct. In G. A. Kohnstamm (Ed.), *Temperament discussed: Temperament and development in infancy and childhood* (pp. 97–106). Lisse, The Netherlands: Swets & Zeitlinger.

Stevenson-Hinde, J., & Hinde, R. A. (1986). Changes in associations between characteristics and interactions. In R. Plomin & J. Dunn (Eds.), *The study of temperament: Changes, continuities and challenges* (pp. 115–129). Hillsdale, NJ: Erlbaum.

Stevenson-Hinde, J., & Simpson, A. E. (1982). Temperament and relationship. In R. Porter & G. M. Collins (Eds.), *Temperamental differences in infants and young children* (Ciba Foundation Symposium No. 89, pp. 51–61). London: Pitman.

Strelau, J. (1983). *Temperament personality activity*. New York: Academic Press.

Tellegen, A. (1982). *Brief manual for the Differential Personality Questionnaire*. Unpublished manuscript, University of Minnesota.

Thomas, A., & Chess, S. (1977). *Temperament and development*. New York: Brunner/Mazel.

Thomas, A., Chess, S., & Birch, H. G. (1968). *Temperament and behavior disorders in children*. New York: New York University Press.

Thomas, A., Chess, S., & Korn, S. J. (1982). The reality of difficult temperament. *Merrill–Palmer Quarterly, 28*, 1–20.

Thomas, A., Chess, S., Birch, H., Hertzig, M., & Korn, S. (1963). *Behavioral individuality in early childhood*. New York: New York University Press.

Thompson, R. A., & Lamb, M. E. (1984). Continuity and change in socioemotional development during the second year. In R. N. Emde & R. J. Harmon (Eds.), *Continuities and discontinuities in development* (pp. 315–338). New York: Plenum Press.

Torgersen, A. M. (1982). Influence of genetic factors on temperament development in early childhood. In R. Porter & G. M. Collins (Eds.), *Temperamental differences in infants and young children* (Ciba Foundation Symposium No. 89, pp. 141–154). London: Pitman.

Trieber, F. A. (1984). Temperament differences between infants who do and do not complete laboratory testing. *Journal of Psychology, 116*, 95–99.

Van den Boom, D. C. (1988). *The developing attachment relationship in mothers with irritable infants: Observation and intervention*. Unpublished doctoral dissertation, Department of Developmental Psychology, University of Leiden, Leiden, The Netherlands.

Vaughn, B. E., Taraldson, B. J., Crichton, L., & Egeland, B. (1981). The assessment of infant temperament: A critique of the Carey Infant Temperament Questionnaire. *Infant Behavior and Development, 4*, 1–17.

Wachs, T. D., & Smitherman, C. (1985). Infant and subject loss in an habituation procedure. *Child Development, 56*, 861–867.

Wilson, R. S., & Matheny, A. P., Jr. (1983). Assessment of temperament in infant twins. *Developmental Psychology, 19*, 172–183.

Wilson, R. S., Brown, A. M., & Matheny, A. P. (1971). Emergence and persistence of behavioral differences in twins. *Child Development, 42,* 1381–1398.

Windle, M. (1988). Psychometric strategies of measures of temperament: A methodological critique. *International Journal of Behavioral Development, 11,* 171–201.

Windle, M., Iwawaki, S., & Lerner, R. M. (1988). *Cross-cultural comparability of temperament among Japanese and American children.* Manuscript submitted for publication.

Windle, M., & Lerner, R. M. (1986). Reassessing the dimensions of temperamental individuality across the life span: The Revised Dimensions of Temperament Survey (DOTS-R). *Journal of Adolescent Research, 1,* 213–230.

Wolkind, S. N., & Desalis, W. (1982). Infant temperament, maternal mental stage and child behavioral problems. In R. Porter & G. M. Collins (Eds.), *Temperamental differences in infants and young children* (Ciba Foundation Symposium No. 89, pp. 221–239). London: Pitman.

12

Assessment of Childhood Depression

MARGARET SEMRUD-CLIKEMAN
Harvard Medical School/Massachusetts General Hospital

Childhood depression has been an area of controversy in recent years. Following a review of the published clinical literature, Lefkowitz and Burton (1978) suggested that the diagnosis of early childhood depression may reflect symptoms that are not statistically atypical or suggestive of psychopathology, but rather reflect normal developmental changes that resolve themselves if given proper time. They based this conclusion on their review of epidemiological studies, which found in a population of normal children a "surprisingly high prevalance of many behaviors generally regarded as symptoms of psychopathology in children" (p. 722). Lefkowitz and Burton (1978) cited studies (Kovacs & Beck, 1977; Lapouse, 1966; Shephard, Oppenheim, & Mitchell, 1966; Werry & Quay, 1971) that found depressive symptoms in 20%–40% of their samples. Conversely other researchers (Brumback, Dietz-Schmidt, & Weinberg, 1977; Brumback & Weinberg, 1977; Reynolds, 1985; Strauss, Forehand, Frame, & Smith, 1984) have felt that the seriousness and prevalence of childhood depression represent a challenge to psychologists and researchers to develop methods for identifying and intervening with children with depressive disorders. A recent study by Anderson, Williams, McGee, and Silva (1987), which utilized a large sample of children from the general population, found that depressive disorders in childhood were the *least* prevalent of all disorders. They utilized *Diagnostic and Statistical Manual of Mental Disorders,* third edition (DSM-III; American Psychiatric Association, 1980) criteria for Depression and gathered data from the children, parents, and teachers.

It appears that there has been growth in the ability to assess depressive symptoms and their severity since the Lefkowitz and Burton (1978) review. Most current studies appear to utilize either the DSM-III or the Weinberg criteria for diagnosis. Cantwell and Carlson (1982), in comparing the two sets of criteria, found a 78% agreement between children who met the DSM-III criteria and those who met the Weinberg criteria, while only 58% of those meeting the Weinberg criteria were also diagnosed by DSM-III criteria. DSM-III/III-R (American Psychiatric Association, 1980, 1987) criteria for a diagnosis of Depression state that a relatively persistent and "dysphoric mood or loss of interest or pleasure in all or almost all usual activities or pastimes" must be present (p. 213). In addition, four of eight additional symptoms must be present for at least 2 weeks. These symptoms include sleep disturbance, loss of energy and appetite change, feelings of self-reproach or guilt, and recurrent thoughts of suicide or death. The DSM-III/III-R criteria may be sufficiently stringent to decrease the identification of children who are in a normal transitional stage, as discussed by Lefkowitz and Burton (1978). It may well have been that earlier studies used different symptomology and/or severity measures, and thus arrived at spuriously high numbers of children with a diagnosis for childhood depression.

Prevalence studies are mixed, but it is generally reported that the rate of childhood depression in the general population is 2%, whereas in clinical populations 28% of outpatient and 50% of inpatient children show signs of depression (Kashani & Simmonds, 1979; Reynolds, 1984; Ryan et al., 1987). Similarly, in a study of 792 children, Anderson (1987) found that one of the least prevalent DSM-III disorders was Depression, as noted above. In addition, Rholes, Blackwell, Jordan, and Walters (1980) found that the incidence of depression appears to increase with age, with younger children showing less susceptibility to depression than adolescent children. These authors speculate that adolescents may well be at a higher risk for experiencing stressors and loss events that would predispose them to depression. Interestingly enough, these researchers found that there were no gender differences in the incidence of depression, unlike the adult literature, which finds a significant gender factor for females.

There has also been much discussion as to the symptomatology of depression in children. Research into developmental differences in expression of depressive behavior by Hodges and Siegel (1985), Kovacs and Paulauskas (1984), Pearce (1978), and Kovacs and Beck (1977) found that children in the age range of 6–12 years often exhibited the following symptoms: headache, abdominal pain, and enuresis as initial signs, with sad affect, sleep problems, and irritability emerging over time. Children aged 12–16 were often found to show restlessness, flight to or from people, and problem behavior. In addition, problems have been noted in inability to tolerate routine, which the authors speculate may well be an attempt to obtain constant stimulation so that unwanted thoughts will not be permitted into awareness. Children in this age group also have been found to become overly involved with their pets and in turn become increasingly socially isolated. Temper tantrums, running away, stealing, truancy, rebelliousness, and antisocial acts are frequently found in the histories of many in this age bracket. In the past, these behaviors were thought to be indicative of what was termed "masked depres-

sion." However, most researchers and clinicians now believe that these behaviors are part of a developmental stage in the expression of depression and term the behaviors "secondary reactions to depression" (Lesse, 1983). Adolescents aged 15–20 often manifest drug abuse, promiscuity, suicidal ideation, and alienation in conjunction with a diagnosis of depression.

Several studies have found that there seems to be a concordance between depression and anxiety, especially school refusal/separation anxiety (Gittelman-Klein & Klein, 1973; Pearce, 1978; Puig-Antich & Rabinovich, 1986; Tisher, 1983), conduct disorders (Chiles, Miller, & Cox, 1980; Kashani et al., 1980; Kovacs, Feinberg, Crouse-Novack, Paulauskas, & Finkelstein, 1984; Puig-Antich, 1982). Therefore, depression in children may be very difficult to assess separately from other forms of psychopathology. However, for the diagnosis of a depressive disorder to be useful, criteria for a separate syndrome needs to be substantiated (Kaslow & Rehm, 1983).

In summary, it can be seen that the study of childhood depression is evolving, with many new and old constructs being investigated. Some of the current investigations are laying to rest such ideas as "masked depression," while fine-tuning diagnostic criteria to be consistent across studies. Anderson et al. (1987) note that many of the earlier studies assessed depression using different criteria in the selection of the subjects, partly accounting for the widely varying rates of prevalence reported. In addition, these studies varied in the age groups examined, degree of psychopathology represented, and type of assessment. All of these methodological problems contribute to the murkiness of the depression data. Not only are the methodological problems worrisome, but difficulty is also present in the various models of depression, which may emphasize different components. These components do not often seem to be integrated into an understandable whole. Models of depression include the following: the cognitive theory (Beck, 1967), a model stressing lack of environmental reinforcement contingencies (Lewinsohn, 1974), the learned helplessness model (Abramson, Seligman, & Teasdale, 1978), the self-control model (Rehm, 1977), and finally the information-processing model of Ingram (1984). Many of these models of depression were developed from adult data; only relatively recently have researchers begun assessing the applicability of these models to children. At this point, little is known about the reliability and validity of the criteria as applied to children. Moreover, most of the studies utilize clinic-referred cases rather than cases from the general population, and this may lead to inaccurate conclusions. To complicate the matter even further, continued difficulty is found in the psychometric instruments purported to measure the construct. This chapter seeks to provide a brief overview of the foremost models of childhood depression. Its major purpose is to review the current measures of childhood depression, with an eye to recommendations for clinical use of these instruments in mental health centers and schools.

PSYCHOLOGICAL MODELS OF DEPRESSION

Beck's Cognitive Theory

Beck's (1967, 1976) theory emphasizes the role of cognitions in depression. He suggests that in depression individuals structure their experience on the basis of cognitions that are often faulty and distorted. These cognitions in turn predispose the individual to misrepresent external events in such a way that loss and deprivation appear most evident in their interactions with the world. These distorted cognitions continue, despite independent or disconfirming evidence to the contrary.

Beck further postulates the following triad of depressive symptoms based on these faulty cognitions:

1. View of self. In cognitive schemas that relate to self-assessment, the self is pictured as unworthy or inadequate.
2. View of the world. The world is seen as making exorbitant demands and as being full of insurmountable obstacles.
3. View of the future. The persons sees the difficulties continuing with no end in sight, which in turn engenders a hopeless attitude.

These cognitions validate themselves in the selective attention of the depressed individual. Hammen and Krantz (1976) found that the degree of improvement in depressive episodes over time was positively correlated with concurrent decreases in depressive distortions and more positive expectations about the future.

Similarly, Abramson et al. (1978) found that depressive cognitions predicted depression at a later date in subjects who were not depressed in the initial testing. Although similar studies have not been conducted with children, Bernard and Joyce (1984) suggest that these negative cognitions are also present in children who experience depressive episodes. Kaslow, Rehm, and Siegel (1984) found that depressed children in contrast to nondepressed children showed lower self-esteem; had negative self-evaluations; made more internal, stable, and global attributions for failure; and made more external, unstable, and specific attribution for success. Further support was found in a study reported by Strauss et al. (1984). They studied children who scored at the extremes on a depression inventory. Their findings were that children with extreme scores showed low self-esteem, social withdrawal, anxiety, unassertiveness, and poor academic achievement. Therefore, some preliminary support with children is provided for Beck's cognitive model.

Information-Processing Model

Similar to the cognitive view of depression is the recent emergence of the information-processing theory espoused by Ingram (1984). This view sees depression as the result of an individual's conceptualization of both external and internal information as negative. Both the overt and covert behavior of individuals is seen as being best understood in reference to the ways in which they collect, transform, encode, access, and utilize information. Kuiper and colleagues (Derry & Kuiper, 1981; Kuiper, Derry, & Macdonald, 1982) found that whereas depressed individuals showed superior memory for negative self-descriptors, nondepressed people showed better memory for positive self-descriptors, and mildly depressed people showed good memory for positive and negative self-descriptors. Hammen and Zupan (1984) suggest that the depressed person possesses a self-schema of negativity and thus more readily encodes negative information provided by the environment, thus generating a depressed mood. These authors sought to evaluate these findings with children; they found that depressed children more readily remembered negative self-descriptors.

Lewinsohn's Behavioral Model

Behavioral models of depression suggest that depression is a result of inadequate or insufficient reinforcers, which can be the result of lack of skill in obtaining reinforcers, lack of reinforcers in the environment for the individual, or inability to utilize reinforcers (Kovacs & Beck, 1977). Relatively little attention is paid to the cognitions of the depressed person in this model. According to Lewinsohn (1974), depressed persons explain their behavior to themselves following the behavior. The depressed persons are unable to identify or utilize contingent reinforcement in the environment. Therefore, attempts are made to assess reinforcement opportunities in the environment and to modify the clients' subsequent behavior so that they will obtain reinforcement.

Self-Control Model

Rehm (1977) postulates that the depressed individual shows deficits in self-monitoring, self-evaluation, self-attribution, and self-reinforcement behavior. Attributions are seen as important motivators of behavior, and depressed individuals are seen as making more internal and stable attributions of failure and attributing their success to more external and unstable forces. This idea is somewhat similar to Beck's component of negative view of self.

Sacco and Graves (1984) found validation for deficits in self-monitoring and self-evaluation with depressed children. When compared with their nondepressed peers, depressed children were found to show more negative self-evaluation, more academic difficulties, and poorer interpersonal skills. In addition, the depressed children showed a negative attributional cognitive style. To

complicate the issue, Mullins, Peterson, Wonderlich, and Reaven (1986) had adults view a videotape of a depressed and a nondepressed child. These authors found that adults evaluated the depressed child more negatively than the nondepressed child. Moreover, the adults showed less willingness to interact with the depressed child, showed more rejection of the depressed child, and predicted a poorer future for the depressed child. The authors postulated that there may well be an interaction among how children present themselves, how they think about themselves, and how significant adults interpret their behavior. Replication and expansion of this type of study would be interesting, especially if control parents, parents with psychopathology, teachers, peers, and clinicians are used as study groups.

Cognitive–Behavioral Model

The cognitive–behavioral model of depression attempts to combine the demonstrated effectiveness of behavior modification with the theories regarding the cognitive processes of the individual. It acknowledges the individual as playing an integral part in the determination of behavior, as well as the part that the environment plays in shaping that behavior. As a result, both cognitive and behavioral variables are seen as important to assess. Kendall and Braswell (1982) suggest that it is important not only to assess the child's observed behavior, but also to assess cognitive processes and their effect on behavior in both its maintenance and its occurrence. It would appear that this suggestion is particularly important in the assessment of depression in children, since much of depression is subjective and may not be readily observable. Puig-Antich, Chambers, and Tabrizi (1983) make the point that inappropriate guilt, obsessions, delusions, depressive mood, self-esteem, anxious worries, and other covert signs may be unknown to all but the child, especially when no overt behaviors are present. Studies on depressed children's behavior seem to have produced mixed results.

A recent study on nonverbal behaviors of depressed children found that the behaviors of sad affect, slowness of movement, and diminished social interaction discriminated depressed girls from nondepressed girls, but were not consistently discriminating for boys (Kazdin, Sherick, Esveldt-Dawson, & Rancurello, 1985). These researchers also found that the relationship was less robust between nonverbal behaviors and depression in children than for adults, leading one to speculate that any complete assessment of childhood depression must include other measures than just behavioral observations in order to arrive at a prudent diagnosis. Additional evidence to support this caution comes from a study by Kazdin, Esveldt-Dawson, Sherick, and Colbus (1985), which found that overt behavioral measures of childhood depression were related to parental reports of depression but not to child reports of depression. In addition, depressive symptoms were found to be expressed in diverse behaviors in day-to-day life; this causes one to question the possibility of consistent behavior observations' leading to correct distinctions of depression in children. Similarly, there have been studies in depression that have at one point or another found attentional factors, short-term as well as long-term memory functions, speed of retrieval, and other variables to be affected or altered by depression (Weingartner, Cohen, Murphy, Martello, & Gerdt, 1981).

In summary, it appears that a comprehensive evaluation of depression in children needs to address not only overt behavior, but also cognitive variables. The cognitive–behavioral approach seems to include cognition, attribution, behavior, and interpersonal variables. The preceding models do not appear to be separate entities; instead, they appear to have much in common with each other. Therefore, assessment of childhood depression needs to address the variables of cognition and behavior in order to present an accurate and complete picture of a child's individual needs.

ISSUES IN ASSESSMENT

Cognitive–behavioral assessment of depression in a child needs to include an accurate and comprehensive list of the situations in which the child's behavior occurs. This includes home, school, community, peers, and any other appropriate environments. In addition, the child's cognitions in these situations need to be studied. There is also the need to compile information from several different significant others in the child's life to complete the picture. Di Giuseppe (1981) suggests three aspects of a complete cognitive–behavioral approach to assessment. These aspects can be readily applied to the assessment of childhood depression. The first aspect is to define the parameters of the current behaviors of the child. This involves recording the frequency and rate of occurrence of the behavior, identifying antecedent and consequent events of the depressed behavior, and gathering information from various sources. In this way, the clinician is able to gain a measure of the severity of the depressive behavior. The second step is to determine the child's cognitions. This involves determination of thoughts that occur while the behavior is being exhibited, the child's self-statements (especially any that may guide behavior), and so on. The third aspect involves assessing the child's problem-solving skills; this aspect is particularly important in developing intervention strategies.

There are two necessary prerequisites for success using cognitive–behavioral techniques; Is the child able to understand cause and effect, and does the child possess the ability to generate alternatives to present behaviors? It is particularly important to assess a child's cognitive and developmental age when determining appropriate interventions. In addition, it is important to assess a child's evaluation of past events. This aspect ties into Beck's triad of depressive symptoms, as these past events may significantly influence a child's view of the world, self, and the future. An additional point of importance for children is that they do not often ask for help, especially in the instance of depression. The child is often referred for help by parents, teachers, or other adults; thus, it becomes very important to assess who exactly has the problem. In short, it is quite clear that a complete and in-depth assessment must utilize as many variables and as much information as possible if an accurate diagnosis of childhood depression is to be achieved.

Hence, the remainder of this chapter discusses various methods of assessing childhood depression using cognitive–behavioral techniques. Assessment techniques reviewed include self-report scales, clinical interviews, peer nomination inventories, behavior rating scales, assessment of cognitions, cognitive style measures, and thought-sampling procedures. Before beginning a discussion of instruments and techniques, it is important to note the obvious but often neglected proposition that children are a special population and that results, conclusions, and measures appropriate to adults may not be appropriate for children. In addition, the clinician needs to be aware of developmental stage considerations and cognitive-developmental changes when assessing a child. Ollendick and Hersen (1984) provide the caution that the child needs to be an integral and active participant in the evaluation. Moreover, assessment with children should be a problem-solving process, with the goal of not only diagnosing the difficulty but also of providing direction for intervention. These cautions fit in well with the cognitive–behavioral approach, as this literature particularly stresses ongoing assessment of the child and the effectiveness of the treatment (Kendall & Korgeski, 1979). With these cautions in mind, each of the different types of cognitive–behavioral assessment of childhood depression is addressed.

SELF-REPORT SCALES

Children's Depression Inventory

The Children's Depression Inventory (CDI; Kovacs & Beck, 1977) evolved from the Beck Depression Inventory (BDI). The CDI contains 27 multiple-choice items that cover an array of overt depressive symptoms, such as sadness, anhedonia, suicidal ideation, and sleep/appetite disturbance. Each CDI item contains three choices; each choice is rated on a 0–2 scale, with a rating of 2 being the most severe. The scale has been administered to children aged 7–17, with clinical control, clinical, and normal groups evaluated (Carlson & Cantwell, 1980; Kazdin, Colbous, & Rodgers, 1986; Kovacs, 1981). Cutoff scores for various levels of severity have been developed. Several studies have found excellent internal consistency ($r = .86$) (Kovacs, 1981); good test–retest reliability ($r = .72$) (Friedman & Butler, 1979); and evi-

dence of construct, content, and criterion validity (Finch & Rogers, 1984; Hodges & Siegel). Cantwell and Carlson (1979) factor-analyzed the CDI and found four factors:

1. Dysphoria/Self-Image—26% of the variance, eight items. Cantwell and Carlson (1979) characterized this as a severity-of-depression measure.
2. Fatigability/Crying/Indecisiveness/Failure—7% of the variance, five items. This was characterized as the self-accusation factor.
3. Somatic Preoccupation/Sleep Disturbance—6% of the variance, two items.
4. Anorexia/Weight Loss—4% of the variance, two items.

Factors 1 and 2 were found to discriminate depressed from nondepressed children (diagnoses based on DSM-III criteria) at the .0001 level for Factor 1 and the .04 level for Factor 2. A discriminant-function analysis of Factors 1 and 2 correctly classified 82.8% of those without affective disorders and 76.2% of those with affective disorders.

However, a study by Carey, Faulstich, Gresham, Ruggiero, and Enyart (1987) found three factors: Depressive Affect, Oppositional Behavior, and Personal Adjustment. On a sample of clinical and non-referred populations, the CDI was found to discriminate between 70.4% and 71.6% in the nonreferred population. None of the factors was found to discriminate between the depressed and conduct-disordered clinical groups. The authors concluded that the CDI may be an excellent screening device for general emotional distress, but they recommend utilizing other measures in conjunction with the CDI to insure the homogeneity of the depressed population. Similar concern as to discriminant validity has been expressed by Saylor, Finch, Spirito, and Bennett (1984), Saylor, Finch, Baskin, et al. (1984), and Nelson, Politano, Finch, Wendel, and Mayhall (1987). All of these studies utilized clinical groups and found that the CDI measured general distress but was unable to discriminate between conduct-disordered and affectively disordered groups. Saylor, Finch, Spirito, et al. (1984) suggest that the best depression measures are those that involve perceptions by the child and employ an interview or self-rating format. In addition, Saylor, Finch, Baskin, et al. (1984) found that a high CDI score generally was indicative of widespread psychopathology.

Further research is certainly warranted on the ability of the CDI to discriminate between clinical groups. At this point, it appears that the CDI measures general distress rather than solely depression. Users of the CDI need to be cognizant of this finding. An additional concern is that many of the newer measures of childhood depression are validated against the CDI, bringing into question all of the rating scales' discriminant validity. Kovacs (1985), in a study of the CDI using clinical and normal populations, recommends that the CDI may be a good discriminator for clinical populations. The CDI is suggested by Kovacs (1985) to be best utilized as a screening device with normal populations until further research as to its discriminant validity is performed.

Short Children's Depression Inventory

The Short CDI is a modification of the Short BDI. Children aged 7–17 have been administered the Short CDI. It includes 13 items rated on a 0–4 scale, with items completed in relation to symptoms experienced in the past week. A score of 8 is considered high and is used to define depression. Carlson and Cantwell (1979) compared results on the Short CDI with clinical interviews of 102 children referred to the UCLA Neuropsychiatric Institute. The findings revealed that 50% of the children were identified as depressed on the Short CDI, whereas only 25% were diagnosed as depressed by clinical interview. Because of the finding of so many false positives, the authors recommend the use of the Short CDI with concurrent systematic history and interview. There are no reports of psychometric properties. The use of this measure for diagnosis would seem to be premature.

Children's Depression Scale

The Children's Depression Scale (CDS) was developed by Lang and Tisher (1978). It is recommended for children aged 9–16 and has 66 items, with 48 items focusing on depressive symptoms and reactions and 18 on positive experiences. The CDS also utilizes a somewhat different different format from the typical paper-and-pencil rating scale. The child is asked to sort statements on cards into one of five boxes, ranging from "very wrong" to "very right." There are alternative forms so that both children and adults can rate the behavior. The subscales themselves were drawn from the literature on depressive symptomatology. The subscales consist of symptoms including pleasure, guilt, affect, social difficulties, thoughts of sickness and death, and low self-esteem. Responses are tallied on a 1–5 scale, with low scores indicating the presence of depression. Factor analysis has found one general factor, so the subscales are not individually reported (Kazdin, 1981).

Psychometric properties of the CDS have been reported only recently. Rotundo and Hensley (1985) found the CDS able to discriminate between depressed and nondepressed adolescents. Kazdin (1987) evaluated the CDS with clinical populations and the concurrence of parent and child ratings on the CDS. Internal consistency was found to be .90 for total depression, .79 for positive affect of the child scales. These correlations were seen as an acceptable level of internal consistency. Concurrent validity was also found to be acceptable. Correlations between the CDS, the CDI, the Bellevue Index of Depression (BID), and the Hopelessness Scale (see below) were found to be significant and positive. Correlation with the Self-Esteem Inventory was found to be negative and significant. Both parent and child ratings were found to show moderate to high correlations between depression and positive experience scores. In addition, Kazdin found that the CDS scales discriminated reliably between children diagnosed as depressed and children diagnosed as nondepressed. Depressed and nondepressed children were found to be equally well differentiated by both the child and adult scales. There remains a need for discriminant validity and test–retest reliability studies using the CDS.

Hopelessness Scale

The Hopelessness Scale was developed by Kazdin, French, Unis, Esveldt-Dawson, and Sherick (1983). It was modeled after the scales developed for adults by Beck, and is designed for children aged 8–13 years. The scale consists of 17 true–false items; it is scored so that the higher the score, the greater the assessed amount of hopelessness or negative view of the future. Acceptable internal consistency ($r = .70$) was found by Kazdin, French, Unis, Esveldt-Dawson, and Sherick (1983). Concurrent validity was assessed using performance on the CDI, the BID, and a depression checklist developed from Weinberg criteria. All of these measures were positively correlated with depression at a moderate level (CDI, $r = .49$; BID, $r = .40$; depression checklist, $r = .22$). Moreover, a further study by Kazdin, Rodgers, and Colbus (1986) found that the Hopelessness Scale was positively correlated with depression and negatively correlated with self-esteem. The Hopelessness Scale was also found to relate to diminished social behavior, especially when children with high hopelessness scores were compared with children with low hopelessness scores. Two factors were identified in the Kazdin, Rodgers, and Colbus (1986) study. They were (1) that the future would be negative and (2) that the child would not be able to alter this fact.

Depression Self-Rating Scale

The Depression Self-Rating Scale (DSRS) was developed by Birleson (1981) on the basis of a literature search for the most common depressive symptoms of childhood depression. The scale is designed for children aged 7–13. It consists of 18 items rated on a 0–2 scale. Birleson found test–retest reliability to be .80 and split-half reliability to be .86, with one major factor identified. He utilized a very small sample of 20 children from a psychiatric residential school and 19 from a local school. Asarnow and Carlson (1985) modified the DSRS by including three items from the Hopelessness Scale and two items assessing the child's capability for empathy, in an attempt to widen the coverage of DSM-III criteria for Depression. Criterion validity of the DSRS was established with the finding that the depressed children scored significantly higher on the DSRS than the nondepressed children. A cutting score of 17 was found to correctly classify 77% of the depressed children. The DSRS scores correlated significantly with the scores on the CDI; however, there was a low and nonsignificant correlation with behavioral observations of the depressed children as measured by the Children's Depression Rating Scale. Asarnow and Carlson (1985) point out that several studies have found low concordance among observable behavior, child reports of depression, and parental reports of depression (Kazdin, French, Unis, & Esveldt-Dawson, 1983; Leon, Kendall, & Garber, 1980). The DSRS is seen as a useful tool for the assessment of children with limited cognitive capacity or younger children, since it only requires a yes–no format. Again, as with other self-report rating scales, the suggestion is made to utilize more measures than just the DSRS in determining depression.

Reynolds Adolescent Depression Scale

The Reynolds Adolescent Depression Scale (RADS) is a 30-item self-report measure intended for use with adolescents. Data reported by the author (Reynolds, 1984) from 3,000 adolescents indicate internal-consistency reliability ranging from .92 to .96. A 6-week test–retest reliability coefficient of .84 was also reported by the author. Reynolds (1984) reports a correlation of .83 between the RADS and the Hamilton Depression Rating Scale with a sample of 126 adolescents. The Hamilton Depression Rating Scale is generally used with adults. No discriminant or convergent validity has been reported. This instrument appears to be in the developmental stage and should be used with other measures of depression until further research can show validation for the RADS.

Conclusions

From the preceding description of the self-rating scales, it can readily seen that the most frequent recommendation is that more than one measure be utilized in diagnosing depression. A complete picture of psychometric properties of these various rating scales is not available at this point. It is not clear that the self-rating scales only measure depression; it may well be that these measures are confounded by general emotional distress. In addition, it is important to assess the child's developmental stage, both emotionally and cognitively. A child's understanding of language is also important in assessing the responses to most of these rating scales. Severity of other types of psychopathology may play into these self-reports as well: For example, Norvell and Towle (1986) found that the CDI was positively correlated with conduct disorder, and that this was a result of responses to CDI items reflecting misconduct rather than depressed mood. The CDI is one of the most frequently used measures and also has been the subject of numerous research delineations of depressed populations; this leads to some concern as to the validity of the studies that utilized the CDI as their sole measure of depression.

TEACHER REPORT SCALES

Teacher Affect Rating Scale

The Teacher Affect Rating Scale was developed by Petti (cited by Cantwell, 1983) to assess depression. It consists of 26 items rated on a scale from 0 to 3 ("not at all" to "very much"). It is based on behavior seen in the last week. Petti identified three factors: Behavior, Learning, and Depression. This scale is still in the developmental stages, but looks promising.

Teacher Nomination Inventory for Depression

The Teacher Nomination Inventory for Depression (TNID) is a modification of the Peer Nomination Inventory for Depression developed by Lefkowitz and Tesiny (1980). It consists of 20 items that the teacher may nominate as representative of the child's behavior. The items were selected from the clinical literature on depression and describe behavior and facial expressions. No psychometric characteristics are provided by the authors. Lefkowitz and Tesiny (1980) found positive, significant correlations between the TNID, self-reports and peer nominations for depression. Saylor, Finch, Spirito, et al. (1984) found no such results with the TNID in comparison to self-reports; however, the TNID did correlate significantly and positively with peer nominations for depression.

Other Scales

As far as could be determined, the scales described above are the only teacher rating measures expressly developed to identify depression. The teacher form of the Child Behavior Checklist (CBCL-T; Achenbach & Edelbrock, 1983) has an identified Depression factor in its Internalizing scale. However, this checklist appears to provide an overall picture of global functioning and not necessarily a diagnosis of depression (Shoemaker, Erickson, & Finch, 1986). Wolfe et al. (1987) found that the CBCL-T Internalizing scale did not distinguish between anxiety and depression disorders. These authors suggest that the CBCL-T is better viewed as a broad-band instrument rather than as one for discrimination of specific disorders. The Personality Inventory for Children (PIC) also has a Depression scale consisting of 46 true–false items. The PIC is a parent rating scale generally completed by the mother. There are few validity studies available at this time as to the PIC Depression scale; this measure should be used with caution, and certainly should not be the sole basis of a diagnosis of depression (Reynolds, 1984; Reynolds, Anderson, & Bartell, in press).

BEHAVIORAL OBSERVATIONS

Behavioral observations are an integral part of cognitive–behavioral assessment. Observations in naturalistic settings can provide invaluable information as to the child's functioning in several different areas. Observation of depression can be somewhat difficult, as children sometimes express depression in different ways. There is increasing evidence that though there is similarity between depressed children and adults, there are features that are unique to children (Leon et al., 1980; Weinberg, Rutman, Sullivan, Penic, & Dietz, 1973). Lefkowitz and Burton (1978) noted the following behaviors occurring with some frequency among depressed children: sadness, unhappiness, apprehension, weepiness, aggression, apathy, withdrawal, listlessness, self-deprecation, poor schoolwork, and somatic complaints of headache and stomachache. It would appear helpful to pinpoint one or two behaviors frequently noted in the child and to observe these target behaviors over time and situations. In addition, there are several behavior checklists that can provide supplemental information. Checklists such as the Quay–Peterson Revised Behavior Problem Checklist (Quay & Peterson, 1975), the CBCL (Achenbach & Edelbrock, 1983), and the Conners Parent and Teacher Rating Scales can be completed by both parents and teachers. In addition, the Devereux Elementary School Behavior Rating Scale (Spivack & Spotts, 1976) has been widely used to indicate possible behavior problems.

INTERVIEWS

Interviews can be helpful in obtaining information in a semistructured manner. There are several clinical interview formats currently being used, with research proceeding on all of them. Interviews can be conducted with the child, either or both parents, or a teacher. Puig-Antich et al. (1983) suggest that interviews conducted with sensitive parents can provide excellent information on observable behaviors and past child verbalizations, and can permit the clinician to establish a chronological framework of concerns and behaviors. They have found that parental communication is most helpful when a younger child is being assessed, altered behavior is present, parents are empathic and relatively free of their own psychopathology, they know the child well, and they have a positive relationship with the child. Puig-Antich et al. suggest interviewing the parents first to obtain a chronology of onset and course of each problem and an overview of the child's development.

Several interviews are reviewed here. This list is not to be considered exhaustive; rather, these interviews were selected on the basis of research available on their ability to evaluate depression in children.

Schedule for Affective Disorders and Schizophrenia for School-Age Children

The Schedule For Affective Disorders and Schizophrenia for School-Age Children (Kiddie-SADS, or K-SADS) is an adaptation of the interview for adults of the Schedule for Affective Disorders and Schizophrenia (SADS). It is intended for children and adolescents. There are two versions: The K-SADS-P is appropriate for present episodes, and the K-SADS-E is appropriate for current and past diagnoses. The K-SADS allows for a diagnosis of Major Depression using the DSM-III/III-R criteria. It also allows for information to be gathered from parents, teachers, and the child. Age range for the K-SADS is 6–16 years old. Kazdin (1981) reports relatively high interrater reliability in interview scoring.

The K-SADS requires familiarity with DSM-III and DSM-III-R criteria for Major Depression. It begins with an unstructured interview and proceeds to a semistructured format. The items begin with a definition of the symptoms and continue with probes designed to determine severity, duration, and frequency of difficulty. The items are clustered together by diagnosis. The K-SADS allows the examiner to reword questions and to query beyond the items if deemed appropriate.

Interview Schedule for Children

The Interview Schedule for Children (ISC) is a structured interview for children aged 8–13 (Kovacs & Beck), 1977). This interview schedule was originally developed to longitudinally assess the occurrence of depression. Symptom probes are concise and are to be applied verbatim. Ratings on the ISC have been found to correlate moderately with the CDI. The ISC follows DSM-III criteria for Depression.

Bellevue Index of Depression—Revised

The Bellevue Index of Depression—Revised (BID-R) was developed on the basis of the Weinberg criteria used to diagnose childhood depression. The interview can be administered to parents, the child, teachers, or other significant adults. The child is asked to answer 40 questions that involve several different problems such as crying, feeling sad, and so on. The child's responses are rated for both severity and duration. In order for a diagnosis of depression to be derived, the child must meet both the severity and duration criteria. The BID-R has spotty validation and reliability studies. Kovacs (1981) found a 83% concordance between the BID-R and a separate clinical diagnosis. She suggests the need for further validation.

Children's Depression Rating Scale—Revised

The Children's Depression Rating Scale—Revised (CDRS-R) was developed by Poznanski, Cook, and Carroll (1979) to assess depression in children aged 6–12. The scale was adapted from the Hamilton Depression Rating Scale for adults. There are 12 items that cover an array of behaviors, including communication, mood disturbance, physical complaints, and vegetive signs. The CDRS-R is completed by pooling information from parents, child, medical personnel, and so on. The interview has a multiple-choice format, with items scaled from 0 to 7 ("unable to rate" to "severe") in the direction of increasing pathology. Agreement among judges is reported as high ($r = .96$), and acceptable correlations have also been reported between interviews and global clinical ratings of depression (Kovacs, 1981). A recent study by Poznanski et al. (1984) found that the CDRS-R measured the severity of depression and was not affected by the age of the child. Test–retest reliability in this study was found to be .81; interrater reliability was .86.

Child's Affective Rating Scale

The Child's Affective Rating Scale (CARS) is an interview for childhood depression in children aged 5–15. There are three subscales: Mood, Verbal Behavior, and Fantasy. These subscales are rated on a 10-point system for severity following the interview. The CARS provides for global clinical ratings rather than self-report of problems by the child. Kazdin and Petti (1982) report test–retest reliability in the moderate and positive range for boys and in the moderate and negative range for girls. A difficulty with this interview schedule is that no cutoff is provided for a diagnosis of depression, nor is there any determination of symptom duration.

Child Assessment Schedule

The Child Assessment Schedule (CAS) is a diagnostic interview that consists of two parts. In the first part, the child is asked approximately 75 questions about school, friends, activities, hobbies, family, fears, worries, mood, thought disorder, and self-image, among other things. The second part consists of a format for the interviewer to record judgments following the interview.

Reliability studies found acceptable interrater reliability for the CAS ($r = .92$) (Hodges, McKnew, Cytryn, Stern, & Kline, 1982). A validity study by Hodges, Stern, Cytryn, and McKnew (1982) found correlations with the CDI of .53 and with the overall pathology score on the CBCL of .57. Similarly, a study by Hodges, McKnew, Burbach, and Roebuck (1987) found good concordance between the CAS and the K-SADS for affective disorders across child and parent informants.

Diagnostic Interview Schedule for Children

The Diagnostic Interview Schedule for Children (DISC), developed at the National Institute of Mental Health, was designed for children aged 6–17. The DISC is a highly structured interview with specified questions. Clinical expertise is not needed, and probes are provided to ask for additional clarification of responses so that experienced clinicians can evaluate the responses at a later date. There are separate forms of the DISC for parents (DISC-P), teachers (DISC-T), and children (DISC-C). The DISC-P and DISC-C yield scores in 27 symptom areas. Most symptoms are coded on a scale of 0–2. The interviews are scorable in terms of DSM-III/III-R criteria.

Reliability and validity data have been provided for overall DISC-P and DISC-C diagnoses. No separate study to date has been found solely for depression. Costello, Edelbrock, and Costello (1984) found that the DISC-C was highly sensitive to disorders (95%) but low in specificity (25%). Children in both a pediatric group and a psychiatric group reported many mild disorders, including dysthymia. Cohen, O'Connor, Lewis, Velez, and Malachowski (1987) found significant but moderate correlations between the DISC interviews and the K-SADS. A study by Edelbrock, Costello, Dulcan, Kalas, and Conover (1985) found the DISC interviews to be reliable for diagnostic paraprofessionals with children aged 10 and older.

Diagnostic Interview for Children and Adolescents

The Diagnostic Interview for Children and Adolescents (DICA) was the first interview designed just for children. It gives both current and past diagnoses. This interview was designed for children aged 6–17 years, and contains separate forms for parent and child; it is to be administered by experienced clinicians. No separate studies on the accuracy of the DICA for diagnosing childhood depression have been reported. However, the DICA has been shown to discriminate between children referred for psychiatric and pediatric care (Herjanic & Campbell, 1977).

An interesting study by Sylvester, Hyde, and Reichler (1987) found that the child and parent forms of the DICA discriminated well as to overall pathology, but as diagnostic specificity increased, parental and parent–child concordances decreased. The authors caution against interviewing just one parent or just the child. Rather, they suggest interviewing both parents and the child to insure diagnostic accuracy.

Related Considerations

Recently, there have been several studies investigating the concordance of diagnosis of depression, using interviews with parents, teachers, and the child. Interestingly enough, these studies found that the informant, be it child, teacher, or parent, was consistent across the different measures as to the evaluation of possible depression. However, there were consistent discrepancies among the informants as to diagnosis. Leon et al. (1980) found that depressed children exhibited different types of behavior problems at home than at school. They used a sample of 138 children in third through sixth grades, diagnosed as depressed or nondepressed on the PIC. They used the CDI, the Conners Parent Rating Scale, and the Conners Teacher Rating Scale. They found

that the depressed children showed more conduct problems, anxiety, impulsive hyperactivity, learning problems, psychosomatic problems, perfectionism, and muscle tension at home than did nondepressed children. Depressed children were rated as more inattentive and passive than nondepressed children. In addition, the authors found that the younger children showed more conduct problems, whereas the older children showed more anxiety. Children with high scores on the CDI were found to attribute negative events more often to internal causes than children with low scores. Moreover, elevated depression scores on the CDI were found to be negatively correlated with the Hyperactivity scale of the PIC ($r = -.04$). The authors also found little consistency between parent and teacher ratings. Leon et al. (1980) recommended further investigation of differential observations in settings, as well as acknowledgment of different behaviors in depressed children in different developmental levels.

Several studies have also addressed the issue of parent–child correspondences on structured interviews. Kazdin, French, and Unis (1980) found that different measures completed by the same person were highly correlated but that correlations between parent and child ratings were poor. The children studied were psychiatric inpatients without neurological impairment, uncontrolled seizure disorders, or confusional states. Children independently diagnosed as depressed rated themselves as less depressed than their parents did, but as more depressed than the nondepressed clinical sample. Parent ratings were found to vary as a function of child IQ, gender, race, and family welfare status. Girls rated themselves as more depressed than boys; whites rated themselves as more depressed than blacks; and white females rated themselves as more depressed than black females. Fathers and mothers on welfare rated their children as less depressed than did nonwelfare parents. However, there was no difference between children as to their self-ratings as a function of welfare status. Mother and father ratings showed statistically significant positive correlations. On the CDI, parent–child reports were not significantly correlated, whereas on the BID there were low but significant correlations ($r = .32$,

$p < .05$). IQ was the only variable found to correlate significantly with mother–child differences, in that the higher the child's IQ, the greater the discrepancy between child and parent. These authors concluded that correspondence between ratings may vary as a function of type of symptoms and disorders, developmental or cognitive stages of the child, and parent characteristics (i.e., their cognitive development and psychopathology). Similar findings were reported by Kazdin, French, Unis, and Esveldt-Dawson (1983) using the CDI, the BID, the Hopelessness Scale, and the CBCL. Their conclusion was that children may underestimate their psychopathology. They found that both child and parent ratings accurately discriminated depressed from nondepressed children, but that the parent ratings more sharply delineated the depressed children.

Herjanic and Reich (1982) found that children reported more often than mothers their feelings of worry, anxiety, and depression. These authors concluded that the child may be the best reporter for these types of subjective feelings, and that when parent and child are given similar structured interviews with symptoms that are concrete, observable, severe, and unambiguous, there is good agreement. There is least agreement on severity of depression when milder forms of behavior are present or when subjective feelings are the delineating factor. An interesting study by Moretti, Fine, Haley, and Marriage (1985) found a moderate correlation between child and parent reports of depression. However, Moretti et al. found that children's reports of depression were consistent with psychiatric diagnosis, while the parents' reports did not discriminate level of depression for affective or nonaffective disorders. In addition, the authors found that the parents were often unaware of the children's subjective feelings. The most interesting finding was that parents' ratings of their own depression were significantly related to their reports of the level of their children's depression. Weissman et al.'s (1987) findings corroborate the Moretti et al. (1985) study.

Therefore, it appears important to assess both a child and his or her parents in regard to the child's depression. In addition, some assessment of possible parental psychopathology would seem to be an important procedure. In line with the cognitive–behavioral philosophy, the child needs to be an active participant in assessment of the presence or absence of depression and its related severity level. Parents appear helpful to delineate time frames, provide behavior observations, and furnish an opportunity to assess family dynamics. Much more research is needed to investigate the contribution of parental factors, developmental and cognitive levels of the child, and other extraneous factors impinging on the diagnosis of depression.

COGNITIVE–BEHAVIORAL MEASURES

Cognitive–behavioral theorists postulate that self-statements play a major role in the creation and maintenance of emotional disorders. Unfortunately, there have been few studies of cognitive–behavioral assessment in depression. Most of the studies cited in Kendall and Braswell (1982) involve behavioral disorders or impulsive children. Kendall and Hollon (1981) suggest four methods of assessing self-statements, adapted from general writings on cognitive–behavioral intervention strategies:

1. Recording of subject's speech. This can be done either as the child completes a task or in reference to direct questioning.
2. Completion of an inventory of self-statements following completion of a task.
3. Listing of thoughts the child had following an event that provoked feelings of depression.
4. Sampling methods that involve the assessment of self-statements at various times and in different settings. Kendall and Korgeski (1979) suggest the use of "in vivo thought sampling," which involves sampling a client's thoughts on the spot and completion of data sheets designed to quantify these thoughts. It would appear that this technique is most likely to be useful for older children.

Bernard and Joyce (1984) provide additional suggestions for assessment of cognitions that are appropriate for different age groups of children. Their discussion of "attribution retraining" appears very relevant in cognitive–behavioral assessment of depression. Attribution retraining revolves around assessing a child's perceptions as to the causes of his or her behavior. According to attribution theory, the view a child constructs about the workings of his or her world has an impact on his or her interactions with the world, and consequently on the child's perception of his or her role in the world. Leon et al. (1980) found that their depressed sample attributed positive events to external causes and negative events to internal causes. Bernard and Joyce (1984) suggest that attribution retraining may be helpful in conjunction with rational–emotive therapy in the treatment of depression, but add that few clinical applications have been documented in the literature. These researchers utilized attribution retraining with an adolescent diagnosed with depression. By changing her self-verbalizations from "I'm hopeless" and "I'll never be as good as Ian [her brother]" to "It is possible to do something about my unhappy feelings and I am the one who can do something about them," the client was able to experience a lessening of her symptoms and consequently rated herself with more acceptance. Of course, therapy was an integral part of this intervention.

The Children's Attributional Styles Questionnaire (KASTAN) is being developed by Kaslow, Tannenbaum, and Seligman (1978) to measure attributions in children. It consists of 48 items, each of which contains a situation and two possible attributions as explanation of the situation. The children are requested to select the statement that best represents why the situation happened to them. Half of the situations represent good outcomes and half bad. There are six subscales with eight items each. Composite scores are given for the good outcomes selected and the bad outcomes selected. Then the bad outcomes are subtracted from the number of good outcomes selected. The lower the score, the more bad attributions are selected and thus the more depressed the child is, according to Abramson et al.'s (1978) theory. This measure is in the developmental stages, but a preliminary study by Kaslow et al. (1984) found that it was able to dis-

criminate depressed from nondepressed children in their sample.

Goldfried and Sobocinski (1975) and Nelson (1976) have postulated that irrational self-statements play a role in children's depression, and found a significant relationship between these statements and depression as measured on rating scales. Obviously, far more research is needed in this area as to the utility of cognitive style. Most of the research currently centers around impulsivity. Cognitive tempo as measured by the Matching Familiar Figures Test may be an alternative method, but validation is scarce for its utility with depressed children. The Porteus mazes were also thought to be a possible measure of lethargy and passivity in depressed children. However, Leon et al. (1980) found that the Porteus did not discriminate depressed from nondepressed children, leading one to believe that cognitive tempo may not be a marker for depression. It appears that these cognitive measures show the weakest research basis in diagnosing depression in children; they may well be useful, but their utility is not well documented.

SOCIOMETRIC MEASURES

The final type of depression assessment to be discussed is the use of peer ratings. There are several sociometric methods open to the practitioner. The foremost instrument for peer identification is the Peer Nomination Inventory for Depression (PNID). This measure consists of 14 items for depressive behaviors, 2 items for popularity, and 2 items for happiness. The items were selected from the literature on childhood depression and from the clinical judgment of nine experts. For each PNID item, the child's score is his or her number of nominations divided by the number in the classroom. These means are then summed across items to yield the child's total score. Lefkowitz and Tesiny (1980) developed the instrument as a possibly more sensitive measure of depression than rating scales. Test–retest reliability was reported by Lefkowitz and Tesiny (1980) as .79 for depression and .74 for happiness. They found four factors when the PNID was factor-analyzed; three of which related to depression (Inadequacy, Loneliness, and Dejection) and the other of which related to happiness. Concurrent validity was demonstrated in moderate but significant correlations with the CDI and teacher-rated depression. Since the PNID found that the children with the highest scores generally were also the same children who were viewed as generally unhappy and unpopular, possessed low self-esteem, and viewed events in the environment as beyond their control, the authors concluded that the PNID showed strong evidence of content and construct validity. A review by Kovacs (1981) suggested that further research is needed on the PNID to show its clinical utility through correlations of its ability to discriminate depressed children with independent psychiatric diagnoses.

SUMMARY

In summary, it appears that the diagnosis of depression in childhood necessitates the use of various measures that tap into different areas of the child's life. From the studies reviewed above, it may well be concluded that the combining of cognitive assessment with behavioral data is necessary for an accurate diagnosis of depression. Particularly important is information from the child as to subjective feelings and thoughts to which parents and teachers may not be privy. Parental input is important in determining time frames and duration of possible depressive symptoms. Of recurring importance is the interaction of parental psychopathology with parental reports of depression in children. Poznanski (1982) found that a high percentage of parents with depressed children were depressed themselves. Her feeling was that such parents either overidentify the problems their children have or withdraw from interaction with the children. It would appear important to obtain information from both parents in order to try to offset this tendency. In addition, it may be a valuable tool in therapy to discuss the various points of view garnered from separate clinical interviews with the parents.

Additional areas of concern are with the psychometric instruments themselves. The instruments reviewed above differ in their definition of depression, the criteria used to diagnose depression, the measurement of severity and duration, standardization on normal populations, and the ability to discriminate depression from other psychopathologies. In fact, this ability to distinguish depressed children from those with other types of psychopathology has repeatedly been cited as one of the weaknesses of most of the measures reported (Kazdin & Petti, 1982). Reliability and validity studies are also needed to ascertain the utility of some of the methods. The cognitive assessment methods of thought sampling, in vivo thought sampling, and attribution measurement have not established a sound empirical basis for use with children, whether depressed or not. Of great concern is the tendency of the various measures to validate one another. The foremost and most widely used instrument, the CDI, is often used to establish the credibility of a new instrument. Unfortunately, the CDI has not been found to discriminate among conduct disorders, anxiety disorders, and depression in psychiatric populations unless the scores are at the extremes. Much of the depression research is based on using groups identified by the CDI, common structured interviews, and similar measures as depressed. This may lead one to question the results of these studies as representative of a population whose major diagnosis is one of depression. The contamination of these samples may be one reason for the conflicting results obtained as to correlates of childhood depression; the research may be based on an empirically shaky foundation, and the postulates taken from this research may well be misdirected. Quay, Routh, and Shapiro (1987) compared Depression, Attention Deficit Disorders, Conduct Disorders, and Autism as defined by DSM-III criteria and found that the differences among these disorders disappeared when subjected to these empirical questions: Are these distinct syndromes? Are these syndromes associated with different causes? Do these syndromes have different outcomes? Do these syndromes require different intervention strategies? Quay et al. (1987) concluded that the disorders needed to be validated more fully by research efforts, rather than just the generating of lists of symptoms as evidenced in DSM-III.

With children, it is especially important to be sensitive to changes in the expression of emotion with developmental stage. Leon et al. (1980) found that different age groups may express depression in different manners. Further research is certainly needed in this area. Moreover, there is a paucity of research in depression in children with academic handicaps (such as learning disabilities), emotional disturbance, mental retardation, and physical handicaps. For the practitioner, these groups are frequently involved in therapy or, at the very least, consultation. Well-controlled research to address these issues would be helpful not only for the clinician, but also for the parents in dealing and coping with these difficulties.

Therefore, it appears that there are numerous researchable questions to be addressed in the area of assessment. Outcome research is scarce, and the comparison of differing types of therapeutic interventions is almost nonexistent. Researchers are beginning to use normal populations in developing norms for their instruments, and this is certainly a step in the right direction. Although the literature generally has concluded that childhood depression exists, the measures of this depression vary according to report source, assessment method used, cutoff scores used to delineate severity, and definition of symptomatology. All of these variables require more careful scrutiny, and studies with broad-based populations, both general and clinical, will aid in our understanding of the underpinnings of childhood depression—and, we may hope in our manner of intervention.

REFERENCES

Abramson, L. Y., Seligman, M. E. P., & Teasdale, J. D. (1978). Learned helplessness in humans: Critique and reformulation. *Journal of Abnormal Psychology, 87*, 40–47.

Achenbach, T. M., & Edelbrock. C. S. (1983). *Manual for the Child Behavior Checklist and Revised Child Behavior Profile*. Burlington: University of Vermont, Department of Psychiatry.

American Psychiatric Association. (1980). *Diagnostic and statistical manual of mental disorders* (3rd ed.). Washington, DC: Author.

American Psychiatric Association. (1987). *Diagnostic and statistical manual of mental disorders* (3rd ed., revised). Washington, DC: Author.

Anderson, J. C., Williams, S., McGee, R., & Silva, P. A. (1987). DSM-III disorders in preadolescent children. *Archives of General Psychiatry, 44*, 69–76.

Asarnow, J. R., & Carlson, G. A. (1985). Depression Self-Rating Scale: Utility with child psychiatric inpatients. *Journal of Consulting and Clinical Psychology, 53*, 491–499.

Beck, A. T. (1967). *Depression: Clinical, experimental, and theoretical aspects*. New York: Hoeber.

Beck, A. T. (1976). *Cognitive therapy and emotional disorders*. New York: International Universities Press.

Bernard, M. E., & Joyce, M. R. (1984). *Rational–emotive therapy with children and adolescents*. New York: Wiley.

Birleson, P. (1981). The validity of depressive disorder in childhood and the development of a self rating scale: A research report. *Journal of Child Psychology and Psychiatry, 22*, 73–88.

Brumback, R. A., Dietz-Schmidt, S. G., & Weinberg, M. A. (1977). Depression in children referred to an educational diagnostic center: Diagnosis and treatment and analysis of criteria and literature review. *Diseases of the Nervous System, 38*, 529–535.

Brumback, R., & Weinberg, W. (1977). Childhood depression: An explanation of a behavior disorder of children. *Perceptual and Motor Skills, 44*, 911–916.

Cantwell, D. P. (1983). Assessment of childhood depression. In D. P. Cantwell & G. A. Carlson (Eds.), *Affective disorders in childhood and adolescence: An update*. New York: Spectrum.

Cantwell, D. P., & Carlson, G. A. (1979). Problems and prospects in the study of childhood depression. *Journal of Nervous and Mental Disease, 167*, 522–529.

Cantwell, D. P., & Carlson, G. A. (1982). Childhood depression. *Journal of Nervous and Mental Disease, 167*, 522–529.

Carey, M. P., Faulstich, M. E., Gresham, F. M., Ruggiero, L., & Enyart, P. (1987). Children's Depression Inventory: Construct and discriminant validity across clinical and nonreferred (control) populations. *Journal of Consulting and Clinical Psychology, 55*, 755–761.

Carlson, G. A., & Cantwell, D. P. (1979). A survey of depressive symptoms in a child and adolescent psychiatric population. *Journal of the American Academy of Child Psychiatry, 18*, 587–589.

Carlson, G. A., & Cantwell, D. P. (1980). A survey of depressive symptoms, syndromes, and disorders in a child psychiatric population. *Journal of Child Psychology and Psychiatry, 21*, 19–25.

Chiles, J., Miller, M. L., & Cox, G. B. (1980). Depression in an adolescent delinquent population. *Archives of General Psychiatry, 37*, 1179–1184.

Cohen, P., O'Connor, P., Lewis, S., Velez, C. N., & Malachowski, B. (1987). Comparison of DISC and K-SADS-P interviews of an epidemiological sample of children. *Journal of the American Academy of Child and Adolescent Psychiatry, 26*, 662–667.

Costello, E. J., Edelbrock, C. S., & Costello, A. J. (1985). Validity of the NIMH Diagnostic Interview Schedule for Children: A comparison between psychiatric and pediatric referrals. *Journal of Abnormal and Child Psychology, 13*, 579–595.

Derry, P. A., & Kuiper, N. A. (1981). Schematic processing and self-reference in clinical depression. *Journal of Abnormal Psychology, 90*, 286–297.

Di Giuseppe, R. A. (1981). Cognitive therapy with children. In G. Emery, S. D. Hollon, & R. C. Bedrosian

(Eds.), *New directions in cognitive therapy*. (pp. 50–98). New York: Guilford Press.

Edelbrock, C., Costello, A. J., Dulcan, M. K., Kalas, R., & Conover, N. C. (1985). Age differences in the reliability of the psychiatric interview of the child. *Child Development, 56,* 265–275.

Finch, A. J., Jr., & Rogers, T. R. (1984). Self report instruments. In T. H. Ollendick & M. Hersen (Eds.), *Child behavioral assessment*. New York: Pergamon Press.

Friedman, R. J., & Butler, L. F. (1979). *Development and evaluation of a test battery to assess childhood depression*. Unpublished manuscript, Ontario Institute for Studies in Education.

Gittelman-Klein, R., & Klein, D. F. (1973). School phobia: Diagnostic considerations in the light of imipramine effects. *Journal of Nervous and Mental Disorders, 156,* 199–215.

Goldfried, M. R., & Sobocinski, D. (1975). The effects of irrational beliefs on emotional arousal. *Journal of Consulting and Clinical Psychology, 43,* 504–510.

Hammen, C. L., & Krantz, S. (1976). Effect of success and failure on depressive cognitions. *Journal of Abnormal Psychology, 85,* 577–586.

Hammen, C. L., & Zupan, B. A. (1984). Self-schemas, depression, and the processing of personal information in children. *Journal of Experimental Psychology, 37,* 598–608.

Herjanic, B., & Campbell, W. (1977). Differentiating psychiatrically disturbed children on the basis of a structured interview. *Journal of Abnormal Child Psychology, 5,* 127–134.

Herjanic, B., & Reich, W. (1982). Development of a structured psychiatric interview for children: Agreement between child and parent on individual symptoms. *Journal of Abnormal Child Psychology, 10,* 307–324.

Hodges, K., McKnew, D., Burbach, D. J., & Roebuck, L. (1987). Diagnostic concordance between the Child Assessment Schedule (CAS) and the Schedule for Affective Disorders and Schizophrenia for School-Age Children (K-SADS) in an outpatient sample using lay interviewers. *Journal of the American Academy of Child and Adolescent Psychiatry, 26,* 654–661.

Hodges, K., McKnew, D., Cytryn, L., Stern, L., & Kline, J. (1982). The Child Assessment Schedule (CAS) diagnostic interview: A report on reliability and validity. *Journal of the American Academy of Child Psychiatry, 21,* 468–473.

Hodges, K., & Siegel, L. J. (1985). Depression in children and adolescents. In E. E. Beckham & W. R. Leber (Eds.), *Handbook of depression*. Homewood, IL: Dorsey Press.

Hodges, K., Stern, L., Cytryn, L., & McKnew, D. (1982). The development of a child assessment interview for research and clinical use. *Journal of Abnormal Child Psychology, 10,* 173–189.

Ingram, R. E. (1984). Toward an information-processing analysis of depression. *Cognitive Therapy and Research, 8,* 443–478.

Kashani, J. H., Manning, G. W., McKnew, D. H., Cytryn, L., Simmonds, J., & Woodperson, P. (1980). Depression in incarcerated delinquents. *Psychiatry Research, 3,* 185–191.

Kashani, J. H., & Simmonds, J. F. (1979). The incidence of depression in children. *American Journal of Psychiatry, 136,* 1203–1205.

Kaslow, N. J., & Rehm, L. P. (1983). Childhood depression. In R. J. Morris & T. R. Kratochwill (Eds.), *The practice of child therapy*. New York: Pergamon Press.

Kaslow, N. J., Rehm, L. P., & Siegel, A. W. (1984). Social-cognitive and cognitive correlates of depression in children. *Journal of Abnormal Child Psychology, 12,* 605–620.

Kaslow, N. J., Tanenbaum, R. L., & Seligman, M. E. P. (1978). *The KASTAN: A children's attributional styles questionnaire*. Unpublished manuscript, University of Pennsylvania.

Kazdin, A. E. (1981). Assessment techniques for childhood depression. *Journal of the American Academy of Child Psychiatry, 20,* 358–375.

Kazdin, A. E. (1987). Children's Depression Scale: Validation with child psychiatric inpatients. *Journal of Child Psychology and Psychiatry, 28,* 29–41.

Kazdin, A. E., Colbus, D., & Rodgers, A. (1986). Assessment of depression and diagnosis of depressive disorder among psychiatrically disturbed children. *Journal of Abnormal Child Psychology, 14,* 499–515.

Kazdin, A. E., Esveldt-Dawson, K., Sherick, R. B., & Colbus, D. (1985). Assessment of overt behavior and childhood depression among psychiatrically disturbed children. *Journal of Consulting and Clinical Psychology, 53,* 201–210

Kazdin, A. E., French, N. H., & Unis, A. S. (1980). Child, mother, and father evaluations of childhood depression in psychiatric inpatient children. *Journal of Abnormal Child Psychology, 11,* 167–180.

Kazdin, A. E., French, N. H., Unis, A. S., & Esveldt-Dawson, K. (1983). Assessment of childhood depression: Correspondence of child and parent ratings. *Journal of the American Academy of Child Psychiatry, 22,* 157–164.

Kazdin, A. E., French, N. H., Unis, A. S., Esveldt-Dawson, K., & Sherick, R. B. (1983). Hopelessness, depression, and suicidal intent among psychiatrically disturbed inpatient children. *Journal of Consulting and Clinical Psychology, 51,* 504–510.

Kazdin, A. E., & Petti, T. A. (1982). Self-report and interview measures of childhood and adolescent depression. *Journal of Child Psychology and Psychiatry, 23,* 437–457.

Kazdin, A. E., Rodgers, A., & Colbus, D. (1986). The Hopelessness Scale for Children: Psychometric characteristics and concurrent validity. *Journal of Consulting and Clinical Psychology, 54,* 241–245.

Kazdin, A. E., Sherick, R. B., Esveldt-Dawson, K., & Rancurello, M. D. (1985). Nonverbal behavior and childhood depression. *Journal of the American Academy of Child Psychiatry, 24,* 303–309.

Kendall, P. C., & Braswell, L. (1982). Assessment for cognitive–behavioral interventions in the schools. *School Psychology Review, 11,* 21–30.

Kendall, P. C., & Hollon, S. D. (1981). *Assessment strategies for cognitive–behavioral interventions*. New York: Academic Press.

Kendall, P.C., & Korgeski, G. P. (1979). Assessment and cognitive–behavioral interventions. *Cognitive Therapy and Research, 3,* 1–21.

Kovacs, M. (1981). Rating scales to assess depression in school-aged children. *Acta Paedopsychiatrica, 46,* 305–315.

Kovacs, M. (1985). Children's Depression Inventory. *Psychopharmacology Bulletin, 21,* 995–998.

Kovacs, M., & Beck, A. T. (1977). An empirical–clinical approach toward a definition of childhood depression. In J. G. Schulterbrandt & A. Raskin (Eds.), *Depression in childhood: Diagnosis, treatment, and conceptual models.* New York: Raven Press.

Kovacs, M., Feinberg, T. L., Crouse-Novack, M. A., Paulauskas, S. L., & Finkelstein, R. (1984). Depressive disorders in childhood: I. A longitudinal prospective study of characteristics and recovery. *Archives of General Psychiatry, 41,* 229–237.

Kovacs, M., & Paulauskas, S. L. (1984). Developmental stage and the expression of depressive disorders in children: An empirical analysis. In D. Cicchetti & K. Schneider-Rosen (Eds.), *New directions for child development: Childhood depression.* San Francisco: Jossey-Bass.

Kuiper, N., Derry, P., & Macdonald, M. (1982). Self-reliance and person perception in depression: A social cognition perspective. In G. Weary & H. Mirels (Eds.), *Integration of clinical and social psychology.* New York: Oxford University Press.

Lang, M., & Tisher, M. (1978). *Children's Depression Scale.* Melbourne: Australian Council for Educational Research.

Lapouse, R. (1966). The epidemiology of behavior disorders in children. *American Journal of Diseases of Children, 111,* 594–599.

Lefkowitz, M. M., & Burton, N. (1978). Childhood depression. *Psychological Bulletin, 85,* 716–726.

Lefkowitz, M. M., & Tesiny, E. P. (1980). Childhood depression. *Journal of Consulting and Clinical Psychology, 48,* 43–50.

Leon, G. R., Kendall, P. C., & Garber, J. (1980). Depression in children: Parent, teacher, and child perspectives. *Journal of Abnormal Child Psychology, 8,* 221–235.

Lesse, S. (1983). Masked depression. *Current Psychiatric Therapy, 22,* 81–87.

Lewinsohn, P. M. (1974). A behavioral approach to depression. In R. J. Friedman & M. M. Katz (Eds.), *The psychology of depression: Contemporary theory and research.* New York: Wiley.

Moretti, M. M., Fine, S., Haley, G., & Marriage, K. (1985). Childhood and adolescent depression: Child report versus parent report information. *Journal of the American Academy of Child Psychiatry, 24,* 298–302.

Mullins, L. L., Peterson, L., Wonderlich, S. A., & Reaven, N. M. (1986). The influence of depressive symptomatology in children on the social responses and perceptions of adults. *Journal of Clinical Child Psychology, 15,* 233–240.

Nelson, W. M., III. (1976). *Cognitive-behavior strategies in modifying an impulsive cognitive style.* Unpublished doctoral dissertation, Virginia Commonwealth University.

Nelson, W. M., III, Politano, P. M., Finch, A. J., Jr., Wendel, N., & Mayhall, C. (1987). Children's Depression Inventory: Normative data and utility with emotionally disturbed children. *Journal of the American Academy of Child and Adolescent Psychiatry, 26,* 43–48

Norvell, N., & Towle, P. O. (1986). Self-reported depression and observable conduct problems in children. *Journal of Clinical Child Psychology, 15,* 228–232.

Ollendick, T. H., & Hersen, M. (1984). An overview of child behavioral assessment. In T. H. Ollendick & M. Hersen (Eds.), *Child behavioral assessment.* New York: Pergamon Press.

Pearce, J. B. (1978). The recognition of depressive disorder in children. *Journal of Research in Social Medicine, 71,* 494–500.

Poznanski, E. O. (1982). The clinical phenomenology of childhood depression. *American Journal of Orthopsychiatry, 52,* 308–313.

Poznanski, E. O., Cook, S. C., & Carroll, B. J. (1979). A depression rating scale for children. *Pediatrics, 64,* 442–450.

Poznanski, E. O., Grossman, J. A., Buchsbaum, Y., Banegas, M., Freeman, L., & Gibbons, R. (1984). Preliminary studies of the reliability and validity of the Children's Depression Rating Scale. *Journal of the American Academy of Child Psychiatry, 23,* 191–197.

Puig-Antich, J. (1982). The use of RDC criteria for major depressive disorder in children and adolescents. *Journal of the American Academy of Child Psychiatry, 18,* 291–293.

Puig-Antich, J., Chambers, W. J., & Tabrizi, M. A. (1983). The clinical assessment of current depressive episodes in children and adolescents. In D. P. Cantwell & G. A. Carlson (Eds.), *Affective disorders in childhood and adolescence: An update.* New York: Spectrum.

Puig-Antich, J., & Rabinovitch, J. (1986). The relationship between affective and anxiety disorders in childhood. In R. Gittelman (Ed.), *Anxiety disorders of childhood.* New York: Guilford Press.

Quay, H. C., & Peterson, D. R. (1975). *Manual for the Revised Behavior Problem Checklist.* Miami: University of Miami Press.

Quay, H. C., Routh, D. K., & Shapiro, S. K. (1987). Psychopathology of childhood: From description to validation. *Annual Review of Psychology, 38,* 491–532.

Rehm, L. P. (1977). A self-control model of depression. *Behavior Therapy, 8,* 787–804.

Reynolds, W. M. (1984). Depression in children and adolescents: Phenomenology, evaluation, and treatment. *School Psychology Review, 13,* 171–182.

Reynolds, W. M. (1985). Depression in childhood and adolescence: Diagnosis, assessment, intervention strategies and research. In T. R. Kratochwill (Ed.), *Advances in school psychology.* Hillsdale, NJ: Erlbaum.

Reynolds, W. M., Anderson, G., & Bartell, N. (in press). Measuring depression in children: A tripartite assessment approach. *Journal of Abnormal Child Psychology.*

Rholes, W. S., Blackwell, J., Jordan, C., & Walters, C. (1980). A developmental study of learned helplessness. *Developmental Psychology, 16,* 616–624.

Rotundo, N., & Hensley, V. R. (1985). The Children's Depression Scale: A study of its validity. *Journal of Child Psychology and Psychiatry, 26,* 917–927.

Ryan, N. D., Puig-Antich, J., Ambrosini, P., Rabinovich, H., Robinson, D., Nelson, B., Iyengar, S., & Twomey, J. (1987). Clinical picture of major depression in children and adolescents. *Archives of General Psychiatry, 44,* 854–861.

Sacco, W. P., & Graves, D. J. (1984). Childhood depression, interpersonal problem-solving, and self-ratings of performance. *Journal of Clinical Child Psychology, 13,* 10–15.

Saylor, C. F., Finch, A. J., Baskin, C. H., Saylor, C. B., Darnell, G., & Furey, W. (1984). Children's Depression Inventory: Investigation of procedures and correlates. *Journal of the American Academy of Child Psychiatry, 23,* 626–628.

Saylor, C. F., Finch, A. J., Spirito, A., & Bennett, B. (1984). The Children's Depression Inventory: A systematic evaluation of psychometric properties. *Journal of Consulting and Clinical Psychology, 52,* 955–967.

Seligman, M. E. P., & Abramson, L. Y. (1981). A learned helplessness point of view. In L. P. Rehm (Ed.), *Behavior therapy for depression.* New York: Academic Press.

Shephard, M., Oppenheim, A. N., & Mitchell, S. (1966). Childhood behavior disorders and the child guidance clinic: An epidemiological study. *Journal of Child Psychology and Psychiatry, 7,* 39–52.

Shoemaker, O. S., Erickson, M. T., & Finch, A. J., Jr. (1986). Depression and anger in third and fourth grade boys: A multimethod assessment approach. *Journal of Clinical Child Psychology, 15,* 290–296.

Spivack, G., & Spotts, J. (1976). *Devereux Child Elementary School Behavior Rating Scale manual.* Devon, PA: Devereux Foundation.

Strauss, C. C., Forehand, R., Frame, C., & Smith, K. (1984). Characteristics of children with extreme scores on the Children's Depression Inventory. *Journal of Clinical Child Psychology, 13,* 227–231.

Sylvester, C. E., Hyde, T. S., & Reichler, R. J. (1987). The Diagnostic Interview for Children and Personality Inventory for Children in studies of children at risk for anxiety disorders or depression. *Journal of the American Academy of Child and Adolescent Psychiatry, 26,* 668–675.

Tisher, M., (1983). School refusal: A depressive equivalent? In D. P. Cantwell & G. A. Carlson (Eds.), *Affective disorders in children and adolescents.* New York: Spectrum.

Weinberg, W. A., Rutman, J., Sullivan, L., Penic, E. C., & Dietz, S. G. (1973). Depression in children referred to an educational diagnostic center. *Journal of Pediatrics, 83,* 1065–1072.

Weingartner, H., Cohen, R. M., Murphy, D. L., Martello, J., & Gerdt, C. (1981). Cognitive processes in depression. *Archives of General Psychiatry, 38,* 42–47.

Weissman, M. M., Wickramarante, P., Warner, V., John, K., Prusoff, B. A., Merikangas, K. R., & Gammon, G. D. (1987). Assessing psychiatric disorders in children. *Archives of General Psychiatry, 44,* 747–753.

Werry, J. S., & Quay, H. C. (1971). The prevalence of behavior symptoms in younger elementary school children. *American Journal of Orthopsychiatry, 41,* 136–143.

Wolfe, V. V., Finch, A. J., Jr., Saylor, C. F., Blount, R. L., Pallmeyer, T. P., & Carek, D. J. (1987). Negative affectivity in children: A multitrait–multimethod investigation. *Journal of Consulting and Clinical Psychology, 55,* 245–250.

13

Objective Assessment of Child and Adolescent Personality: The Personality Inventory for Children (PIC)

DAVID LACHAR
University of Texas Medical School at Houston

The Personality Inventory for Children (PIC) is an objective multidimensional measure of behavior, affect, ability, and family function, which is applied in the assessment of children from preschool through adolescence. Scale scores are derived from adult informants' responses to brief inventory items (e.g., "My child has been difficult to manage," "My child has many friends," "My child worries about things that usually only adults worry about," "My child can tell the time fairly well"). PIC items require a reading proficiency at the sixth- to seventh-grade level (Barad & Hughes, 1984; Harrington & Follett, 1984). Respondents, usually the mothers of the children or adolescents evaluated, answer "true" or "false" to the first 131, 280, or 420 items of the Revised Format administration booklet and record these answers on a hand-scorable or optically scannable answer sheet, or respond to inventory items presented directly to them by a microcomputer.

The items of the 1981 Revised Format administration booklet have been rearranged so that scoring and interpretation options increase with the number of items completed. Responses to the first 131 items generate scores for the Lie scale, a measure of respon-

dent defensiveness, and four broad-band scales derived through factor analysis: (I) Undisciplined/Poor Self-Control; (II) Social Incompetence; (III) Internalization/Somatic Symptoms; and (IV) Cognitive Development (Lachar, 1982; Lachar, Gdowski, & Snyder, 1982). This five-scale format is most useful in research projects when time is extremely limited, when a brief screening device is required to determine the need for a more detailed evaluation, or when respondents' ability to complete a greater number of items is questionable.

Response to the first 280 items of the Revised Format administration booklet (fewer than 50% of the 600 items that comprise the original PIC item pool) provide the 20 scales of the Revised Format Profile Form: the four factor scales, three measures of informant response style, a general screening scale, and 12 scales that measure child ability, behavior, affect, and family status. The relative efficiency of the 280-item format was obtained through item rearrangement and through a process in which 14 of these scales were shortened by removal of an average of 18% of each scale's items, although comparability to their full-length equivalents was retained (Forbes, 1986; Lachar, 1982). The

14 shortened scales are designated with an "–S" suffix, which is also added to each scale's abbreviation.

Completion of the 420 inventory items provides scores for all 20 scales in their full-length format, as well as responses to a critical-item list composed of 162 items that are assigned to 14 mutually exclusive categories: Depression and Poor Self-Concept; Worry and Anxiety; Reality Distortion; Peer Relations; Unsocialized Aggression; Conscience Development; Poor Judgment; Atypical Development; Distractibility, Activity Level and Coordination; Speech and Language; Somatic Complaints/Current Health; School Adjustment; Family Discord; and Other. The other 180 items of the original item pool were removed from the published materials in 1989 to simplify test administration (see Wirt, Lachar, Klinedinst, & Seat, 1984 for a listing of these items and a description of 17 experimental scales that included some of these items).

Selection of the parents as the source of PIC test responses helps overcome two of the major obstacles posed by requesting the referred child or adolescent to respond to numerous self-report descriptions in order to obtain a multiple-scale objective evaluation. The majority of children seen by mental health professionals in a variety of settings appear for such an evaluation because of their noncompliant behaviors and/or documented problems in academic achievement, most notably in the development of reading skills. Therefore, it seems quite unlikely that a technique requiring such children to read and respond to a large set of self-descriptions will find broad acceptance in routine clinical practice. Another difficulty in applying self-report inventory methodology to the assessment of children is the wide variability in verbal comprehension found in such children. If one assumes that the effectiveness of self-report personality descriptors derives from the richness and variety of language, restriction of possible vocabulary to a second- or third-grade reading list would severely limit the options an item writer would have to express the more subtle aspects of child affect and family interaction. It appears, in addition, that several child self-report measures are further restricted in their application by required reading levels that are actually higher than those stated by the test authors (Harrington & Follett, 1984).

The fact that adults respond to PIC items is advantageous in several other ways. When both parents independently complete the PIC, comparison of the profiles generated suggests areas of agreement and disagreement, thereby providing additional information useful in a family or systems-oriented assessment. It should be noted that recent comparison of mother–father PIC pairs suggests that mothers should be selected as primary informants, because fathers may underestimate affect dimensions such as those measured by the Depression and Anxiety scales (Hulbert, Gdowski, & Lachar, 1986). Another study, however, found the application of mother- and father-generated profiles to be quite similar (Clark, 1987).

Because parents provide the item responses, they inherently become involved in their child's assessment—a requirement of Public Law 94-142 (Education for All Handicapped Children Act, 1975), which establishes guidelines for the psychological evaluation of children in need of special education services. Occasionally, linguistic and cultural differences in children obscure the need for a special education placement and make the evaluation of such a need difficult at best. It is possible, however, to translate the PIC into other languages and to establish the validity of these versions. In this manner, a Spanish translation of the PIC might be used by a monolingual school psychologist or social worker to determine whether a child with limited English-language competence will be optimally served by intensive language training, or whether current problems also reflect behavioral, emotional, or family characteristics or deficits in cognitive functioning. Such translations (currently available in Italian, French, Norwegian, and Spanish) also facilitate cross-cultural study of child adjustment and personality development.

A final advantage to be noted is that, as mothers frequently accompany their children when they are tested, the addition of a PIC to an assessment does not increase the professional time needed to complete an evaluation. The 280-item PIC can easily be completed while a child is assessed with a Wechsler Intelligence Scale for Children—

Revised (WISC-R), a Wide Range Achievement Test (WRAT), and a Bender–Gestalt Test. The only additional costs to the clinician are represented by the cost of a reusable administration booklet, an answer sheet, a profile form, and the few minutes needed to score the answer sheet to obtain scale raw scores. Parents not only see this task as a reasonable one, but are often both pleased and actually relieved to have the opportunity to detail their concerns.

Because PIC responses are obtained from informants, concern has been raised that observer distortion could have the potential to compromise scale accuracy. Individuals who have raised these concerns have not taken into account the role of the PIC validity scales, which signal respondent defensiveness or exaggeration. They have also failed to appreciate the documented effectiveness of the PIC profile scales obtained within analyses in which these validity scales were not even used to exclude potentially invalid protocols. Concern has been raised that the PIC profile reflects a mother's intentional distortion (Cronbach, 1984) or actually presents the mother's personality (Achenbach, 1981).

It appears that potential users of informant-derived child evaluation measures may be unable to look beyond their initial reaction to the source of questionnaire responses. This reaction appears to limit their appreciation of the psychometric process by which these responses are transformed into measures that allow the generation of actuarial predictions. In addition to earlier efforts that suggested the lack of a significant relationship between mothers' Minnesota Multiphasic Personality Inventory (MMPI) scales and the PIC descriptions of their children (Lachar & Sharp, 1979; Wirt & Lachar, 1981), recent efforts have suggested that the PICs from mothers who obtain elevated MMPI profiles are comparable to the PICs from mothers who obtain normal-limit MMPI profiles in their ability to predict PIC-independent dimensions of child adjustment (Lachar, Kline, & Gdowski, 1987). That is, informant psychopathology does not appear to compromise PIC profile scale validity significantly.

The objective format of the PIC requires limited professional time for administration and scoring, and interpretive guidelines clarify application (Lachar, 1982; Lachar & Gdowski, 1979; Wirt et al., 1984). The same item pool can be successfully applied from age 3 through adolescence, and family socioeconomic status and cultural background have minimal influence on test interpretation (Lachar & Gdowski, 1979; Wirt et al., 1984). PIC scales may be integrated into a traditional psychometric evaluation, may form the first stage of a sequential assessment process, or may serve to identify children in need of a psychological evaluation. For each scale, higher T-score elevations (generated from 2,390 school-age protocols or 192 preschool descriptions) represent a reduced probability of occurrence among nonreferred children and the increased probability of psychopathology or deficit.

The dimensions represented by scales selected for the PIC profile do not reflect a specific theoretical perspective in regard to personality, psychopathology, or child development, but rather reflect those dimensions routinely assessed by clinicians, regardless of theoretical preference or bias (Achenbach & Edelbrock, 1978; Dreger, 1981). Scale construction methodology has also varied to reflect the specific psychometric characteristics desired, as well as practical issues, such as the availability of appropriate criterion groups. Factor analysis, empirical keying, and rational/content methodologies have been applied to scale item selection in the construction of narrow- and broad-band scales. Characteristic of all the profile scales, however constructed, is their ability to successfully predict non-PIC measures of child adjustment and ability. This established *actuarial* character of the PIC is discussed in some detail later in this chapter.

THE PROFILE SCALES

Informant Response Style

Lie Scale

The rationally developed Lie (L) scale was constructed to identify a defensive response set manifested by a tendency to ascribe the most virtuous of behaviors to, and to deny minor, commonly occurring behavior problems in, the child described. Scale items include "My child sometimes disobeys his (her) parents" and "Sometimes my child will put off doing a chore." Correlations with other PIC scales and ratings of the child suggest that L reflects the absence or denial of behavior problems, especially those classified as delinquent and asocial, as well as the absence or denial of family problems and psychological discomfort. L elevation increases when the respondent intentionally attempts to portray the child as having fewer problems than is actually the case (Daldin, 1985; McVaugh & Grow, 1983). Daldin (1985) found that L scores of $>59T$ increased from 4% to 92% when mothers were asked to complete the PIC as though their children did not have the problems that brought them to a child guidance clinic.

Frequency Scale

The Frequency (F) scale consists of items that were seldom endorsed in the scored direction in the normative sample ($M = 5\%$) or in a sample of preadolescent boys evaluated at child guidance clinics ($M = 14\%$). Item content was varied so that a single pattern of severe disturbance could not account for an extreme scale elevation. The F scale obtains extreme elevations ($120T$) for profiles when inventory items are completed without regard for item content (Wirt et al., 1984). There is evidence that highly elevated F scores may reflect exaggeration of problems. When parents were asked to describe their normal children in such a manner as to convince a psychologist of the presence of psychological disturbance, F increased from $55T$ to $115T$ (McVaugh & Grow, 1983). Mothers of children being evaluated at a child guidance clinic were asked to answer PIC items a second time, exaggerating the difficulties and problems that brought them to the clinic. In this manner, F-S increased from $67T$ to $118T$ (Daldin, 1985). On the other hand, 20% of a child guidance population obtained F elevations in excess of $99T$ (Lachar & Gdowski, 1979), and comparison of profiles for various criterion groups clearly supports the conclusion that F increases with severity of psychopathology (Wirt et al., 1984).

Defensiveness Scale

The empirically constructed Defensiveness (DEF) scale is composed of the inventory items that separated mothers judged to be high in defensiveness from mothers judged to be low in defensiveness on the basis of diagnostic interviews about the children being evaluated. Although a cutting score of $> 59T$ correctly identified 93% of the low-defensiveness and 88% of the high-defensiveness protocols, a recent study under "fake-good" instructions demonstrated that DEF-S T-scores only rose from 35.6 to 54.1. The percentage of profiles with DEF scores of $>59T$ rose from 0% to 40%, although DEF-S never exceeded $60T$ for these 25 profiles (Daldin, 1985). We (Lachar & Gdowski, 1979) suggest that DEF be interpreted to reflect informant resistance and defensiveness starting at $70T$, although only 4% of a heterogeneous child guidance sample obtained scores in this range. Indeed, only an additional 14% obtained scores of 60–69T.

General Adjustment

Adjustment Scale

Item endorsement rates for 600 normal boys 7–12 years of age were compared to the item endorsement rates for 200 maladjusted boys 7–12 years of age to construct this scale. The Adjustment (ADJ) scale is a screening measure that identifies children in need of a psychological evaluation and is a general measure of poor psychological adjustment. Application of a cutting score of $>59T$ correctly classified 86% of normal and 89% of clinic protocols. These classification rates have remained stable through subsequent analyses.

The Cognitive Triad

The first 3 of the 12 substantive scales reflect the cognitive status of the child. Although clinicians may resist a procedure that evaluates child ability without directly assessing the child, the value of such measures on the profile is considerable. These scales may be applied to determine probable need for individual assessment of ability and achievement, and they play a central role in defining relatively homogeneous subgroups of disturbed children through classification of total profile configuration. (See the discussion later in this chapter of classification of special education needs and a PIC profile typology.)

Achievement Scale

The item endorsement rates for second- and third-grade boys who evidenced serious retardation in the development of reading ability were compared with the item endorsement rates of those children whose reading ability was grade-appropriate. These analyses formed the basis of the Achievement (ACH) scale, which assists in the identification of children whose academic achievement is significantly below age expectation regardless of intellectual capacity. A cutting score of $>59T$ correctly identified 97% of construction and 92% of cross-validation protocols. Factor analysis of scale items suggested that ACH not only measures limited academic abilities and poor achievement, but also reflects a dimension of poor psychological adjustment characterized by impulsivity, limited concentration, over- or underassertiveness with peers, and disregard for parental expectations (Wirt et al., 1984).

Intellectual Screening Scale

The Intellectual Screening (IS) scale was constructed to identify children whose difficulties may be related to impaired intellectual functioning or specific cognitive deficits, and for whom an individually administered intellectual assessment would be indicated. Items were identified by contrasting the protocols of retarded children with those of normal, nonretarded disturbed, and psychotic children.

Development Scale

The Development (DVL) scale items, selected through the consensus of experts, primarily reflect retarded development in motor coordination, poor school performance, and lack of any special skill or abilities. Other factors reflect limited motivation to achieve in school, clumsiness and weakness, limited reading skills, and deficient pragmatic skills.

Several investigators have established the relationship between a variety of ability and achievement measures, as well as special education classification, and ACH, IS, and DVL (see Bennett & Welsh, 1981; Clark,

Kehle, Bullock, & Jenson, 1987; DeKrey & Ehly, 1985; DeMoor-Peal & Handal, 1983; Dollinger, Goh, & Cody, 1984; Durrant, 1983; Forbes, 1987; Kelly, 1982; Lachar, Kline, & Boersma, 1986; Newby & Matthews, 1986; Schnel, 1982). Recent efforts suggest that child sex, age, and race do not moderate the relation between scale T-score evaluation and independent individual measurements of ability and achievement (Kline, Lachar, & Sprague, 1985).

Other Clinical Scales

Somatic Concern Scale

The Somatic Concern (SOM) scale is composed of items selected by judges to measure various health-related variables (frequency and seriousness of somatic complaints and illness, adjustment to illness, appetite and eating habits, sleep patterns, energy and strength, and headaches and stomachaches), as well as the physical basis for symptoms. This scale represents a unique and rather small factor when a large number of PIC scales are subjected to factor analysis (Wirt et al., 1984). Two study groups to date have obtained a mean SOM elevation above $60T$: boys exhibiting physical symptoms considered by a physician to be related to experienced stress (Stewart, 1971), and boys and girls with cancer (Armstrong, Wirt, Nesbit, & Martinson, 1982). Pipp (1979) found SOM to be correlated with only one MMPI scale for both male and female adolescent psychiatric patients: Hypochondriasis. Kelly (1982) found that only one Child Behavior Checklist (CBCL) scale correlated with SOM: Somatic complaints. Lachar and Gdowski (1979) found limited but highly appropriate correlates for SOM: fatigue, aches and pains, insomnia, somatic response to stress, and malingering.

Depression Scale

The Depression (D) scale items were judged by experienced clinicians to reflect childhood depression. Factor analysis of scale items yielded dimensions labeled Brooding/Moodiness; Social Isolation; Crying Spells; Lack of Energy; Pessimism/Anhedonia; Concern with Death and Separation; Serious Attitude; Sensitivity to Criticism; Indecisiveness/Poor Self-Concept; and Uncommunicativeness. Leon, Kendell, and Garber (1980) found D to correlate significantly with the Children's Depression Inventory in a sample of elementary school children. Children designated as "depressed" by their D T-score attributed positive events to external causes significantly more often than did children not so identified. Reynolds, Anderson, and Bartell (1985) found D to relate significantly to the Children's Depression Inventory, the Child Depression Scale, and teacher global depression ratings for a sample of 166 elementary school children. Kelly (1982) found D to be most strongly correlated with CBCL scales of Social Withdrawal, Depressed, Uncommunicative, and Social. Pipp (1979) found that D was significantly correlated with the MMPI Social Introversion scale for both male and female adolescent psychiatric patients, but significantly correlated with the MMPI Depression scale for only female adolescents. D has also significantly separated children independently labeled as depressed according to the *Diagnostic and Statistical Manual of Mental Disorders*, third edition (DSM-III) criteria on the basis of maternal interview ($M = 85T$) from children who did not meet this criteria ($M = 61T$); comparable classification performance of the Children's Depression Inventory was no better than that of D applied without the potential incremental validity of other PIC profile scales (Lobovits & Handel, 1985).

Family Relations Scale

The Family Relations (FAM) scale assists in determining the role that family and parental factors play in the development of child psychopathology, and also evaluates the need for in-depth assessment of family and parental characteristics. Scale items were selected from the nominations of experts to assess the following dimensions: parental role effectiveness, ability to cooperate in making family decisions, family involvement in community affairs, presence of feelings of love and happiness in the home, parental emotional adjustment, appropriateness of discipline, and concern for the rights of the child. Lachar and Sharp (1979) found that FAM was the only PIC profile scale that consistently correlated

with a broad range of maternal MMPI scales. FAM elevations are higher for children from divorced than from nondivorced parents (Schreiber, 1982), and FAM obtained the highest mean scale elevation in profiles of children who had a parent in treatment for alcoholism (Anderson & Quast, 1983). Snyder and Gdowski (1980) compared the scores of the Marital Satisfaction Inventory (MSI) from parents when FAM was $>59T$ to the MSI scores when FAM was $<46T$. High-FAM parents obtained significantly higher elevations on 9 of the 11 MSI profile scales. It is also interesting to note that the 1984 manual (Wirt et al., 1984) presents only one criterion group with an elevated mean FAM: adjudicated delinquents.

Delinquency Scale

Item response rates of adjudicated and nonadjudicated adolescents were compared to develop the Delinquency (DLQ) scale, designed to be a concurrent measure of the behavioral characteristics manifested by delinquents and a diagnostic aid in the identification of delinquent children. DLQ obtained a scale score-to-criterion validity of .89 in a cross-validation sample in which a cutting score correctly identified 95% of delinquents and normals. Factor analysis of scale items yielded two substantial factors labeled (1) Disregard for Limits/Interpersonal Insensitivity and (2) Antisocial Tendencies, as well as several small factors labeled Irritability/Limited Tolerance; Sadness; Lack of Interest/Impulsivity; Interpersonal Hostility; and Disrespect for Parents. Pipp (1979) found DLQ to correlate significantly with the MMPI scales Psychopathic Deviate and Hypomania for both male and female adolescents. Kelly (1982) found that DLQ correlated the most highly with the CBCL scales Delinquent and Aggressive. Lachar, Gdowski, and Synder (1984) found DLQ to correlate significantly with parent, teacher, and clinician rating form dimensions of Externalization, Impulsivity, Antisocial Character, and Hostility/Emotional Lability.

Adjudicated delinquents obtained very high T-score elevations, with 58% obtaining DLQ scores of $>99T$. Because DLQ elevations between $70T$ and $100T$ are very frequent for children and adolescents seen at child guidance agencies (Lachar & Gdowski, 1979: 52%), it has been important to identify replicated external correlates of DLQ to guide the interpretation of this scale. McAuliffe and Handal (1984) suggest that DLQ may reflect meaningful variance at much lower T-score elevations. When students attending a parochial high school were divided into two groups at 50T (the majority of the "elevated" sample scored between 50T and 70T), the elevated-DLQ sample scored significantly lower on the Socialization scale of the California Psychological Inventory and higher on a self-report measure of delinquent acts.

Withdrawal Scale

The Withdrawal (WDL) scale items were nominated to measure withdrawal from social contact. Factor analysis to WDL items resulted in content dimensions labeled Social and Physical Isolation; Shyness/Fear of Strangers; Isolation from Peers/Uncommunicativeness; Emotional Distance; Intentional Withdrawal/Distrust; and Isolative Intellectual Pursuits. Psychotic children obtain mean WDL elevations above 69T (Wirt et al., 1984). Kelly (1982) obtained significant correlations between WDL and the CBCL scales Social Withdrawal, Uncommunicativeness, and Social. Pipp (1979) found that WDL correlated significantly with the MMPI scale Social Introversion for both male and female adolescents.

Anxiety Scale

The Anxiety (ANX) scale items were nominated as measuring the various manifestations of anxiety. Factor analysis of scale items resulted in content dimensions labeled Brooding/Moodiness; Fearfulness; Worry; Fear of the Dark; Specific Fears/Crying Spells; Poor Self-Concept; Insecurity/ Fearfulness; and Sensitivity to Criticism/ Pessimism.

Psychosis Scale

The empirically keyed Psychosis (PSY) scale was constructed to discriminate children with psychotic symptomatology from normal, behaviorally disturbed nonpsychotic, and retarded children. Scale score-to-criterion validity was .88 in construction and .84 in cross-validation samples. Psychotic children obtain very high PSY elevations: 84% of the scale construction protocols scored above 99T. Pipp (1979) found that PSY correlated significantly with the MMPI scales Schizophrenia and Social Introversion for both male and female adolescents. PSY was the only PIC scale to correlate significantly with a clinician rating dimension labeled Disorganization/ Limited Reality Testing (Lachar et al., 1984).

Hyperactivity Scale

The Hyperactivity (HPR) scale items were empirically selected so as to separate children seen at guidance clinics who were described by their teachers as hyperactive (and diagnosable according to the revision of DSM-III [DSM-III-R] as having Attention Deficit–Hyperactivity Disorder) from children also evaluated at child guidance clinics who were not seen as hyperactive by their teachers. HPR obtained a scale score-to-criterion validity of .78; and a cutting score of >59T correctly classified 90% of hyperactive and 94% of maladjusted nonhyperactive samples. Breen and Barkley (1983) obtained similar classification rates, and Forbes (1985) found that HPR successfully differentiated between hyperactive and conduct-disordered children. Voelker, Lachar, and Gdowski (1983) found HPR elevation to be related to treatment with methylphenidate and favorable response to such treatment. Kelly (1982) obtained significant correlations between HPR and the CBCL scales Hyperactive, Aggressive, and Delinquent. Clark, Wanous, and Pompa (1982) obtained a considerable number of significant correlations between HPR and teacher ratings of special education students on such rating scale items as "Does not conform to limits," "Easily distracted," "Poor achievement due to distractibility," and "Poor achievement due to impulsivity." Recently, Newby and Mathews (1986) reported a significant relationship between HPR and the Knox Cube Test, a measure highly dependent on attention and concentration.

Social Skills Scale

The Social Skills (SSK) scale is composed of items selected by judges to measure the various characteristics that reflect effective social relations in childhood. SSK item content dimensions reflected in factor groupings suggest that this scale measures both lack of success in social activities (lack of friends; peer rejection; absence of club membership; adults as only social contacts), and the reasons for this lack of success (aggressive behavior with peers; absence of leadership qualities or social influence; social behavior suggesting poor sportsmanship, egocentrism, and obstinacy). SSK has been found to relate significantly to measures of moral judgment and cognitive perspective taking (Kurdek, 1980); to a self-report measure of social competence (Kurdek & Krile, 1983); and to a peer acceptance rating (Kurdek, 1982). SSK has also been found to correlate significantly with the Peer Support scale of the self-report Children's Perception of Social Support Inventory, as well as with parental and self-report measures of the quality of peer support (Schreiber, 1982).

The Factor Scales

Dimensions of child behavior derived through factor analysis have been characterized as either "narrow-band" or "broad-band" in character (Achenbach & Edelbrock, 1978). Narrow-band measures reflect limited dimensions of psychopathology, such as temper tantrums (Dreger, 1981). Broad-band measures, on the other hand, represent general patterns of behavioral disturbance, such as "internalizing" symptomatology (Achenbach & Edelbrock, 1978) or "anxiety turned inward" (Dreger, 1981). Comparison of the relative utility of broad-band versus narrow-band measures is a recurrent theme in the literature. In general, the broad-band measures are viewed as having favorable theoretical and research applications, whereas narrow-band measures with more behavioral specificity are seen as having more clinical utility. The availability of validated broad-band and narrow-band measures within the same instrument allows investigators and clinicians to pursue either or both approaches and facilitates the study of the relative utility of each approach.

The 12 PIC clinical scales (ACH through SSK), although not derived via factor analysis, can be classified in terms of both scale item content and correlate specificity as narrow-band measures. The 313 items of the 12 clinical scales were subjected to a series of factor analyses to identify item dimensions that would reflect a distillation of the variance measured by the PIC profile. Four item content dimensions representing approximately half of the total variance of these 313 items, obtained sufficient discriminative item loadings to facilitate construction of inventory scales.

1. *Undisciplined/Poor Self-Control (I)*. Factor I items appear primarily on scales ADJ, DLQ, and HPR. A factor analysis of scale items resulted in content dimensions labeled Ineffective Discipline; Impulsivity; Problematic Anger; Poor Peer Relationships; Limited Conscience Development; and Poor School Behavior. Correlation with parent, teacher, and clinician ratings provides independent evidence that Factor I reflects hostility/emotional lability, impulsivity, and antisocial behavior (Lachar et al., 1984).

2. *Social Incompetence (II)*. The majority of Factor II scale items are found on ADJ, D, WDL, ANX, PSY, and SSK. A factor analysis of scale items resulted in content dimensions labeled Sadness; Shyness; Peer Rejection; Lack of Leadership Qualities; Social Isolation; Lack of Friends; and Adjustment. Factor II correlates with teacher and clinician ratings of social withdrawal and a parent rating dimension labeled Depressive/Somatic Symptoms (Lachar et al., 1984). The obtained relationship between dysphoric affect and deficient social skills and lack of positive peer relations in children and adolescents is not surprising (Costello, 1981).

3. *Internalization/Somatic Symptoms (III)*. Factor III items appear primarily on SOM, D, and ANX. A factor analysis of scale items resulted in content dimensions labeled Worry/Poor Self-Concept; Somatization; Crying Spells; Insecurity/Fearfulness; Vision Problems; Psychotic Behavior; and Body Temperature. Factor III significantly correlated with parent and clinician dimensions

labeled Depressive/Somatic Symptoms (Lachar et al., 1984).

4. *Cognitive Development (IV)*. The majority of Factor IV items are found on ACH, IS, DVL, and PSY. Factor IV correlates significantly with the parent rating dimensions Developmental Delay and Cognitive/Attentional Deficits, the teacher rating dimension Academic Delay, and the clinician rating dimension Language/Motor Deficits (Lachar et al., 1984). Factor IV has also been found to correlate −.53 with the McCarthy General Cognitive Index and −.63 with the Peabody Picture Vocabulary IQ (Durrant, 1983).

ACTUARIAL INTERPRETATION

"Actuarial interpretation" is that process by which test data are transformed into categories that have been found statistically to be related to meaningful nontest data. In this manner, specific scale values, test indices, or profile scale patterns reliably predict characteristics of the client being evaluated. The meaning of test indices is thereby statistically determined, rather than extrapolated by the clinical process, in which a psychologist integrates personal understanding of a test's ability and performance with theoretical and empirical preferences regarding child development and personality structure to determine the meaning of test results. (An excellent discussion of the process of actuarial interpretation may be found in a chapter by Markes, Seeman, & Haller, 1974.)

Actuarial Interpretation of Individual Profile Scales

Lachar and Gdowski (1979) and Lachar (1982) have detailed the process by which T-scores of the original 16 profile scales were first correlated with ratings from parents, teachers, and clinicians. Rated child characteristics that reliably relate to a specific PIC scale are said to be "correlates" of that scale. Scale correlates were transformed into actuarial interpretation through the process of relating test "catgories" to nontest data. To develop guidelines for interpretation of individual PIC scales, these scales were transformed into T-score ranges of 10 points, and the frequency of established scale correlates was tabulated for these T-score ranges to determine the minimum scale elevation necessary for a correlate to become descriptive.

Lachar and Gdowski (1979) analyzed elaborate data from 431 psychiatric evaluations of children and adolescents; we established interpretive ranges and proposed 37 actuarially determined, interpretive paragraphs for the original 16 profile scales. An important finding of this study was that the minimum elevation necessary to signify clinically meaningful maladjustment differed across these scales. For some scales, a T-score of 60 was significant (L, ADJ, ACH, DVL, FAM, HPR), whereas for other scales a T-score greater than the traditionally assigned value of 70 was necessary to predict clinically meaningful characteristics (F, DLQ, PSY). Lachar (1982) analyzed an expanded sample of 691 psychiatric evaluations and presented 12 actuarially determined interpretive paragraphs for the factor scales. In this study, the factor scales became clinically meaningful at 70T, and each of the four scales was associated with two to four T-score interpretive ranges.

A review of the correlates of a few of the profile scales and their T-score placements suggests the considerable value of actuarial approach to test interpretation. For example, ACH scale correlates form three interpretive bands. Scores above 59T uniformly suggest problematic performance in a variety of academic subjects. When ACH is elevated above 69T, teachers are likley to observe deficiencies in basic abilities that are prerequisite to appropriate achievement, such as verbal comprehension for reading. ACH values above 79T suggest a problematic adjustment, reflecting the effects of either severe and/or chronic academic failure which signals the need for professional intervention. Teacher correlates for this T- score range suggest the presence of a negative self-image: "Frequent daydreaming," "Approaches new tasks and situations with an 'I can't do it' response," and "Gives up easily/expects failure."

Correlates of the D scale appear to be placed within two T-score ranges. Scale values greater than 69T reflect manifestations of dysphoric affect, whereas scores greater than 79T suggest associated disturbances of eating and sleep, as well as suicidal thought and behavior for adolescents. It is interesting to note that D elevations above 79T are related to clinicians' assessment of suicidal content, while D elevations above 89T are related to parents' concern about their children's potential for self-destructuion. Considering that clinicians routinely discuss this topic during an evaluation, and that parents are likely to become concerned about the potential for suicide when their children either threaten or attempt such action, an additional hypothesis that can be drawn from these data is that suicidal ideation is more likely to be associated with threats or attempts within higher scale elevations. FAM correlates appear to fall within three T-score ranges: Scores above 59T reflect family conflict and parental inconsistency; scores above 69T suggest parental emotional disturbance and the possibility of parental alcoholism or substance abuse; and scores above 79T suggest parental rejection and criticism, as well as other behaviors that may justify the label of child abuse.

The actuarial data presented in Lachar and Gdowski (1979) support a conservative interpretation of both the DLQ and PSY scales. Antisocial behaviors and substance abuse were found to be descriptive of DLQ elevations above 109T, and symptoms clearly related to defective reality testing were associated with PSY elevations above 109T. HPR scale values appear to predict two subsets of correlates. HPR values greater than 59T reflect difficulties in classroom adjustment associated with impulsivity, restlessness, distractibility, and an excessive (or perhaps undercontrolled) sociability. HPR elevations above 69T suggest, in addition, the presence of limited frustration tolerance, uncontrolled hostility, and manipulative and perhaps antisocial behaviors that are likely to be associated with poor relationships with peers.

Classification of Special Education Needs

The potential value of acturial assessment in the school setting is perhaps most readily apparent in the classification and placement of children into special education categories and programs, most notably the categories of educable mental retardation, emotional dis-

turbance, and learning disabilities. Recent research using the PIC has also suggested the value of actuarial assessment in the classification of special education needs. Three doctoral dissertations have used the PIC in multiple discriminant-function analyses to place children into various educational classifications (Clark, 1982; DeKrey, 1983; Schnel, 1982). The results of these studies revealed conceptually meaningful differences among the PIC profiles of children in regular education classes and in programs for the learning-disabled, emotionally disturbed, and educable mentally retarded. In addition, substantial percentages of these children were correctly classified by PIC-based discriminant-function rules.

A more recent study (Lachar et al., 1986) has employed the PIC in the construction of an empirically based classification system for special education. Two groups of subjects were included: a derivation sample of 248 children (ages 6–13) in regular and special education placements within public schools in suburban Detroit, Michigan; and three validation samples that had previously comprised the subjects for the Clark (1982), DeKrey (1983), and Schnel (1982) investigations in Michigan, Iowa, and California, respectively. Validation samples were included in this investigation in order to evaluate the generalizability of the proposed PIC-based classification system across school districts in different states.

Derivation sample subjects received special services within six special education placements: (1) learning-disabled/self-contained classroom; (2) learning-disabled/teacher consultant support services; (3) trainable mentally impaired; (4) educable mentally impaired; (5) emotionally impaired; and (6) school social work services. The learning-disabled, mentally impaired, and emotionally impaired placements required certification as educationally handicapped according to criteria established in the *Michigan Special Education Rules* (1980) for this purpose. The school social work classification is not a special education category, but represents a common placement option for children who are referred for evaluation of emotional and/ or behavioral problems but are not eligible for special education services under the emotionally impaired designation. These six special services placements were included in this investigation because they represent the most common placement options considered by the school psychologist in the assessment process. In addition, they are the classifications that rely most often on the types of assessment information typically provided by school psychologists, and are therefore most amenable to the exploration of actuarially based relationships with test data. A seventh sample consisted of students in regular education classes who had never received special education services and were considered by their teachers as not currently requiring such services. These students were matched as closely as possible to the age, grade, and sex distributions of the special education subjects.

Validation samples included the following: students in regular elementary education classes and students in programs for the learning-disabled (Schnel, 1982); students in regular education classes and special education students (ages 6–13) in programs for the learning-disabled, emotionally disturbed, and mentally disabled (DeKrey, 1983); and students (ages 6–16) in programs for the learning-disabled, emotionally impaired, and educable mentally impaired (Clark, 1982). Special education students in these three samples were not classified as to their type of placement (self-contained classroom vs. teacher consultant services).

Like that of McDermott (1982), this investigation sought to develop decision rules that could be applied in a branching decision-tree format to identify children who would profit from inclusion in one classification category as opposed to others. The investigation differed from McDermott's in that the assessment information used in the construction of these decision rules consisted entirely of PIC scale scores. The PIC is ideally suited for this task, because it is multidimensional and assesses many areas relevant to the cognitive and socioemotional problems presented by children who are referred for consideration of a special education placement. It was not intended that the resulting PIC-based classification system would serve as a substitute for traditional assessment practices in the schools; rather, it was hoped that PIC-based actuarial predictions might profitably be used to augment the psychoeducational

assessment process by suggesting areas in need of further assessment.

A branching decision tree of discriminant-function-derived equations most adequately summarizes the first model constructed to place Revised Format PIC profiles into the seven classification options (Lachar et al., 1986). This classification task was defined as a series of successive decisions that allowed progressively finer distinctions to be made about the classification category or placement from which a student would be most likely to profit. The first decision was whether a student would need special education services or would best profit from continued regular education programming. An actuarially based decision rule corresponding to this decision would be applied practically in a screening program such as the "child find" programs currently mandated by P.L. 94-142 (Education for All Handicapped Children Act, 1975) for identifying those preschoolers who might be candidates for later special education programming. Such a rule might also be applied to screen children in regular classes whose problems might suggest the need for special education services.

The second level of this decision tree, applied to the test results of children classified as likely to need special education services, was the determination of whether a child's presenting problems were primarily cognitive or primarily emotional/behavioral in nature. If the child's problems were considered to be primarily cognitive, the next decision was whether these problems were more similar to those presented by mentally impaired children or by learning-disabled children. A final discrimination determined the type of learning disability program or level of mental impairment. If, on the other hand, the child's problems were predicted to be primarily emotional/behavioral, a final decision recommended either school social work services or certification as emotionally impaired, with the special classroom or support services that typically are provided for such children.

Each decision within this classification system was based upon a rule that was a linear combination of PIC profile scale T-scores and could easily be calculated for an individual student. Each rule was constructed on the basis of a discriminant-function analysis of the two categories or groups of derivation sample students relevant to that decision in the classification system. The scales in each classification equation were weighted to reflect the relative importance of each variable's contribution to the decision process. Constants were added to three of the rules to avoid the possibility of negative values.

Once the classification rules had been constructed, cutting scores were established for each rule by examining the distribution of scores obtained in each pair of groups studied. These cutting scores were placed on the branches of this decision-tree model. In order to evaluate the effectiveness of the rules system for classifying individual students according to their educational placement, all subjects in the derivation and validation samples were processed through the system in two stages. The first stage evaluated the PIC as a screening instrument in terms of its ability to separate regular education from special education students. The second stage evaluated the PIC as a classification/placement instrument within special education in terms of its ability to classify known groups of students receiving various types of special education services. Accuracy of placement in derivation and validation samples was assessed at both the level of type of major handicap (emotional/behavioral, learning-disabled, mentally impaired) and at the six endpoints representing the much more narrow specific placements.

Application of the PIC-based classification rules in both the derivation and validation samples suggested considerable value for this actuarial approach to assessing special education needs. Rule 1 (the rule for discriminating regular education from special education students) accomplished its screening purpose with considerable effectiveness, as more than 90% of subjects in the derivation sample (96% in regular education and 89% in special education) were correctly predicted by this rule to be members of either regular or special education programs. When misclassifications did occur on application of Rule 1, examination of actual group membership indicated that most of these misclassifications were for students in the least impaired special education placement groups (learning-disabled/teacher consultant and social work counseling), for which service delivery does not involve special class placement. Similarly impressive classification results were obtained for Rule 1 predictions in the three validation samples (85–90% correct classifications), suggesting considerable generalizability for this rule in assessing the need for special education services.

Application of the remaining rules in both the derivation and validation samples, although less impressive than the results for Rule 1, nevertheless suggest the value of an actuarial approach to the classification of special educational needs. These rules were considerably more effective in predicting the intermediate impairment categories than they were in predicting the more specific special education placements. These rules were most effective in classifying mentally impaired students at both levels of classification, as 90% of trainable mentally impaired and 80% of educable mentally impaired students were correctly classified when processed through the system to their final possible classification. Although it is reasonable to conclude that these students would be more accurately classified using a traditional individual assessment, these results provide rather impressive evidence for classifications based solely on mother-derived Revised Format PIC profile scales in distinguishing these mentally impaired students from children with other educational handicaps.

This branching rules system also performed rather impressively in classifying students for whom emotional/behavioral characteristics were assumed to be the primary handicapping condition. Although classification accuracy was substantially reduced when predictions were extended to the level of specific placement category, the majority of misclassifications for these students were within the same general impairment category, suggesting the value of the actuarial approach at the intermediate level of classification for students presenting with these impairment conditions.

Learning-disabled students were the most difficult to classify at both levels using these rules. The 60% correct classification rate at the intermediate level suggests that a significant proportion of learning-disabled students receive final placement classifications outside of the two learning disability options. For example, the majority of misclassifications for learning-disabled/self-contained classroom students were in the educable mentally impaired category—a result that probably reflects the below-average IQs of many of these students (mean IQ in derivation sample = 85). This finding may also reflect the suggestion in the literature that increasing societal pressures and changing classification standards have led to many educable mentally impaired students' receiving special education services for the learning-disabled (Goldstein, Arkell, Ashcroft, Hurley, & Lilly, 1975; Gottlieb, Alter, & Gottlieb, 1983). The majority of misclassifications for the learning-disabled/teacher consultant students, on the other hand, were in either the emotionally impaired or the social work services category—a finding that probably reflects the frequent observation that emotional/behavioral difficulties are associated with learning disabilities (Porter & Rourke, 1985; Ross, 1976, 1977), as well as the fact that nearly one-third of these students were also receiving school social work services.

Classification of special education students in the three validation samples revealed, in most cases, the reduction in classification accuracy expected on cross-validation. Interestingly, learning-disabled students in the three samples were actually classified more accurately than were learning-disabled students in the derivation sample (64% vs. 87% correct classifications).

The difficulties encountered by this branching system in correctly classifying special education students into finite categories suggest an important limitation of this approach to actuarial classification of special education needs. A characteristic of branching classification rules is that their application for the individual student does not allow comparison of that individual to each of the handicap categories and placement groups that might be considered for the student in a psychoeducational assessment. Once a student's scores place him or her within one branch of the decision tree, classifications positioned on alternative branches cannot be considered. On the basis of the PIC profile scale T-scores, each student is, in effect, considered similar to only one general handicap category and to only one placement group. This approach would be quite satisfactory if each handicap category and special education

placement represented an orthogonal set of child characteristics. That this is not the case is strongly suggested by the school psychology literature (Forness, 1976; Hallahan & Kauffman, 1976, 1977), particularly with regard to the classifications of learning-disabled and emotionally impaired. These current classification rules, therefore, may not accurately capture the characteristics of the student who presents with problems in more than one area. In addition, this approach to classification fails to appreciate the heterogeneity of characteristics that has been demonstrated for children similarly classified both within and across school districts (Hallahan & Kauffman, 1977; McDermott, 1982; Wepman, Cruickshank, Deutsch, Morency, & Strother, 1975).

A second classification approach attempted to improve upon this system by employing an alternative strategy (Boersma, 1985). In this approach, a student's profile was compared with a series of mean profiles representing a special education handicapping condition or specific placement, in order to generate an index of similarity to each mean profile. In this manner, students with multiple problems might appear equally similar to two or more mean profiles. Individual profiles were classified by their similarity to one or more mean profiles using Mahalanobis distance. In an initial application evaluating this similarity approach in assessing the need for special education services, the results were quite comparable to those for the discriminant-function equation, correctly classifying 93% of the 248 derivation profiles. Application to the three replication samples was also similar, obtaining 79%–96% accuracy.

When the similarity measure was applied to identify the one most similar educational classification out of six alternatives, the results were most similar to those obtained by the decision-tree approach. When additional flexibility was added to the system by labeling a profile classification as accurate when actual placement occurred within one of the two most similar categories (a condition resembling actual application of such a system, in which most similar and least similar options would be suggested), classification accuracy within derivation and replication samples improved over the decision-tree approach. A total of 84% of 192 special education students in the derivation sample were correctly placed within one of six options. Of the 280 special education protocols reserved for replication, the classification rate was 57% for the decision-tree approach, 56% for the one most similar mean profile, and 73% for the two most similar profiles. The classification approach that evaluates profile similarity to these seven education categories has been incorporated into the automated interpretation provided by the publisher of the PIC.

A PIC Profile Typology

The wealth of child behavior information provided by multidimensional instruments such as the PIC has stimulated serious consideration of such measures' serving as the basis of classification systems that would represent alternatives to traditional psychiatric diagnostic categories (cf. Lessing, Williams, & Gill, 1982). It has been established that available psychiatric diagnostic systems developed for use with children and adolescents, such as DMS-III (American Psychiatric Association, 1980) and the Group for the Advancement of Psychiatry (1966) system, are problematic because of their unreliability (see Mattison, Cantwell, Russell, & Will, 1979; Werry, Methvan, Fitzpatrick, & Dixon, 1983) as well as their questionable validity (cf. Germezy, 1978; Rutter, 1978). Furthermore, a single diagnostic label (such as Attention Deficit Hyperactivity–Disorder) typically describes a *single* dimension of behavior for an individual child. Children who receive the same global diagnostic label are likely to vary on a significant number of other behavioral dimensions (e.g., ability, social skills, internalization symptomatology) that are also related to their overall adjustment and prognosis (cf. Breen & Barkley, 1983).

As clear as the understanding of the shortcomings of psychiatric diagnostic labels for children has been, there has been relatively little research until very recently that has explored the usefulness of objective, parent-as-informant measures such as the PIC in assigning children within a *classification* system. Although the actuarial systems of Lachar (1982) and Lachar and Gdowski (1979) provide relatively comprehensive descriptions of *individual* children, these systems do not conveniently classify children

into separate *groups*, each with its own unique pattern of problem behavior. The primary goal of any classification typology (which psychiatric diagnostic categories have not yet achieved) is to partition a population of children referred for mental health services into a discrete number of "types" or groups, each with its own characteristic features and symptoms. Children with similar overall ability level, degree of impulse control, external stressors, and areas of poor adjustment should be classified together, and separately from children with other patterns. If children with varying patterns of assets and problems require distinctly different types of intervention (e.g., outpatient vs. inpatient treatment, medication, degree of family participation in therapy) for optimal outcome, a reliable and valid classification system is necessary to make these distinctions.

Identification of PIC Profile Types

The PIC profile scales have recently served as the basis for an empirically derived typology that may offer an alternative to the use of psychiatric diagnostic labels. Gdowski, Lachar, and Kline (1985) used the classification procedure of cluster analysis within a sample of almost 1,800 children and adolescents referred for mental health services to construct such a typology. The total sample included 1,226 evaluations at one child psychiatry facility (67% males; 56% white, 44% black; mean age = 11.6) and six "marker" samples, including psychotic, mentally retarded, adjudicated delinquent, hyperactive, neurologically impaired, and somatizing children. These six samples are fully described in Wirt et al. (1984). These marker samples were included to determine whether the resulting PIC profile typology would classify these cases in a conceptually meaningful way (e.g., the PIC profiles of hyperactive children should not be randomly assigned across profile clusters, nor should the profiles of psychotic children appear in the same clusters with children adjudicated delinquent).

Cluster analysis is a multivariate statistical technique that forms groups of subjects on the basis of their similarity across several measures, such that cases within each group are more similar to one another than to members of other groups. In this study, "similarity" was determined by computer comparisons among the PIC profiles of all children in this large sample. Gdowski et al. (1985) also partitioned this sample into separate halves, to insure that profile groups identified by cluster analysis were stable and replicated across these independent samples. A total of 11 PIC profile types formed by cluster analysis replicated across the Split 1 and 2 samples and classified over 80% of all cases. Subsequent analyses demonstrated that these PIC clusters differed significantly in subject age, sex, and the proportion of the six marker samples classified into each cluster.

Characteristics of Profile Clusters

Inspection of these 11 PIC profile types revealed that they had distinct mean profiles and that the marker sample protocols were not randomly assigned to these groups by the cluster analysis algorithm. PIC profile types included a within-normal-limits mean group (Cluster 1) and clusters with mean elevations suggestive of cognitive impairment (Clusters 3, 4, 5, and 6), behavioral dyscontrol (Clusters 4, 7, 10, and 11), depression and anxiety (Clusters 3, 7, and 9), family conflict (Clusters 7 and 10), and social skills deficits (Clusters 3, 4, 5, 7, and 8). Consistent with problem behavior areas suggested by their mean PIC profiles, Clusters 3, 5, and 8 classified above-base-rate proportions of psychotic children; Clusters 5 and 6 represented high proportions of retarded children; Clusters 7 and 10 contained high proportions of adjudicated delinquents; and Clusters 11 and 12 included relatively high proportions of hyperactive children. The mean ages of Clusters 5 and 6 (characterized by cognitive impairment) were significantly below the sample base rate, whereas the two clusters containing high proportions of adjudicated delinquents (Clusters 7 and 10) were significantly above the base rate. These 11 profile types did not differ with regard to their racial or socioeconomic composition.

Development of Classification Rules

Although these initial results appeared very promising, the actual use of this classification system with individual children was prob-lematic. These PIC profiles were classified into cluster groups by a very complex computer program that evaluated the degree of similarity between individual profiles and the mean profiles of all clusters. This is hardly an activity that clinicians could reasonably hope to duplicate without computer access and expertise. In order to facilitate classification of individual PIC profiles into this typology, a series of objective and easy-to-use rules was developed (Kline, Lachar, & Gdowski, 1987). To classify an individual profile, the clinician scans down a flowchart (Kline, Lachar, & Gdowski, 1987; Lachar et al., 1986) until a complete match between the T-score specifications and the individual profile is obtained. Thus, these rules are sequentially applied, and a profile is classified by the first rule for which all specifications are met. Rule 1 identifies all within-normal-limits PIC profiles that have all 12 PIC substantive profile scales below clinically significant elevations. Rule 2 classifies all profiles having a *single* significantly elevated PIC scale and thus identifies all "spike" profiles. Rules 3 through 6 identify "cognitive deficit" types that all have at least two significant elevations on the scales of the PIC Cognitive Triad (ACH, IS, DVL). Rules 7 through 12 classify "noncognitive deficit" types, which all include IS scores within the normal range. An individual child's profile can be left unclassified at two points in this decision tree.

Kline, Lachar, and Gdowski (1987) demonstrated that the groups generated by the application of the classification rules corresponded very closely with their original cluster counterparts. These rules classified over 90% of the Gdowski et al. (1985) samples.

Interpretation of Profile Types

These two studies demonstrated that PIC profile types identified by cluster analysis replicated across independent samples and classified meaningful proportions of marker sample children. Also individual children could be easily classified into one of these types with the application of a set of sequential rules. However, the major issue for a typology had yet to be addressed: Is this PIC typology valid? Does membership in this profile typology have any relationship to independent and external information about child and adolescent adjustment?

A comprehensive data base has been collected to determine the predictive potential of these profile types, and the results have been of sufficient magnitude to form the basis of actuarial interpretations. Kline, Lachar, and Gdowski (1987) evaluated profile types within a sample of 1,333 children and adolescents who had received a psychiatric evaluation. As part of that evaluation, three forms for each child were completed—one each by parents, teachers, and clinicians. The 365 rating items of these forms were evaluated to identify those items that appeared significantly more or less for a given profile type. An average of 97 correlates was obtained for each of 11 profile types. LaCombe (1985) evaluated a subset of 327 of these 1,333 cases to expand the concurrent data already available through the review of completed medical records. Information regarding presenting complaints, history and chronicity of behavior problems, family functioning, and treatment recommendations was abstracted from medical records, using an 146-item reliable objective coding form. In these analyses, 11 profile types averaged 39 additional correlates.

Two studies (Kline, Lachar, Gdowski, & Boersma, 1987) have extended this profile type data base to include assessment of child intellectual and academic characteristics. In one sample of 329 children and adolescents seen for psychiatric evaluation, their performance on the WISC-R, the Peabody Picture Vocabulary Test, and the Peabody Individual Achievement Test was evaluated. The analyses of each test variable across the 12 profile types were statistically significant. In a second sample of 630 public school children collected by four investigators in three states, the relationship between profile type classification and classroom placement was investigated. These children had been placed in regular classrooms, or were receiving special education services for the emotionally impaired, learning-disabled, educable mentally impaired, or trainable mentally impaired. Of the 10 profile types that were studied, 8 (the other 2 profile types did not reach a minumum sample size) obtained distributions of classroom placements that differed significantly from the overall sample distribution of classroom placements.

In summary, comprehensive interpretive information is available that documents the clinical significance of each profile type classification. Recently, these data have been integrated to form the basis of narrative interpretations that can be found within automated interpretations of the PIC (available from the test's publisher). An example of these automated interpretations is presented in conclusion. Profile Type 7 is the most complex of the noncognitive classifications, reflecting both internalizing and externalizing problems (see Appendix). Profile Type 7 members achieve clinical-range elevations on DLQ and D, as well as at least two clinical-range elevations out of the three scales WDL, PSY, and SSK.

APPENDIX 13.1.

PERSONALITY INVENTORY FOR CHILDREN (PIC)
by David Lachar, Ph.D. and Charles L. Gdowski, Ph.D.
A WPS TEST REPORT by Western Psychological Services
12031 Wilshire Boulevard
Los Angeles, California 90025
Version: 2.00
Copyright (c) 1989 by Western Psychological Services

CLIENT: 000000000   ANSWER SHEET NUMBER: 00000000
SEX: Male   PROCESSING DATE: 08/02/89
AGE: 11 Years   INFORMANT: Mother
SCHOOL GRADE: 5 th   ETHNICITY: White

Form: II (Factor and Shortened Clinical Scales)

* * * * * PIC INTERPRETATION * * * * *

This PIC interpretation is based on the systematic analysis of data obtained in the evaluation of behaviorally disturbed children and adolescents. This report consists of a series of hypotheses that may serve to guide further investigation.

GENERAL ADJUSTMENT AND INFORMANT RESPONSE STYLE:

Inventory responses do not suggest that this informant attempted to minimize or deny any problems that this child may have.

The description of this child's behavior suggests that a psychological/ psychiatric evaluation may assist in the remediation of current problems.

Many infrequent problems and symptoms are described in this protocol. These responses may indicate the presence of highly disruptive behaviors that may require hospitalization for their treatment. Similar response patterns may be obtained by informants who exaggerate child problems or who fail to respond to Inventory items in a conventional manner. The possibilities of exaggeration and atypical response sets should be carefully excluded before credence is given to other profile scale interpretations.

PERSONALITY AND FAMILY EVALUATION:

A history of poor peer relations may lead this child to expect criticism and rejection from others. Parents and teachers frequently observe that similar children have few, if any, friends. Poor social skills may be demonstrated by a failure to initiate relationships, with resulting isolation, or by conflict with peers that reflects poor sportsmanship and limited frustration tolerance.

Current child behavior suggests serious psychological maladjustment, which may be characterized by unusual thoughts and behaviors, social isolation, and emotional lability. Parents frequently note that similar children are "confused or in a daze," and may note excessive daydreaming. Delayed developmental milestones may be reported for social skills, language ability, or motor coordination. Similar children may be resistant to change in the environment, may display rapid mood shifts, or demonstrate poor judgment. Self-destructive behavior (such as head-banging), destruction of objects, difficulty in getting to sleep, or early morning awakening may be present. Current behaviors may include symptoms that are frequently associated with severe emotional disability, such as abnormal motor behavior, echolalic speech, or an associative thought disorder. Evaluation of this child's interpersonal relations and thought processes may reveal a pathological perception of reality.

Child behavior is likely to reflect the presence of depression, anxiety, and fearfulness. Presenting complaints frequently include eating disturbances, trouble falling asleep, nightmares, distrust of others, isolation, emotional lability, fear of school, or excessive worry, self-blame, or self-criticism. Among adolescents, these symptoms may be associated with suicidal thought and behavior. The mothers of these children may be seen as overly permissive and often have difficulty setting limits on the demands of children.

Health-related complaints are likely to require professional attention. Sustained fatigue, aches and pains, or headaches may be present. A careful evaluation will be necessary to determine whether physical symptoms are employed to avoid responsibilities, are used to withdraw from uncomfortable situations, are in response to stress, accompany depression or other emotional states, and/or require medical intervention.

A disregard for rules and societal expectations is likely to be evidenced by behavior displayed at home and at school. Similar children dislike school and demonstrate a poor academic adjustment associated with hostility and defiance or apathy and disinterest. Current behavior is likely to reflect impulsivity, poor judgment, or unmodulated hostility. A character disorder may be suggested by symptoms such as lying, theft, problematic sexual behavior, group delinquent activities, or an established tendency to blame others for current problems.

A history of problematic peer relations is suggested that may be characterized by poorly controlled expression of hostility, fighting, provocation and teasing, or poor sportsmanship. Current and/or past behavior may also suggest hyperactivity, distractibility, restlessness, or impulsivity. Similar children are often inattentive in class, do not complete homework assignments, and may require adult intervention to conform to stated limits. A limited frustration tolerance may be associated with temper tantrums, destruction of objects, projection of blame, direct expression or displacement of anger, or a lack of trust in others. Other problems may include excessive seeking of attention and approval, clumsiness, frequent accidents or fire setting.

A history of marital discord, as well as subsequent separation or divorce, is suggested. One or both parents may be judged to require professional assistance to deal with their emotional instability, alcoholism, or substance abuse. Child behavior problems may result from parenting characterized by inconsistency, undue criticism, rejection, or the use of excessive physical punishment.

NOTE: The studies that form the foundation for this PIC REPORT are presented in three publications published by Western Psychological Services: "Multidimensional Description of Child Personality: A Manual for the Personality Inventory for Children" (WPS Catalog No. W-152G), "Actuarial Assessment of Child and Adolescent Personality: An Interpretive Guide for the Personality Inventory for Children Profile" (W-305), and "Personality Inventory for Children Revised Format Manual Supplement" (W-152GS).

* * * * CRITICAL ITEMS * * * *

These Inventory items were answered by the informant in the direction indicated. Although too much interpretive value should not be placed on individual responses, they may suggest areas for further inquiry.

Relative frequency of item endorsement in male normative and clinic samples is indicated at the end of each statement by this notation: [normative % / clinic %].

--- DEPRESSION AND POOR SELF-CONCEPT ---

132. My child tends to pity himself. (T) [26%/38%]

--- WORRY AND ANXIETY ---

4. My child worries about things that usually only adults worry about. (T) [15%/21%]
21. My child often asks if I love him. (T) [10%/19%]
53. Often my child is afraid of little things. (T) [9%/17%]
76. Sometimes my child's muscles twitch. (T) [5%/15%]
81. Several times my child has spoken of a lump in his throat. (T) [2%/6%]
82. My child frequently has nightmares. (T) [4%/12%]
169. Often my child goes about wringing his hands. (T) [1%/9%]
373. My child often wakes up screaming. (T) [1%/4%]

--- REALITY DISTORTION ---

96. My child gets confused easily. (T) [6%/39%]
120. Frequently my child will put his hands over his ears. (T) [6%/21%]
228. Often my child will laugh for no apparent reason. (T) [7%/20%]
311. My child sometimes hears things others don't hear. (T) [4%/7%]
322. My child sometimes feels things that aren't there. (T) [2%/6%]

--- PEER RELATIONS ---

16. My child is usually rejected by other children. (T) [4%/26%]
36. My child doesn't seem to care to be with others. (T) [4%/18%]
47. My child really has no real friend. (T) [6%/29%]
75. Other children make fun of my child's different ideas. (T) [2%/17%]
160. My child never takes the lead in things. (T) [13%/32%]
239. My child thinks others are plotting against him. (T) [2%/12%]
284. If my child can't run things, he won't play. (T) [5%/14%]
355. My child is very jealous of others. (T) [7%/17%]

--- UNSOCIALIZED AGGRESSION ---

43. My child has been in trouble for attacking others. (T) [2%/16%]
104. Many times my child has become violent. (T) [8%/30%]
143. At times my child has seriously hurt others. (T) [2%/12%]
276. Several times my child has threatened to kill others. (T) [2%/11%]
314. My child is sometimes cruel to animals. (T) [3%/19%]
340. Often my child smashes things when angry. (T) [8%/30%]
404. My child has a terrible temper. (T) [12%/35%]

--- CONSCIENCE DEVELOPMENT ---

30. My child is good at lying his way out of trouble. (T) [14%/38%]
56. My child often disobeys me. (T) [17%/50%]

--- POOR JUDGMENT ---

87. My child will do anything on a dare. (T) [7%/26%]
366. I always worry about my child having an accident when he is out. (T) [16%/33%]

--- ATYPICAL DEVELOPMENT ---

173. My child has had brief periods of time when he seems unaware of everything that is going on. (T) [16%/33%]
255. I had an especially difficult time with temper tantrums in my child at an earlier age. (T) [11%/28%]
391. By the age of five years, my child could dress himself except for tying things. (F) [4%/16%]
419. My child was a premature or overdue baby. (T) [20%/35%]

--- DISTRACTIBILITY, ACTIVITY LEVEL, AND COORDINATION ---

71. My child can't seem to wait for things like other children do. (T) [17%/49%]
295. As a younger child, it was impossible to get my child to take a nap. (T) [16%/20%]
298. My child has had to have drugs to relax. (T) [3%/27%]
349. My child loves to rock back and forth when sitting down. (T) [10%/19%]
356. Five minutes or less is about all my child will ever sit at one time. (T) [6%/22%]

--- SOMATIC COMPLAINTS/CURRENT HEALTH ---

25. My child frequently complains of being hot even on cold days. (T) [6%/12%]
411. My child's headaches usually start with a pain in the back of the neck.
(T) [1%/5%]

--- SCHOOL ADJUSTMENT ---

20. The school says my child needs help in getting along with other children.
(T) [5%/36%]
79. School teachers complain that my child can't sit still. (T) [9%/41%]
198. My child can't sit still in school because of nervousness. (T) [5%/40%]

--- FAMILY DISCORD ---

152. Our marriage has been very unstable (shaky). (T) [12%/25%]
153. The child's father seems jealous of the child. (T) [6%/9%]
170. The child's parents have broken up their marriage several times. (T)
[3%/11%]
188. My child seems unhappy about our home life. (T) [7%/27%]
226. The child's parents disagree a lot about rearing the child. (T) [10%/27%]
245. Several times my child has threatened to run away. (T) [10%/28%]
275. There is a lot of tension in our home. (T) [17%/39%]
335. We often argue about who is the boss at our house. (T) [6%/12%]
345. The child's mother frequently has crying spells. (T) [7%/14%]

--- OTHER ---

357. Neither parent has ever been mentally ill. (F) [10%/15%]

* * * PIC PROFILES * * *

FACTOR SCALES PROFILE

```
                                          T SCORES
          SCORES    CLINICAL  20   30   40   50   60   70   80   90  100  110  120
          T   RAW   LEVEL*    |++++|++++|++++|++++|++++|++++|++++|++++|++++|++++|

Factor Scales

I    96   (27)   Severe                                         X

II   79   (18)   Moderate                                  X

III  116  (21)   Severe                                                   X

IV   46   ( 2)   Normal                     X

     T    RAW    CLINICAL  |++++|++++|++++|++++|++++|++++|++++|++++|++++|++++|
     SCORES      LEVEL*    20   30   40   50   60   70   80   90  100  110  120
                                          T SCORES
```

NOTE: Abbreviations refer to the following scales:

       Factor I : Undisciplined/Poor Self-Control
       Factor II : Social Incompetence
       Factor III: Internalization/Somatic Symptoms
       Factor IV : Cognitive Development

*Degree of recommended clinical interpretation. See Personality Inventory for
Children (PIC): Revised Format Manual Supplement (WPS Cat. No. W-152GS)

CLINICAL SCALES PROFILE

```
                                                 T SCORES
            SCORES   CLINICAL 20   30   40   50   60   70   80   90  100  110  120
          T   RAW    LEVEL*   |++++|++++|++++|++++|++++|++++|++++|++++|++++|++++|
Validity Scales

L        34  ( 1)    Normal               X

F-S     112  (14)    Moderate                                            X

DEF-S    27  ( 7)    Normal            X

ADJ-S   113  (47)    Severe                                                  X

Shortened Clinical Scales |====|====|====|====|====|====|====|====|====|====|

ACH-S    51  (10)    Normal                 X

IS-S     60  (12)    Normal                      X

DVL      49  ( 6)    Normal                X

SOM-S   101  (19)    Severe                                           X

D-S     100  (29)    Severe                                           X

FAM-S    80  (18)    Severe                                    X

DLQ-S   102  (25)    Severe                                           X

WDL-S    68  ( 7)    Normal                          X

ANX-S   102  (20)    Severe                                           X

PSY-S   112  (18)    Severe                                               X

HPR-S    86  (21)    Severe                                     X

SSK-S    93  (26)    Severe                                        X

          T   RAW   CLINICAL |++++|++++|++++|++++|++++|++++|++++|++++|++++|++++|
            SCORES  LEVEL*    20   30   40   50   60   70   80   90  100  110  120
                                                 T SCORES
```

NOTE: Abbreviations refer to the following scales:

L :	Lie	D-S :	Depression-S
F-S :	Frequency-S	FAM-S:	Family Relations-S
DEF-S:	Defensiveness-S	DLQ-S:	Delinquency-S
ADJ-S:	Adjustment-S	WDL-S:	Withdrawal-S
ACH-S:	Achievement-S	ANX-S:	Anxiety-S
IS-S :	Intellectual Screening-S	PSY-S:	Psychosis-S
DVL :	Development	HPR-S:	Hyperactivity-S
SOM-S:	Somatic Concern-S	SSK-S:	Social Skills-S

*Degree of recommended clinical interpretation. See Actuarial Assessment of
 Child and Adolescent Personality (WPS Cat. No. W-305)

              * * SUPPLEMENTAL INTERPRETATION OF THE PIC PROFILE * *

The following descriptions of child functioning are based upon recent empirical study of the PIC profile of children seen in child guidance agencies and child psychiatry departments, as well as children placed into various educational categories by school systems. WPS solicits your evaluation and critique of these new interpretive approaches. Please direct your comments to: David Lachar, Ph.D. c/o Western Psychological Services, 12031 Wilshire Boulevard, Los Angeles, CA 90025

PIC PROFILE CLASSIFICATION SYSTEM

This classification procedure places 90% or more of PIC profiles into one of twelve categories or types--see the back of the PIC ChromaGraph(tm)--by using a series of consecutively applied decision rules. Up to 10% of profiles may remain unclassified. The descriptions of children/adolescents and their families obtained for each profile type are based upon empirically derived correlates, i.e., symptoms, behaviors, and characteristics that have been found to differentiate members of a given profile type from all other profiles. These descriptions may be most appropriate for clients who manifest sufficient problems to warrant an evaluation by a child guidance agency.

Profile Type 7

The pattern of scale elevations in this child's profile is classified as a Profile Type 7. Children who obtain this classification are often significantly older than the average child referred to mental health clinics. Both conduct problems and emotional distress are suggested. These children present with problems involving noncompliance, violation of rules, impulsivity, peer aggression and fighting, lying, stealing, temper tantrums, and/or school dislike. Much of the acting-out of these children appears to have a self-punitive quality and/or is directed toward family members, rather than toward school staff or other authority figures who may not view them as difficult to manage. Parents often describe these children as demonstrating a poor attitude; they are unlikely to trust the child or accept the child's friends. These children often strongly dislike a member of their family. A small number of these children exhibit very serious conduct problems, such as firesetting, drug or alcohol abuse, or other behaviors known to the police.

These children also demonstrate problems reflecting psychological discomfort and emotional conflict: mood lability, sadness, sleep problems, problematic peer relations, and few or no friends. They may be seen as angry or fearful and may demonstrate behavior suggestive of low self-esteem and insecurity. These children should be carefully evaluated for previous or current suicidal ideation or attempts.

Family dysfunction and the child's feelings are often seen as contributing factors to this child's difficulties. These children were typically overly active and difficult to manage from an early age, which was often attributed to inconsistent parental childrearing and ineffective discipline techniques. They often become participants in parental conflict, which causes them to feel angry and insecure. These feelings are often associated with the acting-out of anger and the development of depressive symptoms. These parents may also be viewed as overly critical or rejecting of the child and may not provide consistent nurturance. Patterns of family interaction are often described as causing chronic feelings of anger in the child.

School adjustment may include poor academic performance, although child attitude and motivation are likely to be causal. These children may disobey school rules, fail to complete school work, or may be truant from class or refuse to attend school. Recommendations may include classes for vocational training. As preadolescents, these children may display behavior that requires special education services for the emotionally impaired. When evaluated at clinics, Profile Type 7 children and adolescents obtain mean estimates of ability and achievement within the low average or average range.

Recommendations include family therapy oriented toward improving discipline techniques or conflict resolution. For some cases in which acting-out results in serious consequences (e.g., police involvement), placement outside of the home or inpatient care may be recommended. Consider treatment of substance misuse for some of these cases. This child's problems may meet the criteria for one or more of the following diagnostic categories or diagnoses: Conduct Disorders, Attention-deficit Hyperactivity Disorder, and Depressive Disorders.

While the PIC program has selected the child's most characteristic type using a branching tree procedure, other profile types may also be similar. Similarity indexes matching the child's clinical T-score profile to all types for which similarity can be computed are provided below. Types showing similarity values close to or higher than the one given for this child's selected type should be considered in diagnostic hypotheses. Brief descriptions of all types are given on the back of the PIC ChromaGraph(tm)

		Similarity			Similarity
Type	3	.21	Type	8	.23
Type	4	-.02	Type	9	.39
Type	5	-.18	Type	10	.02
Type	6	-.46	Type	11	-.20
Type	7	.61	Type	12	-.40

CLASSROOM PLACEMENT ANALYSIS

```
-----------------------------------------------------------------------------

   PLACEMENT/INTERVENTION PROGRAM                          SIMILARITY INDEX

   Regular Classroom                                              -.50

   Regular Classroom with Counseling                             -.05

   SPECIAL EDUCATION

   Emotionally Impaired                                           .13

   Learning Disabled, Mainstreamed with Teacher Consultant       -.46

   Learning Disability Self-contained classroom                  -.66

   Educable Mentally Impaired                                     -.56

   Trainable Mentally Impaired                                    -.50

-----------------------------------------------------------------------------
```

In this analysis the child's profile is compared for similarity to seven average profiles obtained from groups of elementary school children found in regular classrooms, receiving counseling, or placed into one of five special education classifications. The index of similarity calculated is comparable to a correlation coefficient, in that larger values indicate those groups with whom this child has the greatest similarity. The table above may be of value in suggesting those educational placements that are the most and the least appropriate.

1(F)	11(F)	21(T)	31(T)	41(T)	51(T)	61(F)	71(T)	81(T)	91(F)
2(F)	12(F)	22(F)	32(F)	42(F)	52(T)	62(F)	72(F)	82(T)	92(F)
3(T)	13(F)	23(T)	33(F)	43(T)	53(T)	63(T)	73(F)	83(F)	93(F)
4(T)	14(T)	24(T)	34(T)	44(F)	54(T)	64(F)	74(T)	84(T)	94(T)
5(F)	15(T)	25(T)	35(T)	45(T)	55(F)	65(T)	75(T)	85(T)	95(F)
6(T)	16(T)	26(T)	36(T)	46(T)	56(T)	66(T)	76(T)	86(F)	96(T)
7(T)	17(F)	27(F)	37(F)	47(T)	57(T)	67(F)	77(T)	87(T)	97(F)
8(T)	18(T)	28(T)	38(T)	48(F)	58(T)	68(T)	78(T)	88(T)	98(T)
9(F)	19(T)	29(T)	39(T)	49(T)	59(F)	69(T)	79(T)	89(F)	99(F)
10(F)	20(T)	30(T)	40(F)	50(T)	60(T)	70(T)	80(T)	90(F)	100(F)
101(T)	111(F)	121(T)	131(T)	141(T)	151(F)	161(F)	171(T)	181(F)	191(T)
102(F)	112(T)	122(F)	132(T)	142(F)	152(T)	162(F)	172(T)	182(T)	192(F)
103(T)	113(T)	123(T)	133(F)	143(T)	153(T)	163(F)	173(T)	183(F)	193(F)
104(T)	114(F)	124(F)	134(F)	144(F)	154(F)	164(T)	174(F)	184(F)	194(F)
105(T)	115(F)	125(T)	135(T)	145(T)	155(T)	165(T)	175(F)	185(F)	195(F)
106(F)	116(T)	126(F)	136(F)	146(T)	156(F)	166(T)	176(T)	186(F)	196(T)
107(T)	117(F)	127(T)	137(T)	147(F)	157(F)	167(T)	177(T)	187(T)	197(T)
108(T)	118(F)	128(T)	138(T)	148(F)	158(F)	168(F)	178(T)	188(T)	198(T)
109(T)	119(F)	129(F)	139(T)	149(T)	159(F)	169(T)	179(F)	189(T)	199(F)
110(T)	120(T)	130(T)	140(F)	150(T)	160(T)	170(T)	180(F)	190(F)	200(F)
201(T)	211(T)	221(T)	231(F)	241(T)	251(T)	261(F)	271(F)		
202(F)	212(T)	222(F)	232(T)	242(F)	252(T)	262(T)	272(T)		
203(F)	213(T)	223(F)	233(F)	243(T)	253(T)	263(T)	273(F)		
204(T)	214(T)	224(T)	234(F)	244(F)	254(F)	264(F)	274(F)		
205(T)	215(F)	225(F)	235(T)	245(T)	255(T)	265(T)	275(T)		
206(T)	216(T)	226(T)	236(F)	246(F)	256(F)	266(F)	276(T)		
207(T)	217(F)	227(F)	237(F)	247(T)	257(F)	267(F)	277(T)		
208(T)	218(T)	228(T)	238(T)	248(F)	258(F)	268(T)	278(F)		
209(F)	219(F)	229(F)	239(T)	249(F)	259(F)	269(F)	279(T)		
210(F)	220(F)	230(T)	240(T)	250(T)	260(T)	270(F)	280(T)		

```
              *   = double response
             ( )  = light mark or response left blank
```

REFERENCES

Achenbach, T. M. (1981). A junior MMPI? (Review of *Multidimensional description of child personality. A manual for the Personality Inventory for Children and Actuarial assessment of child and adolescent personality: An interpretive guide for the Personality Inventory for Children profile*). *Journal of Personality Assessment, 45*, 332–333.

Achenbach, T. M., & Edelbrock, C. S. (1978). The classification of child psychopathology: A review and analysis of empirical efforts. *Psychological Bulletin, 85*, 1275–1301.

American Psychiatric Association. (1980). *Diagnostic and statistical manual of mental disorders* (3rd ed.). Washington, DC: Author.

Anderson, E. E., & Quast, W. (1983). Young children in alcoholic families: A mental health needs-assessment and an intervention/prevention strategy. *Journal of Primary Prevention, 3*, 174–187.

Armstrong, G. D., Wirt, R. D., Nesbit, M. E., & Martinson, I. M. (1982). Multidimensional assessment of psychological problems in children with cancer. *Research in Nursing and Health, 5*, 205–211.

Barad, S. J., & Hughes, H. M. (1984). Readability of the Personality Inventory for Children. *Journal of Consulting and Clinical Psychology, 52*, 906–907.

Bennett, T. S., & Welsh, M. C. (1981). Validity of a configural interpretation of the intellectual screening and achievement scales of the Personality Inventory for Children. *Educational and Psychological Measurement, 41*, 863–868.

Boersma, D. C. (1985). Objective assessment of special needs among elementary students: Applications of the Personality Inventory for Children (Doctoral dissertation, Wayne State University, 1984). *Dissertation Abstracts International, 45*(12B), 3929.

Breen, M. J., & Barkley, R. A. (1983). The Personality Inventory for Children (PIC): Its clinical utility with hyperactive children. *Journal of Pediatric Psychology, 8*, 359–366.

Clark, E. (1982). Construct validity and diagnostic potential of the Personality Inventory for Children (PIC) with emotionally disturbed, learning disabled, and educable mentally retarded children (Doctoral dissertation, Michigan State University, 1982). *Dissertation Abstracts International, 43*(5A), 1473–1474.

Clark, E. (1987). Responses of mothers and fathers on the PIC: Are they significantly different? *Journal of Psychoeducational Assessment, 5*, 138–148.

Clark, E., Kehle, T. J., Bullock, D., & Jenson, W. R. (1987). Convergent and discriminant validity of the Personality Inventory for Children. *Journal of Psychoeducational Assessment, 5*, 99–106.

Clark, E., Wanous, D. S., & Pompa, J. L. (1982, August). *Construct validation of the Personality Inventory for Children (PIC)*. Paper presented at the 90th Annual Convention of the American Psychological Association, Washington, DC.

Costello, C. G. (1981). Childhood depression. In E. J. Mash & L. G. Terdal (Eds.), *Behavioral assessment of childhood disorders* (pp. 305–346). New York: Guilford Press.

Cronbach, L. J. (1984). *Essentials of psychological testing* (4th ed.). New York: Harper & Row.

Daldin, H. (1985). Faking good and faking bad on the Personality Inventory for Children—Revised, shortened format. *Journal of Consulting and Clinical Psychology, 53*, 561–563.

DeKrey, S. J. (1983). Construct validity and educational applications of the Personality Inventory for Children (PIC)—shortened form version (Doctoral dissertation, University of Iowa, 1982). *Dissertation Abstracts International, 43*(12A), 3844.

DeKrey, S. J., & Ehly, S. W. (1985). The Personality Inventory for Children: Differential diagnosis in school settings. *Journal of Psychoeducational Assessment, 3*, 45–53.

DeMoor-Peal, R., & Handal, P. J. (1983). Validity of the Personality Inventory for Children with four-year-old males and females: A caution. *Journal of Pediatric Psychology, 8*, 261–271.

Dollinger, S. J., Goh, D. S., & Cody, J. J. (1984). A note on the congruence of the WISC-R and the cognitive development scales of the Personality Inventory for Children. *Journal of Consulting and Clinical Psychology, 52*, 315–316.

Dreger, R. M. (1981). First-, second-, and third-order factors for the Children's Behavioral Classification Project Instrument and an attempt at reapproachement. *Journal of Abnormal Psychology, 90*, 242–260.

Durrant, J. E. (1983). *Concurrent validity of the narrow-band and broad-band intellectual scales of the Personality Inventory for Children within a preschool population*. Unpublished master's thesis. University of Windsor, Canada.

Education for All Handicapped Children Act of 1975, P. L. 94-142, 42 Fed. Reg. 42474.

Forbes, G. B. (1985). The Personality Inventory for Children (PIC) and hyperactivity: Clinical utility and problems of generalizability. *Journal of Pediatric Psychology, 10*, 141–149.

Forbes, G. B. (1986). Comparison of the short and original scales of the Personality Inventory for Children. *Journal of Clinical Psychology, 41*, 129–132.

Forbes, G. B. (1987). Personality Inventory for Children: Characteristics of learning-disabled children with emotional problems and of emotionally disturbed children with learning problems. *Journal of Clinical Child Psychology, 16*, 133–140.

Forness, S. R. (1976). Behavioristic orientation to categorical labels. *Journal of School Psychology, 14*, 90–96.

Garmezy, N. (1978). DSM-III: Never mind the psychologists: Is it good for the children? *The Clinical Psychologist, 31*, 4–9.

Gdowski, C. L., Lachar, D., & Kline, R. B. (1985). A PIC profile typology of children and adolescents: I. An empirically-derived alternative to traditional diagnosis. *Journal of Abnormal Psychology, 94*, 346–361.

Goldstein, H., Arkell, C., Ashcroft, S. C., Hurley, O. L., & Lilly, M. S. (1975). Schools. In N. Hobbs (Ed.), *Issues in the classification of children* (Vol. 2, pp. 4–61). San Francisco: Jossey-Bass.

Gottlieb, J., Alter, M., & Gottlieb, B. W. (1983). Mainstreaming mentally retarded children. In J. L. Matson & J. A. Mulick (Eds.), *Handbook of mental retardation* (pp. 67–77). New York: Pergamon Press.

Group for the Advancement of Psychiatry. (1966). *Psychopathological disorders in childhood: Theoretical considerations and a proposed classification.* New York: Author.

Hallahan, D. P., & Kauffman, J. M. (1976). *Introduction to learning disabilities.* Englewood Cliffs, NJ: Prentice-Hall.

Hallahan, D. P., & Kauffman, J. M. (1977). Labels, categories, behaviors: ED, LD, and EMR reconsidered. *Journal of Special Education, 11,* 139–149.

Harrington, R. G., & Follett, G. M. (1984). The readability of child personality assessment instruments. *Journal of Psychoeducational Assessment, 2,* 37–48.

Hulbert, T. A., Gdowski, C. L., & Lachar, D. (1986). Interparent agreement on the Personality Inventory for Children: Are substantial correlations sufficient? *Journal of Abnormal Child Psychology, 14,* 115–122.

Kelly, G. T. (1982). A comparison of the Personality Inventory for Children (PIC) and the Child Behavior Checklist (CBCL) with an independent behavior checklist completed by clinicians (Doctoral dissertation, Duke University, 1982). *Dissertation Abstracts International, 43,*(4B), 1257.

Kline, R. B., Lachar, D., & Gdowski, C. L. (1987). A PIC typology of children and adolescents: II. Classification rules and specific behavior correlates. *Journal of Clinical Child Psychology, 16,* 225–234.

Kline, R. B., Lachar, D., Gdowski, C. L., & Boersma, D. C. (1987). A Personality Inventory for Children (PIC) typology: Relationship to cognitive functioning and classroom placement. *Journal of Psychoeducational Assessment, 5,* 327–339.

Kline, R. B., Lachar, D., & Sprague, D. J. (1985). The Personality Inventory for Children (PIC): An unbiased predictor of cognitive and academic status. *Journal of Pediatric Psychology, 10,* 461–477.

Kurdek, L. A. (1980). Developmental relations among children's perspective taking, moral judgment, and parent-rated behaviors. *Merrill–Palmer Quarterly, 26,* 103–121.

Kurdek, L. A. (1982). Long-term predictive validity of children's social-cognitive assessments. *Merrill–Palmer Quarterly, 28,* 511–521.

Kurdek, L. A., & Krile, D. (1983). The relation between third- through eighth-grade children's social cognition and parents' ratings of social skills and general adjustment. *Journal of Genetic Psychology, 143,* 201–206.

Lachar, D. (1982). *Personality Inventory for Children (PIC) Revised Format manual supplement.* Los Angeles: Western Psychological Services.

Lachar, D., & Gdowski, C. L. (1979). *Actuarial assessment of child and adolescent personality: An interpretive guide for the Personality Inventory for Children profile.* Los Angeles: Western Psychological Services.

Lachar, D., Gdowski, C. L., & Snyder, D. K. (1982). Broad-band dimensions of psychopathology: Factor scales for the Personality Inventory for Children. *Journal of Consulting and Clinical Psychology, 50,* 634–642.

Lachar, D., Gdowski, C. L., & Snyder, D. K. (1984). External validation of the Personality Inventory for Children profile and factor scales: Parent, teacher, and clinician ratings. *Journal of Consulting and Clinical Psychology, 52,* 155–164.

Lachar, D., Kline, R. B., & Boersma, D. C. (1986). The Personality Inventory for Children: Approaches to actuarial interpretation in clinic and school settings. In H. M. Knoff (Ed.), *The psychological assessment of child and adolescent personality* (pp. 273–308). New York: Guilford Press.

Lachar, D., Kline, R. B., & Gdowski, C. L. (1987). Respondent psychopathology and interpretive accuracy of the Personality Inventory for Children: The evaluation of a "most reasonable" assumption. *Journal of Personality Assessment, 51,* 165–177.

Lachar, D., & Sharp, J. R. (1979). Use of parents' MMPIs in the research and evaluation of children: A review of the literature and some new data. In J. N. Butcher (Ed.), *New developments in the use of the MMPI* (pp. 203–240). Minneapolis: University of Minnesota Press.

LaCombe, J. A. (1985). Development of a genotypic and phenotypic actuarial interpretive system for the Personality Inventory for Children profile types (Doctoral dissertation, Wayne State University, 1984). *Dissertation Abstracts International, 46*(5A), 1230

Leon, G. R., Kendall, P. C., & Garber, J. (1980). Depression in children: Parent, teacher and child perspectives. *Journal of Abnormal Child Psychology, 8,* 221–235.

Lessing, E. E., Williams, V., & Gill, E. (1982). A cluster-analytically derived typology: Feasible alternatives to clinical diagnostic classification of children? *Journal of Abnormal Child Psychology, 10,* 451–482.

Lobovits, D. A., & Handal, P. J. (1985). Childhood depression: Prevalence using DSM-III criterion and validity of parent and child depression scales. *Journal of Pediatric Psychology, 10,* 45–54.

Marks, P. A., Seeman, W., & Haller, D. L. (1974). *The actuarial use of the MMPI with adolescents and adults.* Baltimore: Williams & Wilkins.

Mattison, M., Cantwell, D. P., Russell, A. T., & Will, L. (1979). A comparison of DSM-II and DSM-III in the diagnosis of childhood psychiatric disorders: II. Interrater agreement. *Archives of General Psychiatry, 36,* 1217–1222.

McAuliffe, T. M., & Handal, P. J. (1984). PIC Delinquency scale: Validity in relation to self-reported delinquent acts. *Criminal Justice and Behavior, 11,* 35–46.

McDermott, P. A. (1982). Actuarial assessment systems for the grouping and classification of school children. In C. R. Reynolds & T. B. Gutkin (Eds.), *The handbook of school psychology* (pp. 243–272). New York: Wiley.

McVaugh, W. H., & Grow, R. T. (1983). Detection of faking on the Personality Inventory for Children. *Journal of Clinical Psychology, 39,* 567–573.

Michigan Special Education Rules as amended August 13, 1980). Lansing: Michigan State Board of Education.

Newby, R. F., & Matthews, C. G. (1986). Relationship between the "Cognitive Triad" from the Personality Inventory for Children and an extended Halstead–Reitan Neuropsychological Battery. *Archives of Clinical Neuropsychology, 1,* 157–163.

Pipp, F. D. (1979). *Actuarial analysis of adolescent personality: Self-report correlates for the Personality Inventory for Children profile scales.* Unpublished master's thesis, Wayne State University.

Porter, J. E., & Rourke, B. P. (1985). Socio-emotional functioning of learning disabled children: A subtypal analysis of personality patterns. In B. P. Rourke (Ed.), *Neuropsychology of learning disabilities in children: Essentials of subtype analysis* (pp. 257–280). New York: Guilford Press.

Reynolds, W. M., Anderson, G., & Bartell, N. (1985). Measuring depression in children: A multimethod assessment investigation. *Journal of Abnormal Child Psychology, 13,* 513–526.

Ross, A. O. (1976). *Psychological aspects of learning disabilities and reading disorders.* New York: McGraw-Hill.

Ross, A. O. (1977). *Learning disability: The unrealized potential.* New York: McGraw-Hill.

Rutter, M. (1978). Diagnostic validity in child psychiatry. *Advances in Biological Psychiatry, 2,* 2–22.

Schnel, J. (1982). The utility of the Student Behavior Checklist and the Personality Inventory for Children to assess affective and academic needs of students with learning disabilities. (Doctoral dissertation, University of San Francisco, 1982). *Dissertation Abstracts International, 43*(10B), 3415.

Schreiber, M. D. (1982). The relationship between extra-familial support networks and coping in children of divorced and non-divorced families. (Doctoral dissertation, Ohio State University, 1982). *Dissertation Abstracts International, 43*(11B), 3742.

Snyder, D. K., & Gdowski, C. L. (1980, October). The relationship of marital dysfunction to psychiatric disturbance in children: An empirical analysis using the MSI and PIC. In *New developments in the actuarial assessment of marital and family interaction.* Symposium conducted at the annual meeting of the National Council of Family Relations, Portland, OR.

Stewart, D. (1971). The construction of a somatizing scale for the Personality Inventory for Children (Doctoral dissertation, University of Minnesota, 1970). *Dissertation Abstracts International, 32,* 572B. (University Microfilms No. 71–18, 824)

Voelker, S., Lachar, D., & Gdowski, C. L. (1983). The Personality Inventory for Children and response to methylphenidate: Preliminary evidence for predictive utility. *Journal of Pediatric Psychology, 8,* 161–169.

Wepman, J. M., Cruickshank, W. M., Deutsch, C. P., Morency, A., & Strother, C. R. (1975). Learning disabilities. In N. Hobbs (Ed.), *Issues in the classification of children* (Vol. 1, pp. 300–317). San Francisco: Jossey-Bass.

Werry, J. S., Methven, R. J., Fitzpatrick, J., & Dixon, H. (1983). The interrater reliability of DSM-III in children. *Journal of Abnormal Child Psychology, 11,* 341–354.

Wirt, R. D., & Lachar, D. (1981). The Personality Inventory for Children: Development and clinical applications. In P. McReynolds (Ed.), *Advances in psychological assessment* (vol. 5, pp. 353–392). San Francisco: Jossey-Bass.

Wirt, R. D., Lachar, D., Klinedinst, J. K., & Seat, P. D. (1984). *Multidimensional description of child personality: A manual for the Personality Inventory for Children* (1984 revision by D. Lachar). Los Angeles: Western Psychological Services.

14

Using the Minnesota Multiphasic Personality Inventory (MMPI) with Adolescents

ROBERT R. REILLEY
Texas A&M University

S everal objective personality inventories are now in common use with adolescents: the Millon Adolescent Personality Inventory, the Sixteen Personality Factor Questionnaire, the Personality Inventory for Children, the High School Personality Questionnaire, and the California Psychological Inventory, among others. All of these inventories attempt to provide a global (or at least broad) picture of the individual's status in terms of significant personality variables. Objective items are employed in the assessment, and results are usually presented in quantitative form for a number of traits or characteristics.

Although the past few years have seen these and other instruments for the assessment of adolescent personality develop and prosper, none can match the Minnesota Multiphasic Personality Inventory (MMPI; Hathaway & McKinley, 1967) in popularity as a clinical or research measure with this young population. The MMPI is the most frequently used personality inventory with both adults and adolescents (Archer, 1987). Yet much of this popularity can be attributed more to the MMPI's success with adult clinical groups than to proven usefulness with younger subjects.

Clinicians and researchers familiar with the MMPI as a measure of adult personality frequently rely on this knowledge in interpreting adolescent profiles. The assumption is made that no important differences exist between adults' and adolescents' responses to the inventory's items. Often, the "art" of test interpretation is employed where the psychologist has no empirical or scientific evidence available to serve as a guide. Exceptions or allowances may be made subjectively for the subject's age or the emotional turbulence of this growth stage.

Although a modification or informed extrapolation of adult data has often served adequately in the past to interpret adolescent MMPI results, a more empirical approach seems overdue. Recent developments, particularly Archer's (1987) timely review of the adolescent MMPI literature, have helped identify situations where adult MMPI data are appropriate and inappropriate in interpreting adolescent profiles. The practitioner or researcher who wishes to adequately understand the MMPI results of adolescent subjects needs both a basic knowledge of the instrument itself and familiarity with recent developments specific to the younger population.

Over the years, several fundamental questions have arisen regarding the validity of adolescent personality assessment by use of the MMPI. Answers to some of these con-

324

cerns are now emerging, and other answers seem imminent. As an example, support for the use of adolescent norms and for the abandonment of the common practice of using adult norms for adolescent subjects has been provided by Archer (1987), who also supplied assistance in applying to adolescents some of the clinically significant descriptive statements associated with certain adult MMPI profiles. Yet research has provided little direction so far as to the appropriate use with adolescents of MMPI short forms, critical item lists, and special scales.

The purpose of this chapter is to provide guidance to professionals interested in using the MMPI with adolescents. Certainly, one chapter can provide no more than an introduction to this topic. Approximately 10,000 articles and books have been written on the MMPI, and about 100 of these are directly relevant to adolescent MMPIs. All of these sources cannot be addressed here. However, pertinent issues are noted, basic information is provided, and sources of additional assistance are presented. This chapter includes (1) a discussion of the development and structure of the MMPI; (2) an overview of the scales, with particular reference to adolescent interpretation; (3) a review of common interpretive strategies as they apply to younger subjects; (4) a presentation of areas of particular concern in working with adolescents; (5) a survey of available literature; and (6) a brief consideration of future trends.

DEVELOPMENT AND CURRENT STRUCTURE

The MMPI is the leading representative of a class of personality tests referred to as "structured" or "paper-and-pencil" instruments. These instruments are self-report questionnaires designed to provide access to a wide band of personality. The term "global" or "general" is often applied to the MMPI and similar inventories because they attempt a comprehensive evaluation of personality functioning, rather than limiting themselves to one or two particular personality traits such as anxiety or depression.

Certain assumptions or opinions underlie the development of structured personality measures. Personality itself is conceptionalized as a unique organization of traits or variables that together characterize the individual and influence his or her relationships with the world. Personality and resulting behavior are seen as mediated by these traits or internal factors, such as feelings, dispositions, or needs. Although the importance of environmental stimuli is recognized, the internal or central factors are given prominence. Unlike the projective techniques (the Rorschach, the Thematic Apperception Test), which are based on the assumption that personality is best evaluated by a holistic approach that allows the dynamic forces in the person to interact in solving a problem, the structured approach provides several more or less independent scale scores that are combined to present a "picture" of the total personality. Empirical data are developed to assist in the interpretation of individual scales and scale combinations.

Advantages cited for structured instruments include the following: economy in collecting large amounts of data quickly, objectively, and in a manner that can be replicated; ease of statistical and computer manipulation of results; and the ready application of such standard measurement concepts as item analysis and reliability evaluations. Of course, for the clinician, the MMPI or other structured inventory is judged as valuable to the degree that it provides valid and useful information about individuals.

Disadvantages frequently mentioned for these instruments generally relate to the structured inventory's written format. Some subjects are not able to read the items well enough to respond accurately. For others, the meaning and intent of the items is only too clear, so that they can and do fake responses. With the MMPI in particular, the time required to read and respond to a large number of items can be a problem. A more general criticism, however, is the question of whether the subject's responses to a variety of printed statements can be converted into a useful evaluation of personality functioning.

Development

The MMPI was developed and first published in the early 1940s, although some inventory items and early work on scales preceded that decade, and additional scales were added at later dates. Originally, items were presented on cards and subjects were asked to sort the cards into three groups: "true," "false," and "cannot say." The convenience of test booklets with separate answer sheets was soon recognized, and this became the dominant form of administration. Hand scoring, machine scoring, and later computer scoring and interpretation were all made easier by the use of the separate answer sheet. Interestingly, some examiners have recently reported that adolescents are more likely to complete the MMPI when it is presented in the older card form (Williams, 1985).

The structure of the MMPI varied somewhat over the first few years of its existence, with new scales and items being added. From the late 1940s until the early 1980s, however, the inventory's form was quite stable: There were 550 different items and 16 repeated items, organized into 4 validity scales and 10 clinical scales. In the early 1980s, the University of Minnesota Press, owner of the MMPI, decided to exert a more active role in the continuing development of the instrument. Although items were not changed, new booklets, answer sheets, profiles, and scoring materials were published, and a new distributor (National Computer Systems, or NCS) was selected. The new profile included space for four "new" scales. These scales were new to the profile, but had each been developed from the MMPI item pool some years previously. Additional changes in the MMPI were also initiated and projected at this time (Kaemmer, 1986).

Currently, two MMPI booklet forms are in common use—the older booklet form and Form R. Identical items are present in these two booklets, but some differences in order or arrangement of items exist. Form R was originally published to provide a booklet with a hard back, so that the inventory can be more conveniently administered where a desk or table is not available. In addition, a "step-down" answer sheet is used with this form, and items have been rearranged so that all 14 traditional scales can be scored if the subject answers only the first 400 items. Items not used in validity and clinical scales have been moved to the end of the booklet.

An increasing number of MMPI adminis-trations are now accomplished without the use of any test booklet or answer sheet. Subjects sit at a computer keyboard and respond to items as they appear on the computer screen. Audiotape versions of the MMPI have also been available for several years, but do not seem to have earned wide acceptance. The comparability of booklet-administered and audiotape-administered inventories is in question. A similar question has recently arisen regarding the computer-administered MMPI (Bresolin, 1984).

The general procedure for personality evaluation with the MMPI begins with the subject responding "true," "false," or "cannot say" to the test items. Responses are recorded by making a separate answer sheet (for printed editions) or by pushing a computer key. In scoring, the responses are counted and recorded on a profile in terms of the particular scale to which they belong. The profile provides standard score (T-score) values for each scale raw score. Interpretation is usually done from the profile, except for computer interpretation, which is based on information stored in the computer memory bank.

Uses

Originally envisioned as an efficient tool to accomplish diagnosis of new clients, the MMPI soon proved inadequate for this purpose but most useful for several related tasks (Graham, 1977). Current uses for this highly popular instrument include (1) assisting in the diagnosis of clinical cases; (2) screening groups for significant psychological conditions; (3) assessing personality within both the normal and abnormal ranges; and (4) serving as an item pool for the development of new scales.

Although the MMPI has not proven successful as a straightforward, uncomplicated method of arriving at the correct diagnostic label for clinical cases, it certainly is a useful aid in this endeavor. Clinicians usually view the MMPI interpretation as important, if not vital, information to be considered in reaching a diagnosis. Other sources of data (interview, mental status examination, history, etc.), however, must also be weighed. Often individuals with particular mental disorders do produce distinctive and identifiable

MMPI profiles, but these profiles are complicated, differing from one another in subtle ways, and exceptions exist. Therefore, the well-trained clinician probably views the MMPI profile as an aid in finding clues to follow up, support for a hypothesis, or evidence for a diagnosis, rather than as proof in and of itself.

The need for a psychological screening device can be appreciated when one considers the difficulty and expense of providing individual diagnostic interviews to large groups of people. Yet it is often important to locate persons with certain personality characteristics, whether positive or negative. Structured or paper-and-pencil tests of personality originated with the Personal Data Sheet by Woodworth, an attempt to aid U.S. military authorities in screening out individuals with serious mental disorders among recruits for World War I. Presently, some universities, training programs, and other groups use the MMPI for this screening function. Along with screening out, "screening in," or the identification of individuals with particularly favorable or desirable personality traits, may be the purpose of these activities. For example, PhD training programs in psychology may use the MMPI to identify potentially good therapists from among a large group of essentially normal and healthy applicants. The MMPI is a useful and economical tool in these screening functions.

Personality assessment probably is the use or purpose most commonly associated with the MMPI. Whether for research or clinical reasons, the MMPI is regularly employed as a means of assessing or evaluating personality characteristics. The inventory and a considerable amount of the research associated with it lend themselves to uncovering the personality functioning of individuals. The MMPI was developed with an orientation toward abnormal or deviant personality functioning; however, this instrument has proven of great value in evaluating the personality of both normal and abnormal individuals. Certainly diagnosis, or labeling a person as having a particular disorder, does not completely describe that individual's personality. All depressed individuals or all anxious individuals are not alike in every aspect of personality. Important differences exist within each mental classification. Similarly, the vast array of

"normals" are not all possessed of the same personality characteristics to an identical degree. Significant differences exist, and the MMPI is effective at distinguishing them.

As an item pool for the development of new scales, the MMPI has been and continues to be eminently successful. Hundreds of useful scales have been developed from these items. Over a decade ago, Dahlstrom, Welsh, and Dahlstrom (1975) published an extensive listing of these "special scales"; however, the 455 they reported probably represent only a fraction of the number now in existence. The empirical approach used in developing the MMPI clinical scales was also applied to the item pool to construct many of the special or research scales. Examples of scales derived in this manner are the Ego Strength *(Es)* scale by Barron and the MacAndrew Alcoholism *(MAC)* scale, both recently added to the MMPI profile. The other two new scales, Conscious Anxiety *(A)* and Conscious Repression *(R)*, were developed by Welsh from a factor analysis of the MMPI items (Graham, 1977).

Current Structure

Currently, the MMPI profile provides the results for 18 scales: 4 validity scales, 10 clinical scales, and the 4 "special" scales just described (see Table 14.1). Validity scales attempt to answer questions about the test-taking behavior of the subject, number of items skipped, attempts to "fake good" or "fake bad," and openness to the assessment. Although primarily intended to aid the examiner in determining how well the profile represents the client's personality, the validity scales also provide useful information regarding personality structure.

The clinical scales, in most cases, were devised empirically by determining sets of items on which normal individuals and specific groups of abnormal individuals differed in their responses. As an example, items on which a group of diagnosed schizophrenics responded differently than a group of normal subjects were selected to form Scale 8, the Schizophrenic *(Sc)* scale. In general, then, the clinical scales were developed to answer this question: How closely do this subject's responses resemble those of individuals who are diagnosed as having cer-

TABLE 14.1. Validity, Clinical, and New Scales of the MMPI

Validity scales

    ?—Cannot Say Scale

    L—Lie

    F—Infrequency

    K—Correction

Clinical scales

    1—Hypochondriasis (*Hs*)

    2—Depression (*D*)

    3—Hysteria (*Hy*)

    4—Psychopathic Deviante (*Pd*)

    5—Masculinity–Femininity (*Mf*)

    6—Paranoia (*Pa*)

    7—Psychasthenia (*Pt*)

    8—Schizophrenia (*Sc*)

    9—Hypomania (*Ma*)

    0—Social Introversion (*Si*)

Special scales

    A—Conscious Anxiety

    R—Conscious Repression

    Es—Ego Strength

    MAC—MacAndrew Alcoholism

tain clinical conditions (hypochondriasis, depression, hysteria, etc.)? Scales 5, Masculinity–Femininity (*Mf*), and 0, Social Introversion (*Si*), were devised somewhat differently (Dahlstrom, Welsh, & Dahlstrom, 1972).

The final four scales were developed at various points in time from the MMPI item pool. As previously noted, the *A* and *R* scales are the factors derived from an early factor analysis of the MMPI; the last two scales were derived empirically, in a manner similar to that used to obtain the clinical scales.

OVERVIEW OF THE MMPI SCALES

The scales were originally designed to be interpreted separately, and their absolute and relative elevations still provide important clinical information. In recent years, however, overall profile shape and, particularly, combinations of scales (discussed below) have been increasingly studied and are now dominant interpretive strategies. Yet a thorough knowledge of the individual scales remains an indispensable foundation for clinical interpretation.

As noted above and in Table 14.1, the MMPI profile, distributed by NCS, presents 18 scales: the 4 validity scales, the 10 traditional clinical scales, and the 4 "new" scales added in the early 1980s. (As also noted earlier, the "new" scales are new to the profile, but not of recent origin.) Scores are expressed as *T*-scores (mean 50, standard deviation 10). A high or abnormal score is usually considered to be a *T*-score of 70 or above, but there are exceptions to this rule of thumb, and the new scales do not fit this general pattern. A discussion of each scale follows.

The Validity Scales

The validity scales contribute both to the evaluation of the profile's validity and, in varying degrees, to the assessment of the individual's personality. These scales attempt to answer questions regarding the subject's ability and willingness to provide a representative picture of himself or herself.

Scale? (Cannot Say Scale)

This validity scale is simply the number of items omitted or double-marked (marked both "true" and "false"). In terms of profile validity, a raw score of 30 or higher—that is, 30 items double-marked or omitted—is used as a strong indication that too many items were skipped for the profile to be adequately interpreted. If the inventory has been properly administered, ? scores this high are quite unusual. Proper administration includes a request that the examinee try to answer all the items.

Some hypotheses regarding personality may be suggested by even moderate scores on this scale (8 or 10 items omitted for adults or over 10 for adolescents). If the test was properly administered, failure to answer items may indicate (1) a degree of hostility or an uncooperative attitude (common among some adolescents); (2) inability to answer some items because of a reading disability, or a problem with attending to the task because of distractibility or confusion (psychotic individuals frequently score high on this scale);

(3) carelessness or lack of motivation to answer the items; or (4) an extremely guarded or compulsive attitude toward answering the items. Inspection of the answer sheet to determine the nature of the particular items omitted may provide additional interpretive hypothesis. Inability to read and understand may be the major reason for skipped items among adolescents.

Scale L (Lie Scale)

Scale L is made up of rather unsophisticated claims to virtue. The naive subject who attempts to "fake good" tends to answer these items in the scored direction. A raw score of 7 or more is often used to suggest such an attempt. Usually, the clinical scales are lowered a bit by the high-L test-taking approach (a denial of problems), but the profile's validity is not seriously altered by even fairly high L scores.

The L score is more likely to reflect personality characteristics than an attempt to present oneself in a good light. Average scores on this scale vary from about 4 for young teenagers to 0–1 for college students; as Graham (1977) points out, intelligence, socioeconomic status, and sophistication must also be considered in determining when the score should be considered high. As a general rule, however, as scores grow beyond the expected average, they are more likely to reflect an individual who is unsophisticated, lacking in self-understanding, moralistic, rigid, and conventional.

Scale F (Infrequency Scale)

Items seldom answered in the scored direction are used to make up this scale. To obtain a high score, the individual must claim a number of very unusual attitudes and beliefs. Adolescents and adults differ markedly in terms of average scores on this scale. Lachar (1974) used the F scale to point out the need for adolescent norms when evaluating individuals younger than 18 years. On the average, adolescents mark many more of these items than adults do. A T-score above 60 for either group could alert the clinician to the possibility of a "fake-bad" set by the examinee. However, Archer (1987) strongly advises flexibility in interpreting validity scales, particularly high F scores among adolescents. Younger subjects may interpret some of these items in a manner different from that of adults. Sex differences may also exist.

Personality characteristics associated with high scores on the F scale range from creative or liberal ideas to eccentricity and bizarre beliefs. Psychopathology, along with faking bad or random marking, must be considered when T-scores on the F scale exceed 60.

Scale K (Correction Scale)

This scale was added to the MMPI to correct five of the clinical scales for differences in openness–defensiveness among test takers. In the construction of the adult profile, fractions of the K score are added to Scales 1, 4, 7, 8, and 9. This "K correction" is not generally used with adolescent norms.

For both adults and adolescents, T-scores on the K scale in excess of 60 often suggest minimizing of problems, with defensiveness and faking good more likely as the score increases. Moderate scores are associated with ego strength, resiliency, and good mental health. Higher scores (T-scores over 60) reflect defensiveness and lack of insight, whereas T-scores much below 50 may indicate a poor self-concept and lack of confidence or trust in self or others. It should be noted that T-scores in the upper 60s on the K scale are often a favorable sign in the profiles of college-educated individuals.

The Clinical Scales

Scale 1: Hypochondriasis

The Hypochondriasis (Hs) scale is primarily a list of physical complaints that the individual can endorse or deny. Rather than identifying persons with actual medical problems, a high score on this scale is associated with a psychological condition in which the individual is overly concerned about bodily functioning. Often the hypochondriac is seen as expressing anxiety in the form of trivial complaints about digestion, elimination, and minor aches and pains.

Higher scorers on Scale 1 are usually described as bothered but not disabled by their reported physical complaints. In addition to being overly concerned with bodily functioning, these individuals tend to be pessimistic, complaining, stubborn, and difficult to deal with. Frequent visits to physicians for vague symptoms are to be expected. Adolescent and adult averages on Scale 1 do not differ greatly; however, Scale 1 does tend to be elevated with older adults.

Scale 2: Depression

Scale 2, the Depression (D) scale, is a fairly uncomplicated measure of the individual's current adjustment. People who feel depressed score high, and people who do not feel depressed score low. High scores are associated with lack of energy, withdrawal from social interaction, sadness, and discouragement. Self-destructive tendencies may be indicated by high scores. The scores on this scale tend to change easily as the subject's mood fluctuates. Younger subjects may score a bit higher than adults.

Scale 3: Hysteria

The Hysteria (Hy) scale was developed to identify individual with symptoms of conversion hysteria; it is associated with denial of shortcomings, narcissistic self-centeredness, demands for attention, and admission of bodily complaints. Individuals who score high on this scale frequently have difficulty with interpersonal relationships because they are self-centered, demanding, immature, and naive. Repression and somatic preoccupation are also part of the clinical picture. Slightly higher scores are often reported with teenagers, and high scores in this population may also reflect achievement motivation and socioeconomic status (Archer, 1987).

Scale 4: Psychopathic Deviate

Scale 4, the Psychopathic Deviate (Pd) scale, measures tendency toward behavior that is usually considered antisocial or criminal. Since a number of traits combine to predict psychopathic behavior, moderate scores on Scale 4 may reflect only part of this syndrome (e.g., feelings of alienation or family conflict), rather than a true antisocial disposition. High scorers are described as impulsive, insen-

sitive to the feelings of others, irresponsible, and likely to have failed in internalizing rules and conventions of society. This scale is related to age, and many young people score in the high range when their behavior and attitudes do not fit the usual description of the high Pd scorer. The need for special adolescent norms and interpretive statements has been particular supported by adult–youth differences on this scale.

Scale 5: Masculinity–Femininity

On the MMPI profile, high scores on the Masculinity–Femininity (Mf) scale for either gender indicate answers judged more appropriate for the opposite sex. Although originally developed as a measure of masculine versus feminine interests and attitudes, Scale 5 interpretation is complicated by a number of factors. Since the 1940s, society's views of the appropriate roles for men and women have changed drastically. These social changes, problems with the original criterion groups for this scale, and other factors have resulted in scores whose true meaning is not well represented by the scale name. High scorers in the masculine direction (independent of gender) are best described as interested in mechanical, scientific, and sports activities, while tending to be adventurous and vigorous. Males or females scoring high in the feminine direction are often described as sensitive, idealistic, warm toward others, intellectually broad in interests, and perhaps passive and dependent.

Scale 6: Paranoia

A predisposition toward oversensitivity, suspiciousness, and hostility is assessed by the Paranoia (Pa) scale. Interpretation differs markedly at different levels. For example, individuals with moderate scores are usually described very favorably. High scorers can be expected to be hostile, argumentative, suspicious, and likely to feel persecuted. Psychotic thinking may also be associated with high scores on this scale, and when Scale 6 is high in combination with Scales 4 and 9, the possibility of violent behavior is suggested. Since interpretation is related to both age and sex, adolescent data are helpful for Scale 6.

Scale 7: Psychasthenia

Scale 7, the Psychasthenia *(Pt)* scale, is an anxiety scale. Unlike Scale 6, this scale has the same meaning at different elevations; the difference is in degree of anxiety. High scorers are often described as anxious, tense, worried, and fearful. Obsessive–compulsive traits may be associated with very high scores. Low-scoring individuals are relatively free from anxiety and quicker to take action. Adolescent scores tend to run higher than those of adults.

Scale 8: Schizophrenia

The Schizophrenia *(Sc)* scale is a long, complicated scale with several types of items. Alienation, isolation, dissatisfaction, creativity, and independence of thought can result in moderately high scores (*T*-scores in the 70s) among individuals who are not mentally ill. However, the scale also includes many items more closely associated with psychosis: delusions, bizarre feelings, and complaints about peculiar bodily dysfunctions. The total profile and other information about the subject help identify the types of items marked and the appropriate interpretation. Scale 8 is another scale on which adolescents usually score higher than adults. Average differences may be highest on this scale, and race may also be a factor (Graham, 1977).

Scale 9: Hypomania

Originally constructed to identify the manic individual, the Hypomania *(Ma)* scale can be considered largely as a measure of energy and enthusiasm. Low scores are often associated with apathy, low energy, and lack of drive, whereas high scorers tend to be energetic, enthusiastic, and outgoing. High scorers may also have some negative characteristics: They may be unproductive, irritable, overactive, and undercontrolled. When combined with a high score on Scale 4, a high Scale 9 score often predicts impulsive and acting-out behavior. Graham (1977) again reported that black subjects and adolescents score higher on this scale.

Scale 10: Social Introversion

The Social Introversion *(Si)* scale attempts to identify the socially withdrawn individual.

High scorers usually take part in few social activities and are anxious, lacking in self-confidence, and shy. Low scorers are outgoing and friendly, but also tend to be immature and impulsive. Individuals who score in the middle ranges are usually rated most favorably. Younger subjects are typically more socially active and score lower on this scale.

The Special Scales

Conscious Anxiety Scale

The Conscious Anxiety *(A)* scale is a measure of overt state anxiety—the amount of anxiety the subject is conscious of at the time of testing. The *A* score is also commonly used as an overall index of maladjustment or mental illness. Scale 7 and the *A* scale are highly correlated, because both measure anxiety. Research has not yet established the usefulness of the *A*, *R*, or *Es* scales with adolescents.

Conscious Repression Scale

The Conscious Repression *(R)* scale is also a scale measuring the individual's conscious state of mind at the time of testing. The *R* scale reflects the degree to which the person feels a need to hold back or repress information about the self. High scorers tend to be formal, cautious people who feel they have something they wish to hide. Low scorers are more open and willing to discuss problems.

Ego Strength Scale

As the name implies, the Ego Strength *(Es)* scale attempts to identify individuals who are psychologically healthy, are able to handle stress, and bounce back from difficulties. Resiliency, strength, and self-confidence are predicted by high scores. Low scorers feel weak and in need of help from others.

MacAndrews Alcoholism Scale

The MacAndrews Alcoholism *(MAC)* scale is a very successful research scale that is now included on the MMPI profile. The *MAC* scale has proven useful in identifying individuals who have an addictive personality;

that is, they have the potential to develop dependence on or to abuse alcohol or other drugs (the *MAC* scale is sometimes referred to as the MacAndrews Addiction Scale). Research indicates that this scale is useful with an adolescent population. Some disagreement exists, however, regarding the best cutoff point to identify adolescents who are addiction-prone (Archer, 1987).

INTERPRETIVE STRATEGIES

Several methods of MMPI interpretation have been developed and have enjoyed popularity over the years. As noted, a scale-by-scale interpretation was originally envisioned as the logical interpretive strategy when the MMPI was first published. Procedures that consider the entire profile, its shape or configuration, later proved useful. More recently, codetypes, usually based on the two or three highest clinical scales, have been recognized as particularly valuable in interpretation. Another procedure involves the ordering of all scales into a "full code" that can be interpreted by referring to an atlas containing descriptions of individuals with similar codes. Also, a variety of special or research scales can be employed to add substantially to the information available about the client or patient.

Fortunately, the professional is not forced to select just one interpretive strategy and to ignore the input of other procedures. In actuality, most MMPI interpretations are the product of several procedures applied to the same data. Computers help immensely in the tedious tasks of scoring and selecting appropriate interpretive statements.

Detailed descriptions of the various MMPI interpretive strategies are beyond the scope of this chapter, but the reader is referred to one of the several texts on the subject (Duckworth & Anderson, 1986; Graham, 1987; Greene, 1980). However, a brief discussion of the most fruitful and popular method, use of codetypes, is appropriate, particularly as this procedure is commonly applied to adolescent profiles. Steps in profile interpretation are discussed below and illustrated by an example. Scoring and profiling of responses are necessary first steps to in-

terpretation unless computer scoring has been employed.

Scoring the Answer Sheet

Once the subject has completed answering the MMPI items, the separate answer sheet is ready for scoring. In general, this is accomplished by placing a transparent scoring key or template over the answer sheet and counting the number of responses indicated for each scale. Different answer sheets and scoring materials are required for the group booklet form and Form R. Detailed directions for scoring, including special directions for some scales, can be obtained from the MMPI manual (Hathaway & McKinley, 1967). Raw scores obtained by counting are recorded on the answer paper. For the group form, responses for some scales are recorded on the back of the answer sheet and must be transferred and added to the scores on the front.

Accuracy of hand scoring is an essential element if a meaningful interpretation is to be obtained. For this reason, the utmost care and careful rechecking are advised in the scoring and profiling procedures. Rechecking of scoring and profiling often clears up the mystery of profiles that "just don't look right."

Profiling

The MMPI profile is obtained by recording and plotting raw scores on a profile form. Separate forms are used for males and females. Some scales are corrected by adding fractions of the score on the K scale before profiling. The traditional adult MMPI norms were used in constructing the profile forms, and the added K values were also considered. Therefore, for adult subjects it is only necessary to plot the raw score or K-corrected raw score on the profile, and the plotting mark will correspond to the correct standard score (T-score) on the edge of the profile.

The plotting of raw scores obtained by adolescents presents special problems. Many authorities believe that neither the adult norms nor the K corrections are appropriate for younger subjects. Therefore, using the procedure described above may result in distorted profiles. One solution is, first, to convert the adolescent's raw scores into T-scores based on a population of individuals the same sex and age as the subject (adolescent norms). These T-score values for both validity and clinical scores can next be recorded on the adult profile forms by entering them from the T-score scale, ignoring the raw score values. Adolescent norms developed by Marks, Seeman, and Haller (1974) are listed in several texts (including Archer, 1987; Dahlstrom et al., 1972; Lachar, 1974).

The availability of adolescent norm profiling sheets from several commercial sources greatly simplifies the task of converting the validity and clinical scale scores to adolescent norm T-scores. These profiles usually are based on the Marks et al. (1974) norms for males and females aged 14 and below to 17 and 18. They are not K-corrected, and raw scores can be directly converted to T-score values by plotting. Adolescent norms for the new scales are not in common use.

Use of the Marks et al. adolescent norms appears generally to result in fewer errors in interpreting MMPI profiles for younger subjects. One disadvantage, however, may be that these norms tend to underestimate psychopathology if a T-score of 70 is used to set the lower limit of the abnormal range. For this reason, a T-score of 65 may prove a more useful critical limit for adolescent profiles (Archer, 1987).

Interpreting the Profile

Several interpretive procedures or strategies are usually applied to any given profile. The experience and training of the interpreter play major roles in the process, and no MMPI interpretation should be considered complete unless it includes the clinical judgment of a competent professional who integrates profile-derived hypotheses with independent data available about the subject. A computer "interpretation," as detailed as it may be, is never a complete interpretation because it lacks clinical judgment and thoughtful application of general information to a specific individual.

In recent years, the use of high-point codetypes has grown to a position of eminence in MMPI interpretation. Although not used exclusively or in isolation from other procedures, the descriptive statements re-

lated to the various codetypes often form the core of the interpretation. Codetypes represent the highest two or three clinical scales and are expressed as the numbers of the scales: For example, 68/86 are the codetypes for profiles with Scales 6 and 8 as the high points. Over the years, research and clinical experience have provided descriptive statements or clinical correlates that commonly fit individuals with the particular codetype. For example, individuals with the 12/21 codetype are frequently described as tense, anxious, and preoccupied with physical complaints. These descriptions are more appropriate when the scores on these scales are high (in or approaching the abnormal range). Of course, some profiles have only one or no scales highly elevated. In these cases, other interpretive strategies may play a more dominant role.

Many of the descriptive data related to codetypes have been derived from adult populations; however, Marks et al. (1974) have provided clinical correlate data for adolescent profile types. Archer (1987) combined the Marks et al. information and appropriate information determined for adult populations with the same codetypes to produce narratives describing adolescents with 29 different high-point codes. These codetype descriptions provide a fruitful source of data for the interpretation of adolescent profiles, as the following case example illustrates.

Case Example

The subject was a 15-year-old white male from a "good family." His parents were both employed at the professional level in a small community where they were active, well known, and respected. The subject's parents reported a number of recent and past problems with their son, including very poor school achievement, incessant quarreling with his siblings, withdrawal, and failure to make or keep friends. Assessment confirmed the school's report that this adolescent had high average intelligence and reading ability two grades above his grade placement.

The MMPI was administered individually by use of the booklet form in a clinical setting after the examiner had spent some time establishing rapport and explaining the need for the test. Figure 14.1 presents the result-

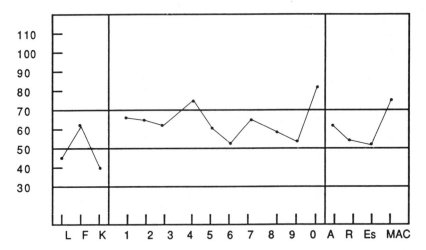

FIGURE 14.1. Sample MMPI profile for a 15-year-old male.

ing profile, using adolescent norms for a 15-year-old male. The scores are not *K*-corrected, and the new scales (*A*, *R*, *Es*, and *MAC*) are expressed in the usual adult *T*-score form.

If the interpretive suggestions from Archer (1987) are used, the validity scales may be viewed as indicating the possibility of faking; most likely, however, they reflect psychopathology, a poor self-concept, inability to cope, and acute distress.

Among the clinical scales, only Scales 4 and 0 exceed a *T*-score of 69 and are in the traditional abnormal range. (However, three additional high scores are identified if 65 is used as the critical *T*-score; these moderately high scores indicate concern about bodily functioning, depression, and anxiety.) The 4-0/0-4 codetype was identified in the Marks et al. (1974) data and is described by Archer (1987) as suggesting more the high Scale 6 personality, with distrust, suspiciousness, and projection common. Overreaction to minor stresses, poor social adjustment, and some grandiose ideas are also associated with this codetype. Shyness, resentment, and argumentativeness complete the description. Note that *K*-corrected adult norms would place both the *F* scale and Scale 8 in the abnormal range, substantially altering the interpretation.

Little can be said about the first three new scales. *A*, *R*, and *Es* seem to support the interpretation based on the clinical scores, but the lack of adolescent norms and adolescent behavioral correlates for these scales makes further analysis risky. The high score (raw score 30) on the *MAC* scale, however, is above the cutoff scores usually recommended for use of the *MAC* (Graham, 1987). Since research does indicate the usefulness of the *MAC* scale with adolescents, a potential for substance abuse could be added to the personality description developed for this young man.

LIMITATIONS AND CAUTIONS

The professional who uses the MMPI with adolescents should be aware of certain limitations of the instrument and cautions to be exercised, in order to avoid errors and other problems. Some of these considerations are discussed below.

Content

The MMPI, perhaps more than most psychological instruments, contains items that some people find objectionable. Items that deal with bodily functions, family relations, religious issues, and sexual practices have considerable potential for sparking conflict. The problem often seems to be more one of public relations than a clinical issue, since the subject who actually is administered the instrument usually can be helped to understand and accept the item content. Others, however, who hear second hand about the nature of the items, may be less accepting. MMPI item content is more likely to result in controversy when groups of normal adolescents are tested in settings such as the public schools. Complaints about invasion of privacy and the like are not unexpected in these situations.

Usually, problems can be avoided or alleviated by the exercise of sound judgment, sensitivity to the concerns of subjects and their parents, and a high standard of professional skill in test administration. The possibility of objections should be considered when the instrument is selected for screening, research, or other purposes. Pros and cons of using the MMPI or any other instrument should be weighed. The advisability of preparing the public for adverse criticism should be considered. Where possible, voluntary rather than compulsory testing may be advisable. General information about the purpose and nature of the evaluation usually can be provided without jeopardizing the research objectives or the test's usefulness. In administering the inventory to individuals or small groups, the experienced examiner is almost always able to establish rapport and to encourage a serious, honest, and cooperative effort.

Subject Reaction

Adolescence is a period of development during which the individual is particularly vulnerable to certain internal and external influences. Sensitivity to peer pressure, concern about "what others will think," and unresolved authority and self-concept issues all can have an influence on the youth's acceptance of the test-taking task. The young subject may react in a defensive and uncooperative manner. Faking good or faking bad are both possible behaviors for the young person who, for one reason or another, does not accept the MMPI administration as a serious and helpful experience.

Again, sensitivity and professional behavior can solve many of these problems. Closely supervised individual or small-group testing may be advisable. Time spent in developing rapport and enlisting cooperation is usually a good investment. Confidentiality is often a major concern of the adolescent, and efforts should be made to help the subject

feel secure that peers will see neither the answer sheet nor the interpretation. Explanations that appeal to the adolescent's self-interest ("What do I get out of this?") and altruism ("How are you going to use this information?") may be of assistance.

Stability of Results

Unlike some measures in the physical sciences, human dimensions are subject to change from time to time. For the young adolescent, height, weight, and shoe size, for example, are expected to change rapidly because of the developmental stage the individual is experiencing. Psychological variables, particularly personality traits, are subject not only to developmental influences, but also to transient personal or environmental factors and to the limitations of the measuring instrument involved. Personality inventories, including the MMPI, tend to be less reliable or stable than measures of intelligence or achievement. This condition may reflect partly the changeable nature of the variables being measured, and partly weaknesses of the instrument.

In interpreting the MMPI profile, particularly that of an adolescent, the professional must keep in mind that scale scores do change in response to both instrument error and actual changes in the variables being measured. Change is to be expected when the subject has had experiences that alter personality characteristics. Psychotherapy has long been recognized as bringing about changes in both personality and MMPI results. The existence of separate MMPI norms for adolescents of differing ages testifies to the personality change potency of the volatile teenage years.

Fortunately, the interpretation of the MMPI usually is not seriously distorted by the limited stability of some individual scales. One reason for this is that interpretation is not limited to or greatly dependent upon the actual magnitude of individual scales. Interpretation usually considers the entire profile, the relationships between and among scales, and relative rather than absolute magnitude of scales. The experienced professional also recognizes that some scales are particularly subject to fluctuation as a result of current mood or developmental status.

Ease of Misinterpretation

Once an individual learns the original names of the scales, the MMPI affords the opportunity for serious mischief. Harm has been done by simplistic, shallow interpretations based on scale names and elevations. A moderate or even pronounced elevation on Scale 8 seldom signifies schizophrenia; a high- or "abnormal"-scoring male on Scale 5 usually is not indicative of homosexuality; and a score above the usual cutoff on the MAC scale does not unerringly identify an alcoholic. A high score on a scale does not necessarily have any meaning in relation to the name of that scale. Time, skill, and experience are required to interpret the MMPI profile adequately to an adolescent, or any subject. Often the damage of misinterpretation is self-inflicted by the curious adolescent, who is given his or her results without proper explanation and "looks it up in a book." At other times, careless or uninformed "experts" have inflicted the hurt on naive subjects. Care should be taken to avoid either situation. The adolescent is particularly vulnerable to misinformation because of lack of experience, oversensitivity to the opinions of others, and many self-doubts resulting from a still uncertain self-concept.

Unjustified Acceptance

The MMPI is properly considered an aid in the diagnosis or understanding of an individual. The profile provides valuable information, and many practitioners find it an indispensable aid. But it is an aid. Final decisions about diagnosis or the nature of an individual's personality are matters of clinical judgment made by professionals using all available information. The MMPI does not diagnose people. It provides information, suggestions, leads, and supporting data.

In addition to suggesting current personality status, the MMPI profile may well reflect potential for the development of a condition, or the profile may be influenced by conditions that once existed but are no longer true of the individual. Erroneous interpretations can be avoided only by an experienced evaluator who includes nontest data in making an analysis.

Most MMPI scales are not linear, pure, or consistent measures of the same variable at all levels; rather, the meaning of the score often varies in quality as it changes in quantity. An example may illustrate this point. Scale 6 *(Pa)* suggests hostility and anger at the high level, but mildly elevated scores are associated with very favorable traits, such as sensitivity, cooperation, and clear thinking. In addition, while an average score may indicate no particular problem in this area, very low scores may be interpreted as suggesting suspiciousness, defensiveness, or delusions. The skilled evaluator must internalize a great deal of information, and must develop personal norms for the scales and a "feel" for the profiles. Although the computer scoring and interpretation programs now available do provide a wealth of information, there is no substitute for the skilled clinician who can interpret these data in terms of the individual they attempt to describe.

Unanswered Questions

Research has not yet answered all questions regarding the use of MMPI-derived data with adolescents, but the findings so far clearly caution against assuming blindly that what is found to be true of adults is true of younger subjects. Short forms, critical items, special scales, and indices that have proven valuable in working with adults may or may not be appropriate for adolescents. In general, these topics have not been sufficiently researched. Even where data do support the usefulness of some scales with adolescents (e.g., the *MAC* scale), doubt still exists regarding appropriate norms or cutoff levels.

It is quite likely that many MMPI items have a different meaning for younger and older subjects, and therefore that they are actually responding to different stimuli. Adolescent norms alone will not ameliorate this difficulty. The use of clinical correlates developed from an adolescent group will help derive meaning for the clinical scales. Understanding the meaning of adolescents' responses to other MMPI scales must await further research.

THE MMPI LITERATURE

The MMPI, in addition to becoming one of the most frequently used of all assessment tools, has inspired an unparalleled flow of literature. Journal articles, books, doctoral dissertations, and assorted other documents relating to the inventory abound. Their number has been estimated as approaching 10,000 (Butcher, 1985), and the literature is continuing to grow.

Although the use of the MMPI with adolescents has been popular almost from the instrument's introduction, research publications with this population have lagged far behind those with adults. Archer (1987) has noted that only about 100 adolescent-related MMPI studies are available to match the many thousands for adults. Therefore, in this section, the discussion must by necessity deal primarily with items based on an adult population. Where possible, publications relating to adolescents are noted.

The vast array of MMPI publications can be categorized or classified in many different ways. The classification system selected for this review stresses the type of treatment attempted by the originator of each publication. Although no one system can equally satisfy the researcher and the practitioner, or the neophyte and the experienced specialist, it is hoped that this approach will prove of some benefit to all. The major divisions used are as follows:

1. General treatments of the MMPI, covering development, uses, interpretation, research, and resource data.
2. Books that address some of the topics listed above by presenting a set of readings, rather than employing a direct narrative approach.
3. Interpretive manuals, including codebooks and "cookbooks," whose primary focus is personality assessment by means of MMPI results.
4. Reference books, including atlases and other resource books that present compiled data.
5. Journals and related publications.

Samples of each type of publication are presented below, with particular note made of publications relating to adolescent MMPIs.

General Treatments

The major conprehensive sources of information about the MMPI have for many years been Dahlstrom et al.'s *An MMPI Handbook: Volume 1. Clinical Interpretation* (1972) and *An MMPI Handbook: Volume 2. Research Applications* (1975). This two-volume text, a revised edition of the 1960 handbook, provides a massive range of pertinent information. Volume 1 treats in detail such topics as administration, scoring, coding, test validity, and several approaches to interpretation. Over 100 pages are devoted to appendices (item lists, score conversions, profile discrimination rules, etc.). These sections are followed by cited references and an index. Volume 2 includes a detailed review of the MMPI literature, organized as follows: (1) several uses of the instrument (applications to mental health problems, medical concerns, criminal justice, etc.); (2) experimental research using the MMPI; and (3) a long series of studies of the instrument itself. The narrative presentations make up only about one-third of Volume 2. Appendices follow for 150 pages; these include the extremely valuable Appendix I, which provides item content, scoring, mean, and standard deviation for 455 special scales of the MMPI. In addition to an index, the last third of the volume contains a 200-page bibliography covering "most of the significant references to the MMPI through the end of 1973" (p. 351).

Although no other single source approaches the comprehensive treatment afforded by *An MMPI Handbook*, other authors have attempted general presentation of the MMPI. Graham's (1987) *The MMPI: A Practical Guide* is a good example of an MMPI publication that is general in scope. Attempting to provide both a textbook for students becoming acquainted with the inventory and a source book for practicing clinicians through this second edition of the popular 1977 text, Graham introduces the reader to the development and rationale of the MMPI before covering basic information about administration, scoring, and the nature and interpretation of the scales.

Graham devotes considerable attention to various interpretive approaches (high-point codetypes, research scales and other special scales, computerized interpretation), as well as a chapter on a general interpretive strategy. This chapter includes suggestions and examples to aid in evaluating specific conditions (e.g., adjustment level) and answering specific referral questions (e.g., the prediction of suicidal behavior). A considerable body of helpful information is among the 40 pages of appendices provided.

The single most important volume relating to adolescent MMPI usage is the comprehensive text recently written by Robert P. Archer. In *Using the MMPI with Adolescents*, Archer (1987) provides an overview of the MMPI literature relating to adolescents, and offers recommendations on the use of the inventory with a young population. This book is and will probably remain for many years the primary source of information for researchers and practitioners working in this area.

For the researcher, Archer reviews the pertinent literature and relates it to such fundamental questions as norm selection, factors affecting interpretation, and more general issues of adolescent development. Practitioners are provided strategies for the clinical interpretation of the adolescent profile and a chapter devoted to codetype correlates or descriptors for adolescents. Also addressed are topics related to the use of the MMPI with 12- and 13-year-olds, short forms, and special scales.

Books of Readings

Books of readings draw together several selections bearing on a particular topic. Often many of the selections have been published earlier in diverse sources or presented at a conference; thus a book of readings is a convenience for the reader. This characteristic is particularly helpful when one is approaching a specific topic within the wide-ranging MMPI literature. Of special note among the MMPI books of readings are the following.

Welsh and Dahlstrom (1956) edited *Basic Readings on the MMPI in Psychology and Medicine*. Many of the early studies that provided the research basis for the development of the MMPI are presented here. This text was updated and expanded in terms of content with the Dahlstrom and Dahlstrom (1979) publication *Basic Readings on the MMPI: A New Selection on Personality Measurement*.

Butcher's (1979) *New Developments in the Use of the MMPI* and Newmark's (1979) *MMPI: Clinical and Research Trends* provide presentations by an array of noted authorities on a number of significant areas of MMPI research. Aging, cross-cultural issues, short forms, special scales, and the application of the MMPI to medical and criminal justice settings are among the topics discussed.

Interpretive Manuals and "Cookbooks"

The MMPI was developed as a tool to aid clinicians in personality assessment. Naturally, a substantial part of the MMPI literature is devoted to this end. Among these aids to interpretation are the various editions of the test manual itself. The manuals by S. R. Hathaway and J. C. McKinley (1942, 1951, 1967) supply basic psychometric data and introduce new forms of the MMPI.

Meehl (1956) called for a "cookbook" suitable for quick and simple MMPI interpretation. The call was answered, and the following decades saw the publication of numerous "cookbooks"—codebooks or interpretive manuals. Marks and Seeman (1963) are usually given credit for devising the first: *The Actuarial Description of Abnormal Personality: An Atlas for Use with the MMPI*. It both provided a model for later interpretive manuals and included considerable empirically based data. Numerous other clinical interpretation manuals and actuarial personality "cookbooks" have since been written to aid the user of the MMPI. These texts vary in several aspects. Some have provided new actuarial data, whereas others have relied more on previous studies or clinical judgment. Different populations of readers (counselors, physicians, etc.) or different client populations (adolescents, college students, etc.) have been addressed.

A popular manual, *A Handbook for Clinical and Actuarial MMPI Interpretation*, was developed by Gilberstadt and Duker (1965). These authors presented a handbook describing 19 MMPI profile types common to the Veterans Administration hospital population they studied; descriptions of individuals fitting into particular types were provided.

Carson, in a 1969 book chapter, presented an excellent and often-quoted interpretive guide for the beginning MMPI user.

Pearson and Swenson (1967) carried the "cookbook" concept one step further with the introduction of an automated MMPI interpretation for use at the Mayo Clinic: *A User's Guide to the Mayo Clinic Automated MMPI Program*. This very basic computer program is presented in a three-page table in their book, but it ushered in an approach to MMPI interpretation that has grown into a sizable industry. Other automated approaches have been described by Manning (1971) in *Programmed Interpretation of the MMPI*, and by Lachar (1974) in *The MMPI: Clinical Assessment and Automated Interpretation*.

At the date of its publication, Lachar's book presented a sophisticated and detailed computer program for MMPI interpretation. Procedures were explained and data were provided so that a clinician could move manually step by step through the program and develop the same interpretation provided with the aid of a computer. Basically, the program is a series of statements found by research to be generally descriptive of individuals who have profiles bearing certain characteristics—scale evaluations, configurations, and others. Limited to the MMPI validity and clinical scales, this program lacks some of the data available in newer computer interpretations, which also employ special scales and other "extraprofile" information. Recently, many concerns regarding uses and abuses of computerized psychological test interpretation have been noted (Matarazzo, 1986).

In the last few years, the publication of MMPI interpretive manuals dwindled, quite likely in anticipation of the publication changes expected. (see section "Future Developments"). But for the reader of this chapter, a few recent texts can be suggested as popular and useful.

The manual by Duckworth and Anderson (1986), *MMPI Interpretation Manual for Counselors and Clinicians*, was designed primarily for practitioners working in mental health centers and university counseling centers. Like other recent sources, this book includes information about the validity scales and clinical scales, and provides suggestions for interpretation based on both single scale elevations and the popular procedure using high-point combinations. In addition, this text includes an extensive treatment of several research scales and discusses the effects of race and culture on MMPI profiles.

The MMPI: An Interpretive Manual, by Roger Greene (1980), is a popular text that provides direction in interpreting the MMPI profile of both adults and adolescents. Short forms, critical items, special scales, and profiles produced by minorities are also discussed.

Vincent et al. (1984) published the *MMPI-168 Codebook*. In this recent text, a well-researched short form of the MMPI is presented with codetypes empirically derived specifically for this instrument. Although adolescent norms are provided, the applicability of the MMPI-168 to adolescents is not yet fully recognized.

In regard to adolescents, the study by Marks et al. (1974), *The Actuarial Use of the MMPI with Adolescents and Adults,* developed the norms and clinical correlate data commonly used with youths at the present time. At least until the completion of normative studies now in progress, the Marks et al. data will continue to be of prime importance. An updated version of the clinical correlates, integrated with the more voluminous information on adult codetypes, is available in Chapter 4 of the Archer (1987) text.

Reference Books

The atlas was once a popular type of MMPI reference book, but its use seems to have diminished. Usually, atlases include case histories of individuals along with their MMPI results. The atlas is typically organized in terms of "profile codes," series of numbers determined by the height of individual profile scales. The purpose of the atlas is to provide a method of comparing an individual with other individuals who have similar MMPI profiles. An example is Hathaway and Meehl's (1951) *An Atlas for the Clinical Use of the MMPI*. As part of their series of studies on youth and delinquency, Hathaway and Monachesi (1961) developed an atlas for use with adolescent clients, *An Atlas of Juvenile MMPI Profiles*.

Lanyon (1968), in *A Handbook of MMPI Group Profiles*, provided another approach to profile comparison that is useful in research and clinical interpretation. Approximately 300 mean profiles are presented for various groups of individuals sharing diagnostic, demographic, or behavioral characteristics. Examples include prisoners, schizophrenics, and delinquents.

A third type of reference book is Swenson, Pearson, and Osborne's (1973) *An MMPI Source Book: Basic Item, Scale and Pattern Data on 50,000 Medical Patients*. This volume presents the MMPI responses of 50,000 medical patients. Originating with a project at the Mayo Clinic, this source book is intended for the use of researchers, students of personality theory, and others concerned with the construction of personality inventories.

MMPI Patterns of American Minorities, by Dahlstrom, Lachar, and Dahlstrom (1986), is a recent reference book providing an evaluation of the research relating to the use of the MMPI with minority groups. New empirical data are also presented.

With a young population, Hathaway and Monachesi (1963) published a detailed work on the characteristics of adolescent MMPI profiles. Although concerned mainly with the prediction of delinquency, this study, *Adolescent Personality and Behavior*, was based on a large sample of adolescents and still represents a major resource for researchers.

Journals and Related Publications

Being immense and diverse, the MMPI literature is naturally found a in wide array of publication. Although the scope, emphasis and even existence of journals vary with time, it is possible to list several periodicals that have published in the past or currently publish substantial amounts of MMPI literature. They include the following:

Dissertation Abstracts International
Educational and Psychological Measurement
Journal of Clinical Psychology
Journal of Counseling Psychology
Journal of Consulting and Clinical Psychology
Journal of Personality Assessment.

Two helpful reviews of the MMPI are found among the chapters of Benjamin B. Wolman's (1978) *Clinical Diagnosis of Mental Disorders: A Handbook*. Chapter 10, "The Minnesota Multiphasic Personality Inventory (MMPI)," by John R. Graham, is a relatively brief introduction to the MMPI written for both students and professionals. In Chapter 15 of the Wolman book, James N. Butcher and Patricia L. Owen discuss "Objective Personality Inventories: Recent Research and Some Contemporary Issues." This long, informative chapter focuses on some of the broader issues involved in using personality inventories, particularly the MMPI. Psychometric considerations rather than clinical applications are stressed.

Bibliographies of the MMPI appear in several of the sources cited above. Perhaps the most extensive of these is the 200-page bibliography in Volume 2 of *An MMPI Handbook* (Dahlstrom et al., 1975). The project by Taulbee, Wright, and Stenmark (1977) provides another comprehensive bibliography. These authors attempted to trace the development of the MMPI from its beginnings up to 1965 by means of an annotated bibliography.

The MMPI literature is obviously extensive and varied. No brief review can do more than sample a portion of the material currently available in print. Another significant body of MMPI literature is much more difficult to tap. It is composed of the unpublished notes, tables, profiles, and related documents that many "MMPI-ers" have collected for their personal use. Only a few of these items eventually reach publication, but they seem to have considerable clinical value.

FUTURE DEVELOPMENTS

The 1980s have witnessed the popularization of a number of innovations in MMPI use with both adults and adolescents. Addition of four scales to the MMPI profile; expanded use of empirically derived critical-item lists; continued research with content scales and short forms; and the increased sophistication of computer scoring and interpretation are among these developments in the adult realm. Clarification of the appropriate application of these developments and more traditional procedures to adolescent subjects has been proceeding in the 1980s and will probably continue to be characteristic of the 1990s.

The next few years appear to promise several developments significant to the assessment of adolescent personality. Four of these likely developments are the following:

1. The continued popularity of personality tests or inventories directed at the adolescent age group. Interest in the adolescent clinical population appears to be growing substantially as noted earlier in this chapter. Several personality tests for adolescents have been developed recently. Further evidence of this growing interest in the assessment of adolescent personality can be found in the other chapters of this section.

2. New MMPI norms and codetype correlates for adolescents. Investigators at the Mayo Clinic have been collecting extensive normative data on the MMPI with normal populations of both adults and adolescents for several years. Preliminary results have been presented by Colligan and Offord (1986). Several other such research efforts (Archer, Gordon, & Kirchner, 1986; Williams, Butcher, & Graham, 1986) are beginning to produce data that will probably result in the eventual replacement of the Marks et al. (1974) adolescent norms and codetype correlates.

3. The publication of an adolescent form of the MMPI. The University of Minnesota renorming project for the MMPI is a far-reaching, major endeavor that was originally envisioned to include the development of two new forms of the MMPI—one for adults, another for adolescents (Kaemmer, 1986). The publication of MMPI-2 was accomplished in 1989 with a new representative standardization sample, some new items, and a few new scales. However, MMPI-2 is not intended for use with subjects below the age of 18. Development of the adolescent form of the MMPI appears to be well advanced and publication is expected in the early 1990s. When carried to fruition, this second phase of the Minnesota project should afford clinicians and researchers an instrument that has many of the advantages of continuity with the MMPI, yet provides some scales and items with special relevance to the younger population.

4. Continued research to clarify the appropriateness of MMPI results for adolescents. A half century of MMPI research and development will soon be completed. This research has doubtless cost millions of dollars, millions of hours, and an inestimable amount of creativity. This legacy cannot easily be dismissed or thrown aside simply because its relevance to the adolescent population has not been established. Rather, research will continue in order to determine the applicability of adult-derived procedures, or, where possible, to adjust them so that they may effectively be used with adolescents.

REFERENCES

Archer, R. P. (1987). *Using the MMPI with adolescents*. Hillsdale, NJ: Erlbaum.

Archer, R. P., Gordon, R. A., & Kircher, F. H. (1986). [MMPI response set characteristics of adolescents]. Unpublished raw data.

Bresolin, M. J. (1984). *A comparative Study of computer administration of the MMPI in an inpatient psychiatric setting*. Unpublished doctoral dissertation, Loyola University of Chicago.

Butcher, J. N. (Ed.). (1979). *New developments in the use of the MMPI*. Minneapolis: Unviversity of Minnesota Press.

Butcher, J. N. (1985). Why use the MMPI? In J. N. Butcher & J. R. Graham (Eds.), *Clinical applications of the MMPI* (pp. 1–2). Minneapolis: University of Minnesota, Department of Conferences.

Butcher, J. N., & Owen, P. L. (1978). Objective personality inventories: Recent research and some contemporary issues. In B. B. Wolman, (Ed.), *Clinical diagnosis of mental disorders: A handbook* (pp. 475–545). New York: Plenum.

Carson, R. C. (1969). Interpretative manual to the MMPI. In J. N. Butcher (Ed.), *MMPI: Research developments and clinical applications* (pp. 279–296). New York: McGraw-Hill.

Colligan, R. C., & Offord, K. P. (1986). *Today's adolescent and the MMPI: Patterns of MMPI responses from normal teenagers of the 80's*. Paper presented at the 32nd Annual Meeting of the Southeastern Psychological Association, Orlando, FL.

Dahlstrom, W. G., & Dahlstrom, L. E. (Eds.). (1979). *Basic readings on the MMPI: A new selection on personality measurement*. Minneapolis: University of Minnesota Press.

Dahlstrom, W. G., Lachar, D., & Dahlstrom, L. E. (1986). *MMPI patterns of American minorities*. Minneapolis: University of Minnesota Press.

Dahlstrom, W. G., Welsh, G. S., & Dahlstrom, L. E. (1972). *An MMPI handbook: Vol. 1. Clinical interpretation*. Minneapolis: University of Minnesota Press.

Dahlstrom, W. G., Welsh, G. S., & Dahlstrom, L. E.

(1975). *An MMPI handbook: Vol. 2. Research applications*. Minneapolis: University of Minnesota Press.

Duckworth, J. C., & Anderson, W. (1986). *MMPI interpretation manual for counselors and clinicians*. Muncie, IN: Accelerated Development.

Gilberstadt, H., & Duker, J. (1965). *A handbook for clinical and actuarial MMPI interpretation*. Philadelphia: W. B. Saunders.

Graham, J. R. (1977). *The MMPI: A practical guide*. New York: Oxford University Press.

Graham, J. R. (1978). The Minnesota Multiphasic Personality Inventory (MMPI). In B. B. Wolman (Ed.), *Clinical diagnosis of mental disorders: A handbook* (pp. 311–331). New York: Plenum.

Graham, J. R. (1985). Interpreting the MacAndrew Alcoholism Scale. In J. N. Butcher & J. R. Graham (Eds.), *Clinical applications of the MMPI* (pp. 27–28). Minneapolis: University of Minnesota, Department of Conferences.

Graham, J. R. (1987). *The MMPI: A practical guide* (2nd ed.). New York: Oxford University Press.

Greene, R. L. (1980). *The MMPI: An interpretive manual*. New York: Grune & Stratton.

Hathaway, S. R., & McKinley, J. C. (1942). *The Minnesota Personality Schedule*. Minneapolis: University of Minnesota Press.

Hathaway, S. R., & McKinley, J. C. (1951). *Minnesota Multiphasic Personality Inventory: Manual* (rev. ed.). New York: Psychological Corporation.

Hathaway, S. R., & McKinley, J. C. (1967). *MMPI manual* (rev. ed.). New York: Psychological Corporation.

Hathaway, S. R., & Meehl, P. (1951). *An atlas for the clinical use of the MMPI*. Minneapolis: University of Minnesota Press.

Hathaway, S. R., & Monachesi, E. D. (1961). *An atlas of juvenile MMPI profiles*. Minneapolis: University of Minnesota Press.

Hathaway, S. R., & Monachesi, E. D. (1963). *Adolescent personality and behavior*. Minneapolis: University of Minnesota Press.

Kaemmer, B. (1986). MMPI restandardization update. *Critical Items, 2,* 8.

Lachar, D. (1974). *The MMPI: Clinical assessment and automated interpretation*. Los Angeles: Western Psychological Services.

Lanyon, R. I. (1968). *A handbook of MMPI group profiles*. Minneapolis: University of Minnesota Press.

Manning, H. M. (1971). Programmed interpretation of the MMPI. *Journal of Personality Assessment, 35,* 162–176.

Marks, P. A., & Seeman, W. (1963). *The actuarial description of abnormal personality: An atlas for use with the MMPI*. Baltimore: Williams & Wilkins.

Marks, P. A., Seeman, W., & Haller, D. (1974). *The actuarial use of the MMPI with adolescents and adults*. Baltimore: Williams & Wilkins.

Matarazzo, J. D. (1986). Computerized clinical psychological test interpretations. *American Psychologists, 41,* 14–24.

Meehl, P. E. (1956). Wanted—a good cookbook. *American Psychologist, 11,* 263–272.

Newmark, C. S. (Ed.). (1979). *MMPI: Clinical and research trends*. New York: Praeger.

Pearson, J. S., & Swenson, W. (1967). *A user's guide to the Mayo Clinic automated MMPI program*. New York: Psychological Corporation.

Swenson, W. M., Pearson, J., & Osborne, D. (1973). *An MMPI source book: Basic item, scale and pattern data on 50,000 medical patients*. Minneapolis: University of Minnesota Press.

Taulbee, E. S., Wright, H. W., & Stenmark, E. E. (1977). *The Minnesota Multiphasic Personality Inventory (MMPI): A comprehensive annotated bibliography (1940–1965)*. Troy, NY: Whitson.

Vincent, K. R., Castillo, I. M., Hauser, R. L., Zapata, J. A., Stuart, H. J., Cohn, C. K., & O'Shanick, G. J. (1984). *MMPI-168 codebook*. Norwood, NJ: Ablex.

Welsh, G. S., & Dahlstrom, W. (Eds.). (1956). *Basic readings on the MMPI in psychology and medicine*. Minneapolis: University of Minnesota Press.

Williams, C. L. (1985). Use of the MMPI with adolescents. In J. N. Butcher & J. R. Graham (Eds.), *Clinical applications of the MMPI* (pp. 37–39). Minneapolis: University of Minnesota, Department of Conferences.

Williams, C. L., Butcher, J. N., & Graham, J. R. (1986, March). *Appropriate MMPI norms for adolescents: An old problem revisited*. Paper presented at the 21st Annual Symposium on Recent Developments in the Use of the MMPI, Clearwater, FL.

Wolman, B. (Ed.). (1978). *Clinical diagnosis of mental disorders: A handbook*. New York: Plenum.

15

Principles of Behavioral Assessment

EDWARD S. SHAPIRO
Lehigh University

CHRISTOPHER H. SKINNER
The University of Alabama

I n the past 15 years, there has been a virtual explosion of research and writing in the area of behavioral assessment. Evidence for this upsurge of interest can be found in the numbers of published texts devoted solely to the topic of behavioral assessment in general (e.g., Cone & Hawkins, 1977; Haynes, 1978). In addition, several texts have appeared in their second or third editions (e.g., Ciminero, Calhoun, & Adams, 1981; Hersen & Bellack, 1987). Others have published texts relating behavioral assessment to specific populations or age groups (e.g., Barlow, 1981; Mash & Terdal, 1988; Powers & Handleman, 1984), and recently applications specific to behavioral assessment in school settings have appeared (e.g., Shapiro, 1987; Shapiro & Kratochwill, 1988). Besides the publication of texts, two journals have also emerged that are devoted primarily to empirical articles on behavioral assessment (*Behavioral Assessment* and the *Journal of Psychopathology and Behavioral Assessment*). Clearly, the principles and methods of behavioral assessment are becoming increasingly integrated into the mainstream of psychological evaluation.

DEFINING BEHAVIORAL ASSESSMENT: ISSUES AND QUESTIONS

To understand clearly how behavioral assessment differs from traditional assessment, one needs to examine the assumptions that underlie the two assessment methodologies. Hartmann, Roper, and Bradford (1979) have provided perhaps one of the most comprehensive comparisons of the two approaches to assessment (see Table 15.1). In their analysis, they examined differences in conceptualizations of personality, identifying causes of behavior, the role of observable behavior in the assessment process, the role of history, consistency of behavior across time, how data are used, and other characteristics that result in critical differences between the two approaches.

Among the many differences noted in Table 15.1 by Hartmann et al. (1979) are key differences in how observable behavior is viewed by each approach. Within traditional assessment, observable behavior is considered important only in that it provides a "window" to intrapsychic conflicts, which are the real source of the behavior seen. For example, a man who repeatedly gets fired from jobs because he is noncompliant to authority may be showing a distinct underlying conflict in dealing with authority figures, stemming from poorly developed relationships with his father. Likewise, a child who is frequently enuretic may be displaying underlying aggressive feelings toward parents and uses the bedwetting as a symbolic act of rebellion. Obviously, these types of interpretations require significant inferences to levels far beyond the observable behavior.

In contrast, observable behavior within

TABLE 15.1. Differences between Behavioral and Traditional Approaches to Assessment

	Behavioral	Traditional
I. Assumptions		
1. Conception of personality	Personality constructs mainly employed to summarize specific behavior patterns, if at all	Personality as a reflection of enduring underlying states or traits
2. Causes of behavior	Maintaining conditions sought in current environment	Intrapsychic or within the individual
II. Implications		
1. Role of behavior	Important as a sample of person's repertoire in specific situation	Behavior assumes importance only insofar as it indexes underlying causes
2. Role of history	Relatively unimportant, except, for example, to provide a retrospective baseline	Crucial in that present conditions seen as a product of the past
3. Consistency of behavior	Behavior thought to be specific to the situation	Behavior expected to be consistent across time and settings
III. Use of data	To describe target behaviors and maintaining conditions	To describe personality functioning and etiology
	To select the appropriate treatment	To diagnose or classify
	To evaluate and revise treatment	To make prognosis; to predict
IV. Other characteristics		
1. Level of inferences	Low	Medium to high
2. Comparisons	More emphasis on intra-individual or idiographic	More emphasis on inter-individual or nomothetic
3. Methods of assessment	More emphasis on direct methods (e.g., observations of behavior in natural environment)	More emphasis on indirect methods (e.g., interviews and self-report)
4. Timing of assessment	More ongoing; prior, during, and after treatment	Pre- and perhaps posttreatment or strictly to diagnose
5. Scope of assessment	Specific measures and of more variables (e.g., of target behaviors in various situations of side effects, context, strengths as well as deficiencies)	More global measures (e.g., of cure, or improvement) but only of the individual

Note. From "Some Relationships between Behavioral and Traditional Assessment" by D. P. Hartmann, B. L. Roper, and D. C. Bradford, 1979, *Journal of Behavioral Assessment, 1,* 3–21. Copyright 1979 by Plenum Press. Reprinted by permission of the authors and the publisher.

behavioral assessment is treated as the problem per se. The behavior is viewed as a sample of a person's behavioral repertoire, but is limited in interpretation to behavior within that situation. The causes of the observable behavior are found in the environmental conditions that maintain the responses, and inferences to underlying intrapsychic determinants are not made. Behavior is simply viewed within the stimuli and consequences that surround the observable response.

Another major difference between the interpretations of behavioral events from traditional and behavioral assessment perspectives revolves around how consistent behavior is across settings. An important assumption in traditional assessment is that behavior observed in one setting is felt to represent stable traits or personality characteristics that reflect one's personality. Because behavior is considered to be cross-situational, observations made in one setting under one set of conditions can easily be generalized to what behavior would be like at other times in other settings. Thus, a child who is noncompliant during an individual testing session with the examiner is inferred to be a "noncompliant child" who is likely to act in similar ways during classroom instruction. Given that behavior is *assumed* to be cross-situational, this prediction is typically made without any direct observation of the person in that setting.

Behavioral assessment assumes behavior to be situationally specific rather than cross-situational. As such, observations made in one setting under one set of conditions are not considered to be generalizable to other settings or time periods without direct verification of responses in those situations. Before any predictions of behavior are made across these situations, individuals must be assessed.

One of the major implications of assuming cross-situationality versus situational specificity of behavior relates to how one interprets many of the traditional psychometric properties of assessment, such as test–retest reliability or concurrent validity. When an assessment instrument is found to have limited test–retest reliability, its continued use is called into question by traditional assessors. This is logical *if* one assumes that behavior *should* be consistent from time to time within the same situation. Calculations of reliability are based upon obtaining the lowest amount of within-subject variance possible. High amounts of within-subject variance found in a measure from a traditional perspective result in a decision that the instrument being employed is faulty and needs to be improved. Thus, poor test–retest reliability is equivalent to problems with the measurement device.

In contrast, if one *does not* assume that behavior should be consistent across time, high amounts of within-subject variance should not necessarily suggest that there is a problem with the measure. If the measurement device is indicating *accurately* that the

subject's behavior is showing significant variation across time, then the key issue is explaining why the variance is present. From a behavioral assessment perspective, the key property for deciding the value of an instrument is not its ability to display similar results across time or setting, but its ability to reflect the behavior accurately each time it is observed.

Similar arguments can be made when examining validity of instruments from traditional and behavioral perspectives. For example, concurrent validation of traditional assessment measures is obtained by correlating measures presumed to be assessing similar traits. When these correlations are low, the measures are considered not to be assessing similar constructs, and therefore the concurrent validation of the measurement devices is reduced. From a behavioral assessment perspective, such low correlations are not surprising, nor should they be anticipated. If behavior is not assumed to be consistent across time and setting, then low correlations on measures presumably assessing the same construct simply suggest a need to look at potential environmental differences that may be resulting in the low cross-measure correlations. Again, the key issue is that cross-situationality is assessed and not assumed.

Nelson and Hayes (1986), Nelson (1983), and Johnston and Pennypacker (1980) have all provided extensive elaboration of the need to evaluate behavioral assessment instruments using a different set of measurement procedures than those typically associated with traditional psychometric measurement. Cone (1977) originally suggested using generalizability theory, as described by Cronbach, Gleser, Nanda, and Rajaratnam (1972), as a conceptual framework for developing a measurement system to evaluate behavioral assessment. Subsequently, Cone (1981) has suggested recasting generalizability theory for behavioral assessment in terms of accuracy of measurement. Essentially, Cone (1981) suggests that one look at the accuracy of behavioral observations in terms of (1) the behavior's occurence, (2) its repeated occurrence, (3) its occurrence in different settings, (4) its measurability by different assessment methods, and (5) its relation to other responses. The degree to which a behavioral assessment device provides information may be determined by the extent to which it has been shown to reflect these five characteristics accurately.

Although some investigators have criticized Cone's (1981) approach to measurement in behavioral assessment (Nelson, Hay, & Hay, 1977), others still maintain that many traditional psychometric concepts should be applied equally to behavioral assessment (Hartmann et al., 1979). In particular, Hartmann et al. (1979) note that the rejection of the assumption of cross-situationality of behavior does not invalidate the use of test–retest reliability, since this type of reliability measure is actually based on temporal stability of behavior rather than cross-situationality. Given that baselines and posttreatment data need to be stable for adequate interpretation, this can be seen as a call for a type of test–retest reliability. Strosahl and Linehan (1986) make a similar argument. Likewise, Hartmann et al. (1979) note that the concepts of validity have the same problems for traditional and behavioral assessment. When behavior cannot be measured through direct observation alone, such as collecting data through parent report, it is important that this source of data as well as others converge on similar findings.

Although the issues of the appropriate measures for evaluating behavioral assessment are far from settled, there does seem to be consistent agreement among investigators regarding the range of methods used in conducting a behavioral assessment. Cone (1978) has provided a conceptual framework for behavioral assessment called the Behavioral Assessment Grid (BAG). His model describes behavioral assessment across three dimensions: contents, methods, and universes of generalization.

Behavioral contents are divided along three modalities of assessment: motor, physiological, and cognitive. Motor contents are those behaviors that are observable and involve various aspects of the striate musculature. These behaviors are considered to be observable without instrumentation and include such activities as walking, talking, hitting, running, raising hands, writing, and so forth. Physiological contents are activities of muscles and glands that are not usually observable without instrumentation. These

include pulse, respiration, galvanic skin response, and muscle tension. Cognitive contents are more difficult to define, but typically refer to private events that affect behavior. Thoughts and feelings obviously cannot be observed directly, and some investigators have viewed the verbal behavior that is the referent of cognitive activity as equivalent to cognitive contents. Clearly, these are *not* equivalent; it is quite possible to have thoughts or feelings that are not expressed (or not expressed the same way) through oral or written modalities.

It has been commonly accepted in behavioral assessment that a complete evaluation should assess behavior across all three content areas (Nelson & Hayes, 1979). However, significant questions have been raised about the potential problems of response covariation when assessing across modalities (Cone, 1979). Still, when one is deciding on the appropriate content areas across which assessment is to be conducted, the triple-response-modality conceptualization of behavior is often used as a conceptual framework for structuring the evaluation (Nelson, 1983).

Cone (1978), in the BAG, has placed the methods of behavioral assessment on a continuum from direct to indirect assessment. The dimension of directness is based on the degree to which the measurement procedure employed assesses the behavior in the setting and under the conditions in which it naturally occurs. The farther one moves away from this type of assessment, the more indirect the assessment method becomes. Methods categorized by Cone (1978) as direct include naturalistic: free behavior; naturalistic: role play; analogue: free behavior analogue: role play and self-observation. Interviews, self-report, and ratings by others are all seen as indirect methods of assessment.

Shapiro and Browder (in press) have provided a similar model of the continuum of behavioral assessment methods, based on Cone's (1978) and displayed in Figure 15.1. In this model, direct observation of behavior in the naturalistic setting is the most direct form of behavioral assessment. As one moves away from this pole of the continuum, assessment conducted under analogue conditions (such as a role-play test) and self-monitoring are also viewed as direct forms of assessment.

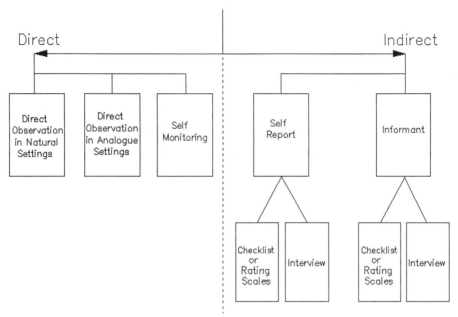

FIGURE 15.1.   A model of the continuum of behavioral assessment methods. From"Behavioral Assessment: Applications for Persons with Mental Retardation" by E. S. Shapiro and D. M. Browder, in press, in J. Matson (Ed.), *The Handbook of Behavior Modification for Persons with Mental Retardation*. New York: Plenum. Copyright by Plenum Press. Reprinted by permission.

These methods are considered direct because they still involve the direct evaluation of the behavior under consideration; however, the behavior may be emitted under conditions that are simulated rather than in the naturalistic setting, or may be influenced by the potential reactivity of self-observation. Nevertheless, all of these methods involve the collection of data as the behavior actually occurs.

In contrast to direct methods, self-report and informant report measures obtain data at a time when the individual is not actually engaging in the specific response. Typically, these methods involve either oral reports (interviews) or written reports (checklists/rating scales). Because the person himself or herself or a significant other is reporting about behavior that is not occurring at the time it is reported, the assessment method is therefore considered indirect.

The third and final dimension of Cone's (1978) BAG involves the universes of generalization. When first conceptualized by Cone (1978), these universes were the degree to which data were consistent across

scorers, items, time, settings, methods, and dimensions. As noted previously, Cone (1981) has subsequently reconceptualized these universes of generalizations as dimensions of accuracy.

The usual context for contrasts between traditional and behavioral assessment, as well as for the development of a conceptual model of behavioral assessment, has been the assessment of social–emotional problems. Recently, however, there have been increasing interest in and development of behavioral assessment methods for children's academic problems (Lentz, 1988; Shapiro, 1987, 1989; Shapiro & Lentz, 1985, 1986). Although a complete discussion of these methods is beyond the scope of this chapter, contrasts between traditional and behavioral methods of assessment can be made for the assessment of academic problems, as well as that of social–emotional problems.

Figure 15.2 displays the types of assessments that may be used to evaluate an academic problem. Individuals presenting with these problems can be assessed through both traditional and behavioral approaches. Tradi-

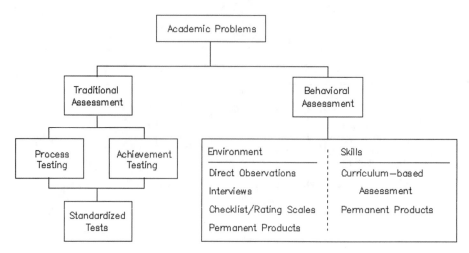

FIGURE 15.2. Types of traditional and behavioral assessments that may be used to evaluate an academic problem.

tional approaches to assessment may involve the evaluation of either psychological processes or general levels of achievement. In both of these cases, standardized tests are typically employed. The use of these measures infers certain assumptions about academic problems. As with traditional personality assessment, the causes of academic problems are considered to be within the child rather than resulting from or in interaction with the instructional environment. Assessments of psychological processes in particular employ a significant degree of inference from observed behavior to unobservable constructs. For example, a student who does poorly on certain subtests of the Wechsler Intelligence Scale for Children—Revised is inferred to have specific deficiencies in information processing. Less inference is employed with tests of general achievement; however, these measures may fail to assess adequately what a child actually has been taught, because of poor overlap between the test content and the curriculum (Jenkins & Pany, 1978; Shapiro & Derr, 1987).

In contrast, behavioral assessment of academic skills incorporates evaluation of both the instructional environment and the individual skills. Thus, academic problems are assumed to lie in an interaction between the instructional conditions and the individual's abilities. Assessment methods linked to the behavioral assessment of academic skills in-

clude direct measures such as observation and administration of skill probes taken directly from the curriculum, as well as indirect methods such as self-report and informant reports.

Overall, behavioral assessment is a methodology based on assumptions that the source of behavioral and academic problems lies in the environmental conditions present when the behavior occurs. In addition, behavioral assessment does not assume persons to have a set of stable, enduring characteristics. Levels of inference are considerably lower than with traditional assessment methodologies. In the next section, the various methods of behavioral assessment are described in more detail.

METHODS OF BEHAVIORAL ASSESSMENT

Direct Methods: Direct Observation

Direct observation requires an independent observer to record overt behaviors of others. Typically, data are obtained on identified behaviors that are likely to be targets for behavior change; however, because behaviors are viewed as situationally specific, it is often useful to record antecedent conditions and consequent events surrounding the behavioral events. Both descriptive and quantitative methods can be used when direct observation is employed.

Descriptive Methods of Recording Data

Descriptive recording involves an independent observer providing a narrative description of observable events. These narrative reports can be used in the initial stage of assessment to identify and operationalize target behaviors, antecedents, and consequences. Descriptive data can also reveal information about the rates and variability of specific behaviors, which can be used when developing and selecting quantitative observational procedures. Daily logs, descriptive time sampling, and antecedent–behavior–consequent (A-B-C) analysis are common forms of descriptive data collection.

Daily logs are often used in narrative recording. For example, a teacher will write a general description of a student's daily behavior. An adult may be asked to describe significant anxiety-provoking incidents that occur between weekly therapy sessions. These reports are useful, in that they can provide general information about the topography, rate, and variability of behaviors.

Another form of narrative recording is an A-B-C analysis. During an A-B-C analysis, the observer provides a written sequential description of the subject's overt behaviors, as well as antecedent conditions and consequent events that immediately surround the subject's behaviors. This type of narrative recording provides more information than a daily log, in that environmental conditions that may be controlling the subjects' behavior are also described. A more quantitative method for conducting an A-B-C analysis by Mace, Yankanich, and West (1988) is described later in this chapter.

Narrative time sampling requires the observer to describe overt behaviors at predetermined intervals (e.g., every minute). This sampling method allows the observer time to record events and may provide a rough estimate of rates of particular behaviors. Although this method of description provides a general indication of behavioral events, some relevant antecedents, behaviors, and consequences that may occur immediately surrounding the momentary observation are not recorded.

Descriptive reports are useful in the initial stage of assessment; however, they are limited in that they are subjective, unquantitative, and difficult to verify empirically. Behaviors recorded are dependent on the observer's vocabulary and subjective judgment. Relevant observations may not be recorded because the observer considers them insignificant or is busy recording other observations. A particular problem with descriptive reports is the failure to provide accurate, operational definitions of behavior to observers. As a result, interobserver agreement is very unlikely, and empirical verification of the observations is nearly impossible.

Quantitative Methods of Recording Behavior

In order for an observer to record behaviors in a quantitative manner, the behaviors must be operationally defined. These definitions must be clear and concise enough that other trained observers can agree on the duration or occurrence rates of these events across extended periods of time. The definitions must have face validity, in that they should include behaviors relevant to the purpose of the assessment. Events to be operationally defined should include the target student's behaviors and surrounding antecedent and consequent events. Data from descriptive reports, interviews, checklists, and rating scales may be used to identify and operationalize target behaviors and relevant environmental events. Event, duration, rate, and time-sampling recording techniques allow one to collect quantifiable direct observation data. Several methods of recording these data have been developed.

Event Recording. Event recording requires the observer to record the number of times a behavior is seen during a specific observational interval. The data can be recorded with any device capable of tallying occurrences. Golf counters, paper and pencil, and counters used by grocery store employees are all appropriate instruments for recording occurrences. The length of the interval is kept consistent across observation periods, allowing one to compare frequency counts across observation periods. Observation periods can range from minutes to days, depending on the behavior being measured and the opportunities for observers to collect data.

Event recording works best with behaviors that have a discrete beginning and end. Raising one's hand, calling out, and completing a mathematics problem are examples of such behaviors. Continuous behaviors with no distinct beginning and end, behaviors that persist for long durations, and high-rate behaviors are difficult to record using frequency counts. Examples of such behaviors include pencil tapping, play, and on-task behavior.

Behaviors that have no clear beginning and end but occur infrequently in response bursts can also be measured using event recording. Tantrums or aggression, for example, can be defined as a response class that includes a large set of related behaviors. Rather than measuring each separate aggressive behavior, an observer can count an outburst as one instance of aggression. In recording response bursts, it is important to define when that specific outburst has ended. For example, an aggressive outburst could be defined as lasting until 1 minute of continuous aggression-free behavior is observed. Any aggressive behavior following that minute would constitute another aggressive event.

Data collected through event recording are usually expressed in terms of rate—the total number of occurrences divided by the amount of observation time (e.g., 0.5 hand raises per minute). Rate measures are preferable to simple frequency counts because they allow one to compare response patterns when observational intervals are not equal. This is important, because observer availability and the possible inability to observe across settings make it difficult to record direct observation data continuously for equal intervals.

Duration Recording. Duration recording requires the observer to record the length of time from the beginning to the end of a response. The starting and finishing points of a response must be precisely defined in order for accurate duration data to be obtained. The goal of assessing many school-related behaviors may be to increase or decrease the duration of particular behaviors. Playing, studying, and time taken to complete a mathematics worksheet are examples of behaviors where duration measures may be employed.

Certain behaviors are critical for duration recording. For example, in reducing child tantrums, it is important to demonstrate that reductions in frequencies of tantrums are simultaneously related to reductions in tantrum durations. It is possible that a child may have tantrums less often but for longer periods of time. Making decisions on the basis of the event-recorded data alone may be misleading. Duration recording does present some practical limitations, however, in that the data require the use of a timing device. This can often become intrusive and result in poor compliance, because parents or teachers find the data collection process disruptive.

Time-Sampling Techniques. When behaviors have no discrete beginnings and ends, accurate recording of the total number of occurrences or the duration of such behaviors is difficult. It is also difficult for observers to continuously record high-frequency behaviors, especially when many separate behaviors are being recorded. Observer availability and the inability to observe subjects in all settings also make continuous observation difficult. For these practical reasons, time-sampling techniques are often used to record observational data.

Time sampling avoids the need for continuous observation by breaking observational periods into shorter timed intervals. The observer merely records the presence or absence of specified behaviors within each timed interval. This also circumvents the need to identify the beginning and end of responses, and allows one to collect accurate and reliable estimates on high-rate behaviors. The percentage of intervals where behavior is observed can then be calculated and reported.

The length of the intervals can vary, depending on the rate of behaviors being recorded and the availability of the observer to perform continuous observations. A teacher may record the absence or presence of a low-rate behavior every 3 hours in the classroom.

An independent observer may be able to continuously record a variety of high-rate behaviors within 15-second intervals. Whole-interval, partial-interval, and momentary recording are three different types of time-sampling techniques. All can be used over any interval length; the primary difference among them is in how behaviors are defined.

In using whole-interval recording, a behavior must be evident for the entire interval to be recorded as "present." If the target behavior is *not* evident at any time during the interval, the interval is scored as "behavior absent." This technique is most appropriate when short intervals are being used to assess behaviors that should be continuous.

Partial-interval recording requires the observer to score an interval as "present" if the target behavior is observed at any time within that interval. The only time the interval is scored as "absent" is when the target behavior is *not* observed at any time during the interval. Once a behavior is evident during an interval, the observer is no longer required to monitor that behavior for that interval. Partial-interval recording is practical for low-rate behaviors because large time intervals can be employed.

When an observer records the presence or absence of a behavior only at the moment an interval ends, momentary recording is being used. With this method of time sampling, the observer disregards any occurrence of the target behavior before or after the interval ends. This method can be used with long- or short-duration intervals.

In choosing a time-sampling method, a number of factors and cautions should be borne in mind. Whole-interval time sampling techniques produce a consistent underestimate of actual behavior rates; partial-interval recording results in consistent overestimates of behavior rates; and momentary recording results in both under- and overestimates of behavior rates (Green & Alverson, 1978; Powell, Martindale, Kulp, Martindale, & Bauman, 1977; Powell & Rockinson, 1978). In comparing partial-interval to momentary time sampling, Lentz (1982) found that the amount of overestimation produced by partial-interval time sampling was variable and could not be predicted. Momentary recording produced un-

der- and overestimates of behavior rates, but with much less error. As the duration of intervals was decreased, the amount of error was also decreased. Based on this research, Lentz (1982) recommended momentary recording over partial-interval.

The rate and variability of the behaviors being measured also influence the method of measurement employed. It is very difficult to obtain an adequate sample of low-rate behaviors such as aggression. Rate or event recording should be employed with behaviors that do not occur at high enough rates for a representative sample to be obtained. Behaviors that display high levels of variability are likely to produce high levels of error, regardless of the sampling technique used; therefore, highly variable behaviors should be observed for long periods of time in order to obtain an accurate picture of the actual rate of occurrences of such behaviors. Because behavior is situationally specific, a child's behavior may be quite different in a small reading group than it is in a large group or during free time activities. Regardless of which sampling procedure is used, observations should be made across situations in order to determine which behaviors occur only in particular situations and which occur more generally.

Observation Systems. Individuals may develop their own observational recording systems based on their own needs. When one is developing a recording system, target behaviors must be identified and operationally defined. In order to choose the appropriate recording method, the rate, topography, and variability of target behaviors must be taken into account. A recording measure should also include assessment of antecedents, consequences, and setting variables that may be influencing target behaviors. The recording system can include any single recording method or a combination of the methods listed above. Interview and narrative reports may also be useful when developing a recording system. Once a recording system is developed, observers should practice using the system in order to insure that they can record events accurately and reliably.

Developing a recording system based on the needs of an individual is useful but time-consuming. Several investigators have developed recording systems that provide accurate, reliable, and sensitive data.

O'Leary, Kaufman, Kass, and Drabman (1970) developed a code used in their study on the effects of loud and soft reprimands. The code has been revised by O'Leary, Romanczyk, Kass, Deitz, and Santogrossi (1979). Nine categories of disruptive behavior are scored on a 20-second observe/10-second record system, using partial- or whole-interval scoring. This coding system has been used in other studies (Kehle, Clark, Jenson, & Wampold, 1986; Santogrossi, O'Leary, Romanczyk, & Kaufman, 1973; Turkewitz, O'Leary, & Ironsmith, 1975), which have showed the system to be a reliable method of collecting data on disruptive behavior in the classroom.

Wahler, House, and Stambaugh (1976) published a recording system designed for home, school, and institutional observations. This system has also been shown to be effective in a number of studies (Wahler, 1980; Wahler & Fox, 1980). The Wahler code employs 24 behavior categories. Whole- and partial-interval recording techniques are used in a 10-second observe/5-second record system. Observers record one of six events that precede the behavior, followed by one or more of the categories of behavior.

Saudargas and Creed (1980) have published a code developed for school psychologists. The State–Event Classroom Observation System (SECOS) employs at least 15 different student and 6 teacher behaviors. These categories of behaviors are divided into states and events. States include 8 behaviors that have varying durations and are therefore scored using a momentary time-sampling procedure (typically every 30 seconds). Events include behaviors that are discrete and can be counted. These behaviors are scored using event recording within each interval. The code also provides room for behavioral categories not defined in the system.

Although research on the SECOS is just beginning to appear (Saudargas & Lentz, 1986; Slate & Saudargas, 1986a, 1986b), it appears to have several advantages over the O'Leary and Wahler codes. The SECOS was specifically designed for use in schools and includes behaviors relevant in instructional situations. Because the Wahler code was developed for use across situations, many variables relevant in instructional settings are not measured. Research also indicates that momentary time sampling is superior to whole- and partial-interval time sampling; the SECOS employs momentary time sampling, whereas the O'Leary and Wahler codes employ only whole- and partial-interval recording. In addition, the O'Leary code does not allow one to record antecedents or teacher–student interactions, but the SECOS and Wahler codes do include these observations.

The practical advantage of these direct observation systems is that once they are learned, the systems can be used to assess a variety of classroom behaviors. Investigators are not required to develop, practice, and evaluate their own observation system every time direct observation is employed. However, despite their practicality, these systems may not be useful for all child-related problems. For example, these systems appear to be geared toward behavior problems typically observed with young students; for secondary students, many relevant antecedents, behaviors, and consequences may not be included in the systems. Likewise, the codes are not designed to assess parent–child interactions. As with all direct observation measures, the choice of recording system must be based on individual problems and environments.

Direct Methods: Self-Monitoring Procedures

Self-monitoring is a form of direct assessment that requires an individual to observe himself or herself and record the occurence of his or her own behavior (Haynes, 1978). Because an independent observer is not needed to collect data, self-monitoring has practical and methodological advantages over direct observation. Self-monitoring allows data to be collected when observers are unavailable. This frees other personnel, such as psychologists, teachers, and caregivers, to perform other duties. Furthermore, self-monitoring can be used to collect data on behaviors that are difficult for others to observe directly, because they occur infrequently, at unpredictable times, or in settings where observation is impossible.

Although narrative, rate, frequency, and time-sampling methods of data collection can all conceivably be employed with self-monitoring, certain practical considerations must be made when children are observing and recording data. Young children may not have the written expression skills or memory capacity to produce narrative reports. When using event or duration recording, children may have difficulty understanding operational definitions of behaviors. Recording a large number of behaviors may also be difficult for children, or children may forget to record behaviors. Time-sampling devices may be too complex, and defining short intervals with a tape may be too intrusive in a classroom. Finally, the method of recording must not be so time-consuming as to compete with the child's school-related behaviors. Watson and Tharp (1972) recommend that self-monitoring recording devices be portable, easy to use, of low cost, and obtrusive enough to serve as a reminder to self-monitor. Typically, event recording is used by students to self-monitor a restricted number of behaviors. Paper and pencil, wrist counters, and stickers have all been used to record self-monitoring data. It is essential that any self-monitoring procedure used with children contain easy-to-interpret definitions of behavior and an uncomplicated recording procedure.

Although self-monitoring has practical and methodological advantages over using an independent observer to record data, research shows that self-monitoring can result in behavioral reactivity and inaccurate data recording (Hayes & Cavoir, 1977; Maletzky, 1974; Nelson, Hay, Devany, & Koslow-Green, 1980). The effects of accuracy and reactivity must be taken into consideration whenever self-monitoring is employed as an assessment procedure.

Accuracy of Self-Monitoring

A number of studies on self-monitoring have determined that individuals do not always accurately record occurrences of behavior (Hayes & Cavoir, 1977; Maletzky, 1974; Shapiro & Ackerman, 1983). A number of variables that may affect the accuracy of self-monitoring have been identified. These are summarized by Nelson (1977) and Shapiro

(1984) and include the following: the valence of the target behavior, training in self-monitoring, awareness of accuracy assessment, reinforcement for accurate self-monitoring, the nature of the recording device, the schedule of self-monitoring, and the requirements to perform other behaviors simultaneously with self-recording.

Nelson, Hay, Hay, and Carsten (1977) and Nelson et al. (1980) found that children self-recorded positive verbalizations more accurately than negative verbalizations. However, Litrownik and Freitas (1980) showed that moderately mentally retarded adolescents self-monitored both positive- and negative-valence behaviors accurately. Nelson, Lipinski, and Boykin (1978) and Shapiro, McGonigle, and Ollendick (1980) found that training in self-observation and self-recording improved the accuracy of self-monitoring. Santogrossi (1974) showed that children's accuracy in self-monitoring improved when the children were told that a teacher or peer was also monitoring their behavior. Fixsen, Phillips, and Wolf (1972) and Risely and Hart (1968) showed that reinforcement contingent upon accurate self-monitoring resulted in increased accuracy of self-monitoring.

The large number of variables that may affect the accuracy of self-recording make it difficult to insure accurate data collection during self-monitoring. Nelson (1977) recommends carrying out frequent and random interobserver checks and using mechanical devices to improve accuracy of self-recording. Providing training in self-monitoring and defining positive-valence behaviors to be recorded may also improve the accuracy of self-monitoring. Although these steps may improve the accuracy of self-recording, more research is clearly needed before investigators can be assured that accurate data are being recorded during self-monitoring.

Reactivity of Self-Monitoring

Self-monitoring often results in behavior change without the aid of other intervention strategies. This behavior change is called "reactivity." Reactivity can also occur when subjects are aware that others are observing and recording their behaviors. This reactivity is of particular interest when individuals serve as both observers and subjects. A number of variables have been identified that may affect the magnitude and/or the direction of behavior change.

Kanfer (1977) suggested that the direction of reactive behavior change in self-monitoring is related to the valence of the measured behavior. He predicted that desirable behaviors should increase and negative behaviors should decrease when self-monitored. Broden, Hall, and Mitts (1971) conducted a study with two eighth-grade students that supported Kanfer's hypothesis. Other variables, such as the experimenters' instructions (Glynn & Thomas, 1974), the nature of the target behavior (Humphrey, Karoly, & Kirschenbaum, 1978), goal setting (Sagotsky, Patterson, & Lepper, 1978), timing of self-recording (Nelson et al., 1980), the nature of the self-recording device (Nelson et al., 1978), and motivational statements (McFall, 1970; McFall & Hammen, 1971), have all been shown to affect the degree of reactivity in self-monitoring.

As with other variables affecting reactivity, the relationship between accuracy and reactivity is unclear. Although Peterson, House, and Alford (1975) argue that only minimal accuracy is needed for reactivity to occur, research shows that this hypothesis may not be accurate. Hayes and Cavoir (1977) correlated individual subjects' accuracy with the amount of relative reactivity and found correlations of .01 and − .02; these indicate that in at least some instances there is no relationship between reactivity and accuracy. Shapiro et al. (1980) showed that one subject who consistently omitted self-recording still displayed reactivity.

Self-monitoring is a practical and useful method of data collection. Although reactive behavior change brought about by self-monitoring may be of therapeutic value, this reactivity can distort preintervention and intervention assessment. Although a large number of variables have been identified that may affect reactivity, the presence or absence of reactivity and the magnitude of reactive behavior change cannot be predicted. When using self-monitoring as an assessment procedure, investigators must recognize that preintervention data may not reflect naturally occurring behavior patterns because of this

reactivity, and that intervention data may be confounded by the interaction between reactivity and the intervention procedure.

Direct Methods: Analogue Assessment

Analogue assessment requires observers to record behaviors in a simulated or altered environment. Inferences must be made from the simulated environment to the natural environment when analogue assessment is employed. Introducing this level of inference may be necessary when accurate and reliable data cannot be collected in the natural environment. Direct observation and self-monitoring data are typically taken in the natural environment. As previously mentioned, direct observation often does not produce reliable and valid measures of low-frequency behaviors that tend to occur at unpredictable times. For example, children may exhibit target behaviors in environments where observation is not always possible. Self-monitoring procedures may be employed for these types of behaviors. However, in some cases children may refuse to self-monitor or may be unable to self-monitor accurately. Furthermore, if assessment data are being collected in order to evaluate the effects of an intervention, the reactivity involved in self-monitoring may confound the results. Role-play measures, problem solving, and descriptive field studies are all assessment methods that address some of these limitations by employing direct observation in a simulated or altered environment.

Role-Play Measures

Perhaps the most common form of analogue assessment is the role-play test. Role-play tests involve presenting subjects with descriptions of a series of hypothetical scenarios, and asking the subjects to imagine themselves in each scenario and to respond. Observers record the absence or presence of various predefined behaviors.

The Behavioral Assertiveness Test for Children (BAT-C) developed by Bornstein, Bellack, and Hersen (1977), and the Behavioral Assertiveness Test for Boys (BAT-B) developed by Reardon, Hersen, Bellack, and

Foley (1979), are examples of existing role-play tests that can be used to assess social skills in children. With these tests, each scenario is described to the child, who has been instructed to respond as he or she would do if actually in the described scenario. The observer records the presence or absence of such responses as eye contact, smiles, and latency of response.

Existing role-play tests are useful; however, investigators are free to develop their own scenarios in order to assess specific target behaviors. The usefulness of role-play tests hinges on the assumption that subjects' responses to the hypothetical scenario are indicative of their responding in the natural environment. Therefore, scenarios developed should be based on events that are likely to occur in the subjects' natural environment. Investigators may find it useful to have teachers or parents participate in developing these scenarios. A number of studies investigating the predictive validity of role-play tests (Michelson, DiLorenzo, Caplin, & Ollendick, 1982; Ollendick, Hart, & Francis, 1985; Van Hasselt, Hersen, & Bellack, 1981; Williamson, Moody, Granberry, Letherman, & Blouin, 1983) show that children often respond differently in the analogue setting than in the natural environment. These studies indicate the need for more research to be conducted in order to further clarify the strengths and limitations of role-play tests.

In response to the problems associated with assessing social skills in an analogue environment, Shapiro, Stover, and Ifkovits (1983) and Shapiro, Gilbert, Friedman, and Steiner (1985) developed a Contrived Test of Social Skills (CTSS). This assessment method also involves constructing a series of scenarios and defining target behaviors. The CTSS differs from traditional role-play tests in that observers prompt teachers to initiate the contrived scenarios in the classroom. Observers are then able to record responses to a contrived situation in the natural environment. Although little research has been conducted on this assessment method, the predictive validity of this procedure is likely to be enhanced when naturally occurring scenarios are designed and prompted unobtrusively.

Problem Solving

Like role-play tests, problem-solving measures involve presenting a series of scenarios and asking the subject to respond orally or in writing. Whereas role-play tests are designed to assess observable behaviors, problem-solving measures are typically designed to assess unobservable cognitive variables that are thought to act as mediators of adjustment. Several problem-solving measures have been developed for measuring specific cognitive skills in different populations.

The Preschool Interpersonal Problem-Solving (PIPS) test was designed by Spivack and Shure (1974) to measure alternative-solution thinking in children 4–5 years old. Children are presented orally with problem scenarios (with accompanying pictures) and are instructed to provide an oral solution to the problems. One set of problems (peers) involves seven scenarios in which a child wants to play with a toy another child is already playing with. When the child gives a solution to the problem, a similar problem scenario (with the children or the toys varying) is presented. The other set of problems (authority) involves five scenarios in which a child has done something wrong and made the mother angry. The child's score on the PIPS is determined by the number of relevant solutions to both sets of items.

The What Happens Next Game (Spivack, Platt, & Shure, 1976) employs the same scenarios as the PIPS to measure consequential thinking. The items are presented in the same way, except that children are asked, "What might happen next in the story?" A child's score is determined by the number of consequences reported across all 12 scenarios.

Spivack et al. (1976) also developed the Children's Means–Ends Problem-Solving Test, which is designed to assess step-by-step means to solving problems in children 10–12 years of age. Here children are provided with the beginning and end of a scenario and are asked to fill in the middle. Six separate themes are used, and the children are scored on the number of means, obstacles, and time references reported.

Feldhusen and Houtz (1975) designed the Purdue Elementary Problem-Solving Inventory to assess disadvantaged elementary school children's problem-solving skills. The test consists of 49 scenarios developed to assess 12 component problem-solving skills, such as defining problems, seeing implications, and verifying solutions. In order to reduce the effects of academic deficits on test performance, items showing experiences of inner-city children are presented with slides and audiotapes. Responses are provided in multiple-choice format.

As with role-play tests, the predictive validity of problem-solving measures hinges on the assumption that the subjects' verbal reports to test stimuli are indicative of their performance in vivo. Yet little research has been conducted to examine the relationship between problem-solving responses and subjects' in vivo behavior. Butler and Meichenbaum (1981) indicate that these measures may be confounded by the subjects' verbal skills. Furthermore, some of the scenarios used in these tests may not reflect many children's real-life situations.

In response to the predictive validity limitations of these verbal reports, McClure, Chinsky, and Larsen (1978) developed the Friendship Club Interaction (FCI) measure. This assessment procedure involves having six children participate in a contest where they are required to answer questions. The contest has specific rules requiring the participants to solve certain interpersonal problems. For example, all six members must be club officers, yet there are only five officer cards. Scores are based on the number of solutions and solution effectiveness.

The FCI is similar to the CTSS, in that children are placed in a contrived situation where behaviors, rather than verbal reports of behaviors, can be directly observed and measured. Although this method of assessing problem solving is more direct than verbal reports, more research is needed to determine the predictive validity of these measures. At present, based on the predictive validity of analogue measures of social skills, it seems likely that analogue measures of problem solving may only have limited predictive validity.

Descriptive Field Studies

Another form of analogue assessment was developed from descriptive field study research described by Bijou, Peterson, and Ault (1968). Mace et al. (1988) describe a six-step process for conducting an assessment of structural and functional conditions that may control aberrant classroom behavior. The six steps are as follows: identifying the problem; collecting data to generate hypotheses; formulating hypotheses regarding structural and functional relations; designing analogue assessment conditions to test the hypotheses; conducting the analysis; and developing and implementing treatment. Direct observations in the natural environment permit investigators to operationalize the target behaviors and to collect data so that hypotheses may be generated regarding structural and functional relations. The data and hypotheses are then used to design analogue conditions, to which the subjects are exposed in order to determine which environmental conditions are controlling the target behaviors.

Iwata, Dorsey, Slifer, Bauman, and Richman (1982) exposed subjects to four analogue conditions (social disapproval, academic demand, unstructured play, and alone) to assess the functional relationship between self-injurious behaviors and specific environmental events. For example, the social disapproval condition required the experimenter to ignore appropriate play behavior and provide oral disapproval statements contingent upon self-injurious behavior. Under the academic demand condition, the experimenter would terminate teaching and turn away from the subject when self-injurious behavior was observed.

After analogue conditions are designed, the subjects are exposed to these conditions in controlled environments following an alternating-treatments design (Barlow & Hayes, 1979). Using direct observation, investigators record and calculate rates of behaviors within each analogue condition. By comparing these rates across conditions, the investigators can determine which environmental conditions may be maintaining the behaviors in the natural environment. For example, in the Iwata et al. (1982) research, high rates of self-injurious behaviors under the social disapproval condition indicated that negative attention might be reinforcing self-injurious behavior in the natural environment. This suggested the use of an extinction program coupled with differential reinforcement of appropriate responses as an intervention for self-injurious behavior in this environment. High rates of self-injurious behavior under the academic demand condition suggested that negative reinforcement (escaping academic demands) might be maintaining self-injurious behavior in academic settings. It was thought that requiring the subjects to participate and complete the academic task might reduce this behavior in the natural environment.

Descriptive field studies have been used to assess conditions that may maintain a variety of other aberrant behaviors in children, including tantrums (Carr & Newsome, 1985), stereotypy (Mace, Browder, & Lin, 1987), pica (Mace & Knight, 1986), aggressive and disruptive behavior (Mace, Page, Ivancic, & O'Brien, 1986), and reluctant speech (Mace & West, 1986). Although the process is somewhat time-consuming, descriptive field studies are useful in that they provide empirical evidence for determining environmental conditions that may be maintaining target behaviors in the natural environment. This evidence indicates intervention strategies that are likely to produce the desired changes in behaviors.

Indirect Methods: Self-Report and Informant Report

Indirect assessment methods do not require direct observation, but rely on retrospective reporting of the subject or significant others, such as teachers, parents, spouses, or caregivers. The indirect nature of these assessment procedures makes all findings suspect unless empirically verified. Indirect assessment data are typically collected by interviews or by paper-and-pencil devices such as checklists and rating scales.

Interviews

Interviewing is probably the most widely used assessment procedure. Interviews can be employed to gather information about client concerns; to build interpersonal relationships between clients and professionals; to identify and define target behaviors, antecedents, consequences, and possible reinforcers; to assess nonverbal behaviors; and to obtain historical information that may be related to the present problem.

The flexibility of an interview allows one to collect a wide variety of information. Yet the reliability and validity of oral report data are questionable. Linehan (1977) and Witt et al. (1988) note that the ability of the person being interviewed to remember and accurately describe past events; the person's motivation to provide accurate information; and the person's perception of his or her role can all have an impact on the information gathered during an interview.

Little research has been conducted to investigate the reliability and validity of interviewing techniques (Gresham, 1984; Haynes & Wilson, 1979). One reason for this is that the interview process typically lacks standardization or structure, which makes it difficult to evaluate specific interviewing techniques. Perhaps the one exception to this is a behavioral interviewing technique developed by Bergan and his associates (Bergan, 1977; Bergan & Tombari, 1975, 1976; Kratochwill & Bergan, 1978) as part of a behavioral consultation model.

The Bergan consultation model is a structured four-step process consisting of problem identification, problem analysis, plan implementation, and problem evaluation. The problem identification, analysis, and evaluation interviews each have specific goals. For example, two of the goals of the problem identification interview are to obtain a description of the problem behavior and to determine the environmental conditions under which this behavior occurs.

The statements made in the interviews are coded according to context of the statement, process or intention of the statement, whether or not the statement called for a response, and who made the statement. Using this coding system, research has determined that the data gathered are directly affected by the interviewer's verbal behavior (Bergan & Tombari, 1976). For example, a verbal response defined as a behavior specification elicitor, such as "What makes you think Joey is aggressive?", provides the interviewer with information that he or she can use to arrive at operational definitions of problem behaviors and controlling variables.

The structure and the coding system provided in the Bergan interviews makes it possible to assess the effects of interviewer behavior on the type of information gathered. More research is needed in order to determine which interviewer behaviors result in the collection of the most useful and accurate data. As this research continues, it may be possible to develop structured interview procedures that produce more reliable and valid data.

Other interviewing systems have been developed for use in psychiatric settings. Paget (1984) reviewed several of these measures used for diagnosing childhood problems. She found that although the use of structured instruments had significant advantages over more informal approaches to interviewing, the measures were all very lengthy and time-consuming, and had questionable value beyond diagnosis.

Checklists and Rating Scales

Checklists and rating scales are typically paper-and-pencil instruments that are completed by the subject (self-report) or by someone familiar with the subject's behaviors (informant report). Walls, Werner, Bacon, and Zane (1977), Haynes and Wilson (1979), and Hoge (1983) provide extensive lists of these measures. Some of these instruments have been designed to screen a large range of behaviors; others are used to assess a more specific class of behaviors, such as social skills or assertiveness. Both broad-band and narrow-band instruments are useful at different stages of the assessment process.

Broad-Band Instruments. Broad-band or global instruments require an individual to rate a large number of potential behavior problems. This global approach is useful in narrowing the wide range of potential target behaviors that may be selected for intervention. Because such a large range of behaviors is assessed with global measures, the information can be used to supplement or confirm interview data.

The Child Behavior Profile and the Child Behavior Checklist (Achenbach, 1978; Achenbach & Edelbrock, 1978, 1979; Edelbrock & Achenbach, 1984) constitutes an example of a broad-band instrument that can be completed by parents, teachers, or children (11–18 years old). Although the different ver-

sions of the profile vary, depending on who is completing the instrument and the age of the child being assessed, the overall structure of the profile is similar. It consists of two sections, one for assessing social competence and the other for assessing potential behavior problems. On the parent form, scores on the Social Competence section are combined to form a Social Competence Index in three possible areas: Social, Activities, and School. The Social Competence section of the teacher form is similar to the parent version, but elicits responses regarding the child's general school behaviors, such as whether the child is working hard, behaving appropriately, and so forth.

The Behavior Problem portion of the profile requires the individual completing the form to rate the presence or absence of potential behavior problems on a scale from 0 ("not true about subject") to 2 ("very true about subject"). The parent and teacher versions each contain 113 analogous or identical items; the self-report version contains 90 items identical to those in the teacher and parent versions.

Subscales were developed across age and sex, based on an extensive factor analysis of items from each scale on 2,300 clinic-referred children. Scores on the various subscales are derived by summing the items identified by the factor analysis. These subscale scores can then be compared to the normative subscale scores that were derived from assessing 1,300 randomly selected, non-clinic-referred children.

Several advantages of this instrument are directly related to its norm-referenced base. It allows one to determine the degree to which the referred child resembles a sample of nonreferred children across the subscales. An individual's general strengths and weaknesses can also be evaluated by comparing scores across the subscales. Because of the extensive psychometric development of the Child Behavior Profile and Child Behavior Checklist, school psychologists can use the results to assist in making diagnostic classifications, which are often required when making eligibility decisions for special education placement. Although a variety of other checklist and rating scales are available, investigators should exercise caution when using any of these instruments for diagnostic classification. Many of these instruments have been normed on small, homogeneous samples and do not have the psychometric properties needed for making diagnostic classifications.

Global checklist and rating scales are useful screening instruments because they sample such a wide variety of potential behavior problems; however, they provide very minimal information on specific behavior problems. A rating scale may place a student in a particular category, but this labeling does not indicate which specific behaviors should be targeted for intervention. Because behaviors are defined and rated in nonobjective terms, an item-by-item analysis is unlikely to indicate these target behaviors. Therefore, these global measures should be used primarily as screening instruments to identify general areas or classes of behavior problems to be further assessed.

Narrow-Band Instruments. A variety of checklist and rating scales have been developed to assess specific classes of behavior problems. These instruments are similar to global checklist and rating scales; however, the items are designed to assess a particular problem area in more depth than global measures can. For example, the Children's Assertiveness Behavior Scale (Wood, Michelson, & Flynn, 1978) consists of 27 items, each of which describes a situation where assertive responses are desired. The child is given five different responses and is instructed to choose the one that matches the way the child would usually behave in that particular situation. Responses range from passive (-2) to aggressive ($+2$).

Other scales have been developed to assess a variety of classes of behaviors, including self-control (Kendall & Wilcox, 1979; Kendall, Zupan, & Braswell, 1981), fear (Ollendick, Matson, & Helsel, 1985), anxiety (Castaneda, McCandless, & Palmero, 1956), and depression (Kovacs & Beck, 1977). These scales are useful in that they help indicate which specific behaviors should be targeted for treatment. For example, a global inventory may indicate that a child may be unassertive. An assertiveness rating scale should provide more information about the topography of the unassertive behavior and

which conditions elicit unassertive responding.

Considerations When Using Checklist or Rating Scales. Ciminero and Drabman (1977) indicate that checklist and rating scales have several advantages over other assessment procedures. They are practical in that a variety of information can be gained without involving the investigator's time. Global measures can be used to eliminate time spent on evaluating behaviors not relevant to the problem. Furthermore, a comprehensive assessment of a client's general strengths and weaknesses can be obtained through these global measures.

Although checklist and rating scales have a number of distinct advantages, they rely on individuals to report on and rate behaviors that have occurred in the past. Because of this retrospective reporting, these measures suffer from many of the same limitations as interviews. The data reported can be influenced by the individual's memory, motivation, perception about reasons for completing the instrument, and subjective judgment.

Most checklists and rating scales are not standardized, provide no norms, and lack any type of psychometric evaluation. Although the concurrent validity between some of these measures is strong, research indicates that data collected through checklists and interviews may not correlate with observed levels of behavior (Kendall & Wilcox, 1979; Kendall et al., 1981; Shapiro, Lentz, & Sofman, 1985). This lack of predictive validity severely limits the use of assessment measures. Clearly, more research is needed to improve the psychometric properties and the predictive validity of checklist and rating scales.

CONCLUSIONS

Behavioral assessment offers several advantages over more traditional psychological assessment methods. Whereas the primary purpose of traditional measures is to provide diagnostic and classification decisions, behavioral assessment is designed to provide a much broader range of potential information. In addition to providing data that can assist in making a classification decision, behavioral assessment methods are designed to suggest potential intervention procedures that may be successful in remediating the person's problem. In addition, the data collected through behavioral assessment should serve as a baseline against which any subsequent change in behavior can be measured. Thus, behavioral assessment can provide an empirical, ongoing means for evaluating client progress.

Despite these very positive potential uses of behavioral assessment data, the methodology of behavioral assessment is not as widely accepted and employed in clinical practice as one would expect (Wade & Baker, 1977; Wade, Baker, & Hartmann, 1979; Wade, Baker, Morton, & Baker, 1978). This appears to be equally true in school settings (Anderson, Cancelli, & Kratochwill, 1984). One likely explanation for the limited use of behavioral assessment in clinical practice may be related to the nature of current knowledge of assessment techniques. Although many of the strategies of behavioral assessment have been available for a long time, significant research on behavioral assessment per se is in its infancy. By contrast, research in traditional assessment has a long, well-known history. Given the range of potential uses of behavioral assessment, increased future use in clinical practice should be anticipated.

Overall, understanding the full range of human abilities and responses must include integration of differing conceptualizations of the assessment process. Not surprisingly, some investigators have suggested ways in which traditional and behavioral assessment methodologies can be incorporated (e.g., Nelson, 1980; Prout & Ferber, 1988). Although such integration is probably useful, it may present conceptual problems as investigators attempt to interpret and communicate the results of evaluations. Continued efforts to examine more carefully the potential advantages and limitations of both traditional and behavioral assessment are surely needed.

REFERENCES

Achenbach, T. M. (1978). The Child Behavior Profile: I. Boys ages 6–11. *Journal of Consulting and Clinical Psychology, 46,* 478–488.

Achenbach, T. M., & Edelbrock, C. S. (1978). The classification of child psychopathology: A review and analysis of empirical efforts. *Psychological Bulletin, 85,* 1275–1301.

Achenbach, T. M., & Edelbrock, C. S. (1979). The Child Behavior Profile: II. Boys aged 12–16 and girls aged 6–11 and 12–16. *Journal of Consulting and Clinical Psychology, 47,* 223–233.

Anderson, T. K., Cancelli, A. A., & Kratochwill, T. R. (1984). Self-reported assessment practices of school psychologists: Implications for training and practice. *Journal of School Psychology, 22,* 17–29.

Barlow, D. H. (1981). *Behavioral assessment of adult disorders.* New York: Guilford Press.

Barlow, D. H., & Hayes, S. C. (1979). Alternating treatment designs: One strategy for comparing the effects of two treatments in a single subject. *Journal of Applied Behavior Analysis, 12,* 319–325.

Bergan, J. R. (1977). *Behavioral consultation.* Columbus, OH: Charles E. Merrill.

Bergan, J. R., & Tombari, M. L. (1975). The analysis of verbal interactions occurring during consultation. *Journal of School Psychology, 13,* 209–226.

Bergan, J. R., & Tombari, M. L. (1976). Consultant skill and efficiency and the implementation and outcomes of consultation. *Journal of School Psychology, 14,* 3–14.

Bijou, S. W., Peterson, R. F., & Ault, M. H. (1968). A method of integrating descriptive and experimental field studies at the level of data and empirical concepts. *Journal of Applied Behavior Analysis, 1,* 175–191.

Bornstein, M. T., Bellack, A. S., & Hersen, M. (1977). Social skills training for unassertive children: A multiple-baseline analysis. *Journal of Applied Behavior Analysis, 10,* 183–195.

Broden, M., Hall, R. V., & Mitts, B. (1971). The effect of self-recording on the classroom behavior of two 8th grade students. *Journal of Applied Behavior Analysis, 4,* 191–199.

Butler, L., & Meichenbaum, D. (1981). The assessment of interpersonal problem-solving skills. In P. C. Kendall & S. D. Hollon (Eds.), *Assessment strategies for cognitive–behavioral interventions* (pp. 197–225). New York: Academic Press.

Carr, E. G., & Newsome, C. (1985). Demand-related tantrums: Conceptualization and treatment. *Behavior Modification, 9,* 403–426.

Castaneda, A., McCandless, B., & Palmero, D. (1956). The children's form of the Manifest Anxiety Scale. *Child Development, 27,* 317–326.

Ciminero, A. R., Calhoun, K. S., & Adams, H. E. (Eds.). (1981). *Handbook of behavioral assessment* (2nd ed.). New York: Wiley.

Ciminero, A. R., & Drabman, R. S. (1977). Current developments in the behavioral assessment of children. In B. B. Lahey & A. E. Kazdin (Eds.), *Advances in clinical child psychology* (Vol. 1, pp. 47–84). New York: Plenum.

Cone, J. D. (1977). The relevance of reliability and validity for behavioral assessment. *Behavior Therapy, 8,* 41–426.

Cone, J. D. (1978). The Behavioral Assessment Grid (BAG): A conceptual framework and a taxonomy. *Behavior Therapy, 9,* 882–888.

Cone, J. D. (1979). Why the "I've got a better agreement

measure" literature continues to grow: A commentary on two articles by Birkimer and Brown. *Journal of Applied Behavior Analysis, 12,* 571–572.

Cone, J. D. (1981). Psychometric considerations. In M. Hersen & A. S. Bellack (Eds.), *Behavioral assessment: A practical handbook* (pp. 38–68). New York: Pergamon Press.

Cone, J. D., & Hawkins, R. P. (Eds.). (1977). *Behavioral assessment: New directions in clinical psychology.* New York: Brunner/Mazel.

Cronbach, L. J., Gleser, G. S., Nanda, H., & Rajaratnam, N. (1972). *The dependability of behavioral measures.* New York: Wiley.

Edelbrock, C. S., & Achenbach, T. M. (1984). The teacher version of the Child Behavior Profile: I. Boys aged 6–11. *Journal of Consulting and Clinical Psychology, 52,* 207–217.

Feldhusen, J., & Houtz, J. (1975). Problem solving and the concrete–abstract dimension. *Gifted Child Quarterly, 19,* 122–129.

Fixsen, D. L., Phillips, E. L., & Wolf, M. M. (1972). Achievement Place: The reliability of self-reporting and peer-tutoring and their effects on behavior. *Journal of Applied Behavior Analysis, 5,* 19–30.

Glynn, E. L., & Thomas, J. D. (1974). Effects of cueing on self-control of classroom behavior. *Journal of Applied Behavior Analysis, 7,* 299–306.

Green, S. B., & Alverson, L. G. (1978). A comparison of indirect measures for long duration behaviors. *Journal of Applied Behavior Analysis, 11,* 530.

Gresham, F. M. (1984). Behavioral interviews in school psychology: Issues in psychometric adequacy and research. *School Psychology Review, 13,* 17–25.

Hartmann, D. P., Roper, B. L., & Bradford, D. C. (1979). Some relationships between behavioral and traditional assessment. *Journal of Behavioral Assessment, 1,* 3–21.

Hayes, S. C., & Cavoir, N. (1977). Multiple tracking and the reactivity of self-monitoring: I. Negative behaviors. *Behavior Therapy, 8,* 819–831.

Haynes, S. N. (1978). *Principles of behavioral assessment.* New York: Gardner Press.

Haynes, S. N., & Wilson, C. C. (1979). *Behavioral assessment: Recent advances in methods, concepts, and applications.* San Francisco: Jossey-Bass.

Hersen, M., & Bellack, A. S. (Eds.). (1987). *Behavioral assessment: A practical handbook* (3rd ed.). New York: Pergamon Press.

Hoge, R. D. (1983). Psychometric properties of teacher-judgement measures of pupil aptitudes, classroom behaviors, and achievement levels. *Journal of Special Education, 17,* 401–429.

Humphrey, L. L., Karoly, P., & Kirschenbaum, D. S. (1978). Self-management in the classroom: Self-imposed response cost versus self-reward. *Behavior Therapy, 9,* 592–601.

Iwata, B. A., Dorsey, M. F., Slifer, K. J., Bauman, K. E., & Richman, G. S. (1982). Toward a functional analysis of self-injury. *Analysis and Intervention in Developmental Disabilities, 2,* 3–20.

Jenkins, J. R., & Pany, D. (1978). Standardized achievement tests: How useful for special education? *Exceptional Children, 44,* 448–453.

Johnston, J. M., & Pennypacker, H. S. (1980). *Strategies and tactics of human behavioral research.* Hillsdale, NJ: Erlbaum.

Kanfer, F. H. (1977). The many faces of self-control. In R. B. Stuart (Ed.), *Behavioral self-management: Strategies, techniques, and outcomes* (pp. 1–48). New York: Brunner/Mazel.

Kehle, T. J., Clark, E., Jenson, W. R., & Wampold, B. E. (1986). Effectiveness of self-observation with behavior disordered elementary school children. *School Psychology Review, 15,* 289–295.

Kendall, P. C., & Wilcox, L. E. (1979). Self-control in children: Development of a rating scale. *Journal of Consulting and Clinical Psychology, 47,* 1020–1029.

Kendall, P. C., Zupan, B. A., & Braswell, L. (1981). Self-control in children: Further analysis of the Self-Control Rating Scale. *Behavior Therapy, 12,* 667–681.

Kovacs, M., & Beck, A. T. (1977). An empirical approach toward a definition of childhood depression. In J. G. Schulterbrandt & A. Raskin (Eds.), *Depression in childhood: Diagnosis, treatment, and conceptual models* (pp. 1–25). New York: Raven Press.

Kratochwill, T. R., & Bergan, J. R. (1978). Evaluating programs in applied settings through behavioral consultation. *Journal of School Psychology, 16,* 375–386.

Lentz, F. E., Jr. (1982). *An empirical examination of the utility of partial interval and momentary time sampling as a measure of behavior.* Unpublished doctoral dissertation, University of Tennessee.

Lentz, F. E., Jr. (1988). Direct observation and measurement of academic skills: A conceptual review. In E. S. Shapiro & T. R. Kratochwill (Eds.), *Behavioral assessment in schools: Conceptual foundations and practical applications* (pp. 76–120). New York: Guilford Press.

Linehan, M. M. (1977). Issues in behavioral interviewing. In J. D. Cone & R. P. Hawkins (Eds.), *Behavioral assessment: New directions in clinical psychology* (pp. 30–51). New York: Brunner/Mazel.

Litrownik, A. J., & Freitas, J. L. (1980). Self-monitoring in moderately retarded adolescents: Reactivity and accuracy as a function of valence. *Behavior Therapy, 11,* 245–258.

Mace, F. C., Browder, D. M., & Lin, Y. (1987). Analysis of demand conditions associated with stereotypy. *Journal of Behavior Therapy and Experimental Psychiatry, 18,* 25–31.

Mace, F. C., & Knight, D. (1986). Functional analysis and treatment of severe pica. *Journal of Applied Behavior Analysis, 19,* 411–416.

Mace, F. C., Page, T. J., Ivancic, M. T., & O'Brien, S. (1986). Analysis of environmental determinants of aggression and disruption in mentally retarded children. *Applied Research in Mental Retardation, 7,* 1–19.

Mace, F. C., & West, B. J. (1986). Analysis of demand conditions associated with reluctant speech. *Journal of Behavior Therapy and Experimental Psychiatry, 17,* 285–294.

Mace, F. C., Yankanich, M. A., & West, B. J. (1988). Toward a methodology of experimental analysis and treatment of aberrant classroom behaviors. *Special Services in the Schools, 4*(3/4), 71–88.

Maletzky, B. M. (1974). Assisted covert sensitization in the treatment of exhibitionism. *Journal of Consulting and Clinical Psychology, 42,* 34–40.

Mash, E. J., & Terdal, L. G. (Eds.). (1981). *Behavioral assessment of childhood disorders* (2nd ed.). New York: Guilford Press.

McClure, L. F., Chinsky, J. M., & Larsen, S. W. (1978). Enhancing social problem-solving performance in an elementary school setting. *Journal of Educational Psychology, 70,* 504–513.

McFall, R. M. (1970). Effects of self-monitoring on normal smoking behavior. *Journal of Consulting and Clinical Psychology, 35,* 135–142.

McFall, R. M., & Hammen, C. L. (1971). Motivation structure and self-monitoring: The role of non-specific factors in smoking reduction. *Journal of Consulting and Clinical Psychology, 37,* 80–86.

Michelson, L., DiLorenzo, T. M., Caplin, J. P., & Ollendick, T. H. (1982). Situational determinants of the Behavioral Assertiveness Role-Play Test for Children (BAT-CR). *Behavior Therapy, 13,* 724–734.

Nelson, R. O. (1977). Methodological issues in assessment via self-monitoring. In J. D. Cone & R. P. Hawkins (Eds.), *Behavioral assessment: New directions in clinical psychology* (pp. 217–240). New York: Brunner/Mazel.

Nelson, R. O. (1980). The use of intelligence tests in behavioral assessment. *Behavioral Assessment, 2,* 417–423.

Nelson, R. O. (1983). Behavioral assessment: Past, present, and future. *Behavioral Assessment, 5,* 195–206.

Nelson, R. O., Hay, L. R., Devany, J., & Koslow-Green, L. (1980). The reactivity and accuracy of children's self-monitoring: Three experiments. *Child Behavior Therapy, 2,* 1–24.

Nelson, R. O., Hay, L. R., & Hay, W. M. (1977). Comments on Cone's "The relevance of reliability and validity for behavioral assessment." *Behavior Therapy, 8,* 427–430.

Nelson, R. O., Hay, L. R., Hay, W. M., & Carsten, C. B. (1977). The reactivity and accuracy of teachers' self-monitoring of positive and negative classroom verbalizations. *Behavior Therapy, 8,* 972–985.

Nelson, R. O., Hayes, S. C. (1979). Some current dimensions of behavioral assessment. *Behavioral Assessment, 1,* 1–16.

Nelson, R. O., & Hayes, S. C. (Eds.). (1986). *Conceptual foundations of behavioral assessment.* New York: Guilford Press.

Nelson, R. O., Lipinski, D. P., & Boykin, R. A. (1978). The effects of self-recorders' training and the obtrusiveness of the self-monitoring device on the accuracy and reactivity of self-monitoring. *Behavior Therapy, 9,* 200–208.

O'Leary, K. D., Kaufman, K. F., Kass, R., & Drabman, R. (1970). The effects of loud and soft reprimands on the behavior of disruptive students. *Exceptional Children, 37,* 145–155.

O'Leary, K. D., Romanczyk, R. G., Kass, R. E., Dietz, A., & Santogrossi, D. A. (1979). *Procedures for classroom observation of teachers and children.* Stony Brook: State University of New York at Stony Brook, Department of Psychology.

Ollendick, T. H., Hart, K. J., & Francis, G. (1985). Social validation of the Revised Behavioral Assertiveness Test for Children (BAT-CR). *Child and Family Behavior Therapy, 7,* 17–33.

Ollendick, T. H., Matson, J. L., & Helsel, W. J. (1985). Fears in children and adolescents: Normative data. *Behaviour Research and Therapy, 23,* 465–467.

Paget, K. D., (1984). The structured interview: A psychometric review. *Journal of School Psychology, 22,* 415–426.

Peterson, G. L., House, A. E., & Alford, H. F. (1975, March). *Self-monitoring: Accuracy and reactivity in patients' recording of their clinically targeted behavior.* Paper presented at the meeting of the Southeastern Psychological Association, Atlanta, GA.

Powell, J., Martindale, B., Kulp, S., Martindale, A., & Bauman, R. (1977). Taking a closer look: Time sampling and measurement error. *Journal of Applied Behavior Analysis, 10,* 325–332.

Powell, J., & Rockinson, R. (1978). On the inability of interval time sampling to reflect frequency of occurrence data. *Journal of Applied Behavior Analysis, 11,* 531–532.

Powers, M. D., & Handleman, J. S. (1984). *Behavioral assessment of severe developmental disabilities.* Rockville, MD: Aspen Systems.

Prout, H. T., & Ferber, S. M. (1988). Analogue assessment: Traditional personality assessment measures in behavioral assessment. In E. S. Shapiro & T. R. Kratochwill (Eds.), *Behavioral assessment in schools: Conceptual foundations and practical applications* (pp. 322–383). New York: Guilford Press.

Reardon, R. C., Hersen, M., Bellack, A. S., & Foley, J. M. (1979). Measuring social skills in grade school boys. *Journal of Behavioral Assessment, 1,* 87–105.

Risely, T. R., & Hart, B. (1968). Developing correspondence between the non-verbal and verbal behavior of school children. *Journal of Applied Behavior Analysis, 1,* 267–281.

Sagotsky, G., Patterson, G. L., & Lepper, M. R. (1978). Training children's self-control: A field experiment in self-monitoring and goal setting in the classroom. *Journal of Experimental Child Psychology, 25,* 242–253.

Santogrossi, D. A. (1974, October). *Self-reinforcement and external monitoring of performance on an academic task.* Paper presented at the Fifth Annual Conference on Applied Behavior Analysis in Education, Kansas City, KS.

Santogrossi, D. A., O'Leary, K. D., Romanczyk, R. G., & Kaufman, K. F. (1973). Self-evaluation by adolescents in a psychiatric hospital school token program. *Journal of Applied Behavior Analysis, 6,* 277–287.

Saudargas, R. A., & Creed, V. (1980). *State–Event Classroom Observation System.* Knoxville: University of Tennessee, Department of Psychology.

Saudargas, R. A., & Lentz, F. E. (1986). Estimating percent of time and rate via direct observation: A suggested observational procedure and format. *School Psychology Review, 15,* 36–48.

Shapiro, E. S. (1984). Self-monitoring. In T. H. Ollendick & M. Hersen (Eds.), *Child behavior assessment: Principles and procedures* (pp. 148–165). New York: Pergamon Press.

Shapiro, E. S. (1987). *Behavioral assessment in school psychology.* Hillsdale, NJ: Erlbaum.

Shapiro, E. S. (1989). *Academic skill problems: Direct assessment and intervention.* New York: Guilford Press.

Shapiro, E. S., & Ackerman, A. M. (1983). Increasing productivity rates in adult mentally retarded clients: The failure of self-monitoring. *Applied Research in Mental Retardation, 4,* 163–181.

Shapiro, E. S., & Browder, D. M. (in press). Behavioral assessment: Applications for persons with mental retardation. In J. Matson (Ed.), *The handbook of behavior modification for persons with mental retardation*. New York: Plenum.

Shapiro, E. S., & Derr, T. F. (1987). An examination of overlap between reading curricula and standardized achievement tests. *Journal of Special Education, 21,* 59–67.

Shapiro, E. S., Gilbert, D., Friedman, J., & Steiner, S. (1985, December). *Concurrent validity of role-play and contrived tests in assessing social skills in disruptive adolescents.* Paper presented at the annual meeting of the Association for Advancement of Behavior Therapy, Houston, TX.

Shapiro, E. S., & Kratochwill, T. R. (Eds.). (1988). *Behavioral assessment in schools: Conceptual foundations and practical applications*. New York: Guilford Press.

Shapiro, E. S., & Lentz, F. E. (1985). Assessing academic behavior: A behavioral approach. *School Psychology Review, 14,* 325–338.

Shapiro, E. S., & Lentz, F. E. (1986). Behavioral assessment of academic behavior. In T. R. Kratochwill (Ed.), *Advances in school psychology* (Vol. 5, pp. 87–139). Hillsdale, NJ: Erlbaum.

Shapiro, E. S., Lentz, F. E., & Sofman, R. (1985). Validity of rating scales in assessing aggressive behavior in classroom settings. *Journal of School Psychology, 23,* 69–80.

Shapiro, E. S., McGonigle, J. J., & Ollendick, T. H. (1980). An analysis of self-assessment and self-reinforcement in a self-managed token economy with mentally retarded children. *Applied Research in Mental Retardation, 1,* 227–240.

Shapiro, E. S., Stover, J. E., & Ifkovits, G. A. (1983, November). *Predictive and concurrent validity of role-play and naturalistic assessment of social skills in kindergarten children.* Paper presented at the annual meeting of the Association for Advancement of Behavior Therapy, Washington, DC.

Slate, J. R., & Saudargas, R. A. (1986a). Differences in the classroom behavior of behaviorally disordered and regular class children. *Behavior Disorders, 11,* 45–53.

Slate, J. R., & Saudargas, R. A. (1986b). Differences in learning disabled and average students' classroom behaviors. *Learning Disabilities Quarterly, 9,* 61–67.

Spivack, G., Platt, J., & Shure, M. B. (1976). *The problem-solving approach to adjustment*. San Francisco: Jossey-Bass.

Spivack, G., & Shure, M. B. (1974). *Social adjustment of young children*. San Francisco: Jossey-Bass.

Strosahl, K. D., & Linehan, M. M. (1986). Basic issues in behavioral assessment. In A. Ciminero, K. Calhoun, & H. Adams (Eds.), *Handbook of behavioral assessment* (2nd ed., pp. 12–46). New York: Wiley.

Turkewitz, H., O'Leary, K. D., & Ironsmith, M. (1975). Generalization and maintenance of appropriate behavior through self-control. *Journal of Consulting and Clinical Psychology, 43,* 577–583.

Van Hasselt, V. B., Hersen, M., & Bellack, A. S. (1981). The validity of role-play tests for assessing social skills in children. *Behavior Therapy, 12,* 202–216.

Wade, T. C., & Baker, T. B. (1977). Opinions and use of psychological tests: A survey of clinical psychologists. *American Psychologist, 32,* 874–882.

Wade, T. C., Baker, T. B., & Hartmann, D. P. (1979). Behavior therapists' self-reported views and practices. *The Behavior Therapist, 2,* 3–6.

Wade, T. C., Baker, T. B., Morton, T. L., & Baker, L. J. (1978). The status of psychological testing in clinical psychology: Relationships between test use and professional activities and orientations. *Journal of Personality Assessment, 42,* 3–10.

Wahler, R. G. (1980). The insular mother: Her problems in parent–child treatment. *Journal of Applied Behavior Analysis, 13,* 207–220.

Wahler, R. G., & Fox, J. J., III. (1980). Solitary toy play and time out: A family treatment package for children with aggressive and oppositional behavior. *Journal of Applied Behavior Analysis, 13,* 23–40.

Wahler, R. C., House, A. E., & Stambaugh, E. E., II. (1976). *Ecological assessment for child problem behaviors: A clinical package for home, school, and institutional settings*. New York: Pergamon Press.

Walls, R. T., Werner, T. J., Bacon, A., & Zane, T. (1977). Behavior checklists. In J. D. Cone & R. P. Hawkins (Eds.), *Behavioral assessment: New directions in clinical psychology* (pp. 77–146). New York: Brunner/Mazel.

Watson, D. L., & Tharp, R. G. (1972). *Self-directed behavior: Self-modification for personal adjustment*. Monterey, CA: Brooks/Cole.

Williamson, D. A., Moody, S. C., Granberry, S. W., Letherman, V. R., & Blovin, D. C. (1983). Criterion-related validity of a role-play social skills test for children. *Behavior Therapy, 14,* 466–481.

Witt, J. C., Cavell, T. A., Heffer, R. W., Carey, M. P., & Martens, B. K. (1988). Child self-report: Interviewing techniques and rating scales. In E. S. Shapiro & T. R. Kratochwill (Eds.), *Behavioral assessment in schools: Conceptual foundations and practical applications* (pp. 384–454). New York: Guilford Press.

Wood, R., Michelson, L., & Flynn, S. (1978, November). *Assessment of assertive behavior in elementary school children.* Paper presented at the annual meeting of the Association for Advancement of Behavior Therapy, Chicago.

16

Structured Rating Scales: A Review of Self-Report and Informant Rating Processes, Procedures, and Issues

JOSEPH C. WITT
Louisiana State University

ROBERT W. HEFFER
Children's Hospital, New Orleans

JAN PFEIFFER
Louisiana State University

T he profession of psychology is associated with the science of behavior. In practice, psychologists are concerned with helping to resolve human problems. But the practitioner does not select just any problem as the focus of attention. Typically psychologists react not to problems per se, but to *complaints* about problems (Baer, 1987; Witt, in press). People have many problems, but usually choose to complain about only a few of these problems. They choose to complain to neighbors, friends, and psychologists. It is the complaint and not the problem itself that serves as the antecedent for the problem-solving activities of psychologists.

A psychologist confronted wtih someone complaining about a problem needs to know as much as possible about the problem and the factors contributing to it. How big a problem is it? How long has it been occurring? What solutions have already failed? Do other people think this is a problem? Are there other problems (related or unrelated to the problem complained about) that might also be having an affect? The oldest and most durable assessment device for learning the answers to these questions is the interview.

With the interview, an assessor can probe flexibly all the factors that may be contributing to the problem and that are causing the person to complain. In addition, the interview can be used to elicit the perceptions of other people about the problems being complained about. Often these other people are the ones who have initiated a referral about the problem. With most problems, for the purpose of intervention planning, it would be difficult to defend any other assessment device as better than a thorough interview conducted by a competent clinician with a willing and articulate client. But the clinician is not always competent, the interview is not always thorough, and the client is not always willing and articulate. Therefore, problems are missed or are not understood, inaccurate information is reported, and data gleaned from an interview must be brought into question. As Burke and DeMers (1979) have suggested, "the same characteristics which make the assessment interview so widely used (e.g., its flexibility, spontaneity, and ease of administration) are also the interview's greatest liabilities when the psychometric qualities of reliability and validity are considered" (p. 51).

Rating scales are obviously derivatives of the unstructured interview. They represent an evolution of the interview in the direction of increasing structure. This additional structure has several advantages, because rating scales make the collection of data more systematic and objective; this allows for (1) the comparison of data obtained across time, (2) the comparison of responses obtained to those of some norm group, and (3) the determination of the psychometric underpinnings of the assessment device (Page, 1984). The advantages of rating scales over the interview come at the cost of decreased flexibility and possibly a decrease in breadth and depth.

In a comprehensive assessment of child functioning, there is a need to use a variety of assessment modes and sources, and there is a need to gather data via both rating scales and interviews, as well as direct observation, formal tests, and other sources of information. This process of conducting assessment using a number of methods, settings, and information sources has been termed "multiple operationalism" (Witt, Elliott, Gresham, & Kramer, 1988); its purpose is to examine the data obtained for convergence. To the extent that data from multiple sources agree, one can be more certain of the validity of the data. To the extent that there is a lack of convergence, there is a need for additional assessment.

The purpose of this chapter is to provide a review of the processes, procedures, and issues surrounding the use of rating scales. Two types of rating scales are discussed: ratings by others and self-report rating scales. For both types of rating scales, the discussion is limited to those instruments that apply to school-age children.

INFORMANT RATINGS

Children, especially young children, are rarely self-referred; instead, they are identified by adults who are concerned about them. Upon referral of a child, it is both logical and necessary to elicit information about the child from the referring adult. In addition to obtaining information from the referral source, the principle of multiple operationalism requires the collection of data from other adults who have frequent contact with the child in various settings. Traditionally, this information has been obtained through an interview; however, for reasons mentioned above, it is becoming increasing popular to provide adult (and, in some cases, peer) informants with ratings scales and checklists that pertain to the problems and competencies of the referred child. This section begins with a brief discussion of issues related to the selection and use of informant rating scales and concludes with a review of selected rating scales.

Advantages of Informant Rating Scales

Rating scales completed by adults who have frequent contact with a child offer several advantages over the interview and other assessment methodologies (Ciminero & Drabman, 1977). A major advantage over the interview is convenience, in that multiple viewpoints can be elicited in a manner that is time- and cost-efficient for the assessor. If the rating scale is comprehensive enough, then it helps insure that assessment has "touched all the bases" and mentioned most of the significant problem areas. The unstructured interview may delve deeply into some areas of functioning but may ignore other areas completely, thus increasing the probability of missing a significant problem. Rating scales, by providing a structured response format and operationalizing behavior, can reduce the subjectivity inherent in adults' judgments of children. Thus, when an adult believes a child to be a "good kid," a "bad kid," or "hyperactive," these global beliefs can be clarified if the informant is asked to rate specific component behaviors.

To the extent that rating scales increase the likelihood that significant adults in a child's environment will be asked about the child, rating scales increase the ecological validity of assessment by moving away from more traditional child-based assessment activities. A psychologist working alone with a child in an office for a couple of hours obtains a paltry bit of information, compared to the rich data available from parents and teachers, which derive from their extended acquaintance and observations of the child both with other people and alone. If the psychologist wants to know how a child does out in the world, then it is valuable to ask people who are out in the world with the child. Data obtained from teachers are especilly important, because they have the opportunity to observe children in a more or less standard classroom situation and to compare children who are at the same developmental level.

It is often assumed, and sometimes rightly so, that teacher and parent ratings are biased. Because of this, some have chosen to abandon information from such informants in favor of more "objective" child-based assessment. This is a mistake for two reasons. For one thing, there is considerable evidence, at least for teachers, that rating scales can provide information that is superior to so-called "objective" data. The Teacher Rating of Academic Performance (Gresham, Reschly, & Carey, 1987), which asks teachers only seven questions, was superior in predicting special education placement to both the Wechsler Intelligence Scale for Children—Revised and the Peabody Individual Achievement Test. And this study focused upon the *academic* functioning of children, a bastion of psychometric excellence for test producers.

The second reason to downplay the criticism that informant ratings are too biased to be of any use is that it is because of their very bias that valuable information can be obtained. Even though informant ratings are undeniably biased, they are also "correct" in a very important way. By definition, a problem is a *perception* that a discrepancy exists between what one wants a situation to be and what the situation actually is. All the objective data in the world may point to the fact that a particular child has no problems whatsoever. Despite this evidence, one of the child's teachers believes the child does have a problem. A psychologist in this situation must understand and deal with the teacher's perception of the problem, and rating scales provide one means of learning more about the teacher's perception. Toward this end, a welcome change in some new rating scales is the addition of an importance dimension: The informant is asked to rate not only the extent to which a child has a particular problem, but also the extent to which that problem is important to the rater. In this way, the rater can indicate that a problem such as nail biting occurs frequently but is not very important, whereas fighting also occurs frequently and is of high importance to the rater. This allows an assessor to get quickly at the issue of fit between what is expected and important and what is actually occurring or not occurring as expected.

All too frequently, behavior rating scales are needed because the child is unable to respond to other measures that require direct interaction with an assessor. This is true of some infants and/or severely handicapped individuals whose ability to respond to questions or other stimuli is limited. In these situations, ratings by others who know the individuals provide a means of obtaining data on the children's functioning.

Problems and Issues with Informant Ratings

Despite the rise in popularity and obvious advantages of rating scales, there remains some well-founded skepticism about informant ratings. At the core of the issues surrounding the use of rating scales is simply this common question: "Do you believe everything everyone tells you?" That is, rating scale data are based upon perceptions that are colored and biased. A teacher wanting a child to receive some treatment (e.g., special education) may complete a rating scale about the child so as to make the child appear as needy as possible. As mentioned above, the perceptions are important in their own right. However, the assessor is also interested in learning the "truth" about a particular child. The best measurement science has to offer in defining truth is the convergence of data from multiple sources. Each piece of assessment data needs to be understood in its own right, but it also becomes part of a larger mosaic that provides a more stable and valid picture of a child.

The subjectivity inherent in rating scales may be compounded by sloppy scale construction. Subjectivity varies as a function of the level of analysis, the type of item, and the manner in which the item is scaled (Edelbrock, 1983, 1988). Consider, for example, the following hypothetical item that asks the rater to indicate the degree to which a child is "hyperactive," using the 5-point scale provided without indicating a time frame:

	Not true of student			Very true of student	
Is hyperactive	1	2	3	4	5

A rater examining this item has several questions to ask. What does hyperactive mean? What does "Not true of student" mean in terms of actual frequency, duration, and intensity of hyperactivity? What time frame should be used? Perhaps the child was hyperactive 6 months ago but is doing better today. Contrast the item above with the following item, where the rater has been given specific instructions to consider only the child's behavior over the past 1-week time period:

	Number of times behavior has occurred				
Gets out of seat without permission	0	1–3	4–6	7–10	11+

With this type of item, subjectivity is reduced because the "behavior" being evaluated is better operationalized, and there is less opportunity for different raters to misinterpret the item. In addition, the rater is asked to indicate the number of times a behavior occurred within a 1-week time period, rather than to provide a global interpretation of the behavior. Since most people will not have an exact count of this behavior, the item still reflects a perception, but the perception is more focused and there is less chance for misinterpretation. Obviously, it is possible to be overly specific and to construct items that are so trivial that they fail to have relevance to the typical case. Rating scale users must determine how the data will be applied and select a rating scale that has the time frame, level of analysis, and response format best suited to their needs.

The issue of bias and subjectivity in the use of rating scales can be understood better through a consideration of three specific types of bias: (1) halo effects, (2) leniency or severity, and (3) central tendency (Martin, Hooper, & Snow, 1986b; Saal, Downey, & Lahey, 1980). "Halo effects" pertain to the rater's failure to discriminate among independent aspects of the ratee's behavior (Saal et al., 1980). In other words, if a rater assumes that a particular child is "good," then all aspects of that child's functioning may be evaluated positively.

Whereas halo effects are noticeable within the individual being rated, the second type of bias, "leniency/severity bias," applies most frequently *within* the rater across people being rated. Just as it is common for some teachers to grade more leniently than others, so too it is possible for raters to be more lenient or more difficult across ratees. Saal et al. (1980) have described three versions of this type of bias:

a tendency to assign higher or lower ratings to an individual than is warranted by the ratee's behavior; a response set attributed to "easy" or "hard-nosed" raters whose ratings are consistently higher or lower than is warranted . . . ; and . . . a shift in mean ratings from the midpoint of the rating scale in the favorable or unfavorable direction. (p. 417)

The third type of bias, "central tendency bias," is related to a reluctance on the part of some raters to assign ratings at one extreme or another (Saal et al., 1980). Some raters are unwilling to go out on a limb and assign extreme ratings, even when such ratings are warranted (DeCotiis, 1977). This results in a restriction of range that causes both truly outstanding and truly atrocious children to appear more average than is actually the case.

Another issue facing the users of rating scales is who the informant should be. Obviously, the type and frequency of informants' contact with a child will affect their perceptions of a child's behavior. Cross-situational assessment of children with rating scales has produced varying results; this has led to concerns about validity (Achenbach, McConaughy, & Howell, 1987). For example, the correlations between mothers', fathers', and teachers' ratings of the same children are frequently reported to be in the low to middle .30s (Achenbach et al., 1987). Although such results have been construed as casting doubt on one or both informants, Achenbach et al. (1987) argue that different informants validly contribute different information. That is, "low correlations between informants may indicate that the target variables differ from one situation to another, rather than that the informants' reports are invalid or unreliable" (p. 213). Such differences may result from the focus by the respondent on different dimensions of behavior. For example, teachers may be more oriented to a behavior such as paying attention, while parents may key in on whether the child is responsible in his or her daily activities.

Convenience and efficiency are primary reasons for the widespread use of rating scales. However, it should be kept in mind that rating scales are convenient to the assessor but may be very inconvenient to the person completing the rating scale. It may be disturbing for some teachers to find a mailbox full of rating scales after having referred a child. They may correctly believe that the completion of the forms does not tell the whole story about a child. Problems in this area can be averted by providing raters with a rationale for using rating scales and by giving them an opportunity to add further information in person. In addition, a continuing relationship with the raters will be facilitated by providing feedback concerning the results of the ratings. These simple courtesies help to establish a more favorable cost–benefit ratio for the raters by insuring that they get something in return for the time spent completing the rating forms.

Review of Selected Informant Rating Scales

Our discussion of informant rating scales concludes with brief reviews of selected rating scales. The instruments identified for review have been selected on the basis of being widely used in both research and practice. It is relatively safe to assume that the scales are widely used, because they are technically sound and/or they have proven valuable in the diagnosis or treatment of behavior and emotional problems.

Child Behavior Checklist

The Child Behavior Checklist (CBCL; Achenbach & Edelbrock, 1983) offers two primary advantages to potential consumers of informant rating scales. First, the technical foundation on which it is based provides perhaps the strongest empirical support of all the informant rating scales. Second, the authors have provided both parent and teacher versions of the scale, thus allowing for comparisons across settings and thereby facilitating the goal of multiple operationalism. In addition to the teacher and parent informant rating versions, there is also a Youth Self-Report Form (Achenbach & Edelbrock, 1986) and a Direct Observation Scale. Completing either the teacher or parent versions of the CBCL requires approximately 15 minutes; this is time well spent in the identification of behaviors that informants view as being a high priority for intervention.

The parent and teacher versions differ slightly. Parents rate their child across 20 Social Competence and 118 Behavior Problem items. Behavior Problem items are rated using a 0–1–2 indexing of how true the item is of the child now and within the past 6 months (0, behavior "not true" of child; 1, behavior "sometimes or somewhat true" of child; and 2, behavior "very true or often true" of child). The Teacher Report Form of the CBCL (Achenbach & Edelbrock, 1986) has approximately an 80% overlap with the parent version, with items from the parent version pertaining only to home problems (e.g., bedwetting) being replaced by items related to school problems. Within the Behavior Problem section, 91 items have counterparts rated by parents. The Teacher Report Form is designed to obtain reports of children's academic performance, adaptive functioning, and behavior problems. The same 0–1–2 scaling format used in the parent version is also used for the Behavior Problem section of the teacher version.

TABLE 16.1. Syndromes Derived from the Parent Version of the Child Behavior Checklist

Group	Internalizing syndromes	Mixed syndromes	Externalizing syndromes
Boys age 6–11	1. Anxious 2. Social Withdrawal	3. Unpopular 4. Self-Destructive 5. Obsessive– Compulsive	6. Inattentive 7. Nervous–Overactive 8. Aggressive
Boys age 12–16	1. Social Withdrawal 2. Anxious	3. Unpopular 4. Obsessive– Compulsive 5. Immature 6. Self-Destructive	7. Inattentive 8. Aggressive
Girls age 6–11	1. Anxious 2. Social Withdrawal	3. Depressed 4. Unpopular 5. Self-Destructive	6. Inattentive 7. Nervous–Overactive 8. Aggressive
Girls age 12–16	1. Anxious 2. Social Withdrawal	3. Depressed 4. Immature 5. Self-Destructive	6. Inattentive 7. Unpopular 8. Delinquent 9. Aggressive

Note. From "Informant Reports" by C. S. Edlebrock, 1988, in E. S. Shapiro and T. R. Kratochwill (Eds.), *Behavioral Assessment in Schools: Conceptual Foundations and Practical Applications* (p. 368), New York: Guilford Press: Copyright 1988 by the Guilford Press. Reprinted by permission.

Data Obtained. The CBCL has two broad-bond factors, Externalizing and Internalizing. Under each are several narrow-band syndromes for each age and sex group. Table 16.1 presents the various syndromes derived for the parent version, and Table 16.2 presents syndromes for the teacher version of the CBCL. In general, "internalizing" syndromes pertain to problems within an individual such as anxiety and depression, whereas "externalizing" syndromes consist of acting-out behaviors such as hyperactivity and aggression. For internalizing disorders, self-report instruments are usually a better choice than informant rating scales (Witt, Cavell, Carey, Heffer, & Martens, 1988). Although not based on a national sample, adequate norms do exist for both the teacher and parent forms of the CBCL and can be used to derive T-scores for each age and sex group.

Reliability and Validity. Both the parent and teacher forms of the CBCL have adequate reliability. For the parent version, the test's authors reported test–retest reliability coefficients for the narrow-band factors to range from .61 (Obsessive–Compulsive) to .96 (Hyperactive), with a median 1-week test–retest reliability coefficient of .81. The broad-band factors had 1-week stability coefficients of .82 for Internalizing and .91 for Externalizing. Reliability coefficients for the total scales were generally in the low .90s. On the teacher version, Pearson correlations for 1-week test–retest reliabilities ranged from .86 for Adaptive Behavior to .93 for School Performance.

Support for the validity of the CBCL is encouraging. The teacher version has been shown to discriminate between clinical and nonclinical populations, including specific diagnostic subgroups as well as children who are in special education versus regular class placement (Edelbrock, 1988). Especially noteworthy, for users of the CBCL in particular and of informant ratings in general who have the general concern that ratings are biased *perceptions*, are the very high correlations between the teacher version and *observations* of children's behavior (Edelbrock, 1988). The parent version also has considerable data to suggest that it is measuring what it is supposed to measure. More specifically, the parent version has been shown to correlate significantly with similar instruments, such as the Conners Parent Rating Scale (Conners, 1973) and the Revised Behavior Problem Checklist (Quay & Peterson, 1983).

TABLE 16.2. Syndromes Derived from the Teacher Version of the Child Behavior Checklist

Group	Internalizing syndromes	Mixed syndromes	Externalizing syndromes
Boys age 4–5	1. Social Withdrawal 2. Depressed 3. Immature 4. Somatic Complaints	5. Sex Problems	6. Schizoid 7. Aggressive 8. Delinquent
Boys age 6–11	1. Schizoid or Anxious 2. Depressed 3. Uncommunicative 4. Obsessive– Compulsive 5. Somatic Complaints	6. Social Withdrawal	7. Hyperactive 8. Aggressive 9. Delinquent
Boys age 12–16	1. Somatic Complaints 2. Schizoid 3. Uncommunicative 4. Immature 5. Obsessive– Compulsive	6. Hostile Withdrawal	7. Delinquent 8. Aggressive 9. Hyperactive
Girls age 4–5	1. Somatic Complaints 2. Depressed 3. Schizoid or Anxious 4. Social Withdrawal	5. Obese	6. Aggressive 7. Sex Problems 8. Hyperactive
Girls age 6–11	1. Depressed 2. Social Withdrawal 3. Somatic Withdrawal 4. Schizoid–Obsessive		5. Hyperactive 6. Sex Problems 7. Delinquent 8. Aggressive

Girls age 12–16	1. Anxious–Obsessive
	2. Somatic Complaints
	3. Schizoid
	4. Depressed
	   Withdrawal
		5. Immature–
		   Hyperactive
			6. Delinquent
			7. Aggressive
			8. Cruel

Note. From "Informant Reports" by C. S. Edlebrock, 1988, in E. S. Shapiro and T. R. Kratochwill (Eds.), *Behavioral Assessment in Schools: Conceptual Foundations and Practical Applications* (p. 367), New York: Guilford Press. Copyright 1988 by the Guilford Press. Reprinted by permission.

Concluding Comments. Both the parent and teacher versions of the CBCL are well-designed instruments that have amassed an impressive foundation of empirical support. Although lacking a nationally representative sample, the CBCL is still one of the most technically sound instruments of its kind. The real value of both versions is in describing children's behavior in a concise but comprehensive and meaningful fashion in a short amount of time.

The Conners Rating Scales

The Conners Rating Scales represent another informant rating instrument with both teacher and parent versions available. Both of these scales have been used extensively in the diagnosis of hyperactivity in children and in treatment efficacy studies. In fact, both instruments have been included in a standard assessment battery recommended by the National Institute of Mental Health for research in childhood psychopharmacology (Martin, Hooper, & Snow, 1986a).

The Conners Teacher Rating Scale is composed of 39 items on which teachers are asked to indicate the extent to which behaviors or problems (e.g., defiant, excitable) are present in the child being evaluated. A 4-point scale ranging from "not at all present" to "very much present" is used to scale the ratings. The Conners Parent Rating Scale is a 48-item instrument, with some versions of the instrument scaled in the same way as the teacher scale and some requiring parents to rate items on a 4-point scale ranging from "not at all" (0) to "very much" (3).

A major shortcoming of both instruments is the presence of numerous versions. Some versions are simply shorter versions of the originals, whereas others have incorporated wording variations. For the test consumer, this means that care must be exercised in the selection of the instrument, because norms for one version may not be applicable to slightly different versions.

Data Obtained. Data from the Teacher Rating Scale can be interpreted using the six scales derived by Trites, Blouin, and La Prade (1979): Hyperactivity, Conduct Problem, Emotional Overindulgent, Anxious–Passive, Asocial, and Daydream–Attendance Problem. Norms based upon an extremely limited sample are available in the manual for each of these scales. The Parent Rating Scale yields scores on six primary factors: Conduct Problem I (e.g., fighting), Learning Problem, Psychosomatic, Impulsive–Hyperactive, Conduct Problem II (e.g., disobedience), and Anxiety (Goyette, Conners, & Ulrich, 1978). In addition, a 10-item Hyperactivity index can be derived from both the parent and teacher versions; however, the two may not be comparable (Edelbrock, 1988).

Reliability and Validity. Evaluating the psychometric underpinnings of the Conners scales is a difficult task because of the number of different versions of the scales and the varying content, items, and length of the subscales. Fortunately, for most versions, reliability and validity data are adequate, given that Conners Rating Scales are most frequently used for screening or in combination with other, more psychometrically sound methods of assessment.

Reliability coefficients for both the parent and teacher versions have ranged from the low .30s for 1-year test–retest to the middle .90s for more short-term test–retest coefficients (Conners, 1973; Glow, Glow, & Rump, 1982). Internal consistency of both scales is typically about .70 (Goyette et al., 1978). Given that reliability coefficients for the subscales have been shown to be questionable (Edelbrock, 1988), their use in making important diagnostic or treatment decisions would be difficult to defend.

The original factor-analytic work conducted with the Teacher Rating Scale by Conners (1969) employed 103 children with attention deficit disorder or behavior disorder, and yielded five orthogonal factors: Conduct Problem, Inattentive–Passive, Tension–Anxiety, Hyperactivity, and Social Ability. This last factor was not included in the scoring. The composition of some of the factors and wording of five items were changed by Conners (1973) in order to have 10 items in common with the Parent Rating Scale (Conners, 1970).

A second factor-analytic study was conducted by Werry, Sprague, and Cohen (1975) with this revised Teacher Rating Scale on 291 normal children in New Zealand. Of the original four factors, Werry et al. found concordance with Conners's first factor, Conduct Problem. The Inattentive–Passive factor and Hyperactivity factor presented as one factor, and the Tension–Anxiety factor appeared highly unstable. Trites et. al. (1979) performed another factor analysis on the revised scale (Conners, 1973). This study was completed on 19,583 elemenary school children (English-speaking) in Canada. The results produced similar findings, with Hyperactivity and Conduct Disorder factors extracted and four additional factors accounting for smaller percentages of the variance. The children in this normative sample ranged in age from 4 to 12. A revised 28-item Teacher Rating Scale was developed by Goyette et al. (1978), and three factors were extracted accounting for 61.7% of the variance. These were identified as Conduct Problem, Hyperactivity, and Inattentive–Passive. The normative group consisted of 383 children ranging in age from 3 to 17.

Trites et al. (1979) generated interitem correlations for each of the six derived Teacher Rating Scale factors. These correlations ranged form .27 to .52. Alpha coefficients for each of the scales fell into the moderate range of .61 on Daydreams/Attendance Problems to .95 on Hyperactivity. Using a five-factor solution, Lahey, Green, and Forehand (1980) found moderate correlations between the Conduct Problem, Hyperactivity, Inattentive–Passive, and Social Ability scales. Generally, the internal consistency of the 39-item Teacher Rating Scale has been adequate, and Conners (1973) reported test–retest reliability ranging from about .70 to

.90 over a 1-month interval. Glow et al. (1982) found that test–retest correlations ranged from .01 for Anxious to Please subscale to .57 for the total score on the Adelaide version of the Teacher Rating Scale, over a 1-year period.

Validity for the Conners Rating Scales has been established by "(1) highly significant correlations with many other measures of child behavior and psychopathology, (2) the ability to discriminate well between normal and hyperactive children, (3) significant discrimination between diagnostic subgroups of children, and (4) proven sensitivity to drug effects" (Edelbrock, 1988, p. 365). There is a noticeable absence of any relationship between rating data and observational data, thus bringing into question whether informant perceptions correspond to reality (Kivlahan, Siegel, & Ullman, 1982; Martin et al., 1986b).

Concluding Comments. The Conners Rating Scales continue to remain a relatively popular choice for both researchers and practitioners. This is somewhat surprising, given the availability of instruments (e.g., the CBCL) that appear to be superior in content, format, psychometric adequacy, and ease of use. In the past, consumers have had to tolerate a confusing array of alternative versions of the scale; this fact, combined with the lack of an organized manual, has made it difficult to use, compare, and correctly interpret scores. Given the large research base for the Conners, the discrepancy is very large between what is and what could be for this instrument.

Walker Problem Behavior Identification Checklist

The Walker Problem Behavior Identification Checklist (WPBIC; Walker, 1983) is a 50-item checklist designed for use with elementary school children for the purpose of identifying behavior problems. Informants are asked to indicate whether specific behaviors (e.g., temper tantrums) have or have not occurred during a 2-month period preceding the rating. An interesting addition to the WPBIC is the weighting of behaviors in terms of the degree to which they interfere with classroom adjustment. Obviously, some

behaviors are more detrimental to classroom functioning than others, and the WPIC provides a means of incorporating this into a total score. In addition, the items were generated by classroom teachers, thus further increasing the social validity of the instrument.

Data Obtained. The WPBIC yields scores on each of five empirically derived factors. These factors are listed below, along with examples of behaviors that correspond to the factors:

1. *Acting Out*—complains about unfairness and/or discrimination toward self; becomes upset when things don't go his or her way; has temper tantrums.
2. *Withdrawal*—does not engage in group activities; has no friends; does not initiate relationships with others.
3. *Distractibility*—overactive, restless, and continually shifts body position; continually seeks attention; easily distracted.
4. *Disturbed Peer Relations*—babbles to self; comments that nobody likes him or her; refers to self as dumb, stupid, or incapable.
5. *Immaturity*—reacts to stressful situations with body aches, headaches, or stomachaches; has nervous tics; weeps or cries without provocation.'

Scores can be calculated for each of these factors by comparing the weighted raw scores (i.e., weighted in terms of importance) to a normative sample to obtain a T-score with a mean of 50 and a standard deviation of 10. The norms are not based upon a nationally representative sample of children, and this represents a major weakness of the instrument.

Reliability and Validity. Traditional measures of test reliability have yielded good results of the WPBIC, with split-half reliabilities of .98 reported in the manual and test–retest coefficients (over approximately a 1-month period) reported to be in the .80s. Reliability data for the subscales are lacking.

Minimal validity data have been reported in the test manual. Total scores have been shown to be significantly different for children classified as behavior-disordered versus a normal comparison group. When WPBIC total score were correlated with three criteria (i.e., whether or not the child had been examined by a psychologist or been referred to a clinical psychiatric facility; whether or not the child was receiving special education programming; or whether or not the child was receiving homebound instruction because of his or her inability to profit from classroom instruction due to behavior problems), the biserial correlation was .68, indicating that the WPBIC is predictive of behavioral disturbance in elementary school children (Witt, Cavett, et al., 1988).

Concluding Comments. Mace (1985) has noted that the limitations of the WPBIC include "regionally restricted and unspecified characteristics [of the] normative samples, a lack of interrater agreement measures, many items that refer to mentalistic constructed rather than observable behavior, . . . and no validation of the correspondence between checklist items and directly observed behavior" (p. 1691). These problems also obviously apply to other instruments and are partially counterbalanced by the WPBIC's ability to differentiate children with known problems from normal children. The weighing of various behaviors in terms of importance is a noteworthy strength.

SELF-REPORT RATING SCALES

Historically, child self-report rating scales have not been routinely included in the psychological or educational assessment of children. Developmentally and behaviorally oriented psychologists, however, have come to recognize the merit of including child self-ratings in the assessment process (Garber, 1984; Mash & Terdal, 1981; Ollendick & Hersen, 1984; Witt, Cavell, et al., 1988). Utilizing information from children in a multiple-source approach to assessment often has involved obtaining children's *verbal* self-report via structured or unstructured clinical interviews. Although problems do exist in using self-ratings with children (e.g., linguistic and cognitive differences in children because of uneven developmental changes across and within age groups), such objective

data are more conducive to empirical studies of reliability and validity than are informally collected verbal self-report data. Child self-report rating scales should appeal, therefore, to an assessor interested in a scientific approach to measuring overt and covert behavior in children.

In this section, developmental issues pertaining to child self-rating scales are discussed first. Next, an overview of some of the more psychometrically sound and/or frequently used self-rating instruments available for children and adolescents is provided. A substantial portion of this section will be devoted to a table (see Table 16.3) in which descriptive and evaluative information with regard to various self-rating scales is presented. Further information on some of the self-ratings described in this section can be found in *Tests and Measurements in Child Development: Handbook II* (Johnson, 1976) or *The Ninth Mental Measurements Yearbook* (Mitchell, 1985). Some of the information presented in this section was first discussed in Witt, Cavell, et al. (1988).

Assessment and Developmental Issues in Child Self-Ratings

A number of problems have been identified with regard to child self-ratings (Witt, Cavell, et al., 1988). Although some researchers have reported agreement between child self-ratings and parent ratings of childhood behavior problems such as fears (Bondy, Sheslow, & Garcia, 1985), low levels of convergence between child self-ratings and parent ratings or observed behavior have generally been reported (Finch & Rogers, 1984; Ollendick & Meador, 1984). Given the complex skills required for responding to self-ratings, it is not surprising that discrepancies between child self-reports and other assessment methods have been found. For example, variables associated with a given child, such as impulse control or written and receptive language skills, interact with the age-appropriateness of an instrument's grammar, vocabulary, and choice format to influence responses obtained from self-ratings.

To resolve some of the difficulties with child self-ratings, practitioners using such instruments should attend to developmental considerations with regard to stimulus and response complexity. For example, test stimuli should be appropriate for the age and skill level of the population of interest (Byrd & Gholson, 1984). In addition, response formats for child self-ratings should be chosen with an appreciation of how cognitive skills, such as seriation or continuous quantities (Inhelder & Piaget, 1964; Inhelder, Sinclair, & Bovet, 1974), influence a child's ability to understand the units and anchors of a given self-rating scale.

Self-Ratings of Global Personality Characteristics and Behavior

Behavior checklists and personality self-report inventories allow the assessor to obtain information with regard to a child's or adolescent's personal perspective on a number of variables simultaneously. Comparison to data obtained from such self-report instruments to information obtained from other informants (e.g., parents, teachers, peers, other professionals) provides the assessor with a multisource representation of the child's problems. However, the length of these instruments often inhibits their frequent use, and the theoretical underpinnings of some of them may not appeal to all psychologists.

Personality Inventories

As shown in Table 16.3, several self-report personality inventories are available for use with children and adolescents. The Millon Adolescent Personality Inventory (MAPI; Millon, Green, & Meager, 1982) was developed in accordance with Millon's personality theory, which postulates eight styles of functioning. These eight personality styles are based on two dimensions that form a 4 × 2 matrix. The first dimension relates to adolescents' pursuit of positive reinforcement and the avoidance of emotional pain and distress, whereas the second dimension represents coping behaviors used to maximize reinforcement and minimize pain or discomfort. A large ($n = 2,157$) representative sample was used to standardize the MAPI. Two strengths of the MAPI are that the items have been written at a sixth-grade reading level and that the manual is comprehensive. Computer reports for the MAPI provide a descriptive profile of an adolescent's thoughts and feelings. One limitation of the MAPI is a lack of empirical validation to confirm the underlying structure of the inventory. The MAPI is recommended for research in which aspects of adolescent personality are a concern.

Two other personality inventories are the Minnesota Multiphasic Personality Inventory (MMPI; Hathaway & Monachesi, 1963) and the Children's Personality Questionnaire (CPQ; Porter & Cattell, 1979). Although the MMPI was developed originally for use with adults, adolescent norms have been developed (Marks, Seeman, & Haller, 1974). The MMPI has been used extensively with adolescents; however, its length and scoring time have severely restricted its utility. The MMPI is recommended as a research instrument for the assessment of broad categories of personality. (For a more detailed discussion, see Chapter 14, this volume.)

The CPQ was developed for young children and was derived from the adult personality inventory developed by Cattell. The CPQ is easily scored, but it has a lengthy administration time, and the manual is overly jargonistic. Although extensive normative data are available, no information is provided with regard to demographic variables. In addition, the manual does not effectively facilitate interpretation of CPQ scores. The CPQ is not recommended for general clinical use by psychologists.

Behavior Checklists

The Behavior Rating Profile (BRP; Brown & Hammill, 1978), as described in Table 16.3, is a relatively short instrument designed to assess a child's behavior at home, at school, and with peers, as opposed to his or her personality characteristics. A large representative sample ($n = 1,326$) was used to standardize the BRP. Parent and teacher report forms are available. Although further validation of the BRP is required, its attention to the situational specificity of a child's behavior may assist in treatment planning.

Another promising scale is the CBCL Youth Self-Report Form (CBCL-YSRF; Achenbach & Edelbrock, 1986). CBCL par-

TABLE 16.3. Self-Report Rating Scales for Use with Children and Adolescents

Instrument	Age range	Response format	Subscales	Reliability and validity data
Personality inventories				
Millon Adolescent Personality Inventory (MAPI; Millon, Green, & Meagher, 1982)	13–19 years	150 items; true–false	Introversion; Inhibited; Cooperative; Sociable; Confident; Forceful; Respectful; Sensitive	Internal consistency = .67–.82. Test–retest = .69–.88 (5-mo.); .55–.68 (1-yr.). MAPI has been evaluated in relation to other personality scales (e.g., California Psychological Inventory, Edwards Personal Preference Survey). MAPI also has been factor-analyzed.
Minnesota Multiphasic Personality Inventory (MMPI [adolescent norms]; Hathaway & Monachesi, 1963)	14–16 years	550 items (alternate forms, 168 items); true–false	Cannot Say; Correction; Lie; Infrequency; Hypochondriasis; Depression; Hysteria; Psychopathic Deviate; Masculinity–Femininity; Paranoia; Psychasthenia; Schizophrenia; Hypomania; Social Introversion	Test–retest = .32–.56 (3-yr.). MMPI has extensive concurrent and predictive validity with adolescents. The shortened form (n = .68) has been used frequently with adolescents, although this scale diminishes in validity and reliability.
Children's Personality Questionnaire (CPQ: Porter & Cattell, 1979)	8–12 years	Two forms; 140 items per form	14 dichotomous scores (e.g., dull vs. bright; sober vs. enthusiastic)	Alternate form = .20–.29. Test–retest = .28–.87 (1-wk.). Numerous validity studies have been conducted assessing low and high achievers, delinquents, and children with personality disorders.
Behavior checklists				
Children Behavior Checklist, Youth Self-Report Form (CBCL-YSRF; Achenbach & Edelbrock, 1986)	11–18 years	120 items; not true–very true	Not available	Test–retest = .69 (6-mo.). Limited data are available at this time. Convergent validity has been demonstrated between the CBCL-YSRF total score and CBCLs completed by mothers and clinicians for a sample of thirty 12- to 17-year-olds seen at a community mental health center.

(continued)

TABLE 16.3. (*continued*)

Instrument	Age range	Response format	Subscales	Reliability and validity data
Behavior Rating Profile (BRP [self-report form]; Brown & Hammill, 1978)	6–13 years	60 items; three scales, 20 items per scale; true–false	Peer; Home; School	Internal consistency = .74–.87. Concurrent validity of BRP with other behavior rating scales and Vineland Social Maturity Scale across three groups of behaviorally handicapped youths (inpatient psychiatric patients, public school emotionally disturbed, learning-disabled students). Convergent validity with BRP as rated by parents and teachers. BRP distinguishes psychiatrically disturbed from nondisturbed youths.
			Anxiety	
Revised Children's Manifest Anxiety Scale (RCMAS; Reynolds & Richmond, 1978, 1985)	6–17 years	37 items; true–false	Lie; Worry; Physiological; Concentration; Total Anxiety	Internal consistency = .78–.85. Test-retest = .68 (9-mo.); .98 (3-wk.). Concurrent validity with STAIC; convergent validity with Walker Problem Behavior Identification Checklist (Walker, 1983); coefficients of congruence = .96–.99 between gender and ethnic groups; no relation to State Anxiety on STAIC.
State–Trait Anxiety Inventory for Children (STAIC; Spielberger, 1973)	9–12 years	40 items (20 State and 20 Trait); 3-point scale	State Anxiety; Trait Anxiety	Internal consistency = .78–.87, Test-retest median = .68 for Trait and .39 for State (6-wk.). Concurrent validity with RCMAS, GASC, California Achievement Test, STAI scores, and teacher-assigned grades. Scores on State version change in response to stressful situations.
State–Trait Anxiety Inventory (STAI; Spielberger, 1983)	13 years and above	40 items (20 State and 20 Trait); 3-point scale	State Anxiety; Trait Anxiety	Internal consistency = .86–.90. Test-retest median = .73 for Trait and .48 for State (30-day). Concurrent validity with BDI and Children's Depression Adjective Checklist scores of adolescent psychiatric inpatients; stable factor structure.

Measure	Age/Grade	Format	Factors/Content	Reliability/Validity
Generalized Anxiety Scale for Children (GASC; Sarason, Davidson, Lighthall, Waite, & Ruebush, 1960)	Grades 1–9	45 items; yes–no	Generalized Anxiety; Lie	Test–retest = .64–.79 (4-mo.), dependent on type of administrator. Concurrent validity coefficients with test anxiety, achievement, and IQ. Zero order correlations with Lie scale of CMAS.
Test Anxiety Scale for Children (TASC; Sarason et al., 1960)	Grades 1–9	30 items; yes–no	Not applicable	Internal consistency = .82–.89. Test–retest = .65–82 (2-mo.); .55–.78 (4-mo.). Same validity coefficients as with the GASC.

Fears

Measure	Age/Grade	Format	Factors/Content	Reliability/Validity
Fear Survey Schedule for Children (FSSC; Scherer & Nakamura, 1968)	9–12 years	80 items; 5-point scale (none–very much)	Failure; Major and Minor Fears; Medical; Death; Dark; Home–School; Miscellaneous Fears	Internal consistency (Spearman–Brown formula) = .94. Test–retest = .63–.83, depending on gender and grade of child. Concurrent validity with CMAS. Factor analysis indicated eight fear content areas. Convergent validity with mothers' report of children's fears.
Fear Survey Schedule for Children—Revised (FSSC-R; Ollendick, 1983)	8–18 years	80 items; 3-point scale (none–a lot)	Failure and Criticism; Unknown; Injury and Small Animals; Danger and Death; Medical Fears	Internal consistency = .92–.95. Test–retest = .81–.89 (1-wk.); .55–.62 (3-mo.). Concurrent validity with Trait Anxiety on STAIC, self-concept, and locus of control. Factor analyses indicated five factors. In addition, FSSC-R distinguished a matched control group from a clinical group of school-phobic youths.
Children's Fear Survey Schedule (CFSS; Ryall & Dietiker, 1979)	4–12 years	48 items; 3-point scale (not afraid–very afraid)	Not applicable	Test–retest (K–6th grade) = .79–.91 (1-wk.). CFSS was able to distinguish 24 outpatient children from 24 nonreferred public school children matched on age, sex, and grade.

(continued)

TABLE 16.3. (*continued*)

Instrument	Age range	Response format	Subscales	Reliability and validity data
			Depression	
Children's Depression Inventory (CDI; Kovacs & Beck, 1977)	8–17 years	27 items; child chooses best of three sentences	Not applicable	Internal consistency - .70–.89. Test–retest = .51 (2-wk.); .74–77 (3-wk.); .43 (1-mo.); .41–.69 (1-yr.). The CDI has been evaluated in numerous validation studies. Concurrent validity has been established with social skills, dysphoric mood, problem solving, academic achievement, overt behavior, anxiety, stress, and life events. Some evidence of convergent validity has been obtained with parental report. Factor analyses have indicated that the CDI is multidimensional. In addition, the CDI has been able to distinguish depressed from nondepressed youths and is sensitive to treatment effects.
Beck Depression Inventory (BDI; Beck, Ward, Mendelson, Mock, & Erbaugh 1961)	12 years and above	21 items; person chooses best of four sentences	Not applicable	Internal consistency = .79–.90. Test–retest (inpatient youths) = .69 (5-day); .75 (6-wk.). The BDI has been used extensively with normal and psychiatric adolescents. Concurrent validity has been obtained with other depression measures, assertion, dysphoric mood, anxiety, problem solving, academic achievement, self-esteem, locus of control, and life events. The BDI is also able to distinguish depressed from nondepressed adolescents and is sensitive to treatment effects for depression.

Reynolds Adolescent Depression Scale (RADS; Reynolds, 1985b)	12–17 years	30 items; 4-point scale	Not applicable	Internal consistency = .91–.96. Split-half = .91. Test–retest = .80 (6-wk.); .79 (3-mo.); .63 (1-yr.). The RADS has been extensively validated. Concurrent validity has been established with other depression measures, self-esteem, loneliness, anxiety, and stressful life events. Moreover, convergence validity has been obtained between the RADS and a semistructured interview of depression. The RADS has also been shown to be sensitive to treatment effects.
Center for Epidemiological Studies Depression Scale For Children (CES-DC; Weissman, Orvaschel, & Padian, 1980)	6 years and above	20 items; 4-point scale (none–a lot)	Not applicable	Internal consistency (inpatient youths) = .77–.86. Test–retest = .12–.69 (2-wk.). The CES-DC has been used infrequently by researchers. Concurrent validity is limited to a modest correlation with the CDI and to distinguishing children of high and low risk for depression. Also, the CES-DC has obtained equivocal results concerning its ability to distinguish clinically depressed from nondepressed youths.
Depression Self-Rating Scale (DSRS; Birleson, 1980)	6–13 years	18 items; 3-point scale	Not applicable	Internal consistency = .73–.86. Split-half = .61–.67. Test–Retest = .80 (duration unspecified). The DSRS has preliminary concurrent validation with the CDI. Also, convergent validity has been reported with a semistructured interview of depression. The DSRS has some support for its ability to distinguish depressed from nondepressed children.

Reinforcement/activities

Children's Reinforcement Survey Schedule (CRSS; Cautela & Kastenbaum, 1967)	Grades K–3 use first form; grades 4–6 use 75-item form	Two forms, each 25 items; third form, 75 items (dislike–like very much)	Not applicable	Test–Retest (141 elementary school children) = .48–.72. Male responses were less stable than those of females. The CRSS has been used primarily to identify reinforcing stimuli and their associated valences.

(continued)

TABLE 16.3. (*continued*)

Instrument	Age range	Response format	Subscales	Reliability and validity data
Adolescent Activity Checklist (AAC; Carey, Kelley, Buss, & Scott, 1986)	Grades 7–12	100 items rated for frequency and valence; 50 pleasant and 50 unpleasant items	Pleasant Events; Unpleasant Events	Internal consistency = .94–.95. Homogeneity median = .48 for Pleasant Events; .53 for Unpleasant Events. Criterion-related validity with self-ratings of depressive behaviors. No significant differences in age, grade, race, or socioeconomic status.
			Major life events	
Junior High Life Experiences Survey (JHLES; Swearingen & Cohen, 1985)	Grades 7–8	39 items; 7-point scale	Not applicable	Reliability data not reported. Initial concurrent validity has been established with the STAIC and BDI. Gender differences were found on the JHLES, with males scoring lower than females on the number of negative and uncontrollable events and negative impact ratings.
Life Event Record (LER; Coddington, 1972)	Grades K–12 (four forms)	30–42 items, depending on age	Not applicable	Reliability data not reported. Concurrent validity with rating of health status, problem-solving, depression, locus of control, accident frequency, and other related constructs.
Life Events Checklist (LEC; Johnson & McCutcheon, 1980)	10–17 years	44 items (frequency, valence, and impact)	Not applicable	Test–retest = .69–.72 (2-wk.). Concurrent validity with BDI, locus of control, Trait Anxiety on STAIC, reports of school days missed, and health problems. No relation was found between social desirability and LEC scores.

Self-evaluation

Measure	Age/Grade	Format	Subscales	Psychometric properties
Self-Esteem Inventory (SEI; Coopersmith, 1967)	8–15 years	58 items; like me–unlike me	General Self; Home–Parents; School–Academic; Social Self–Peers; Lie (School Form)	Internal consistency = .80–.92. Test–retest = .88 (5-wk.); .64 (12-mo.); .42–.70 (3-yr.). Concurrent validity with SPPC, other measures of self-concept, and measures of social desirability. Factor analyses have yielded five to nine factors somewhat related to School Form subscales.
Self-Perception Profile for Children (SPPC; Harter, 1982)	Grades 3–7	36 items; structured alternative format	Scholastic Competence; Social Acceptance; Athletic Competence; Physical Appearance; Conduct/Behavior; Self-Worth	Internal consistency (for subscales) = .72–.87. Test–retest = .70–.87 (3-mo.); .69–.80 (9-mo.). Concurrent validity with SEI. Factor analyses indicated five factors, thus supporting subscale structure. Grade and gender differences found for some subscales.
Self-Observation Scales (SOS; Stenner & Katzenmeyer, 1979)	Grades K–12	50–72 items across forms; yes–no	Self-Acceptance; Self-Security; Social Maturity; School Affiliation; Teacher Affiliation; Peer Affiliation; Social Confidence; Self-Assertion	Internal consistency (K–6th grade) = .65–.85. Test–retest = .73–.91 (1-wk.). Validity studies reported only for K–3 and 4–6 forms. SOS scores discriminated between groups of teacher-rated "socially insecure," "aggressive," and "very healthy" children. Factor analyses used to derive subscales for each form.
Piers–Harris Self-Concept Scale (PHSCS; Piers & Harris, 1969)	Grades 4–12	80 items; yes–no	Behavior; School and Intellectual Status; Physical Appearance and Attributes; Anxiety; Popularity; Satisfaction; Happiness cluster scores	Internal consistency (for total score) = .88–.90; (for cluster scores) = .73–.81. Test–retest = .42–.96. Convergent validity with SEI and other measures of self-concept. Factor analyses have inconsistently supported structure of cluster scores. PHSCS has discriminated between racial, age, and clinical groups in numerous studies.
Offer Self-Image Questionnaire for Adolescents (OSIQ; Offer & Howard, 1972)	13–19 years	130 items; 6-point scale (describes me very well–does not describe me at all)	12 subscales within five categories (Psychological Self, Sexual Self, Social Self, Familial Self, Coping Self, Total	Internal consistency = .30–.91. Test–retest = .49–.81. Concurrent validity with measures of self-concept, "mental health," and "adjustment." Numerous studies have found OSIQ discriminates between age and gender groups and distinguishes clinical from normal groups.

(continued)

TABLE 16.3. (*continued*)

Instrument	Age range	Response format	Subscales	Reliability and validity data
Social behavior				
Children's Self-Efficacy for Peer Interaction Scale (CSPIS; Wheeler & Ladd, 1982)	Grades 3–5	22 items; 4-point scale (hard–easy)	Total score; Conflict and Nonconflict factors	Internal consistency = .73–.85. Test–retest = .80–.90 (2-wk.). Concurrent validity with PHSCS subscales (Physical), peer ratings, sociometrics, and teacher ratings of social self-efficacy. Two factors obtained (Conflict and Nonconflict situations).
Children's Action Tendency Scale (CATS; Deluty, 1979)	Grades 3–6	39 items; three paired-comparison alternatives	Total score; Aggressiveness, Submissiveness, and Assertiveness scores	Internal consistency = .63–.77. Test–retest = .48–.57 (4-mo.). Concurrent validity of subscale scores with respective peer and teacher ratings. Assertiveness and Aggressiveness scores correlated with peer report of behavioral adjustment, sociometric measures of popularity, and PHSCS (depending on gender) in expected directions.
Children's Assertive Behavior Scale (CABS; Michelson & Wood, 1982)	Grades 4–6	27 items; 5-point scale (passive–assertive-aggressive responses)	Total Assertive Behavior; Passive and Aggressive scores	Internal consistency = .77–.80. Test–retest = .66–.86 (4-wk.). Concurrent validity with behavioral observations and peer, parent, and teacher ratings of social skill. Convergent validity with measures of social competence. Factor analyses revealed homogeneous factor structure. Discriminated children trained in social skills from untrained children.
Children's Inventory of Anger (CIA; Nelson & Finch, 1973)	Grades 4–8	71 items; 4-point scale ("I don't care"–"I'm furious" faces)	Six factor scores	Internal consistency = .96. Test–retest = .82 (3-mo.). Concurrent validity with peer and "blind" staff ratings of anger control problems in hospitalized (psychiatric) children. Modestly correlated with Acting-Out factor of Walker Problem Behavior Identification Checklist (teacher rating). Factor analyses yielded six factors reflecting sources of anger.

Measure	Age	Format	Factors/Score	Psychometric properties
Matson Evaluation of Social Skills with Youngsters (MESSY; Matson, Rotatori, & Helsel, 1983)	4–18 years	62 items; 5-point scale (not at all–very much)	Five factors	Internal consistency = .80–.95. Test–retest = ? (2 wk.). Factor analyses yielded five factors related to appropriateness of social behavior. Low correlation with structured child interview. Not correlated with behavioral role play, sociometrics, or teacher ratings of popularity, social skills, and social adjustment. Gender, grade-level, and handicapped–nonhandicapped group differences found with some MESSY factors.

Locus of control

Measure	Age	Format	Factors/Score	Psychometric properties
Children's Nowicki–Strickland Internal–External Control Scale (CNS-IE; Nowicki & Strickland, 1973)	Grades 3–12	40 items; yes–no	Three to nine factors found across studies	Internal consistency (split-half method) = .63–.81. Test–retest = .63–.71 (6-wk.). Concurrent validity with two other locus of control measures. Internal control correlated with academic achievement and PHSCS for males. Factor analyses yielded three to nine factors.
Children's Locus of Control Scale (CLCS; Bialer, 1961)	6–14 years	23 items; yes–no	Total score	Split-half = .49–.87. Test–retest = .84 (7-day); .68 (2- to 3-wk.). Convergent validity with CNS-IE, but not other locus of control measures. Correlated with intelligence and delay-of-gratification measures and with response to cues of success–failure.
Multidimensional Measures of Children's Perceptions of Control (CPC; Connell, 1980)	8–14 years	48 items; 4-point scale (very true–not at all true)	Source of Control (Internal, External, Unknown); Competency Domain; Outcome; Realm of Reference	Item-total correlation = .28–.89. Higher External scores of epileptic children relative to diabetic and healthy peers. Unknown Control score in academic domain related to school achievement.

ent and teacher versions and a system for direct observation of classroom behavior are also available, as discussed earlier in this chapter; parent reports of toddler (2–3 years) behavior is currently being developed as well. The CBCL-YSRF, however, is in its preliminary stages of development and, therefore, is not recommended for routine clinical use.

Self-Ratings of Specific Behavior Problems or Other Factors

Behavior-specific child self-ratings are best employed to fine-tune an assessment, to screen for particular behavior problems, and to evaluate intervention effects as outcome or ongoing assessment measures. "In general, these types of measures are more focused than the global checklists and include more contextual information" (Mash & Terdal, 1981, p. 49). Behavior-specific self-ratings typically are developed to measure cognitive controlling stimuli from the child's perspective (Evans & Nelson, 1977; Staats, 1972) and often are incorporated in an assessment when one or more distinct behavior problems are identified via more global measures, such as a behavior checklist or clinical interview. A selective review of self-report instruments relevant to assessing attitudes, perceptions, and behaviors in children and adolescents follows.

Anxiety

As shown in Table 16.3, a number of self-report instruments are available to assess anxiety and fears in children. One of the most widely used instruments of general anxiety is the Revised Children's Manifest Anxiety Scale (RCMAS; Reynolds & Richmond, 1978, 1985), a revision of the Children's Manifest Anxiety Scale (CMAS; Costaneda, McCandless, & Palermo, 1956). The original scale was revised to reduce the difficulty of the vocabulary, and thus to make the scale appropriate to a wider age range (i.e., 1st through 12th grades). The RCMAS has a large ($n = 4,200$) normative sample and is easily administered and scored. In line with Cone's (1978) Behavioral Assessment Grid, the RCMAS subscales facilitate the assessment of two modes of anxiety (i.e., physiolog-

ical and cognitive). The Lie scale serves as a check on the accuracy of information reported by the child or adolescent. Like several other measures of anxiety, the RCMAS lacks situation specificity. As described in Table 16.3, the RCMAS appears to be a reliable and valid measure of general anxiety.

Two other frequently used scales are the State–Trait Anxiety Inventory for Children (STAIC; Spielberger, 1973) and the State–Trait Anxiety Inventory (STAI; Spielberger, 1983). As shown in Table 16.3, both instruments have been developed with considerable methodological rigor. The STAIC is a downward extension of the STAI; however, the STAIC should not be considered as a parallel form of the STAI, because the two scales only correlate moderately in adolescents and have distinctive factor structures (Faulstich & Carey, 1985). The STAIC has been used cross-culturally, and preliminary normative data are available for fourth- to sixth-graders. The STAI has been employed in over 2,000 studies; however, few studies have been conducted with youths, and adolescent norms are limited to a small sample ($n = 424$) of high school students. A unique feature of the STAIC and the STAI is their incorporation of State and Trait scales. The State form is particularly useful for assessing situation specific behaviors. For instance, the State form can be used as an outcome measure of anxious behaviors associated with test taking. Like the RCMAS, the STAI and STAIC have been subjected to considerable empirical evaluation and are recommended for clinical and research purposes.

Also presented in Table 16.3 are the Generalized Anxiety Scale for Children (GASC) and the Text Anxiety Scale for Children (TASC), which were both developed by Sarason, Davidson, Lighthall, Waite, and Ruebush (1960). Both scales are lacking data with regard to their reliability and validity; therefore, the GASC and TASC are recommended only for research purposes.

Fears

Three of the instruments most frequently used to assess childhood and adolescent fears are shown in Table 16.3: the Fear Survey

Schedule for Children (FSSC; Scherer & Nakamura, 1968); The Fear Survey Schedule for Children—Revised (FSSC-R; Ollendick, 1983); and the Children's Fear Survey Schedule (CFSS; Ryall & Dietiker, 1979). The FSSC was developed by asking professionals and school personnel about children's fears and by using items from the Wolpe–Lang Scale. The FSSC is appropriate for only a narrow age range and apparently does not take into account the developmental and cognitive limitations of young children. In addition, it lacks adequate ($n = 99$) normative data (Bondy et al., 1985). The FSSC was later revised to address these weaknesses (i.e., the FSSCR; Ollendick, 1983; Ollendick, Matson, & Helsel, 1985). The FSSC-R was scaled to take into account the developmental and cognitive level of normal, clinic-referred, and mentally retarded children aged 8–18 years. The FSSC-R is a considerable improvement over the FSSC; however, a large representative normative sample is still needed for the FSSC-R.

The CFSS was developed by asking children aged 4–12 years to report frequently feared stimuli. This approach to item development assured greater domain sampling than that of the FSSC and the FSSC-R. Similar to the problems observed with the FSSC, the CFSS has a restricted age range, has not been evaluated adequately with regard to its reliability and validity, and has not been developed with a representative normative sample. Thus, all three fear survey schedules have limitations, and therefore are recommended only for research purposes. The FSSC-R has received the most systematic empirical evaluation, however, and may be used clinically if caution is demonstrated in its interpretation.

Depression

Self-rating scales are particularly well suited to the assessment of depression because a child or adolescent's subjective experience of distress may not be apparent to his or her parents or teachers (Reynolds, Anderson, & Bartell, 1985; Saylor, Finch, Spirito, & Bennett, 1984). As shown in Table 16.3, several instruments are currently available to assess depression in children and adolescents.

One of the most widely used and validated self-ratings of depression in childhood is the Children's Depression Inventory (CDI; Kovacs & Beck, 1977). The CDI measures depressive affect, oppositional behavior, and personal adjustment (Carey, Faulstich, Gresham, Ruggiero, & Enyart, in press) and can be read by children as young as first-graders (Kazdin & Petti, 1982). As described in Table 16.3, the CDI's reliability and validity have been studied extensively (Carey et al., 1985; Kovacs, 1983; Saylor et al., 1984; Smucker, Craighead, Craighead, & Green, 1986). Moreover, the CDI has extensive normative data with school, medical, and inpatient and outpatient psychiatric populations (Finch, Saylor, & Edwards, 1985; Smucker et al., 1986) and is sensitive to treatment effects (Stark, Reynolds, & Kaslow, in press). At present, the CDI, a downward extension of the Beck Depression Inventory (BDI), appears to be the most appropriate self-rating instrument for assessing depression in childhood. It is used best as a research instrument and a clinical screening device.

The BDI (Beck, Ward, Mendelson, Mock, & Erbaugh, 1961) and the Reynolds Adolescent Depression Scale (RADS; Reynolds, 1985b) have been utilized frequently with adolescents. The BDI was originally developed to be used with adults; however, a number of investigations have indicated that the BDI is a reliable and valid measure with adolescents (Chiles, Miller, & Cox, 1980; Kaplan, Hong, & Weinhold, 1984; Strober, Green, & Carlson, 1981; Teri, 1982a, 1982b). In contrast, the RADS was developed specifically to assess depression in adolescence. Like the BDI, the RADS (see Table 16.3) has been subjected to rigorous empirical evaluation and appears to be a reliable and valid measure of the severity of adolescent depression (Reynolds, 1985a, 1985b; Reynolds & Coats, in press). The RADS has the added advantage of extensive normative data ($n = 8,000$) by gender and grade. Both the BDI and the RADS have been demonstrated to be sensitive to treatment outcome (Reynolds & Coats, in press) and are easy to administer and score. The BDI and the RADS are recommended as research instruments and clinical screening devices. Tentative cutoff scores for levels of depression have been established for both the BDI (Beck & Beck, 1972) and the RADS.

Two other instruments discussed in Table 16.3 are the Center for Epidemiological Studies Depression Scale for Children (CES-DC; Weissman, Orvaschel, & Padian, 1980) and the Depression Self-Rating Scale (DSRS; Birleson, 1980). Currently, favorable results have been reported with regard to the DSRS's reliability; however, only limited validation and normative data ($n = 73$) are available (Asarnow & Carlson, 1985; Birleson, 1980). In contrast, unfavorable results have been reported for the test–retest reliability and criterion-related validity of the CES-DC (Faulstich, Carey, Ruggiero, Enyart, & Gresham, 1985). Therefore, neither the CES-DC nor the DSRS can be recommended for general clinical practice, although they may be useful as research tools.

Reinforcers and Activities

Relatively few instruments exist that quantify reinforcers and routine activities of children and adolescents. As shown in Table 16.3, two measures that quantify reinforcers and activities are the Children's Reinforcement Survey Schedule (CRSS; Cautela & Kastenbaum, 1967) and the Adolescent Activity Checklist (AAC; Carey, Kelley, Buss, & Scott, 1986). Such scales may be useful for identifying reinforcers or target behaviors for intervention (e.g., reduction of specific aversive events).

The CRSS consists of three lists of age-specific reinforcers, rated in terms of how well the student likes a specific reinforcer. The CRSS may facilitate the identification of reinforcers that may be used to reinforce behaviors targeted for intervention. Preliminary results have been promising, although additional data is needed with regard to the CRSS's practical utility. Because few reinforcement scales exist, the CRSS is recommended as an idiographic survey of stimuli that a child identifies as reinforcing.

The AAC is an activity checklist developed to quantify pleasant and unpleasant events that frequently occur in adolescence. The AAC was developed by asking adolescents and professionals to report pleasant and unpleasant activities, and in its present form, the adolescent rates the valence (pleasantness–unpleasantness) of 100 events. Norma-

tive data are available for 900 adolescents (Carey et al., 1986). Like the CRSS, the AAC is in need of further validation before it can be recommended for general clinical use; however, it may be a useful tool for assessing behaviors associated with adolescent depression and daily hassles.

Major Life Events

Whereas the scales just discussed measure concrete reinforcers and routine life events, other scales have been developed to assess major life events. Such instruments have been used frequently to quantify the level of stress an individual has experienced over an extended time interval. Schedules of major life events, therefore, can assist the assessor in the development of a thorough learning history. As described in Table 16.3, three of the most frequently used schedules are the Junior High Life Experiences Survey (JHLES; Swearingen & Cohen, 1985), the Life Event Record (LER; Coddington, 1972), and the Life Events Checklist (LEC; Johnson & McCutcheon, 1980). For an excellent review of life events as stressors for children and adolescents, see Johnson (1982).

The JHLES is a new instrument in which items were adapted from existing life events scales in a small pilot study with youths. Currently, the instrument developers have yet to report data on its reliability; furthermore, limited validity data have been reported. The JHLES, therefore, is not recommended for general clinical use. In contrast, the LER is the most frequently used major life events schedule with children and adolescents. Although the LER has a substantial normative sample ($n = 3,526$), it has several problems that limit its utility at present. For example, it does not adequately sample child and adolescent life events; scores do not reflect positive or negative impact of items; and it relies on outdated weighted unit scores.

LEC items were generated from the Life Experiences Survey (Brand & Johnson, 1982) and from questioning adolescents about life events. In contrast to the JHLES and LER, the authors of the LEC have reported results with regard to its temporal stability and have constructed items so that valence, frequency, and impact of events are obtained. Moreover, as described in Table 16.3, the LEC has demonstrated concurrent validity with a variety of related behaviors and constructs (Brand & Johnson, 1982; Johnson, 1982). The major limitation of the LEC is its lack of adequate normative data. In summary, the JHLES is not recommended for general use, whereas the LER and LEC are recommended for research purposes and limited clinical use.

Self-Evaluation

A plethora of research has centered on a construct alternately labeled "self-concept," "self-worth," "self-esteem," "self-perception," "self-image," and "self-evaluation." Typically, the choice of a label for this construct is a function of one's theoretical orientation and views regarding the etiological course of normal and problem behavior. Common to all definitions of this construct, however, is the concept of a judgment, perception, or attitude about one's own abilities to function in society. We refer to this construct as "self-evaluation" and define it as self-appraisal of competence in specific skill domains related to cognitive, affective, and interpersonal efficacy (Karoly, 1981; Kendal & Braswell, 1985).

Listed in Table 16.3 are five self-rating instruments reported to assess self-evaluation in children and adolescents. The Self-Esteem Inventory (SEI; Coopersmith, 1967) was designed "to measure evaluative attitudes toward the self in social, academic, family, and personal areas of experience" (Coopersmith, 1984, p. 2). The SEI School Form, which offers four subscale scores, consists of 50 items related to antecedents, consequences, and correlates of self-esteem, as well as eight Lie scale items. A 25-item School Short Form is available as an alternate to the School Form. A total score correlation of .86 was found between these two alternate forms. In addition, an Adult Form, appropriate for persons over age 15, has recently been developed. The SEI is easily scored and was developed using a large ($n = 1,748$) normative sample. Based on data from over 100 studies, the SEI is recommended as a reliable and valid measure of self-evaluation in children.

Two other generally reliable self-ratings of self-evaluation are the Self-Perception Profile for Children (SPPC; Harter, 1982) and the Self-Observation Scales (SOS; Stenner & Katzenmeyer, 1979). The SPPC, a recent revision of the Perceived Competence Scale for Children (Harter, 1982) in which a sample of 748 children was used, yields subscale scores representing six competency or skill domains. An abbreviated teacher form is available. Respondents to the SPPC complete a form entitled "What I Am Like" by marking "really true for me" or "sort of true for me" on one of two alternate statements per item. For example, item 11 requires a choice between "Some kids usually do the *right* thing BUT other kids often *don't* do the right thing." This response format may be difficult for some children to understand, and therefore limits the utility of the SPPC.

The SOS provides factor-analytically derived subscale scores that differ for each of four forms (i.e., grades K–3, 4–6, 7–9, and 10–12). Reading level and response format vary across forms and are age-appropriate. For example, the Grades K–3 form is administered orally to the child, who responds by marking the nose of a happy or sad face. In spite of exemplary attention to developmental issues in constructing the SOS, its clinical use is limited because of a paucity of validity studies and restricted circulation of information (i.e., the descriptive reports, computer scoring, standardized national norms, and manual are available only through the National Testing Service). The SPPC and the SOS are recommended for research use and for limited clinical use.

The two remaining measures of self-evaluation listed in Table 16.3, the Pier–Harris Self-Concept Scale (PHSCS; Piers & Harris, 1969) and the Offer Self-Image Questionnaire for Adolescents (OSIQ; Offer & Howard, 1972), have enjoyed widespread use. The PHSCS, or "The Way I Feel About Myself," was written at a third-grade reading level and provides an overall self-concept score or a profile of six cluster scores. Factor-analytic research has inconsistently supported the structure of PHSCS cluster scores. The PHSCS was developed using a normative sample ($n = 1,183$) from a school district in Pennsylvania. Computer scoring is available from the publisher. The recently revised manual (Piers, 1984) reports two new scores—the Response Bias Index, which assesses negative response sets or acquiescence, and the Inconsistency Index, which identifies random response patterns—used to facilitate judgments with regard to the validity of a child's report on the PHSCS. Numerous investigations of the reliability and validity of the PHSCS support use of the overall self-concept score for research and clinical purposes.

The OSIQ has undergone several revisions and has been translated into numerous languages for international distribution (Offer, Ostrov, & Howard, 1981; Wisniewski, 1985; Young, 1984). An OSIQ parent rating form is currently available, and a newsletter describing recent developments with the OSIQ is published several times a year. Computer scoring is available from the author. Although the OSIQ is a well-promulgated instrument, inadequate psychometric properties (e.g., some reports of poor reliability) and length (i.e., 130 items) limit its practical utility.

Social Behavior

Behavioral assessment of social behavior in children and adolescents typically has relied on information culled from sociometric measures, ratings by others, behavioral role-play tests, and naturalistic observations. Within the past decade, however, child self-ratings of interpersonal behaviors have been added to the psychologist's assessment armamentarium.

All the self-ratings of social behavior presented in Table 16.3 have the same basic goal: to measure a child's perspective on his or her social competence. Most authors agree that identification of cognitive and overt behaviors related to social relations is critical to a conceptualization of social competence (Eisenberg & Harris, 1984). We endorse Gresham's (1986) conceptualization of social competence as being comprised of (1) adaptive behavior and (2) social skills. In this definition, the term "social skills" refers to interpersonal behaviors, self-related cognitions, and task-related behaviors (e.g., attending behavior, following directions). Each of the social behavior self-ratings described in this section attempts to measure various aspects of social competence in children (e.g., self-efficacy, assertiveness). Although some of these self-ratings show potential, most are not currently recommended for general clinical use because of a need for further validation.

The Children's Self-Efficacy for Peer Interaction Scale (CSPIS) was developed to measure a child's self-report of "ability to enact prosocial verbal persuasive skills in specific peer situations" (Wheeler & Ladd, 1982, p. 796). The CSPIS was developed from a sample ($n = 245$) of third- to fifth-graders. A total self-efficacy score is derived by summing scores across 22 items that are divided into conflict and nonconflict social situations. Scores range from 22 to 88, with higher scores representing greater perception of efficacy. The CSPIS is well grounded in the literature on children's social cognitions and, with additional validation, may become a useful tool for psychologists.

Two measures purported to assess a child's self-perception of aggressive, assertive, and submissive or passive behaviors are the Children's Action Tendency Scale (CATS; Deluty, 1979, 1981), and the Children's Assertive Behavior Scale (CABS; Michelson & Wood, 1982). The CATS was developed following the behavioral-analytic model described by Goldfried and D'Zurilla (1969). Informants read an item in which a social conflict situation is presented and then choose a response from three pairs of alternatives, representing all possible pairs of submissive, assertive, and aggressive responses. Although the author believes that such a response format avoids providing respondents with the opportunity to give only socially desirable answers, it may tax the comprehension skills of children for whom the CATS is targeted (i.e., third- to sixth-graders). Deleting items 3, 12, and 13 improves the validity of the CATS; norms, based on a sample of over 600 children, are available (Deluty, 1979, 1981).

The CABS presents social situations involving assertive behaviors (e.g., initiating conversations, making requests), each with five possible answers that vary along a scrambled continuum of very passive, passive, assertive, aggressive, and very aggressive responses. The respondent is instructed to choose the response most like the one he or she would usually give in each situation. This response format appears more age-appropriate than the paired-comparison alternatives employed in the CATS. The response format and the reading level of the CABS were socially validated in pilot studies. A sample of 319 fourth- to sixth-graders was employed in the development of this instrument. Although Hobbs and Walle (1985) present results suggestive of its validity, the CABS is currently recommended for research and limited clinical uses.

The Children's Inventory of Anger (CIA; Nelson & Finch, 1973) is an exemplar of sensitivity to developmental issues in the construction of self-ratings for children. For example, reading specialists were consulted to insure that the CIA was written on a fourth-grade reading level; in addition, because pilot work suggested that impulsive and aggressive children tend to think in pictures more than in words (Stein, Finch, Hooke, Montgomery, & Nelson, 1975), symbolic anchors were used in the 4-point rating scale for each item. These symbolic anchors range from a smiling, nonchalant face, labeled "I don't care. That situation doesn't even bother me," to an intensely angry face, described as "I can't stand that! I'm furious!" Respondents use these symbolic anchors to respond to 71 anger-provoking situations, derived from interviews with normal and emotionally disturbed children with regard to what made them angry. Large samples were used (n's = 376–1,000) to develop the CIA, which appears to be a promising instrument for assessing anger in children. Its clinical utility is hindered at present, however, by its length and by a need for more studies investigating its validity.

The Matson Evaluation of Social Skills with Youngsters (MESSY; Matson, Rotatori, & Helsel, 1983) was developed, using a relatively large sample of children from a normal population (n = 422) and samples of visually impaired and hearing-impaired children, as a measure of social behavior excesses and deficits in children. Factor analyses on the 64-item teacher report form have yielded two factors (i.e., Inappropriate Assertiveness/Impulsiveness and Appropriate Social Skills), whereas five factors have been found to underlie the 62-item self-report form (i.e., Appropriate Social Skills, Inappropriate Assertiveness, Impulsive/Recalcitrant/Overconfident, and Jealousy/Withdrawal).

Matson and his colleagues should be commended for basing the MESSY on a behavioral conceptualization of social skills, as well as for adapting the MESSY for use with handicapped children (Matson, Heinze, Helsel, Kappermann, & Rotatori, 1986; Matson, Macklin, & Helsel, 1985). The MESSY cannot be recommended currently for clinical purposes, however, because of its length and because concurrent and convergent validity with other measures of social behavior have not yet been sufficiently demonstrated (see Table 16.3).

Locus of Control

The construct labeled "locus of control of reinforcement" alludes to one's perception of the degree of influence he or she exerts over the outcome of events. Rotter (1966) described an "internal–external" continuum, in which "internal locus of control" refers to a belief that reinforcers are completely within one's power and "external locus of control" refers to a perception that reinforcers are determined by factors outside of one's influence. Listed in Table 16.3 are three instruments intended to measure children's attributions of control over environmental events. Although direct assessment of locus of control has little clinical value per se, locus of control has been studied as a moderator variable and as a predictor of treatment outcome (Rogers & Finch, 1984).

Two of the earliest measures constructed to assess generalized locus of control in children and adolescents are the Children's Nowicki–Strickland Internal–External Control Scale (CNS-IE; Nowicki & Strickland, 1973) and the Children's Locus of Control Scale (CLCS; Bialer, 1961). The CNS-IE was written at a fifth-grade reading level and was based on data from a large sample (n = 1,017) of 3rd- to 12th-graders. For third and fourth grades, oral administration is recommended. Higher scores represent perception of more external control over events. CNS-IE items are intended to assess attribution of control in multiple situations (e.g., belief in chance or luck, interpersonal relations, school achievement). Two CNS-IE short forms are available: a 20-item primary form for third- to sixth-graders, and a 21-item secondary form for 7th- to 12-graders. Nowicki and Duke

(1974) developed a downward extension of the CNS-IE, the Preschool and Primary NS-IE (PPNS-IE), which is appropriate for children 4–8 years old. The 34 items of the PPNS-IE are worded at a 4-year-old level and are illustrated using cartoon drawings. Although the PPNS-IE is appealing because of its consideration of developmental issues, its clinical use cannot currently be recommended because of psychometric inadequacies (Herzbergen, Linney, Seidman, & Rappaport, 1979). However, extensive empirical analyses support clinical and research use of the CNS-IE as a measure of generalized locus of control in children (Rogers & Finch, 1984).

The CLCS was developed using small samples of mentally retarded individuals (aged 17–28 years) and normal children (first through third grades), and is administered orally. Higher scores represent perception of more internal control over events. Gozali and Bialer (1968) designed an alternate form of the CLCS in which the positively and negatively keyed items are reversed. A correlation of .67 was found between the two CLCS forms, leading the authors to discount potential effects of a response set on CLCS scores. Gorsuch, Heringhan, and Bernard (1972) found a relationship between verbal ability and reliability of the CLCS. These researchers cited evidence suggesting that children with lower verbal ability responded randomly because they failed to understand the CLCS items.

Although the CLCS has been found to correlate significantly with the CNS-IE (Bialer, 1961), Bachrach and Peterson (1976) reported that the CLCS did not correlate significantly with two other measures of locus of control in a sample of 25 first- to third-graders. As also found with the CNS-IE, internal control as measured by the CLCS increases with age. In spite of years of general use, the CLCS is not to be preferred over the psychometrically superior CNS-IE when one is studying nonhandicapped children.

In contrast to the CNS-IE and the CLCS, which are measures of general locus of control, the Multidimensional Measure of Children's Perceptions of Control (CPC; Connell, 1980) assesses children's attributions of control across success outcomes and failure outcomes in three competency domains (i.e., social, physical, and academic) and a general domain. The CPC, or "Why Things Happen," also assesses three sources of control (i.e., Internal, Powerful Others, and Unknown), as well as children's beliefs with regard to why they succeed or fail (i.e., personal realm of reference). The CPC was developed using a relatively large sample ($n = 521$). An attractive feature of the CPC is the manner in which it taps children's situation-specific perspectives on control. The CPC's psychometric inadequacies, however, preclude its present use other than as a research instrument.

Acknowledgment. Portions of this chapter are adapted from "Child Self-Report: Interviewing Techniques and Rating Scales" by J. C. Witt, T. Cavell, M. Carey, R. Heffer, and B. K. Martens, 1988, in E. S. Shapiro and T. R. Kratochwill (Eds.), *Behavioral Assessment in Schools: Conceptual Foundations and Practical Applications* (pp. 384–454). New York: Guilford Press. Copyright 1988 by The Guilford Press. Adapted by permission.

REFERENCES

Achenbach, T. M., & Edelbrock, C. S. (1983). *Manual for the Child Behavior Checklist and Revised Child Behavior Profile*. Burlington: University of Vermont, Department of Psychiatry.

Achenbach, T. M., & Edelbrock C. S. (1986). *Youth Self-Report Profile*. (Available from T. M. Achenbach, Center for Children, Youth, and Families, University of Vermont, 1 S. Prospect St., Burlington, VT 05401)

Achenbach, T. M., McConaughy, S. H., & Howell, C. T. (1987). Child/adolescent behavior and emotional problems: Implications of cross-informant correlations for situational specificity. *Psychological Bulletin, 101,* 213–232.

Asarnow, J., & Carlson, G. A. (1985). Depression Self-Rating Scale: Utility with child psychiatric inpatients. *Journal of Consulting and Clinical Psychology, 53,* 491–499.

Bachrach, P., & Peterson, R. A. (1976). Test–retest reliability and interrelation among three other laws of control measures for children. *Perceptual and Motor Skills, 43,* 260–262.

Bauer, D. M. (1987). The difference between basic and applied behavior analysis in one behavior. *Behavior Analysis, 22,* 101–106.

Beck, A. T., & Beck, R. W. (1972). Screening depressed patients in family practice: A rapid technique. *Postgraduate Medicine, 52,* 81–85.

Beck, A. T., Ward, C., Mendelson, M., Mock, J., & Erbaugh, J. (1961). An inventory for measuring depression. *Archives of General Psychiatry, 4*, 53–63.

Bialer, I. (1961). Conceptualization of success and failure in mentally retarded and normal children. *Journal of Personality, 29*, 303–320.

Birleson, P. (1980). The validity of depressive disorder in childhood and the development of a self-rating scale: A research report. *Journal of Child Psychology and Psychiatry, 22*, 73–87.

Bondy, A., Sheslow, D., & Garcia, L. T. (1985). An investigation of children's fears and their mother's fears. *Journal of Psychopathology and Behavioral Assessment, 7*, 1–12.

Brand, A. H., & Johnson, J. H. (1982). Note on reliability of the Life Events Checklist. *Psychological Reports, 50*, 1274.

Brown, L. L., & Hammill, D. D. (1978). *The Behavior Rating Profile: An ecological approach to behavioral assessment*. Austin, TX: Pro-Ed.

Burke, J. P., & DeMers, S. (1979). A paradigm for evaluating assessment interviewing techniques. *Psychology in the Schools, 16*, 51–60.

Byrd, D. M., & Gholson, B. (1984). A cognitive-developmental model of reading. In B. Gholson & T. L. Rosenthal (Eds.), *Applications of cognitive-developmental theory* (pp. 21–48). New York: Academic Press.

Carey, M. P., Faulstich, M. E., Gresham, F. M., Ruggiero, L., & Enyart, P. (in press). The Children's Depression Inventory: Construct and discriminant validity across clinical and normal populations. *Journal of Consulting and Clinical Psychology*.

Carey, M. P., Kelley, M. L., Buss, R. R., & Scott, O. (1986). Relationship of activity to depression in adolescents: Development of the Adolescent Activity Checklist. *Journal of Consulting and Clinical Psychology, 54*, 320–322.

Castaneda, A., McCandless, B. R., & Palermo, D. S. (1956). The children's form of the Manifest Anxiety Scale. *Child Development, 27*, 317–326.

Cautela, J. R., & Kastenbaum, R. (1967). A reinforcement survey for use in therapy. *Psychological Reports, 20*, 1115–1130.

Chiles, A., Miller, M. L., & Cox, G. B. (1980). Depression in an adolescent delinquent population. *Archives of General Psychiatry, 37*, 1179–1184.

Ciminero, A. R., & Drabman, R. S. (1977). Current developments in the behavioral assessment of children. In B. B. Lahey & A. E. Kazdin (Eds.), *Advances in clinical child psychology* (Vol. 1, pp. 47–84). New York: Plenum.

Coddington, R. D. (1972). The significance of life events as etiological factors in the diseases of children: I. A survey of professional workers. *Journal of Psychosomatic Research, 16*, 205–213.

Cone, J. D. (1978). The Behavioral Assessment Grid (BAG): A conceptual framework and taxonomy. *Behavior Therapy, 9*, 882–888.

Connell, J. P. (1980). *A Multidimensional Measure of Children's Perceptions of Control: Manual*. Unpublished manuscript, University of Denver.

Conners, C. K. (1969). A teacher rating scale for use in drug studies with children. *American Journal of Psychiatry, 126*, 884–889.

Conners, C. K. (1970). Symptom patterns in hyperkinetic, neurotic and abnormal children. *Child Development, 41*, 667–682.

Conners, C. K. (1973). Rating scales for use in drug studies with children. *Psychopharmacology Bulletin, 14*, 24–42.

Coopersmith, S. (1967). *The antecedents of self-esteem*. Palo Alto, CA: Consulting Psychologists Press.

Coopersmith, S. (1984). *Self-Esteem Inventories*. Palo Alto, CA: Consulting Psychologist Press.

DeCotiis, T. A. (1977). An analysis of the external validity and applied relevance of three rating formats. *Organizational Behavior and Human Performance, 19*, 247–266.

Deluty, R. H. (1979). Children's Action Tendency Scale: A self-report measure of aggressiveness, assertiveness, and submissiveness in children. *Journal of Consulting and Clinical Psychology, 41*, 1061–1071.

Deluty, R. H. (1981). Alternative thinking ability of aggressive, assertive, and submissive children. *Cognitive Therapy and Research, 5*, 309–312.

Edelbrock, C. (1983). Problems and issues in using rating scales to assess child personality and psychopathology. *School Psychology Review, 12*, 293–299.

Edelbrock, C. (1983). Informant reports. In E. S. Shapiro & T. R. Kratochwill (Eds.), *Behavioral assessment in schools: Conceptual foundations and practical applications* (pp. 351–383). New York: Guilford Press.

Eisenberg, N., & Harris, J. D. (1984). School competence: A developmental perspective. *School Psychology Review, 8*, 267–277.

Evans, I. M., & Nelson, R. O. (1977). Assessment of child behavior problems. In A. R. Ciminero, K. S. Calhoun, & H. E. Adams (Eds.), *Handbook of behavioral assessment* (pp. 603–608). New York: Wiley.

Faulstich, M. E., & Carey, M. P. (1985). *Assessment of anxiety in adolescents: Psychometric comparison of Spielberger's Trait Anxiety Inventories for children (STAIC) and adults (STAI)*. Unpublished manuscript.

Faulstich, M. E., Carey, M. P., Ruggiero, L., Enyart, P., & Gresham, F. M. (1986). *Assessment of depression in childhood and adolescence: An evaluation of the Center for Epidemiological Studies Depression Scale for Children*. American Journal of Psychiatry, 143, 1024–1027.

Finch, A. J., Jr., & Rogers, T. R. (1984). Self-report instruments. In T. H. Ollendick & M. Herson (Eds.), *Child behavioral assessment: Principles and procedures*. (pp. 106–123). New York: Pergamon Press.

Finch, A. J., Jr., Saylor, C. F., & Edwards, G. L. (1985). Children's Depression Inventory: Sex and grade norms for normal children. *Journal of Consulting and Clinical Psychology, 53*, 424–425.

Garber, J. (1984). Classification of childhood psychopathology: A developmental perspective. *Child Development, 55*, 30–48.

Glow, R. A., Glow, P. H., & Rump, E. E. (1982). The stability of child behavior disorders: A one-year test–retest study of the Adelaide versions of the Conner Teacher and Parent Rating Scales. *Journal of Abnormal Child Psychology, 10*, 33–60.

Goldfried, M., & D'Zurilla, T. J. (1969). A behavioral-analytic model in assessment and research. In C. D. Spielberger (Ed.), *Current topics in clinical and com-*

munity psychology, (Vol. 1, pp. 151–196). New York: Academic Press.

Gorsuch, R. L., Herighan, R. P., & Barnard, C. (1972). Locus of control: An example of dangers in using children's scales with children. *Child Development, 43,* 579–590.

Gozali, J., & Bialer, I. (1968). Children's Locus of Control Scale: Independence from response set bias among retardates. *American Journal of Mental Deficiency, 72,* 622–625.

Goyette, C. H., Conners, C. K., & Ulrich, R. F. (1978). Normative data on the revised Conners Parent and Teacher Rating Scales. *Journal of Abnormal Child Psychology, 6,* 221–236.

Gresham, F. M. (1986). Conceptual and definitional issues in the assessment of children's social skills: Implications for classification and training. *Journal of Clinical Child Psychology, 15,* 3–15.

Gresham, F. M., Reschly, D. J., & Carey, M. P. (1987). Teachers as "tests": Classification accuracy and learning disabled children. *School Psychology Review, 16,* 543–553.

Harter, S. (1982). The Perceived Competence Scale for Children. *Child Development, 53,* 3–15.

Hathaway, S. R., & Monachesi, E. D. (1963). *Adolescent personality and behavior: MMPI patterns of normal delinquent, dropout and other outcomes.* Minneapolis: University of Minnesota Press.

Herzbergen, S. D., Linney, J. A., Seidman, E., & Rappaport, T. (1979). Preschool and Primary Locus of Control Scale: Is it ready for use? *Developmental Psychology, 15,* 320–324.

Hobbs, S. A., & Walle, D. L. (1985). Validation of the Children's Assertive Behavior Scale. *Journal of Psychopathology and Behavioral Assessment, 1,* 145–153.

Inhelder, B., & Piaget, J. (1964). *The early growth of logic in the child.* New York: Norton.

Inhelder, B., Sinclair, H., & Bovet, M. (1974). *Learning and the development of cognition.* Cambridge, MA: Harvard University Press.

Johnson, J. H. (1982). Life events as stressors in childhood and adolescence. In B. B. Lahey & A. E. Kazdin (Eds.), *Advances in clinical child psychology* (Vol. 4, pp. 222–253). New York: Plenum Press.

Johnson, J. H., & McCutcheon, S. (1980). Assessing life stress in older children and adolescents: Preliminary findings with the Life Events Checklist. In I. G. Sarason & C. D. Spielberger (Eds.), *Stress and anxiety* (Vol. 7, pp. 61–104). Washington, DC:

Johnson, O. G. (1976). *Tests and measurements in child development: Handbook II* (Vols. 1 & 2). San Francisco: Jossey-Bass.

Kaplan, S. L., Hong, G. E., & Weinhold, C. (1984). Epidemiology of depressive symptomatology in adolescents. *Journal of the American Academy of Child Psychiatry, 23,* 91–98.

Karoly, P. (1981). Self-management problems in children. In E. J. Mash & L. G. Terdal (Eds.), *Behavioral assessment of childhood disorders* (pp. 79–126). New York: Guilford Press.

Kazdin, A. E., & Petti, T. A. (1982). Self-report and interview measures of childhood and adolescent depression. *Journal of Child Psychology and Psychiatry, 23,* 437–457.

Kendall, P. C., & Braswell, L. (1985). *Cognitive-*

behavioral therapy for impulsive children. New York: Guilford Press.

Kivlahan, D. R., Siegel, L. J., & Ullman, D. G. (1982). Relationship among measures of activity in children. *Journal of Pediatric Psychology, 7,* 331–334.

Kovacs, M. (1983). *The Children's Depression Inventory: A self-rated depression scale for school-aged youngsters.* Unpublished manuscript.

Kovacs, M., & Beck, A. T. (1977). An empirical–clinical approach toward a definition of childhood depression. In J. G. Shulterbrandt & A. Raskin (Eds.), *Depression in childhood: Diagnosis, treatment, and conceptual models* (pp. 1–25). New York: Raven Press.

Lahey, B. B., Green, K. D., & Forehand, R. (1980). On the independence of ratings of hyperactivity, conduct problems, and attention deficits in children: A multiple regression analysis. *Journal of Consulting and Clinical Psychology, 48,* 566–574.

Mace, F. C. (1985). Review of the Walker Behavior Problem Checklist. In J. V. Mitchell (Ed.). *The ninth mental measurements yearbook* (pp. 1689–1691). Lincoln, NE: Buros Institute of Mental Measurements.

Marks, P. A., Seeman, W., & Haller, D. L. (1974). *The actuarial use of the MMPI with adolescents and adults.* Baltimore: Williams & Wilkins.

Martin, R. P., Hooper, S., & Snow, J. (1986a). Behavior checklist for males 6–12 years of age. *Psychological Reports, 21,* 885–896.

Martin, R. P., Hooper, S., & Snow, J. (1986b). Behavior rating scale approaches to personality assessment in children and adolescents. In H. Knoff (Ed.), *The assessment of child and adolescent personality* (pp. 309–351). New York: Guilford Press.

Mash, E. J., & Terdal, L. G. (1981). Behavioral assessment of childhood disturbance. In E. J. Mash & L. G. Terdal (Eds.), *Behavioral assessment of childhood disorders* (pp. 3–76). New York: Guilford Press.

Matson, J. L., Heinze, A., Helsel, W. J., Kappermann, G., & Rotatori, A. F. (1986). Assessing social behavior in the visually handicapped: The Matson Evaluation of Social Skills with Youngsters (MESSY). *Journal of Child Psychology, 15,* 78–87.

Matson, J. L., Macklin, G. F., & Helsel, W. J. (1985). Psychometric properties of the Matson Evaluation of Social Skills with Youngsters with emotional problems and self concept in deaf children. *Journal of Behavior Therapy and Experimental Psychiatry, 16,* 117–123.

Matson, J. L., Rotatori, A. F., & Helsel, W. J. (1983). Development of a rating scale to measure social skills in children: The Matson Evaluation of Social Skills with Youngsters (MESSY). *Behaviour Research and Therapy, 21,* 335–340.

Michelson, L., & Wood, R. (1982). Development and psychometric properties of the children's Assertive Behavior Scale. *Journal of Behavioral Assessment, 4,* 3–13.

Millon, T., Green, C. J., & Meger, R. B. (1982). *Millon Adolescent Personality Inventory manual.* Minneapolis: National Computer Systems.

Mitchell, J. V. (Ed.). (1985). *The ninth mental measurements yearbook* (Vols. 1 & 2). Lincoln: University of Nebraska Press.

Nelson, W. M., III, & Finch, A. J., Jr. (1973). *The Children's Inventory of Anger.* Unpublished manuscript, Xavier University.

Nowicki, S., & Duke, M. P. (1974). A preschool and

primary internal–external control scale. *Developmental Psychology, 10,* 874–880.

Nowicki, S., & Strickland, B. R. (1973). A locus of control scale for children. *Journal of Consulting and Clinical Psychology, 40,* 148–154.

Offer, D., & Howard, K. I. (1972). An empirical analysis of the Offer Self-Image Questionnaire for adolescents. *Archives of General Psychiatry, 27,* 744–746.

Offer, D., Ostrov, E., & Howard, K. I. (1981). *The Offer Self-Image Questionnaire for adolescents: A manual.* Chicago: Michael Reese Hospital.

Ollendick, T. H. (1983). Reliability and validity of the Revised Fear Survey Schedule for Children (FSSC-R). *Behaviour Research and Therapy, 21,* 685–692.

Ollendick, T. H., & Hersen, M. (1984). An overview of child behavioral assessment. In T. H. Ollendick & M. Hersen (Eds.), *Child behavioral assessment: Principles and procedures* (pp. 3–19). New York: Pergamon Press.

Ollendick, T. H., Matson, J. L., & Helsel, W. J. (1985). Fears in visually-impaired and normally-sighted youths. *Behaviour Research and Therapy, 23,* 375–378.

Ollindick, T. H., & Meador, A. E. (1984). Behavioral assessment of children. In G. Goldstein & M. Hersen (Eds.), *Handbook of psychological assessment* (pp. 351–368). New York: Pergamon Press.

Paget, K. D. (1984). The structured assessment interview: A psychometric review. *Journal of School Psychology, 22,* 415–427.

Piers, E. V. (1984). *A manual for the Piers–Harris Children's Self-Concept Scale.* Los Angeles: Western Psychological Services.

Piers, E. V., & Harris, D. B. (1969). *A manual for the Piers–Harris Self-Concept Scale.* Nashville, TN: Counselor Recordings and Tests.

Porter, R. B., & Cattell, R. B. (1979). *What you do and what you think.* Champaign, IL: Institute for Personality and Ability Testing.

Quay, H. C., & Peterson, C. (1983). *Manual for the Revised Behavior Problem Checklist.* Coral Gables, FL: Authors.

Reynolds, C. R., & Richmond, B. O. (1978). What I think and feel: A revised measure of children's manifest anxiety. *Journal of Abnormal Psychology, 6,* 271–280.

Reynolds, C. R., & Richmond, B. O. (1985). *Revised Children's Manifest Anxiety Scale (RCMAS).* Los Angeles: Western Psychological Services.

Reynolds, W. M. (1985a). Depression in childhood and adolescence: Diagnosis, assessment, intervention strategies and research. In T. R. Kratochwill (Ed.), *Advances in school psychology* (Vol. 4, pp. 187–204). Hillsdale, NJ: Erlbaum.

Reynolds, W. M. (1985b). *Development and validation of a scale to measure depression in adolescents.* Paper presented at the annual meeting of the Society for Personality Assessment, Berkeley, CA.

Reynolds, W. M., Anderson, G., & Bartell, N. (1985). Measuring depression in children: A multimethod assessment investigation. *Journal of Abnormal Child Psychology, 13,* 513–526.

Reynolds, W. M., & Coats, K. I. (in press). A comparison of cognitive–behavioral therapy and relaxation training for the treatment of depression in adolescents. *Journal of Consulting and Clinical Psychology.*

Rotter, J. E. (1966). Generalized expectancies for internal versus external control of reinforcement. *Psychological Monographs, 80,* (1, Whole No. 609).

Ryall, M. R., & Dietiker, K. E. (1979). Reliability and clinical validity of the Children's Fear Survey Schedule. *Journal of Behavior Therapy and Experimental Psychiatry, 10,* 303–309.

Saal, F. E., Downey, R. G., & Lahey, M. A. (1980). Rating the ratings: Assessing the psychometric quality of rating data. *Psychological Bulletin, 88,* 413–428.

Sarason, S. B., Davidson, K. S., Lighthall, F. F., Waite, R. R., & Ruebush, B. (1960). *Anxiety in elementary school children.* New York: Wiley.

Saylor, C. F., Finch, A. J., Spirito, A., & Bennett, B. (1984). The Children's Depression Inventory: Systematic evaluation of psychometric properties. *Journal of Consulting and Clinical Psychology, 52,* 955–967.

Scherer, W. M., & Nakamura, C. Y. (1968). A Fear Survey Schedule for Children (FSS-FC): A factor analytic comparison with manifest anxiety (CMAS). *Behaviour Research and Therapy, 6,* 173–182.

Smucker, M. R., Craighead, W. E., Craighead, L. W., & Green, B. J. (1986). Normative and reliability data for the Children's Depression Inventory. *Journal of Abnormal Child Psychology, 14,* 25–39.

Spielberger, C. D. (1973). *Manual for the State–Trait Anxiety Inventory for Children.* Palo Alto, CA: Consulting Psychologists Press.

Spielberger, C. D. (1983). *Manual for the State–Trait Anxiety Inventory (rev.).* Palo Alto, CA: Consulting Psychologists Press.

Staats, A. W. (1972). Language behavior therapy: A derivative of social behaviorism. *Behavior Therapy, 3,* 165–192.

Stark, K. D., Reynolds, W. M., & Kaslow, N. J. (in press). A comparison of the relative efficacy of self-control and behavior therapy for the reduction of depression in children. *Journal of Abnormal Child Psychology.*

Stein, A. B., Finch, A. J., Jr., Hooke, J. F., Montgomery, L. E., & Nelson, W. M., III. (1975). Cognitive tempo and the mode of representation in emotionally disturbed children and normal children. *Journal of Psychology, 90,* 197–201.

Stenner, A. J., & Katzenmeyer, W. G. (1979). *Self-Observation Scales: Technical manual and user's guide.* Durham, NC: NTS Research.

Strober, M., Green, J, & Carlson, G. (1981). Utility of the Beck Depression Inventory with psychiatrically hospitalized adolescents. *Journal of Consulting and Clinical Psychology, 49,* 482–483.

Swearingen, E. M., & Cohen, L. H. (1985). Measurement of adolescent's life events: The Junior High Life Experiences Survey. *American Journal of Community Psychology, 13,* 69–85.

Teri, L. (1982a). Depression in adolescence: Its relationship to assertion and various aspects of self-image. *Journal of Clinical Child Psychology, 13,* 69–85.

Teri, L. (1982b). The use of the Beck Depression Inventory with adolescents. *Journal of Abnormal Child Psychology, 10,* 277–284.

Trites, R. L., Blouin, A. G., & La Prade, K. (1979). Factor analysis of the Conners Teacher Rating Scale based on a normative sample. *Journal of Consulting and Clinical Psychology, 80,* 615–623.

Walker, H. M. (1983). *Walker Problem Behavior Identification Checklist.* Los Angeles: Western Psychological Services.

Weissman, M., Orvaschel, H., & Padian, N. (1980). Children's symptom and social functioning: Self reports scales. *Journal of Nervous and Mental Disease, 168,* 736–740.

Werry, J. S., Sprague, R. L., & Cohen, M. N. (1975). Conners Teacher Rating Scale for use in drug studies with children: An empirical study. *Journal of Abnormal Psychology, 3,* 217–229.

Wheeler, V. A., & Ladd, G. W. (1982). Assessment of children's self-efficacy for social interactions with peers. *Developmental Psychology, 18,* 795–805.

Wisniewski, S. (Ed.). (1985, May). *OSIQ Newsletter, 1*(2). (Available from Michael Reese Hospital and Medical Center, Adolescent Research Center, De-

partment of Psychiatry, Lake Shore Drive, Chicago, IL 60616)

Witt, J. C. (in press). Face-to-face verbal interaction in school-based consultation: A review of the research. *School Psychology Quarterly.*

Witt, J. C., Cavell, T., Carey, M., Heffer, R., & Martens, B. K. (1988). Child self-report: Interviewing techniques and rating scales. In E. S. Shapiro & T. R. Kratochwill (Eds.), *Behavioral assessment in schools: Conceptual foundations and practical applications* (pp. 384–454). New York: Guilford Press.

Witt, J. C., Elliott, S. N., Gresham, F. M., & Kramer, J. J. (1988). *Assessment of special children: Tests and the problem-solving process.* Glenview, IL: Foresman/Little, Brown.

Young, S. (Ed.). (1984, March). *OSIQ Newsletter, 1*(1). (Available from Michael Reese Hospital and Medical Center, Adolescent Research Center, Department of Psychiatry, Lake Shore Drive, Chicago, IL 60616)

17

Computer-Assisted Assessment of Adolescent and Child Personality: What's Available

KEVIN L. MORELAND
National Computer Systems,
Professional Assessment Services, Minneapolis

SOME HISTORY

The use of machines to process psychological test data is not a recent innovation (Fowler, 1985). A progression from a variety of mechanical and electronic "scoring machines" to the digital computer has freed successive generations of beleaguered secretaries and graduate students from laborious hand scoring of objective tests. The first information concerning scoring machines for the Strong Vocational Interest Blank (SVIB) appeared in 1930 (Campbell, 1971). The SVIB was first scored by a Hollerith card sorter in the late 1920s. This primitive method required that 420 Hollerith cards corresponding to the responses for a single test be selected from among 1,260 possible cards. Those cards were then run through the sorter three times to score the 22 scales then composing the SVIB. Elmer Hankes, a Minneapolis electrical engineer, first used a computer to score the SVIB in 1946. Hankes's analog computer employed keypunched cards like the Hollerith card sorter, but his equipment required far fewer cards per test. A year later, he adapted the same technology to the scoring of the Minnesota Multiphasic Personality Inventory (MMPI; Dahlstrom, Welsh, & Dahlstrom, 1972).

In the mid-1950s, E. F. Lindquist's Measurement Research Center (MRC) in Iowa City began to use optical mark-reading devices to "scan" answer sheets. These "scanners" permitted the processing of test answer sheets themselves, thus avoiding the cumbersome, error-prone process of keypunching test responses onto cards. The central test-processing equipment in use at this writing is a refinement of the MRC system developed over 35 years ago. In 1962, National Computer Systems (NCS) linked an optical scanner with a digital computer and began scoring both the SVIB and the MMPI (Campbell, 1971; Dahlstrom et al., 1972). Most computer-assisted[1] test scoring still employs optical scanning/digital computer technology, and the number and types of tests scored by this method have grown ex-

---

[1] The term "computer-*based* test interpretation" is commonly used to refer to computer-generated narratives describing the meaning of test scores. Sampson (1987) feels that this kind of terminology may cause the practitioner to misunderstand the role of the computer in the assessment process. In particular, he fears that practitioners may lose sight of the importance of human supervision and, possibly, intervention whenever a computer is being used as a tool in the assessment process. He has recommended that the term "computer-*assisted*" be used to emphasize the fact that the computer supports, rather than replaces, human efforts in the assessment domain. That recommendation is followed in this chapter.

ponentially during the last three decades. Though computer-assisted scoring is most easily accomplished for objective tests with a limited number of response alternatives, sophisticated computer programs have also been developed to score the narrative responses elicited by projective techniques (e.g., Gorham, 1967). Prior to the advent of these programs, extensive training, if not professional expertise, was required to score projective tests. Similar programs have also been developed to evaluate other types of complex verbal productions (e.g., Tucker & Rosenberg, 1980).

In addition to keeping nerves from becoming frayed, computer-assisted scoring frees psychologists to spend more time in other functions, such as psychotherapy, where computer technology is not so advanced (see, however, Colby, 1980). It also enables more individuals to undergo psychological assessment. Finally, though not completely immune from the slings and arrows of human imperfections (e.g., Fowler & Coyle, 1968; Grayson & Backer, 1972; Weigel & Phillips, 1967), computer-assisted scoring appears to be more reliable than that done solely by humans (Greene, 1980, pp. 25–26; Klett, Schaefer, & Plemel, 1985). A computer, once correctly programmed, will apply scoring rules with slavish consistency, whereas fatigue and other human frailties may render the psychologist, graduate student, or secretary inconsistent in the application of even the most objective scoring rules (Kleinmuntz, 1969).

In the late 1950s, a group of psychologists and psychiatrists decided that similar advantages might accrue if tests were interpreted by computer. Thus the first computer-assisted test interpretation (CATI) system was developed at the Mayo Clinic in Rochester, Minnesota (Pearson, Swenson, Rome, Mataya, & Brannick, 1965; Rome, Mataya, Pearson, Swenson, & Brannick, 1965). The MMPI was administered on special IBM™ cards that could be marked by the patient and read into the computer by an optical mark reader ("scanner"). The computer then scored the MMPI and printed a series of descriptive statements from among a library of 62 statements, most of which were associated with elevations on single MMPI scales. Soon after the Mayo system was reported in

the literature, the first CATI system to receive widespread professional use was developed by Fowler (1966) at the University of Alabama. In 1965, the Roche Psychiatric Service Institute (RPSI), established by Roche Laboratories to make the Fowler system commercially available to psychologists and psychiatrists, initiated the first national mail-in MMPI CATI service. During the 17 years RPSI operated, approximately one-fourth of the eligible psychiatrists and psychologists in the United States used the service.

The Behaviordyne system (Finney, 1966) and the Caldwell report (Caldwell, 1970) have received wide use in the United States, and are still available. Later MMPI interpretation systems were developed by Lachar (1974) and Butcher (University of Minnesota, 1982, 1984). Other prominent CATI systems that have been marketed commercially in the United States interpret the Sixteen Personality Factor Questionnaire (16PF; Karson & O'Dell, 1975, 1987); the Rorschach (Exner, 1987); and the Millon instruments—the Millon Multiaxial Clinical Inventory, the Millon Behavioral Health Inventory, and the Millon Adolescent Personality Inventory (NCS, 1988), among others. The assessment of child and adolescent personality is dominated by projective instruments that do not lend themselves to large-scale computer processing (cf. Elbert & Holden, 1987). Therefore, computer assistance in the assessment of child and adolescent personality is of relatively recent origin.

This chapter provides an overview of the types of computer-assisted assessment products and services that are currently available for the assessment of adolescent and child personality. The first part of the chapter deals with input—that is, the various ways in which personality assessment data can be entered into a computer. The pros and cons of each of the available methods are highlighted. This is followed by a brief digression into the technical issues surrounding one of the hot topics in computer-assisted assessment today: test administration by computer. The next section of the chapter discusses the output side of computer-assisted assessment—in other words, the types of reports that are currently available. The validity of CATI systems, which is perhaps the most talked-about topic in computer-assisted asseessment today, receives detailed attention. The chapter winds up with some advice for the would-be consumer of computer-assisted personality assessment products for adolescents and children.

INPUT

There are several means of entering assessment data into a computer. All have important implications for the cost of computer processing and the time it takes to receive results.

Central Processing

Central test processing requires that tests be administered in the usual fashion. The answer sheets that have been completed using pencil and paper are then sent to a remote central location for processing. Test protocols are ordinarily sent to the processing site through the mail, but electronic facsimile machines are also beginning to be used for this purpose.[2] Test results are returned to the examiner in the same fashion, with the written report sometimes preceded by a telephoned oral report.

Central test processing flourished initially because the equipment required was very large and costly. Many universities and other large institutions acquired such equipment in the 1960s, but it remained beyond the means of individual practitioners until the mid-1980s. With the increasing availability of inexpensive microcomputers and optical mark-reading equipment, computer-assisted test processing is being decentralized, though the demise of central processing is not yet in sight. Central processing will continue to be attractive when test results are not needed quickly or when a large number of tests must be processed. Academic achievement tests, entrance and competency examinations, licensing and certification examinations, and vocational interest inventories will continue to be processed centrally for the foreseeable

future. At present, many thousands of personality inventories are processed centrally each year too. Most of the MMPIs processed by computer are mailed to NCS. When clients are being seen only once a week, central processing provides test results quickly enough.

Central processing is also economical in the short-run, because the practitioner need not purchase any computer equipment. With the cost of powerful microcomputers near $1,000 and falling, and the price of data communication terminals considerably less than that, central processing, with its associated mailing costs, cannot maintain even this short-run cost advantage for long. Central processing also forces practitioners to stay with tests that have a fixed item sequence. Although there are as yet no psychometric personality tests in general use that are administered using a variable item sequence, there are a number of useful interviews wherein item responses determine which questions will subsequently be asked and in what order (see below).

Virtually all major test publishers in the United States maintain a central processing service for one or more of their tests. NCS maintains the largest such service, with 34 different reports available for 27 different tests.[3]

Teleprocessing

Like central processing, teleprocessing makes use of a remote computer. However, teleprocessing differs from central processing in that raw data are entered locally (e.g., in the practitioner's office) and results are printed locally. In between, the raw data (in electronic form) are transmitted to the computer over the telephone; the data are processed; and results are returned via telephone. Teleprocessing is a relatively new means of processing test data, having been commercially available only since the early 1980s. Because of the advantages detailed

---

[2]Data from facsimiles of answer sheets must currently be keypunched into the computer, placing a practical limitation on the usefulness of this method of transmitting test protocols. However, there is no such limitation when it comes to returning reports to the examiner.

[3]When considering figures like these, the reader needs to keep in mind that new companies and products appear every month (if not more often) and that this chapter was completed in August 1988. Consult Appendix 17.1 of this chapter for a useful listing of many of the computer-assisted products for the assessment of adolescent and child personality available as of early 1988.

below, teleprocessing is becoming an increasingly popular means of processing personality assessment data.

Teleprocessing is an attractive alternative to central processing because test results are available within minutes. It is an attractive alternative to local processing (see the next section) because start-up costs can be lower. The only equipment needed is a data communications terminal. Communications terminals with a built-in printer and 300-baud modem[4] can be purchased for less than $500. Terminals tend to be inexpensive because they are "dumb"; all they will do is send and receive information. By contrast, microcomputers with enough intelligence to allow local test processing cost about twice as much as a terminal. Teleprocessing has the added advantage of allowing the use of virtually any microcomputer (in lieu of a data communications terminal). Software for use in local test processing is typically available for only the most popular brands of microcomputers, such as IBM™.

Furthermore, there are currently some computer-assisted assessment services available via teleprocessing that are not available locally. Services other than test processing can also be obtained via teleprocessing. For example, a number of teleprocessing services are available for use in conducting literature searches. The American Psychological Association's PsychInfo is one example of such a service. The Buros Institute for Mental Measurements maintains its data base of test reviews on a computer that can be accessed by teleprocessing. (See Lieff, 1984, and Pressman, 1984, for examples of other services that can be obtained via teleprocessing.)

The main disadvantage of teleprocessing is that the test user has to pay for the telephone call to the central computer. Fortunately, these charges tend to be modest. My experience is that they currently range from about 50¢ to about $2.00 per test processed. These charges vary according to the test, the type of results desired, and the teleprocessing service being used. There is always a charge for the telephone hookup, though it may be "bundled" with the charge for test processing.

At present two American test publishers maintain teleprocessing services: NCS and the Institute for Personality and Ability Testing (IPAT). NCS's ARION II™ service is the larger of the two, offering 31 different reports for 24 different tests. ARION II can be accessed by virtually any 300- or 1,200-baud data communications terminal, or by most microcomputers using a modem and communications software. Raw test data may be entered into ARION II for teleprocessing in two ways: by entering item responses from an answer sheet via a keyboard, or by processing answer sheets through local optical mark-reading equipment. Raw scores, standard scores, and derived scores (e.g., produced by regression equations) are then calculated by NCS's central computer. Those scores and, in many cases, a CATI are then returned to the practitioner's office via telephone. The test results can then be printed immediately or, if the practioner is using a microcomputer, stored for later use.

The Teletest™ service can be accessed with either a 1,200-baud telecommunications terminal or a microcomputer. Data can be entered into the Teletest system in two ways. All the available tests and reports can be accessed by entering raw scale scores into the system via a keyboard. Standard scores and derived scores are then calculated by IPAT's central computer and returned to the user's terminal or microcomputer. IPAT has also developed the Teledisk™ to allow adolescent and adult clients to take the 16PF and the Adult Personality Inventory on-line on an IBM personal computer. That is, the computer presents test items to the client on the screen, and the client responds by pressing the appropriate key on the computer keyboard. The item endorsements are then processed and the results are reported via telephone. As of this writing, IPAT is considering expanding the Teledisk to accommodate more tests and different brands of microcomputers. A third American test publisher, Consulting Psychologists Press, is also preparing to open a teleprocessing service.

---

[4]"Baud" refers to the speed at which data are transmitted. For example, 300 baud is 30 characters per second. The faster data are transmitted, the lower the telephone charges for teleprocessing. A "modem" is an electronic device that translates (or modulates) signals from a computer into signals that can be transmitted over ordinary telephone lines. A modem will also demodulate signals received over the telephone so that a computer can read them.

Local Processing

With local test processing, nothing has to be sent through the mail or over the telephone in order to accomplish all the steps necessary to receive computer-assisted personality assessment results. For the individual practitioner, this means using a microcomputer. Local processing may involve an optical mark reader, but it need not. A microcomputer used for local test processing can also be configured to teleprocess, but need not be.

Two big advantages of local processing are practitioner control and flexibility. The local system will never be unavailable because of routine maintenance at an inconvenient time. If the optical mark reader is on the blink, the responses can always be key-entered. If, for any reason, the local system cannot be used to process tests (perhaps because the appropriate software is unavailable), it may be possible to teleprocess those tests. If that is not possible, the practitioner can fall back on central test processing. Hand scoring is an option for many tests, but, as is noted in the section on output (below), hand scoring often means giving up much of the information that is provided by the computer. On the other hand, local software is available to assist in the scoring and interpretation of instruments (such as the Rorschach) that must be administered and, to some extent, scored by hand (see Exner, 1987).

Another advantage of local test processing is that it forces the practitioner to own a computer. If the computer is configured for teleprocessing, the practitioner can enjoy the nontesting services, such as those described earlier, that are available over the telephone. Optical mark readers also have many nontesting applications, such as processing of client intake forms. In addition, the computer owner can use local software for everything from billing to word processing.

The ability to administer tests on-line is another advantage usually touted for local test processing, although, as noted, on-line administration is also compatible with teleprocessing. There is some professional controversy about the administration of tests by computer, which I discuss in more detail later. There are also some practical advantages and disadvantages to be considered.

One often hears anecdotal claims that obstreperous youths who refuse to complete ordinary tests can be seduced by the computer. A number of useful structured interviews must be administered by a human or a computer—that is, they are not amenable to the paper-and-pencil format (cf. Stein, 1987). The reason why a computer is necessary is that these interviews use branching logic. For example, if a parent indicates that he or she is married, the computer may then ask whether this is the parent's first marriage. If the parent, on the other hand, indicates that he or she has never been married, no further questions about marriage are asked. This is obviously quite different from paper-and-pencil tests, which have a fixed item pool presented in a fixed sequence. Branching logic allows the use of a very large item pool without exhausting clients with too many inquiries or irritating them with irrelevant questions. Tests that branch on the basis of the psychometric characteristics of the items (rather than rational considerations, as in the case of interviews) have been under development by ability testers for many years (e.g., Weiss & Vale, 1987). Such "computer-adaptive" tests are not yet available for personality assessment, but clinically oriented researchers are working on the development of such instruments (see Butcher, Keller, & Bacon, 1985). This is surely the wave of the not-too-distant future.

There is one big disadvantage of on-line test administration that typically occurs to people once the high-tech glamor of using the computer to administer an instrument has worn off: Administration monopolizes a microcomputer. As long as a parent or child is completing an instrument on-line, a microcomputer cannot be used to write reports, update patient records, send out bills, reconcile accounts, or do anything else. And some popular instruments take a long time to complete on-line. Some parents can complete the 600 items of the full Personality Inventory for Children (PIC; Wirt, Lachar, Klinedinst, & Seat, 1984) on-line in 45 minutes; however, others may take as long as 2 hours. It is doubtful that this is a cost-effective use of the computer equipment. By contrast, an experienced clerk can easily type in all 600 PIC responses from an answer sheet in less than 5 minutes. An optical mark reader can process an answer sheet in a few seconds.

Currently, there exists an embarrassment of riches when it comes to assessment software for local use. Paradoxically, this may be a disadvantage to the potential consumer of computer-assisted assessment. The advent of cheap microcomputers and easy-to-learn computer programming languages has changed things greatly from that time not too long ago when tens of thousands of dollars' worth of equipment and highly specialized knowledge were needed to open a computer-assisted assessment business. Gone are the days when the tremendous investment necessary to develop and market computer-assisted assessment products virtually guaranteed that they had been carefully developed by experts. Much of the software now available for local computer-assisted assessment has been developed by individuals who have no special qualifications. Many of the assessment software companies that have sprung up in the last few years appear to be located in someone's basement. Furthermore, an alarming number of computer software companies spring up overnight, only to disappear just as quickly (Larson, 1984).

This is not to say that none of the new companies can deliver and support a high-quality product. Every company was young once. Psychological Assessment Resources is an example of a company that 5 years ago could have been fairly described as a basement operation; today it is one of the major competitiors in the field of computer-assisted assessment. Other new companies appear to produce high-quality assessment tools that are not psychometric in nature—for example, structured interviews and problem checklists. However, my feeling is that practitioners are on safer ground dealing with established test publishers if their product meets their needs. The established publishers generally have more personnel and expertise to devote to critical issues such as quality assurance of software before it is sold and support of that software in the field after it is sold. They also tend to command the best software authors. And, most importantly, they are unlikely to disappear overnight.

Technical "Input" Issues: On-Line Administration of Tests and Interviews

In the abstract, computer administration of tests and interviews appears to be a nonissue. Procedures for computer administration of tests are developed in the same way that administration procedures for conventional tests are developed, are they not? The answer is yes, in principle. As a matter of fact, most assessment tools that are currently available for on-line administration were developed for conventional administration. Therefore, as a practical matter, practitioners must be concerned that factors indigenous to on-line administration but irrelevant to the purposes of the test may alter test performance. These computer-linked factors may change the nature of the task so dramatically that the computer-administered and conventional versions of a test cannot be said to be measuring the same construct. For example, scores on a test of divergent thinking (e.g., listing uses for common objects within a time limit) will depend heavily on typing ability if administered via a computer keyboard, but will be completely independent of typing skill if administered in the conventional fashion. In such cases, normative, reliability, and validity data cannot be generalized from the conventional to the computer-administered version of the test.

There are a number of plausible reasons to believe that differences may be found between computer-assisted and conventional item presentation. First, the computer presents items a few at a time, at most. On conventional tests respondents often have access to all the questions at the same time; this causes some to skip around looking for questions they can answer. This may be a boon to the test respondent, as when a later question provides a clue to the answer for a question that was skipped. Skipping around in a personality inventory may create a more consistent response pattern than would otherwise be the case. For example, adolescents who describe themselves as "hostile" on an adjective checklist may be more likely to endorse "angry" if the first answer can be reviewed. The computer usually does not permit such item interconnections.

Another difference between administration methods is that the computer usually requires a response—though not necessarily an answer—to each item. The test respondent who wishes to skip an item usually pushes a button to do so. As just noted, the computer does not present an entire test at once, so the respondent has no way of knowing how many items are on the test. On many conventional tests the respondent can see all the items, and the prospect of taking a long test may lead to hurried answers or even omissions. The computer may force more careful attention to each item, which may affect the meaning of individual responses, thus affecting the results.

In both of these instances, it is reasonable to suppose that computer-assisted administration may be psychometrically superior to conventional administration. However, it may also cause the results to differ enough from those obtained from conventional administration to make data developed in that mode inapplicable when the instrument is administered via computer.

There is evidence that certain types of items may function differently depending on the mode of administration, regardless of how carefully they were adapted to the computer. Greaud and Green (1986) found large differences in scores on speeded tests between computer-assisted and paper-and-pencil administrations. Their tests involved very simple arithmetic problems, so it is not surprising that the time needed to record a response—a variable that differed greatly as a function of administration mode—significantly affected scores. Hoffman and Lundberg (1976) found the two modes to be equivalent on multiple-choice and true–false items; however, the computer presentation of items requiring matching responses resulted in significantly lower scores, different numbers of changed answers, and different patterns of changed answers.

There is also evidence that rather subtle differences between on-line and conventional test administrations can produce large differences in test scores produced by the two modes. Studies of on-line administration of the MMPI indicate that providing an explicit "Cannot Say" option often produces a greater number of item omissions than is found when the option is less obvious (Hona-

ker, 1988). Allred and Harris (1984) indicated that a similar phenomenon is encountered when the Adjective Checklist is administered by computer and respondents must therefore actively reject an adjective rather than passively fail to endorse it.

The content of items may also have an effect. Many years ago, Smith (1963) hypothesized that "confession-type" questions might be answered more honestly on the impersonal computer. This is not a very appealing hypothesis where comparisons with apparently impersonal paper-and-pencil questionnaires are concerned. There is no *a priori* reason to believe that questionnaires are any more "invasive" than computers. However, three studies have found some evidence that this is the case (Evan & Miller, 1969; Hart & Goldstein, 1985; Koson, Kitchen, Kochen, & Stodolsky, 1970). Skinner and Allen (1983), on the other hand, found no differences between subjects' willingness to describe their alcohol and illegal drug use on a paper-and-pencil questionnaire and on a computer. To muddy the waters further, one study of on-line administration of the MMPI found patients producing more pathological profiles when the test was administered in the usual fashion than when it was administered via computer (Bresolin, 1984). The data from automated interviews are not consistent in this regard, though the hypothesis that people might respond more honestly to an impersonal computer than to a human interviewer is intuitively appealing. Seven studies have found individuals admitting more socially undesirable behaviors to a computer than to an interviewer (Carr, Ghosh, & Ancil, 1983; Duffy & Waterton, 1984; Greist & Klein, 1980; Angle, Johnson, Grebenkemper, & Ellinwood, 1979; Angle, Ellinwood, & Carroll, 1978; Greist, Klein, Van Cura, & Erdman, 1975; Lucas, Mullins, Luna, & McInroy, 1977), whereas two have not (Reich, Robins, Woodruff, Taibelson, Rich, & Cunningham, 1975; Skinner & Allen, 1983). Unfortunately, it is not clear whether the former results are due to an increased willingness to admit things to a computer, to the fact that computers can be counted on to ask everyone the same questions while interviewers cannot, or to both.

On the other hand, it seems fair to conclude that people tend to be more willing to deal frankly with sensitive material when interacting with an impersonal computer than when talking with another person. This may be a problem even if, as seems likely, the data gathered during a computer interview are more accurate than those gathered in a face-to-face encounter (Greist et al., 1973; compare the conclusions of Lucas et al., 1977, with those of Pernanen, 1974). For example, it seems likely that the developers of the revised third edition of the *Diagnostic and Statistical Manual of Mental Disorders* (DSM-III-R; American Psychiatric Association, 1987) were using implicit norms based on years of experience in evaluating patients when they decided that one must possess X number of symptoms of a certain type in order to be diagnosed as suffering Y disorder. Those "cutting scores" may result in overdiagnosis if applied to data from the structured psychiatric interview schedules that are now being computerized (see Stein, 1987).

Despite these inconsistencies, the bulk of the evidence on computer adaptations of paper-and-pencil questionnaires points to the conclusion that nonequivalence is typically small enough to be of no practical consequence, if it is present at all (see also Beaumont & French, 1987; Blankenship, 1976; Harrell & Lombardo, 1984; Katz & Dalby, 1981a, 1981b; Lukin, Dowd, Plake, & Kraft, 1985; Ridgway, MacCulloch, & Mills, 1982; Wilson, Thompson, & Wylie, 1982). Rezmovic (1977) found that computer administration caused extreme scorers to become even more extreme, suggesting that nonequivalence in questionnaires may occur mainly at points in the distribution of scores where measurement is already imprecise. The only consistent finding in the literature is that provision of an obvious "Cannot Say" option on the computer changes MMPI and California Psychological Inventory (CPI) scores (Honaker, 1988; Scissons, 1976).[5] This finding appears to be due to the change in response format between computer-administered and conventional versions of the tests. When care is taken to keep the

two administration formats as similar as possible, this problem disappears (Honaker, 1988).

These conclusions can only be tentative because of the paucity of studies and the fact that all used adult subjects. Moreover, only a few of these investigations took individual differences into account. There is some evidence—both direct and indirect—that individual differences may be important. As noted, Rezmovic (1977) found mode effects mainly for extreme scorers. Koson et al. (1970) found that only their female subjects tended to be more honest on the computer. In addition to this direct evidence, there is a large and rapidly growing body of literature on attitudes toward computer-administered tests and interviews, as well as on the affective reactions engendered by computer test administration. Adults are generally favorable to being questioned by computer; indeed, many prefer interaction with a computer to conventional assessment (see Bresolin, 1984; Coddington & King, 1972; Greist, 1975; Honaker, 1988; Lucas, 1977). Adults have rated interacting with the computer as at least as relaxing as other methods of assessment (Coddington & King, 1972; Honaker, 1988; Skinner & Allen, 1983), even if the computer initially was somewhat more anxiety-provoking than a traditional questionnaire (Lushene, O'Neil, & Dunn, 1974). However, a significant minority of subjects in these same studies report a persistent negative reaction to the computer. The elderly compose one demographic group that is, in general, uncomfortable being questioned by a computer (Carr, Wilson, Ghosh, Ancil, & Woods, 1982; Volans & Levy, 1982).[6] It is reasonable to speculate that such negative reactions may adversely affect the quality of computer-administered assessments. Perhaps people who are frustrated by having a cold, unresponsive computer ask questions or who are daunted by the technology may respond carelessly or be too nervous to devote proper attention to the assessment task.

In summary, most data collected on adults indicate that if a computer-assisted adminis-

---

[5]See Hofer and Green (1985) and Honaker (1988) for somewhat different interpretations of these data.

[6]It is only fair to point out that we do not know how the elderly feel about traditional assessment; they may not like that much, either.

tration procedure is comparable to the conventional one, comparable results will be obtained. The data are a little more shaky with regard to personality inventories and interviews than ability tests. This is not surprising, given the widely held belief that responses to the former have more complex determinants than responses to the latter, regardless of mode of administration. Ability testers have never concerned themselves with issues such as social desirability! Furthermore, it is important to keep in mind that none of the studies reviewed in this section involved adolescent or child subjects, and only one involved parent responses about children (Coddington & King, 1972). Responses from these respondents may be even more complicated. The assessor needs to be familiar with the different types of test equivalence and their respective implications for the use of interpretive data. Hofer and Green (1985) provide a brief, practical synopsis of this complex topic. If an individual expresses reluctance to interact with the computer, the test or interview should probably be administered in the conventional fashion. In any case, extra care should be taken to insure that individuals understand the task at hand and are able to respond appropriately. Johnson and White (1980) found that elderly people who received 1 hour of training in the use of a terminal prior to testing scored significantly higher on the Wonderlic Personnel Test than did those who received no training. Practitioners may find it beneficial to develop several samples of different item types for training in the use of the computer. Equipment and other conditions of testing are important determinants of the quality of any assessment, but computer administration places an extra burden on the assessor to see that testing conditions are optimal. Properly functioning equipment (including a clean, glare-free display with adequate resolution) and clear response devices (perhaps with covers over unused keys) are important.

OUTPUT

As with input, there are several output options available to the consumer of computer-assisted personality assessment. Choice of the best option depends mainly on the amount of information necessary to discharge the assessment task at hand. Time may also be a consideration. The more detailed the computer-assisted report, the less time and effort a practitioner must put forth to work up a case. In reading what follows, one should keep in mind the fact that the taxomony of report types is merely a heuristic device. In practice, reports are frequently a combination of the pure types discussed in the following section; in particular, interpretive reports usually report scores. Computer-assisted personality assessment systems can be usefully characterized along two dimensions: the amount of information they provide and the method used to develop them.

Information Provided

Scoring Reports

Scoring reports present just what their name implies: test scores. The scores may be simply listed or they may be drawn on a profile, but scores are all that such reports provide. Some tests—notably vocational interest inventories with well over 100 scales, such as the Kuder Occupational Interest Survey and the Strong Interest Inventory—are much too long to score by hand. Thus, computer-assisted scoring reports are a necessity rather than an option for those tests. Even in cases where the test may be scored by hand, scoring reports will be useful when a practitioner desires to use a large number of scores. One can, for example, get by with hand-scoring the 16 PIC scales that have been part of the basic profile since the test was first published (Wirt, Lachar, Klinedinst, & Seat, 1977). However, some practitioners feel that they get more out of the test if they have scores on some of the special scales available for the test. It takes roughly a minute to hand-score and plot one PIC scale. Thus one need not use many special scales before computer-assisted scoring becomes cost-effective. This is to say nothing about the increase in scoring accuracy that can be expected from computer-assisted scoring (see Greene, 1980, p. 25; Klett et al., 1985).

Extended Scoring Reports

Zachary (1984) defined extended scoring reports as "usually involving the addition [to a scoring report] of detailed statistical output but little or no case-specific narrative" (p. 9). One does not often see test profiles that include statistical confidence intervals plotted around scores, and statistical significance tests. These kinds of data make it possible for practitioners to identify especially meaningful scores at a glance. They should also increase the practitioner's confidence that those scores are, in fact, important. Everyone ought to be willing to admit that statistical significance tests are bound to beat old-fashioned clinical "eyeballing" of profiles! And what busy practitioner is going to calculate confidence intervals by hand—especially for tests with dozens of scales? On the other hand, as Zachary was careful to point out, it is still up to the practitioner to determine the clinical significance of the statistical significance.

The possibilities for reports of this kind are legion. For example, different confidence intervals might be computed for use in interscale and test–retest comparisons (see Dudek, 1979). Jackson (1984) provides statistical indices of similarity between Jackson Vocational Interest Survey profiles and mean profiles for a number of occupational clusters and college majors. This kind of report is widely available for popular ability measures, such as the Wechsler, Stanford–Binet, and Kaufman instruments. George Huba and his colleagues at Western Psychological Services (WPS) are applying similar techniques to many inventories, including the Developmental Profile II for children (WPS, 1988).

Descriptive Reports

Descriptive reports may be distinguished from other types of CATIs by two factors: Each scale on the instrument is interpreted without reference to the others, scale by scale; and comments on any one scale are usually quite cryptic. These interpretations often involve no more than an adverb modifying the adjectival form of the scale name. Such an interpretation of a high score on an anxiety scale might, for example, read: "Johnny's parents report that he is very anxious." Thus, the interpretive comments directly reflect empirical data. If one discounts the ambiguity introduced by the use of words

in place of numbers, the interpretive statements are as valid as the scales themselves. At first blush, this kind of report may seem so simple-minded as to be unhelpful; this is not the case. This type of report can be especially helpful when a test has a large number of scales or when a large number of tests need to be interpreted in a short period of time. They allow the practitioner to identify the most deviant scores quickly and easily. This kind of report is most helpful if an instrument contains scales that are reported in terms of different types of standard scores (e.g., Ripley & Ripley, 1979) or different normative samples (e.g., Hansen, 1987). The MMPI report developed at the Mayo Clinic was the first report of this type. Many structured interviews completed by parents yield this kind of report (see Stein, 1987).

Screening Reports

Screening reports, like descriptive reports, are cryptic. They are distinguished from descriptive reports in that relationships among scales are usually considered in the interpretation, and the interpretive comments are not usually couched in terms of a single scale name. The Minnesota Personnel Screening Report for the MMPI (University of Minnesota, 1984) is a screening report in this sense. The main body of that report is very cryptic—five 6-point rating scales. None of the rating scales corresponds directly to an MMPI scale, however. In fact, the rating on each of the five scales is determined by the configuration of a number of MMPI scales. The rules governing the "Content Themes" presented in that report are also complex. The comment that the client "may keep problems to himself or herself too much" results from consideration of the following set of rules:

L and K are greater than F and
F is less than $55T$ and
D, Pa, Pt, and Sc are less than $65T$ and
    Hy is greater than $69T$ or
    $Hy2$ is greater than $63T$ or
    Hy is greater than $64T$, and $Hy1$ or $Hy5$ is greater than $59T$ or
    R is greater than $59T$ or
    $D5$ is greater than $59T$

Screening reports are most helpful in situations where the same decision can be reached by multiple paths. Take the example of screening prospective foster parents for emotional fitness. A screening report like the Minnesota Personnel Screening Report may deem a candidate's emotional fitness "suspect" if he or she (1) seems to be a thrill-seeking individual; (2) is so neurotic that he or she is likely to be preoccupied with his or her own needs, to the detriment of the child; or (3) may have a drinking problem.

Many of the structured interviews for children and adolescents cited by Stein (1987) can be classified as screening reports as well as descriptive reports. While not psychometric in the sense of the MMPI, they do use complex decision rules to arrive at a narrow conclusion, usually a proposed psychiatric diagnosis.

Like that of descriptive reports, the output of screening reports is limited. However, unlike that of descriptive reports, the validation of screening reports is not simple and straightforward. As illustrated above, the simple output may be generated by extensive, complex sets of rules, each of which may have to be validated.

Consultative Reports

Dahlstrom et al. (1972) contrasted consultative reports for the MMPI with screening reports in the following fashion: "The intent [of consultative reports] is to provide a more detailed analysis of the test data in professional language appropriate to communication between colleagues" (p. 313). In other words, consultative reports are designed to mimic as closely as possible the reports generated every day by human test interpreters. Well-developed reports of this type are characterized by the smoothly flowing prose and detailed exploitation of the data that are expected from an expert human consultant. Indeed, the chief advantage of these reports is that they can provide busy practitioners with a consultation from someone who has spent years studying and using the instrument in question—an expert to whom the average practitioner would not ordinarily have access. Fowler's system for the MMPI produced the first CATIs of this type. Lachar's (1987) system for the PIC is an example of a consultative report describing adolescents and children. These types of reports are what come to most practitioners' minds upon hearing the phrase "computer-based test interpretations." Consultative reports are the subject of most of the rest of this chapter.

How Computer-Assisted Test Interpretations Are Developed

In 1956 Paul Meehl called for a good "cookbook" for test interpretation. He was advocating the actuarial approach to prediction and description defined by Sines (1966) as "the empirical determination of the regularities that may exist between specified psychological test data and equally clearly specified socially, clinically, or theoretically significant non-test characteristics of the persons tested" (p. 135). This approach to CATI development can best be illustrated through the example of one such system.

Unlike the MMPI and most other popular psychological tests, which were published prior to the computer age, Lachar's CATI system for the PIC was developed without a considerable "clinical lore" concerning the performance of the PIC scales (Lachar, 1987). (Fowler, 1987, considers the concurrent development of test and interpretive system an "ideal" strategy, in which test development efforts enrich the evolving interpretation system.)

Efforts to compile a data base that would allow the development of empirically supported interpretive guidelines were initiated before the PIC was published. Criterion data collection forms (see Appendix A in Lachar & Gdowski, 1979) were accepted by the staff of an active psychiatry teaching service as performing clinically meaningful functions. An application form gathered presenting complaints, developmental history, and facts concerning pregnancy and birth. A form mailed to the child's school recorded teacher observations, estimates of achievement, and judgments about the causes of observed problems, as well as suggested solutions. A final form was completed by the psychiatry resident or psychology intern who conducted the initial evaluation of the child or adolescent and parents. This last form allowed the collection of dichotomous ratings (present–

absent) of descriptors that could be, for the most part, arrayed under the following headings: affect, cognitive functioning, interpersonal relations, physical development and health, family relations, and parent description. Psychiatric diagnoses and ideal treatment recommendations were also recorded. Collection of data using these three forms resulted in an actuarial analysis of the PIC scores of 431 children and adolescents (Lachar & Gdowski, 1979).

The actuarial data base that provided the interpretive paragraphs and paragraph assignment to scores was generated in two phases. In the first phase, the 322 descriptive variables from the parent, teacher, and clinician forms were correlated with each of 20 basic profile scales to develop scale correlates. In the second phrase, each identified correlate was studied to determine the relationship between the correlate and PIC scale T-score ranges. That is, correlate frequency was tabulated within a number of contiguous T-score ranges, usually 10 points in width. The goal of this process was to identify appropriate T-score ranges to which a given correlate could be applied, as well as to obtain an estimate of the frequency of each correlate within the T-score ranges. Rules were established to lead to correlate classification rates similar to their base rates within the study sample. A similar analysis determined frequent patterns of elevated T-score ranges and allowed the development of narrative paragraphs that reflected the elevation of two or more profile scales. Those efforts produced interpretive correlates like those in Table 17.1. Those correlates form the basis of the CATI system for the PIC sold by WPS (WPS, 1988). It is easy to see that this system conforms to Sines's (1966) definition of an actuarial system. It is also easy to understand Meehl's (1956) enthusiasm for the actuarial approach to test interpretation: The interpretations are, *ipso facto*, valid within known limits.[7]

The combination of automated scoring and computer-assisted, actuarial interpretation would seem to be a marriage made in Assessment Heaven. Unfortunately, this relationship remains in the courtship stage. In spite of the fact that this is the way CATI systems *should* be developed, only three such CATI systems are commercially available: those for the PIC and the Marital Satisfaction Inventory (MSI; WPS, 1988), and Gough's interpretive system for the CPI (Consulting Psychologists Press, 1988). After Meehl published his article, there were several major attempts to produce actuarial "cookbooks" for the MMPI (Drake & Oetting, 1959; Gilberstadt & Duker, 1965; Gynther, Altman, & Sletten, 1973; Marks & Seeman, 1963), including one for adolescents (Marks, Seeman, & Haller, 1974). These herculean efforts have fared poorly outside the settings in which they were developed. Application of the complex profile classification rules necessary for actuarial interpretation causes the bulk of the tests to go unclassified (e.g., Briggs, Taylor, & Tellegen, 1966). Even when the adult "cookbooks" published by Marks and Seeman and by Gilberstadt and Duker have been combined, the majority of tests have failed to find an interpretive niche (e.g., Payne & Wiggins, 1968). Although ignoring some of the classification rules allowed a greater number of tests to be classified, Payne and Wiggins still could not classify all of their sample. This is to say nothing of the decrement in validity that has been shown to occur when the actuarial correlates are generalized to populations differing in base rates of psychopathology, demographic characteristics, and other important factors (see Fowler & Athey, 1971; Gynther & Brilliant, 1968; Palmer, 1971). This state of affairs led some psychologists who were determined to exploit the advantages of CATI, such as Fowler (1969), to advocate the "automated

---

[7]Lanyon (1987, p. 228), however, recently noted: At the narrative level of interpretation, what is presented is likely to depart significantly from the simple statement level. There are two kinds of departures. First, there are a very large number of possible combinations of statements, and each combination, together with its associated verbs and conjunctions, has unique meaning beyond the contribution of each statement.

Second, the narrative product as a whole conveys to the reader an overall impression that transcends individual statements and sentences. Therefore, for a narrative to be valid, demonstration of the validity of individual statements in an objective or automated context is necessary but not sufficient. It must be shown that the overall narrative itself correctly represents the respondent (p. 228).

TABLE 17.1. Actuarial Correlates of the Personality Inventory for Children Delinquency Scale

Descriptor[a]	Correlations[b]	Base rate	T-score ranges								Decision rule	True positive rate
			30–59	60–69	70–79	80–89	90–99	100–109	110–119	>120		
Impulsive behavior	.25, .39	68[c]	40	57	61	72	76	72	84	100	>79T	79%
Temper tantrums	.27, .25	43	18	42	40	38	44	63	64	69	>99T <60T	66% 47%
Involved w/police	.44, .49	17	0	4	6	10	21	19	58	63	>109T	15%
Dislikes school	.18, .38	39	28	28	28	30	48	55	63	70	>89T	57%
Mother inconsistent in setting limits	.26, .30	59	27	45	61	59	64	82	89	67	>99T <60T	79% 63%

Note. From *Actuarial Assessment of Child and Adolescent Personality: An Interpretive Guide for the Personality Inventory for Children Profile* by D. Lachar and C. G. Gwodski, 1979, Los Angeles: Western Psychological Services. Copyright 1979 by Western Psychological Services, Inc. Adapted by permission.

[a]Clinician ratings.

[b]n's = 215 and 216, respectively.

[c]Percentage of children rated as displaying the characteristic.

clinician . . . until the actuary comes" (pp. 109–110).

The essential difference between the computer-assisted actuarial and computer-assisted clinical approaches is that the former method assigns interpretive statements on the basis of their statistical association with test data, whereas statements chosen by the latter approach are a function of human decision making (cf. Wiggins, 1973). The psychologist who devises the statements and assignment rules in the computer-assisted clinical approach typically makes use of available actuarial data, but, as suggested by the fate of the actuarial "cookbooks" discussed above, is sometimes forced to rely on his or her practical experience in order to insure that all tests are interpreted (Fowler, 1969). Fowler assumed that even though practical experience must sometimes be resorted to, the psychologist developing the interpretive statements usually possesses greater experience and, presumably, expertise than the average psychologist. (Unfortunately, the advent of microcomputers has made that assumption less tenable than it was when Fowler was writing; see Moreland, 1987.) Although undoubtedly not as good as actuarial interpretation, computer-assisted clinical interpretation possesses several advantages over human interpretation. In addition to those advantages noted above in the discussion of computer-assisted scoring of test data, computer-assisted interpretation has an advantage over human interpretation when large and varied populations are involved. Fowler (1969) noted that computers can store tremendous volumes of material and can retrieve them more rapidly and reliably than humans. Thus, whereas the average psychologist is typically limited in the research literature and population samples to which he or she is exposed and the information about them he or she can retain, the expert human interpreter can see to it that the computer adjusts for relevant demographic and other nontest variables.

The promise of the "automated clinician" has been realized in a number of studies, some employing the MMPI (e.g., Goldberg, 1965, 1970; Kleinmuntz, 1963) and many involving other types of clinical judgments (e.g., DeDombal, 1979; Greist et al., 1973, 1974; McDonald, 1976; but see Blois, 1980;

Kleinmuntz, 1968; and Weizenbaum, 1976 for counterexamples). It comes as no surprise, then, that "automated clinicians" to interpret psychological tests have proliferated. Several CATI systems have been developed that interpret, but do not score, the Rorschach (Century Diagnostics, 1980; Exner, 1987; Harris, Niedner, Feldman, Fink, & Johnson, 1981; Piotrowski, 1964). There has also been work on an interpretive program for the Holtzman Inkblot Technique (Holtzman, 1975), which can also be computer-scored (Gorham, 1967). Computer-assisted clinical prediction systems have also been developed for the Halstead–Reitan Neuropsychological Battery (Adams, 1975; Finkelstein, 1977; Golden, in press). By far the majority of computer-assisted interpretive systems have, however, been developed for objective tests. Fowler (1969) has suggested that this is because the administration, scoring, and interpretation of projective techniques is often highly individualistic and based heavily on intuition and clinical experience (cf. Exner & Exner, 1972). Scoring of many ability tests, such as the Halstead–Reitan, often requires professional judgment. By contrast, objective tests have traditionally emphasized standardized administration and scoring, and have emphasized an objective, empirical approach to interpretation.

Of the objective tests, personality inventories have most often been the subjects of computer-assisted interpretation. The reasons for this are unclear, but I would speculate that one reason is the fact that data from many scales and indices, as well as nontest data (e.g., demographic characteristics), are often combined to arrive at complex and lengthy interpretations (cf. Kleinmuntz, 1975). The complexity of this task allows for the fullest use of the advantages conferred by the computer, described above.

WHAT DO THE DATA SHOW?

With very few exceptions, current CATI systems use the method of computer-assisted clinical prediction. Thus, many of the available CATI systems need to be validated, just as a test needs to be validated. The issue with actuarial interpretations is not validity per se—they are necessarily valid in the setting in which they were developed—but generalizability (see, however, footnote 7). As already noted, David Lachar and his colleagues have expended a great deal of creative effort in developing an actuarial CATI system for the PIC. However, most of the empirical correlates used in this system were developed in one clinical setting. Will they be equally applicable in other settings? The jury is out. The same is not true of the decision-tree "key" approach to the interpretation of neuropsychological data (mainly the Halstead–Reitan Battery) developed by Russell, Neuringer, and Goldstein (1970). Several studies have called into question the generalizability of Russell et al.'s initial findings (Anthony, Heaton, & Lehman, 1980; Goldstein & Shelly, 1982; Swiercinsky & Warnock, 1977). This is not too surprising when one considers the fact that the "key" approach was developed in a hospital serving only U.S. military veterans—a rather select population. Comparative studies have found that the computer-assisted clinical prediction systems developed by Adams (1975) and Finkelstein (1977) are about as accurate as the Russell et al. "key" approach (Adams, Kvale, & Keegan, 1984; Anthony et al., 1980). They are not, however, as accurate as expert human interpreters (Heaton, Grant, Anthony, & Lehman, 1981). It is also worth noting that there are numerous instances in which neurologists' (Kleinmuntz, 1968) and other physicians' (Blois, 1980) clinical judgment has bested the computer.

A very different state of affairs exists with regard to computer-assisted clinical interpretation of personality tests. Both the means of assessing system validity and the results of validity studies differ from those in neuropsychology and medicine. This may reflect the primitive state of personality assessment relative to neuropsychology and medicine; criterion information is much more definitive in the latter two areas. It may also reflect the comparatively primitive state of computer programs for neuropsychological assessment (cf. Adams & Heaton, 1985) and in some areas of medical diagnosis. Time will tell.

In the United States, far more CATI systems have been developed—and sold—for objective personality inventories for adolescents and adults than for any other kind of psychological test. Yet, viewed in proportion to their availability, far fewer validity studies have been completed on those systems. As will be seen shortly, the validity studies that have been completed on those systems are also far less scientifically adequate than those reviewed above.

The MMPI is used all over the world (see Butcher & Pancheri, 1976; Butcher & Spielberger, 1985). No other test has given rise to as many CATI systems (see Butcher & Owen, 1978; Butcher & Pancheri, 1976), and these systems have been the subject of most of the attempts to validate CATIs. These investigations of the MMPI appear to be representative of the methods used to study the validity of CATIs for personality inventories (cf. Green, 1982). Hence, studies of MMPI CATIs are the focus of attention here. Those studies have involved several experimental approaches. A few studies have compared CATIs with human interpretations, using rigorous experimental designs (e.g., Bringmann, Balance, & Giesbrecht, 1972; Glueck & Reznikoff, 1965; Johnson, Giannetti, & Williams, 1978). The "criterion" reports, since they are prepared by human interpreters, may provide a poor standard against which to judge the validity of computer-assisted interpretations of the MMPI. The validity of a clinician's interpretation of the MMPI is often low enough that a CATI can be at serious variance with it and still be accurate (e.g., Graham, 1967). Labeck, Johnson, and Harris (1983) asked three experts to rate the quality and accuracy of interpretive rules and interpretive statements for the MMPI CATI system developed by Labeck. Though suffering from the same problem as those studies using clinicians' reports as criteria, this study does highlight a useful means of evaluating and improving CATI systems. This is especially true in light of the fact that most CATI systems are developed by one individual.

Most of the published studies of MMPI CATI validity have involved asking the recipients of CATIs to rate the accuracy of the interpretations on the basis of their knowledge of the test respondents (Green, 1982; Moreland, 1985; Vincent & Castillo, 1984). Though disparaged by some writers (Lanyon, 1984; Matarazzo, 1983), these studies are considered promising by other experts (see Adair, 1978)—especially if slightly modified (see Butcher, 1978; Webb, Miller, & Fowler, 1970)—and therefore merit further consideration.

The "customer satisfaction" (Lanyon, 1984) studies have been overwhelmingly supportive of CATIs, as indicated by the median accuracy rating of 78.5% found in one review of that literature (Moreland, 1987). The one such study involving adolescents yielded an accuracy rating of 58% when the MMPI was scored using adolescent norms (Lachar, Klinge, & Grisell, 1976). The accuracy rating dropped to 32% when the MMPI was scored using adult norms. Ehrenworth and Archer (1985) replicated Lachar et al.'s (1976) findings for adolescent norms using interpretations that, while not computer-assisted, were amenable to computer processing. On the other hand, they found that adult norms yielded equally accurate interpretations. Interestingly, Ehrenworth and Archer (1985) found that the combination of adolescent norms and interpretive correlates developed especially for adolescents by Marks et al. (1974) yielded the *least* accurate interpretations.

Reviewers appear to agree that one should be skeptical of all these figures because of what Webb et al. (1970) characterized as the lack of information on base rate accuracy of the reports (see Butcher, 1978). Webb and his colleagues were concerned that raters characterized reports as accurate not because the reports were pointed descriptions of the individuals at issue, but rather because they contained glittering generalities (cf. O'Dell, 1972). However, some of the "customer satisfaction" studies have been useful in guiding authors' efforts to improve their CATI systems for the MMPI (see Moreland, 1985). Furthermore, one study of adults addressed the issue of base rate accuracy by having clinicians rate two CATIs—one of which was closely matched to the genuine CATI but was, nevertheless, bogus—for each test respondent (Moreland & Onstad, 1985). Wimbish (1985) has conducted a similar study using adolescent subjects. Both of the latter two studies have demonstrated that clinicians rate computer-assisted MMPI interpretations sold by several American commercial firms as being considerably more accurate

than bogus reports. A study of the Millon Clinical Multiaxial Inventory yielded similar results (Moreland & Godfrey, 1987). Eyde, Kowal, and Fishburne (in press) were recently able to demonstrate significant differences in the accuracy of *genuine* reports on the same patient produced by different CATI systems for the MMPI. (This model study should be carefully examined by everyone interested in this topic.) However, these studies have also demonstrated that critics like Lanyon and Matarazzo have a right to be concerned about the base rate accuracy of CATIs. The (Moreland & Onstad, 1985) incremental validity figure of 41%, although very encouraging, does not provide the potential CATI consumer with the same degree of comfort as Lushene and Gilbertstadt's (1972) "customer satisfaction" rating of 93%.

A few researchers have asked consumers of computer-assisted MMPI interpretations to complete symptom checklists or Q-sorts based on the computer-generated reports, and have subsequently compared those ratings with analogous ones made by clinicians familiar with each patient (see Moreland, 1985).

The "external criterion" studies have typically dealt with the base rate accuracy problem by comparing the accuracy of report-based ratings with "stereotypical patient" ratings or by presenting multireport–multirating intercorrelation matrices. These studies have been plagued by small samples of test respondents, CATIs, and criterion variables, calling into question the generalizability of the results. Furthermore, the results of these studies have been decidedly mixed. Two studies have indicated that CATIs enjoy modest validity, similar in magnitude to that found for interpretations generated in the traditional fashion (Chase, 1974; Crumpton, 1974). Two other studies have found computer-assisted MMPI interpretations to manifest chance accuracy (Anderson, 1969; Hedlund, Morgan, & Master, 1972). And one study found CATIs to be valid for one set of criterion variables, but no more valid than "stereotypical patient" ratings for another set of criterion variables (Moreland, 1983). The Moreland (1983) and Chase (1974) studies found that the ratings made directly from MMPI profiles were more valid than those based on CATIs. Anderson (1969) found no differences between profile- and CATI-based ratings, in spite of the fact that his profile judges were well-known MMPI experts. Chase's (1974) CATIs were at least as accurate as clinician-generated reports. None of these studies focused on adolescents.

Attempting to draw a summary conclusion from these mixed results may be a fool's errand, but, in the interest of helping the potential CATI consumer, an attempt will be made. The results of the "external criterion" studies—validity coefficients mainly in the .20s and .30s for both CATIs and clinician-generated interpretations—should not leave one sanguine about the efficacy of clinical assessment. However. it appears that computer-assisted MMPI interpretations are about as accurate as interpretive inferences made from the MMPI in the usual clinical fashion. These tentative conclusions may not generalize beyond the MMPI, since no other test enjoys such a large empirical base from which interpretations may be drawn. Furthermore, these conclusions are based mainly on adult data.

ADVICE TO THE
WOULD-BE CONSUMER

All of the foregoing can be distilled into a few questions that prospective consumers of computer-assisted assessment should ask themselves before deciding what to buy. Questions related to output should be asked first: "What kind of assessment information do I need?" Once potential consumers narrow the range of possibilities to such categories as "psychometric evaluation of the severity of child psychiatric patients' presenting problems," they can ask, "In what form do I need the information (e.g., scores or interpretation)?" Input options should not be considered until these questions about the kind and form of information required are settled. Information needs should dictate choice of computer services, rather than the other way around. Once output needs are decided upon, the sort of computer service to use can be chosen.

Assuming that a practitioner does not desire technology-dependent information (e.g., a social history that requires on-line administration because it uses branching logic), a variety of options will still be available at this point. Would-be consumers can now ask, "What kind of turnaround time do I need? Can I afford to wait for central processing or do I need immediate results?" Practitioners who need immediate processing will need to consider the volume of assessment they do: "Do I process enough tests to make me want to avoid the telephone charges involved in teleprocessing? Is my assessment practice small enough to make on-line administration an attractive option, or will I need an optical mark reader to handle everything?" Finally, potential consumers should ask themselves some important practical questions about the company they are thinking of dealing with: "Do their products evidence good craftsmanship? What kind of technical support do they offer to their customers? Is the company financially sound, or is it likely to be gone tomorrow?"

I believe that these questions will help practitioners to choose the right computer-assisted assessment products and services. I hope that considering the issues in this order will also help them to make the right choices quickly and efficiently. Obviously, if a practitioner needs an interpretive report and none exists, it is fruitless to worry about how to get the data into the computer!

How to Choose a Computer-Assisted Test Interpretation System

If one elects to use the computer to administer or score tests, assessing the adequacy of a product is relatively straightforward. Before putting one's faith in a CATI, however, one should ask a number of additional questions.

Unfortunately, unless one is interested in the CPI, Halstead–Reitan, MMPI, MSI, or PIC, available empirical data offer little guidance to the potential consumer of CATIs. It would be foolish to try to generalize to other tests from so few data, many of which are also of poor quality and few of which are based on children or adolescents. When studies of CATI validity become more numerous, prospective CATI consumers should check them to see how many of the following criteria for an ideal study are met. This should help determine the weight to assign any given study when deciding whether to use a CATI system. In the meantime, these criteria can serve as guidelines for those planning studies of CATIs. The data contemplated in these criteria are difficult to collect, so neither consumers nor researchers need despair if a study does not meet all these guidelines.

1. Did raters have prior experience with the interpretive systems under study?
2. Were raters given experience with the rating system prior to the beginning of the study?
3. Was the sample of raters representative of those using the interpretation in applied contexts?
4. Was the sample of test respondents unbiased?
5. Was the content of the criterion instruments representative of the content covered by the interpretive system?
6. Were ratings completed keeping the appropriate time frame in mind? (For example, the adequacy of inferences about transient affective states should not be rated on the basis of observations conducted weeks after the test was administered.)
7. Was discriminant validity of the interpretations assessed? (This can be accomplished in "customer satisfaction" studies by obtaining ratings of both genuine and bogus reports [see Moreland & Onstad, 1985] or genuine reports generated by different CATI systems [see Eyde et al., in press]; multireport–multirating intercorrelations can be used for this same purpose in "external criterion" studies [see Chase, 1974].)
8. Was *inter*rater reliability assessed?
9. Was *intra*rater reliability assessed?
10. Was reliability of the interpretations themselves, across time, assessed?
11. Could raters indicate contradictory elements of interpretations?
12. Could raters indicate useless elements of interpretations?
13. Could raters indicate when interpretations omitted significant information?
14. Were interpretive statements produced by different rules assessed independently? (Ideally, if different rules produce different paragraphs, accuracy ratings should be obtained for each paragraph.)

As a practical matter, those interested in using CATIs at present will need to rely on four sources of data that are not supposed to be accorded much credibility when it comes to making decisions about the adequacy of assessment tools: the credentials of the system author; documentation of the system (e.g., manuals); scholarly reviews of the CATI system; and brief trials. The potential CATI customer should take the following steps and ask the following questions prior to settling on a system:

First, the customer should find out who developed the CATI and investigate that person's qualifications. Does the developer have a record of scholarship with the instrument in question? In the general area of CATI? Does the system author have any credential that indicates special expertise as a practitioner? If the answer to all of these questions is no, one would be well advised to look elsewhere.

Next, it is also important to examine the published documentation for the interpretive system. Documentation providing decision rules for interpretive statements is almost unheard of, because most CATI developers are concerned less their work be stolen (exceptions include Lachar, 1974; Lachar & Alexander, 1978). However, the general interpretive approach is usually documented. That is, one is told something like this: "PIC system Z generates its interpretations from one, two, and three scale elevations of the basic profile scales at five different levels of elevation." The potential customer should try to determine whether the interpretive approach is orthodox; idiosyncratic scoring methods and unusual approaches to interpretation indicate that caution is necessary. A significant minority of CATI developers seem to be creative people who feel that the world will benefit from some special approach to scoring and/or interpretation they have developed. They are seldom able to document the utility of their special approach. In most cases, a list of references consulted to develop the interpretive rules and statements is provided. Do the referenced sources appear in peer-reviewed publications? Or are they unpublished "research reports" and the like? One should be especially wary of the latter, discounting them as evidence unless copies can be obtained for evaluation.

It is particularly important to find out whether there are any scholarly reviews of the system. Good sources for such reviews are *The Mental Measurements Yearbook* (e.g., Mitchell, 1985) and journals such as *Computers in Psychiatry/Psychology* and *Computers in Human Behavior*. New publications are appearing in this area almost as fast as computer software, so other sources of reviews may soon be available. The reviews will provide a dispassionate opinion from someone who may have been given access to proprietary interpretive information that is not available to potential consumers. One caution: The customer should check the reviewer's credentials, asking the same questions raised above about the system author.

Finally, the practitioner should try the CATI system on a set of cases about which much is known and for which he or she need not rely on the CATI in practical decision making. Insofar as possible, these trials should be performed according to the suggestions for CATI research I have given above. This will cost a few dollars in the short run, but may save a great many in the long run.

How to Use Computer-Assisted Test Interpretations

Like the tests that give rise to them, CATIs can be used well and they can be used poorly. Assuming that the CATI system is generally sound, the issue boils down to when one should have faith in a CATI and when one should be skeptical of it. The limits of an actuarial system's utility are relatively easy to identify. Knowledge of the population on which such a system was developed will afford reliable clues about its limitations. Take, for example, the neuropsychological "key" system of Russell et al. (1970), which was developed using male veterans of the U.S. military. One is justified in being skeptical about that system's utility with women. Furthermore, patients with penetrating head wounds are more common in U.S. Veterans Administration Medical Centers than in civilian medical settings. The actuarial CATI system for the PIC was developed, for the most part, in an inner-city psychiatric facility serv-

ing a large population of ethnic minorities and individuals of low socioeconomic status, many with severe psychiatric problems (Lachar & Gdowski, 1979). Thus, that system may not generalize to expensive private psychiatric settings specializing in long-term psychotherapy of neurotic problems.

It is more difficult to decide when to be wary of the output of computer-assisted clinical prediction systems. The following tentative set of suggestions based on the clinical judgment literature may be useful to the CATI consumer:

1. *Low-probability events*. Suicide comes most easily to mind here. It goes without saying that one cannot depend on CATI results alone to confirm the presence or absence of something as rare as suicidal intent.

2. *Rare score combinations*. The more unusual the combination of scores, the more the author of a clinical CATI system has had to rely on clinical lore and his or her idiosyncratic experience in developing an interpretation. And, of course, he or she will have less experience with unusual configurations than with common ones. For example, it seems unlikely that a CATI developer would have much experience with children having elevations on both the Depressed and Hyperactive scales of the Child Behavior Profile (Achenbach & Edelbrock, 1983).

3. *Extreme scores*. CATIs are more likely to be off the mark in the presence of extreme scores. This is especially likely to be the case if the interpretive system employs coarse groupings. Many CATI systems for multiscore inventories group profiles solely according to the one or two highest scale scores; yet a child whose PIC profile includes elevations only on the Achievement and Development scales must differ markedly from a child who, in addition, has an elevation on the Delinquency scale.

4. *Scores near cutoffs*. Related to the problem of extreme scores is the problem of scores near cutting points. Here the rigidity and reliability of the computer becomes a hindrance rather than a help. Unfortunately, a difference of 1 T-score point can sometimes make a big difference in a computer-assisted interpretation. To return to the example just

given, a PIC profile with Achievement and Development at their respective cutoff scores and Delinquency 1 T-score point below the cutoff may yield an interpretation emphasizing the possibility of learning disability. An increment of 1 T-score point on Delinquency may change the interpretation drastically, causing it to focus more on antisocial acting out than on psychoeducational problems.

5. *Unusual response sets/styles.* Many of the currently extant CATI systems do not deal well with the test respondent who is motivated to respond in an unusual manner. For example, none of the systems for interpreting the Halstead–Reitan Battery cited above have provisions for detecting those who are motivated to look bad in an effort to collect compensation for an injury. Many CATI systems come closer to being adequate in this regard, but all too many will grind out an interpretation for any kind of input that is submitted.

FINAL THOUGHTS

At present, it is especially important that consumers of computer technology for psychological assessment use sound professional judgment and not abdicate to the computer. The computer is likely eventually to replace the professional for many, but not all, assessment functions (see Meehl, 1954, for instances in which the professional is indispensable). Until Meehl's (1956) advertisement for a good interpretive "cookbook" (i.e., actuarial system) is answered, the professional will need to be especially circumspect in the use of CATIs. The actuarial CATI systems for the CPI, Halstead–Reitan, MSI, and PIC come close to Meehl's ideal. But most CATI systems now available rely heavily on the judgment of a single clinician. Therefore, CATIs should also be used as only one element in the assessment process, and especially not as a substitute for informed professional judgment.

APPENDIX 17.1. COMPUTER-ASSISTED PRODUCTS FOR THE ASSESSMENT OF CHILD AND ADOLESCENT PERSONALITY

Instrument name	Supplier
Adolescent Diagnostic Screening Battery	Reason House
Adolescent Multiphasic Personality Inventory	Pacific Psychological
ASIEP Computerized Scoring and Interpretation	ASIEP Program Education Co.
Barclay Classroom Assessment System	Western Psychological Services
Bender Report 3.0	Psychometric Software
Child and Adolescent Diagnostic Screening Inventory	Psychologistics
Child Behavior Checklist	University of Vermont, Department of Psychiatry
Child Diagnostic Screening Battery	Reason House
Children's Personality Questionnaire Narrative Report	Institute for Personality and Ability Testing
Children's State–Trait Anxiety Inventory Computer Program	Multi-Health Systems
Computer-Generated Bender Clinical Assessment	Precision People
Computer-Generated H-T-P Clinical Assessment	Precision People
Conners Parent Rating Scale Computer Program	Multi-Health Systems
Conners Teacher Rating Scale Computer Program	Multi-Health Systems
Diagnostic Interview for Children and Adolescents Computer Program: Child Version	Multi-Health Systems
Diagnostic Interview for Children and Adolescents Computer Program: Parent Version	Multi-Health Systems
Eysenck Personality Questionnaire (Junior)	Educational and Industrial Testing Service
High School Personality Questionnaire Narrative Report	Institute for Personality and Ability Testing
Jesness Behavior Check List	Consulting Psychologists Press
Jesness Inventory	Consulting Psychologists Press
Kinetic Family Drawing Tests: Computer Analysis	Reason House
Louisville Behavior Checklist	Western Psychological Services
MAPI Narrative Report	Sienna Software
Marks Adolescent MMPI Report	Applied Innovations
Millon Adolescent Personality Inventory: Clinical Interpretive Report	National Computer System (NCS), Professional Assessment Services (PAS) Division
Millon Adolescent Personality Inventory: Guidance Interpretive Report	NCS, PAS Division
Personality Inventory for Children (PIC)	Western Psychological Services
PIC Narrative Report	Sienna Software
Piers–Harris Children's Self-Concept Scale	Western Psychological Services
Projective Drawing Tests: Computer Analysis	Reason House
Projective Drawing Tests: School Version	Reason House
Rorschach Comprehensive System—Exner Report	Psychological Assessment Resources
Rorschach Data Summary and Narrative Report	Psychologistics
Symptom History for Children	Integrated Professional Systems
Tennessee Self-Concept Scale	Western Psychological Services

Note. Descriptions of most of these products can be found in *Psychware Sourcebook* (Krug, 1987). See *Tests in Print III* (Mitchell, 1983) for the address and telephone number of suppliers not listed in *Psychware Sourcebook*.

REFERENCES

Achenbach, T. M., & Edelbrock, C. S. (1983). *Manual for the Child Behavior Checklist and Revised Child Behavior Profile*. Burlington: University of Vermont, Department of Psychiatry.

Adair, F. L. (1978). Computerized scoring and interpreting services [Re: Minnesota Multiphasic Personality Inventory]. In O. K. Buros (Ed.), *Eighth mental measurements yearbook* (Vol. 1, pp. 940–942, 945–949, 952–953, 957–960). Highland, NJ: Gryphon Press.

Adams, K. M. (1975). Automated clinical interpretation of the neuropsychological test battery: An ability based approach. *Dissertation Abstracts International, 35*, 6085B. (University Mircofilms No. 75–13, 289)

Adams, K. M., Kvale, V. I., & Keegan, J. R. (1984). Relative accuracy of three automated systems for neuropsychological interpretation based on two representative tasks. *Journal of Clinical Neuropsychology, 6*, 413–431.

Adams, K. M., & Heaton, R. K. (1985). Automated interpretation of neuropsychological test data. *Journal of Consulting and Clinical Psychology, 53*, 790–802.

Allred, L. J., & Harris, W. G. (1984). *The nonequivalence of computerized and conventional administrations of the Adjective Checklist*. Unpublished manuscript, Johns Hopkins University.

American Psychiatric Association. (1987). *Diagnostic and statistical manual of mental disorders* (3rd ed., rev.). Washington, DC: Author.

Anderson, B. N. (1969). *The utility of the Minnesota Multiphasic Personality Inventory in a private psychiatric hospital setting*. Unpublished master's thesis, Ohio State University.

Angle, H., Ellinwood, E., & Carroll, J. (1978). Computer interview problem assessment of psychiatric patients. *Proceedings of the Second Annual Symposium on Computer Applications in Medical Care* (pp. 137–148). New York: Institute of Electrical and Electronics Engineers.

Angle, H. V., Johnson, T., Grebenkemper, N. S., & Ellinwood, E. H. (1979). Computer interview support for clinicians. *Professional Psychology, 10*, 49–57.

Anthony, W. Z., Heaton, R. K., & Lehman, R. A. W., (1980). An attempt to cross-validate two actuarial systems for neuropsychological test interpretation. *Journal of Consulting and Clinical Psychology, 48*, 317–326.

Beaumont, J. G., & French, C. F. (1987). A clinical field study of eight automated psychometric procedures: The Leicester/DHSS Project. *International Journal of Man-Machine Studies, 26*, 311–320.

Blankenship, L. L. (1976). Computer-conducted assessment of life-change psychological stress. *Dissertation Abstracts International, 37*, 2495B. (University Microfilms No. 76–24, 045)

Blois, M. S. (1980). Clinical judgment and computers. *New England Journal of Medicine, 303*, 192–197.

Bresolin, M. J., Jr. (1984). A comparative study of computer administration of the Minnesota Multiphasic Personality Inventory in an inpatient psychiatric setting. *Dissertation Abstracts International, 46*, 295B. (University Microfilms No. 85-06,377).

Briggs, P. F., Taylor, M., & Tellegen, A. (1966). *A study of the Marks and Seeman MMPI profile types as applied to a sample of 2,875 psychiatric patients* (Research Laboratories Report No. PR-66-S). Minneapolis: University of Minnesota, Department of Psychiatry.

Bringmann, W. G., Balance, W. D. G., & Giesbrecht, C. A. (1972). The computer vs. the technologist: Comparison of psychological reports on normal and elevated MMPI profiles. *Psychological Reports, 31*, 211–217.

Butcher, J. N. (1978). Computerized scoring and interpreting services [Re: Minnesota Multiphasic Personality Inventory]. In O. K. Buros (Ed.), *The eighth mental measurements yearbook* (Vol. 1, pp. 942–945, 947–956, 958, 960–962). Highland Park, NJ: Gryphon Press.

Butcher, J. N., Keller, L. S., & Bacon, S. F. (1985). Current developments and future directions in computerized personality assessment. *Journal of Consulting and Clinical Psychology, 53*, 803–815.

Butcher, J. N., & Owen, P. L. (1978). Objective personality inventories: Recent research and some contemporary issues. In B. Wolman (Ed.), *Clinical diagnosis of mental disorders: A handbook* (pp. 475–545). New York: Plenum Press.

Butcher, J. N., & Pancheri, P. (Eds.). (1976). *A handbook of cross-national MMPI research*. Minneapolis: University of Minnesota Press.

Butcher, J. N., & Spielberger, C. D. (Eds.). (1985). *Advances in personality assessment* (Vol. 4). Hillsdale, NJ: Erlbaum.

Caldwell, A. B. (1970). *Recent advances in automated interpretation of the MMPI*. Paper presented at the Fifth Annual Symposium on Recent Developments in the Use of the MMPI, Mexico City.

Campbell, D. P. (1971). *Handbook for the Strong Vocational Interest Blank*. Stanford, CA: Stanford University Press.

Carr, A. C., Ghosh, A., & Ancil, R. J. (1983). Can a computer take a psychiatric history? *Psychological Medicine, 13*, 151–158.

Carr, A. C., Wilson, S. L., Ghosh, A., Ancil, R. J., & Woods, R. T. (1982). Automated testing of geriatric patients using a microcomputer-based system. *International Journal of Man–Machine Studies, 17*, 297–300.

Century Diagnostics. (1980). *Computer interpreted Rorschach*. Tempe, AZ: Author.

Chase, L. L. S. (1974). An evaluation of MMPI interpretation systems. *Dissertation Abstracts International, 35*, 3009B. (University Microfilms No. 74–26, 172)

Coddington, R. D., & King, T. L. (1972). Automated history taking in child psychiatry. *American Journal of Psychiatry, 129*, 276–282.

Colby, K. M. (1980). Computer psychotherapists. In J. B. Sidowski, J. H. Johnson, & T. A. Williams (Eds.), *Technology in mental health care delivery systems* (pp. 109–117). Norwood, NJ: Ablex.

Consulting Psychologists Press. (1988). *1988 catalog*. Palo Alto, CA: Author.

Crumpton, C. A. (1974). An evaluation and comparison of three automated MMPI interpretive reports. *Dissertation Abstracts International, 35*, 6090B. (University Microfilms No. 75-11, 982)

Dahlstrom, W. G., Welsh, G. S., & Dahlstrom, L. E.,

(1972). *An MMPI handbook: Vol. 1. Clinical applications*. Minneapolis: University of Minnesota Press.

DeDombal, F. T. (1979). Computers and the surgeon: A matter of decision. *The Surgeon, 35,* 57.

Drake, L. E., & Oetting, E. R. (1959). *An MMPI codebook for counselors*. Minneapolis: University of Minnesota Press.

Dudek, F. J. (1979). The continuing misinterpretation of the standard error of measurement. *Psychological Bulletin, 86,* 335–337.

Duffy, J. C., & Waterton, J. J. (1984). Under-reporting of alcohol consumption in sample surveys: The effect of computer interviewing in fieldwork. *British Journal of Addictions, 79,* 303–308.

Ehrenworth, N. V., & Archer, R. P. (1985). A comparison of clinical accuracy ratings of interpretive approaches for adolescent MMPI responses. *Journal of Personality Assessment, 49,* 413–421.

Elbert, J. C., & Holden, E. W. (1987). Child diagnostic assessment: Current training practices in clinical psychology internships. *Professional Psychology: Research and Practice, 18,* 587–596.

Evan, W. M., & Miller, J. R. (1969). Differential effects on response bias of computer vs. conventional administration of a social science questionnaire. *Behavioral Science, 14,* 216–227.

Exner, J. E., Jr. (1987). Computer assistance in Rorschach interpretation. In J. N. Butcher (Ed.), *Computerized psychological assessment: A practitioner's guide* (pp. 218–235). New York: Basic Books.

Exner, J. E., Jr., & Exner, D. E. (1972). How clinicians use the Rorschach. *Journal of Personality Assessment, 36,* 403–408.

Eyde, L. D., Kowal, D. M., & Fishburne, F. J., Jr. (in press). The validity of computer-based test interpretations of the MMPI. In S. Wise & T. B. Gutkin (Eds.), *The computer as adjunct to the decision making process*. Lincoln, NE: Buros Institute of Mental Measurements.

Finkelstein, J. N. (1977). BRAIN: A computer program for interpretation of the Halstead–Reitan Neuropsychological Test Battery. *Dissertation Abstracts International, 37,* 5349B. (University Microfilms No. 77–88, 8864)

Finney, J. C. (1966). Programmed interpretation of MMPI and CPI. *Archives of General Psychiatry, 15,* 75–81.

Fowler, R. D. (1966). *The MMPI notebook: A guide to the clinical use of the automated MMPI*. Nutley, NJ: Roche Psychiatric Service Institute.

Fowler, R. D. (1969). Automated interpretation of personality test data. In J. N. Butcher (Ed.), *MMPI: Research developments and clinical applications* (pp. 105–126). New York: McGraw-Hill.

Fowler, R. D. (1985). Landmarks in computer-assisted psychological assessment. *Journal of Consulting and Clinical Psychology, 53,* 748–759.

Fowler, R. D. (1987). Developing a computer-based test interpretation system. In J. N. Butcher (Ed.), *Computerized psychological assessment: A practitioner's guide* (pp. 50–63). New York: Basic Books.

Fowler, R. D., & Athey, E. B. (1971). A cross-validation of Gilberstadt and Duker's 1-2-3-4 profile type. *Journal of Clinical Psychology, 37,* 238–240.

Fowler, R. D., & Coyle, F. A. (1968). Scoring error on the MMPI. *Journal of Clinical Psychology, 24,* 68–69.

Gilberstadt, H., & Duker, J. (1965). *A handbook for clinical and actuarial MMPI interpretation*. Philadelphia: W. B. Saunders.

Glueck, B. C., Jr., & Reznikoff, M. (1965). Comparison of computer-derived personality profile and projective psychological test findings. *American Journal of Psychiatry, 121,* 1156–1161.

Goldberg, L. R. (1965). Diagnosticians vs. diagnostic signs: The diagnosis of psychosis vs. neurosis from the MMPI. *Psychological Monographs, 79* (9, Whole No. 602).

Goldberg, L. R. (1970). Man vs. model of man: A rationale, plus some evidence, for a method of improving on clinical inferences. *Psychological Bulletin, 73,* 422–432.

Golden, C. J. (in press). *Interpretive report for the Halstead–Reitan Neuropsychological Battery*. Minneapolis: National Computer Systems.

Goldstein, G., & Shelly, C. (1982). A further attempt to cross-validate the Russell, Neuringer, and Goldstein neuropsychological keys. *Journal of Consulting and Clinical Psychology, 50,* 721–726.

Gorham, D. R. (1967). Validity and reliability studies of computer-based scoring system for ink-blot responses. *Journal of Consulting Psychology, 31,* 65–70.

Graham, J. R. (1967). A Q-sort study of the accuracy of clinical descriptions based on the MMPI. *Journal of Psychiatric Research, 5,* 297–305.

Grayson, H. H., & Backer, T. E. (1972). Scoring accuracy of four automated MMPI interpretation report agencies. *Journal of Clinical Psychology, 28,* 366–370.

Greaud, V. A., & Green, B. F. (1986). Equivalence of conventional and computer presentation of speed tests. *Applied Psychological Measurement, 10,* 23–34.

Green C. J. (1982). The diagnostic accuracy and utility of MMPI and MCMI computer interpretive reports. *Journal of Personality Assessment, 46,* 359–365.

Greene, R. L., (1980). *The MMPI: An interpretive manual*. New York: Grune & Stratton.

Greist, J. H. (1975). The computer interview as a medium for collecting questionnaire data on drug use: Predicting adolescent drug abuse. In D. J. Lettieri (Ed.), *Predicting adolescent drug use: A review of issues, methods and correlates* (pp. 147–164). Washington, DC: U.S. Government Printing Office.

Greist, J. H., Gustafson, D. H., Strauss, F. F., Rowse, G. L., Laughren, T. P., & Chiles, J. A. (1973). A computer interview for suicide risk prediction. *American Journal of Psychiatry, 130,* 1327–1332.

Greist, J. H., Gustafson, D. H., Strauss, F. F., Rowse, G. L., Laughren, T. P., & Chiles, J. A. (1974). Suicide risk prediction: A new approach. *Suicide and Life-Threatening Behavior, 4,* 212–223.

Greist, J. H., & Klein, M. H. (1980). Computer programs for patients, clinicians, and researchers in psychiatry. In J. B. Sidowski, J. H. Johnson, & T. A. Williams (Eds.). *Technology in mental health care delivery systems* (pp. 161–182). Norwood, NJ: Ablex.

Greist, J. H., Klein, M. H., Van Cura, L. J., & Erdman, H. P. (1975). Computer interview questionnaires for drug use/abuse. In D. J. Lettieri (Ed.), *Predicting adolescent drug abuse: A review of issues, methods, and correlates* (pp. 147–164). Rockville, MD: National Institute of Drug Abuse.

Gynther, M. D., Altman, H., & Sletten, I. W. (1973). Replicated correlates of MMPI two-point code types:

The Missouri actuarial system. *Journal of Clinical Psychology, 28,* 263–286.

Gynther, M. D., & Brilliant, P. J. (1968). The MMPI K+ profile: A reexamination. *Journal of Consulting and Clinical Psychology, 32,* 616–617.

Hansen, J. C. (1987). Computer-assisted interpretation of the Strong Interest Inventory. In J. N. Butcher (Ed.), *Computerized psychological assessment: A practitioner's guide* (pp. 292–321). New York: Basic Books.

Harrell, T. H., & Lombardo, T. A. (1984). Validation of an automated 16PF administration procedure. *Journal of Personality Assessment, 48,* 638–642.

Harris, W. G., Niedner, D., Feldman, C., Fink, A., & Johnson, J. H. (1981). An on-line interpretive Rorschach approach: Using Exner's Comprehensive System. *Behavior Research Methods and Instrumentation, 13,* 588–591.

Hart, R. R., & Goldstein, M. A. (1985). Computer-assisted psychological assessment. *Computers in Human Services, 1,* 69–75.

Heaton, R. K., Grant, I., Anthony, W. Z., & Lehman, R. A. W. (1981). A comparison of clinical and automated interpretation of the Halstead–Reitan Battery. *Journal of Clinical Neuropsychology, 3,* 121–141.

Hedlund, J. L., Morgan, D. W., & Master, F. D. (1972). The Mayo Clinic automated MMPI program: Cross-validation with psychiatric patients in an Army hospital. *Journal of Clinical Psychology, 28,* 505–510.

Hofer, P. J., & Green, B. F. (1985). The challenge of competence and creativity in computerized psychological testing. *Journal of Consulting and Clinical Psychology, 53,* 826–838.

Hoffman, K. I., & Lundberg, G. D. (1976). A comparison of computer monitored group tests with paper-and-pencil tests. *Educational and Psychological Measurement, 36,* 791–809.

Holtzman, W. H. (1975). New developments in the Holtzman Inkblot Technique. In P. McReynolds (Ed.), *Advances in psychological assessment* (Vol. 3, pp. 243–274). San Francisco: Jossey-Bass.

Honaker, L. M. (1988). The equivalency of computerized and conventional MMPI administration: A review. *Clinical Psychology Review, 8,* 561–577.

Jackson, D. N. (1984). *Jackson Vocational Interest Survey manual* (2nd ed.). Port Huron, MI: Research Psychologists Press.

Johnson, D. F., & White, C. B. (1980). Effects of training on computerized test performance in the elderly. *Journal of Applied Psychology, 65,* 357–358.

Johnson, J. H., Giannetti, R. A., & Williams, T. A. (1978). A self-contained microcomputer system for psychological testing. *Behavior Research Methods and Instrumentation, 10,* 579–581.

Karson, S., & O'Dell, J. W. (1975). A new automated interpretation system for the 16PF. *Journal of Personality Assessment, 39,* 256–260.

Karson, S., & O'Dell, J. W. (1987). Computer-based interpretation of the 16PF: The Karson Clinical Report in contemporary practice. In J. N. Butcher (Ed.), *Computerized psychological assessment: A practitioner's guide* (pp. 198–217). New York: Basic Books.

Katz, L., & Dalby, J. T. (1981a). Computer and manual administration of the Eysenck Personality Inventory. *Journal of Clinical Psychology, 37,* 586–588.

Katz, L., & Dalby, J. T. (1981b). Computer-assisted and traditional assessment of elementary-school-aged children. *Contemporary Educational Psychology, 6,* 314–322.

Kleinmuntz, B. (1963). MMPI decision rules for the identification of college maladjustment. *Psychological Monographs, 77*(14, Whole No. 577).

Kleinmuntz, B. (Ed.). (1968). *Formal representation of human judgment.* New York: Wiley.

Kleinmuntz, B. (1969). Personality test interpretation by computer and clinician. In J. N. Butcher (Ed.), *MMPI: Research developments and clinical applications* (pp. 97–104). New York: McGraw-Hill.

Kleinmuntz, B. (1975). The computer as clinician. *American Psychologist, 30,* 379–387.

Klett, B., Schaefer, A., & Plemel, D. (1985, May). Just how accurate are computer-scored tests? *The VA Chief Psychologist,* p. 7.

Koson, D., Kitchen, C., Kochen, M., & Stodolsky, D. (1970). Psychological testing by computer: Effect on response bias. *Educational and Psychological Measurement, 30,* 803–810.

Krug, S. E. (Ed.). (1987). *Psychware sourcebook* (2nd ed.). Kansas City, MO: Test Corporation of America.

Labeck, L. J., Johnson, J. H., & Harris, W. G. (1983). Validity of an automated on-line MMPI interpretive system. *Journal of Clinical Psychology, 39,* 412–416.

Lachar, D. (1974). *The MMPI: Clinical assessment and automated interpretation.* Los Angeles: Western Psychological Services.

Lachar, D. (1987). Automated assessment of child and adolescent personality: The Personality Inventory for Children (PIC). In J. N. Butcher (Ed.), *Computerized psychological assessment: A practitioner's guide* (pp. 261–291). New York: Basic Books.

Lachar, D., & Alexander, R. S. (1978). Verdicality of self-report: Replicated correlates of the Wiggins MMPI content scales. *Journal of Consulting and Clinical Psychology, 46,* 1349–1356.

Lachar, D., & Gdowski, C. G. (1979). *Actuarial assessment of child and adolescent personality: An interpretative guide for the Personality Inventory for Children profile.* Los Angeles: Western Psychological Services.

Lachar, D., Klinge, V., & Grisell, J. L. (1976). Relative accuracy of automated MMPI narratives generated from adult norm and adolescent norm profiles. *Journal of Consulting and Clinical Psychology, 44,* 20–24.

Lanyon, R. I. (1984). Personality assessment. *Annual Review of Psychology, 35,* 667–701.

Lanyon, R. I. (1987). The validity of computer-based personality assessment products: Recommendations for the future. *Computers in Human Behavior, 3,* 225–238.

Larson, E. (1984, January 6). Many firms seek entry into software. *The Wall Street Journal,* p. 23.

Lieff, J. D. (1984). *Computers and other technological aids for psychiatric private practice.* Washington, DC: American Psychiatric Press.

Lucas, R. W. (1977). A study of patients' attitudes to computer interrogation. *International Journal of Man–Machine Studies, 9,* 69–86.

Lucas, R. W., Mullins, P. J., Luna, C. B., & McInroy, D. C. (1977). Psychiatrists and a computer as interrogators of patients with alcohol-related illnesses: A comparison. *British Journal of Psychiatry, 131,* 160–167.

Lukin, M. E., Dowd, E. T., Plake, B. S., & Kraft, R. B. (1985). Comparing computerized versus traditional psychological assessment. *Computers in Human Behavior, 1,* 49–58.

Lushene, R. E., & Gilberstadt, H. (1972, March). *Validation of VA MMPI computer-generated reports.* Paper presented at the Veterans Administration Cooperative Studies Conference, St. Louis.

Lushene, R. E., O'Neil, H. H., & Dunn, T. (1974). Equivalent validity of a completely computerized MMPI. *Journal of Personality Assessment, 38,* 353–361.

Marks, P. A., & Seeman, W. (1963). *The actuarial description of personality: An atlas for use with the MMPI.* Baltimore: Williams & Wilkins.

Marks, P. A., Seeman, W., & Haller, D. L. (1974). *The actuarial use of the MMPI with adolescents and adults.* Baltimore: Williams & Wilkins.

Matarazzo, J. M. (1983). Computerized psychological testing. *Science, 221,* 323.

McDonald, C. J. (1976). Protocol-based computer reminders, the quality of care and the non-perfectibility of man. *New England Journal of Medicine, 295,* 1351–1355.

Meehl, P. E. (1954). *Clinical versus statistical prediction: A theoretical analysis and a review of the evidence.* Minneapolis: University of Minnesota Press.

Meehl, P. E., (1956). Wanted—a good cookbook. *American Psychologist, 11,* 263–272.

Mitchell, J. V., Jr. (Ed.). (1983). *Tests in print III.* Lincoln, NE: Buros Institute of Mental Measurements.

Mitchell, J. V., Jr. (Ed.). (1985). The *ninth mental measurements yearbook.* Lincoln, NE: Buros Institute of Mental Measurements.

Moreland, K. L., (1983, April). *A comparison of the validity of two MMPI interpretation systems: A preliminary report.* Paper presented at the 18th Annual Symposium on Recent Developments in the Use of the MMPI, Minneapolis.

Moreland, K. L. (1985). Validation of computer-based test interpretations: Problems and prospects. *Journal of Consulting and Clinical Psychology, 53,* 816–825.

Moreland, K. L. (1987). Computer-based test interpretations: Advice to the consumer. *Applied Psychology: An International Review, 36,* 385–399.

Moreland, K. L., & Godfrey, J, O. (1987). Validity of Millon's computerized interpretation system for the MCMI: A controlled study. *Journal of Consulting and Clinical Psychology, 55,* 113–114.

Moreland, K. L., & Onstad, J. A. (1985, March). *Validity of the Minnesota Report: 1. Mental health outpatients.* Paper presented at the 20th Annual Symposium on Recent Developments in the use of the MMPI, Honolulu.

National Computer Systems (NCS). (1988). *Professional Assessment Services 1988 catalog.* Minneapolis: Author.

O'Dell, J. W. (1972). P. T. Barnum explores the computer. *Journal of Consulting and Clinical Psychology, 38,* 270–273.

Palmer, W. H. (1971). Actuarial MMPI interpretation: A replication and extension. *Dissertation Abstracts International, 31,* 6265B. (University Microfilms No. 71–09, 128)

Payne, F. D., & Wiggins, J. S. (1968). Effects of rule relaxation and system combination on classification rates in two MMPI "cookbook" systems. *Journal of Consulting and Clinical Psychology, 32,* 734–736.

Pearson, J. S., Rome, H. P., Swenson, W. M., Mataya, P., & Brannick, T. L. (1965). Development of a computer system for scoring and interpretation of MMPI in a medical clinic. *Annals of the New York Academy of Sciences, 126,* 684–692.

Pernanen, K. (1974). Validity of survey data in alcohol use. In R. J. Gibbins, Y. Israel, H. Kalant, R. E. Popham, W. Schmidt, & R. C. Smart (Eds). *Research advances in alcohol and drug problems* (Vol. 1, pp. 355–374). New York: Wiley.

Piotrowski, Z. A. (1964). A digital computer administration of inkblot test data. *Psychiatric Quarterly, 38,* 1–26.

Pressman, R. M. (1984). *Microcomputers and the private practitioner.* Homewood, IL: Dow Jones–Irwin.

Reich, T., Robins, L. E., Woodruff, R. A., Jr., Taibelson, M., Rich, C., & Cunningham, L. (1975). Computer-assisted derivation of a screening interview for alcoholism. *Archives of General Psychiatry, 32,* 847–852.

Rezmovic, V. (1977). The effects of computerized experimentation on response variance. *Behavior Research Methods and Instrumentation, 9,* 144–147.

Ridgway, J., MacCulloch, M. J., & Mills, H. E. (1982). Some experiences administrating a psychometric test with a light pen and microcomputer. *International Journal of Man-Machine Studies, 17,* 265–278.

Ripley, R. E., & Ripley, M. J. (1979). *Career families: Interpretation manual for the World of Work Inventory* (rev. ed.). Scottsdale, AZ: World of Work.

Rome, H. P., Mataya, P., Pearson, J. S., Swenson, W., & Brannick, T. L. (1965). Automatic personality assessment. In R. W. Stacy & B. Waxman (Eds.), *Computers in biomedical research* (Vol. 1, pp. 505–524). New York: Academic Press.

Russell, E. W., Neuringer, C., & Goldstein, G. (1970). *Assessment of brain damage: A neuropsychological key approach.* New York: Wiley.

Sampson, J. P., Jr. (1987). "Computer-assisted" or "computerized": What's in a name? *Journal of Counseling and Development, 66,* 116–118.

Scissons, E. H. (1976). Computer administration of the California Psychological Inventory. *Measurement and Evaluation in Guidance, 9,* 22–25.

Sines, J. O. (1966). Actuarial methods in personality assessment. In B. Maher (Ed.), *Progress in experimental personality research* (Vol. 3, pp. 133–193). New York: Academic Press.

Skinner, H. A., & Allen, B. A. (1983). Does the computer make a difference? Computerized versus face-to-face versus self-report assessment of alcohol, drug, and tobacco use. *Journal of Consulting and Clinical Psychology, 51,* 267–275.

Smith, R. E. (1963). Examination by computer. *Behavioral Science, 8,* 76–79.

Stein, S. J. (1987). Computer-assisted diagnosis for children and adolescents. In J. N. Butcher (Ed.), *Computerized psychological assessment: A practitioner's guide* (pp. 145–160). New York: Basic Books.

Swiercinsky, D. P., & Warnock, J. K. (1977). Comparison of the neuropsychological key and discriminant analysis approaches in predicting cerebral damage and localization. *Journal of Consulting and Clinical Psychology, 45*, 808–814.

Tucker, G. J., & Rosenberg, S. D. (1980). Computer analysis of schizophrenic speech: An example of computer usage in the study of psychopathologic processes. In J. B. Sidowski, J. H. Johnson, & T. A. Williams (Eds.), *Technology in mental health care delivery systems* (pp. 109–117). Norwood, NJ: Ablex.

University of Minnesota. (1982). *User's guide for the Minnesota Report*. Minneapolis: National Computer Systems.

University of Minnesota. (1984). *User's guide for the Minnesota Report: Personnel Selection System*. Minneapolis: National Computer Systems.

Vincent, K. R., & Castillo, I. M. (1984). A comparison of two MMPI narratives. *Computers in Psychiatry/ Psychology, 6*(4), 30–32.

Volans, P. J., & Levy, R. (1982). A re-evaluation of an automated tailored test of concept learning with elderly psychiatric patients. *British Journal of Psychology, 21*, 93–101.

Webb, J. T., Miller, M. L., & Fowler, R. D. (1970). Extending professional time: A computerized MMPI interpretation service. *Journal of Clinical Psychology, 26*, 210–214.

Weigel, R. G., & Phillips, M. (1967). An evaluation of MMPI scoring accuracy by two national scoring agencies. *Journal of Clinical Psychology, 23*, 101–103.

Weiss, D. J., & Vale, C. D. (1987). Computerized adaptive testing for measuring abilities and other psychological variables. In J. N. Butcher (Ed.), *Computerized psychological assessment: A practitioner's guide* (pp. 325–343). New York: Basic Books.

Weizenbaum, J. (1976). *Computer power and human reason: From judgment to calculation*. San Francisco: W. H. Freeman.

Western Psychological Serivces (WPS). (1988). *1988–1989 catalog*. Los Angeles: Author.

Wiggins, J. S. (1973). *Personality and prediction: Principles of personality assessment*. Reading, MA: Addison-Wesley.

Wilson, S. L., Thompson, J. A., & Wylie, G. (1982). Automated psychological testing for the severely physically handicapped. *International Journal of Man-Machine Studies, 17*, 291–296.

Wimbish, L. G. (1985). The importance of appropriate norms for the computerized interpretation of adolescent MMPI profiles. *Dissertation Abstracts International, 46*, 3234B. (University Microfilms No. 85–26, 277).

Wirt, R. D., Lachar, D., Klinedinst, J. K., & Seat, P. D. (1977). *Multidimensional description of child personality: A manual for the Personality Inventory for Children*. Los Angeles: Western Psychological Services.

Wirt, R. D., Lachar, D., Klinedinst, J. K., & Seat, P. D., (1984). *Multidimensional description of child personality: A manual for the Personality Inventory for Children* (rev. ed. by D. Lachar). Los Angeles: Western Psychological Services.

Zachary, R. (1984, August). Computer-based test interpretations: Comments and discussion. In J. D. Matarazzo (Chair), *Computer-based test interpretation: Prospects and problems*. Symposium conducted at the annual convention of the American Psychological Association, Toronto.

IV

ASSESSMENT OF SOCIAL SKILLS, STATUS, AND MATURITY

18

Assessment of Social Skills: Sociometric and Behavioral Approaches

JAN HUGHES
Texas A&M University

DEFINITION OF SOCIAL COMPETENCE AND SOCIAL SKILLS

Research interest in children's social development has a long and distinguished history, with important empirical investigations and theoretical developments occurring in the 1930s and 1940s (Koch, 1933; Piaget, 1932). After three decades of relative lack of interest in research on social development, research began to increase dramatically in the 1960s and continues unabated today.

Several reasons contribute to the current interest among both psychologists and educators in children's social competence. First, social interactions are important in everyday life, and the possibility of making social interactions more satisfying and of reducing loneliness, conflict, and other interpersonal problems is appealing. Second, disenchantment with the use of intelligence as the major outcome measure of educational intervention programs such as Head Start stimulated the search for other socially valid outcome measures to be used with intelligence tests (Putallaz & Gootman, 1982). The view of personal competence as consisting of competence in intellectual, social, and physical spheres has gained prominence (Greenspan, 1981). Third, a large body of research provides evidence that peer relationship problems in childhood are predictive of a variety of negative outcomes in adolescence and adulthood. Childhood unpopularity predicts juvenile delinquency (Roff, Sells, & Golden, 1972), dropping out of school (Ullmann, 1957), bad-conduct discharges from the military service (Roff, 1961), and mental health problems in adulthood (Cowen, Pederson, Barbigian, Izzo, & Trost, 1973; Kohn, 1977; Strain, Cooke, & Apollini, 1976). Concurrently, unpopular children demonstrate lower levels of academic achievement and score below average on measures of cognitive and emotional development (Green, Forehand, Beck, & Vosk, 1980; Kauffman, 1985; Laughlin, 1954; Muma, 1965; Patterson, 1964; Porterfield & Schlinchting, 1961). Fourth, intervention studies attempting to remediate social skill deficits in unpopular children have resulted in treatment gains on measures of specific social skills, as well as on measures of peer acceptance and teacher ratings (for reviews, see Conger & Keane, 1981; Gresham, 1985; Gresham & Lemanek, 1983; Hughes & Sullivan, 1988; Urban & Kendall, 1980).

Despite the growing interest among psychologists and educators in topics related to children's social competence, no consensus on the definition of "social competence" exists. Recently, several researchers have suggested that one obstacle to achieving definitional consensus has been the failure to distinguish between the terms "social competence" and "social skills" (Gresham & Elliot, 1984; Putallaz & Gottman, 1982). According to this view, "social competence" is an evaluative term referring to the overall effectiveness of social behaviors, and the term "social skills" refers to specific behaviors leading to judgments of competence. Judgments of peers via sociometric measures and judgments of teachers via rating scales are measures of social competence. Their use is supported by evidence linking them to socially important outcomes, such as academic achievement, special class placements, and psychological adjustment. Because sociometric procedures and most teacher rating scales do not provide information on a child's social behaviors, they are not useful in identifying specific social skills to be targeted in an intervention. They are best considered indicator variables, in the sense that they are an index of psychological risk (Hops & Greenwood, 1981; Putallaz & Gottman, 1982).

Social skills are behaviors that increase the probability that others (teachers, peers) will evaluate the individual as socially competent.

> Social skills are those behaviors which, within a given situation, predict important social outcomes such as (a) peer acceptance or popularity, (b) significant others' judgments of behavior, or (c) other social behaviors known to correlate consistently with peer acceptance or significant others' judgments. (Gresham & Elliot, 1984, pp. 292–293)

This approach to defining social skills, referred to as the "social validity approach," "allows for specification of behaviors in which a child is deficient or socially skilled based upon the behavior's relationship to a socially important outcome" (Gresham & Elliott, 1984, p. 293). Ladd and Mize's (1983) definition of social skills also distinguishes between skilled behaviors and socially important outcomes, while also recognizing cognitive mediators of social behaviors: "Social skills . . . refer to children's ability to organize cognitions and behaviors into an integrated course of action directed toward culturally acceptable social or interpersonal goals" (p. 127).

Certainly these definitional problems have interfered with developments in the assessment of social competence and social skills. Several additional problems further interfere with the assessment of social skills. First, it is often difficult to ascertain whether poor skill performance is a result of a skill deficit or a performance deficit. A child may not engage in a particular social behavior either because he or she does not know how to perform the behavior (skill deficit), or because the child lacks motivation to perform the behavior (performance deficit). A child's outcome expectancies and self-efficacy for performing the behavior may affect the child's motivation. Second, even when motivational reasons for inept performance can be ruled out, the assessor does not know which particular component skills are deficient. That is, topographically identical behaviors may have different causes (McFall, 1982). For example, aggressive behaviors may result from a lack of knowledge of effective strategies for resolving conflicts or from a lack of impulse control. Third, when information is obtained from a child's teachers and parents as well as from the child, the agreement among raters may be quite low. Fourth, given the importance of situational determinants of social behavior, assessment results obtained in one setting cannot be assumed to generalize to a different setting. Thus, the setting as well as the behavior should be assessed.

Despite these problems, significant progress has occurred in the assessment of children's social competence and social skills. This chapter critically reviews measures of social competence and social skills. Particular emphasis is given to school-based assessment procedures. This decision is based on the fact that most child psychological assessment occurs in schools. These child assessments are usually performed for the purpose of determining child eligibility for special education services. Because handicapped learners are likely to experience social skills problems that interfere with their academic performance, the assessment of social skills should be a routine part of the assessment of children suspected of being handicapped. This recommendation is based on research documenting social skills deficits in handicapped learners, including samples of learning-disabled (Bryan, 1978; Hallahan & Kauffman, 1986; Waterman, Sobesky, Silvern, Aoki, & McCaulay, 1981), emotionally disturbed (Hallahan & Kauffman, 1986; Kauffman, 1985; Morgan, 1978; Quay, Morse, & Cutler, 1966; Stumme, Gresham, & Scott, 1982), and mentally retarded (Hallahan & Kauffman, 1986) children.

Four major approaches to the assessment of social competence and social skills are reviewed: sociometric approaches, behavior ratings, direct observation, and behavioral self-report scales. For each approach, applications are reviewed, strengths and weaknesses are noted, and recommendations are offered.

SOCIOMETRIC APPROACHES

History

Although there are a variety of sociometric procedures, an element common to all sociometric measures is the involvement of peers in the evaluation of children's social competence. Developed in the 1930s (Koch, 1933), sociometric procedures have frequently been used to evaluate children's peer acceptance, as well as to evaluate the social organization or social–emotional structure of classrooms (Gronlund, 1959). Literally hundreds of published studies during the last half century have used sociometric procedures to investigate children's peer relationships and social adjustment. Furthermore, the number of research studies using sociometric procedures has increased dramatically during the past 10 years, partially as a result of research demonstrating the long-term negative consequences of early peer rejection (e.g., Cowen et al., 1973; Roff et al., 1972). Despite this increased activity, the most commonly used type of sociometric procedure, peer nomination, is nearly identical to that used by Koch (1933) and later by Gronlund (1959). Developments in sociometric assessment have included additional peer evaluation procedures (e.g., rating scales and peer behavioral descriptions), refinements in the peer nomination procedure (e.g., the use of pictures in obtaining nominations from young children), additional evidence of the stability and validity of sociometric procedures, and new typologies of peer acceptance status. The heightened research interest in sociometric assessment is reflected in several recent reviews (Asher & Hymel, 1981; Bierman, 1987; Hops & Lewin, 1984; Hymel, 1983; Puttallaz & Gottman, 1982).

The term "sociometric assessment" refers to a range of specific procedures that can be grouped for discussion purposes into three types: peer nominations, peer behavioral descriptions, and Likert-type rating scales. This section of the chapter describes and evaluates each type, and suggests guidelines for selecting an approach that best meets the purposes of the assessment.

Peer Nomination Approach

The peer nomination approach is probably the most frequently used sociometric procedure, and it certainly has the longest history (e.g., Gronlund, 1959; Koch, 1933). Each child in a classroom (or other socially defined group) is asked to select a restricted number of classmates with respect to a given criterion (e.g., "like the most," "most like to have as a best friend," "most like to play with"). A child's score is the number of nominations received. Positive-nomination scores are considered indices of the child's popularity or peer acceptance.

A common practice is combining a positive-nomination criterion with a negative criterion. Negative-nomination procedures include asking children to nominate three peers whom they like the least or three children whom they would least prefer as playmates. For ethical reasons, the phrasing "like least" is preferred to the phrasing "dislike." Children who receive a high number of negative nominations are considered rejected.

Researchers, educators, and parents have been reluctant to use negative nominations because their use may increase the saliency of peer rejection in a group. That is, rejected children as well as their peers may become more aware of rejected children's status, and this increased awareness may alter behavior in a way that is detrimental to rejected children. If children discuss their choices with one another, a consensus that a particular child is disliked may build. Although these concerns are legitimate ones, children are already very aware of the rejected child's status. In an empirical investigation of the effect of negative-choice sociometric procedures on children's interaction, Hayvren and Hymel (1984) observed preschool children before and after the administration of positive and negative sociometric questions. The children did not discuss their choices and did not interact differently after the sociometric measure. Although providing evidence to support the conclusion that sociometric procedures are not reactive in preschool populations, these results cannot be generalized to older populations. Ratiner, Weissberg, and Caplan (1986) found that many of the 32 sixth-grade students who completed sociometric ratings later reported in individual interviews that students discussed their ratings.

Given the possible detrimental consequences of negative-choice nominations, it would be ill advised to use them unless they make an important and unique contribution to the assessment of a child's social competence. In this regard, the data suggest that positive and negative nominations are measuring different dimensions of social competence. For example, positive- and negative-nomination scores are only moderately negatively correlated (Gottman, 1977; Hymel & Asher, 1977; Landau, Milich, & Whitten, 1984) or not at all (Hartup, Glazer, & Charlesworth, 1967). Thus, one cannot predict a child's rejection score on the basis of knowledge of the child's positive-nomination score. When only positive nominations are used, it is not possible to distinguish between two types of unpopular children, "neglected" and "rejected" children. Both types of children receive few positive nominations. The neglected child also receives few negative nominations, whereas the rejective child receives many negative nominations. Evidence of behavioral differences between rejected and neglected children (Coie, Dodge, & Coppotelli, 1982; Dodge, Coie, & Brakke, 1982; Dodge, Schlundt, Schocken, & Delugach, 1983) and evidence that rejected status is more stable (Coie & Dodge, 1983) support the use of negative nominations for purposes of selecting children for social skills interventions programs, as well as for selecting the skills to be taught in a social skills intervention program.

When negative nominations are used, certain precautions should be taken to minimize possible deleterious effects. The examiner should tell the children that their choices are private and should not be discussed among themselves. The sociometric measure should not be administered before an activity that permits conversing, such as before recess or lunch.

Several authors have suggested that a more useful measure of children's social competence could be achieved by developing a typology of sociometric types based on a consideration of both positive- and negative-choice nominations (Gronlund, 1959; Puttallaz & Gottman, 1982; Hymel, 1983). The utility of a classification system is evaluation by evidence of the system's concurrent and predictive validity (Hymel, 1983). One recently proposed system (Coie et al., 1982) has provided evidence of concurrent and predictive validity as well as evidence of long-term stability. (Reliability and validity of nomination procedures are discussed below.) In this system, which refines a system proposed by Peery (1979), two new sociometric scores are derived from the "like most" (LM) and "like least" (LL) scores. Raw score nominations for LM and LL are standardized within classrooms. The standard scores for the LM and LL items are used to generate social preference ($z_{LM} - z_{LL}$) and social impact ($z_{LM} + z_{LL}$) scores. The derived social preference and social impact scores are used to identify children for five distinct social status groups (i.e., popular, average, controversial, neglected, and rejected; see Coie et al., 1982, for classification formulas). In an initial validation study (Coie et al., 1982), 486 of 848 third-, fifth-, and eighth-graders were classified into one of the five status types.

Reliability of Peer Nominations

Elementary school children's nomination scores have been found to be reliable over periods from 6 weeks to 5 years (Bonney, 1943; Feinberg, 1964; Horrocks & Benimoff, 1966; Roff et al. 1972; Wasik, 1987). In an excellent recent longitudinal study, Coie and Dodge (1983) collected yearly sociometric data on a sample of third- and fifth-graders across a 5-year period. In a departure from earlier studies, Coie and Dodge permitted nominations to be made across the entire grade level rather than within classrooms.

Because the children in a given grade shared parts of the day and maintained friendships from year to year across classrooms, Coie and Dodge believed that within-classroom nominations would distort the real picture of relationships in the school. For example, a child might receive no positive nominations in a particular year because his or her friends were in another classroom, rather than because he or she was friendless. For the third-grade sample, test–retest correlations for the LM criterion were .57 for year 1 to year 2 and .28 for year 1 to year 5. The test–retest correlations for the LL nominations tended to be higher than for the LM nominations. For the third-grade sample, these correlations were .54 for year 1 to year 2 and .35 for year 1 to year 5; for the fifth-grade sample, LL correlations were .71 for year 1 to year 2 and .32 for year 1 to year 5.

Nomination measures are less reliable at the preschool level than at the elementary level (Hymel, 1983). In an effort to improve the test–retest reliability of sociometric measures with preschoolers, McCandless and Marshall (1957) modified the nomination procedure to include photographs of all the children who could be nominated. In a 10- to 15-minute individual interview, children are shown photographs of all of their classmates and are asked to point to the picture of their best friends (or the three children whom they like the most). This modification attempts to avoid memory problems, such as a child's failing to nominate a classmate due to difficulty in remembering a name or remembering all potential nominees. Despite this modification, studies using this procedure have reported only moderate test–retest reliabilities with preschoolers (Asher, Singleton, Tinsley, & Hymel, 1979; Hartup et al., 1967; McCandless & Marshall, 1957). Although rejection scores are more reliable than acceptance scores for elementary school children (Coie & Dodge, 1983), acceptance scores are more reliable than either rejection scores or combined acceptance and rejected scores for preschoolers (Asher et al., 1979; Hartup et al., 1967).

Although some researchers have suggested a weighted scoring of nominations, such that the child's first nomination is weighted more heavily than the child's second or third nominations (e.g. Hartup et al., 1967), weighted and unweighted scores are highly correlated (see Hymel, 1983). Furthermore, as Hymel (1983) suggests, unless the child is instructed to list his or her very best friend first, to list his or her next best friend second, and so forth, a weighted scoring system is not justifiable. Some researchers do instruct children to order nominations and use weighted scoring (e.g., Foster & Ritchey, 1985).

Coie and Dodge (1983) provide both evidence of the stability of social preference and social impact scores and evidence of the reliability of the five sociometric types over a 5-year period for a sample of third- and fifth-graders. With respect to the reliabilities of status categories, status as popular was moderately stable over a 1-year period (36% of all popular children in a given year were also popular the following year). Stability of popularity was slightly lower over longer intervals. The rejected status was the most stable category: over a 1-year period, 45% of rejected children remained rejected; after a 4-year period, this figure was 30%. Whereas rejected children were unlikely to change to average or popular status, the neglected and controversial status groups were less stable. Furthermore, neglected children were likely to move toward positive or average status. Considering the length of time and the dramatic change in composition of the peer group (each cohort was followed from elementary to junior high school), the stability of the rejected status is remarkable. A clue as to why rejected status is stable is found in the peer behavioral descriptions used by Coie and Dodge. Children who became (or remained) rejected were perceived by peers as uncooperative, as not being leaders, as disruptive, and as starting fights. These results are consistent with studies on behavioral correlates of rejected status (Coie & Kupersmidt, 1983; Dodge et al., 1982; Hartup et al., 1967; Wasik, 1987), as well as with research on behavioral antecedents of rejected status (Coie & Kupersmidt, 1983; Dodge, 1983).

Validity of Peer Nominations

Many of the studies frequently cited as supportive of the premise that low peer acceptance leads to adjustment difficulties are retrospective rather than longitudinal studies (e.g., Strain et al., 1976). Of the few longitudinal studies, only the Roff et al. (1972) study used peer nominations. In a 5-year longitudinal study, Roff and colleagues found that third- and sixth-grade children's peer acceptance (computed as the number of LM minus the number of LL nominations) predicted delinquency and in 9th and 10th grades among middle- and upper-class boys, but not among lower-class boys. Although these results offer important evidence of the predictive validity of peer nominations, these results need to be replicated on a different sample of children. As Hymel (1983) notes, there are no data for the predictive validity of peer nominations with preschool children.

In contrast to the few studies on the predictive validity of nomination measures, there are many studies of concurrent validity. Many of these studies investigate behavioral correlates of sociometric status. The picture that consistently emerges, from samples of preschool children to adolescents, is one of popular children giving and receiving more positive reinforcement and rejected children giving and receiving more negative reinforcement (Dodge et al., 1982; Dodge et al., 1983; Gottman, Gonso, & Rasmussen, 1975; Greenwood, Walker, Todd, & Hops, 1979; Hartup et al., 1967; Ladd, 1983; Landau et al., 1984; Marshall & McCandless, 1957; Putallaz, 1983). Positive-nomination scores predict elementary school children's knowledge of friendship-making strategies (Gottman et al., 1975). Peer acceptance scores also correlate with teacher ratings (e.g., Vosk, Forehand, Parker, & Richard, 1982) and measures of academic achievement (e.g., Bonney, 1971; Green et al., 1980).

A limit of earlier studies on behavioral correlates of peer acceptance was the use of designs that did not permit a determination of the causal relationships between social behavior and peer acceptance or rejection. Researchers first identified the sociometric status of children in already existing peer groups and then conducted observations to determine the correlates of status. These designs did not permit a determination of whether the negative behaviors associated with peer rejection were the result of status or the cause of it. A child who is disliked by peers, perhaps for such attributes as physical attractiveness or economic status, may behave differently toward peers as a result of the rejection. Recently, researchers have demonstrated that behavioral interaction style is a cause of status and not just a result (Coie & Kupersmidt, 1983; Dodge, 1983; Putallaz, 1983). The Dodge (1983) study is illustrative of this new generation of research on behavioral antecedents of peer social status. Forty-eight previously unacquainted second-grade boys were brought together in six play groups of eight boys each. Unstructured play groups met in a laboratory setting under supervision. Observers and video cameras recorded interactive behaviors. At the conclusion of the eighth session, a positive- and negative-choice sociometric measure was administered to each boy, and status groups of popular, rejected, neglected, controversial, and average boys were identified, according to the Coie et al. (1982) procedure. Behavioral antecedents of rejected and neglected status were identified. The children who became rejected were those who engaged in a great deal of aggression and inappropriate behaviors and who engaged in less social conversation than average children. The children who became neglected spent significantly more time in solitary play than average children and engaged in more inappropriate (but not more aggressive) behaviors.

Additional evidence of the concurrent validity of peer nominations is found in the Coie and Dodge (1983) study. Peer behavioral descriptions as well as peer nomination data were collected of 486 third- and fifth-graders. Significant differences in peer perceptions of the behaviors of the different groups emerged. Rejected children were described by peers as disruptive and aggressive; controversial children were described as disruptive and aggressive, but also as social leaders (like the popular children).

Recent research studies on social-cognitive correlates have offered additional evidence of the concurrent validity of peer nominations and the Coie et al. (1982) classification system. For example, popular and average elementary school children, compared to their rejected and neglected peers, are less likely to attribute hostile intentions for a peer's accidental or prosocial provocation (Dodge, Murphy, & Buchsbaum, 1984).

Peer Behavioral Descriptions

A limit of the most frequently used peer nomination approach is that knowledge of a child's acceptance or rejection status does not permit a specification of those personal attributes or skills that determine the child's status. Therefore, a more structured approach to peer nominations has been suggested. The peer behavioral description method is an example of a more structured nomination procedure. The best known example of this sociometric procedure is the Class Play (Bower, 1969; Lambert & Bower, 1961). Children pretend to be directors of an imaginary play and "cast" their classmates in a variety of positive and negative roles. Examples of roles are "Someone who is the leader when children do something in class or on the playground—someone everybody listens to" and "A bully—someone who picks on smaller boys and girls." Each child receives a visibility score (based on the combined nominations for positive and negative roles), a positive score, and a negative score. Masten, Morison, and Pellegrini (1985) revised the original Class Play in order to improve the sampling of positive aspects of social competence and to eliminate items referring directly to academic and/or intellectual ability. The resulting Revised Class Play consists of 30 roles, 15 positive and 15 negative. Other minor modifications in content and in administration were made to correct methodological problems. Importantly, children are provided with a roster listing all children eligible for casting, as opposed to the fill-in-the-blank format of the Lambert–Bower version.

Reliability of Behavioral Descriptions

The original Class Play evidenced good short-term stability (Lambert & Bower, 1961). The Revised Class Play (Masten et al., 1985) yields three factors identified through factor analysis: Sociability–leadership, Aggressive–disruptive, and Sensitive–isolated. For each factor, Masten et al. (1985) report good internal consistency as well as good stability for intervals of 6 and 17 months.

Coie and Dodge (1983) used behavioral descriptions in their 5-year longitudinal study with third- and fifth-graders. In the first year of the study, children were asked to name three children who best fit each of 24 behavioral descriptions. In subsequent years, only 5 of the original 24 behavioral descriptions were employed because of time constraints. These five descriptions, selected on the basis of cluster analysis, described five behavioral types: "cooperative," "disruptive," "acts shy," "starts fights," and "leader." The "starts fights" description was the most stable across years (correlation coefficient of third to fourth grades = .83; of fifth to sixth grades = .84). All behavioral descriptions revealed moderately high stability across each year.

Validity of Behavioral Descriptions

In an ambitious and widely cited study, Cowen and his colleagues at the Rochester Mental Health Project in New York (Cowen et al., 1973) correlated test data collected on third-grade children in the year 1961 with listings in a community psychiatric register 11–13 years later. Extensive data were collected on the third-grade children, including absenteeism, grades, intelligence scores, achievement test performance, teacher ratings, and a peer behavioral description procedure (i.e., the Class Play). Eleven years later, the research team examined a community mental health register to learn which of these children were being seen by mental health professionals. The Class Play was the best predictor of later emotional difficulties. Also using the Class Play procedure, Lambert (1972) found that peer nominations made in the second and third grades predicted high school adjustment status.

Only in recent years have researchers investigated the concurrent validity of peer behavioral descriptions. The majority of these studies have investigated social-cognitive correlates of aggressive peer nominations. For example, in a series of studies, Dodge and his colleagues found that children receiving a high number of aggressive peer nominations as well as a low number of "play with" nominations had social-cognitive deficits that presumably underlay their peer relationship difficulties (Dodge & Frame, 1982; Dodge & Newman, 1981; Richard & Dodge, 1982; Steinberg & Dodge, 1983). Perry, Perry, and Rasmussen (1986) found that peers receiving a high number of nominations on nine aggressive items of a peer nomination inventory reported that it was easier to perform aggression and more difficult to inhibit aggressive impulses. Also, aggressive children were more confident that aggression would result in positive consequences and would reduce aversive treatment by others.

Rating Scales

The roster-and-rating sociometric questionnaire presents each child in a classroom (or other social group, such as cabinmates at camp) with an alphabetical class roster. Next to each child's name is a 5- or 7-point Likert-type scale. The respondent is asked to rate his or her degree of liking for each person on the roster. An example of a "play with" rating scale used with elementary school children is given in Table 18.1.

When such a scale is used with preschool and kindergarten children, the child rates his or her degree of liking by assigning photographs of classmates to boxes represented by one of three faces: happy face ("children you like a lot"), neutral face ("children you kind of like"), and sad face ("children you don't like"). A child's score is the average of all the ratings he or she receives. One advantage of the roster-and-rating approach is that the ethical concerns associated with a negative-nomination question are minimized. In addition, ratings are believed to be more stable than nomination scores because each child is rated by all classmates. Whereas one or two persons' changing their nominations will have a relatively large effect on nomination scores, rating scores are less affected by a few individuals' changing their minds (Asher et al., 1979). Also, ratings decrease the likelihood that a student will not be selected because of being momentarily forgotten or because other children cannot spell his or her name (Asher et al., 1979).

Ratings and nomination scores are significantly correlated. Asher et al. (1979) found that "play with" ratings correlated .74 and −.73 with positive and negative nominations, respectively, in a preschool sample. Ladd and Oden (1979) found similar results with elementary students. Nevertheless, rating questionnaires and nomination questionnaires measure different aspects of social relationships. Ratings tend to measure peer acceptance or likability, whereas nominations measure friendship patterns (Schofield & Whitley, 1983). In both a meta-analytic study of the effect of race on socioeconomic preferences and a field-based study, Schofield and Whitley (1983) found stronger within-in-group preferences for peer nominations than for ratings. They concluded that "peer nominations reveal friendships, whereas the roster-and-rating technique assesses interpersonal acceptance, a much less intimate form of relationship" (p. 243).

Several researchers recommend using same-sex ratings because children's ratings show sex bias (Hayden-Thomson, Rubin, & Hymel, 1987; Singleton & Asher, 1977). The relative reliability of same-sex versus both-sex ratings has not been empirically determined.

Reliability of Ratings

Roster-and-rating scores are more reliable than nomination scores. The median reliability coefficients over a 6-week retest interval across 11 elementary school classrooms were .82 for "play with" ratings, .84 for "work

TABLE 18.1. "Play with" Rating Scale Used with Elementary School Children

	I like to play with this person a lot	I like to play with this person	Don't know very well	Don't like to play with this person	Don't like to play with this person at all
Lucy					
Sam					
Kevin					
Beth					

with" ratings, and .69 for "best friend" nominations (Oden & Asher, 1977). In a sample of preschool children, Asher et al. (1979) found retest reliability coefficients of .56 for positive nominations, .42 for negative nominations, and .81 for "play with" ratings.

Compared to the considerable evidence of the long-term stability of nominations, there are few extant data on the long-term stability of ratings. Rubin and Daniels-Beirness (1983) found the stability of "play with" ratings over a 1-year period from kindergarten to first grade to be moderately high ($r = .48$). Because these children did not move as a group from kindergarten to first-grade classrooms, this level of stability suggests that child characteristics rather than reputational factors accounted for the stability.

Validity of Ratings

A great deal of evidence supports the concurrent validity of peer ratings. Ratings correlate significantly and positively with positive peer interaction and significantly and negatively with negative peer interaction (Hymel, 1983; Rubin & Daniels-Beirness, 1983). Furthermore, children who receive high ratings demonstrate more sophisticated social-cognitive skills (Ladd & Oden, 1979; Renshaw, 1981; Renshaw & Asher, 1983; Rubin & Daniels-Beirness, 1983).

Primarily because the roster-and-rating approach is a relatively new type of sociometric measure, there is little evidence of its predictive validity. However, several studies have found that ratings can be predicted from social behaviors. First-grade children's sociometric status, based on "play with" ratings, could be predicted by observations of social interaction taken 1 year earlier, when they were in kindergarten (Rubin & Daniels-Beirness, 1983). Putallaz (1983) found that observational measures of children's strategies for entering a new play group during the summer before first grade predicted sociometric status derived from "play with" ratings in first grade, 4 months later. Their predictive studies offer support for the construct validity of ratings, because they support the view that sociometric status is a result of social interactions and not a cause of it.

Comparisons among Sociometric Procedures

Because of the higher reliability and concurrent validity of roster-and-ratings with preschool and kindergarten children, the roster-and-rating approach is recommended over the nomination approach for young ages (Asher et al., 1979; Hymel, 1983). In the elementary and secondary grades, ratings, nominations, and peer behavioral descriptions have demonstrated good reliability and validity. Therefore, the choice of sociometric approach depends on the purpose of the assessment as well as on practical considerations. Because behavioral and social-cognitive differences have been related to the classifications based on Coie's formula (Coie et al., 1982), the use of positive and negative nominations to derive both social preference and social impact scores is recommended when the purpose of the study is to select children for a skills training intervention program. If the purpose of assessment is to study acceptance of persons on the basis of race, sex, or handicapped condition, ratings are preferred because they reflect acceptance, whereas nominations reflect friendship patterns. Also, if the purpose of assessment is to evaluate outcomes of a social skills intervention program designed to increase children's social acceptability, ratings are recommended, because they are more sensitive to treatment effects (Gresham & Nagle, 1980; Oden & Asher, 1977). However, if the purpose of an intervention is to teach friendship-making skills, a positive-nominations questionnaire would be preferable. If teachers, administrators, or parents object to the use of negative nominations, a combination of roster-and-ratings and positive nominations would permit discrimination between two types of children, both of whom receive few positive nominations. The child who is friendless but who is rated as moderately liked is not as great a clinical concern as is the friendless child who is rated as disliked.

If the examiner is interested in identifying a special subpopulation of unpopular peers, a combination of peer behavioral descriptions and positive peer nominations is recommended. For example, Dodge (1980) classified children as aggressive if they received a low number of positive peer nominations and a high number of aggressive descriptions.

BEHAVIORAL ASSESSMENT

Rating Scales

Overview

Behavior checklists and rating scales completed by teachers and parents are common components in the assessment of children's social competence (Cartledge & Milburn, 1986; Gresham, 1982a; Michelson, Sugai, Wood, & Kazdin, 1983). Both checklists and rating scales require an adult to make judgments regarding a child's behavior or characteristics. It is important to note that teachers' perceptions of children's social behaviors can be obtained through nominations, rankings, checklists, and rating scales.

A checklist requires the adult to make a dichotomous decision as to whether the child demonstrates a behavior (e.g., "participates in group") or characteristic (e.g., "thinks others pick on him or her"). A rating scale requires the adult to indicate the degree to which a behavior or characteristic describes a child. Thus, a ratings scale has three or more response options, such as "never," "sometimes," and "often" (Cone & Hawkins, 1977; Humphrey & Ciminero, 1979). Because the psychometric properties and uses of checklists and rating scales are similar, the term "rating scale" is used here to refer to both types of instruments.

Nominations require the teacher to select a certain number of children who fit a description, such as "withdrawn." Rankings require the teacher to rank all children in a class in terms of a single characteristic or status. Bolstad and Johnson (1977) asked elementary teachers to nominate boy and girl pairs who were "best-behaved," "average," and "least well-behaved" in classroom conduct. These teacher-labeled groups differed on several categories of direct observations of classroom behavior. Working with preschool populations, Greenwood et al. (1979) found that teachers' rankings of children on frequency of peer verbal interaction correctly identified the least interacting child and were significantly correlated with rate of observed interaction. Preschool teacher rankings of popularity are significantly correlated with both peer nomination scores and observed social behavior (Connolly & Doyle, 1981). Although rankings and nomination procedures have proven useful in screening children, they are not widely used in the assessment of social competence, probably because of the global nature of the information these yield.

Several characteristics of rating scales contribute to their popularity. They are economical, are easy to administer and score, and demonstrate good test–retest and interrater reliabilities (Behar & Stringfield, 1974; Bolstad & Johnson, 1977; Connolly & Doyle, 1981; Edelbrock, Greenbaum, & Conover, 1985). With respect to validity issues, teacher ratings predict direct behavior observations (Algozzine, 1977; Balou, 1966; Bolstad & Johnson, 1977; Kohn & Parnes, 1974; Marshall & McCandless, 1957; Quay, 1979; Schachar, Sandbery, & Rutter, 1986), as well as diagnostic classification (Behar & Stringfield, 1974; Stumme et al., 1982; Waksman, 1985) and peer sociometric measures (Green et al., 1980; Greenwood et al., 1979; Greenwood, Walker, & Hops, 1977; Van Hasselt, Hersen, & Bellack, 1981; Vosk et al., 1982). The use of multiple raters permits a determination of the cross-situational consistency of a child's behavior. Consistency at school can be assessed by having two teachers complete a scale, and home–school consistency can be assessed by having a parent and a teacher complete parallel forms of a scale that provides norms for both teacher and parent forms (e.g., the Child Behavior Checklist [CBCL]; Achenbach & Edelbrock, 1983, 1986). Differences between parent and teacher raters, rather than being a limitation of rating scales, are generally the result both of setting differences and of differences in standards for behavior (Hops & Greenwood, 1988). In addition to providing information concerning a child's behavior, rating scales provide important information about the child's impact on significant others. Thus, multiple raters help to determine the influence of the setting on a child's behavior and the child's impact on social agents (Hops & Greenwood, 1988). The fact that these social agents (i.e., teachers and parents) refer children for special services on the basis of their perceptions of the normality of the chilren's behavior argues for the importance of including these perceptions in the assessment of children's social behaviors. In addition, teachers' and parents' perceptions of a child will affect their interactions with the child.

Although behavior rating scales have many advantages, they also have limitations. First, rating scales are useful in identifying children who may have social competence problems and in evaluating the impact of intervention programs, but they do not specify problem behaviors or skilled behaviors. This distinction between global evaluative data and specific behavioral data has been made by several researchers (Gresham, 1982a; Hops & Greenwood, 1981; Hughes & Sullivan, 1988).

Second, rating scales are limited by the inadequate opportunities teachers and parents have to observe those social behaviors that are crucial to peer acceptance (Reardon, Hersen, Bellack, & Foley, 1979). Much of the social interaction of elementary school children occurs outside the purview of adults (Asher & Hymel, 1981), and secondary school teachers probably have even fewer opportunities to observe crucial social interactions.

Third, rating scales are subject to rater bias. Both the specificity of the items and characteristics of the rater affect interrater agreement. For example, inexperienced teachers consistently overrate maladjustment (Clarfield, 1974). Also, scales that require teachers to rate global behaviors are less reliable than scales that require teachers to rate fairly specific behaviors (Shuller & McNamara, 1976).

In the next section, several dimensions on which rating scales vary are delineated, examples are presented, and implications for the assessment of social skills are discussed.

Dimensions

Specificity. Although most teacher and parent rating scales obtain the rater's global perception of the child's social competence, some scales obtain perceptions of specific social behaviors. Those scales that measure global evaluations are useful for purposes of

(1) screening children for the presence of social competence problems and (2) evaluating the social validity of intervention programs intended to improve a child's social competence (Gresham, 1982a; Hughes & Sullivan, 1988). Because significant adults' perceptions of a child are frequently the basis for referral for mental health services and predict other socially important outcomes, they are important indices of the impact or social validity of intervention programs. Measures that access these socially valued outcomes are termed "impact assessment measures" (Kendall & Morison, 1984). Teacher ratings are not useful for measuring specific social behaviors that may contribute to others' judgments of the child's overall social competence. Thus, rating scales do not permit a specification of the nature of a social competence problem or, in the case of popular children, the nature of their social skills.

Examples of ratings scales that measure significant others' global evaluations of children include the Revised Behavior Problem Checklist (RBPC; Quay & Peterson, 1983; 1984), the CBCL (Achenbach & Edelbrock, 1983, 1986), and the Conners Parent and Teacher Rating Scales (Goyette, Conners, & Ulrich, 1978). These scales tend to be norm-referenced and comprehensive, and yield factor scores in addition to a total score. These tests' principal use is classifying children based on standardized factor and total scores. In over 20 years of research on the original BPC (Quay & Peterson, 1979) and 6 years of research on the RBPC (Quay & Peterson, 1983), the scales and total score have consistently discriminated clinical from normal children. Statistically significant and clinically meaningful correlations between subscale scores and behavioral observations, peer nominations, and diagnostic classification have consistently been found (Lahey, Shaughency, Frame, & Strauss, 1985; Quay & Peterson, 1983).

The individual items on the RBPC and similar scales (e.g., the CBCL, the Conners) are not directly useful. Items are averaged to form scales, and a child's score on that scale is compared with age norms. Although the behavioral specificity of items varies, most items refer to a class of behaviors rather than to a specific behavior. The following items from the RBPC illustrate the range in item specificity: "lacks self-confidence," "loyal to delinquent friends," "sulks and pouts," "steals from people outside the home," "generally fearful."

Examples of rating scales that measure specific social skills include the Social Behavior Assessment (SBA; Stephens, 1978, 1981), the Teacher Rating of Social Skills (TROSS; Clark, Gresham, & Elliott, 1985), and the Matson Evaluation of Social Skills with Youngsters (MESSY; Matson, Rotatori, & Helsel, 1983). Items on these scales are behaviorally specific and are interpreted from a criterion-referenced perspective. Items are frequently derived from social skills training curriculum (Stephens, 1978). If a child is rated as not demonstrating a specific social behavior (i.e., giving a peer a compliment), that behavior may be targeted in a social skills intervention. Behaviorally specific rating scales are relatively new, and evidence pertaining to their psychometric properties is meager. Because the items require a low level of inference, it is expected that the scales would demonstrate higher interrater reliabilities than scales requiring larger inferences (Waksman, 1985). However, the empirical support for this expected greater reliability is lacking. A criticism of the MESSY, the TROSS, and other specific scales is that inadequate attention is given to developmental differences. Without norms, it is difficult to determine whether a particular social behavior is expected at a given age level.

The purpose of behaviorally specific scales is to delineate the nature of a child's difficulties or specific behavior deficits, so that these deficits can be targeted for an intervention. The assumption is that the child's skill deficits contribute to his or her social competence problems, as identified by sociometric testing or teacher global ratings. Therefore, evidence that scale items predict observations of specific behavior as well as peer and teacher ratings is necessary to establish the scale's validity. To date, this evidence has not been forthcoming for scales that attempt to measure a wide range of specific social behaviors.

Some teacher rating scales were designed to measure a more limited aspect of social behavior, such as aggressiveness (Walker et al., 1978) or withdrawal (Hops et al., 1978). The Reprogramming Environmental Contingencies for Effective Social Skills instrument (RECESS; Walker et al., 1978) is specific to aggressive behaviors and discriminates aggressive from normal children (Walker, et al., 1981). The Social Interaction Rating Scale (SIRS; Hops et al., 1978) requires teachers to rate behaviors specific to social withdrawal. The SIRS discriminates between children referred for withdrawal and nonreferred classmates, and items correlate with observed time engaged in social behavior (Hops & Greenwood, 1988).

Informant. There are advantages and disadvantages of using parents and teachers as informants. Because teachers have the opportunity to rate children in comparison to other children of the same age in a standardized environment, their ratings are likely to provide more objective and accurate information than parent ratings. Conversely, parents have opportunities to observe their children in many different settings across a long period of time. Because much of children's social behavior occurs at school, teachers may be in a better position than parents to observe social interactions. However, this relative edge teachers enjoy may disappear in secondary school, because those social behaviors that are most important to peer acceptance and rejection occur outside adult purview.

One advantage of teacher ratings is the opportunity to have more than one teacher rate a child's behavior. If the child's ratings are different in different classrooms, characteristics of settings that facilitate or interfere with the child's social behavior can be investigated, as can the possibility of rater bias.

Although most rating scales were developed for use with specific raters, some scales have parallel forms and separate norms for teacher-completed and parent-completed scales (e.g., Achenbach & Edelbrock, 1983, 1986; Goyette et al., 1978; Quay & Peterson, 1983). The advantage of obtaining both teacher and parent ratings is the opportunity to assess home–school continuity in the child's behavior, as well as the child's differential impact on important social agents.

Scope. Rating scales vary in their level of comprehensiveness. Scales like the CBCL (Achenback & Edelbroch, 1983) are broadband, low-fidelity measures developed for purposes of screening for broadly based child psychopathology. These scales vary with respect to their relevance to social competence. For example, the Social Withdrawal and Aggressive scales of the CBCL are highly relevant to social competence assessment, whereas the Obsessive–Compulsive and Somatic Complaints scales are less directly relevant. Some scales were developed for purposes of assessing a more restricted range of child behavior, such as hyperactivity (Conners, 1969) or self-control (Humphrey, 1982). Scales specifically designed to assess social skills, include the Waksman Social Skills Rating Scale (WSSRS; Waksman, 1985), the MESSY (Matson et al., 1983), the Walker Problem Behavior Identification Checklist (WPBIC; Walker, 1976), the SIRS; (Hops et al., 1978), and the RECESS (Walker et al., 1978).

Item Format. Scales differ with respect to whether the informant rates a child on problem behaviors (or classes of problem behaviors) or on socially skilled behaviors (or classes of skilled behaviors). The problem behavior format is characteristic of the norm-referenced, standardized, comprehensive scales, whereas the skilled behavior format is characteristic of criterion-referenced, nonstandardized scales. The problem behavior format is most useful for purposes of screening and classification; the skilled behavior format is most useful for purposes of specifying positive social behavioral deficits that might be targeted in a social skills intervention program.

Support for rating both problem and skilled behaviors is provided by studies on behavioral correlates of peer acceptance and rejection (Dodge & Murphy, 1984: Putallaz & Gottman, 1982). Compared to unpopular children, popular children not only engage in fewer negative social behaviors, but also engage in more prosocial behaviors. Thus, the assessment of positive and negative behaviors permits a more complete description of socially consequential behavioral excesses and deficits.

Direct Observation

Overview

Direct observation is the hallmark of behavioral assessment (Bellack, 1979). Barton and Ascione (1984) define direct observation as "the process by which human observers, using operational definitions as their guide, record the overt motor and/or verbal behavior of other humans" (p. 167). This definition includes recordings that are made at the same time or immediately following the observation of behavior; it excludes recordings made after an observational period, in the form of a narrative, rating form, or checklist.

Direct observation of children's social performance has several advantages. First, the resulting data require little inference for interpretation. For example, the knowledge that a child engaged in physical aggression (i.e., hitting, pushing, pinching) three times during a 30-minute unstructured-play period is important in its own right. Second, direct observation permits the specification of both target behaviors and important contextual variables (i.e., antecedents and consequences). Thus, the resulting data are useful in selecting treatment targets and determining the changes needed in the child's environment to effect a desired change in child behavior. Third, because direct observation procedures are relatively nonreactive, they can be used repeatedly to permit continuous recording of target behaviors. Thus, they are very useful in experimental designs that require continuous recording of the subject's behavior (Barlow & Hersen, 1984).

Fourth, direct observations have proven sensitive to treatment effects in social skills intervention programs (e.g., Bierman & Furman, 1984; Bornstein, Bellack, & Hersen, 1980; Cook & Apolloni, 1976). Fifth, when researchers combine direct observation of target behaviors with socially valid criterion measures in assessing outcomes of social skill interventions, it is possible to establish the functional relationship between specific behaviors and socially valid criteria (e.g., peer and teacher ratings). Thus, researchers can document which behavioral changes resulted in improvement in peer acceptance or teacher global ratings.

Sixth, direct observation procedures that code sequential social interactions permit a more precise definition of social–interactional difficulties. For example, knowing that a socially withdrawn child responds to peers' initiatives at the same frequency as other children but seldom initiates social interactions has important implications for selecting the specific skills to target in a social skills intervention. Similarly, knowing that a child's aggressive responses follow criticism from peers and are rewarded by teacher attention has implications for treatment.

Seventh, direct observation procedures permit the documentation of behavioral "constellations" (Kazdin, 1985). Behaviors that co-occur comprise constellations, and a change in one of the behaviors in the constellation is likely to affect the occurrence of other behaviors. Observational codes that encompass several different behaviors can help to determine which behaviors covary. This information is useful in selecting treatment targets, because changes in those behaviors that are likely to result in the greatest "ripple effect" are preferred treatment targets. Finally, observations obtained by trained observers are highly reliable and not as susceptible to biasing information as ratings (Cunningham & Tharp, 1981; Shuller & McNamara, 1976).

Direct observation also has certain important limitations. As Asher and Hymel (1981) point out, schools, the most common settings in which direct observations are conducted, do not provide good opportunities to observe behaviors related to peer acceptance and liking. Second, the critical interactions for friendship formation and maintenance and for peer rejection may occur at too low a frequency to permit reliable observation, especially with older children. In this regard, Asher and Hymel (1981) suggest that developmental changes in friendship skills account for the failure of several researchers to find relationships between direct observation and peer acceptance at ages beyond the preschool years. Behaviors important to developing friendships differ at different ages (Eisenberg & Harris, 1984): Overt, easily observed behaviors are more important at younger ages, and more complex and subtle behaviors are more important at older ages. Thus, verbal behaviors, which are more important to older children's friendship choices, are more difficult to observe unobtrusively than is sharing, an important social skill at the preschool level (Barton & Ascione, 1979). An additional complicating factor in observing older children's social behaviors is the likelihood that older children will be less natural in the presence of an adult observer.

Third, direct observation procedures may be expensive. Many procedures reported in the social skills literature require highly trained observers. Gresham (1982b) trained observers for 5 hours in order to achieve interrator agreement of 80%. In order to obtain reliable and useful observations, more than one observation period in several settings is usually necessary, increasing the cost of this approach.

Fourth, direct observations may be insensitive to qualitative aspects of social behavior. In a recent study with adolescents, Panella and Henggeler (1986) found that observation methods that measured the quality of behaviors correlated more highly with other indices of social competence than methods that measured the quantity of social behaviors. However, most direct observation methods assess quantity versus quality of social behaviors. In this regard, Barton and Ascione (1984) suggest ways to code the quality or intensity of behavior while not decreasing the method's objectivity.

Dimensions of Direct Observations

Settings. Direct observation of behavior may occur in the child's natural setting (e.g., Gottman et al., 1975; Foster & Ritchey, 1985), in a contrived setting (e.g., Putallaz, 1983; Panella & Henggeler, 1986), or in a role-playing setting (Bornstein et al., 1980). Contrived settings avoid some of the disadvantages of direct observations discussed above, providing an economical and practical alternative to direct observation in the natural environment. Because contrived settings permit greater standardization of observational procedures, differences between children are more likely to be a result of child variables than of setting differences.

An example of an observation in a contrived setting that is practical for practitioners is offered by Franco, Christoff, Crimmins, and Kelly (1983). An extremely shy 14-year-old boy was taught conversation skills using behavioral interventions. The effectiveness of training was assessed by coding the child's performance during contrived, unstructured conversations with a variety of unfamiliar persons. The observational categories included asking questions, making reinforcing comments, and eye contact. A multiple-baseline design across behaviors permitted the documentation of changes in the taught skills as a result of the behavioral intervention.

Role-play observations differ from observations in contrived settings in the amount of structure or standardization employed. A typical role-play test presents children with a standard set of scenes or situations. Children are presented with a live or recorded prompt and are asked to respond to the prompt as they would if actually in that situation. By selecting different scenes, the examiner can observe a variety of skills that might require days of observation in the natural environment.

Given the promise of role-play assessment, it is not surprising that several researchers have investigated the validity of role-play observations. Although role-play observations are sensitive to treatment (Berler, Gross, & Drabman, 1982; Bornstein et al., 1980), there is no evidence that improved role-play performance of taught skills generalizes to the child's everyday social interactions or enhances peer or teacher ratings (Hughes & Sullivan, 1988). Observations of specific role-play behaviors made from videotapes do correlate with adults' global ratings of assertion, also based on role-play performance (Ollendick, 1981; Ollendick, Hart, & Francis, 1985; Reardon et al., 1979). However, the social validity of adult ratings of role-play assertion has yet to be demonstrated. A recent study casts doubt on the social validity of role-play measures of assertion. Child judges viewed videotaped role-play performances and indicated how much they would like to play with the child. Children's global ratings of likability did not correlate with observations of specific assertive behaviors (Ollendick et al., 1985).

Essential to the validity of role-play tests is evidence that role-play performance predicts children's naturalistic social interactions, diagnostic classification, peer acceptance, or teacher ratings. With very few exceptions (Gaffney & McFall, 1981; Hughes & Hall, 1985), role-play performance fails this test of criterion-related validity (Beck, Forehand, Neeper, & Baskin, 1982; Kazdin, Matson, & Esveldt-Dawson, 1984; Matson, Esveldt-Dawson, & Kazdin, 1983; Ollendick, 1981; Reardon et al., 1979; Van Hasselt et al., 1981; Vosk et al., 1982).

Customized versus Standardized Systems. One advantage of direct observations is their flexibility. The examiner can select which behaviors, antecedents, and consequences to observe, according to the idiosyncrasies present in the situation. Each child's behavioral topography and responsiveness to environmental contingencies and events are idiosyncratic. For example, one child's social approach may be controlled by the proximity of adults, whereas another child's social approach may be controlled by the nature of the activity (dramatic play vs. construction). Because not all potentially controlling antecedents and consequences can be simultaneously observed, the observer must develop hypotheses regarding significant behavioral antecedents and consequences. These hypotheses are based on referral information, a behavioral interview, or a narrative recording of behavior. Next, the observational instrument is tailored to these hypotheses.

Standardized observational instruments are necessary for certain research purposes, because they permit comparisons among groups of children and replication by other researchers.

Molecular versus Molar Categories. Some observation procedures code discrete, molecular behaviors, such as eye contact, speech latency, and smiling (Bornstein et al., 1980). Other procedures code global behaviors, such as initiating positive peer interaction (Gresham & Nagle, 1980; Hartup et al., 1967). Both highly molecular and highly molar categories have limitations. Molecular systems either select a small segment of social interaction to observe or are unmanageable and unreliable. Molar systems run the risk of lumping together behaviors that are functionally dissimilar. In addition, global behavioral categories are more susceptible to rater subjectivity (Siegel, Dragovich, & Marholin, 1976).

Sequential versus Unilateral Behaviors. Most published observational systems record behavior of an individual child; however, some systems record sequential interactions (Dodge, 1983; Putallaz, 1983). In a sequential system, a child's behaviors are recorded in relation to peer initiations and peer responses. For example, Putallaz and Gottman (1982) found that unpopular children differed in their response to a disagreement with a peer. Popular children responded by stating a general rule as a basis for their disagreement and suggesting alternatives, whereas unpopular children responded negatively and did not recommend alternatives. Because sequential observation systems record the effects produced by a behavior, they permit the identification of socially skilled behaviors. Socially skilled behaviors "maximize the probability of maintaining or enhancing positive effects for the interaction" (Foster & Ritchey, 1979, p. 626). Using sequential analyses, Dodge et al. (1983) determined the probability that a child's entry attempt would be reacted to positively or negatively by the peer group. The probability depended on both the child's status and the entry behavior.

Reliability

Test–retest, interrater, and internal-consistency reliability are relevant to direct observation. Interrater reliability is the type of reliability most closely attended to in direct observation, with most researchers reporting good interrater reliabilities. Researchers report test–retest reliability less frequently, which is a measure of the adequacy of the sampling of behavior. If the observer is assessing the child's prosocial behavior in unstructured-play activities, the observation should occur on more than one day and should last longer than a few minutes in order to adequately sample the behavior of interest. Evidence of internal consistency is important when specific categories of behavior are later grouped together to yield a single score, such as positive social interaction. Before categories are grouped, it is important to present evidence that the categories are interrelated and that a single score is justified.

Validity

Despite the assertion that direct observations have face validity, the issue of validity needs to be empirically established. With respect to criterion-related validity of the direct observation of social skills, the observed behaviors should correlate with socially valid criteria, such as peer acceptance or teacher ratings. Because observations of children's assertive behaviors do not correlate with children's peer acceptance or teacher ratings, the observation procedure is not a valid measure of social skills. Similarly, there is unequivocal support for selection of rate of interaction as an index of social skill, in that several researchers have found that rate of interaction does not predict sociometric status (Hops & Greenwood, 1988).

In creating operational definitions of behavior, researchers are creating behavioral constructs (Foster & Ritchey, 1979). Thus, it is important to provide evidence of the construct validity of the observational categories. The observational categories are an attempt to break up streams of behavior into categories. The categories impose meaning on this behavioral stream. If behaviors that are functionally different are assigned to the same behavior code, the construct validity of that code is weakened. For example, researchers typically lump together several behaviors into the code "positive peer interaction." Are these behaviors functionally similar? If the code "complies with others' requests" is lumped into the category "positive peer interaction," compliance should correlate more highly with other positive peer interactions than with negative peer interactions. In addition, evidence that compliance enhances peer relationships is necessary. Does compliance occur more often between friends than between nonfriends? Additional evidence of construct validity of direct observations is provided by studies demonstrating that the target behavior increases as a result of a social skills intervention.

Self-Report Instruments

Numerous self-report instruments purport to measure a variety of constructs related to children's social skills and social competence, including self-concept (Harter, 1982), loneliness (Asher, Hymel, & Renshaw, 1984; Asher & Wheeler, 1985), locus of control (Nowicki & Strickland, 1973), anxiety (Reynolds & Richmond, 1978), anger (Nelson & Finch, 1978), self-efficacy (Wheeler & Ladd, 1982), and assertion (Deluty, 1979). Self-report instruments differ on several dimensions, including item specificity, item format, scope, and focus. Three self-report measures of social behaviors are reviewed here: the Children's Action Tendency Scale (CATS; Deluty, 1979, 1981), the Children's Assertive Behavior Scale (CABS; Michelson & Wood, 1982), and the youth self-report form of the MESSY (Matson et al., 1983).

The CATS requires a child to report how he or she would respond in 13 conflict situations. Each of the 13 situations is followed by three response alternatives (one aggressive, one submissive, and one assertive), which are presented in a paired-comparison format such that all possible combinations of the alternatives are presented. The child's score on the Aggressive, Submissive, and Assertive scales can range from 0 to 26. The CATS has moderate test–retest, split-half, and internal-consistency reliability coefficients (Deluty, 1979, 1981; Scanlon & Ollendick, 1986). The Assertive and Aggressive scales discriminate children nominated by teachers as aggressive from normal children (Deluty, 1979), as well as from assertive and submissive children (Scanlon & Ollendick, 1986); however, assertive and submissive children do not differ on the CATS. Thus, the scale has some clinical utility for assessing aggressive children, but is not useful for assessing passive or withdrawn children. CATS scores correlated with naturalistic observations of assertive behaviors for third- to fifth-grade boys, but not for girls. Evidence for the construct validity of the CATS is provided by Scanlon and Ollendick (1986), who found significant correlations between CATS scale scores and similar scales on the CABS (see below).

The CABS (Michelson & Wood, 1982) consists of 27 items assessing children's self-reported responses to positive and negative interpersonal situations. The measure yields a Passive, an Aggressive, and a Total Assertion score. The scale has moderate test–retest and internal-consistency reliability (Michelson & Wood, 1982; Scanlon & Ollendick, 1986). The CABS Assertion score discriminates aggressive boys from nonaggressive boys, but the instrument does not discriminate between assertive and passive/withdrawn boys or girls (Scanlon & Ollendick, 1986). The CABS scales correlate significantly and positively with similar scales on the CATS. To date, no data exists on the relationship of CABS scores to naturalistic behavior, sociometric status, or teacher global ratings of social competence.

The MESSY (Matson et al., 1983) is broader in scope than the CABS or CATS, focusing on a range of social behaviors as well as feelings and cognitions. Children rate themselves on a 5-point scale on 92 items. The scale samples diverse areas of social functioning, including social isolation, expression of hostility, conversation skills, and making friends. The measure yields scores for Positive Social Behaviors, Negative Social Behaviors, and Total Overall Skills (positive minus negative scores). A parallel teacher report form (discussed earlier in this chapter) is available. In an initial validation study, MESSY scores correlated with teachers' overall popularity ranking and two teacher social skills ratings (Matson et al., 1983). However, MESSY scores did not predict sociometric scores. Results of a second validation study (Kazdin et al., 1984) found that MESSY scores did not significantly correlate with several child measures or with staff or teacher measures; however, it did significantly correlate with parent-reported aggression. Thus, evidence for the predictive validity of the MESSY is mixed but generally negative.

FINAL WORDS

The assessment of children's social competence and social skills is an active research topic, with significant developments occurring within the last 10 years. This chapter has reviewed developments in sociometric and behavioral approaches to assessing social competence and social skills. It is important to note that developments in the assessment of children's social cognition are worthy of attention from cognitive–behavioral researchers and practitioners. Children's attributions for social interactions, knowledge of effective social strategies, goals for social interactions, and perspective-taking ability all influence their social behaviors and social effectiveness. The maximum benefit from sociometric and behavioral assessment approaches is gained when they comprise part of a multicomponent assessment that also includes social-cognitive assessment methodologies. Examples of information-processing models for assessing social skills that combine these three assessment methodologies are detailed in Hughes and Hall (1987) and Dodge and Murphy (1984).

REFERENCES

Achenbach, T. M., & Edelbrock, C. S. (1983). *Manual for the Child Behavior Checklist and Revised Child Behavior Profile*. Burlington, VT: University Associates in Psychiatry.

Achenbach, T. M., & Edelbrock, C. S. (1986). *Manual for the Teacher's Report Form and Teacher's Version of the Child Behavior Profile*. Burlington, VT: University Associates in Psychiatry.

Algozzine, B. (1977). The emotionally disturbed child: Disturbed or disturbing? *Journal of Abnormal Child Psychology*, 5, 205–211.

Asher, S. R., & Hymel, S. (1981). Children's social competence in peer relations: Sociometric and behavioral assessment. In J. D. Wine & M. D. Smye (Eds.), *Social competence* (pp. 125–157). New York: Guilford Press.

Asher, S. R., Hymel, S., & Renshaw, P. D. (1984). Loneliness in children. *Child Development*, 55, 1456–1464.

Asher, S. R., Singleton, L. C., Tinsley, B. R., & Hymel, S. (1979). A reliable sociometric measure for preschool children. *Developmental Psychology*, 15, 443–444.

Asher, S. R., & Wheeler, V. A. (1985). Children's loneliness: A comparison of rejected and neglected peer status. *Journal of Consulting and Clinical Psychology*, 53, 500–505.

Balou, B. (1966). The emotionally and socially handicapped. *Review of Educational Research*, 36, 120–133.

Barlow, D. H., & Hersen, M. (1984). *Single case experimental designs: Strategies for studying behavior change* (2nd ed.). New York: Pergamon Press.

Barton, E. J., & Ascione, F. R. (1979). Sharing in preschool children: Facilitating stimulus generalization, response generalization, and maintenance. *Journal of Applied Behavior Analysis*, 12, 417–430.

Barton, E. J., & Ascione, F. R. (1984). Direct observation. In T. H. Ollendick & M. Hersen (Eds.), *Child*

behavioral assessment (pp. 166–194). New York: Pergamon Press.

Beck, S., Forehand, R., Neeper, R., & Baskin, C. H. (1982). A companion of two analogue strategies for assessing children's social skills. *Journal of Consulting and Clinical Psychology*, 50, 596–597.

Behar, L. B., & Stringfield, S. (1974). A behavior rating scale for the preschool child. *Developmental Psychology*, 10, 601–610.

Bellack, S. A. (1979). A critical appraisal of strategies for assessing social skills. *Behavioral assessment*, 1, 157–176.

Berler, E. S., Gross, A. M., & Drabman, R. S. (1982). Social skills training with children: Proceed with caution. *Journal of Applied Behavior Analysis*, 15, 41–53.

Bierman, K. L. (1987). The clinical significance and assessment of poor peer relations: Peer neglect versus peer rejection. *Journal of Developmental and Behavioral Pediatrics*, 8, 233–240.

Bierman, K. L., & Furman, W. (1984). The effects of social skills training and peer involvement on the social adjustment of preadolescents. *Child Development*, 55, 151–162.

Bolstad, O. P., & Johnson, S. M. (1977). The relationship between teachers' assessment of students and students' actual behavior in the classroom. *Child Development*, 48, 570–578.

Bonney, M. E. (1943). The relative stability of social, intellectual and academic status in grades 11 to 12, and the interrelationships between these various forms of growth. *Journal of Educational Psychology*, 34, 88–102.

Bonney, M. R. (1971). Assessment of efforts to aid socially isolated elementary school pupils. *Journal of Educational Research*, 64, 345–364.

Bornstein, M., Bellack, A. S., & Hersen, M. (1980). Social skills training for highly aggressive children. *Behavior Modification*, 4, 173–186.

Bower, E. M. (1969). *Early identification of emotionally handicapped children in school* (2nd ed.). Springfield, IL: Charles C Thomas.

Bryan, J. H. (1978). Social relationships and verbal interactions of learning disabled children. *Journal of Learning Disabilities*, 11, 107–115.

Cartledge, G., & Milburn, J. F. (1986). *Teaching social skills to children: Innovative approaches* (2nd ed.). New York: Pergamon Press.

Clarfield, S. P. (1974). The development of a teacher referral form for identifying early school maladaption. *American Journal of Community Pscyhology*, 2, 199–210.

Clark, L., Gresham, F. M., & Elliott, S. N. (1985). Development and validation of social skills assessment measure: The TROSS-C. *Journal of Psychoeducational Assessment*, 4, 347–356.

Coie, J. D., & Dodge, K. A. (1983). Continuities and changes in children's social status: A five-year longitudinal study. *Merrill–Palmer Quarterly*, 29, 261–282.

Coie, J. D., Dodge, K. A., & Coppotelli, H. (1982). Dimensions and types of status: A cross-age perspective. *Developmental Psychology*, 18, 557–570.

Coie, J. D., & Kupersmidt, J. B. (1983). A behavioral analysis of emerging social status in boys' groups. *Child Development*, 54, 1400–1416.

Cone, J. E., & Hawkins, R. P. (Eds.). *Behavioral assessment: New directions in clinical psychology*. New York: Brunner/Mazel.

Conger, J. C., & Keane, S. P. (1981). Social skills intervention in the treatment of isolated or withdrawn children. *Psychological Bulletin, 90*, 478–495.

Conners, C. K. (1969). A teacher rating scale for use in drug studies with children. *American Journal of Psychiatry, 126*, 884–888.

Connolly, J., & Doyle, A. (1981). Assessment of social competence in preschoolers: Teachers versus peers. *Developmental Psychology, 17*, 454–462.

Cook, T. P., & Apolloni, T. (1976). Developing positive social–emotional behaviors: A study of training and generalization effects. *Journal of Applied Behavior Analysis, 9*, 65–78.

Cowen, E. L., Pederson, A., Barbigian, H., Izzo, L. D., & Trost, M. A. (1973). Longterm follow up of early detected vulnerable children. *Journal of Consulting and Clinical Psychology, 41*, 438–446.

Cunningham, T. R., & Tharp, R. G. (1981). The influence of settings on accuracy and reliability of behavioral observation. *Behavioral Assessment, 3*, 67–78.

Deluty, R. H. (1979). Children's action tendency scale: A self-report measure of aggressiveness, assertiveness, and submissiveness in children. *Journal of Consulting and Clinical Psychology, 47*, 1061–1071.

Deluty, R. H. (1981). Adaptiveness of aggressive, assertive and submissive behavior for children. *Journal of Clinical Child Psychology, 10*, 149–155.

Dodge, K. A. (1980). Social cognition and children's aggressive behavior. *Child Development, 51*, 162–170.

Dodge, K. A. (1983). Behavioral antecedents of peer social status. *Child Development, 54*, 1386–1399.

Dodge, K. A., Coie, J. D., & Brakke, N. P. (1982). Behavior patterns of socially rejected and neglected preadolescents: The roles of social approach and aggression. *Journal of Abnormal Child Psychology, 10*, 389–410.

Dodge, K. A., & Frame, C. L. (1982). Social cognitive biases and deficits in aggressive boys. *Child Development, 53*, 620–635.

Dodge, K. A., & Murphy, R. R. (1984). The assessment of social competence in adolescents. In P. Karoly & J. J. Steffen (Eds.), *Adolescent behavior disorders: Foundations and contemporary concerns* (Vol. 3, pp. 61–96). Lexington, MA: Lexington Books.

Dodge, K. A., Murphy, R. R., & Buchsbaum, K. (1984). The assessment of intention-cue detection skills in children: Implications for developmental psychopathology. *Child Development, 55*, 163–173.

Dodge, K. A., & Newman, J. P. (1981). Biased decision-making processes in aggressive boys. *Journal of Abnormal Psychology, 90*, 375–379.

Dodge, K. A., Schlundt, D. C., Schocken, I., & Delugach, J. D. (1983). Social competence and children's sociometric status: The role of peer group entry strategies. *Merrill–Palmer Quarterly, 29*, 309–336.

Edelbrock C., Greenbaum, R., & Conover, N. C. (1985). Reliability and concurrent relations between the teacher version of the Child Behavior Profile and the Conners Revised Teacher Rating Scale. *Journal of Abnormal Child Psychology, 13*, 295–304.

Eisenberg, N., & Harris, J. O. (1984). Social competence: A developmental perspective. *School Psychology Review, 13*, 267–277.

Feinberg, M. R. (1964). Stability of sociometric status in two adolescent class groups. *Journal of Genetic Psychology, 104*, 83–87.

Foster, S. L., & Ritchey, W. L. (1979). Issues in the assessment of social competence in children. *Journal of Applied Behavior Analysis, 12*, 625–638.

Foster, S. L., & Ritchey, W. L. (1985). Behavioral correlates of sociometric status of fourth-, fifth-, and sixth-grade children in two classroom situations. *Behavioral Assessment, 7*, 79–93.

Franco, D. P., Christoff, K. A., Crimmins, D. B., & Kelly, J. A. (1983). Social skills training for an extremely shy young adolescent: A case study. *Behavior Therapy, 14*, 568–575.

Gaffney, L. R., & McFall, R. M. (1981). A comparison of social skills in delinquent and nondelinquent adolescent girls using a behavioral role playing inventory. *Journal of Consulting and Clinical Psychology, 49*, 959–997.

Gottman, J. M. (1977). The effects of a modeling film on social isolation in preschool children: A methodological investigation. *Journal of Abnormal Child Psychology, 5*, 69–78.

Gottman, J., Gonso, J., & Rasmussen, B. (1975). Social interaction, social competence, and friendship in children. *Child Development, 46*, 709–718.

Goyette, C. H., Conners, C. K., & Ulrich, R. F. (1978). Normative data on the Revised Conners Parent and Teacher Rating Scales. *Journal of Abnormal Child Psychology, 6*, 221–236.

Green, K. P., Forehand, R., Beck, S. J., & Vosk, B. (1980). An assessment of the relationship among measures of children's social competence and children's academic achievement. *Child Development, 51*, 1149–1156.

Greenspan, S. (1981). Defining childhood social competence: A proposed working model. In B. K. Keogh (Ed.), *Advances in special education: Socialization influences on exceptionality* (pp. 1–40). Greenwich, CT: JAI Press.

Greenwood, C. R., Walker, H. M., & Hops, H. (1977). Some issues in social interaction/withdrawal assessment. *Exceptional Children, 43*, 490–499.

Greenwood, C. R., Walker, H. M., Todd, N. M., & Hops, H. (1979). Selecting a cost effective screening device for the assessment of preschool social withdrawal. *Journal of Applied Behavioral Analysis, 12*, 639–652.

Gresham, F. M. (1982a). A model for the behavioral assessment of behavior disorders in children: Measurement considerations and practical application. *Journal of School Psychology, 20*, 131–143.

Gresham, F. M. (1982b). Social interactions as predictors of children's likability and friendship patterns: A multiple regression analysis. *Journal of Behavioral Assessment, 4*, 39–53.

Gresham, F. M. (1985). Utility of cognitive–behavioral procedures for social skills training with children: A critical review. *Journal of Abnormal Child Psychology, 13*, 411–423.

Gresham, F. M., & Elliott, S. N. (1984). Assessment of children's social skills: A review of methods and issues. *School Psychology Review, 13*, 292–301.

Gresham, F. M., & Lemanek, K. L. (1983). Social skills:

A review of cognitive–behavioral training procedures with children. *Journal of Developmental Psychology, 4,* 239–261.

Gresham, F. M., & Nagle, R. J. (1980). Social skills training with children: Responsiveness to modeling and coaching as a function of peer orientation. *Journal of Consulting and Clinical Psychology, 48,* 718–729.

Gronlund, N. E. (1959). *Sociometry in the classroom.* New York: Harper.

Hallahan, D. P., & Kauffman, J. M. (1986). *Exceptional children* (3rd ed.). Englewood Cliffs, NJ: Prentice-Hall.

Harter, S. (1982). The Perceived Competence Scale for Children. *Child Development, 53,* 87–97.

Hartup, W. W., Glazer, J. A., & Charlesworth, R. (1967). Peer reinforcement and sociometric status. *Child Development, 38,* 1017–1024.

Hayden-Thomson, L., Rubin, K. H., & Hymel, S. (1987). Sex preferences in sociometric choices. *Developmental Psychology, 23,* 558–562.

Hayvren, M., & Hymel, S. (1984). Ethical issues in sociometric testing: Impact of sociometric measures on interaction behavior. *Developmental Psychology, 20,* 849–884.

Hops, H., Fleischman, D. H., Guild, J., Paine, S., Street, H., Walker, H. M., & Greenwood, C. P. (1978). *Program for Establishing Effective Relationship Skills (PEERS): Consultant manual.* Eugene: University of Oregon, Center for Research in the Behavioral Education of the Handicapped.

Hops, H., & Greenwood, C. R. (1981). Social skills deficits. In E. J. Mash & L. G. Terdal (Eds.), *Behavioral assessment of childhood disorders* (pp. 347–384). New York: Guilford Press.

Hops, H., & Greenwood, C. R. (1988). Social skill deficits. In E. J. Mash & L. G. Terdal (Eds.), *Behavioral assessment of childhood disorders* (2nd ed. pp. 263–314). New York: Guilford Press.

Hops, H., & Lewin, L. (1984). Peer sociometric forms. In T. H. Ollendick & M. Hersen (Eds.), *Child behavioral assessment* (pp. 124–147). New York: Pergamon Press.

Horrocks, J. E., & Benimoff, M. (1966). Stability of adolescents' nominee status. *Adolescence, 3,* 224–229.

Hughes, J. N., & Hall, D. M. (1985). Performance of disturbed and nondisturbed boys on a role play test of social competence. *Behavioral Disorders, 11,* 24–29.

Hughes, J. N., & Hall, R. (1987). A proposed model for the assessment of children's social competence. *Professional School Psychology, 2,* 247–260.

Hughes, J. N., & Sullivan, K. (1988). Outcome-assessment in social skills training with children. *Journal of School Psychology, 26,* 167–183.

Humphrey, L. L. (1982). Children's and teacher's perspectives on children's self-control: The development of two rating scales. *Journal of Consulting and Clinical Psychology, 50,* 624–633.

Humphrey, L. L., & Ciminero, A. R. (1979). Parent report measures of child behavior: A review. *Journal of Clinical Child Psychology, 8,* 56–63.

Hymel, S. (1983). Preschool children's peer relations: Issues in sociometric assessment. *Merrill–Palmer Quarterly, 29,* 237–260.

Hymel, S., & Asher, S. R., (1977, March). *Assessment and training of isolated children's social skills.* Paper presented at the biennial meeting of the Society for Research in Child Development, New Orleans. (ERIC Document Service Reproduction Service No. ED136930)

Kauffman, J. M. (1985). *Characteristics of children's behavior disorders.* Columbus, OH: Charles E. Merrill.

Kazdin, A. E. (1985). Selection of target behaviors: The relationship of treatment focus to clinical dysfunction. *Behavioral Assessment, 7,* 33–47.

Kazdin, A. E., Matson, J. L., & Esveldt-Dawson, K. (1984). The relationship of role-play assessment of children's social skills to multiple measure of social competence. *Behaviour Research and Therapy, 22,* 129–139.

Kendall, P. C., & Morison, P. (1984). Integrating cognitive and behavioral procedures for the treatment of socially isolated children. In A. W. Meyers & W. E. Craighead (Eds.), *Cognitive behavior therapy with children* (pp. 261–288). New York: Plenum.

Koch, H. L. (1933). Popularity in preschool children: Some related factors and a technique for its measurement. *Child Development, 4,* 164–175.

Kohn, M. (1977). The Kohn Social Competence Scale and Kohn Symptom Checklist for the preschool child. A follow-up report. *Journal of Abnormal Child Psychology, 5,* 249–263.

Kohn, M., & Parnes, B. (1974). Social interaction in the classroom: A comparison of apathetic–withdrawn and angry–defiant children. *Journal of Genetic Psychology, 125,* 165–175.

Ladd, G. W. (1983). Social networks of popular, average, and rejected children in school settings. *Merrill–Palmer Quarterly, 29,* 282–307.

Ladd, G. W., & Mize, J. (1983). A cognitive–social learning model of social-skill training. *Psychological Review, 90,* 127–157.

Ladd, G. W., & Oden, S. (1979). The relationship between peer acceptance and children's ideas about helpfulness. *Child Development, 50,* 402–408.

Lahey, B. B., Shaughency, E. A., Frame, C. C., & Strauss, C. C. (1985). Teacher ratings of attention problems in children experimentally classified as exhibiting attention deficit disorder with and without hyperactivity. *Journal of the American Academy of Child Psychiatry, 24,* 613–616.

Lambert, N. M. (1972). Intellectual and nonintellectual predictors of high school status. *Journal of Special Education, 6,* 247–259.

Lambert, N. M., & Bower, E. M. (1961). *A process for in-school screening of children with emotional handicaps.* Princeton, NJ: Educational Testing Service.

Landau, S., Milich, R., & Whitten, P. (1984). A comparison of teacher and peer assessment of social status. *Journal of Clinical Child Psychology, 13,* 44–49.

Laughlin, F. (1954). *The peer status of sixth- and seventh-grade children.* New York: Teachers College, Columbia University.

Marshall, H. R., & McCandless, B. R. (1957). A study in prediction of social behavior of preschool children. *Child Development, 28,* 49–59.

Masten, A. S., Morison, P., & Pellegrini, D. S. (1985). A revised class play method of peer assessment. *Developmental Psychology, 21,* 523–533.

Matson, J. L., Esveldt-Dawson, K., & Kazdin, A. E. (1983). Validation of methods for assessing social skills in children. *Journal of Clinical Child Psychology, 12,* 174–180.

Matson, J. L., Rotatori, A. F., & Helsel, W. J. (1983). Development of a rating scale to measure social skills in children: The Matson Evaluation of Social Skills with Youngsters (MESSY). *Behaviour Research and Therapy, 21,* 335–340.

McCandless, B. R., & Marshall, H. R. (1957). A picture sociometric technique for preschool children and its relation to teacher judgments of friendship. *Child Development, 28,* 139–147.

McFall, R. M. (1982). A review and reformulation of the concept of social skill. *Behavioral Assessment, 4,* 1–33.

Michelson, L., Sugai, D. P., Wood, R. P., & Kazdin, A. E. (1983). *Social-skills assessment and training with children.* New York: Plenum.

Michelson, L., & Wood, R. (1982). Development and psychometric properties of the Children's Assertive Behavior Scale. *Journal of Behavioral Assessment, 4,* 3–13.

Morgan, S. R. (1978). A descriptive analysis of maladjusted behavior in socially rejected children. *Behavioral Disorders, 4,* 23–30.

Muma, J. R. (1965). Peer evaluation and academic achievement performance. *Personnel Guidance Journal, 44,* 405–409.

Nelson, W. M., III, & Finch, A. J., Jr. (1978). *The Children's Inventory of Anger.* Unpublished manuscript, Xavier University.

Nowicki, S., Jr., & Strickland, B. R. (1973). A locus of control scale for children. *Journal of Consulting and Clinical Psychology, 40,* 148–154.

Oden, S. L., & Asher, S. R. (1977). Coaching children in social skills for friendship making. *Child Development, 48,* 495–506.

Ollendick, T. H. (1981). Assessment of social interaction skills in school children. *Behavioral Counseling Quarterly, 1,* 277–243.

Ollendick T. H., Hart, K. J., & Francis, G. (1985). Social validation of the revised Behavioral Assertiveness Test for Children (BAT-CR). *Child and Family Behavior Therapy, 7,* 17–33.

Panella, D., & Henggeler, S. W. (1986). Peer interactions of conduct-disordered, anxious–withdrawn, and well-adjusted black adolescents. *Journal of Abnormal Child Psychology, 14,* 1–11.

Patterson, G. P. (1964). An empirical approach to the classification of disturbed children. *Journal of Clinical Psychology, 20,* 326–337.

Peery, J. C. (1979). Popular, amiable, isolated, rejected: A reconceptualization of sociometric status in preschool children. *Child Development, 50,* 1231–1234.

Perry, D. G., Perry, L. C., & Rasmussen, P. (1986). Cognitive social learning mediators of aggression. *Child Development, 57,* 700–711.

Piaget, J. (1932). *Moral judgment of the child.* New York: Harcourt, Brace.

Porterfield, O. V., & Schlinchting, G. (1961). Peer status and reading achievement. *Journal of Educational Research, 54,* 291–297.

Putallaz, M. (1983). Predictive children's sociometric status from their behavior. *Child Development, 54,* 1417–1426.

Putallaz, M., & Gottman, J. (1982). Conceptualizing social competence in children. In P. Karoly & J. J.

Steffen (Eds.), *Improving children's social competence.* Lexington, MA: Lexington Books.

Quay, H. C. (1979). Classification. In H. C. Quay & J. S. Werry (Eds.), *Psychopathological disorders of childhood* (2nd ed., pp. 1–42). New York: Wiley.

Quay, H. C., Morse, W. C., & Cutler, R. L. (1966). Personality patterns of pupils in special classes for the emotionally disturbed. *Exceptional Children, 32,* 297–301.

Quay, H. C., & Peterson, D. R. (1979). *Manual for the Behavior Problem Checklist.* Highland Park, NJ: Authors.

Quay, H. C., & Peterson, D. R. (1983). *Interim manual for the Revised Behavior Problem Checklist.* Coral Gables, FL: University of Miami.

Quay, H. C., & Peterson, D. R. (1984). *Appendix I to the interim manual for the Revised Behavior Problem Checklist.* Coral Gables, FL: University of Miami.

Ratiner, C., Weissberg, R., & Caplan, M. (1986, August). *Ethical considerations in sociometric testing: The reactions of preadolescent subjects.* Paper presented at the meeting of the American Psychological Association, Washington, DC.

Reardon, R. C., Hersen, M., Bellack, A. S., & Foley, J. M. (1979). Measuring social skill in grade school boys. *Journal of Behavioral Assessment, 1,* 87–105.

Renshaw, P. D. (1981). *Social knowledge and sociometric status: Children's goals and strategies for peer interaction.* Unpublished doctoral dissertation, University of Illinois.

Renshaw, P. D., & Asher, S. R. (1983). Children's goals and strategies for social interaction. *Merrill–Palmer Quarterly, 29,* 353–374.

Reynolds, C. R., & Richmond, B. O. (1978). "What I Think and Feel": A revised measure of children's manifest anxiety. *Journal of Abnormal Child Psychology, 6,* 271–280.

Richard, B. A., & Dodge, K. A. (1982). Social maladjustment and problem solving in school-aged children. *Journal of Consulting and Clinical Psychology, 50,* 226–233.

Roff, M. (1961). Childhood social interactions and young adult bad conduct. *Journal of Abnormal and Social Psychology, 63,* 331–337.

Roff, M., Sells, S. B., & Golden, M. M. (1972). *Social adjustment and personality development in children.* Minneapolis: University of Minnesota Press.

Rubin, K. H., & Daniels-Beirness, T. (1983). Concurrent and predictive correlates of sociometric status in kindergarten and grade 1 children. *Merrill–Palmer Quarterly, 29,* 337–351.

Scanlon, E. M., & Ollendick, T. H. (1986). Children's assertive behavior: The reliability and validity of three self-report measures. *Child and Family Behavior Therapy, 1,* 9–21.

Schachar, R., Sandberg, S., & Rutter, M. (1986). Agreement between teachers' ratings and observations of hyperactivity, inattentiveness, and defiance. *Journal of Abnormal Child Psychology, 14,* 331–345.

Schofield, J. W., & Whitley, B. E. (1983). Peer nomination vs. rating scale measurment of children's peer preference. *Social Psychology Quarterly, 46,* 242–251.

Shuller, D. Y., & McNamara, J. R. (1976). Expectancy factors in behavioral observation. *Behavior Therapy, 7,* 519–527.

Siegel, L. J., Dragovich, S. L., & Marholin, P. (1976). The effects of biasing information on behavioral observations and rating scales. *Journal of Abnormal Child Psychology, 4,* 221–233.

Singleton, L. C., & Asher, S. K. (1977). Peer preferences and social interaction among third-grade children in an integrated school district. *Journal of Educational Psychology, 69,* 330–336.

Steinberg, M. D., & Dodge, K. A. (1983). Attributional bias in aggressive adolescent boys and girls. *Journal of Social and Clinical Psychology, 1,* 312–321.

Stephens, T. M. (1978). *Social skills in the classroom.* Columbus, OH: Cedars.

Stephens, T. M. (1981). *Technical information: Social Behavior Assessment.* Columbus, OH: Cedars.

Strain, P. S., Cooke, T. P., & Apollini, T. (1976). *Teaching exceptional children.* New York: Academic Press.

Stumme, V. S., Gresham, F. M., & Scott, V. A. (1982). Validity of social behavioral assessment in discriminating emotionally disabled from nonhandicapped students. *Journal of Behavioral Assessment, 4,* 327–341.

Ullman, C. A. (1957). Teachers, peers, and tests as predictors of adjustment. *Journal of Educational Psychology, 48,* 257–267.

Urbain, E. S., & Kendall, P. C. (1980). Review of social cognitive problem solving interventions with children. *Psychological Bulletin, 88,* 109–143.

Van Hasselt, V. B., Hersen, M., & Bellack, A. S. (1981). The validity of role play tests for assessing social skills in children. *Behavior Therapy, 12,* 202–216.

Vosk, B., Forehand, R., Parker, J. B., & Richard, K. (1982). A multimethod comparison of popular and unpopular children. *Developmental Psychology, 18,* 571–575.

Waksman, S. A. (1985). The development and psychometric properties of a rating scale for children's social skills. *Journal of Psychoeducational Assessment, 3,* 111–121.

Walker, H. M. (1976). *Walker Problem Behavior Identification Checklist manual.* Los Angeles: Western Psychological Services.

Walker, H. M., Street, A., Garrett, B., Crossen, J., Hops, H., & Greenwood, C. R. (1978). *Reprogramming Environmental Contingencies for Effective Social Skills (RECESS): Consultant manual.* Eugene: University of Oregon, Center at Oregon for Research in the Behavioral Education of the Handicapped.

Wasik, B. H. (1987). Sociometric measures and peer descriptors of Kindergarten children: A study of reliability and validity. *Journal of Clinical Child Psychology, 16,* 218–224.

Waterman, J. B., Sobesky, W. E., Silvern, L., Aoki, B., & McCaulay, M. (1981). Social perspective-taking and adjustment in emotionally disturbed, learning disabled, and normal children. *Journal of Abnormal Child Psychology, 9,* 133–148.

Wheeler, V. A., & Ladd, G. W. (1982). Assessment of children's self-efficacy for social interaction with peers. *Developmental Psychology, 18,* 795–805.

19

Adaptive Behavior: The Construct and Its Measurement

LIZANNE DeSTEFANO
DEBRA S. THOMPSON
University of Illinois

The notion of "adaptive behavior" has been of central importance in psychological assessment and treatment for almost half a century. An essential element in the diagnosis of mental retardation, the assessment of adaptive behavior is increasingly recognized as having utility in the diagnosis, treatment, and evaluation of a wide range of psychological, medical, and educational problems.

Despite the wide acceptance of the concept, problems still exist with the definition, measurement, and interpretation of adaptive behavior. In this chapter, we begin by attempting to find common ground among the many definitions of the construct. Following a historical review of these uses, issues in the measurement of adaptive behavior are presented, including reviews of the most commonly used measures of adaptive behavior. The uses of adaptive behavior information are then discussed. The chapter ends by outlining needs and future trends in the assessment of adaptive behavior.

DEFINITION OF THE CONSTRUCT

Current conceptions of adaptive behavior are not new. The terms "social competence" and "social maturity" have been used over the last 50 years to refer to the same construct. During this time, a number of influential definitions of "adaptive behavior" have been offered. Several of these are quoted below. Careful examination of these quotes reveals commonalities and differences among the various interpretations; these can lead to a broader understanding of the definition of adaptive behavior.

Social competence is the functional ability of the human organism for exercising personal independence and social responsibility. (Doll, 1953, p. 10)

Adaptive behavior refers primarily to the effectiveness of the individual in adapting to the natural and social demands of the environment. (Heber, 1961, p. 3)

Adaptive behavior is the degree to which an individual meets the standards of personal and social responsibility expected of their [sic] age and cultural group. (Grossman, 1973, p. 11)

Simply stated, adaptive behavior refers to the way an individual performs those tasks expected of someone his (her) age in his (her) culture. (President's Committee on Mental Retardation, 1975, p. 6)

[Adaptive behavior is] the degree to which a student is able to function and participate effec-

445

tively as a responsible member of his family and community. (Office of Civil Rights, 1972, quoted in Oakland, 1977, p. 150)

More recently, Sparrow, Balla, and Cicchetti (1984) have defined "adaptive behavior" as the performance of the daily activities required for personal and social sufficiency. Three characteristics are critical in this concept of adaptive behavior. First, adaptive behavior is an age-related construct. As normally developing children grow older, adaptive behavior increases and becomes more complex. Second, adaptive behavior is determined by the standards of significant others—namely, those who live, work, play, teach, and interact with an individual. Finally, adaptive behavior is defined as an individual's typical performance or what an individual does day by day, not an individual's ability or potential to perform a task. If a person has the ability to perform a daily task, but does not demonstrate it when required, adaptive behavior is considered to be inadequate.

Common Elements across Definitions

Examining the definitions of adaptive behavior as we have done reveals two things. First, the construct has remained relatively unchanged over time. Second, there are several common elements across definitions that can be examined collectively to arrive at a global description of the construct. Across definitions, it is commonly recognized that adaptive behavior is developmental in nature; that it should be viewed within a cultural context; and that it may have greater meaning when viewed from a situational perspective rather than a generalized one.

Developmental Nature

Every major definition of adaptive behavior implies different standards, depending on the age of the individual. Expectations of adaptive behavior vary for persons of different ages. Deficits in adaptive behavior will vary for different age groups, as Grossman (1983, p. 25) makes clear.

During infancy and early childhood, sensory–motor skills, communication skills (speech and language), self-help skills, and primary socialization skills develop sequentially as the child matures. The adaptive behavior of the young child is measured using the status of these skills as indicators. Delays in the acquisition of these skills represent potential deficiencies in adaptive behavior for this age group, according to Grossman (1983).

Although self-care and communication remain important parts of adaptive behavior at any age, the skills required for adaptation during childhood and early adolescence are characterized largely by complex learning processes. As Grossman (1983) notes, this learning is evidenced in the acquisition and application of basic academic skills; in the demonstration of appropriate reasoning and judgment in mastery of the environment; and in the quality of the child's interpersonal relationships and participation in group activities.

In the late adolescent and adult years, vocational performance and social responsibilities assume primary importance in assessing adaptive behavior. Grossman (1983) states that these can take the form of the degree to which individuals are able to maintain themselves independently in the community and in gainful employment, as well as by their ability to meet and conform to community standards.

Cultural Context

In addition to developmental aspects, most definitions of adaptive behavior include recognition of cultural influences. The expectations for competence depend on cultural context. Different expectations exist and different competencies are expected in different cultural milieus (Mercer, 1977). In the assessment of adaptive behavior, it is important to assure sensitivity to cultural context by obtaining information from a primary caregiver who is familiar with the adaptive behavior demands of the individual's culture.

Situational versus Generalized Perspective

Most conceptions of adaptive behavior imply a situational perspective rather than a generalized trait view. As we have seen, expectations for behavior vary with age and culture. Likewise, demands on adaptive behavior differ, depending on the specific situation in which the individual is functioning. As we discuss later in the "History and Evolution" section, part of the rationale for including assessment of adaptive behavior outside of school as part of the procedure in the diagnosis of mental retardation was to prevent the labeling of the "6-hour retarded child" (President's Committee on Mental Retardation, 1970)—a child whose learning ability and adaptive behavior are subaverage in the school setting, but who functions within normal limits in his or her family and community. When assessing adaptive behavior, it is important to obtain information across a variety of settings (i.e., home, school, peer group, and community), in order to obtain a clear picture of the stability and variability of an individual's adaptive behavior and the situational factors affecting it.

Domains

The domains of behavior specified in various conceptions of adaptive behavior reflect some commonalities as well as some differences. Nearly every conception includes the notion of self-maintenance, or independent functioning having to do with one's physical needs. Skills in this area include fine and gross motor development, toileting, feeding, dressing, and personal hygiene.

Most conceptions of adaptive behavior include dimensions of interpersonal relationships—getting along with others, both peers and adults. This is evidenced by the quality of peer relationships, compliance with authority, coping skills, social awareness, and leisure time activities.

Social responsibility, defined as the ability of the individual to accept responsibility as a member of a community group and to carry out appropriate behaviors in terms of these group expectations, is often included as an aspect of adaptive behavior. This is reflected in levels of conformity, socially positive creativity, social adjustment, emotional maturity, and acceptance of some levels of civic responsibility, leading to complete or partial economic independence (Leland, 1973, p. 91–92). Activities or social roles that are included in this domain are vocational/career competencies; constructive participation in family, neighborhood, and community; and assumption of responsibility for care of others.

Cognitive competencies and communication skills are often included as domains of adaptive behavior. These processes include the acquisition of knowledge as a function of the experiences of the individual, the retention of that knowledge in memory, and the recall and use of stored knowledge in response to familiar or new stimuli. During childhood, difficulties in learning are usually manifested in academic learning in school. For this reason, many tests of adaptive behavior include items dealing with reading, math, and written language. During the school years, academic role performance is an important expectation that is common to all cultures in our society. To ignore this aspect in a measure of adaptive behavior would be a serious deficiency. It is important to remember, however, that during an evaluation of adaptive behavior, attention should focus not only on basic academic skills and their use, but also on skills essential in coping with the environment, including concepts of time and money, decision making, peer relations, and self sufficiency (Grossman, 1977, pp. 11–14). As we discuss in the next section, whether or not this domain is included in a conception of adaptive behavior has large significance in terms of the relationship of adaptive behavior and intelligence (Heber, 1962, p. 77; Reschly, 1982).

The Relationship between Adaptive Behavior and Intelligence

Once the definition and scope of the adaptive behavior construct have become fairly clear, its relationship to another popular descriptor of human functioning, intelligence, comes into question. The independence of these two constructs is often debated (Heber, 1962; Leland, Shellhaas, Nihira, & Foster, 1967; Reschly, 1982).

The quality of general adaptation is mediated by level of intelligence; thus the two concepts overlap in meaning. It is evident, however, from our consideration of the definition of adaptive behavior, with its stress on everyday coping in response to concrete, environmental demands, that "adaptive behavior" refers to what people do to take care of themselves and to relate to others in daily living and that it is quite different from the abstract potential implied by "intelligence."

Measurement of the two constructs differs in significant ways. Most measurements of adaptive behavior are designed to determine a person's common and typical performance, whereas intelligence tests seek to determine the highest potential for performance. Adaptive behavior items reflect everyday proficiencies of self-care in such areas as eating, dressing, toileting, communicating needs, and meeting ordinary social responsibility. Items on intelligence tests sample receptive and expressive language, academic skills, reasoning, and abstract abilities. Adaptive behavior information is usually secured through interviews with informants, this being an efficient way to gather information that is sensitive to setting, culture, and the typical daily activities of the individual. Intelligence tests are administered in a controlled clinical testing interview, with the subject and examiner in an one-to-one situation.

A comprehensive review of research on adaptive behavior and intelligence reveals a great deal of variability among the studies (Harrison, 1987; Leland et al., 1967; Sparrow et al., 1984). The correlations between scores on various measures of adaptive behavior and intelligence vary significantly, depending on measures used, type of subjects, and variability within samples. However, in most studies, correlations were in the moderate range (about .40–.60). These correlations, though substantial, indicate that adaptive behavior and intelligence are quite different for a sizable number of persons (Kazimour & Reschly, 1980). Although adaptive behavior scales yield information that is sometimes closely correlated with IQ, especially for persons at very low levels of functioning, this close correlation is not always present (Reschly, 1982). The choice of adaptive behavior measures appears to be a major influence on the relationship between adaptive behavior and intelligence (Reschly, 1982). When the content of the adaptive behavior measure includes many items pertaining to learning and academic skills, the correlations increase.

HISTORY AND EVOLUTION OF THE CONSTRUCT

Present concepts of adaptive behavior can be traced to early attempts to describe persons with mental retardation. As early as the Renaissance and the Reformation, language and law defined mental retardation in terms of adaptive behavior, or a person's ability to take care of himself or herself and get along with others (Harrison, 1985; Kagin, 1968).

Legal reforms for persons with mental retardation during the 1800s resulted in continued attention to adaptive behavior and a greater effort to understand the differences between persons with mental retardation and other community members (Robinson & Robinson, 1976). In the 1900s the development of the Binet intelligence scale and its counterparts led to the pervasive practice of defining mental retardation on the basis of intelligence test scores alone. This practice continued for over half a century.

Edgar Doll, the major pioneer in the objective assessment of adaptive behavior, disagreed with the use of intelligence test scores as a sole criterion. Among his six criteria of mental deficiency, Doll (1940) listed social incompetence as the first and most important. Doll's ideas formed the basis of present definitions of mental retardation and practices in the assessment of adaptive behavior. For many years after Doll's development of the Vineland Social Maturity Scale in the 1930s, however, intelligence test scores continued to receive major emphasis in the classification of mental retardation.

It was not until 1959 that the American Association on Mental Deficiency (AAMD) published its first official manual and formally included deficits in adaptive behavior, associated with subaverage intelligence, as an integral part of the definition of mental retardation (Heber, 1959). Subsequent editions of the manual (Grossman, 1973, 1977, 1983; Heber, 1961) have further emphasized the importance of adaptive behavior.

The 1960s and 1970s saw a trend toward the normalization of individuals with handicaps and the awareness that effective programs for teaching adaptive skills should allow individuals with handicaps to participate as fully as possible in normal environments. In addition to this trend, the courts had an enormous influence on psychological assessment and special education services during this time period (Bersoff, 1981). Nearly all of the major principles codified in special education legislation of the mid- and late 1970s appeared earlier in judicial opinions or consent decrees (Turnbull, 1978). In several of these cases, concern arose about "6-hour retarded children," or children of minority groups and/or low socioeconomic status (SES) who were labeled as retarded in the public schools but exhibited adequate adaptive behavior at home and in the community (*Diana v. State Board of Education*, 1970; *Guadalupe v. Tempe Elementary School District*, 1972). Mercer (1970) attributed the overrepresentation of minorities and students of low SES in special education classrooms to the use of a higher cutoff point for intelligence test scores by schools; the failure of the schools to assess adaptive behavior; and the bias of intelligence tests, favoring verbal tasks over nonverbal or performance items. Appropriate assessment and educational services for "6-hour retarded children" were among the most important issues in litigation in the early 1970s.

Litigation emphasized the need for a nonbiased and multifaceted assessment of all children with handicaps, to increase the fairness of educational decisions based on the results of tests and to investigate functioning in all areas related to a particular handicap. This concern eventually led to court decisions that results of intelligence tests cannot be the primary basis for classifying children as mentally retarded and that adaptive behavior must be assessed.

The increased importance of adaptive behavior was reflected in the 1973 and 1977 versions of the AAMD manual, where the words "existing concurrently" replaced the 1961 wording of "associated with"; this change implies that the assessment of adaptive behavior is of the same importance as the assessment of intelligence in diagnoses of mental retardation. In addition, the 1977 version broadened the conception of adaptive behavior for school-age children by stressing that performance outside of school is at least as important as performance inside school when one is making placement decisions in special education.

The passage of the Education for All Handicapped Children Act of 1975 (P.L. 94-142) represented the culmination of the issues of the 1960s and 1970s. P.L. 94-142 has stringent guidelines for the assessment of children with handicaps, and stipulates that deficits in adaptive behavior must be substantiated before a child is classified as mentally retarded. The rules and regulations regarding P.L. 94-142 (Regulations Implementing Education for All Handicapped Children Act, 1977) imply that adaptive behavior should be considered in all special education classification decisions, regardless of the nature of the handicap. Adaptive behavior is a prominent area in the outline of the multifactorial assessment process that is advocated for all children being considered for classification and placement in programs for students with mild handicaps. Since the passage of the law, most states have developed guidelines for adaptive behavior assessment and many have strict criteria for the types of adaptive behavior instruments and scores to be used (Harrison, 1987).

Subsequent revisions of this act, the Education for all Handicapped Children Act Amendments of 1983 (P.L. 98-199) and 1986 (P.L. 99-457), have extended public education's responsibility to serving children in early childhood, as well as to assisting students with the transition from secondary school to community life. Adaptive behavior holds special significance for these two age groups. As we have said earlier, during school years, the delays in acquisition of academic skills are the most common indicators of mental retardation or other learning problems addressed by special education. During early childhood, before the onset of formal learning, deficits in adaptive behavior become the salient indicators of problems in development. Likewise, for a student leaving school and entering adult life, the important issues may no longer be the student's reading or math level, but the proficiency with which the student meets the demands of the adult world—namely, his or her adaptive behavior.

In the future, the role of adaptive behavior in the identification of special populations will probably increase in importance because of the variety of influences discussed here. The increased emphasis now placed on the use of the adaptive behavior concept in special education and programs for persons with handicaps is resulting in attempts to clarify the characteristics of adaptive behavior and in the publication of many new instruments for measuring adaptive behavior.

ASSESSMENT OF ADAPTIVE BEHAVIOR

The kind of instrument or data collection method for adaptive behavior information that is appropriate depends upon its intended use. In a national survey of federally funded special education programs, DeStefano and Linn (1987) identified four major uses of assessment information: identification/placement, program planning, monitoring or progress, and program evaluation. In cases where adaptive behavior information is needed for identification, placement, or program evaluation purposes, the selection of norm-referenced, standardized measures is warranted. For purposes of program planning or monitoring student progress, norm-referenced tests may still be useful, but information may also be obtained more effectively by using informal assessment or criterion-referenced measures. The special qualities and uses of these types of tests are discussed below.

Informal Assessment

Adaptive behavior assessment is informally employed each time a teacher, parent, or multidisciplinary team requests a clinical assessment to determine whether a child is handicapped. The referring party has already observed that the behavioral development of that child is different from that of peers or siblings, and/or that he or she has difficulty meeting simple demands in daily life. Informal appraisals may be made by observations or by asking people who are in daily contact with the child to note the extent to which self-care needs are met; to determine whether the person can come and go in the home and neighborhood; and to observe whether he or she displays basic social amenities, communicates needs, takes direction, and so on. Those best qualified to describe adaptive behavior are people who are fully acquainted with the everyday life of the subject—teachers, parents, or other care providers. Even when an instrument is appropriate for a child being evaluated, clinical judgment and data collected through informal means should be used. This may take the form of short interviews with each of the persons familiar with the child. Observations of the child in different settings can also provide important information on adaptive behavior. This additional information can validate test results and aid in the interpretation of standardized test data.

Standardized Assessment

Over the last 15 years, several popular standardized measures of adaptive behavior have been developed. These instruments permit clinicians to make determinations that may be more objective than those based on unstructured interviews or limited observations (Sattler, 1982). Most of these scales, like measures of intelligence, are standardized in administration and scoring. Some have information on psychometric properties of the test, such as reliability, standard error of measurement, and validity. Many have adequate norms, and most have interpretive manuals.

The measures of adaptive behavior that are currently available vary greatly, not only in quality and norming, but also in intended application. For example, some have been intentionally limited for use with persons with profound or severe mental retardation, or with young children; others have been designed to measure readiness for independent living. Still others are intended not to assist in the diagnosis of mental retardation or other handicapping conditions, but rather to determine the current status of a person's competencies in a particular area in order to set goals for training. Because of the differing properties of different tests, clinicians must be careful to select those scales most suited to their particular needs.

Much more experience must be accumulated in the utilization of adaptive behavior scales and their scores for the same degree of confidence to be placed in them as is currently placed in the use of intelligence measures. Although there are similarities in the two areas of measurement, certain properties of the construct of adaptive behavior create measurement issues that are different from those usually encountered in the measure of intelligence or academic achievement (Meyers, Nihira, & Zetlin, 1979; Witt & Martens, 1984). These shared and unique concerns are discussed below.

Norms

As will become clear from the reviews of adaptive behavior measures that follow, the quality of norms varies from test to test. Unfortunately, national samples have not been used in most standardizations. Of the tests reviewed, only the Scales of Independent Behavior (SIB) and the Vineland Adaptive Behavior Scales (VABS) can boast of national standardization samples. Geographic specificity of norms can bias test results. Both the AAMD Adaptive Behavior Scale, Public School Version (ABS-PS) and the Adaptive Behavior Inventory for Children (ABIC) use norms based exclusively on children in California. The accuracy of the ABIC norms for children in other locations has been investigated. Buckley and Oakland (1977) studied the accuracy of California norms for two samples of Mexican-American children in Texas. The California mean scores were higher for both samples, with a difference as large as one-third of a standard deviation. In a study using four groups of children from other regions, Kazimour and Reschly (1980) also found that the California means on the ABIC were higher than the other groups.

Age range of the subjects is also an important issue in the standardization of some measures of adaptive behavior. It is recommended that an examiner check both the age ranges of the subjects in the standardization sample and the number of subjects at each age level before choosing a measure of adaptive behavior for a particular case. For example, the VABS is claimed to be appropriate for use with persons from birth to adulthood. In reality, complete norms and scoring options are available through 18 years, 11 months of age, and for adults in special norm groups. Valid scores cannot be obtained for nonhandicapped adults or those outside the special norm groups.

Maximum versus Typical Performance

A traditional distinction among types of tests is that between maximum-performance and typical-performance instruments (Cronbach, 1970). Maximum-performance items are designed to measure an individual's best effort or potential to perform a task. Typical-performance items measure how the individual customarily, habitually, or usually performs. The emphasis is not on whether the individual "can" perform the behavior, but rather on whether the individual "does" perform the behavior (Sparrow et al., 1984). Most measures of adaptive behavior attempt to measure typical performance.

A number of special problems exist with typical-performance constructs and measures (Reschly, 1982; Witt & Martens, 1984). The instruments are subject to faking and other response sets. Some measures of adaptive behavior attempt to control for response bias through the use of a semistructured interview rather than a multiple-choice or yes–no format (Sparrow et al., 1984). Use of multiple respondents provides one means of triangulating and validating data and of detecting response bias. It is also important that each respondent's credibility be evaluated. In an interview, the respondent may reveal his or her own attitudes toward the child and toward the various areas of adaptive behavior and social competence included in the scale.

The situation-specific nature of many adaptive behaviors, particularly those that involve attitudes, social behaviors, or interpersonal competencies, creates additional measurement problems. It is difficult to ascertain the impact of internal motivational and external situational contingencies on an individual's adaptive behavior score in a single interview. Most respondents do not have opportunities to observe children in all of the settings and roles included in the adaptive behavior scales. The respondent's approach to those items where his or her knowledge base is incomplete may make a large difference in the overall score. Once again, multiple respondents, each of whom is familiar with different aspects of the individual's life (home, school, peer group), can alleviate this problem.

Use of a Composite Score

There is some controversy surrounding the use of a single score to represent an individual's general level of social competence, as opposed to the reporting of multiple scores for each domain or content area. Although the idea of a composite score analogous to the IQ is a boon to diagnosis and criteria for entry into special programs, the meaning of such a score should be considered. Adaptive behavior tests measure many more and different facets of a person's everyday functioning than intelligence tests. For this reason, we see more within-subject variation in adaptive behavior scores than in intelligence test scores (Coulter & Morrow, 1978). Given this fact, aggregation of scores from very distinct subtests to create a composite score may not be a fair representation of the adaptive behavior construct.

TEST REVIEWS

In this section, reviews of eight of the most popular or promising measures of adaptive behavior are presented. The reviews are intended to aid an examiner in determining the appropriateness of an instrument for a particular assessment task. Information from the reviews is summarized in Appendix 19.1 to this chapter.

Adaptive Behavior Inventory for Children

Overview

The Adaptive Behavior Inventory for Children (ABIC; Mercer & Lewis, 1978) assesses a child's role behavior in a variety of non-school settings, including the home, community, and neighborhood, in order to provide a socioecological view of the child based on the family's perspective and norms. The test provides a profile of the child's adaptive fit on

242 items in areas that the test's authors consider critically important for children from 5 to 11 years of age: Family, Community, Peer Relations, Nonacademic School Roles, Earner/Consumer, and General Self-Maintenance Skills. The ABIC is derived from the social systems model. It serves as one component of the System of Multicultural Pluralistic Assessment (SOMPA).

The ABIC kit consists of an extensive parent interview manual, scoring keys, and parent interview record forms. The parent interview manual is available in English and Spanish and contains clear administration and scoring rules, good examples of scoring, the interview items, and tables for converting raw scores into scaled scores.

Practical Applications/Uses

The ABIC is an individually administered, structured interview with one parent (usually the mother) or most knowledgeable adult who has the best opportunity to observe the child's activities outside of school. The ABIC interview is divided into two parts. The first section consists of the first 35 items, which are not age-graded and are asked of all informants. The second section contains the rest of the items, which are age-graded; only those items necessary to establish a basal and a ceiling level are administered. The interviewer is usually a trained professional. However, a teacher aide or paraprofessional who has been thoroughly trained can be an effective interviewer, especially if he or she comes from an environment similar to the child's.

As an integral component of the SOMPA, the ABIC is designed to allow educators and mental health professionals to meet the federal nondiscriminatory assessment requirements of P.L. 94-142. The ABIC is designed to provide a measure of current adaptive functioning to differentiate the comprehensively retarded child (i.e., the child who does poorly in all areas of functioning) from the "pseudoretarded" or "6-hour retarded" child (i.e., the child who demonstrates significant intellectual deficits as measured by IQ, but who functions adequately outside of class, as measured by an adaptive scale). The ABIC has been used widely to establish that large numbers of school-age children do *not* merit the label of "mild mental retardation" and are thus ineligible to receive special education services. Its primary purpose, therefore, has been for placement.

The ABIC is also designed to ascertain whether the behavior of children aged 5–11 years meets the social expectations of their groups from the perspective of their families. The resulting profile for each child represents a description of the child's social behaviors in these subsystems at a given point in time. Organizing items in this manner represents a significant contribution to the measurement of adaptive behavior. Previous adaptive measures organize items in terms of domains of functionally related behaviors (e.g., communication skills) within either a single environment (e.g., the ABS-PS) or in unspecified environments (e.g., the VABS). But subscales reflecting important social antecedents (e.g., Peer Relations) seem to be a much more appropriate way to describe global adaptive functioning of the noninstitutionalized child. The ABIC profile not only emphasizes that adaptive behaviors are situationally influenced, but also facilitates identification of environmental impediments to successful adaptation.

Technical Aspects

The ABIC items were generated by interviewing (1) parents of children with retardation and (2) other parents recruited and paid for the task, as well as through the authors' previous research. The initial item pool was pretested with 1,259 parents. The final standardization sample, collected during the 1972–1973 academic school year, consisted of responses from 2,085 interviews: 696 black respondents, 690 Hispanic, and 699 white. Although equal ethnic group representation in the standardization sample is demonstrated, equal representation of ethnic groups certainly does not exist in the California population where the research was conducted, nor is it likely to exist in any other location where the ABIC would be used.

Reliability of the ABIC is very good; split-half data are provided for the total score and for each ethnic group at each age level from 5 to 11 years. A standard error of measurement

is provided for each reliability coefficient, a commendable practice. Total score reliabilities for the entire standardization sample and for each ethnic group were .95 or higher. The separate scale reliabilities varied from .76 (Peer Relations at 10 and 11 years). Total group coefficients range from a high of .83 (Family and General Self-Maintenance) to a low of .66 (Peer Relations and Earner/Consumer), with a median of .76.

In terms of validity, the authors argue that the usual practice of correlating the inventory scores with measures of intelligence, achievement, aptitude, or school performance is inappropriate, because the ABIC is designed to assess the degree to which a child successfully meets the expectations of others in the social systems measured. However, the ABIC does not offer any method for developing information regarding those expectations or for making judgments regarding adaptive behavior on the basis of such comparisons. The SOMPA technical manual provides correlations between the ABIC and the Wechsler Intelligence Scale for Children—Revised (WISC-R), which range from .05 (Performance IQ and Earner/Consumer) to .19 (Verbal IQ and Nonacademic School Roles).

Critique

One of the greatest contributions of the ABIC is that many of the various statistical, political, and social assumptions guiding its construction and use are made explicit; this is a tremendous help to potential users in deciding whether the ABIC is suitable for their particular testing purposes.

The nondiscriminatory assessment of adaptive functioning of school-age children has become one of the most important measurement goals facing educational and mental health professionals. The ABIC is widely used for this purpose and, because of its controversial nature and immense social impact, has probably attracted more research interest than any other adaptive scale.

The most significant limitations of the ABIC are that (1) like most other adaptive measures, it relies exclusively on informant reports; (2) scores are unstable over long test–retest time intervals; (3) norms exclude such minorities as Asian and Native American children and overrepresent other minorities in the total norm group; (4) there is limited presentation of psychometric data in the manual, particularly with regard to construct or predictive validity; and (5) the manuals do not provide examples for interpreting "at-risk" profiles.

The major strengths are that (1) its underlying assumptions are explicitly stated; (2) item content is unbiased with respect to the three ethnic groups, gender, and SES; (3) items are empirically derived and selected based on a large sample from the normal population; (4) administration and scoring procedures are clear; (5) it possesses good internal-consistency reliability; and (6) there does exist some evidence for criterion-related validity.

Despite the drawbacks listed above, the ABIC appears to be a reliable and useful measure for the unbiased assessment of most middle-SES white, black, and Hispanic school-age children.

AAMD Adaptive Behavior Scale, School Edition

Overview

The AAMD's Adaptive Behavior Scale, School Edition (ABS-SE; Nihara et al., 1981) can be used to assess children whose adaptive behavior indicates possible mental retardation, emotional disturbance, or other learning handicaps. The scale is divided into two parts and covers 21 areas of adaptive behavior. Part One evaluates personal independence in daily living tasks, such as eating, dressing, and shopping, that are considered adaptive. Part Two measures personality and behavior disorders, such as teasing others, damaging property, and disrupting class activities, that are considered maladaptive. The 21 areas covered in the 95 test items fall into five domains: Personal Self-Sufficiency, Community Self-Sufficiency, Personal–Social Responsibility, Personal Adjustment, and Social Adjustment. The ABS-SE is intended for school children aged 3 through 16.

An administration manual, diagnostic manual, assessment booklet, instructional planning profile, diagnostic profile, and two parent guides are available from the publisher.

Practical Applications/Uses

This test is of primary use in making public school classification decisions for students with mild and moderate mental retardation. For each student, a Comparison Score based on all of the adaptive domains, together with IQ and other information, is compared to expectations for regular, mildly handicapped, and moderately handicapped students. Each scale item consists of a list of statements, each of which describes a behavior. The person completing the paper-and-pencil scale rates the child on 95 items. The scale is usually completed by the child's teacher or the school psychologist, based on school and home information. However, it is recommended that ratings be obtained from both teachers and parents so that comparisons among home, community, and school environments can be drawn. It provides a global index of adaptive behavior with a variety of scores that can help in prioritizing behavioral objectives. The analysis of items can also yield objectives for inclusion in student individual education programs (IEPs) required by P.L. 94-142.

Technical Aspects

Revised norms for the 1981 revision were based on a standardization sample that was increased from 2,600 to 6,500 students with mild and moderate retardation and nonhandicapped students; the age range was from 3 to 16, and the sample was drawn from California and Florida. Norm frequencies have been tabled for the usual demographic parameters, but no effort has been made to compare percentages to expectancies for the population at large.

Among the five domains covered in the ABS-SE, Community Self-Sufficiency, Personal–Social Responsibility, and Social Adjustment are the most reliable, with a majority of coefficient alpha values at or above .80. Personal Self-Sufficiency and Personal Adjustment are less reliable, with values in the moderate to low ranges across age and classification levels. Standard errors of measurement are reported for the factor raw scores.

According to the manual, the assumption underlying construct validity for adaptive behavior is that it is separate from but related to intelligence (since both measures provide evidence of psychological development). Low to moderate correlations between domains on Parts One and Two and IQ scores from a variety of measures tend to support this description of the construct. Also, predictive validity is evident in the normative research, which shows significant effects for class status (regular, mildly retarded, and moderately retarded) across age levels. Multiple-regression analyses are interpreted by the manual as evidence that the scale is valid for differentiating among nonhandicapped children and children with mild and moderate retardation, aged 7–12.

The studies of validity and reliability conducted using the normative data on this scale raise several questions. If validity of the scale is satisfactory only through age 12, should the scale be used for making decisions about the placement of adolescents between ages 13 and 16? Does the scale demonstrate concurrent validity with other established measures of adaptive behavior, such as the VABS and the ABIC? Until these validity studies have been conducted, caution should be exercised in making decisions based on test results with older children.

Critique

The use of the predecessor to the ABS-SE, the ABS-PS (the Public School Version), for placement decisions was challenged on the grounds that its original and intended purpose was program planning, not identification. This revised School Edition includes considerable evidence that the scale can be used for identification and placement decisions, as noted previously in the review.

The renormed ABS-SE is one of the most widely used school measures of adaptive behavior. Revisions in the latest manuals have clarified procedures for interpreting the scale, but the test is not entirely free from clinical judgment demands. The scale is extremely time-consuming to administer and score, and the demanding calculations and score conversions invite clerical errors. Norms might be developed for other handicapped groups, such as the blind or deaf, but this has not been done to date.

Another consideration is the extent to which the scale identifies the presence of retardation, especially mild to moderate degrees, within differing social contexts. Although the test items do sample school, home, and community behaviors, there are no guidelines for distinguishing the "6-hour retarded child" at school from the child who is significantly below expectations across all settings, although the examiner is encouraged to make these comparisons in the manual.

Software for the ABS-SE, called ABSOFT, has been developed to allow for ready access to norm-referenced scores. After recording the responses for each item, the profiles of students can be produced. Derived scores relate the examinees to the various reference groups (regular, mildly retarded, moderately retarded).

Balthazar Scales of Adaptive Behavior I: Scales of Functional Independence

Overview

The Balthazar Scales of Adaptive Behavior I: Scales of Functional Independence (BSAB-I; Balthazar, 1971) was designed to measure very small differences in the self-care experiences of children and adults with profound or severe mental retardation. One use of the BSAB-I is to assess individual behavior in self-care skills and to compare these scores with scores in normative groups. These scale measurements are also used to identify weaknesses in eating, dressing, and toileting skills in order to give appropriate training or treatment, after which the scales can be used again to determine the amount of improvement in the skills where inadequacies were identified.

The BSAB-I contains three scales, with several sections included within each one. First, the Toileting scale contains three daytime toileting sections (bladder, bowel, and general) and a nighttime supplementary section. Second, the Eating scale has six sections: dependent feeding, finger foods, spoon usage, fork usage, drinking, and an eating checklist. The third scale, the Dressing scale, includes both a male and a female section to accommodate differences in clothing.

The test is administered as a multiple-item paper-and-pencil observational inventory assessment. Personnel in residential treatment facilities can be trained within a week to become observers and raters. The BSAB-I is administered individually. The Toileting scale requires interviewing of aides on the day and night shifts in a residential setting. The Eating scale requires unobtrusive observations of a subject by a rater/technician during one or more mealtime periods. The Dressing scale is administered in a manner to elicit optional performance with encouragement by a rater/technician.

A manual and scoring booklets are available from the publisher. The BSAB-I items are arranged conveniently in a four-page scoring booklet.

Practical Application/Uses

The BASB-I was designed to measure achievement in basic skills (eating, dressing, and toileting). The manual suggests four uses for which the BSAB-I is appropriate: (1) as a baseline measure of specific skills or groups of skills in which the subject is weak, in order to focus on training and treatment, with posttraining measures used to indicate the degree of progress in weak skill areas; (2) as an instrument on which examinees' profiles may be compared with those of normative groups (the BSAB-I may be used for this purpose in association with global intelligence scales for mentally retarded subjects or with social intelligence scales); (3) as a means of developing programs for the retarded in residential centers and in community referral systems; and (4) as the key measuring instrument in research programs in institutions.

The author claims that the BSAB-I is appropriate for only children and adults with severe or profound mental retardation (those whose IQs range from 20 to 35 on global intelligence tests). The use of the BSAB-I for persons with higher IQs, or for those who are blind or are otherwise physically handicapped, is not recommended. Because the age range for the standardization sample (discussed below) was 5–57 years, it is not advisable to deviate too far from this range.

Technical Aspects

The author's conception of validity of the BSAB-I is construct validity (i.e., the

observed behavior is the criterion measure itself). There are no reported external-validity studies. However, statistical relationships of the BSAB-I and indicators of general social coping behavior and language proficiency in the BSAB-II were established without using Kendall's tau, a nonparametric technique, as was used in establishing this association between BSAB-I and BSAB-II. The relationships between the two scales were statistically significant, but this is by no means external validation; it is an association between the BSAB-I and social/language scales on the BSAB-II.

Reliabilities reported were of two kinds: proportion agreements and correlation coefficients across all scale items of the paired rater scores. The reliability coefficient was .873 for the Eating scale, .965 for the Dressing scale, and .939 for the Toileting scale, resulting in respectable interrater reliability.

Observational studies in developing the BSAB-I began in 1964 and continued through 1968. The normative sample consisted of institutionalized residents at the Central Wisconsin Center for the Developmentally Disabled in Madison, Wisconsin. Additional samples were obtained from other institutions in the United States and abroad. A great majority of the normative sample were ambulatory residents, although some were semiambulatory. The age range of the normative sample was 5–57 years, with a median age of 17.3. Data obtained from observing behaviors of the more severely retarded group constituted an item pool, from which items were selected and transformed into subscales. For standardization, 122 subjects were tested on the Eating scale, 200 on the Dressing scale, and 129 on the Toileting scale.

Critique

Although the BSAB-I represents a successful attempt to identify some basic self-help skills, some of the customary psychometric requirements are missing in accounts of the early development and standardization of the instrument. For example, there are no established patterns of relationships with well-known reference instruments. Although early versions of the BSAB-I (which included language and social aspects) were correlated with the Vineland Social Maturity Scale (+.63), the present version was correlated with another Balthazar instrument only—the BSAB-II.

The lack of external criteria in the validation process is not particularly disturbing, especially with a self-help skill instrument. However, the establishment of norms beyond the original standardization sample in Wisconsin would be helpful to the BSAB-I user. Perhaps some of the local studies that Balthazar recommends in his manual have been completed but not yet published. In addition, it is rather presumptuous to pass judgment on the BSAB-I with the same array of requirements and standards that one uses for evaluating instruments designed to cut across a complete range of skills and abilities.

Balthazar Scales of Adaptive Behavior II: Scales of Social Adaptation

Overview

The Balthazar Scales of Adaptive Behavior II: Scales of Social Adaptation (BSAB-II) was constructed as an observational system to measure the adaptiveness of social coping behaviors of persons with severe or profound retardation or emotonal disturbance in residential institutional settings. The purpose of the BSAB-II is to evaluate individual children and adults, and to provide a system for specifying, describing, and evaluating the goals of treatment or training programs for persons with mental retardation. Focused only on social skills, the BSAB-II (Balthazar, 1973) was designed as a supplement to the BSAB-I, which Balthazar developed in 1971 to assess more basic self-care skills (eating, dressing, and toileting behaviors).

The test consists of 74 subscale items within 19 scales and drawn from seven global behavior categories representative of a comprehensive domain of behaviors indicative of social adaptation. The seven broad behavior categories include the following: Unadaptive Self-Directed Behaviors (five ratings); Unadaptive Interpersonal Behaviors (two ratings); Adaptive Self-Directed Behaviors (one rating); Adaptive Interpersonal Behaviors (three ratings); Verbal Communication (two ratings); Play Activities (three ratings); and Response to Instructions (three

ratings). In addition, there is a nine-item checklist of behaviors related to personal care, such as toileting, drinking, and clothing adjustment.

The test is administered as a multiple-item paper-and-pencil observational inventory assessment. According to the manual, rater/technicians need not have a professional background to administer or score the scales. The only requisites are that the rater be articulate, alert, accurate, and thoroughly acquainted with the subscale items prior to the onset of evaluation activities. Instructions are provided for use by rater/technicians, teachers, and paraprofessionals.

The manual accompanying the BSAB-II is divided into two sections: one for professional supervisors and a second for rater/technicians. Extensive information for both is provided. The test package also includes scoring sheets for the observation sessions and a summary sheet to display the social coping behavior profile.

Practical Applications/Uses

The behaviors represented by the subscale items and the scales are intended to provide specific objectives for treatment and training programs for persons with severe and profound mental retardation, on either an individual or a group basis. Subjects are observed during typical activities in a residential, institutional setting (e.g., state school, hospital, etc.). The BSAB-II can be administered either wholly or in part; it provides a system for developing and evaluating programs and a means of obtaining clinical information useful to professional staff and researchers. Methods for observation are provided in the manual.

Scores on the BSAB-II are interpreted in the context of the purpose for the evaluation. On an individual basis, scores yield a profile of the subject's skills and deficits in social situations. The manual reports mean subscale item scores on the standardization sample ($n = 102$) described later in this review, although neither percentile rank nor standard score norms are available for interpreting scores. The mean scores are of questionable clinical utility to researchers, professional supervisors or therapists, however, because standard deviations and distributional characteristics are not reported. Despite the lack of emphasis on norm-referenced interpretation of scores, the BSAB-II appears to be much like a criterion-referenced test. As such, profiles can be used much in the manner of an IEP, as mandated by P.L. 94-142, for structuring the treatment or training program of students with handicaps. Alternately, the BSAB-II can be a system for developing institutional goals for programs, and it also provides a built-in means for summative and formative program evaluation by assessing profile changes over time.

Technical Aspects

The BSAB-II manual does not present extensive information on the psychometric properties of the instrument. The author emphasizes the need for "serious" researchers, program evaluators, and professional supervisors to conduct their own reliability studies, especially with regard to interrater agreement and interrater stability over time. The appendix to the manual reports the results of two interrater reliability studies conducted with an earlier version of the current scale, but the number of subjects was quite small and results were not consistent between the two studies.

In addition, there is no evidence reported in favor of test–retest reliability (stability) or internal consistency (homogeneity). In light of the fact that only 5 of the 19 scales are composed of more than four items, internal consistency may pose a problem, given the well-known relationship between reliability and test length. It would appear that the author has addressed this issue; he argues that parametric and even nonparametric correlation coefficients cannot be computed with the BSAB-II. However, because the subscale item scores are sums of the number of behaviors observed, there is no sound reason why conventional item-analytic strategies cannot be applied to BSAB-II data.

No specific mention is made of any effort to establish content validity. As with the BSAB-I, the author adheres to the argument that behavior observations constitute the criterion measure itself; in other words, validity is perfect! This assumption seems highly sus-

pect. Also, examination of the content of the subscale items reveals considerable room for subjective interpretation. In summary of the validity evidence reported, it is safest to say that there simply is none.

The BSAB-II was developed from observations of 288 residents with severe or profound mental retardation in nursery and infirmary wards at the Central Wisconsin Colony and Training School in Madison, Wisconsin. On the basis of 5 years of observation of these subjects, and 2 years of additional study at two other sites, an item pool representative of a broad variety of coping behaviors was generated. The age range of the individuals under observation was 5–57 years, with a median age of 17 years. Their global IQ scores were in the profound to severe classifications, ranging from 20 to 35.

Critique

Although numerous "rating scales" have been standardized and validated, the BSAB-II is probably the most systematically developed "observation scale" for the purpose of measuring social adaptation. Researchers and clinical professionals wishing to conduct observational studies of persons with mental retardation will find that the BSAB-II provides useful information about the social behavior and functioning of their target population.

Practitioners will find the BSAB-II appealing because it can be administered by non-professional personnel in a relatively short period of time; a comprehensive behavior profile is obtained for treatment or training on an individual basis; a broad age range of subjects can be assessed; and built-in procedures are offered for program development and evaluation. Drawbacks to the use of the BSAB-II are psychometric concerns. If the BSAB-II is viewed as a test, there is limited evidence of reliability and no evidence of validity. Rating scales, such as the AAMD Adaptive Behavior Scales, have far superior psychometric properties. If, on the other hand, the BSAB-II is viewed as an observational system, researchers and practitioners need to concern themselves primarily with the problem of training observers to achieve a fair degree of objectivity in their ratings.

Children's Adaptive Behavior Scale

Overview

The Children's Adaptive Behavior Scale (CABS; Richmond & Kicklighter, 1979) is a norm-referenced instrument for the evaluation of adaptive behavior skills in children aged 5 years through 10 years, 11 months. In contrast to other adaptive behavior scales, which obtain their data through methods such as parent and teacher interviews, the items of the CABS are administered directly to the child. Thus, the constructs are measured by noting the child's own behavior and responses. The CABS consists of five domains, each requiring verbal responses to orally administered questions, with the number of items within a set varying from 16 to 30. The specific domains are as follows: Language Development, Independent Functioning, Family Role Performance, Economic/Vocational Activity, and Socialization. The test is administered individually by a skilled psychological examiner, with 30–40 minutes being the approximate testing time. The purpose of the CABS is to provide a nonbiased assessment that distinguishes those children who are retarded in all aspects of development from those who test within retarded ranges on intelligence measures but whose adaptive skills are not in the retarded ranges.

A test kit is available that includes a manual, a picture book for students, and record forms.

Practical Applications/Uses

The CABS requires direct assessment of the child rather than an interview with a third-party respondent. Although this may have advantages over adaptive behavior measures that depend on data from informants gathered retrospectively, it cannot be assumed that data obtained from the child in an one-to-one setting with an examiner will be reflective of adaptive performance outside the testing situation. Information obtained on the CABS should be confirmed by obtaining direct samples of behavior in other natural settings (e.g., home, community). This is an important issue, inasmuch as a primary reason for obtaining measures of adaptive functioning is to go beyond individual testing situations. This becomes especially relevant when one considers that some of the item content of the CABS is similar to that included within intelligence tests. Thus, by contrast with other adaptive behavior measures, the CABS appears to emphasize the cognitive competencies that are required for various adaptive behaviors. Rather than being used for screening and placement, its primary purpose is for teachers to plan program remediation on the basis of test results.

Technical Aspects

The CABS was standardized on a sample of 250 children with mild mental retardation (IQ range 55–70) from South Carolina and Georgia. Fifty children were included at each age level from ages 6 through 10. These data are quite limited, considering the purpose of the scale. Given this small and unrepresentative standardization sample (i.e., no breakdown for SES, race, etc.), the norms may not be representative of the general population of children with mild retardation. Therefore, the authors rightly urge test users to develop their own local norms. The normative data contain large standard deviations on individual subtests at each age level. Therefore, reporting a range of age scores, rather than using a precise age-equivalent score, is recommended for individual domains. The most emphasis should be placed on the total test score.

Test–retest data gathered at a 2-week interval on a sample of 36 black, nonretarded children yielded reliability coefficients ranging from .97 to .99 for individual subtests and the total score. This sample consisted of only three males and three females at each age level from ages 5 through 10. Although the sample size was small, the results suggest excellent reliability.

The validity and reliability data presented raise concerns with regard to selection of item content, small sample sizes, and other areas. Until further validity and reliability studies are conducted and the normative sample is expanded, the test user will remain uncertain as to the precise skills and abilities that the CABS is tapping. The test user, then, will also be on questionable grounds in interpreting a low score on one domain as indicating a need to strengthen that particular ability, or a high score as definitely indicating that a child is not retarded. The authors wisely advise the test user to seek corroborating evidence for such judgments from parent/teacher interviews and further observational data.

Critique

Some of the positive features of the CABS include the following: It appears to be economical in terms of the clinician and client time involved for administration; it is designed for use in an educational setting; and the test is administered directly to the child.

This review suggests that individuals using the CABS should consider a few issues. First, the CABS still has rather limited data on norming, reliability, and validity. Certainly, a larger and more nationally representative normative population is needed, as are test–retest reliability data on a sample of retarded children. Second, the CABs should probably be supplemented by other measures of adaptive functions to obtain a broader picture of performance across settings and individuals.

In summary, the CABS holds promise for identifying children whose poor performance on an intelligence test is not indicative of true adaptive potential. At this point, individual CABS items are best used as criterion-referenced indices for instructional planning, while the five domain scores should be ignored. CABS total scores are best used to suggest additional assessment questions.

Scales of Independent Behavior

Overview

The Scales of Independent Behavior (SIB; Bruininks, Woodcock, Weatherman, & Hill, 1984) is a relatively new instrument that represents a multidimensional measure of functional independence and adaptive behavior. The Broad Independence Scale of the SIB consists of four clusters of independence, including 14 subscales containing 226 items and covering the following areas: (1) Motor Skills, (2) Social Interaction and Communication Skills, (3) Personal Independence Skills, and (4) Community Independence Skills. The Broad Independence Scale is adminis-

tered individually through a structured interview in about 45–60 minutes and is intended for ages infant through adult (including 40 years and above). A Short Form Scale provides a brief measure of broad independence. Consisting of 32 tasks selected from the 14 subscales in the Broad Independence Scale, the Short Form can be used for quick screening to identify examinees who are at risk for problems in adaptive behavior and need to be administered the entire Broad Independent Scale. The Short Form takes about 10–15 minutes to administer. The Early Development Scale provides a developmental measure of adaptive behavior from infancy to 3 years. The scale is also useful for assessing the adaptive functioning of children and adults with severe or profound handicaps. Composed of 32 tasks sampled from 12 of the 14 developmental areas covered in the SIB, the scale takes about 10–15 minutes to administer. The Inventory for Client and Agency Planning (ICAP; Bruininks, Hill, Weatherman, & Woodcock, 1986), an abbreviated form of the SIB, offers a quick, convenient way to assess client characteristics, determine service needs, and monitor progress over time.

Information gained from a parent, caregiver, or teacher is used in a multiple-item interview format. According to the authors, SIB examiners do not necessarily need formal training or experience. The procedures and instructions have been designed so that experienced interviewers can become proficient in administering the SIB through study and practice on their own. Inexperienced examiners will require supervised practice. The SIB interviewer's manual contains complete descriptions for administering, scoring, and interpreting the SIB, and also includes the norms tables.

A unique feature of the SIB is its Problem Behaviors Scale. This scale permits the examiner to assess eight critical areas of problem behavior, which are scored in four useful indices. The dual rating system employed on the Problem Behaviors Scale allows the examiner to compare not only the frequency but also the severity of the maladaptive behavior, providing more substantive interpretive data.

The intent of the authors of the SIB was to develop a test that met a number of content and design specifications. The test administration and scoring were intended to be objective enough that novices in testing could administer the SIB without difficulty. To increase clarity and reliability, the test items were written as precise behavioral objectives tapping a broad range of practical skills from the areas of functional independence and adaptive behavior. In addition, the test items were arranged to sample significant aspects of development among children and adults with profound to mild handicaps, as well as nonhandicapped persons. The test items were designed to maximize the differences among subjects with varying degrees of proficiency and ability, and to minimize verbal comprehension and memory requirements as much as possible for respondents. Descriptions of significant strengths and weaknesses in functioning in the home, school, and community settings were intended to be major outcomes of administering the SIB, along with descriptions of training needs.

Practical Application/Uses

Because of the organization of the SIB into scales, clusters, and subscales, examiners should find that the SIB has maximum flexibility and utility in testing. The SIB may be used for screening, individual diagnostic evaluation, individualized program planning, selection and placement, guidance, monitoring of educational progress, program evaluation, and research.

Technical Aspects

The SIB was standardized on a sample of nearly 1,800 subjects, randomly selected from over 40 communities distributed across the United States. The normative sample covered an age range from infancy to over 40 years. In order to obtain additional technical data, over 1,000 handicapped and nonhandicapped people were also sampled; these included samples of persons with mental retardation, learning disabilities, behavior disorders, and hearing impairments.

The reliability of the SIB has been reported using internal-consistency and test–retest procedures. Median corrected split-half reliability coefficients on the SIB cluster scores across handicapped age levels were generally in the high .80s and .90s, and were in the high .90 range for the Broad Independence Scale across all age levels. When the median corrected split-half reliabilities for all 14 subscales and the Short Form Scale were examined using a special sample of subjects with handicaps, the median coefficients across groups and age levels were found to be high, mostly in the .90s. The median composite reliabilities for the four SIB clusters and for the Broad Independence Scale scores for special samples of handicapped subjects were mostly in the high .90s.

The test–retest reliability coefficients for the Short Form Scale, the four clusters, the Broad Independence Scale, and the four indices of problem behaviors were assessed using two elementary school-age samples of nonhandicapped subjects. Of the 20 coefficients, 16 were in the .80s and .90s; the other 4 were in the .70 range. These coefficients indicate high test–retest reliability. The SIB shows good content validity, in that its structure and content cover a broad range of skills and traits included in current models of adaptive and maladaptive behavior. Obtained scores include the following: age scores, percentile ranks, standard scores, relative performance index, expected range of independence, and instructional range.

Critique

Since the assessment of adaptive functioning is important not just for persons with mental retardation, but also for subjects who may have emotional disturbances, behavior disorders, and so forth, the SIB has many features to recommend it as a measure of adaptive behavior in subjects' current functioning in real-life situations. Because the SIB is statistically and conceptually linked to the Woodcock–Johnson Psycho-Educational Battery, it is part of a comprehensive assessment system that permits comparisons of a subject's functional independence, problem behaviors, cognitive ability, achievement, and interests. The SIB has several administration options and is therefore very flexible. In addition, it is one of the few currently available adaptive behavior scales that is nationally standardized for infants to adults (over 40 years).

The SIB has been criticized for incomplete

technical data in terms of the absence of factor-analytic studies and predictive-validity studies. Although the SIB is easy to administer and score, the actual item scoring and score conversion can be rather tedious because of the number of tables and scoring options available. To remedy these problems, a SIB Compuscore program is available.

Tests for Everyday Living

Overview

Tests for Everyday Living (TEL; Halpern, Irvin, & Landman, 1979) is described as a competency-based instrument intended to measure "knowledge of life skills necessary to successfully perform everyday life tasks" (Halpern et al., 1979, p. 16). Seven tests are included: Purchasing Habits, Banking, Budgeting, Health Care, Home Management, Job Search Skills, and Job-Related Behaviors. Each test contains between 33 and 37 items, with the total score based on all 245 items. Each of the seven tests takes about 20–30 minutes to administer. TEL tests are orally administered in the form of multiple-choice items (three choices) to individuals or to groups of 20 or less. Of the 245 items, 209 require no reading ability on the part of the students; this oral format allows poor readers to show their knowledge in life skills areas. The other 36 items (5–8 from each of the seven tests) do require some reading skill, and a separate Reading Scale score can be computed for the items requiring reading.

Components of the test include a 24-page test booklet (useable only once) and a lengthy examiner's manual that contains an answer key and technical report. Administration requires no special training and can be performed by classroom teachers or counselors.

Practical Application/Uses

At the junior high level, it is suggested that the TEL can be used effectively with all regular, remedial, and learning-disabled students. At the senior high level, it is best used with average or low-achieving students, including students in remedial classes and students with learning disabilities. However,

the examiner's manual states that the use of the TEL is *not* recommended with persons with mental retardation. The same authors have developed three other similar test batteries for use with persons with mental retardation to measure similar life skills competencies: the Social and Provocational Information Battery (SPIB); the SPIB, Revised Edition (SPIB-R); and the SPIB-T, the "trainable" version, which is suitable for examinees with moderate retardation.

The tests have been designed to be useful in several ways: as a means of individual student diagnosis or classroom group placement in life skills content areas; as a content outline of life skills competencies for instructional development and planning; and as a means for evaluation of student progress or the impact of life skills instruction. In addition, the TEL includes the applied Reading Scale to permit assessment of students' "survival" reading skills.

Technical Aspects

During standardization, initial versions of 40–50 items per test were tried out on 100 secondary students. On the basis of item means and item–test point biserials, a few items were revised or eliminated. The remaining 40–45 items per test were then tried out on a sample of 525 junior high and middle school students and 325 senior high school students. The tryouts were in four school districts: Anchorage, Alaska; Springfield, Oregon; and two in Los Angeles County, California. Final item selection was based on (1) point biserial correlations of items and the total test; (2) item difficulty; and (3) preservation of content integrity. It is important to note that all point biserials and all other test statistics were recomputed for the subset of items determined to be acceptable. There was no cross-validation sample.

Coefficient alphas are reported separately for junior high and senior high samples for each of the seven tests, the total battery, and the Reading Scale. For the seven tests, these range from .68 to .83; for the Reading Scale, they are .81 and .76 (junior and senior high); and for the total battery, they are .92 for each sample. It must be remembered that these are very high values because they were recomputed alphas from a select set of items partly chosen for their high point biserials from a larger set of items.

The validity evidence is limited to content validity. By examining the content structures presented in the manual, users can discern whether the domains as sampled are of interest to them.

Critique

In summary, the TEL appears to be well constructed and has good content validity. Reliabilities of the tests are fair, but are based on a subset of items that were selected from initial tryouts and not cross-validated. Intercorrelations are not reported. There are no norms, which may be a serious limitation for many users. The TEL's strengths include early identification of life skills inadequacies and the diagnosis of individual strengths and weaknesses of students and programs. Also, the tests are administered and scored easily to provide immediate feedback.

Vineland Adaptive Behavior Scales

Overview

The latest revision of the Vineland Social Maturity Scale, the Vineland Adaptive Behavior Scales (VABS; Sparrow et al., 1984), is a system for assessing personal and social adaptability of individuals from birth to adulthood. Like the original scale, the present VABS is not a test in the usual sense of the word. It is a scorable structured interview, conducted by a trained interviewer, with a respondent who is familiar with the subject's everyday behavior. The interview can be conducted in approximately 1 hour. The scales are applicable to both handicapped and nonhandicapped individuals.

There are three versions of the newly revised VABS: (1) Interview Edition, Survey Form; (2) Interview Edition, Expanded Form; and (3) Classroom Edition. Four general areas and 11 subdomain areas are sampled: Communication (Receptive, Expressive, and Written); Daily Living Skills (Personal, Domestic, and Community); Socialization (Interpersonal Relationships, Play and Leisure Time, and Coping Skills), and Motor Skills (Gross and Fine). These four domains are combined to provide an Adaptive Behavior Composite score.

The Survey Form is the most similar to the original Vineland scale, includes 297 items, and provides a general assessment of adaptive behavior. It is available in Spanish.

The Expanded Form contains 577 items, including 297 from the Survey Form, and is also available in Spanish. This longer version provides not only a more comprehensive and detailed assessment of adaptive behavior, but also a systematic basis for preparing educational, habilitative, and treatment programs through use of a separate booklet, the program planning report.

An optional Maladaptive Behavior domain is included in the Survey Form and Expanded Form. Part 1 describes minor maladaptive behaviors; Part 2 rates more serious maladaptive behaviors in the moderate to serious range in terms of degree of frequency of occurrence.

The Classroom Edition is a questionnaire of 244 items and assesses adaptive behavior in the classroom for students from 3½ to 13 years of age. Some items are from the Survey and Expanded Forms, and additional items relate to basic academic functioning. It is a checklist, completed independently by teachers.

A number of scores are obtainable: standard scores for the whole test and four domains; percentiles; stanines; and age equivalents. Guidelines for profile analysis and interpretation are provided in the manual.

Among the three versions of the VABS, the publisher provides extensive materials in the form of manuals, record booklets, program planning reports, reports to parents, score summary and profile booklets, and a technical supplement. The test and reports to parents are available in both English and Spanish.

Practical Applications/Uses

The most important use of the VABS continues to be provision of up-to-date standards for social and adaptive behavior of children from birth to 18 years of age. Social competency scores can be compared to intellectual development as measured by such tests as the Bayley Mental and Motor Scales, the revised Stanford–Binet, the Wechsler Preschool and Primary Scale of Intelligence

(WPPSI), and the WISC-R. The VABS is not limited to use with persons with mental retardation, but can also be useful in assessing children with physical handicaps, emotional disturbance, hearing impairments, or visual handicaps. Each of these groups is represented in special national samples providing supplementary norms for the scale.

The VABS can be used to develop individual educational, habilitative, and treatment programs. Strengths and weaknesses in specific areas can be pinpointed in order to select the most suitable program for the individual or to zero in on specific activities in the program that might be most beneficial.

Technical Aspects

The VABS was standardized using a national sample that was highly representative of 1980 census figures. A total of 21,876 parental participation forms provided a pool from which a sample of 3,000 standardization subjects was randomly selected. The standardization group comprised 100 subjects in each of 30 age groups between birth and 18 years, 11 months. It consisted of 1,500 males and 1,500 females from four geographical regions (Northeast, North Central, South, and West) and four racial groups (white, black, Hispanic, and other). Items for the standardization of the scale were selected from 529 items used in a national pretest sample.

Three types of reliability estimates were developed: split-half (or internal consistency), test–retest, and interrater reliability. Split-half correlations ranged from a low of .83 for the Motor Skills domain to .94 for the Adaptive Behavior Composite score on the Survey Form. On the Expanded Form, median split-half correlations were considered very satisfactory. Test–retest reliability obtained by testing 484 individuals from the ages of 6 months to 18 years, 11 months at 2- to 4-week intervals (mean, 17 days) varied by age groups: Correlations were in the .90s for ages 6 months through 6 years, 11 months, and in the .80s for ages 7 through 18 years, 11 months.

Over the whole age range, however, domain test–retest correlations ran from .98 to .99; reliability was thus considered to be excellent. Interrater reliability for 160 individuals interviewed twice by different in-

terviewers resulted in correlations ranging from .96 to .99 for different domains, also excellent.

Extensive validity data are provided in the examiner's manual. Construct, content, and concurrent validity appear to be well established.

Critique

The VABS is a well-standardized, reliable, and valid means of assessing adaptive behavior. The Survey Form and Expanded Form area appropriate for persons from birth to 18 years of age. Older adults with mental retardation can also be evaluated using these forms. The Classroom Edition is a measure of school-related adaptive behavior for elementary students. The development of remediation plans, intended by the authors to be a special use of the Expanded Form, is subject to limitations at certain age ranges and at certain classes of behaviors. The major caution to be emphasized would seem to be that the structure, recommended uses, and methods of developing derived scores differ considerably among the three forms. The potential user, then, is advised to know the properties of each quite well and to fit those properties to the assessment needs of a specific client. Without computer assistance, hand scoring of a multitude of domains and a variety of scores can be a lengthy, tedious, and time-consuming process. The complicated scoring and the use of a difficult semistructured interview technique make training sessions for examiners highly desirable.

THE INTERPRETATION AND USE OF ADAPTIVE BEHAVIOR INFORMATION

Persons who are delayed or deficient in development are likely to have more difficulty in adapting to the environment than normally developing persons and will be less able to meet societal demands. It is these deficiencies in adaptive behavior that usually determine the individual's needs for programs or services and/or for legal actions. For this reason, adaptive behavior information is useful for a variety of clinical, educational, and habilitative purposes. In our discussion, we have organized the use of adaptive behavior information according to four broad areas (DeStefano & Linn, 1987): identification/placement; program planning; monitoring of student/client progress; and program evaluation/research.

Identification and Placement

Assessment of adaptive behavior can identify behavioral and affective strengths and deficiencies in an individual or group. This pattern of strengths and deficiencies is a useful tool when making a diagnosis of a specific handicapping condition or determining whether an individual meets the criteria of a target group. The use of adaptive behavior scores, in addition to intelligence or achievement test data, provides information on the impact of the handicap of on individual's day-to-day life, which can then be compared with intellectual potential and/or academic performance for full information in making a diagnosis.

Patterns of adaptive behavior often suggest the most suitable service placement for an individual. In infancy and early childhood, deficits in sensory–motor development, in acquisition of self-help and communication skills, and in development of socialization skills point to needs for medical services, early childhood education, and/or family counseling. During childhood and early adolescence, deficits in learning and coping skills indicate needs for specialized educational, psychological, prevocational, and recreational programs. In late adolescence and adult years, deficits indicate needs for vocational training and placement, independent living skills training, and a variety of supportive services.

Diagnosing Mental Retardation

As discussed earlier, deficits in adaptive behavior must exist concurrently with significantly subaverage (IQ of 70–75 or below) intellectual functioning before a diagnosis of mental retardation can be made (Grossman, 1983). Deficits in adaptive behavior are determined by clinical assessment and, usually, the administration of standardized scales. According to these criteria, children who

have normal social development outside of school should not be classified as mentally retarded, regardless of IQ or academic achievement. It is absolutely necessary, therefore, that each initial diagnosis of mental retardation include some measure of adaptive behavior.

The importance of the construct does not end there. Within the framework of the definition of mental retardation, an individual may meet the criterion of mental retardation at one time in life and not at some other time. He or she may change status as a result of changes in intellectual functioning, adaptive behavior, societal expectations, or other known and unknown factors. The decision to classify an individual as mentally retarded at any given time should always be made in relation to behavioral standards and norms and in comparison to the individual's chronological age group (Grossman, 1983). For this reason, assessment of adaptive behavior remains a necessary part of all psychological re-evaluations throughout a person's lifespan.

Declassification

Strict adherence to the use of existing adaptive behavior scales may lead to large numbers of students' being "declassified" (i.e., rendered ineligible for special education programs for the mildly retarded). Depending on the adaptive behavior measure used, research indicates that adaptive behavior assessment does reduce overrepresentation of minorities in special classes for mental retardation. Fisher (1978) reported a high rate of declassification among all groups as a result of the direct use of the ABIC in classification/placement decisions. Serious questions exist concerning whether these changes are beneficial to children.

Studies of the characteristics of children declassified through the use of adaptive behavior have produced these findings (Fisher, 1978; Scott, 1979): One-half of the declassified students were eligible for other special education or remedial classes; however, the other half were not eligible for any existing special services, even though their intellectual and academic performance was below average. Simply returning these students to regular classes does nothing about their aptitude and achievement problems. To deny or ignore the educational problems experienced by declassified children would be naive and inhumane.

Progress is being made toward refining the classification system to resolve this dilemma. Some programs have chosen to maintain traditional classification systems, but base placement decisions upon need rather than degree of deviation from normal. Others have introduced behavioral descriptors such as "educationally disadvantaged" or "educationally handicapped" to describe those programs delivering remedial and compensatory services to students who do not meet criteria for admission into programs for the mildly mentally retarded because of adequate adaptive behavior (quasi-retarded or "6-hour retarded" children).

Use with Other Special Populations

Although the salience of the adaptive behavior construct is most often associated with the identification of persons with mental retardation, adaptive behavior information is useful in the understanding of a number of other handicapping conditions. In the case of persons with physical handicaps or health impairments, adaptive behavior scores indicate the degree to which the handicaps interfere with daily functioning. Changes in adaptive behavior scores can result from the introduction of a new prosthetic device or piece of adaptive equipment, the acquisition of alternate methods of performing the task, or (in the case of a decrease in scores) a worsening of physical condition. In the case of emotional disturbance or chronic mental illness, adaptive behavior scores can indicate the extent to which the disorder affects socialization or self-maintenance, and changes in scores over time can be used to monitor the effectiveness of psychotherapy, drug treatment, or other interventions.

It is apparent that the way in which adaptive behavior is conceptualized and measured, along with the available service options, will have a significant influence on the identification/placement decisions that are made. Because many of the skill areas in which behavioral and educational interventions are used are also skill areas measured with adaptive behavior scales, the classification of an individual is directly related to program planning for service delivery.

Program Planning

Item analysis of an individual's performance on criterion-referenced and some norm-referenced measures of adaptive behavior can provide a basis for developing objectives for individualized education, treatment, and habilitation plans. In order to maximize normalization and integration for persons with handicaps, consideration of communication skills, daily living skills, socialization skills, sensory–motor skills, and level of independence should be a part of every program-planning session. The use of a profile of scores makes it possible to set priorities for the most needed training and to utilize client strengths when designing intervention strategies. Some adaptive behavior scales have been constructed specifically for the purpose of establishing training targets and of measuring progress before and after training (Sparrow et al., 1984).

The use of information on maladaptive behavior is also relevant to program planning. Tendencies to run away, be aggressive, engage in self-abuse, or express undesirable sexual behavior are behaviors that interfere with integration and optimal functioning and should be addressed in program plans.

Monitoring of Students/Client Progress

As stated in earlier sections, information obtained from standardized measures of adaptive behavior can provide an objective basis for comparisons of an individual's level of functioning over time; these enable a clinician to plot progress or to evaluate a training program. Comparisons can be made using scores on individual items, changes in raw scores, and (in some cases) changes in standard scores or percentile ranks. It is also possible to compare ratings of the same individual under different situations, to help determine situational influences on adaptive functioning.

Program Evaluation/Research

Adaptive behavior test scores provide a standardized way of reporting information between and within organizations. When one is describing a progam in an evaluation report or research article, adaptive behavior information, along with other assessment data, can be used to summarize the level of functioning of individuals in a program. In that way, persons unfamiliar with that program can quickly get a sense of the population served and of the relevance of findings from the program to their own student/client group. Adaptive behavior information is also valuable in reports for the purpose of governmental or agency planning. Establishing the number of people who are ambulatory, who can or cannot communicate needs, who have impaired sensory–motor functioning, or who can function in the community without supervision provides essential information for program development and budgeting. In addition to providing a description of the population served by a program, changes in adaptive behavior scores as a result of programmatic intervention can be used as an indicator of program effectiveness. Progress can be measured on an individual basis to provide information on how effectively an individualized program plan is meeting its goals and to suggest areas for future planning. Longitudinal data on adaptive behavior can also be collected and summarized for all individuals in a program as a measure of overall program success. Adaptive behavior data from similar instruments can be compared across programs to determine which intervention produced the greatest changes in adaptive behavior. Cross-group data can also be aggregated and used to represent the characteristics of the population served in similar programs in a state or region of the country.

In research, adaptive behavior scores are helpful in describing the characteristics of a group of subjects. Test scores can be used as independent variables, to stratify a sample, or as dependent variables, to measure impact of an intervention on various aspects of the construct.

NEEDS AND FUTURE DIRECTIONS

Data cited in the *Larry P. v. Riles* (1979) case indicated that the records for most children placed in programs for students with mild retardation in California did not include adaptive behavior data. At the same time, Smith and Polloway (1979) found that most of the recently published research in mental retardation did not report on the adaptive behavior levels of students. Coulter and Morrow (1978) stated that part of the problem was that quite a few states did not require adaptive behavior assessment, and those that did require it did not clearly define the concept or provide guidelines for selecting and using adaptive behavior measures.

There is evidence that this situation has improved in the last decade. Since the full implementation of P.L. 94-412 and its successors, P.L. 98-199 and 99-457, most states have developed guidelines for the assessment of adaptive behavior, and many have strict criteria regarding the adaptive behavior instruments and scores to be used (Harrison, 1987; Patrick & Reschly, 1982). In a survey of over 100 federally funded special education programs, DeStefano and Linn (1987) found that next to intelligence testing, adaptive behavior assessment was the type of assessment most frequently carried out by the programs.

As the use of adaptive behavior information has become more prevalent, the number of instruments available has also grown, and their quality has improved. A few of the newer instruments have national norms based on 1980 census data. Their standardizations were carried out with a rigor previously associated only with the development of intelligence tests. Despite these points of progress, there is still work to be done concerning the measurement of adaptive behavior. First, the reliability and validity of assessing "typical" performance through third-party interviews versus clinical or naturalistic observation must still be tested. Ways of improving interview methods must also be tried. Second, we need to better understand the advantages of obtaining adaptive behavior information from several informants, each of whom is familiar with a particular setting in an individual's life, over the current practice of using a single respondent to provide information across a number of settings. Third, the relationship of adaptive behavior scores to other educational and independent living variables, such as classroom behavior, peer relations, teacher ratings, employability, and independent living status, is necessary to clarify the importance of the construct for identification, placement, and program planning. Finally, the fate of "declassified" children, or those who fail to qualify for special assistance on the basis of adaptive behavior scores, must be investigated, and the relative effectiveness of the various strategies for serving these students should be documented and disseminated so that local education agencies can move quickly to accommodate this underserved group.

The 1970s and 1980s were a time when concern with providing more effective and fairer assessment and interventions for children and adults with handicaps resulted in a reawakening of interest in adaptive behavior. This new energy has increased and improved our technology to assess this construct. Given the recent federal legislation that identifies successful transition from school and adjustment to adult life as the primary goal of education in general and special education in particular (Will, 1983), the importance of adaptive behavior assessment has never been greater and should increase in the years to come.

REFERENCES

Balthazar, E. E. (1971). *Scales of Functional Independence*. Palo Alto, CA: Consulting Psychologists Press.

Balthazar, E. E. (1973). *Scales of Social Adaptation*. Palo Alto, CA: Consulting Psychologists Press.

Bersoff, D. (1981). Testing and the law. *American Psychologist, 36*(10), 1047–1056.

Bruininks, R. J., Hill, B. K., Weatherman, R. F., & Woodcock, R. N. (1986). *Inventory for client and agency planning*. Allen, TX: DLM Teaching Resources.

Bruininks, R. J., Woodcock, R. W., Weatherman, R. F., & Hill, B. K. (1984). *Scales of Independent Behavior*. Allen, TX: DLM Teaching Resources.

Buckley, K., & Oakland, T. (1977, August). *Contrasting localized norms on Mexican–American children on the*

ABIC. Paper presented at the annual meeting of the American Psychological Association, San Francisco.

Coulter, A., & Morrow, H. (1978). *The concept and measurement of adaptive behavior*. New York: Grune & Stratton.

Cronbach, L. J. (1970). *Essentials of psychological testing*. New York: Harper & Row.

DeStefano, L., & Linn, R. (1987). *Review of student assessment instruments and practices*. Urbana: Transition Institute, University of Illinois.

Diana v. State Board of Education, No. C-7037 RFP (N.D. Cal. 1970).

Doll, E. A. (1940). A social basis of mental diagnosis. *Journal of Applied Psychology, 24,* 160–169.

Doll, E. A. (1953). *Measurement of social competence: A manual for the Vineland Social Maturity Scale*. Circle Pines, MN: American Guidance Services.

Education for All Handicapped Children Act of 1975, P.L. 94-142, 20 U.S.C. §1401 (1975).

Education for All Handicapped Children Act Amendments, P.L. 98-199 (1983).

Education for All Handicapped Children Act Amendments, P.L. 99-457 (1986).

Fisher, A. (1978, August). *Four approaches to classification of mental retardation*. Paper presented at the annual meeting of the American Psychological Association, Toronto.

Grossman, H. J. (Ed.). (1973). *Manual on terminology and classification in mental retardation*. Washington, DC: American Association on Mental Deficiency.

Grossman, H. J. (Ed.). (1977). *Manual on terminology and classification in mental retardation*. Washington, DC: American Association on Mental Deficiency.

Grossman, H. J. (Ed.). (1983). *Classification in mental retardation*. Washington, DC: American Association on Mental Deficiency.

Guadalupe v. Tempe Elementary School District, No. 71-435 (D. Ariz. 1972).

Halpern, A., Irvin, L., & Landman, J. (1979). *Tests for Everyday Living*. Monterey, CA: CTB/McGraw-Hill.

Harrison, P.L. (1985). *Vineland Adaptive Behavior Scales, Classroom Edition Manual*. Circle Pines, MN: American Guidance Service.

Harrison, P. L. (1987). Adaptive behavior. In C. R. Reynolds & L. Mann (Eds.), *Encyclopedia of special education* (pp. 34–35). New York: Wiley.

Heber, R. (1959). A manual on terminology and classification in mental retardation (2nd ed.). [Monograph supplement]. *American Journal of Mental Deficiency*.

Heber, R. (1961). Modification in the manual of terminology and classification in mental retardation. *American Journal of Mental Deficiency, 65,* 499–500.

Heber, R. (1962). Mental retardation: Concept and classification. In E. Trapp & P. Himelstein (Eds.), *Readings on the exceptional child* (pp. 69–81). New York: Appleton-Century-Crofts.

Kagin, E. F. (1968). Adaptive behavior and mental retardation during the Renaissance and Reformation. *Proceedings of the 76th Annual Convention of the American Psychological Association, 3,* 687–688.

Kazimour, K., & Reschly, D. (1980). *The relationship of the ABIC to ability, achievement, and sociocultural background*. Unpublished manuscript, Iowa State University.

Leland, H. (1973). Adaptive behavior and mentally retarded behavior. In R. Eyman, E. Myers, & G. Targan (Eds.), *Sociobehavioral studies in mental retardation* (pp. 91–100). Washington, DC: American Association on Mental Deficiency.

Leland, H. (1978). Theoretical considerations on adaptive behavior. In A. Coulter & H. Morrow (Eds.), *The concept and measurement of adaptive behavior*. New York: Grune & Stratton.

Leland, H., Shellhaas, M., Nihira, K., & Foster, R. (1967). Adaptive behavior: A new dimension in the classification of the mentally retarded. *Mental Retardation Abstracts, 4*, 359–387.

Mercer, J. R. (1970). Sociological perspectives on mild mental retardation. In H. Haywood (Ed.), *Sociocultural aspects of mental retardation*. New York: Appleton-Century-Crofts.

Mercer, J. R. (1977). The struggle for children's rights: Critical juncture for school psychology. *School Psychology Digest, 6*, 4–18.

Mercer, J. R., & Lewis, J. E. (1978). *Adaptive Behavior Inventory for Children*. New York: Psychological Corporation.

Meyers, C. E., Nihira, K., & Zetlin, A. (1979). The measurements of adaptive behavior. In N. R. Ellis (Ed.), *Handbook of mental deficiency: Psychological theory and research* (2nd ed., pp. 215–253). Hillside, NJ: Erlbaum.

Nihira, K., Foster, R., Shellhaas, M., Leland, H., Lambert, N., & Windmiller, M. (1981). *AAMD Adaptive Behavior Scale, School Edition*. Monterey, CA: Publisher's Test Service.

Oakland, T. (Ed.). (1977). *Psychological and educational assessment of minority children*. New York: Brunner/Mazel.

Patrick, J. L., & Reschly, D. J. (1982). Relationship of state educational criteria and demographic variables to school systems prevalence of mental retardation. *American Journal of Mental Deficiency, 86*, 351–360.

President's Committee on Mental Retardation. (1970). *The six-hour retarded child*. Washington, DC: U.S. Government Printing Office.

President's Committee on Mental Retardation. (1975). *Mental retardation: The known and unknown*. Washington, DC: U.S. Government Printing Office.

Regulations Implementing Education for All Handicapped Children Act of 1975, P.L. 94-142. Fed. Reg. 42,474 (1977).

Reschly, D. (1982). Assessing mild mental retardation: The influence of adaptive behavior, socioeconomic status and prospects for nonbiased assessment. In C. R. Reynolds & T. B. Gutkin (Eds.), *Handbook of school psychology* (pp. 209–242). New York: Wiley.

Richmond, B. O., & Kicklighter, R. H. (1979). *Children's Adaptive Behavior Scale*. Atlanta: Humanics Limited.

Robinson, N. M., & Robinson, H. B. (1976). *The mentally retarded child*. New York: McGraw-Hill.

Sattler, J. M. (1982). *Assessment of children's intelligence and special abilities* (2nd ed.). Boston: Allyn & Bacon.

Scott, S. (1979). *Identification of declassified students: Characteristics and needs of the population*. Paper presented at the annual meeting of the American Psychological Association, New York.

Smith, J., & Polloway, E. (1979). The dimensions of adaptive behavior in mental retardation research: An analysis of recent practices. *American Journal of Mental Deficiency, 84*, 203–206.

Sparrow, S. S., Balla, D. A., & Cicchetti, D. V. (1984). *Vineland Adaptive Behavior Scales*. Circle Pines, MN: American Guidance Service.

Turnbull, H. (1978). The past and future impact of court decisions in special education. *Phi Delta Kappan, 60*, 523–527.

Will, M. (1983). *OSERS programming for the transition of youth with disabilities: Bridges from school to working life*. Washington, DC: Office of Special Education and Rehabilitative Services, U.S. Department of Education.

Witt, J. C., & Martens, B. K. (1984). Adaptive behavior: Test and assessment issues. *School Psychology Review, 13*, 478–484.

APPENDIX 19.1. SUMMARY OF ADAPTIVE BEHAVIOR ASSESSMENT INSTRUMENTS

Name of instrument; author(s); date of publication	Publisher	Age range	Population type			Competencies assessed								
			Clinical	School	Residential	Physical development/sensory–motor/locomotion	Language and communication	Academic skills	Vocational and occupational skills	Economic/budgetary skills	Social skills	Self-direction	Self-help/independent maintenance/daily living skills	Maladaptive behavior
AAMD Adaptive Behavior Scale, School Edition (ABS-SE; Nihira et al., 1981)	CTB/McGraw-Hill	3–16 years	×	×		×	×		×	×	×	×	×	×
Adaptive Behavior Inventory for Children (ABIC; Mercer & Lewis, 1978)	Psychological Corporation	5–11 years		×					×	×	×		×	
Balthazar Scales of Adaptive Behavior I: Scales of Functional Independence (BSAB = I; Balthazar, 1971)	Consulting Psychologists Press	All ages, profoundly and severely handicapped	×	×	×								×	
Balthazar Scales of Adaptive Behavior II: Scales of Social Adaptation (BSAB = II; Balthazar, 1973)	Consulting Psychologists Press	All ages, profoundly and severely retarded and emotionally disturbed	×		×		×				×	×	×	
Children's Adaptive Behavior Scale (CABS; Richmond & Kicklighter, 1979)	Stoelting	5–10 years		×			×		×	×	×	×	×	
Scales of Independent Behavior (SIB; Bruininks, Woodcock, Weatherman, & Hill, 1984)	DLM Teaching Resources	Infants–adults (including 40 years and above)	×	×	×	×	×		×	×	×		×	×
Tests for Everyday Living (TEL; Halpern, Irvin, & Landman, 1979)	CTB/McGraw-Hill	Adolescents (grades 7–12) and young adults, especially low-functioning students		×				×	×	×			×	
Vineland Adaptive Behavior Scales (VAB; Sparrow, Balla, & Cicchetti, 1984)	American Guidance Service	Survey Form and Expanded Form, birth to 18 years, 11 months and low-functioning adults; Classroom Edition, 3 years to 12 years, 11 months	×	×	×	×	×	×	×	×	×	×	×	×

[a]With extensive training in interviewing

Identification	Placement/programming	Monitoring progress	Program evaluation	Teacher	Diagnostician/psychologist	Paraprofessional	Teacher	Parent/caregiver	Child	Administration time	Individual	Group	Reliability and validity data available?	Grade equivalent/age	Percentile	Standard score	Norming/standardization information available?
×	×	×		×	×	×	×	×		Minimum 1 hour	×		Yes		×	×	Yes
×	×			×	×	×[a]		×		45 minutes	×		Yes		×	×	Yes
	×	×		×	×	×		×	×	Varies	×		Yes, but limited		×		Yes
	×	×		×	×	×			×	Varies	×		Yes, but limited			×	Yes
	×				×				×	Approximately 30–40 minutes	×		Yes		×	×	Yes
×	×	×	×	×	×	×	×	×		Broad Independence Scale, 45–60 minutes; Short Form Scale, 10–15 minutes; Early Development Scale, 10–15 minutes	×		Yes	×	×	×	Yes
	×			×	×				×	20–30 minutes for each of seven tests	×	×	Yes		×	×	Norming, No; standardization, yes
×	×	×	×		×	×[a]	×	×		Survey Form, 20–60 minutes; Expanded Form 60–90 minutes; Classroom Edition, 20 minutes	×		Yes	×	×	×	Yes

20

Assessment with the Vineland Adaptive Behavior Scales

PATTI L. HARRISON
The University of Alabama

T he Vineland Adaptive Behavior Scales (Sparrow, Balla, & Cicchetti, 1984a, 1984b, 1985) constitute a revision of the Vineland Social Maturity Scale (Doll, 1935, 1965), an instrument that paved the way for modern thought about mental retardation and adaptive behavior. Edgar A. Doll, author of the original Vineland, was a major pioneer in the field of mental retardation, as well as the objective assessment of adaptive behavior. His work at the Vineland Training School in Vineland, New Jersey focused on the relationship between mental deficiency and social competence. His concept of social competence, which he defined as "the functional ability of the human organism for exercising personal independence and social responsibility" (Doll, 1953, p. 10), later came to be called "adaptive behavior." Of Doll's (1940) six criteria of mental deficiency, he listed social incompetence as the first and most important criterion. He wrote that, because a social circumstance leads to the suspicion of mental deficiency, a mental diagnosis is incomplete if it does not begin with a sound estimate of the person's social competence and end with a prediction of what the person's social competence will be following prognosis or treatment.

Doll (1953) contributed many ideas to the understanding and measurement of adaptive behavior that remain important parts of current conceptions of adaptive behavior and modern adaptive behavior scales. One of the most important ideas is that adaptive behavior is developmental in nature; what is considered to be adequate adaptive behavior is dependent on the age of the person under evaluation. A second enduring contribution of Doll is that adaptive behavior is multidimensional and encompasses a variety of domains. He identified eight categories of items on the Vineland Social Maturity Scale: Self-Help General, Self-Help Dressing, Self-Help Eating, Communication, Self-Direction, Socialization, Locomotion, and Occupation. Current ideas about adaptive behavior continue to reflect its multidimensional nature. Another of Doll's ideas that has withstood the test of time concerns the method of administering adaptive behavior scales. The Vineland Social Maturity Scale was designed to be administered to a third-party informant who is familiar with the activities of the person being evaluated. The third-party method of administration is particularly appropriate for the assessment of adaptive behavior. Because adaptive behavior is generally conceptualized as the daily activities in which a person engages to take care of himself or herself and get along with other people, the information supplied by a third party will be more valid than the direct administration of tasks. The third-party method also allows for the assessment of individuals who cannot participate in the administration of many tests, such as the severely handicapped and young children. Most modern adaptive behavior scales are administered to third parties, such as parents, caregivers, and teachers.

Doll's ideas about adaptive behavior were undoubtedly important for present-day concepts about adaptive behavior. However, for many years after his development of the Vineland Social Maturity Scale in the 1930s, intelligence test scores served as the first (and usually only) criterion of mental retardation. It was not until the 1960s that there began to be increased interest in the assessment of adaptive behavior. According to Meyers, Nihira, and Zetlin (1979), interest began to increase at this time for two reasons. First, there was growing criticism over the use of intelligence tests to classify minority individuals as mentally retarded, because of the potential bias in intelligence tests. Second, concerns about characteristics of mentally retarded people in institutions led to the need to teach these people adaptive skills for placement in community settings, or deinstitutionalization. These two issues resulted in litigation and legislation that focused on the assessment of adaptive behavior.

In 1959, the American Association on Mental Deficiency (AAMD) published its first manual and officially included deficits in adaptive behavior, in addition to subaverage intellectual functioning, as an integral part of the definition of mental retardation (Heber, 1959). Revised editions of the manual (Grossman, 1973, 1977, 1983) further emphasized the importance of adaptive behavior in the classification of mental retardation. However, the assessment of adaptive behavior of children probably received its greatest influence from the passage of the Education for All Handicapped Children Act of 1975 (P.L. 94-142), which followed a similar act—the Rehabilitation Act of 1973, a law to promote the education, employment, and training of the handicapped. P.L. 94-142 requires that deficits in adaptive behavior be substantiated before a child is classified as mentally retarded. Furthermore, it recognizes the importance of adaptive behavior for children with handicaps other than mental retardation.

Currently, adaptive behavior assessment is routine before a person is classified as mentally retarded. Although the history of adaptive behavior assessment lies in the field of mental retardation, adaptive behavior scales are being used more and more often with individuals with handicaps other than mental retardation, to determine the extent to which the handicaps affect daily functioning (Harrison, 1985; Sparrow, Balla, & Cicchetti, 1984c, 1984d). For instance, adaptive behavior assessment is commonly conducted with emotionally disturbed children (Sparrow et al., 1986), hearing-impaired and visually handicapped children (Meacham, Kline, Stovall, & Iceman, 1987), learning-disabled children (Weller & Strawser, 1981), physically handicapped children (Pollingue, 1987), and brain-injured children (Harrison, 1984).

Adaptive behavior scales are typically used for two primary purposes with children (Coulter, 1980). The first purpose is to obtain data for the identification of handicaps (e.g., educable mental retardation) and placement of children in special education programs. The second purpose is to obtain information to plan educational and treatment programs for children, in order to include social and self-help skills as part of interventions.

Adaptive behavior, according to the authors of the Vineland Adaptive Behavior Scales, is defined as "the performance of the daily activities required for personal and social sufficiency" (Harrison, 1985, p. 6; Sparrow et al., 1984a, p. 6, and 1984b, p. 6). The Vineland authors indicate that three important characteristics are inherent to the definition of adaptive behavior, as well as to the use of the Vineland. The first is that adaptive behavior is age-related; the activities necessary for self-sufficiency increase and become more complex as individuals grow older. The second characteristic is that adaptive behavior is judged according to the expectation and standards of a person's society, as well as those of people in the society. Thus, adaptive skills required in the United States may not be the same as the skills required in other countries, and a person's adaptive behavior is considered to be adequate if those people who live, work, play, and otherwise interact with him or her believe that it is. The third characteristic, perhaps the most important when using the Vineland and most other adaptive behavior scales, is that adaptive behavior is defined by performance, not ability. If a person has the ability to use adaptive skills, but does not do so because of lack of motivation or some other reason, his or her adaptive behavior is considered inadequate.

OVERVIEW OF THE VINELAND ADAPTIVE BEHAVIOR SCALES

The Vineland Adaptive Behavior Scales consists of three versions, which can be used together or separately: the Survey Form, the Expanded Form, and the Classroom Edition. Each version measures adaptive behavior in four domains. An overview of the three versions and their content and organization is provided in this section of the chapter.

Content

Each of the three versions of the Vineland measures four domains of adaptive behavior, and each of the domains contain two or three subdomains. The Communication domain has three subdomains: Receptive, oral communicated used by others that an individual understands; Expressive, the oral communication used by an individual; and Written, an individual's understanding and use of the basic reading and writing skills necessary for daily functioning. The three subdomains of the Daily Living Skills domain are Personal, or eating, dressing, grooming, and health care skills; Domestic, or cooking and housekeeping skills; and Community, or money, safety, telephone, time, and job skills. The Socialization domain consists of three subdomains: Interpersonal Relationships, or getting along with others; Play and Leisure Time, or an individual's performance of activities such as games, hobbies, and watching television; and Coping Skills, an individual's responsibility and sensitivity to others. The two subdomains of the Motor Skills domain are Gross, or an individual's use of the arms and legs for movement and coordination; and Fine, a individual's use of hands and fingers for manipulating objects. (Because motor skills required for adaptive behavior reach a peak at a relatively young age, the Motor Skills domain is optional for individuals age 6 and

older and is administered only if a motor deficit is suspected.) The four adaptive behavior domains are combined to form the Adaptive Behavior Composite, a measure of general adaptive behavior. The Vineland Survey Form and Expanded Form also include the optional Maladaptive Behavior domain, which contains items dealing with negative behavior that may interfere with adaptive functioning. Table 20.1 contains samples of items from the Vineland domains.

Three item scores are used with the Vineland. An item is scored 2 if an individual usually and successfully performs the activity described by the item. A score of 1 indicates that the activity is emergent, or sometimes performed or performed with partial success. An item is score 0 if the activity is seldom or never performed. The Survey Form and Expanded Form have two additional scores. A score of N may be used if the activity is not performed because of limiting circumstances—for instance, the individual's household does not have a telephone or television. A score of DK may be used if the parent or caregiver has no knowledge of the individual's performance of the activity.

Versions

The Interview Edition, Survey Form provides a norm-referenced approach to the measurment of adaptive behavior and assesses strengths and weaknesses in specific areas of adaptive behavior. It is administered to a parent or other primary caregive of an individual from birth to 18 years, 11 months of age, or to the parent or primary caregiver of a low-functioning adult. Administration requires 20–60 minutes. The method of administration used with the Survey Form is a semistructured clinical interview. Instead of reading questions to the respondent, the interviewer uses his or her own probes and questions to elicit descriptions of the individual's activites from the respondent. The interviewer uses more specific probes and questions as necessary to obtain information to score the items. This method which was originally developed by Doll (1953) for use with the Vineland Social Maturity Scale, is felt to create a more positive atmosphere and to yield more accurate results than reading the questions to the respondent or asking the

TABLE 20.1. Samples of Items from the Vineland Adaptive Behavior Scales

Domain	Subdomain	Item
Communication	Receptive	Follows instructions requiring an action and an object.
		Listens to a story for at least 5 minutes.
	Expressive	Speaks in full sentences.
		Gives complex directions to others
	Written	Prints or writes own first and last name.
		Reads adult newspaper stories.
Daily Living Skills	Personal	Bathes or showers without assistance.
		Covers mouth and nose when coughing or sneezing.
	Domestic	Makes own bed when asked.
		Uses household cleaning products appropriately and correctly.
	Community	Tells time by 5-minute segments.
		Manages own money without assistance.
Socialization	Interpersonal Relationships	Has a group of friends.
		Initiates conversations on topics of particular interest to others.
	Play and Leisure Time	Follows rules in simple games without being reminded.
		Watches television or listens to radio for information about a particular area of interest.
	Coping Skills	Uses appropriate table manners without being told.
		Apologizes for mistakes or errors in judgment.
Motor Skills	Gross	Walks down stairs with alternating feet without assistance.
		Climbs on high play equipment.
	Fine	Opens doors by turning and pulling doorknobs.
		Draws more than one recognizable form with pencils and crayons.
Maladaptive Behavior		Has temper tantrums.
		Runs away.

Note. From *Vineland Adaptive Behavior Scales* by S. S. Sparrow, D. A. Balla, and Domenic V. Cicchetti, 1984/1985, Circle Pines, MN: American Guidance Service. Copyright 1984/1985 by the American Guidance Service. Reprinted by permission.

respondent to complete a questionnaire. It also allows the interviewer to use clinical skills when discussing sensitive issues with parents or caregivers.

The 297 items of the Survey Form are arranged by domain. Within each domain, items are listed in developmental order, and subdomains are identified. The administration of items in each domain begins at the item designated for the individual's age. Then basal and ceiling rules are established that restrict administration and scoring of the items in the domain to the items appropriate for the individual's level of functioning.

The primary purpose of the Interview Edition, Expanded Form is to provide a systematic basis for planning objectives and activities for intervention programs. Like the Survey Form, the Expanded Form also yields norm-referenced information and an assessment of strengths and weaknesses in adaptive behavior. The Expanded Form is administered to parents or caregivers of individuals from birth to 18 years, 11 months of age, or to parents of caregivers of low-functioning adults. Administration requires 60–90 minutes, and the semistructured method is used for interviewing. The Expanded Form can be used in several ways. For example, the Expanded Form can be administered as a follow-up to the Survey Form to acquire specific program-planning information for deficits in adaptive behavior indicated by the Survey Form. The Expanded Form may also be used independently of the Survey Form when it is shown that an individual has deficits in adaptive behavior and specific plans are needed for intervention.

The Expanded Form has a total of 577 items, including all of the 297 items from the Survey Form. Items are arranged by subdomain. Within each subdomain, items are arranged in clusters of two to eight items, listed in developmental order. The items of the clusters represent sequential skills needed to master the highest level, or target, of the cluster. For example, a cluster in the Personal subdomain of the Daily Living Skill domain is "Using Tableware." The items in this cluster are as follows:

1. Feeds self with spoon.
2. Feeds self with fork.
3. Feeds self with spoon without spilling.
4. Holds spoon correctly.
5. Holds fork correctly.
6. Spreads food with table knife without assistance.
7. Cuts with table knife.
8. Uses spoon, fork, and knife competently.

A basal rule is applied during administration of the Expanded Form to limit administration to those clusters appropriate for the individual's functional level.

The Classroom Edition provides a norm-referenced measure of general adaptive behavior in the classroom, as well as of strengths and weaknesses in classroom adaptive behavior. This version of the Vineland consists of a questionnaire completed by a teacher. The age range for the Classroom Edition is from 3 years to 12 years, 11 months. The Classroom Edition requires about 20 minutes for a teacher to complete. An examiner is not required, but a qualified professional is needed to compute and in-

terpret the derived scores. The Classroom Edition may be used in conjunction with the Survey Form when it is necessary to assess a child's adaptive behavior from two points of view, a parent's and a teacher's. The Classroom Edition may also be used instead of the Survey Form when it is necessary to assess an individual's classroom rather than home behavior or when a parent is not available for a Survey Form interview.

The Classroom Edition contains a total of 244 items. About 80% of the items are also on the Survey Form. Additional items on the Classroom Edition measure academic activities related to survival skills (e.g., recognizing "$" and "%" symbols, adding and subtracting numbers). Items are arranged by subdomains. There are no basal and ceiling rules; teachers respond to all items in the questionnaire. However, teachers assign item scores of 2, 1, and 0 in one of two ways. If a teacher has sufficient opportunity to observe the activity described by the item, then an item score is assigned in a column labeled "Observed Performance." If a teacher is unsure of performance or has little opportunity to observe the activity, the teacher is required to estimate performance of the activity and assign an item score in a column labeled "Estimated Performance." The professional who scores the Classroom edition uses the information about "Observed Performance" and "Estimated Performance" to determine whether the teacher knows enough about the child's adaptive activities to be a valid respondent to the questionnaire.

TECHNICAL DATA

The Vineland Social Maturity Scale was characterized by a limited norm sample and inadequate support for reliability and validity. Many of the more recent adaptive behavior scales have unfortunately used small standardization samples as well, and their developers have not seemed to make many efforts to meet psychometric standards for assessment instruments. The Vineland Adaptive Behavior Scales, however, were developed with the philosophy that an adaptive behavior instrument should reflect the same painstaking methods used with and expected for intelligence and achievement tests.

Development and Standardization

The development of the Vineland Survey Form, Expanded Form, and Classroom Edition was a 6-year process that began with the writing and field testing of over 3,000 items. The items were reduced after the application of a series of criteria by the authors. These criteria included the representativeness of the items for daily activities, the lasting relevance of the items, and the amenability of the items to objective scoring procedures. The remaining items were included in a national item tryout with over 700 individuals. The national tryout provided the basis for item statistics and interrater reliability coefficients needed to construct the standardization version of the instrument.

The Survey Form of the Vineland was standardized with a national sample of 3,000 individuals from birth to 18 years, 11 months of age. Standardization took place in 24 states, and the standardization sample was stratified in order to match U.S. census figures according to sex, race or ethnic group, community size, region of the country, and parents' level of education. Supplementary norms for the Survey Form were provided by the following seven samples:

1,050 ambulatory and nonambulatory mentally retarded adults in residential facilities
800 ambulatory mentally retarded adults in residential facilities
250 nonambulatory mentally retarded adults in residential facilities
90 mentally retarded adults in nonresidential or community facilities
150 emotionally disturbed children in residential facilities
300 hearing-impaired children in residential facilities
200 visually handicapped children in residential facilities

The Expanded Form was not used in a standardization program. Instead, Rasch–Wright item calibration estimates permitted the generation of norms for the Expanded Form utilizing the Survey Form normative data.

The Classroom Edition was standardized with a national sample of 2,984 individuals in 38 states. The standardization sample was selected to match U.S. census figures for sex, race or ethnic group, community size, region of the country, and parents' level of education.

Reliability

The Vineland manuals summarize the results of three types of reliability studies: internal consistency, test–retest, and interrater (Harrison, 1985; Sparrow et al., 1984b, 1984c). Internal-consistency reliability coefficients, based on data from the national standardization sample, were determined using the split-half method. For the Survey Form, median internal-consistency coefficients ranged from .83 to .90 for the domains, and the median coefficient for the Adaptive Behavior Composite was .94. The median coefficients for the Expanded Form domains ranged from .86 to .95, and the median coefficient for the Adaptive Behavior Composite was .97. Median internal-consistency coefficients for the Classroom Edition domains ranged from .80 to .95, and the median coefficient for the Adaptive Behavior Composite was .98.

During a test–retest reliability study, the Survey Form was administered twice to the parents of 484 children. The same interviewers readministered the Survey Form to the same parents after a 2- to 4-week interval. Correlations between domain standard scores from the first and second administrations ranged from .81 to .86, and the correlation for the Adaptive Behavior Composite was .88.

Parents of a total of 160 children participated in an interrater reliability study with the Survey Form. Each parent in the study was interviewed twice by different interviewers, with a 1- to 14-day interval between the interviews. Correlations between scores from the two administrations ranged from .62 to .75 for the domains, and the correlation for the Adaptive Behavior Composite was .74.

Validity

Research conducted with the Vineland during its development and after its publication support its validity for a variety of uses. This research, which includes developmental progression of scores, factor analysis, profile of scores for groups of handicapped individuals, and correlations with other tests, is summarized in this section.

The mean domain raw scores obtained from the national standardization samples (see Harrison, 1985; Sparrow et al., 1984c, 1984d) show a systematic developmental progression. The raw scores for Vineland subdomains do not show the same increase with age; this is expected, because performance on many subdomains is expected to begin at certain ages and peak at other ages. For example, receptive communication peaks at about age 6 or 7, and written communication begins at about age 5. However, the subdomains show a developmental increase through the ages for which the items of a subdomain are developmentally appropriate.

Factor analyses were conducted for the Vineland domains and subdomains (Harrison, 1985; Sparrow et al., 1984c, 1984d). Principal components analyses of the domains produced one significant factor, supporting the Adaptive Behavior Composite as a measure of general adaptive behavior. Principal factor analysis of the subdomains generally confirmed the organization of the subdomains into their respective domains.

Profiles of handicapped individuals on the Vineland indicate that groups who would be expected to have different levels of adaptive behavior from those of normal individuals do, in fact, demonstrate these differences. Investigations indicated that the following groups have a lower level of performance than the national standardization sample on the Vineland Survey Form: institutionalized mentally retarded adults (Childers & Bolen, 1985), developmentally delayed preschoolers (Harrison & Ingram, 1984), and developmentally handicapped children (Ronka, 1984). Furthermore, Rainwater-Bryant (1985) found that learning-disabled children had higher Survey Form scores than mentally retarded children. Sparrow et al. (1984c) reported that hearing-impaired and emotionally disturbed children had higher scores on the Survey Form than visually handicapped children, and Sparrow et al. (1986) reported that a group of normal children had higher scores than a group of children with atypical mild personality development. Wald et al. (1986) found that a group of normal children had higher Survey Form scores than a group of

children who had meningitis during the first 6 months of life.

Similar findings were reported for the Classroom Edition. Behaviorally disordered (Mealor & Olson, 1986) and developmentally handicapped children (Ronka, 1984) exhibited lower performance than the Classroom Edition standardization sample. Rainwater-Bryant (1985) reported that learning-disabled children had higher scores than mentally retarded children.

Studies investigating the relationship between the Vineland and other measures of adaptive behavior generally found moderate correlations. However, as indicated elsewhere (Harrison, 1987), most adaptive behavior scales exhibit moderate correlations with each other, perhaps because adaptive behavior scales are generally not developed on the basis of a unitary concept of general adaptive behavior. Sparrow et al. (1984c) reported moderate correlations between the Survey Form and the Vineland Social Maturity Scale for a group of normal children. (It should also be noted that Sparrow et al., 1984c, found that the mean Survey Form Adaptive Behavior Composite was about 24 points lower than the mean Social Quotient of the Vineland Social Maturity Scale, highlighting the effect of the 50 years' difference between the norming of the two instruments.) Childers and Bolen (1985), Altepeter and Moscato (1982), and Britton and Eaves (1986) reported moderate to high correlations between the Vineland Survey Form or Classroom Edition and the Vineland Social Maturity Scale for samples of institutionalized mentally retarded adults, hearing-impaired children, and educable and trainable mentally retarded children, respectively. Other investigators reported low to moderate correlations between the Vineland and the Adaptive Behavior Inventory for Children or the AAMD Adaptive Behavior Scale for samples of normal children, developmentally handicapped children, trainable mentally retarded children, and institutionalized mentally retarded adults (Bensberg & Irons, 1986; Bolen, Durham, Childers, & Johnson, 1984; Bracken et al., 1984; Mealor, 1986; Rolka, 1984).

Several studies have compared the Vineland Survey Form and Classroom Edition for samples of normal children, children participating in Head Start programs, developmentally handicapped children, mentally retarded children, and learning-disabled children (Arffa, Rider, & Cummings, 1984; Harrison, 1985; Rainwater-Bryant, 1985; Ronka, 1984). Although the investigators generally found no significant differences between the scores on the two instruments, they also found low to moderate correlations. These findings suggest that the Survey Form and Classroom Edition are measuring two different aspects of adaptive behavior, and that both instruments should be administered to obtain a complete picture of children's adaptive functioning.

There have been several investigations of the relationship between the Vineland and measures of intelligence. The correlations between the Survey Form or Classroom Edition and various measures of intelligence were generally low to moderate for samples of normal children, children in Head Start programs, developmentally delayed preschool children, behaviorally disordered children, and institutionalized mentally retarded adults (Arffa et al., 1984; Durham, 1982; Guidubaldi, Cleminshaw, Perry, & Kehle, 1983; Harrison, 1985; Harrison & Ingram, 1984; Harrison & Kamphaus, 1984; Kopp, Rice, & Schumacher, 1983; Mealo & Olson, 1986). Moderate correlations between adaptive behavior and intelligence are expected because, as noted by Meyers et al. (1979), measurement of the two constructs differs in several respects. Keith, Fehrman, Harrison, and Pottebaum (1987) further investigated the nature of the relationship between intelligence and adaptive behavior, and used factor analysis to support the contention that adapted behavior (as measured by the Vineland Survey Form) and intelligence (as measured by the Kaufman Assessment Battery for Children) are two separate but related constructs.

USING THE VINELAND IN CHILD ASSESSMENT

As indicated earlier in this chapter, adaptive behavior scales have two primary uses: (1) identification of handicaps and placement of children in special education programs, and (2) planning of intervention programs. The use of the Vineland for these two purposes is discussed in this section of the chapter. In addition, three case studies are presented as examples of the use of the Vineland for child assessment.

Identification and Placement

The norm-referenced scores available for the Vineland Survey Form, Expanded Form, and Classroom Edition allow a determination of a child's general adaptive functioning, as well as strengths and weaknesses in different areas of adaptive behavior. The derived scores provide a basis for substantiating either deficits in adaptive behavior or adequate adaptive behavior. Deficits in adaptive behavior, as well as in intelligence, must be supported before a child can be classified as mentally retarded, according to P.L. 94-142. Vineland scores can be also used for the identification of other handicaps or problems. For example, Mercer (1973) hypothesized that children with emotional and behavioral disturbances have average intelligence and deficits in adaptive behavior, and Sparrow et al. (1986) provided some evidence that this pattern is found among children with mild atypical personality development. Adaptive behavior assessment of children with physical and sensory handicaps is important for the identification of the effects of these handicaps on daily functioning, although it is not necessarily important for identification of the handicaps (Meacham et al., 1987; Pollingue, 1987; Sparrow et al., 1984c, 1984d). Weller and Strawer (1987) suggested that different subtypes of learning-disabled children have characteristic patterns in adaptive behavior. Adaptive behavior scales are often used with learning-disabled children to rule out the possibility that mental retardation is the cause of their school-related problems.

Although the use of adaptive behavior scales is extending beyond the area of mental retardation, their primary use is still with mentally retarded children. However, there are several issues concerning the use of adaptive behavior scales for a mental retardation classification. First, there is no clear consensus on what constitutes a deficit in adaptive behavior (Reschly, 1986). In most states, guidelines give specific intelligence test scores that classify a child as mentally retarded (e.g., scores below 70), but there are usually no "cutoff" scores for adaptive behavior scales. Some professionals have developed their own "cutoff" scores similar to those for intelligence test scores (e.g., adaptive behavior scores below 70); others classify a child as mentally retarded if adaptive behavior is below average in one area, but average in other areas.

The second issue in using adaptive behavior for classification of mental retardation is declassification. Declassification occurs when children who are eligible for a mental retardation classification because of subaverage intellectual functioning are no longer eligible because they exhibit adequate adaptive behavior. Declassification may prevent children from receiving the negative label of "mentally retarded," but may also prevent children from receiving special education services they need. Reschly (1985) has suggested two levels of educable mental retardation to handle the issue of declassification. The first level, "educational retardation," would consist of children who have subaverage intelligence and school achievement, but average adaptive behavior. The second level, "mental retardation," would consist of children who have subaverage intelligence, school achievement, *and* adaptive behavior. Unfortunately, most states do not provide funding for education programs to serve children meeting Reschly's definition of educational retardation.

The norm-referenced information for the Vineland Survey Form, Expanded Form, and Classroom Edition provides a variety of ways to assess performance on the domains and subdomains. The primary type of score for the domains and the Adaptive Behavior Composite is a normalized standard score, with a mean of 100 and standard deviation of 15. The standard scores range from 20 to 160, or from about 5½ standard deviations below the mean to 4 standard deviations above the mean. Bands of error for five different confidence levels (68, 85, 90, 95, and 99) are provided to take into account the effects of measurement error when interpreting standard scores. National percentile ranks, stanines, and age equivalents are also available for the domains and the Adaptive Behavior Composite; in addition, performance may be described in terms of "adaptive levels" or descriptive categories (high, moderately high, adequate, moderately low, and low).

The primary norm-referenced information obtained for the Survey Form, Expanded Form, and Classroom Edition subdomains consists of adaptive levels (the descriptive categories of high, moderately high, adequate, moderately low, and low). Age equivalents are also available, but it is recommended that these be used sparingly, if at all, for the subdomains. Although age equivalents have long been used in psychological and educational testing, they leave much to be desired because the scale units are unequal; 1 year's growth has different meaning at different points in the age continuum and for different areas of adaptive behavior. In addition, the developmental nature of the Vineland subdomains discussed earlier often yields age equivalents that can be misleading because of the beginning and peaking of performance on the subdomains. For example, the highest possible age equivalent for the Receptive subdomain of the Survey Form is 7 years, 10 months.

The Maladaptive Behavior domain of the Survey Form and Expanded Form yields "maladaptive levels." Maladaptive levels are descriptive categories (nonsignificant, intermediate, significant) that indicate the frequency of maladaptive behavior.

The scores described above allow comparison between a child and the national normative sample of the Vineland. The Survey Form and Expanded Form also include supplementary norms to allow comparison between a child and the supplementary norm groups listed earlier in this chapter. The supplementary norms provide additional useful information about a handicapped child's performance on the Vineland. For example, when the Vineland Survey Form is administered for a hearing-impaired child and the child is compared to the national sample of "normal" children, his or her performance may be low in all areas. However, the child can be compared to the supplementary norm group of hearing-impaired children to obtain perhaps a more meaningful interpretation of his or her performance in relation to peers with the same handicap. Supplementary norm group percentile ranks and adaptive levels (descriptive categories of above average, average, and below average) are available for the domains and the Adaptive Behavior Composite. Subdomain performance may be described with supplementary norm group adaptive levels (above average, average, below average). The Maladaptive Behavior domain may be interpreted with supplementary norm group maladaptive levels of nonsignificant, intermediate, and significant.

The national and supplementary norms yield "interindividual" comparisons between a child and a norm group. After norm-referenced scores are obtained, fluctuations in the domain standard scores may be explored with "intraindividual" or "ipsative" comparisons, which provide comparisons of the child's performance in one area with his or her performance in another area. Three types of ipsative comparisons are included with the Vineland Survey Form, Expanded Form, and Classroom Edition interpretive systems. The first method requires determining the difference between each domain standard score and the average domain standard score, and indicates relative strengths and weaknesses in performance. This method is recommended over the other two methods because it provides the most succinct overview of domain score fluctuations. The second method requires determining differences between each pair of domain standard scores. The third method indicates the difference between the highest and lowest domain standard scores, or the range of domain standard scores.

The significance of any differences may be determined in two ways for each of the three methods of investigating domain standard score fluctuations. Statistical significance indicates that standard score differences are larger than chance fluctuations and may not be attributed to errors in measurement. Values required for statistical differences in Vineland domain standard scores are reported for the .05 and .01 levels of significance. The second method for determining significance is to compare a child's differences to differences actually obtained by the norm sample to determine whether the child's differences are abnormal or unusual. Values required to denote unusual differences are reported for five different levels: differences that occurred in only the extreme 16%, 10%, 5%, 2%, and 1% of the norm samples. The method of determining whether differences are unusual, as well as statistically significant, has been used increasingly with psychological tests since Kaufman (1976) found that statistically significant Verbal–Performance differences were in fact quite common in the Wechsler Intelligence Scale for Children—Revised (WISC-R) standardization sample. Thus, differences may be statistically significant, or may be "true" differences between different levels of performance, but may not be unusual or abnormal.

Intervention Planning

The norm-referenced information obtained from the Vineland Survey Form, Expanded Form, and Classroom Edition provides extensive information about a child's performance or lack of performance on daily behavior expected of others the same age. The norm-referenced information can be used in several ways to plan useful interventions. The profile of scores on the domains and the child's domain strengths and weaknesses can be used to select the areas that need to be addressed in an intervention program. For example, if Jessie's performance on the Motor Skills domain is low and relatively weak in comparison to her performance on other domains, a program that includes physical activities would appear to be needed. Review of a child's performance on the subdomains provides more specific information for planning programs. For example, David may have low performance on the Personal subdomain in comparison to adequate performance on other subdomains. His intervention program should probably then include training in skills such as dressing and grooming. Additional information can be obtained by reviewing individual items in the domains and subdomains.

The Vineland Expanded Form, unlike the Survey Form and Classroom edition, was specifically designed to yield systematic and comprehensive information for planning intervention programs. Among the key features of the Expanded Form are program-planning profiles. The program-planning profiles provide a means of graphing performance on each cluster of the Expanded Form and determining which clusters represent deficits for a child. If a child's performance on a cluster is found to be deficient, his or her performance on the individual items in the cluster can be reviewed to determine which activities are being performed adequately and which activities should form the objectives from an intervention program. For example, the "Listening and Attending" cluster of the Receptive domain contain items measuring increasing amounts of time spent listening to stories, educational presentations, and lectures. If Nancy, who is found to have a deficit in this cluster, only listens to an educational presentation for 5 minutes, an objective for Nancy's intervention program would be to increase her listening time until she has mastered the activity described by the target item of this cluster, "Attends to school or public lecture more than 15 minutes." The Expanded Form also includes a program-planning report, which may be used to develop an individual program plan for a child.

Case Illustrations

The cases of Heather, Andy, and Chad are used to illustrate the use of the Vineland Survey Form, Expanded Form, and Classroom Edition for identification and program planning.

Heather

Heather, aged 9 years, 2 months, has been referred for evaluation because of poor school performance. She is in the third grade for the second time. Heather's parents and teacher indicate that she is performing below grade level in all subjects, although she appears to be motivated when performing classroom activities. Her teacher reports that she is a nice but shy and withdrawn child, who is often teased by other children because she is rather large for her age. Heather has been administered the WISC-R and the Kaufman Test of Educational Achievement. Her WISC-R IQs are well below average: Verbal, 65; Performance, 62; and Full Scale, 62. Her scores on the achievement test support her parents' and teacher's reports: She is per-

forming well below others her age and grade in reading, spelling, and arithmetic. Previous testing indicates that she has no vision, hearing, or speech difficulties.

Heather's mother has been administered the Vineland Survey Form, and the results are reported in Table 20.2. Her general adaptive functioning is in the moderately low adaptive level, as seen by her Adaptive Behavior Composite of 80. However, the composite scores masks a range of performance of low to adequate on the adaptive behavior domains. Heather's functioning on the Daily Living Skills domain, with a standard score of 104, is in the adequate range. Her Socialization standard score of 84 is moderately low, and her score of 67 on the Communication domain is low. Her standard scores for each domain have been compared with her average standard score to determine areas of relative strengths and weaknesses. She exhibits a statistically significant strength ($p < .01$) in Daily Living Skills; the difference between her Daily Living Skills standard score and average standard score is unusual as well, occurring in only the extreme 5% of the standardization sample. Communication is a statistically significant weakness ($p < .01$) for Heather, and the difference between her Communication standard score and average standard score is unusual, occurring in only the extreme 10% of the standardization sample. Thus, Heather's moderately low score on the Adaptive Behavior Composite is less meaningful when one considers that she has a statistically significant and unusual strength in Daily Living Skills and weakness in Communication, relative to her own average level of functioning.

A review of Heather's subdomain adaptive levels provides more specific information about her adaptive functioning. In the area of her greatest strength, Daily Living Skills, she has adequate adaptive levels on the Personal and Community subdomains and a moderately high level on the Domestic subdomain. A review of her item scores on the Domestic subdomain indicates that she performs many household tasks not performed by most children her age, such as cooking and cleaning. In fact, Heather's mother reports that Heather has sole responsibility for her younger brother and sister while her parents are at work. On the Socialization do-

TABLE 20.2. Vineland Survey Form Results for Heather, Aged 9 Years, 2 Months

Domain standard sources with bands of error at 90% confidence level:
Communication: 67 ± 9
Daily Living Skills: 104 ± 8
Socialization: 84 ± 9
Adaptive Behavior Composite: 80 ± 6

Subdomain adaptive levels:

Communication	Receptive: Moderately low	
	Expressive: Moderately low	
	Written: Low	
Daily Living Skills	Personal: Adequate	
	Domestic: Moderately high	
	Community: Adequate	
Socialization	Interpersonal Relationships: Adequate	
	Play and Leisure Time: Adequate	
	Coping Skills: Moderately low	

Maladaptive Behavior domain maladaptive level: Intermediate

main, Heather has adequate adaptive levels on Interpersonal Relationships and Play and Leisure Time, but a moderately low adaptive level on Coping Skills. Her item scores in the Coping Skills subdomain suggest that Heather has problems in controlling her anger and hurt feelings. Finally, in the Communication domain, Heather's area of relative weakness, she has moderately low adaptive levels in the Receptive and Expressive subdomains and low performance in the Written subdomain. Her low performance in the Written subdomain is not unexpected, because the items measure skills in using reading and writing for daily functioning, and Heather's problems in these areas have been documented elsewhere.

Heather's score on the Maladaptive Behavior domain has been given an intermediate maladaptive level. A review of the items in this domain indicates that Heather laughs or cries too easily and is frequently withdrawn.

After this review of Heather's performance on the Vineland, the major question is whether or not she should be classified as mentally retarded. Undoubtedly, Heather's problems with academic activities have been clearly documented. However, she performs adequately in many areas of adaptive behavior. Her weakness on the Vineland Communication domain probably reflects her

poor academic skills and not necessarily poor general adaptive behavior. The professionals who evaluate a child such as Heather must make a difficult decision: Should Heather be declassified and denied the special educational services she so obviously needs, or should she be classified as mentally retarded despite her strengths in adaptive behavior? Whatever decision is made about Heather, any intervention plan made for her should include activities directed toward increasing her coping skills as well as her academic skills, and decreasing her withdrawal and her laughing and crying.

Andy

Andy, aged 15 years, 2 months, has participated in a program for the educable mentally retarded since he was 7 years old. His scores on the WISC-R, administered 2 years ago, are Verbal IQ, 62; Performance IQ, 65; and Full Scale IQ, 62. Andy's mother has been administered the Vineland Expanded Form so that objectives for interventions in adaptive behavior can be developed for the new school year. As seen in Table 20.3, his Adaptive Behavior Composite rates his general adaptive functioning as low. However, his functioning on the Communication and Daily Living Skills domains is low, while his performance on the Socialization domain is

TABLE 20.3. Vineland Expanded Form Results for Andy, Aged 15 Years, 2 Months

Domain standard scores with bands of error at 90% confidence level:

Communication: 64 ± 10

Daily Living Skills: 52 ± 7

Socialization: 92 ± 7

Adaptive Behavior Composite: 64 ± 6

Subdomain adaptive levels:

Communication	Receptive: Adequate
	Expressive: Moderately low
	Written: Moderately low
Daily Living Skills	Personal: Low
	Domestic: Low
	Community: Low
Socialization	Interpersonal Relationships: Adequate
	Play and Leisure Time: Adequate
	Coping Skills: Adequate

Maladaptive Behavior domain maladaptive level: Nonsignificant

---

adequate. His Socialization domain standard score is a statistically significant ($p < .01$) and unusual strength when compared to his own average level of functioning, occurring in only the extreme 1% of the standardization sample. On the other hand, his Daily Living Skills standard score is a statistically significant ($p < .01$) and unusual weakness, occurring in only the extreme 10% of the standardization sample.

His subdomain performance is fairly consistent with his domain performance. In the area of his greatest strength, Socialization, the subdomains are rated as adequate. In Communication, his subdomain performance is rated as adequate. In the area of his greatest weakness, Daily Living Skills, the subdomains are all rated as low. Andy's maladaptive behavior is rated as nonsignificant.

Because Andy's lowest level of performance is in Daily Living Skills, it has been decided that intervention plans should concentrate on this area. The program-planning profiles of the Expanded Form have been completed to determine the adaptive behavior clusters that represent specific deficits for Andy. A list of the clusters in the Personal subdomain that have been determined to be deficits is shown in Table 20.4. A list of intervention objectives obtained form the items of each of the clusters is presented in Table 20.5. As seen in Table 20.5, the clusters provide hierarchical objectives; the first objective for each cluster must be achieved before the second objective is started, and so on.

Chad

Chad, aged 10 years, 9 months, has been referred for evaluation because of acting-out behaviors at school. Chad's teacher reports that he often teases other children, starts fights, and disrupts the class with tantrums or laughter. The teacher feels that Chad has average or higher intelligence, but that he has poor academic performance because he does not attend to directions from the teacher or to his classroom work. Chad's school grades have been steadily falling since he entered school, although his standardized achievement tests show that he is performing at grade level; he is in danger of being retained in fifth grade.

Chad has been adminstered the Kaufman Assessment Battery for Children. His global scale scores are Sequential Processing, 98; Simultaneous Processing, 105; Mental Processing Composite, 102; and Achievement, 95. Thus, his intelligence is in the average range. Andy's teacher has completed the Vineland Classroom Edition, and the results are summarized in Table 20.6.

Chad's general adaptive functioning, as measured by the Classroom Edition, falls in

TABLE 20.4. Vineland Expanded Form Cluster Deficits in the Personal Subdomain for Andy

Caring for nose

Putting on shoes

Using tableware

Putting on clothes

Wearing clothing appropriate for weather

Beginning health care

Caring for hair

Caring for fingernails

Advanced health care

the moderately low range and is much lower than his intelligence. His scores on the domains indicate that his functioning on the Communication and Daily Living Skills domains is at adequate adaptive levels. His functioning on the Socialization domain, however, is low. He exhibits a relative strength on the Daily Living Skills that is both statistically significant ($p < .01$) and unusual, occurring in the extreme 16% of the standardization sample. As expected, his

functioning on the Socialization domain represents a relative weakness. The difference between his Socialization standard score and average domain standard score is statistically significant ($p < .01$) and unusual, occurring in the extreme 5% of the standardization sample.

Chad's functioning on the subdomains is consistent with his domain performance. All Communication and Daily Living Skills subdomains are ranked as adequate. The Socialization subdomains are ranked as moderately low or low. A review of the items in the Socialization subdomains indicates that Chad is not performing many activities appropriate for his age. For example, in the Interpersonal Relationships subdomain, his teacher reports that he does not have friends or initiate and respond to social exchanges. Item scores in the Play and Leisure Time subdomain indicate that he does not follow rules in games, share his possessions with others, or have hobbies. In the Coping Skills subdomain, Chad does not apologize for mistakes or follow school and community rules.

TABLE 20.5. Intervention Objectives Indicated by Vineland Expanded Form Cluster Deficits in the Personal Subdomain for Andy

Caring for nose
  1. Andy will care for nose without assistance.

Putting on shoes
  1. Andy will correctly lace shoes without assistance.
  2. Andy will tie shoelaces into a bow without assistance.

Using tableware
  1. Andy will cut with table knife.
  2. Andy will use spoon, fork, and knife competently.

Putting on clothes
  1. Andy will dress self completely, except for tying shoelaces.
  2. Andy will dress self completely, including tying shoelaces and fastening all fasteners.

Wearing clothing appropriate for weather
  1. Andy will dress in anticipation of changes in weather without being reminded.

Beginning health care
  1. Andy will avoid persons with contagious illnesses without being reminded.

Caring for hair
  1. Andy will care for hair without assistance.
  2. Andy will care for hair without being reminded and without assistance.

Caring for fingernails
  1. Andy will clean fingernails when asked.
  2. Andy will trim or file fingernails when asked.
  3. Andy will care for fingernails without being reminded and without assistance.

Advanced health care
  1. Andy will take own medicine appropriately.
  2. Andy will use oral thermometer without assistance.

TABLE 20.6. Vineland Classroom Edition Results for Chad, Aged 10 Years, 9 Months

Domain standard scores with bands of error at 90% confidence level:
  Communication: 85 ± 7
  Daily Living Skills: 87 ± 5
  Socialization: 63 ± 6
  Adaptive Behavior Composite: 75 ± 4

Subdomain adaptive levels:

Communication	Receptive: Adequate
	Expressive: Adequate
	Written: Adequate
Daily Living Skills	Personal: Adequate
	Domestic: Adequate
	Community: Adequate
Socialization	Interpersonal Relationships: Low
	Play and Leisure Time: Moderately low
	Coping Skills: Low

In conclusion, Chad, a boy with average intellectual functioning, appears to be exhibiting behavioral problems in the classroom that are interfering with his classroom academic performance. The results of the Vineland Classroom Edition suggest that he has a socialization weakness that is fairly pervasive in all areas of socialization. It is recommended that further evaluation of Chad's personality and behavior in a variety of settings at home and school be conducted, to obtain a total picture of his difficulties and determine the need for his placement in a special class for the behaviorally disordered.

Conclusion

The examples of Heather, Andy, and Chad provide brief illustrations of how the Vineland can be used to identify problems and plan interventions for the problems. When interpreting results from the Vineland, it is important to keep the following in mind: Although the Vineland is a well-standardized instrument, it should never be the sole source of information used to make decisions about handicaps or educational decisions. No instrument should ever be used in that way. Vineland results should be interpreted along with results from other tests, behavioral observations, and background information to obtain a complete picture of a child's functioning. Second, the Vineland requires a third party (parent, caregiver, or teacher) to supply information about a child's activities. The results should always be interpreted in light of the accuracy of the respondent's information. Third, one of the most important variables that affects information yielded by the Vineland is the age of the child being evaluated. For preschool children, the Vineland emphasizes behaviors such as following instruction, language skills, eating, toileting, dressing, getting along with playmates, drawing, and cutting. Skills such as basic reading and writing, grooming, beginning domestic skills, skills in using the telephone, time, and money, and extracurricular activities are the focus for elementary school-age children. For junior and senior high school students, the Vineland includes skills such as managing money, writing letters, job-related skills, and keeping appointments. Finally, parents play important roles in the intervention plans that result from the Vineland. Adaptive behavior, by definition, consists of activities required for daily functioning at home, as well as school. Any interventions planned for adaptive behavior must be communicated to parents and must take place *both* at home and school.

REFERENCES

Altepeter, T., & Moscato, E. M. (1982, March). *An equating study of the revised Vineland: Hearing-impaired sample.* Paper presented at the meeting of the National Association of School Psychologists, Toronto.

Arffa, S., Rider, L., & Cummings, J. A. (1984). [An investigation of cognitive and adaptive functioning of Head Start children]. Unpublished raw data.

Bensberg, G. J., & Irons, T. (1986). A comparison of the AAMD Adaptive Behavior Scales and the Vineland Adaptive Behavior Scales within a sample of persons classified as moderately and severely retarded. *Education and Training of the Mentally Retarded, 21*, 220–228.

Bolen, L. M., Durham, T. W., Childers, J. S., & Johnson, G. (1984). *Convergent and discriminant validation of the Vineland Adaptive Behavior Scales by the multitrait–multimethod matrix*. Unpublished manuscript.

Bracken, B., Brock, G., Ehlenbach, J., Gissal, T., Haas, M., Jernigan, V., Murray, A., Pedriani, A., & Stoiber, K. (1984). *The correlation between the revised Vineland and ABIC for school-age children*. Unpublished manuscript.

Britton, W. H., & Eaves, R. C. (1986). Relationships between the Vineland Adaptive Behavior Scales, Classroom Edition and the Vineland Social Maturity Scale. *American Journal of Mental Deficiency, 91*, 105–107.

Childers, J. S., & Bolen, L. M. (1985, April). *The Vineland scales: Comparing the old and new*. Paper presented at the convention of the National Association of School Psychologists, Las Vegas, NV.

Coulter, W. A. (1980). Adaptive behavior and professional disfavor: Controversies and trends for school psychologists. *School Psychology Review, 9*, 67–74.

Doll, E. A. (1935). A genetic scale of social maturity. *American Journal of Orthopsychiatry, 5*, 180–188.

Doll, E. A. (1940). A social basis of mental diagnosis. *Journal of Applied Psychology, 24*, 160–169.

Doll, E. A. (1953). *Measurement of social competence*. Circle Pines, MN: American Guidance Service.

Doll, E. A. (1965). *Vineland Social Maturity Scale*. Circle Pines, MN: American Guidance Service.

Durham, T. W. (1982, August). The relationship of the Vineland Adaptive Behavior Scales to intelligence among the institutionalized mentally retarded. In J. C. Childers (Chair), *Vineland Adaptive Behavior Scales: A measure of adaptive functioning*. Symposium conducted at the meeting of the American Psychological Association, Washington, DC.

Education for All Handicapped Children Act of 1975, P.L. 94-142, 20 U.S.C. § 1401 (1975).

Grossman, H. J. (Ed.). (1973). *Manual on terminology and classification in mental retardation* (1973 rev.). Washington, DC: American Association on Mental Deficiency.

Grossman, H. J. (Ed.), (1977). *Manual on terminology and classification in mental retardation* (1977 rev.). Washington, DC: American Association on Mental Deficiency.

Grossman, H. J. (Ed.), (1983). *Classification in mental retardation* (1983 rev.). Washington, DC: American Association on Mental Deficiency.

Guidubaldi, J., Cleminshaw, H., Perry, J., & Kehle, T. J. (1983, August). *Factors affecting the adjustment of children from divorced families*. Paper presented at the meeting of the American Psychological Association, Anaheim, CA.

Harrison, P. L. (1984, March). Assessment with the Vineland Adaptive Behavior Scales. In *Integrated functional assessment*. Symposium conducted at the Fourth International Symposium of Models and Techniques of Cognitive Rehabilitation, Indianapolis.

Harrison, P. L. (1985). *Vineland Adaptive Behavior Scales: Classroom Edition manual*. Circle Pines, MN: American Guidance Service.

Harrison, P. L. (1987). Research with adaptive behavior scales. *Journal of Special Education, 21*, 37–68.

Harrison, P. L., & Ingram, R. P. (1984, May). Performance of developmentally delayed preschoolers on the Vineland Adaptive Behavior Scales. In S. S. Sparrow (Chair), *The Vineland Adaptive Behavior Scales: Results of national standardization and clinical and research applications*. Symposium conducted at the meeting of the American Association on Mental Deficiency, Minneapolis.

Harrison, P. L., & Kamphaus, R. W. (1984, April). *Comparison between the K-ABC and Vineland Adaptive Behavior Scales*. Paper presented at the meeting of the National Association of School Psychologists, Philadelphia.

Heber, R. F. (1959). A manual on terminology and classification in mental retardation [Monograph suppl.]. *American Journal of Mental Deficiency, 64*.

Kaufman, A. S. (1976). Verbal–Performance IQ discrepancies on the WISC-R. *Journal of Consulting and Clinical Psychology, 44*, 739–744.

Keith, T. S., Fehrman, P. G., Harrison, P. L., & Pottebaum, S. M., (1987). The relation between adaptive behavior and intelligence: Testing alternative explanations. *Journal of School Psychology, 25*, 31–43.

Kopp, J. T., Rice, V. L., & Schumacher, K. M. (1984). *Test–retest reliability and concurrent validity of the Vineland Adaptive Behavior Scales*. Unpublished manuscript.

Meacham, F., Kline, M., Stovall, J., & Iceman, D. (1987). Adaptive behavior and sensory handicaps. *Journal of Special Education, 21*, 183–196.

Mealor, D. J. (1986). *A comparative analysis of adaptive behavior for elementary students*. Unpublished manuscript, University of Central Florida, Orlando.

Mealor, D. J., & Olson, J. L. (1986). *An analysis of intellectual functioning and adaptive behavior of behaviorally disordered students*. Unpublished manuscript, University of Central Florida, Orlando.

Mercer, J. (1973). *Labeling the mentally retarded*. Berkeley: University of California Press.

Meyers, C. E., Nihira, K., & Zetlin, A. (1979). The measurement of adaptive behavior. In N. R. Ellis (Ed.), *Handbook of mental deficiency: Psychological theory and research* (2nd ed., pp. 215–253). Hillsdale, NJ: Erlbaum.

Pollinger, A. (1987). Adaptive behavior and physical handicaps. *Journal of Special Education, 21*, 117–126.

Rainwater-Bryant, F. (1985). *Comparisons of parent-obtained and teacher-obtained adaptive behavior scores for handicapped children*. Unpublished doctoral dissertation, Memphis State University.

Rehabilitation Act of 1973, 29 U.S.C. § 794 (1973).

Reschly, D. J. (1985). Best practices: Adaptive behavior. In A. Thomas & J. Grimes (Eds.). *Best practices in school psychology* (pp. 353–368). Stratford, CT: National Association of School Psychologists.

Reschly, D. J. (1986, August). Adaptive behavior: Issues in classification, placement, program planning, and intervention. In F. M. Gresham (Chair), *Social com-

petence characteristics of the mildly handicapped. Symposium conducted at the 94th Annual Convention of the American Psychological Association, Washington, DC.

Ronka, C. S. (1984). *A comparison of adaptive behavior ratings: Vineland Adaptive Behavior Scales and AAMD Adaptive Behavior Scales—School Edition*. Unpublished doctoral dissertation, University of Cincinnati.

Sparrow, S. S., Balla, D. A., & Cicchetti, D. V. (1984a). *Vineland Adaptive Behavior Scales: Interview Edition, Survey Form*. Circle Pines, MN: American Guidance Service.

Sparrow, S. S., Balla, D. A., & Cicchetti, D. V. (1984b). *Vineland Adaptive Behavior Scales: Interview Edition, Expanded Form*. Circle Pines, MN: American Guidance Service.

Sparrow, S. S., Balla, D. A., & Cicchetti, D. V. (1984c). *Vineland Adaptive Behavior Scales: Interview Edition, Survey Form manual*. Circle Pines, MN: American Guidance Service.

Sparrow, S. S., Balla, D. A., & Cicchetti, D. V. (1984d). *Vineland Adaptive Behavior Scales: Interview Edition, Expanded Form manual*. Circle Pines, MN: American Guidance Service.

Sparrow, S. S., Balla, D. A., & Cicchetti, D. V. (1985). *Vineland Adaptive Behavior Scales: Classroom Edition*. Circle Pines, MN: American Guidance Service.

Sparrow, S. S., Rescorla, L. A., Provence, S., Condon, S. O., Goudreau, D., & Cicchetti, D. V. (1986). A follow-up of "atypical" children. *Journal of the American Academy of Child Psychiatry, 25,* 181–185.

Wald, E. R., Bergman, I., Taylor, H. G., Chiponis, D., Porter, C., & Kubek, K. (1986). *Long-term outcome of Group B streptococcal meningitis*. Unpublished manuscript.

Weller, C., & Strawser, S. (1981). *Weller–Strawser Scales of Adaptive Behavior*. Novato, CA: Academic Therapy Publications.

Weller, C., & Strawser, S. (1987). Adaptive behavior of subtypes of learning disabled individuals. *Journal of Special Education, 21,* 101–116.

V

SPECIAL TOPICS IN CHILDHOOD PERSONALITY ASSESSMENT

21

Interpretation in Cross-Cultural Personality Assessment

ROGELIO DIAZ-GUERRERO
ROLANDO DIAZ-LOVING
Universidad Nacional de Mexico

It was 1964. The Holtzman, Diaz-Guerrero, and Swartz (1975) cross-cultural, longitudinal, and overlapping study of school children in Mexico and the United States was underway. Many members of the American and Mexican teams were observing through a large Gessell chamber at the University of Texas while a typical assistant from each team—first the American group, then the Mexican group—applied the cross-cultural battery to a subject of his or her own culture. The atmospheres of the two assessment situations were strikingly different. The American tester was detached and, to the Mexican observers, cold. The American child was absorbed, challenged, and involved with the tasks. He/she gave to most of the observers the impression of competing with the tester. The noise level and commotion were minimal. The Mexican tester was vehement and expressive—to the American observers, overly warm. The Mexican child was responsive and involved in the interpersonal relation; it seemed that he/she wanted to please the tester with good answers to the tests. The noise level and commotion seemed high to the American observers.

The occasion was part of a systematic joint training in the administration and interpretation of the battery by the two groups of assistants. What should be done? Train the assistants to produce equivalence in the testing atmosphere? The decision was that the total atmosphere, including the contribution of the subjects, was a genuine expression of each culture and should be left alone. Many later studies with varied samples of Americans and Mexicans have shown that these atmospheres in the assessment situation result from behavioral dispositions, attitudes, and the different sociocultural premises of the two groups.

Interpretation in cross-cultural personality assessment, it can be seen, is not simple. In what follows, we deal with some broad perspectives and end with what appears the most precise. However, it should be clear also that for different pragmatic purposes, different perspectives may be more helpful.

UNIVERSAL CULTURAL PERSPECTIVES

The Search for Universal Dimensions

The first universal cultural perspective was undoubtedly the original assumption of many pioneers in psychological testing that tests and procedures would be universally reliable and valid. It is by now well known that this attitude led to historical statements and un-

491

avoidably heated controversies (Cronbach, 1975; Yerkes, 1921).

The search for universal dimensions has become, in recent years, far more sophisticated. It purports to find those aspects of human nature that remain reasonably constant across most cultures and that will finally permit fairer and universally significant comparative assessments.

Lonner (1980) is an excellent source for the discussion of psychological universals. In his effort to define the concept of universals, he said:

> A major problem hindering the understanding of behavior throughout the world is related to competing epistemologies both within psychology and across her sister disciplines. There are different definitions of universals as well as different units, constructs and methods that are used in an attempt to pin them down. For a contrasting example, physicists and chemists are to be envied. One does not study gravity cross-culturally; neutrons are undoubtedly as unambiguously "universals" in Nepal as they are in Cambridge. Variability in measurement and in observation in the so-called "hard" sciences is virtually non-existent when compared with the various "softer sciences." (p. 148)

Lonner goes on to cite Bruner (1974), who, while contemplating Mendeleief's periodic table of elements, remarked, "Wouldn't it be marvelous if at one stroke all the different elements that constitute the cultures of the world could be tied together?" (p. 392).

In his comprehensive analysis, Lonner specifies that it is possible to search for universal behavioral dimensions from four perspectives: those of anthropology, biology, language and linguistics, and psychology. In view of the complexity of the definition of universals, and the varied perspectives and sources of possible behavioral universals, it would appear from the start that finding valid, professionally useful procedures for cross-cultural assessment would be practically impossible. Lonner's thoughtful chapter is, however, indispensable reading for anyone interested in the basic conceptualizations needed for the development of lists of possible universals and the ways to approach them in either anthropology, biology, liguistics, or psychology.

It is timely to observe here that the exploration in this chapter is theoretically more limited and has more pragmatic goals. Also, this is certainly not a handbook of cross-cultural assessment, but an attempt to identify examples of such assessment and to illustrate—this is our fundamental objective—what may be considered valid approaches to interpretation in this realm.

In this understanding, we continue this section by describing a recent and ambitious attempt to discriminate some universal psychological dimensions. The following sections present four examples of possibly universal assessment procedures. These four have been selected not only because of their psychological significance, but because we can provide specific examples of their use. We conclude the chapter with a discussion of the beginnings of a new discipline, ethnopsychology.

Hofstede's Culture Dimensions

In his studies of work-related values among employees of a multinational corporation in as many as 53 countries and regions, Hofstede (1980, 1983) has repeatedly found four cultural dimensions. Although his methodology should be examined more closely than it has been, there is little doubt that Hofstede's four factors are intriguing. Since they are the result of research rather than speculation, these are dimensions to be kept in mind when trying to interpret cross-cultural assessment results.

Hofstede's first dimension is called "power distance." He defines it as the extent to which the less powerful members of institutions and organizations accept the fact that power is distributed unequally. He points out that the basic anthropological/societal issue related to this factor is social inequality and the amount of authority that one person has over others. The second dimension he labels "uncertainty avoidance." The definition for this as is follows: "The extent to which people feel threatened by ambiguous situations, and have created beliefs and institutions that try to avoid this" (Hofstede & Bond, 1984, p. 419). The way in which a society deals with conflicts and aggression and with life and death is the basic anthropological/societal issue to which this dimension relates. It will probably be harder for the reader to accept that there is as much of a relationship between this dimension and its related social issue as there is in the power distance dimension.

Hofstede calls the third dimension "individualism versus collectivism." It is interesting that Marin and Triandis (1985) have defined a similar dimension as the result of much comparative work between Latin/Hispanic Americans and Anglo-Americans. The one pole of this continuum, individualism, is defined as a situation in which people are supposed to look after themselves and their immediate families only; the opposite pole, collectivism, is defined as a situation in which people belong to in-groups or collectivities that are supposed to look after the people in exchange for loyalty. The basic anthropological/societal issue that is related to this dimension is the individual's dependence on the group—his or her self-concept as "I" or "we."

The fourth dimension has been labeled "masculinity versus femininity." This dimension has been extensively studied in the United States by Spence and Helmreich (1978); more recently, we have found that with certain modifications (see "The Ethnopsychological Approach," below), it works also for Mexicans. However, Hofstede's dimension is broader than ours. Thus, masculinity is defined as a situation in which the dominant values in society are success, money, and things; on the contrary, femininity is defined as a situation in which the dominant value in society is caring for others and for the quality of life. The important issues to which this dimension relates, according to Hofstede, are the choice of social sex roles and their effects on people's self-concept.

Hofstede and Bond (1984) open their article on Hofstede's dimensions with a plea for the need for "synergy" among cross-cultural studies:

> Cross-cultural psychology relates psychological characteristics to "culture," that is, a state of the surrounding social system. Different studies exploring different psychological characteristics but covering the same set of cultural environments can be expected to show synergy: that is, to be partly complementary, to be like pieces in a large jigsaw puzzle that shows how culture conditions psychological functioning. (p. 417)

Hofstede and Bond found synergy—that is, high correlations between these four universal dimensions and the results in a study by Ng et al. (1982). Ng and colleagues collected data from students in nine Asian and Pacific countries, using a modified version of the Rokeach Value Survey. Since six of the nine countries covered in that study were also covered in Hofstede's (1980, 1983) studies, a correlation analysis was done for the overlapping countries between the five factors emerging from Ng et al.'s reanalysis[1] and the four dimensions of Hofstede. This comparative synergical study broadens our understanding of the four avowedly universal cultural dimensions, in a way that is best expressed by the authors:

> In the factor analytical comparison, power distance is associated with "salvation," "courageous," "capable," "social recognition" and "imaginative." These are terms that evoke the ideal of a charismatic leader who is socially recognized and points the road to salvation. Uncertainty avoidance is associated with "cheerful," "happiness" and "a comfortable life." This suggests the ideal of a cozy, risk-avoiding, "don't-rock-the-boat" life. Individualism, in the factor analytical comparison, is associated with an "exciting life" and "a world of beauty." Hofstede (1980, pp. 230–231) found as correlations of individualism in correlated studies: "variety," "enjoyment in life" and "pleasure." Individualism appears to be associated with an epicurean life ideal. (Hofstede & Bond, 1984, p. 430)

Hofstede and Bond found some discrepancy between the masculinity–femininity dimension and the results of Ng et al., but all in all there was a good degree of correspondence.

This is, at any rate, the most notable effort to ascertain universal cultural dimensions as they affect psychological functioning. Any professional involved in cross-cultural assessment should keep in mind these broad dimensions, their possible correlates, and their quantitative variable impact across cultures when trying to understand the results of personality assessment in different cultures.

[1]Each of these factors contains coherent combinations of Rokeach's values. Interestingly, Factor 1, with highest loadings on "world of peace" and "equality," did not correlate unequivocally with any of Hofstede's dimensions.

OSGOOD'S SEMANTIC DIFFERENTIAL TECHNIQUE

What is behind the thousands of adjectives used to qualify experience? Are there equal numbers of irreducible meanings (semantic features) behind the adjectives? In an informal conversation at the side of a pool in Merida, Yucatan, Mexico, one of us (Diaz-Guerrero) was telling Charlie Osgood that his contribution to the discovery of a limited number of fundamental dimensions in human qualifying was comparable to the limited number of logical forms of thinking discovered by Aristotle. With modesty and good humor, Charlie answered: "Well, perhaps, but I had an advantage that Aristotle never had—the electronic computer."

As Osgood, Suci, and Tannenbaum (1957) describe, it took 6–7 years for a team of researchers at the University of Illinois to develop an objective measure of meaning, the Semantic Differential (SD). The SD is a measurement tool composed of 13 bipolar scales, each of which has seven spaces between its endpoints, as in these examples.

Good _ _ _ _ _ _ _ Bad
Strong _ _ _ _ _ _ _ Weak
Fast _ _ _ _ _ _ _ Slow

For a concept such as "power," the individuals being studied place a cross in the space between the adjectives on each scale that expresses their best guess about the meaning of the concept in reference to the adjectives. The adjectival scales were derived by factor analysis from about 10,000 original adjectives. Four of these scales provide the composite score for the factor of Evaluation, and four of each for Potency and Activity. The 13th scale, "Familiar _ _ _ _ _ _ _ Unfamiliar," provides a measure of how well the concept is known to the individual. The entire effort to develop the SD is described in the book *The Measurement of Meaning* (Osgood et al., 1957). The book sparked many applications of the SD technique to a large number and variety of problems; this led to the publication of a volume entitled *Semantic Differential Technique: A Source Book* (Snyder & Osgood, 1969). In his introduction to this book, Osgood has the following to say:

I must confess that sometimes I feel like the Geppetto of a wayward Pinocchio who has wandered off into the Big City, and Lord knows what mischief he is getting into. Some people think Pinocchio is a specific standardized test; he is not, of course, being subject to concept/scale interaction. Some think he is a measure of meaning-in-general; he is not, of course, reflecting primarily affective meaning by virtue of the metaphorical usage of his scales. And in recent years Pinocchio has been trotting around the world, introducing himself to people who speak different languages and enjoy different cultures; but in these travels, Geppetto has at least been able to keep a hand on the puppet's strings. (p. ix).

As observed in the last lines, beginning in February 1960 with a conference at the University of Illinois and for 15 years afterward, Osgood and his team—with the help and cooperation of first 23 and finally over 30 principal investigators in many culture/language communities around the world—developed indigenous SD techniques in each of these communities. The original finding was that in all of these communities, the same three major factor dimensions of Evaluation, Potency, and Activity (abbreviated as E, P, and A in the quotation that follows) were repeatedly found. This led to a sufficiently well-founded statement of the universality of affective meaning. To clarify the meaning of these three dimensions further, it is useful to quote again from Osgood (1971):

But why E, P, and A? . . . I believe it was M. Brewster Smith who first pointed out to me the essential identity of our E-P-A factors to the dimensions of feeling as described in introspective studies of feeling by Wundt in the last century and in studies of communication via facial expressions by Schlosberg and many others, including myself (Osgood, 1966) in the present century. Consistent with my behavioristic theory of meaning, it is these pervasive affective features which dominate much of our behavior, including language behavior; we really are—Chomsky and the mentalists to the contrary—still animals at base. I simply refer you to the latest news for confirmation. What is important to us now, as it was way back in the age of Neanderthal Man, about the sign of a thing is: First, does it refer to something *good* or *bad* for me (Is it an antelope or a saber-toothed tiger?). Second, does it refer to something which is *strong* or *weak* with respect to me (Is it a saber-toothed tiger or a mosquito?), and third, for behavioral purposes, does it refer to something which is *active* or *passive* (Is it a saber-toothed tiger or merely a pool of quicksand, which I can simply walk around?). These "gut" reactions to things and their signs, by every criterion used by linguists, lexicographers and philosophers, have the properties of semantic features; to deny their importance is to fly in the face of everyday common sense as well as much scientific data. (pp. 37–38)

Once each culture had developed its indigenous, emic SD scales based on a cross-culturally *common* procedure, each principal investigator had a cross-culturally equivalent tool that delivered the same three underlying affective features that would be found in every other culture community. Pancultural factor analysis conducted on the SD ratings of the same 100 concepts across some 29 language/culture communities provided the best and most comparable scales for all cultures involved (Osgood, May, & Murray, 1975). These scales were then used to measure the affective meaning of some 620 concepts in each of the culture communities for a reasonably comparable cross-cultural study. The ratings compiled in the *Atlas of Affective Meanings* were obtained from about 400 male ninth-graders attending public high school[2] in each of the culture communities. A specific characteristic of Osgood's early quest to determine the universality of affective meaning was that his subjects were drawn from educated groups. (It is fortunate for our purposes that cross-cultural assessment is usually done on more or less educated groups.) Admittedly, also, the subjects were not randomly selected from all cultures. Osgood pointed out that a cross-cultural researcher can opt for representativeness within countries (vertical probing) or equivalence across countries (horizontal probing). He used to say that the more you maximize representativeness within, the more you minimize equivalence between, and vice versa. In his studies he purposely opted for

maximizing the equivalence across countries, since his research objective was to compare semantic systems across overall differences in language and culture.

In order to illustrate the complexities of cross-cultural comparisons, as well as the importance to cross-cultural assessment of the development of the SD technique, we now examine the *Atlas* data for one of the concept categories that is relevant to Hofstede's universals. This category is labeled "Supraordinate–Subordinate." It includes the following 19 concepts: "leader," "policeman," "authority," "power," "rich people," "master," "professor," "king," "hero," "student," "most people," "middle class," "follower," "beggar," "illiterate," "borrowing money," "poor people," "servant," and "I (myself)."

Tables 21.1 and 21.2 show the intracultural ranks of these concepts on the basic measures of Evaluation and Potency for 29 culture/language communities. Before we go any further, let us explain that all of the samples of ninth-graders were taken from urban centers, since the principal investigators in the different countries were usually attached to large universities. The only sample that was different in age and education from the rest was that of Yucatan, Mexico (YC in the tables). The subjects in this sample were rural adults in a small village in Yucatan. In the tables, the stub column gives the 19 concepts of the Supraordinate–Subordinate category. Each of the next 29 columns is headed by a two-letter abbreviation indicating the name of the country or culture/language community and the name of the language spoken. The column before the last gives the mean ranking for each of the concepts, and the last column indicates whether the concept has a universally high (U+) or a universally low (U−) score. Each of the columns presents the intracultural rank of the concept from 1 through 19.

Let us make some comparisons based on the Table 21.1 data, regarding Evaluation of the concepts in this category. It can be seen, for instance, that the American–English (AE) adolescents agreed on the rank of only one concept, "illiterate," with the Mexican–Spanish (MS) adolescents. An important and large discrepancy in ranking is in the concept "I (myself),": The AE adolescents ranked this concept 4th, whereas the MS group ranked it

TABLE 21.1. Evaluation Rankings for the Supraordinate–Subordinate Category of Concepts

Concept	FR	BF	ND	GG	SW	FF	AE	BE	YC	MS	CS	BP	HM	YS	IT	GK	IH	TK	LA	IF	AD	AP	DH	CB	MK	MM	TH	HC	JP	Mean	Universal value[a]
LEAD	4	5	4	7	1+	9	5	1+	17−	8	9	9	6	4	7	6	7	3	9	2+	2+	1+	1+	4	10−	6	7	4	4	5.6	U+
POLI	18−	16−	14	10	8	6+	7+	16−	19−	15	8	10	13	9	12	2+	6+	8	14−	10	9	9	18−	17−	7+	8	11	13	13	10.7	
AUTH	11	11	18−	11	13	15−	12	13	8	10	13	2+	12	7	6+	11	8	14−	10	9	8	8	5+	15−	5+	9	14−	13	12	10.4	
POWE	6	14−	11	9	18−	16−	2+	6	11	7	1+	8	4+	5	9	4+	8	9	4+	9	7	7	8	9	8	12−	7	14−		8.4	
RICH	17−	13	9+	13	17−	13	14	8+	7+	16	15	19−	18−	17−	11	15	15	10	12	14	15	16	13	16	7+	5+	2+	15	5+	12.7	
MAST	15	12	15	15	10	0	17−	4+	3+	13	14	3+	4+	18−	18−	16−	16−	5+	11	16−	14	15	14	10	8+	0	13	14	1+	11.6	U+
PROF	8	7	3	4	4	7	8	9−	2	2	6	1+	8	10−	8	4	3	6	2	8	1+	3	3	3	2	3	3	5	9−	4.9	U+
KING	7	10	6	12	2+	10	15−	10	14−	7	12	15−	14−	14−	14	9	13−	15−	13−	6	5+	5+	6	6	1+	4+	1+	18−	10	9.4	
HERO	2	1	2	1	3	1	1	2	5	3	1	8−	5	1	1	1	2	7−	1	4	6	4	5	13−	2	1	4	2	6	3.4	U+
STUD	1	6	5	6	6	5	4	1	2	18−	2	3	2	3	5	1	1	3	6	2	2	1	3	1	3	1	4	2	6	3.9	U+
PEOP	13	8	12	8	9	8	10	11	6+	6+	5+	5+	7	11	13	14−	9	15−	12	11	10	8	13	12	12	11	10	8		9.7	
MIDD	9	4+	7	5+	12	4+	9	15−	10	5+	7	11	11	12	13	10	12	11	6+	11	12	11	15−	9	6+	14−	9	6+	11	9.6	
FOLL	19−	9	10	16−	16−	12	11	3+	1+	4+	10	5+	10	11	5+	19−	11	4+	13	14	13	16−	12	10	12	11	15−	15−	12	11.1	
BEGG	14	19	16	18	19	18	17	12+	17	17	13+	17	15	17	19	16	18	17	19	19	18	17	16	14	16	18	19	16	18	16.9	U−
ILLI	16	18	17	17	15	17	18	19	16	18	18	16	19	18	17	19	19	19	18	17	18	19	19	17	18	19	17	17	17	17.7	U−
BORR	10+	15	19	19	14	19	13	14	15	19	4+	15	19	15	14	11+	18	19	17	18	17	16	19	19	16	9+	16	19	19	16.2	U−
POOR	12	17	13	14	11	14	16	18−	13	11	14	16	13	16	12	17	16	16	15	13	17	13	17	7+	15	16	18−	9+	16	14.3	U−
SERV	5+	3+	8	2+	7	3+	3+	7	18−	14−	4+	17−	9	6	9	8	10	12	5+	10	7	14−	12	11	14−	13−	5+	8	7	8.7	
I(MY)	3	2	1+	3	5	2	4	12−	9−	12	3	12−	3	2	3	7	2	7	4	11−	2	4	10−	6	1+	3	4	10−	6	5.0	U+

Note. Abbreviations for concepts: LEAD, leader; POLI, policeman; AUTH, authority; POWE, power; RICH, rich people; MAST, master; PROF, professor; KING, king; HERO, hero; STUD, student; PEOP, most people; MIDD, middle class; FOLL, follower; BEGG, beggar; ILLI, illiterate; BORR, borrowing money; POOR, poor poeple; SERV, servant; I(MY), I (myself).

Abbreviations for culture/language communities: FR, France–French; BF, Belgium–Flemish; ND, Netherlands–Dutch; GG, West Germany–German; SW, Sweden–Swedish; FF, Finland–Finnish; AE, United States (white Americans)–English; BE, United States (black Americans)–English; YC, Yucatan (Mexico)–Spanish; MS, Mexico–Spanish; CS, Costa Rica–Spanish; BP, Brazil–Portuguese; HM, Hungary–Magyar; YS, Yugoslavia–Serbo-Croatian; IT, Italy–Italian; GK, Greece–Greek; IH, Israel–Hebrew; TK, Turkey–Turkish; LA, Lebanon–Arabic; IF, Iran–Farsi; AD, Afghanistan–Dari; AP, Afghanistan–Pashtu; DH, Delhi (India)–Hindi; CB, Calcutta (India)–Bengali; MK, Mysore (India)–Kannada; MM, Malaysia–Malay; TH, Thailand–Thai; HC, Hong Kong–Cantonese; JP, Japan–Japanese

The data are from Osgood, May, and Murray (1975).

[a] U+, universally high; U−, universally low.

12th. This corresponds to a very significant difference in the evaluation of the self-concept in the two cultures, with the AE rating it more highly. Another large discrepancy comes in regard to the ranking of "policeman," which was 7th for the AE group and only 15th for the MS adolescents. A third important discrepancy is in the concept of "power": The AE adolescents ranked it 2nd, while the MS adolescents ranked it 9th. It is interesting that the MS adolescents ranked the concept of "professor" 2nd, whereas the AE adolescents placed it 8th, and that the concept of "student" was ranked 1st by the MS group and 6th by the AE group. The MS adolescents placed "follower" 4th, while the AE group placed it 11th; "poor people" was ranked 11th by the MS adolescents and 16th by the AE youths. It is interesting that the same Mexican adolescents who gave "I (myself)" such a low rating, both in this ranking and in their actual evaluative scores on the SD as compared with most other cultural groups (Diaz-Guerrero, 1982a), should have ranked "student" so high. They were themselves students, but the word "student" in Mexico is reserved for university students, who receive (both from high-schoolers and from the population in general) a very high evaluation. These differences illustrate that although the power distance of the Supraordinate–Subordinate dimension may be universal, the power hierarchies across countries differ greatly, as does the meaning of each of the power roles. In the present example, the fact alone that the Mexicans rate themselves lower in general, as well as among the various Supraordinate–Subordinate concepts, provides a dramatic difference to be taken into account in personality assessment. The difference becomes still more dramatic when it is found (Diaz-Guerrero, 1982a) that this low self-esteem means (among other things) modesty and the desire to highlight, in contrast, the value of the family, religious figures, institutions, and society.

But even more striking than these differences between the AE and MS groups are the cross-ethnic differences within the same nation in the case of white Americans (the AE group) and black Americans (BE in the tables). In this case, there is not a single agreement in rank. Understandably, there is a striking difference in the evaluation of "policeman": The AE adolescents ranked it 7th, a significantly high rank among the 19 concepts, whereas the BE youths ranked it 16th, a significantly low rank for their own ranking of the 19 concepts. Another significant difference is in the evaluation of "master," which was placed 17th by the AE group but 4th by the BE group. The reader may make some other comparisons, but he or she will find that outside some tendencies toward agreement in ranking of certain power distance concepts, such as "poor people," "beggar," and "illiterate," the subjective ranking of these Supraordinate–Subordinate concepts is as different between white and black Americans as it is between white Americans and Mexicans. Much that is said in this chapter regarding cross-cultural assessment applies to cross-ethnic assessment as well.

Beyond these vertical comparisons, it is important to see similarities and differences in the horizontal plane. As shown in the last column of Table 21.1, there are five concepts agreed by all culture/language groups to be affectively positive, and four concepts agreed by all groups to be affectively negative. "Leader," "professor," "hero," "student," and "I (myself)" are universally positively evaluated; "beggar," "illiterate," "borrowing money," and "poor people" are universally negatively evaluated. But even in these generally agreed evaluations, some communities' rankings differ noticeably. Thus, the Brazil–Portuguese (BP) group ranked "beggar" significantly less negatively than did the other nations; there are similar trends in the Netherlands–Dutch (ND) and the France–French (FR) groups for "borrowing money" and in the BE group for "poor people" and "illiterate."

Now let us examine the ranking of "power" across all of these culture/language communities with regard to evaluation. In the following list, the numbers represent the rankings, and the group or groups following each number are those that gave "power" that ranking.

1. Hungary–Magyar (HM).
2. AE.
4. Italy–Italian (IT), Turkey–Turkish (TK), and Iran–Farsi (IF).
5. Greece–Greek (GK).

6. FR, BE.
7. Hong Kong–Cantonese (HC) BP, Afghanistan–Pashtu (AP), and Delhi (India)–Hindi (DH).
8. Yugoslavia–Serbo-Croatian (YS), Lebanon–Arabic (LA), Calcutta (India)–Bengali (CB), and Malaysia–Malay (MM).
9. West Germany–German (GG), MS, Israel–Hebrew (IH), Afghanistan–Dari (AD), and Mysore (India)–Kannada (MK).
11. YC, Costa Rica–Spanish (CS), and ND.
12. Thailand–Thai (TH).
14. Belgium–Flemish (BF) and Japan–Japanese (JP).
16. Finland–Finnish (FF).
18. Sweden–Swedish (SW).

The concept of "power" may certainly be universal. However, not only was it evaluated as good in some places and as bad in others, according to the actual mean scores recorded in this study; there are also great variations across cultures and even cross-ethnically within the same culture in the ranking of "power," compared with 18 other concepts in the category of Supraordinate–Subordinate.

Many differences can be expected in regard to the Evaluation of these 19 Supraordinate–Subordinate concepts, but one would ordinarily expect that regarding their strength or Potency, there should be a much greater agreement across cultures. As can be seen from the last column of Table 21.2, however, there is only universal agreement for nine of the concepts as far as Potency is concerned. "Leader," "authority," "power," and "hero" are universally potent concepts; "beggar," "illiterate," "borrowing money," "poor people," and "servant" are universally weak concepts. But Table 21.2 also, again, shows exceptions in the rating of each of these nine concepts. The cross-cultural differences, as well as the cross-ethnic differences within the same culture, for the ranking of the Potency of these concepts show separate subjective worlds. It must, of course, be recalled that in the assessment of personality we are fundamentally assessing subjective worlds.

In cross-cultural assessment, it may become indispensable to determine the subjective meaning to individuals or groups of, for instance, the personality traits or needs that we are measuring by personality inventories. It is here that the SD technique, particularly when scales derived from a pancultural analysis are available (Osgood et al., 1975), will help clarify and often broaden the meaning of scores obtained in the different traits or needs studied. This meaning, as we shall see later, may be different from one culture to another.

CROSS-CULTURAL ANXIETY MEASUREMENT

The momentous question of which cultures provoke more and which provoke less anxiety in their subjects could be answered scientifically if we had a culture-free measure of anxiety. Politically, it is perhaps a blessing that even measures such as Spielberger, Gorsuch, and Lushene's (1970) State–Trait Anxiety Inventory (STAI)—and not because of theory or methodological limitations—fall short of this ideal. This is at least true of the measurement of trait anxiety. State anxiety—that is, the amount of anxiety aroused by specific objective stresses, such as a university exam in mathematics—is certainly more amenable to a cross-cultural research design or to a cross-cultural assessment.

The nature of anxiety, its conceptualization, and its measurement are anything but simple. As pointed out by Holtzman (1976), anxiety as a human process implies a sequence of cognitive, affective, physiological, and behavioral events. It is also dependent upon environmental stimuli or stimulating situations. Furthermore, Holtzman and Bitterman (1956) found that large-scale, multivariate studies of anxiety and reactions to stress have mostly revealed a very low order of intercorrelation among sociometric, self-report, perceptual, physiological, and biochemical measures professing to quantify anxiety.

But it is precisely through the persistent efforts of Spielberger and his many national and international colleagues that theory and measurement have come closest to producing a meaningful understanding of anxiety across methods, across populations, and—what is important here—across cultures.

TABLE 21.2. Potency Rankings for the Supraordinate–Subordinate Category of Concepts

Concept	FR	BF	ND	GG	SW	FF	AE	BE	YC	MS	CS	BP	HM	YS	IT	GK	IH	TK	LA	IF	AD	AP	DH	CB	MK	MM	TH	HC	JP	Mean	Universal value[a]
LEAD	3	6	3	2	9-	3	2	1	3	2	3	4	5	3	6	2	3	1	6	3	6	5	2	3	12-	5	1	3	1	3.7	U+
POLI	4	3	5	4	2+	1+	8	18-	11	9	6	3	14-	10	7	5	7	5	3	6	2+	4	8	12-	8	9	7	9	4	6.7	
AUTH	8	4	7	5	11-	6	5	11-	1+	3	2	5	3	9	3	3	4	8	7	5	7	9	6	11-	7	3	2	5	9	5.8	U+
POWE	2	5	1	3	10-	4	1	7	7	1	1	1	1	10-	2	1	2	3	8	2	5	7	1	2	2	8	8	1	7	3.8	U+
RICH	12	14-	13	11	15-	9	2+	2+	14-	9	8	10	17-	11	11	9	9	6	12	7	8	16-	5	10	3+	1+	6	16-	6	9.4	
MAST	7	7	4+	9	7	0	4+	6	6	11	5	11	7	6	14-	13	12	9	5	12	7	8	17-	13	7	8	2+	13	8	8.6	
PROF	15-	13	19-	13	8	7	12	12	9	4+	15-	7	13	14-	8	7	6	2+	1+	10	1+	6	9	7	10	10	3+	7	3+	8.7	
KING	6	16-	11	6	3+	2+	6	13-	10	7	4	14-	15-	10	8	10	4	11	9	4	3+	4	5	4	7	4	6	5		7.7	
HERO	1	1	2	1	1	5	3	3	5	5	7	1	2	1	1	10-	4	1	3	8-	3	1	5	6	5	4	2			3.2	U+
STUD	9	12	12	7	6	17-	10	4+	16-	8	12	2+	6	8	4+	10	13	12	9	8	10	11	14	1+	10	9	12	11	10	9.1	
PEOP	16-	11	6+	15	13	13	16-	15	4+	12	13	13	8	5+	12	12	8	14	14	11	14	10	12	9	12	11	10	15		11.5	
MIDD	11	8	9	12	16-	8	11	19-	14	10	8	6+	11	12	13	6+	15	7	10	15	12	12	14	15	13	8	10	11	13	11.3	
FOLL	5+	9	17-	10	12	12	14	8	8	6+	10	19-	9	11	9	14	11	13	16	14	6+	14	19-	12	12	12				11.9	
BEGG	19	19	18	19	16	19	14	12+	19	18	9+	19	19	19	19	19	19	18	19	18	19									17.8	U-
ILLI	17	18	14	17	15	17	10+	19	18	17	18	18	17	19	19	15	18	18	17											17.1	U-
BORR	14	15	10+	16	14	10+	13	16	17	16	16	16	14	15	18	11	12	14	14											14.9	U-
POOR	18	17	16	18	19	18	9+	15	17	19	12	17	13	18	17	16	17	13	17	18										16.0	U-
SERV	13	10	15	8+	4+	19-	15	17	18	15	11	18	12	7+	15	16	13	13	9+	15	11	13	15	14	15	16				13.7	U-
I(MY)	10	2+	8	14-	5	14-	7	5	13	13	14-	15-	4+	4+	5	9	5	16-	2+	4+	13	2+	13	6	17-	13	16-	2+	11	9.0	

Note. Abbreviations for concepts: LEAD, leader; POLI, policeman; AUTH, authority; POWE, power; RICH, rich people; MAST, master; PROF, professor; KING, king; HERO, hero; STUD, student; PEOP, most people; MIDD, middle class; FOLL, follower; BEGG, beggar; ILLI, illiterate; BORR, borrowing money; POOR, poor poeple; SERV, servant; I(MY), I (myself).

Abbreviations for culture/language communities: FR, France–French; BF, Belgium–Flemish; ND, Netherlands–Dutch; GG, West Germany–German; SW, Sweden–Swedish; FF, Finland–Finnish; AE, United States (white Americans)–English; BE, United States (black Americans)–English; YC, Yucatan (Mexico)–Spanish; MS, Mexico–Spanish; CS, Costa Rica–Spanish; BP, Brazil–Portuguese; HM, Hungary–Magyar; YS, Yugoslavia–Serbo-Croatian; IT, Italy–Italian; GK, Greece–Greek; IH, Israel–Hebrew; TK, Turkey–Turkish; LA, Lebanon–Arabic; IF, Iran–Farsi; AD, Afghanistan–Dari; AP, Afghanistan–Pashtu; DH, Delhi (India)–Hindi; CB, Calcutta (India)–Bengali; MK, Mysore (India)–Kannada; MM, Malaysia–Malay; TH, Thailand–Thai; HC, Hong Kong–Cantonese; JP, Japan–Japanese

The data are from Osgood, May, and Murray (1975).

[a]U+, universally high; U−, universally low.

Definitions of Terms

Fundamental to a more adequate theory of anxiety has been the clear definition of terms that have been used quite ambiguously in the literature. The crucial terms in this connection are "stress," "threat," and "anxiety."

Spielberger (1976) notes that the term "stress" has been used to refer not only to dangerous stimulus conditions (stressors) that produce anxiety reactions, but also to the cognitive, affective, behavioral, and physiological changes (stress reactions) that are produced by the stressful stimuli. In agreement with theoretical developments and findings of research, Spielberger (1972) proposes that the terms "stress" and "threat" be used to refer to different aspects of the temporal sequence of events that results in the evocation of an anxiety reaction. Thus, "stress" should refer to the objective, consensually validated stimulus properties of a situation characterized by a degree of physical or psychological danger. Spielberger (1976) says:

> Stress denotes the objective stimulus properties of a situation, threat refers to an individual's perception of a situation as more or less dangerous or personally threatening to him or her. Situations that are objectively stressful are likely to be perceived as threatening by most people, but whether or not a particular person will interpret a specific danger situation as threatening will depend upon that individual's subjective (idiosyncratic) appraisal of the situation. Thus, a stressful situation may not be perceived as threatening by an individual who either does not recognize the inherent danger, or has the necessary skills and experience to cope with it. (p. 5)

Particularly important in cross-cultural assessment is the affirmation that situations that are objectively stressful are likely to be perceived as threatening by most people; however, whether or not a particular person will interpret a specific danger situation as threatening will depend upon the individual's subjective (idiosyncratic) appraisal of the situation. This is uniquely applicable to cross-cultural assessment. Even evidently stressful situations such as sickness or death are perceived as differentially threatening across cultures. In the Osgood et al. (1975) study described earlier, the concept of "cancer" was significantly less bad and powerful (i.e., less threatening) for the Japan–Japanese (JP) adolescents than it was either for the France–French (FR) or the white American–English (AE) adolescents. The subjective concept of "death," in spite of the fact that it was perceived as more dynamic by the Brazilian–Portuguese (BP) adolescents, was significantly less threatening to them than to almost all of the other groups in Osgood's et al. pancultural study. Thus, the concept of threat implies necessarily that objectively nonstressful situations may be also subjectively appraised as dangerous by individuals who, for any reason, will see them as personally threatening. With these limitations, however, the appraisal of a specific situation as threatening should be determined by the objective stimulus characteristics, the individual's cultural and personal experience with similar situations, and any memories or thoughts instigated or evoked by the situation. Spielberger adds:

> If a situation or thought is perceived as threatening, irrespective of the presence of real or objective danger (stress), the person who perceives the situation as threatening will experience an increase in state anxiety (A-State). Thus: stress → perception of danger (threat) → increase in A-State. (1976, p. 5)

It is important to observe, as Holtzman (1976) does, that when an individual (or a group) is placed under high stress, the relationships among the cognitive, perceptual, affective, physiological, and behavioral events of anxiety become clearer. Here the organism will respond in a more coordinated fashion to stress. Behavioral observations of the objective situation, verbal self-reports of state anxiety, content of fantasy and perception as revealed by projective techniques, physiological indices of muscle tension and autonomic nervous system lability, and biochemical indicators of stress reaction will intercorrelate, reflecting a total response of the threatened organism. The components that appear isolated in a relaxed state become synergistic if the threat is high.

For Spielberger and his associates, the cognitive–perceptual system is the fundamental one for the measurement of anxiety. Thus, the self-report inventory becomes the key method to be used in extracting information about the individual's perception of his or her own inner feelings, bodily sensations, and cognitive as well as emotional reactions to stress. To measure state anxiety, it is necessary to have a precise conceptual definition of the pattern of responses characterizing the inner feelings as a transitory state. Since state anxiety is clearly unequivocal, a good and valid measure of it is certainly a precondition for meaningful intra- and cross-cultural research about anxiety phenomena. But besides anxiety as a state, there is much use in the psychological literature of the term "anxiety" to refer to a more stable personality disposition—that is, a trait. One would have to imagine that through time, individuals or groups are subject to a variety of stresses from life and that their corresponding appraisal of the degree of threat that these stresses entail leads to a degree of constant state anxiety. This is why Spielberger sees the need to consider both state and trait anxiety. In theory, trait anxiety becomes logically and statistically connected to unequivocal state anxiety by being defined as the *proneness* of an individual to develop state anxiety. Spielberger has the following to say:

> Trait anxiety (A-Trait) refers to relatively stable individual differences in anxiety proneness that are manifested in behavior in the frequency with which an individual experiences A-State elevations over time. Persons who are high in A-Trait, for example, psychoneurotic patients, are more strongly disposed to perceive the world as dangerous or threatening than low A-Trait persons. Consequently, high A-Trait individuals are more vulnerable to stress and tend to experience A-State reactions of greater intensity and with greater frequency over time than persons who are low in A-Trait. (1976, p. 6)

The State–Trait Anxiety Inventory

The STAI A-State scale contains 20 statements (e.g., "I am tense," "I feel nervous") that induce people to describe how they feel at the particular moment by rating themselves on a 4-point scale (1, "not at all"; 2, "Somewhat"; 3, "moderately so"; 4, "very much so"). Construct validity was utilized as the fundamental criterion for including each individual A-State item in the scale. Pilot

subjects had higher mean scores on the items selected for the A-State scale in a stressful situation (taking an exam, giving a speech) than in a neutral situation, and lower mean scores in a relaxed situation. The cardinal qualities measured by the STAI A-State scale are tension, apprehension, and nervousness as these phenomenological feeling states vary along a continuum of increasing levels of intensity. Lower scores are anticipated to reflect the states of calmness, serenity, and relaxation; intermediate scores indicate moderate levels of tension and apprehensiveness; and high scores correspond with intense states of fright or apprehension.

The STAI A-Trait scale contains 20 statements that induce people to describe how they generally feel (e.g., "I feel that difficulties are piling up so that I cannot overcome them," "I take disappointments so keenly that I can't put them out of my mind"). Subjects respond to each item by rating themselves on a 4-point scale 1, "almost never"; 2, "sometimes"; 3, "often"; 4, "almost always"). Whereas the A-State scale is an intensity scale based on a quantity range, individual items were selected for the STAI A-Trait scale on the basis of the concurrent validity of each item as determined from correlations with two widely accepted measures of trait anxiety, the Taylor Manifest Anxiety Scale and the IPAT anxiety scales (Cattell & Scheier, 1963). Each A-Trait item was also determined to be impervious to situational stress and relatively stable over time.

Spielberger and Diaz-Guerrero (1976, 1983, 1986) report that in at least 13 culture/language groups, including Hindi, Spanish, Portuguese, French, Turkish, Russian, Hungarian, Kiswahili, Lugandan, Polish, Arabic, Bengali, and Korean, the construction, norming, and validation of the STAI have been sufficiently developed to permit important indigenous use in a variety of health, educational, personality, social-psychological, and even sport applications. It also permits far more meaningful cross-cultural research and, to a certain extent, cross-cultural assessment of anxiety than heretofore was possible.

After reviewing the steps taken in the research for the development of the Hindi, Spanish, and Portuguese versions of the STAI, Holtzman has the following to say:

"Few indeed are the verbally based psychological techniques that have been handled as rigorously in cross-cultural, cross-language research" (1976, p. 177). It is the painstaking work carried out by the cross-cultural researches in these 13 culture/language groups that permits us to include the STAI among the four examples presented in this chapter as *q*uasi-universal measurement techniques. Interestingly, this is the only clearly self-report method included.

I believe it is possible to say that measurement with the A-State scale of the STAI, in the 13 culture/language communities that have complied with most of the steps advised by Spielberger and Sharma (1976), will prove very useful as a sensitive indicator of the transitory anxiety experienced by clients in counseling, psychotherapy, and behavior therapy; of the degree of state anxiety provoked by tests and examinations (although the Test Anxiety Inventory [see Bauermeister, Collazo, & Spielberger, 1983] should be more precise in the future); of individual differences among surgeons while operating; and of changes in transitory anxiety over time. As an independent measure of the perceived threat posed by specific situational stresses in each culture/language group, the A-State scale can produce the very first bona fide cross-cultural comparisons of reactive anxiety.

Several studies have put to a drastic test the theoretical expectation that an independent dimension of trait anxiety exists. It is now generally accepted by all that such a dimension does exist. The cross-cultural assessment of trait anxiety is, however, a target for the usual criticisms of any self-report questionnaire—that is, faking, social desirability, response set, and so on. Paradoxically, it is precisely the A-Trait scales's very meaningful correlation with the measure of anxiety state at rest and while under duress that provides an important source of validity for this self-report device.

It has been a finding common to many culture/language groups that males obtain lower mean scores on the A-Trait scale than females. It has been argued, convincingly, that males have many more reasons to deny or minimize anxiety proneness than women do. Cross-culturally, this is an immense question. It would be very difficult to state

that males' need to minimize anxiety proneness in different cultures is the same. However, the development of norms for each of the culture/language groups minimizes the risk of arriving at premature clinical conclusions regarding trait anxiety in these groups; furthermore, one can think of the possibility of cross-cultural assessment studies in which an independent measure of defense or tendency to minimize or "fake good" in regard to trait anxiety would be given together with the A-Trait scale.

At any rate, intraculturally, wherever the normalization of the STAI has been properly developed, the A-Trait scale will provide a means of screening patients and normal populations for individuals with neurotic anxiety problems, and can certainly serve in the selection of persons with different degrees of anxiety proneness. In the conditions noted above, the presence of the indigenous STAIs has opened the door for a number of studies relating anxiety proneness to the performance of many different activities.

One caveat to keep in mind when utilizing the A-Trait scale in the assessment of psychopathology, particularly cross-culturally, is this: Although it certainly appears that the source of most psychopathology in the United States is anxiety, it is plausible that even in countries like the United States there may be individuals for whom the main source of mental suffering is depression, as it appears to be in some cultures. As will be seen later, there is some evidence that in Mexico, the main source of psychopathology is not anxiety but depression.

THE HOLTZMAN INKBLOT TECHNIQUE

In discussing the cross-cultural use of psychological tests, Brislin, Lonner, and Thorndike (1973) observe that the inkblot stands alone, not only among psychological tests but among projective tests, as a genuinely ambiguous stimulus. They feel that all other techniques, including projectives, bear clear traces of the culture in which they have been originated. About the Holtzman Inkblot Technique (HIT), they have the following to say:

The HIT thus has all the features of the Rorschach, including most of the scoring categories, plus many of its own features (such as anxiety, pathognomic verbalization, space and hostility), and can thus be considered a careful attempt to meet the standards of psychometric instruments. Cronbach (1970) notes that "the test construction and standardization was carried out with a degree of attention to technical detail no other personality test can match" (p. 637). Although HIT and Rorschach scores have much the same meaning, the HIT offers more promise in the validation of inkblot hypotheses, and the standardized method of administration is, from a cross-cultural standpoint, a most welcome characteristic. (p. 139)

The fundamental reason for the development of the HIT was to overcome the major defects of the Rorschach as a projective method for the assessment of personality and for differential diagnosis. As indicated by Holtzman (1980a), preliminary work made him realize that a complete new set of inkblots could be constructed on sound psychometric principles only by embarking on a major program of developmental research. Holtzman and his assistants experimented with thousands of inkblots until the final version of the technique was completed in 1958. After this, again with the help of his assistants, a standardization program on thousands of individuals was conducted across the United States on populations ranging all the way from preschool children to superior adults. Also included were samples of schizophrenics, mentally retarded individuals, and depressed patients (Holtzman, Thorpe, Swartz, & Herron, 1961).

The HIT consists of two parallel forms, A and B, each containing 45 matched inkblots of various color, form, and shading nuances, together with 2 trial inkblots common to both forms. Everything indicates that greatly improved psychometric properties were achieved without losing the rich symbolic quality of the projective responses for which the Rorschach had proven so valuable. However, the HIT differs from the Rorschach in that each subject gives only one response for each card, and the examiner uses a simple, standardized scoring system containing 22 variables that are designed to capture most of the aspects of inkblot perceptions according to Rorschach, but in such

a way as to permit more reliable, unidimensional quantitative treatment. Beginning with 1 of the 2 trial inkblots, the 47 inkblot plates are given serially with instructions that stress the following points: (1) The inkblots were not made to look like anything in particular; (2) different people see different things in them; and (3) only one response for each card is desired. The tester includes the essential feature of each verbal response on a record form, together with notes on the location of the response and the reaction time to each blot. It is important to note that the inkblots in the parallel version of the test, Form B, are remarkably similar in their general characteristics to Form A but differ in specific details. The means and the standard deviations for each of the 22 inkblot scores in the test are identical in both forms, regardless of the populations studied. This assures their interchangeability for repeated testing. Swartz and Holtzman (1963), with a standard set of slides, developed a group administration method for the HIT that proved to have response characteristics similar to those of the standard individual version, at least for normal individuals. Gorham and his colleagues developed a computer program for 17 of the HIT variables, simulating hand scoring to deal with large samples using a streamlined record form (Gorham, 1967, 1970; Gorham, Moseley, & Holtzman, 1968; Moseley, Gorham, & Hill, 1963). All of these features make the HIT attractive for cross-cultural assessment. It has been utilized in many cross-cultural studies. Three of these are summarized here to illustrate the potentialities of the technique.

The Seven-Culture Study

After Gorham (1967) ascertained the validity and generally high reliability of the computer scoring system for HIT group responses in the English language, Diaz-Guerrero, Fernandez Davila, and Fernandez Pardo (1967) followed in his footsteps by developing a similar comparability between individual and computer-based Spanish-language scores for the HIT with Mexican and Panamanian subjects. With the help of local psychologists, Moseley (1967) then carried out a multivariate comparison of HIT scores in seven cultures: Argentina, Colombia (Bogota), Colombia (Cartagena), Mexico, Panama, the United States, and Venezuela.

Table 21.3 presents the means of the 17 computer-scored HIT variables by cultures, together with the number of university students that were studied in each of the seven cultures. As Moseley suggests, geography appears to have something to do with degree of similarity of responses to the HIT. The impact of one culture upon another appears to be directly related to the difference in the masses (number of inhabitants) of the cultures and inversely related to the square of the geographic distance between the cultures. This generalization is modified by such factors as having boundaries in common or not and the size of these boundaries. At any rate, Table 21.3 has been modified from Moseley's (1967) original version by placing the countries in sequence according to their geographic nearness to the United States.

The first observation is that the Mexican sample is much closer in almost every score to the American sample than to the faraway Argentinian sample. Next, it is quite clear that there is a strong tendency for the samples of the countries closer to the United States to be more alike, at least in profile. Using the 17 computer-based inkblot scores in a multiple discriminant-function analysis, Moseley made predictions for the cultural identities of the 714 college students in this seven-culture study. The students' actual cultural identities were then compared with those predicted exclusively from inkblot responses. The results are most interesting. On the basis of patterns of inkblot scores alone, in one analysis of the Latin-American cultures, Moseley found not a single college student from Argentina, Colombia, or Venezuela—the three South American countries—misclassified as a Mexican or Panamanian (see Table 21.4). Nor were any of the Mexicans or Panamanians misclassified as Argentinians. Only two Mexicans and five Panamanians were misclassified as Colombians, and only one Mexican and no Panamanians were misidentified as Venezuelans.

It is even more interesting to note which countries in the multiple discriminant-function analysis are closest to others in their patterns of responses. When the United States is compared with four Latin-American cultures (see Table 21.5), only Mexico appears similar to the United States. As many as 21% of the Americans were misclassified as Mexicans, compared to fewer than 2% of Americans misclassified as being from any other culture. As for the Mexicans, 17% were misclassified as Americans, and 24% (see Table 21.4) appeared as Panamanians. It is clear from this study that Mexico and the United States share more characteristics, probably because of their geographic closeness and a shared extensive boarder, on the HIT that either shares with the cultures of South America.[3]

Regarding these results, Holtzman (1980a) has the following to say:

> This type of global analysis across major cultures of the Americas is difficult to interpret in any depth. It is clear from Moseley's study that the degree of cultural exchange and diffusion between two countries is strikingly parallel to the degree of similarity in personality patterns as measured by inkblot scores. (p. 107)

A Two-Culture, Longitudinal, Overlapping Study of Child Development

Beginning in 1963, Holtzman, Diaz-Guerrero, and Swartz, in collaboration with Laosa, Lara Tapia, Morales, Reyes-Lagunes, and Witzke, and close to 100 research assistants and helpers, initiated what may be the most ambitious cross-cultural longitudinal study of child development available (Holtzman et al., 1975). A total of 450 Mexican children from Mexico City and 450 Ango-American children from Austin, Texas, were carefully sampled in order to be representative of the educational institutions and school populations in each country and culture; representative also of two local social classes; and still overlapping to the extent that about 150 pairs had parents with an identical or

---

[3]The large percentage of reciprocal misidentification of Mexican and American university students is, in our opinion, also a result of the fact that the two traditional cultures are almost at opposite ends of a continuum with regard to coping. The American culture emphasizes active coping, and the Mexican culture stresses passive, self-modifying coping. University students are probably most opposed to their traditional culture, with the Mexicans becoming active in coping and the Americans passive. As a result, they may become far more similar than other types of subjects.

TABLE 21.3. Means and Standard Deviations of Computer-Scored HIT Variables by Cultures

HIT variables	U.S. mean	Mexico mean	Panama mean	Venezuela mean	Colombia (C) mean	Colombia (B) mean	Argentina mean	U.S. SD	Mexico SD	Panama SD	Venezuela SD	Colombia (C) SD	Colombia (B) SD	Argentina SD
Location	42.2	35.1	37.6	31.8	44.8	51.3	27.6	14.2	13.0	15.6	15.6	18.4	17.7	13.6
Rejection	1.7	2.7	1.6	1.8	5.6	1.2	0.8	3.2	3.5	3.3	4.4	7.1	2.8	1.5
Form definiteness	79.5	74.8	65.9	56.7	58.8	62.4	61.0	11.7	13.3	12.0	14.5	12.0	13.1	11.3
Color	8.3	6.4	5.6	8.2	3.1	3.8	6.3	5.1	4.1	4.0	4.8	2.9	4.0	4.0
Shading	3.8	4.0	5.8	5.4	2.2	2.8	4.3	2.3	3.0	4.8	4.1	2.1	2.9	3.5
Movement	27.8	23.6	15.2	20.4	9.1	13.1	20.2	12.0	12.1	8.0	10.9	6.4	9.2	8.9
Integration	2.0	1.5	1.4	4.0	1.7	3.2	4.5	1.6	1.2	1.3	1.6	1.5	1.4	1.4
Human	25.2	23.6	17.0	20.1	14.5	20.9	20.0	8.5	7.9	6.4	6.9	6.1	8.3	6.0
Animal	25.1	25.4	24.4	21.9	19.3	22.3	20.1	7.1	7.2	5.8	8.4	6.6	7.4	6.2
Anatomy	2.0	2.3	2.6	3.2	3.5	1.7	1.6	2.0	2.7	2.4	2.8	3.1	1.9	1.7
Sex	0.6	0.3	0.3	0.4	0.2	0.5	0.1	1.8	0.9	0.6	0.7	0.4	1.0	0.4
Abstract	1.3	1.3	0.6	1.1	0.6	0.5	1.2	1.7	1.8	0.9	1.1	0.8	1.0	1.3
Anxiety	8.6	7.2	4.9	5.5	4.0	4.1	7.1	4.5	5.0	3.8	4.0	3.0	2.7	3.7
Hostility	6.5	4.0	3.6	2.9	2.4	3.5	4.0	3.3	2.8	2.8	2.8	2.0	2.0	2.9
Barrier	10.2	12.0	9.5	9.0	7.5	8.5	9.6	3.9	3.9	3.4	4.0	3.4	2.8	3.3
Penetration	3.7	2.9	1.8	1.8	1.0	1.3	2.2	2.3	1.9	1.8	1.5	1.1	1.3	1.7
Popular	9.5	6.9	4.9	5.5	3.7	4.5	4.8	3.0	2.6	2.4	2.4	2.1	2.2	2.3

Note. Colombia (B), Bogotá; Colombia (C), Cartagena. Adapted from "Multivariate Comparison of Seven Cultures: Argentina, Colombia (Bogotá, Cartagena), Mexico, Panama, United States and Venezuela" by E. C. Moseley, 1967, in C. Hereford and L. Natalicio (Eds.), *Aportaciones de la Psicología a la Investigación Transcultural* (pp. 291–304), Mexico City: Trillas. Copyright 1967 by Editorial Trillas of Mexico City. Adapted by permission.

TABLE 21.4. Discriminant-Function Classification Matrix for Central and South American Cultures

Actual	Argentina	Colombia (C)	Venezuela	Mexico	Panama	Total
			Predicted			
Argentina	68	7	16	0	0	91
Colombia (C)	7	89	4	0	0	100
Venezuela	19	10	77	0	0	106
Mexico	0	2	1	73	24	100
Panama	0	5	0	14	75	94
Total						491

Note. Colombia (B), Bogotá; Colombia (C), Cartagena. Adapted from "Multivariate Comparison of Seven Cultures: Argentina, Colombia (Bogota, Cartagena), Mexico, Panama, United States and Venezuela" by E. C. Moseley, 1967, in C. Hereford and L. Natalicio (Eds.), *Aportaciones de la Psicología a la Investigación Transcultural* (pp. 291–304), Mexico City: Trillas. Copyright 1967 by Editorial Trillas of Mexico City. Adapted by permission.

TABLE 21.5. Discriminant-Function Classification Matrix for Selected North, Central, and South American Cultures

Actual	United States	Colombia (B)	Colombia (C)	Venezuela	Panama	Total
			Predicted			
United States	111	1	1	2	31	146
Colombia (B)	0	56	11	10	0	77
Colombia (C)	0	26	66	8	0	100
Venezuela	0	20	9	77	0	106
Mexico	17	0	1	1	81	100
Total						529

Note. Colombia (B), Bogotá; Colombia (C), Cartagena. Adapted from "Multivariate Comparison of Seven Cultures: Argentina, Colombia (Bogota, Cartagena), Mexico, Panama, United States and Venezuela" by E. C. Moseley, 1967, in C. Hereford and L. Natalicio (Eds.), *Aportaciones de la Psicología a la Investigación Transcultural* (pp. 291–304), Mexico City: Trillas. Copyright 1967 by Editorial Trillas of Mexico City. Adapted by permission.

similar level of education and occupation. Utmost care was exercised regarding the training (often in the same combined group) of the American and Mexican research assistants, to insure that the application of a battery of measuring instruments and interviews would be as homogeneous as possible. When the tests were not objective, much effort was spent in order to make the scoring criteria the same. Much work was done in order to try to adapt the objective tests, which were mostly developed in the United States, to the Mexican culture. Originally there were the same number of boys and girls, and there were three groups of 150 children each in Mexico City and in Austin, Texas. The study began when these children were in the first, fourth, and seventh grades and when they were 6.7, 9.7, and 12.7 years of age; the actual testing took place within 30 days of the age as specified.

A large battery of tests (see Table 2.2 in Holtzman et al., 1975) was given yearly, sometimes repeatedly for the entire 6 years

of the study and in others for a lesser number of years. The HIT was applied individually every year for the 6 years in the three samples in both cultures, yielding many replications for analysis. Forms A and B of the HIT were alternately used (i.e., Form A in one year, Form B in the next).

A brief definition of 12 HIT scores is necessary for a better understanding of the results. Reaction Time is the average time in seconds from the presentation of an inkblot to the beginning of the response. Pathognomic Verbalization is a score reflecting the degree of autistic, bizarre thinking evident in responses to the inkblots. Location is a score measuring the tendency to break down the inkblot into smaller fragments when reporting a perception. Movement reflects the energy level of movement or potential movement ascribed to the percept regardless of content. Integration is scored when two or more adequately perceived blot elements are organized into a large whole. Anxiety is based upon signs of anxiety in fantasy con-

TABLE 21.6. Cross-Cultural Mean Comparisons on the HIT for which Uniformly Significant Differences Were Found between Mexican and Anglo-American Children

Score	Mexican	Anglo-American	Interpretation for Mexican
Reaction time	21.7	17.9	Slower respose time to inkblots.
Pathognomic verbalization	3.1	6.4	Less pathology in fantasy.
Location	43.3	33.0	More small details.
Movement	14.1	25.7	Less movement in fantasy.
Integration	2.0	3.3	Lower integration of parts into whole.
Anxiety	5.6	9.1	Less anxiety in fantasy.
Hostility	6.3	10.1	Less hostility in fantasy.

Note. The data are from Holtzman, Diaz-Guerrero, and Swartz (1975).

tent, as indicated by emotions and attitudes, expressive behavior, symbolism, or cultural stereotypes of fear. Hostility is based upon signs of hostility in the fantasy content. Barrier is a score based upon references to any protective covering, membrane, shell, or skin that might be symbolically related to a perception of body image boundaries in inkblot responses. Penetration is indicative of symbolic penetration of the exterior of the body. Anatomy is scored for responses referring to any part of the body, x-rays, and medical drawings. Color measures the apparent primacy of color (including black, grey, or white) as a determinant of a person's response to inkblots. Shading is a similar score dealing with the apparent primacy of shading as a determinant of texture, depth, or vista in a person's inkblot responses.

Table 21.6 shows the HIT scores for which consistent differences were found between Mexican and Anglo-American children in the 18 replications. Beyond the differences shown in Table 21.6, the Mexican children rejected an average of 3.2 inkblots, while the American children rejected an average of 2.2. Although this difference failed to reach significance uniformly, it was significant in most of the 18 replications.

In Form Definiteness, there was no difference in the mean score for the two cultures, but highly significant differences appeared for age group and social class. Thus, Form Definiteness increased with age and grade, and upper-class children obtained higher mean scores than lower-class children in both cultures. The complexity of the comparison

for some variables such as Form Definiteness is shown in Figure 21.1, in an interaction among culture, sex, and year of repeated testing. It can be noted that when tested initially, boys reported more specific perceptions than did girls in both cultures. Although this difference (higher Form Definitiveness for boys) continued to hold up fairly well throughout the 6 years of repeated testing for American children, the sex difference gradually narrowed and then reversed for the Mexicans. In the last 2 years, the Mexican girls received higher scores on Form Definiteness than did the Mexican boys.

As far as Form Appropriateness is concerned for the two younger groups (6.7 and 9.7), Mexicans had significantly higher scores than Americans. The differences disappeared in the oldest group (12.7). In Barrier, there were quite consistently significant differences: American children had higher scores than Mexican children. While Mexican children obtained an average score of 8.7 in Color, American children scored nearly twice as high (16.07); only upper-class Mexican children in the youngest age group scored higher than their American counterparts, and this difference was slight and insignificant. The mean score on Shading also proved to be considerably higher for the American children in general (4.39) than for the Mexican children (2.54). However, among the oldest children (who had reached college age by the end of the study) of the two countries, these differences disappeared. It is important to note that the mean score for Anatomy increased with age in Mexico while

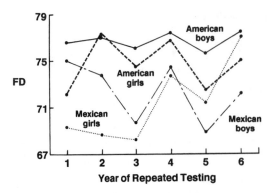

FIGURE 21.1.   Scores on the Form Definiteness variable of the HIT for Mexican and Anglo-American children by culture, sex, and year of repeated testing. The data are from Holtzman, Diaz-Guerrero, and Swartz (1975). From *Personality Development in Two Cultures* (p. 215) by W. H. Holtzman, R. Diaz-Guerrero, and J. D. Swartz, 1975, Austin: University of Texas Press. Copyright 1975 by University of Texas Press. Reprinted by permission.

it consistently decreased in the United States, producing significantly higher scores in Anatomy for the older groups in Mexico. It is clearly important for personality assessment in children that the younger children showed far more and larger inkblot score differences than older adolescents and college students.

Finally, on Penetration, the American children obtained a higher mean score (3.43) than did the Mexican children (2.05). In this case, American children showed no significant differences across the three groups, whereas the Mexican children increased from 0.79 for the youngest children to 2.22 for Group II and 3.14 for Group III.

It is important to report that almost all of these cross-cultural differences were found independently by Tamm (1967a, 1967b). Tamm designed a study involving bilingual Mexican and American children attending the American School in Mexico City. Thirty children in the first, fourth, and seventh grades were tested at 6.7 years, 9.7 years, and 12.7 years of age, respectively, in order to provide precise parallels to the experimental design employed in the larger cross-cultural study between the United States and Mexico. In Tamm's study, half of the children were native Mexicans for whom Spanish was the primary language;

they generally came for upper-class Mexican families, with probably a strong desire on the part of the parents for their children to obtain an American-style education. The other half of the children were Americans whose fathers were in Mexico on business or as government representatives. These American families probably wanted their children to develop bilingual/bicultural skills and attitudes. (It is important to know that the curriculum in the American School is taught half in English and half in Spanish.) Besides the HIT, Tamm administered all the subtests of the Wechsler Intelligence Scale for Children (WISC). In the larger cross-cultural study there were significant differences favoring the Americans on the WISC subtests, but in this setting only Digit Span proved significant across cultures, with the Mexican children scoring higher than the Americans. On the other hand, in responding to the HIT, the Mexican children used much more small detail and less human content, and had lower Color, Movement, Pathognomic Verbalization, Anxiety, and Hostility scores than the American children, the same as in the larger study.

The Mexican/Mexican-American Cross-Cultural Study

Beginning in 1978 with a grant from The Hogg Foundation for Mental Health, the Institute of Family Studies of the University of Texas and the National Institute for the Behavioral Sciences in Mexico launched a research program to study the impact of Mexican culture and economic stress upon mental and physical health (Diaz-Guerrero, 1986a; Diaz-Guerrero & Iscoe, 1984). The sample design included 60 Mexican and 60 Mexican-American families. In addition to the parents (the mothers were tested for the study), each family had three children—a 15- to 16-year-old adolescent, an 11- to 12-year-old preadolescent, and a 5- to 6-year-old child (the sexes were almost equally represented)—who were tested or interviewed. All families belonged to one of two social classes (semiskilled-worker and skilled-worker families, as measured by education and occupation of the fathers). No statistical differences appeared in the results for social class between the Mexican and Mexican-American families, but economic differences

TABLE 21.7. *F* Values and/or Student *t* Values for Differences in HIT Variables between Mexicans and Mexican-Americans

	Preadolescents		Adolescents		Mothers	
	n = 60 Monterrey	*n* = 60 San Antonio	*n* = 60 Monterrey	*n* = 60 San Antonio	*n* = 60 Monterrey	*n* = 60 San Antonio
HITFDC ($\bar{x}$)	72.05	84.50***	67.07	83.80***	62.73	76.60***
HITFAC ($\bar{x}$)	40.10	34.47***	41.92	35.10***	40.30	36.70***
HITRT ($\bar{x}$)	17.98	14.57***	22.57	14.98***	20.85	18.27***
HITR ($\bar{x}$)	4.45	0.78***	4.37	0.92***	7.33	0.77***
HITC ($\bar{x}$)	7.23	8.32***	8.13	21.83***	7.17	12.98***
HITSh ($\bar{x}$)	0.25	4.58***	0.47	8.20***	0.27	7.08***
HITM ($\bar{x}$)	10.08	16.82***	12.68	33.02***	8.05	21.07***
HITI ($\bar{x}$)	1.38	2.18***	2.52	3.48***	1.33	3.40***
HITH ($\bar{x}$)	15.62	18.53*	14.77	20.72***	13.13	17.63***
HITA ($\bar{x}$)	28.23	34.57***	26.62	30.41**	21.72	32.23***
HITAX ($\bar{x}$)	3.57	4.43	3.72	5.68	4.35	6.17
HITHS ($\bar{x}$)	4.23	5.67*	4.47	11.73**	3.83	5.30*
HIRBR	—	—	—	—	—	n.s.
HITLoc	—	—	—	—	—	n.s.
HITVC	—	—	—	—	—	—
HITP	4.85	5.57	5.37	6.65*	4.15	5.33*

Note. From "Holtzman Inkblot Technique (HIT) Differences across Mexican, Mexican-American and Angloamerican Cultures" by R. Diaz-Guerrero. In E. E. Roskam (Ed.), *Measurement and Personality Assessment: Vol. 8. Proceedings of the XXIII International Congress of Psychology* (p. 254), 1985, Amsterdam: Elsevier Science Publishers. Copyright 1985 by Elsevier Science Publishers. Reprinted by permission. HITFDC, Form Definiteness corrected for Rejection; HITFAC, Form Appropriateness; HITRT, Reaction Time; HITR, Rejection; HITC, Color; HITSh, Shading; HITM, Movement; HITI, Integration; HITH, Human; HITA, Animal; HITAX, Anxiety; HITHS, Hostility; HITBR, Barrier; HITLoc, Location; HITVC, Pathognomic Verbalization: HITP, Popular.
  *$p < .05$.
  **$p < .01$.
  ***$p < .001$.

that favored the Mexican-American families were clear in the number of rooms in the household and home appliances. Monterrey, in northern Mexico, and San Antonio, Texas, in the southwestern United States, were the cities for the study. One of the instruments in the battery of tests and interviews was the HIT.

Table 21.7 displays the significant differences found between Mexican and Mexican-American preadolescents, adolescents, and their mothers in this study. It is abundantly clear again that for the majority of HIT scores, strikingly consistent differences were found between Mexicans and Mexican-Americans—almost the same differences as those previously found between Mexicans and Anglo-Americans. A degree of acculturation to the Anglo-American pattern is evident in many of the scores; it fails, however, to

appear on some variables such as Barrier, Location and Pathognomic Verbalization, in which the Mexican-Americans are indistinguishable from their counterparts. Anxiety and to a lesser extent Hostility show the same trend, though it is not statistically significant. These data substantiate the findings of the earlier studies concerning differences between the Mexican and the Anglo-American cultures. On the basis of such overwhelming evidence in which differences remain across time in so many subcultural variables, we must conclude that they are real cross-cultural differences. However, even then, to say that they are due to culture may be an incomplete and vague interpretation, since the entire ecosystem of each city from which subjects were drawn in these studies may be involved.

The Meaning of the Differences

What is the psychological meaning of the differences found in these three studies? There are at least two ways in which these differences in psychological meaning can be approached. One is in terms of normal cultural behavior, and the other in terms of (we hope) a universal clinical viewpoint. Holtzman et al. (1975) interpreted normal cultural differences in terms of an active versus passive cross-cultural dichotomy of coping styles. Anglo-Americans, when facing a problem, will try to solve it by modifying the physical, the interpersonal, and/or the social environment. Mexicans, when facing a problem, will try to solve it by modifying themselves (Diaz-Guerrero, 1965, 1967). In what follows, taking advantage of the results of many other cross-cultural and intracultural studies of the populations under study, we try to spell out some further ways in which coping styles affect each one of the differentiating HIT scores. In particular, we try to describe the way a Mexican child would cope with the task represented by the HIT and with the examiner.[4]

The following is hypothesized for the actual responses of the Mexican child. The Mexican is less conscious of time than the American, and he perceives time as passing more slowly. He takes the HIT card and observes it carefully. He wants more than anything else to please the examiner. He searches the inkblot in such a way that he can find either in the whole or in a small area a very appropriate form; the younger the individual, the stronger this tendency will be. Because he is coping more passively with the task, he will tend to reject more cards than the American. In addition, social relations in Mexico are formal, and color, omnipresent in the Mexican ecosystem, will be taken for granted. Therefore, the child will place more emphasis on the formal aspects of the inkblot than on the color and the shading. His passive world, and certainly the world of the inkblots, is far more static than that of the American. Consequently, the Mexican child will see much less movement in the inkblots. His effort in the task, beyond that of pleasing the

examiner, will be very much in accordance with his more passive dealing with the task, and he will have lower scores in Integration and Animal. His lower scores in Anxiety, Hostility, and Pathognomic Verbalization, each representing aspects of fantasy life, are partially due to this more passive view of life; moreover, anxious, hostile, or bizarre statements might be displeasing to the examiner and are definitely at odds with the courteous, pleasing, perhaps even formalistically polite pattern of the Mexican. The Mexican child's higher score on Anatomy appears to go along with a greater preoccupation with the inner organs, as was found through the SD technique (Holtzman et al., 1975, p. 343); this is consistent with the passive, self-modifying coping style. The generally lower scores on Barrier and the increasing scores on Penetration with age in the Mexican may signify the greater openness, adaptability, and flexibility of the Mexican to outside influence (field sensitivity?) and his apparently greater ability to find humor in everything.

Holtzman et al. (1975) noted that for a few variables (i.e., Reaction Time and Shading), the oldest, most educated Mexican children had the same scores as their American counterparts. In Mexico it has been found repeatedly, as we shall see later, that the more formal education a subject has (particularly higher education), the lower the subject's scores in several scales measuring traditional cultural beliefs. When one is testing advanced university students, cultural differences will tend to diminish—particularly if such students belong to geographically close cultures, as shown in the study by Moseley (1967). Amount of formal education must always be taken into account in personality assessment, cross-cultural or not. There are variables, however, where cross-cultural differences remain, regardless of age/grade level or geographical proximity. A striking example is Movement on the HIT. Here the difference (with the American children clearly scoring higher) remains across all ages, both sexes, and the two socioeconomic levels. Nevertheless, it was found that boys saw significantly more Movement than girls in both cultures.

The second large question that can be raised, and one that is often taken for granted intuitively, is this: What clinical meaning can be attached to these differences? If we can

---

[4]For the sake of simplicity, masculine pronouns ("he," "his," etc.) are used in the discussion that follows. All of what is said, of course, applies to females as well, except where sex differences are plainly indicated.

TABLE 21.8. The HIT Scores That Frequently Differentiate Mexicans and Anglo-Americans

Mexican pattern	Anglo-American pattern
More HIT Anatomy	Less HIT Anatomy
Less HIT Animal	More HIT Animal
Less HIT Anxiety	More HIT Anxiety
Less HIT Barrier	More HIT Barrier
Less HIT Color	More HIT Color
More HIT Form Appropriateness	Less HIT Form Appropriateness
Less HIT Human	More HIT Human
Less HIT Hostility	More HIT Hostility
Less HIT Integration	More HIT Integration
More HIT Location	Less HIT Location
Less HIT Movement	More HIT Movement
Less HIT Pathognomic Verbalization	More HIT Pathognomic Verbalization
Less HIT Penetration	More HIT Penetration
More HIT Rejection	Less HIT Rejection
More HIT Reaction Time	Less HIT Reaction Time
Less HIT Shading	More HIT Shading

Note. From "Holtzman Inkblot Technique (HIT) Differences across Mexican, Mexican-American and Angloamerican Cultures" by R. Diaz-Guerrero. In E. E. Roskam (Ed.), *Measurement and Personality Assessment: Vol. 8. Proceedings of the XXIII International Congress of Psychology* (p. 256), 1985, Amsterdam: Elsevier Science Publishers. Copyright 1985 by Elsevier Science Publishers. Reprinted by permission.

hold on to somewhat universal meanings of psychopathology, it may be stated that a good number of the scores that differentiate Mexicans and Americans consistently (see Table 21.8) are often considered by clinicians as signs of depression. Hill (1972, p. 161) enumerates HIT scores that identify dejected attitudes and depression as high scores on Reaction Time and Rejection, and low scores on Color, Shading, and Form Definitiveness. On the other hand, she also considers high scores on Pathognomic Verbalization, Penetration, and Anxiety as part of the self-punitive attitude. The passive pattern, being one where self-modification rather than the modification of the environment is prevalent, should actually tend to provoke depression in the members of a culture that hold to this pattern of coping. It is interesting that in a recent study (Diaz-Guerrero, 1984a), a low Evaluation factor and high Potency and Activity factors in the SD for the concept of "sadness" in Mexico correlated highly with 20 crucial clinical concepts surveying mental pathology in the Mexicans.

These results have led us to the tentative conclusion that, while anxiety may be the main source of psychopathology in the United States, depression is the fundamental source of pathology in Mexico. The facts that there is a very large drinking problem among Mexicans, and that drug addiction is relatively higher among Mexican-Americans than among Anglo-Americans, seem to back the idea that the cultural pattern prevalent in Mexico tends to lead to a normal depressive *cultural* attitude in Mexicans. At the same time, however, when a culture imposes a patterning on individuals—in this case, a depressive patterning—many of the efforts of both individuals and groups, particularly families and other societal institutions, are aimed dialectically at counterbalancing this initial patterning. Therefore, the usual atmosphere that can be perceived in the Mexican culture tends to be somewhat hypomanic. In such an ecosystem, there is an accent on everything that will lift the somewhat depresssive outlook—in this case, fiestas, siestas, ceremonies, entertainment, movie going, and sporting events; highly, deeply, and lengthy communicative interpersonal relations (friendship, love, romantic activities); music and singing; and so on.

It is important to realize that when the statements "Life is to be endured" and "Life is to be enjoyed" were placed on a forced-choice questionnaire for Mexicans and Anglo-Americans of different ages, the Americans selected the "Life is to be enjoyed" alternative close to 80% of the time, whereas just the opposite was found for the Mexicans. This apparently means that while the Mexicans start out believing that "Life is to be endured," they employ much creativity and time in order to make it agreeable and actually find it not as bad as anticipated. On the other hand, first-hand contact with American individuals and groups gives the feeling of sadness and depression. Although their culture starts with an unbounded optimism and the idea that life is to be enjoyed, the many realities of life seem to reduce the enthusiasm of the Americans greatly, and the general atmosphere tends to be more on the depressive side, sometimes brimming with cynicism; in turn, and for different reasons, this leads Americans to drinking, drug use, and so on.

Thus, concurrently, and apparently in a contradictory fashion, the cognitive attitude of Americans is one of optimism, of hope, and of interested achievement (Holtzman et al., 1975). On the contrary, there is a general trend in the Mexicans to perceive the future with pessimism and also to look down at the potentialities of their fellow citizens as compared with foreign groups; the Mexican style of achievement is often far more connected to affiliative networks than to oneself as a standard (Diaz-Guerrero, 1975, p. 143).

Abel (1973) reported a number of studies with the Rorschach showing the sensitivity of inkblots to cross-cultural differences. Given, however, that the psychometric weakness of this tool would be multiplied in cross-cultural assessment, the more promising instrument for this task is the HIT. Holtzman (1975, 1980b) reviews a number of new developments, including technological advances, variations of the standard form, and results of cross-cultural studies with the HIT. Particularly important are the development of configurational patterns, the clinical statements associated with them, and their use in differential diagnosis. The HIT can be very useful when those employing it have substantial knowledge of the main psychosocial dimensions or sociocultural premises prevalent in each country.

The reader, however, must carefully ponder the following thoughts from Holtzman (1980b):

> The assumption of a complex but direct relationship between an individual's personality and his responses when taking a projective test leads to three corollaries that are rarely made explicit: a) Belief that a test record is a sufficiently extensive sampling of the personality to warrant making judgements about it; b) belief that the psychological determinants of the responses are basic and general; and c) belief that projective techniques tap the durable essence of personality equally in different individuals across a wide range of ethnic, socioeconomic and cultural variations. (pp. 246–247)

Holtzman generally cautions against over-interpretation of any type of projective test protocol. He agrees with the usual clinical practice of employing a variety of other techniques along with the projectives whenever interpretation is to be attempted.[5]

WITKIN'S MEASUREMENTS

Witkin et al. (1954) opened up what Werner (1962) would undoubtedly have called an "unknown territory"; they devised a series of procedures, some of which are relatively simple measurements, that give access to various aspects of both normal and abnormal personality. It must be added that the setting up of procedures was guided by a flexible but systematic and frequently brilliant conceptualization that colleagues and followers have often emulated.

In the first of the series of laboratory procedures developed by Witkin and colleagues, an erect subject in a totally darkened room views a tilted luminous rectangular frame, and his or her task is to adjust to an upright position a tilted luminous rod centered within the tilted frame. This Rod-and-Frame Test (RFT) was followed by the Body Adjustment Test (BAT); its companion, the Room Adjustment Test (RAT); and a psychometric device, the Articulation of Body Concept Scale

---

[5]Even physicists are excruciatingly aware that phenomena such as electricity are never fully exposed. Each method or technical procedure reveals only a facet of the total phenomenon or process.

(ABC), which uses a figure-drawing approach.

As Witkin (1978) points out, when the need arose for other assessment procedures to determine an individual's or a group's standing on the dimension of field dependence–independence, he and his colleagues were able to draw on the laboratory work to develop a battery of tests. Among these were the original, individually applied Embedded Figure Test (EFT), which was followed by the Group (GEFT) and Children's (CEFT) versions. Witkin et al. (1954) and Witkin, Dyk, Fatterson, Goodenough, and Karp (1962/1974) are the major sources for information on the laboratory and the ABC measures. For the EFT and related tests, there is a manual (Witkin, Oltman, Raskin, & Karp, 1971).

The dimension of field dependence–independence is a cognitive style or specific form of processing external information, but it is also connected with the degree of "psychological differentiation." This latter term refers to the complexity of structure of a psychosocial system. The crucial aspect of differentiation, for our purposes, is explained by Witkin (1978) as follows:

I am going to focus on the self–nonself segregation aspect of differentiation because that is where field dependence–independence has its conceptual home. Development of a segregated self carries with it the formation of internal frames of reference. The availability of internal referents and the greater polarity between self and others, which self–nonself segregation implies, contribute to greater determination of behavior from within. On the other hand, the lesser repertoire of internal standards and the continued connection with others associated with limited self–nonself segregation are likely to encourage reference to external sources as guides of behavior. . . . The tendency to rely primarily on internal referents in a self-consistent way we designate as *field-independent* cognitive style. The tendency to give greater credit to external referents is a *field-dependent* cognitive style. (pp. 15–16)

Innumerable studies have demonstrated that to have a high score in field independence or in field dependence is associated with many expressions and behaviors of personality. These range all the way from vocational facilitation through several aspects of social behavior to typical mechanisms of defense and psychopathology. Table 21.9, taken from Brislin et al. (1973), is a good summary. The authors warn, however, that although support for most of those statements has been provided by a number of intra- and cross-cultural studies, the statements should be viewed as hypotheses. Latter studies have continued to reinforce and extend a number of these hypotheses for the interpretation of results on the Witkin measures. Berry's (1976) systematic study has clearly related field dependence and independence to several important ecological factors.

The program of study by Holtzman et al. (1975), described earlier, included many replications of the individually applied EFT. A short, 12-item form of the EFT (Witkin et al., 1971) was used in that study. Each item in this test presents the subject with a complex, geometric, variously colored figure, in which the subject is to locate and trace a simple figure that he or she has inspected previously. Successful performance on the task requires selective attention only to relevant aspects of the complex stimulus, in order to avoid the effects of distracting cues. From each subject's performance on the 12 items, four scores were derived: number of errors, number of items correct, reaction time to correct solution average over the 12 items, and number of re-exams. For the sample utilized in this study, each Mexican child was paired with an American child on sex, age/grade, and socioeconomic status of the family until all closely matched cases were exhausted. The procedure yielded 196 precisely matched pairs, 56 in the youngest group (6.7), 75 in the middle group (9.7), and 65 in the oldest group (12.7)—a total of 392 children.

We present the results of this part of the study through two types of analyses that are pertinent to the issue of cross-cultural development of cognitive–perceptual style: (1) stability coefficients across 5 years of repeated testing by culture and age group; and (2) a complex analysis of variance design with five main factors—(a) socioeconomic level, (b)

TABLE 21.9. Traits and Abilities Associated with Field Independence and Dependence

Field-independent (parts of the field are experienced as discrete from organized ground)	Field-dependent (perception dominated by organization of surrounding field, and parts of field are experienced as fused)
"Fluid" or analytic ability	"Crystallized" or trained ability
More differentiated perception	Less differentiated perception
Males tend to be higher	Females tend to be higher
Increases with age plateau in young adulthood	Geriatrics "return to field dependence"
"Articulated" cognitive style	"Global" cognitive style
"Articulated" body concept (body has definite limits)	"Global" body concept (body is less separated from environment)
Sense of separate identity high	Low sense of separate identity
Nonconforming, less easily influenced socially	Conforming, more easily influenced socially
Isolation as a major defense	Massive repression and primitive denial as major defenses
Pathologically, delusions and other means to struggle for maintenance of identity	Pathologically, tend to show severe identity problems
Permissively raised	Strictly raised

Note. From *Cross-Cultural Research Methods* by R. W. Brislin, W. J. Lonner, and R. M. Thorndike, 1973, New York: Wiley. Copyright 1973 by John Wiley and Sons, Inc. Reprinted by permission.

sex, (c) age group, (d) culture, and (e) years of repeated testing.

The Stability Coefficients

Although all four of the EFT scores showed sufficient stability across time, here we deal only with one of the two best: mean reaction time to correct solution, the other being number of items correct. Mean time to correct solution (Table 21.10) consistently yielded high test–retest correlations, regardless of the interval between testing periods. The highest stability coefficients, however, were obtained for the oldest children with shorter intervals of time between testing. The average stability with an interval of only 1 year between tests was .79, which was the highest for any of the tests utilized in the Holtzman et al. (1975) study. The average stability coefficients for 2 and 3 years were .72 and .62, respectively. Although there was a slight tendency for these scores to be more stable among the American children, particularly in the oldest group, than among the Mexican children, the difference is not large.

Analysis of Variance

The EFT was given initially only to children in Groups II and III (the two older groups) because it proved too difficult for first-graders. Later, however, it was possible to obtain test data from the children in Group I in Years 4 and 5 of the study, when they were sufficiently mature to cope with the task. (At the time, the CEFT was not available.) Scores for Groups II and III in the first year were analyzed separately from scores from all three groups in Years 4 and 5. In each analysis, four summary scores were analyzed systematically. The number-of-errors score (EFT error) consisted of the total number of errors across the 12 figures; an error occurred when a child offered as a solution a completed but incorrect tracing. The number of items correct out of the 12 figures (EFT correct) constituted a second score. The third score consisted of the average time taken per figure (EFT time). The number of times during the test that a child re-examined the simple figure (the simple and complex figures are never shown simultaneously), in order to refresh his or her memory of what he or she was searching for in the complex figure, con-

TABLE 21.10. Test–Retest Correlations for Mean Reaction Time to Correct Solution on the EFT across 5 Years of Repeated Testing, by Culture and Age Group

Years correlated	Mexico City		Austin	
	Group II	Group III	Group II	Group III
12	.57	.72	.69	.83
13	.59	.68	.66	.74
14	.56	.56	.52	.75
15	.32	.57	.53	.73
23	.78	.84	.80	.82
24	.70	.63	.71	.87
25	.60	.61	.70	.84
34	.84	.74	.75	.85
35	.73	.72	.82	.85
45	.83	.74	.76	.90

Note. Children in Group II were 9.7 years old at the beginning of the study; children in Group III were 12.7 years old at the beginning. From *Personality Development in Two Cultures* (p. 84) by W. H. Holtzman, R. Diaz-Guerrero, and J. D. Swartz, 1975, Austin: University of Texas Press. Copyright 1975 by University of Texas Press. Reprinted by permission.

stituted the number of re-exam scores (EFT re-exam).

Highly significant differences were obtained for all four of the summary scores on the EFT in the comparison of children in Mexico and the United States. The American children made fewer errors than did the Mexican children (means of 8.7 and 11.8, respectively), regardless of age, socioeconomic status, or sex. Consistent with this result were the findings that the American children obtained higher scores on EFT correct (8.1 compared to 7.1), lower scores on EFT time (91 seconds compared to 106 seconds), and lower scores on EFT re-exam (8.7 compared to 13.9).

Analysis of similar data for the second and third years of repeated testing for the two older age groups revealed essentially the same outcome. In Years 4 and 5, a slightly different analysis was undertaken, since by that time the children in the youngest group were old enough to take the EFT, comparisons across all three age groups were then possible. Year 5, however, probably was the most appropri-

ate one in which to make a comparison across all three age groups, because it was the first year in which any possible practice and adaptation effects would have been present for all three groups. Interestingly, in light of the results of the earlier analysis of only the two older groups, the differences between the Mexican and American children had diminished by Year 5 to the point where they were no longer significant, regardless of the score analyzed. There were, expectedly, significant differences evident in Group I (the youngest group), but these were overshadowed completely by the fact that the mean number of errors for the total group had dropped to 5.8 while the number of items correct had risen to 9.6 (out of 12 figures). The average reaction time per item for all children had dropped to 59 seconds, and the number of re-examinations had fallen to 3.0. It appears that the task had become too easy for the older children, particularly in Group III.

Mean EFT time scores for the 5 years of repeated testing for Groups II and III (see Figure 21.2) show the improvement in performance with increasing age that one would expect from a developmental function. While Mexican girls, regardless of age, were generally the slowest in finding the hidden figures, the Mexican boys caught up with the Americans by the age of 13 and thereafter were indistinguishable from them. Contrary to previous findings, one can see in Figure 21.2 that few if any practice effects due to repeated testing were evident. At the two ages where Groups II and III overlapped, the mean scores for identical ages were strikingly similar except for the 12-year-old Americans; even these differences disappeared 1 year later.

Discussion of These Results

The stability or degree of invariance shown by the Witkin EFT is its most remarkable feature. If there are stable characteristics in people, this test appears to come closest to their measurement. Furthermore, evidence has accumulated from a number of studies that such personality attributes as differentiation of self-concept, articulateness of body image, and method of impulse regulation

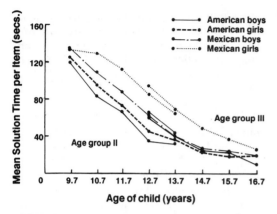

FIGURE 21.2.   Time score on the EFT as a function of age, age group, sex, and culture. From *Personality Development in Two Cultures* (p. 188) by W. H. Holtzman, R. Diaz-Guerrero, and J. D. Swartz, 1975, Austin: University of Texas Press. Copyright 1975 by University of Texas Press. Reprinted by permission.

form an interrelated cluster that includes field independence as measured by Witkin's tests. Such psychological differentiation is closely tied to developmental change from undifferentiated early states to more highly differentiated and integrated adult states. It is also clear from research, that high differentiation (field independence) or low differentiation (field dependence) has no relationship to general intelligence, personal adjustment, or other aspects of the individual that are often judged to be good or bad within the value system of a culture.

Witkin et al. (1962/1974) reviewed a series of studies that had been carried out in a trial to identify the socialization variables related to a relatively less developed or more developed level of differentiation. A number of the findings in Holtzman et al. (1975, pp. 322–323) concerning attitudes, values, family life style, and socialization practices in the Mexican home resemble the variables utilized in the studies reviewed by Witkin. None of the measures representing them at the time, however, correlated with the results of the EFT testing. It was regretted then that there had been no systematic or standardized application of questionnaires to assess sociocultural premises pertinent to both cultures, so that these important relationships could be fully investigated. Later, however,

this was done in more limited but clearly significant studies.

In February 1976, Diaz-Guerrero and Castillo Vales organized a research conference at the School of Psychology of the University of Yucatan in Mexico. With monetary assistance from the Ford Foundation of Mexico, and important institutional help from the National University of Mexico and the University of Yucatan, this conference brought teachers and students of the School of Psychology together with a group of cross-cultural psychologists. Among these latter were Michael Cole, Gordon Finley, Wayne Holtzman, Walter Lonner, Luiz Natalicio, Harold Pepinsky, Donald Sharp, and Charles Spielberger. The fundamental objective of the conference was to establish important dimensions to be included in a local research program. Lonner (as part of his sabbatical year) and Sharp were to carry out the fieldwork, and Castillo Vales and Diaz-Guerrero would serve as advisors. Local teachers and students were to participate in the work. Among the dimensions considered important were Witkin's measures; Rotter's externality–internality; and Diaz-Guerrero's historic–sociocultural premises (HSCPs; see next section), as assessed by an instrument called the Filosofia de Vida.

Diaz-Guerrero and Castillo Vales (1981) reported some of the results. The study was carried out in Yucatecan school children from elementary and high schools. Among the relevant results was a moderate correlation ($-.48$, $p < .01$) between the Self-Assertion factor of the Filosofia de Vida and total time on the EFT (applied individually). Another interesting finding was that among all the tests, including the Raven Matrices, two of the factors of the Filosofia de Vida (Active Self-Assertion and Active Internal Control) correlated most strongly with age, proving to be a better developmental measure even than the Raven. Another interesting finding was that Witkin's, Rotter's, and the Filosofia de Vida dimensions all correlated significantly with each other, but that the Filosofia de Vida dimensions correlated more highly with Rotter's and Witkin's dimensions than the latter did between themselves. Clearly, the Filosofia de Vida was more pertinent to the subjects.

A little later, Diaz-Guerrero (1982b) re-

TABLE 21.11. Intercorrelations between the Nine Factorial Scales of the HSCPs and Selected Scores of the EFT, Personally Administered to Mexico City Mothers of Upper-Lower and Lower-Middle Classes

HSCPs of the Mexican Family	EFT total mean time	EFT number correct	EFT re-exams
Machismo	.42***	−.35**	.22
Affiliative Obedience	.17	−.13	.15
Virginity	.35**	−.31*	.17
Abnegation	.33**	−.31*	.21
Fear of Authority	−.04	.01	.08
Family Status Quo	.20	−.17	.30*
Respect/Love	.45***	−.41***	.09
Family Honor	.34**	−.31*	.02
Cultural Rigidity	.44***	−.38**	.25*
EFT total mean time	1.00	−.92***	.41***
EFT number correct	−.92***	1.00	−.43***
EFT errors	.54***	.47***	.41***
EFT re-exams	.41***	−.42***	1.00
EFT mean time per figure	.42***	.20	−.19

Note. The data are from Diaz-Guerrero (1982b).
  *$p < .05$.
 **$p < .01$.
***$p < .001$.

ported on the results of a study carried out with 67 mothers, who were carefully selected to represent the upper-lower and lower-middle classes in Mexico City. In this case, the factors of a test called the HSCPs of the Mexican Family, were correlated with the scores obtained from the EFT applied individually. Table 21.11 presents the results. It is evident that the factor scales of Respect over Love, Cultural Rigidity, and Machismo correlated most highly with the two most reliable scores of the EFT. The fact that Affiliative Obedience, with the exception of Fear of Authority, showed the lowest correlations may help clarify the meaning of field dependence–independence.[6] It does not appear to go so much with authority or obedience in Mexico as it goes with strictness, severity, and awed respect. A degree of fanatic conformity with cultural commands, which is one part of the HSCPs of the Mexican Family, goes well with some ideas expressed by Witkin about the meaning of field dependence. It is worthwhile pointing out that several of the factors of the HSCPs correlate as highly with EFT total time as the

latter correlates with some of the EFT secondary scores such as re-examination. As we shall see in the next section of this chapter, another convergence between the HSCPs and Witkin's measures is the fact that they have been found to be significantly and meaningfully related to a number of personality, vocational, and cognitive constructs.

The evidence thus far accumulated for Witkin's measures, particularly the EFT, indicates that they should be considered important tools in cross-cultural personality assessment. At least for Mexico, they have shown what we consider a *sine qua non* characteristic: They have shown significant and meaningful correlations with scales that measure locally developed cultural and personality dimensions.

THE ETHNOPSYCHOLOGICAL APPROACH

In their comprehensive article on cross-cultural and cross-ethnic assessment, Sundberg and Gonzalez (1981) have the following to say:

> In sum, assessment involves the collection, organization, interpretation, evaluation and communication of psychological information

---

[6]In Mexico, it is much more common among psychologists and others to refer to this dichotomy as "field sensitivity versus field independence." This choice of words has fewer pejorative connotations.

about a person, a group, or an identified population for the purposes of description and decision making in clinical and community programs or for related research. The psychological assessor is always part of a larger system, which will be important in setting specific goals. That system, for our purposes here, is assumed to be representative of the dominant culture in some way. To achieve a full cross-cultural perspective, the psychologist must be aware of how assessment activities express the values and customs of the dominant culture and guard against unfair usage. (pp. 463–464)

These authors agree with Berry (1980) that cross-cultural assessment does not refer only to the use of tests and techniques that have been translated, normed, and applied to every group. They insist that it should also include the development of procedures that are particularly useful for understanding a given culture on its own terms. Sundberg and Gonzalez provide a particularly acute discussion of the many methodological pitfalls that attend the use of "another culture's" test in cross-cultural assessment. A careful reading of their article is important for the professional cross-cultural psychologist.

In 1971, Diaz-Guerrero set forth the following blueprint:

The psychologist in a developing country must therefore dedicate his attention to his own culture; paralleling the empirical constructs developed in the Anglo-American culture, he must pore over the peculiarities of his own people and develop concepts that will fit their specific and idiosyncratic nature. . . . He must think about how he can construct tests that are valid totally and specifically to the mental characteristics of his own people. (p. 13)

The first dimension typical of the Mexican culture was reported a year later (Diaz-Guerrero, 1972). The article was ponderously titled "A Factorial Scale of Historic–Sociocultural Premises of the Mexican Family" (translated from the Spanish). The story since then is long, but it has ended in the need to start developing a new discipline, an ethnopsychology.

An ethnopsychology should begin by accepting that the developing human being is subject to an extremely varied stimulation. He is growing

and interacting in nothing less than a very complex ecosystem. The human ecosystem, beyond all of the variables that biologists enumerate for other species, includes a powerful subjective ecosystem—that is, the way the individual and the various groups perceive themselves and the objective ecosystem to function, and, in addition, objective anthropological, sociological–structural, and economic variables. (Diaz-Guerrero, 1986b, p. 3).

In this paper (of which a revised version is being considered for a book on indigenous psychologies, sponsored by the International Association of Cross-Cultural Psychology), an attempt is made to formulate tenets, corollaries, and goals of a systematic ethnopsychology, and the effort is illustrated by a series of ethnopsychological studies in the Mexican culture. At the heart of the effort is the concept of the HSCP. It is pointed out that the most significant part of the human subjective ecosystem can be given in generalized statements that bear the characteristics of platonic ideas; that are defended by an operational majority or a significant minority of the people of a given culture; and that govern the thinking, the feeling and, if the situation permits, the behavior of individuals of a given culture. Earlier papers (Diaz-Guerrero, 1982b, 1984b) have described the 13 factorial dimensions of HSCPs so far discovered for the Mexican culture.

Paramount for the understanding of the impact of culture on personality development is the culture–counterculture hypothesis developed by Diaz-Guerrero (Diaz-Guerrero, 1980; Diaz-Guerrero & Castillo Vales, 1981). This is considered fundamental in cross-cultural assessment. The hypothesis is as follows: The older an individual in a given culture is, and in particular the more liberal education he or she has received, the less the individual's thinking, feeling, and behavior will be governed by the HSCPs premises of his or her culture. A number of intracultural studies have confirmed this hypothesis. The important finding in the Holtzman et al. study (1975) reported in an earlier section—that a number of the cultural differences between Mexicans and Americans tended to disappear as the subjects became older and more educated—is one more demonstration of the importance of the hypothesis.

A proper ethnopsychology, it is believed (Diaz-Guerrero, 1986b), must show that the factorial cultural dimensions discovered for a given community relate at least moderately significantly and meaningfully to independent measures of cognitive, personality, and moral development; to vocational interests; and to important sociological and economic variables measured in the same subjects. That paper presented a number of tables with data obtained in previous studies, confirming various aspects of this assertion. An ethnopsychological approach would fundamentally demand that studies be carried out to discover the crucial dimensions for every culture. The method to be followed— in this case, an HSCP approach—is not as important as the fact that the discovered dimensions are cogent, valid, and (one hopes) bear meaningful relationships to psychological and other social science constructs in the given culture.

Parallel to the efforts in the direction of a theoretically rigorous and systematic ethnopsychology, there have recently been a number of studies in Mexico dealing with the importance of a culture-specific operationalization of possibly universal psychological concepts and constructs. Beginning in 1981, a group of psychologists and graduate students of the Graduate Department of Social Psychology at the National University of Mexico—conscious of the lengthy and crucial debate about these matters in the crosscultural literature (i.e., Berry, 1969; Davidson, Jaccard, Triandis, Morales, & Diaz-Guerrero, 1976; Triandis, Vassiliou, Vassiliou, Tanaka, & Shanmugan, 1972)—have carried out research germane to these problems. The following patterns have emerged to be taken into consideration for an ethnopsychological approach:

1. The proper translation of an instrument from English to Spanish revealed similar dimensions in the Spanish version applied to Mexican subjects, although individual traits sometimes appeared on different dimensions.
2. The proper translation of an instrument from English to Spanish revealed an incoherent structure in Mexican subjects. Nevertheless, using the original Anglo-American definition of the concepts, an instrument was developed to measure this construct in the Mexican culture.
3. Psychometric analyses of the proper translation of an instrument applied to Mexican subjects revealed an additional independent, local, culture-bound dimension (Diaz-Loving & Andrade Palos, 1984).
4. Based on sociocultural premises, culture-specific constructs and measurement instruments have been advanced.
5. The construct has been extracted from specific local populations. Content analysis of the responses serves as a basis for the forging of concepts and their subsequent operationalization (La Rosa, 1986).

Specific illustrations of the first two of these patterns will exemplify this surging ethnopsychological approach.

Spence, Helmreich, and Stapp (1974) developed the Personal Attributes Questionnaire (PAQ), a measure of masculine (instrumental) and feminine (expressive) traits, which are divided into socially desirable and undesirable characteristics for both sexes. Although instrumentality and expressivity may be universal human traits, their desirability is normative, and thus may be culture-specific. The original PAQ scales were created for and by Anglo-Americans; the generalizability of the instrument, as well as its use and psychometric qualities, must therefore be tested in each new language or culture.

We (Diaz-Loving, Diaz-Guerrero, Helmreich, & Spence, 1981) translated and backtranslated the PAQ from English to Spanish, trying as much as possible to preserve the original scales' connotative meaning in the process. The translated instrument was given to 594 Mexican males and females, and extensive psychometric analyses were conducted on the data obtained (Diaz-Loving et al., 1981). These analyses revealed that the general constructs of positive and negative instrumental as well as positive and negative expressive traits fround in the United States were also present in the Mexican instrument. However, several traits changed from one dimension to another in the Mexican culture. For example, being dominant and dictatorial, which is perceived as an undesirable instrumental characteristic for U.S. subjects—

bad for both sexes, but worse for females—were perceived in Mexico as positive instrumental traits, desirable in both sexes but better in males. The importance given in Mexico to showing respect and affectionate obedience toward parents and older people in general seems not only to make it acceptable to be authoritarian, but actually encourages it.

Other traits, such as being aggressive, which in the United States is desirable for males and not for females, are seen as generally negative in both sexes in Mexico, although more undesirable in females. It is interesting to note that in recent research Flores-Galaz, Diaz-Loving, and Rivera-Aragon (1987) found that even assertiveness is not a positive characteristic in Mexico. Factor analysis of a multidimensional assertivity scale developed by these authors revealed that the first factor, which explained over 30% of the instrument's variance, measured nonassertiveness; further analysis of the scales' means confirmed the importance of nonassertive behavior. Diaz-Guerrero (1967) postulated, and we and others have found much evidence, that Mexicans tend to be self-modifying rather than other-modifying. Aggression, and even assertiveness, are other-modifying behaviors. Further evidence of the self-modifying tendency in Mexico is provided by the fact that the item "servile," which is a negative expressive trait in the United States, is a positive expressive characteristic in Mexico.

In spite of these and other changes dictated by cultural-specific socialization of instrumental and expressive traits, it should be noted that although more or less desirable in one or the other country, expressive traits were always expressive and instrumental traits were always instrumental.

In other instances, however, an instrument has been translated from English to Spanish, and no resemblance has been found between the results from the original instrument and the translated version. Helmreich and Spence's (1978) Work and Family Orientation Questionnaire (WOFO) was translated and back-translated from English to Spanish and applied to Mexican samples by Diaz-Loving and Andrade Palos (1985). The WOFO is a multidimensional achievement orientation measure that includes Mastery, Work, and Competition subscales. The Spanish translation of the WOFO was given to two samples, one of 594 and the other of 300 male and female subjects in Mexico City. Factor analysis, both with an orthogonal and a nonorthogonal rotation, gave more than 20 factors with eigenvalues higher than 1 and no single factor with more than three items with factor weights of ±.20.

Given the immense dispersion of the variance of the items, and the absence of any logical or conceptual reason to add factors or items, a new instrument was developed with culturally based asseverations that conceptually mirrored the definitions of mastery, work, and competition given by Helmreich and Spence (1978). The new instrument was given to 401 males and female subjects (Diaz-Loving, Andrade Palos, & La Rosa, in press), and factor analysis of their responses uncovered three factors, which explain 46.71% of the total variance, measuring Mastery, Work, and Competition.

The fact that the same construct and definition can lead to different linguistic operationalizations, depending on the culture, alerts us to the importance of the universality of some psychological constructs and at the same time to the culture-specific representation of such characteristics. Although having parallel instruments does not permit a quantitative comparison between two cultures, it does permit intracultural comparisons and qualitative intercultural comparisons.

CONCLUSIONS

We have tried to maintain a constant theme throughout this chapter. In the interpretation of results of cross-cultural assessments, it is obvious that we must rely on cultural understanding. Helpful cultural understanding may be obtained by grasping the implications embodied in possible cultural universals. Importantly, there are a number of measurement techniques—four have been described in this paper—that if used adequately can provide important information for cross-cultural assessment. More basically, measurable, specific indigenous or ethnic dimensions will provide a very important conceptual framework for cultural interpretation. Finally, whenever possible, culture-specific universals—here referred to as factorial dimensions of HSCPs—that are significantly correlated intraculturally to measures of personality and cognitive development and other social science constructs appear to provide an even stricter avenue for the clinical or other type of interpretation of cross-cultural results. Cross-cultural psychology, more than any other discipline, has opened up many unknown worlds. By itself and by the disciplines that it will inspire, it will provide in time very basic answers.

REFERENCES

Abel, T. M. (1973). *Psychological testing in cultural contexts*. New Haven, CT: College and University Press.

Bauermeister, J. J., Ollazo, J. A., & Spielberger, C. D. (1983). The construction and validation of the Spanish form of the Test Anxiety Inventory: Inventario de Evaluacion sobre Examenes (IDASE). In C. D. Spielberger & R. Diaz-Guerrero (Eds.), *Cross-cultural anxiety* (Vol. 2, pp. 67–88). Washington, DC: Hemisphere.

Berry, J. W. (1969). On cross-cultural comparability. *International Journal of Psychology, 4,* 119–128.

Berry, J. W. (1976). *Human ecology and cognitive style: Comparative studies in cultural and psychological adaptation*. Beverly Hills, CA: Sage/Halsted.

Berry, J. W. (1980). Introduction to methodology. In H. C. Triandis & J. W. Berry (Eds.), *Handbook of cross-cultural psychology: Vol. 2. Methodology* (pp. 1–28). Boston: Allyn & Bacon.

Brislin, R. W., Lonner, W. J., & Thorndike, R. M. (1973). *Cross-cultural research methods*. New York: Wiley.

Bruner, J. S. (1974). Concluding comments. In J. Dawson & W. J. Lonner (Eds.), *Readings in cross-cultural psychology*. Hong Kong: University of Hong Kong Press.

Cattell, R. B., & Scheier, I. H. (1963). *Handbook for the IPAT Anxiety Scale*. Champaign, IL: Institute for Personality and Ability Testing.

Cronbach, L. J. (1970). *Essentials of psychological testing* (3rd ed.). New York: Harper & Row.

Cronbach, L. J. (1975). Five decades of public controversy over mental testing. *American Psychologist, 30,* 1–14.

Davidson, A. R., Jaccard, J. J., Triandis, H. C., Morales, M. L., & Diaz-Guerrero, R. (1976). Cross-cultural model testing: Toward a solution of the etic–emic dilemma. *International Journal of Psychology, 11,* 1–13.

Diaz-Guerrero, R. (1965). Sociocultural and psychodynamic processes in adolescent transition and mental health. In M. Sherif & C. W. Sherif (Eds.), *Problems of youth* (pp. 156–181). Chicago: Aldine.

Diaz-Guerrero, R. (1967). Sociocultural premises, attitudes and cross-cultural research. *International Journal of Psychology, 2,* 79–87.

Diaz-Guerrero, R. (1971). La enseñanza de la investigac-ión psicológica en Latinoamérica: Un paradigma. *Revista Latinoamericana de Psicología, 3,* 5–36.

Diaz-Guerrero, R. (1972). Una escala factorial de premisas historico–socioculturales de la familia Mexicana. *Revista Interamericana de Psicología, 6,* 235–244.

Diaz-Guerrero, R. (1975). *Psychology of the Mexican: Culture and personality*. Austin: University of Texas Press.

Diaz-Guerrero, R. (1980). The culture–counterculture theoretical approach to human and social system development: The case of mothers in four Mexican subcultures. *Proceedings of the XXIInd International Congress of Psychology* (pp. 55–60). Leipzig: International Union of Scientific Psychology.

Diaz-Guerrero, R. (1982a). El Yó del Mexicano y la Piramide. In R. Diaz-Guerrero (Ed.), *Psicología del Mexicano* (pp. 195–241). Mexico City: Trillas.

Diaz-Guerrero, R. (1982b). The psychology of the historic–sociocultural premise: I. *Spanish Language Psychology, 2,* 383–410.

Diaz-Guerrero, R. (1984a). Tristeza y psicopatología en México. *Salud Mental, 7*(2), 3–9.

Diaz-Guerrero, R. (1984b). La psicología de los Mexicanos: Un paradigma. *Revista Mexicana de Psicología, 1,* 95–104.

Diaz-Guerrero, R. (1986a). *El ecosistema sociocultural y la calidad de la vida*. Mexico City: Trillas.

Diaz-Guerrero, R. (1986b, July). A Mexican ethnopsychology. In J. W. Berry & U. Kim (Chairs), *Indigenous psychology*. Symposium presented at the 8th Congress of the International Society of Cross-Cultural Psychology, Istanbul, Turkey.

Diaz-Guerrero, R., & Castillo Vales, V. M. (1981). El enfoque cultura–contracultura y el desarrollo cognitivo y de la personalidad en escolares yucatecos. *Enseñanza e Investigacion en Psicologia, 7,* 5–26.

Diaz-Guerrero, R., Fernandez Davila, M. L., & Fernandez Pardo, G. (1967). Grado de comparabilidad entre la calificacion individual del HIT y la de la computadora en sujetos de habla española. In C. F. Hereford & L. Natalicio (Eds.), *Aportaciones de la psicología a la investigacion transcultural* (pp. 305–310). Mexico City: Trillas.

Diaz-Guerrero, R., & Iscoe, I. (1984). El impacto de la cultura Iberoamericana tradicional y del estres económico sobre la salud mental y física: Instrumentacíon y potencial para la investigacion transcultural, I. *Revista Latinoamericana de Psicología, 16,* 167–211.

Diaz-Loving, R., & Andrade Palos, P. (1984). Una escala de locus de control para niños mexicanos. *Interamerican Journal of Psychiatry, 18,* 21–33.

Diaz-Loving, R., & Andrade Palos, P. (1985). *Motivacion de logro y orientacion hacia la familia y el trabajo*. Paper presented at the Primer Congreso Interamericano de Psicología Laboral, Oaxaca, México.

Diaz-Loving, R., Andrade Palos, P., & La Rosa, J. (in press). Orientacion de logro. Desarrollo de una escala multidimensional (EOL) y su relacíon con aspectos sociales y de personalidad. *Revista Mexicana de Psicología*.

Diaz-Loving, R., Diaz-Guerrero, R., Helmreich, R. L., & Spence, J. T. (1981). Comparación transcultural y análisis psicometrico de una medida de rasgos masculinos (instrumental) y femininos (expresivos). *Revista de la Asociación Latinoamericana de Psicología Social, 1,* 3–38.

Flores-Galaz, M., Diaz-Loving, R., & Rivera-Aragon, S. (1987). MERA: Una medida de asertividad para la cultura Mexicana. *Revista Mexicana de Psicología, 4,* 29–35.

Gorham, D. R. (1967). Validity and reliability of a computer scoring system for inkblot responses. In C. F. Hereford & L. Natalicio (Eds.), *Aportaciones de la psicologia a la investigacion transcultural* (pp. 276–290). Mexico City: Trillas.

Gorham, D. R. (1970). Cross-cultural research based on the Holtzman Inkblot Technique. In *International Congress of the Rorschach and Other Projective Techniques* (Vol. 7, pp. 158–164).

Gorham, D. R., Moseley, E. C., & Holtzman, W. H. (1968). Norms for the computer scored Holtzman Inkblot Technique [*Monograph supplement*]. *Perceptual and Motor Skills, 26,* 1279–1305.

Helmreich, R., & Spence, J. (1978). The Work and Family Orientation Questionnaire: An objective instrument to assess components of achievement motivation and attitudes toward family and career. *JSAS: Catalog of Selected Documents in Psychology, 8,* 35–77.

Hill, F. H. (1972). *The Holtzman Inkblot Technique.* San Francisco: Jossey-Bass.

Hofstede, G. (1980). *Cultures and consequences: International differences in work-related values.* Beverly Hills, CA: Sage.

Hofstede, G. (1983). Dimensions of national cultures in 50 countries and 3 regions. In J. B. Deregowksi, S. Dziurawis, & R. C. Annis (Eds.), *Explications in cross-cultural psychology.* Lisse, The Netherlands: Swets & Zeitlinger.

Hofstede, G., & Bond, M. H. (1984). Hofstede's culture dimensions: An independent validation using Rokeach's Value Survey. *Journal of Cross-Cultural Psychology, 15,* 417–433.

Holtzman, W. H. (1975). New developments in the Holtzman Inkblot Technique. In P. McReynolds (Ed.), *Advances in psychological assessment* (Vol. 3, pp. 243–274). San Francisco: Jossey-Bass.

Holtzman, W. H. (1976). Critique of research on anxiety across cultures. In C. D. Spielberger & R. Diaz-Guerrero (Eds.), *Cross-cultural anxiety* (Vol. 1, pp. 175–187). Washington, DC: Hemisphere.

Holtzman, W. H. (1980a). Cultures and personality development in the Americas. In *Proceedings of the XXIInd International Congress of Psychology* (pp. 106–113). Leipzig: International Union of Psychological Science.

Holtzman, W. H. (1980b). Projective techniques. In H. C. Triandis & J. W. Berry (Eds.), *Handbook of cross-cultural psychology: Vol. 2. Methodology.* Boston: Allyn & Bacon.

Holtzman, W. H., & Bitterman, M. E. (1956). A factorial study of adjustment to stress. *Journal of Abnormal and Social Psychology, 52,* 179–185.

Holtzman, W. H., Diaz-Guerrero, R., & Swartz, J. D. (1975). *Personality development in two cultures.* Austin: University of Texas Press.

Holtzman, W. H., Thorpe, J. S., Swartz, J. D., & Herron, E. W. (1961). *Inkblot perception and personality: Holtzman Inkblot Technique.* Austin: University of Texas Press.

La Rosa, J. (1986). *Escalas de locus de control y autoconcepto: Construcción y validación.* Unpublished doctoral dissertation, University of Mexico, Mexico City.

Lonner, W. J. (1980). The search for psychological universals. In H. C. Triandis & W. W. Lambert (Eds.), *Handbook of cross-cultural psychology: Vol. 1. Perspectives* (pp. 143–204). Boston: Allyn & Bacon.

Marin, G., & Triandis, H. C. (1985). Allocentrism as an important characteristic of the behavior of Latinamericans and Hispanics. In R. Diaz-Guerrero (Ed.), *Cross-cultural and national studies in social psychology: Proceedings of the XXIIIrd International Congress of Psychology* (Vol. 2, pp. 85–104). Amsterdam: Elsevier/North-Holland.

Moseley, E. C. (1967). Multivariate comparison of seven cultures: Argentina, Colombia (Bogotá, Cartagena), Mexico, Panama, United States and Venezuela. In C. Hereford & L. Natalicio (Eds.), *Aportaciones de la psicologia a la investigacion transcultural* (pp. 291–304). Mexico City: Trillas.

Moseley, E. C., Gorham, D. R., & Hill, E. (1963). Computer scoring of inkblot. *Perceptual and Motor Skills, 17,* 498.

Ng, S. H., Hossain, A. B., Ball, P., Bond, M. H., Hayashi, K., Lim, S. P., O'Driscoll, M. P., Sinha, D., & Yang, K. S. (1982). Human values in nine countries. In R. Rath, H. S. Asthana, D. Sinha, & J. B. H. Sinha (Eds.), *Diversity and unity in cross-cultural psychology.* Lisse, The Netherlands: Swets & Zeitlinger.

Osgood, C. E. (1966). Dimensionality of the semantic space for communication via facial expressions. *Scandinavian Journal of Psychology, 7,* 1–30.

Osgood, C. E. (1971). Exploration in semantic space: A personal diary. *Journal of Social Issues, 27*(4), 5–64.

Osgood, C. E., May, W. H., & Murray, S. M. (1975). *Cross-cultural universals of affective meaning.* Urbana: University of Illinois Press.

Osgood, C. E., Suci, G. J., & Tannenbaum, P. H. (1957). *The measurement of meaning.* Urbana: University of Illinois Press.

Snyder, F., & Osgood, C. E. (Eds.). (1969). *Semantic differential technique: A source book.* Chicago: Aldine.

Spence, J. T., & Helmreich, R. L. (1978). *Masculinity and femininity: Their psychological dimensions, correlates and antecedents.* Austin: University of Texas Press.

Spence, J. T., Helmreich, R. L., & Stapp, J. (1974). The Personal Attributes Questionnaire: A measure of sex role stereotypes and masculinity–femininity. *JSAS: Catalog of Selected Documents in Psychology, 4,* 43.

Spielberger, C. D. (1972). Anxiety as an emotional state. In C. D. Spielberger (Ed.), *Anxiety: Current trends in theory and research* (Vol. 1, 23–49). New York: Academic Press.

Spielberger, C. D. (1976). The nature and measurement of anxiety. In C. D. Spielberger & R. Diaz-Guerrero (Eds.), *Cross-cultural anxiety* (Vol. 1, pp. 3–12). Washington, DC: Hemisphere.

Spielberger, C. D., & Diaz-Guerrero, R. (Eds.). (1976). *Cross-cultural anxiety* (Vol. 1). Washington, DC: Hemisphere.

Spielberger, C. D., & Diaz-Guerrero, R. (Eds.). (1983). *Cross-cultural anxiety* (Vol. 2). Washington, DC: Hemisphere.

Spielberger, C. D., & Diaz-Guerrero, R. (Eds.). (1986). *Cross-cultural anxiety* (Vol. 3). Washington, DC: Hemisphere.

Spielberger, C. D., Gorsuch, R. L., & Lushene, R. E.

(1970). *State–Trait Anxiety Inventory*. Palo Alto, CA: Consulting Psychologists Press.

Spielberger, C. D., & Sharma, S. (1976). Cross-cultural measurement of anxiety. In C. D. Spielberger & R. Diaz-Guerrero (Eds.), *Cross-cultural anxiety* (Vol. 1, pp. 13–28). Washington, DC: Hemisphere.

Sundberg, N. D., & Gonzalez, L. R. (1981). Cross-cultural and cross-ethnic assessment: Overview and issues. In P. McReynolds (Ed.), *Advances in psychological assessment* (Vol. 5, pp. 460–541). San Francisco: Jossey-Bass.

Swartz, J. D., & Holtzman, W. H. (1963). Group method of administration of the Holtzman Inkblot Technique. *Journal of Clinical Psychology, 19*, 433–441.

Tamm, M. (1967a). *El Holtzman Inkblot Test, el Wechsler Intelligence Scale for Children y otros tests en el estudio psicologico transcultural de niños de habla expañola e inglesa residentes en Mexico*. Unpublished doctoral dissertation, Universidad Nacional Autonoma de Mexico, Mexico City.

Tamm, M. (1967b). Resultados preliminares de un estudio transcultural y de desarrollo de la personalidad de niños mexicanos y norteamericanos. In C. F. Hereford & L. Natalício (Eds.), *Aportaciones de la psicología a la investigacion transcultural* (pp. 159–164). Mexico City: Trillas.

Triandis, H. C., Vassiliou, V., Vassiliou, G., Tanaka, Y., & Shanmugan, A. (1972). *The analysis of subjective culture*. New York: Wiley.

Werner, H. (1962). The significance of general experimental psychology for the understanding of abnormal behavior and its correction or prevention. In T. Denbo & G. Leviton (Eds.), *The Relationship between Rehabilitation and Psychology: A conference held at the Institute of Human Development, Clark University, 1959* (pp. 62–74). Washington, DC: Department of Health, Education and Welfare.

Witkin, H. A. (1978). *Cognitive styles in personal and cultural adaptation*. Worcester, MA: Clark University Press.

Witkin, H. A., Dyk, R. B., Fatterson, H. F., Goodenough, D. R., & Karp, S. A. (1974). *Psychological differentiation*. Potomac, MD: Erlbaum. (Original work published 1962)

Witkin, H. A., Lewis, H. B., Hertznan, M., Machover, K., Meissner, P. B., & Wapner, S. (1954). *Personality through perception*. New York: Harper.

Witkin, H. A., Oltman, P. K., Raskin, E., & Karp, S. A. (1971). *A manual for the Embedded Figures Test*. Palo Alto, CA: Consulting Psychologists Press.

Yerkes, R. M. (Ed.). (1921). Psychological examining in the U.S. Army [Special issue]. *Proceedings of the National Academy of Sciences USA, 15*, 890.

22

The Problem of Cultural Bias in Personality Assessment

MICHELLE P. MORAN
Private Practice, San Antonio, Texas

The study of bias in psychological testing is a relatively new area for empirical research, spurred largely by issues related to the Civil Rights movement. Allegations of cultural test bias were initially leveled against intelligence tests and based largely upon findings of ethnic group differences in mental test scores. Coupled with findings of disproportionate numbers of minority students in special education classes (admission to which was largely determined by use of IQ tests) and the desire to curb racial inequality, these factors led to serious criticism of psychological testing in general and of IQ tests in particular.

The most vocal criticisms of psychological testing with minority groups have been leveled by the Association of Black Psychologists, which, at its annual meeting in 1969, requested that the American Psychological Association call a moratorium on the use of educational and psychological tests with the "culturally different." The Association of Black Psychologists alleged that psychological testing was being used to label blacks as uneducable, to place black children in special classes, to perpetuate inferior education in blacks by denying higher educational opportunities, and to destroy the positive growth and development of black people (Williams, 1971); the issue of cultural test bias thus became and remains a hotly debated and emotionally laden one. In support of the group's

views of psychological testing as demeaning to blacks, biased, and unfair, Rosenthal's (1966) data on the self-fulfilling prophecy of labeling and the lack of homogeneity of the black and white sociocultural experience were cited.

These allegations, while leading to much heated debate and controversy among professionals, laypeople, and legislative officials, did spur a great deal of research, particularly with ability tests. Impetus to conceptualize test bias and to develop research methodology was promoted by the substantial controversy. Meanwhile, the use of psychological tests had increased greatly, particularly in the schools, following the introduction of Public Law 94-142, the Education for All Handicapped Children Act of 1975; this law mandated that special education services be provided to handicapped children. Specifying procedures and due process methods to be used in identifying handicapped children, the act required evaluations by psychologists, educational diagnosticians, and other qualified personnel in diagnosing the handicaps of children for possible special education services. Such handicaps as mental retardation, learning disability, and severe emotional disturbance included under P. L. 94-142 could be determined only through the use of psychological testing by qualified professionals. Partially as a result of the increased use of tests and their increased practical importance, the tests themselves ultimately came under increased scrutiny. Special education classes, designed to provide additional support in the form of individualized instruction and materials for children with learning and/or emotional problems, also came under scrutiny, particularly since these classes were found to have disproportionate numbers of minority students.

Just as other social institutions were being desegregated through court decisions, efforts toward halting what was called the "inferior education" of minorities in special education classes were made through the judicial system. Criticism of the special education identification and remediation model reached a peak in the 1970s in a controversial class action suit (*Larry P. v. Riles,* 1979) in San Francisco. The plaintiffs on behalf of Larry P., a black student placed in a classroom for the educable mentally retarded, asserted that special education classes were not desirable forms of treatment but were rather "dead-end" and "stigmatizing," and alleged that public school special education classes contained disproportionate numbers of minority students as a result of unfair testing practices. The judge ruled in favor of the plaintiffs, labeling IQ tests as biased and enjoining the state against further placement of black children in special classes if that placement was determined primarily through use of IQ tests (Bersoff, 1982). Appeal of this case in 1979 yielded similar results and provided legal mandates against test bias, although a case involving similar issues in Chicago (*PASE v. Hannon,* 1980) led to the diametrically opposed finding that major IQ tests in use are *not* biased and do *not* discriminate against black children.

As these contrasting legal positions illustrate, judicial decisions regarding test bias led to no resolution of the debate. Their involvement did, however, provide a strong judicial mandate against test bias, a factor that served to heighten the need for research into the test bias issue. In addition to judicial mandates to eliminate bias in psychological testing (e.g., *Diana v. State Board of Education,* 1970; *Guadelupe v. Tempe Elementary School,* 1972, cited in Bersoff, 1982; *Hobson v. Hobson,* 1967, cited in Bersoff, 1982; *Larry P. v. Riles,* 1979), federal legislation also re-

quired that tests be valid for the purposes for which they are used and that fairness be maintained (Civil Rights Act of 1964; Education for All Handicapped Children Act of 1975; Vocational Rehabilitation Act of 1973). Ethical mandates of the profession (American Psychological Association, 1979) added fervor to the issue, demanding the most complete, accurate, and fair use of and interpretation of test results for any individual or group of individuals. These forces served to increase the professional attention devoted to the examination of test bias and to its elimination.

PSYCHOLOGICAL TEST BIAS AS A SCIENTIFIC ISSUE

Many of the objections to the use of psychological tests with minorities that have been raised by minority psychologists and plaintiffs in class action suits have been potentially legitimate and do require empirical investigation and resolution. Frequently, however, the objections lack empirical evidence (e.g., Hilliard, 1979), and are based on opinions formed through reviewing test items or race/ethnic group differences. The objections have often been regarded as proof that the tests are indeed biased. From a scientific standpoint, it is imperative that the objections and the question of test bias be addressed through empirical investigation.

That race differences in mental test scores exist has been accepted by some test critics as evidence of test bias. Such acceptance precludes scientific investigation of the presence or absence of bias. Just as minority groups assert that there is no basis for determining that differences among racial and ethnic groups do exist, there is no documented reason to believe that the differences do *not* exist. Believing that such differences are not real but are mere artifacts of the tests used exemplifies what Jensen (1980) calls the "egalitarian fallacy." This view posits that all human populations are in fact identical on all mental traits—a notion that removes the investigation of race or ethnic differences in mental abilities from scientific inquiry through *a priori* acceptance of the null hypothesis with regard to cross-group differences in mental ability. This logic disregards the fact that mental test score differences among ethnic groups have been among the best-researched phenomena in cross-cultural psychology, with differences persisting over time at relatively constant levels (Reynolds & Gutkin, 1980).

As in all areas of science, empirical investigation must supersede personal testimonial or beliefs in the pursuit of knowledge. The study of bias is no different and requires study of the tests as they relate to the demographic variables involved, rather than the mere examination of mean score differences among demographic groups. Such a view necessarily leads to the conceptualization of bias as the presence of systematic (as opposed to random) error that serves to raise or lower the mean scores for a particular demographic group. The presence of such error would lead to artifactual differences among groups as a result of test use, instead of "true" difference in test scores among the groups. The view of "test bias" as a statistical term rather than one referring to mean differences among groups has been the one accepted by most leading researchers in the area of test bias (Berk, 1982; Jensen, 1980; Reynolds, 1982b). This conceptualization of "cultural test bias" as a statistical term is used throughout this chapter in reference to the examination of bias in intelligence and personality assessment.

The objections not empirically addressed but raised by minority and other investigators into the issue of test bias have generally dealt with specific problems they see as existing within the tests themselves. Although these objections have been leveled against IQ and other ability tests, they are important to consider with some distinctions in the issue of bias in affective tests. The following categories have been presented previously (Reynolds, 1982b) and include the following:

1. *Inappropriate content.* Tests geared toward middle-class values contain content areas to which minority children have not been exposed. As a result, some critics suggest that the content of most standardized tests today insures that the results reflect the subjects' degree of Anglocentrism, rather than their intelligence or other real cognitive abilities (Mercer, 1984).

2. *Inappropriate standardization sam-*

ples. Since tests are normed on primarily white middle-class children, minorities are underrepresented in the normative reference group data. Although such tests as the Wechsler Intelligence Scale for Children—Revised (WISC-R) have included blacks and other minorities in direct proportion to their representation in the U.S. population, critics contend that such small numbers have no impact on the tests. Harrington (1975) has gone so far as to state that tests primarily normed on a certain reference group can be *none other* than biased against an underrepresented group in terms of actual numbers included in the normative data. Harrington's work is reviewed in detail in Reynolds (1982b).

3. *Examiner and language bias.* Psychologists who are primarily white and standard-English-speaking may tend to intimidate and fail to communicate accurately with minority children. Lower test scores may thus reflect communication difficulties and intimidation rather than lower ability.

4. *Inequitable social consequences.* The labeling and channeling into various educational tracts that occur as a result of allegedly biased tests result in a disadvantage to minority children in both educational and vocational pursuits.

5. *Measurement of different constructs.* Tests may be measuring different qualities, skills, and attributes when used with children from other than the white middle-class culture.

6. *Differential predictive validity.* Tests are reported to have different levels of accuracy in terms of the prediction of some outcomes (grades, pass–fail rate in schools, level of educational attainment achieved, occupational level, etc.). The difficulty with this objection relates to the difficulty in selecting a common criterion against which to validate tests for different culture groups. Inherent in this position are also the difficulties relating to the predictive validity of the tests themselves, regardless of the differences in prediction among different groups.

Although these objections raise serious concerns regarding virtually all areas of test use and fairness, they have been helpful in directing the empirical study of bias. In scientific research, each objection can be conceptualized as a hypothesis and investigated to determine the relative effects of the variables (language effects, measurement of different constructs, influence of standardization data, etc.) upon test scores. Examination of each of these factors provides needed information in determining the presence or absence or test bias in scientific terms.

Over the past decade, considerable research has been conducted in addressing each of these areas with respect to the use of the major intelligence tests (i.e., the WISC-R, the Wechsler Adult Intelligence Scale—Revised [WAIS-R], and the Wechsler Preschool and Primary Intelligence Scale [WPPSI] in use today. This body of literature is reviewed in some detail in Reynolds (1982b) and in Chapter 26, Volume 1 of the present work by Reynolds and Kaiser. The results of this considerable research appear to indicate that the major, well-standardized intelligence tests in wide use today are not biased against different minority groups. Application of sophisticated research methodology in examining such research hypotheses as differential validity, language effects, and the measurement of different constructs for different ethnic groups has evolved through this research. The use of these techniques and the conceptualization of bias as it relates to various areas of concern in test use had led to the development of empirically definable and testable definitions of bias in the areas of content, construct, and predictive validity (Reynolds, 1982a).

Although much research has been ongoing in the areas of cognitive or ability tests, the same degree of fervor has not arisen in the investigation of personality test bias. Since psychometric theory for test development is highly similar for ability and personality tests, then it follows that the same type of empirical conceptualization and methodology could be used in the investigation of personality test bias. With some modifications, many widely used personality tests could be studied using the conceptual framework pioneered in studies of ability tests. These possibilities are discussed in the chapter in terms of their conceptual "fit" into the existing theoretical and research design frameworks pioneered in the study of ability tests.

GENERAL CONSIDERATIONS FOR PERSONALITY ASSESSMENT

Before the issues of bias can be thoroughly reviewed with respect to personality tests, a discussion of their basic theoretical distinctions, the general types of tests in use, types of data yielded, and criticisms often directed at their use is in order. "Personality assessment" is the general term used to refer to instruments that measure emotional, motivational, attitudinal, and interpersonal characteristics of an individual. There are in print several hundred personality tests that address many different theoretical constructs with respect to an individual's functioning. This chapter confines itself to the discussion of widely used personality tests for the assessment of emotional disturbance in individuals—that is, personality tests that are used by clinicians to distinguish between healthy or "normal" functioning and behavior patterns, and pathological patterns that suggest the need for treatment. These are the tests generally used by psychologists when a psychological test battery is administered.

Test development, like that for cognitive assessment, begins with a theory of personality functioning and maintains the goal of describing the examinee in terms of that theoretical framework, in one way or another. In conjunction with other factors involved in the assessment technique (length of test, manner of administration, cost factors, etc.), a scaling method is adopted and a pool of test items is developed. Ideally, according to psychometric theory, this process includes a tryout phase for the items, study of the psychometric properties of the items, and redevelopment of the test. Norms are developed on the completed form of the test, and the normative comparison provides the descriptive information about the examinee's personality.

At present, there exists a multitude of personality theories, and there are at least as many ways of constructing a test to address various facets of an individual. One of the most important distinctions is whether the constructs employed in the test are capable of being elicited and measured in an objective format (either self-report or observer-based), or whether they are to be elicited indirectly through projective techniques.

Objective tests are generally self-report questionnaires in which the examinee responds to true–false or multiple-choice questions. The items are generally scored according to an expected "correct" direction (i.e., one that does not reflect pathology); according to a direction that identifies the presence of the trait being measured; or in some other way, depending upon the rationale of the test.

The score after normative comparison is generally regarded as an index of the relative amount of the trait or other characteristic being measured. Some scores are not quantitatively meaningful, but rather reflect descriptive data about the person in a categorical or nominal fashion. The data yielded by the test are important for the investigation of test bias, since, as in other statistical applications, the techniques employed vary with respect to the data used in the research.

An additional factor is the complexity of the test in terms of the number of traits or other personality components that are being measured. Unidimensional tests address a single facet of affective functioning. Examples include the Beck Depression Inventory (BDI), the Revised Children's Manifest Anxiety Scale (RCMAS), the State–Trait Anxiety Inventory, the Children's Depression Inventory, and others. Objective unidimensional tests are the most psychometrically sound in terms of validity and reliability estimates, because the relatively narrow focus of the test necessarily excludes some other sources of variance or error. These psychometric properties are important in terms of practical test use, although personality tests as a whole have not fared well in this regard. Reliability and validity are important to the study of bias as well, since empirical investigation of bias involves examination of error and its sources, whether in the test itself or as a functiin of differential error due to demographic differences among the groups in question. Tests low in validity and reliability necessarily lead to difficulty in determining the relative amount of error that is attributable to demographic variables as opposed to random error, simply because the test score includes more error and less "true score."

In addition to unidimensional tests, there exist multidimensional tests that aim to describe an individual's total personality functioning and his or her interaction with the environment from a given theoretical vantage point. Scores yield description of the relative strengths of the individual's various traits or tendencies in comparison to those of others in his or her reference group. These tests may yield a total measure of adjustment (e.g., total mean or weighted mean score), as well as scores of the subscales involved. Examples of such multidimensional tests include the Minnesota Multiphasic Personality Inventory (MMPI); the Sixteen Personality Factor Questionnaire (16PF); the California Psychological Inventory (CPI); the Early School, High School, and Children's Personality Questionnaires; the California Test of Personality (CTP); and others. The psychometric sophistication of these tests varies greatly, and their statistical properties also yield highly discrepant and generally not very favorable reliability and validity estimates.

Another objective type of personality test that is gaining popularity is the behavior rating scale, generally used in describing children's behavior. A teacher or parent rates the child's behavior along various dimensions that yield descriptions of typical behavior patterns or response styles. Often interpretations of pathology are made on the basis of data describing aberrant types of behavior. Although behavior has often been regarded as situation-specific, several multidimensional rating scales that describe an examinee's behavior and related personality traits have been developed that are psychometrically sound and often improve considerably upon the statistical properties of objective self-report and projective measures. Examples of these are the Achenbach Child Behavior Checklist (CBCL), the Conners Parent and Teacher Rating Scales, the Eyberg Child Behavior Inventory, Burk's Behavior Rating Scales, and the Personality Inventory for Children (PIC).

Projective or unstructured tests are perhaps the oldest and most widely used personality assessment techniques. These tests are based upon the projective hypothesis, which posits that an individual, when presented with ambiguous material, will structure the stimulus in a way that reflects fundamental aspects of his or her psychological functioning (Anastasi, 1976). These perceptual, cognitive, and emotional factors are interpreted from the responses provided by an individual. Underlying conflicts, thought processes, emotional needs, anxieties, and other personality issues are supposedly reflected in the response data. One group of such tests consists of the widely used inkblot techniques, such as the Rorschach and the Holtzman Inkblot Technique (HIT). Several scoring methods for evaluating various qualities of the responses, which are interpreted to describe an examinee, exist for these methods. Exner's (1974) scoring method is a quantifiable system upon which interpretations are based.

The Thematic Apperception Test (TAT), the Children's Apperception Test, the Roberts Apperception Test for Children (RATC), and others are also widely used projective tests. These techniques focus on the development of stories or themes to ambiguous picture cards, which are then evaluated for an individual's needs, conflicts, and other environmental stressors indicated in the thematic material. The scoring systems are generally categorical or descriptive rather than norm-referenced, although the RATC has an objectively scored and quantifiable, norm-referenced scoring system for evaluating the thematic content provided by the examinee. Other verbal projective techniques include word association methods and sentence completion blanks, such as the Rotter and Willerman forms. Although some scoring systems are employed, responses are generally interpreted by clinical impression, and these techniques are often used as structured interviewing techniques.

Drawing tests, which include the House–Tree–Person (H-T-P), Draw-A-Person (DAP), and Kinetic Family Drawing (K-F-D), constitute yet another group of widely used projective techniques. Although there exists an objective, quantifiable scoring system for the DAP, which yields a cognitive measure sometimes regarded as analogous to an IQ, these tests are generally scored for various indicators of pathology in a nominal fashion. The scorings and their interpretations, however, appear to have little interrater reliability or validity with overt behavior.

Generally, the psychometric statistical properties of all personality tests are not nearly as strong as those for cognitive measures. Often, there are serious concerns with regard to reliability, validity, and interpretive meaning of the measures employed. Some techniques (i.e., the Rorschach and other projectives) have been so widely criticized for their lack of psychometric soundness that various authors have questioned whether they should be used at all (Anastasi, 1976). These concerns, however, have not appeared to decrease the practical use of these tests with adults and children in clinical and school settings. In fact, the Rorschach remains one of the most widely used psychological tests in the world.

The criticisms of these tests in regard to reliability and validity estimates, when they exist, are often valid. The lack of objective scoring often precludes the development of reliability and validity indices, as is the case with drawing tests scored for signs of pathology, which appear highly disputed among raters. Interrater reliability estimates for various measures reflect the lack of consistency with which items are scored across raters even when a scoring system does exist. Anastasi (1976) has suggested that the tests appear as projective for the examiner as they do for the examinee, and that interpretations may reflect the influence of the examiner's needs and conflicts as much as those of the examinee.

Internal-consistency estimates for reliability are difficult to make, since the tests, particularly multidimensional ones, are specifically developed to measure many different areas of personality rather than one narrowly defined and hence more accurately measured area of examination. As a result, unidimensional tests such as the BDI and the RCMAS have fared best in this regard. Test–retest methods of determining reliability have also proven ineffective in providing stability estimates of these tests, since there often appear to be significant personality changes over time; these may result either from situational or environmental factors, or from some type of treatment. Development of parallel forms has been the most meaningful way to investigate personality test reliability, although few tests have capitalized on this methodology.

With respect to validity, there are limitations as well. Methodological flaws seem to mar most of the research aimed at identifying criterion-related validity for various personality measures. Although criteria are difficult to specify for some measures, such criteria as diagnosis, occupational level, sociometric ratings, and other estimates of general well-being or pathology can be used. Difficulties with the interrater reliability of these criterion variables (e.g., diagnosis) further complicate this type of research. In addition, some of the constructs examined by the personality tests (e.g., morbid fantasy) have no behavioral referent upon which to base a validity study. This has led to increased criticism, particularly of projective tests, because their constructs may not reflect actual behavior but underlying thoughts and feelings that can never be observed. Whether such unobservable constructs can be measured remains an issue of debate. Other factors besides those relevant to the personality trait under investigation (verbal or general intellectual abilities; psychomotor skill; frustration or other physical state; etc.) confound personality test scores and their meanings, and add further confusion to the issue of what the tests measure and what their results mean.

The deficiency of norms has also been cited as a difficulty with personality tests. When norms do exist, they are often based on inpatient or psychiatric populations rather than on an appropriate reference group for an examinee. Often, incomplete standardization samples are used, and age, sex, and race/ethnicity factors are not taken into account. Of greatest concern to the issue of cultural bias is the fact that standardization samples often omit minority subjects entirely, leading to serious questions about their applicability for those groups.

The psychometric difficulties of personality assessment techniques are very important to the investigation of cultural test bias in these measures, for it is the statistical properties of the test that are investigated in a scientific inquiry about test bias. The test score distributions, reliability and validity estimates, factor-analytic results, comparisons, and other statistical properties are the subjects of investigation in test bias study. When these properties themselves are problematic or undefinable in a test, then it follows that there are difficulties when statistical techniques are applied to them. For example, when reliability is low, comparison of test reliability between groups in a study of bias yields questionable results, since there is a high degree of error inherent in the test itself. The same type of problematic situation is true of low validity estimates when predictive accuracy of the test is compared between race or ethnic groups. When norms or objective scoring methods do not exist for a technique, then statistical procedures for examining bias are often inapplicable. In order to use the statistical methods pioneered in bias study with cognitive measures, it is necessary that each test under consideration meet the following criteria: (1) The test should have objective scoring; (2) there should exist norms from an appropriate reference group for the test in question; (3) reliability estimates should exist and should be adequate to warrant use of the test; (4) validity estimates should also exist and should also reach an appropriate level for test use.

Although the psychometric properties of personality tests generally lead to serious concerns regarding their usefulness, they continue to be widely used. The continued zealous use of personality testing does, however, increase the need for further study of the tests and improved test development. It is quite likely that the tests in use today, although failing to meet the expectations for psychometric properties found in ability tests, are better predictors of an individual's functioning than is mere clinical judgment. Given the widespread use of personality testing and the importance of decisions based upon their use (e.g., diagnosis, labeling, qualification for various services or programs, assistance in decision making for hiring or promoting employees, etc.), continued investigation into the accuracy of the test scores themselves and the validity of their interpretations is sorely needed. The issue of bias is one of the larger issues surrounding the use of personality tests, and study is needed in order to understand the meanings and accuracy of these tests for the various individuals and groups with whom they are so widely used.

THE IMPORTANCE OF CULTURAL INFLUENCES ON PERSONALITY

In addition to concerns regarding the psychometric properties of personality tests and how they affect the investigation of test bias, cross-cultural theories address the differences among demographic groups that probably influence personality development. Such factors as child-rearing patterns, gender roles, motivations, values, life goals, and other cultural experiences are suggested in theory as differing among various ethnic/race groups (Padilla & Ruiz, 1975; Williams, 1971). Given the relevance of these factors to personality development, it is intuitively likely that one's cultural experience influences the development of one's personality. Since it is the outcome of these varied experiences in conjunction with inborn individual differences that personality tests purport to measure, it is imperative that the meaning of the test results be clear for all groups with whom the test is used.

A number of studies have been conducted that explore cultural differences in performance on objective personality tests. Most of the research in this area has focused on mean differences between and among cultural groups—usually whites (Anglos), blacks, Mexican-Americans, and American-Indians—on the clinical scales of the MMPI (Butcher, Ball, & Ray, 1964; Gynther, Fowler, & Erdberg, 1971; Harrison & Kass, 1967; Holcomb & Adams, 1982; Holland, 1979; McCreary & Padilla, 1977; Padilla, Olmedo, & Loya, 1982; Plemons, 1977; Pollack & Shore, 1980). Such comparisons indicate that minority groups, on the average, earn more deviant scale elevations than do Anglos. On the MMPI, blacks and American Indians are generally found to have elevated Frequency *(F)* and Schizophrenia *(Sc)* scales, while blacks show additional elevations in Lie *(L)*, Hypochondriasis *(Hs)*, and Hypomania *(Ma)*. Mexican-Americans have been found to have even higher *L* scales than do blacks, and to possess significant *Hs* scale elevations in comparison to Anglos. Anglos, in contrast, have been found to have higher Depression *(D)* and Hysteria *(Hy)* scales, although these levels are generally not clinically significant.

Only one study (Plemons, 1977) found no mean scale differences among the cultural groups studied.

Although some scale elevations have been replicated frequently enough to warrant the generalization that cultural group differences in MMPI performance do exist, the quality of this body of research is relatively poor. Most sample sizes are extremely small, and samples consist of inmate or inpatient populations. Frequently, such variables as socioeconomic status (SES), IQ, educational level, and psychiatric diagnosis are not addressed in the analyses. When such variables are included in the analyses, it appears that they mediate the differences to some degree (which is not unexpected, since the frequency of specific mental disorders is reported to vary by ethnic group; Pasamanick, 1963). However, significant differences persist on some scales in virtually all of the samples.

Investigations of cultural differences on other objective tests or tests that are used more routinely with children are rare. Investigators have documented cultural group differences in performance on the RCMAS (Reynolds & Paget, 1981); the CPI (Mason, 1967); the Bender–Gestalt (Fanibanda, 1973; Peixotte, 1954); the Eysenck Personality Inventory (EPI; Lowe & Hildman, 1972); the 16PF and Personal Orientation Inventory (POI; Brown, 1979); and measures of self-concept (Carpenter & Busse, 1969; Lefley, 1975). Like the research on adult samples, these studies are generally of poor quality and are characterized by small samples and lack of controls for extraneous variables. The results of this body of research on personality tests other than the MMPI again reflect differences among various cultural groups. On the CPI, Anglos respond in a way that indicates them to be more flexible and socially effective, whereas Mexican-Americans' responses indicate higher levels of responsibility and self-control. American Indians' mean profiles reflect a lower sense of well-being and intellectual efficiency. The results of comparisons on the EPI indicate that Anglos have elevated Extraversion scales while blacks have lower Neuroticism scales. Comparisons on the 16PF and the POI reflect significant differences on the 16PF, with Mexican-Americans responding in a manner that describes them as being more humble, dependent upon a group, and practical, whereas Anglos appear more self-assured and trusting. No differences have been found on the POI. No overall race differences have been found for measures of self-concept, but differences were found when one sample was divided by grade and sex, with first-grade black females having a lower self-concept than first-grade white females. The group comparisons of performance on the Bender–Gestalt also reflect differences in performance on the various stimuli figures as well as on total scores.

Comparisons have also been conducted on the RCMAS, an objective measure of anxiety for use with children and adolescents using a national normative sample and examining additional demographic variables. Reynolds and Paget (1981) found mean differences between blacks and whites, with blacks typically scoring higher than whites on the Total Anxiety scale of the RCMAS. More importantly, their analyses found a significant triple-order interaction (age × race × sex) for the Total Anxiety scale, as well as for the component Physiological, Worry/Oversensitivity, Concentration, and Lie scales. Such an interaction suggests that although main effects or significant differences between blacks and whites exist on the RCMAS, this significant interaction precludes a clear analysis of the effects of the age, race, and sex variables on test performance. For this reason, the authors included separate age × race × sex norms for the Total Anxiety scale as well as for the four subscales of the RCMAS.

Few comparisons of performance on projective measures can be found in the literature. Differences in performance between various cultural groups have been documented on the Rorschach (Kaplan, 1955; Kaplan, Rickers-Ovsiankina, & Joseph, 1956) and on the HIT (Holtzman, Diaz-Guerrero, & Swartz, 1975; Laosa, Lara-Tapia, & Swartz, 1974; Miller, 1982; Scott, 1981). Mexican-American respondents have been found to be underproductive in terms of the mean number of Rorschach percepts (Kaplan, 1955; Kaplan et al., 1956). The authors, however, were unable to determine whether such a response pattern reflected personality characteristics or stereotyped attitudes in the

culture. Distinct differences on the Rorschach appeared on measures of Hostility in one study (Johnson & Sikes, 1965). The black group was high on Victim Hostility. They apparently felt they were victims—vulnerable and surrounded by impending violence. The Mexican-American group was high on Potential Hostility, seeing much latent hostility in the world. The Anglos occupied a middle position in their handling of hostility, but showed greatest internal tension together with more flexible control.

The HIT has been used extensively in cross-cultural research and seems to have overcome many of the psychometric weaknesses of other projective techniques (Sundberg & Gonzales, 1981). Significant differences between blacks and whites were found on 3 of the 22 HIT scores (Megargee, 1967): Pathognomic Verbalization (whites > blacks), Anatomy (blacks > whites), and Popular (whites > blacks). Cross-cultural comparison of mean scores on seven variables indicated significant differences between Mexican and American children (Holtzman et al., 1975). Mexican children had a slower response time to the inkblots; had less pathology in fantasy; gave more small details; had less movement, less anxiety, and less hostility in fantasy; and were less likely to integrate parts into a whole.

In addition, differences have been reported using apperception tests. Differences on the TAT were found on three scoring categories: family unity, mother–son relationships, and father–son relationships (Johnson & Sikes, 1965). The Mexican-American group had a more consistent view of the family as unified. Blacks achieved the lowest scores in these categories, offering stories in which there was no interaction or in which trouble was being experienced. Mexican-Americans described the mother as self-sacrificing and the father as authoritarian and dominant; this is consistent with views of the Hispanic culture (Johnson & Sikes, 1965). Cowan and Goldberg (1967), using experimental black TAT stimulus material with blacks, found that higher "need for achievement" scores were expressed for black stimulus figures and for male figures. The use of black TAT stimuli tends to enhance the individual's ratings of the test, and this facilitates story production (Bailey &

Green, 1977). Differences on TAT scores are not identified when whites and blacks are matched for IQ (Megargee, 1967).

The results of this type of research with projective instruments are similar to those obtained for objective instruments: Minority groups have generally been found to respond in ways that would be interpreted as being more deviant than would the responses of Anglos. These differences have been regarded less as evidence of bias in this body of research than as indications of differences in value orientations and general personality dynamics between various cultural groups (Olmedo, 1977; Padilla & Ruiz, 1973, 1975). These theoretical explanations, however, have not been supported empirically. Again, these differences no more provide support for the theoretical explanations than they do for the presence or the absence of bias; they simply indicate that different cultural groups respond differently to such stimuli.

In addition to mean test score differences in support of the importance of cultural factors in personality assessment, some interesting studies have been conducted examining race differences in the rates of occurrence of, and symptoms demonstrated for, various mental disorders. Pasamanick (1963), in an early study, found that blacks had higher rates of mental deficiency, whereas whites were found to have rates of neurotic, autonomic, and psychophysiological disorders twice as high as those of blacks, as well as slightly higher rates of psychoses. The differences in rates of mental illness reported were further elaborated by Pasamanick as apparently due to public versus private modes of treatment: Blacks usually seek public services more often, with the result that more black mental illness is reported in the literature. Similarly, DeHoyos and DeHoyos (1965), in a study comparing the symptoms of blacks and whites diagnosed as schizophrenic, found that blacks demonstrated fewer symptoms than whites. They were found to demonstrate more hallucinations; however, this finding was not significant. Simon, Fliess, Garland, Stiller, and Sharpe (1973) compared rates of depression and schizophrenia between blacks and whites. Their results indicated no differences between blacks and whites on the degree of pathology as demonstrated by hallucinations,

disturbed thought processes, or behavior. However, hospital diagnoses indicated that 50% of these white patients were diagnosed as having affective disorders, whereas no blacks were diagnosed as such; rather, blacks appeared to be diagnosed more frequently as schizophrenic. The only differences evident in the Simon et al. study were that blacks demonstrated more frequent symptoms of worry, anxiety, and physical complaints.

In a similar study, using a health opinion survey and social history in making diagnoses, Warheit, Holzer, and Arey (1975) found that blacks scored higher on pathology in the areas of phobias, anxiety symptoms, and depression when mean groups were compared. Their regression analysis, however, indicated that race accounted for only 8% of the variance in diagnosis; thus, race appears to contribute little practical significance in the determination of these disorders. In a single study comparing Mexican-Americans and Anglos, Fabrega, Swartz, and Wallace (1968) found no differences in the frequency of schizophrenic diagnoses in their study of inpatients. They did find, however, that Mexican-Americans had lower educational levels and Anglos higher IQs—factors that probably influence personality test scores.

These studies have dealt primarily with adult samples, but some provocative studies have been conducted examining bias in the diagnosis and evaluation of psychopathology and behavior in adolescents. Lewis, Balla, and Shanok (1979) reported that when black adolescents were seen in community mental health settings, behavioral indications of schizophrenia, paranoia, or other psychoses or neuroses were often dismissed as "cultural aberrations." These unusual behaviors in black adolescents were then explained as being appropriate to coping with frustrations created by the antagonistic white culture. Lewis and colleagues (1979) found that white adolescents exhibiting similar behaviors were given psychiatric diagnoses and referred for therapy and/or residential placement. These same behaviors were not seen as requiring treatment in black adolescents. These authors assert that this failure to diagnose mental illness in the black population is actually a form of bias in the denial of treatment. A subsequent study (Lewis, Shanok, Cohen,

Kligfeld, & Frisone, 1980) found that "many seriously psychiatrically disturbed, aggressive black adolescents are being channeled into correction facilities while their equally aggressive white counterparts are directed toward psychiatric treatment facilities" (p. 1216). Such failures to diagnose blacks as emotionally disturbed may be credited to the critics of psychological testing with minorities, who state that such aggressive behaviors are acceptable and even necessary in the black culture (Reynolds, 1982b).

For example, the plaintiffs' witnesses in the *Larry P.* (1979) and *PASE* (1980) cases indicated in discussing items from the WISC-R that while it may be appropriate for a white middle-class child to respond to a much smaller child who starts a fight by not fighting back, black children must respond by fighting back because this may well be the only way of protecting oneself in a black ghetto. Such criticisms suggest that aggression and violence are not pathological amoung certain groups and that, as such, their behavior, judgments, and personality test scores should be interpreted differently. In fact, no clear empirical evidence exists for differential interpretation in intelligence or personality test scores across race. Although this issue has been empirically investigated for IQ tests, it has not been well researched for personality tests. Professionals must make diagnostic and placement decisions on the basis of empirical data, rather than testimony of "expert witnesses," differential diagnosis or placement rates, or mean differences in actual test scores (Jensen, 1980; Reynolds & Brown, 1984).

The above-described studies, while questioning whether commonly used personality tests are appropriate for various ethnic/race groups, do not address the question of cultural test bias. None of the studies mentioned here provide data suggesting either that the differences are due to artifactual differences in the tests themselves or that they are due to real differences among groups. As with other types of mental tests, the fact that differences exist does not "prove" that a test is biased, any more than it "proves" that minority groups have more deviant personalities. What is needed to address the bias question accurately is study of

whether the tests measure the same constructs with equivalent accuracy in the prediction of some outcome or other. This is, of course, a question related to the test's validity.

MODELS OF TEST BIAS

The most important areas in need of investigation with regard to the presence or absence of cultural test bias are those of differential content, construct, and predictive validity. That is, the most important issues involve questioning whether items on the tests reflect subjects' abilities across groups with similar accuracy, whether the tests measure the same constructs, and whether the results yield similar predictions based on test scores across racial or ethnic groups. The tripartite notion of validity so often used in scholarly communication allows the formulation of directly testable hypotheses in the investigation of test bias.

Bias in Content Validity

The contention that psychological tests were developed for a white middle-class population and do not reflect the values and cultural experiences (and subsequently the knowledge) common to minority cultures is perhaps the objection most frequently raised to the use of tests with minorities (Hilliard, 1979; Williams, 1971). Review of specific items of a test that are singled out and identified as biased by "expert judges" is a method that has been widely employed in the investigation of this type of alleged bias. This manner of investigation, while lacking in empirical soundness, has been widely publicized as "proof" that various tests are indeed biased. Items are generally singled out for reasons that relate to perceived differences between cultures and are based on the following concerns: (1) Items may ask for information that minority children have not had an equal opportunity to learn; (2) scoring is inaccurate because of an arbitrary decision on one correct answer that is correct for the mainstream culture, but that unfairly penalizes minority children, who may provide answers that would be correct in their culture;

(3) the language of the question is unfamiliar to minority children and may preclude their giving the correct answer because of difficulties in understanding the question. Each of these criticisms contributes to the same conclusion: that the test items are more difficult for children from minority groups than for children from the white middle-class culture upon which they are normed. This notion leads to an empirically defined and testable definition for content bias in aptitude tests:

An item or subscale of a test is considered to be biased in content when it is demonstrated to be relatively more difficult for members of one group than another, when the general ability level of the groups being compared is held constant and no reasonable, theoretical rationale exists to explain group differences on the item (or subscale) in question. (Reynolds, 1982b, p. 188)

Hypothesis testing with regard to content bias should then proceed to determine whether minority groups fail to respond in the correct direction more frequently than do white middle-class groups (or the group upon which the test is standardized and most widely used) when the total score of the test or subtest is constant. That is, when there are no apparent group differences in overall ability level (or other construct employed in test development), there should exist no difference in the proportion of correct versus incorrect responses to a given item across subgroups. IQ tests and other ability tests have been investigated using this type of logic, with the application of various statistical techniques.

Many psychometrically sophisticated techniques have been applied to the investigation of item bias in aptitude measures. These include chi-square analyses of item performance by group (Ironson, 1982); cross-group comparisons of difficulty and discrimination indices (Angoff, 1982); comparisons of latent trait parameters or item characteristic curves across groups (Ironson, 1982); partial-correlation procedures (Reynolds, Chatman, & Willson, 1983; Stricker, 1982); and applications of analysis of variance (ANOVA) where a significant item × group interaction denotes item bias (Jensen, 1980; Plake & Hoo-

ver, 1979; Reynolds, 1982a, 1982b). An investigation comparing the merits of each of these item bias methodologies was conducted by Burrill (1982). Her findings, based upon review of numerous studies comparing item bias techniques, suggest that the chi-square, ANOVA, transformed item difficulty, Rasch models, and partial-correlation procedures all produce acceptable evaluations of item bias. However, the methods vary greatly in terms of practical concerns (sample size required, costliness, degree of statistical sophistication, etc.). In addition, the techniques often identify different items as biased even when identical data are evaluated, so the question of preferred methodology remains unanswered and continues to generate additional debate in the discipline. Burrill advises researchers to evaluate both practical and empirical issues in selecting the methodology, and she advocates the use of more than one technique simultaneously to improve the reliability of the results. In applications to ability tests, these methods have not found significant amounts of bias in specific items. When bias is found, it appears equally balanced for both groups (majority and minority) under study and accounts for very small amounts of variance in total test scores (Reynolds, 1982b).

Given the notions of "difficulty" and "general ability level" stated in the definition above, the issue of content bias for personality tests appears somewhat more complex. Personality tests are generally not developed upon a scale of "difficulty" in the same sense as aptitude and other ability tests are; rather, they are developed to measure various qualitative dimensions of an individual's personality. However, they generally yield quantifiable scores that reflect varying degrees or relative amounts of a given trait in comparison to those of other individuals. Such tests as the MMPI, the 16PF, the CTP, the BDI, and others are developed to be scored in a keyed or correct–incorrect fashion, with total scores reflecting the relative amount of a given trait, indicator of pathology, or level of adjustment. These quantifiable scores do lend themselves to application of the same type of logic identified in the research hypothesis above. That is, if the demographic groups under study do not differ in overall score (or are equal in the trait measured by the test), then specific items should not be answered in the incorrect or nonkeyed direction more frequently by one group than by another.

Application of the available statistical techniques identifies items performing differentially (e.g., items that are more "difficult" or more frequently scored as incorrect for one group than for another) across groups, and the identified items are considered biased. Review of these items could potentially answer the question of why specific items perform differently for a given group, and could serve to promote the elimination of items that differ across groups. In addition, the practical importance of the biased items to the total test score (amount of variance accounted for by those identified items) may be examined, and this may help test users make decisions regarding the applicability of the test to the group in question. If, in practice, there are biased items but they account for only a small percentage of the variance in test score, then the test may remain useful with that group, at least from an item bias standpoint.

Conceptual differences between item bias studies of ability and personality tests are somewhat more pointed in investigations using projective techniques (e.g., inkblot techniques, thematic apperception tests, or projective drawings), where qualitative differences reflect different personality tendencies of a categorical or descriptive nature rather than the relative amount of a given trait in a quantitative sense. Examining the cultural test bias hypothesis in these tests demands that decisions be based upon the type of scoring of the test and design of the research. Statistics that can be used with nominal data (e.g., chi-square) are applicable for these tests, and research indicates that this method produces acceptable results (Burrill, 1982).

Investigations of item bias, regarded as the study of content validity, have been widely undertaken with ability tests, but have also been conducted with some objective personality instruments. Most of this research has used the chi-square technique for item bias detection (Schueneman, 1979). Both the MMPI and the CPI have been found to have a high percentage of items that perform differentially across race. Miller, Knapp, and

Daniels (1968) found identifiable clusters of items that were biased on the MMPI. These clusters included items dealing with physical symptoms, reliance on conventional standards, denial of anxiety, and mistrust of society, with the result that minority students' responses to such items generally promoted more deviant scale scores. Costello (1977) also found differences in the endorsement rates of various MMPI items, which also clustered into meaningful groups. Generally, black females' responses to such items indicated them to feel greater loss of control, feelings of alienation, physical symptoms, hallucinations, pessimism, and religiosity. Black inmates' item responses suggested that they were more likely to feel angry and misunderstood, to lack leadership, and to distrust society. Harrison and Kass (1967) found no identifiable clusters in their chi-square analysis of MMPI items, which identified 213 of 550 items as performing differently for black and white pregnant women. However, approximately equal numbers of pathological items were endorsed by each group; as a result, a balance in the degree of bias was found, with little adverse affect on overall test use.

Jones (1978) conducted analyses of the CPI and the Embedded Figures Test that identified about one-third of the CPI items as functioning differently across racial groups, with blacks scoring in the "correct" or keyed direction on 23% of the items, while whites responded in the keyed direction to 61% of the items. Sex differences were found as well. Furthermore, 83 of the items clustered into 10 patterns accounting for 83% of the variance in test scores. Blacks' responses suggested that they possess greater field dependence, more assertiveness, more power orientation, and less risk-taking tendencies than whites. The analysis of the Embedded Figures Test found that the items clustered into 10 groups, with ethnic differences on these clusters indicating that blacks expressed a more field-dependent style and whites expressed a more field-independent cognitive style. Cross and Burger (1982) found about one-third of CPI items to discriminate significantly between blacks and whites. Factor analysis of these items reflected ethnic differences within each sex grouping. Blacks as a whole were identified as showing less social extraversion and anxiety, more cynicism, and more fear of water. Black males appeared to be more rigid and conventional with higher mechanical interests, whereas white females had fewer adjustment difficulties, greater happiness and social morality, and less interest in politics. Gonzales (1973) also found that a significant number of DAP scoring items changed scoring category with minority status when performance was compared to Koppitz norms. This sample of Mexican-American, white, black, Navajo, and Pueblo children had higher frequencies in the scoring categories of hair, fingers, feet, and two-dimensional drawings, while the normative sample was higher in the frequency of eyebrows, elbows, and profile view. Such findings suggest that item-level differences exist even on routinely used drawing tests.

Only one study of item bias on personality scales has employed the ANOVA methodology, a technique widely used in the study of item bias on ability tests. Reynolds, Plake, and Harding (1983) found a significant race × item interaction on the RCMAS. However, the interaction accounted for less than 1% of the variance in test scores, suggesting little practical effects of the race differences in overall scores. In addition, the direction of bias appeared to be balanced across groups, with only a slight remaining bias against black males.

Using the CTP with a large sample of normal-functioning Mexican-American and Anglo children in south Texas, I (Moran, 1985) conducted item bias research using both the ANOVA and partial-correlation methods. The ANOVA identified significant race × item interactions on all 12 scales of this instrument. Interaction contrasts identified 13 of the 144 items (9%) as performing differentially, all in the keyed or correct direction for Anglos. Six scales had no biased items, while five scales had one or two biased items (with the exception of the Social Standards scale, on which 5 of the 12 possible items were biased).

Partial-correlation procedures on these data examined item × race correlations with total scale score held constant. This method identified 41 items (28%) as performing differentially between the two groups. In-

terestingly, 23 (16%) were found to favor Mexican-Americans (e.g., to be relatively less difficult), while 18 (12%) favored Anglos. Additional analyses of correlation between race and total scale score with total test score partialed out were computed to examine profile patterns. Performance on 7 of the 12 scales was found to be significantly different for the two groups when they were statistically equated on total scale score. Again, however, a balance in the direction of the differences was found: Four scales favored Mexican-Americans (Belonging, Freedom from Withdrawing Tendencies, Family Relationships, and School Relationships), whereas three favored Anglos (Self-Reliance, Personal Worth, and Social Standards). Overall, these results raised some questions regarding possible social value differences between the two groups, and supported the need for investigation of construct and predictive validity in order to determine the applicability of the test for these groups.

In terms of the differences in actual items and numbers of items identified as biased by the different item bias detection methods, Burrill (1982), Stricker (1982), and Reynolds, Chatman, and Willson (1983) find no clear superiority of one method over the others. Work continues with various samples and tests to determine what factors (sampling error, sample size, etc.) influence these differences in practice. Currently, it is recommended that one's choice of method be based upon practical considerations as well as the type of study being conducted; use of more than one method is advocated, in order to improve the reliability of the results.

The current status of item bias investigations conducted in the personality test literature can be best described as yielding equivocal results. The investigations have not been conducted with many of the widely used tests; even when they have been done, many questions, particularly that of the practical significance of the group differences in content at the item level, remain unanswered. The need appears clear for further item bias investigations, using a combination of methods to assure reliable results. In addition, investigation of construct and predictive validity are needed to fully address the presence or absence of bias and its applicability for various groups.

Bias in Construct Validity

"Construct validity," the term referring to whether or not a test measures what it was designed to measure, is perhaps the most important area of test investigation, given its practical importance. It is clear that similar constructs must be measured for different groups if the test is to have the same meaning across groups. There is no single method for the accurate determination of the construct validity of a psychological test. The definition of bias, then, requires a general statement that may be researched through a variety of methodologies. Reynolds offers the following definition: "Bias exists in regard to construct validity when a test is shown to measure different hypothetical traits (psychological constructs) for one group than another or to measure the same trait but with differing degrees of accuracy" (1982b, p. 194).

Investigation of this type of bias in personality tests appears most analogous to investigation of aptitude tests in terms of conceptualization in the existing methodology. According to cross-cultural theory, it is also most intuitively likely that differences may occur, since personality tests may indeed tap very real sociocultural differences among subgroups. However, if a test is to be used with various groups and its scores are to be interpreted similarly across groups, then it must be measuring the same construct for those groups. If not, the meaning of the score will not be the same for members of different groups, and bias (or systematic error raising or lowering the scores for a given group) necessarily exists. Should differences in the identified constructs of the test occur among groups and be found to be based upon some real difference between the groups or upon test error, then use of that test for the group in question would be unethical without substantial alteration in scoring, norm use, or interpretation for the group.

A wide variety of techniques is available for the investigation of a test's construct validity. These methods include factor analysis, which, when applied to studies of test bias, involves the comparison of factor structures across racial groups (Reynolds, 1982a); investigation of the consistency of correlations between age and raw scores across race (Jensen, 1980); examination of cross-group multi-trait–multimethod test validation matrices (Reynolds, 1982a); comparisons of reliability coefficients across groups (Reynolds, 1982a); and comparison of item discrimination indices (item–total correlations) across races (Reynolds, 1982a). These methods, when results are compared across groups, are all regarded as acceptable methods for studying test bias, although factor-analytic and reliability comparisons are most widely regarded as important (Berk, 1982; Gordon, 1984; Jensen, 1980; Mercer, 1984; Reynolds, 1982a, 1982b). In actual research, the choice of methodology is generally determined by practical considerations, as well as by the type of test under study and the data yielded by the specific design of the research.

It is likely that comparison of factor structures and reliability estimates across groups are the best means of investigating construct bias in personality tests. These methodologies answer two important questions with regard to bias: (1) Are the constructs (factor structures) measured in the same way for the groups in question? (2) Are the constructs measured with equal accuracy (reliability) for the groups? Multitrait–multimethod validation matrices and item–total correlations are also acceptable methods for use with affective measures. Investigation of the consistency of correlations between age and raw scores across race would be inappropriate, since personality tests are not developed on the principle that test performance should increase linearly with age.

Some studies of the cross-group construct validity of personality tests have been conducted, although they are meager, given the practical significance of the results of this research: If factor structures differ across groups, it is inappropriate to compare group means or to give the same interpretation of profiles of scores across groups. Studies comparing factor structures of personality tests across various groups have examined various tests, including the MMPI, the 16PF, the HIT, the RCMAS, and the Intermediate Self-Observation Scale. Holland's (1979) factor-analytic study of the MMPI with inmates found that three factors emerged for Anglos whereas four emerged for blacks and Mexican-Americans, suggesting that different constructs were being measured for the ethnic groups. Philip (1972) examined the factor structure of the 16PF and concluded that only the factor of anxiety was similar between British and American samples, with a measure of factorial similarity, rc, yielding values in the .89–.94 range. The value of rc should exceed .90 for the factors to be considered similar (Harman, 1976; Mulaik, 1972). Other factors were less similar across these groups, but the authors concluded that the existing differences held little practical significance and recommended continued use of American norms for the 16PF in Britain.

Factorial invariance of the Intermediate Self-Observation Scale for blacks and whites was supported in research by Katzenmeyer and Stenner (1977). Reynolds and Paget (1981) reported the equivalence of a five-factor solution for blacks and whites and for males and females on the RCMAS, with rc values in the high .90s. A study of the HIT indicated equivalent factors for Mexican children from Mexico City and Texas and for Anglo children (Holtzman et al., 1975). In research on the CTP (Moran, 1985), two factors were found to be similar for Anglos and Mexican-Americans, with coefficients of congruence exceeding .90. However, it was interesting to note that the factors did not load into the clean distinctions of Personal Adjustment and Social Adjustment, according to test theory and development. Rather, a general Personal Adjustment factor emerged, and scales theoretically developed to measure social adjustment in relationships and maintaining appropriate behavior toward others loaded more substantially on the Personal Adjustment factor, encompassing self-esteem, acceptance, independence, and freedom from stress-related symptoms. A smaller Social Adjustment factor did emerge and was supported by both statistics and theory.

Burns (1986), in a study of the factorial similarity of the RATC (an objectively scored and norm-referenced projective technique) for Mexican-American and Anglo children, found that the constructs were not equivalent across ethnic groups or sex. Individual subscales contributed differentially to the three factors being measured, and the meaning of the test for Mexican-American children and its use with this group were questioned.

Comparisons of internal-consistency estimates across groups are also important in investigation of an instrument's cross-group construct validity (Clarizio, 1982; Duffy, Salvia, Tucker, & Ysseldyke, 1981; Feldt, 1969; Linn & Werts, 1971; Oakland & Feigenbaum, 1979; Reynolds, 1982a, 1982b). These comparisons provide information regarding the accuracy with which the test measures a trait across groups. Although some cross-cultural comparisons have been carried out between American and South African and German samples with objective personality tests (Orpen, 1972; Runge, Frey, Gollwitzer, Helmreich, & Spence, 1981), and more frequently with ability tests such as the WISC-R and the Bender–Gestalt (Oakland & Feigenbaum, 1979), studies of this nature with widely used personality tests are nearly nonexistent. In addition, the use of a statistical technique for comparing the significance of the differences in internal-consistency estimates (Feldt, 1969) has been largely ignored in the study of personality tests. Use of such a statistic appears necessary in order to assure that any existing differences in reliability are indeed real rather than artifactual.

Plake, Piersel, Harding, and Reynolds (1982), Reynolds and Piersel (1983), and Reynolds and Paget (1981) did use the Feldt technique in their investigations of the cross-group construct validity of the Estes Reading Attitude Scale, the Boehm Test of the Basic Concepts, and the RCMAS, respectively. Their results indicated congruent internal-consistency estimates between Anglo and Mexican-American subjects on the Estes and Boehm instruments. On the RCMAS, congruent internal-consistency estimates for white males and females and black males were found at ages 6 through 19. However, black females' performance was significantly less reliable than that of white females aged 6, 8, 10, and 11.

The investigation of the CTP (Moran, 1985) included cross-group reliability comparisons for Mexican-Americans and Anglos. The reliability estimates from this sample, based on use of the Feldt technique, were significantly higher for Anglos on every subscale and on the three composite scales (Personal, Social, and Total Adjustment). The significant difference in reliability (Anglo mean $r_{xx} = .68$; Mexican-American mean $r_{xx} = .58$)

indicated that the CTP is less accurate for Mexican-Americans than for Anglos.

It is quite likely that the generally poor reliability of personality tests in general has limited some of the work in cross-group reliability comparisons. Arguments have been presented that the traditional methods for assessing reliability and validity are not applicable to projective instruments (Lanyon & Goodstein, 1982), and this may provide an explanation for the nonexistence of bias studies in the area of projective personality tests. The following explanations have been offered as to why the classical tests of reliability do not apply to projective techniques: (1) the difficulty in obtaining comparable halves; (2) sensitivity of the projective techniques to slight changes in the individual; (3) inadequate representation by the stimulus of various scoring categories; (4) lack of standardization of instructions; and (5) subjective scoring systems (Lanyon & Goodstein, 1982). These conditions assuredly affect measured reliability and, subsequently, cross-group comparisons of reliability coefficients. Awareness of the poor psychometric properties of these instruments does not, however, diminish the need both for continued efforts to improve the quality of the tests themselves and for increased understanding of the meaning of the results for various demographic groups.

Bias in Predictive Validity

Bias may also occur in predictive validity when the relationship of a test score to some external criterion differs across groups. Reynolds's definition of bias in predictive validity is a slight restatement of the Cleary, Humphreys, Kendrick, and Wesman (1975) definition and can be empirically investigated:

> A test is considered biased with respect to predictive validity when the inference drawn from the test score is not made with the smallest feasible random error or if there is constant error in an inference or prediction as a function of membership in a particular group. (Reynolds, 1982b, p. 201)

For a test to be unbiased with regard to prediction, the criterion predicted by use of the test (e.g., achievement, occupational level, diagnosis, indicator of pathology, personality trait, level of adjustment, etc.) should be predicted equally well for different racial or ethnic groups. Errors in prediction should be minimal and approximately equal for each group if the test is to be used in a similar fashion for all groups. As is the case when differences in construct validity occur, differences in predictive validity suggest the need for use of the test in a different manner, revision of the test to reflect the real differences inherent among the groups, or cessation of the use of that test for the minority groups in question.

The methodology used for examination of differential criterion-related validity essentially involves the cross-group comparison of regression lines derived from the relationship of test scores with performance on a criterion measure. The regression equations may be developed from criterion measures obtained either concurrently with test administration or at a later time. For a test to be nonbiased with regard to criterion-related validity, the regression lines for two groups should be the same. Although many widely used intelligence and achievement tests have been examined via comparison of regression lines, relatively little examination of possible bias in personality tests using this methodology has occurred.

Studies have been most prolific in cross-validation of subscales of the MMPI with various criterion measures for blacks and whites. Newmark, Gentry, Warren, and Finch (1981) found no race or sex bias in their MMPI index for schizophrenia when this index was related to criterion measures of behavioral observations, social history, and diagnosis based on mental status. Lothstein and Jones (1978) did find that high scores for blacks on the psychopathic Deviate (Pd), Sc, and Ma scales of the MMPI did not predict assaultiveness at the same level of prediction found with prisoners of other races. Gilberstadt and Duker's 8-6 profile type was validated against symptom checklists and judges' ratings of hospital and social histories for whites and blacks (Clark & Miller, 1971). Clark and Miller's findings suggested that both race groups were similar in the presence of hallucinations, confusion, memory and concentration impairment, flat affect, and thought disorder. Zager (1981) found bias against blacks in a validation of seven MMPI alcohol/drug abuse scales, although the scales were found to have little validity in predicting abusers regardless of race. Validation of the *Pd* scale was sought for black males in a study with inmates and students (Elion & Megargee, 1975). Results indicated that *Pd* elevations did discriminate black inmates from college students, although blacks had significantly higher *Pd* scale scores than usually found with the MMPI.

Methodological weaknesses similar to those found in the studies of mean differences are present in these studies of external bias. The studies used small samples, and individuals were drawn primarily from prisons and psychiatric facilities. Further confounding the interpretation of the results are the low reliabilities of the criterion measures used (e.g., psychiatric diagnosis, level of violence exhibited, degree of substance abuse, etc.). Potential moderator variables (e.g., SES, IQ, and educational level) were often not included in the analyses. When IQ was used in the analyses, a multiple discriminant function identified the first and second variables on the MMPI as discriminators of high and low IQ, differentiating low-IQ whites from low-IQ blacks rather than indicating differences in personality variables (Rosenblatt & Pritchard, 1978). In similar fashion, Davis and Jones (1974) found that low educational level acts as a moderator variable to raise MMPI scores on the *Sc* and Paranoia *(Pa)* scales for blacks, although no race differences were found when educational level and diagnosis were controlled. These MMPI studies, then, yield equivocal results with regard to the differential predictive validity of the various scales for blacks and whites.

The only predictive validity study of a projective test, the RATC, was conducted by Burns (1986), who used behavior ratings on the Achenbach CBCL as a criterion. The results indicated that there was no constant error in the prediction of behavior (CBCL scores) as a function of Mexican-American versus Anglo group membership. Evidence was, however, provided for bias in the predictions of the Internalizing score as a function of ethnic group membership, as teachers rated Mexican-American students higher than predicted on the Internalizing scale of

the CBCL. Of note was the finding that RATC variables accounted for between 6% and 14% of the variance of the CBCL scores, suggesting little relationship between overt behavior and projective test responses.

A recent study (Kline, Lachar, & Sprague, 1985) of the PIC sought to examine race, sex, and age bias in its prediction of the cognitive status of white and black children. No race bias was found in the prediction of achievement and IQ by the PIC Cognitive Triad profile scales. Unfortunately, the relationship of affective scales with a criterion measure was not addressed in this work, although the PIC is a widely used personality assessment technique.

As this review of the literature suggests, the cross-group predictive accuracy for a variety of widely used personality tests remains an unanswered question. It is a question urgently in need of research, since personality tests are widely used with minority groups, and some studies have indicated that differential predictive validity exists for various groups.

CONCLUSIONS AND FUTURE DIRECTIONS

Although the controversy over bias in personality tests has not been as spirited as that regarding bias in ability tests, the widespread use and practical importance of personality tests in labeling and decision making suggests the need for widespread study of the cultural bias question. The issues involved in cultural bias in personality assessment are, of course, extremely complex and not likely to be resolved for some time.

The research addressing this question has been extremely limited and rather inconclusive. Results have shown limited evidence for content or item bias on some objective personality tests. Research with the MMPI has been methodologically poor but has identified significant proportions of items as biased. The need is clear for a well-designed study of this widely used instrument to further examine the issue and the relative impact of the biased items on test scores. The RCMAS and CTP have been found to have small proportions of biased items, although the practical significance of these items to the total test score is extremely small and does not indicate that these tests are inappropriate for the minorities involved. Other objective tests remain in need of study. Projective techniques will be extremely difficult to study with current methodology because of their subjective nature, although chi-square techniques could be applied and are likely to be meaningful in a well-developed study.

Perhaps more importantly, the issue of differential construct validity remains urgently in need of study for various race and ethnic groups. The question of whether the test measures the same constructs across groups is a fundamental one in determining the applicability of the test for the major ethnic/racial groups in this country. Research on this point has again been methodologically flawed in studies of the MMPI and could well be conducted with an appropriate sample. The HIT, CTP, and RCMAS have demonstrated factorial equivalence, although the RATC has not. Use of the RATC from a quantitative standpoint is thus questionable, while use of the other tests appears supported. Further study of the accuracy of the measurements across groups is warranted to fully address the issue of bias in construct validity.

In terms of predictive accuracy across groups, little study has been conducted. Significant concerns remain, given the substantial void in this body of research and the equivocal nature of existing results. The initial investigations should probably focus on objective tests, since the selection of an appropriate criterion is more readily accomplished than with projective tests, whose constructs may lack behavioral referents. Even projective tests could, however, be validated against multidimensional behavior rating scales; diagnosis; or presence or absence of thought disorder, depression, anxiety, or other psychopathology.

The methodologies used with ability tests and applied to some personality tests appear highly useful. With only minor alterations in the ways these methods are applied or the way in which scores are analyzed for various measures, future study would appear well within the bounds of current scientific methods. As criteria for emotional disturbance and diagnosis become more objective, the task should become somewhat more focused. Tests that provide information relevant to these or identifiable treatment issues could be identified, adding confidence to use of test results.

Of particular importance is the application of this methodology in the development phase of the construction of new tests or revisions of old ones. Revision of norms with more appropriate standardization samples appears needed for most personality tests, and it is incumbent upon test publishers to undertake these challenges. Bias studies that address differential validity issues and the applicability of the test for various groups should be presented in test manuals. Should study indicate differences, then separate norms should be provided for the group(s) in question. Methodological advances in test development and validation may promote some resolution of the cultural test bias issue and other psychometric issues relevant to personality assessment. It appears, however, that current bias methodology, when applied to the more psychometrically sound personality assessment techniques, should lead to some resolution of this important question for the individuals with whom these tests are so widely used.

REFERENCES

American Psychological Association. (1979). *Ethical standards of psychologists*. Washington, DC: Author.

Anastasi, A. (1976). *Psychological testing* (4th ed.). New York: Macmillan.

Angoff, W. H. (1982). Use of difficulty and discrimination indicies for detecting item bias. In R. A. Berk (Ed.), *Handbook of methods for detecting test bias* (pp. 96–116). Baltimore: Johns Hopkins University Press.

Bailey, B. E., & Green, J. (1977). Blacks' Thematic Apperception Test stimulus material. *Journal of Personality Assessment, 41,* 25–30.

Berk, R. A. (Ed.). (1982). *Handbook of methods for detecting test bias*. Baltimore: Johns Hopkins University Press.

Bersoff, D. N. (1982). The legal regulation of school psychology. In C. R. Reynolds & T. B. Gutkin (Eds.), *The handbook of school psychology* (pp. 1043–1074). New York: Wiley.

Brown, C. E. (1979). *Impact of sex, socioeconomic status, and examiners' ethnicity and sex on response patterns of Anglo and Hispanic subjects on the 16PF and the POI* (Doctoral dissertation, New Mexico State University, 1978). *Dissertation Abstracts International, 39,* 5513B.

Burns, C. W. (1986). *The validity of the Roberts Apperception Test for Children across ethnic groups and between sexes*. Unpublished doctoral dissertation, Texas A&M University.

Burrill, L. E. (1982). Comparative studies of item bias methods. In R. A. Berk (Ed.), *Handbook of methods for detecting test bias* (pp. 161–179). Baltimore: John Hopkins University Press.

Butcher, J. M., Ball, B., & Ray, E. (1964). Effects of socioeconomic level on MMPI differences in Negro–white college students. *Journal of Counseling Psychology, 11,* 83–87.

Carpenter, T. R., & Busse, T. V. (1969). Development of self-concept in Negro and white welfare children. *Child Development, 40,* 935–939.

Civil Rights Act of 1964, 7 U.S.C. § 713 (1964).

Clarizio, H. F. (1982). Intellectual assessment of Hispanic children. *Psychology in the Schools, 19,* 61–71.

Clark, C. G., & Miller, H. L. (1971). Validation of Gilberstadt & Duker's 8-6 profile type on a black sample. *Psychological Reports, 29,* 259–264.

Cleary, T. A., Humphreys, L. G., Kendrick, S. A., & Wesman, A. (1975). Educational uses of tests with disadvantaged students. *American Psychologist, 30,* 15–41.

Costello, R. M. (1977). Construction and cross-validation of an MMPI black–white scale. *Journal of Personality Assessment, 41,* 514–519.

Cowan, G., & Goldberg, F. (1967). Need achievement as a function of the race and sex of figures in selected TAT cards. *Journal of Personality and Social Psychology, 5,* 245–249.

Cross, D. T., & Burger, G. (1982). Ethnicity as a variable in responses to California Psychological Inventory items. *Journal of Personality Assessment, 46,* 153–153.

Davis, W. E., & Jones, M. H. (1974). Negro versus Caucasian psychological test performance revisited. *Journal of Consulting and Clinical Psychology, 42,* 675–679.

DeHoyos, A., & DeHoyos, G. (1965). Symptomatology differentials between Negro and white schizophrenics. *International Journal of Social Psychiatry, 11,* 245–255.

Diana v. State Board of Education, No. C-70 37 RFP (N. D. Cal. 1970).

Duffy, J. B., Salvia, J. Tucker, J., & Ysseldyke, J. E. (1981). Nonbiased assessment: A need for operationalism. *Exceptional Children, 47,* 427–434.

Education for All Handicapped Children Act of 1975, P. L. 94-142, 34 C.F.R. § 300. (1975).

Exner, J. E. (1974). *The Rorschach: A comprehensive system*. New York: Wiley.

Elion, V. H., & Megargee, E. I. (1975). Validity of the MMPI *Pd* scale among black males. *Journal of Consulting and Clinical Psychology, 43,* 166–172.

Fabrega, H., Swartz, J., & Wallace, C. A. (1968). Ethnic differences in psychopathology. *Archives of General Psychology, 19,* 218–226.

Fanibanda, D. K. (1973). Cultural influence on Hutt's adaptation of Bender Gestalt test: A pilot study. *Journal of Personality Assessment, 37,* 531–536

Feldt, L. S. (1969). A test of the hypothesis that Cronbach's alpha or Kuder–Richardson coefficient twenty is the same for two tests. *Psychometrika, 34,* 363–373.

Gonzales, E. (1973). A cross-cultural comparison of the development items of five ethnic groups in the

Southwest. *Journal of Personality Assessment, 37,* 531–536.

Gordon, R. A. (1984). Digits backward and the Mercer–Kamin law: An empirical response to Mercer's treatment of internal validity of IQ tests. In C. R. Reynolds & R. T. Brown (Eds.), *Perspectives on bias in mental testing* (pp. 357–506). New York: Plenum.

Guadalupe v. Tempe Elementary School District, 71-435 (District Court of Arizona, January 1972).

Gynther, M. D., Fowler, R. D., & Erdberg, P. (1971). False positives galore: The application of standard MMPI criteria to a rural isolated Negro sample. *Journal of Clinical Psychology, 27,* 234–237.

Harman, H. (1976). *Modern factor analysis* (2nd ed.). Chicago: University of Chicago Press.

Harrington, G. M. (1975). Intelligence tests may favour the majority groups in a population. *Nature, 258,* 708–709.

Harrison, R. H., & Kass, E. H. (1967). Differences between Negro and white pregnant women on the MMPI. *Journal of Consulting Psychology, 31,* 454–463.

Hilliard, A. G. (1979). Standardization and cultural bias as impediments to the scientific study and validation of "intelligence." *Journal of Research and Development in Education, 12,* 47–58.

Hobson v. Hansen, 269 F. Supp. 401 (D.D.C. 1967).

Holcomb, W. R., & Adams, N. (1982). Racial influences in intelligence and personality measures of people who commit murder. *Journal of Clinical Psychology, 38,* 793–796.

Holland, T. R. (1979). Ethnic group differences in MMPI profile pattern and factorial structure among adult offenders. *Journal of Personality Assessment, 43,* 72–77.

Holtzman, W. H., Diaz-Guerrero, R., & Schwartz, J. D. (1975). *Personality development in two cultures: A cross-cultural longitudinal study of school children in Mexico and the United States*. Austin: University of Texas Press.

Ironson, G. H. (1982). Use of chi-square and latent trait approaches for detecting item bias. In R. A. Berk (Eds.), *Handbook of methods for detecting test bias* (pp. 117–160). Baltimore: Johns Hopkins University Press.

Jensen, A. R. (1980). *Bias in mental testing*. New York: Free Press.

Johnson, D. L., & Sikes, M. P. (1965). Rorschach and TAT responses of Negro, Mexican American, and Anglo psychiatric patients. *Journal of Projective Techniques, 29,* 183–188.

Jones, E. E. (1978). Black–white personality differences: Another look. *Journal of Personality Assessment, 42,* 244–252.

Kaplan, B. P. (1955). Reflections of the acculturation process in the Rorschach test. *Journal of Projective Techniques, 19,* 30–35.

Kaplan, B. P., Rickers-Ovsiankina, M. A., & Joseph, A. (1956). An attempt to sort Rorschach records from four cultures. *Journal of Projective Techniques, 20,* 172–180.

Katzenmeyer, W. G., & Stenner, A. J. (1977). Estimation of the invariance of factor structures across sex and race with implications for hypothesis testing. *Educational and Psychological Measurement, 37,* 111–119.

Kline, R. B., Lachar, P., & Sprague, D. J. (1985). The Personality Inventory for Children (PIC): An unbiased predictor of cognitive and academic status. *Journal of Pediatric Psychology, 10,* 461–477.

Lanyon, R. I., & Goodstein, L. D. (1982). *Personality assessment.* New York: Wiley.

Laosa, L. M., Lara-Tapia, S., & Swartz, J. (1974). Pathognomic verbalizations, anxiety, and hostility in normal Mexican and United States Anglo-American children's fantasies: A longitudinal study. *Journal of Consulting and Clinical Psychology, 42,* 73–78.

Larry P. v. Riles, 343 F. Supp. 1306 (N.D. Cal. 1979).

Lefley, H. P. (1975). Differential self-concept in American Indian children as a function of language and examiner. *Journal of Personality and Social Psychology, 31,* 36–41.

Lewis, D. O., Balla, D. A., & Shanok, S. S. (1979). Some evidence of race bias in the diagnosis and treatment of the juvenile offender. *American Journal of Orthopsychiatry, 49,* 53–61.

Lewis, D. O., Shanok, S. S., Cohen, R. J., Kligfield, M., & Frisone, G. (1980). Race bias in the diagnosis and disposition of violent adolescents. *American Journal of Psychiatry, 137,* 1211–1216.

Linn, R. L., & Werts, C. E. (1971). Considerations for studies of test bias. *Journal of Educational Measurement, 8,* 1–4.

Lothstein, L. M., & Jones, P. (1978). Discriminating violent individuals by means of various psychological tests. *Journal of Personality Assessment, 42,* 237–243.

Lowe, J. D., & Hildman, L. K. (1972). EPI scores as a function of race. *British Journal of Social and Clinical Psychology, 11,* 191–192.

Mason, E. P. (1967). Comparison of personality characteristics of junior high students from American Indian, Mexican, and Caucasian ethnic backgrounds. *Journal of Social Psychology, 73,* 145–155.

McCreary, C., & Padilla, E. (1977). MMPI differences among black, Mexican-American, and white male of offenders. *Journal of Clinical Psychology, 33,* 171–177.

Megargee, E. I. (1967). Hostility on the TAT as a function of defensive inhibition and stimulus situation. *Journal of Projective Techniques and Personality Assessment, 31,* 73–79.

Mercer, J. R. (1984). What is a racially and culturally nondiscriminatory test? A sociological and pluralistic perspective. In C. R. Reynolds & R. T. Brown (Eds.), *Perspectives on bias in mental testing* (pp. 293–356). New York: Plenum.

Miller, C., Knapp, S. C., & Daniels, C. W. (1968). MMPI study of Negro mental hygiene clinic patients. *Journal of Abnormal Psychology, 73,* 168–173.

Miller, F. E. (1982). *Level of perceptual development in normal achieving Mexican-American children as measured by responses on the Holtzman Inkblot Technique: A normative study.* Unpublished doctoral dissertation, Texas A&M University.

Moran, M. P. (1985). *An evaluation of internal bias on the California Test of Personality.* Unpublished doctoral dissertation, Texas A&M University.

Mulaik, S. A. (1972). *The foundation of factor analysis.* New York: McGraw-Hill.

Newmark, C. S., Gentry, L., Warren, N., & Finch, A. J. (1981). Racial bias in an MMPI index of schizophrenia. *British Journal of Clinical Psychology, 20,* 215–216.

Oakland, T., & Feigenbaum, D. (1979). Multiple sources of test bias on the WISC-R and the Bender Gestalt test. *Journal of Consulting and Clinical Psychology, 47,* 968–974.

Olmedo, E. L. (1977). Psychological testing and the Chicano: A reassessment. In J. L. Martinez, Jr. (Ed.), *Chicano psychology* (pp. 176–195). New York: Academic Press.

Orpen, C. (1972). The cross-cultural validity of the EPI: A test in Afrikaans-speaking South Africa. *British Journal of Social and Clinical Psychology, 11,* 244–247.

Padilla, E. R., Olmedo, E. L., & Loya, F. (1982). Acculturation and the MMPI performance of Chicano and Anglo college students. *Hispanic Journal of Behavioral Sciences, 4,* 451–466.

Padilla, A. M., & Ruiz, R. A. (1973). *Latino mental health: A review of the Literature* (DHEW Publication No. HSM 73-9143). Washington, DC: U.S. Government Printing Office.

Padilla, A. M., & Ruiz, R. A. (1975). Personality assessment and test interpretation of Mexican-Americans: A critique. *Journal of Personality Assessment, 39,* 103–109.

Pasamanick, B. (1963). Some misconceptions concerning differences in the racial prevalence of mental disease. *American Journal of Orthopsychiatry, 33,* 72–86.

PASE v. Hannon, 506 F. Supp. 831 (N.D. Ill. 1980).

Peixotte, H. E. (1954). The Bender Gestalt Visual Motor Test as a culture-free test of personality. *Journal of Clinical Psychology, 10,* 369–372.

Philip, A. A. (1972). Cross-cultural stability of second-order factors in the 16PF. *British Journal of Social and Clinical Psychology, 11,* 276–283.

Plake, B. S., & Hoover, H. D. (1980). An analytic method for identifying biased items. *Journal of Experimental Education, 48,* 153–154.

Plake, B. S., Piersel, W. C., Harding, R. E., & Reynolds, C. R. (1982). The relationship of ethnic group membership to the measurement and meaning of attitudes toward reading: Implications for validity of test score interpretations. *Educational and Psychological Measurement, 42,* 1259–1267.

Plemons, G. (1977). A comparison of MMPI scores of Anglo and Mexican-American psychiatric patients. *Journal of Consulting and Clinical Psychology, 45,* 194–150.

Pollack, D., & Shore, J. H. (1980). Validity of the MMPI with Native Americans. *American Journal of Psychiatry, 137,* 946–950.

Reynolds, C. R. (1982a). Methods for detecting construct and predictive bias. In R. A. Berk (Ed.), *Handbook of methods for detecting test bias* (pp. 199–227). Baltimore: Johns Hopkins University Press.

Reynolds, C. R. (1982b). The problem of bias in psychological assessment. In C. R. Reynolds & T. B. Gutkin (Eds.), *The handbook of school psychology* (pp. 178–208). New York: Wiley.

Reynolds, C. R., & Brown, R. T. (1984). Bias in mental testing: An introduction to the issues. In C. R. Reynolds & R. T. Brown (Eds.), *Perspectives on bias in mental testing* (pp. 1–40). New York: Plenum.

Reynolds, C. R., Chatman, S. R., & Willson, V. L. (1983, April). *Item bias on the 1981 revised edition of* the Peabody Picture Vocabulary Test using a new method of detecting bias. Paper presented at the annual meeting of the American Educational Research Association, Montreal.

Reynolds, C. R., & Gutkin, T. B. (1980, September). WISC-R performance of blacks and whites matched on four demographic variables. Paper presented at the annual meeting of the American Psychological Association, Montreal.

Reynolds, C. R., & Paget, K. D. (1981). Factor analysis of the Revised Children's Manifest Anxiety Scale for blacks, whites, males, and females with a national normative sample. Journal of Consulting and Clinical Psychology, 49, 349–352.

Reynolds, C. R., & Piersel, W. C. (1983). Multiple aspects of bias on the Boehm Test of Basic Concepts (Forms A & B) for white and Mexican-American children. Journal of Psychoeducational Assessment, 1, 135–142.

Reynolds, C. R., Plake, B. S., & Harding, R. E. (1983). Item bias in the assessment of children's anxiety: Race and sex interaction on items of the Revised Children's Manifest Anxiety Scale. Journal of Psychoeducational Assessment, 1, 17–24.

Rosenblatt, A. I., & Pritchard, D. A. (1983). Moderators of racial differences on the MMPI. Journal of Consulting and Clinical Psychology, 46, 1572–1573.

Rosenthal, R. (1966). Experimenter effects in behavioral research. New York: Appleton-Century-Crofts.

Runge, T. E., Frey, D., Gollwitzer, P. M., Helmreich, R. L., & Spence, J. T. (1981). Masculine (instrumental) and feminine (expressive) traits: A comparison between students in the United States and West Germany. Journal of Cross-Cultural Psychology, 12, 142–162.

Schueneman, J. (1979). A method of assessing bias in test items. Journal of Educational Measurement, 16, 143–152.

Scott, R. (1981). FM: Clinically meaningful Rorschach index with minority children. Psychology in the Schools, 18, 143–152.

Simon, R. L., Fliess, J. S., Garland, B. J., Stiller, P. R., & Sharpe, L. (1973). Depression and schizophrenia in hospitalized black and white mental patients. Archives of General Psychiatry, 28, 509–512.

Stricker, L. J. (1982). Identifying test items that perform differentially in population subgroups: A partial correlation index. Applied Psychological Measurement, 6, 261–273.

Sundberg, N. D., & Gonzales, L. R. (1981). Cross-cultural and cross-ethnic assessment: Overview and issues. In P. McReynolds (Ed.), Advances in psychological assessment (Vol. 5, pp. 460–529). San Francisco: Jossey-Bass.

Vocational Rehabilitation Act of 1973, Section 504, U.S.C. § 504 (1973).

Warheit, G., Holzer, C., & Arey, S. (1975). Race and mental illness: An epidemiological update. Journal of Health and Social Behaviors, 16, 243–256.

Williams, R. L. (1971). Testing and dehumanizing black children. School Psychologist, 25, 11–13.

Zager, L. D. (1981). Seven MMPI alcohol and drug abuse scales: An empirical investigation of their interrelationships, convergent and discriminant validity and degree of racial bias. Journal of Personality and Social Psychology, 40, 532–544.

23

Assessing the Family Context

CINDY I. CARLSON
University of Texas at Austin

I t has been argued that the family context exerts the most pervasive, continuous, and personal influence on the development of children. Empirical studies confirm the critical significance of the family environment. Numerous family process and status variables have been found to mediate children's adjustment, including marital confict (O'Leary, 1984), family structure (Guidabaldi, Cleminshaw, Peery, & McLoughlin, 1983; Hetherington, Cox, & Cox, 1982; Wallerstein & Kelly, 1980), parenting style (Maccoby & Martin, 1983), parental mental health (Baldwin, Cole, & Baldwin, 1982; Billings & Moos, 1983), family communication patterns (Grotevant & Cooper, 1985), and extrafamilial stressors (McCubbin & Patterson, 1985). It is surprising, given the critical significance of the family context to children's development and subsequent school adjustment, that the assessment practices of psychologists have remained primarily child-centered (Carlson & Sincavage, 1987).

This chapter addresses the importance of assessing the family context in the evaluation of children's psychological and educational functioning. The purpose of the chapter is to review methods of family assessment relevant to the task of child evaluation and to place these methods within a conceptual framework that permits flexible utilization of methods. The chapter begins with an overview of the theoretical forces that have led to the current interest in studying the family within the social sciences and that have in-

fluenced family assessment methodology. Next, a framework for classifying family measurement procedures is introduced in which three major dimensions are emphasized: perspective, level, and construct assessed. The third section provides a broad conceptual framework for evaluating the family context. Reviews of selected family measurement techniques follow; measurement techniques are broadly grouped into interview, observation, and self-report methods. Finally, a concluding section addresses the strengths and limitations of various types of family assessment methods, with recommendations for use in practice.

FAMILY ASSESSMENT: THEORETICAL STREAMS OF INFLUENCE

In order to give the reader an appreciation of the multiple theoretical perspectives, disciplines, and methodological perspectives, a brief review follows of the major research traditions that have influenced the development of current family assessment procedures. These research traditions include family sociology, systems/communication theory, child and developmental psychology, and social learning theory (Jacobs, 1987), as well as ecological psychology. Although these streams of research have not developed in isolation from one another, family assessment measures will vary to some extent, depending upon the theoretical tradition from which they most clearly derive.

Family Sociology

The study of the family is considered to have its origins in sociology with the publication of Ernest Burgess's (1926) paper, "The Family as a Unit of Interacting Personalities." Burgess's ideas can be seen as important forerunners to current conceptualizing about the family. Specifically, Burgess (1) emphasized the process versus the content of family interaction, (2) conceptualized the family as the unit of study, and (3) analyzed the family in terms of family patterns and roles (Jacobs, 1987).

Subsequent to Burgess, several major sociological perspectives can be distinguished with respect to study of the family context (Jacobs, 1987). Parsons's structural–functional model of group process was influential in the development of clinical models of family functioning that emphasize the fit between role performance and family organization (e.g., the family process model—Steinhauer, Santa-Barbara, & Skinner, 1984; the structural family therapy model—Minuchin, 1974). Social exchange theory viewed social interaction in terms of such concepts as rewards and costs, and influenced, in particular, marital interaction research and therapy. The focus on conflict and power within social groups spurred the development of marital and family conflict and satisfaction measures. Finally, the concept of family development originated within the sociological tradition (Hill, 1949, 1958).

In addition to these major theoretical streams, sociology also contributed significantly to the methodology of family assessment. Parsons's and Bale's development of the interaction process analysis, an observational coding scheme for analyzing small-group process, provided both the methodology and key variables for subsequent family process coding schemes (see Grotevant & Carlson, 1987). Strodtbeck's revealed-difference technique (Strodtbeck, 1951) continues to be the stimulus situation for many studies of family process and clinical evaluations of families.

Although sociology provided critical impetus to the family studies tradition, and particularly to the development of marital measures, the most significant contributions to current whole-family assessment practice have derived from the more recently formulated systems/comunications theory.

Systems/Communications Theory

Beginning in the 1950s, clinical researchers (e.g., the Palo Alto group [Jackson, Bateson, Haley, and Weakland], Lidz, Wynne, and Bowen) turned their attention to the role of the family in the etiology of severe adult psychopathology. Common to this research was a focus on family communication patterns; theoretical models that emphasized the primacy of the interactional context in understanding deviant behavior; and, over time, acceptance of the explanatory power of general systems theory (Bertalanffy, 1968).

At the core of a systems orientation is the concept that elements exist in a state of active communicative interrelatedness and interdependence within a bounded unit (e.g., the individual, the family, the classroom, the organization), such that the activities of one element cannot help having a direct or indirect influence on the other elements of the system; this results in a whole that is greater than the sum of the elements (Koman & Stechler, 1985). The properties of the system, as well as the mechanisms that maintain problem behavior, are evident in the repeated interactional or communication sequences between members (elements) of the system who are in a mutual and interdependent relationship with one another.

The systems/communication perspective has significant implications for the methodology required for family assessment. First, the dysfunctional behavior of an individual child is viewed as meaningless without a view to the systemic context in which it is embedded. Second, a systems orientation implies a relational as opposed to an individual focus to assessment. A relational focus demands techniques that measure the interactions of elements within systems and between systems, in contrast with traditional techniques, which focus on individual variability across systems such as the home and school. Third, this orientation underscores the complexity of relationships that can exist within and between systems, and between children's dysfunctional behavior and their systemic contexts. Thus, this perspective encourages the utilization of family assessment procedures that go beyond single variables aimed at only one level of the family matrix (Jacobs, 1987).

Child and Developmental Psychology

A third influence on the development of measures of the family derives primarily from research in child and developmental psychology that has had as its goal the explication of parenting variables that systematically vary with children's cognitive and social–emotional development. This research on the parent–child relationship has shifted over the past several decades from a "social mold" theoretical viewpoint, in which parent influences were viewed as unidirectional from the parent to the child, to a transactional view (see Sameroff, 1987), in which the parent and child are viewed as establishing organized, reciprocal patterns of interaction that characterize their relationship (Hartup, 1978). Thus, within this perspective, the origins of children's personalities are viewed as the direct outcome of their social relationships. More specifically, children are viewed as internalizing relationship "wholes" —that is, the roles, attitudes, and behaviors both of their parents and of themselves as respondents (Sroufe & Fleeson, 1986). Developmental research on the parent–child relationship has spurred the identification of key parenting dimensions and the creation of numerous parent–child measures. Furthermore, it has heightened awareness of the critical importance of assessing the child and family within a temporal context. Thus, child behaviors surrounding family interaction patterns are expected to shift with age and stage. The deviance of behavior is thus evaluated with a view both to the systemic context and to its developmental appropriateness.

A second influence of developmental psychology has been the inclusion of a lifespan perspective. The lifespan perspective has focused attention on the individual development of parents and the role of parent developmental status in subsequent parenting capacity. Extension of the developmental perspective across the lifespan has also en-

couraged the formulation of family life cycle theory (Carter & McGoldrick, 1980; Terkelsen, 1980) (see later discussion on family development).

Social Learning Theory

Yet another major influence on family measurement has been behavioral psychology, particularly social learning theory. Although far from a homogeneous discipline, the research tradition of social learning can be characterized by the following: (1) a continuing view that behavior and its variation are functions of the reinforcement contingencies of the environment; (2) a concern with illuminating the reciprocal, bidirectional chains of interaction or social exchange that comprise the environment; (3) a preference for naturalistic observation as an assessment methodology; (4) a commitment to scientific, methodologically rigorous procedures and the clinical application of findings; and (5) concern with the macroenvironmental contingencies that affect the family (Conger, 1981, 1983; Jacobs, 1987; Patterson, 1982). The social learning researchers concerned with child problems (e.g., Forehand & McMahon, 1981; Patterson, 1982; Patterson & Reid, 1984; Patterson, Reid, Jones, & Conger, 1975; Reid, 1978) have made substantial methodological contributions to family assessment with the provision of valid and reliable observation and quasi-observation procedures.

Ecological Psychology

Ecological psychology, associated with the work of Lewin (1951), is essentially concerned with the relationship between individual behavior and the total life space (Barker, 1968). Much of the early research in ecological psychology was concerned with the study of the inextricably linked behavior–environment interface, such that behavior of participants and the surrounding environment formed a bounded unit, the behavior setting (Barker, 1968; Wicker, 1979). More recently, ecological theory has been integrated with developmental psychology (e.g., Bronfenbrenner, 1979) and in clinical practice with systems theory (e.g., Jasnowski, 1984); however, the distinctions between the two perspectives are salient. "Ecology" is a broader construct that includes the concept of "system," but the concept of "system" does not necessarily include the concept of "ecology" (Mannino & Shore, 1984). With regard to family assessment, "system" refers to the family context, while "ecology" refers to the relationships of the family system with relationship systems beyond the family (e.g., the school, church, neighborhood). The primary contributions of ecological psychology to assessment of the family context have been a theoretical framework for assessment and measures for evaluating the family–environment interface.

ISSUES IN ASSESSING THE FAMILY CONTEXT

Constructs Assessed

Family assessment methods are driven by their theoretical origins. The theoretical foundation of a family assessment procedure determines assumptions regarding the role of family process in the development of children's problems, and thus guides the choice of constructs or dimensions to be included in a measure. Existing methods, which have been derived from the various disciplines previously discussed, as well as from the specific interests of family researcher/clinicians, represent a considerable array of theoretical premises. (See Grotevant & Carlson, 1989, and Jabob, 1987, for reviews of existing measures with greater consideration of theoretical issues.) Furthermore, the state of the art in family theory development and test validation is such that no single model of family functioning or treatment can be considered to be *the* choice for specific child psychological or educational problems. Given that family assessment measures demonstrate considerable variation in the dimensions that are assessed, it is incumbent upon the clinician or researcher to carefully ascertain the theoretical base of these measures and to choose one that is congruent with his or her perspective.

The challenge of selecting a measure that evaluates the specific family context constructs of interest to the family researcher or clinician is increased by the conceptual heterogeneity observed in measures (Gro-

tevant & Carlson, 1989). Careful reviews of measures find that subscales of measures are not always labeled consistently with their content. For example, the construct of expressiveness on one scale might refer to family members' hugging and touching one another and to their feelings of closeness; on another measure, this dimension might contain items reflecting willingness to discuss problems and express opinions. The lack of consistent construct correspondence across measures reflects the lack of consensus within the family study field regarding the meaning and operationalization of theoretical variables.

A second construct-related issue in family assessment is the validity of constructs assessed. The construct validity of the majority of measures of family assessment has not, as yet, been well established (Grotevant & Carlson, 1989). Furthermore, researchers have found that separate measures purporting to measure the same construct (e.g., cohesion) and using the same method of measurement (e.g., objective self-report) still show low correspondence between scores (Beavers & Voeller, 1983). Once again, clinicians and researchers must examine available validity studies regarding their measure of choice, and must be cautious in interpretation of data regarding particular dimensions of family functioning across measures.

Level

Family systems theory indicates that the family is organized into complex interrelated and interdependent components that are hierarchically nested. These nested levels or subsystems, from bottom to top, are as follows: the individual subsystem (child and adult); the sibling subsystem; the parent–child subsystem; the parental subsystem; the marital subsystem; and the whole family unit. When family systems theory is combined with ecological theory to provide a framework for assessing the family, assessment becomes even more complex. The ecological–systems framework views the ecological levels of individual, family, and community as a reciprocally determined, interactive system (Anderson, 1983; Conger, 1981; Wilson, 1986). An ecological–systems approach to the assessment of the family context would integrate information from the following sources: individual, individual–family interface, dyadic or subsystem family relationships, whole family system, whole family–social system(s) interface, and broad social context. Although this comprehensive family assessment approach has much to recommend it, it also poses dilemmas of cost and complexity. Few researchers or clinicians have the resources to obtain data from all of the above-mentioned sources. Furthermore, no single measurement technique has yet been designed that captures the multiple ecological–systems levels of the family. Thus, the correspondence of data across multiple measures poses problems for the family researcher/clinician. Unfortunately, empirical data are, as yet, unavailable to answer the questions of which levels and which measures of family functioning provide the most valid predictive information regarding child psychological and education problems.

Although empirical support is lacking, family clinicians have made recommendations regarding which family systems levels to assess in child referrals. Although the specifics of the presenting problem deserve consideration, Gurman and Kniskern (1981) assert that in families with an identified problem child, evaluation of the child, the marital subsystem, and the whole family unit is essential.

Perspective

A variety of methods have been utilized to evaluate the family context. These include self-report questionnaires, interviews, formal and informal observation, behavior ratings of self or others, projective methods, and structured tasks. One major distinction among these methods involves differentiating procedures based upon reports of family members from procedures based upon the direct observation of the interactions of family members. This distinction has often been characterized as the "insider" versus the "outsider" perspective in family relationships—that is, the ways in which viewpoints of members within the family system differ from the views of members outside the system (Cromwell, Olson, & Fournier, 1976; Gurman & Kniskern, 1981). The insider–

outsider distinction appears similar to the distinction between subjective and objective assessment; however, both insider and outsider procedures vary substantially along a continuum of objectivity. A more useful view is to acknowledge that the insider and outsider perspectives tap distinct realities of family relationships that have been found to have a low correspondence with one another (Olson, 1977). For example, a family's perception of its level of closeness or cohesion may be only weakly correlated with a clinician's rating of the same dimension.

A second useful methodological distinction relevant to family assessment is provided by Huston and Robins (1982), who differentiate the measurement of interpersonal events, subjective events, subjective conditions, and relationship properties, each of which can be the focus of an assessment of family relationships. "Interpersonal events" (or event sequences) refer to the overt, observable behaviors of family members that can be measured with formal and informal observation methods. "Subjective events" refer to the covert and momentary ideas, thoughts, and emotions of each family member. Subjective events can be elicited during an interview. When a relationship endures over time, as family relationships do, stable attributions, attitudes, and beliefs about family members, their relationships, and characteristics of the whole family unit emerge. These relatively stable emotions and cognitions are termed "subjective conditions" and are measurable primarily by self-report methods. Once subjective conditions are in place, they can affect patterns of interpersonal and subjective events. These recurrent patterns of interpersonal or subjective events reflect "relationship properties." Relationship properties, by definition, must be observed or recorded as a repetition of behavior or subjective response over time. Relationship patterns can be measured with various observation methods and are particularly suitable for clinical rating scales. How do these various characteristics of family relationships, in fact, relate to one another? Huston and Robins (1982) assert:

> The fundamental characteristic of a relationship is behavioral interdependence; that is, each

person's overt behavior affects the overt behavior and subjective events of the other. In addition, any relationship that endures long enough to allow both partners to form attitudes and beliefs about each other and the relationship (subjective conditions) can be viewed as exhibiting psychological interdependence. . . . Subjective conditions, once developed, have a controlling or constraining effect on each person's behavior. In turn, ongoing interpersonal and subjective events, particularly when they form a pattern over time, affect the subjective conditions of each partner. (p. 903)

The Huston and Robins position provides a theoretical framework for considering the controlling effect of subjective conditions in behavior that is congruent with the reciprocal deterministic views of social learning theory (Bandura, 1977). The acknowledged importance of both the overt behavior and covert cognitive processes of self and others as controllers of the child's behavior supports the value of evaluating both the subjective conditions and the observed behavioral patterns within the family.

Psychometric Quality

The value of any family assessment method is ultimately limited by its reliability, its validity, and the normative data available for the interpretation of scores. Within the family assessment field, few measures have as yet received adequate empirical validation. No measure has been comprehensively evaluated regarding its concurrent and predictive validity for the differential diagnosis of children's psychological and educational problems. The importance, therefore, of closely examining available psychometric data on a particular measure is underscored, as is the cautious interpretation of scores regarding children's problems. For additional discussion of psychometric issues, the interested reader is referred to the *Standards for Educational and Psychological Testing* (American Psychological Association, 1985), as well as to available reviews of family assessment methods (Filsinger, 1983; Forman & Hagan, 1983; Grotevant & Carlson, 1989).

Summary

The multiple aspects of family relationships that can be assessed leave the family researcher or diagnostician faced with two basic decisions: choosing which aspects of the family to measure, and selecting a satisfactory method of measurement (Huston & Robins, 1982). The process of deciding which aspects of the family context to measure is likely to differ for researchers versus clinicians (Grotevant & Carlson, 1989). In a typical research project, the investigator has one or more questions or hypotheses to test that have been determined prior to the onset of the study. Thus, the primary steps involved in selecting a family assessment focus include (1) clear specification of the construct(s) of interest, which may be interpersonal or subjective events, subjective conditions, or relationship properties, and which may emphasize a particular aspect of the family milieu, such as power or conflict; (2) clear specification of the level of family relationship of interest (i.e., an individual, a particular dyad, the whole family unit); and (3) specification of the rules for unitizing and aggregating data (Grotevant & Carlson, 1989; Huston & Robins, 1982). Furthermore, the requirements for reliability in research are somewhat lower than in clinical settings, where an assessment measure may influence decision making regarding treatment (Nunnally, 1978).

In contrast with the clearly specified questions of the research setting, the psychologist conducting a child-oriented evaluation in the clinical or school setting is more likely to be engaged in "detective work" regarding the role of the family context in the child's problem. For example, in a child-oriented family assessment, the questions to be answered may include the following: Is the presenting problem the real problem? Is family functioning inextricably linked with the child's presenting problem? If yes, what aspects of family functioning and what key family relationships underlie the problem? What treatment plan can be derived from identified family dysfunction? Is treatment effective in a changing family context? Thus, an assessment of the family context associated with a child referral calls for an initial broad scope. In the following section, a broad framework for a clinical evaluation of the family context is provided.

CLINICAL FRAMEWORK FOR ASSESSING THE FAMILY CONTEXT

In a clinical assessment of the family context there are five principal areas to examine: (1) family transactional patterns; (2) family developmental stage; (3) family stress and coping; (4) the family's subjective reality; and (5) the presenting problem of the child as a reflection of systemic dysfunction.

Family Transactional Patterns

The primary focus of an assessment of the family context from a family systems perspective is on the repeated transactional patterns that characterize the family system, and, in particular, that surround the problem behavior of the child. When transactional patterns are relatively enduring such that they organize the components of the family into somewhat stable and predictable relationships, the "structure" of the family emerges (Minuchin, 1974). Transactional patterns that define structure are characterized by invisible rules and operational routines that define how the interdependent parts or members of the family relate to one another and how they in turn influence the family system. For example, in the typical parent–child relationship, repeated transactions occur that are centered upon limit setting for the child by the parent, such that both members of the family system learn about their power and role in relation to each other.

Assessment of family structure is facilitated by attention to principles of system organization. In general, systems are organized hierarchically. The family system's hierarchical organization is determined by both universal and idiosyncratic constraints (Minuchin, 1974). Universal social norms, for example, expect an authoritative executive subsystem within the family, usually comprised of the parent(s), that has greater power and authority than the less competent and less experienced child subsystem. Each family, however, because of its unique composition, sociocultural heritage, and history, develops an idiosyncratic family organization in which roles customarily accomplished by the parent subsystem may be carried out by another subsystem (e.g., grandparents, eldest child, aunts or uncles, neighbors). Critical to "good enough" family functioning is a family organization or structure that permits the accomplishment of roles necessary to the survival of the family unit and that fosters the individual development of family members.

Although endless variations of workable family structures may exist, the adequacy of a family's organization is strongly related to the clarity of boundaries or rules regarding participation in different roles (Haley, 1987; Minuchin, 1974). Boundaries serve to protect the differentiation of the family system, such that each individual or subsystem can accomplish its essential task with assistance from other family members when needed, but without intrusion that compromises autonomy. Families that have developed overly intrusive, unclear boundaries, with lower levels of differentiation between family members and subsystems, are labeled "enmeshed"; families with overly rigid boundaries and excessive levels of autonomy between family members and subsystems are labeled "disengaged" (Minuchin, 1974). Child problems associated with enmeshed family systems typically involve compromised development of competence, independence, and mastery, whereas disengaged families are associated with child problems involving limited monitoring or nurturance (Hoffman, 1981).

A second target of family system assessment consists of the discrete, time-limited sequences of behavior that constitute a particular transaction, especially transactions that surround the identified problem of the child. The goal is to identify the feedback loops that are operating in a homeostatic manner to maintain the child's problem. "Feedback loops" refer to the communication pathway across boundaries within the family that signal to members their degree of conformity to or discrepancy from the overall purpose of the system. Feedback loops that promote stability, equilibrium, and a reduction of behavior are termed "constancy" or "deviation-countering" loops. Feedback loops that promote growth, diversity, change, or an increase in activity are termed "variety" or "deviation-amplifying" loops. Both types of feedback are essential to functional families; however, overreliance upon one type of feedback loop, either as a family style or in coping with a particular child problem, may exacerbate the difficulty, and thus may point to the need for an intervention that disrupts the ineffective feedback loop and replaces it with an alternative action (Hoffman, 1981).

Transactional process and structure are interrelated properties of family systems. The expression of process between family members over time gives that process the status of structure. Either a dysfunctional structure or a dysfunctional sequence of behavior can serve to maintain a child's difficulty. From a measurement perspective, family transactional patterns are typically evaluated with observation of family interaction.

Family Development and the Family Life Cycle

Identifying the family's developmental stage, as characterized by family life cycle theory (Carter & McGoldrick, 1980), provides a mechanism by which the "goodness of fit" between the family's structure or organization and children's developmental needs can be evaluated. According to the family life cycle framework, alterations in family organization are required in response to the development of individual family members. Family organizational change is believed to occur through a process of insertion (recognition of the change), destabilization (temporary instability of behavior), and resolution (integration of stable behavioral sequences) (Terkelsen, 1980). Given the maturation rate of children, family dynamics can be viewed as a process of continuous change and adaptation. Much of children's development is incremental and requires only the gradual addition and deletion of behaviors to and from stable transactional patterns by family members. In contrast, some aspects of child development, termed "second-order developments," demand a whole new ensemble of behavioral sequences within the family, as well as readjustments in the identity and self-concept of family members. These major developmental shifts occur infrequently and characterize the family life cycle as depicted in Table 23.1. The family life cycle is characterized by the major normative process and structure transformations required of the family, primarily in response to child-rearing functions. In addition to these universal family developmental stages, some families may experience paranormative or idiosyncratic events that interrupt the normative progress of the family along the life cycle (e.g., divorce, remarriage, chronic illness). The life cycles for the common paranormative life events of divorce and remarriage appear in Table 23.2. Family developmental stage is identified by the first occurrence of an event, as this is believed to have the most pronounced impact on family adaptation (Terkelsen, 1980). Given disruptions in the normative family life cycle, a family can be in several developmental stages simultaneously.

According to family life cycle theory, child symptomatology appears when a family does not sufficiently transform its structure to adapt to a second-order developmental change. For example, adolescent dysfunction may occur in response to parents' failure to alter patterns of child-rearing (e.g., close monitoring and affective involvement), such that the adolescent's individuation and autonomy are compromised (see Haley, 1980, for an informative discussion of this phenomenon). The goal of a developmental assessment of the family context, therefore, includes the following: (1) identification of the ages and developmental stages of children; (2) identification of ages and developmental stages of parents; (3) placement of the family in a life cycle, determined by the phase of the eldest child or by a paranormative event; (4) examination of child-rearing practices and family organizational structure; (5) determination of the goodness of fit between existing child-rearing practices and supportive structure with developmental stage, particularly of the symptomatic child. This information can be gained with parent questionnaires, interviews, or structured interview methods such as the genogram.

Family Stress and Coping

Stress is viewed as a normal part of the developmental process of individuals and families (McCubbin & Figley, 1983). As individuals make developmental changes, other family members and the family system must adapt. Similarly, family members and

TABLE 23.1. The Stages of the Family Life Cycle

Family life cycle stages	Key transition task	Family changes required to proceed developmentally
Unmarried adult	Parent–child separation	a. Differentiation of self from family of origin b. Development of intimate peer relationships c. Establishment of self in work
Married couple	Commitment to the new system	a. Formation of married system b. Realignment of relationships with extended families and friends to include new spouse
Family with young children	Accept new members into the system	a. Adjustment of marital system to make space for children b. Assumption of parenting roles c. Realignment of relationships with extended family to include parenting and grandparenting roles
Family with adolescents	Increase flexibility of family boundaries to include children's independence	a. Adjustment of parent–child relationships to permit adolescent movement in and out of the system b. Refocus on midlife marital and career issues
Launching children	Accept a multitude of exits and entries into the family	a. Renegotiate marital system as a dyad b. Develop adult-to-adult relationship with grown children
Family in later life	Shift generational roles	a. Maintain functioning in face of physical decline b. Dealing with loss of loved ones and preparing for death c. More central role for middle generation in maintaining the family system

Note. Adapted from *The Family Life Cycle: A Framework For Family Therapy,* edited by E. A. Carter and M. McGoldrick, 1980, New York: Gardner Press. Copyright 1980 by E. A. Carter and M. McGoldrick. Adapted by permission.

the family system must adapt to external stressors, such as economic decline or geographic relocation. The response of the family to stressful events is considered "coping."

The earliest family-based conceptual model of families and stress, which emerged from the field of sociology, was Hill's (1949, 1958) "ABCX" family crisis model. In this model, A (stressor event) was hypothesized to interact with B (family's crisis-meeting resources) and with C (family's definition of the crisis) to produce the magnitude of X (the crisis). This model has recently been expanded by McCubbin and Patterson (1983) to include a multilevel analysis of precrisis variables and to add postcrisis variables. The "double-ABCX" model provides a framework with which to organize the collection of information regarding extent of family crises and the family style of coping.

Family stress and coping can be evaluated with the use of objective self-report measures. McCubbin and associates have developed a number of self-report measures to capture the dimensions of the double-ABCX model, including the Family Inventory of Life Events and Change (McCubbin, Patterson, & Wilson, 1983), which also has an adolescent version (McCubbin, Patterson, Bauman, & Harris, 1981). For reviews of these and other family stress and coping measures, the reader is referred to Grotevant and Carlson (1989) and Paget (1987). Family stress and coping can also be derived less systematically from information collected with dynamic interview stimuli such as the genogram or ecomap (described later in this chapter).

Family Subjective Reality

Although the identification of behavior sequences is essential to determining the contingencies operating to exacerbate or maintain a child's problematic behavior within the family system, family members' subjective perceptions are expected to be informative regarding the relatively stable and enduring beliefs and attitudes that serve to constrain behavioral patterns. Gottman's (1979) study of distressed and nondistressed couples, for example, found no significant between-group differences in behavior, but rather differences in their perceptions of the meaning of their partners' behavior. Olson and Wilson (1985) found that perceived family satisfaction was more closely related to symptomatology than was a dysfunctional family organization pattern as assessed by self-report measures. Thus, evaluation of the perceptions of family members regarding the quality of their family life can serve to highlight behavior–attitude discrepancies, to identify covert processes, and to provide a focus for intervention. The subjective reality of family members is measured primarily via self-report methods, but can also be derived from interviews.

The Presenting Problem

A key assumption of family systems theory applied to psychology is that problem behavior is developed and maintained within the context of an interpersonal system and that, in order for the disturbing behavior to change, some element within that system must change (Kral, 1986). The focus of problem identification from a family systems perspective is the identification of the repeated sequence of behavior between persons involved in the problem that maintain the child's dysfunctional behavior (Haley, 1987).

It is important to keep in mind that the "problem" as presented by parents and teachers is seldom the "real problem" as viewed from a family systems orientation. The adults in a child's environment are likely to view the problem as internal to the child, rather than as a function of their interactions with the child. Obviously, if the adults in a child's world understood how to shift their behavior to alleviate the child's difficulties, then no problem would exist. In fact, some family theorists assert that persons have "difficulties" that only become "problems" when the difficulties are mishandled, when they remain unresolved, and when more of the same "solution" is applied by parents or professionals (Fisch, Weakland, & Segal, 1982). The increased application of a well-intended solution escalates the original difficulty, by a vicious-circle process, into a problem that may bear little resemblance to the original difficulty. The problem is thus maintained by the very behavior intended to resolve it! Given the critical role of interactive sequences in the maintenance of dysfunctional behavior, it becomes critical to obtain an adequate amount of information about the problem in order to break the cycle. Interviews are the family assessment method of choice for obtaining a "motion picture" of the problem.

METHODS OF FAMILY ASSESSMENT

Three principal assessment strategies have been used in assessment of the family context: (1) interview, (2) observation, and (3) self-report questionnaires. Within each of these broad categories, numerous variations exist. In this section, each strategy and related variations are discussed. (In addition to the three main strategies, projective methods are also discussed briefly.) Strengths and limitations of each method are noted, and particular techniques are recommended.

Interview Techniques

The interview is considered by family therapists to be the most useful family assessment strategy. Preference for this strategy has emerged as a result of the emphasis in family systems theory on the role of transactional patterns in the maintenance of problem behavior. Thus, the primary goal of an interview, from a family systems perspective,

TABLE 23.2. Dislocations of the Family Life Cycle

Family life cycle stage	Psychological task(s)	Family changes required to proceed developmentally
		Divorce
1. Decision to divorce	Acceptance of inability to resolve marital tensions sufficiently to continue relationship	a. Adult: Accept role in marital breakup b. Communication of decision to children and provision of emotional support c. Child: Acknowledge marital disruption
2. Planning the breakup of the system	Supporting viable arrangements for all parts of the system	a. Working cooperatively on problems of custody, visitation, finances b. Dealing with extended family about the divorce
3. Separation	Willingness to continue cooperative coparental relationship	a. Restructuring marital and parent–child relationships b. Realignment of extended-family relationships: staying connected with spouse's family
	Begin resolution of attachment to spouse	c. Mourning the loss of intact family d. Providing emotional support for children
4. The divorce	More work on resolution of feelings: overcoming hurt, anger, guilt, rejections, etc.	a. Giving up fantasies of reconciliation b. Regaining sense of direction and freedom to pursue customary activities c. Staying connected with extended families
		Postdivorce single-parent family
1. Custodial single parent	Willingness to maintain contact with ex-spouse and support contact of children with ex-spouse and family	a. Making flexible visitation arrangements b. Maintaining clear boundaries between the ex-spousal and coparental relationships
	Creation of a stable environment	c. Establishing authoritative parenting patterns d. Meeting multiple family role needs: economic, child care, recreational, etc. e. Rebuilding social support network
2. Noncustodial single parent	Willingness to maintain contact with ex-spouse and support custodial parent's relationship with children	a. Finding ways to continue effective parenting relationship with children b. Rebuild own social network

TABLE 23.2. (*continued*)

Family life cycle stage	Psychological task(s)	Family changes required to proceed developmentally
	Remarried family	
1. Entering a new relationship	Resolution of relationship issues and emotional loss from first marriage	a. Openness to new relationship b. Recommitment to marriage and formation of a new family system
2. Conceptualizing and planning of new family	Accepting mixed emotions on the part of self and other family members	a. Work on open communication b. Plan for maintenance of cooperative coparental relationships with ex-spouses c. Plan to help children deal with fears, loyalty conflicts, and membership in two systems
	Accepting need for time and patience for adjustment to complexity of new roles	d. Realignment of relationships with extended family to include new spouse and children e. Plan for maintenance of connections for children with extended family of ex-spouse
3. Remarriage	Final resolution of attachment to previous spouse and ideal of "intact" family	a. Restructuring family boundaries to allow for inclusion of new stepparent b. Realignment of relationships throughout subsystems to permit meshing of several systems
	Acceptance of a different model of families with permeable boundaries	c. Making room for relationships of all children with biological (noncustodial) relatives d. Sharing memories and histories to enhance family integration

Note. Adapted from *The Family Life Cycle: A Framework for Family Therapy*, edited by E. A. Carter and M. McGoldrick, 1980, New York: Gardner Press. Copyright 1980 by E. A. Carter and M. McGoldrick. Adapted by permission.

is to gather information in a way that clarifies the family's transactions centering around the child's difficulty. Many family theorists contend that an assessment interview with the whole family is essential to clarifying these patterns of interaction (e.g., Minuchin, 1974), whereas others believe that patterns can be discerned and changed with a single-member focus in assessment and intervention (Fisch et al., 1982). However, as Haley (1987) asserts, the way in which the child's problem is examined is the beginning of intervention. Thus, a whole family interview not only enhances the validity of an assessment of the family context, but also serves to "frame" the situation as a family problem.

Structural–Strategic Interviewing

Excellent guidelines for conducting a family interview are provided by Haley (1987), with a step-by-step elaboration of Haley's method by Weber, McKeever, and McDaniel (1985). These interview guidelines are based theoretically in the structural–strategic family therapy framework, which emphasizes the role of present family transactions versus past history in problem formation and maintenance; a therapeutic goal of resolving the problem while altering family structures that support the problem; and brief, action-oriented intervention. A key focus, therefore, of the family interview is to create a situation in which family members can interact with one another in such a way that the interviewer can observe and evaluate the transactions. Although the literature noted above provides clear guidelines for conducting the interview, familiarity with strategic–structural family therapy theory will enhance the interviewer's competence in assessing the meaning of transactions. Recommended readings include Minuchin (1974), Minuchin and Fishman (1981), Minuchin, Rosman, and Baker (1978), Haley (1987), Umbarger (1983), Stanton (1981), and Aponte and Van Deusen (1981).

Circular Questioning

Another interview technique derived from family systems theory is circular questioning. This strategy is based theoretically in the systemic or brief therapy model that has been developed at the Mental Research Institute (e.g., Fisch et al., 1982). This theoretical model concurs with the strategic–structural model in viewing the etiology of symptoms within interpersonal transactions. In contrast with the preceding model, brief or systemic therapists believe that one small change in the system's transactions, located anywhere in the circular process identified as sustaining the problem, will change the entire sequence. Thus, the focus of change within this model is considerably narrower. Critical to the success of this model of family intervention, however, is the initial assessment interview, which must be conducted in such a way as to facilitate a change in the family system. One interview technique is the use of circular questioning, in which the interviewer repeats similar questions throughout the interview, with a slightly different focus each time in response to the answers provided by family members (Tomm, 1987a, 1987b). Examples of questions that have been recommended to be included in an interview specifically focused on family-school problems include the following (Kral, 1986):

"Please describe the problem."
"What happens next?" (Repeat as often as necessary.)
"When don't you have this problem?"
"Who does what differently?"
"What will have to happen for that to happen more often?"
"How will you know when the problem is solved?"
"If a miracle happens and the problem were solved, what will be different?"

"Are there times when this already happens—if only for a little bit?"
"Who will have to do what to have it happen again?" (pp. 8–9)

It is important to note that questions regarding "why" the problem exists are avoided. Rather, the focus of questioning is on the positive—what is working—as well as on specifying the behavioral interactions maintaining the problem, so that interventions can be implemented. Furthermore, as noted, circular questioning is viewed as a simultaneous process of assessment and intervention.

Several strategies can be used in conjunction with the interview to assist in the collection of information about the family context. A description of two commonly used methods, the genogram and the ecomap, follows. The genogram (Bowen, 1978) is most useful for collecting information about the extended-family and family-of-origin systems; the ecomap (Hartmann, 1979) provides an indicator of extrafamilial stress, coping, and resources. Both techniques engage family members in a nonthreatening, collaborative, data-collecting effort, which can also facilitate expression of subjective perceptions and feelings regarding issues contextually related to the problem.

Genogram and Ecomap

The genogram is a diagram, visually similar to a family, that depicts the family's three-generational relationship system. The genogram was developed by Murray Bowen (1978) as a method of evaluating the generational transmission process of dysfunction in families; however, it is currently used more broadly to clarify family relationships. The genogram uses a consistent set of symbols for depicting family relationships across time (see Figure 23.1). When the collection of pertinent factual data accompanies diagram construction, a family's genogram can provide information regarding family coping style, the number and nature of life cycle transitions, current and previous stressors, existing and historical interpersonal boundaries, and the role of the extended family in the child's problem. Comprehensive guide-

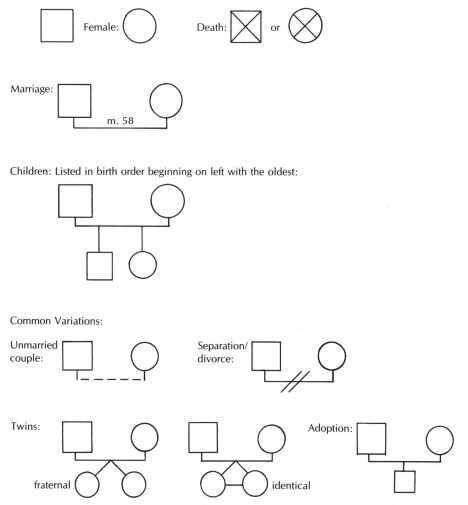

FIGURE 23.1. Key to constructing a genogram. A genogram is a graphic depiction of how family members are biologically and legally related across generations. As with any map, the communicative value of the representation lies in the consistent use of symbols, as shown in the figure. A complete genogram should include (1) names and ages of all family members; (2) dates of significant life events (e.g., birth, marriage, divorce, death, major geographic moves); (3) notations of occupations, illnesses, etc.; (4) information on a minimum of three generations; (5) household compositions designated by a dotted line surrounding the family members' symbols. This figure draws on information contained in Bowen (1978), Carter and McGoldrick (1980), and McGoldrick and Gerson (1985).

lines for the construction and interpretation of genograms are provided by McGoldrick and Gersen (1985). In summary, the genogram provides a visual historical record of family relationships and coping that has communicative value across clinicians.

The ecomap is similar to the genogram in that it is a collaborative data collection method that provides a visual representation of the family system. Whereas the focus of the genogram is the family in the context of time, the focus of the ecomap is the family in the context of space. The ecomap, which is based on ecological theory (Hartmann, 1979), uses universal symbols to depict relationships between the family and extrafamilial social systems. In short, the ecomap provides data on the availability and the family's use of extrafamilial resources in coping with the child' problem. As such, it provides data on environmental stressors that may exacerbate or be more focal than resolution of the child's problem, family problem-solving capacity, and directions for intervention.

Summary

The interview method of family assessment has both strengths and limitations. Its strengths lie in its economy and breadth of focus. The interview is perhaps the most efficient means of obtaining both objective data about family transactional patterns and subjective data about perceptions and feelings of family members. On the other hand, the interview is subject to multiple sources of error. One source of error derives from family members, whose reports of retrospective events may be inaccurate or intentionally falsified; their reports of subjective events may be biased by social desirability or lack of insight. A second source of error derives from the exclusive reliance upon the clinical skill and judgment of the interviewer. The limitations of clinical judgment versus statistical prediction have been well documented (Meehl, 1954); however, clinical methods remain essential for obtaining information when adequate objective measurement techniques are not available (Anastasi, 1982). Within the family assessment field at present, the lack of coherence across theorists regarding the essential family processes to evaluate, as well as the lack of psychometrically validated objective measures, assures that the interview will remain a key family assessment method. However, its limitations should be acknowledged, and, when feasible, it should be used in conjunction with more objective data collection methods.

Observation Methods

Observation has increasingly become the method of choice among family researchers and clinicians for identifying dysfunctional patterns of family interaction. The move toward observation methods has been stimulated by early criticism of the validity of family self-report methods (Strauss & Brown, 1978); by empirical evidence for the relatively low correspondance between what people say they do and their actual behavior (Deutscher, 1973, cited in Conger, 1983; Gottman, 1979); and by research that successfully differentiates distressed from nondistressed families when interaction patterns are the criteria (Gottman, 1979; Minuchin, Rosman, & Baker, 1978; Patterson, 1982). Observation is frequently recommended as requiring fewer inferences and, therefore, as providing a more objective view of family functioning than other assessment methods. In reality, observation methods vary in type, methodological rigor, level of inference required, and susceptibility to bias, and therefore, vary in both the type and quality of the data they yield. Informal observation procedures, in which no systematic coding scheme is used, have been found to yield no greater than chance levels of discrimination between distressed and nondistressed families (Conger, 1981). Formal observation schemes, in contrast, which provide systematic monitoring and recording of behavioral events, can provide a precise description of interactive patterns that can be the key for identifying how a child's problem behavior is elicited, maintained, and organized within the family (Cairns & Green, 1979; Patterson, 1982). However, formal observation methods can be notoriously labor-intensive and time-consuming, and this usually limits their usefulness for the practitioner. In the following discussion of formal observation schemes, only those that appear useful for practitioners are discussed. In addition, methods for increasing the systematic focus of informal observations are identified. Researchers of family interaction who seek information regarding family interaction coding schemes and related issues are referred to Filsinger (1983), Gilbert and Christensen (1985), Grotevant and Carlson (1987, 1989), Jacob, Tennenbaum, and Krahn (1987), and Markman and Notarius (1987).

Formal Observation

Formal observation methods can be categorized as (1) "naturalistic," in which behavior is observed as it naturally occurs in the environment; (2) "analogue," in which behavior is observed in a controlled environment designed to elicit behavior of interest; and (3) "participant," in which family members monitor their own or another member's behavior (Wilson, 1986). Coding schemes that derive from the behavioral theoretical tradition emphasize naturalistic observation (often dinner in the home setting), whereas the family therapy tradition has tended to use analogue observation, with families assigned discussion tasks focusing on family decision making, revealed differences, or unresolved conflicts in a clinic setting. The correspondance between naturalistic and analogue observation is currently undetermined, and thus it cannot be presumed (Wilson, 1986). Participant observation has infrequently been used in family context assessment. It has more commonly been used to determine marital partners' assessment of their interaction or a parent's (usually the mother's) assessment of child behavior (Margolin, 1987). Although greater use of this method for assessing the whole family context has been encouraged (Margolin, 1987), and the psychometric quality of this method of data collection has been ascertained for parent reports of child behavior (Patterson, 1982), the lack of data on participant observation with family systems limits further discussion of this method.

Patterson and his colleagues at the Oregon Social Learning Center have been leaders in the establishment of reliable and valid methods of naturalistic observation. These clinician/researchers developed the Family Interaction Coding System (FICS) to measure aggressive behavior patterns within the family (Reid, 1978). The FICS consists of 29 code categories (14 aversive, 14 prosocial, and 1 summary coercion index) and represents perhaps the most carefully developed and researched coding system available. Patterson (1982) provides an excellent summary of the coding system and its empirical support, as well as treatment guidelines for working with coercive family systems. A review of the FICS indicates that it is most useful for assessing the family environments of conduct-disordered, preadolescent children.

A useful adolescent complement to the FICS is the family observation system developed by James Alexander and his colleagues at the University of Utah. Their coding system identifies defensive and supportive communication behaviors in the family that have been found to differentiate families with delinquent adolescents (Alexander, 1973a, 1973b). This observation method elicits family interaction in an analogue situation, with families asked to discuss topics of disagreement. The interaction is videotaped and coded every 6 seconds for one of four defensive behaviors or one of four supportive behaviors. An advantage of this coding system is that it is simple, relative to other observation schemes; a disadvantage is the equipment requirement for reliable coding. Like Patterson, Alexander has developed a problem-solving treatment program for families that blends behavioral and family systems theoretical traditions; thus, findings based upon the observation can readily be linked with intervention (Barton & Alexander, 1981).

Informal Observation

Although formal observation procedures have the advantage of significantly enhanced reliability and validity, a primary disadvantage is the high cost of both data collection and analysis. For many practitioners, therefore, informal observation that is systematically focused may be the method of choice. Several family systems intervention models (e.g., structural, strategic, systemic) use informal observation of family interaction, often within an interview situation, to establish hypotheses regarding the communication patterns underlying individual symptomatology. These models serve to guide an informal observation of family interaction.

An initial focus of observation is the "power hierarchy" within the family. According to Haley (1987), child problems most frequently derive from a confused hierarchy in the family. In Western culture, parents are expected to be authoritative with regard to their children; yet out-of-control children often have more control of the situation than do their parents. Determination of a confused hierarchy is made by observing repeated patterns of interaction between parents and child for rule establishment, rule clarity, monitoring, rule enforcement, consistency, and follow-through. Patterson's (1982) descriptions of coercive family process are excellent examples of inverted parent–child power hierarchies. Confusion of hierarchy, however, is not limited to the parent–child dyad. Role confusion or role conflict, evidenced in repeated behavioral transactions among family members, may also occur between parents, between parents and grandparents, between parents and other child caretakers, or between siblings, all with potentially negative effects upon the symptomatic child. Key to the evaluation of the role of confused family hierarchy in a child's problems is an assessment of the extent to which the operative transactional rules limit or impair the child's development or adaptability to contexts beyond the family. For example, in a household composed of a single-parent, mother, a grandmother, and male child, the observed difficulty of the mother in asserting herself with her own mother (the grandmother) would not be viewed as problematic unless coupled with an observed difficulty of the mother in establishing limits for her son and reports of behavioral difficulties in the school setting.

A second related focus of observation of family interaction patterns is the behavioral proximity versus distance between family members. Who is too close (enmeshed) with whom, and who is too distant (disengaged) from whom (Fishman, 1983)? Parameters of distance and proximity can be observed by noting physical contact, amount of verbal communication, communication content (e.g., support or criticism, mind reading, talking for another person), pronoun use and referents (e.g., "I" vs. "we"), distribution of gaze, personal physical space as evident in seating, and personal emotional space as evident in tolerance of individual differences in thoughts and feelings.

The closeness and distance between family members is equivalent to an assessment of the boundaries of the system from a structural family therapy perspective. Individuals or subsystems within the family may have overly permeable, diffuse boundaries, in which too much information or activity between members is exchanged, and mastery or autonomy of functioning of both parties is compromised. Examples of overly permeable or intrusive boundaries between parents and children include parents' continuing to exert excessive influence over an adolescent's wardrobe; parents' sharing intimate details regarding their sexual or emotional life with a child; and children's sleeping with parents or failing to respect parents' privacy in other ways, such as with unabated demands for attention. In contrast, boundaries between family members may be too distant or rigid, so that essential assistance and responsiveness are unavailable and individual functioning is compromised. Examples of too-distant boundaries include parents' failure to monitor the whereabouts of their children; parents' lack of response to a child's chronic failures; and children's refusal over time to establish a relationship with a "good enough" stepparent. It is not uncommon for a boundary between family members or subsystems to alternate between enmeshed and disengagement, as the frustration and anxiety associated with an overly cohesive relationship may lead to interpersonal tension and a resulting distance or withdrawal (Minuchin, 1974).

A third focus of observation, which combines the elements of power and boundary, is the identification of pathological "triangles." Haley (1987) notes that most child problems involve both a malfunctioning hierarchy and a triangle. Bowen (1978) is credited with first observing dysfunctional triangular arrangements in families. He observed that triangles often emerge when the tension between two family members is intolerable and a third party (often the child, if symptomatic) is brought in to diffuse it. Four pathological triadic arrangements, depicted in Figure 23.2, have been implicated in children's dysfunction: triangulation, parent–child coalition, detouring–attacking, and detouring–supportive (Umbarger, 1983).

In triangulation, each parent vies for the loyalty of the child against the remaining parent. This pattern is commonly observed in conflictual divorce situations (Isaacs, Montalvo, & Abelsohn, 1987; Wallerstein & Kelly, 1980). In the parent–child coalition, the child joins in alliance with one parent against the "outsider" parent. This arrangement often underlies the problem of the seemingly un-

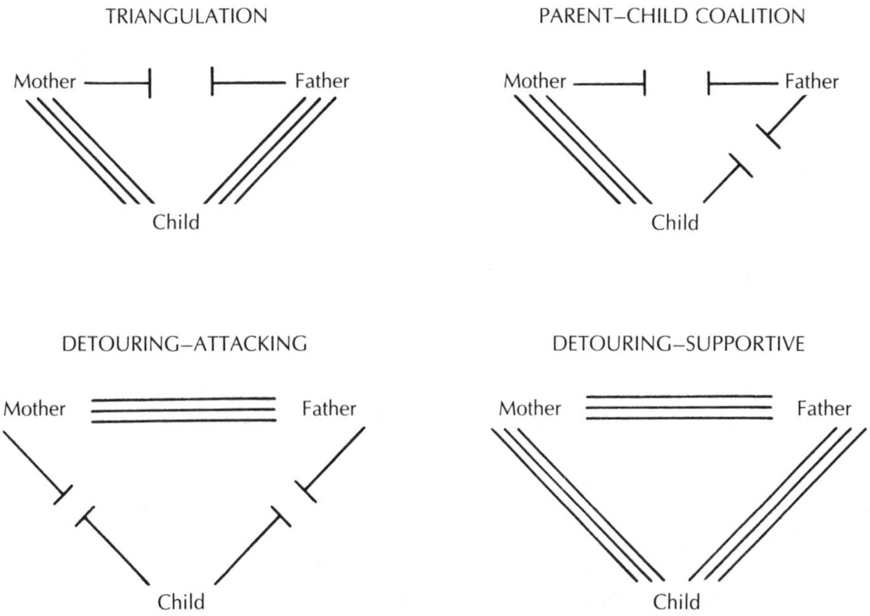

TRIANGULATION

PARENT–CHILD COALITION

DETOURING–ATTACKING

DETOURING–SUPPORTIVE

FIGURE 23.2. Pathological triangles. A set of three lines indicates an enmeshed relationship; a broken line indicates a conflictual relationship. Reprinted from *Structural Family Therapy* by C. C. Umbarger, 1983, New York: Grune & Stratton. Copyright 1983 by C. C. Umbarger. Reprinted by permission.

involved father. Detouring triangles have in common an intense focus upon the child, not another parent, as the problem. In the attacking triangle the child is scapegoated as "bad," whereas in the supportive triangle the child is the recipient of overconcern and is viewed as "sick." Clearly, child characteristics play a role in these triangles: Children with hyperactivity or other types of externalizing disorders are often the focus of an attacking triangle, whereas psychomatic or handicapped children may become the focus of a supportive triangle. Once again, triangle patterns will be reflected in the repeated patterns of transaction that occur within the family interaction.

Summary of Formal and Informal Observations

In summary, formal observation methods can be expected to reliably identify specific behavioral contingencies that may underlie problematic behavior of the child; however, these are more labor-intensive than many family assessment methods. Informal observation methods, in contrast, can be used during an interview or home visit with

the family and thus are cost-effective. Unless observation is systematic, however, it may provide meaningless data. One method of enhancing the reliability of informal methods of observation of family interaction is to complete a clinical rating scale of the family following an interview or home visit. A description of this method follows.

Clinical Rating Scales

Clinical rating scales of family dynamics provide a cost-efficient method of objectifying observations of family interactions, so that enhanced prediction, treatment evaluation, and communication among professionals are possible. Rating methodology takes advantage of the complex information-processing capabilities of the interviewer/rater to abstract and synthesize relevant pieces of information to arrive at a summary judgment. As such, given the complexity of family dynamics, this method may be uniquely suited for assessment of family relationship properties.

Numerous family clinical rating scales have been developed (see Carlson & Grotevant, 1987a and 1987b, for a comprehensive review). Particularly useful are rating scales derived from a clear theoretical base that have accompanying self-report measures; these permit a multimethod (clinical and statistical) family evaluation. Family rating scales that meet these criteria include the following: the Beavers–Timberlawn Family Evaluation Scale and Family Style Scale (Beavers, n.d.); the McMaster Clinical Rating Scale (Epstein, Baldwin, & Bishop, 1982); the Family Assessment Measure Clinical Rating Scale (Skinner & Steinhauer, 1986); and the Clinical Rating Scale for the Circumplex model of marital and family systems (Olson & Killorin, 1985). Most of these clinical rating scales were developed in conjunction with or following the development of a self-report measure. The self-report measures for many of these scales, and their theoretical origins, are described in the next section and thus, are not be elaborated here. In contrast, the Beavers family assessment procedure, next described, originated with a rating scale methodology, and thus has amassed the most empirical support.

The Beavers–Timberlawn family assessment process rests on two clinical rating scales, the Family Evaluation Scale and the Family Style Scale (formerly the Centripetal/Centrifugal Family Style Scale) (Beavers, n.d.). These scales are based on the Beavers system model of family functioning, which is based on a clinical interpretation of general systems theory and emphasizes the key challenge of the developmental processes of separation and individuation within the family (Lewis, Beavers, Gossett, & Phillips, 1976). The Family Evaluation Scale consists of six major scales rated on a 9-point Likert response format: Family Structure; Mythology; Goal-Directed Negotiation; Autonomy; Family Affect; and Global Health/Pathology. All but two of the subscales, Mythology and Invasiveness (under Autonomy), can be reliably rated (Green, Kolevson, & Vosler, 1985; Hulgus, 1985). This rating scale has significantly differentiated healthy from clinic families (Lewis et al., 1976). The Family Style Scale is a seven-item rating scale designed to evaluate the family's "manner of being together." Family Style subscales include Social Presentation, Verbal Expression of Closeness, Positive Expression of Feelings, Parental/Adult Conflict, Parental Control–Clinging, and Parent Control–Aggres-

sive, as well as a General scale. Subscale reliability for the measure is mixed (Hulgus, 1985). Thus, the primary advantage of the Family Style Scale is its complementarity with the Family Evaluation Scale. When both rating scales are used, a family may be located on a "map" of family functioning in accordance with the Beavers system model.

Summary of Clinical Rating Scales

The key advantage of using a clinical rating scale following the family interview is the objective recording of observations in a summary form that (1) has communicative value for other professionals and (2) permits evaluation of the reliability of clinical judgments. Disadvantages of rating scales include their susceptibility to numerous rater errors or biases, as well as the fact that their communicative value is limited by the "shared reality" across professionals of the meaning of rated constructs (Cairns & Green, 1979; Carlson & Grotevant, 1987a). Thus, it is advised that within a setting, the following steps be taken to assure reliability of ratings: (1) that a particular theoretical viewpoint be adopted; (2) that rater training be conducted; (3) that family interviews be video- or audio-recorded; (4) that recorded interviews be rated by two or more raters; and (5) that acceptable interrater reliability be established. Although interrater reliability should be re-evaluated periodically, completion of ratings by multiple raters should not be essential in clinical settings once reliable ratings have been obtained. For research purposes, of course, multiple raters and reliability determinants remain essential.

Self-Report Methods

Self-report measures are useful for assessing the interior or insider perspective of family relationships. This assessment method evaluates the subjective condition within the family context. Although numerous standardized family assessment measures are available, research on the validity of existing measures, particularly with regard to differential prediction of child symptomatology, remains seriously limited (Grotevant & Carlson, 1989). Instrument selection must currently be governed by available relevant criteria, including data on psychometric validation, ease of use (e.g., item length, reading level of questions, instructions for administration and interpretation of scores), appropriateness for the setting, and the expected utility of the measure for the purpose identified. It is beyond the scope of this chapter to review all available measures. (For comprehensive discussion, the reader is referred to the following evaluative reviews: Filsinger, 1983; Forman & Hagan, 1983; Grotevant & Carlson, 1989; Markman & Notarius, 1987.) In the following discussion, measures are described that appear to have particular utility for assessment of the family context of children. Both measures of whole-family functioning and measures of specific dyadic relationships within the family are included. Measures have been selected on the basis of demonstrated psychometric quality or significance with regard to one or more of the criteria noted. Strengths and limitations of the measures are also discussed.

Measures of the Whole Family System

Family Environment Scale. The Family Environment Scale (FES; Moos & Moos, 1986) is a 90-item, true–false questionnaire designed to provide researchers and clinicians with a systematic assessment of the social environment or climate of the family unit. The measure is theoretically based in ecological psychology and general systems theory. The FES includes 10 subscales that assess three underlying dimensions: (1) Interpersonal Relationships (subscales— Cohesion, Expressiveness, Conflict); (2) Personal Growth (subscales—Independence, Achievement, Orientation, Intellectual– Cultural Orientation, Active–Recreational Orientation, and Moral–Religious Emphasis); (3) System Maintenance (subscales— Organization, Control). Three forms of the FES are available: The Real Form evaluates the current environment; the Ideal Form evaluates the desired environment; and the Expectations Form measures perceptions of a new environment, such as may occur with adoption or remarriage. The FES is appropriate for family members over 11 years of age.

Strengths of the FES include the adequacy of its psychometric validation, the availability

of normative data, and its widespread use in clinical research, which provides a large comparative data base. The FES (Real Form), demonstrates adequate reliability, has been standardized and normed on a sample of 1,125 normal and 500 distressed families, and has had its validity established in over 200 studies (Moos, Clayton, & Max, 1979; Moos & Moos, 1986; Moos & Spinrad, 1984). Furthermore, the nonintrusive nature of the FES questions assures its appropriateness for nonclinical settings. Length (and thus completion time) is one limitation of the FES. A short version of the FES is available for use in research with large samples; however, the reliability of the shortened version is not well documented. In addition to length, limitations of the FES include the instability of the factor structure (e.g., Fowler, 1981), concern regarding the generalizability of normative data across heterogeneous populations, and the limitations of a forced-choice design format.

Children's Version of the Family Environment Scale. The Children's Version of the Family Environment Scale (CVFES; Pino, Simons, & Slawinowski, 1984) is a 30-item, pictorial, multiple-choice measure designed to assess children's (ages 5–12) perceptions of their family's social climate. The CVFES is conceptually equivalent to the FES, with identical dimensions and subscales (see FES discussion). The CVFES represents an important potential contribution to the family assessment field, both as an extension downward in age of the widely used FES and also as a means of objectively measuring family functioning with young children, for whom the majority of family assessment instruments are inappropriate. In fact, the ability of young children to evaluate the "whole" of the family is an unanswered empirical question. Unfortunately, the psychometric properties of the CVFES have not been carefully examined, and thus the utility of this instrument cannot be assured at this time (Grotevant & Carlson, 1989).

Family Adaptability and Cohesion Evaluation Scales III. The Family Adaptability and Cohesion Evaluation Scale III (FACES III; Olson, Portner, & Lavee, 1985) measures family cohesion and adaptability as well as perceived and ideal family functioning within the Circumplex model of family functioning (Olson, Sprenkle, & Russell, 1979). Family members above age 11 complete the 20-item, 5-point Likert scale twice, once to measure present perception of family functioning and again to measure desired family functioning. Scores from the two sub-scales of Adaptability and Cohesion are placed on a circumplex grid, which classifies the family into one of 16 types. Location on the typology indicates level and direction of dysfunction, degree of incongruence between family members' perceptions, degree of satisfaction with current functioning, and the desired goal of intervention (i.e., movement toward the "balanced family" center of the circumplex grid).

The advantages of FACES III are ease of use and strong psychometric support (Olson et al., 1985). Furthermore, a clinical rating scale compatible with the FACES III is also available, permitting multimethod family assessment from both an insider and an outsider viewpoint. As with other measures, the utility of FACES III is limited by the need for acceptance of its theoretical foundation, which has been criticized in the family psychology literature (see Beavers & Voeller, 1983). In addition, although the authors of FACES III have indicated that this revision of the FACES is psychometrically sound, previous versions have been problematic. Replication of the psychometric data reported by the authors will be welcome, and should not as yet be assumed.

Family Assessment Measure III. The Family Assessment Measure III (FAM-III; Skinner, Steinhauer, & Santa-Barbara, 1984) is a measure of family strengths and weaknesses based theoretically on the process model of family functioning (Steinhauer et al., 1984). The FAM-III is a unique family assessment measure in providing a multilevel (within-family) assessment of functioning across identical dimensions of Task Accomplishment, Role Performance, Communication, Affective Expression, Affective Involvement, Control, and Values and Norms. Three scales comprise the FAM-III: a 50-item General Scale, which measures overall level of family health; a 42-item Dyadic Relationship Scale, completed separately for each designated dyadic relationship, which measures each members's view of the quality of that relationship; and a 42-item Self-Rating Scale, in which each family member rates his or her own functioning. Items and subscales are consistent across the three family levels of individual, dyadic, and whole-family functioning. The additional items in the General Scale reflect the inclusion of Social Desirability and Defensiveness subscales. Items have a 4-point Likert-type response format, and the measure is appropriate for family members above age 10.

The FAM-III was standardized on 475 families (28% problem families); the reliability and validity of the overall ratings of the three scales were supported, but the internal consistency of the within-scale dimensions was variable, particularly for the Self-Rating Scale (Skinner, Steinhauer, & Santa-Barbara, 1983). The key advantage of the FAM-III is the opportunity to obtain a family assessment that is dimensionally consistent across multiple levels of family organization. In addition, a theoretically congruent structured clinical interview and clinical rating scale are available, permitting multimethod family assessment. Limitations of the FAM-III are the psychometric problems associated with the subscales; these are acknowledged by the authors, who indicate that the instrument remains in the developmental phase.

Family Process Scales (Form E). The purpose of Form E of the Family Process Scales (FPS; Barbarin & Gilbert, 1979), which is based on family systems theory, is to assess the interdependence of family members, the dynamic homeostasis in the family, and the family's ability to provide an environment that fosters healthy psychological development and promotes a sense of well-being in its members. The scale, based on family systems theory, includes 50 items, each of which is responded to on a 5-point Likert scale ranging from "strongly agree" to "strongly disagree." Five factor-analytically derived scales (10 items each) are included: Enmeshment, Mutuality, Flexibility, Support, and Satisfaction. Cronbach alpha reliability coefficients for the five scales range from .74 to .96, and tests for concurrent validity indicate moderate correlations between FPS scale scores and those of similar constructs on other measures (Barbarin & Tirado, 1985).

Structural Family Interaction Scale—Revised (Form A). Form A of the Structural Family Interaction Scale—Revised (SFIS-R; Perosa, 1986) represents the only available self-report measure developed from structural family therapy theory; thus, it is a particularly useful measure for clinicians or counselors practicing this model of family treatment. It contains eight subscales, derived from factor analysis: Spouse Conflict, Parent Coalition versus Cross-Generational Triads, Father–Child Cohesion–Estrangement, Mother–Child Cohesion–Estrangement, Enmeshment–Disengagement, Family Conflict Avoidance–Expression, Flexibility–Rigidity, Overprotection–Autonomy. Alpha reliabilities for the eight scales range from .76 to .93 with test–retest reliabilities exceeding .80 for every scale (Perosa, Hansen, & Perosa, 1981).

Clinical Measurement Package. The Clinical Measurement Package (CMP; Hudson, 1982) consists of nine brief (25-item) scales developed for use as a repeated measurement of treatment progress, as well as a measure of the magnitude of severity of an individual or family problem. The nine scales are as follows: Index of Family Relations; Index of Parental Attitudes; Index of Marital Satisfaction; Child's Attitude toward Mother; Child's Attitude toward Father; Index of Self-Esteem; Index of Peer Relations; and the Generalized Contentment Scale (nonpsychotic depression index). The construct validity and criterion validity of the scales have been established (Hudson, 1982; Saunders & Schuchts, 1987). Although clinical cutoff scores are provided, normative data are unavailable; thus it would be inappropriate to base diagnostic or classification decisions on this instrument. As a screening device and a repeated measure of intervention success, the CMP has numerous advantages—ease of administration, scoring, completion, and interpretations, as well as demonstrated resistance to response decay over repeated administrations (Hudson, 1982). In addition, the multiple scales in the package provide a multiple-perspective view of a problem that encompasses the individual, relational, and family systems levels. Limitations of the CMP include its lack of reliability with children under 12 years of age and failure to evaluate the social desirability of the measure.

Summary and Discussion. A number of self-report measures of whole-family functioning have been described here. Several issues regarding the use of these measures are salient. One issue is the degree to which these measures are interchangeable. Common to all the measures is (to a greater or lesser degree) reliance upon the theoretical foundation of family systems theory, which would suggest interchangeability. However, the measures frequently rest only secondarily on family systems theory, and thus their interchangeability is limited. Unfortunately, to date, no studies have evaluated the convergent validity of the measures described, and the question of interchangeability cannot be answered. Users of the whole-family self-report measures, therefore, are advised to carefully evaluate the psychometric properties, item content, and theoretical basis of a measure to assure its utility for the particular question of interest in clinical evaluation or research.

A second self-report method issue is the lack of objective child measures of family functioning. Only one self-report measure of family functioning, the CVFES, is currently available for children of elementary school age (Grotevant & Carlson, 1989). It is possible that the cognitive-developmental capacities of the younger child are not capable of reliable measurement of phenomena as complex as family relationships; however, this is certainly a hypothesis worthy of investigation. Currently, the field of family assessment is forced to rely upon projective techniques (e.g. Kinetic Family Drawing; Burns & Kaufman, 1970) or child reports of specific parent behavior (see discussion below).

Third, although assessment of whole-family functioning may be desirable and is certainly congruent with family systems theory, multilevel assessment may be even more informative. The majority of the measures reviewed permit evaluation of the whole family system, albeit from multiple respondent viewpoints. Only two measures, the FAM-III and the CMP, permit both evaluation of the whole family system and dyadic relational levels. Recent research suggests that each level of analysis (e.g., the individual, parent–child dyads, the marital dyad, sibling dyads, the whole family) adds explanatory power to understanding family phenomena that is not captured by one superordinate measurement (Cowan, 1987). At present, a multilevel assessment of family functioning requires the use of the FAM-III or the use of multiple measures. Self-report measures of different types of dyadic relationships within the family are described next.

Measures of the Parent–Child Relationship

Self-reports of the parent–child relationship include measures with the parent as respondent, measures with the child as respondent, and a few measures with both the parent and the child as respondents. Parent-as-respondent measures are first described, followed by measures in which the child or both parties are respondents. Again, measures have been selected for inclusion on the basis of their proven psychometric quality or their particular unique perspective. For a comprehensive review of parent–child relationship measures, see Johnson (1976) and Grotevant and Carlson (1989).

Parent as a Teacher Inventory. The Parent as a Teacher Inventory (PAAT; Strom, 1984) is designed to measure parents' attitudes about their role in their children's creativity, play, and learning, as well as to measure parents' levels of frustration and need for control over their children's behavior. The PAAT, intended for parents of children between the ages of 3 and 9, includes five subscales: Creativity, Frustration, Control, Play, and Teaching–Learning. The reliability and validity of the PAAT have been established (Johnson, 1975). This measure has also demonstrated sensitivity to changes in parent behavior following a parent education intervention. The measure is available in several languages, including Spanish.

Child-Rearing Practices Report. The Child-Rearing Practices Report (CRPR;

Block, 1965) measures maternal and paternal child-rearing attitudes, values, and goals. It uses a *Q*-sort format (91 items), which reduces the problem of response set bias. Twenty-eight scales have been derived from the 91-item CRPR pool (Roberts, Block, & Block, 1984). Both first-person (parent's evaluation of self) and third-person (adolescent's evaluation of parents) forms are available. The CRPR has been standardized and normed on a diverse sample of over 6,000 people in diverse settings. Reliability and validity of the measure have been well established (Block, Block, & Morrison, 1981). The CRPR has also been translated into numerous languages, including Spanish.

Parenting Stress Index. The Parenting Stress Index (PSI; Abidin, 1983) is a self-report questionnaire designed for screening and diagnosis of parental stress in parents of children under age 10. It is based on attachment, temperament, and stress theories. The PSI includes both a Parent and a Child domain to evaluate perceptions of the parent regarding self and child. Subscales in the Child domain include Adaptability; Acceptability of the Child to the Parent; Child Demandingness; Child Mood; Child Distractibility/Hyperactivity; and Child Reinforces Parent. Subscales in the Parent domain include Parent Depression/Unhappiness; Parent Attachment; Restrictions Imposed by the Parental Role; Parent's Sense of Competence; Social Isolation; Relationship with Spouse; and Physical Health. Data regarding norms, reliability, and validity are available for the PSI.

Child Abuse Potential Inventory. The Child Abuse Potential Inventory (CAP; Milner, 1986) is designed as a screening tool for the detection of physical child abuse. The CAP include 77 items, written at a third-grade reading level, which tap six scales: Distress; Rigidity; Unhappiness; Problems with Child and Self; Problems with Family; and Problems from Others. It also includes three validity scales: a Lie scale, a Random Response scale, and an Inconsistency scale. The CAP has been carefully validated and normed.

Parent Perception Inventory. The Parent Perception Inventory (PPI; Hazzard, Christensen, & Margolin, 1983) assesses children's perceptions of positive and negative behaviors by their mothers and fathers. It is a short instrument, designed for oral administration, and thus appropriate for the school-age child. Measured positive parental behaviors include positive reinforcement, comfort, talk time, involvement in decision making, time together, positive evaluation, allowing independence, assistance, and nonverbal affection. Identified negative parental behaviors include privilege removal, criticism, command, physical punishment, yelling, threatening, time out, nagging, and ignoring. The PPI has demonstrated high reliability and promising validity (Hazzard et al., 1983).

Parent Acceptance–Rejection Questionnaire. The Parent Acceptance–Rejection Questionnaire (PARQ; Rohner, 1984) has both a parent and a child form. Thus, the PARQ provides a measure of the reciprocal views of the parent and child on the same dimensions of acceptance–rejection in the relationship. The PARQ is a 60-item instrument with four scales: Warmth/Affection; Aggression/Hostility; Neglect/Indifference; and Undifferentiated Rejection. Reliability and validity of the PARQ have been established. Although descriptive data, which include means and standard deviations, are available, norms are not. The PARQ has been used with children as young as fourth grade. The PARQ was designed for use cross-culturally, and therefore has been translated into many languages, including Spanish. It should be noted that the PARQ is primarily a research tool and that its clinical utility has not been established.

Measures of the Marital Relationship

Assessment of the marital relationship may seem inappropriate in the evaluation of the family context surrounding a child's psychoeducational problem; however, the relationship between marital interaction and child psychopathology has been consistently demonstrated (Emery & O'Leary, 1982; Margolin, 1981; O'Leary, 1984). As noted previously, the marital dyad is one of three family systems levels recommended for assessment in children's problems (Gurman & Kniskern, 1981). Below is a description of one measure, the Dyadic Adjustment Scale (DAS), which assesses marital satisfaction and yet does not contain items that intrude upon the privacy of the marital relationship (e.g., questions regarding sexual functioning) in a manner inappropriate to child-oriented assessment. Two additional marital measures may be of interest. These include the Marital Adjustment Test (MAT; Locke & Wallace, 1959) and the Marital Satisfaction Inventory (MSI; Snyder, 1979). Many of the items in the MAT have been incorporated into the DAS, and therefore it is not discussed. The MSI is a lengthy instrument (280 items) with excellent reliability but less than satisfactory validity at this time. The marital relationship can also be evaluated with two of the whole-family self-report measures previously described, the FAM-III (Skinner et al., 1983) and the Index of Marital Relations scale in the CMP (Hudson, 1982).

The DAS (Spanier, 1976) is perhaps the most popular measure of marital adjustment. The 32-item questionnaire measures four components of the marital relationship: Dyadic Consensus; Dyadic Cohesion; Dyadic Satisfaction; and Affectional Expression. The DAS demonstrates good internal reliability and validity. Normative data are not available, although mean scores and standard deviations for distressed and nondistressed groups provide clinical guidelines. The four-factor solution of the DAS has been replicated across some but not all samples; therefore, the total dyadic adjustment score at this time appears the most reliable index.

Measures of the Sibling Relationship

Although interest in sibling relations is increasing, much of the research focus has been on younger children, particularly the response of the first-born child to the birth of a sibling (e.g., Dunn & Kendrick, 1981), and has utilized direct observation methodology. Only one self-report measure of sibling relationships, described here, has been identified for school-age children.

The Sibling Relationship Questionnaire (SRQ; Furman & Buhrmester, 1985) is a 51-item questionnaire that measures two key aspects of the sibling relationship, satisfaction and importance. A factor analysis of the instrument yielded four factors that accounted for 71% of the variance: Warmth/Closeness; Relative Status/Power; Conflict; and Rivalry. Reliability, both internal consistency and test–retest, for the SRQ was high. The measure is too recently developed to have accumulated substantial validity evidence. The SRQ has been used with children in the fourth and fifth grades, with items read aloud to assure comprehension.

Projective Methods

Given the limited number of objective self-report measures for middle childhood, clinicians frequently use projective techniques. Kinetic Family Drawing (Burns & Kaufman, 1970) is perhaps the most widely used projective method of evaluating the child's perceptions of his or her family context. With this method, the child is instructed to draw a picture of the family, with each member engaged in some activity. Drawings are clinically evaluated for themes such as acceptance/rejection, conflict, self-concept, insecurity, anxiety, defensiveness (Burns & Kaufman, 1970; Reynolds, 1983). The advantages of projective techniques include their usefulness in capturing the perceptions of younger children, their resistance to faking, and their cost-effectiveness. The commonly acknowledged disadvantages of projective techniques are their lack of normative data and lack of standardized administration and scoring procedures, particularly for the final integrative and interpretive stages; these limitations seriously affect reliability and validity (Anastasi, 1982).

GENERAL SUMMARY AND DISCUSSION

Research consistently documents a relationship between the family context and children's psychological and educational functioning; this underscores the critical importance of including an assessment of the family's functioning in child-oriented assessments. In this chapter, numerous methods and specific techniques of family assessment have been described. Methods, broadly

categorized, include the use of interviews, observation, self-report questionnaires, and semistructured or projective stimuli. Each method has noteworthy strengths and limitations for the family researcher and clinician. Furthermore, the family diagnostician has a considerable choice of techniques or measures to use within each methodological group. In general, observation, either naturalistic or within an analogue or interview setting, is viewed as the essential methodology for determining contingencies of behavior; self-report methods, in contrast, most reliably capture the interior of family members' social reality. Currently, limited empirical data exist to support the predictive differential validity of particular methods or tests for particular children's psychological and educational problems.

In addition to choice of method, the family researcher/clinician is faced with several issues unique to conducting an assessment of the family context. These include determining which levels of the family system to assess, which perspectives to evaluate (insider vs. outsider), and which constructs to measure (i.e., which aspects of family functioning are critical to the referral problem). As noted throughout this chapter, there exist few empirical data to guide these decisions. Current research suggests that the insider–outsider perspective provides unique views of family relationships, and, similarly, that assessment of each different level of the family system provides unique information. There does not currently exist a theoretical consensus within the family psychology field regarding the salient characteristics of the family to be assessed to predict psychopathology. This would suggest that the family researcher/clinician should employ multiple measures that tap multiple perspectives and cut across family system levels. This strategy of multisystem–multimethod assessment has been recommended by Cromwell and Peterson (1983).

Cromwell and Peterson (1983) indicate that in a multisystem–multimethod assessment of the family context, the following steps are appropriate: (1) Conceptualize the family in terms of hierarchical levels; (2) identify the system level(s) hypothesized to be most involved in the child's problem behavior; and (3) identify methods that correspond with the system level to be evaluated. I would add a fourth step, which is to include measures that capture both the insider and outsider perspectives at each system level to be assessed. In a multisystem–multimethod analysis, data from each system level are juxtaposed and examined across system levels, with a view to divergent information about targeted levels of the family system and to convergent information or themes that are common throughout the family. For example, one might find that levels of affective involvement vary considerably across dyadic relationships within a family, but that dissatisfaction with the accomplishment of roles is a consistent theme among family members. These data, if viewed as contributing to the child's psychological or educational difficulty, might be interpreted to indicate a whole-family intervention of increasing organization within the family and restructuring family relationships to balance distance and proximity in such a way that the child can optimize development and reduce symptomatic behavior.

The multisystem–multimethod assessment provides a helpful framework for organizing the numerous aspects of the family context that may be appropriate to evaluate in a child-oriented assessment. As such, it appears particularly useful for the clinician assessing a single family. In the clincial setting, discrepancies between family members and across subsystems, as noted in the example above, can suggest treatment goals. The multisystem–multimethod strategy remains problematic for the family researcher, however, as it raises difficult questions regarding the investigator's interpretation and use of test data obtained from different family members and across different methods. Unfortunately, the complex issues of intermember discrepancy and intermethod correspondance appear to have no quick answers; systematic examination of these questions will require time and effort (Grotevant & Carlson, 1989).

For readers of this chapter, although freedom of choice and the opportunity for decision making are valued professional roles, limited choices and more evident guidelines may at times have appeared desirable with regard to conducting an assessment of the family context. As noted elsewhere (Gro-

tevant & Carlson, 1989), the family assessment field has proliferated rapidly and in an uncoordinated fashion. It somewhat resembles the nine-headed monster of Greek mythology, Hydra, which Hercules was challenged to slay. Whenever one of Hydra's heads was cut off, two new ones grew in its place. Thus, my attempt in this chapter to impose order on this young and somewhat unruly field has been limited to a large extent by the emergence of the field. Patience will be required as the family assessment field continues to develop and test theories of family functioning, and to identify the most reliable and valid measures of theoretical constructs. In the meantime, family researchers and clinicians are cautioned to attend carefully to the psychometric properties of existing measures, to use multiple methods and measures when feasible, and to generalize with caution. In particular, no family assessment measure has yet demonstrated adequate psychometric quality or validation studies to warrant its sole use in determining diagnosis or labeling for treatment. On a more positive note, however, numerous family context methods and measures have been developed that demonstrate more than adequate reliability and validity for use in research, in supporting clinical decisions regarding the child, and in guiding treatment.

REFERENCES

Abidin, R. R. (1983). *Parenting Stress Index (PSI)*. Charlottesville, VA: Pediatric Psychology Press.

Anastasi, A. (1982). *Psychological testing* (rev. ed.). New York: Macmillan.

Alexander, J. F. (1973a). Defensive and supportive communication in family systems. *Journal of Marriage and the Family, 35,* 613–617.

Alexander, J. F. (1973b). Defensive and supportive communication in normal and deviant families. *Journal of Consulting and Clinical Psychology, 40,* 223–231.

American Psychological Association. (1985). *Standards for educational and psychological testing*. Washington, DC: Author.

Aponte, H. J., & Van Deusen, J. M. (1981). Structural family therapy. In. A. S. Gurman & D. P. Kniskern (Eds.), *Handbook of family therapy* (pp. 310–360). New York: Brunner/Mazel.

Baldwin, A. L., Cole, R. E., & Baldwin, C. P. (1982). Parental pathology, family interaction, and the competence of the child in school. *Monographs of the Society for Research in Child Development, 47*(5), Serial no. 197).

Bandura, A. (1977). *Social learning theory*. Englewood Cliffs, NJ: Prentice-Hall.

Barbarin, O. A., & Gilbert, R. (1979). *Family Process Scales*. Ann Arbor, MI: Family Development Project.

Barbarin, O. A., & Tirado, M. (1985). Enmeshment, family processes, and successful treatment of obesity. *Family Relations, 34*, 115–121.

Barker, R. G. (1968). *Ecological psychology: Concepts and methods for studying the environment of human behavior*. Stanford, CA: Stanford University Press.

Barton, C., & Alexander, J. F. (1981). Functional family therapy. In A. S. Gurman & D. P. Kniskern (Eds.), *Handbook of family therapy* (pp. 403–443). New York: Brunner/Mazel.

Beavers, W. R. (n.d.). *Beavers–Timberlawn Family Evaluation Scale and Family Style Evaluation Manual*. (Available from the Southwest Family Institute, Dallas, TX 75230)

Beavers, W. R., & Voeller, M. N. (1983). Family models: Comparing and contrasting the Olson circumplex model with the Beavers system mode. *Family Process, 22*, 85–98.

Bertalanffy, L. von. (1968). *General systems theory*. New York: Braziller.

Billings, A. G., & Moos, R. H. (1983). Comparisons of children of depressed and nondepressed parents: A social–environmental perspective. *Journal of Abnormal Child Psychology, 11*, 463–486.

Block, J. H. (1965). *The Child-Rearing Practices Report (CRPR): A set of Q items for the description of parental socialization attitudes and values*. Unpublished manuscript, University of California at Berkeley.

Block, J. H., Block, J., & Morrison, A. (1981). Parental agreement–disagreement on childrearing orientations and gender-related personality correlates in children. *Child Development, 52*, 965–974.

Bowen, M. (1978). *Family therapy in clinical practice*. New York: Jason Aronson.

Bronfenbrenner, U. (1979). *The ecology of human development*. Cambridge, MA: Harvard University Press.

Burgess, E. W. (1926). The family as a unit of interacting personalities. *Family, 7*, 3–9.

Burns, R. C., & Kaufman, S. H. (1970). *Kinetic Family Drawings (K-F-D): An introduction to understanding children through kinetic drawing*. New York: Brunner/Mazel.

Cairns, R. B., & Green, J. A. (1979). How to assess personality and social patterns: Observations or ratings? In R. B. Cairns (Ed.), *The analysis of social interactions: Methods, issues, and illustrations* (pp. 209–226). Hillsdale, NJ: Erlbaum.

Carlson, C. I., & Grotevant, H. D. (1987a). A comparative review of family rating scales: Guidelines for clinicians and researchers. *Journal of Family Psychology, 1*, 23–47.

Carlson, C. I., & Grotevant, H. D. (1987b). Rejoinder: The challenges of reconciling family theory with method. *Journal of Family Psychology, 1*, 62–65.

Carlson, C. I., & Sincavage, J. (1987). Family-oriented school psychology practice: Results of a national survey of NASP members. *School Psychology Review, 16*, 519–526.

Carter, E. A., & McGoldrick, M. (Eds.). (1980). *The family life cycle: A framework for family therapy*. New York: Gardner Press.

Conger, R. D. (1981). The assessment of dysfunctional family systems. In B. B. Lahey & A. E. Kazdin (Eds.), *Advances in clinical child psychology* (Vol. 4, pp. 199–243). New York: Plenum.

Conger, R. D. (1983). Behavioral assessment for practitioners: Some reasons and recommendations. In E. E. Filsinger (Ed.), *Marriage and family assessment* (pp. 137–152). Beverly Hills, CA: Sage.

Cowan, P. A. (1987). The need for theoretical and methodological integrations in family research. *Journal of Family Psychology, 1*, 48–50.

Cromwell, R. D., Olson, D. H. L., & Fournier, D. G. (1976). Tools and techniques for diagnosis and evaluation in marital and family therapy. *Family Process, 15*, 1–49.

Cromwell, R. E., & Peterson, G. W. (1983). Multisystem–multimethod family assessment in clinical contexts. *Family Process, 22*, 147–171.

Dunn, J., & Kendrick, C. (1981). Social behavior of young siblings in the family context: Differences between same-sex and different-sex dyads. *Child Development, 52*, 1265–1273.

Emery, R. E., & O'Leary, K. D. (1982). Children's perceptions of marital discord and behavior problems of boys and girls. *Journal of Abnormal Child Psychology, 10*, 11–24.

Epstein, N. B., Baldwin, L. M., & Bishop, D. (1982). *McMaster Clinical Rating Scale* (Available from Brown/Butler Family Research Center, Providence, RI 02906)

Filsinger, E. E. (Ed.). (1983). *Marriage and family assessment*. Beverly Hills, CA: Sage.

Fisch, R., Weakland, J. H., & Segal, L. (1982). *The tactics of change*. San Francisco: Jossey-Bass.

Fishman, H. C. (1983). Reflections on assessment in structural family therapy. In B. Keeney (Ed.), *Diagnosis and assessment in family therapy*. Rockville, MD: Aspen.

Forehand, R., & McMahon, R. J. (1981). *Helping the noncompliant child: A clinician's guide to parent training*. New York: Guilford Press.

Forman, B. D., & Hagan, B. J. (1983). A comparative review of total family functioning measures. *American Journal of Family Therapy, 11*, 25–40.

Fowler, P. C. (1981). Maximum likelihood factor structure of the Family Environment Scale. *Journal of Clinical Psychology, 37*, 160–164.

Furman, W., & Buhrmester, D. (1985). Children's perceptions of the qualities of sibling relationships. *Child Development, 56*, 448–461.

Gilbert, R., & Christensen, A. (1985). Observational assessment of marital and family interaction: Methodological considerations. In L. L'Abate (Ed.), *The handbook of family psychology and therapy* (Vol. 1, pp. 961–988). Homewood, IL: Dorsey Press.

Gottman, J. (1979). *Marital interaction: Experimental investigation*. New York: Academic Press.

Green, R. G., Kolevson, M. S., & Vosler, N. R. (1985). The Beavers–Timberlawn model of family competence and the circumplex model of family adaptability and cohesion: Separate but equal? *Family Process, 24*, 385–398.

Grotevant, H. D., & Carlson, C. I. (1987). Family interaction coding schemes: A descriptive review. *Family Process, 26*, 49–74.

Grotevant, H. D., & Carlson, C. I. (1989). *Family*

assessment: A guide to methods and measures. New York: Guilford Press.

Grotevant, H. D., & Cooper, C. R. (1985). Patterns of interaction in family relationships and the development of identity exploration in adolescence. *Child Development, 56*, 415–428.

Guidabaldi, J., Cleminshaw, H. K., Peery, J. D., & McLoughlin, C. S. (1983). The impact of parental divorce on children: Report of the nationwide NASP study. *School Psychology Review, 12*, 300–323.

Gurman, A. S., & Kniskern, D. P. (1981). Family therapy outcome research: Knowns and unknowns. In A. S. Gurman & D. P. Kniskern (Eds.), *Handbook of family therapy* (pp. 742–776). New York: Brunner/Mazel.

Haley, J. (1980). *Leaving home*. New York: McGraw-Hill.

Haley, J. (1987). *Problem-solving therapy* (rev. ed.). San Francisco: Jossey-Bass.

Hartmann, A. (1979). *Finding families: An ecological approach to family assessment in adoption*. Beverly Hills, CA: Sage.

Hartmann, D. P. (Ed.), (1982). *Using observers to study behavior: New directions for methodology of social and behavior science*. San Francisco: Jossey-Bass.

Hartup, W. W. (1978). Perspectives on child and family interaction: Past, present, and future. In R. M. Lerner & G. B. Spanier (Eds.), *Child influences on marital and family interaction: A life-span perspective* (pp. 23–46). New York: Academic Press.

Hazzard, A., Christensen, A., & Margolin, G. (1983). Children's perceptions of parental behaviors. *Journal of Abnormal Child Psychology, 11*, 49–60.

Hetherington, E. M., Cox, M., & Cox, R. (1982). Effects of divorce on parents and children. In M. E. Lamb (Ed.), *Non-traditional families: Parenting and child development*. Hillsdale, NJ: Erlbaum.

Hill, R. (1949). *Families under stress*. New York: Harper & Row.

Hill, R. (1958). General features of families under stress. *Social Casework, 49*, 139–150.

Hoffman, L. (1981). *Foundations of family therapy: A conceptual framework for systems change*. New York: Basic Books.

Hudson, W. W. (1982). *The Clinical Measurement Package: A field manual*. Homewood, IL: Dorsey Press.

Hulgus, Y. F. (1985). *Scoring guide for the Beavers–Timberlawn Family Evaluation Scale and the Centripetal/Centrifugal Family Style Scale*. (Available from Southwest Family Institute, 12532 Nuestra, Dallas, TX 75230)

Huston, T. L., & Robins, E. (1982). Conceptual and methodological issues in studying close relationships. *Journal of Marriage and the Family, 44*, 901–925.

Isaacs, M. B., Montalvo, B., & Abelsohn, D. (1986). *The difficult divorce*. New York: Basic Books.

Jacob, T. (Ed.). (1987). *Family interaction and psychopathology*. New York: Plenum.

Jacob, T., Tennenbaum, D. L., & Krahn, G. (1987). Factors influencing the reliability and validity of observation data. In T. Jacob (Ed.), *Family interaction and psychopathology* (pp. 297–328). New York: Plenum.

Jasnowski, M. L. (1984). The ecosystemic perspective in clinical assessment and intervention. In W. A. O'Connor & B. Lubin (Eds.), *Ecological approaches to clin-ical and community psychology* (pp. 41–56). New York: Wiley.

Johnson, A. (1975). *An assessment of Mexican–American parent childrearing feelings and behaviors*. Unpublished doctoral dissertation, Arizona State University, Tempe.

Johnson, O. G. (1976). *Tests and measurements in child development: Handbook* (Vols. 1 & 2). San Francisco: Jossey-Bass.

Koman, S. L., & Stechler, G. (1985). Making the jump to systems. In M. P. Mirkin & S. L. Koman (Eds.), *Handbook of adolescents and family therapy* (pp. 1–20). New York: Gardner Press.

Kral, R. (1986). *Strategies that work: Techniques for solution in the schools*. Milwaukee, WI: Brief Therapy Center.

Lewin, K. (1951). *Field theory in social science*. New York: Harper.

Lewis, J. M., Beavers, W. R., Gossett, J. T., & Phillips, V. A. (1976). *No single thread: Psychological health in family systems*. New York: Brunner/Mazel.

Locke, H. J., & Wallace, K. M. (1959). Short marital-adjustment and prediction tests: Their reliability and validity. *Marriage and Family Living, 21*, 251–255.

Maccoby, E. E., & Martin, J. A. (1983). Socialization in the context of the family: Parent–child interaction. In E. M. Hetherington (Ed.), *Handbook of child psychology: Vol. 4. Socialization, personality and social development* (pp. 1–102). New York: Wiley.

Mannino, F. V., & Shore, M. F. (1984). An ecological perspective on family intervention. In W. A. O'Connor & B. Lubin (Eds.), *Ecological approaches to clinical and community psychology* (pp. 75–93). New York: Wiley.

Margolin, G. (1981). The reciprocal relationship between marital and child problems. In J. P. Vincent (Ed.), *Advances in family intervention assessment and theory: An annual compilation of research* (Vol. 2). Greenwich, CT: JAL Press.

Margolin, G. (1987). Participant observation procedures in marital and family assessment. In T. Jacobs (Ed.), *Family interaction and psychopathology* (pp. 391–426). New York: Plenum.

Markman, H. J., & Notarius, C. I. (1987). Coding marital and family interaction: Current status. In T. Jacobs (Ed.), *Family interaction and psychopathology* (pp. 329–390). New York: Plenum.

McCubbin, H. I., & Figley, C. R. (1983). *Stress and the family: Vol. 1. Coping with normative transitions*. New York: Brunner/Mazel.

McCubbin, H. I., & Patterson, J. M. (1983). Stress: The Family Inventory of Life Events and Changes. In E. E. Filsinger (Ed.), *Marriage and family assessment* (pp. 275–298). Beverly Hills, CA: Sage.

McCubbin, H. I., & Patterson, J. M. (1985). Family transitions: Adaptation to stress. In H. I. McCubbin & C. R. Figley (Eds.). *Stress and the family: Vol. 1. Coping with normative transitions* (pp. 5–25). New York: Brunner/Mazel.

McCubbin, H. I., Patterson, J. M., Bauman, E., & Harris, L. H. (1981). *Adolescent–Family Inventory of Life Events and Changes* (A-FILE). St Paul, MN: Family Social Science.

McCubbin, H. I., Patterson, J. M., & Wilson, L. (1983). *Family Inventory of Life Events and Changes (FILE) Form C*. St. Paul, MN: Family Social Science.

McGoldrick, M., & Gerson, R. (1985). *Genograms in family assessment*. New York: Norton.

Meehl, P. E. (1954). *Clinical versus statistical prediction: A theoretical analysis and a review of the evidence*. Minneapolis: University of Minnesota Press.

Milner, J. S. (1986). *The Child Abuse Potential Inventory manual* (2nd ed.). Webster, NC: Psytech.

Minuchin, S. (1974). *Families and family therapy*. Cambridge, MA: Harvard University Press.

Minuchin, S., & Fishman, H. C. (1981). *Family therapy techniques*. Cambridge, MA: Harvard University Press

Minuchin, S., Rosman, B., & Baker, L. (1978). *Psychosomatic families*. Cambridge, MA: Harvard University Press.

Moos, R. H., Clayton, J., & Max, W. (1979). *The Social Climate Scales: An annotated bibliography*, Palo Alto, CA: Consulting Psychologists Press.

Moos, R. H., & Moos, B. S. (1986). *Family Environment Scale manual* (rev. ed.). Palo Alto, CA: Consulting Psychologists Press.

Moos, R. H., & Spinrad, S. (1984). *The Social Climate Scales: An annotated bibliography, 1979–1983*. Palo Alto, CA: Consulting Psychologists Press.

Nunnally, J. C. (1978). *Psychometric theory* (2nd ed.). New York: McGraw-Hill.

O'Leary, K. D. (1984). Marital discord and children: Problems, strategies, methodologies and results. In A. Doyle, D. Gold, & D. S. Moskovitz (Eds.), *New directions for child development: No. 24. Children in families under stress* (pp. 35–47). San Francisco: Jossey-Bass.

Olson, D. H. (1977). Insiders' and outsiders' views of relationships: Research studies. In G. Levinger & H. Rausch (Eds.), *Close relationships: Perspectives on the meaning of intimacy*. Amherst: University of Massachusetts.

Olson, D. H., & Killorin, E. (1985). *Clinical Rating Scale for the circumplex model of marital and family systems*. (Available from Family Social Science, University of Minnesota, St. Paul, MN 55108)

Olson, D., Portner, J., & Lavee, Y. (1985). *FACES III*. (Available from Family Social Science, University of Minnesota, St. Paul, MN 55108)

Olson, D., & Wilson, M. (1985). *Family satisfaction*. Unpublished manuscript, Family Social Science, University of Minnesota.

Patterson, G. R. (1982). *A Social learning approach to family intervention: Vol. 3. Coercive family process*. Eugene, OR: Castalia.

Olson, D., Sprenkle, D. H., & Russell, C. S. (1979). Cimcumplex Model of Marital and Family Systems I: Cohesion and adaptability dimensions, family types, and clinical applications. *Family Process, 18*, 3–28.

Paget, K. D. (1987). Systemic family assessment: Concepts and strategies for school psychologists. *School Psychology Review, 16*(4), 429–442.

Patterson, G. R., & Reid, J. B. (1984). Social interaction processes within the family: The study of the moment-by-moment family transactions in which human social development is embedded. *Journal of Applied Developmental Psychology, 5*, 327–362.

Patterson, G. R., Reid, J. B., Jones, R. R., & Conger, R. E. (1975). *A social learning approach to family intervention: Vol. 1. Families with aggressive children*. Eugene, OR: Castalia.

Perosa, L. M. (1986). *The revision of the Structural Family Interaction Scale*. Unpublished manuscript.

Perosa, L. M., Hansen, J., & Perosa, S. (1981). Development of the Structural Family Interaction Scale. *Family Therapy, 8*, 77–90.

Pino, C. J., Simons, N., & Slawinowski, M. J. (1984). *Children's Version/Family Environment Scale*. Palo Alto, CA: Consulting Psychologists Press.

Reid, J. B. (Ed.). (1978). *A social learning approach to family intervention: Vol. 2. Observation in home settings*. Eugene, OR: Castalia.

Reynolds, C. R. (1983). A quick-scoring guide to the interpretation of children's Kinetic Family Drawings (KFD). *Psychology in the Schools, 15*, 489–492.

Roberts, G. C., Block, J. H., & Block, J. (1984). Continuity and change in parents' child-rearing practices. *Child Development, 55*, 586–597.

Rohner, R. P. (1984). *Handbook for the study of parental acceptance and rejection* (rev. ed.). Storrs: Center for the Study of Parental Acceptance and Rejection, University of Connecticut.

Sameroff, A. (1987). The social context of development. In N. Eisenberg (Ed.), *Contemporary topics in developmental psychology* (pp. 90–215). New York: Wiley.

Saunders, B. E., & Schuchts, R. B. (1987). Assessing parent–child relationships: A report of normative scores and revalidation of two clinical scales. *Family Process, 26*, 373–381.

Skinner, H. A., & Steinhauer, P. D. (1986). *Family Assessment Measure Clinical Rating Scale*. Toronto: Addiction & Research Foundation.

Skinner, H. A., Steinhauer, P. D., & Santa-Barbara, J. (1983). The Family Assessment Measure. *Canadian Journal of Community Mental Health, 2*, 91–105.

Skinner, H. A., Steinhauer, P. D., & Santa-Barbara, J. (1984). *The Family Assessment Measure: Administration and interpretation guide*. (Available from Addiction Research Foundation, Toronto, Ontario, Canada)

Snyder, D. K. (1979). Multidimensional assessment of marital satisfaction. *Journal of Marriage and the Family, 41*, 813–823.

Spanier, G. B. (1976). Measuring dyadic adjustment: New scales for assessing the quality of marriage and similar dyads. *Journal of Marriage and the Family, 38*, 15–28.

Sroufe, L. A., & Fleeson, J. (1986). Attachment and the construction of relationships. In W. W. Hartup & Z. Rubin (Eds.), *Relationships and development* (pp. 51–72). Hillsdale, NJ: Erlbaum.

Stanton, M. D. (1981). Strategic approaches to family therapy. In A. S. Gurman & D. P. Kniskern (Eds.), *Handbook of family therapy* (pp. 361–402). New York: Brunner/Mazel.

Steinhauer, P. D., Santa-Barbara, J., & Skinner, H. (1984). The process model of family functioning. *Canadian Journal of Psychiatry, 29*, 77–88.

Straus, M. A., & Brown, B. W. (1978). *Family measurement techniques: Abstracts of published instruments, 1935–1974* (rev. ed.). Minneapolis: University of Minnesota Press.

Strodtbeck, F. L. (1951). Husband–wife interaction over revealed differences. *American Sociological Review, 16*, 468–473.

Strom, R. D. (1984). *Parent as a Teacher Inventory manual*. Bensenville, IL: Scholastic Testing Service.

Terkelsen, K. G. (1980). Toward a theory of the family life cycle. In E. A. Carter & M. McGoldrick (Eds.), *The family life cycle: A framework for family therapy* (pp. 21–52). New York: Gardner Press.

Tomm, K. (1987a). Interventive interviewing: Part I. Strategizing as a fourth guideline for the therapist. *Family Process, 26*, 3–14.

Tomm, K. (1987b). Interventive interviewing: Part II. Reflexive questioning as a means to enable self-healing. *Family Process, 26*, 167–184.

Umbarger, C. C. (1983). *Structural family therapy*. New York: Grune & Stratton.

Wallerstein, J., & Kelly, J. B. (1980). *Surviving the breakup*. New York: Basic Books.

Weber, T., McKeever, J. E., & McDaniel, S. H. (1985). A beginner's guide to the problem-oriented first family interview. *Family Process, 24*, 356–364.

Wicker, A. W. (1979). *An introduction to ecological psychology*. Monterey, CA: Brooks/Cole.

Wilson, C. C. (1986). Family assessment in preschool evaluation. *School Psychology Review, 15*, 166–179.

24

Issues in Child Custody Evaluation and Testimony

PATRICE MCCLURE-BUTTERFIELD
Georgia Southern University

Louis Nizer, the well-known divorce lawyer, states in his book *My Life in Court:* "All litigations evoke intense feelings of animosity, revenge, and retribution. Some of them may be fought ruthlessly. But none of them, even in their most aggravated form, can equal the sheer, unadulterated venom of a matrimonial contest" (1968, p. 153). Gardner adds: "And of all the forms of matrimonial litigation, the most vicious and venomous by far is custody litigation" (1976, p. 381).

It may be that psychologists and other mental health professionals are requested to become involved in matrimonial problems most frequently when the issues include child custody. But psychologists, as a rule, are reluctant to enter into therapy situations when they know that litigation is involved and a court appearance is likely. Indeed, psychologists refuse so often under these circumstances that clients sometimes misrepresent their reasons for seeking therapy. Once so involved, psychologists can be subpoenaed and then must testify.

The experience of being on the witness stand can be humiliating, frightening, and confidence-destroying if the psychologist is unprepared. In spite of the many pitfalls, however, psychologists should not shy away from the opportunity to utilize their skills, especially as those skills relate to expertise in the personality and behavior assessment of children and their parents. There exists a moral and an ethical responsibility to assess individuals as accurately and completely as possible in order to determine appropriate treatment and recommendations. In cases involving legal disputes over child custody, the psychologist's expertise in assessment can provide a valuable service to help determine placements in the best interests of the child(ren) in question.

The inexact nature of the field of psychology (often described as more of an art or developing clinical field than a science) makes psychologists feel vulnerable to attack, especially when subjective test instruments are used to help formulate an opinion or diagnosis. This chapter begins by providing a brief history of the bases for custodial decisions, the reasons why evaluations may be requested, and criteria for custodial evaluations. Models of evaluations and the evaluation report itself are then described and discussed. In addition, suggestions on how to prepare to be an expert witness and some guidelines for dealing with specific problems on the witness stand are provided. This information should help to alleviate the stress and the ambivalence reported by many psychologists in accepting cases that expose them to the legal system, especially cases associated with the highly emotionally charged issues in child custody disputes.

HISTORY OF CUSTODIAL DECISIONS

Ninety percent of child custody arrangements are made through stipulated agreements between parents; in 85% of these cases, the mother gets custody without the father contesting it (Weitzman & Dixon, 1979). In only 10% of the cases does a judge or jury decide who gets custody (Hodges, 1986). As Weiss (1979) points out, even though judges decide a small proportion of custody cases, the criteria used are important to know, so that lawyers and mental health professionals can determine what custody and visitation arrangements are reasonable to expect or demand if custody is contested. Historical antecedents guide and shape judges in their determinations.

Prior to 1920, children were considered the property of the father, and if parents divorced the father typically retained custody. The general reasoning was that the father was best for the child because he could provide physical protection, nurturing, financial maintenance, and education (Weiss, 1979). However, as the United States moved from an agrarian to an industrial society during the late 1800s and early 1900s, fathers entered the labor force often in factories, leaving mothers as the primary child care providers (Clingempeel & Reppucci, 1982). Mother love became an important aspect of a child's development because of the emerging attitude that one purpose of the family was to protect the child from an impersonal world (Weiss, 1979). Freud's influence in the early 1900s was also an important factor. Emotional bonding between mother and child was recognized increasingly as a strong influence in the young child's development.

Tender Years Doctrine

The "tender years" doctrine related to the assumption that a young child's best interests are served by the mother. In the United States this belief began to be voiced as early as 1830 (Foster & Freed, 1978), but did not become common until the 1920s. The age defined as "tender" varied. Some courts set the range from birth to 6 years of age; others extended it to age 9 or even age 12 (Hodges, 1986). The upper age to which the tender years doctrine applied seemed to increase over time (Weiss, 1979).

Under the tender years doctrine, in a disputed custody case, the father had to prove the mother unfit rather than simply prove that he was the better parent. It was not until the 1960s and 1970s that several states repealed the tender years doctrine because (1) it clearly discriminated against fathers; (2) there was a growing recognition that fathers could be very adequate parents even for young children (Orthner & Lewis, 1979; Santrock & Warshak, 1979); and (3) increasingly, divorced mothers became employed, and therefore not able to remain at home with their children at all times (Hodges, 1986).

Best Interests of the Child

A child custody opinion based on "the best interests of the child" was written in the late 1920s, which rapidly replaced the tender years doctrine and became accepted throughout the country (Hodges, 1986). Today this criterion as a legal basis for child custody decisions has been adopted by most states.

The doctrine of the best interests of the child gives a judge a great deal of discretionary power. Issues of which parent is "at fault" ostensibly were removed from decision criteria by the advent of "no-fault" divorce. However, in spite of the Uniform Marriage and Divorce Act (National Conference of Commissioners on Uniform State Laws, 1971) adopted by many states, the view that one parent is at fault in the dissolution of a marriage (e.g., has had an affair) and should be punished is still common. The act specifically enjoins that the conduct of a parent that did not directly influence the child should not be considered as part of the custody decision. Nonetheless, judges still seem to be influenced by evidence of immorality (Weiss, 1979). Giving custody to such a parent may be perceived as rewarding immoral behavior (Hodges, 1986), and therefore not in the best interests of the child.

A second living situation—cohabitation, which should be protected by another uniform code, the Uniform Custody Code (National Conference of Commissioners on

Uniform State Laws, 1971)—also still seems to affect judges' decisions in custody battles. Given the increase in cohabitation in the United States in recent years, custody decisions considering this factor have far-reaching implications. The Illinois Supreme Court, for example, ruled that such living conditions have the potential to do future harm to the characters of children and that their mental and emotional health may be affected adversely (Hodges, 1986). These issues of morality do not take into consideration the quality of the relationships among the adults and the children in question. It is the quality of relationships that psychologists and other mental health professionals often find themselves attempting to evaluate.

Current Perspectives

It should be noted that the best interests of the child doctrine seldom is used as the *sole* criterion in custody decisions (Hodges, 1986). For example, Derdeyn (1975) reported that the interests of the biological parents are given greater weight than the child's. A more recent study (Felner et al., 1985) reported that in one state only 15% of the lawyers and only half of the judges included the best interests of the child as one of the five most critical factors in deciding custody. Many other factors seem to take precedence in the mind of the court when it comes to custody issues. Some of these include the persistence of the notions that the sex of the child and parent should match and that the parent with the better economic resources should have custody.

Today, two different types of custodial arrangements seem to be the most common alternatives to the mother having sole legal responsibility and residential custody. These are joint custody and father custody.

Joint Custody

The general public often confuses legal responsibility with physical location of the child. It is possible for parents to have joint responsibility for raising children, even if the children physically reside with one parent. In the past 5–10 years, joint custody has been the custody decision of choice when neither parent is considered inappropriate in terms of quality of parenting. This approach seems to work best with parents who can communicate fairly well and generally agree on parenting style (Reppucci, 1984).

Although "joint custody" technically means shared legal responsibility for child welfare, in practical terms it also usually means more equal distribution of the time the children spend with the parents. Some children switch homes every 6 months (with visitation with the other parent during this time), and some children switch every day or every few days. Four primary patterns of shared physical custody have been described in the literature by Atwell, Moore, Nielsen, and Levite (1984): (1) long-term (summer–winter; school year–vacations; alternating full years); (2) short-term (alternate months, alternate weeks, split week, every other day, and split day); (3) "bird's nest" (parents move in and out of children's home); and (4) free access (children go back and forth from parent to parent at will). All these combinations work best if the parents both reside within the same school district. Problems noted by Ramos (1979) include the possible perception by the children of transience and instability, the increased costs of maintaining two households, and changes in children's and parents' needs over time. The issue of transience for children has received a great deal of attention from the media in the late 1980s. Lack of consistency by parents appears to be exacerbated by the maintenance of two entirely separate sets of living conditions. Irving, Benjamin, and Trocme (1984) voiced concerns about joint physical custody for very young children, for emotionally unstable children, for parents who might use their children as a weapon, or for parents for whom joint custody is court-ordered rather than a desired custody outcome.

Father Custody

Fathers' parenting styles have become the subject of several recent studies, as the father as the sole physical custodian (with either joint or sole legal responsibility) becomes a more acceptable and common outcome of custody disputes. Lewis, Feiring, and Weintraub (1981) note that fathers' patterns of parenting do differ from mothers'. As a group, fathers in intact families spend less one-to-one time with children, are more concerned than mothers with sex-role development, spend less time in caregiving activities, and spend more time in play. Lewis et al. (1981) concluded that although fathers' styles may differ, they appear to be as sensitive and as concerned with child rearing as mothers.

The most extensive direct-measure research (as opposed to case study research) on father custody has been done by Warshak and Santrock (Santrock & Warshak, 1979; Warshak & Santrock, 1983a, 1983b). Results suggest a clear relationship between type of custody and adjustment of the child. Children living with the same-sex parent were better adjusted than those living with the opposite-sex parent. For mother custody, there was little difference in these children's adjustment when compared with that of children in intact homes. It should be noted that the children in this study were between 6 and 11 years of age, and that fathers and mothers may be differentially beneficial to children of each gender over time. This is a research question that is as yet unanswered (Hodges, 1986). However, there seems to be no evidence to date suggesting that fathers who want custody and obtain it are in general inferior to mothers who obtain custody. For psychologists and mental health professionals who will be asked to assist in making recommendations based upon research in child custody cases, this is an important area of research to monitor in the coming years.

REASONS FOR CHILD AND FAMILY EVALUATION

There are a number of reasons related to child custody for which a mental health practitioner may be asked to evaluate individuals and provide testimony. Each requires the ability to formulate and articulate expert opinions based upon sound psychological foundations. The psychologist must know how to select appropriate instruments for evaluation; this requires a knowledge of the validity, reliability, and general strengths and weaknesses of a wide variety of assessment techniques. (This aspect of child custody evaluation is discussed in more detail later in this chapter.) These issues must be kept in mind as each of the reasons for evaluation is enumerated below.

Parental Fitness

The question of the mental health of adults caring for children may not be asked solely in relation to custody issues arising from divorce. Parental fitness issues may be raised by social agencies, as in the case of mentally handicapped or mentally ill parents of a physically or mentally handicapped child. Although mental handicaps or controlled (or recurrent) mental illness in itself does not constitute a reason for removal of a child into foster or institutional care, a professional psychologist may need to perform intellectual, personality, and behavioral assessments to help determine custody that is in the best interests of the child.

Custody Changes

Just as in initial custody proceedings, parents sometimes request changes in custody based on what is termed "change of circumstances." Financial, geographical, or health (physical and/or mental) considerations; wishes of the child; and many other factors may precipitate a request for legal changes in custody by either parent. The issues are much the same as in initial custody battles and often are just as emotion-charged. After all, if the parties were in agreement, custody changes would probably simply be made without any need for court involvement.

Visitation Rights

Visitation schedules often are a source of continuing conflict even after custody is determined. A parent may be discouraging visitation with the noncustodial parent, often in subtle and sometimes unconscious ways. If mediation is not required by the original custody decision for solution of conflicts, then the parties must return to court. Often, psychological evaluation of all parties is necessary. Blau (1984) recommends specific visitation schedules and environmental arrangements for children under age 5. The reader is referred to this excellent source for more details on this issue.

Child Abuse/Neglect

If abuse or neglect is charged by one parent to another, court intervention may be required. Indeed, if abuse is suspected and reported, social agencies automatically initiate procedures that may result in legal intervention. In such cases, evaluation of all parties and adjustments in visitation and/or custody may well be required. Children have been removed from parents who are chronic alcoholics (nonresponsive to treatment), sexually promiscuous, or mentally incompetent if the parents have not arranged for appropriate alternative care when they are indisposed or otherwise unavailable.

Juvenile Misbehavior

Juvenile court services often employ mental health workers and psychologists in cases where children under the age of 17 (16 in some states or for some offenses) are involved in violations of the law. Juveniles and their families may be evaluated for psychopathology, parental fitness, and likelihood of responsiveness to treatment. The testimony of psychologists weighs heavily in determining disposition of such cases, including the possibility of foster care.

Adoption

Following the establishment of the fact that the parental rights of the natural parents have been severed, a determination must be made as to whether a proposed adoptive family can meet the physical and emotional needs of a specific child or children. Many of the factors to be taken into account are similar to those in criteria for custody—the age and health of the adoptive child; the age and health of the prospective parents; religious preferences; financial stability; emotional climate; and marital status (Shapiro, 1984).

Marital Reconciliation/Mediation

In cases where separated or divorced individuals reconcile, child custody issues may be handled out of court, but often will require the assistance of a therapist. However, issues (which perhaps contributed to the initial marital conflict) concerning children, their care, handling, discipline, school problems, and the like will all require the same kind of careful, complete evaluation utilized in custody conflicts. The largest difference is that communication with both parents is direct, rather than through an attorney or in a courtroom. Reconciliation evaluation obviously also requires a careful assessment of the parents' relationships with each other. A prospect of future court appearances should always be considered.

Regardless of the purpose of the requested evaluation, be it court-ordered or family-initiated, the issues of careful test selection, administration, scoring, and interpretation are the same. Clinical interviews may be challenged in court and must be clearly differentiated from simply "talking to the patient." Subjective test instruments must be qualified as such and supported by behavioral observations. Questionnaires should be selected for their ability to obtain specific types of information about the individual. Standardized tests must be administered strictly according to manual directions. All of the psychologist's skills in personality and behavior assessment must be utilized in order to assist in the making of a clear, concise, and sound decision that can affect the lives of the individuals for a long time to come.

CRITERIA FOR CUSTODY EVALUATIONS

Charnas (1981) noted that there is a lack of guidelines or criteria in the law and social science literature for defining "the best interests of the child" in the child custody decision-making process. This makes the psychologist's job a more difficult one. Hodges (1986) explains that in the absence of criteria, an assessment of parent–child bonding, or of which parent is the "psychological parent," has been used as a guide for child placement. The term "psychological parent" refers to the parent who better fulfills lthe child's psychological and physical needs (Goldstein, Freud, & Solnit, 1973). Judges and lawyers are uncomfortable using the bond as a criterion because they prefer to use objective rather than subjective evidence. This is one major reason why psychologists and their test instruments come under such close scrutiny in the court-room.

Although the order of the lists that follow may vary among judges, lawyers, and mental health practitioners, criteria for custody seem to include the same major issues. Chasin and Grunebaum (1981) summarize these points well. They recommend favoring the parent with the following characteristics:

1. Is more likely to foster visitation and shows the more objective attitude toward the other parent.
2. Will maintain the greater continuity of child contact with relatives, friends, neighborhood, schools, etc.
3. Has the better child-rearing skills.
4. Shows the greater humanity, consistency, and flexibility in handling the child(ren).
5. Is the one to whom the child is more deeply attached.

Other criteria for custody decisions, provided by Benedek (1972), Woody (1977), and Fine (1980), include the following:

1. The reasonable preference of the child (if the child is of sufficient age).
2. Support for the parent who will provide geographic stability.
3. Support for the parent with capacity to provide the child with food, clothing, and medical care.
4. Support for the parent willing to provide continued religious training.
5. Avoidance of separation of siblings.

Awad (1978) notes that mental fitness (implying degree of adjustment) of the parent is rarely relevant to child custody evaluations and that diagnosis tends not to be a useful criterion. The issue for the psychologist is to determine whether any existing mental incapacity interferes with parenting abilities and affects the child directly. For example, a diagnosis of schizophrenia in a parent is, in and of itself, not sufficient reason to decide against this individual in a custody case.

Using any of the criteria listed above, one is struck immediately with the awareness of the obvious difficulties associated with evaluation in these areas. McDermott,

Tseng, Char, and Fukunaga (1978) identified four major problem areas in conducting a custody evaluation. First, they noted that it was difficult to obtain evidence on the natural parent–child relationship or natural home environment. This is probably because a custody evaluation home visit by a psychologist invariably creates high anxiety or a forced tolerance in the home that would not exist otherwise. Second, McDermott et al. remind the reader that research indicates that women look less well adjusted at the time of the separation decision, whereas men look worse some time after the separation. Discovering children's real preference for either parent is also difficult, as loyalty conflicts often exist. Third, data in other areas often conflict or are inconclusive, and psychologists have difficulty predicting the future effects of certain factors on children's later development or over time (e.g., custody award of infants to fathers; cross-sex parent–child combinations; alcoholism recurrence; and religious fervor). The last major problem noted by this study was the difficulty in choosing between "poisons." The more available parent may not have the better skills.

CUSTODY EVALUATION PROCEDURES

"Custody evaluation" refers to the process of gathering information, interpreting data, and forming and communicating recommendations concerning child custody. As stated above, there are no national standards for such evaluations. Given the complexity of family relationships, the problem of predicting future stability in the midst of the upset over a divorce, and the problem of changing developmental needs over time, a judge needs the wisdom of Solomon (Hodges, 1986). The psychologist needs the courage of Samson to explore this minefield and avoid the pitfalls of bias to arrive at a decision in the best interests of the child.

Precustody Evaluation Negotiations

Hodges (1986) recommends that the first responsibility of the mental health professional is the welfare of the child. Therefore, he cautions that the professional should avoid representing one parent against the other in a child custody dispute, regardless of who is paying. In addition, it should be made clear in advance (in writing) that the evaluation report will be made available to the court and to both attorneys, not just the attorney requesting the evaluation. One attorney should not be permitted to decide whether or not to use the report after it is read. (This caution is not necessary, of course, if the evaluation is a court-ordered one.) Parents should sign a permission-for-evaluation form (if not under court order) and should be informed about the evaluation process, the limits of confidentiality, and the procedure for billing. Hodges also recommends obtaining fees in advance and placing them in an escrow account, to avoid the difficulty of collecting fees from the "losing party" after the court decision is made.

Agency versus Private Practitioner Evaluations

Custody evaluations conducted by social service agencies, probation departments, or the court itself are probably shorter than those done by private practitioners. Watson (1979) describes the Denver District Court procedure as including the following steps:

1. An interview with each parent, including information about education, number of marriages, number of children, and military service.
2. Employment and police check.
3. Evaluation of the physical and emotional health of each parent, including physician and therapist reports.
4. Interviews with neighbors and other witnesses if appropriate.
5. Background information from school principal, teachers, social workers, nurses, or other school personnel.

Children are interviewed at school by an agency social worker.

A private evaluation will probably take place in an office, and ideally includes the following, according to Blau (1984):

1. Several interviews with each parent alone. Parents need to be reminded that nothing in the interview is confidential.

2. Several interviews with each child alone. Gardner (1976) recommends observing preschool children two or three times, and older children three or more times. Children also need to be informed that the interview is not confidential.
3. Interviewing the parent and children together.
4. Interviewing teachers, babysitters, and other significant people in the children's lives. Grandparents may be seen, as well as any new person to whom the children will be exposed who is involved with either parent. Chasin and Grunebaum (1981) suggest also seeking out housekeepers, friends, neighbors, physicians, and psychotherapists.
5. A home visit. This allows determination of the safety of the home setting and information about the sensitivity of the parents to the children's needs.

In addition, Chasin and Grunebaum (1981) tell parents that the practitioner is willing to read any material parents would like to submit, and to talk to anyone the parents feel has information that would help the court make a decision about custody.

The type of private evaluation described above may take up to 40 staff hours in a two-child-family situation, plus staff meetings and report-writing time. The time obviously increases with the complexity of the case. Added to actual court appearance time, such an evaluation can cost anywhere from $1,000 to $5,000. Since parents are already paying substantial legal fees, private evaluations are not possible for many families. Sometimes this results in the briefer evaluation procedures described earlier or in noncontested court battles.

The British Columbia, Canada, Service Delivery Standards

In 1985, the British Columbia Department of Corrections developed a set of standards for custody and access assessment. This is most unusual and serves as an important model for custody evaluation procedures in the United States. These guidelines provide for a specially trained family court counselor to perform the assessment, but permits private evaluation also. The best interests of the child are the primary consideration for custody determination, and British Columbia law specifically excludes from consideration behavior of a parent that does not affect the child (Blau, 1984).

All parties to the assessment are notified that nothing is confidential. The family court counselor initially sees both parents together in the home, if possible. The child is observed in the parents' presence, regardless of the child's age. The child's views are obtained and his or her feelings may be expressed, but the child is not asked to make a choice as to with which parent he or she wishes to reside. The report must be made available to all parties 5 days before the hearing. Although evaluators still have wide discretion as to how to collect data, guidelines do exist for minimum specific information requirements. This data base allows for a common set of criteria and permits a research basis for effectiveness of this procedure.

Test Selection

Psychological testing is most commonly done as part of an evaluation of the children and parents only. Projective techniques may be used to assess bonding. For example, the Children's Apperception Test, a sentence completion test, and/or the Kinetic Family Drawing procedure may be used with children, while the Thematic Apperception Test may be used with adults. The Minnesota Multiphasic Personality Inventory may alert the psychologist to some borderline pathology missed in an interview. Other tests may be used at the evaluator's discretion. However, no custody evaluation should be based on the results of psychological testing only. Projective test results, in particular, are meaningful only in the light of other information obtained in interviews, questionnaires, and direct behavioral observation. Hodges (1986) warns psychologists never to answer questions in court about the interpretation of a single response, since conclusions reported in writing should be based on the evaluation of *patterns* of responses.

Blau (1984) recommends close inspection of school adjustment and the child's status, special abilities, needs, and problems. Such an examination should include a thorough evaluation of (1) intellectual status and potential, (2) neuropsychological factors, (3) academic achievement, and (4) personality and personal adjustment. Specific tests and procedures obviously depend upon the age and background of the child.

Interview Techniques

The reader is referred to a very helpful review by Hodges (1986) for numerous lists of potential questions to ask in interviews with parents, children, and parent–child dyads or triads. He also outlines play situations for interviewing young children. He cautions psychologists to make careful notes of all observations, interactions, and test information. Memory has been shown to be highly unreliable, especially when there is (as is almost always the case) a long time delay before reaching court. Another excellent, detailed description of the interview process is offered by Gardner (1976), who is well known for his work in psychotherapy with children of divorce.

THE CUSTODY EVALUATION REPORT

Writing the Report

The custody evaluation report is a major instrument used by opposing attorneys to formulate court tactics; as mentioned above, this report should be available to all parties before the court date. It is imperative that this written document be accurate, concise, and clear. The report should be written by the major evaluator if a team approach has been employed. It should begin with a statement of the purpose of the evaluation (e.g., "to determine custody placement in the child's best interests") and a summary of the data, techniques, and instruments used in the evaluation. Writing should be clear, simple, and free from professional jargon. If possible, both parents' strengths should be cited, but the report should state the facts, the opinions formulated from the facts, and the conclusions, avoiding biases. Awad (1978) recommends that for situations in which there is no clear-cut recommendation, it is useful to report the situation as precisely as possible and to list the advantages and disadvantages of each possible recommendation.

Gardner (1976) reminds the reader that a diagnosis is *not* necessary in a report. The purpose of the report is to recommend custody placement, and a diagnostic label may serve to distract and confuse the court, thereby clouding the main issue. Gardner also warns against making statements (e.g., quoting a parent) as if they were proven facts. The court views this as hearsay, and they are not admissible. For example, instead of saying, "Mr. X drinks one case of beer daily," the psychologist should say, "If the court accepts as true Mrs. X's allegation that her husband consumes, on the average, one case of beer daily, then I would consider this an argument against his receiving custody of the children." It is important to remember that although the custody evaluation report is a critical factor, the *court* has the ultimate responsibility for deciding placement.

Clawar (1984) has proposed criteria for evaluating the scientific respectability of a custody report. These criteria serve as useful guides to the custody evaluator. The following points should be kept in mind and included in a written custody evaluation report:

1. A full history of the family and situation(s) with all appropriate data is required.
2. Credentials of the writer (expertise) should be in line with the testimony needed.
3. The amount of time involved in the evaluation should be stated.
4. Sources should be cited, including referral source.
5. The report should focus on patterns or themes rather than isolated incidents or responses.
6. Conclusions supported by other professionals or research should be noted.
7. Appropriate tests should be used for the questions asked.
8. Clarity of the report is crucial.
9. Language of the report should be neutral, not adversarial. Technical terms should be avoided.
10. The context in which observations were made (office, home) should be described, and the writer should state whether the conclusions can be generalized.
11. The limitations of the report should be indicated.
12. Conclusions should be drawn from the material used in the evaluation.

Feedback to Parents

Depending on the adversarial level of contesting parents, the custody evaluator may take one of two stances regarding direct feedback to parents and their attorneys after the evaluation is complete. The evaluator may meet with the opposing attorneys to explore constructive alternatives to litigation. However, if this outcome is improbable, then Gardner (1976) recommends that the evaluator maintain a strictly neutral position. The written report should be sent to the court, which will give a copy to both lawyers. Any meetings should be avoided. The place to air differences of opinion with regard to the psychologist's report should be in court.

PSYCHOLOGICAL TESTS IN THE COURTROOM

Psychologists' expertise in the area of testing is what makes them unique among professionals and in demand for testimony in many types of legal disputes. The development, standardization, and use of psychological tests have had much to do historically with the emergence of psychology as a scientific field. Since 1954, the American Psychological Association (APA) has formally recognized the importance of scientific standards in the development and application of test instruments. In 1974, APA published the original *Standards for Educational and Psychological Tests;* these were published in revised form in 1985. The standards specify in detail the qualifications of test users; methods of choosing tests for specific purposes; administration and scoring standards to be followed; and acceptable procedures and limitations for the interpretation of psychological tests.

This last point is particularly important, especially during cross-examination in child custody cases. Psychologists who testify about the meaning of psychological tests should realize, warns Blau (1984), that their opinions will be subjected to minute scrutiny by competent opposing counsel (Poythress, 1980; Ziskin, 1981). Reports and depositions will probably be reviewed by other psychologists specifically for the purpose of identifying errors, distortions, improprieties, and inaccuracies. The psychologist who testifies in court must adhere to the highest standards in order to serve his or her client properly, avoid embarrassment, and protect the good name of psychology. Readers are encouraged to become very familiar with the APA *Standards* for these reasons. Similarly, the *Ethical Principles of Psychology* (APA, 1981) and the *Standards for Providers of Psychological Services* (APA, 1977) should be well known and practiced by any licensed psychologist, especially before going on the witness stand. Studies have indicated (e.g., Ash & Guyer, 1984) that judges are influenced heavily by the testimony of expert witnesses (more so than juries are), and this is why opposing counsel will try so hard to discredit a psychologist on the witness stand. It is very important for a psychologist to avoid having his or her entire testimony lose credence because of ignorance of the standards upon which professional clinical psychology is founded.

PREPARING AS AN EXPERT WITNESS

There are many details about which to be concerned when preparing for testimony in court. However, there are a few important points to consider before even meeting a proposed client. If an attorney contacts a psychologist to request expert testimony in a child custody case, as mentioned earlier in this chapter, the psychologist should obtain assurance in writing that he or she is appearing as an advocate for the child's best interests and are not in support of either parent. Moreover, in the initial interview with the attorney (often conducted by telephone for 15–30 minutes), the psychologist should obtain the pertinent facts of the case sufficiently clearly to determine that his or her unique and specific professional skills can be applied appropriately to the case. In addition, some attorneys are unaware of the time needed by an expert witness to conduct a thorough examination (as described earlier),

to prepare reports, and to research the literature, so an anticipated court date is a critical piece of information to have before accepting a case. Availability of records and willingness of family members to participate in the evaluation are also helpful to know about, before committing time and energy to such an undertaking.

Once a case is accepted and the evaluation is complete, much time may pass before actual court testimony is required. Detailed records of dates, time, facts, and documentation must be catalogued carefully for easy retrieval when needed. No detail is too small to record. Blau (1984), in his book *The Psychologist as Expert Witness*, has many useful forms to aid in data organization, and the reader is referred to this excellent source.

Prior to the court appearance, the attorney should be briefed by the psychologist as well as vice versa, in order to assist in the planning of the kinds of questions that should and will be asked in court. The attorney can help the psychologist understand the best way to present his or her data; the psychologist can assist the lawyer in formulating questions that will elicit the opinion the psychologist wishes to express. In addition, the expert needs to anticipate in advance what some of the challenges to his or her opinion might be, and should attempt to deal with any weaknesses frankly during *direct* examination. This avoids the appearance of defensiveness upon cross-examination if such weaknesses should be pinpointed by the opposing counsel. Many problems can be avoided if psychologists train the attorneys who will examine them (Denton, 1987).

Psychologists on the Witness Stand

Psychologists often are ignorant of courtroom dynamics and the rules of courtroom performance. These rules cover who can be spoken to, by whom, when, and how. They also structure what can and what cannot be said in court. In an adversarial situation, these requirements lead attorneys to manipulate the rules to present evidence in support of their case, to discredit the evidence of the other side, and to prevent the other attorney from doing the same (Hodges, 1986).

Attorneys have different styles just as psychologists do (Girdner, 1985). Some are principled bargainers who attempt to negotiate a fair agreement. A few are soft bargainers and like to avoid conflict and risk. Others are hard bargainers who have winning as their primary goal and rarely negotitate except in an aggressive manner (Hodges, 1986). Regardless of the opposing attorney's style in cross-examining an expert witness, the psychologist should keep several points in mind:

1. The expert witness should be prepared to state professional qualifications clearly and in a well-articulated voice. These include educational level, clinical experience, experience as an expert witness, professional organizations to which the professional belongs or in which he or she holds office, membership on any local committees (especially when they may have to do with the case, such as a council on child abuse), and any other relevant information. The opposing counsel may challenge the credentials, but the judge will determine the witness's status as an expert. A licensed psychologist in clinical practice generally will be considered qualified to serve as an expert, or it is unlikely that he or she would be on the witness stand.

2. Professional dress is a requirement to avoid offending judges or suggesting lack of respect for the court, as well as to protect professional credibility.

3. The witness should speak slowly and clearly, avoiding jargon. This is an area of criticism of attorneys as well as expert witnesses. One should avoid continually defining words, or worse, ignoring the need for their definition.

4. Joking or wisecracking should be avoided, even if the attorney does this. The witness should be relaxed and unintimidated, but should show that he or she takes the role of expert witness seriously (Gardner, 1976).

5. The witness should address the judge as "Your Honor" and learn the names of all attorneys, so that responses to questions may be prefaced with the correct name.

6. The witness may restate an attorney's questions, changing small words he or she may have used to get the witness to contradict an earlier statement. The question may then be answered as restated (e.g., "If

you mean . . . , then I would have the following opinion . . .").

7. The witness should feel free to take notes and/or books on the stand and should not be afraid to use them. However, he or she should be familiar with the location of the information to avoid delays and fumbling. Also, anything taken on the stand may be entered as an exhibit, so only those items should be taken that the witness would not be uncomfortable having the court see.

8. If an attorney asks a multiple-part question and wants a "yes" or "no" answer, the witness should not be afraid to say that the question cannot be answered with a simple "yes" or "no."

9. At the end of testimony, if an expert witness feels that an important piece of information has not been revealed, he or she may request of the judge an opportunity to present evidence felt to be vital to the court's decision. In family court, this may well be permitted.

10. If asked about his or her fee, the witness should not be apologetic. Expert witnesses are paid for their time, not their support. Fees in court should be charged at the same hourly rate as fees for office visits.

It is a wise professional who reads as much as possible concerning courtroom etiquette and procedure before going on the witness stand. A valid evaluation and a valuable opinion could well be lost in attorney manipulation. Being prepared helps to assure that such damage is held to a minimum in the best interests of the child in a custody dispute. Several additional valuable courtroom tips are offered by Brodsky (1977), Gardner (1976), Hodges, (1986), MacHovec (1985), and Melton, Petrila, Poythress, and Slobogin (1987).

Testifying under Protest

Any therapist who has had any association with a case can be subpoenaed to testify. Sometimes a therapist is involved because a parent mentions to his or her attorney that he or she or a child was in therapy with the practitioner. Child therapists are particularly loath to testify because of confidentiality, which is controlled by the parent, and which can be damaged sufficiently to destroy benefits achieved by therapy. The child psychologist can request that the judge keep the child's welfare protected by avoiding testimony of information obtained from therapy sessions with the child. If that request is denied, the therapist can request that such evidence be given in chambers so that the parents will not be informed about the child's concerns.

SUMMARY

As psychologists become more aware of the opportunities to serve as expert witnesses, and are more willing to do so, a broadening involvement between psychology and the law can be expected. The increasing numbers of psychologists who have served as expert witnesses or in a consultation role with attorneys suggests that such interaction indeed has grown over the last decade (Kerr & Bray, 1982; Saks & Hastie, 1978; Sales, 1981). Judges appointed or elected to serve judicial roles in family matters now enter their jobs with broader backgrounds in psychology from their undergraduate training and in law school. It is probable that psychologists will be called upon in even greater numbers in the future to meet the ever-growing demands placed on the legal system, especially as they relate to family matters and children.

In the past, courts have understood little about family dynamics or child development; as a result, experts could be qualified from a wide range of backgrounds in the behavioral sciences. However, with the growing sophistication of attorneys and judges in family practice, experts will find it harder to qualify without true ability to field the sophisticated cross-examination coming from more knowledgeable attorneys, who are aware of the existence of the relevant body of literature and expect the experts also to be knowledgeable.

There exists a great need for training and continuing education programs to improve psychologists' preparation to meet the challenges most certainly to be presented by family court and child custody issues (as well as other forensic work). With the continually increasing divorce rates in the United States, and the increase in the numbers of cases where fathers succeed in winning custody, the likelihood of increased need for expert witnesses is great. Too few psychologists feel prepared to meet the demands placed on them by today's legal system. We must meet these demands in order to continue to be advocates for the best interests of children. Internship experiences and coursework need to be directed at this important and growing aspect of psychological service, lest we be considered negligent in meeting our moral and ethical standards of training and competence.

REFERENCES

American Psychological Association (APA). (1977). *Standards for providers of psychological services*. Washington, DC: Author.

American Psychological Association (APA). (1981). Ethical principles of psychologists. *American Psychologist, 36*, 633–638.

American Psychological Association (APA). (1985). *Standards for educational and psychological tests* (rev. ed.). Washington, DC: Author.

Ash, P., & Guyer, M. (1984). Court implementation of mental health professionals' recommendations in contested child custody and visitation cases. *Bulletin of the American Academy of Psychiatry and the Law, 12*, 137–147.

Atwell, A. E., Moore, U. S., Nielsen, E., & Levite, Z. (1984). Effects of joint custody on children. *Bulletin of the American Academy of Psychiatry and the Law, 12*, 149–157.

Awad, G.A. (1978). Basic principles in custody assessments. *Canadian Psychiatric Association Journal, 23*, 441–447.

Benedek, E. P. (1972). Child custody laws: Their psychiatric implications. *American Journal of Psychiatry, 129*, 326–328.

Blau, T. H. (1984). *The psychologist as expert witness*. New York: Wiley.

Brodsky, S. (1977). A mental health professional on the witness stand: A survival guide. In B. D. Sales (Ed.), *Psychology in the legal process* (pp. 269–276). New York: Spectrum.

Charnas, J. F. (1981). Practice trends in divorce related to child custody. *Journal of Divorce, 4*(4), 57–67.

Chasin, R., & Grunebaum, H. (1981). A model for evaluation in child custody disputes. *American Journal of Family Therapy, 9*, 43–49.

Clawar, S. S. (1984). How to determine whether a family report is scientific. *Conciliation Courts Review, 22*(2), 71–76.

Clingempeel, W. G., & Reppucci, N. D. (1982). Joint custody after divorce: Major issues and goals for research. *Psychological Bulletin, 91*, 102–127.

Denton, L. (1987, December). Expert testimony: Law and science. *APA Monitor*, p. 24.

Derdeyn, A. P. (1975). Child custody consultation. *American Journal of Orthopsychiatry, 45*, 791–801.

Felner, R. D., Terre, L., Goldfarb, A., Farber, S. S., Primavera, J., Bishop, T. A., & Abner, M. S. (1985). Party status of children during marital dissolution: Child preference and legal representation in custody decisions. *Journal of Clinical Child Psychology, 14*, 42–48.

Fine, S. (1980). Children in divorce, custody, and access situations: The contributions of the mental health professional. *Journal of Child Psychology and Psychiatry, 21*, 353–361.

Foster, H. H., & Freed, D. J. (1978). Life with father: 1978. *Family Law Quarterly, 11*, 321–342.

Gardner, R. A. (1976). *Psychotherapy with children of divorce*. New York: Jason Aronson.

Girdner, L. K. (1985). Strategies of conflict: Custody litigation in the United States. *Journal of Divorce, 9*(1), 1–15.

Goldstein, J., Freud, A., & Solnit, A. (1973). *Beyond the best interests of the child*. New York: Free Press.

Hodges, W. F. (1986). *Interventions for children of divorce: Custody, access, and psychotherapy*. New York: Wiley.

Irving, H. H., Benjamin, M., & Trocme, N. (1984). Shared parenting: An empirical analysis using a large data base. *Family Process, 23*, 561–569.

Kerr, N. L., & Bray, R. M. (Eds.). (1982). *The psychology of the courtroom*. New York: Academic Press.

Lewis, M., Feiring, C., & Weintraub, M. (1981). The father as a member of the child's social network. In M. E. Lamb (Ed.), *The role of the father in child development* (pp. 259–294). New York: Wiley.

MacHovec, F. (1985, October). Courtroom survival. *NASP Communique*, p. 8.

McDermott, J. F., Tseng, W., Char, W. F., & Fukunaga, C. S. (1978). Child custody decision making. *Journal of the American Academy of Child Psychiatry, 17*, 104–116.

Melton, G. B., Petrila, J., Poythress, N. G., & Slobogin, C. (1987). *Psychological evaluations for the courts: A handbook for mental health professionals and lawyers*. New York: Guilford Press.

National Conference of Commissioners on Uniform State Laws. (1971). Uniform marriage and divorce act. *Family Law Quarterly, 5*, 205–251.

Nizer, L. (1968). *My life in court*. New York: Pyramid.

Orthner, D. K., & Lewis, K. (1979). Evidence of single father competence in child rearing. *Family Law Quarterly, 13*, 27–47.

Poythress, N. G. (1980). Coping on the witness stand: Learned responses to "learned treatises." *Professional Psychology, 11*, 139–149.

Ramos, S. (1979). *The complete book of child custody*. New York: Putnam.

Reppucci, N. D. (1984). The wisdom of Solomon: Issues in child custody determination. In N. D. Reppucci, L. A. Weithorn, E. P. Mulrey, & J. Monahan (Eds.), *Children, mental health, and the law* (59–78). Beverly Hills, CA: Sage.

Saks, M. J., & Hastie, R. (1978). *Social psychology in court*. New York: Van Nostrand Reinhold.

Sales, B. D. (Ed.). (1981). *The trial process*. New York: Plenum Press.

Santrock, J. W., & Warshak, R. A. (1979). Father custody and social development in boys and girls. *Journal of Social Issues, 35*(4), 112–115.

Shapiro, D. L. (1984). *Psychological evaluation and expert testimony: A practical guide to forensic work*. New York: Van Nostrand Reinhold.

Warshak, R. A., & Santrock, J. W. (1983a). The impact of divorce in father-custody and mother-custody homes: The child's perspective. In L. A. Kurdek (Ed.), *New directions for child development: No. 19 Children and divorce* (pp. 29–46). San Francisco: Jossey-Bass.

Warshak, R. A., & Santrock, J. W. (1983b). Children of divorce: Impact of custody disposition on social development. In E. J. Callahan & K. A. McCluskey (Eds.), *Life-span developmental psychology: Nonnormative life events*. New York: Academic Press.

Watson, E. (1979, June 23). *Custody investigation as conducted by the Denver District Court Probation Department*. Paper presented at the Fourth Annual Child Custody Workshop, sponsored by Continuing Legal Education in Colorado, Inc., and the Interdisciplinary Committee on Child Custody, Keystone, CO.

Weiss, R. S. (1979). Issues in the adjudication of custody when parents separate. In G. Levinger & O. C. Moles (Eds.), *Divorce and separation: Context, causes, and consequences* (pp. 324–336). New York: Basic Books.

Weitzman, L. J., & Dixon, R. B. (1979). Child custody awards. *University of California–Davis Law Review, 12*, 473–521.

Woody, R. H. (1977). Behavioral science criteria in child custody determinations. *Journal of Marriage and Family Counseling, 3*, 11–17.

Ziskin, J. (1981). *Coping with psychiatric and psychological testimony* (3rd ed.). Marina del Rey, CA: Law and Psychology Press.

25

Measuring Student Motivation

PAMELA R. CLINKENBEARD
SUE C. MURPHY
University of Georgia

AN OVERVIEW OF THE CHAPTER

The purpose of this chapter is to present information on a number of instruments in use to measure academic-achievement-related motivation. It is expected that this information will be of use both to researchers interested in measuring motivation variables, and to school administrators and teachers who want to assess group motivation and evaluate programs where some change in motivation is a goal. Some of the instruments are available for purchase from test publishers; many are research instruments and are available for research use with permission of the authors.

Selection of Instruments

A number of sources were searched for mention of instruments that clearly or apparently measured motivation. These sources included *The Ninth Mental Measurements Yearbook* (Mitchell, 1985), *Tests in Print III* (Mitchell, 1983), *Tests* (Sweetland & Keyser, 1986), *Test Critiques* (Keyser & Sweetland, 1986), *Tests and Measurements in Child Development: Handbook II* (Johnson, 1976), *Directory of Unpublished Experimental Mental Measures* (Goldman & Osborne, 1985), *The ETS Test Collection Catalog* (Educational Testing Service, 1986), recent issues of the *Journal of Educational Measurement* and of *Educational and Psychological Measure-*ment, and recently published articles and books addressing achievement motivation. As test titles were collected, references to technical manuals or articles discussing the development of the test were investigated.

The final selection of the instruments discussed below was based on several criteria. First, the final version of the instrument had to be developed within the last 15 years, or used as a research instrument in a journal article published within the last 15 years. Second, the instrument must have been developed for, or used in research with, students below college age. Finally, there had to be some minimal technical information available (many unpublished motivation instruments do not provide validity, reliability, or norming information of any kind). Although our list is not exhaustive, it is a wide representation of motivation measures currently or recently in use in schools or in research on student motivation. It should be noted that most of the authors of these instruments caution the user that their instrument should only be used in research, or for group assessment, rather than for making educational decisions about individuals or for use in individual counseling.

Instrument Categories

The categorization of instruments, while somewhat arbitrary, was made along primarily theoretical lines (see Dweck & Elliott,

1983; Stipek, 1988). The "Measures of Need for Achievement" section describes instruments developed mostly by McClelland and his students (see Atkinson & Litwin, 1960; McClelland, Atkinson, Clark, & Lowell, 1953). The two "motive to achieve success" measures (the Thematic Apperception Test [TAT] and the Children's Apperception Test [CAT]), the test anxiety measures, and the resultant achievement motivation measures are theorectically interrelated. McClelland's scoring system uses the TAT (Murray, 1983) to measure the motive to achieve success (Mas), or the desire to approach achievement situations. Test anxiety instruments have been developed to measure the motive to avoid failure (Maf), or the desire to avoid achievement situations. Resultant achievement motivation instruments measure what is left—that is, Maf subtracted from Mas.

The "General Achievement Motivation Measures" section discusses instruments purporting to measure need for achievement or achievement motivation, but not directly tied to achievement motivation theory as outlined above. Some of these instruments are based on their own theories of achievement motivation (e.g., the Prestatie Motivatie Test); others are not based on any one theory, but are based on behavioral and teacher information (e.g., the Motivation Scale of the Scales for Rating the Behavioral Characteristics of Superior Students).

The "Personality Batteries" section describes major personality assessments that have one or more motivation subscales. In these cases, there is no separate theory of motivation guiding the construction of the motivation items; motivation is seen as one part of a theory of personality. These personality batteries have technical information available for their motivation-related subscales.

The "Intrinsic Motivation Measures" section describes instruments that assess desire to engage in learning activities for their own sake, rather than for some extrinsic reward or goal (see Stipek, 1988; White, 1959). The items on these measures tend to be highly classroom-oriented.

The "Causality Measures" section presents measures of locus of control and measures of attributions. These instruments assess beliefs about the causes of achievement outcomes: Locus of control makes the distinction between internal (one's own ability or effort) and external (teacher, the task) causes (see Lefcourt, 1976); attribution measures tend to offer four or more choices (ability, effort, task difficulty, luck) as to cause for a particular outcome (see Weiner, 1974). The relationship of these measures to motivation is that certain attributional belief patterns will make it more likely that a student will put forth continuing effort to achieve.

Finally, the section on "Measures of Cognitive/Affective Aspects of Motivation" describes instruments that assess students' beliefs or feelings about their own competence in the classroom. A student who believes that he or she is not good at schoolwork compared to classmates, or who feels like a failure, is not likely to be motivated to achieve, since achievement may appear to be impossible.

MEASURES OF NEED FOR ACHIEVEMENT

Thematic Apperception Test

The TAT is used with children aged 11 through adults. Its purpose, as McClelland et al. (1953) present it, is to measure "need for achievement" (nAch)—that is, themes that show a goal of "success in competition with some standard of excellence" (p. 110). In their samples in the early 1950s, men's nAch was in the domain of leadership capacity and intelligence, and women's use was in the domain of social acceptability. (The TAT was developed with college men, but has been used in research with many different groups.)

As a personality test, the TAT consists of 30 pictures or selected combinations thereof. As McClelland et al. (1953) standardized the procedure in motivation research, four pictures were projected on a screen, with four questions for each picture asking about the people and the situation. Subjects were instructed to use the questions to help make up a story about each picture for a "test of creative imagination." Interrater reliability of this format was reported as .95; for a 6-month score–rescore, it was .95. Inexperienced raters usually correlated .90 with experienced raters after scoring the protocols of 90–120 subjects. Corrected alternate-form reliability was .65; this figure was highly affected by the situation at time of testing.

Validity is complex and subject to situational factors. Correlations with grades, Scholastic Aptitude Test scores, or a combination ranged from .39 to .51. With a different set of pictures, the correlation with grades was .05. In another study, the TAT significantly discriminated between subjects with high grades and those with low grades.

The TAT is scored for several different types of "achievement imagery" (AI). AI must be present; then several other interdependent subcategories of achievement activity are scored. The nAch score is the algebraic sum of the scores from the four stories. Responses are scored by classifications of response elements by objective criteria, rather than by clinical judgments, as in other uses of the TAT. McClelland et al. (1953) recommend that if one wants to assess nAch in order to correlate it with other variables, more pictures should be used and perhaps fewer themes should be scored.

Children's Apperception Test

The CAT (Bellak & Bellak, 1980), for children aged 3–10 years, is a projective method of describing personality. It was developed as an alternative to the TAT for younger children. When used in motivation research, it is scored for motives such as need for achievement.

The CAT is individually administered orally by a psychologist trained in its use. Administration takes about 30 minutes. Ten scenes are presented showing animal figures in human social settings. The examiner asks the child to tell a story about what is going on in the picture. Stories are rated on the presence or absence of 10 themes; those most pertinent to motivation are (1) main needs and drives of the hero, and (2) anxieties.

The CAT is not "scored." The presence or absence of thematic elements is recorded. The CAT does not have, and does not claim to have, psychometric precision; hence, no technical information is provided. Its use is primarily clinical.

Test Anxiety Scale for Children

The Test Anxiety Scale for Children (TASC) is a self-report instrument to measure students' propensity to experience anxiety in evaluative situations (Saranson, Davidson, Lighthall, Waite, & Ruebush, 1960). It was developed for use with elementary-age students (but has been used with older students), and consists of 30 questions read aloud to a class; the examiner waits until all children answer (by circling "yes" or "no") before reading the next item. All "yes" answers indicate anxiety. A sample item is "Do you think you worry more about school than other children?" A Lie scale, to locate subjects who engage in "defensive distortion," is also available.

Hill and Sarason (1966) note that over time, anxiety scores become increasingly and negatively related to both intellectual (measured by IQ) and achievement performance. They report correlations between the TASC and IQ ranging from −.31 to −.46, and correlations between the TASC and achievement ranging from −.36 to −.51. Test–retest reliability across 2 years ranged from .33 for younger students to .58 for older students. For further research on the TASC, see Nicholls (1976).

Test Anxiety Scale for Children—Revised

The Test Anxiety Scale for Children-Revised (TASC-Rx; Feld & Lewis, 1969) is a revision of the TASC that controls for response bias and multidimensionality; items are phrased positively (the reverse of the TASC items), so that a "yes" response indicates absence of anxiety. Like the TASC, it contains 30 items to be read to the class and answered by circling a "yes" or a "no." A sample item is "Do you feel relaxed while you are taking a test?" A factor analysis found four subscales in the TASC-Rx: Somatic Signs, Signs of Anxiety, Test Anxiety, and Poor Self-Evaluation.

Research on the TASC-Rx has been conducted with children of various races and sociocultural backgrounds. A strong relationship between it and reading and math achievement test scores was demonstrated in 4th, 8th, and 11th grades. For more information, see Hill (1980).

Test Comfort Index

The Test Comfort Index (TCI) was developed for quick, easy assessment of test anxiety in classrooms for diagnostic and research purposes (Harnisch, Hill, & Fyans, 1980). TCI items are selected from the TASC-Rx; the seven items selected are primarily from the Test Anxiety items on the TASC-Rx. A sample item is "Do you feel relaxed before taking a test?" The TCI was normed on more than 600 students in Illinois in the 4th, 8th, and 11th grades. For more information, see Hill and Wigfield (1984).

State–Trait Anxiety Inventory

The purpose of the State–Trait Anxiety Inventory (STAI) is to measure both transitory and persistent anxiety (Spielberger, Gorsuch, & Lushene, 1970). The STAI can be used with high school students through adults. It has two scales of 20 items each. The A-State scale measures feelings of anxiety at a particular moment in time (transitory). The A-Trait scale measures persistent or generalized anxiety experienced over time. Items on the A-State scale require one of four intensity responses ranging from "not at all" to "very much so." Items on the A-Trait scale require a frequency response ranging from "almost never" to "almost always."

Internal consistency (Cronbach's alpha), ranged from .89 to .91 for A-Trait and from .86 to .95 for A-State. Test–retest reliabilities (ranging from 1 hour to 104 days) for A-Trait were .65 to .86, and for A-State were .16 to .62. The authors note that the lower test–retest correlations for A-State contributed to its construct validity. In a validity study with 126 college women, A-Trait correlated with the Institute for Personality and Ability Testing's Anxiety Scale .75 and .80 with the Manifest Anxiety Scale. Validity has been demonstrated with a wide variety of studies.

State–Trait Anxiety Inventory for Children

The State–Trait Anxiety Inventory for Children (STAIC) is a downward extension of the STAI for fourth through sixth grades (Spielberger, Edwards, Montouri, & Lushene, 1970). Its purpose is to measure both transitory and persistent anxiety. Like the STAI, the STAIC has two scales of 20 items each, an A-State scale and an A-Trait scale. For each item, subjects select one of three choices regarding how they feel.

The STAIC was normed on black and white males and females in fourth through sixth grades. For A-State, internal consistency (Cronbach's alpha) was .82 and .87 for boys and girls, respectively; for A-Trait, it was .78 and .81, respectively. Test–retest reliabilities for A-Trait were .65 and .71, respectively; for A-State, they were .31 and .47, respectively. With regard to concurrent validity, both A-State and A-Trait were significantly correlated with locus of control as measured by the Nowicki–Strickland Locus of Control Scale, with higher anxiety related to more externality ($r = .31–.36$). A-Trait correlated .75 with the Children's Manifest Anxiety Scale and .63 with the General Anxiety Scale for Children. For recent research using the STAIC, see Nunn (1988).

Resultant Achievement Motivation Test

The Resultant Achievement Motivation Test (RAM), normed on college students (Mehrabian, 1968), has also been used with high school students. Its purpose is to discriminate those individuals whose motive to achieve is stronger than their motive to avoid failure, from individuals whose motive to avoid failure is stronger than their motive to achieve. "Resultant achievement motivation" is defined as motive to avoid failure subtracted from motive to achieve. The RAM has separate Male and Female scales with 34 items each. Possible responses to each item range on a 7-point scale from "very strong agreement" to "very strong disagreement."

Test–retest reliability for the Male scale after 10 weeks was .78. For the Female scale, the correlation was .72. With regard to validity, correlations between the Male scale and other motivation instruments were as follows: with the TAT nAch score, .28; with the Test Anxiety Questionnaire (TAQ), which measures motive to avoid failure, −.16; with TAT − TAQ, .29; and with the Rotter Internal–External Locus of Control Scale, .64. Correlations between the Female scale and the same instruments were .17, −.11, .13, and .41, respectively.

For more information and research with the RAM, see Mehrabian (1969) and Brinkman (1973).

Resultant Achievement Motivation Test (Short Form)

A modified version of the RAM, though developed on college students, has been used with younger students. Its purpose, like that of the RAM, is to discriminate individuals whose motive to achieve is stronger than their motive to avoid failure, from individuals whose motive to avoid failure is stronger than their motive to achieve. The short form contains 26 of the original 34 items from the Male and Female scales, with responses on a 9-point scale.

Schultz and Pomerantz (1974), for their modification of the short form, found an internal consistency of .55 and subscale reliabilities ranging from .52 to .57. The same version of the RAM short form was correlated with the Bass Task Orientation Scale ($r = .20$, $p < .05$) and with the Jackson Achievement Scale ($r = .62$). It was correlated .40 with the Debilitating Anxiety subscale of the Prestatie Motivatie Test; .41 with the Comprehensive Test of Basic Skills; .29 with IQ; and .48 with grades.

GENERAL ACHIEVEMENT MOTIVATION MEASURES

Academic Achievement Motivation Scale

The Academic Achievement Motivation Scale (AAM; Lehrer & Hieronymous, 1977), developed for junior high students, is an objective measure of academic achievement motivation designed to investigate the two subcategories of "achievement via conformance" and "achievement via independence." Items are drawn from the California Psychological Inventory, the Edwards Personal Preference Schedule, the Kuder Vocational Interest Inventory, and the Michigan State M-Scales. Part I contains seven biographical questions; Part II, 59 questions forming the actual AAM; Part III, 93 questions from the Children's Report of Parental Behavior Inventory. There are four kinds of items on the actual AAM: (1) trait-related sentences rated "like me," "somewhat like me," or "not like me"; (2) triads in which the student has to choose the item most closely related to his or her interests; (3) items requiring a choice of one of two behavior patterns; and (4) vocabulary items. Items were judged by a panel of educators and psychologists in terms of academic achievement motivation, and each item used had a mean rating of 3.6 or more on a 5-point scale.

The AAM was normed on eigth-graders in southeast Iowa. Split-half reliability was .92. With regard to validity, in a multiple-regression analysis, "achievement via independence" contributed significantly to the final multiple R for the composite score of the Iowa Test of Basic Skills.

Achievement Motivation Test

The Achievement Motivation Test, an objective measure of school motivation (Russell, 1969), is appropriate for students in all secondary grades and possibly for younger students as well. Most research has been done with ninth-graders. It is made up of 30 items with yes–no responses drawn from the context of school life. A sample item is "Would you ever enter a contest with other students knowing you had a very slight chance of winning?"

The Achievement Motivation Test was normed on rural ninth-grade students in Appalachian Kentucky and on urban Kentucky high school students. Split-half reliability was .95. It correlated from .60 to .72 with various total scores on achievement test batteries; it significantly discriminated between volunteers and nonvolunteers for an academic contest. For research using the Achievement Motivation Test, see Rowley (1974).

Animal Crackers: A Test of Motivation to Achieve

Animal Crackers (Adkins & Ballif, 1972) was designed to measure the achievement motivation (particularly academic motivation) of preschool through first-grade students. It gives six component scores: School Enjoyment, Self-Confidence, Purposiveness, Instrumental Activity, Self-Evaluation, and Total. There are 60 items (12 per component). Individual administration takes 30–40 minutes, and group administration 45–60 minutes. The test employs an "objective–projective" technique: Each item is a pair of identical animals, where descriptions of the animals' different behavior or attitudes show differences in motivation. The child selects the animal that likes what the child likes or does what the child does.

Animal Crackers was normed on a national sample of students in kindergarten and first grade from 32 states (there are no preschool norms). For internal consistency, Kuder–Richardson 20 correlations ranged, for subtests, from .69 to .92; for the total test they ranged from, .94 to .98. Content validity was claimed through construction of items according to a general theory of motivation. Correlations with teacher ratings were .45 for kindergarten and .23 for first-grade. For research using Animal Crackers, see Ziraba (1976).

Classroom Behavior Inventory

The Classroom Behavior Inventory (CBI; Cicirelli et al., 1971) was designed to measure children's motivation to achieve in school learning and can be used in first through third grades. It was originally developed for a Head Start evaluation. It assumes that teachers can observe and judge motivation based on classroom performance and behavior. Motivation is operationalized as a child's investment of energy, effort, and attention in attempting to learn, to attain higher goals, to compete with himself or herself and others, and to master classroom tasks. Teachers rate students on a continuum on 22 subjective items, using a 5-point scale from "never" to "almost always." A sample item is "Is he easily distracted by things going on around him?"

The CBI was "field-tested with experienced teachers" (p. 387). Norms are available for disadvantaged groups in first through third grades, including black, white, Mexican-American, and other students. The interrater coefficient of concordance was .65; the Kuder–Richardson 20 internal consistency was .95. Correlations of the CBI with California Achievement Test subtests ranged from .45 to .63. For a disadvantaged

group, correlations with achievement tests ranged from .45 to .54. Cole (1974) found correlations with various achievement test scores ranging from .20 to .32, and a correlation with self-concept of .21.

Junior Index of Motivation

The Junior Index of Motivation (JIM; Frymier, 1970) was developed to measure general academic motivation in young people (primarily junior high school students). It assumes that motivation to do well in school comes primarily from within and is rooted in personality, values, and curiosity. The JIM is a paper-and-pencil measure taking about 30 minutes. It consists of 80 statements (30 of which are fillers); responses range from –2 to +2 (with no 0 response), meaning slight or strong agreement or disagreement. Sample items are "Most people would like school better if teachers did not give grades"; "Not many people in the world are really kind." The items cover three general areas: Personality, Values, and Curiosity.

The JIM was normed on students in seventh through ninth grades in various states and on Ohio college students. Split-half reliabilities with various groups ranged from .63 to .83. Test–retest reliability was .70. The JIM significantly discriminated between students rated, by teachers, as being very motivated or having low motivation. It also significantly discriminated between high and low achievers on the Sequential Tests of Educational Progress (STEP) tests (controlling for ability). For predictive validity, it significantly discriminated between seventh-graders who did and did not later attend college (Frymier, Henning, Henning, West, & Norris, 1975). The items are not very *school*-oriented, and the language is a bit dated.

Motivational Checklist

The Motivational Checklist (Kowalski, Stipek, & Daniels, 1987) was developed to help teachers in first through sixth grades become better diagnosticians of the variety of motivational patterns and problems in the elementary classroom. The checklist is for teachers to complete on students. Descriptive statements require responses on a 5-point scale from "not at all true" to "very true"; the 36 items are grouped into seven categories (Intrinsically Motivated, Self-Protective, Alienated, Extrinsically Motivated, Helpless, Unchallenged, Anxious). A sample items is "Is not interested in learning anything that is not required."

Subscale reliabilities range from .65 to .89. The checklist is available from Kowalski at the University of West Florida's Educational Research and Development Center.

Prestatie Motivatie Test

The Prestatie Motivatie Test (PMT; Hermans, 1970) was developed for college students and adults, but has been used with younger students. (Some items require rewording with younger students.) It measures characteristics that distinguish high from low achievers; items in 10 areas were drawn from the literature on personality and motivation in an attempt to compile a heterogeneous group. The PMT has 29 Guttman-scaled items with Likert-format responses to each stem. It is somewhat academically oriented. A sample item is "When doing something difficult:"; responses for this item range from "I give it up very quickly" to "I usually see it through."

The PMT was originally normed on males in colleges in the Netherlands. Kuder–Richardson 20 reliabilities of .85 and .88 (in neutral and achievement-oriented research conditions) have been demonstrated. The PMT was significantly correlated with performance tasks under achievement conditions, but not under neutral conditions. It was correlated .20 with the TAT in achievement conditions and .13 with the TAT in neutral conditions. For use of the PMT with young adolescents, see Prawat (1976); for more information on validity, see Morris and Snyder (1978).

Scales for Rating the Behavioral Characteristics of Superior Students, Motivation Scale

The Scales for Rating the Behavioral Characteristics of Superior Students (Renzulli, Smith, White, Callahn, & Hartmen, 1976) were developed to provide objective checklists to help teachers identify students for gifted programs. The system was developed with children in fourth through sixth grades but is appropriate for all school-age children. The Motivation Scale contains nine descriptive items on which a teacher rates the student from "seldon or never" to "almost always." A sample item is "Needs little external motivation to follow through in work that initially excites him."

Interrater reliability was .85; the coefficient of stability was .91. Items were chosen from a literature review on the characteristics of gifted children; each item had to have been stressed in three different studies. The scale significantly discriminated between a gifted group and an average group. The Motivation Scale correlated .36 with intelligence, and from .42 to .60 with various achievement scores.

Work and Family Orientation Questionnaire

The Work and Family Orientation Questionnaire (WOFO; Helmreich & Spence, 1979) is a measure of achievement motivation (conceived of as a set of related components influenced by outside concerns and by masculinity–femininity), as well as a measure of attitudes toward family and career. It was developed for college students and adults, but has been used in research with high school students.

The WOFO is a self-report instrument; the motivation section consists of statements with possible responses ranging on a 5-point scale from "strongly agree" to "strongly disagree." Subscales include Work, Mastery, and Competitiveness.

The WOFO has been normed on various groups, including a large high school group. Cronbach's alpha for the three subscales ranged from .61 to .76. It significantly discriminated between groups assumed to be different on the achievement motivation subscales—for example, between scientists, college athletes, and other college students. West Point cadets scored higher on all three subscales than university students (Adams, Priest, & Prince, 1985). For more research using the WOFO, see Hollinger and Fleming (1985).

PERSONALITY BATTERIES

School Motivation Analysis Test

The School Motivation Analysis Test (SMAT; Krug, Cattell, & Sweney, 1976) is a downward extension of the Motivation Analysis Test for ages 12–17. It assesses 10 dynamic traits—6 primary drives and 4 acquired interest patterns. It is based on Cattell's "dynamic calculus" model of motivation; its purpose is to measure motivations and interests in adolescents. The SMAT is an objective paper-and-pencil test with 190 items. The Uses subtest has 45 items; respondents select one of two alternatives regarding how to use a resource. Paired Choices, 45 items, requires selecting one of two words that goes better with a key word. The 100-item Knowledge subtest is multiple-choice. The entire test requires 50–60 minutes to administer. The handbook contains scoring instructions for the 20 Primary scores, 20 Secondary scores, and 5 Derivative scores.

The standardization sample varied by geography, community size, race/ethnicity, and occupation of principal wage earner in the family. Test-retest reliability after 1 week ranged from .39 to .99. Internal consistency (Kuder–Richardson 21) for the five Derivative scores ranged from .86 to .94. With regard to validity, linear regression analysis showed that adding the Integrated Motivation scores to a battery increased efficiency in predicting school achievement. Incremental validity was greatest for reading and least for mathematics. For more information on the SMAT, see Child (1984).

California Psychological Inventory

The California Psychological Inventory (CPI; Gough, 1975) predicts how people will behave in certain circumstances of social interaction. It assesses not traits, but "folk concepts" of social behavior. It is appropriate for ages 13 and older. Two of the scales measure motivation to achieve: Achievement via Conformance (Ac) and Achievement via Independence (Ai). The CPI is self-administered with no time limit and is a paper-and-pencil measure. There are 480 true–false items in the entire CPI; the Ac scale has 38 items and the Ai scale has 32 items.

Test–retest reliability after 1 year was .69 for Ac and .63 for Ai. Ac was correlated with high school grades (.35–.40); Ai was correlated with college grades (.19–.44). For more information on the CPI, see Gough (1968); see also Waddell (1984).

Orientation and Motivation Inventory

The Orientation and Motivation Inventory (OMI; Youniss, Lorr, & Stefic, 1979) is intended to measure "preferred ways people have of thinking about, orienting, and responding to the world around them," (p. 555) which are assumed to represent underlying motivations. One scale title is Achievement-Motivated vs. Nonambitious. The OMI is appropriate for late high school students or older. There are 20 true–false items per scale; administration time is 30–45 minutes. The 12 scales intercorrelate to produce four "higher-order" factors: Status Seeking, People Seeking, Experience Seeking, and Seeking Understanding.

The OMI was normed on high school and college females and males. Internal-consistency reliability ranged from .67 to .84 for subscales, computed separately for females and males. Test–retest reliability ranged from .69 to .91 across 3 weeks. The OMI is significantly correlated with similar self-report measures and with student self-ratings.

INTRINSIC MOTIVATION MEASURES

Children's Academic Intrinsic Motivation Inventory

The Children's Academic Intrinsic Motivation Inventory (CAIMI), developed for fourth through eighth grades (Gottfried, 1985), measures students' academic intrinsic motivation for school learning across four subject areas, as well as general orientation toward school. It is a self-report measure with 44 main questions, for a total of 122 items in five scales: Reading, Math, Science,

Social Studies, and General School Orientation. A sample question is "I enjoy learning things in: reading, math, social studies, science" (four separate items). Possible responses range from "strongly agree" to "strongly disagree" along a 5-point Likert scale.

The CAIMI was normed, in various studies, on black and white children in fourth through eighth grades at public and private schools. Internal-consistency reliability ranged from .83 to .93. Test–retest reliability after 2 months ranged from .66 to .76. With regard to validity, correlations with the motivational subscales of the Harter Scale of Instrinsic versus Extrinsic Orientation ranged from .17 ($p < .05$) to .64. The CAIMI was significantly correlated with achievement (with IQ partialed out): The Math scale was significantly correlated with math achievement, and the Reading scale was significantly correlated with language and science achievement. The CAIMI was significantly and negatively related to academic anxiety.

Children's Academic Intrinsic Motivation Inventory—Primary

The CAIMI-Primary (Gottfried, 1985) is a downward extension of the CAIMI for first through third grades. It measures students' academic intrinsic motivation for school learning in two subject areas (reading and math), as well as general orientation toward school. The items are the same as those on the CAIMI (though reading and math only are assessed), but the language is sometimes simplified. Possible responses to each item are "very true," "a little true," and "not true."

The CAIMI-Primary was first normed on white first- and second-graders (Gottfried, 1985). Research is being conducted with children in first through third grades from a variety of ethnic backgrounds. Internal-consistency reliability ranged from .80 to .88 across scales. Correlations with the Woodcock–Johnson Psychoeducational Battery and with teacher ratings of student achievement ranged from .27 to .61.

Intrinsic Intellectual Motivation Scale

The Intrinsic Intellectual Motivation Scale (IIM; Lloyd & Barenblatt, 1984) is designed for high school students and measures intrinsic intellectual motivation, defined as the tendency to pursue intellectual tasks for their own sake. The IIM has 44 items with Likert scale responses. A sample item is "When using the encyclopedia, I find myself reading articles that have nothing to do with the subjects I am looking up."

Tenth-grade samples were used for reliability data; internal-consistency reliability ranged from .85 to .90. A correlation of .04 with the Need for Achievement subtest of the Edwards Personal Preference Schedule indicated that the IIM measures a different construct from need for achievement. A partial correlation for IIM and achievement (controlling for IQ) was significant. IIM was second only to IQ in proportion of variance accounting for achievement (Bergin, 1987).

Scale of Intrinsic versus Extrinsic Orientation in the Classroom

The Scale of Intrinsic versus Extrinsic Orientation in the Classroom was developed for third through ninth grades (Harter, 1981) and taps children's orientation toward learning and mastery. There are five dimensions within the scale: (1) Preference for Challenge versus Easy Work; (2) Curiosity/Interest versus Teacher Approval; (3) Independent Mastery versus Dependence on Teacher; (4) Independent Judgment versus Reliance on Teacher Judgment; and (5) Internal versus External Criteria for Success and Failure. There are six items per scale (30 total), with a structured-alternative format in which the child first chooses the description of the "kid most like me" (of two choices), and then indicates whether the description is "sort of true" or "really true" for him or her.

The scale was normed on New York and California students. Internal consistency (Kuder–Richardson 20) on average was .80; for the subscales, it ranged from .54 to .84. Test–retest reliability after 9 months and 1 year ranged from .48 to .63 across subscales; for a 5-month interval, it ranged from .58 to .76. For validity, the average loading for the five factors was .58. Predictive validity for the Preference for Challenge subscale was .72. The scale shows systematic developmental trends. For research using the scale, see Silon and Harter (1985).

CAUSALITY MEASURES: LOCUS OF CONTROL AND ATTRIBUTIONS

Nowicki–Strickland Locus of Control Scale

The Nowicki–Strickland Locus of Control Scale (sometimes referred to as the Children's Nowicki–Strickland Internal–External Control Scale) measures generalized locus of control in 3rd through 12th grades (Nowicki & Strickland, 1973). It contains 40 questions written at a fifth-grade reading level in an agree–disagree format. A higher score reflects a more external locus.

The Nowicki–Strickland was normed on over 1,000 mostly white children in a Southern suburban county. Internal consistency ranged from .63 to .81 (increasing with the age of the children). Test–retest reliability after 6 weeks ranged from .63 to .71. The Nowicki–Strickland correlations with the Intellectual Achievement Responsibility Questionnaire (IAR) ranged from .31 to .71; its correlation with the Bialer–Cromwell was .41. For more information, see Weisz and Stipek (1982).

Intellectual Achievement Responsibility Questionnaire

The IAR was developed for third grade and above to measure children's beliefs in "reinforcement responsibility" in intellectual/academic achievement situations—that is, the amount of control children feel they have over rewards and punishments in those situations (Crandall, Katkovsky, & Crandall, 1965). It gives scores for Internality for Success (I+) and Internality for Failure (I–). Of 34 forced-choice items, there are equal numbers of positive and negative events. A sample item is "When you forget something you heard in class, is it (a) because the teacher didn't explain it very well, or (b) because you didn't try very hard to remember?" External response options are limited to parents, teachers, and peers (not luck, fate, etc.), because it was felt that these would be the most salient externals to children. The IAR should be given individually and orally to students below sixth grade.

The IAR was normed on students from a variety of types of schools and socioeconomic status levels, and in 3rd through 6th grades and 8th, 10th, and 12th grades. Split-half reliability ranged from .54 to .60 (based on the correlation between eight and nine items within the I+ and the I– items). Test–retest correlations ranged from .47 to .74. Correlations between I+ and I– event items ranged from .11 to .43. The authors recommend not using total score, since I+ and I– items seem to measure different constructs. For more information, see Bauer (1975).

Intellectual Achievement Responsibility Questionnaire— Modified

A modified version of the IAR was developed to measure locus of control in adolescents (Lifshitz & Ramot, 1978). Of the original 34 IAR items, 15 were changed from school activities to work and social interactions by altering the wording. The 34 items are clustered into three groups: Intellectual Achievement, Social Interactions, and Work.

Reliability of the subscales ranged from .25 to .35. Correlations of the intellectual achievement items with parental locus of control orientations ranged from –.22 to .32.

Locus of Control Inventory for Three Achievement Domains

The Locus of Control Inventory for Three Achievement Domains (LOCITAD), for ages 12 and up, assesses locus of control orientation in three achievement domains: Intellectual, Social, and Physical (Bradley, Stuck, Coop, & White, 1977). Items in each of the three domains (48 total) are answered with a yes or no. Half the items refer to successful outcomes and the other half to unsuccessful outcomes.

The LOCITAD was normed on students aged 12–18; subscale intercorrelations ranged from .44 to .57. Internal consistency (Kuder–Richardson 20) ranged from .52 for the Physical subscale to .75 for the total scale. Correlations with the IAR ranged from .45 to .78; correlations with the Nowicki–Strickland ranged from .43 to .49. For more information, see Omizo, Omizo, and Michael (1987).

The Multidimensional Measure of Children's Perceptions of Control

The Multidimensional Measure of Children's Perceptions of Control (Connell, 1985) measures children's understanding of the locus of the cause for success and failure outcomes. This measure, for third through ninth graders, assesses three dimensions of perceptions of control (Internal, Powerful Others, and Unknown) within three behavioral domains (Cognitive, Social, and Physical). Success and failure outcomes are assessed separately, and general items are also included. A sample item is "If I want to get good grades in school, it's up to me to do it"; the child responds on a 4-point scale from "not at all true" to "very true." There are 48 items on the scale.

Reliability estimates with coefficient alpha ranged from .43 to .70, with ¾ of the subscales above .60. Test–retest data after 9 months from a New York sample ranged from .30–.48; for a California sample after 17 months, the range was .25–.50. For validity in the cognitive domain, correlations with achievement test scores and teacher ratings were in the low to moderate significance range. Connell (1985) presents detailed information on validity estimates for the Cognitive, Social, and Physical domains.

Multidimensional–Multiattributional Causality Scale

The Multidimensional–Multiattributional Causality Scale (MMCS; Lefcourt, von Baeyer, Ware, & Cox, 1979) is designed to measure goal-specific locus of control (in Achievement and Affiliation domains). It is appropriate for high-achieving high school students (it was developed for college use). For both Affiliation and Achievement, there are 24 Likert-type scale items (12 success and 12 failure statements). Responses range from 0 ("disagree") to 4 ("agree"). The items are divided evenly among four possible attributions. The externality score can range from 0 to 96; any specific attribution can range from 0 to 24.

For internal consistency, Cronbach's alpha ranged from .58 to .81. Spearman–Brown split-half correlations ranged from .61 to .76. Test–retest reliability ranged from .50 to .70.

Correlations between the MMCS and the Rotter Internal–External Scale ranged from .23 to .62. With the Crowne–Marlow Need for Approval scale, the MMCS correlated −.33 for Achievement items and .01 for Affiliation items (evidence that it is not biased due to social desirability). Factorial validity was demonstrated with a sample of academically gifted high school students (Powers, Douglas, & Choroszy, 1983).

Preschool and Primary Nowicki–Strickland Internal–External Control Scale

The Preschool and Primary Nowicki–Strickland Internal–External Control Scale (PPNS-IE; Nowicki & Duke, 1974) was developed to measure generalized locus of control in preschool and primary-age children (4–8 years). There are 26 items in cartoon format, with an additional 8 social desirability items; children answer yes or no to each item.

Test–retest reliability after 6 weeks was .79. The correlation of the PPNS-IE with the Nowicki–Strickland was .78; its correlation with achievement (Iowa Test of Basic Skills) was significant for females ($r = -.34$ to $-.45$). For more information, see Weisz and Stipek (1982).

Rotter Internal–External Control Scale

The Rotter Scale (Rotter, 1966) was developed for adolescents to adults and measures generalized locus of control—the extent to which individuals believe they are internally or externally controlled. There are 29 items, 6 of which are filler items. Responses require a choice between internal and external alternatives. Higher scores reflect greater externality.

Internal consistency ranged from .69 to .73 for combined-sex samples. Test–retest reliability (1-week to 2-month intervals) ranged from .49 to .83. A recent study of construct validity (Marsh & Richards, 1987) indicates multidimensionality (five to six distinguishable factors) rather than the unidimensionality proposed by the author.

Stanford Preschool
Internal–External Scale

The Stanford Preschool Internal–External Scale (SPIES) was developed to measure locus of control in preschool (Mischel, Zeiss, & Zeiss, 1974) and kindergarten (Chartier, Lankford, & Ainley, 1976) children. It is a forced-choice instrument, with 14 items asking about events with successful or unsuccessful outcomes.

The SPIES was normed on 211 children aged 3–5 years. Test–retest reliability across a 2- to 3-week interval averaged .59; for children in first through third grades, it ranged from .36 to .81. Split-half reliabilities were .14 and .20 for the subscales (significant at the .05 level). The correlation between the SPIES and the Bialer Scale for Children was .18. For more information, see Bachrach and Peterson (1976).

Survey of Achievement Responsibility

The Survey of Achievement Responsibility (SOAR; Ryckman, Sprague, & Peckham, 1985) assesses attributions for success and failure in Language Arts, Math/Science, and Physical Education domains for students in 4th through 12 grades. It consists of 40 items—20 success outcome items and 20 "mirror" failure outcome items. There are eight success and failure items each for Language Arts and for Math/Science, and four success and four failure items for Physical Education. Each item presents four causal options: effort, ability, task difficulty, and luck.

Internal consistency (alpha coefficients) for the Language Arts and Math/Science scales ranged from .39 to .75; test–retest reliability ranged from .44 to .75. For recent research using the SOAR, see Ryckman and Peckham (1987).

Tel Aviv Locus of Control Scale

The Tel Aviv Locus of Control Scale was developed to measure locus of control for students in fourth through eighth grades (Milgram & Milgram, 1975). It assesses across three dimensions: time, content, and success–failure orientation. There are 48 items overall, 24 for the Past scale and 24 for the Future scale. Half of the items in each of these scales (12) refer to successful outcomes and half to unsuccessful outcomes. Each scale's items are divided into six loci: teacher and academics, parents and siblings, and familiar and unfamiliar same-age peers.

The Tel Aviv scale was normed on 298 children from five schools in Tel Aviv. Split-half reliability ranged from .31 to .67 for the Past scale and from .74 to .93 for the Future scale. The correlation between children in fourth through sixth grades and children in seventh and eighth grades was .84, indicating consistency across grade level. It was found that the assumption of responsibility rose with age, and that the Past scale was more valid than the Future scale.

MEASURES OF COGNITIVE AND AFFECTIVE ASPECTS OF MOTIVATION

Motivational Orientation Scales

These Motivational Orientation Scales (Nicholls, Patashnick, & Nolen, 1985) measure students' personal goals in school. Research on the scales has looked at their relationship to scales measuring students' views of the purposes of schooling and students' perceptions of the causes of school success. The original version of the Motivational Orientation Scales, developed for adolescents, included subscales for Avoidance of Work, Ego and Social Orientation, and Task Orientation. A sample item for Task Orientation is "I feel most successful if something I learned really makes sense." Subscales of the related Purposes of Schooling Scale include Wealth and Status, Commitment to Society, Understanding the World, and Achievement Motivation.

Coefficient alphas for the Motivational Orientation subscales ranged from .68 to .89. For more research using these scales, see Nicholls, Cheung, Lauer, and Patashnick (in press) and Nicholls (1989).

Self-Perception Profile for Children

Formerly the Perceived Competence Scale for Children (Harter, 1982), the Self-Perception Profile for Children (Harter, 1985) assesses children's sense of competence across different domains: Scholastic Competence, Social Acceptance, Athletic Competence, Physical Appearance, Behavioral Conduct, and Global Self-Worth. It can be used with students in the third through sixth grades. The format is one of structured alternatives: The child chooses one of two descriptions as "most like me," then indicates "sort of true for me" or "really true for me"; there are 36 items, 6 for each domain. The profile is group administered.

Although the original version was normed on students in the third through sixth grades from four states in three different regions of the country, the psychometric information presented in the most recent manual was based on four samples drawn from Colorado. Approximately 90% of the nearly 1500 subjects were Caucasion, ranging from lower-middle to upper-middle class.

Internal consistency reliability for the 6 subscales ranged from .71 to .86. Test–retest reliability was not reported for the 36-item version, but ranged from .69 to .87 (3- to 9-month intervals) for the earlier 28-item version. Factor loadings ranged for .33 to .82, but may have varied from sample to sample.

Other versions available from the author include: an adolescent version with 3 additional subscales (Romantic Appeal, Close Friendship, and Job Competence); a 13-domain college version; a 12-domain adult version; pictorial versions, one for preschool/kindergarten and another for first/second grade; and special versions for mentally retarded and learning disabled children. For more information, see Silon and Harter (1985).

Perception of Ability Scale for Students

Formerly the Student's Perception of Ability Scale (Boersma, Chapman, & Maguire, 1979), the Perception of Ability Scale for Students (PASS) is designed to assess academic self-concept, or feelings and attitudes about school performance, in five academic areas: reading, spelling, language arts, arithmetic, and printing/writing. It is appropriate for children in second through sixth grades.

The PASS has 70 forced-choice, yes–no items covering six subscales: Perception of

General Ability, Perception of Arithmetic Ability, General School Satisfaction, Perception of Reading and Spelling Ability, Perception of Penmanship and Neatness (all 12 items each), and Confidence in Academic Ability (10 items).

The PASS was normed on Canadian and New Zealand elementary students. Internal-consistency reliability was .92. The median Cronbach's alpha for the subscales was .80. Test–retest reliability (after 4–6 weeks) was .83, with the subscale median .77. Intercorrelations between total and subscale scores and the Piers–Harris Self-Concept Scale ranged from –.03 to .08, providing evidence that the PASS does discriminate more than general self-concept. Its correlation with grades was .49. For more information, see Chapman and Boersma (1986).

Self-Concept of Academic Ability

The Self-Concept of Academic Ability Scale, designed for junior high school students, assesses academic self-concept (Brookover, Thomas, & Paterson, 1964). Parallel forms assess general self-concept of ability, and specific self-concept of ability in each of four subjects: arithmetic, English, social studies, and science. The format is an eight-item Guttman scale multiple-choice questionnaire, with responses along a 5-point continuum.

The Self-Concept of Academic Ability was normed on over 1,000 students (white only) in seventh grade. Internal-consistency reliability ranged from .77 to .82; the reproducibility coefficient was .95–.96. The correlation between this scale and the Self-Perception of Attainment Scale (SPAS) was .56. The correlation with grades (controlling for IQ) was .34–.37 ($p < .05$). For more information, see Burke, Ellison, and Hunt (1985).

The Self-Efficacy for Academic Tasks

The Self-Efficacy for Academic Tasks (SEAT; Owen & Baum, 1985) is a 34-item measure of children's perceptions of self-efficacy, that is, confidence in their ability to organize and carry out school tasks. It also measures attributions for success or failure on school tasks. For each item, the child marks either a happy face, an unhappy face, or a neutral face indicating how good he or she is at, for example, "answering when a teacher calls on you." Then, for each item where a happy (success) or unhappy (failure) face was marked, the child checks one of five attributions: smart/not smart, try hard/don't try, lucky/unlucky, easy/too hard, and, for failure only, too shy.

The SEAT gives 10 scores: one self-efficacy score, and nine percentage scores reflecting how often a child uses the various attributions. Stability estimates across a 6-month interval for the self-efficacy score ranged from .24 to .68. Originally developed for upper elementary age students, the SEAT is now available in high school and college versions and in domains other than academic. For more information, see Baum (1985).

Self-Perception of Attainment Scale

The SPAS, for ages 5–13, was developed to measure a child's ranking of his or her own ability relative to that of classmates (Nicholls, 1978). It is a schematic depiction of 30 faces representing children in the class, ranked from the poorest student (30) to the best (1). The child marks an X on the face representing his or her perception of rank in class.

The SPAS was normed on New Zealand children. Its test–retest reliability after 2 weeks was .83. Correlations with teacher ratings of reading achievement ranged from .67 to .76. The correlation with the Self-Concept of Academic Ability, as noted above, was .56. Correlations of the SPAS with actual achievement and teacher ratings increased with age. For more information, see Burke et al. (1985).

The Self-Regulatory Style Questionnaire

The Self-Regulatory Style Questionnaire (Connell & Ryan, 1987) measures four styles of regulation children employ in school situations. Children endorse different reasons for doing homework, doing classwork, wanting to do well in school, and answering questions in class; there are 26 items in all. The measure is designed primarily for upper elementary school children. The four dimensions of style include External Regula-

tion (for example, working to avoid getting yelled at), Introjected Regulation (for example, being ashamed if one doesn't do homework), Identified Regulation (e.g., because it's important), and Intrinsic Motivation (e.g., because it's fun). Alpha reliabilities for the four subscales range from .75 to .88.

Self-Concept and Motivation Inventory

There are four different age versions of the Self-Concept and Motivation Inventory (SCAMIN) (subtitled "What Face Would You Wear?"), which measures academic self-concept and motivation (Milchus, Farrah, & Reitz, 1968). The preschool/kindergarten version contains 24 items with three faces (sad, happy, neutral) each. A typical question is "What face would you wear if your forgot your story or song in front of the whole class?" The student responds by blackening the "nose" on the appropriate face. The version for first through third grades has five faces for responses. The version for third through sixth grades has 48 items, and the secondary version has 64 items.

The SCAMIN was normed on over 1,000 Detroit students. Split-half reliability ranged from .73 to .93. A recent study of the preschool/kindergarten version, with over 5,000 Tennessee kindergarten students, found Cronbach's alphas for subscales as follows: Academic Self-Concept, .67; Achievement Investment, .60; and Achievement Needs, .60. Concurrent validity of the scales was demonstrated by comparisons with teacher judgment, with coefficients ranging from .54 to .91.; the scales have good "logical validity." For more information on factor structure and reliability, see Davis, Sellers, and Johnston (1988).

REFERENCES

Adams, J., Priest, R. F., & Prince, H. T. (1985). Achievement motive: Analyzing the validity of the WOFO. *Psychology of Women Quarterly, 9,* 357–370.

Adkins, D. C., & Ballif, B. L. (1972). A new approach to response sets in analysis of a test of motivation to achieve. *Educational and Psychological Measurement, 32,* 559–577.

Atkinson, J. W., & Litwin, G. H. (1960). Achievement motive and test anxiety conceived as motive to approach success and motive to avoid failure. *Journal of Abnormal and Social Psychology, 60,* 52–63.

Bachrach, R., & Peterson, R. A. (1976). Test–retest reliability and interrelation among three locus of control measures for children. *Perceptual and Motor Skills, 43,* 260–262.

Bauer, D. H. (1975). The effect of instructions, anxiety, and locus on control on intelligence test scores. *Measurement and Evaluation in Guidance, 8,* 13–19.

Baum, S. (1985). *Learning disabled students with superior cognitive abilities: A validation study of descriptive behavior.* Unpublished doctoral dissertation, University of Connecticut, Storrs.

Bellak, L., & Bellak, S. (1980). *A manual for the Children's Apperception Test* (7th ed.) Larchmont, NY: C.P.S.

Bergin, D. A. (1987, April). *Achievement, out-of-school activities, and intrinsic motivation for learning.* Paper presented at the annual meeting of the American Educational Research Association, Washington, DC.

Boersma, F. J., Chapman, J. W., & Maguire, T. O. (1979). *Technical data on the Student's Perception of Ability Scale* (Report No. TM 008 213). Edmonton: University of Alberta. (ERIC Document Reproduction Service No. ED 166 233)

Bradley, R. H., Stuck, G. B., Coop, R. H., & White, K. P. (1977). A new scale to assess locus of control in three achievement domains. *Psychological Reports, 41,* 656.

Brinkman, E. H. (1973). Personality correlates of educational set in the classroom. *Journal of Educational Research, 66,* 221–223.

Brookover, W. B., Thomas, S., & Paterson, A. (1964). Self concept of ability and school achievement. *Sociology of Education, 37,* 271–278.

Burke, J. P., Ellison, G. C., & Hunt, J. P. (1985). Measuring academic self-concept in children: A comparison of two scales. *Psychology in the Schools, 22,* 260–264.

Chapman, J. W., & Boersma, F. J. (1986). Student's Perception of Ability Scale: Comparison of scores for gifted, average, and learning disabled students. *Perceptual and Motor Skills, 63,* 57–58.

Child, D. (1984). Motivation and the dynamic calculus: A teacher's view. *Multivariate Behavioral Research, 19,* 288–298.

Chartier, G. M., Lankford, D. A., & Ainley, C. (1976). The Stanford Preschool Internal–External Scale: Extension to kindergarteners. *Journal of Personality Assessment, 40,* 431–433.

Cicirelli, V. G., Granger, R., Schemmel, D., Cooper, W., Helms, D., Holthouse, N., & Nehls, J. (1971). Measures of self-concept, attitudes, and achievement motivation of primary grade children. *Journal of School Psychology, 9,* 383–392.

Cole, J. L. (1974). The relationship of selected personality variables to academic achievement of average aptitude third graders. *Journal of Educational Research, 67,* 329–333.

Connell, J. P. (1985). A new multidimensional measure of children's perceptions of control. *Child Development, 56,* 1018–1041.

Connell, J. P., & Ryan, R. (1987). A developmental theory of motivation in the classroom. *Teacher Education Quarterly, 11,* 64–77.

Crandall, V. C., Katkovsky, W., & Crandall, V. J. (1965). Children's beliefs in their own control of reinforcements in intellectual–academic achievement situations. *Child Development, 36,* 91–109.

Davis, T. M., Sellers, P. A., & Johnston, J. M. (1988). The factor structure and internal consistency of the Self-Concept and Motivation Inventory: What Face Would Your Wear? (preschool/kindergarten form). *Educational and Psychological Measurement, 48,* 237–246.

Dweck, C. S., & Elliott, E. S. (1983). Achievement motivation. In E. M. Hetherington (Ed.), *Handbook of child psychology: Vol. 4. Socialization, personality, and social development* (pp. 643–691). New York: Wiley.

Educational Testing Service. (1986). *The ETS test collection catalog: Vol. 1. Achievement tests and measurement devices.* Phoenix: Oryx Press.

Feld, S. C., & Lewis, J. (1969). The assessment of achievement anxieties in children. In C. P. Smith (Ed.), *Achievement-related motives in children* (pp. 151–199). New York: Russell Sage Foundation.

Frymier, J. R. (1970). Development and validation of a motivation index. *Theory into Practice, 9,* 56–85.

Frymier, J. R., Henning, M. J., Henning, W., West, S. C., & Norris, L. (1975). A longitudinal study of academic motivation. *Journal of Educational Research, 69,* 63–66.

Goldman, B. A., & Osborne, W. L. (Eds.). (1985). *Directory of unpublished experimental mental measures* (Vol. 4). New York: Human Sciences Press.

Gottfried, A. E. (1985). Academic intrinsic motivation in elementary and junior high school students. *Journal of Educational Psychology, 77,* 631–645.

Gough, H. G. (1968). An interpreter's syllabus for the California Psychological Inventory. In P. McReynolds (Ed.), *Advances in psychological assessment* (Vol. 1). Palo Alto, CA: Science and Behavior Books.

Gough, H. G. (1975). *California Psychological Inventory manual.* Palo Alto, CA: Consulting Psychologists Press.

Harnisch, D., Hill, K., & Fyans, L. (1980, April). *Development of a shorter, more reliable and more valid measure of test motivation.* Paper presented at the annual meeting of the National Council on Measurement in Education, Boston.

Harter, S. (1981). A new self-report scale of intrinsic versus extrinsic orientation in the classroom: Motivational and informational components. *Developmental Psychology, 17,* 300–312.

Harter, S. (1982). The Perceived Competence Scale for Children. *Child Development, 53,* 87–97.

Harter, S. (1985). *Manual for the Self-Perception Profile for Children.* Denver: University of Denver.

Helmreich, R. L., & Spence, J. T. (1979). The Work and Family Orientation Questionnaire: An objective instrument to assess components of achievement motivation and attitudes toward family and career. *JSAS: Catalog of Selected Documents in Psychology, 8,* 35. (Ms. No. 1677)

Hermans, J. J. M. (1970). A questionnaire measure of achievement motivation. *Journal of Applied Psychology, 54,* 353–363.

Hill, K. T. (1980). Motivation, evaluation and educational testing policy. In L. J. Fyans (Ed.), *Achievement motivation: Recent trends in theory and research* (pp. 34–95). New York: Plenum.

Hill, K. T., & Sarason, S. B. (1966). The relation of test anxiety and defensiveness to test and school performance over the elementary-school years: A further longitudinal study. *Monographs of the Society for Research in Child Development, 31*(2, Serial No. 104).

Hill, K. T., & Wigfield, A. (1984). Test anxiety: A major educational problem and what can be done about it. *Elementary School Journal, 85,* 105–126.

Hollinger, C. L., & Fleming, E. S. (1985). Social orientation and the social self-esteem of gifted and talented female adolescents. *Journal of Youth and Adolescence, 14,* 389–399.

Johnson, O. G. (1976). *Tests and measurements in child development: Handbook II.* San Francisco: Jossey-Bass.

Keyser, D. J., & Sweetland, R. C. (Eds.). (1986). *Test critiques* (Vol. 5). Kansas City, MO: Test Corporation of America.

Kowalski, P., Stipek, D., & Daniels, D. (1987, April). *The relationship between teachers' ratings and students' self-reported motivation.* Paper presented at the annual meeting of the American Educational Research Association, Washington, DC.

Krug, S. E., Cattell, R. B., & Sweney, A. B. (1976). *Handbook for the School Motivation Analysis Test: SMAT.* Champaign, IL: Institute for Personality and Ability Testing.

Lefcourt, H. M. (1976). *Locus of control.* Hillsdale, NJ: Erlbaum.

Lefcourt, H. M., von Baeyer, C. L., Ware, E. E., & Cox, D. J. (1979). The Multidimensional–Multiattributional Causality Scale: The development of a goal specific locus of control scale. *Canadian Journal of Behavioural Science, 11,* 286–304.

Lehrer, B., & Hieronymous, A. (1977). Predicting achievement using intellectual academic–motivational and selected nonintellectual factors. *Journal of Experimental Education, 45,* 44–51.

Lifshitz, M., & Ramot, L. (1978). Toward a framework for developing children's locus-of-control orientation: Implication from the kibbutz system. *Child Development, 49,* 85–95.

Lloyd, J., & Barenblatt, L. (1984). Intrinsic intellectuality: Its relations to social class, intelligence, and achievement. *Journal of Personality and Social Psychology, 46,* 646–654.

Marsh, H. W., & Richards, G. E. (1987). The multidimensionality of the Rotter I-E Scale and its higher-order structure: An application of confirmatory factor analysis. *Multivariate Behavioral Research, 22,* 39–69.

McClelland, D. C., Atkinson, J. W., Clark, R. A., & Lowell, E. L. (1953). *The achievement motive.* Englewood Cliffs, NJ: Prentice-Hall.

Mehrabian, A. (1968). Male and female scales of the tendency to achieve. *Educational and Psychological Measurement, 28,* 493–502.

Mehrabian, A. (1969). Measures of achieving tendency. *Educational and Psychological Measurement, 29,* 445–451.

Milchus, N., Farrah, G., & Reitz, W. (1968). *The Self-Concept and Motivation Inventory: What Face Would You Wear? Preschool/Kindergarten Form.* Dearborn Heights, MI: Person-O-Metrics.

Milgram, N. A., & Milgram, R. M. (1975). Dimensions of locus on control in children. *Psychological Reports, 37,* 523–538.

Mischel, W., Zeiss, R., & Zeiss, A. (1974). Internal–external control and persistence: Validation and implications of the Stanford Preschool Internal–External Scale. *Journal of Personality and Social Psychology, 29,* 265–278.

Mitchell, J. V., Jr. (Ed.). (1983). *Tests in print III.* Lincoln, NE: Buros Institute of Mental Measurements.

Mitchell, J. V., Jr. (Ed.). (1985). *The ninth mental measurements yearbook.* Lincoln, NE: Buros Institute of Mental Measurements.

Morris, J. H., & Snyder, R. A. (1978). Convergent validities of the Resultant Achievement Motivation Test and the Prestatie Motivation Test with Ac and Ai scales of the CPI. *Educational and Psychological Measurement, 38,* 1151–1155.

Murray, H. A. (1938). *Explorations in personality.* New York: Oxford University Press.

Nicholls, J. G. (1976). When a scale measures more than its name denotes: The case of the Test Anxiety Scale for Children. *Journal of Consulting and Clinical Psychology, 44,* 976–985.

Nicholls, J. G. (1978). The development of the concepts of effort and ability, perception of academic attainment, and the understanding that difficult tasks require more ability. *Child Development, 49,* 800–814.

Nicholls, J. G. (1989). *The competitive ethos and democratic education.* Cambridge: Harvard University Press.

Nicholls, J. G., Cheung, P. C., Lauer, J., & Patashnick, M. (in press). *Learning and individual differences.*

Nicholls, J. G., Patashnick, M., & Nolen, S. B. (1985). Adolescents' theories of education. *Journal of Educational Psychology, 77,* 683–692.

Nowicki, S., Jr., & Duke, M. P. (1974). A preschool and primary internal–external control scale. *Developmental Psychology, 10,* 874–880.

Nowicki, S., Jr., & Strickland, B. R. (1973). A locus of control scale for children. *Journal of Consulting and Clinical Psychology, 40,* 148–154.

Nunn, G. D. (1988). Concurrent validity between the Nowicki–Strickland Locus of Control Scale and the State–Trait Anxiety Inventory for Children. *Educational and Psychological Measurement, 48,* 435–438.

Omizo, M. M., Omizo, S. A., & Michael, W. B. (1987). Relationship of Locus of Control Inventory for Three Achievement Domains (LOCITAD) to two other locus of control measures: A construct validity study. *Educational and Psychological Measurement, 47,* 737–742.

Owen, S. V., & Baum, S. M. (1985). *Development of an academic self-efficacy scale for upper elementary school children.* Unpublished manuscript, University of Connecticut, Storrs.

Powers, S., Douglas, P., & Choroszy, M. (1983). The factorial validity of the Multidimensional–Multiattributional Causality Scale. *Educational and Psychological Measurement, 43,* 611–615.

Prawat, R. S. (1976). Mapping the affective domain in young adolescents. *Journal of Educational Psychology, 68,* 566–572.

Renzulli, J. S., Smith, L. H., White, A. J., Callahan, C.

M., & Hartmen, R. K. (1976). *Scales for rating the behavioral characteristics of superior students.* Wethersfield, CT: Creative Learning Press.

Rotter, J. B. (1966). Generalized expectancies for internal versus external control of reinforcement. *Psychological Monographs, 80*(1, Whole No. 609).

Rowley, G. (1974). Which examinees are most favored by the use of multiple choice tests? *Journal of Educational Measurement, 11,* 15–23.

Russell, I. L. (1969). Motivation for school achievement: Measurement and validation. *Journal of Educational Research, 62,* 263–266.

Ryckman, D. B., & Peckham, P. (1987). Gender differences in attributions for success and failure situations across subject areas. *Journal of Educational Research, 81,* 120–125.

Ryckman, D. B., Sprague, D. G., & Peckham, P. D. (1985, April). *The Survey of Achievement Responsibility (SOAR): Some reliability and validity data on a new academically oriented attribution scale.* Paper presented at the annual convention of the American Educational Research Association, Chicago.

Sarason, S., Davidson, K., Lighthall, R., Waite, R., & Ruebush, B. (1960). *Anxiety in elementary school children.* New York: Wiley.

Schultz, C. B., & Pomerantz, M. (1974). Some problems in the application of achievement motivation to education: The assessment of motive to succeed and probability of success. *Journal of Educational Psychology, 66,* 599–608.

Silon, E. L., & Harter, S. (1985). Assessment of perceived competence, motivational orientation, and anxiety in segregated and mainstreamed educable mentally retarded children. *Journal of Educatonal Psychology, 77,* 217–230.

Spielberger, C. D., Edwards, C. D., Montouri, J., & Lushene, R. (1970). *The State–Trait Anxiety Inventory for Children (How I Feel Questionnaire).* Palo Alto, CA: Consulting Psychologists Press.

Spielberger, C. D., Gorsuch, R. L., & Lushene, R. E. (1970). *Manual for the State–Trait Anxiety Inventory.* Palo Alto, CA: Consulting Psychologists Press.

Stipek, D. J. (1988). *Motivation to learn: From theory to practice.* Englewood Cliffs, NJ: Prentice-Hall.

Sweetland, R. C., & Keyser, D. J. (Eds.). (1986). *Tests: A comprehensive reference for assessments in psychology, education, and business* (2nd ed.). Kansas City, MO: Test Corporation of America.

Waddell, K. J. (1984). The self-concept and social adaptation of hyperactive children in adolescence. *Journal of Clinical Child Psychology, 13,* 50–55.

Weiner, B. (1974). *Achievement motivation and attribution theory.* Morristown, NJ: General Learning Press.

Weisz, J. R., & Stipek, D. J. (1982). Competence, contingency, and the development of perceived control. *Human Development, 25,* 250–281.

White, R. W. (1959). Motivation reconsidered: The concept of competence. *Psychological Review, 66,* 297–333.

Youniss, R. P., Lorr, M., & Stefic, E. C. (1979). Assessment of motives and orientations. *Psychological Reports, 45,* 555–561.

Ziraba, S. (1976). The relationship of achievement motivation to sex, locus of control, anxiety and type of school environment among kindergarten children. *Dissertation Abstracts International, 37,* 5460A.

Index